THE LAW OF SECURITIES REGULATION

Revised Fifth Edition

By

Thomas Lee Hazen
Cary C. Boshamer Distinguished Professor of Law
The University of North Carolina at Chapel Hill

HORNBOOK SERIES®

Mat #40530513

Hornbook Series, *WESTLAW*, and West Group are trademarks
registered in the U.S. Patent and Trademark Office.

COPYRIGHT © 1985, 1990, 1996 WEST PUBLISHING CO.
© West, a Thomson business, 2002, 2005
© 2006 Thomson/West
      610 Opperman Drive
      P.O. Box 64526
      St. Paul, MN 55164–0526
      1–800–328–9352
Printed in the United States of America

ISBN–13: 978–0–314–17245–7
ISBN–10: 0–314–17245–9

*TEXT IS PRINTED ON 10% POST
CONSUMER RECYCLED PAPER*

To: Lisa, George, Elliott, and Lucie

*

Preliminary Note on the Scope of the One Volume Hornbook

This Hornbook is a one volume version and a substantial abridgement of my six volume Treatise on Securities Regulation (Practitioner's Edition). The Hornbook is designed for students but can also serve as a desk book for lawyers desiring an overview of the law. The Fifth Edition was revised in 2006 to reflect some important recent developments including the 1933 Act offering reform rules.[.5]

The Hornbook omits many sections of the Practitioner's Edition that the reader may want to consult for more in-depth analysis or for topics reserved for the Practitioner's Edition, which provides more extensive footnoting, directing the reader to primary and other secondary sources. The Hornbook provides an entry into the world of securities regulation. The Practitioner's Edition provides significantly more depth, insight, and footnoting of sources.

The Hornbook retains the section numbers[1] and footnote numbering as they appear in the multi-volume Practitioner's Edition in order to help user who decides to consult the more comprehensive treatise. The index includes all references to the Practitioner's Edition even if the sections do not appear in this Hornbook.

PREFACE

Securities law, especially at the federal level, was once considered a specialty that only the large Wall Street law firms had to worry about. That is certainly no longer the case. Lawyers all over the country are finding themselves in contact with many aspects of the federal securities laws. There is hardly a lawyer who himself or herself does not have either directly or indirectly some investment in the stock or bond markets. Furthermore, our clients are likely to have similar investments. There is also ever-increasing number of participants in the options, futures, and derivatives markets.

Because of the widespread possibility of federal remedies that exist for investors who are injured in the securities markets, every lawyer should have at least a passing familiarity with the federal securities laws. Conscientious lawyers should keep abreast of developments due to the burgeoning alternative investment opportunities including options, index futures and the like. Also, since the definition of securities is an expansive one, a large number of investment opportunities that are not in the traditional forms of stock or bonds may still be subject to the regulatory and protective provisions of both federal and state securities law. It follows that securities law has become relevant to general practitioners as well as specialists.

Additionally there are large numbers of lawyers who have a general corporate and commercial practice which touches upon both state and federal securities laws. No matter how small the business, if it is in corporate or limited partnership form, the antifraud provisions and attendant potential civil liabili-

---

[.5] Readers desiring additional recent developments should consult the pocket part of the Practitioner's Edition.

[1] Some subheadings have been deleted from the Hornbook for the convenience of the reader.

ties loom in the background as something for the corporate planner to keep in mind. On occasion, the securities laws may also apply to limited liability company and limited liability partnership investments.[2] Any time a company issues stock, the securities laws are implicated. The exemptions from federal and state registration requirements are not as straightforward as they may seem[3] and thus any corporate planner should be aware of the necessary precautions to secure the desired exemption.

This Hornbook, and the more comprehensive Practitioner's Edition of this treatise, is designed both for students and attorneys needing an introduction to the securities laws as well as for specialists dealing with these issues on a daily basis who seek more in-depth analysis of the law and current developments. This Hornbook, which is now in its fifth edition, is designed to give an overview of the securities laws with the understanding that the space limitations do not permit an in-depth treatment of all aspects of federal and state law. The multi-volume Practitioner's Edition has evolved and grown over the twenty years and five editions that it has been in existence. Over the years various chapters have been expanded and added to reflect the changes in the dynamic field of securities regulation.

This Hornbook is not merely a primer. The hope is to provide a firm understanding of the basics of securities law and adequate guidance as to further sources for the more esoteric aspects of the law of securities regulation.

Many areas of federal regulation are sufficiently complex so as to preclude an adequate surface treatment. The coverage of both the Hornbook and Treatise represents an attempt to strike a balance between the need for sufficient depth and the space limitations. In many instances choices have been made to allow in-depth treatment of some of the more common areas and to limit the details of the more specialized areas.

Towards these ends, a large portion of the Hornbook is devoted to discussion of the federal Securities Act of 1933[4] and the Securities Exchange Act of 1934.[5] Primary emphasis is placed upon the regulation of the securities markets as it applies to issuers of securities and to most investors. Lawyers who do not specialize in securities law are likely to come into contact with a number of areas covered by the Securities Act of 1933 and the Securities Exchange Act of 1934. These include the registration requirements for securities distributions and the various exemptions from registration. Both the 1933 and 1934 Acts provide a wide range of remedies for investors injured by fraudulent practices and material misstatements and omissions.[6] Shareholder suffrage is a major thrust of the Exchange Act's proxy regulations.[7] The Exchange Act also includes the Williams Act Amendments that contain the federal regulation of tender offers[8]—a topic often in the forefront of the financial news of the day.

---

[2] *See* §§ 1.6[10], 1.6[11] *infra.*

[3] *See* chapter 4 *infra.*

[4] 15 U.S.C.A. §§ 77a *et seq. See* chapters 1–7 *infra.*

[5] 15 U.S.C.A. §§ 78a *et seq. See* chapters 10–16 *infra.*

[6] *See* chapter 12 *infra.*

[7] *See* chapter 10 *infra.*

[8] *See* chapter 11 *infra.*

Another topic of current concern is the sanctions against insider trading based on nonpublic information.[9] A major developing area has been the creation of mechanisms for a national market system in order to help eliminate many of the inefficiencies of the traditional exchange and over-the-counter markets.[10]

Although regulation of the broker-dealer industry is a very important aspect of securities law, the treatment in both the Hornbook and Treatise is somewhat selective.[11] Formerly, broker-dealer law was primarily a subspecialty of interest to a relatively small number of lawyers. However, that has changed. There has been rampant fraud in many sectors of the securities industry and this has resulted in increased widespread significance of broker-dealer law. Accordingly, in the Fifth Edition, there is a significantly expanded treatment of broker-dealer regulation both by the SEC and self regulatory organizations. The previous editions' treatment of the markets generally has been revised to reflect dramatic changes that have taken place, not the least of which are due to technological developments.

In addition, there is only brief treatment of the state securities laws, in part because of the ever-increasing importance of the federal laws and also because of the high degree of jurisdictional variation and the need to consult the law of each applicable state. The Hornbook and Treatise also examine the other federal acts administered by the SEC: the Public Utility Holding Company Act of 1935,[12] the Trust Indenture Act of 1939,[13] the Investment Company Act of 1940,[14] and the Investment Advisers Act of 1940.[15] The Practitioner's Edition also contains some materials on related laws including the Securities Investor Protection Act[16] that governs broker-dealer insolvency, Article 8 of the Uniform Commercial Code[17] which governs securities transactions, the Foreign Corrupt Practices Act,[18] the Racketeering Influenced and Corrupt Organizations Act,[19] and the ever-increasing blurring of the lines of demarcation

---

[9] *See* § 12.17 *infra.*

[10] *See* chapter 14 *infra.*

[11] *See* chapters 14–15 *infra.* For additional discussion of the aspects of broker-dealer regulation. See Jerry W. Markham & Thomas L. Hazen, Broker-Dealer Operations Under Securities and Commodities Law: Financial Responsibilities, Credit Regulation, and Customer Protection (2d ed. 2002).

[12] Pub. Law No. 74–333, 49 Stat. 803 (1935), codified as amended at 15 U.S.C.A. §§ 79–79z–6, discussed in chapter 18 *infra* [Practitioner's Edition only].

[13] Act of August 3, 1939, 53 Stat. 1149, which is discussed in chapter 19 *infra.*

[14] Act of Aug. 22, 1940, 54 Stat. 789, codified in 15 U.S.C.A. §§ 80a–1 through 80a–52, discussed in chapter 20 *infra.*

[15] Act of Aug. 22, 1940 54 Stat. 847, codified in 15 U.S.C.A. §§ 80b–1 *et seq.,* discussed in chapter 21 *infra.*

[16] Codified as amended 15 U.S.C.A. §§ 78aaa–78*lll,* discussed in § 14.24 *infra.*

[17] *See* chapter 23 *infra* [Practitioner's Edition only].

[18] Pub. Law 95–213, 95th Cong., 1st Sess., 91 Stat. 1494 (1977), codified in 15 U.S.C.A. §§ 78m(b), 78dd–1, 78dd–2, discussed in §§ 9.3, 22.2 *infra.*

[19] Pub. Law No. 91–452, 84 Stat. 922 (1970), codified in 18 U.S.C.A. §§ 1961–1968, discussed in § 22.3 *infra.*

between investment banking and commercial banking.[20] There is also a brief overview of federal regulation of the commodities markets.[21]

As is always the case in the fast-changing world of securities regulation, there have been major changes in the law since the last edition. This Practitioner's Edition has grown from one volume in its first edition to its current six volume length.

A few of the developments over the past twenty years deserve specific mention here. The Internet has made securities investing more readily available. At the same time, it has opened up new avenues for those unscrupulous market participants wanting to engage in fraud. The changes in the law resulting from the Internet are discussed throughout both the Hornbook and the Practitioner's Edition. There have been two federal litigation reform Acts plus a total rearrangement of the jurisdictional allocation between the federal law and the states regarding securities regulation.

Disclosure obligations in many areas have changed dramatically. For example, the regulators have become increasingly concerned with the role analysts play in the securities markets and a new system has been put in place. The SEC has also instituted a new requirement of "plain English" in disclosure.

The ever-changing nature of the financial markets has also resulted in significant change. In 1999, Congress repealed the barriers that formerly existed between investment banking, commercial banking, and other financial services.[22] In 2000, Congress made revolutionary changes to commodities regulation and the law relating to derivative investments. The changes brought about by the Commodity Futures Modernization Act of 2000[23] that have had an impact on securities regulation are addressed in the Fifth Edition. Also, the terror attack of 2001 created increased focus on money laundering.[24]

The corporate scandals that emerged at the turn of the twenty-first century have had a profound impact on securities regulation. For example, in 2002, Congress adopted the Sarbanes-Oxley Act[25] in reaction to infamous corporate scandals including Enron's, Tyco's and WorldCom's. The Sarbanes-Oxley Act introduced a new federal focus on corporate governance—an area of the law that was traditionally reserved to the states. The Sarbanes-Oxley Act is discussed throughout both the Hornbook and Treatise where applicable.

The foregoing are but examples of the major changes that lead to the Fifth Edition. These major changes are supplemented by the significant refinements in existing doctrines in all aspects of securities regulation.

---

[20] *See* § 22.6 *infra.*

[21] *See* § 22.7 *infra.* For more detailed discussion of the commodities laws and the derivatives markets, see Phillip McBride Johnson & Thomas Lee Hazen, Derivatives Regulation (2004).

[22] *See* the Gramm-Leach-Bliley Act, Pub. Law 106–102, 1999 U.S.C.C.A.N. (113 Stat.) 1338 (1999).

[23] Commodity Futures Modernization Act of 2000, Pub. Law 106–554, 114 Stat. 2763 (December 21, 2000).

[24] *See* § 22.5 *infra.*

[25] Sarbanes-Oxley Act of 2002, Pub. Law 107–204 (July 30, 2002).

The Practitioner's Edition contains four Appendices. Appendix A contains guides to the SEC's new plain English disclosure requirements. Appendix B contains materials relating to the SEC's Regulation FD which abolished selective disclosure practices that formerly had been employed by many public companies. Appendix C consists of a helpful SEC summary of its interpretations in administering the "shareholder proposal rule" which governs the inclusion of shareholder proposals in management's proxy statement. Finally, Appendix D (which also appears as the Appendix to the Hornbook) is designed to provide an overview to researching securities law through Westlaw.

The Fifth Edition contains developments through August 2004. As was the case with previous editions, the Practitioner's Edition will be twice each year. The one-volume student Hornbook edition is considerably abridged but contains references to the Practitioner's Edition in order to facilitate further study.

The federal securities statutes along with SEC rules and forms, including the disclosure guides in Regulation S-K and S-B are found in a separate statutory supplement which is published annually by Thomson-West.

ACKNOWLEDGMENTS

As with any work of this size there are a number of people whose hard work and support made this endeavor possible. In addition to my family, which has endured the long nights and short weekends, this treatise would never have been produced without the support from the University of North Carolina School of Law. In particular I would like to thank former Dean Kenneth S. Broun for his support and encouragement as well as the support and encouragement of my current Dean Gene Nichol. During the preparation of the first edition, my former colleague and very good friend Marianne K. Smythe was most patient with my ignorance and provided me with much insight into the workings of the Securities and Exchange Commission. I would like to acknowledge the great help I received from the late Professor N. Ferebee Taylor for the hours spent parsing the intricacies of SEC Rule 10b-5 and Professor Robert G. Byrd for his insights on the law of fraud and on remedies. There also was a number of support staff whose hard work made this treatise possible and the many student assistants who have helped me over the years.

I especially want to thank my wife Lisa for her help, support, and patience.

RESEARCH AIDS[26]

Researching the law in the area of securities regulation is not an easy task since a vast body of law is contained in administrative rules, interpretations and no-action letters that are not officially reported. In addition to the database of Westlaw which contains all of the pertinent information, Thomson-West publishes a securities law library on cd-rom. The Federal Securities Law Reporter, a multiple volume looseleaf reporter published by Commerce Clearing House (CCH) is another comprehensive source; a companion CCH resource is the Blue Sky Law Reporter which addresses the various state securities regulation statutes and administrative law. The Bureau of National Affairs' Secu-

---

[26] *See also* § 1.0[2] *infra.*

rities Regulation and Law Reporter can be very helpful in keeping lawyers up-to-date with the rapidly changing law of securities regulation. Prentice–Hall also publishes a looseleaf service. Looseleaf services in related fields include the Commodity Futures Law Reporter and the Federal Banking Law Reporter, both of which are published by Commerce Clearing House.

In addition to the Practitioner's Edition of this Treatise, secondary sources for more detail on some of the matters dealt with in this Hornbook include: James D. Cox & Thomas Lee Hazen, Cox and Hazen on Corporations (Aspen Law & Business, 2d ed.2003); Phillip McBride Johnson & Thomas Lee Hazen, Derivatives Regulation (Aspen Law & Business, 2004); and Jerry W. Markham & Thomas Lee Hazen, Broker Dealer Operations and Regulation Under Securities and Commodities Law: Financial Responsibilities, Credit Regulation, and Customer Protection (Thomson-West, 2d ed. 2002).

THOMAS LEE HAZEN

Chapel Hill, North Carolina,
August, 2006

Westlaw® Overview

The Law of Securities Regulation offers a detailed and comprehensive treatment of principles and issues in securities law practice. To supplement the information contained in this book, you can access Westlaw, West's computer-assisted legal research service. Westlaw contains a broad array of legal resources, including case law, statutes, expert commentary, current developments, and various other types of information.

Learning how to use these materials effectively will enhance your legal research abilities. To help you coordinate the information in the book with your Westlaw research, this volume contains an appendix listing Westlaw databases, search techniques, and sample problems.

The instructions and features described in this Westlaw overview are based on accessing Westlaw via westlaw.com® at **www.westlaw.com**.

THE PUBLISHER

*

Summary of Contents

*

Table of Contents

THE LAW OF SECURITIES REGULATION

Revised Fifth Edition

*

Chapter 1

THE BASIC COVERAGE OF
THE SECURITIES ACT

Table of Sections

---

§ 1.0   Overview of Treatise; Sources of Securities Law; Overview of this Chapter

§ 1.0[1]   Overview of Treatise

Securities regulation is an extremely complicated field. At the federal level, it is implemented by a myriad of statutes and regulatory rules. The statutes and rules are extremely complex and detailed. The case law is particularly perplexing because of the degree of detail and complexity the law imposes. However, it is not only the law that is difficult and elaborate. The transactions that implicate the securities laws are extremely intricate as well. This treatise tries to distill the law and its application to these transactions in an understandable manner.

The treatise begins with a general discussion of the securities markets and an overview of the regulatory scheme.[9] This is followed by a discussion of the various securities and related investment instruments that are regulated by the securities laws.[10] The book then embarks on a discussion of the registration and disclosure process for public offerings of securities.[11] This is followed by detailed discussion of exemptions from this registration process for publicly offered securities.[12] Civil liabilities arising out of this 1933 Act registration process are also discussed in detail.[13] Then, there is a brief analysis of the state securities laws.[14]

---

§ 1.0

9.   *See* §§ 1.1–1.4 *infra.*

10.   *See* §§ 1.5–1.7 *infra.*

11.   *See* chapters 2–3 *infra. See also* chapters 5–6 *infra.*

12.   *See* chapter 4 *infra.*

13.   *See* chapter 7 *infra. See also* chapter 12 *infra.*

14.   *See* chapter 8 *infra.*

1

After discussing the registration requirements and exemptions for public offerings, this treatise analyzes the periodic reporting and disclosure obligations applicable to public companies generally.[15] This includes discussion of federal regulation of shareholder voting and the proxy process[16] as well as corporate takeovers.[17] This is followed by discussion of the anti-manipulation and antifraud rules that apply to all securities transactions, as well as to civil liabilities arising thereunder.[18] There then is discussion of special rules applicable to transactions by certain insiders of publicly held companies.[19]

A significant portion of the securities laws is devoted to market regulation—the regulation of the securities markets and the broker-dealers who trade in securities. That regulation is discussed in a subsequent chapter,[20] which is followed by a discussion of the arbitration of disputes involving securities broker-dealers.[21]

The Securities and Exchange Commission administers the federal securities laws. An entire chapter is devoted to the structure and operation of the SEC.[22] Complex jurisdictional issues arise in connection with the administration and enforcement of the securities laws. These jurisdictional issues are addressed in a subsequent chapter of this treatise.[23] This is followed by discussion of some of the more specialized securities regulation including the former regulation of public utility holding companies,[24] publicly traded debt securities,[25] investment companies (including mutual funds),[26] and professional investment advisers.[27]

There is a large body of related regulation beyond the securities laws themselves. There is a chapter devoted to discussion of these laws as well.[28]

§ 1.0[2] Sources of Securities Law[29]

Securities Laws

Although originating as a matter of state law,[30] the vast majority of securities regulation in the United States is a matter of federal law. State law

---

15. *See* chapter 9 *infra.*

16. *See* chapter 10 *infra.*

17. *See* chapter 11 *infra.*

18. *See* chapter 12 *infra.*

19. *See* chapter 13 *infra. See also* § 12.17 *infra.*

20. *See* chapter 14 *infra.*

21. *See* chapter 15 *infra.*

22. *See* chapter 16 *infra. See also* §§ 1.3–1.4 *infra.*

23. *See* chapter 17 *infra. See also* § 1.5 *infra.*

24. *See* chapter 18 *infra.*

25. *See* chapter 19 *infra.*

26. *See* chapter 20 *infra.*

27. *See* chapter 21 *infra.*

28. *See* chapter 22 *infra* (The Foreign Corrupt Practices Act, RICO, Mail and Wire Fraud, regulation of financial services generally, and the commodities laws).

29. This subsection is adapted from Thomas Lee Hazen & David L Ratner, Securities Regulation Cases and Materials 11–16 (6th Ed. 2003).

30. *See* § 1.2[2] *infra.*

remains significant with respect to some transactions, but federal law clearly has the most significant impact on securities regulation. The discussion that follows is designed to give a brief overview of the sources of federal law that are discussed throughout this treatise.

The starting point in analyzing any question of federal securities law is of course the statutes. In the strictest sense, there is no federal "common law" of securities,[31] and any rights or liabilities must find their source in the statutes themselves. The statutes are, however, quite sketchy or ambiguous in many important areas, so that it is necessary to resort to supplemental sources of law. These sources are of two kinds: rules and other statements of general applicability issued by the SEC (or self-regulatory organizations) and reports of decided cases.

The SEC has broad rule-making powers under the various statutes it administers and has exercised its authority by prescribing at least three different kinds of rules. One category is procedural rules, setting forth the steps to be followed in proceedings before the Commission, as well as such mundane matters as the hours the Commission is open, where papers should be filed, what size type to use, and so forth. A second important category is the type of rule the Commission writes where Congress has given it the power to fill in the terms of the statute. For example, section 14 of the 1934 Act[32] provides that no person shall solicit proxies from shareholders of a registered company "in contravention of such rules and regulations as the Commission may prescribe * * *." Pursuant to that authority, the SEC has adopted a detailed set of rules (Regulation 14A) prescribing the form of proxy, the contents of the proxy statement, the procedures to be followed in proxy contests and in responding to proposals submitted by shareholders, and other matters. A third important category of rules defines some of the general terms used in the laws. A significant example of this definitional power are the rules adopted under the 1933 Act, defining the circumstances in which secondary offerings, mergers, nonpublic offerings, and intrastate offerings, will be exempt from 1933 Act registration requirements.

Supplementing the SEC's rules are its forms for the various statements and reports which issuers, broker-dealers and others are required to file under the Acts. Since disclosure is such an important part of the regulatory pattern, these forms (which have the legal force of rules) play an important part in defining the extent of the disclosure obligation.

Beyond the rules and forms, the SEC goes in for a good deal of "informal lawmaking," setting forth the views of the Commission or its staff on questions of current concern, without stating them in the form of legal requirements. The principal media for these statements are SEC "Releases" which, as the name implies, are simply statements distributed to the press, to companies and firms registered with the Commission, and to other interested persons. While Releases are also used for the proposal and adoption of rules or to meet other formal notice requirements, they are often used to set forth Commission or staff views through general statements of policy or recitation

---

31. However, the essence of most securities litigation is grounded upon SEC Rule 10b–5 (17 C.F.R. § 240.10b–5), which is very brief and sketchy. Thus, it is fair to say that the vast body of case law under this section is a type of de facto federal common law of securities fraud. These cases and Rule 10b–5 are discussed in chapter 12 *infra*.

32. 15 U.S.C.A. § 78n.

of the position taken by the Commission in various specific cases. Examples of both types will be found in this treatise. An overview of the SEC's lawmaking process is discussed below in section 1.4 of this treatise. A more detailed analysis of the SEC's operations is found in chapter 16.

In addition to general public statements of policy, the staff has, since the Commission's early days, been willing to respond to individual private inquiries as to whether a certain transaction could be carried out in a specified manner. These responses are known as "no-action" letters, because they customarily state that "the staff will recommend no action to the Commission" if the transaction is done in the specified manner.[33] Prior to 1970, these letters were not made public, leading to complaints that the large law firms which frequently corresponded with the SEC had access to a considerable body of "secret law" which was unavailable to other lawyers and their clients. As a result of these complaints, as well as recommendations from the Administrative Conference of the United States, the SEC now makes these letters and responses public, adding to the burdens of lawyers who wish to make sure they have thoroughly researched a particular point.

As noted above, technology has led to changes in the market place for securities. For example, Electronic Communication Networks (ECNs)[34] may operate like exchanges and thus present a competing mechanism for trading securities listed on the more traditional stock exchanges. In addition, in 2006, the NASDAQ national market was registered as a national securities exchange. In that same year, the New York Stock Exchange merged with Archipelago, a major ECN.[35]

In some areas of federal securities law, notably in the registration provisions of the 1933 Act, most of the "law" is found in the rules, forms, and policy statements of the Commission, and very little in the form of decided "cases." In other areas, however, notably under the general anti-fraud provisions of the 1934 Act,[36] there is very little in the way of formal rules, and the law has developed in the traditional "common law" manner, with courts and other tribunals deciding each case on the basis of precedents.

The SEC materials include reports of decisions in several different types of proceedings. The SEC itself may proceed in a number of ways if it discovers what it believes to be a violation of the law.

If the alleged violator is a broker-dealer or investment adviser required to register with the SEC, the Commission can bring a proceeding to revoke or suspend the firm's registration or take other disciplinary action.[37] If the alleged violator is an issuer seeking to sell securities under a 1933 Act registration statement, the Securities and Exchange Commission can bring a proceeding to suspend the effectiveness of the statement.[38] And, under power granted to the Commission in 1990, it can bring a proceeding against any alleged violator of the securities laws to require that person to cease and

---

33. No action letters are discussed in §§ 16.2, 16.32 *infra.*

34. *See* 17 C.F.R. §§ 240. 11Ac–1–1, 11Ac–4. Island and Instinet are two of the more well-known ECNs.

35. *See, e.g.,* Nasdaq Readying New Marketplace Meant to Replace OTC Bulletin Board, 35 Sec. Reg. & L. Rep. (BNA) 185 (Feb. 3, 2003).

36. Section 10(b) of the 1934 Act, 15 U.S.C.A. § 78j(b). *See* chapter 12 *infra.*

37. Broker-dealer regulation is discussed in chapter 14 *infra.*

38. SEC powers generally are discussed in chapter 16 *infra.*

desist from further violations. In any of these proceedings, the Commission staff acts as "prosecutor" and the Commission itself makes the final decision (after initial findings by an administrative law judge). The Commission's decision is appealable to the United States Court of Appeals in the District of Columbia or to the circuit where the registrant's principal place of business is located.

The Commission also has authority to go to court to obtain relief against alleged securities law violators. The most common type of Commission proceeding is an application to a federal district court for an injunction against future violations. In a particularly egregious case, however, the Commission may refer the matter to the Department of Justice for prosecution as a criminal violation.

The Securities and Exchange Commission is not a "collection agency." It has no statutory power to require a securities law violator to make restitution to people who have been injured by his or her violations. In a number of injunction actions, however, the SEC has requested, and the courts have granted, as "ancillary relief," an order directing the violator to "disgorge" his profits to a depository for distribution to persons entitled to recovery. In addition, this type of ancillary disgorgement relief may be ordered as part of an SEC administrative order against someone who violates the securities laws.

People who believe they have been injured by a violation of the securities laws can bring a civil action in the courts for damages. Injured investors may sue either under the specific civil liability provisions of those laws or assert an "implied" right of action under a provision prohibiting the activity in question. There have been an enormous number of private damage actions under the federal securities laws, particularly actions asserting an implied right of action under the general anti-fraud provisions. While many of these actions relate to distinctive securities law problems, such as misleading statements or "insider trading," a substantial number have involved allegations of corporate mismanagement which might also constitute violations of state corporation law. Plaintiffs usually bring these actions under the federal securities laws to avoid restrictive state court decisions or state procedural obstacles to stockholders' derivative suits.

Prior to 1975, the United States Supreme Court reviewed very few securities cases, and when it did, it generally construed the law broadly and gave great deference to the views of the SEC. Since that time, however, the Court has taken a very restrictive view of federal securities law, particularly with respect to implied private rights of action, and has rejected the views of the SEC in a number of important cases.

Another consequence of this litigation "explosion," and the resulting uncertainties surrounding civil liability under the federal securities laws, has been increased pressure for "codification" of those laws. The American Law Institute in 1978 completed work on a nine-year project to prepare a "Federal Securities Code," designed to replace all of the federal securities laws now on the books, and to give more certainty and predictability to the provisions for civil liability. However, the proposed Securities Code was never introduced in Congress. Nevertheless, many of the proposed Code's concepts have been introduced into the current regulatory system.

Where to Find the Law

Thomson/West's "Securities Regulation: Selected Statutes, Rules and Forms" should meet most lawyers' needs in studying the materials in this treatise. For advanced research, the most comprehensive and up-to-date sources for all of the federal securities laws, SEC rules, forms, interpretations and decisions, and court decisions on securities matters are the Westlaw and Lexis federal securities law libraries, and the loose-leaf Federal Securities Law Reporter published by Commerce Clearing House (CCH). Copies of the 1933 and 1934 Acts, and of the rules and forms governing the preparation of disclosure documents under those two acts, are also available through the SEC website (www.sec.gov).

The official version of the federal securities laws is of course found in the United States Code (and in the United States Code Annotated) as sections 77 through 80 of Title 15. Unfortunately, whoever was in charge of numbering the Code decided that the sections of the 1933 Act (15 U.S.C. § 77) should be numbered 77a, 77b, 77c, etc. Thus 5(b)(1) of the Act becomes 15 U.S.C. § 77e(b)(1), and § 12(a)(2) becomes § 77*l*(a)(2). The 1934 Act is handled in similar fashion in 15 U.S.C. § 78. Since everyone connected with securities regulation uses the section numbers of the Acts, rather than the Code references, this treatise refers to those sections in addition to providing the official citations. If you want to find a section of the 1933 or 1934 Act in the Code you can do so easily, provided you remember the alphabet and have enough fingers to count to 26 (sections of the 1934 Act after section 26 are rendered as §§ 78aa, 78bb, and so forth). In addition, when Congress adds entirely new sections, they may be incorporated into the midst of the existing statutes with letters. Thus, for example there is a Section 8A of the 1933 Act (15 U.S.C. § 77h–1) which appears between sections 8 and 9 of that Act.

The official version of the SEC rules can be found in volume 17 of the Code of Federal Regulations. Here the numbering system is more rational. 1933 Act rules are found in 17 C.F.R. § 230.___ under the rule number, and 1934 Act rules can be found in 17 C.F.R. § 240.___ in the same manner. Thus 1933 Act Rule 144 is 17 C.F.R. § 230.144, and 1934 Act Rule 10b–5 is 17 C.F.R. § 240.10b–5.

SEC Releases announcing the proposal or adoption of new rules, as well as those containing significant interpretations of the law, can be found in the Federal Register for the day on which the release was issued. Other Releases are not systematically or officially published in any form other than the mimeographed releases actually distributed by the Commission, numbered serially by reference to the Act or Acts to which they related, such as Securities Act Release No. 4434. Compilations of "significant" releases under certain of the Acts are available through a number of official and unofficial compilations.

The SEC's "no-action" letters, as noted above, are now publicly available. They can be examined at the SEC office in Washington, and selected letters are published or summarized in the CCH Federal Securities Law Reporter or the BNA Securities Regulation and Law Reports (described below). Complete texts of all letters are available from several sources, including Westlaw and Lexis.

The official texts of SEC decisions in administrative proceedings brought before it are distributed as "Releases" at the time they are handed down, and are eventually printed and compiled in bound volumes of "SEC Decisions and Reports." The reports of these proceedings are available on Westlaw and Lexis and also on the SEC website (www.sec.gov).

Useful statistical and narrative information concerning the SEC's activities can be found in the Commission's "Annual Reports" to Congress. These reports are customarily available through the Government Printing Office for several years back. They are also available through the SEC's website and on Westlaw and Lexis.

Court decisions involving the federal securities laws are generally reported promptly and in full text in the CCH Federal Securities Law Reporter. Decisions of the Courts of Appeals, of course, also appear in West's Federal Reporter (F.2d & F.3d), and the more significant District Court decisions appear in the Federal Supplement (F.Supp. & F.Supp.2d). SEC briefs in cases involving the securities laws, which often contain significant statements of Commission policy, are sometimes excerpted in the CCH Reporter. Formerly, these statements of policy were otherwise available only by request to the Commission's Office of General Counsel. Today, they are made available on the SEC website and are also collected on Westlaw and Lexis.

Up-to-date compilations of the constitutions, rules and interpretations of the major stock exchanges and the National Association of Securities Dealers (the "NASD") can be found in the loose-leaf stock exchange "Guides" and the "NASD Manual" published by CCH. They also can be found on the exchanges or NASD's websites.

As far as state securities law is concerned, the most current and comprehensive compilation of statutes, rules, and administrative and court decisions is the CCH Blue Sky Law Reporter, which contains separate sections covering the law of each of the 50 states. Westlaw and Lexis also have comprehensive state securities law libraries. The securities law of any particular state can also be obtained through its published statutes, published administrative regulations (if any), and official and unofficial reports of its court decisions.

As noted above, there is a great deal of information on the Internet. For example, the official websites of the Securities and Exchange Commission all provide very useful information including regulatory rules and decisions.

Secondary sources include books, articles and current periodicals. In addition to articles and notes in the general law reviews published by law schools and bar associations, there are several publications devoted specifically to securities and related matters, including "Securities Regulation Law Journal," published by Thomson/West. Relevant secondary sources are cited throughout this treatise.

A number of programs on securities law for practicing lawyers, generally lasting two or three days but sometimes longer, are sponsored each year by various organizations. The transcripts of some of these programs, featuring lectures and panel discussions by SEC officials, securities law specialists, and others, are published in book form, and are useful sources of discussion of current problems. The outlines for many of these programs are available on Westlaw and Lexis.

Publications summarizing current developments in securities regulation on a weekly basis include Securities Regulation and Law Report, published by Bureau of National Affairs (BNA), and the summaries accompanying the weekly supplements to the CCH Federal Securities Law Reports. Of the daily newspapers, The Wall Street Journal provides the most thorough coverage, with frequent lengthier stories providing useful background information.

The Securities Bar

There are no formal prerequisites for a lawyer to engage in securities practice.[39] The SEC's rules of practice provide that any member of the bar of any state may practice before it. There are a substantial number of lawyers specializing in securities matters, and many thousands of others who deal with securities matters in the course of their practice.

As a field of practice, securities regulation is more a series of sub-specialties than a single specialty. While there are common threads of doctrine and approach which run through the entire subject, securities practice tends to be divided in roughly the same way as the division in the SEC staff: disclosure, enforcement, and regulation.

Disclosure practice revolves around the preparation of the various documents that have to be filed with the SEC. Because of the great amount of time and care that goes into 1933 Act registration statements, and the substantial fees that lawyers charge for this kind of work, drafting disclosure documents has become an important sub-specialty. Legal representation of underwriters in 1933 Act offerings tends to be concentrated in a relatively small number of firms in the major financial centers. On the other hand, many lawyers who have not specialized in securities work may find themselves representing the issuer in a 1933 Act registration when a privately-owned company they have represented decides to "go public."

The second major branch of "disclosure" work grows out of general representation of publicly-owned corporations. This work may include preparation of proxy statements and other documents in connection with annual meetings or mergers, advice to corporate officers, directors and "insiders" regarding their transactions in the corporation's securities, and preparation of other documents required by the 1934 Act.

Whereas "disclosure" work falls generally into the province of the office lawyer, "enforcement" work falls more within the province of the litigator. Enforcement work may consist of representing broker-dealers or others charged by the SEC with violations of the securities laws, but it also includes representation of plaintiffs and defendants in the rapidly increasing numbers of private damage actions alleging similar violations.

A relatively small number of lawyers specialize in the "regulation" side of the SEC's activity, representing the interests of individual firms or trade groups in SEC rule-making proceedings, Congressional hearings, and other policy-making activities.

In addition to the lawyers specializing in one or another branch of securities work, there are many thousands more engaged in general business practice who from time to time face a question of securities law, such as whether a particular transaction requires registration under the 1933 Act, or

---

39. In 2002, Congress required the SEC to define what constitutes proper conduct before the SEC. *See* Section 307 of the Sarbanes–Oxley Act of 2002, Sarbanes–Oxley Act of 2002, Pub. Law 107–204 (July 30, 2002) and applicable SEC Rules which are discussed in §§ 7.15, 9.8, *infra*. These rules impose heightened requirements on many attorneys engaged in securities law practice.

whether a defrauded client can get into federal court by adding a 1934 Act claim to his state law claims. This treatise is designed to provide a basic groundwork for the lawyers specializing in the securities field, as well as a basic familiarity with the coverage and concepts of the securities laws for those who anticipate less frequent encounters with those concepts.

§ 1.1 Overview of the Securities Markets and Their Operation

§ 1.1[1] Securities Markets and Regulation in Context[1]

Securities[2] occupy a unique and important place in American life. Securities are the instruments which evidence the financial rights, and in some instances, the power to control, the corporations which own the great majority of our nation's and the world's productive facilities. Securities are the instruments through which business enterprises and governmental entities raise a substantial portion of the funds that are used to finance new capital. Securities are the instruments in which many millions of Americans (and investors all over the world) invest their savings in order to provide for their retirement income, education for their children, or in the hopes of achieving a higher standard of living for themselves and their family. And, inevitably, securities are the instruments by which unscrupulous promoters and sales people prey on those hopes and desires by selling overvalued (or even worthless) paper to many thousands of people every year.

Taken literally, the concept of a security is based on the condition of being secure and free from danger;[3] in reality this is anything but the case with respect to investment securities. The feature which distinguishes securities from most other commodities in which people deal is that securities have no intrinsic value in themselves—securities represent rights in something else. The value of a bond, note, or other promise to pay depends upon the financial position of the promisor. The value of a share of stock depends on the profitability or future prospects of the corporation or other entity which issued it. The market price of stock depends on how much other people are willing to pay for the stock, based on their evaluation of the company's prospects.

The foregoing features of securities give a distinctive coloration to the regulation of transactions in securities, in contrast to the regulation of transactions in goods or commodities. Most goods are produced, distributed, and used or consumed. Governmental regulation of goods generally focuses on protecting the ultimate consumer against dangerous articles, misleading ad-

---

§ 1.1

1. Portions of this subsection have been adapted from David L. Ratner & Thomas Lee Hazen, Securities Regulation: Cases and Materials ch. 1 (5th ed. 1996).

2. A "security, in business economics, [is] a written evidence of ownership conferring the right to receive property not currently in possession of the holder. The most common forms of securities are stocks (or shares) and bonds." The New Encyclopaedia Britannica (15th ed. Micropaedia 1998). *See also, e.g.,* Oxford English Dictionary (2d ed. 1989) (a security is "[a] document held by a creditor as guarantee of his right to payment. Hence, any particular kind of stock, shares, or other form of investment guaranteed by such documents"). The statutory definition of security is discussed in § 1.6 *infra.*

3. Security has thus been defined as "the condition of being protected from or not exposed to danger; safety." Oxford English Dictionary (2d ed. 1989). *See also* footnote 2 *supra.*

vertising, and unfair or non-competitive pricing practices. Securities are different.

The first difference is that securities are created rather than produced. Securities can be issued in unlimited amounts and virtually without any costs since securities are nothing in themselves but rather represent only an interest in something else. Therefore, an important focus of securities regulation is assuring that when securities are created and offered to the public, investors have an accurate idea of what that "something else" is and how much of an interest in that "something else" the security in question represents.

The second difference is that unlike goods, securities are not used or consumed by their purchasers. Securities become a kind of currency,[4] traded in the so-called "secondary markets"[5] at fluctuating prices. These "secondary" transactions[6] far outweigh, in number and volume, the offerings of newly created securities (frequently referred to as initial public offerings or IPOs). A second important focus of securities regulation, therefore, is to ensure that there is a continuous flow of information about the corporation or other entity that is represented[7] by the securities being actively traded in the secondary markets.

The third difference between securities and goods involves the intangible and complex nature of securities. Since the complexity of securities invites unscrupulous people to attempt to cheat or mislead investors and traders, the securities laws contain provisions prohibiting a wide variety of fraudulent, manipulative, or deceptive practices.[8] These provisions have been applied to a wide range of activities, including trading on inside information,[9] misleading corporate publicity,[10] and improper dealings by corporate management.[11]

Fourth, and finally, since a large industry has grown up to buy and sell securities for investors and traders, securities regulation is concerned with the regulation of people and firms engaged in the business,[12] in order to assure that they do not take advantage of their superior experience and access to overreach their nonprofessional customers.

§ 1.1[2]　The Securities Markets

Securities are traded through facilities known as "markets." These markets may have physical locations, but in many instances are simply formal

---

4.　In fact, securities are treated similarly to other cash-like "negotiable instruments under the Uniform Commercial Code." *See* Article 8 of the Uniform Commercial Code.

5.　"Secondary" markets is the term used to refer to the trading of securities between buyers and sellers as opposed to investors who initially purchase the security directly from the company issuing the securities. The securities exchanges and over-the-counter markets are the secondary markets for publicly traded securities. The regulation of these markets is discussed in chapter 14 *infra.*

6.　Secondary transactions are discussed in various sections throughout this treatise. *See, e.g.,* § 4.26 *infra.*

7.　Securities regulation describes the corporation or entity as the "issuer" of the securities. *See, e.g.,* section 2(a)(4) of the Securities Act of 1933, 15 U.S.C.A. § 77b(a)(4).

8.　*See, e.g.,* sections 9, 10, and 15 of the Securities Exchange Act of 1934, 15 U.S.C.A. §§ 78i, 78j, 78o, which are discussed in § 12.1 *infra.*

9.　*See* § 12.17 *infra.*

10.　*See, e.g.,* § 12.19 *infra.*

11.　*See, e.g.,* § 12.20 *infra.*

12.　*See* chapter 14 *infra* for discussion of broker-dealers and their regulation.

or informal systems of communication through which buyers and sellers make their interests known and consummate transactions. There are many different markets for securities.

Publicly held securities in the United States are traded both on formally centrally organized securities exchanges, which are operated as auction markets, and in the more loosely organized "over-the-counter" markets[13] which operated through a more fragmented "market maker" system.[14] The largest and most prestigious national securities exchange is the New York Stock Exchange which is followed both in size and in prestige by the American Stock Exchange.[15] Both of these national exchanges are recognized and regulated pursuant to section 6 of the Securities Exchange Act of 1934[16] and thus are subject to supervision and oversight by the Securities and Exchange Commission.[17] The exchanges, which are modeled on an auction system, provide investor protection through the minimum standards for securities as imposed by their listing requirements and also through their requirements for broker-dealer membership. Beyond the two national exchanges, there are seven other exchanges, many of them referred to as regional exchanges: the Boston Stock Exchange, the Chicago Board Options Exchange, the Cincinnati Stock Exchange, the Inter–Mountain Exchange, the Midwest Stock Exchange, the Pacific Stock Exchange, and the Philadelphia Stock Exchange.[18] A number of the stocks traded on some regional exchanges are also traded on the New York Stock Exchange. Commencing in the 1970s, some of the regional exchanges began to focus more on options than on equity securities.[19] The American Stock Exchange became active as a securities options market. The New York Stock Exchange subsequently began listing options as well. Although the physical floor of the exchange is in theory the focus of the auction process, technology has removed a significant number of transactions from the floor of the exchange to computers.

In 2000, the SEC approved the application of the International Securities Exchange to be registered as a national securities exchange.[20] The ISE is the first attempt to adapt the auctions system applicable to securities exchange to

---

13. The over-the-counter markets are operated under the aegis of the National Association of Securities Dealers (NASD). *See* § 14.3 *infra.*

14. Market makers are discussed in § 14.10 *infra.*

15. Although for a large part of its history the American Stock Exchange was generally considered the second most prestigious exchange, the overall prestige of the American Stock Exchange has yielded to the over-the-counter markets and, in particular, the National Market System and the National Association of Securities Dealers' Automated Quotation system (NASDAQ). In fact, a number of companies, particularly in technology related industries, which could qualify for listing on the New York Stock Exchange have elected to remain in the over-the-counter markets. Notwithstanding its apparently waning prestige in some circles, the American Stock Exchange, which as noted below, was acquired by the NASD, continues to list the securities of a number of well known companies, particularly those in energy-related industry.

16. 15 U.S.C.A. § 78f.

17. *Id. See* § 14.3 *infra* for a discussion of the markets' structure and regulation.

18. Prior to 1991, there was a tenth registered exchange; however, the Spokane Stock Exchange became a casualty of the SEC's increased enforcement efforts with regard to penny stocks. The SEC's penny stock rules are discussed in § 14.19 *infra.*

19. For discussion of the options markets *see* SEC, Report of the Special Study of the Options Markets, 96th Cong. 1st Sess. (1978). *See also* §§ 1.5, 1.7 *infra* for discussion of the explosion of stock options and other derivative investments.

20. Approval of Application for Exchange Registration International Securities Exchange LLC, SEC News Digest 2000–36, 2000 WL 218366 (S.E.C.) (SEC February 25, 2000).

an entirely electronic environment.[21] The number of registered securities exchanges is likely to increase even further. In 2001, the NASDAQ filed an application with the SEC to be recognized as a national securities exchange.[22] In 2006, the NASDAQ stock market became a registered national securities exchange. That same year, the New York Stock Exchange expanded its electronic order execution capabilities when it merged with Archipelago which had been one of the largest electronic communications networks (ECNs). Subsequently, the NYSE expanded internationally with its move to merge with Euronext, a major offshore trading facility. Also, as a result of the Commodity Futures Modernization Act of 2000,[23] there are likely to be new exchanges recognized for the limited purpose of trading securities futures products.[24]

The largest number of issuers have their securities traded on the over-the-counter markets although exchange listed securities generally have greater trading volume or turnover. In the 1980s and 1990s, the over-the-counter markets, especially through the National Association of Securities Dealers' National Market System,[25] have become a much more serious factor in United States capital markets. Unlike the national exchanges, the over-the-counter markets merely provide a forum for brokers and dealers to arrange their own securities trades. Much of the trading on over-the-counter markets has been facilitated by the National Association of Securities Dealers Automated Quotation System (NASDAQ). In addition to the automated quotation system, the most frequently traded over-the-counter stocks are listed in the national market system which has many attributes of a securities exchange.[26] As is the case with the NASDAQ, the national market system is operated under the supervision of the National Association of Securities Dealers. A number of smaller over-the-counter companies listed in NASDAQ which do not qualify for the national market system have their securities listed in the NASDAQ small capitalization system.[27] Less frequently traded and many low priced

---

21. *See* Notice of Filing of Proposed Rule Change by the International Securities Exchange LLC, 66 FR 36353–01, 2001 WL 768983 (F.R.) (SEC July 11, 2001); Commission Grants ISE Exemption to Accommodate its Electronic Market in the Marketwide Data System, SEC News Digest 2000–101, 2000 WL 681095 (S.E.C.) (SEC May 26, 2000).

22. Fed. Sec. L. Rep. (CCH) Report Bulletin No. 1981 p. 4 (June 13, 2001).

23. Pub. Law 106–554, 114 Stat. 2763 (December 21, 2000).

24. *See* Registration of National Securities Exchanges Pursuant to Section 6(g) of the Securities Exchange Act of 1934 and Proposed Rule Changes of National Securities Exchanges and Limited Purpose National Securities Associations, Sec. Exch. Act Rel. No. 34–44279 2001 WL 491727 (SEC May 8, 2001).

25. Although NASDAQ is may be referred to in some circles as an exchange, it is not a national securities exchange within the meaning of the securities laws. Fezzani v. Bear, Stearns & Co., Inc., 384 F.Supp.2d 618 (S.D.N.Y.2004) ("Section 9 prohibits certain acts of manipulation with regard to securities traded on a national securities exchange. *See* 15 U.S.C. § 78i(a). Here, the complaint alleges that the manipulated securities were traded through the National Association of Securities Dealers Automated Quotations System ("NASDAQ"). This is the only allegation regarding the markets on which the manipulated securities were traded. NASDAQ has been held not to be a national securities exchange within the meaning of section 9") *See* Connolly, 763 F.Supp. at 12 n. 4; Martin v. Prudential–Bache Secs., Inc., 820 F.Supp. 980, 983–84 (W.D.N.C. 1991); Cowen & Co. v. Merriam, 745 F.Supp. 925, 930–31 (S.D.N.Y.1990); Cammer v. Bloom, 711 F.Supp. 1264, 1277 n. 18 (D.N.J.1989); Garvin v. Blinder Robinson & Co., 115 F.R.D. 318, 320 n. 3 (E.D.Pa.1987).

26. The NASD's national market system is discussed in § 14.2 *infra.*

27. In an attempt to remain competitive with NASDAQ, the American Stock Exchange created a two-tiered market by relaxing some of its listing requirements for qualifying smaller capitalization companies. This second tier is known as AMEX emerging issues. Under the new

over-the-counter securities used to be relegated to the "pink sheets" which were lists of quotations that were circulated daily. Today, technological advancements have led to listing these "pink sheet" securities on an electronic bulletin board.

The National Association of Securities Dealers (NASD) is a self-regulatory organization which is organized and governed under the oversight of the Securities and Exchange Commission pursuant to section 15 of the Securities Exchange Act of 1934.[28] Following up on what had become a growing concern, in the 1980's there was a concerted movement towards a consolidated, national market system which would replace the current exchange system.[29] Although there have been proposals, there has not been a consolidation of the national exchanges with the over-the-counter markets. There has been some limited movement in this direction as there is now off-exchange trading in many listed securities. In light of the power and prestige of the leading national exchanges, it is unlikely that they will disappear. On the other hand, it is clear that the expansion of the NASD's national market has become an increasingly important factor in the American securities markets. These markets have become the home of many of the more glamorous "go-go" high technology stock issues. In fact, in many newspapers today, the NASDAQ stock listings are given more prominence than the previously more prestigious American Stock Exchange.

The operation of the market place, whether through a centralized national exchange or the over-the-counter markets, is dependent on the broker-dealer industry. The stock exchanges limit access to their trading floor to members who have purchased "seats" on the exchange. The exchanges have rules and regulations covering the conduct of member brokers and dealers, including minimum capital requirements. These rules are designed to increase public trust and strengthen the integrity of the market place. Similarly, the National Association of Securities Dealers has membership requirements and regulatory rules of conduct. The Securities and Exchange Commission regulates broker-dealers directly as well as indirectly through its oversight responsibilities for the exchange rules and National Association of Securities Dealers. This oversight responsibility extends to the self-policing activities of the securities exchanges and the NASD. Securities regulation thus consists not only of direct SEC involvement but also a massive self-regulatory system operating under SEC oversight.

As noted above, since the early 1970s, from time to time there has been increasing movement toward establishing a truly national market system.[30] The development of a true national market system would avoid variations among the national and various regional exchanges in the quotation of securities. Also, it was believed by some observers that a true national market system would greatly save on the "paper crunch" and would provide a more

listing criteria, the AMEX provided an exchange-based auction marketplace for smaller companies that were not able to meet the exchange's more rigorous first-tier listing criteria. *See* Creation of New AMEX Marketplace for Smaller Companies Approved by SEC, 24 Sec.Reg. & L.Rep. (BNA) 295 (March 6, 1992); William Power & Herb Block, Amex's New Home for "Start–Ups" Wins SEC Nod, Wall.St.J. p. C1 (March 6, 1992). The Amex is discontinuing this second tier. See Wall St.J. p. C11 (May 12, 1995).

28. 15 U.S.C.A. § 78*o*.

29. *See* § 14.2 *infra.*

30. The statutory concept of a national market system is not the same thing as the NASD's National Market System which lists its most widely traded over-the-counter securities.

efficient exchange mechanism. Technological advancements generally, and increased computer capability in particular, have paved the way for more efficient markets both on the exchanges and through the NASD's over-the-counter facilities. These increased efficiencies, although accomplishing some of the goals urged by proponents of a national market system, exist in the continuing environments of multiple securities markets. Regulation of the securities markets and the broker-dealers operating in these markets is discussed in a subsequent chapter.[31]

§ 1.1[3] The Securities Industry[32]

The securities industry is characterized by great diversity, both in size and function. There are several thousand firms engaged in one or more types of securities activities, ranging from large multi-service firms engaged in brokerage, market-making, underwriting, investment advice, and fund management, as well as commodities, real estate dealings, and a variety of other financial services including banking and insurance. There also are small or even one-person firms engaged solely in selling mutual fund shares or dealing in a few securities of local or regional interest.

From the passage in 1933 of the former Glass–Steagall Act,[33] which prohibited banks from dealing in securities (except government bonds), the securities industry consisted of a relatively separate and well-defined group of firms. However, with the increasing tendency for individuals to make their equity investments indirectly through institutions, rather than trading directly in stock for their own account, securities firms came increasingly into competition with banks, insurance companies, and other financial institutions. At the same time that securities firms began offering their customers an increasing number of financial services that traditionally had been associated with commercial banking, commercial banks entered into many areas that formerly were reserved for investment bankers and securities firms. This competition placed severe strains on the existing regulatory structure under which securities firms, banks, and insurance companies are regulated by different agencies with entirely different concerns and approaches. In 1999, Congress repealed Glass–Steagall[34] and paved the way for even more competition among and between financial institutions that can now offer a wide variety of financial services to their customers.

§ 1.1[4] The Regulatory System[35]

In addition to regulation of the securities markets, the federal securities laws regulate the companies issuing securities ("issuers"[36]) as well as purchasers and sellers of securities. Securities trading activities can be divided into

---

31. *See* chapter 14 *infra.*

32. This subsection is adapted from David L. Ratner & Thomas Lee Hazen, Securities Regulation: Cases and Materials 3–4 (5th ed. 1996).

33. The Banking Act of 1933, Ch. 89, 48 Stat. 184 (1933), codified in various sections of 12 U.S.C.A. (1999) *See* in particular 12 U.S.C.A. §§ 24, 378(a) (1999).

34. The Glass–Steagall Act was repealed by Pub. Law. 106–102, 1999 U.S.C.C.A.N. (113 Stat.) 1338. *See generally* Symposium, 4 N.C. Banking Inst. 1 (2000); Michael K. O'Neal, Summary and Analysis of the Gramm–Leach–Bliley Act, 28 Sec. Reg. L.J. 95 (2000).

35. *See also* § 1.2 *infra.* For discussion of the impact of the regulatory system on the applicability of the antitrust laws, *see* § 14.1[9] *infra.*

36. Section 2(a)(4) of the 1933 Act defines "issuer". 15 U.S.C.A. § 77b(a)(4). *See* § 4.26[1] *infra.*

two basic subgroups. Most of the day-to-day trading on both the securities exchanges and over-the-counter markets consists of "secondary" transactions between investors and involve securities that have previously been issued by the corporation or other issuer. All of the proceeds from these secondary sales, after applicable commissions to the securities brokers handling the transaction, go to the investors who are parting with their securities. None of these proceeds from secondary transactions in the securities markets flow back to the companies issuing the securities. This aspect of the secondary securities markets is frequently referred to as "trading" (as opposed to "distribution" of securities) and is regulated primarily by the provisions of the Securities and Exchange Act of 1934.[37] The regulation of the securities trading markets is termed market regulation.

The process by which securities are first offered to the public, frequently referred to as primary offerings or distributions, is governed primarily by the Securities Act of 1933.[38] This is the way in which corporate capital is raised in the public equity markets. Also covered by the Securities Act of 1933 and included within the concept of securities distributions are so-called secondary "distributions"[39] which occur, for example, when an extremely large block of securities has been placed in the hands of a private investor, institution, or group of investors and is subsequently offered by the selling shareholders to the members of the general public. As is the case with secondary transactions generally, the proceeds from secondary distributions inure to the benefit of the selling shareholder(s). In the case of both primary and secondary distributions,[40] unless an appropriate exemption is applicable, registration of the securities will be required under the Securities Act of 1933.[41] This, then, is the focus of the 1933 Act: initial public offerings, primary, and secondary distributions of securities; although some selected provisions of the Act apply to more private, non-open-market transactions. Whereas the distribution process triggers the registration provisions of the 1933 Act, for the most part the extent to which securities are widely held and actively traded triggers the jurisdictional requirements of the Securities Exchange Act of 1934.[42] Registration and periodic reporting by issuers under the 1934 Exchange Act depend generally upon the degree to which the securities are widely held.[43]

In addition to the securities markets, investors may look to the various commodities and derivatives markets and the trading of commodity futures.

---

37. 15 U.S.C.A. § 78a *et seq.*

38. 15 U.S.C.A. § 77a *et seq.*

39. In contrast to the secondary trading that takes place in the securities markets on a daily basis.

40. Primary and secondary distributions can occur as separate transactions or can be "piggy backed" into one registered offering. It is not uncommon for an offering to be a combination of a primary and secondary distribution. *Cf.* Moffat v. Harcourt Brace & Co., 892 F.Supp. 1431 (M.D.Fla.1994) (issuer's delay in applying for registration did not violate agreement with holder of "piggy back" registration rights).

41. *See* chapters 2, 3 *infra.*

42. An important exception is found in the general antifraud Rule 10b–5, 17 C.F.R. § 240.10b–5, the reach of which extends to purchases or sales of any securities where the facilities of interstate commerce are implicated. Rule 10b–5 and the implied private right of action thereunder are discussed in chapter 12 *infra.* In addition to Rule 10b–5, the general antifraud proscription in connection with tender offers, section 14(e), is not limited to companies subject to the 1934 Act's registration and periodic reporting requirements. 15 U.S.C.A. § 78n(e), which is discussed in § 11.6 *infra.*

43. *See* § 9.2–9.3 *infra.*

At one time, the commodities markets were limited to agricultural and other tangible commodities such as precious metals and fossil fuels. Today, more than seventy percent of all commodity futures transactions involve financial futures. There thus has developed a wide range of overlapping or hybrid investments that have attributes of both commodities and securities. Although there have been a number of jurisdictional disputes,[44] the commodities futures markets generally are regulated by the Commodity Futures Trading Commission pursuant to the Commodity Exchange Act.[45] Beginning in the 1970s and carrying through the 1980s and 1990s, the futures and commodity options markets regulated by the CFTC and the options markets regulated by the SEC have become increasingly competitive with the increased trading in derivative financial instruments, including treasury bill, foreign currency and stock index futures (as compared, for example, with the trading of stock index and foreign currency options).[46] Options on securities are regulated by the SEC, but futures and commodity options (including options on futures) are not subject to SEC regulation[47] but rather are left to the Commodity Futures Trading Commission.[48]

A technological development that has caused significant regulatory concern and concern about abuses has been the emergence of the use of the Internet for securities trading. For example, in the mid 1990s, an increasing number of small companies began to make a market for their own shares through the facilities of the Internet.[50] The SEC seriously questioned this unregulated online offering of securities and put a halt to the activities of a small brewery. However, after negotiations with the company, the Commission permitted online trading to resume with certain safeguards. Additionally, the Commission subsequently issued a No Action Letter permitting a company to make a market in its own shares using the Internet.[51] A collateral consequence of some Internet offerings has been raising money that in turn was invested in securities of other companies, thus subjecting the company undertaking the Internet offering to the provisions of the Investment Company Act of 1940.[52] The potential of becoming an inadvertent investment company, of course, is not limited to securities offered over the Internet.[53]

The SEC also became concerned about companies relying on the 1933 Act

---

44. For example, one area of current dispute is whether managed commodities accounts are securities. *See* § 1.7 *infra*.

45. 7 U.S.C.A. § 1–24. *See generally* Philip M. Johnson & Thomas L. Hazen, Derivatives Regulation (2004); Commodities Futures L.Rep. (CCH).

46. Although the form of a futures contract may differ from a listed option, their operational effect and investment strategies are very similar, if not identical, when dealing with financial options and futures.

47. In a controversial ruling, the SEC granted securities exchanges' applications to list index participation units which have some characteristics of futures but were found to be securities. Sec. Exch. Act Rel. No. 34–26709 (April 11, 1989). *See* §§ 1.5, 1.7 *infra*.

48. *See generally* Philip M. Johnson & Thomas L. Hazen, Derivatives Regulation (2004).

50. *E.g.,* StockPower, Inc., [1998 Transfer Binder] Fed. Sec. L. Rep. (CCH) ¶ 77,479 (SEC No Action Letter Nov. 3, 1998) (company could post company-sponsored direct stock purchase plan on the Internet); Terzah Ewing, Online, From New York, Those Dusty Pink Sheets Are Taking Their Obscure Stocks to the Internet, Wall St. J. C1 (Sept. 2, 1999).

51. Real Goods Trading Corp., 1996 WL 422670, 28 Sec. Reg. & L. Rep. (BNA) 850 (SEC No Action Letter June 25, 1996).

52. 15 U.S.C.A. §§ 80a–1 through 80a–52. *See* chapter 20 *infra*.

53. Inadvertent investment companies are discussed in § 20.3 *infra*.

registration exemption provided by Rule 504[54] as a vehicle for effecting a public distribution of securities via the Internet without registration under the Securities Act of 1933.[55] A pattern emerged whereby companies would issue stock on the Internet and then provide a bulletin board or other online trading vehicle whereby initial purchasers could sell their shares to other investors. Frequently, these unregistered offerings were accompanied by a good deal of sales hype about the newly issued securities. In large part as a response to these so-called "pump and dump" schemes, the SEC amended Rule 504's exemption from registration to prohibit a general solicitation and to impose restrictions on resale unless the securities are registered under state law or issued under a state law exemption permitting a general solicitation.[56]

Of course, securities fraud over the Internet is actionable under the securities laws.[57] The use of the Internet has also raised international implications as well. Specifically, the SEC is concerned about website offerings that are intended to remain offshore but may reach United States residents.[58]

The foregoing description sets forth a few representative examples of the impact of the Internet. Internet-related issues are considered throughout this treatise in connection with the types of conduct that implicate the securities laws.

§ 1.2 History, Scope, and Coverage of Federal and State Securities Regulatory Schemes

§ 1.2[1] The Antecedents of Securities Regulation in the United States

As pointed out in the preceding section of this treatise,[1] securities are complex investment instruments that differ significantly from other things that are traded in commerce to the extent that securities are intangible and are neither produced nor consumed. Additionally, in large part because of their very nature, securities and the securities markets have been particularly susceptible to fraud and manipulation. The various laws that regulate securities transactions have been designed to address this susceptibility. These laws have a rich history and predate regulation in the United States.

---

54. 17 C.F.R. § 230.504; *see* § 4.21 *infra*.

55. *See* Sec. Act Rel. No. 33–7644 (SEC Feb. 25, 1999).

56. Rule 504(b)(1), 17 C.F.R. § 230.504(b)(1). While the Internet can still be used for exempt offerings of securities, the ability to create a public secondary market without registration has been severely limited, if not eliminated.

57. *See, e.g.,* SEC v. Western Executive Group, Inc., 28 Sec. Reg. & L. Rep. (BNA) 1343 (C.D.Cal.1996) (granting preliminary injunction); Robert A. Prentice, The Future of Corporate Disclosure: The Internet, Securities Fraud, and Rule 10b–5, 47 Emory L.J. 1 (1998); Comment, Securities Fraud Over the Internet: The Flies in the Ointment and the Hope of Fly Paper, 30 Case Wes. Res. J. Int'l L. 489 (1998); SEC Files Civil Fraud Complaint Against Internet Stock Touting Operation, 32 Sec. Reg. & L. Rep. (BNA) 7 (Jan. 10, 2000).

58. *See* Statement of the Commission Regarding Use of Internet Websites to Offer Securities, Solicit Securities Transactions or Advertise Investment Services Offshore, International Series Release No. 1125, Sec. Act Rel. No. 33–7516, 1998 WL 135626 (F.R.) (SEC March 27, 1998). The SEC Release suggests a disclaimer that the website offering is not available to United States residents, and further, that there be some procedures to assure that offers are not made to United States residents.

§ 1.2

1. *See* § 1.1[1] *supra*.

The regulation of securities transactions began with the regulation of the dealers in securities. Over time the regulation expanded to cover the companies issuing the securities as well as the market place itself. Today there is widespread regulation of all aspects of securities transactions and the market place.

Regulation of securities brokers dates back to the thirteenth century. This early regulation authorized licensing securities brokers in London.[2] Stock exchange dealings, with speculation subject to alternate booms and panics, became a part of the English markets in the latter part of the seventeenth century. Trading in shares of stock led to periods of speculation and wild fluctuations in the market.[3] This was followed by English legislation by the end of the seventeenth century, which was enacted to protect investors against unscrupulous manipulation by stock jobbers and stock brokers.[5] Investment schemes throughout Europe led to many frauds including the infamous South Sea Bubble.[6]

The South Sea Company was one of the arch speculators in, and manipulators of, its own shares.[7] These manipulations eventually caused a great increase in the market price of its shares. The huge increase in the price of South Sea Company shares led to a tremendous wave of company promotions and to speculation in the securities of newly formed companies. On one day, for example, one thousand persons subscribed to shares in a company "for carrying on an undertaking of great importance, but nobody to know what it is."[8] In 1719, the South Sea Company launched an ambitious program to persuade investors holding government bonds and annuities to exchange them for shares of its stock. To make some funds available for speculation in its shares and to check the floatation of new companies competing for public funds, the South Sea Company inspired passage of the Bubble Act of 1720.[9] The purported objective of the Bubble Act was to prevent unwary persons from investing in fraudulent projects or undertakings. It prohibited unincorporated companies from acting as though they were corporate bodies or pretending that their shares were transferable. The South Sea Company and certain other existing companies were exempted from its prohibitions. The Bubble Act was not well drafted and failed to define clearly the practices and offenses it sought to prevent.[10] The Bubble Act was eventually repealed in 1825.[11]

---

2. Statute of Edward I, in 1285. *See* S. Killik, The Work of the Stock Exchange 12 (2d ed. 1934); 1 Louis Loss & Joel Seligman, Securities Regulation § 1–A (3d ed. 1989).

3. Promoters of both incorporated and unincorporated companies foisted doubtful schemes on the investing public. *See* 1 James D. Cox & Thomas Lee Hazen, Cox & Hazen on Corporations § 2.2 (2d ed. 2002).

5. 8 & 9 Wm. 3, ch. 32 (1697) ("An act to restrain the number and ill practice of brokers and stock jobbers"); *see* Lane, The Years Before the Stock Exchange, 7 Hist. Today 760, 761 (1957); 1 Louis Loss & Joel Seligman, Securities Regulation § 1–A (3d ed. 1989).

6. *See* 1 Louis Loss & Joel Seligman, Securities Regulation § 1–A (3d ed. 1989).

7. This paragraph is adapted from 1 James D. Cox, Thomas Lee Hazen & F. Hodge O'Neal, Corporation § 2.2 (2000).

8. William Searle Holdsworth, A History of English Law 214–215 (5th ed. 1942); Leslie W. Melville, South Sea Bubble 97 (1921). *See also* John Carswell, The South Sea Bubble (1960); Virginia Cowles, The Great Swindle: The Story of the South Sea Bubble (1960).

9. 6 Geo. I, ch. 18. 2 Wood's Collyer on the Law of Partnership §§ 826, 827 at 1200, 1203 (Horace G. Wood ed. 1878).

10. The Bubble Act was a product of haste and self-interest. This ambiguous and incoherent legislation long caused great uncertainty and confusion and raised unnecessary doubts about the validity of the issuance of transferable shares by legitimate unincorporated companies. *See* 1 James D. Cox & Thomas Lee Hazen, Cox & Hazen on Corporations § 2.2 (2d ed. 2002).

11. 6 Geo. 4, ch. 91. *See* A. Dubois, The English Business Company after the Bubble Act 1720–1800 (1938).

The Joint Stock Companies Registration Act of 1844,[12] entitled "An Act for the Registration, Incorporation, and Regulation of Joint Stock Companies," was the first general companies act under which a joint stock company could become incorporated in England.[13] The Companies Act of 1844 also enacted the first modern prospectus requirement.[14] And one of its descendants formed the basis for legislation in the United States.[15] As discussed in the next subsection of this treatise,[16] securities regulation in the United States began with the states.[17] This was followed twenty-six years later with the enactment of this nation's first federal regulation of securities transactions.

The first federal securities regulation was contained in the Securities Act of 1933 which grew out of the New Deal. The initial push for regulation in this country started years earlier in reaction to the Panic of 1907. In October 1907:

> depositors lost confidence in several New York banks which were thought to be part of a group of stock market operators who met with financial ruin when they failed to corner the market in the stock of a copper mining company they controlled. Prices on the New York Stock Exchange fell precipitously, and the bank run spread. By the time confidence was restored, the country was in a recession, many banks had closed, and many small investors had been ruined. Before long, many people came to believe that stock market operators who stood to profit from lower stock prices had engineered the price collapse. Believing that the price collapse precipitated widespread panic across the economy, these people demanded that the government intervene.
>
> In January 1908, President Theodore Roosevelt informed Congress that it would be desirable to adopt measures "to prevent at least the grosser forms of gambling in securities and commodities, such as making large sales of what men do not possess and 'cornering' the market."[18]

---

12. 7 & 8 Vict., ch. 110.

13. "Joint stock company" was defined as a commercial partnership with more than 25 members or with capital divided into freely transferable shares. The 1844 Act compelled such companies to incorporate by registering their names, addresses, and purposes, and granted registered companies the corporate privilege of suing and being sued as entities. A company's members, however, remained subject to unlimited liability and could not absolve themselves from such liability to third parties even by provisions in their agreement of organization. *See* 1 James D. Cox & Thomas Lee Hazen, Cox & Hazen on Corporations § 2.2 (2d ed. 2002).

14. 7 & 8 Vict., ch. 110. *See* 1 Louis Loss & Joel Seligman, Securities Regulation § 1–A (3d ed. 1989).

15. The definition of prospectus in the Securities Act of 1933 (1933 Act § 2(a)(10), 15 U.S.C.A. § 77b(a)(10)) was patterned on the British Companies Act of 1929. *See* Gustafson v. Alloyd Co., 513 U.S. 561, 599–600, 115 S.Ct. 1061, 131 L.Ed.2d 1 (1995) (Ginsburg, J., dissenting).

16. *See* § 1.2[2] *infra*.

17. Kans.Laws 1911, c. 133. Selective regulation predated the Kansas enactment. Some more limited securities regulation existed before the Kansas statute. For example, in 1852 Massachusetts was regulating securities issued by common carriers. *See* Harry G. Henn & John R. Alexander, Laws of Corporations 843 (3d ed. 1983).

State securities regulation was challenged as beyond the power of the states but was held to be constitutional as a valid use of police power of the states to protect the public against "speculative schemes." Hall v. Geiger–Jones Co., 242 U.S. 539, 550, 37 S.Ct. 217, 220, 61 L.Ed. 480 (1917).

18. Steve Thel, The Original Conception of Section 10(b) of the Securities Exchange Act, 42 Stan. L. Rev. 385, 395–396 (1990).

As pointed out above, the roots of the Securities Act of 1933 predated these events. The 1933 Act borrowed heavily from regulation that was adopted in England.[19] Federal securities regulation in the United States followed state regulation of securities[20] and several centuries of legislation in England. It has thus been observed that "the problems at which modern securities regulation is directed are as old as the cupidity of sellers and the gullibility of buyers."[21]

The discussion that follows provides an overview of the development of state[22] and federal[23] securities regulation in the United States. This is followed by an overview of the federal agency that is charged with administering the federal securities laws—the Securities and Exchange Commission[24]

§ 1.2[2] The Regulatory Era Begins—State Securities Laws

Beginning in the late nineteenth century, industrialists located primarily in the eastern part of the United States found fertile ground for securities in the developing American frontier. There were many questionable promotional practices and, as a consequence, pressures arose to regulate the marketing of fraudulently valued securities. Accordingly, in 1911, Kansas passed the first state securities statutory regulatory scheme. This, like subsequent securities legislation in other states, has come to be known as a "blue sky law."

There are a number of explanations for the derivation of the "blue sky" appellation, the most common of which was because of the Kansas statute's purpose to protect the Kansas farmers against the industrialists selling them a piece of the blue sky. A number of states followed suit and blue sky laws began to spring up throughout the country. Today, all states have blue sky legislation.

As enacted, the state blue sky laws not only focused on providing investors with full disclosure of relevant facts, but also required that all securities registered thereunder "qualify" on a merit basis, evaluating the substantive terms of the securities to be offered. Blue sky laws continue to retain this dual regulatory focus. In order to rule on the merits of such investments, the state securities commissioner or administrator typically was given the power to determine whether the securities were suitable for sale. Notwithstanding the broad regulatory potential of the merit approach, the blue sky laws proved to be relatively ineffective in stamping out securities frauds, especially on a national level.[26] Following enactment of the early state securities laws, federal legislation was successfully resisted for a while. However, the stock market crash of 1929 is properly described as the straw that

---

19. *See, e.g.,* Stuart Banner, Anglo–American Securities Regulation: Cultural and Political Roots, 1690–1860 (1998); Paul G. Mahoney, Essay and Review: The Pernicious Art of Securities Regulation, 66 U. Chi. L. Rev. 1373 (1999).

20. *See* § 1.2[2] *infra.* State laws are also discussed in chapter 8 *infra.*

21. 1 Louis Loss & Joel Seligman, Securities Regulation § 1–A (3d ed. 1989). *See also, e.g.,* J. Carswell, The South Sea Bubble (1960); J. Francis, History of the Bank of England, Its Times and Traditions ch. 8 (1862); L. Melville, The South Sea Bubble viii (1921).

22. *See* § 1.1[2] *infra.*

23. *See* § 1.1[3] *infra.*

24. *See* §§ 1.3–1.4 *infra.* For more detail, *see* chapter 16 *infra.*

26. Although such a merit analysis exists in many states in limited form, it has not had a significant impact in eliminating unduly speculative securities from the public markets.

broke the camel's back. The era that followed ushered in federal securities regulation.[27]

The scope of state blue sky laws was significantly curtailed in 1996 with the enactment of the National Securities Markets Improvement Act of 1996.[28] These 1996 amendments to the federal securities laws reversed the pattern established under the first sixty-three years of federal securities regulation of concurrent state and federal regulation. The former regime of concurrent state and federal regulation was narrowed since the 1996 amendments explicitly preempted state law in many areas of securities regulation.[29] Particularly affected were the registration and reporting requirements applicable to securities transactions. State regulation of broker-dealers[30] and investment advisers[31] was also curtailed. The National Securities Markets Improvement Act preempts the states from imposing the specified regulatory provisions but does not preclude state law fraud actions.[32] In contrast, the Securities Litigation Uniform Standards Act of 1998 preempts certain securities fraud class actions involving publicly traded securities.[33]

§ 1.2[3] The New Deal and Federal Regulation

Although the general economic conditions played a considerable role leading up to the Wall Street crash of 1929, the number of fraudulently floated securities that contributed to the great crash should not be underestimated. In fact, the congressional hearings which culminated in the first federal securities legislation are replete with examples of outrageous conduct by securities promoters that most certainly had a disastrous impact on our nation's economy. In relatively short order, Congress entered into the regulatory arena with its first major New Deal legislation–the Securities Act of 1933, which became known as the "Truth in Securities" Act.[34] The federal legislation, which has been characterized as the first true consumer protection law,[35] contained many of the features of state blue sky laws, except that it did not (and, as amended, still does not) establish a system of merit regulation. Instead, under the guidance of a federal agency, the Act focuses on disclosure. The focus on disclosure was based on the conclusion that sunlight is the best disinfectant.[36] At the time of enactment, the 1933 Act was administered by the Federal Trade Commission. The FTC's securities law jurisdiction was replaced

---

27. *See* § 1.2[3] *infra.*

28. Pub. L. No. 104–290, 110 Stat. 3416 (1996). *See, e.g.,* Symposium, The National Securities Markets Improvements Act–One Year Later, 53 Bus. Law. 507 (1998); Comment, The National Securities Market Improvement Act: How Improved is the Securities Market?, 36 Duq. L. Rev. 365 (1998).

29. The preemptive legislation is discussed throughout this treatise. *See* in particular the discussion in § 8.1[2] *infra.*

30. Broker-dealer regulation is discussed in chapter 14 *infra.*

31. Investment adviser regulation is discussed in chapter 21 *infra.*

32. Zuri–Invest AG v. Natwest Finance Inc., 177 F.Supp.2d 189 (S.D.N.Y.2001).

33. *See* §§ *7.17[2], 12.15[2]* infra.

34. 15 U.S.C.A. § 77a–77aa; Milton H. Cohen, "Truth in Securities" Revisited, 79 Harv. L.Rev. 1340 (1966). *See generally* Francis Pecora, Wall Street Under Oath (1939).

35. In fact, when he signed the bill into law, President Franklin Roosevelt observed that this nation was moving from a period of *caveat emptor* into one of *caveat vendor.*

36. This is the oft-cited phrase of Louis D. Brandeis. Louis D. Brandeis, Other People's Money ch. 5 (1914) ("sunlight is said to be the best of disinfectants; electric light the most efficient policeman").

in 1934 with the creation of the Securities and Exchange Commission.[37] The 1933 Act quite properly has been characterized as a great success in balancing the needs of investors and the public generally against the desire to maintain free and efficient markets.[38]

§ 1.2[3][A] The Securities Act of 1933

The Securities Act of 1933, as noted in the preceding section, is directed primarily at the distribution of securities. Subject to certain enumerated exemptions, the 1933 Act generally requires the registration of all securities being placed in the hands of the public for the first time, regardless of whether this is accomplished through a primary or secondary offering.[39] After considerable debate, Congress decided not to follow the pattern of the state acts and eschewed the idea of a merit approach, opting instead for a system of full disclosure. The theory behind the federal regulatory framework is that investors are adequately protected if all relevant aspects of the securities being marketed are fully and fairly disclosed. The reasoning is that full disclosure provides investors with sufficient opportunity to evaluate the merits of an investment and fend for themselves. It is a basic tenet of federal securities regulation that investors' ability to make their own evaluations of available investments obviates any need that some observers may perceive for the more costly and time-consuming governmental merit analysis of the securities being offered.

The Securities Act of 1933 contains a number of private remedies for investors who are injured due to violations of the Act.[40] There are also general antifraud provisions which bar material omissions and misrepresentations in connection with the offer or sale of securities.[41] The scope of the Securities Act of 1933 is limited; first, insofar as its registration and disclosure provisions cover only distributions of securities and second, as its investor-protection reach extends only to purchasers (and not sellers) of securities.

§ 1.2[3][B] The Securities Exchange Act of 1934

In 1934, Congress enacted the Securities Exchange Act of 1934 which is a more omnibus regulation. The Securities Exchange Act of 1934 is referred to alternatively as the 1934 Act or as the Exchange Act. The extent of the regulation introduced by the Exchange Act was so vast that Congress felt it was not possible to continue overburdening the Federal Trade Commission with this new administrative responsibility and thus established the Securities and Exchange Commission which is now one of the most influential and

---

37. The organization and operation of the Securities and Exchange Commission is discussed in §§ 1.2[3][C], 1.3,–1.4, and chapter 16 *infra*.

38. *See, e.g.,* Paul G. Mahoney, The Political Economy of the Securities Act of 1933, 30 J. Leg. Stud. 1, 31 (2001) ("The Securities Act accordingly provides a useful cautionary tale about the efficacy of economic regulation. The act is generally regarded as one of the greatest success stories of the New Deal. Unlike many regulatory statutes, it has been largely untouched by claims that it raises entry barriers or enforces cartel agreements among members of the regulated industry").

39. *See* chapters 2, 3 *infra.* This includes not only primary distributions (sold by the issuer), but also secondary distributions wherein the securities are sold by individuals or institutions who did not acquire the securities in a public offering. *See* §§ 4.26–4.28 *infra*.

40. These are: section 11, 15 U.S.C.A. § 77k, for material misstatements and omissions in registration statements; section 12(a)(1), 15 U.S.C.A. § 77*l*(a)(1), for securities sold in violation of the registration requirements, and section 12(a)(2), 15 U.S.C.A. § 77*l*(a)(2), creating an action by purchasers against their sellers for material misstatements or omissions. *See* §§ 7.2, 7.6 *infra*.

41. Section 17(a), 15 U.S.C.A. § 77q(a). *See* § 7.11[1] *infra*.

well respected federal agencies, although it is relatively modest in size. The Securities Exchange Act of 1934 is directed at regulating all aspects of public trading of securities.[43] The Act does not focus only on securities, their issuers,[44] purchasers, and sellers;[45] it also regulates the marketplace, including the exchanges, the over-the-counter markets, and broker-dealers generally.[46]

In terms of its investor-protection thrust, the Securities Exchange Act of 1934 has a much broader reach than the Securities Act of 1933. To begin with, the 1934 Act's protections extend to sellers as well as purchasers of securities. There are two distinct jurisdictional triggers for the 1934 Act's investor-protection provisions. First, the 1934 Act contains a general provision that bars fraud and material misstatements or omissions of material facts in connection with any purchase or sale of security.[47] The only jurisdictional limitation on this provision is that there must be the use of an instrumentality of interstate commerce.[48] Although these general antifraud proscriptions have a broad reach, the vast majority of the 1934 Act's regulation of securities issuers derives from the second jurisdictional trigger that is found in the Act's periodic reporting and disclosure requirements which emanate primarily from the fact that securities traded on a national exchange (and now most of those traded in the over-the-counter markets) must be registered with the Securities and Exchange Commission.[49]

Registration of a company's securities under the Exchange Act involves full disclosure of the company's business, financial position, and management as well as numerous periodic reporting requirements.[50] The Exchange Act also includes special provisions dealing with stock manipulation,[51] improper trading while in possession of non-public material information,[52] insider short swing profits,[53] and misstatements in documents filed with the Securities and Exchange Commission.[54] Further, because of the importance of shareholder suffrage in public issue corporations, Congress included regulation of the proxy machinery of all publicly traded corporations that are subject to the Act's reporting requirements.[55] Most of the foregoing provisions have been part of the regulatory scheme since the Act's inception in 1934. Subsequently,

---

43. For discussion of the impact of securities regulation on the antitrust laws application to securities transactions, *see* § 14.1[9] *infra.*

44. *See* Chapter 9 *infra. See also* chapters 10 (proxy regulation), Chapter 11 (takeovers and tender offers), and Chapter 13 (insider reporting and short-swing profits) *infra.*

45. *See* chapter 12 *infra.*

46. *See* chapter 14 *infra.*

47. Section 10(b), 15 U.S.C.A. § 78j(b). Most notable is Rule 10b–5 promulgated thereunder. 17 C.F.R. § 240.10b–5. *See* §§ 12.3, 12.4 *infra.*

48. The interstate commerce requirement has been broadly construed so as to make it highly doubtful that a case will ever be dismissed on the absence of this jurisdictional basis. *See* § 17.2 *infra.*

49. For purposes of the Act, the regional exchanges are regulated as national exchanges. *See* chapters 9, 14 *infra.* There is a class of securities which although not registered under the 1934 Act, are subject to the periodic reporting requirements. *See* § 9.3 *infra.*

50. *See* §§ 9.2, 9.3 *infra.*

51. Section 9, 15 U.S.C.A. § 78i; § 12.1 *infra.*

52. In addition to Rules 10b–5 and 14e–3, 17 C.F.R. §§ 240.10b–5, 240.14e–3, *see, e.g.,* sections 20A and 21(d)(2)(A), 15 U.S.C.A. § 78t–1, 78u(d)(2)(A). For a discussion of insider trading *see* § 12.17 *infra.*

53. Section 16(b), 15 U.S.C.A. § 78p(b); §§ 13.2–13.4 *infra.*

54. Section 18(a), 15 U.S.C.A. § 78r(a); § 12.19 *infra.*

55. Sections 14(a)-(c), 15 U.S.C.A. § 78n(a)-(c); chapter 10 *infra.*

in 1968, Congress added the Williams Act Amendments which impose candid disclosure and reporting requirements on tender offers and on other attempts to purchase control of publicly traded corporations.[56] Each of these provisions of the Exchange Act is taken up in more detail in subsequent sections of this treatise.

§ 1.2[3][C] The Securities and Exchange Commission

Since its inception, the Securities and Exchange Commission has played an important role in maintaining the efficiency and integrity of the American securities markets. However, the system is far from perfect. As the market crash of October 1987 and the market "break" of 1989 demonstrated, wild market gyrations can seriously harm investors who get caught in the squeeze. Just as the market crash of 1929 triggered the current regulatory frameworks, the 1987 crash has led to some regulatory changes, and the continued aftershocks are likely to lead to some more. The SEC, Congress, and others undertook numerous studies and investigated various ways to regulate market mechanisms in a manner that will preserve the market's efficiency and help prevent a repeat of the events of October 1987. Under the leadership of the SEC, the stock exchanges installed circuit breakers to help minimize the effect of sharp volatility in the securities markets. The 1990s brought in an expansion of trading in various types of derivative investments which resulted in struggles between the SEC and CFTC regarding jurisdiction over these investments. Also, the 1990s ushered in a new era—the use of the Internet for securities trading. This resulted in additional regulatory concerns that are considered throughout this treatise.

While no system is perfect, the SEC has had significant beneficial impact on the American securities markets and our regulatory framework has become a model for other countries. Needless to say, however, the SEC has not been without its critics.

§ 1.2[3][D] Other Federal Securities Laws

§ 1.2[3][D][1] The Public Utility Holding Company Act of 1935; the Trust Indenture Act of 1939; the Investment Company and Investment Advisers Acts of 1940; the Securities Investor Protection Act of 1970; and the Sarbanes–Oxley Act of 2002

Following the Securities Exchange Act of 1934, Congress enacted a number of additional securities laws that form part of the federal regulatory scheme. These additional five securities laws are as follows.

Public Utility Holding Company Act of 1935. The Public Utility Holding Company Act of 1935 which dealt with the special problems raised by financing public issue utilities and, in particular, regulating the activities of large public utility holding company systems.[58] The Public Utility Holding Company Act was repealed in 2005.

Trust Indenture Act of 1939. The Trust Indenture Act of 1939[60] addresses

---

56. Sections 13(d), (e), 14(d), (f), 15 U.S.C.A. § 78m(d)(e), n(d)(f); chapter 11 *infra*.

58. Pub.L. No. 74–333, 49 Stat. 803 (1935), codified as amended at 15 U.S.C.A. §§ 79–79z–6, discussed in chapter 18 *infra*.

60. Act of August 3, 1939, 53 Stat. 1149.

debt financing by issuing bonds to the public.[61] The substantive provisions of the Trust Indenture Act that apply to the both the indenture and debenture that comprise the corporate debt are in addition to any registration requirements under the Securities Act of 1933 or reporting or other disclosure requirements imposed by the Securities Exchange Act of 1934.

Investment Company Act of 1940. The Investment Company Act of 1940[62] provides for regulation of mutual funds and other investment companies. The Investment Company Act imposes governance and other structural requirements as well as various antifraud and disclosure provisions.[63] The Investment Company Act supplements the disclosure and reporting provisions of the Securities Act of 1933 and the Securities Exchange Act of 1934.

Investment Advisers Act of 1940. The Investment Advisers Acts of 1940,[64] regulates professional investment analysts in the business of generating and providing financial advice to investors.[65] This Act covers investment advisers to institutional investors such as mutual funds, as well as investment advisers offering their services to investors generally.

Securities Investor Protection Act of 1970. In 1970, Congress added the Securities Investor Protection Act[66] which was enacted to address the increasing concern over the then increasing number of insolvent brokerage firms and broker-dealer firm failures.

Periodic Amendments to Securities Laws. The foregoing seven securities laws are amended periodically. Sometimes those amendments are ushered in by Acts with their own names. A few examples of these amending Acts are: the Williams Act[67] of 1968 which addressed tender offers,[68] the Insider Trading Sanctions Act of 1984[69] which enhanced enforcement of insider trading prohibitions, the Private Securities Litigation Reform Act of 1995[70] which addressed many areas of private securities litigation,[71] and the Securities Litigation Uniform Standards Act of 1998[72] which prevents most class actions based on securities fraud from being brought in state court.[73] In 2002, Congress made massive amendments when it enacted the Sarbanes–Oxley Act[74] that not only amended many provisions of the Securities Act of 1933 and

---

61. *See* chapter 19 *infra.*

62. Act of Aug. 22, 1940, 54 Stat. 789, codified in 15 U.S.C.A. §§ 80a–1 through 80a–52, discussed in chapter 20 *infra.*

63. *See* chapter 20 *infra.*

64. Act of Aug. 22, 1940 54 Stat. 847, codified in 15 U.S.C.A. § 80b–1 *et seq.,* discussed in chapter 21 *infra.*

65. *See* chapter 21 *infra.*

66. 15 U.S.C.A. § 78aaa–78*lll. See* § 14.24 *infra.*

67. Pub.L. No. 90–439, 82 Stat. 454 (1968) (codified at 15 U.S.C. §§ 78m(d)–(e), n(d)–(f)). *See generally* Edward R. Aranow & Herbert A. Einhorn, Tender Offers For Corporate Control (1973); Alan R. Bromberg, The Securities Law of Tender Offers, 15 N.Y.L.F. 462 (1962); Robert W. Hamilton, Some Reflections on Cash Tender Offer Legislation, 15 N.Y.L.F. 269 (1969).

68. *See* chapter 11 *infra.*

69. Pub. L. No. 98–376, 98 Stat. 1264 (1984).

70. Pub. Law No. 104–67, 109 Stat. 737 (104th Cong. 1st Sess. December 22, 1995) (HR 1058).

71. *See* § 12.15[1] *infra.*

72. Pub. Law No. 105–353, 112 Stat. 3227 (105th Cong.–2d Sess. November 3, 1998) (S 1260).

73. *See* § 12.15[2] *infra.*

74. Sarbanes–Oxley Act of 2002, Pub. Law 107–204 (July 30, 2002). *See* Senate Report No. 107–205 (July 3, 2002).

the Securities Exchange Act of 1934, but also introduced some scattered stand-alone provisions into the United States Code.[75] Since the Sarbanes–Oxley Act contained sweeping changes, it is likely that at least some observers and commentators will refer to it as the eighth federal securities law.

§ 1.2[3][D][2] The Proposed Federal Securities Code

In 1968, the Council of the American Law Institute began work on the Proposed Federal Securities Code project. Professor Louis Loss was named as the Code's chief reporter. After six tentative drafts and various revisions, in 1980, the American Law Institute endorsed the final draft of its Proposed Federal Securities Code.[76] The Proposed Securities Code certainly was not without its critics.[77] Although at one time the Code was endorsed by the SEC,[78] it was not even formally introduced into Congress; with the passage of time, it has become evident that the Proposed Code will not become law.[79] Nevertheless, the Proposed Code proved to be a worthy project for a number of reasons. First, many of its suggestions have since become embodied in the existing regulatory scheme. Second, the drafter's comments provide an excellent analysis of the case law as of that time. In deciding cases under the existing law, some courts looked for guidance both to the body of the Proposed Code and to its comments.

§ 1.2[3][D][3] The Sarbanes–Oxley Act of 2002

The Sarbanes–Oxley Act of 2002,[86] which is discussed throughout this treatise where applicable, adopted comprehensive corporate governance reforms in response to various corporate scandals including Enron and Worldcom. Many of the Sarbanes–Oxley provisions are disclosure provisions combined with enhanced criminal penalties for violations, but the clear thrust of these amendments is to improve corporate governance. The Sarbanes–Oxley Act goes further than any of the earlier securities laws and amendments in dealing directly with corporate governance—an area that had traditionally been reserved to the states.[87] For example, the Sarbanes–Oxley Act addressed accounting and auditing reforms, the role of public corporations' audit committees,[88] increased accountability of executive officers,[89] and corporate attorneys,[90] in addition to increased criminal penalties for violations of the securi-

---

75. *See* § 1.2[2][D][3] *infra.*

76. A.L.I., Proposed Federal Securities Code (1980).

77. *See* Lewis D. Lowenfels, The Case Against the Proposed Federal Securities Code, 65 Va.L.Rev. 615 (1979); BNA Interview: Pollack Questions the Advisability of Passing Federal Securities Code at the Time, 484 Sec.Reg. & L.Rep. (BNA) AAB1 (Jan. 3, 1979).

78. Sec. Exch. Act Rel. No. 34–17153 (Sept. 18, 1980). A year and a half later the Commission reaffirmed its endorsement. Sec. Act Rel. No. 33–6377 (Jan. 21, 1982).

79. *See* Richard W. Jennings & Harold Marsh, Jr. Securities Regulation: Cases and Materials xvii (5th ed. 1982); C. Edward Fletcher, Rise Phoenix: A Guide to the Defunct Federal Securities Code, 11 Am.J. Trial Ad. 103 (1987); Plan to Revise Securities Laws Lies Dormant, Wall St. Journal p. 31 (Oct. 8, 1981).

86. Sarbanes–Oxley Act of 2002, Pub. Law 107–204 (July 30, 2002). *See* Senate Report No. 107–205 (July 3, 2002).

87. *See, e.g.,* the discussion of the inability to use SEC antifraud rules to regulate corporate mismanagement in § 12.20 *infra.*

88. *See* § 9.6 *infra.*

89. *See* § 9.3[2][A] *infra.*

90. Sarbanes–Oxley Act of 2002, Pub. Law 107–204 § 307 (July 30, 2002), which mandates SEC rulemaking to define what constitutes proper representation by attorneys practicing before

ties laws. The Sarbanes–Oxley Act created an accounting oversight board to oversee the accounting profession and to police the self-regulatory system that previously existed.[91] The Sarbanes–Oxley Act also addressed auditor independence requirements.[92]

The Sarbanes–Oxley Act may prove to be more than a one-time reaction to major corporate scandals. It could be the beginning of a sea change by focusing federal law more and more on corporate governance and other areas of corporate law that have traditionally been left to the states.

Title III of the Sarbanes–Oxley Act addressed various corporate governance concerns including the audit committee, requiring personal certifications of accuracy by the chief executive and chief financial officers of public companies.[93] The Act further prohibits loans to high ranking executives, subject to certain exceptions to be elaborated upon in SEC rulemaking. The Act also calls for enhanced financial disclosures by public companies.[94]

Titles VIII and IX of the Sarbanes Oxley Act[95] provide for enhanced criminal penalties for violations of the Act generally, and in particular, for frauds perpetrated upon shareholders of public companies. The Act provides protection to corporate whistle-blowers.[96] The Act also covers other areas, including heightened controls over securities analysts' conflicts of interest[97] and a sense of the Senate that federal corporate tax returns should be signed by a corporation's chief executive officer.[98]

§ 1.2[3][E] Federal Preemption of State Law

In 1996, Congress significantly limited the role of state law in securities regulation. The National Securities Markets Improvement Act of 1996[99] explicitly preempts state law in many areas. An amended section 18 of the 1933 Act now provides that a number of securities offerings will be exempted from state law regulation.[100] The 1996 amendments specifically preempt state regulation that would require registration or qualification of several categories of covered securities. Those covered securities include most publicly traded securities: securities listed on the New York Stock Exchange, the American Stock Exchange, or the NASD's National Market.[101] Although

---

the SEC. The rules must require, *inter alia*, that once an attorney has evidence of serious corporate wrongdoing, he or she, must climb the corporate ladder, possibly to the audit committee and to the board of directors, until satisfied that the problem has been attended to. *See* § 9.8 *infra*.

91. Sarbanes–Oxley Act of 2002, Pub. Law 107–204 tit. I (July 30, 2002). *See* § 9.6 *infra*.

92. Sarbanes–Oxley Act of 2002, Pub. Law 107–204 tit. II (July 30, 2002).

93. Sarbanes–Oxley Act of 2002, Pub. Law 107–204 tit. III (July 30, 2002). *See* § 3.9[9] *infra*.

94. Sarbanes–Oxley Act of 2002, Pub. Law 107–204 tit. IV (July 30, 2002). *See* § 3.9[9] *infra*.

95. Sarbanes–Oxley Act of 2002, Pub. Law 107–204 tits. VIII, IX (July 30, 2002). *See also id.* tit. 11.

96. Sarbanes–Oxley Act of 2002, Pub. Law 107–204 § 1107 (July 30, 2002).

97. Sarbanes–Oxley Act of 2002, Pub. Law 107–204 § 501 (July 30, 2002). *See* § 14.16[6] *infra*.

98. Sarbanes–Oxley Act of 2002, Pub. Law 107–204 § 1001 (July 30, 2002).

99. Pub. L. No. 104–290, 110 Stat. 3416 (1996). The impact on state laws is discussed further in Chapter 8 *infra. See, e.g.*, Symposium, The National Securities Markets Improvements Act— One Year Later, 53 Bus. Law. 507 (1998); Comment, The National Securities Market Improvement Act: How Improved is the Securities Market?, 36 Duq. L. Rev. 365 (1998).

100. 15 U.S.C.A. § 77r.

101. Section 18(b)(1)(A), 15 U.S.C.A. § 77r(b)(1)(A). The Act also gives the SEC rulemaking power to expand the exemption to other listed securities on a securities exchange that has listing

precluding the states from imposing registration or reporting requirements on issuers of covered securities, the federal act expressly preserves the states' right to require filing of documents solely for notice purposes.[102] In addition to the preemption of state laws with regard to the foregoing publicly traded securities, a number of exempt securities are also exempted from state regulation.[103] Furthermore, even for those securities and transactions not otherwise preempted and thus exempted from state regulation, sales to "qualified purchasers" as defined by the SEC are also exempted.[104]

§ 1.3 The Securities and Exchange Commission; Structure of the SEC

The Securities and Exchange Commission is a highly departmentalized federal agency, which is reflected in its wide range of authority and various types of administrative responsibilities.[1] The Commission is a true "super agency," notwithstanding its relatively small size as compared with other federal regulatory agencies. In spite of the SEC's broad range of authority and the general criticism of governmental overregulation, the Commission has been recognized as one of the most efficient and effective federal agencies.

§ 1.3[1] The SEC Commissioners

The Commission consists of five commissioners serving five-year terms.[2] They are appointed by the President, subject to the normal confirmatory action by Congress. One of the five commissioners is designated as Commission Chairman. Of the five commissioners, no more than three can be from the same political party.

The five commissioners comprise what is sometimes referred to as the full Commission, as compared with division heads and SEC staff members. The full Commission, in addition to exercising its supervisory power over all of its divisions, has direct review power of rulings and hearings before an administrative judge as well as the final authority on the promulgation of all SEC rules. The commissioners as a group necessarily fulfill the function of the final arbiter of overall SEC policy. Since there is no specific statutory provision to the contrary, SEC action is governed by common law quorum and voting rules.[3]

---

standards similar to those identified in subsection (b)(1)(A). Section 18(b)(1)(B), 15 U.S.C.A. § 77r(b)(1)(B). Also exempted are securities of the same issuer with equal seniority or that are senior to the securities exempted from state regulation under subsections (1)(A) and (1)(B). Section 18(b)(1)(C), 15 U.S.C.A. § 77r(b)(1)(C).

102. Section 18(c)(2), 15 U.S.C.A. § 77r(c)(2).

103. Section 18(b)(4), 15 U.S.C.A. § 77r(b)(4).

104. Section 18(b)(3), 15 U.S.C.A. § 77r(b)(3). The SEC is empowered to define categories of qualified purchaser "consistent with the public interest and the protection of investors." *Id.*

§ 1.3

1. For a more detailed discussion of the SEC *see* chapter 16 *infra* wherein the SEC, its Rules of Practice, and its structure are discussed more fully. Descriptions of current SEC activities and structure can be found in the Commission's annual reports.

2. *See* § 16.43 *infra.*

3. *See, e.g.,* Falcon Trading Group v. SEC, 102 F.3d 579 (D.C.Cir.1996) (upholding SEC rule designating two out of three commissioners to be a quorum, in the absence of all five commission positions being filled).

The Securities Exchange Act of 1934 permits the SEC to delegate many of its decisions, and thus a vote of the full Commission is not necessary to authorize a specific enforcement

§ 1.3[2] The Divisions of the Commission

The adjudicatory responsibilities of the Commission are carried out through the administrative law judges, while the rest of the Commission's administrative powers are handled through its four divisions and five regional offices.

The Division of Enforcement is responsible for the investigation of all suspected securities laws violations.[4] Once it is believed that a violation has been committed, the result may be SEC judicial enforcement actions, reference to the Justice Department for criminal prosecution, or administrative sanctions imposed after a hearing. These actions may be taken against registered issuers, their officers and employees, registered broker-dealers, and members of exchanges or self-regulatory associations, such as the NASD. The Division of Corporation Finance[5] has primary responsibility for examining all registration documents for compliance with the securities laws' disclosure requirements. The Division of Corporation Finance, or "Corp Fin," also prepares various disclosure guides that are promulgated by the Commission. The Division of Corporation Finance is also extremely helpful in aiding the preparation of first-time or difficult disclosure documents, especially through the Commission's regional and district offices. The Division of Market Regulation[6] is devoted to regulatory practices and policies relating to the exchanges, the over-the-counter markets, and broker-dealers. There is some overlap with the Division of Investment Management,[7] which is concerned with the regulation under the two 1940 Acts of the investment company industry and investment advisers.

In the Commission's hierarchy, there are various offices below the four divisions. The Office of the General Counsel[9] is charged with the responsibility of advising both the Commission and all of its divisions on questions of law. The General Counsel also represents the Commission in litigation, both at the trial and appellate court levels, and is instrumental in preparing Commission sponsored legislation. In 1989, the Commission consolidated the functions of the Office of Opinions and Review into the Office of the General Counsel. The Office of the Accountant[10] generates Commission policy on various accounting practices; it also represents the Commission when dealing with self-regulatory organizations, such as the Financial Accounting Standards Board (FASB). The Chief Economist and Directorate of Economic and Policy Analysis[11] as their names imply, are in charge of generating various economic studies used by the Commission and its divisions. The Office of Policy Planning formerly had the task of coordinating the Commission's long term goals; this function has been transferred to the Directorate of Economic and Policy Analysis. Each Division and Office in the Washington, D.C. headquarters of the Commission has

proceeding; accordingly, the enforcement proceeding was valid even though the Commission had only two commissioners at the time it was instituted. SEC v. Feminella, 947 F.Supp. 722 (S.D.N.Y.1996).

4. SEC enforcement is discussed in 16.2 *infra.* The Division of Enforcement is discussed in § 16.46 *infra.*

5. *See* § 16.44 *infra.*

6. *See* § 16.45 *infra.*

7. *See* § 16.47 *infra.*

9. *See* § 16.53 *infra.*

10. *See* § 16.54, *infra.*

11. *See* § 16.55 *infra.*

responsibility for the development, direction, and policy guidance for all operating programs under its jurisdiction.[12]

The next level of Commission hierarchy contains the offices that handle the day-to-day operation of the Commission's activities: administrative services, controller, data processing, personnel, public information, records, registrations, and reports. Under the direct supervision of the Executive Director,[13] the five regional offices set forth below (and their respective district offices), along with the district offices that exist in the four busier regions, carry out the work of the Commission on a regional level.[14]

Each of the Regional Directors (formerly called regional administrators), is responsible for the implementation of all programs and for supervision of all employees in his or her region.[15] In 1993, the nine regional office were reduced to five, while some of the former regional offices were redesignated as branch offices. Prior to 1993, the Regional Administrators were located in New York, Boston, Atlanta, Chicago, Fort Worth, Denver, Los Angeles, Seattle, and Philadelphia.[16] Some of the larger regional offices have branch offices.[17] Under the 1993 reorganization plan, the number of regional offices was reduced from nine to five and the former regional offices were redesignated as district offices. As a result of the reorganization, Chicago, Denver, Los Angeles, and New York remain regional offices; their regional administrators were redesignated as regional directors. The Seattle office became a district of the Los Angeles regional office which continues to oversee the San Francisco district; the Salt Lake City office became a district office, under the Denver regional office, as did the Fort Worth office; while the Philadelphia and Boston offices were made district offices of the New York regional office. In the second stage of the plan, the Atlanta office became a district office and Miami was designated the regional office that will oversee the Atlanta district.[18]

---

12. 17 C.F.R. § 200.11(a)(1). The Headquarters Office is located at 450 Fifth Street, N.W., Washington, DC 20549. *Id.*

13. *See* § 16.62 *infra.*

14. *See* § 16.49 *infra.*

15. 17 C.F.R. § 200.11(a)(2).

16. 17 C.F.R. § 200.11(b). *See id.* for complete addresses of each of the Regional Administrators.

17. The Chicago Regional Office has a branch office in Detroit, the Fort Worth Regional Office has a branch office in Houston, the Denver Regional Office has a branch office in Salt Lake City, and the Los Angeles Regional Office has a branch office in San Francisco.

18. For more detailed description of the regional and district offices, *see* § 16.49 *infra.*

§ 1.4 The Work of the SEC

§ 1.4[1] Overview of SEC Authority

With the creation of the Securities and Exchange Commission in 1934, Congress gave the Securities and Exchange Commission the responsibility of administering the regulation provided by all seven of the securities laws.[1] The Commission acquits that responsibility with each of the four basic administrative agency powers: rule-making, adjudicatory, investigatory, and enforcement.[2] During the late twentieth century, the Commission's enforcement powers expanded significantly. In addition to now having the ability to seek treble damage penalties for insider trading violations,[3] the Commission can impose civil penalties in administrative procedures[4] and has been given cease and desist authority.[5] The only administrative authority that the Commission does not have is the power to adjudicate disputes between individual litigants.[6]

§ 1.4[2] SEC Rulemaking

As with administrative agencies generally, there are two varieties of rule-making authority: delegated and interpretative. Much of the Commission's legislative or rule-making power derives from the certain sections of the securities laws which specifically empower the SEC to promulgate rules that have the force of statutory provisions.[7]

§ 1.4[2][A] Delegated Rulemaking

Rule-making by direct legislative delegation necessarily has the effect of law so long as the rule-making has been in compliance with the process set forth in the Administrative Procedure Act[8] and the scope of the rule does not exceed the grant of authority in the organic statute that created this administrative rule-making power.

The validity of SEC rulemaking is dependent upon the scope of the authorizing statute. Rules that go beyond the scope of the statute are therefore invalid. Major questions involving the validity of SEC rules are frequently raised in connection with rules that touch upon corporate governance, which is a matter that has traditionally been left to state law. The

---

§ 1.4

1. The SEC's activities are described each year in the Commission's annual report. *See generally* SEC, A Twenty Five Year Summary of the Activities of the Securities and Exchange Commission 1934–1959 (1961); SEC, The Work of the Securities and Exchange Commission (1974).

2. *See* Thomas L. Hazen, Administrative Enforcement: An Evaluation of the Securities and Exchange Commission's Use of Injunctions and Other Enforcement Methods, 31 Hastings L.J. 427 (1979).

3. Section 21A of the Exchange Act, 15 U.S.C.A. § 78u–1. *See* §§ 9.5, 13.9 *infra*.

4. Section 21B of the Exchange Act, 15 U.S.C.A. § 78u–2.

5. *E.g.*, section 21C of the Exchange Act, 15 U.S.C.A. § 78u–3. *See* § 16.5 *infra*.

6. *Compare, e.g.*, the Commodity Futures Trading Commission which through its reparations procedures can adjudicate customer/broker disputes. Section 14 of the Commodity Exchange Act, 7 U.S.C.A. § 18.

7. *See e.g.*, section 3(b) of the 1933 Act giving the Commission power to promulgate exemptions from registration, 15 U.S.C.A. § 77c(b); and section 10(b) of the 1934 Act which delegates to the Commission the responsibility to promulgate rules determining the scope of anti-fraud liability, 15 U.S.C.A. § 78j(b).

8. 5 U.S.C.A. §§ 551 *et seq.*

securities laws provide an "intelligible conceptual line excluding the Commission from corporate governance."[9] Accordingly, the D.C. Circuit Court of Appeals invalidated the Commission's attempt to regulate substantive voting rights of shareholders.[10]

§ 1.4[2][B] Interpretative Rulemaking

Commission rule-making is not limited to legislatively delegated rules. The SEC has also promulgated a number of interpretive rules which are designed to aid corporate planners and attorneys in complying with the statutes' requirements.[11] Unlike the rules promulgated pursuant to specific statutory delegation, interpretative rules do not carry with them the force of law; they simply reflect the Commission's interpretation of the law created by the statute. Nevertheless, interpretative rules are extremely important in guiding practitioners through the regulatory maze. Equally important is that fact that when interpreting the scope of a statute, federal courts traditionally give deference to administrative interpretation.[12] The reasoning underpinning this deference is the reliability of the agency's expertise as compared to the court's general knowledge and authority.

§ 1.4[2][C] Safe Harbor Rules

A special variety of SEC interpretative rules are the so-called safe harbor rules. A safe harbor rule sets forth conditions under which the SEC will take the position that the law has been complied with. A person's compliance with a safe harbor rule will thus assure that he or she is safe from SEC prosecution with regard to the transaction in question. The SEC safe harbor rules, which are discussed throughout this treatise are designed to help provide for certainty in planning transactions in order to comply with the applicable securities laws.

§ 1.4[3] SEC Interpretive Releases; Staff Legal Bulletins

Beyond its expressly delegated and interpretative rule-making activities, the Securities and Exchange Commission disseminates unsolicited advisory opinions in the form of SEC Releases,[14] which may include guidelines or suggest interpretation of statutory provisions and rules. In addition to periodic interpretative releases, each time the Commission proposes a new rule or rule amendment, the proposal is accompanied by a release. Similarly, when new rules or amendments are adopted, the SEC's formal adoption is accompanied by an interpretative release. The SEC positions announced in interpretative releases necessarily provide less precedential and predictive value than do

---

9. Business Roundtable v. SEC, 905 F.2d 406 (D.C.Cir.1990).

10. *Id. See* discussion in § 10.1 *infra.* Another example of the SEC's clash with corporate governance issues arose in the context of the regulation of "going private" transactions. *See* § 11.8[2] *infra.*

11. The current versions of the rules are compiled annually in volume 17 of the Code of Federal Regulations (hereinafter cited as "17 C.F.R. § ___"). Since the Commission has many rule changes each year, looseleaf services should also be consulted. *See, e.g.,* Fed.Sec.L.Rep. (CCH). A WESTLAW check will help reveal the most current versions of the SEC's rules.

All of the Commission's activities are reported in the SEC Digest and SEC Docket which are published weekly and daily by the Commission. This information also is available on WESTLAW.

12. Chevron U.S.A. v. Natural Resources Defense Council, 467 U.S. 837, 104 S.Ct. 2778, 81 L.Ed.2d 694 (1984).

14. The Commission's releases are published in the Federal register and also appear in the various looseleaf services. This information also is available on WESTLAW.

rules that are promulgated as a result of the more formal interpretive rule-making process.

In addition to the SEC Releases described above, the Commission will from time to time issue Accounting Releases which deal with various matters involving disclosure and presentation of financial information. Some Accounting Releases also discuss the SEC auditing requirements that apply to registered public companies. The SEC also publishes Litigation Releases which announce filings, settlements, and judgments in SEC enforcement actions that are brought in federal court.

Although having less precedential effect than the formal SEC Releases, from time to time the SEC publishes Staff Legal Bulletins. These Bulletins, which are available on the SEC's website, provide further insight into the SEC's approach to selected issues. As is the case with SEC Releases, Staff Legal Bulletins are mentioned throughout this treatise where appropriate.

§ 1.4[4] SEC No Action Letters

One step below interpretative releases, in terms of precedential hierarchy, are the Commission's "no action" letters. These no action letters are analogous to IRS private letter rulings. No action letters are SEC staff responses to private requests for indication of whether certain contemplated conduct is in compliance with the appropriate statutory provisions and rules. Most requests for a no action letter are compliance oriented and thus are handled by the Division of Corporation Finance; although, on occasion the other divisions may render similar assistance in their areas of expertise. No action letters can be very helpful to practitioners.[15] However, it must be kept in mind that the SEC's responses are staff interpretations rather than formal Commission action and thus have extremely limited, if any, precedential weight.[16] The SEC staff position in a no action letter has been described as a statement to the effect that:

> This is my view based on the facts as you describe them. You may not rely on it as if it were a Commission decision. If you don't like it, you are at liberty to disregard it and follow your own construction, subject to the risk that I may recommend appropriate action to the Commission and the Commission may institute proceedings or take other steps if the Commission agrees with my view.[17]

A no action letter is purely a matter between the SEC staff and the party requesting it. The request for a no action letter does not bind the party requesting it to act in a certain way so as to create any protectable expectations in third parties. Accordingly, it has been held that a corporation's shareholders cannot force management to frame a transaction according to the terms of its no action request.[18] Conversely, when the Commission has responded favorably to a request for a no action letter, the SEC's interpretation will not preclude a third party from challenging the transaction. The no

---

15. *See, e.g.,* Thomas P. Lemke, The SEC No–Action Letter Process, 42 Bus.Law. 1019 (1987).

16. *See, e.g.,* Roosevelt v. E.I. Du Pont de Nemours & Co., 958 F.2d 416, 427 n. 19 (D.C.Cir.1992) (principle of deference to agency views does not apply to no action letters as they are not formal agency positions).

17. Professional Care Services, Inc., [1973–74 Transfer Binder] Fed.Sec.L.Rep. (CCH) ¶ 79,770 at p. 84,080 (SEC No Action Letter April 15, 1974) (quoting 3 Louis Loss, Securities Regulation 1895 (2d ed. 1961)).

18. Beaumont v. American Can Co., 797 F.2d 79 (2d Cir.1986), *affirming* 621 F.Supp. 484 (S.D.N.Y.1985).

action position may, of course, have some persuasive effect insofar as it represents the Commission's interpretation and exhibits the SEC's current thinking on particular matters.[19] The limited precedential effect of no action letters was reinforced with the Commission's initiation of administrative proceedings to address conduct that had previously been the subject of favorable no action responses.[20] In conjunction with the initiation of the administrative proceeding, Commissioner Fleischman issued a written statement emphasizing that since no action responses are limited to the particular facts in the requesting letter, it is risky to make general conclusions from specific responses.[21] It is clear that a court will not give the same deference to a no action response as it would to formal rulemaking or interpretative pronouncements.[22]

A number of commentators have criticized the "no action" letter as an inefficient method of lawmaking.[23] The no action letter as an ad hoc method of advising has been attacked as too time-consuming and cumbersome. Further, no action letters fail to provide practitioners with significant precedential or predictive aid. The value of no action letters and other mechanisms of informal Commission action is even further diminished, as described more fully below in a discussion of the registration process under the Securities Act of 1933,[24] by the availability of comment letters and less formal telephone conferences provided by the Division of Corporation Finance and various regional offices as guides for revision of documents filed with the Commission.

Nevertheless, given all of its shortcomings, the no action letter process has been an influential one in forming securities law. No action letters can be of great help in shedding light on the SEC's current view of many significant issues. Relevant no action letter positions are discussed as appropriate throughout this treatise.

§ 1.4[5] SEC Oversight and Regulatory Authority

Aside from the foregoing quasi-legislative responsibilities, the Commission also has regulatory oversight and quasi-judicial power over brokers,

---

19. On occasion, the full Commission has been willing to reconsider the position taken by the staff in a no action response. *See, e.g.,* United Brotherhood of Carpenters and Joiners of America, 2002 WL 31749942 (SEC No Action Letter Dec. 6, 2002). If the Commission takes the position that the staff erred, it may nevertheless permit the company's management that relied in good faith on the staff response to act in accordance with the initial no action response. *Id.*

20. Morgan Stanley & Co., Sec.Exch.Act Rel. No. 34–28,990, Admin.Proc.File No. 3–7473 (March 20, 1991) (charging violations of limits on sale of control person stock in connection with stock sale to satisfy margin requirements).

21. As stated by Commissioner Fleischman, "since the particular letter under discussion states that it's limited to the facts of its own case and that only the addressee is protected by it, others claiming to be similarly situated can't be allowed to reason from the letter to derive general propositions on which the addressee itself could not rely." *Id.* (written statement of Commissioner Fleischman).

22. Amalgamated Clothing & Textile Workers Union v. Wal–Mart Stores, Inc., 821 F.Supp. 877 (S.D.N.Y.1993) (no action responses do not represent official agency positions), *relying on* Roosevelt v. E.I. Du Pont de Nemours & Co., 958 F.2d 416, 427 n. 19 (D.C.Cir.1992) (principle of deference to agency views does not apply to no action letters as they are not formal agency positions); New York City Employees' Retirement System v. Dole Food Co., 795 F.Supp. 95, 100–101 (S.D.N.Y.1992), *vacated as moot* 969 F.2d 1430 (2d Cir.1992) (courts are not bound by no action responses).

23. Louis Loss, Summary Remarks (ABA National Institute: Advisors to Management), 30 Bus.Law. 163, 164–65 (Special Issue 1975); Lewis D. Lowenfels, SEC No Action Letters: Conflicts with the Existing Statutes, Cases and Commission Releases, 59 Va.L.Rev. 303 (1973).

24. *See* chapter 3 *infra.*

dealers, and exchanges that it licenses under the Exchange Act of 1934.[25] From time to time, questions have arisen concerning the effect of the SEC's regulatory and self-regulatory oversight authority on the impact of the antitrust laws. Where there is pervasive regulation either by the SEC directly or by the self regulatory organizations under the direct oversight and supervision of the SEC, then the Securities Exchange Act will operate as an implied repeal of the antitrust laws.[26] Not all SEC regulated conduct will have such a preemptive effect on the antitrust laws. Conduct that is not permitted by SEC Rule, self-regulatory rule, or regulation generally may be scrutinized under the antitrust laws.[27]

Correlative to the SEC's oversight responsibility is the agency's ability to impose administrative disciplinary sanctions upon those subject to its licensing authority. The SEC's disciplinary authority covers broker-dealers, investment advisers, and investment companies, as well as professionals such as attorneys or accountants who practice before the Commission. The Commission also has the power to impose administrative sanctions against other persons who violate the securities laws. In addition to direct enforcement authority, the Commission may in its discretion publish the results of its investigations.[28] One of the more controversial areas of the Commission's disciplinary authority has been exerted under Rule 102(e) of the Commission's Rules of Practice which relates to practice before the Commission and thus allows the SEC to discipline professionals such as attorneys and accountants who appear before the Commission in a representative capacity.[29] Disciplinary proceedings under Rule 102(e) relate only to practice before the Commission; more general disbarment proceedings are left to the states in their regulation of the legal and accounting professions.

§ 1.4[6] SEC Enforcement Authority

The third major administrative function carried out by the SEC, in addition to rulemaking and adjudication, is that of enforcement. Through the Division of Enforcement, the Commission investigates all potential violations of each act that it administers. Where appropriate, such violation will be addressed through the SEC's administrative sanctions referred to above, or forwarded to the Department of Justice for criminal prosecution. The Commission also performs a direct prosecutorial function by virtue of its authority

25. 15 U.S.C.A. § 78o. *See, e.g.,* Paul G. Mahoney, The Exchange as Regulator, 83 Va. L. Rev. 1453 (1997). *See* chapter 14 *infra.*

26. *See* United States v. NASD, 422 U.S. 694, 95 S.Ct. 2427, 45 L.Ed.2d 486 (1975); Gordon v. New York Stock Exchange, Inc., 422 U.S. 659, 95 S.Ct. 2598, 45 L.Ed.2d 463 (1975); In re Stock Exchanges Options Trading Antitrust Litigation, 317 F.3d 134 (2d Cir. 2003) (Sherman Antitrust Act's restraint of trade provisions were impliedly repealed with respect to claim challenging listing of options on securities exchanges); Friedman v. Salomon/Smith Barney, Inc., 313 F.3d 796 (2d Cir. 2002) (implied repeal of antitrust laws precluded antitrust suit challenging alleged price fixing with respect to IPO shares). *But see* In re Public Offering Fee Antitrust Litigation, 2003 WL 21496795, 2003–2 Trade Cases ¶ 74114 (S.D.N.Y. 2003) (no implied repeal of antitrust laws with respect to investor suit). *See also, e.g.,* Silver v. New York Stock Exchange, 373 U.S. 341, 83 S.Ct. 1246, 10 L.Ed.2d 389 (1963). The impact of the antitrust laws generally is discussed in § 14.1[9] *infra.*

27. *See* In re Nasdaq Market–Makers Antitrust Litigation, 1999 WL 395407 (S.D.N.Y.1999); In re Nasdaq Market–Makers Antitrust Litigation, 184 F.R.D. 506 (S.D.N.Y.1999).

28. 15 U.S.C.A. § 78u(a). *See* Sec.Exch.Act Rel. No. 34–15664 (March 21, 1979). For criticism of the publication of investigations *see* In re Spartek, Inc., 491 Sec.Reg. 8 L.Rep. (BNA) EB1 (SEC Feb. 21, 1979) (Karmel, dissenting).

29. 17 C.F.R. § 201.2(e).

to seek injunctions against alleged violators, as well as appropriate ancillary relief in the federal district courts. Originally, the ability to secure ancillary relief was implied from the court's inherent equity authority.[31] The Commission has since been given express statutory authority to seek disgorgement of ill-gotten gains,[32] imposition of civil penalties,[33] and bar orders[34] as part of its judicial enforcement arsenal.

Congress enacted legislation in 1990 that expanded significantly the role of the Commission in enforcement matters. As part of the Securities Enforcement and Penny Stock Reform Act of 1990,[35] the Commission was given cease and desist power.[36] The law that gave the SEC cease and desist authority further empowers the Commission to impose civil penalties in administrative proceedings.[37] The legislation also increased civil penalties for violations of the securities laws generally,[38] and empowers the SEC to go to court to secure an order barring officers and directors from associating with issuers under the Commission's jurisdiction.[39] The penalties for numerous securities violations were increased again in 2002 when Congress enacted the Sarbanes–Oxley Act[40] in reaction to many notorious corporate frauds and failures.

§ 1.5   The SEC's Subject–Matter Jurisdiction; The CFTC–SEC Division of Regulatory Authority; Financial Services

§ 1.5[1] Jurisdictional Concerns

As discussed directly above, the Securities and Exchange Commission has wide-ranging responsibility with regard to the securities markets. The expanded sophistication of the securities markets has led to sweeping changes in the regulatory role of the Commission. As discussed in the preceding sections, the heart of the Securities and Exchange Commission's jurisdiction is the regulation of securities markets and securities trading. Beginning in the 1970s, the development and diversification of derivative investment products have created overlapping jurisdiction between the SEC and the Commodity Futures Trading Commission (CFTC).

---

31. *See generally* Thomas L. Hazen, Administrative Enforcement: An Evaluation of the Securities and Exchange Commission's Use of Injunctions and Other Enforcement Methods, 31 Hastings L.J. 427 (1979).

32. Section 21A of the Exchange Act, 15 U.S.C.A. § 78u–1.

33. *Id.*

34. Under appropriate circumstances, a court may order that a violator of the securities law be barred from association with a company subject to the SEC's registration and reporting requirements. Section 21(d)(2) of the Exchange Act, 15 U.S.C.A. § 78u(d)(2).

35. Pub.L. No. 101–429.

36. Securities Act of 1933 § 8A, 15 U.S.C.A. § 77h–1; Securities Exchange Act of 1934 § 21C, 23(d), 15 U.S.C.A. § 78u–3, 78w(d); Investment Company Act of 1940 § 9(f), 15 U.S.C.A. § 80a–9(f); Investment Advisers Act of 1940 § 203(k), 15 U.S.C.A. § 80b–3(k). *See* discussion in § 16.32 *infra.*

37. Securities Exchange Act of 1934 § 21B, 15 U.S.C.A. § 78u–2; Investment Company Act § 9(d), (e), 15 U.S.C.A. § 80a–9(d), (e); Investment Advisers Act § 203(i), 15 U.S.C.A. § 80b–3(i). *See* discussion in § 16.2 *infra.*

38. Securities Act of 1933 § 20(d), 15 U.S.C.A. § 77t(d); Securities Exchange Act of 1934 § 21(d)(3), 15 U.S.C.A. § 78u(d)(3); Investment Company Act § 42(e); 15 U.S.C.A. § 80a–41(e); Investment Advisers Act § 209(e); 15 U.S.C.A. § 80b–9(e). *See* discussion in § 16.2 *infra.*

39. Securities Exchange Act of 1934 § 21(d)(2), 15 U.S.C.A. § 78u(d)(2). *See* discussion in § 16.2 *infra.*

40. Sarbanes–Oxley Act of 2002, Pub. Law 107–204 (July 30, 2002).

Traditionally, the futures markets were devoted to agricultural and other tangible commodities. However, those markets began to trade financial futures and other derivative instruments wherein the underlying commodities were instruments more commonly associated with the securities markets, including treasury bonds or stock index futures. When combined with foreign currency contracts and other related futures and options, it is estimated that more than seventy percent of the volume on the commodities exchanges is attributable to financial instruments as opposed to tangible commodities.

§ 1.5[5] Index Participations and Other Hybrids as Securities or Commodities

In 1988, three securities exchanges filed applications to permit trading of stock index participation instruments (also known as stock baskets). A stock basket (like an index futures or option contract) allows investors to participate in gains (or losses) derived from an index based on the collective price of the underlying securities. In March 1989, the SEC granted the applications and approved trading of three types of stock baskets on the applicant securities exchanges.[46] Stock index futures have been trading on the commodities exchanges for a number of years. The SEC's recognition of these novel index participation units as securities has opened another round of the SEC/CFTC jurisdictional struggle.[47] The Chicago Mercantile Exchange challenged the SEC action, claiming that these investment instruments were futures contracts and as such were subject to the exclusive jurisdiction of the CFTC.[48] The Seventh Circuit ruled that index participations were subject to the exclusive jurisdiction of the CFTC.[49]

In holding that the CFTC had exclusive jurisdiction over these index participation units, Judge Easterbrook explained that the basic premise underlying the jurisdictional accord was that if an instrument could be classified as both a security and a futures contract, exclusive jurisdiction of its trading lies with the CFTC.[50] In the wake of the decision, the first Bush administration introduced legislation that would transfer jurisdiction over all stock index futures to the SEC.[51] Other proposals for regulatory reform that have been suggested include giving the SEC oversight responsibility with regard to the CFTC's financial and stock index jurisdiction.[52] It is thus fair to say that Congress has been reexamining the jurisdictional accord for years. For a long time, it seemed doubtful that any adjustments to the jurisdiction of the SEC and CFTC would be the result of another accord between the two agencies.[53] However, in 1999, the two agencies were close to an agreement on massive changes, including the repeal of the prohibition on futures of individ-

§ 1.5

46. Sec. Exch. Act. Rel. No. 34–26709 (SEC March 14, 1989).

47. *See* Ricks, Stock Basket Approval Stirs Court Action, Wall St. J. p. C1 (Wednesday, March 15, 1989).

48. *Id.*

49. Chicago Mercantile Exchange v. SEC, 883 F.2d 537 (7th Cir.1989), *cert. denied* 496 U.S. 936, 110 S.Ct. 3214, 110 L.Ed.2d 662 (1990).

50. *See also* the discussion in § 1.7 *infra.*

51. *See* 22 Sec.Reg. & L.Rep. (BNA) 731 (May 11, 1990).

52. *E.g.,* Report of the Presidential Task Force on Market Practices (Jan. 8, 1988).

53. *See* Brady Rules Out any Compromise on SEC–CFTC Jurisdictional Dispute, 22 Sec.Reg. & L.Rep. (BNA) 1031 (July 13, 1990).

ual securities. The legislation that was eventually enacted permits the trading of futures on individual securities and further provides that jurisdiction over securities-based swap agreements remains primarily with the CFTC.[54]

At the same time that the CFTC was contesting the applicability of the securities laws to index participations, it exempted a number of hybrid instruments (having characteristics of both securities and commodities-related investments) from the coverage of the Commodity Exchange Act.[55] Hybrid investments qualifying for the exemption from the bulk of federal commodities law regulation include instruments that combine commodity options or futures characteristics with debt instruments, preferred equity instruments, and depository transactions.

§ 1.5[6] Registration of Exchanges

Another aspect of the jurisdictional dispute arose in connection with two commodities exchanges' challenge to SEC registration of a clearing agent for an electronic trading system for options on government securities.[57] The Seventh Circuit reversed the SEC order granting clearing agent registration for an agent of an electronic system for trading options on government securities.[58] However, the victory was short-lived. On remand, the SEC ruled that the agent did not have to register as a securities exchange and reaffirmed its earlier position that it could be registered as a clearing agent.[59] The Seventh Circuit upheld the SEC's ruling.[60]

As a result of the Commodity Futures Modernization Act of 2000,[61] security futures products[62] may be traded on either securities exchanges subject to SEC regulation, or commodities contract markets or derivatives transaction execution facilities that are subject to CFTC oversight.[63]

§ 1.5[7] Financial Services

In the same year that Congress enacted the Securities Act of 1933, it also enacted the Glass–Steagall Act[64] in order to erect a barrier between commercial banking and securities activities (also known as investment banking). During the latter part of the twentieth century, banks, brokerage firms, insurance companies, and other financial institutions pushed for increased competition between the formerly separate industries. The barriers between

54. Commodity Futures Modernization Act of 2000, Pub. Law No. 106–554, 114 Stat. 2763 (Dec. 21, 2000).

55. CFTC Regulations §§ 34.1–34.3, 17 C.F.R. §§ 34.1–34.3. *See* Statutory Interpretation Concerning Certain Hybrid Instruments, [1990–1992 Transfer Binder] Comm.Fut.L.Rep. (CCH) ¶ 24,805 (CFTC April 11, 1990).

57. The SEC has the responsibility for registering clearing agencies for exchanges. 15 U.S.C.A. § 78q–1. *See* § 14.3 *infra.*

58. Board of Trade of City of Chicago v. SEC, 883 F.2d 525 (7th Cir.1989), *appeal after remand* 923 F.2d 1270 (1991).

59. *See* 22 Sec.Reg. & L.Rep. (BNA) 56 (Jan. 12, 1990).

60. Board of Trade of City of Chicago v. SEC, 923 F.2d 1270 (7th Cir.1991).

61. Pub. Law No. 106–554, 114 Stat. 2763 (Dec. 21, 2000).

62. Futures on individual equity securities and narrow based stock index futures. *See* § 1.7[7] *infra.*

63. *See* Philip McBride Johnson & Thomas Lee Hazen, Derivatives Regulation Chapter 1 (2004).

64. The Banking Act of 1933, Ch. 89, 48 Stat. 184 (1933), codified in various sections of 12 U.S.C.A. *See* in particular 12 U.S.C.A. §§ 24, 378(a).

these activities began to crumble, culminating in 1999, when Congress repealed[65] the structural impediments that were formerly imposed by the Glass–Steagall Act.

The barriers that formerly existed between commercial banking, insurance, and investment banking activities no longer exist. The current regime imposes functional regulation. This means that securities activities of banks and other financial institutions are subject to SEC jurisdiction. Banking activities are regulated by the appropriate federal or state banking agency.[66] Insurance activities are regulated by state insurance regulators.[67]

§ 1.6 Definition of "Security"

§ 1.6[1] Statutory Definition of "Security"

What do the following have in common: scotch whiskey,[1] self-improvement courses,[2] cosmetics,[3] earthworms,[4] beavers,[5] muskrats,[6] rabbits,[7] chinchillas,[8] animal breeding programs,[9] cattle embryos,[10] fishing boats,[11] vacuum cleaners,[12] cemetery lots,[13] coin operated telephones,[14] master recording con-

65. Gramm–Leach–Bliley Act, Pub. Law. 106–102, 1999 U.S.C.C.A.N. (113 Stat.) 1338 (1999). *See generally* Symposium, 4 N.C. Banking Inst. 1 (2000); Michael K. O'Neal, Summary and Analysis of the Gramm–Leach–Bliley Act, 28 Sec. Reg. L.J. 95 (2000).

66. *See, e.g.,* Jonathan B. Macey, The Business of Banking: Before and After Gramm–Leach Bliley, 25 J. Corp. L. 691 (2000); Michael P. Malloy, Banking in the Twenty–First Century, 25 J. Corp. L. 787 (2000).

67. *See generally* Lissa L. Broome & Jerry W. Markham, Banking and Insurance: Before and After the Gramm–Leach–Bliley Act, 25 J. Corp. L. 723 (2000).

§ 1.6

1. SEC v. Glen–Arden Commodities, Inc. [1973 Transfer Binder] Fed.Sec.L.Rep. (CCH) ¶ 94,142 (E.D.N.Y.1973); SEC v. M.A. Lundy Associates, 362 F.Supp. 226 (D.R.I.1973); SEC v. Haffenden–Rimar International, Inc., 362 F.Supp. 323 (E.D.Va.1973), *affirmed* 496 F.2d 1192 (4th Cir.1974).

2. SEC v. Glenn W. Turner Enterprises, Inc., 474 F.2d 476 (9th Cir.1973), *cert. denied* 414 U.S. 821, 94 S.Ct. 117, 38 L.Ed.2d 53 (1973).

3. SEC v. Koscot Interplanetary, Inc., 497 F.2d 473 (5th Cir.1974).

4. In re Worm World, Inc., 3 Blue Sky L.Rep. (CCH) ¶ 71,414 (S.D. Dept. of Commerce & Consumer Affairs 1978).

5. Continental Marketing Corp. v. SEC, 387 F.2d 466 (10th Cir.1967).

6. State v. Robbins, 185 Minn. 202, 240 N.W. 456 (1932).

7. Stevens v. Liberty Packing Corp., 111 N.J.Eq. 61, 161 A. 193 (1932).

8. SEC v. Chinchilla, Inc., Fed.Sec.L.Rep. (CCH) ¶ 90,618 (N.D.Ill.1953); Hollywood State Bank v. Wilde, 70 Cal.App.2d 103, 160 P.2d 846 (1945).

9. United States v. Freiberg, 34 Fed.Appx. 281 (9th Cir.2002) (interests in ostrich breeding program were securities under California law); Bailey v. J.W.K. Properties, Inc., 904 F.2d 918 (4th Cir.1990) (cattle breeding program was an investment contract and hence a security; investors had little or no control over breeding operations or success of investment).

10. Eberhardt v. Waters, 901 F.2d 1578 (11th Cir.1990) (sale of cattle embryos was a security under Georgia blue sky law).

11. SEC v. Pyne, 33 F.Supp. 988 (D.Mass.1940). *But cf.* Deckebach v. La Vida Charters, Inc., 867 F.2d 278 (6th Cir.1989) (yacht purchase and management agreement lacked a horizontal common enterprise and thus was not a security).

12. Bell v. Health–Mor, Inc., 549 F.2d 342 (5th Cir.1977).

13. Holloway v. Thompson, 112 Ind.App. 229, 42 N.E.2d 421 (1942); In re Waldstein, 160 Misc. 763, 291 N.Y.S. 697 (1936). *But cf.* Memorial Gardens of the Valley v. Love, 5 Utah 2d 270, 300 P.2d 628 (1956) (burial lots not securities in absence of purchase for speculative investment).

14. *See* SEC v. Edwards, 540 U.S. 389, 124 S.Ct. 892, 157 L.Ed.2d 813 (2004) (pay telephone leasing program could be a security even though investors were promised a fixed rather than variable return).

tracts,[15] pooled litigation funds,[16] and fruit trees?[17] The answer is that they have all been held to be securities within the meaning of federal or state securities statutes. The vast range of such unconventional investments that have fallen within the ambit of the securities laws' coverage is due to the broad statutory definition of a "security;"[18] section 2(a)(1) of the Securities Act of 1933 is representative.[19]

The statutory definition includes certain derivative investments as securities.[20] For example, options on securities are themselves securities.[21] In 2000, Congress amended the securities laws to exclude a security-based swap agreement from the definition of security.[22] However, securities-based swap agreements are nevertheless subject to the antifraud provisions of the securities laws.[23] Futures on individual securities are within the definition of security and can now be traded in the commodities markets provided that there has been compliance with applicable regulatory provisions.[24]

In determining the basic coverage of the securities laws, the slightly different definitions of a security in the 1933 and 1934 Acts[25] are to be treated as "virtually identical," according to the Supreme Court.[26] The statutory language is expansive and has been interpreted accordingly. The broadly drafted statutory definition has continued to give the courts problems in providing predictable guidelines. Nevertheless, an attorney's failure to advise a client of the possibility of an investment offering being classified as a security can constitute legal malpractice.[28] Furthermore, it is not necessary to establish that the defendant knew that the instrument he or she was marketing was a security.[29]

---

15. *E.g.,* Kolibash v. Sagittarius Recording Co., 626 F.Supp. 1173 (S.D.Ohio 1986).

16. B.J. Tannenbaum, Jr., 18 Sec.Reg. & L.Rep. (BNA) 1826 (SEC No Action Letter Dec. 4, 1986).

17. *E.g.,* SEC v. W.J. Howey Co., 328 U.S. 293, 66 S.Ct. 1100, 90 L.Ed. 1244 (1946); SEC v. Tung Corp. of America, 32 F.Supp. 371 (N.D.Ill.1940).

18. The dictionary definition of the term is not very helpful. In fact, it is deceptive since taken literally, the concept of a security is based on the condition of being secure and free from danger (Oxford English Dictionary (2d ed. 1989)) and in reality is anything but.

19. 15 U.S.C.A. § 77b(a)(1). *See also, e.g.,* 15 U.S.C.A. § 78c(a)(10) (1976); Unif.Sec.Act § 401(e).

20. *See* In re Commission Guidance on Application of Certain Provisions of Securities Act of 1933, Securities Act of 1934, Rules thereunder to Trading in Security Futures Products, Sec. Act Rel. No. 33–8107, Sec. Exch. Act Rel. No. 34–46101, 2002 WL 1357820 (SEC June 21, 2002).

21. *See, e.g.,* Wharf (Holdings) Ltd. v. United International Holdings, Inc., 532 U.S. 588, 121 S.Ct. 1776, 149 L.Ed.2d 845 (2001) (oral option is a security subject to the federal securities laws).

22. Pub. Law 106–554, 114 Stat. 2763 (December 21, 2000). *See* 15 U.S.C.A. §§ 77b–1(b)(1), 78c–1(b)(1) (excluding "security-based swap agreements" from the definition of "security"); 15 U.S.C.A. §§ 77b–1(a), 78c–1(a) (excluding "non-security-based swap agreements" from the definition of "security"). *See also* 15 U.S.C.A. §§ 77b(a)(1), 78c(a)(10) (definition of security).

23. 1933 Act § 17(a), 1934 Act § 10(b); 15 U.S.C.A. §§ 77q(a), 78j(b).

24. 7 U.S.C.A. § 1a(31), added in Pub. Law 106–554, 114 Stat. 2763 (December 21, 2000).

25. For example, the 1934 Act excludes short-term commercial paper from the definition. Section 3(a)(10), 15 U.S.C.A. § 78c(a)(10). In contrast, although included in the 1933 Act's definition of security, short-term commercial paper is exempt from that Act's registration requirements. Sections 2(a)(1), 3(a)(3), 15 U.S.C.A. § 77a(1), 77c(a)(3).

26. Tcherepnin v. Knight, 389 U.S. 332, 335, 88 S.Ct. 548, 552, 19 L.Ed.2d 564 (1967).

28. Popham, Haik, Schnobrich, Kaufman & Doty, Ltd. v. Newcomb Securities Co., 751 F.2d 1262 (D.C.Cir.1985).

29. *See, e.g.,* SEC v. Current Financial Services, Inc., 100 F.Supp.2d 1, 5–6 (D.D.C.2000) (defendant violated the securities laws even though he did not know that the investment vehicle he was marketing was a security).

In deciding whether a particular investment vehicle is a security, a number of generalizations can be made. The investors' perceptions and expectations will be a significant factor.[33] Thus, if the investment is marketed by a securities broker, it is more likely to fall under the securities laws.[34] In a close case, the existence of a parallel federal regulatory scheme may lead a court to find that the securities laws are not necessary for investor protection.[35] It must be remembered, however, that the existence of a parallel regulatory scheme subjecting the investments in question to some other regulatory agency will not preclude a finding that a security exists. Rather, the existence of such a parallel regulatory scheme simply may tip the balance against finding a security in a case that is very close to the margins.

The courts have used various tests for determining whether a security exists. One court has indicated that if the issuer registers an investment instrument as a security merely to be cautious, the investment will still not be subject to the securities laws if it fails to meet the statutory definition.[36] The issuer's determination of the character of the investment being offered thus will not alone determine whether the investments qualify as securities. Similarly, the fact that interests are characterized as investments will not in itself classify them as securities.[37]

§ 1.6[2] Judicial Interpretation of "Investment Contract"— The *Howey* Test

The judicial definition of security has developed primarily from interpretation of the statutory phrase "investment contract." With the lead of the Supreme Court, federal and state courts have strived to arrive at a workable definition and have formulated various tests and approaches. Throughout the history of struggling for an appropriate definition, courts have been mindful of the fact that the bottom-line question is whether the particular investment or instrument involved is one that needs or demands the investor protection of the federal (or state) securities laws.[38]

In its first pronouncement on this issue, the United States Supreme Court focused on the general character of the investment vehicle in question.[39] Specifically, in determining whether a security existed, the Court looked to (1) the terms of the offer; (2) the plan of distribution; and (3) the economic inducements that were held out to the prospective purchaser. Just three years later, the Court set forth the test that survives to this day.

---

33. *E.g.,* Reves v. Ernst & Young, 494 U.S. 56, 110 S.Ct. 945, 108 L.Ed.2d 47 (1990) (short-term notes were securities). *See also, e.g.,* SEC v. I–2001, SEC News Digest 2002–4 January 7, 2002 SECDIG 2002–4–3, 2002 WL 14394 (SEC 2002) (complaint charging online solicitation of investor funds for "guaranteed" investment).

34. *E.g.,* Pollack v. Laidlaw Holdings, Inc., 27 F.3d 808 (2d Cir.1994) (mortgage participations sold by securities broker were securities).

35. Reves v. Ernst & Young, 494 U.S. 56, 110 S.Ct. 945, 108 L.Ed.2d 47 (1990) (explicitly identifying this as a factor in determining whether a note can be excluded as short-term commercial paper); Marine Bank v. Weaver, 455 U.S. 551, 102 S.Ct. 1220, 71 L.Ed.2d 409 (1982) (bank-issued certificate of deposit not a security subject to federal securities laws since it is already federally insured and purchasers therefore do not need that extra layer of protection the laws afford).

36. Great Rivers Co–op. v. Farmland Industries, Inc., 198 F.3d 685 (8th Cir.1999) ("Notwithstanding the fact that Farmland registered these instruments as securities, a registration it states was made out of caution, we agree that the characterization of the capital credits as 'rights to purchase' stock did not transform the capital credits into securities").

37. *Id.;* Teague v. Bakker, 139 F.3d 892 (4th Cir. 1998) (unpublished, text in Westlaw).

38. Marine Bank v. Weaver, 455 U.S. 551, 102 S.Ct. 1220, 71 L.Ed.2d 409 (1982) (bank-issued certificate of deposit not a security subject to federal securities laws since it is already federally insured and purchasers therefore do not need that extra layer of protection the laws afford).

39. SEC v. C.M. Joiner Leasing Corp., 320 U.S. 344, 64 S.Ct. 120, 88 L.Ed. 88 (1943).

In SEC v. W.J. Howey Co.[40] the Court announced: "An investment contract for purposes of the Securities Act means a contract, transaction or scheme whereby a person [1] invests his money [2] in a common enterprise and [3] is led to expect profits [4] solely from the efforts of the promoter or a third party."[41] The *Howey* case arose from the promotion of small lots of fruit trees when the offeror also offered a "management" contract by which an affiliate of the issuer would pick and market the fruit with the profit inuring to the investor. In finding the promotional scheme to be a security, the Court pointed out that not only are formal stock certificates not required, but a nominal ownership interest in the physical assets of the enterprise, such as actually owning fruit trees, does not preclude the determination that a security in fact exists. The Court in *Howey* did not present any single determinative factor in defining "security," but rather looked to the investment package as a whole, including the ways in which the investment was marketed to investors. This aspect of the *Howey* decision is most significant since a reading of all of the relevant cases leads to the conclusion that what is being offered may not be as important as how it is being presented.

The existence of an investment contract depends not so much on what is actually being offered but how it is being offered, and what is being promised. Thus, for example, offering and receiving money for investments that do not in fact exist violate the securities laws.[42] It is sufficient that the essential ingredients of an investment contract are being offered.[43] Fraud in describing an investment opportunity which bears the characteristics of a security can create a security even if there is no substance to the business enterprise that is described. Thus, a Ponzi scheme,[44] which resembles a chain letter, pyramid scheme, or similar fraud will implicate the federal securities laws.[45]

§ 1.6[2][A] The Investment of Money

The Supreme Court in the *Howey* decision spoke in terms of an investor in securities being someone who "invests his money."[56] Does this mean that avoiding an upfront investment of cash or the equivalent will avoid subjecting the investment to the securities laws? The clear answer is that it will not. Subsequent case law has taken the position that the investment of services or property, as opposed to money, can also suffice.[57] However, the mere fact that

---

40. 328 U.S. 293, 298–99, 66 S.Ct. 1100, 1102–03, 90 L.Ed. 1244 (1946).

41. *Id.*

42. SEC v. Lauer, 52 F.3d 667 (7th Cir.1995); SEC v. Gallard, 1997 WL 767570, [1998 Transfer Binder] Fed. Sec. L. Rep. (CCH) ¶ 90,144 (S.D.N.Y. 1997) (fact that securities did not exist did not preclude Rule 10b–5 claim).

43. SEC v. Unique Financial Concepts, 196 F.3d 1195, 1200 (11th Cir.1999), relying on SEC v. W. J. Howey Co., 328 U.S. 293, 301, 66 S.Ct. 1100, 1104, 90 L.Ed. 1244 (1946).

44. *See, e.g.,* Stuart R. Cohn, The Impact of Securities Laws on Developing Companies: Would the Wright Brothers Have Gotten Off the Ground?, 3 J. Small & Emerging Bus. L. 315, 350 n.99 (1999).

45. *See, e.g.,* S.E.C. v. Credit Bancorp, Ltd., 290 F.3d 80 (2d Cir.2002) *affirming* 195 F.Supp.2d 475 (S.D.N.Y.2002) (SEC established antifraud violations in connection with Ponzi scheme).

56. *See* § 1.6[2][A] *supra.*

57. *See, e.g.,* Popovice v. Milides, 11 F.Supp.2d 638, 643 (E.D.Pa.1998) ("several courts have held that an agreement exchanging services for stock constitutes a 'sale' under the Securities Exchange Act").

an employment agreement contains a profit sharing arrangement will not be enough to create a security.[58] On the other hand, stock appreciation rights[59] or other instruments giving the recipient the functional equivalent of stock will be a security.[60]

§ 1.6[2][B] In a Common Enterprise

Another factor under the *Howey* test for identifying an investment contract that has undergone subsequent scrutiny is the requirement that there be a common enterprise. The common enterprise requirement focuses on the question of the extent to which the success of the investor's interest rises and falls with others involved in the enterprise.[62] In contrast to the generally accepted *Howey* test, the existence of a common enterprise is not necessary under the risk capital analysis[63] that has been adopted in many states and has received at least lip service in some federal decisions.[64]

A pooling of interests among more than one investor is the clearest example of a common enterprise. However, courts have also been asked to find a common enterprise when only one investor may be involved. Courts have developed the concept of "horizontal commonality" to describe the pooling of like interests among investors,[65] in contrast to "vertical commonality" where the promoter shares risk with the investor.[66] Horizontal commonality clearly satisfies the *Howey* common enterprise requirement but the courts are divided as to whether vertical commonality will suffice.[67] However, it is equally clear that when there is no common enterprise, the *Howey* test will not be satisfied.[68]

The cases examining whether vertical commonality will suffice have taken varying approaches. The Fifth Circuit has adopted a broad test of vertical commonality that is satisfied by a showing that the fortunes of the investor are inextricably tied to the promoter's efforts.[69] The broad approach

---

58. *E.g.*, Peyton v. Morrow Electronics, Inc., 587 F.2d 413 (9th Cir.1978).

59. *E.g.*, Sanderson v. H.I.G. P–XI Holding, Inc., 2000 WL 1042813 [1999–2000 Transfer Binder] Fed. Sec. L. Rep. (CCH) ¶ 91,047 (E.D.La.2000) (stock appreciation rights are securities).

60. *See, e.g.*, Aiena v. Olsen, 69 F.Supp.2d 521, 534 (S.D.N.Y.1999) (certificates entitling former directors payments equivalent to stock dividends could be securities).

62. *See, e.g.*, SEC v. The Infinity Group Co., 212 F.3d 180 (3d Cir.2000), *affirming* 993 F.Supp. 321, 993 F.Supp. 324 (E.D.Pa.1998) (finding an investment contract based on pooling of investments where investors were promised fixed return).

63. King v. Pope, 91 S.W.3d 314 (Tenn. 2002) (sale-leaseback arrangement was a security under risk capital test even though there was no common enterprise).

64. The risk capital test is discussed in § 1.6[3] *infra*.

65. *See, e.g.*, SEC v. Infinity Group Co., 212 F.3d 180, 187–188 (3d Cir.2000) ("Horizontal commonality is characterized by 'a pooling of investors' contributions and distributions of profits and losses on a pro-rata basis among investors").

66. Many of the cases involving horizontal and vertical commonality arose in the context of deciding whether a managed brokerage account is a security.

67. *Ibid.* Vale Natural Gas America Corp. v. Carrollton Resources 1990, Ltd., 795 F.Supp. 795 (E.D.La.1992).

68. *See, e.g.*, V.F. Associates, Inc. v. Reissman, 1991 WL 49733, [1990–1991 Transfer Binder] Fed.Sec.L.Rep. (CCH) ¶ 95,917 (E.D.Pa.1991), *appeal dismissed* 958 F.2d 366 (3d Cir.1992) (agreement concerning compensation of agent selling life insurance policies to financial planning clients was not a security since it was not an agreement made between a number of passive investors but rather was negotiated by each of the parties individually).

69. Long v. Shultz Cattle Co., 881 F.2d 129, 140–41 (5th Cir.1989); Walther v. Maricopa International Investment Corp., 1998 WL 186736, [1998 Transfer Binder] Fed. Sec. L. Rep. (CCH) ¶ 90,203 (S.D.N.Y. 1998) (vertical commonality was sufficient where investor's returns were tied

to vertical commonality merely requires that the success of the investment be linked to the *efforts* of the promoter.[70] The Fifth Circuit is not alone in finding vertical commonality sufficient.[71] The Eleventh Circuit similarly recognizes a broad concept of when vertical commonality will satisfy the common enterprise requirement.[72] The court explained that the common enterprise requirement is satisfied when the investor's fortunes are tied to the success of the promoter or other third party.[73] Some courts have rejected a broad definition of vertical commonality.[74] The narrower test of vertical commonality requires that the investor's fortunes be tied to the *fortunes* of the promoter.[75] A number of courts have utilized the narrow view to find that managed commodities accounts are not securities.[76] The Ninth Circuit similarly has adopted a narrow test of vertical commonality.[77]

§ 1.6[2][C] With an Expectation of Profit

The absence of a profit expectation will preclude finding that a security exists.[82] In United Housing Foundation, Inc. v. Forman,[83] the Supreme Court established that an insignificant profit motive will not satisfy the expectation of profit requirement. This was echoed in the Court's later decision in

to the success of the investment adviser); DeWit v. Firstar Corp., 904 F.Supp. 1476 (N.D.Iowa 1995) (vertical commonality was sufficient).

70. Revak v. SEC Realty Corp., 18 F.3d 81, 87–88 (2d Cir.1994), *relying on* Long v. Shultz Cattle Co., 881 F.2d 129, 140–41 (5th Cir.1989); SEC v. Comcoa, Ltd., 855 F.Supp. 1258 (S.D.Fla.1994) (finding vertical commonality with regard to service to assist application and development of FCC licenses).

71. McGill v. American Land & Exploration Co., 776 F.2d 923, 924–25 (10th Cir.1985) (finding vertical commonality sufficient with regard to joint venture and that lack of horizontal commonality with other investors did not preclude a finding of a security).

72. SEC v. Unique Financial Concepts, 196 F.3d 1195, 1199 (11th Cir.1999); SEC v. Comcoa, Ltd., 855 F.Supp. 1258 (S.D.Fla.1994).

73. SEC v. Unique Financial Concepts, 196 F.3d 1195, 1199 (11th Cir.1999) ("a common enterprise exists where 'the fortunes of the investor are interwoven with and dependant on the efforts and success of those seeking the investment or of third parties' "), quoting from Villeneuve v. Advanced Business Concepts Corp., 698 F.2d 1121, 1124 (11th Cir.1983). *See also, e.g.*, SEC v. Koscot Interplanetary, Inc., 497 F.2d 473, 479 (5th Cir.1974) ("the fact that an investor's return is independent of that of other investors in the scheme is not decisive. Rather, the requisite commonality is evidenced by the fact that the fortunes of all investors are inexorably tied to the efficacy of the [promoter]").

74. Schofield v. First Commodity Corp., 638 F.Supp. 4 (D.Mass.1985), *judgment affirmed* 793 F.2d 28 (1st Cir.1986); Mechigian v. Art Capital Corp., 612 F.Supp. 1421, 1427 (S.D.N.Y.1985). *Accord* Silverstein v. Merrill Lynch, Pierce, Fenner & Smith, Inc., 618 F.Supp. 436 (S.D.N.Y. 1985).

75. Revak v. SEC Realty Corp., 18 F.3d 81, 88 (2d Cir.1994) (holding that interests in a condominium were not securities); SEC v. Pinckney, 923 F.Supp. 76 (E.D.N.C.1996) (to establish vertical commonality, investor's profits must be linked to promoters; question of fact as to whether "strict vertical commonality" test was satisfied).

76. Mordaunt v. Incomco, 686 F.2d 815 (9th Cir.1982), *cert. denied* 469 U.S. 1115, 105 S.Ct. 801, 83 L.Ed.2d 793 (1985); Brodt v. Bache & Co., Inc., 595 F.2d 459 (9th Cir.1978); Milnarik v. M–S Commodities, Inc., 457 F.2d 274 (7th Cir.1972), *cert. denied* 409 U.S. 887, 93 S.Ct. 113, 34 L.Ed.2d 144 (1972); Popham, Haik, Schnobrich, Kaufman & Doty, Ltd. v. Price, 1984 WL 2395, [1983–1984 Transfer Binder] Fed.Sec.L.Rep. (CCH) ¶ 99,682 (D.D.C.1984); Wasnowic v. Chicago Board of Trade, 352 F.Supp. 1066 (M.D.Pa.1972), *affirmed mem.* 491 F.2d 752 (3d Cir.1973), *cert. denied* 416 U.S. 994, 94 S.Ct. 2407, 40 L.Ed.2d 773 (1974).

77. SEC v. Goldfield Deep Mines Co., 758 F.2d 459 (9th Cir.1985).

82. *See, e.g.*, CanAccord Capital Corp., 2002 WL 126572 (SEC No Action Letter Jan. 18, 2002) (a "Term Note" accompanying a guarantee issued under the Quebec Immigrant Investor Program for Assistance to Business was not a security).

83. 421 U.S. 837, 95 S.Ct. 2051, 44 L.Ed.2d 621 (1975) (stock in residential housing cooperative was not a security).

International Brotherhood of Teamsters v. Daniel.[84] In a questionable unpublished decision, the Fourth Circuit affirmed a district court decision holding that it is not enough that the profit motive be a significant factor, it must be the primary factor in the marketing of the investment.[85] A substantial profit motive should be sufficient to support this aspect of the *Howey* test, even if it is not the only factor motivating investors.

The expectation of a profit is not limited to participation in the proceeds of a business or enterprise. Thus, the Supreme Court has made it clear that a promise of a fixed income stream can satisfy the profit requirement.[86] In an earlier decision the Court had identified the "touchstone" of an investment contract as "the presence of an investment in a common venture premised on a reasonable expectation of profits to be derived from the entrepreneurial or managerial efforts of others," and then laid out two examples of investor interests that had previously found to have been "profits."[87] The Court in its decision in SEC v. Edwards then made it clear that this was not an exclusive list of what constitutes a profit[88] in holding that a fixed return instrument can be an investment contract under the *Howey* test.

§ 1.6[2][D]　From the Efforts of Others

Under the original formulation of the *Howey* test in order to have a security the profits must have been expected "solely from the efforts of the promoter or a third party."[89] Subsequent case law in the circuit courts have diluted the requirement that the profits be secured "solely" from the efforts of others has been diluted to one that the profits be expected to be derived "primarily" or "substantially" from the efforts of others.[90] Where the investor's efforts are significant in the success of the enterprise, an investment contract (and hence a security) will not be found to exist.[91] Where the efforts of others are *de minimis* in assuring the success of the investment, the *Howey* test will not be satisfied.[92] In contrast, the fact that investors retain some control will not be sufficient to defeat the efforts of others requirement so long as the "efforts of others" are primarily significant.[93] Thus, the fact that

---

84.　439 U.S. 551, 99 S.Ct. 790, 58 L.Ed.2d 808 (1979) (involuntary noncontributory pension plan was not a security).

85.　Teague v. Bakker, 139 F.3d 892, 1998 WL 168876 (4th Cir.1998) (unpublished, text in Westlaw).

86.　SEC v. Edwards, 540 U.S. 389, 124 S.Ct. 892, 157 L.Ed.2d 813 (2004) (holding that a promise of a fixed return from a sale-leaseback arrangement satisfied *Howey's* profit requirement).

87.　United Housing Foundation, Inc. v. Forman, 421 U.S. 837, 852, 95 S.Ct. 2051, 44 L.Ed.2d 621 (1975).

88.　540 U.S. at 394–395, 124 S.Ct. at 897–898.

89.　SEC v. W.J. Howey Co., 328 U.S. 293, 298–99, 66 S.Ct. 1100, 1102–03, 90 L.Ed. 1244 (1946).

90.　*See, e.g.,* SEC v. Glenn W. Turner Enterprises, Inc., 474 F.2d 476 (9th Cir.1973), *cert. denied* 414 U.S. 821, 94 S.Ct. 117, 38 L.Ed.2d 53 (1973).

91.　*E.g.,* Steinhardt Group v. Citicorp, 126 F.3d 144 (3d Cir.1997) (limited partnership interest in securitization transaction was not a security where limited partner's retention of "pervasive control" meant that he was relying extensively on his own efforts).

92.　*E.g.,* SEC v. Life Partners, Inc., 87 F.3d 536 (D.C.Cir.1996), *rehearing denied* 102 F.3d 587 (D.C.Cir.1996) (viatical settlements, whereby investor receives death benefits of life insurance policy taken out on AIDS victim, were not securities since efforts of others was ministerial rather than substantive).

93.　*See, e.g.,* SEC v. Unique Financial Concepts, 196 F.3d 1195, 1201–1202 (11th Cir.1999).

some efforts of the investor are necessary for the success of the operation, such as with pyramid sales arrangements,[94] licensing agreements,[95] founder-membership contracts and customer referral agreements,[96] including those denominated, at least in form, as franchise contracts,[97] does not change the scheme's character from that of an investment contract. It is clear, however, that a bona fide franchise agreement is not a security.[98] Similarly, a contract to provide bona fide services is not the sale of a security. Nevertheless, a security exists when a so-called service involves a common enterprise in addition to a significant investment risk and the promoter's efforts are necessary to make the investment a success.[100] Thus, the fact that an investment may resemble a franchise in form will not insulate it from the securities laws if in substance it is a passive investment.[101]

A promoter cannot simply provide some minimum level of involvement for the investor and thereby avoid the application of the securities laws. As the foregoing discussion indicates, it is clear that the efforts of the investor must in some way be significant to the success of the enterprise in order to negate the reliance on the significant efforts of others. As noted earlier, this will depend not so much on the structure or form of the investment as it does on the expectations of investor participation that are created by the marketing efforts.

Not every effort of the promoter (or others) will render an investment subject to the securities laws. Although in one instance, a district court held that assignments of future insurance benefits, or other contract rights, were securities where the promoter's efforts are necessary to maintain a secondary market and to assure the investor of his or her profit,[102] the ruling was reversed on appeal. The court of appeals reversed, holding that the post-purchase services of others were merely ministerial and thus not sufficient to satisfy the "efforts of others" prong of the *Howey* test.[103] In the course of its opinion the court of appeals further indicated that the efforts of others must be significant for success after the instrument is marketed. Accordingly, the fact that others efforts were significant in defining and promoting the investment vehicles was not sufficient to classify viatical[104] agreements or settle-

94. *E.g.,* SEC v. Glenn W. Turner Enterprises, Inc., 474 F.2d 476 (9th Cir.1973), *cert. denied* 414 U.S. 821, 94 S.Ct. 117, 38 L.Ed.2d 53 (1973) (pyramid scheme based on self-improvement course); SEC v. Koscot Interplanetary, Inc., 497 F.2d 473 (5th Cir.1974) (pyramid scheme based on cosmetic sales distributorships was a security).

95. SEC v. Aqua–Sonic Products Corp., 524 F.Supp. 866 (S.D.N.Y.1981).

96. *See, e.g.,* United States v. Holtzclaw, 950 F.Supp. 1306 (S.D.W.Va.1997) (customer referral agreement in connection with gold investment program was not a security), *affirmed on other grounds,* 131 F.3d 137 (4th Cir. 1997).

97. *See* Mitzner v. Cardet International, Inc., 358 F.Supp. 1262 (N.D.Ill.1973).

98. *E.g.,* Martin v. T.V. Tempo, Inc., 628 F.2d 887 (5th Cir.1980).

100. *E.g.,* SEC v. Comcoa Ltd., 855 F.Supp. 1258 (S.D.Fla.1994).

101. SEC v. Friendly Power Co., 49 F.Supp.2d 1363 (S.D.Fla.1999) (interests in a limited liability company for a franchise were securities where investors had no significant control over the enterprise).

102. *See* SEC v. Life Partners, Inc., 898 F.Supp. 14 (D.D.C.1995) (viatical settlements of life insurance policies on AIDS victims), *s.c.* 912 F.Supp. 4 (D.D.C.1996), reversed 87 F.3d 536 (D.C.Cir.1996), rehearing denied 102 F.3d 587 (D.C.Cir.1996).

103. SEC v. Life Partners, Inc., 87 F.3d 536 (D.C.Cir.1996), rehearing denied 102 F.3d 587 (D.C.Cir.1996).

104. A viatical agreement permits a terminally ill patient to receive a present discounted payment on his or her life insurance benefits in return for giving up the death benefits when the

ments as securities since the promoter's activities did not bear upon the fundamental success or failure of the underlying investment.[105] There is some authority, however, to the contrary which holds viatical contracts are securities under federal law,[106] at least where investors were sold fractional interests in the underlying insurance policies.[107]

§ 1.6[3] Alternative Interpretation of "Investment Contract"—Risk Capital Analysis

The general principles of the *Howey* investment contract analysis set forth broad guidelines as to when a security will be found to exist. Many of the cases are best understood not only in terms of the general principles but in the context of the particular type of investment involved. Accordingly, after a discussion of the alternative "risk capital" test that may have some applicability under federal law, there is discussion addressing various types of investment vehicles which have been held to be securities. Supplementing the *Howey* test, many state courts and a few federal courts have followed the so-called risk capital test.[113]

Although couched in different terminology, the risk capital analysis is aimed at similar criteria as the *Howey* test, although, as noted above, under the risk capital analysis, it may not be necessary to find a common enterprise. The key is the dependency upon others for the success of the enterprise and the promotion of the activity as an investment vehicle.

The risk capital approach can be defined in terms of a four factor analysis.[114] The risk capital test will result in the finding of an investment contract when (1) the offeree provides initial value to the enterprise;[115] (2) the initial value is subject to the risks of the enterprise; (3) the initial value is induced by representations leading to a reasonable understanding that the offeree will realize a valuable benefit[116] beyond the initial value; and (4) the offeree does not exercise practical and managerial control over the enterprise.[117]

---

patient dies. These arrangements have been marketed widely, especially to H.I.V. and aids victims. A number of governments agencies have challenged these arrangements as unfair or deceptive as has the North American Securities Administrators Association. *See* Special Report, Betting on Death: Insurance Settlements Intended to Help the Dying Have Short–Changed Them and Fleeced Many Investors Instead, Consumer Reports (Feb. 2001); Viaticals Not Sure Thing, http://cnnfn.cnn.com/2001/01/16/insurance/q_viatical/.

105. *E.g.,* SEC v. Life Partners, Inc., 87 F.3d 536 (D.C.Cir.1996), *rehearing denied* 102 F.3d 587 (D.C.Cir.1996) (viatical settlements, whereby investor receives death benefits of life insurance policy taken out on AIDS victim, were not securities since efforts of others was ministerial rather than substantive).

106. SEC v. Mutual Benefits Corp., 323 F.Supp.2d 1337 (S.D. Fla. 2004) (viatical contract was a security).

107. *See* Wuliger v. Christie, 310 F.Supp.2d 897, 903–904 (N.D. Ohio 2004).

113. *E.g.,* Silver Hills Country Club v. Sobieski, 55 Cal.2d 811, 13 Cal.Rptr. 186, 361 P.2d 906 (1961).

114. Hawaii v. Hawaii Market Center, 52 Haw. 642, 485 P.2d 105, 109 (1971), *relying on* Coffey, The Economic Realities of a "Security": Is There a Meaningful Formula?, 18 W. Res. L. Rev. 366, 367 (1967).

115. This phraseology indicates that that investment of value is not limited to money or cash equivalents.

116. This language seems to make clear that a benefit other than traditional profits can satisfy the test. This is in contrast to the expectation of profit requirement under the *Howey* test.

117. This parallels *Howey's* efforts of others requirement.

While addressing the same basic concepts as the *Howey* test, the risk capital analysis provides more flexibility and does not lead to so stringent an application as to raise questions of whether vertical commonality is sufficient or whether the profit is limited to economic benefit. Thus, for example, a managed commodities account would clearly fall within the risk capital test, while many federal circuits hold that it will not be a security under the *Howey* test without some element of vertical commonality.[118] This is the case because the elements of the risk capital test can be satisfied even though the investment does not involve a common enterprise.[119] Another example of the risk capital test's inclusiveness is demonstrated in comparison with *Howey's* expectation of profit requirement. Under the *Howey* analysis, the profit expectation must be substantial if not the primary focus of the transaction.[120] In contrast, the risk capital approach looks for a "substantial benefit." Thus, for example, an equity interest in a golf course or country club can satisfy the risk capital test when it would not be a security under the *Howey* test.[121]

§ 1.6[4] Leasing Programs as Securities

A number of decisions have found that interests in leases of master video and audio recordings are investment contracts and thus have held that they are securities under both federal and state law.[124] Similarly, a video production program has been held to be a security.[125] However, when the leasing program lacks a common enterprise or is dependent upon the investor's managerial efforts, a security will not be found to exist.

In SEC v. Edwards,[129] the Supreme Court held that a sale-leaseback program involving pay telephones could be a security under the *Howey* test.[130] The Court reached this result even though the arrangement promised a fixed rather than variable return.[131]

§ 1.6[5] Franchises and Distributorships—Pyramid Schemes as Securities

As is the case with leasing programs, franchises and distributorships are not ordinarily securities.[136] This is so because in a true franchise or distribu-

---

118. *See, e.g.*, Brodt v. Bache & Co., 595 F.2d 459 (9th Cir.1978) (managed commodities account is not a security).

119. King v. Pope, 91 S.W.3d 314 (Tenn. 2002) (sale-leaseback arrangement was a security under risk capital test even though there was no common enterprise).

120. *See, e.g.*, Teague v. Bakker, 139 F.3d 892 (4th Cir. 1998) (unpublished, text in Westlaw).

121. *Compare, e.g.*, Silver Hills Country Club v. Sobieski, 55 Cal.2d 811, 13 Cal.Rptr. 186, 361 P.2d 906 (1961) (country club interest held to be a security under risk capital analysis), *with, e.g.*, Manchester Country Club, 31 Sec. Reg. & L. Rep. (BNA) 730 (SEC No Action Letter May 13, 1999) (country club equity interest would not be treated as a security under federal law); Bent Creek Country Club, 1993 WL 380731 (SEC No Action Letter Sept. 23, 1993) (country club equity interests did not have to be registered under federal law; no action letter was also secured from the state securities regulator).

124. *E.g.*, Kolibash v. Sagittarius Recording Co., 626 F.Supp. 1173 (S.D.Ohio 1986) (holding that promised tax benefits satisfied the requirement that there be an expectation of a profit).

125. Nottingham v. General American Communications Corp., 811 F.2d 873 (5th Cir.1987).

129. 540 U.S. 389,, 124 S.Ct. 892, 157 L.Ed.2d 813 (2004). *See also, e.g.*, State v. Pace, 677 N.W.2d 761 (Iowa 2004) (pay telephone sale-leaseback was a security under Iowa law);

130. As eloquently state by Justice O'Connor: "Opportunity doesn't always knock ... sometimes it rings. App. 113 (ETS Payphones promotional brochure). And sometimes it hangs up. So it did for the 10,000 people who invested a total of $300 million in the payphone sale-and-leaseback arrangements touted by respondent under that slogan." 540 U.S. at 391, 124 S.Ct. at 895.

131. 540 U.S. at 394–395, 124 S.Ct. at 897–898.

136. *E.g.*, Martin v. T.V. Tempo, Inc., 628 F.2d 887 (5th Cir.1980); Nash & Associates, Inc. v. Lum's of Ohio, Inc., 484 F.2d 392 (6th Cir.1973).

tion, the efforts of the franchisee or distributor are extremely significant in the success of the enterprise.[137] However, when the efforts of the promoter or someone associated with the promoter are the undeniably significant ones, a security will exist. If the efforts of the promoter are so significant, the fact that *some* efforts of the investor are necessary for the success of the operation will not preclude a security from being found. Thus, pyramid sales arrangements,[138] licensing agreements,[139] founder-membership contracts and customer referral agreements,[140] including those denominated, at least in form, as franchise contracts,[141] have all been found to be securities under an economic reality analysis. It is clear that simply because an investment may resemble a franchise in form, the investment will not be insulated from the securities laws if in substance it is passive and its success is substantially dependent on the efforts of others.[142]

§ 1.6[6] Commodities and Managed Accounts as Securities

Another fertile area of litigation has involved the classification of commodities—related investments. Based upon the extent of managerial and market-making activities offered by the seller, a gold investment has been held to be a security.[143] However, when all that is offered is the underlying commodity combined with storage and marketing services there is no security as the investor is relying upon the market price of the commodity rather than the seller's marketing or managerial efforts.[144] In contrast, when the object underlying the futures contract is itself a security, the futures contract may also be classified as a security.[145] This type of arrangement is in economic reality more like a securities option contract, which is clearly a security. However, where the subject of the futures contract is not a security but merely an index based on securities prices, a security has been held not to exist.[146] In 2000, Congress resolved some of these issues in amending the securities and commodities laws to provide that trading can now take place in futures on individual securities; and these futures contracts may be traded in

---

137. *See* the discussion of the efforts of others § 1.6[2][D] *supra.*

138. *E.g.,* SEC v. Glenn W. Turner Enterprises, Inc., 474 F.2d 476 (9th Cir.1973), *cert. denied* 414 U.S. 821, 94 S.Ct. 117, 38 L.Ed.2d 53 (1973) (pyramid scheme based on self-improvement course); SEC v. Koscot Interplanetary, Inc., 497 F.2d 473 (5th Cir.1974) (pyramid scheme based on cosmetic sales distributorships was a security).

139. SEC v. Aqua–Sonic Products Corp., 524 F.Supp. 866 (S.D.N.Y.1981).

140. *See, e.g.* Florida Discount Centers, Inc. v. Antinori, 232 So.2d 17 (Fla.1970); Hawaii v. Hawaii Market Center, Inc., 52 Hawaii 642, 485 P.2d 105 (1971).

141. *See* Mitzner v. Cardet International, Inc., 358 F.Supp. 1262 (N.D.Ill.1973).

142. SEC v. Friendly Power Co., 49 F.Supp.2d 1363 (S.D.Fla.1999) (interests in a limited liability company for a franchise were securities where investors had no significant control over the enterprise).

143. SEC v. International Mining Exchange, Inc., 515 F.Supp. 1062 (D.Colo.1981).

144. *See, e.g.,* Noa v. Key Futures, Inc., 638 F.2d 77 (9th Cir.1980). *Cf.* Dahl v. English, 578 F.Supp. 17 (N.D.Ill.1983) (artwork held not to be a security).

145. Abrams v. Oppenheimer Government Securities, Inc., 737 F.2d 582 (7th Cir.1984).

146. Mallen v. Merrill Lynch, Pierce, Fenner & Smith Inc., 605 F.Supp. 1105 (N.D.Ga.1985). *See generally* David J. Gilberg, Regulation of New Financial Instruments Under the Federal Securities and Commodities Laws, 39 Vand.L.Rev. 1599 (1986). *See* § 1.7 *infra.*

both the securities and commodities markets.[147] That same legislation also provided that securities-based swap agreements are not securities, although they are subject to the securities laws' antifraud provisions.[148] Swap agreements have been held not to be securities under state securities laws.[149]

The Fifth[150] and Eighth[151] Circuits have held that a managed brokerage account is a security. The pivotal issue is the existence of a common enterprise. The courts have analyzed this in terms of vertical or horizontal commonality. The Fifth Circuit has adopted a broad test of vertical commonality that is satisfied by a showing that the fortunes of the investor are inextricably tied to the promoter's efforts.[152] The Second Circuit has rejected the broad view of vertical commonality in favor of a stricter view.[153] The broad test of vertical commonality simply requires that the success of the investment be linked to the *efforts* of the promoter.[154] In contrast, the narrower test of vertical commonality requires that the investor's fortunes be tied to the *fortunes* of the promoter.[155] Utilizing this test, the Seventh,[156] Third[157] and Ninth Circuits have held that managed commodities accounts are not securities.

§ 1.6[7] Employee Benefit Plans as Securities

The Howey test has been refined to include significant investment of valuable consideration other than money (such as goods or services) with the expectation of a profit as a means for finding an investment vehicle subject to federal securities laws. Viewing services as a sufficient investment leads to the conclusion that employee benefit plans can constitute securities.

In International Brotherhood of Teamsters v. Daniel,[170] the Supreme Court ruled that a compulsory noncontributory defined benefit employee pension plan is not a security under the 1933 Act's definition. The Court made note of not only the involuntary nature of the plan, but also the fact

---

147. Commodity Futures Modernization Act of 2000, Pub. Law No. 106–554, 114 Stat. 2763 (Dec. 21, 2000).

148. *Id.*

149. Lehman Bros. Commercial Corp. v. Minmetals Intern. Non–Ferrous Metals Trading Co., 179 F.Supp.2d 159 (S.D.N.Y.2001).

150. SEC v. Continental Commodities Corp., 497 F.2d 516 (5th Cir.1974). *See also e.g.,* Taylor v. Bear Stearns & Co., 572 F.Supp. 667 (N.D.Ga.1983); Westlake v. Abrams, 565 F.Supp. 1330 (N.D.Ga.1983).

151. Booth v. Peavey Co. Commodity Services, 430 F.2d 132, 133 (8th Cir.1970) (indicating the presence of a remedy under the securities acts for churning in a discretionary commodities account).

152. This broad test has been rejected by other courts. *E.g.,* Schofield v. First Commodity Corp., 638 F.Supp. 4 (D.Mass.1985), *judgment affirmed* 793 F.2d 28 (1st Cir.1986).

153. Revak v. SEC Realty Corp., 18 F.3d 81 (2d Cir.1994).

154. *Id.* at 87–88, *relying on* Long v. Shultz Cattle Co., 881 F.2d 129, 140–41 (5th Cir.1989); SEC v. ETS Payphones, Inc., 123 F.Supp.2d 1349, 1353 (N.D.Ga.2000)*reversed* 300 F.3d 1281 (11th Cir.2002) (sale-leaseback agreement involving pay telephones constituted a security where the fortunes of the investors were tied to the efforts of the promoter).

155. *See, e.g.,* Revak v. SEC Realty Corp., 18 F.3d 81, 88 (2d Cir.1994) (holding that interests in a condominium were not securities).

156. Milnarik v. M–S Commodities, Inc., 457 F.2d 274 (7th Cir.1972), *cert. denied* 409 U.S. 887, 93 S.Ct. 113, 34 L.Ed.2d 144 (1972).

157. Wasnowic v. Chicago Board of Trade, 352 F.Supp. 1066 (M.D.Pa.1972), *affirmed mem.* 491 F.2d 752 (3d Cir.1973), *cert. denied* 416 U.S. 994, 94 S.Ct. 2407, 40 L.Ed.2d 773 (1974).

170. 439 U.S. 551, 99 S.Ct. 790, 58 L.Ed.2d 808 (1979).

that there was no employee contribution (*i.e.*, no investment of money); these factors strongly negated any inference that a security was involved. The Court also noted that insofar as it was faced with a defined benefit plan, the pay-out to the employee upon retirement bore no relation to the employee's contribution in terms of time in service. Another factor considered by the Supreme Court in *Daniel* was that there was no substantial expectation of a profit. Since a large part of the eventual retirement benefits were to be derived from the employer's contribution, rather than from the reinvestment income derived from the efforts of pension plan managers, the profit aspects of the plan were too insubstantial to fall within the concept of an investment contract. Moreover, the Court focused on a number of contingencies to the plan's vesting, which in turn rendered any "profit" too speculative to justify a reasonable expectation. Because of the multiplicity of factors involved in the *Daniel* decision, it cannot be safely said that a pension plan will never be characterized as a security. In fact, benefit plans that have the investment characteristics of securities will fall under the Act. For example, a voluntary contributory plan with a variable annuity might well be found to be subject to the securities laws.[172] Similarly, interests in a voluntary employee stock option plan clearly are securities.[173] In contrast, a mandatory stock option plan completely funded by the employer is not a security.[174]

There are public policy reasons to minimize the impact of the securities laws on certain types of employee compensation plans in order to encourage employers to offer employees a share in the profits of the business. Accordingly, stock compensation plans of non-public companies can qualify for an exemption from the 1933 Act's registration requirements.[175] Compensation to executives and other key employees of both privately held and publicly traded companies may also qualify for an exemption from registration.[176] Additionally, stock offerings to employees of publicly held companies can qualify for a very short registration form.[177]

§ 1.6[8] Variable Annuities as Securities

While variable annuity contracts come within the ambit of the securities laws,[178] fixed annuities, as is the case with insurance policies, generally do not.[179] However, the Seventh Circuit held an annuity with a minimum guarantee to be a security.[180] The Commission has adopted a safe harbor rule

---

172. *Cf.* SEC v. Variable Annuity Life Insurance Co., 359 U.S. 65, 79 S.Ct. 618, 3 L.Ed.2d 640 (1959) (variable annuity held to be a non-exempt security).

173. *E.g.,* Uselton v. Commercial Lovelace Motor Freight, Inc., 940 F.2d 564 (10th Cir.1991), *cert. denied* 502 U.S. 983, 112 S.Ct. 589, 116 L.Ed.2d 614 (1991) (contributory voluntary employee stock ownership plan was a security; ERISA did not provide sufficient protection to displace the application of federal securities laws); Hood v. Smith's Transfer Corp., 762 F.Supp. 1274, 1290–1291 (W.D.Ky.1991).

174. Matassarin v. Lynch, 174 F.3d 549 (5th Cir.1999).

175. SEC Rule 701, 17 C.F.R. § 230.701, which is discussed in § 4.18 *infra.*

176. The applicable exemption here would be the one for transactions by issuers not involving a public offering. 1933 Act § 4(2), 15 U.S.C.A. § 77d(2), which is discussed in §§ 4.24, 4.25 *infra.*

177. 1933 Act Form S–8, 17 C.F.R. § 239.16b.

178. *See, e.g.,* SEC v. Variable Annuity Life Insurance Co., 359 U.S. 65, 79 S.Ct. 618, 3 L.Ed.2d 640 (1959) (variable annuity held to be a non-exempt security).

179. Allen v. Lloyd's of London, 94 F.3d 923 (4th Cir.1996) (settlement of disputes and formation of reinsurance entity did not involve securities since the participants in the settlement did not stand to make any profit from the reinsurance enterprise).

180. Otto v. Variable Annuity Life Ins. Co., 814 F.2d 1127 (7th Cir.1986) (the court noted that the minimum was low and there was an expectation of a higher payout).

under which qualifying annuities need not be registered as securities.[181] Those annuities qualifying for the safe harbor include annuities with guaranteed purchase benefits based on the purchase price and interest credited thereto, provided further that the annuity contracts are not marketed as investments.[182] The safe harbor thus depends on the investment risk falling on the insurer rather than the insured.

§ 1.6[9] Real Estate Interests as Securities

In a decision that predated *Daniel*, the Supreme Court, in United Housing Foundation, Inc. v. Forman, ruled that shares of stock in a cooperative residential housing project did not fall within the Securities Act's definition.[183] Although "stock" is expressly included in the Act's definition of security, the fact that the shares were denominated as stock by the corporation was not considered dispositive of the matter since the shares had none of the traditional characteristics which stocks generally possess.[184] The Court upheld substance over form and focused upon the economic reality of the investment venture. The Court distinguished resort condominium cases in which someone might well be induced to purchase the property primarily for investment, since the buildings in *Forman* were used as bona fide primary residences. Although the other criteria of the four-factor *Howey* test may have been met, there was no expectation of a profit, despite promised rent deductions through profits rebated from commercial leasing. The Court found that this "return" on the commercial properties was, at best, tangential to the stock and thus the residential lease agreements were properly characterized as residential housing contracts rather than as investment contracts.[186]

Generally, a conveyance of real estate will not be subject to the securities laws.[187] Thus, for example, a condominium interest will not ordinarily be a security.[188] However, when a transaction has the investment type indicia normally associated with investment contracts, a security may be found to exist.[189] Sale of a real estate interest for commercial purposes will be a security when the profit potential is dependent upon management of the real estate by the promoter of the real estate program.[190] Residential real estate can also be a

---

181. 17 C.F.R. § 230.151. *See* § 4.9 *infra*.

182. 17 C.F.R. § 230.151.

183. 421 U.S. 837, 95 S.Ct. 2051, 44 L.Ed.2d 621 (1975). *Accord* Hackford v. First Security Bank of Utah, 464 U.S. 827, 104 S.Ct. 100, 78 L.Ed.2d 105 (1983) (shares of "stock" in range land entitling owners to grazing privileges held not a security since there was no profit expectation).

184. "Despite their name, they lack what the court in Tcherepnin deemed the most common feature of stock: the right to receive 'dividends contingent upon an apportionment of profits'. 389 U.S. at 339. Nor do they possess the other characteristics traditionally associated with stock: they are not negotiable; they cannot be pledged or hypothecated; they confer no voting rights in proportion to the number of shares owned; and they cannot appreciate in value." 421 U.S. at 851, 95 S.Ct. at 2060.

186. 421 U.S. at 855–58, 95 S.Ct. at 2061–63.

187. *E.g.,* Wals v. Fox Hills Development Corp., 24 F.3d 1016 (7th Cir.1994) (sale of time share unit was not sale of a security); Rodriguez v. Banco Central Corp., 990 F.2d 7 (1st Cir.1993) (sale of residential real estate did not involve a security).

188. Revak v. SEC Realty Corp., 18 F.3d 81 (2d Cir.1994).

189. Hocking v. Dubois, 885 F.2d 1449 (9th Cir.1989), *cert. denied* 494 U.S. 1078, 110 S.Ct. 1805, 108 L.Ed.2d 936 (1990) (question of fact as to whether rental pool arrangement was a security).

190. *See, e.g.,* Triple Net Leasing, LLC, 2000 WL 1221859 (SEC No Action Letter Aug. 23, 2000) (exchange of net real estate interest with net lease arrangement would be a security).

security when marketed for investment purposes. Thus, for example, a security will exist where residential condominium interests are marketed with collateral agreements giving rise to a profit expectation.[191] Similarly, the currently fashionable marketing of real estate interests through time-share or shared equity programs raises securities law issues because of the possibility of finding an investment contract.[192] However, properly marketed as a vacation residence, time-share interests will not be securities.[193] Nevertheless, when the time-share interest is offered more as an investment than a place to stay, the securities laws are more likely to be implicated.

Fractional undivided interests in oil and mineral rights are expressly covered by the statutory definition of security.[195] However, a leasehold interest has been held to be an interest in realty and thus not a security.[196]

Country club memberships can be seen as analogous to real estate interests. Frequently country clubs raise funds through founder-memberships or the issuance of stock in lieu of an initiation fee. Country club interests may be classified as securities under some state laws,[198] but ordinarily will not be subject to federal law because of the absence of a profit expectation.[199] However, if there is a profit potential, then the federal definition may be invoked.[200]

Outside of the real estate context, it has been held that a syndication agreement will not be subject to the securities laws where "the agreement is designed to allow the investor to *use* or *consume* the item purchased."[201] However, the result should be otherwise if the shares are marketed as an investment rather than simply a consumable.

§ 1.6[10] Partnership Interests as Securities

Another type of arrangement that clearly falls into the reach of the securities law is the limited partnership. In some instances, joint ventures and general partnerships might also fall under the securities laws' coverage. In the

---

191. *See* Hocking v. Dubois, 839 F.2d 560 (9th Cir.1988).

192. *See, e.g.,* David M. Fields, Real Estate Interests as Investment Contracts: An Update and a New Application:The Shared Equity Program, 12 Real Est. L.J. 307 (1984).

193. So long as there is no pooling of profits, the fact that there is a pooling of weeks with regard to residential occupancy does not create a security. *See* Wals v. Fox Hills Development Corp., 24 F.3d 1016 (7th Cir.1994), *affirming* 828 F.Supp. 623 (E.D.Wis.1993) (the court pointed out that each time share owner's interest was a separate slice of an interest in realty).

195. *See* Cascade Energy & Metals Corp. v. Banks, 896 F.2d 1557 (10th Cir.1990), *cert. denied* 498 U.S. 849, 111 S.Ct. 138, 112 L.Ed.2d 105 (1990).

196. Deutsch Energy Co. v. Mazur, 813 F.2d 1567 (9th Cir.1987); Coal Resources, Inc. v. Gulf & Western Indus., Inc., 756 F.2d 443 (6th Cir.1985).

198. *E.g.,* Silver Hills Country Club v. Sobieski, 55 Cal.2d 811, 13 Cal.Rptr. 186, 361 P.2d 906 (1961).

199. *E.g.,* Rice v. Branigar Organization, Inc., 922 F.2d 788 (11th Cir.1991), (sale of membership and undeveloped lots in beach club development was not the sale of a security); WA Golf Company, L.L.C., 2004 WL 1713749 (SEC No Action Letter July 30, 2004) (sale of country club memberships did not have to be registered under the 1933 Act).

200. Club at Pelican Bay, Inc., 26 Sec. Reg. & L. Rep. (BNA) 104 (SEC no action letter available Jan. 7, 1994) (refusing to issue a no action response for transferable country club interests).

201. Wabash Valley Power Association v. Public Service Co. of Indiana, 678 F.Supp. 757 (S.D.Ind.1988) (contract for construction of nuclear power plant held not a security since investor planned to use resulting power); Kefalas v. Bonnie Brae Farms, Inc., 630 F.Supp. 6, 8 (E.D.Ky. 1985) (thoroughbred breeding syndication was not a security even though purchaser did not own mares and hoped for price appreciation in breeding rights).

case of a limited partnership interest, the Uniform Limited Partnership Act requires that, at least to some extent, the investment be a passive one. Any significant degree of control or management in the enterprise may transform the limited partner into a general partner.[203] Accordingly, any time there is a bona fide limited partnership interest, by definition, the investor puts his or her funds at risk depending primarily upon the efforts of others, *i.e.,* the managing partners. It follows that unless the limited partner exercises an unusual amount of control over the business,[204] his or her limited partnership interest will be a security.

Some state securities acts expressly include limited partnership interests in the definition of security.[208] Under the case law, there is a presumption that general partnership interests do not qualify as securities.[209]

A growing number of states have recognized a new variety of limited partnership known as the limited liability limited partnership.[210] This variation permits partners to become general partners and still stand behind a limited liability shield. Accordingly, in a limited liability limited partnership a limited partner may become a general partner without losing his or her limited liability. This permits limited partners to become general partners and have significant say in the day-to-day operations of the partnership business and would likely not be subject to the securities laws for the same reason that a general partnership interest ordinarily is not a security.

Since a general partnership interest and most joint ventures will ordinarily carry with them a substantial say in the management of the enterprise, they will not fall under the securities laws' purview unless there is substantial reliance on the efforts of others. However, where a joint venturer or general partner does not exercise control and in essence is a passive investor, a security will be found to exist.[214] The fact that partners in a general partnership have the potential to exercise control in the enterprise will not preclude any general partnership interest from being a security. The ultimate determination will depend on the ways in which the partnership interests are marketed to the investors. If it is contemplated that the partners will play a passive role while the business is managed by someone else, then the securities laws are likely to be implicated.

§ 1.6[11] Limited Liability Company Interests as Securities

In the 1980s the limited liability company emerged as a new form of doing business and has continued to become increasingly popular. In fact, in

203. *See, e.g.,* Weil v. Diversified Properties, 319 F.Supp. 778 (D.D.C.1970).

204. *See, e.g.,* David v. L.A. Presidential Management II, L.P., 2000 WL 1207157 (E.D.Pa. 2000) (control by limited partner meant that his limited partnership interest was not a security).

208. *See* Rivlin v. Levine, 195 Cal.App.2d 13, 15 Cal.Rptr. 587 (1961) (California statute at that time excluded limited partnerships from security laws except if the partnership interest was offered to the public, West's Ann.Cal.Corp. Code § 25100(e)).

209. *See, e.g.,* D & D Management Inc. v. Gulftex Energy Corp., 35 Sec. Reg. & L. Rep. (BNA) 189 (N.D. Ga. 2003).

210. *E.g.,* Ark. Code Ann. § 4–43–1111; Colo. Rev. Stats. Ann. §§ 7–64–101 *et seq.*; Del. Code Ann. tit. 6 § 17–214; West's Fla. Stats. Ann. § 608.402; Ga. Code §§ 14–8–62 *et seq.*; Minn. Stats. Ann. § 322A.88; Vernon's Annot. Mo. Stats. § 359.172; No. Dak. Cent. Code §§ 45–23–01 *et seq.*; Va. Code § 50–73.78.

214. *See, e.g.,* Stone v. Kirk, 8 F.3d 1079 (6th Cir.1993) (joint venture interests were securities where the investors relied substantially on the expertise and managerial skills of the promoter); Reeves v. Teuscher, 881 F.2d 1495 (9th Cir.1989) (general partnership interest in real estate venture was a security).

many instances, the limited liability company has become the entity of choice in forming a new business. Limited liability companies are designed to give investors the benefit of pass-through tax treatment that applies to limited partnerships without imposing the limitation that limited partners may not exert too much control in the day-to-day management lest they be declared general partners and thereby lose their limited liability shield. The limited liability company has become the form of choice for noncorporate business entities.[218] Since neither partnership interests nor shares in limited liability companies are expressly listed in the Act's definition of "security," unlike corporate stock, they qualify as securities only if they fall within the definition of an "investment contract."[219] Many limited liability companies (and hence shares in those companies) have corporate attributes, including possibly the centralization of management. Nevertheless, limited liability companies can be set up without centralized management and in such cases should be treated like a general partnership which ordinarily is not a security. However, if the limited liability company agreement provides a centralized management, for the same reasons that a limited partnership interest ordinarily will be a security, interests in limited liability companies will implicate the securities laws. A number of states have dealt with this nontraditional form of doing business by expressly treating limited liability companies as securities.[222]

§ 1.6[12] Beneficial Interests in Business Trusts and Real Estate Investment Trusts as Securities

In addition to the partnership form of doing business and limited liability companies which are discussed directly above, business trusts can be used as an investment vehicle. A very common example is a real estate investment trust. Although the statutory definition of security does not expressly include a business trust,[232] beneficial interests in a business trust satisfy the *Howey* for classifying an investment contract as a security. As a passive investment in a business carried on by others, it is clear that a beneficial interest in a business trust is a security.[233] Furthermore, in its definition of equity security under the Securities Exchange Act of 1934, a business trust is expressly included.[234]

§ 1.6[13] Stock as a Security

Stock is one of the enumerated instruments in section 2(a)(1)'s definition of a security. Thus, there is a strong presumption that stock is a security.

---

218. A form of doing business that may be analogized to a limited liability company with a centralized management is a business trust. Beneficial interests in business trusts are generally treated as securities. *Cf., e.g.,* Sheppard v. TCW/DW Term Trust 2000, 938 F.Supp. 171 (S.D.N.Y.1996) (securities fraud action dismissed for lack of materiality and scienter).

219. *E.g.,* Robinson v. Glynn, 349 F.3d 166 (4th Cir. 2003) (applying investment contract analysis based on the particular company involved rather than trying to craft an across-the-board conclusion for all LLCs).

222. *See, e.g.,* N.H. Rev. Stat. Ann. § 421–B:13 (requiring limited liability companies to indicate whether they are registering their interests as securities or are relying on an exemption); Indiana Code § 23–2–1 (including limited liability company within the definition of security).

232. It does, however, include a voting trust certificate or collateral trust certificate. 15 U.S.C.A. §§ 77b(a)(1), 78c(a)(10).

233. *See, e.g.,* SEC v. Banner Fund International, 211 F.3d 602, 614–615 (D.C.Cir.2000) (interests in offshore business trust were securities). *See also, e.g.,* Melton v. Unterreiner, 575 F.2d 204 (8th Cir.1978).

234. 1934 Act Rule 3a–11, 17 C.F.R. § 240.3a–11.

In United Housing Foundation v. Forman,[235] the Supreme Court held that stock in residential housing cooperative was not a security. The Court pointed out that although stock is expressly included in the definition of security, the stock in *Forman* was not stock as that term is generally understood. The stock merely evidenced an interest in the cooperative building and a right to occupy the residential unit attached to the lease. The Court also noted that the stock was not transferable without the lease, and there was no profit incentive.[236] Thus, as a matter of the economic realities, the stock represented an interest in real estate rather than a business venture. Other certificates that are labeled stock or equity interests have been held not to be securities on similar grounds. Thus, for example, interests in an agricultural cooperative that represent the holders right to reap the commercial benefits in the cooperative are not securities.[237] Stock in other cooperative ventures has been held not to be securities. Stock in a credit association has been held not to be a security.[239] Also, stock in a country club that entitled the holder to membership is not a security because it is something other than conventional investment stock.[240] Memberships in retail cooperatives are not securities if there is no investment incentive.[242]

The courts in the foregoing cases and SEC no action letters holding that something labeled stock was not a security pointed out that the shares in question did not possess the characteristics of stock in business corporations.[244] It would follow that corporate stock (as well as options[245] on such stock) is a security. Nevertheless, utilizing the economic reality test of earlier cases, it was held that the sale of stock in a closely held corporation may not be a "security" especially if it is, in essence, a transfer of the ownership and management of the corporation's assets.[246] The circuits were in conflict as to the validity of this "sale of business" exception for including stock as a

---

235. 421 U.S. 837, 95 S.Ct. 2051, 44 L.Ed.2d 621 (1975).

236. The stock in *Forman* did not permit the holder to realize any appreciation in value. Even in more traditional cooperatives where the seller of the stock will be entitled to an appreciation in value, this appreciation would derive from the increase in the value of the real estate interest rather than any business enterprise. And, as discussed above, real estate ordinarily is not a security.

237. Great Rivers Co–op. v. Farmland Industries, Inc., 198 F.3d 685 (8th Cir.1999) (capital credits in agricultural cooperative that had been received in exchange for equity interests and were exchangeable into equity interests were not securities).

239. Seger v. Federal Intermediate Credit Bank of Omaha, 850 F.2d 468 (8th Cir.1988) (Class B stock in production credit association was held not to be a security).

240. *E.g.,* Manchester Country Club, 31 Sec. Reg. & L. Rep. (BNA) 730 (SEC No Action Letter May 13, 1999) (country club equity interest would not be treated as a security).

242. NBF Acquisition, Inc., 1997 WL 157493 (SEC No Action Letter April 1, 1997) (stock and patronage notes were not securities).

244. United Housing Foundation v. Forman, 421 U.S. 837, 95 S.Ct. 2051, 44 L.Ed.2d 621 (1975); Great Rivers Co–op. v. Farmland Industries, Inc., 198 F.3d 685 (8th Cir.1999); Seger v. Federal Intermediate Credit Bank of Omaha, 850 F.2d 468 (8th Cir.1988).

245. It is clear that an option on a security is itself a security. *See, e.g.,* Fry v. UAL Corp., 84 F.3d 936, 937–38 (7th Cir.1996), *relying on* Blue Chip Stamps v. Manor Drug Stores, 421 U.S. 723, 750–51, 95 S.Ct. 1917, 1932–33, 44 L.Ed.2d 539 (1975); Fenoglio v. Augat, Inc., 50 F.Supp.2d 46 (D.Mass.1999). *See also, e.g.,* Section 3(a)(11) of the 1934 Act, 15 U.S.C.A. § 78c(a)(10), which defines equity security to clearly include an option on stock. *Compare, e.g.,* Morales v. New Valley Corp., 968 F.Supp. 139 (S.D.N.Y.1997) (assignment of right to receive fees based on appreciation of company's stock was not a derivative security so as to subject it to section 16(b) of the Securities Exchange Act of 1934).

246. *E.g.,* Landreth Timber Co. v. Landreth, 731 F.2d 1348 (9th Cir.1984) *reversed* 471 U.S. 681, 105 S.Ct. 2297, 85 L.Ed.2d 692 (1985).

security. One court went so far as to hold that the sale of fifty percent of the outstanding shares is not a sale of securities subject to either state or federal securities regulation.[248] The Tenth Circuit has held that transfer of eighty-one percent of the stock to a purchaser who was to manage the business was a sale of the business and thus not subject to the securities laws.[249] The Seventh Circuit, in an even more questionable decision, imposed a rebuttable presumption that no security is involved when more than fifty percent of the stock is purchased.[250]

In companion decisions, the Supreme Court rejected outright the sale of business doctrine, reasoning that when a business enterprise elects the corporate form and offers shares with the traditional indicia of ownership, the statutory definition is satisfied.[252] The Court's holding in *Landreth Timber* confirms that it will not aggressively utilize the economic reality test to limit applicability of the securities acts to transactions falling within a literal reading of the statute. It therefore appears that the Court's earlier restrictive ruling in *Forman* relating to stock in a government subsidized residential housing cooperative may well be *sui generis* (or close to it) and thus entitled to relatively little precedential effect except on facts very similar to those in *Forman*.[253] Otherwise, the shares of stock will be characterized as securities.[254]

Notwithstanding the rejection of the sale of business doctrine, a corporate acquisition that is not structured in terms of a stock transaction will not implicate the securities laws.[255] The form of a corporate acquisition will generally determine the extent to which the securities laws are implicated.

§ 1.6[14] Notes as Securities

Section 2(a)(1) expressly includes "any note" within the definition of a security.[265] As discussed in the discussion that follows, most of the concern over the application of the securities laws has centered around short term notes. This is because there is no exemption for long-term obligations. The broad concept of note means that even a personal loan can qualify as a security if it is not covered by the exemption for short term commercial paper. Thus, for example, one state court has held that a when a stock broker issued a promissory note in exchange for a loan from a customer, that note was a security.[266] It is noteworthy that the loan was by a customer to his stock broker thus providing a securities-related nexus. However, the decision did not expressly limit its application to that context. As such the decision could have far-reaching implications. Although personal nature of loans help qualify

---

248. Oakhill Cemetery of Hammond, Inc. v. Tri–State Bank, 513 F.Supp. 885 (N.D.Ill. 1981).

249. Christy v. Cambron, 710 F.2d 669 (10th Cir.1983).

250. Sutter v. Groen, 687 F.2d 197 (7th Cir.1982).

252. Landreth Timber Co. v. Landreth, 471 U.S. 681, 105 S.Ct. 2297, 85 L.Ed.2d 692 (1985); Gould v. Ruefenacht, 471 U.S. 701, 105 S.Ct. 2308, 85 L.Ed.2d 708 (1985).

253. *Ibid.*

254. *See, e.g.,* Jeanne Piaubert, S.A. v. Sefrioui, 208 F.3d 221 (9th Cir. 2000) (unpublished opinion) (sufficiently alleging that stock was a security).

255. Coal Resources, Inc. v. Gulf & Western Industries, Inc., 756 F.2d 443 (6th Cir.1985), *on remand* 645 F.Supp. 1028 (S.D.Ohio 1986), *reversed* 865 F.2d 761 (6th Cir.1989).

265. 15 U.S.C.A. § 77b(a)(1).

266. Mosley v. State, 253 Ga.App. 710, 560 S.E.2d 305 (2002) (criminal conviction, treating note as unregistered security).

for the exemption for short term commercial paper;[267] this is not the case with longer term notes. Nevertheless, it is conceivable that a court might interpret the statutory definition in section 2(a)(1) not to apply to notes issued in exchange for personal loans. The court could reach this result in much the same way that the Supreme Court decided that stock issued in connection with residential cooperative housing was not a security.[268] The rationale for such a result excluding long-term promissory notes from the definition, would be that the preamble to section 2(a) provides that the definition apply "unless the context otherwise requires."[269] The proper interpretation would seem to be that a purely personal loan (outside of the context of securities transactions) was not intended to be covered by the securities loans even if that loan is secured by a note.

Section 3(a)(3) of the Securities Act of 1933 exempts any "note * * * aris[ing] out of a current transaction" with a maturity not exceeding nine months.[272] In contrast section 3(a)(10) of the Securities Exchange Act of 1934 excludes such short term notes from the definition of a security.[273] For a long time the courts employed the economic reality test by asking whether the transaction under scrutiny is an investment vehicle which would trigger the securities acts' coverage or whether it is more properly characterized as a commercial venture which should not be subjected to the securities laws.[274] This became known as the investment/commercial dichotomy. Then, in 1990, the Supreme Court focused on the economic reality and employed a similar "family resemblance test" in holding that a variable rate demand note issued by a farmers' cooperative was a security.[275]

Even in the face of the family resemblance test or the commercial-investment dichotomy, the fact that the issuer of a short-term note is a bank does not preclude the finding that a security exists.[276] Thus, when notes or loan agreements have investment attributes, the courts have found securities to exist.[277] However, the courts have been willing to find a commercial rather than investment context, especially when bank financing is involved. The statutory definition of security has been held not to be implicated when the loan agreement is purely commercial, is relatively short term, and has a rate of interest comparable to the applicable prevailing commercial rate which is not varied with the profitability of the lender.[278] Further, the fact that there is

---

267. *See* the discussion of the family resemblance test that follows in the text.

268. United Housing Foundation, Inc. v. Forman, 421 U.S. 837, 95 S.Ct. 2051, 44 L.Ed.2d 621 (1975). *See* the discussion in § 1.6[13] *supra*.

269. 15 U.S.C.A. § 77b(a).

272. 15 U.S.C.A. § 77c(a)(3).

273. 15 U.S.C.A. § 78c(a)(10).

274. *See, e.g.,* Arthur Young & Co. v. Reves, 856 F.2d 52 (8th Cir.1988), *reversed* 494 U.S. 56, 110 S.Ct. 945, 108 L.Ed.2d 47 (1990) (demand note was not a security).

275. Reves v. Ernst & Young, 494 U.S. 56, 110 S.Ct. 945, 108 L.Ed.2d 47 (1990).

276. Exchange National Bank of Chicago v. Touche Ross & Co., 544 F.2d 1126 (2d Cir.1976).

277. *E.g.,* SEC v. Eurobond Exchange, Ltd., 13 F.3d 1334 (9th Cir.1994) (Eurobond investment program held to be a security); McGill v. American Land & Exploration Co., 776 F.2d 923, 925 (10th Cir.1985) (note issued in connection with joint venture held to be a security).

278. *E.g.,* Union National Bank of Little Rock v. Farmers Bank, 786 F.2d 881 (8th Cir.1986) (bank's purchase of 100% interest in an unsecured note was not a security); James v. Meinke, 778 F.2d 200 (5th Cir.1985) (guarantee of commercial loan held not to be a security).

a profit expectation will not be sufficient to warrant the finding of a security when the transaction is purely commercial.[279]

In Reves v. Ernst & Young,[280] the Supreme Court attempted to resolve some of the issues relating to the question of when a note will be a security. *Reves* involved variable rate demand notes that were issued by a farmers' cooperative. The Court eschewed application of the *Howey* four-factor test, reasoning that this test is limited to the definition of investment contract.[281] The investment contract analysis is inapplicable to the other items specifically enumerated in the Act's definition of security. Instead, there is a presumption that an instrument which falls within one of the enumerated categories is a security. It follows that there is a presumption that a note is a security.

The Court in *Reves* applied the "family resemblance" test in holding that certain demand notes were securities.[283] The family resemblance test that was adopted in *Reves* to a large extent is a different way of articulating the investment-commercial dichotomy that has been employed by the circuit and district courts. In applying the family resemblance test, the Court identified four types of "notes" that do not fit within the definition of security: (1) notes delivered in connection with consumer financing, (2) a note secured by a home

---

279. James v. Meinke, 778 F.2d 200, 204–205 (5th Cir.1985); Moy v. Warren, 1984 WL 2453, [1984 Transfer Binder] Fed.Sec.L.Rep. (CCH) ¶ 91,601 (D.Or.1984). *See also, e.g.* Arthur Young & Co. v. Reves, 856 F.2d 52 (8th Cir.1988) (Farmers' Cooperative's demand notes were not securities), *reversed* 494 U.S. 56, 110 S.Ct. 945, 108 L.Ed.2d 47 (1990).

280. 494 U.S. 56, 110 S.Ct. 945, 108 L.Ed.2d 47 (1990), *rehearing denied* 494 U.S. 1092, 110 S.Ct. 1840, 108 L.Ed.2d 968 (1990). *See, e.g.,* Steinberg, Notes as Securities: *Reves* and its Implications, 51 Ohio St.L.J. 675 (1990).

281. It has been suggested that the family resemblance test is nothing more than a restatement of the *Howey* test. Consider the following analysis, suggesting that the Court's opinion in *Reves* does not truly provide a new method of analysis:

[A]fter dismissing the *Howey* test out of hand, the Court adopted a reformulation of the *Howey* test. It even listed the *Reves* factors in basically the /same order as the prongs of the *Howey* test:

Howey	*Reves*
1. An investment of money	1. The motives are investment, not commercial or consumer.
2. in a common enterprise (under the multiple-investors test)	2. The notes are offered and sold to a broad segment of the public.
3. with an expectation of profits	3. The public reasonably expects the notes to be investments.
4. solely from the efforts of others.	4. [This is inherent in notes.]
5. The absence of an alternative regulatory scheme.	5. The absence of an alternative regulatory scheme or other risk-reducing factor.

. . . . The Court failed to realize what it had done, even though it said the family resemblance test applied the "same factors" that the Court had applied in the past, and even though all the cases but one that the Supreme Court cited for the *Reves* factors were investment contract cases. The Court even cited *Howey* itself. However, notwithstanding its overwhelming reliance on investment contract cases, the Court still insisted that "the *Howey* test is irrelevant to the issue before us today."

James D. Gordon III, Interplanetary Intelligence About Promissory Notes as Securities, 69 Tex. L. Rev. 383, 403 (1990).

283. *See* Reves v. Ernst & Young, 494 U.S. 56, 110 S.Ct. 945, 108 L.Ed.2d 47 (1990). *See also, e.g.,* SEC v. Global Telecom Services, LLC, 2004 WL 1638045 (D. Conn. 2004) (notes were securities).

mortgage, (3) short-term notes to a small business secured by the business' assets, and (4) bank character loans.[287] The more closely any particular note resembles any of these four categories, the more likely it is that the securities laws are not to be invoked.

The Court in *Reves* held that since "note" is one of the items enumerated in the Act's definition, there is a presumption that a note is a security.[289] However, the presumption may be rebutted by evaluation of the following four factors:

(1) an examination of the transaction in order to assess the motivations that would prompt a reasonable lender (buyer) and creditor (seller) to enter into it—for example, was the transaction in question an investment transaction or a commercial or consumer transaction?

(2) the plan of distribution used in offering and selling the instrument— for example, is the instrument commonly traded for investment or speculation?

(3) the reasonable expectations of the investing public—are the notes generally perceived as investment opportunities? and

(4) whether some factor such as the applicability of a parallel regulatory scheme significantly reduces the risk and thereby renders the protection of the federal securities laws unnecessary.[293]

In applying these factors, the Supreme Court Justices in *Reves* were all in agreement in finding that the uncollateralized, uninsured, unregulated notes at issue in that case were securities. However, the court was split as to whether they fell within the exemption for notes with maturities of less than nine months from the date of issuance. The majority held that although the notes were payable on demand, the demand might not come for "years or decades" in the future and accordingly, the short-term exemption should not apply.[294] The four dissenters took the position that the demand feature meant that the notes reached their maturity at issuance.[295]

The family resemblance test that was applied in *Reves* does not provide as much of a bright line as one might have hoped. Yet it does establish that since there is a presumption that a note is a security, the burden of persuasion falls on the party seeking to exclude the note from the Act's coverage.[296] The Court in *Reves* thus announced a rule that will exclude only those instruments which, because of their terms and the way in which they are issued, do not have the basic characteristics of investment securities.[297] If the notes have

---

287. The Court was relying on the Second Circuit's analysis in Exchange National Bank of Chicago v. Touche Ross & Co., 544 F.2d 1126, 1138 (2d Cir.1976).

289. 494 U.S. at 64–66, 110 S.Ct. at 951–52, 108 L.Ed.2d at 60–61.

293. 494 U.S. at 67, 110 S.Ct. at 952. The absence of a parallel regulatory scheme will not in itself result in a finding that a security exists. LeBrun v. Kuswa, 24 F.Supp.2d 641 (E.D.La.1998) (promissory notes were not securities).

294. 494 U.S. at 67, 110 S.Ct. at 952. *See, e.g.,* Roer v. Oxbridge Inc., 198 F.Supp.2d 212 (E.D.N.Y.2001) (short-term notes did not fall within one of the categories qualifying for the exclusion from the definition of security).

295. 494 U.S. at 76, 110 S.Ct. at 957, 108 L.Ed.2d at 67 (Rehnquist dissenting in part; Justice Rehnquist was joined by Justices White, O'Connor & Scalia).

296. *See, e.g.,* Arthur Children's Trust v. Keim, 994 F.2d 1390 (9th Cir.1993) (notes were securities).

297. *See, e.g.,* Pollack v. Laidlaw Holdings, Inc., 27 F.3d 808 (2d Cir.1994) (mortgage participations sold by securities brokers were properly characterized as investment rather than commercial and thus were securities).

been issued in a consumer or commercial context, they are not likely to fall within the definition of security. The test therefore necessarily becomes highly individualized to the facts of the particular case. As the presumption indicates, issuers and sellers of notes must be aware of the potential securities law ramifications.

Under the family resemblance test announced in *Reves* test, securities that most closely resemble purely commercial or banking transactions will not be classified as securities. The Second Circuit, applying the *Reves* analysis, has ruled that under the family resemblance test, participation interests in short-term commercial loans were not securities.[302] The presumption that a security exists thus may be rebutted, but the burden is on the party seeking to be excluded from the securities laws' purview. It follows that absent evidence that the note does not contain any of the benchmarks of a security as identified by the Court in *Reves,* the securities laws will apply. This presumption carries forward to commercial paper as well as to notes issued by savings and loan institutions.[304] Therefore, for example, in the ordinary case commercial paper issued by a corporation will be a security.[305]

§ 1.6[15] Certificates of Deposit as Securities

Related to the issue of when a note is subject to the securities laws, is the applicability of those laws to bank certificates of deposit. Section 2(a)(1)'s definition of security expressly includes "certificate of deposit for a security" within its list of investments that are subject to the 1933 Act.[309] A "certificate of deposit for a security" is similarly listed in the definition found in section 3(a)(1) of the Securities Exchange Act of 1934.[310] Nevertheless, the Supreme Court has ruled that a federally insured certificate of deposit issued by a bank is not subject to the securities laws.[311] When, however, an investment firm markets certificates of deposit as liquid investments and maintains a secondary market for the certificates of deposit, their sale has been held to be subject to the securities acts.[312] Some subsequent and prior lower court decisions have held that certificates of deposit issued by foreign banks are deemed to be securities.[313] The reasoning is that United States government-regulated banks and federally insured commitments do not require the protection of the securities laws whereas foreign instruments may.[314] Similarly, certificates of deposit that are not subject to either United States or foreign regulation have

---

302. Banco Espanol de Credito v. Security Pacific National Bank, 973 F.2d 51 (2d Cir.1992), *cert. denied* 509 U.S. 903, 113 S.Ct. 2992, 125 L.Ed.2d 687 (1993).

304. Bradford v. Moench, 809 F.Supp. 1473 (D.Utah 1992) (thrift certificates issued by a savings and loan association were securities).

305. In re NBW Commercial Paper Litigation, 813 F.Supp. 7 (D.D.C.1992), relying on Securities Industry Association v. Board of Governors, 468 U.S. 137, 104 S.Ct. 2979, 82 L.Ed.2d 107 (1984) and the *Reves* decision.

309. 15 U.S.C.A. § 77b(a)(1).

310. 15 U.S.C.A. § 78c(a)(10).

311. Marine Bank v. Weaver, 455 U.S. 551, 102 S.Ct. 1220, 71 L.Ed.2d 409 (1982), *on remand* 683 F.2d 744 (3d Cir.1982).

312. Gary Plastic Packaging Corp. v. Merrill Lynch, Pierce, Fenner & Smith, Inc., 756 F.2d 230 (2d Cir.1985).

313. *E.g.,* Meason v. Bank of Miami, 652 F.2d 542 (5th Cir.1981), *rehearing denied* 659 F.2d 1079 (5th Cir.1981) (Grand Cayman bank).

314. The Court in *Marine Bank* looked to the preamble to section 2's definitions ("unless the context otherwise requires") as justifying excluding a certificate of deposit which otherwise would fall within section 2(3)'s definition of security.

been held to be securities.[315] Enhancements to United States certificates of deposit may also implicate the securities laws.[316]

§ 1.7 Derivative Investments: Stock Options, Index Options, and Futures

The statutory definitions in both the 1933 and 1934 Acts make it clear that securities include not only stocks and bonds but also "any put, call, straddle, option, or privilege on any security."[1] Thus, an investment that is derivative of a security is itself a security. Derivative investments—both those based on securities and those based on commodities or other underlying values—have become a significant segment of the investment markets. Regulation of derivative investments is more fragmented than securities regulation generally. The discussion that follows addresses the applicability of the securities laws to derivative investment.

§ 1.7[1] Derivative Investments: An Overview

Over the past four decades, the securities markets have been infused with options trading in order to provide an alternative way to participate in short term investments in securities. Put and call options on individual securities allow investors to hedge their positions and thereby limit risk. While reducing risk may be the motivation for some investors, much options trading has been on a speculative basis. Since its inception, public trading of options on securities exchanges has been an active financial market. The success of the options markets for individual securities paved the way for expansion into markets for index options which are subject to Securities and Exchange Commission regulation and markets for futures based on stock indexes, which are subject to the jurisdiction of the Commodity Futures Trading Commission. The index markets permit investors to diversify their holdings by not tying their investments to the stock of a particular issuer. Index options and futures are broadly-based indexes the value of which is dependent upon the current per share price of the stocks comprising the index. By utilizing the index markets investors can take positions in groups of stocks tied to a publicly traded index option or futures contract. The index markets also have provided additional opportunities for the breed of arbitrageurs known as risk arbitrageurs.[3]

Options provide an important way to hedge long positions in securities.[4] A long position exists when an investor owns securities, as opposed to a short position when an investor has sold options or securities thereby obligating him or her to purchase them at a later date. For example, an investor owning

---

315. SEC v. Randy, 38 F.Supp.2d 657 (N.D.Ill.1999).

316. *See, e.g.,* Bruce F. Fein, PC, 32 Sec. Reg. & L. Rep. (BNA) 1081, 2000 WL 963337 (SEC No Action Letter July 11, 2000) (the staff declined to issue a no action response for a certificate of deposit with an enhanced interest rate to induce additional deposits to the bank).

§ 1.7

1. 1933 Act § 2(a)(1), 1934 Act § 3(a)(11); 15 U.S.C. § 77b(2), 78c(a)(10).

3. *See* Thomas L. Hazen, Volatility and Market Inefficiency: A Commentary on the Effects of Options, Futures, and Risk Arbitrage on the Stock Market, 44 Wash. & Lee L.Rev. 789 (1987); Janet E. Kerr & John C. Maguire, Program Trading: A Critical Analysis, 45 Wash. & Lee L.Rev. 991 (1988).

4. It is clear that an option on a security is itself a security. See, e.g., Fry v. UAL Corp., 84 F.3d 936, 937–38 (7th Cir.1996), *relying on* Blue Chip Stamps v. Manor Drug Stores, 421 U.S. 723, 750–51, 95 S.Ct. 1917, 1932–33, 44 L.Ed.2d 539 (1975).

1000 shares of ABC Co. stock which is currently trading at $12 per share may want to limit the risk of a price decline. In such a case, an appropriate hedge strategy would be to buy put options with a strike price of $10 per share. This would guarantee that at any time until the expiration date the investor could sell the stock for $10 per share. Buying the puts will cause the investor to incur the cost of the premium that the market has placed on the put and thereby the investor increases his or her total cost but limits the risk of loss.

Another example of an option strategy occurs when the investor believes that the market is likely to decline and therefore he or she maintains a large cash balance. In order to hedge against the possibility that their negative market outlook is wrong, investors may want to purchase call options, in selected stocks or broader-based index options, which would allow participation in a market rise. The purchase of call options involves less cash than investing in the underlying stocks but also is much more speculative as the investor stands to lose his or her entire investment if the option expires when the stock price is below the option exercise price. Options on individual securities are themselves securities.[6]

In 2000, Congress opened the door for a futures market place to parallel the securities option markets that are subject to SEC regulation. The 2000 amendments to the Commodity Exchange Act granted for the first time to the Commodity Futures Trading Commission jurisdiction over futures contracts on individual securities.[7] This has opened the door for a futures market in securities subject to CFTC jurisdiction that will parallel the securities options markets that are regulated by the SEC.

Options and futures are not limited to individual securities. As discussed directly below, options and futures contracts can also be based on groups of individual securities. These groups may be established according to well established stock indexes or alternatively by a group of securities characterized by industry or other identifying factors.

§ 1.7[5] "New Exotics"—Swaps and Other Hybrids

During the 1980s a host of novel and exotic investment products developed. A number of commercial banks and investment banks began to develop specialized financial products geared to the investment objectives of particular clients.[37] Among these "new exotics" were interest-rate swaps, followed by foreign currency swaps and, eventually, by equity- or commodity-based swaps. Also, during the 1980s, these hybrid and derivative instruments flourished, interrelating all sorts of financial variables to permit sophisticated hedging strategies. At the same time, many institutional investors got in over their heads. One of the most infamous incidents involved Orange County California's tremendous losses as a result of these investments.

Swap transactions have become an important part of the international economy. For example, interest rate swaps are frequently used to manage credit risks. The prevalence of swap agreements means that there are large

---

6. *See, e.g.,* Wharf (Holdings) Ltd. v. United International Holdings, Inc., 532 U.S. 588, 121 S.Ct. 1776, 149 L.Ed.2d 845 (2001) (oral option is a security subject to the federal securities laws).

7. 7 U.S.C.A. § 1a(31) as added by Pub. Law 106–554, 114 Stat. 2763 (December 21, 2000). Previously, the CFTC only had jurisdiction over stock index futures.

37. For a detailed discussion of the new exotics, *see* 1 Phillip McBride Johnson & Thomas Lee Hazen, Derivatives Regulation § 1.02[8][A] (2004).

amounts of money tied up in these arrangements most of which are largely unregulated.

Most of these over-the-counter derivative and swap transactions are virtually unregulated (except to the limited extent that some of the underlying instruments are securities). Even if some of the underlying instruments are regulated, the regulations do not address the complex relationships that exist as a result of the swap or derivative formulas. It is these formulas that create the risks that are not easily understood even by the most sophisticated investors. In addition to the absence of meaningful securities regulation (other than the antifraud rules), these over-the-counter derivatives and swaps are generally excluded or exempt from the coverage of the commodities laws. For the most part, these exotic derivatives are not subject to regulation as securities because they involve contracts between the creator and the investor where the gains of one are the losses of the other; thus, swaps and the like do not involve a common enterprise.[41] Although promoters of these derivative instruments put substantial efforts into their design and marketing, standing alone, this is not sufficient to classify them as securities.

In 2000, Congress amended the securities and commodities laws regarding hybrid investments.[45] Among other things, these amendments resulted in securities-based swap agreements being excluded from the definition of security but nevertheless subjected to the securities laws antifraud provisions.[46] Also, swaps that are not security-based do not fall with either the registration or antifraud provisions of the securities laws. Furthermore, there is authority to support the proposition that the 2000 modernization legislation does not preclude the states from regulating swap transactions as securities.[47] These amendments were part of a massive overhaul of the Commodity Exchange Act and the regulation provided by the CFTC.

Even though they are not subject to direct SEC regulation, the securities laws nevertheless can impact investments in various commodities-related derivative instruments. Item 305 of Regulation S-K requires that filings with the SEC reveal the extent of a company's exposure to risks due to derivative investments.[48] Also, brokers' failure to disclose risks of securities related derivative investments can also result in liability.[49]

§ 1.7[6] Unregulated Over-the-Counter Derivatives

At the heart of the Commodity Exchange Act was the contract market monopoly required by section 4 of that Act.[54] This meant that commodity–

41. Procter & Gamble Co. v. Bankers Trust Co., 925 F.Supp. 1270 (S.D.Ohio 1996) (interest rate swaps lacked commonality and thus were not investment contracts).

45. Pub. Law 106–554, 114 Stat. 2763 (December 21, 2000). The 2000 amendments also placed futures contracts on individual securities within the jurisdiction of the CFTC. This permits individualized securities futures to trade in the commodities markets under CFTC regulation as investments that parallel the securities options market that is regulated by the SEC.

46. See 15 U.S.C.A. §§ 77b–1(b)(1), 78c–1(b)(1) (excluding "security-based swap agreements" from the definition of "security"); 15 U.S.C.A. §§ 77b–1(a), 78c–1(a) (excluding "non-security-based swap agreements" from the definition of "security").

47. Integrated Research Services, Inc. v. Illinois Secretary of State, Securities Dept., 328 Ill.App.3d 67, 262 Ill.Dec. 304, 765 N.E.2d 130 (2002) (foreign currency contracts were held to be securities under the Illinois Securities Act).

48. 17 C.F.R. § 229.305. See Note, Baring's Ghost: Item 305 in SEC Regulation SBK and "Market Risk" Disclosures of Financial Derivatives, 34 Ga. L. Rev. 1417 (2000).

49. See, e.g., Former BT Broker Settles SEC Case Over Transactions with Gibson Greetings, 28 Sec. Reg. & L. Rep. (BNA) 754 (June 14, 1996).

54. 7 U.S.C.A. § 6. See 1 Philip McBride Johnson & Thomas Lee Hazen, Derivatives Regulation § 1.07 (2004).

related instruments that fall within the exclusive jurisdiction of the CFTC had to be traded on a registered commodities contract market or exchange absent some exemption or exclusion from the Act. As a result, unlike the securities markets, there was no public over-the-counter market for commodity-related investments. If an instrument fell within the Act's exclusive jurisdiction but was exempt from the contract market monopoly requirement, then the instruments could be traded off-exchange. However, since such exempt commodity-related investments still fall under the Act's exclusive jurisdiction, the SEC cannot assert jurisdiction. As discussed more fully elsewhere in this treatise,[55] the Commodity Futures Modernization Act of 2000[56] created a revolution in commodities regulation when it largely eliminated the contract market monopoly. In addition to various exemptions from CFTC regulation, there are exclusions from the Commodity Exchange Act's coverage, such as for forward contracts[57] as opposed to futures contracts. As such forward contracts are not subject to the act and thus may be traded over-the-counter, other than through an organized contract market.

As discussed above, swap transactions have been the subject of regulatory controversy. Swap transactions, like any hybrid instruments containing commodities components, are likely to be categorized as subject to the CFTC's exclusive jurisdiction. The CFTC and Congress provided exemptions from the Act for many swap transactions involving institutional and other sophisticated participants.[59] This created an over-the-counter market among sophisticated participants for certain commodity-related investments. In 2000, the CFTC proposed additional rules for certain swap transactions that would have the effect of extending the exemption to other commodities products and thus would truly open up an over-the-counter market for futures.[60] These proposals became moot when Congress enacted a massive overhaul of the Commodity Exchange Act that includes expansion of the unregulated over-the-counter derivatives markets.[61]

---

55. *See* § 22.7 *infra.*

56. Pub. Law 106–554, 114 Stat. 2763 (December 21, 2000).

57. A forward contract is a contract calling for a future delivery where the parties to the contract engage in a trade or business that utilizes the underlying commodity. See 1 Phillip McBride Johnson & Thomas Lee Hazen, Derivatives Regulation § 1.02[5], 1.02[8][B] (2004). For example, a farmer who sells his or her crops to a distributor with a future delivery date and delivery of the farmer's crops is in fact anticipated, then the contract is classified as a forward rather than futures contract and thus not subject to the Act's regulatory provisions.

59. 7 U.S.C. § 16(e)(2). Parts 34, 35 of the CFTC Regulations, 17 C.F.R. §§ 34.1–34.2, 35.1–35.2.

60. A New Regulatory Framework for Multilateral Transaction Execution Facilities, Intermediaries and Clearing Organizations, 65 FR 39039–01, 2000 WL 795027 (CFTC June 22, 2000); Exemption for Bilateral Transactions, 65 FR 39033, 2000 WL 795026 (CFTC June 22, 2000). *See* 1 Phillip McBride Johnson & Thomas Lee Hazen, Derivatives Regulation § 2.02[7] (2004).

61. Commodity Futures Modernization Act of 2000, Pub. Law No. 106–554, 114 Stat. 2763 (Dec. 21, 2000). These amendments to the Commodity Exchange Act codified the previously existing unregulated over-the-counter markets for swap and other hybrid transactions between qualified institutional investors. The new regulatory regime also introduced a new category of futures markets for certain commodities-based products and is open not to retail investors generally (unless participating through a registered futures commission merchant) but only to specified qualified investors. The over-the-counter futures market exists as an "exempt board of trade" which takes the form of a derivatives transaction execution facility ("DTEF").

§ 1.7[7] Security Futures Products

In a striking reversal of prior law, the Commodity Futures Modernization Act of 2000[62] permits the trading of futures contracts on single stocks and narrow-based security indexes. Securities futures products may be traded on either securities or commodities exchanges. In establishing this co-regulatory system, the Commodity Futures Modernization Act directs the SEC and CFTC to coordinate their regulatory oversight over securities futures. A stock future is defined as a security, which makes the Securities Exchange Act of 1934 generally applicable to trading in securities futures.[63] Securities futures can be traded only on common stock registered under section 12 of the Securities Exchange Act of 1934.[64] Those securities are subject to the detailed SEC periodic reporting requirements.[65]

The Commodity Futures Modernization Act permits trading of securities futures either on a national securities exchange registered with the SEC or a commodities contract market that is registered with the CFTC. A commodities contract market that trades security futures must be cross-registered with the SEC. Conversely, a securities exchange that trades securities futures has its primary regulation by the SEC but must be cross-registered with the CFTC.

Additional regulations are imposed as a prerequisite to trading in securities futures. For example suitability requirements are imposed on a commodities contract market.[66] The suitability requirements for securities futures traded on a contract market must be comparable to the suitability requirements imposed by a national securities association.[67]

---

62. Pub. Law 106–554, 114 Stat. 2763 (December 21, 2000).

63. State gambling laws and blue sky laws are preempted with respect to stock futures.

64. 15 U.S.C. § 78*l*.

65. *See* chapter 9 *infra* for general discussion of the 1934 Act's registration and periodic reporting requirements.

66. Pub. Law 106–554, 114 Stat. 2763 (December 21, 2000).

67. Pub. Law 106–554, 114 Stat. 2763 (December 21, 2000). The suitability requirements for securities are discussed in § 14.16 *infra*.

Chapter 2

REGISTRATION REQUIREMENTS OF THE SECURITIES ACT OF 1933

Table of Sections

---

§ 2.0   Overview of 1933 Act Registration

When companies go public and register their offerings of securities under the 1933 Act, they must pay attention to both the process and the law. In particular, this means that participants in the offering must be familiar with mechanics of the offering process as well with the law's requirements regarding the disclosures that must be made in the registration statement that is filed for the offering and also the disclosure obligations that follow once the company is public.

These requirements that are imposed by section 5[2] impose limits on what companies and their representatives can say during the registration process. As part of this process there is a mandated disclosure document, known as the prospectus.[7] Section 5 of the Act thus restricts both oral and written communications and also limits actual sales to the post-effective period. In addition to the mechanics of the offering process, the 1933 Act imposes significant disclosure obligations. The preparation of the registration statement and applicable disclosures is discussed in a subsequent chapter of this treatise.[8]

§ 2.1   The Underwriting Process

Underwriters form an essential link in the process of offering securities for public consumption. Underwriting practices have varied over time. There is no single universally accepted underwriting mechanism; instead, there are a variety of underwriting arrangements. The particular underwriting arrange-

---

§ 2.0

2.   15 U.S.C. § 77e.

7.   "Prospectus" is defined in section 2(a)(10) of the Act, 15 U.S.C.A. § 77b(a)(10). The contents of the prospectus is dictated by section 10 of the Act and the registration requirements generally. 15 U.S.C.A. § 77b. *See also* sections 6 and 7, 15 U.S.C.A. §§ 77f, 77g. The prospectus delivery requirements are discussed in §§ 2.4, 2.5 *infra*.

8.   *See* chapter 3 *infra*.

ment for any offering will generally be a reflection of the financial exigencies of the situation.

This section discusses the basic types of underwriting arrangements. In contrast to this description of practices in the securities industry, a later section of this treatise examines the 1933 Act definition of underwriter[1] which may bring within the Act's reach individuals and entities who are not underwriters in the generic sense of the word. Classification as a statutory underwriter can result in the imposition of civil liability.[2] Additionally, the presence of underwriter status may preclude an exemption from the Act's registration requirements.[3] Those issues are discussed in subsequent sections of this treatise.[4] The discussion that follows addresses formal underwriting arrangements that are commonly found in public offerings (and in some cases in private offerings).

There are a number of methods by which an issuer can raise capital, both for starting out its business and for expansion and/or continuation of an existing concern. Financing can be carried out by the issuer directly or through an intermediary or underwriter. Perhaps the simplest method is direct financing: that is, without an investment banker, underwriter, promoter, or other intermediary. Although direct financing may be simpler, the vast majority of public offerings are underwritten.

§ 2.1[1] Direct Offerings

While it is relatively rare, direct financing does have its place in the securities markets, albeit a small one. Generally, there are said to be five basic methods of direct financing, although additional variations may exist.

First, there can be a direct public offering by the issuer. Such a direct offering can be used for both small and large public offerings. Traditionally, direct public offerings have been especially rare because most issuers do not have the wherewithal or expertise in the financial industry to market their shares to a large number of investors. Marketing a full-scale public offering ordinarily requires a broker-dealer network and sales persons registered with the SEC and National Association of Securities Dealers (NASD).[6] Accordingly, public offerings traditionally have been not suitable for direct distribution by the issuer. However, the increased availability of the Internet has made many direct offerings more feasible.[7] As a result of the increased use of the Internet

---

§ 2.1

1. Section 2(a)(11), 15 U.S.C.A. § 77b(a)(11). *See* § 4.27 *infra.*

2. Section 11 of the 1933 Act imposes liability on underwriters for material misstatements and omissions in a public offering's registration statement. 15 U.S.C.A. § 77k. *See* § 7.3 *infra.*

3. Section 4(1) of the 1933 Act sets forth an exemption for transactions not involving an issuer, underwriter, or a dealer. 15 U.S.C.A. § 77d(1). *See* §§ 4.26–4.27 *infra.*

4. *See* §§ 4.26, 4.27, 7.3 *infra.*

6. The federal regulatory framework for broker-dealers is taken up in chapter 14 *infra.*

7. In 1996, an issuer used the Internet for a direct public offering for what may have been the first time. The SEC was concerned about a small brewery that used the Internet to accomplish an initial public offering and then make a market in its shares. The SEC seriously questioned this, and the activities were subsequently halted. But, after negotiations, the Commission permitted online trading to resume with certain safeguards. Additionally, the Commission has since issued a no action letter permitting a company to make a market in its own shares using the Internet. Real Goods Trading Corp., 28 Sec. Reg. & L. Rep. (BNA) 850 (SEC No Action Letter available June 25, 1996).

for offering securities, the SEC has taken steps to clarify the applicability of the 1933 Act's registration provisions to Internet offerings.[8]

A second variation of the direct offering by an issuer, and one that traditionally has been slightly more common than general direct offerings, is an offering to existing security holders where it is contemplated that only existing shareholders will purchase the new securities being offered, thus eliminating the necessity for a promotional or retailing sales effort. A variation is a direct offering exclusively to employees of the issuer.

The third and perhaps most common type of direct financing utilizing traditional debt and equity securities is the direct private placement whereby the issuer turns to a bank, financial institution, or significant private investor to raise all desired capital. For many endeavors, especially established concerns with good track records, such qualified willing investors are readily available and the issuer need not avail itself of an underwriter or promoter in order to stimulate investor interest. The fourth, relatively rarely used technique is the distribution of securities through public sealed bidding. The fifth and final type of direct financing is generally associated with commercial lenders and consists of directly secured bank loans, mortgage loans, equipment loans, and sale-leaseback arrangements.

The viability of direct offerings has been increased significantly by technological advances. In particular, the Internet offers an opportunity for issuers to offer their shares directly to investors rather than use an underwriter. This development has raised a number of issues for securities regulation. For example, can the Internet be used for the 1933 Act's prospectus delivery requirements? The SEC's current position is that it can so long as there is some assurance that once an investor enters a website offering securities, he or she cannot subscribe to the issue being offered without first viewing the required prospectus.[13] There also has been concern about the use of exemptions from registration (in particular the exemption provided by Rule 504 or Regulation D[14]) as a vehicle for creating a public market over the Internet without registration.[15] Another abusive practice has been the use of stock "giveaways" by companies to try to promote their stock.[16]

§ 2.1[2] Nature and Varieties of Underwriting Arrangements

As noted above, most financing that involves any significant selling effort will be conducted through promoters, investment bankers, or underwriters. Although generally associated with public offerings, underwriting arrangements are also common with relatively wide-spread unregistered exempt

---

8. For example, the SEC narrowed the scope of the exemption provided by SEC Rule 504 in order to curb abuses in connection with the use of the exemption for direct offerings by issuers using the Internet. 17 C.F.R. § 230.504. *See* Sec. Act Rel. No. 33–7644 (SEC Feb. 25, 1999). *See also, e.g.,* Use of Electronic Media, Sec. Act Rel. No. 33–7856, 2000 WL 502290 (SEC April 28, 2000);, Note, Regulation A: Direct Public Offerings and the Internet, 79 Denver U.L. Rev. 229 (2001).

13. *See, e.g.,* Internet Capital Corp., 1997 WL 796944, *1 (S.E.C.) (SEC No Action Letter Dec. 24, 1997).

14. 17 C.F.R. § 230.504; *see* § 4.21 *infra.*

15. *See* Sec. Act Rel. No. 33–7644 (SEC Feb. 25, 1999); Sec. Act Rel. No. 33–7300 (May 31, 1996).

16. Internet "Free Stock" Offerings Mostly Illegal, SEC's Walker Says, 31 Sec. Reg. & L. Rep. (BNA) 458 (April 9, 1999).

Investment Banker

offerings.[17] There are various ways in which an investment banker's expertise and services may be used in connection with the raising of capital. First, and most common with regard to public offerings of securities in this country, is the negotiated underwriting agreement with an investment banker, or group of investment bankers, to handle a public offering, which is usually conducted pursuant to full-fledged federal registration. The negotiated underwriting agreement is also common in connection with a limited or qualified public offering that may take place in reliance upon one of the qualified exemptions from the registration requirements of the 1933 Act.[18] Another less frequently used method of securing an underwriter for public offering is the use of sealed bids. A variation on the competitive bidding is the "Dutch auction," wherein prospective underwriters bid for a portion of an upcoming offering. The Dutch auction is also used as a method for selling and pricing securities to the public. Under a Dutch auction, the issuer typically sets a price range and potential investors submit their bids, reflecting the price at which they are willing to purchase the securities. Dutch auction offerings are more common in Europe but have been used in the U.S.[20]

The term "underwriter" derives its meaning from former British insurance practices. When insuring their cargo shippers would seek out investors to insure their property. The insurers would add their signatures and would write their names under those of the shippers; hence the term "underwriters." Both in terms of the insurance industry and the securities markets, the concept of underwriting has expanded significantly since its inception. In many instances, underwriting no longer reflects pure insurance but may be in the form of various types of either best efforts or firm commitment agreements.

Most, if not all, underwriters of any securities offering will generally be broker-dealers who are members of the National Association of Securities Dealers (NASD). Underwriting agreements are subject to the NASD's Rules of Fair Practice which deal, *inter alia*, with the distribution of shares, over allotment options (also known as "green shoe" provisions), and "compensation factors." Underwriting agreements and registration materials must be filed with the NASD's Corporate Financing Department in Washington, D.C. Upon filing, the NASD may respond with a letter of comment.

There are three basic varieties of negotiated underwriting arrangements in the securities industry. Those three are: (1) strict underwriting, (2) firm-commitment underwriting, and (3) best efforts underwriting.

§ 2.1[2][A]   Strict Underwriting

Strict underwriting, also known as "old-fashioned" or "stand by" underwriting, is insurance in its strictest sense. In lieu of utilizing an investment banker as an agent to resell the securities to the public, the issuer turns to an

---

17. *See* Sec. Act Rel. No. 33–1256 (1937). *See generally* chapter 4 *infra*.

18. *See* sections 3 and 4 of the 1933 Act, 15 U.S.C.A. §§ 77c, 77d.

20. In the spring of 2004, Google announced that it planned to conduct an IPO via a Dutch auction. The IPO took place in August 2004. There have been successful "Dutch auctions" such as the one held for American Express Co.'s adjustable rate preferred stock (also referred to as "money market preferred"). *See* Securities Week p. 5 (October 22, 1984). *See also, e.g.,* Lucas C. Townsend, Global Resolution "Prevent Spinning? A Critical Evaluation of Current Alternatives," 34 Seton Hall L. Rev. 1121 (2004) (recommending increased use of the Dutch auction); *See also* Note, Auctioning New Issues of Corporate Securities, 71 Va.L.Rev. 1381 (1985).

"insuring house" which will advertise and receive subscriptions and applications for shares from the public. When the subscription lists are closed, the issuer in turn allots the securities to the applicants secured by the insuring house. In a strict underwriting arrangement, the underwriters guarantee to purchase the unsold portion of the allotment. This strict underwriting method is relatively rare in the United States and is generally found only in connection with offerings to existing security holders.

§ 2.1[2][B]   Firm–Commitment Underwriting

The second type and most common arrangement in this country is firm-commitment underwriting. Under a typical firm commitment agreement the issuer sells the entire allotment outright to a group of securities firms represented by one or more managers, managing underwriters or principal underwriters. In a firm-commitment underwriting agreement, the underwriting group, headed by the managing or principal underwriters, agrees to purchase the securities from the issuer. The term "firm commitment" is somewhat misleading since it is common practice to have a "market out" clause which excuses the underwriters from the obligation to purchase in the event of a substantial change in the issuer's financial condition.[26] Typically, the principal underwriters will sign the firm-commitment underwriting agreement. These managers or principal underwriters in turn contact other broker-dealers to become members of the underwriting group who are to act as wholesalers of the securities to be offered. In many instances the securities distribution network will include the use of a selling group of other investment bankers or brokerage houses. Members of the selling group generally do not share the underwriters' risk and are thus retailers who are compensated with agents' or brokers' commissions rather than by sharing in the underwriting fee.

Section 2(a)(3) of the 1933 Act[27] excludes from its definition of "offer to sell" preliminary negotiations and agreements between the underwriter and the issuer and among underwriters in privity with the issuer. However, absent an exemption, prior to the filing of the registration statement, no offers can be made to members of the investing public; nor can there be sales or contracts for sale prior to the effective date. Although section 2(a)(3)'s exclusion probably includes the final contract between the underwriter and the issuer, it may be wise not to have more than an understanding and to reserve formal execution of the final contract until immediately after the filing of the registration statement. In fact, the typical practice is to follow such a course.

There is no definitive ruling on how "preliminary" the negotiations and agreements must be in order to qualify for exclusion.[28] Generally, the issue

---

26. A typical "market out" clause provides that the underwriters are excused from their firm commitment should there be "a material adverse event affecting the issuer that materially impairs the investment quality of the offered securities." *See, e.g.,* First Boston Corp., [1985–1986 Transfer Binder] Fed.Sec.L.Rep. (CCH) ¶ 78,152 (SEC No Action Letter Sept. 2, 1985). *Compare* Walk–In Medical Centers, Inc. v. Breuer Capital Corp., 818 F.2d 260 (2d Cir.1987) (affirming $33 million judgment against an underwriter who claimed that "adverse market conditions" excused performance of underwriting agreement).

27. 15 U.S.C.A. § 77b(a)(3). *See* § 5.3 *infra.*

28. The legislative history explains that "the sole purpose * * * is to make clear that the usual agreement among underwriters as well as the agreement between the underwriters and the issuer (or controlling person, as the case may be) may be made before the registration statement will be a question of fact depending upon the participants in the negotiations.[29] Also, the construction of the statutory language may raise the question as to what agreements between the issuer and underwriter or among underwriters will qualify as "preliminary." In most instances, questions regarding "agreements" are merely academic since it is common practice for the final underwriting agreement not to be signed until the eve of the offering. Prior to that time, the issuer and managing underwriter generally operate under a nonbinding letter of intent.[30]

[handwritten margin note: Nonbinding letter of intent.]

Underwriting arrangements may contain an escape clause which permits the underwriting group to terminate the underwriting agreement if there has been a substantial change in the issuer's operation or, for example, if there has been a change in "operating political or marketing conditions." While this is broader than the traditional force majeure clause found in other industries, it is not generally abused. The underwriter's ability to exit from an offering is protected even beyond such escape clauses. For example, where the issuer's prospectus is misleading, the underwriting contract has been held unenforceable, thus entitling the underwriter to withdraw from the distribution.[31]

[handwritten margin note: Escape clause]

§ 2.1[2][C] Best Efforts Underwriting

The third basic type of underwriting arrangement commonly used in the United States is known as a "best efforts" underwriting and does not put the underwriter at risk in the event that investors do not purchase the entire allotment being offered to the public.[32] Best efforts underwriting is generally used by less established issuers that cannot find an investment banker who is willing to make a firm commitment because of the speculative nature of the distribution. In some instances, even established companies may try to avail themselves of best efforts underwriting arrangements in order to save on the cost of distribution since the underwriter's fee may be lower in an offering where the underwriter is not taking the risk of absorbing all or part of an unsold allotment. With a best efforts underwriting agreement, the investment banker or brokerage firm, rather than buying the securities from the issuer for resale to the public, sells them for the issuer merely as an agent. Under such best efforts arrangements, the underwriter is generally paid in the form of an agent's commission on actual sales rather than from a dealer's profit or a fee based on a percentage of the overall proceeds of the offering.

§ 2.1[2][D] Underwriting by Auction

There are numerous variations on the foregoing three basic types of underwriting arrangements.[33] For example, competitive bidding by potential

---

has been filed." S.Rep. No. 1036, 83 Cong., 2d Sess. 11 (1954). *See* Richard W. Jennings & Harold Marsh, Jr., Securities Regulation 47–49 (6th ed. 1987).

29. SEC v. Cavanagh, 155 F.3d 129, 135 (2d Cir.1998) (upholding district court's determination that the exclusion for preliminary negotiations did not apply to the negotiations in question).

30. A letter of intent containing an agreement to underwrite an offering is not a binding contract for the sale of securities. Cafe La France, Inc. v. Schneider Securities, Inc., 281 F.Supp.2d 361 (D.R.I. 2003) (letter of intent regarding underwriting of planned IPO was not a binding contract; underwriter could withdraw prior to IPO and did not owe a fiduciary duty to the company since the underwriting agreement clearly permitted withdrawal).

31. Kaiser-Frazer Corp. v. Otis & Co., 195 F.2d 838 (2d Cir.1952), *cert. denied* 344 U.S. 856, 73 S.Ct. 89, 97 L.Ed. 664 (1952).

32. *See* Harold I. Freilich & Ralph S. Janvey, Understanding "Best Efforts" Offerings, 17 Sec.Reg.L.J. 151 (1989).

33. Delayed registered offerings (shelf registrations) have been a relatively new development in the history of public offerings and are examples of practices that were generated by the

underwriters traditionally has been the most common method for offerings involving financing by municipalities, other state governmental agencies, and public utilities.[34] A variation of this in the private sector is the relatively infrequently used "Dutch auction."

§ 2.1[3] Underwriters' Compensation; NASD Review

As discussed above, the underwriting agreement is the result of negotiations between the managing or lead underwriter and the company issuing the securities to be offered. Setting the underwriters' compensation is an important part of the process. The National Association of Securities Dealers (NASD), the self-regulatory organization that is intimately involved with broker-dealer regulation generally,[36] requires that it receive a filed copy of most 1933 Act registration statements for public offerings in order to allow the NASD to review the underwriters' compensation.

The NASD's standards for underwriters' compensation are found in its corporate and financing rules.[37] The standards are complex and, at the same time, leave a great deal to the NASD's discretion.

§ 2.2   The Operation of Section 5 of the Securities Act of 1933

§ 2.2[1] Operation of Section 5—Overview

Section 5

The core of the 1933 Act's registration requirements are found in section 5 of the Act.[1] Section 5's prohibitions are implemented by regulating the scope of all offers as well as sales of securities so long as there is sufficient use of interstate commerce unless there is an applicable exemption.

Absent an exemption from the 1933 Act's registration requirements,[2] section 5(c) of the Securities Act of 1933 strictly prohibits all selling efforts by making it unlawful to offer a security for sale unless a registration statement has been filed.[3] Section 5 also restricts selling efforts and absolutely prohibits sales until the registration statement has become effective. Section 5's prohibitions thus continue after the registration statement has been filed. Even after a registration statement has been filed, it remains unlawful to sell the securities until the registration statement has become effective.[4] Further, once

---

investment banking industry. *See* 1 Louis Loss & Joel Seligman, Securities Regulation 353–372 (1987). *See also* § 3.11 *infra*.

34.   *See* 1 Louis Loss & Joel Seligman, Securities Regulation 343–352 (1987). *See* § 14.6 *infra* for a discussion of municipal securities dealers.

36.   *See* § 14.3 *infra*.

37.   NASD Rule 2710 (Underwriting Terms and Arrangements).

§ 2.2

1.   15 U.S.C.A. § 77e.

2.   Section 3 of the Act sets forth a list of securities that are exempt from the 1933 Act's registration provisions. 15 U.S.C.A. § 77c. Section 4 sets forth transactions that are exempt from registration. 15 U.S.C.A. § 77d. Section 28 gives the SEC the power to exempt persons, transactions, and securities from any of the Act's provisions. 15 U.S.C.A. § 77z–3. Exempt securities and exempt transactions are discussed in chapter 4 *infra*.

3.   Section 5(c), 15 U.S.C.A. § 77e(c). *See* § 2.3 *infra* for discussion of the restrictions during the pre-filing period.

4.   Section 5(a), 15 U.S.C.A. § 77e(a). *See* § 2.4 *infra* for discussion of the waiting period.

the registration statement has been filed, and even after it has become effective, there are restrictions on the types of written offers to sell that may be made.[5] Offers and sales in contravention of section 5 result in a violation even if the defendant did not know that he or she was marketing securities in violation of the Act.[6] This is the case because section 5 is not based on common law fraud[7] and thus does not require that the defendant have acted with scienter.[8] All that is required is that a defendant willfully offer securities. The Act does not expressly require an intent to violate the registration requirement. Nevertheless, a criminal conviction would appear to require at least a minimal amount of *mens rea*.[9]

Section 5 thus divides the registration process into three time periods: the pre-filing, waiting, and post-effective periods. Once the public offering is contemplated, the time prior to the completion of the initial registration statement and filing is known as the *pre-filing period*.[10] After the registration statement has been filed with the SEC, there is a statutory twenty-day *waiting period*[11] prior to the effective date of the registration statement at which time sales of the securities can take place. The statutory language is not reflective of what really happens since the actual waiting period is rarely the twenty-day period specified in the statute.[12] Section 5's requirements do not end with the effective date as they continue through the *post-effective* period until the distribution of securities has been completed.[13] These limitations take the form of the prospectus requirements which are discussed below.

The basic purpose of the 1933 Act's registration requirement, as well as section 5's prohibitions and limitations on permissible offers to sell securities, is to assure that the investor has adequate information upon which to base his or her investment decision. It is generally conceded to be a fiction that each investor or potential investor reads the prospectus from cover to cover; and thus, it has been suggested by some observers that most disclosures that are required by the securities laws are not in fact relevant to the majority of investors.[14] However, investment professionals, such as research analysts,

5. This emanates from the prospectus delivery requirements of section 5(b), 15 U.S.C.A. § 77e(b). *See* section 2(a)(10) of the Act, 15 U.S.C.A. § 77b(a)(10) for the definition of prospectus. *See also* the discussion in §§ 2.3, 2.4 *infra*.

6. *See, e.g.*, SEC v. Current Financial Services, Inc., 100 F.Supp.2d 1, 5–6 (D.D.C.2000) (defendant violated the securities laws even though he did not know that the investment vehicle he was marketing was a security).

7. In contrast, SEC Rule 10b–5 is limited to fraudulent conduct. *See, e.g.*, Santa Fe Industries, Inc. v. Green, 430 U.S. 462, 476, 97 S.Ct. 1292, 1302, 51 L.Ed.2d 480 (1977); Ernst & Ernst v. Hochfelder, 425 U.S. 185, 96 S.Ct. 1375, 47 L.Ed.2d 668 (1976).

8. *See e.g.*, SEC v. Current Financial Services, Inc., 100 F.Supp.2d 1, 5–6 (D.D.C.2000); SEC v. Friendly Power Co., 49 F.Supp.2d 1363, 1367 (S.D.Fla.1999); SEC v. Parkersburg Wireless LLC, 991 F.Supp. 6, 8–9 (D.D.C.1997). For discussion of the derivation of the scienter requirement in securities fraud actions, *see* § 12.8 *infra*.

9. *See, e.g.*, United States v. Lindo, 18 F.3d 353 (6th Cir.1994) (upholding conviction for sale of unregistered securities where defendant had reason to know that he was involved in an illegal transaction).

10. *See* § 2.3 *infra*.

11. Section 8(a) of the 1933 Act, 15 U.S.C.A. § 77h(a).

12. *See* § 2.4 *infra*.

13. *See* § 2.5 *infra*.

14. *See, e.g.*, Homer Kripke, A Search for a Meaningful Securities Disclosure Policy, 31 Bus.Law. 293 (1975); Symposium, New Approaches to Disclosure in Registered Securities Offerings: A Panel Discussion, 28 Bus.Law. 505 (1973).

investment advisers and broker-dealers, when viewed as a group, read all publicly disseminated information in addition to other information which is otherwise available. The opinions of these market professionals, frequently reflected in terms of buy or sell recommendations, create an informed and supposedly efficient market which, in turn, prices the securities at an appropriate level. Accordingly, it is asserted that notwithstanding the absence of significant lay investor interest in the bulk of the SEC disclosure documents, the relevant information nonetheless is filtered into the market and is reflected by the price established by an informed market.[15] Others observers are of the view that the disclosure requirements are directly meaningful to individual investors.[16]

A widespread readership of disclosure documents among investors generally is not absolutely crucial to the justification for the securities laws' truth in securities requirements. Another justification for requiring disclosure, even though many investors may not ever read the information in question, is that the market participants' knowledge that full disclosure has been made instills investor confidence and hence stability which would otherwise be lacking, as has been the case with many foreign securities markets. To this end, it is noteworthy that lack of investor confidence was a major factor in the great Wall Street crash of 1929. All of section 5's prohibitions must be viewed and understood in the context of the informational goals of the Securities Act of 1933.

§ 2.2[2] Operation of Section 5—The Basic Prohibitions of the Pre–Filing, Waiting, and Post–Effective Periods

As noted above, section 5 divides the registration process into three parts: the pre-filing period,[28] the waiting period, and the post-effective period.[29] Section 5(a)(1) prohibits the use of the mails or other facility of interstate commerce to sell a security prior to the effective date of the 1933 Act registration statement.[30] Taken literally, section 5(a)(1)'s language could possibly be read to include the mere the making of offers to sell. However, when section 5(a)(1) is read in conjunction with sections 5(b) and 5(c), it is clear that section 5(a)(1) was designed to prevent the use of the mails or other

---

15. *Cf.* Wielgos v. Commonwealth Edison Co., 892 F.2d 509 (7th Cir.1989) (indicating that at least with a well seasoned, actively followed issuer, the more important audience for the registration disclosures is the sophisticated analyst and that disclosures may be tailored accordingly).

16. In one influential decision it was held that there are three audiences to whom the registration statement is directed, and that the disclosures must be understandable for each of the following audiences: (1) the amateur investor who reads only for the broadest types of information, (2) the professional advisor and/or manager who makes a close study of the prospectus and bases his or her decisions on the conclusions drawn from this study, and (3) the analyst who relies on the prospectus as one of several sources in forming an opinion. *See* Feit v. Leasco Data Processing Equipment Corp., 332 F.Supp. 544, 565–66 (E.D.N.Y.1971).

28. *See* § 2.3 *infra.* Section 5(c) applies to all transactions unless a registration statement has been filed. It is not necessarily limited to transactions that occur in contemplation of a registered public offering. However, most transactions that take place outside of the context of a public offering are exempt from section 5's prohibitions. For example, section 4(1) exempts transactions not involving an issuer, underwriter, or a dealer. 15 U.S.C.A. § 77d(1); *see* § 4.26[1] *infra.* Section 4(2) exempts transaction by an issuer not involving a public offering. 15 U.S.C.A. § 77d(2); *see* §§ 4.24, 4.25 *infra.* Section 4(3) exempts most dealer transactions in securities. 15 U.S.C.A. § 77d(3); *see* 4.31 *infra.* Section 4(4) of the Act exempts unsolicited brokers' transactions. 15 U.S.C.A. § 77d(4); *see* § 4.26[2] *infra.*

29. *See* chapter 3 *infra* for discussion of the entire registration process.

30. 15 U.S.C.A. § 77e(a)(1).

instrumentalities to make a binding contract (as opposed something less, such as simply an offer to sell). Section 5(a)(1)'s prohibitions cover the use of the mails, "through the use or medium of any prospectus or otherwise."[31] As discussed more fully below, the Act defines prospectus to include a written offer to sell,[32] and section 5(b)(1)[33] expressly permits the use of certain forms of prospectus during the waiting period.[34] Accordingly, it would not make sense to read section 5(a)(1) as prohibiting any form of prospectus prior to the effective date.

Section 5(a)(2)[35] prohibits the delivery of any security for sale unless a registration statement is in effect and thus extends its prohibitions into the waiting period. Section 5(b)[36] imposes prospectus requirements and thereby prescribes the types of prospectuses that may be used for both offers during the waiting period[37] and for offers and sales during the post-effective period.[38] Section 5(c),[39] which is the broadest in prohibitions, applies only to the pre-filing period. The following diagram depicts the operation of section 5:

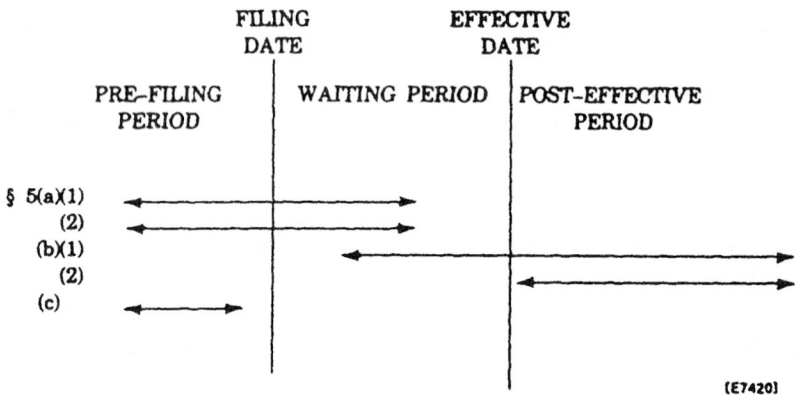

Section 5(c) prohibits all offers to sell as well as all offers to buy prior to the filing of a registration statement. This necessarily includes oral as well as written offers. Section 5(c) contains the only prohibition on oral offers[41] and is also the only restriction on offers to buy. Since it covers both offers to sell and offers to buy securities, section 5(c) on its face would seem to be applicable to

---

31. *Id.*

32. 15 U.S.C.A. § 2(a)(10).

33. 15 U.S.C.A. § 77e(b)(1).

34. The 1933 Act's prospectus requirements were modeled on the English Companies Act and its predecessors which date back to 1844. *See* Joel Seligman, The Transformation of Wall Street, 62–63 (1982). The concept of the waiting period was new to the 1933 Act. *Id. See also, See* Harold S. Bloomenthal and Samuel Wolf, Securities and Federal Corporate Law § 27:37.3 (2d ed. 2000).

35. 15 U.S.C.A. § 77e(a)(2). *See* § 2.5 *infra.*

36. 15 U.S.C.A. § 77e(b). *See* §§ 2.4–2.5 *infra.*

37. The waiting period is discussed in § 2.4 *infra.*

38. The post-effective period is discussed in § 2.5 *infra.*

39. 15 U.S.C.A. § 77e(c). *See* § 2.3 *infra.*

41. Although oral offers are not covered by section 5 after the commencement of the waiting period, an oral contract of sale would violate section 5(a) of the Act. In another context, the Supreme Court has made it clear that an oral contract of sale is a security subject to federal regulation. Wharf (Holdings) Ltd. v. United International Holdings, Inc., 532 U.S. 588, 121 S.Ct. 1776, 149 L.Ed.2d 845 (2001) (oral option is a security subject to the federal securities laws).

negotiations between issuers and underwriters. However, section 2(a)(3)[42] of the Act expressly provides an exclusion from the definition of offer to sell for preliminary negotiations between an issuer and an underwriter or among underwriters in privity with the issuer. Without such an exclusion, it would be impossible to negotiate a public offering, as the issuer would have to file the registration statement prior to even establishing either the terms of the offering or the underwriting agreement. The exclusion of preliminary underwriter negotiations and agreements is a major exception to the pre-filing prohibitions; although, as will be seen in subsequent sections of this treatise, even beyond the exclusion for preliminary underwriting negotiations and agreements, limited pre-filing publicity is permissible.[43] Section 5(c)'s prohibition[44] on offers operates during the pre-filing period, and violations of these quiet period limitations have come to be known as illegal "gun jumping."

By virtue of section 5(b) of the Act,[45] all written offers or prospectuses must conform with the statutory prospectus requirement. Section 2(a)(10) of the Act[46] defines prospectus to include any written offer[47] in addition to offers made over radio or television.[48] Accordingly, oral offers to sell are not covered by section 5(b) nor are offers to buy, whether oral or in writing. Oral offers to sell and all offers to buy are thus unregulated during the waiting period; they are also unregulated during the post-effective period. Sections 10(a) and 10(b) of the 1933 Act[49] set out the requirements for permissible written offers during both the waiting and post-effective periods.[50]

Under the express terms of section 8 of the Act,[55] a registration statement becomes effective twenty days after the last amendment has been filed. This twenty-day waiting period is subject to the Commission's authority to issue a stop order which postpones the effective date until removal of the stop order, and also is subject to the Commission's willingness to grant acceleration of the effective date upon application by the registrant.[56] The drafters of section 8 may have contemplated that ordinarily a registration statement will become

42. 15 U.S.C.A. § 77b(a)(2).

43. *See, e.g.,* 17 C.F.R. § 230.135 which is discussed in § 2.3 *infra.* In 1998, the Commission introduced a proposal for a major overhaul of the registrations process. One of the changes would involve the expansion of permissible pre-filing communications. *See* Sec. Act Rel. No. 33–7606 (SEC Nov. 3, 1998). *See* § 3.4 *infra.*

44. 15 U.S.C.A. § 77e(c).

45. 15 U.S.C.A. § 77e(b).

46. 15 U.S.C.A. § 77b(a)(10). *See, e.g.,* SEC v. Thomas D. Kienlen Corp., 755 F.Supp. 936 (D.Or.1991) (brochure describing "safety", "improved performance", and "lower costs" of mutual fund was a prospectus and thus violated section 5(b)(1) when used during the waiting period).

47. Although not expressly covered by the statute, computer email, computer disks, and other digitally encoded communications would appear to and certainly should fall within the definition of prospectus. Such an interpretation is bolstered by the fact that radio and television communications are expressly included. The SEC has not addressed the issue directly but has indicated that electronically transmitted messages would qualify as prospectuses. Sec. Act Rel. No. 33–6982; 57 FR 16141 (March 19, 1993) ("Some electronic media, such as computer bulletin boards, may provide the capacity to read the disclosure for a sufficient period of time and to reproduce the disclosure and order form in print").

48. The definition as adopted in 1933 was patterned on the British Companies Act of 1929. *See* Gustafson v. Alloyd Co., 513 U.S. 561, 599–600, 115 S.Ct. 1061, 131 L.Ed.2d 1 (1995) (Ginsburg, J., dissenting).

49. 15 U.S.C.A. § 77j(a), (b).

50. *See* §§ 2.4–2.5 *infra.*

55. 15 U.S.C.A. § 77h.

56. *See* the more detailed discussion of acceleration procedures and requirements in § 3.6[2] *infra.* Compliance with the plain English requirements is now a factor that the SEC will consider

effective within twenty days of its filing and that in rare cases this period would be extended by amendment to the registration statement or by the issuance of a stop order or a refusal order. However, this apparent statutory pattern is not reflective of actual SEC practice. As a practical matter, the SEC reserves the formal stop order and refusal order proceedings for woefully deficient filings. For example, where a registration statement has many material misstatements and/or omissions of material fact, the SEC is more likely to issue a formal stop order.[57] In rare instances, the SEC will use the stop order even after the registration statement has become effective.[58] The institution of stop order proceedings has collateral consequences such as imposing disclosure obligations on the registrant and also disqualifying the registrant from the use of certain exemptions from registration.[59] In addition to the use of stop and refusal order proceedings for extremely defective registration statements, the SEC has used these proceedings to issue public opinions and thereby explain its views on important disclosure issues.[60]

The registration review process generally consists of correspondence between the Commission staff and the registrant.[61] Typically, the Commission staff will respond to an initial filing with a detailed letter of comments.[62] Especially in the case of first-time registrants, this informal give and take with the SEC will generally go beyond the twenty-day statutory period. It is common for issuers to file delaying amendments in order to give adequate time to respond to the SEC staff's suggestions.[63] When the informal discus-

---

in deciding whether to grant acceleration of the effective date of the registration statement. *See* Rule 461, 17 C.F.R. § 230.461.

57. *See, e.g.*, In the Matter of Toks Inc. SEC News Digest 2002–6, 2002 WL 22165 (SEC Initial Decision Jan. 9, 2002) (stop order issued).

58. *Id. See, e.g.*, SEC ALJ Suspends Effectiveness of Registration Statement for IPO, 34 Sec. Reg. & L. Rep. (BNA) 49 (Jan. 14, 2002).

59. *See, e.g.*, Rules 262 and 505 which provide that a section 8 proceeding (as well as other actions under the securities laws) will disqualify registrants and underwriters from participation in Regulation A and Rule 505 offerings. 17 C.F.R. §§ 230.262, 230.505.

60. *See, e.g.*, In the Matter of Franchard Corp., 42 S.E.C. 163 (SEC 1964); In the Matter of Universal Camera Corp., 19 S.E.C. 648 (1945).

61. *E.g.*, Universal Camera Corp., 19 S.E.C. 648, 658 (1945); Sec. Act Rel. No. 33–5231, 1 Fed.Sec.L.Rep. (CCH) ¶ 057 (Feb. 3, 1972). *See* § 3.5 *infra*.

Although this is the way in which the SEC normally proceeds, it may depart from the informal review process and initiate formal section 8 proceedings. *See, e.g.*, Doman Helicopters, Inc., 41 S.E.C. 431 (SEC 1963) (rejecting the registrant's argument that the SEC must first resort to the informal review process before instituting formal proceedings). In *Doman Helicopters* it was claimed that a stop order was not warranted since the initial filing was only a "preliminary filing" and the SEC never initiated its informal review. Once the section 8 hearings began, the registrant filed an amendment to delay the effective date which was claimed to have avoided the necessity of stop order proceedings. The Commission ruled that in light of the serious deficiencies in the registration statement as originally filed, section 8 proceedings were warranted. The seriousness of the deficiencies in *Doman Helicopters* was exacerbated by the fact that there were already more than 8,000 public investors. The SEC, thus, is not required to resort first to the more usual informal methods of review.

62. Until 2004, these comment letters have been publicly available only in response to requests under the Freedom of Information Act. In April 2004, the SEC announced that effective August 1, 2004, the comment letters will be made available on the SEC website but no sooner than 45 days after the SEC's review of the filing is completed. *See* SEC Staff to Publicly Release Comment Letters and Responses, SEC Press Rel. No. 2004–89, http://www.sec.gov/news/press/2004–89.htm (June 23, 2004). In addition to the SEC letters of comment, company responses will also be posted on the website. *Id.* The company may request confidential treatment under appropriate circumstances. *Id.*

63. SEC Rule 473 formally recognizes the propriety of delaying amendments. 17 C.F.R. § 230.473. However, not all forms are eligible for delaying amendments. Forms F–7, F–8, F–9,

sions between the registrant's counsel and the Commission staff result in a registration statement that the SEC will find acceptable, it is not uncommon for the registrant to seek acceleration of the effective date.[64] The SEC's plain English requirements for disclosure documents added a new dimension to the review process.[65] In addition to substantive disclosure rules, documents are now reviewed with an eye toward plain English compliance. The SEC had always voiced a concern with the clarity of disclosures but the plain English requirements mandate particular care with respect to specified portions of the registration statement. Violations of plain English requirements will not in and of themselves render the registration statement materially misleading. However, plain English deviations may result in an enhanced SEC review process and thus a delay in the effective date.

Frequently, the pricing of an offering[66] will not take place until just before the effective date. Although the participants planning a public offering will generally have at least a "ball park" figure for the planned offering price, general market fluctuations often require leaving the determination of a precise figure until the effective date. In these cases, it is necessary to file an amendment to the registration statement which relates to the price. Under the terms of section 8 of the Act, the filing of an amendment would ordinarily trigger an additional twenty-day statutory waiting period before the effective date. However, when such price amendments are filed, the Commission will consent to immediate effectiveness, thus, avoiding the statutory twenty-day period from running anew.[67]

The filing of a registration statement is not a step to be taken lightly. Once a registration statement has been filed, it cannot be withdrawn without Commission approval.[68] Formerly, the Commission had to act affirmatively in order to approve the request to withdraw the registration statement.[69] In 2001, the SEC amended Rule 477 to provide for automatic withdrawal of the registration statement unless the Commission objects to the request for withdrawal within fifteen days after the registrant's filing of an application to withdraw the registration statement.[70]

---

and F–10 for use by private foreign issuers are not eligible for delaying amendments. Delaying amendments are not expressly authorized for Forms S–3, S–4, F–4, and S–8. The various registration forms are described briefly in § 3.4 *infra.*

64. SEC Rule 461 sets out the requirements for acceleration. 17 C.F.R. § 230.461. *See* § 3.6[2] *infra.*

65. The plain English requirements include: use of the active rather than passive voice, short sentences, use of definite, concrete everyday words, presentation of information in tabular form or with bullet lists, the avoidance of legal jargon and highly technical business terminology, as well as the avoidance of multiple negatives. Rule 421, 17 C.F.R. § 230.421. *See* § 3.10[2] *infra.*

66. *Cf.* Friedman v. Salomon/Smith Barney, Inc., 2000 WL 1804719, [2000–2001 Transfer Binder] Fed. Sec. L. Rep. (CCH) ¶ 91,273, 2000–2 Trade Cases ¶ 73,115 (S.D.N.Y. 2000), *rehearing denied*, 2001 WL 64774 (S.D.N.Y.2001) (antitrust claim against broker dealers and underwriters alleging collusive inflated prices in connection with public offerings was preempted by SEC regulation).

67. 15 U.S.C.A. § 77h(a); 17 C.F.R. § 230.430A;.17 C.F.R. § 230.475.

68. 17 C.F.R. § 230.477.

69. Former 17 C.F.R. § 230.477 (this approval requirement was amended in 2001).

70. 17 C.F.R. § 230.477. Integration of Abandoned Offerings, Sec. Act Rel. No. 33–7943, 2001 WL 68771 (SEC Jan. 26, 2001). This change was made in conjunction with the adoption of Rule 155 which provides a safe harbor from integration for private offerings following an abandoned registered offering. 17 C.F.R. § 230.155 which is discussed in § 4.36[4][B] *infra.* Rule 155 also provides a safe harbor from integration for registered public offerings following an abandoned private offering. 17 C.F.R. § 230.477.

Although withdrawal is not guaranteed, most frequently it will be permitted. It is stated Commission policy to permit withdrawal of the registration statement if "consistent with the public interest and protection of investors."[71] In the normal course of events, the Commission will ordinarily approve a request for withdrawal. However, when it is believed that the registration process warrants imposing sanctions against the participants, the Commission might elect to refuse permission for withdrawal and go ahead with formal proceedings under section 8.[72] The SEC has been willing to use withdrawal of the registration statement as a condition to dismissal of stop order proceedings.[73]

The sections that follow examine the impact of technology on the offering process. This is followed by sections[74] describing the effects of SEC regulation during the pre-filing, waiting, and post-effective periods.

§ 2.2[3] Impact of Technology and the Internet on the Operation of Section 5

The Internet has opened up additional avenues for the offer and sale of securities. Online access gives issuers and underwriters a much broader and inexpensive exposure to potential investors. A number of issues have arisen concerning the impact of online activities and the 1933 Act's registration, prospectus, and exemptive provisions. A major issue, for example, is the fact that the Securities Act is drafted in terms of written disclosures. It thus becomes important to what extent online communications can comply with the Act.[75]

§ 2.2[3][A] Online Offerings

The ease with which potential investors can access the online resources has made the Internet fertile ground for securities offerings. In 1999, the Commission approved the use of the Internet for a public offering using online communications.[76] The approval was conditioned on safeguards designed to assure that appropriate disclosure documents were sent and received. Further, the SEC required reconfirmation of purchases by emails in order for an investor to effect a purchase of the securities.[77] In 2000, the SEC issued an interpretative release on the use of electronic media.[78] In this release, the Commission confirmed policies that it had established since the beginning of the use of online communications. For example, the SEC has permitted online auctions for securities provided there is electronic delivery of the necessary disclosure documents.[79] The SEC has reaffirmed the necessity of taking

---

71. 17 C.F.R. § 230.477.

72. *See* the discussion of section 8 proceedings in § 3.6 *infra*.

73. *E.g.*, In the Matter of a Registration Statement of Jonathan Aerospace Materials Corp., 2001 WL 1662289, Sec. Act Rel. No. 33–8050 (SEC Dec. 31, 2001).

74. *See* §§ 2.3–2.5 *infra*.

75. *See* Use of Electronic Media, Sec. Act Rel. No. 33–7856, 2000 WL 502290 (SEC April 28, 2000).

76. Wit Capital Corp., 31 Sec. Reg. & L. Rep. (BNA) 993, 1999 WL 498545 (SEC No Action Letter July 14, 1999).

77. *Id.*

78. Use of Electronic Media, Sec. Act Rel. No. 33–7856, 2000 WL 502290 (SEC April 28, 2000).

79. Wit Capital Corp., 2000 WL 1013585 (SEC No Action Letter July 20, 2000); W.R. Hambrecht & Co. 2000 WL 987735 (SEC No Action Letter July 12, 2000).

precautions so that online offerings do not run afoul of the disclosure mandates of the 1933 Act.[80] It is clear, for example, that email communications will be treated as written communications for purposes of section 5.[81]

§ 2.2[3][B] Electronic Delivery of "Written" Materials

As part of its public offering reform in 2005,[81.5] the SEC clarified that most online communications qualify as written communications.[81.10] There is an exception for live or real-time communications.[81.15]

In 1995, the SEC issued its initial interpretative release addressing the use of electronic delivery format for documents under the Securities Act of 1933, the Securities Exchange Act of 1934, and the Investment Company Act of 1940.[82] A subsequent SEC interpretative release was issued to deal with electronic delivery by broker dealers and investment advisers.[83] Another SEC release issued in 2000 summarized and updated its online delivery policies.[84]

To begin with, many observers contended that access to information online should be sufficient to satisfy delivery requirements. The SEC disagrees, however, and currently requires something more than simply making information available online.[85] The Commission believes that access to the Internet is not so widespread as to assume delivery from access but, at the same time, the SEC solicited additional comments as to whether to implement at least a piecemeal "access equals delivery" policy.

The SEC has confirmed that consent for receipt of electronic delivery may be obtained in writing, online via email, or over the telephone. This consent to electronic delivery can be limited to selected documents or it can be global and thereby apply to all documents to be delivered to the investor or potential investor. The Commission has not, however, accepted the suggestion that the widespread use of the Internet justifies an implied consent to electronic delivery or a rule that availability of information online will be treated as delivery of that information.[89]

Another issue is the format of the information that is being used to satisfy a delivery obligation. The Commission has made it clear that use of portable delivery format (PDF files) is not too burdensome on the investing public and thus is permitted.[90]

---

80. Use of Electronic Media, Sec. Act Rel. No. 33–7856, 2000 WL 502290 (SEC April 28, 2000).:

81. *See, e.g.* In the Matter of Goldman, Sachs & Co., Admin. Proc. No 3–11533, Sec. Act Rel. No. 33–8434, Sec. Exch. Act Rel. No. 34–49953, 2004 WL 1476147 (S.E.C. Release No. Jul 01, 2004)(emails during waiting period violated section 5(b); settlement of administrative proceedings).

81.5 *See* Securities Offering Reform, Sec. Act Rel. No. 33–8591, Sec. Exch. Act Rel. No. 34–52056, Inv. Co. Act Rel. No. IC–26993 70 Fed. Reg. 44722–01, 2005 WL 1692642 (SEC July 19, 2005).

81.10 17 C.F.R. § 230.405 ("definition of "graphic communication", which is incorporated by reference into the definition of "written communication).

81.15 *Id. See* § 2.2[3][C] *infra.*

82. Use of Electronic Media for Delivery Purposes, Sec. Act Rel. No. 33–7233, 60 Fed. Reg. 53458, 1995 WL 600083 (SEC Oct. 6, 1995).

83. Use of Electronic Media by Broker–Dealers, Transfer Agents, and Investment Advisers for Delivery of Information; Additional Examples Under the Securities Act of 1933, Securities Exchange Act of 1934, and Investment Company Act of 1940, Sec. Act Rel. No. 33–7288, 61 Fed. Reg. 24644, 1996 WL 251581 (SEC May 9, 1996).

84. Use of Electronic Media, Sec. Act Rel. No. 33–7856, 2000 WL 502290 (SEC April 28, 2000).

85. Use of Electronic Media, Sec. Act Rel. No. 33–7856, 2000 WL 502290 (SEC April 28, 2000).

89. *Id.*

90. *Id.*

If an issuer decides to use a web site for prospectus delivery, the issuer must take precautions in order to assure that only permissible material is included. The issuer must clearly define on the web site the document that purports to be the section 10 prospectus. Any hyperlinks within that portion of the web site designated as part of the prospectus will be considered part of the prospectus. Hyperlinks that may appear elsewhere on the web site that are clearly not embodied in the prospectus will not be considered part of the prospectus. As explained by the Commission, "[i]nformation on a web site would be part of a Section 10 prospectus only if an issuer (or person acting on behalf of the issuer, including an intermediary with delivery obligations) acts to make it part of the prospectus."[94] While the issuer is "in registration" there is an increasing likelihood that information in any third party web sites that are hyperlinked to the issuer's web site will be deemed to have been adopted by the issuer. Additionally, the prominence of any such hyperlinks, as well as the way the information is presented will be factors in deciding whether to treat the information on the hyperlinked third party web site as having been adopted or endorsed by the issuer.

§ 2.2[3][C] Electronic Road Shows

Section 2(a)(10) of the Securities Act of 1933 defines prospectus as a written or radio or television communication.[97] Oral communications are not within the definition of prospectus and so are not regulated by section 5(b) of the Act.[98] Thus, during the waiting and post-effective periods there are no restrictions on oral communications other than those imposed by the anti-fraud rules. Accordingly, promoters of public offerings frequently make statements over the telephone or in person that they would not be able to make in writing during the waiting and post-effective periods.[99] It is also common for promoters of public offerings to hold meetings, known as road shows, to discuss the securities being offered.[100] The SEC has also permitted road shows over the Internet without being classified as a prospectus.[101] The Commission has conditioned no action letter relief for Internet road shows as follows: (1) the road show may not exclude any material information; (2) only one version of the road show is captured for subsequent Internet transmission; and (3) the content of the road show is consistent with the information contained in the statutory prospectus.[102]

---

94. *Id.*

97. 15 U.S.C.A. § 77b(a)(10).

98. 15 U.S.C.A. § 77e(b). However, section 5(c) prohibits oral offers to sell and oral offers to buy during the pre-filing period. 15 U.S.C.A. § 77e(c). *See* § 2.3 *infra.*

99. *Cf.* Carr v. CIGNA Securities, 95 F.3d 544 (7th Cir.1996) (documents warning investors that investment was risky precluded claim based on oral assurances that the investment was safe and conservative).

100. *See, e.g.,* Private Financial Network, [1997 Transfer Binder] Fed. Sec. L. Rep. (CCH) ¶ 77,332 (SEC No Action Letter March 12, 1997) (video transmissions of road shows were not prospectuses). *See also, e.g.,* Note, Watch Your Mouth: Section 12(a)(2) Liability for Oral Statements Made at Road Shows, 23 J. Corp. L. 541 (1998).

101. *See* Charles Schwab & Co., 31 Sec. Reg. & L. Rep. (BNA) 1560 (SEC No Action Letter Nov. 12, 1999) (live presentations via Internet in password protect areas were permissible).

102. Charles Schwab & Co., 32 Sec. Reg. & L. Rep. (BNA) 235 (SEC No Action Letter Feb. 9, 2000), *clarifying* Charles Schwab & Co., 31 Sec. Reg. & L. Rep. (BNA) 1560 (SEC No Action Letter Nov. 12, 1999).

In 2005, the SEC codified its interpretations regarding electronic road shows.[106.5] Specifically, an electronic road show that consists of a "live" broadcast is not consider a prospectus whereas other electronic road shows constitute a writing and therefore may be permissible under as a "free writing prospectus."[106.10]

§ 2.3　The Pre–Filing Period

§ 2.3[1]　Basic Prohibitions of the Pre–Filing Period

As written, section 5(c)[1] prohibits offers to sell and offers to buy[2] regardless of whether a public offering and registration is contemplated in the foreseeable future. It follows that section 5(c)'s prohibitions are not limited to transactions that may occur in contemplation of a registered public offering. Nevertheless, the commonly used terminology "pre-filing period" indicates that a public offering is contemplated. As discussed elsewhere in this treatise, most securities transactions that take place outside of the context of a public offering are exempt from section 5's prohibitions.[3]

Once a public offering is contemplated, section 5(c)'s prohibitions on offers to sell and offers to buy clearly come into play. When does the pre-filing period begin? There is no statutory time period to help us answer this question. The mere contemplation of a public offering in the future will not by itself trigger the 1933 Act's pre-filing obligations. The pre-filing period begins once a company decides to take concrete steps toward a public offering.[4] As a practical matter, in planning transactions, planners should consider the prohibitions applicable to the pre-filing period to apply at least the thirty days immediately preceding the filing of the registration statement.

Section 5(c)[5] sets forth the basic prohibitions for the pre-filing period. There can be neither legal offers to buy nor offers to sell securities until a registration statement has been filed. Section 5(c) is the broadest proscription as it covers all offers—whether written or oral and whether to buy or to sell—with offer to sell being described broadly as any conduct that is reasonably

---

106.5　*See* Securities Offering Reform, Sec. Act Rel. No. 33–8591, Sec. Exch. Act Rel. No. 34–52056, Inv. Co. Act Rel. No. IC–26993 70 Fed. Reg. 44722–01, 2005 WL 1692642 (SEC July 19, 2005).

106.10　*See* 1933 Act Rules 164 and 433, 17 C.F.R. §§ 230.164, 230.433; Securities Offering Reform, Sec. Act Rel. No. 33–8591, Sec. Exch. Act Rel. No. 34–52056, Inv. Co. Act Rel. No. IC–26993 70 Fed. Reg. 44722–01, 2005 WL 1692642 (SEC July 19, 2005).

§ 2.3

1.　15 U.S.C.A. § 77e(c).

2.　Section 5(c) is the only portion of section 5 that covers offers to buy as well as offers to sell. *See* Richard J. Morgan, Offers to Buy Under The Securities Act of 1933, 1982 Ariz. St. L.J. 809.

3.　These exemptions are found in section four of the Act. For example, section 4(1) exempts transactions not involving an issuer, underwriter, or a dealer. 15 U.S.C.A. § 77d(1); *see* § 4.26[1] *infra*. Section 4(2) exempts transaction by an issuer not involving a public offering. 15 U.S.C.A. § 77d(2); *see* §§ 4.24, 4.25 *infra*. Section 4(3) exempts most dealer transactions in securities. 15 U.S.C.A. § 77d(3); *see* 4.31 *infra*. Section 4(4) of the Act exempts unsolicited brokers' transactions. 15 U.S.C.A. § 77d(4); *see* § 4.26[2] *infra*. Of course, absent an applicable exemption, section 5(c)'s prohibitions will apply even if no public offering is contemplated.

4.　The SEC has not addressed the duration of the pre-filing period but it has indicated that "in registration" means "at least from the time an issuer reaches an understanding with the broker-dealer which is to act as managing underwriter prior to the filing of a registration statement." Guidelines for Release of Information by Issuers Whose Securities are in Registration, Sec.Act Rel. No. 33–5180, 1971 WL 11224, Fed.Sec.L.Rep. (CCH) ¶ 3056 (Aug. 16, 1971).

5.　15 U.S.C.A. § 77e(c).

calculated to generate a buying interest. A violation of section 5(c) does not depend upon an actual sale so long as there have been illegal offers.[7]

In contrast to section 5(c)'s prohibitions on offers to sell and offers to buy in the absence of a registration statement having been filed, the prohibitions for both the waiting and post-effective periods apply only to written, radio, or television offers to sell as defined by section 2(a)(10) of the Act,[8] and not to oral offers to sell nor to any offers to buy. In addition to the prohibition against offers during the pre-filing period, section 5(a)[9] bars all sales of securities during both the pre-filing and waiting periods.

Preliminary negotiations and agreements between an issuer and underwriters (and among underwriters who are to be in privity with the issuer) are excluded from section 2(a)(3)'s definition of sell or offer to sell[10] and thus do not violate the "gun jumping" prohibitions contained in section 5(c); nor do they implicate the prospectus requirements of section 5(b) or the sale prohibition of section 5(a).

Therefore, absent an exemption or the exclusion for underwriters' preliminary negotiations and agreements, offers to buy, offers to sell (whether written or oral), and sales are all prohibited during the pre-filing period. Accordingly, the 1933 Act's broadest prohibitions take effect prior to filing of the registration statement. This broad reach of section 5(c) makes sense to the extent that during this time there is absolutely no public information about the upcoming offering, except for information which may have been disclosed if the issuer is already a public company and therefore subject to the 1934 Act's periodic reporting requirements. In light of the absence of reliable up-to-date information about the issuer and/or the terms of the upcoming offering, any premature sales-related activity or "gun jumping" would circumvent the purpose of the 1933 Act's registration and prospectus requirements. Such a circumvention would thus amount to a violation of section 5.

As part of its securities offering reform that was adopted in 2005, the SEC adopted rules explicitly permitting additional communications during the quiet period by qualifying preexisting public companies. The new rules also clarify application of section 5 to first time issuers and non-reporting companies. All companies, including first time issuers are permitted to publicly disseminate information that does not refer to a securities offering and provided the issuer takes reasonable steps to prevent further distribution of the information during the thirty days immediately preceding the public offering.[14.5] There is an additional, more expansive safe harbor for preexisting public companies that explicitly includes both "factual business information or forward-looking information."[14.10] This exemption applies to the types of

---

7. SEC v. Cavanagh, 155 F.3d 129, 135 (2d Cir.1998) ("Section 5(c) requires the filing of a registration statement prior to any offer, regardless of whether a sale occurs or the conditions of that sale").

8. 15 U.S.C.A. § 77b(a)(10).

9. 15 U.S.C.A. § 77e(a).

10. 15 U.S.C.A. § 77b(a)(3). A letter of intent to underwrite an offering is not a binding contract for the sale of securities. Cafe La France, Inc. v. Schneider Securities, Inc., 281 F.Supp.2d 361 (D.R.I. 2003).

14.5 1933 Act Rule 163A, 17 C.F.R. 230.163A.

14.10 1933 Act Rule 168(a), 17 C.F.R. § 230.168(a). Rule 168 provides a safe harbor from the definition of offer as used in section 5(c)'s gun-jumping prohibition as well as a safe harbor from section 2(a)(10)'s definition of "prospectus" thereby preventing the application of the prohibition

information that the company had been disseminating in the regular course of business.

Rule 163A provides a safe harbor from a section 5(c) violation for communications made by or on behalf of the issuer provided the statement is made more than 30 days before the registration statement is filed. This safe harbor, among other things, is conditioned upon the absence of any reference to the upcoming offering. Statements referencing the upcoming offering must fall within the parameters of the SEC *Loeb Rhodes* decision that is discussed below,[14.15] Rule 135's safe harbor,[14.20] or, with respect to well known seasoned issuers qualify as a permissible prefiling free writing prospectus under Rule 163.[14.25]

[handwritten margin note: Rule 163A 30 day safe harbor...]

As a practical matter, most of section 5(c)'s gun-jumping prohibitions do not apply to the largest public companies that qualify as well-known seasoned issuers ("WKSIs"). A WKSI is a company that qualifies for registration on 1933 Act Form S–3 or F–3 and either: (A) As of a date within 60 days of the determination date, has a worldwide market value of its outstanding voting and non-voting common equity held by non-affiliates of $700 million or more; or (B)(1) As of a date within 60 days of the determination date, has issued in the last three years at least $1 billion aggregate principal amount of non-convertible securities, other than common equity, in primary offerings for cash, not exchange, registered under the Act; and (2) Will register only non-convertible securities, other than common equity, and full and unconditional guarantees permitted pursuant to paragraph (1)(ii) of this definition unless, at the determination date, the issuer also is eligible to register a primary offering of its securities relying on General Instruction I.B.1. of Form S–3 or Form F–3.[14.30] Also, Rule 168 is a safe harbor for preexisting public companies that explicitly includes both "factual business information or forward-looking information" which applies to the types of information that the company had been disseminating in the regular course of business.[14.35]

---

in Securities Act section 5(b)(1) on the use of a prospectus that is not a statutory prospectus. The prospectus requirements for the waiting period are discussed in § 2.4 *infra*. 17 C.F.R. § 230.168(c) ("A communication containing information about the registered offering or released or disseminated as part of the offering activities in the registered offering is excluded from the exemption").

14.15 In the Matter of Carl M. Loeb, Rhoades & Co., 38 S.E.C. 843, Sec. Exch. Act Rel. No. 34–5870, 1959 WL 59531 (SEC Feb. 9, 1959); *see* § 2.3[2] *infra*.

14.20 17 C.F.R. § 230.135; *see* § 2.3[3] *infra*.

14.25 *See* § 2.4[2][E] *infra*.

14.30 17 C.F.R. § 230.405. A seasoned issuer, other than a WKSI, is an issuer that uses Form S–3 or Form F–3 to register primary offerings of securities. Securities Offering Reform, Sec. Act Rel. No. 33–8591, Sec. Exch. Act Rel. No. 34–52056, Inv. Co. Act Rel. No. IC–26993 70 Fed. Reg. 44722–01, 2005 WL 1692642 (SEC August 3, 2005). "An unseasoned issuer is an issuer that is required to file reports pursuant to Sections 13 or 15(d) of the Exchange Act, but does not satisfy the requirements of Form S–3 or Form F–3 for a primary offering of its securities." *Id.*

14.35 17 C.F.R. § 230.168. The safe harbor applies to information disseminated by broker-dealers as agent of the issuer but is not available to investment companies. *Id.* The new rules introduced by the offering reform may not be invoked by certain ineligible issuers. In eligible issuers include: companies that are not current in their 1934 Act reports over the preceding twelve months; companies that are or during the preceding three years were blank check or shell companies or penny stock issuers; limited partnerships offering and selling their securities other than through a firm commitment underwriting; companies that have filed for bankruptcy or insolvency within the preceding three years; companies that have bee the subject of 1933 Act stop or refusal orders; and companies the during the preceding three years have been convicted of specified felonies or misdemeanors, have been found to have violated the federal securities laws' anti-fraud provisions, or have been the subject of an administrative decree for violating the

§ 2.3[2] What is an Offer to Sell?: Generating a Buying Interest

Section 2(a)(3) of the Act[15] defines offer to sell in terms of any activity that is reasonably calculated to solicit or generate a buying interest. The determination of whether there is an offer is not a matter of state contract law but rather is a question of federal law depending upon whether the challenged conduct has conditioned the offeree's or public's mind by generating a buying interest.[16] The fact that negotiations fall short of an enforceable offer to sell under state law thus does not prevent the person negotiating to sell the securities in question from offering to sell the securities in violation of section 5 of the Securities Act of 1933 Act.[17] A letter or other communication that solicits investor interest prior to the filing of the registration statement will ordinarily be a illegal offer to sell.[18] The SEC has indicated that it is possible to generate a buying interest and therefore have an offer to sell in promotional material that does not even mention the upcoming offering, especially where the materials are used as part of a plan to prepare the market in advance of the dissemination of offering materials.[19] Dissemination of information in the ordinary course of business is permissible but it becomes questionable when the timing of such activities seems to be gearing up to an impending public offering.[20]

Definitional problems frequently arise in connection with inadvertent "gun jumping" publicity that may violate section 5(c) of the Act. One of the most frequent context for "gun jumping" problems involves publicity about an upcoming offering or about the company itself prior to the filing of a 1933 Act registration statement. The courts have construed section 2(a)(3)'s definition of offer to sell quite broadly. The concept of offer is not limited to contract law doctrine but rather includes a communication of a character calculated to arouse investor interest in the securities to be offered.[21]

---

federal securities laws' antifraud provisions. *See* Securities Offering Reform, Sec. Act Rel. No. 33–8591, Sec. Exch. Act Rel. No. 34–52056, Inv. Co. Act Rel. No. IC–26993 70 Fed. Reg. 44722–01, 2005 WL 1692642 (SEC August 3, 2005).

15. 15 U.S.C.A. § 77b(a)(3).

16. *E.g.,* SEC v. Cavanagh, 155 F.3d 129, 135 (2d Cir.1998) (the definition of offer to sell "extends beyond the common law contract concept of an offer and clearly covers [defendants'] negotiations"); Diskin v. Lomasney & Co., 452 F.2d 871, 875 (2d Cir. 1971).

17. *See, e.g.,* SEC v. Cavanagh, 155 F.3d 129, 135 (2d Cir.1998); Diskin v. Lomasney & Co., 452 F.2d 871, 875 (2d Cir. 1971).

18. *See, e.g.,* SEC v. Commercial Investment & Development Corp., 373 F.Supp. 1153 (S.D.Fla.1974). *See also, e.g.,* SEC v. Thomas D. Kienlen Corp., 755 F.Supp. 936 (D.Or.1991).

19. Sec. Act Rel. 33–3844 Example 1, 1957 WL 3605 (1957) (the mailing in question "obviously was designed to awaken an interest which later would be focused on the specific financing to be presented in the prospectus shortly to be sent to the same mailing list").

20. *See, e.g.,* Georgeson & Co., 1977 WL 13861 [1977–1978 Transfer Binder] Fed. Sec. L. Rep. (CCH) ¶ 81,118 (SEC No Action Letter Feb. 3, 1977, available Mar. 3, 1977) ("it would seem prudent and appropriate for those issuers that do not have a consistent history of such activities to defer commencing them until the registration process has been completed" and thereby avoid the inference "that an issuer is engaging in them for the purpose of priming the market for an impending securities offering").

21. In the Matter of Carl M. Loeb, Rhoades & Co., 38 S.E.C. 843, Sec. Exch. Act Rel. No. 34–5870, 1959 WL 59531 (SEC Feb. 9, 1959). *See also, e.g.,* Chris–Craft Industries, Inc. v. Bangor Punta Corp., 426 F.2d 569 (2d Cir.1970); Guidelines for Release of Information by Issuers Whose Securities are in Registration, Sec.Act Rel. No. 33–5180, 1971 WL 11224, 1 Fed.Sec.L.Rep. (CCH) ¶ 3056 (Aug. 16, 1971).

The initial leading authority on this point is the SEC decision, In the Matter of Carl M. Loeb, Rhoades & Co.[22] In that administrative proceeding, the underwriter prepared and disseminated a press release six weeks prior to the filing of the registration statement. The press release announced that a hitherto one-person real estate venture owning over one hundred thousand acres "in the area of the gold coast" in Florida was about to go public. The press release went on to identify the investment banker that would be handling the underwriting arrangements and further named the issuer's principal officers. The press release generated a buying interest, as evidenced by the fact that over one hundred securities dealers contacted the named managing underwriter asking that they be included in the underwriting syndicate.[23] The SEC examined the press release and held that although in the form of a news item, the release disclosed much more information than was necessary to simply alert the public of a newsworthy event and thus constituted an offer to sell within section 2(a)(3)'s definition. The key to the Commission's decision seemed to be not only the fact that more than one hundred securities firms had shown a buying interest but further that the press release identified the name of the principal underwriter, hence directing potential buyers to the selling source. The SEC has specifically cautioned that including the underwriter's name in pre-filing publicity is likely to generate a buying interest and therefore trigger the definition of "offer to sell."[24] Naming the underwriter will disqualify a communication from the protections of Rule 135's safe harbor for pre-filing publicity.[25]

Following the *Loeb, Rhoades* decision, there was concern that the line of demarcation between legitimate pre-filing publicity and an illegal offer to sell was a murky one. Accordingly, the SEC tried to clarify the issue when it amended Rule 135.[26] The current version of the rule enumerates the types of pre-filing publicity that will not be considered in violation of section 5(c)'s "gun jumping" prohibitions. Rule 135 is silent on the extent of its reach: that is, whether it is a safe harbor or an exclusive harbor. Nevertheless, one court[27] has indicated it to be the exclusive method for disseminating permissible pre-filing information. Presumably, this view of exclusivity is limited to press releases and other announcements geared solely to the impending public offering. The SEC has explained, for example, that the issuer should continue to make full disclosure in its 1934 Act periodic reports as well as to continue the types of publicity that the issuer undertakes as a matter of its ordinary course of business.[28]

---

22.   38 S.E.C. 843, Sec. Exch. Act Rel. No. 34–5870, 1959 WL 59531 (SEC Feb. 9, 1959), noted in 1959 Duke L.J. 460; 54 Nw.L.Rev. 131 (1959). *Cf.* SEC v. Arvida Corp., [1957–1961 Transfer Binder] Fed. Sec. L. Rep. (CCH) ¶ 90,883 (S.D.N.Y. 1958) (refusing to dismiss the complaint but also refusing the SEC's request for a preliminary injunction).

For summary of the gun jumping prohibitions, *see* Joseph P. Richardson & Joseph E. Reece, Gun Jumping, 26 Rev.Sec. & Commod.Reg. 1 (1993).

23.   The press release also announced the issuer's intent to embark upon a "comprehensive statement of orderly development."

24.   Sec. Act Rel. 33–4697, 1964 WL 68261 (1964). *See also, e.g.,* Chris–Craft Industries, Inc. v. Bangor Punta Corp., 426 F.2d 569 (2d Cir.1970).

25.   17 C.F.R. § 230.135. *See* § 2.3[3] *infra.*

26.   17 C.F.R. § 230.135.

27.   Chris-Craft Industries, Inc. v. Bangor Punta Corp., 426 F.2d 569 (2d Cir.1970).

28.   *See, e.g.,* Guidelines for Release of Information by Issuers Whose Securities are in Registration, Sec.Act Rel. No. 33–5180, 1971 WL 11224, 1 Fed.Sec.L.Rep. (CCH) ¶ 3056 (Aug. 16, 1971).

As noted above, Rule 163A provides a safe harbor from a section 5(c) violation for communications made by or on behalf of the issuer provided the statement is made more than 30 days before the registration statement is filed.[28.5] This safe harbor, among other things, is conditioned upon the absence of any reference to the upcoming offering. Prefiling publicity that references the upcoming offering must fall within one of the permissible statements discussed in the sections that follow.

Factual Information and gun-jumping; forward-looking statements by reporting companies.

Rule 169[28.95] provides a safe harbor for "factual business information" that is not directed to investors but is issued as part of the company's ordinary business. Thus, for example, product advertisements are protected by the safe harbor.[28.100] Rule 169's safe harbor applies to non-reporting companies as well as to reporting companies. The safe harbor does not apply to communications made as part of the offering and also is limited to the types of information the company had made in the past. 1934 Act reporting companies are given a broader safe harbor in Rule 168[28.105] which permits not only the dissemination of factual information but also forward looking information. As is the case with Rule 169, Rule 168's safe harbor for reporting companies applies only if "the timing, manner, and form in which the information is released or disseminated is consistent in material respects with similar past releases or disseminations"[28.110] and also excludes from the safe harbor communications "containing information about the registered offering or released or disseminated as part of the offering activities in the registered offering."[28.115] The safe harbors in Rules 168 and 169 apply both to section 5(c) gun jumping and to information during the waiting and post effective periods as the rules refer to section 2(a)(10)'s definition of prospectus as well.

Even after the expiration of the pre-filing period, participants must be careful not to make written offers unless they are in compliance with the prospectus requirements of section 5(b) of the Act.[29] Thus, once the decision to go public has been made and continuing through the waiting and post-effective periods when prospectuses must be delivered, participants in a registered offering must be very careful in not making statements that will be regarded as conditioning the market.

28.5   17 C.F.R. § 230.163A.

28.95   17 C.F.R. § 230.169.

28.100   17 C.F.R. § 230.169 (b) ("(1) Factual business information means some or all of the following information that is released or disseminated under the conditions in paragraph (d) of this section: (i) Factual information about the issuer, its business or financial developments, or other aspects of its business; and (ii) Advertisements of, or other information about, the issuer's products or services. (2) For purposes of this section, the release or dissemination of a communication is by or on behalf of the issuer if the issuer or an agent or representative of the issuer, other than an offering participant who is an underwriter or dealer, authorizes or approves such release or dissemination before it is made.").

28.105   17 C.F.R. § 230.168.

28.110   17 C.F.R. § 230.168(d)(2).

28.115   17 C.F.R. § 230.168(c).

29.   15 U.S.C.A. § 77e(b). *See* § 2.4 *infra*.

§ 2.3[3] Safe Harbor for Permissible Pre–Filing Announcements—SEC Rules 135, 168 and 169

Rule 135 provides that, solely for the purpose of section 5 of the Act, a notice given by an issuer or selling shareholder to the effect that it proposes to make a registered public offering is not an offer for sale if the notice contains only the information specified in the rule and further states that an offer can be made only through the use of a prospectus. The rule, which as written reads like a safe harbor rule,[31] applies to "a notice of a proposed offering to be registered under the Act" published by "an issuer or a selling security holder (and any person acting on behalf of either of them)."[32] It is noteworthy that the rule does not address itself to press releases by promoters, underwriters or other participants unless they are issuing the statement on behalf of the issuer or selling shareholders. It is quite possible that the omission of underwriters and promoters from Rule 135 reflects a view that any publicity initiated by an underwriter or promoter is likely to be viewed as the type of sales effort that section 5(c) was designed to prevent.[33] It would certainly seem to make sense to limit pre-filing publicity to the information sent out by the issuer whose interest in disseminating the information may be other than initiating the sales effort. Furthermore, limiting pre-filing publicity to the issuer is consistent with Rule 135's goal of balancing the right to disseminate newsworthy information against the risks of generating a buying interest in the security which will be registered, before adequate information is available. Notwithstanding this reading of Rule 135, it should be remembered that the prohibition is limited to participants in the offering and securities professionals in light of the exemption for transactions by persons other than issuers, underwriters, and dealers.[34]

Rule 135 publicity can legitimately contain (1) the name of the issuer; (2) the title, amount, and basic terms of the offering; (3) in the case of a rights offering to existing security holders, the subscription ratio, record date and approximate date of the proposed rights offering, as well as the subscription price; (4) where securities are exchanged for securities of another issuer, the nature and "basis" of the exchange;[35] (5) in the case of an offering to employees of the issuer or any affiliate, the class of employees and the amount proposed to be offered, including the offering price; and (6) any statement required by state law or administrative authority.

Rule 135 does not expressly permit mention of the offering price in the pre-filing publicity for most public offerings. Only Rule 135 subsections 3 and 5, which deal with rights offerings to existing securities holders and offerings to employees, expressly permit mention of price. There is authority supporting the exclusivity of these provisions permitting reference to price. For example, within the tender offer context, in the announcement of a proposed exchange

---

31. Although at least one decision has indicated that the rule is not merely a safe harbor but is an exclusive list of permissible pre-filing notices. Chris–Craft Industries, Inc. v. Bangor Punta Corp., 426 F.2d 569 (2d Cir.1970).

32. 17 C.F.R. § 230.135.

33. The naming of the underwriter in pre-filing publicity has in fact been held to be a significant factor in finding an illegal selling effort. *See* In the Matter of Carl M. Loeb, Rhoades & Co., 38 S.E.C. 843, Sec. Exch. Act Rel. No. 34–5870, 1959 WL 59531 (SEC Feb. 9, 1959). *See also, e.g.,* Chris–Craft Industries, Inc. v. Bangor Punta Corp., 426 F.2d 569 (2d Cir.1970).

34. Section 4(1), 15 U.S.C.A. § 77d(1), which is discussed in § 4.26 *infra*.

35. Rule 135(a)(4) in allowing the basis of the exchange is in contrast to subsections (3) and (5) which permit mentioning the offering price.

offer for which no registration statement had been filed, a valuation of securities not yet issued that were to be distributed as part of the exchange package went beyond the terms of Rule 135 and was thus held to render the press release an offer to sell the securities in violation of section 5(c).[36] The "gun jumping" problem in the course of exchange offers has to a large extent been remedied by Rule 165,[37] which was promulgated in connection with the SEC's adoption of Regulation M–A.[38] Rule 165 permits announcements of tender offers prior to the filing of the 1933 Act registration statement. Rule 165 applies not only to tender offers, but also to other business combinations, such as mergers, where the shares issued will be covered by a 1933 Act registration statement.[39] These pre-filing announcements permitted by Rule 165 need to be filed with the SEC.[40] Once the registration statement is filed, any written communications to shareholders must comply with the 1933 Act's prospectus requirements.[41]

SEC Rule 135, as noted above, refers only to pre-filing publicity by issuers and says nothing about information provided by others. By virtue of section 4(1)'s exemption,[42] persons who are not issuers, underwriters, or dealers may issue any pre-filing information. This exemption, of course, is subject to the caveat that anyone acting on behalf of the issuer, its affiliates, or other participants in the offering will be considered one of the underwriters[43] or their agents according to common law agency principles.[44] If Rule 135 is in fact exclusive,[45] then neither underwriters nor dealers can issue any pre-filing publicity without an exemption such as those found in Rules 137, 138, and 139,[46] which are discussed directly below.[47] It is arguable that any other publicity would be a selling effort or at least reasonably calculated to stimulate a buying interest and thus within section 2(a)(3)'s definition. Even if Rule 135 is deemed not to be exclusive, any non-exempt underwriter or dealer generating pre-filing publicity would be subject to careful factual scrutiny along the lines of the *Loeb, Rhoades* analysis as to whether an illegal selling effort has taken place. In any event, the safest course is to adhere strictly to Rule 135 and thus make no disclosures beyond its terms, as well as limit the dissemination of such information to the public.[48]

---

36. Chris-Craft Industries, Inc. v. Bangor Punta Corp., 426 F.2d 569 (2d Cir.1970). The SEC has since indicated that mentioning price in the context of a takeover will not always be an offer to sell. Sec.Act Rel.No. 33–5927, 3 Fed.Sec.L.Rep. (CCH) ¶ 24,284(H) (April 24, 1978).

37. 17 C.F.R. § 230.165.

38. Regulation of Takeovers and Security Holder Communications, Sec. Exch. Act Rel. No. 34–42055, 70 S.E.C. Docket 2229, 1999 WL 969596 (SEC Oct. 22, 1999).

39. This includes, for example, combinations effectuated through registration on Form S–4 that combines the 1933 Act proxy statement with the 1934 Act Schedule 14A that is required for soliciting proxies.

40. 1933 Act Rules 135(b), 425, 17 C.F.R. §§ 230.135(b), 230.425.

41. The prospectus requirements are discussed in §§ 2.4, 2.5 *infra*.

42. 15 U.S.C.A. § 77d(1). *See* § 4.26 *infra*.

43. *See* section 2(a)(11); 15 U.S.C.A. § 77b(a)(11).

44. *See also* section 15's liability of controlling persons. 15 U.S.C.A. § 77o discussed in § 7.12 *infra*.

45. *See* Chris–Craft Industries, Inc. v. Bangor Punta Corp., 426 F.2d 569 (2d Cir.1970).

46. 17 C.F.R. §§ 230.137–230.139.

47. *See* § 2.3[6] *infra*.

48. Even where the offering is purely a secondary one, a literal reading of the rule would limit the press release to the issuer as opposed to the actual registrants. Secondary distributions are discussed in §§ 4.26–4.29 *infra*.

§ 2.3[4] Exchange Offers and Business Combinations Subject to the Exchange Act

In 1999, the Commission liberalized its rules relating to tender offers governed by the Securities Exchange Act of 1934.[49] These liberalized rules permit parties to communicate more freely about planned tender offers and business combinations without triggering the gun jumping provisions of the 1933 Act. As discussed above, the gun jumping provisions would otherwise apply to statements regarding tender offers and business combinations when the new shares being issued will be subject to a 1933 Act registration. The increased communication provisions apply once the tender offer has been publicly announced. The concept of a "public announcement" encompasses all communications that put the market on notice of a proposed transaction. "Public announcement" means any communication by a party to the transaction, or any person authorized to act on a party's behalf, which is reasonably designed to, or has the effect of, informing the public or security holders in general about the transaction.[50] The gun jumping rules permit increased communication not only during the pre-filing but also during the waiting and post-effective periods so long as they are made after public announcement of the exchange offer and written communications are filed with the SEC on the date that they are first used.[51] Rule 135(a)(4) permits a limited amount of information about a pending tender offer prior to the filing of the 1933 Act registration statement.[54] With regard to business combinations, Rule 166[55] and Rule 145(b)(1) provide a similar approach by stating that certain communications will not constitute either an offer to sell or a prospectus under the 1933 Act.[56] The SEC points out, however, that technical compliance with these gun jumping rules will not provide an exemption if in fact there is a scheme to precondition the market for a capital raising transaction.[57]

§ 2.3[5] The Impact of Exchange Act Reporting Requirements and Other Disclosure Obligations on the Pre–Filing Quiet Period

The pressure for affirmative disclosure that may result from the 1934 Act reporting requirements, including the proxy rules and the tender offer provisions,[58] or in the case of non-reporting companies from Exchange Act Rule 10b–5,[59] may be at odds with section 5(c)'s limitations on publicity. In such a case "[t]he Commission * * * emphasizes that there is no basis in the securities acts or in any policy of the Commission which would justify the

---

49. Regulation of Takeovers and Security Holder Communications, Sec. Act Rel. No. 33–7760, 1999 WL 969596 (SEC Oct. 22, 1999).

50. 1933 Act Rule 165(f)(3), 17 C.F.R. § 230.165(f)(3).

51. 1933 Act Rule 425, 17 C.F.R. § 230.425.

54. 17 C.F.R. § 230.135(a)(4).

55. Rule 166, 17 C.F.R. § 230.166.

56. Rule 145(b)(1), 17 C.F.R. § 230.145(b)(1). Rule 145 is discussed in § 5.2 *infra*.

57. Rule 166 "is available only to communications relating to business combinations. The exemption does not apply to communications that may be in technical compliance with this section, but have the primary purpose or effect of conditioning the market for another transaction, such as a capital-raising or resale transaction." Preliminary note to Rule 166, 17 C.F.R. § 230.166.

58. *See* Chris–Craft Industries, Inc. v. Bangor Punta Corp., 426 F.2d 569 (2d Cir.1970).

59. 17 C.F.R. § 240.10b–5. *See* chapter 12 *infra*.

practice of non-disclosure on the grounds that it has the securities in registration under the Securities Act of 1933."[60] By "in registration," the SEC means "at least from the time an issuer reaches an understanding with the broker-dealer which is to act as managing underwriter prior to the filing of a registration statement and [continues through] the period ... during which dealers must deliver a prospectus."[61] The balance that permits the issuer to continue normal publicity[62] during the pre-filing period is a delicate one. It accordingly has been held that too much disclosure will nevertheless violate section 5(c),[63] thus frequently placing the issuer between a rock and a hard place in deciding the extent of permissible pre-filing publicity. Close questions necessarily require careful examination of the gun jumping prohibitions in conjunction with the materiality requirements of the applicable affirmative disclosure requirements. For example, the shareholders who are asked in a proxy statement to approve authorization of shares for future distribution must be given more pre-filing information than would otherwise be permissible under Rule 135.

Even beyond the conflicting pulls of the 1933 Act's "gun jumping" prohibitions and the Exchange Act's call for full disclosure, "gun jumping" tensions can arise in other areas in which the issuer is engaged in the public dissemination of information. The SEC suggests that issuers establish internal controls to protect against improvident release of information while securities are in registration.[64]

The SEC's 2005 offering reform rules gave more certainty to the issues facing existing public companies. The rules in essence divide existing public companies into two categories—seasoned issuers and well-known seasoned issuers ("WIKSIs") which are larger more widely held public companies.[64.5] As noted above, a practical matter, most of section 5(c)'s gun-jumping prohibitions do not apply to the largest public companies that qualify as well-known seasoned issuers.

[For discussion of SEC Rules 137–139 dealing with broker-dealer recommendations, see § 2.3[6] of the Practitioner's Edition.]

§ 2.4   The Waiting Period

§ 2.4[1]   Prohibitions During the Waiting Period

Once the registration statement has been filed, the waiting period begins. Since section 5(c) is no longer in effect after filing, anyone is free to make an offer to buy the security in registration, as well as to make oral offers to sell,

---

60. Guidelines for Release of Information by Issuers Whose Securities are in Registration, Sec.Act Rel. No. 33–5180, 1971 WL 11224, Fed.Sec.L.Rep. (CCH) ¶ 3056 (Aug. 16, 1971).

61. *Id.* fn. 1 *Accord* Use of Electronic Media, Sec. Act Rel. No. 33–7856, 2000 WL 502290 fn. 10 (SEC April 28, 2000).

62. The pre-filing "gun jumping" prohibitions "are not intended to restrict the normal communications between an issuer and its stockholders or the announcement to the public generally of information with respect to important business and financial developments." Sec. Act Rel. 33–4697, 1964 WL 68261 (1964).

63. Chris-Craft Indus., Inc. v. Bangor Punta Corp., 426 F.2d 569 (2d Cir.1970).

64. Guidelines for Release of Information by Issuers Whose Securities are in Registration, Sec.Act Rel. No. 33–5180, 1971 WL 120474, 1 Fed.Sec.L.Rep. (CCH) ¶ 3056 (Aug. 16, 1971). *Accord* Use of Electronic Media, Sec. Act Rel. No. 33–7856, 2000 WL 502290 (SEC April 28, 2000).

64.5 *See* footnote 14.30 *supra* and accompanying text.

provided that no sale is consummated, lest there be a violation of section 5(a).[2] In addition to section 5(a)'s ban on sales prior to the effective date, the key to both the waiting and post-effective periods is found in the prospectus requirements of the 1933 Act. Section 5(b)(1)[3] makes it unlawful to utilize the mails or any instrumentality of transportation in interstate commerce to transmit any prospectus with regard to a security for which a registration statement has been filed, unless the prospectus meets the requirements of section 10 of the Act.[4] Section 5(b)(2)[5] prohibits the delivery of a security for sale unless accompanied or preceded by a prospectus meeting the requirements of section 10(a).[6]

The broad definition of prospectus gives significant impact to section 5(b)(1)'s requirements. Section 2(a)(10)[9] defines "prospectus" to include all written offers to sell the security, in addition to any offer to sell transmitted by means of radio or television. Although section 2(a)(10) does not address the issue directly, it is now clear that web-based communications (excerpt certain real-time communications) are written communications[10.5] which means, for example, that an offer to sell transmitted through electronic mail, appearing on a website, or delivered on computer disk or other digitally encoded manner would qualify as a prospectus.[11] The SEC has examined the status of electronically transmitted offers to sell and has indicated that there is a strong argument that they should be treated the same as written, television, and radio communications (as opposed to oral or telephone communications). The Commission has since made it clear that the prospectus delivery requirements apply to electronic communications.[13] Issuers must take care to assure that the electronic communications comply with the prospectus delivery requirements. A web site can be used to identify prospectus materials. Any hyperlinks within that area of the web site will be considered part of the prospectus, whereas hyperlinks appearing elsewhere on the web site will not.[14]

In 1997, the SEC proposed Rule 154, which, among other things, included an Internet address within the definition of addresses for the purposes of prospectus delivery (as well as delivery of annual reports to the shareholders).[15] The rule as adopted, not only permits delivery to an electronic mailbox,

---

§ 2.4

2. 15 U.S.C.A. §§ 77e(a), 77e(c). *See* § 2.3 *supra.*

3. 15 U.S.C.A. § 77e(b)(1).

4. 15 U.S.C.A. § 77j. Rule 154 permits single delivery to two or more investors living in one household provided the recipients have consented to a single delivery format. Rule 154, 17 C.F.R. 230.154. *See* Sec. Act Rel. No. 33–7766, 64 Fed. Reg. 62540 (Nov. 16, 1999); Sec. Act Rel. No. 33–7475 (SEC 1997). This process is known as "householding."

5. 15 U.S.C.A. § 77e(b)(2). Since section 5(a) prohibits sales during the waiting period, the practical impact of section 5(b)(2) is during the post-effective period.

6. The section 10(a) prospectus is discussed in §§ 2.5, 3.2 *infra.*

9. 15 U.S.C.A. § 77b(a)(10).

10.5 *See* 17 C.F.R. § 230.405 (definition of "graphic communication", which is incorporated by reference into the definition of "written communication").

11. *See, e.g.* In the Matter of Goldman, Sachs & Co., Admin. Proc. No 3–11533, Sec. Act Rel. No. 33–8434, Sec. Exch. Act Rel. No. 34–49953, 2004 WL 1476147 (S.E.C. Release No. Jul 01, 2004) (emails during waiting period violated section 5(b); settlement of administrative proceedings).

13. Use of Electronic Media, Sec. Act Rel. No. 33–7856, 2000 WL 502290 (SEC April 28, 2000).

14. Use of Electronic Media, Sec. Act Rel. No. 33–7856, 2000 WL 502290 (SEC April 28, 2000).

15. *See* Sec. Act Rel. No. 33–7475 (SEC 1997).

it also permits delivery by traditional means to multiple people at the same address so long as they sign an appropriate consent.[16]

In line with the expansive definition applicable to offers to sell generally, the definition of prospectus is far-reaching.[18] For example, written statements that condition the market can run afoul of the prospectus requirements. Also, a contract for sale falls within the definition. Section 2(a)(10)'s definition not only includes advertisement circulars and notices which offer the securities for sale but also expressly covers communications confirming sales of securities in registration. This is an especially significant aspect of the definition of prospectus since, by virtue of Rule 10b–10 of the 1934 Act,[21] all transactions by a broker for a customer's account must be preceded by a written confirmation, which pursuant to section 5(b)(1) must conform to section 10's disclosure requirements unless an applicable exemption can be established. Section 2(a)(10) further sets forth an important exclusion from the definition of prospectus which permits use of "identifying statements" and "tombstone ads," which are considered directly below.[22]

Section 10 of the 1933 Act sets out the requirements of a statutory prospectus—*i.e.*, one that is sufficient to avoid violation of section 5(b)'s prohibitions. Section 10(a) requires the prospectus to include all relevant information about the issuer.[23] Section 10(a)(3) further provides that whenever the prospectus is used more than nine months after the registration statement's effective date, the information must be updated so as to be accurate within a time frame of not more than sixteen months prior to *use* of the prospectus.[24]

In addition to section 10(a)'s statutory prospectus, section 10(b)[25] permits the Commission to promulgate rules that allow the use of a "summary prospectus" so as to satisfy section 5(b)(1)'s prospectus requirement. Although most section 10(b) summary prospectuses can be used during both the waiting and post-effective periods, they are valid only for section 5(b)(1)'s prospectus requirements and do not extend to section 5(b)(2)'s delivery for sale proscriptions. The Commission has exercised its rulemaking power under section 10(b) to authorize summary prospectuses under Rule 430 (the preliminary or "red herring" prospectus),[26] and Rule 431[27] which permits a summary prospectus prepared by the issuer and filed with the registration statement. The preliminary or "red herring" prospectus which is permitted pursuant to Rule 430[28] is not explicitly grounded upon section 10(b)[29] but obviously is based upon that statutory grant of rulemaking authority.

---

16. Rule 154, 17 C.F.R. § 230.154.

18. *See, e.g.*, SEC v. Graystone Nash, Inc., 820 F.Supp. 863 (D.N.J.1993) (magazine article was reasonably calculated to generate a buying interest and thus was an offer and prospectus that violated section 5(b)).

21. 17 C.F.R. § 240.10b–10.

22. *See* § 2.4[2] *infra.*

23. 15 U.S.C.A. § 77aa. *See* chapter 3 *infra.*

24. 15 U.S.C.A. § 77j(a)(3). These time periods contemplate that the information in the prospectus may be as of a date several months before the prospectus was prepared.

25. 15 U.S.C.A. § 77j(b).

26. 17 C.F.R. § 230.430.

27. 17 C.F.R. § 230.431.

28. 17 C.F.R. § 230.430.

29. *See* 1 Louis Loss, Securities Regulation 232–34 (2d ed. 1961).

§ 2.4[2] Permissible Offers to Sell During the Waiting Period

Since prospectus is defined as an offer to sell, unlike during the pre-filing period, offers to buy are permitted during the waiting (and post-effective period). With regard to offers to sell, there are, in essence, five types of permissible offers to sell that may be made during the waiting period: oral communications, identifying statements, qualifying preliminary prospectuses, certain summary prospectuses, and a "free-writing" prospectus.

§ 2.4[2][A] Oral Offers to Sell

Section 5(b) applies only to prospectuses as defined in section 2(a)(10) which, as noted above, is limited to written, radio, and television offers to sell and thus does not include oral communications. Since section 5(c)'s prohibition on all offers to sell expressly expires upon the filing of the registration statement, there are no prohibitions on oral offers after the filing. The waiting period thus permits selling efforts with regard to securities in registration. For example, brokers, and even dealers who are members of the underwriting group, may make all offers to sell either on a face-to-face basis or over the telephone, so long as there is no final contract to purchase the security prior to the effective date. Notwithstanding the absence of section 5 implications, oral offers to sell during the waiting and post-effective periods are, of course, subject to the securities acts' general antifraud provisions.

Since oral communications are not within the definition of prospectus, there are no restrictions other than those imposed by the antifraud rules. Accordingly, it is common for promoters of public offerings and brokers to make statements over the telephone or in person that they would not be able to make in writing.[30] It is also common for promoters of public offerings to hold meetings, known as road shows, to discuss the securities being offered.[31] Slide and video presentations at live road shows are permissible so long as the investor is not provided with copies of the materials since such copies would qualify as a "prospectus" under the Act.[32] A video broadcast that is transmitted into a live road show is also permissible for similar reasons.[33]

The SEC has also permitted road shows over the Internet.[34] The Commission has given no action letter relief for Internet road shows on three conditions: (1) the road show may not exclude any material information; (2) only one version of the road show is captured for subsequent Internet transmission; and (3) the content of the road show is consistent with the information contained in the statutory prospectus.[35] It must be remembered

30. *Cf.* Carr v. CIGNA Securities, 95 F.3d 544 (7th Cir.1996) (documents warning investors that investment was risky precluded claim based on oral assurances that the investment was safe and conservative).

31. *See, e.g.,* Private Financial Network, [1997 Transfer Binder] Fed. Sec. L. Rep. (CCH) ¶ 77,332 (SEC No Action Letter March 12, 1997) (video transmissions of road shows were not prospectuses). *See also, e.g.,* Note, Watch Your Mouth: Section 12(a)(2) Liability for Oral Statements Made at Road Shows, 23 J. Corp. L. 541 (1998).

32. See Exploration, Inc., 1986 WL 67374 (SEC No Action Letter Nov. 10, 1986).

33. Private Financial Network, 1997 WL 107175 (SEC No Action Letter March 12, 1997).

34. *See* Charles Schwab & Co., 31 Sec. Reg. & L. Rep. (BNA) 1560 (SEC No Action Letter Nov. 12, 1999) (live presentations via Internet in password protect areas were permissible).

35. Charles Schwab & Co., 32 Sec. Reg. & L. Rep. (BNA) 235 (SEC No Action Letter Feb. 9, 2000), *clarifying* Charles Schwab & Co., 31 Sec. Reg. & L. Rep. (BNA) 1560 (SEC No Action Letter Nov. 12, 1999).

that statements made at road shows (regardless of how the presentation is conducted) are subject to the securities laws' antifraud provisions.[36]

It thus is clear that oral offers do not have section 5 implications during the waiting and post-effective periods. However, where oral communications progress to an enforceable contract under state law, then there will be section 5 consequences since section 5(a)[37] prohibits sales prior to the registration statement's effective date. In another context, the Supreme Court expressly held that oral contract for sale are subject to the federal securities laws.[38]

§ 2.4[2][B] The "Tombstone Advertisement" and Other Identifying Statements

Section 2(a)(10)(b) of the 1933 Act expressly excludes from the definition of "prospectus" a communication if it "does no more than identify the security, state the price thereof, state by whom orders will be executed, and contains such other information as [may be required by Commission rules and regulations]" and if it specifies from whom a statutory prospectus may be obtained.[39] The Commission promulgated Rule 134[40] which specifies twelve categories of information that may be included in the tombstone ad (or other identifying statement) without running afoul of the 1933 Act's prospectus requirements.[41] Tombstone ads may appear in newspapers or other hard print media, they may be mailed,[42] and they may appear online.[43] It is also perfectly permissible to follow up tombstone ads by making telephone or other oral communications to the potential investors.[44]

Inclusion of any information not specifically permitted by Rule 134 renders the rule unavailable and thus can result in a prospectus that fails to comply with section 10's requirements. This, in turn, will result in a violation of section 5 of the Act.

§ 2.4[2][C] The Preliminary ("Red Herring") Prospectus

The preliminary prospectus or so-called "red herring" is authorized by Rule 430.[52] The preliminary or "red herring" prospectus may contain substantially the same information as a full-blown section 10(a) statutory prospectus,

---

36. Krim v. pcOrder.com, Inc., 2002 WL 1185913, Fed. Sec. L. Rep. ¶ 91786 (W.D.Tex.2002).

37. 15 U.S.C.A. § 77e(a).

38. Wharf (Holdings) Ltd. v. United International Holdings, Inc., 532 U.S. 588, 121 S.Ct. 1776, 149 L.Ed.2d 845 (2001) (oral option is a security subject to the federal securities laws).

39. 15 U.S.C.A. § 77j(b)(10).

40. 17 C.F.R. § 230.134. *See also* Rule 142 which defines the meaning of participating in a distribution. 17 C.F.R. § 230.142.

41. *See, e.g.,* The Securities Transfer Association, Inc., 1994 WL 698256 (SEC No Action Letter Dec. 1, 1994). *See also* Rule 482, 17 C.F.R. § 230.482 which permits investment company advertising to contain information beyond that which is permitted by Rule 134. *See* § 20.8[4] *infra.*

42. *See, e.g.,* Hartford Life Insurance Co., 1988 WL 234496 (SEC No Action Letter July 1, 1988).

43. *See, e.g.,* StockPower Inc., 1998 WL 767495 (SEC No Action Letter July 13, 1998 available Nov. 3, 1998) (tombstone ad in website).

44. *See, e.g.,* Capital Supervisors, Inc., 1983 WL 28567 (SEC No Action Letter June 27, 1983 available August 27, 1983).

52. 17 C.F.R. § 230.430. *See also* John J. Jenkins, Recalculation of a Preliminary Prospectus: Statutory Basis and Analytical Techniques for Resolving Recirculation Issues, 55 Bus. Law. 155 (1999).

"except for the omission of information with respect to the offering price, underwriting discounts or commissions, discounts or commissions to dealers, amount of proceeds, conversion rates, call prices, or other matters dependent upon the offering price."[53] Rule 430 thus permits, but does not require, the mention of price which may also be included in the tombstone ad used during the waiting period. In addition to the possible price exclusion, the preliminary prospectus must include a legend in red ink to the effect that a registration statement has not yet become effective and that a formal offer to sell can only be made subsequent to the effective date.

§ 2.4[2][D] The Summary Prospectus

SEC Rule 431[55] permits an additional type of summary prospectus which operates solely for the purpose of section 5(b)(1) and thus not for the delivery for sale requirements of section 5(b)(2).[56] Communications complying with Rule 431 may be used during the post-effective period for section 5(b)(1) purposes.[57] The Rule 431 prospectus must be filed with the registration statement and can be used only if the issuer is a 1934 Act registered reporting company.[58] In addition, the Exchange Act reports must be current.[59] The summary prospectus permitted by Rule 431 must contain all of the information that is specified in the official SEC form accompanying the applicable registration statement form and further may not include any information which is not permitted in the tombstone ad, as spelled out in Rule 134(a).[60] The Rule 431 summary prospectus must also contain a caption similar to that required for the preliminary prospectus as well as a statement setting forth that copies of a more complete prospectus may be obtained from designated brokerage firms. Eight copies of the Rule 431 summary prospectus must be filed with the commission at least five working days prior to the use thereof. Issuers which qualify for use of the Rule 431 summary prospectus may use a *preliminary* summary prospectus during the waiting period.

§ 2.4[2][E]   The Free Writing Prospectus

In 2005, the SEC overhauled its public offering rules and significantly expanded the types of information that may be publicly disseminated during a

---

53. 17 C.F.R. § 230.430(a). In the case of an offering by an issuer which is not subject to the 1934 Act periodic reporting requirements, the preliminary prospectus must contain a good faith estimate of the range of the offering price and the number of shares to be offered. Reg. S–K, Item 501(b)(6).

55. 17 C.F.R. § 230.431. The Commission has proposed expanding the category of issuers who can use the summary prospectus. *See* 22 Sec.Reg. & L.Rep. (BNA) 899 (June 15, 1990).

56. 15 U.S.C.A. §§ 77e(b)(1), (2).

57. 15 U.S.C.A. § 77e(b)(1). However, the rule 431 summary prospectus may not be used to satisfy section 5(b)(2). 15 U.S.C.A. § 77e(b)(2). *See* § 2.5 *infra*.

58. 17 C.F.R. § 230.431(b).

59. In order to be eligible for use of the Rule 431 summary prospectus, the issuer must: (1) either (a) be organized under the laws of the United States, any state, territory or the District of Columbia or (b) be a foreign private issuer which qualifies for use of 1933 Act registration Form F–2; (2) be a registered reporting company pursuant to section 12 of the Securities Exchange Act of 1934; (3) have been subject to the Exchange Act's registration and periodic reporting requirements for thirty-six months prior to the filing of the 1933 Act registration statement; and (4) have not failed to pay any dividend or sinking fund installment on preferred stock and have not defaulted on any debt or long-term lease payments (unless the aggregate of such defaults are not material to the issuer's financial position) since the end of its last fiscal year. 17 C.F.R. § 230.431(b).

60. 17 C.F.R. § 230.134(a).

1933 Act registration.[60.5] In Rules 163 and 164, the SEC introduced the concept of a free writing prospectus that may be used by qualifying issuers during the prefiling and waiting periods.[60.10] These rules permit many issuers to use **a** free writing prospectus that has been filed with the SEC. In some cases, the free writing prospectus must be accompanied or proceeded by a statutory prospectus. If the requirements of Rule 163 or 164 are satisfied, written communications that otherwise would constitute an illegal offer to sell may be used during the pre-filing and waiting periods. As pointed out earlier,[60.15] Rule 163 permits well-known seasoned issuers (WKSIs)[60.20] to use a free writing prospectus during the pre-filing period providing that the offer is filed with the SEC and contains a legend that offering will be by prospectus.[60.25] The safe harbor is not available for business combinations nor is it available for investment companies.[60.30] The safe harbor applies to the company itself and to broker-dealers acting as agent for the company in disseminating information.[60.35]

A free writing prospectus is a written communication (including graphic and electronic communications) that constitutes an offer to sell.[60.40] A free writing prospectus may not, however, contain in formation that contradicts information in current SEC filings (including the 1933 Act registration statement). In addition, as a general proposition, a precondition to a company's use of a free writing prospectus is that it contain a statement to the effect that the offering is being made pursuant to a registration statement. The free writing prospectus should also indicate how the registration statement or statutory prospectus can be obtained or accessed.

A company's classification based on the public trading of its securities affect the availability of the free writing prospectus. Well-known seasoned issuers are generally free to use free writing prospectuses regardless of whether a registration statement has been filed. The use of a free writing

---

60.5 *See* Securities Offering Reform, Sec. Act Rel. No. 33–8591, Sec. Exch. Act Rel. No. 34–52056, Inv. Co. Act Rel. No. IC–26993 70 Fed. Reg. 44722–01, 2005 WL 1692642 (SEC August 3, 2005).

60.10 17 C.F.R. §§ 230.163, 230.164. The new rules introduced by the offering reform may not be invoked by certain ineligible issuers. In eligible issuers include: companies that are not current in their 1934 Act reports over the preceding twelve months; companies that are or during the preceding three years were blank check or shell companies or penny stock issuers; limited partnerships offering and selling their securities other than through a firm commitment underwriting; companies that have filed for bankruptcy or insolvency within the preceding three years; companies that have bee the subject of 1933 Act stop or refusal orders; and companies the during the preceding three years have been convicted of specified felonies or misdemeanors, have been found to have violated the federal securities laws' anti-fraud provisions, or have been the subject of an administrative decree for violating the federal securities laws' antifraud provisions. *See* Securities Offering Reform, Sec. Act Rel. No. 33–8591, Sec. Exch. Act Rel. No. 34–52056, Inv. Co. Act Rel. No. IC–26993 70 Fed. Reg. 44722–01, 2005 WL 1692642 (SEC August 3, 2005).

60.15 *See* § 2.3[2] *supra*.

60.20 17 C.F.R. § 230.405. A WKSI is a company that qualifies for registration on 1933 Act Form S–3 or F–3 and either: (A) As of a date within 60 days of the determination date, has a worldwide market value of its outstanding voting and non-voting common equity held by non-affiliates of $700 million or more; or (B)(1) As of a date within 60 days of the determination date, has issued in the last three years at least $1 billion aggregate principal amount of non-convertible securities, other than common equity, in primary offerings for cash, not exchange, registered under the Act; and (2) Will register only non-convertible securities, other than common equity, and full and unconditional guarantees permitted pursuant to paragraph (1)(ii) of this definition unless, at the determination date, the issuer also is eligible to register a primary offering of its securities relying on General Instruction I.B.1. of Form S–3 or Form F–3. *Id.*

60.25 17 C.F.R. § 230.163.

60.30 17 C.F.R. § 230.163(b)(3).

60.35 17 C.F.R. § 230.163.

60.40 17 C.F.R. § 230.405.

prospectus for other issuers is generally limited to after filing of the registration statement. With respect to non-reporting[60.50] and unseasoned reporting companies,[60.55] a free writing prospectus must be accompanied or preceded by a hard copy of the most recent statutory prospectus if (1) the free writing prospectus was prepared by or on behalf of the issuer or an offering participant, (2) payment or other consideration is provided by the issuer or an offering participant for the publication or broadcast of the free writing prospectus, or (3) section 17(b) of the 1933 Act[60.60] otherwise requires disclosure of consideration given in exchange for dissemination of the free writing prospectus.[60.65] In the case of a free writing prospectus that is delivered electronically, a hyperlink to an electronic statutory prospectus satisfies the physical delivery requirement.[60.70] In contrast, WKSIs and seasoned issuers[60.75] need not make physical delivery of a statutory prospectus.[60.80] Instead, it is sufficient if the person disseminating the free writing prospectus relating to a WKSI or seasoned issuer includes a legend notifying the recipient that a registration statement has been filed, the web address or hyperlink to the SEC website, and a toll-free number for requesting a statutory prospectus.[60.85]

In many instances, before it is used, a free writing prospectus must be filed with the SEC.[60.90] An immaterial inadvertent failure to file the free writing prospectus with the SEC will not automatically render the communication in violation of section 5(b) of the Act.[60.95]

§ 2.4[2][F] Safe Harbors for Factual Information and Forward–Looking Statements by 1934 Act Reporting Companies; Rules 168 and 169

As is the case during the prefiling-filing period,[60.100] Rules 168 and 169 provide safe harbors for dissemination of factual information by 1933 Act

---

60.50 "A non-reporting issuer is an issuer that is not required to file reports pursuant to Section 13 or Section 15(d) of the Exchange Act, regardless of whether it is filing such reports voluntarily." Securities Offering Reform, Sec. Act Rel. No. 33–8591, Sec. Exch. Act Rel. No. 34–52056, Inv. Co. Act Rel. No. IC–26993 70 Fed. Reg. 44722–01, 2005 WL 1692642 (SEC August 3, 2005).

60.55 "An unseasoned issuer is an issuer that is required to file reports pursuant to Section 13 or Section 15(d) of the Exchange Act, but does not satisfy the requirements of Form S–3 or Form F–3 for a primary offering of its securities." Securities Offering Reform, Sec. Act Rel. No. 33–8591, Sec. Exch. Act Rel. No. 34–52056, Inv. Co. Act Rel. No. IC–26993 70 Fed. Reg. 44722–01, 2005 WL 1692642 (SEC August 3, 2005).

60.60 15 U.S.C.A. § 77q(b); *see* §§ 7.11[2], 14.14[4] *infra*.

60.65 17 C.F.R. § 230.433(b)(2)(i).

60.70 Note 1 to 17 C.F.R. § 230.433(b)(2)(i). ("The condition that a free writing prospectus shall be accompanied or preceded by the most recent prospectus satisfying the requirements of section 10 of the Act would be satisfied if a free writing prospectus that is an electronic communication contained an active hyperlink to such most recent prospectus").

60.75 " A seasoned issuer is an issuer that uses Form S–3 or Form F–3 to register primary offerings of securities." Securities Offering Reform, Sec. Act Rel. No. 33–8591, Sec. Exch. Act Rel. No. 34–52056, Inv. Co. Act Rel. No. IC–26993 70 Fed. Reg. 44722–01, 2005 WL 1692642 (SEC August 3, 2005).

60.80 17 C.F.R. § 230.433.

60.85 *Id.* An immaterial and inadvertent failure to provide the legend will not be fatal. *See* 17 C.F.R. § 230.164.

60.90 17 C.F.R. § 230.433(d).

60.95 17 C.F.R. § 230.164(b).

60.100 *See* § 2.3[2] *supra*.

registrants and of forward-looking information by 1934 Act reporting companies.[60.105] These rules provide sage harbors from section 2(a)(10)'s definition of
prospectus and thus apply during the waiting and post-effective periods. Rule
169 provides a safe harbor for "factual business information" that is not
directed to investors but is issued as part of the company's ordinary business.[60.110] This includes, for example, product advertisements directed to customers.[60.115] The safe harbor does not apply to communications made as part of
the offering and also is limited to the types of information the company had
made in the past. 1934 Act reporting companies are given a broader safe
harbor in Rule 168 which permits not only the dissemination of factual
information but also forward looking information.[60.120] Like Rule 169, Rule
168's safe harbor for reporting companies applies only if "the timing, manner,
and form in which the information is released or disseminated is consistent in
material respects with similar past releases or disseminations"[60.125] and also
excludes from the safe harbor communications "containing information about
the registered offering or released or disseminated as part of the offering
activities in the registered offering."[60.130]

§ 2.4[3] Limited Statements After Public Announcement of Tender Offer or Business Combination

In 1999, the SEC liberalized its rules concerning communications relating
to a tender offer or business combination requiring the registration of shares
under the 1933 Act.[61] Under Rule 165, communications after the effective date
of a registration statement that are made prior to the public announcement[62]
of a business combination will not be deemed a prospectus for the purposes of
section 5(b)(1) of the 1934 Act.[63]

§ 2.4[4] Broker–Dealer Recommendations

Rules 137, 138, and 139, which are discussed earlier in this treatise,[64]
permit publication of certain recommendations by dealers, provided that each
of the appropriate rule's conditions are met.[65] Aside from the foregoing
exceptions or pursuant to an exemption in sections 3 or 4 of the 1933 Act,
only the above-mentioned four types of offers may be made during the waiting
period.

§ 2.4[5] Suspension of Prospectus Delivery Requirements for Certain Transactions by Dealers

SEC Rule 174 suspends the prospectus delivery requirements for certain
securities transactions with regard to transactions by dealers not participating

---

60.105   17 C.F.R. §§ 230.168, 169.

60.110   17 C.F.R. § 230.169.

60.115   17 C.F.R. § 230.169 (b).

60.120   17 C.F.R. § 230.168.

60.125   17 C.F.R. § 230.168(d)(2).

60.130   17 C.F.R. § 230.168(c).

61. *See* Regulation of Takeovers and Security Holder Communications, Sec. Act Rel. No. 33–7760, 1999 WL 969596 (SEC Oct. 22, 1999).

62.   17 C.F.R. § 230.165(f)(3).

63.   Rule 165(b).

64.   *See* § 2.3[6] *supra*.

65.   17 C.F.R. §§ 230.137–139.

in the distribution.[67] Rule 174, as is the case with Rules 137 through 139, which are discussed in the preceding section, applies to those companies subject to the 1933 Act's registration and periodic reporting requirements.[68] Rule 174 dispenses with the prospectus delivery requirements for offers and sales by nonparticipating dealers after the effective date.[69]

§ 2.4[6] Broker–Dealer Standard of Conduct With Regard to Prospectus Delivery Requirements

Exchange Act Rule 15c2–8[70] sets forth standards of conduct for broker-dealers with regard to the 1933 Act's prospectus delivery requirements. The rule makes it a deceptive act or practice for a broker or dealer to participate in a distribution covered by a 1933 Act registration statement and not to make available to each associated person sufficient copies of the preliminary prospectus prior to any customer solicitation.[71] The rule also provides that the managing underwriter must take "reasonable steps" to assure that all participating brokers and dealers are furnished with sufficient copies of the preliminary prospectus, each amended preliminary prospectus and the final prospectus.[72] The rule further requires a participating broker or dealer to take reasonable steps to comply with written requests for a copy of the latest preliminary prospectus.[73]

As a 1934 Act rule, Rule 15c2–8 does not directly affect compliance with section 5. Violations of the rule's prospectus delivery obligations do not automatically result in a violation of section 5 of the 1933 Act. However, this does not take away from the importance of broker-dealers' complying with Rule 15c2–8.

§ 2.5 The Post–Effective Period

§ 2.5[1] Prohibitions During the Post–Effective Period

Section 5(a) of the 1933 Act[1] prohibits all sales of securities facilitated by the use of the mail or other instrumentalities of interstate commerce to effect a sale prior to the effective date of the registration statement. Once the registration statement becomes effective, section 5(a)'s prohibitions cease to apply, and the only limitation on securities sales, aside from the disclosure

---

67. 17 C.F.R. § 230.174. Rule 174 is discussed in more detail in the next section; § 2.5 *infra.*

68. *See* § 2.3 *supra.* The 1934 Act registration requirements are set forth in section 12 of the 1934 Act, 15 U.S.C.A. 78*l*. *See* § 9.2 *infra.*

69. Section 4(3) of the Act exempts the prospectus delivery requirements for dealers after the expiration of a forty or ninety day period following the effective date. *See* § 4.31 *infra.* Rule 174 dispenses with the prospectus delivery requirements prior to the expiration of the forty or ninety day period so long as the dealer is not participating in the distribution and where the issuer is subject to the 1934 Act's periodic reporting requirements. 17 C.F.R. § 230.174. The rule also reduces the so-called "quiet period" to twenty-five days for issuers whose securities are traded on a national exchange or through the NASD's Automated Quotation system (NASDAQ). 17 C.F.R. § 230.174(d). *See* § 2.5 *infra.*

70. 17 C.F.R. § 240.15c2–8.

71. 17 C.F.R. § 240.15c2–8(d). The rule further provides that all such persons shall immediately be sent copies of any amended preliminary prospectus.

72. 17 C.F.R. § 240.15c2–8(f).

73. 17 C.F.R. § 240.15c2–8(b).

§ 2.5

1. 15 U.S.C.A. § 77e(a).

and anti-fraud provisions, are those contained in the prospectus requirements of section 5(b) of the Act.[2] Section 5(b)(1) requires that all prospectuses (*i.e.*, written, radio, or television offers to sell) must comply with the statutory prospectus requirements of section 10.[3] Delivery via the Internet will satisfy section 5(b)(1)'s requirements, so long as the potential investor must see the prospectus before placing any orders.

The operation and effect of section 5(b)(1) are much the same as for the waiting period except that some of the methods of permissible offers during the waiting period are not allowed during the post-effective period. The summary prospectus that has been filed as part of the registration statement as defined in Rule 431[6] may be used during both the waiting and post-effective periods, but solely for the purpose of satisfying section 5(b)(1)'s requirements and not for the delivery before sale requirement contained in section 5(b)(2). However, the preliminary prospectus or "red herring" that is permitted by Rule 430 during the waiting period is expressly limited "for use prior to the effective date."[7] Accordingly, the "red herring" may not be used during the post-effective period either for subsection (b)(1) or (b)(2).

§ 2.5[2] Supplementary Sales Literature ("Free Writing")

Section 2(a)(10)(a) of the 1933 Act permits the use of supplementary sales literature after the effective date even if such literature is neither in conformance to nor contained in the statutory prospectus.[8] This is known as "free writing," which is expressly permitted by statute only during the post-effective period. Unrestricted free writing is not permitted during the waiting period. In 2005, as part of its public offering reform,[9.5] the SEC adopted Rules 163 and 164 which allow the use of a "free writing prospectus."[9.10] As discussed above,[9.15] with respect to non-reporting[9.20] and unseasoned reporting companies,[9.25] a free writing prospectus must be accompanied or preceded by a hard copy of the most recent statutory prospectus under most circum-

---

2. 15 U.S.C.A. § 77e(b).

For a visual depiction of the operation of section 5 *see* the chart in § 2.2 *supra*.

3. 15 U.S.C.A. § 77j.

6. 17 C.F.R. § 230.431. *See* § 2.4 *supra*.

The Commission proposed expanding the category of issuers who can use the summary prospectus. *See* 22 Sec.Reg. & L.Rep. (BNA) 899 (June 15, 1990).

7. 17 C.F.R. § 230.430.

8. 15 U.S.C.A. § 77b(a)(10). This is sometimes referred to as "free writing."

9.5 *See* Securities Offering Reform, Sec. Act Rel. No. 33–8591, Sec. Exch. Act Rel. No. 34–52056, Inv. Co. Act Rel. No. IC–26993 70 Fed. Reg. 44722–01, 2005 WL 1692642 (SEC August 3, 2005).

9.10 117 C.F.R. §§ 230.163, 230.164.

9.15 *See* § 2.4[2][E] *supra*.

9.20 "A non-reporting issuer is an issuer that is not required to file reports pursuant to Section 13 or Section 15(d) of the Exchange Act, regardless of whether it is filing such reports voluntarily." Securities Offering Reform, Sec. Act Rel. No. 33–8591, Sec. Exch. Act Rel. No. 34–52056, Inv. Co. Act Rel. No. IC–26993 70 Fed. Reg. 44722–01, 2005 WL 1692642 (SEC August 3, 2005).

9.25 "An unseasoned issuer is an issuer that is required to file reports pursuant to Section 13 or Section 15(d) of the Exchange Act, but does not satisfy the requirements of Form S–3 or Form F–3 for a primary offering of its securities." Securities Offering Reform, Sec. Act Rel. No. 33–8591, Sec. Exch. Act Rel. No. 34–52056, Inv. Co. Act Rel. No. IC–26993 70 Fed. Reg. 44722–01, 2005 WL 1692642 (SEC August 3, 2005).

stances.[9.30] In contrast, WKSIs and seasoned issuers need not make physical delivery of a statutory prospectus.[9.35] In many instances, before it is used, a free writing prospectus must be filed with the SEC.[9.40]

Unlike the free writing prospectus, free writing materials contemplated by the statute during the post-effective period, need not be filed with the SEC. A significant limitation upon use of statutorily permitted supplementary sales literature during the post-effective period is that it must be proven by the registrant, or other person relying on the permissible use of such literature, that prior to or at the same time as receiving it, a section 10(a) statutory prospectus had been sent or given to a person receiving the supplementary sales literature.

There are no explicit statutory restrictions on the types of information that may be included in the supplementary sales literature. It must not be forgotten, however, that unduly optimistic promotional sales talk will render the supplementary sales literature in violation of the anti-fraud provisions of both the 1933 and 1934 Acts.[10] The use of electronic media for prospectus delivery raises questions concerning free writing with respect to other material that may be on or linked to the website. The SEC has taken the position that with respect to an area of a website denominated as a prospectus, hyperlinks included within that designated area will be considered part of the prospectus whereas hyperlinks that may exist elsewhere on the web site will not be considered part of the prospectus.[11]

§ 2.5[3] Updating the Registration Statement and Prospectus During the Post–Effective Period

Another aspect of the post-effective period is that although the registration statement need not be updated for most developments subsequent to the

---

9.30 Delivery is required if (1) the free writing prospectus was prepared by or on behalf of the issuer or an offering participant, (2) payment or other consideration is provided by the issuer or an offering participant for the publication or broadcast of the free writing prospectus, or (3) section 17(b) of the 1933 Act. 17 C.F.R. § 230.433(b)(2)(i). In the case of a free writing prospectus that is delivered electronically, a hyperlink to an electronic statutory prospectus satisfies the physical delivery requirement. *Id.* The new rules introduced by the offering reform may not be invoked by certain ineligible issuers. Ineligible issuers include: companies that are not current in their 1934 Act reports over the preceding twelve months; companies that are or during the preceding three years were blank check or shell companies or penny stock issuers; limited partnerships offering and selling their securities other than through a firm commitment underwriting; companies that have filed for bankruptcy or insolvency within the preceding three years; companies that have bee the subject of 1933 Act stop or refusal orders; and companies the during the preceding three years have been convicted of specified felonies or misdemeanors, have been found to have violated the federal securities laws' anti-fraud provisions, or have been the subject of an administrative decree for violating the federal securities laws' antifraud provisions. *See* Securities Offering Reform, Sec. Act Rel. No. 33–8591, Sec. Exch. Act Rel. No. 34–52056, Inv. Co. Act Rel. No. IC–26993 70 Fed. Reg. 44722–01, 2005 WL 1692642 (SEC August 3, 2005).

9.35 17 C.F.R. § 230.433. Instead, it is sufficient if the person disseminating the free writing prospectus relating to a WKSI or seasoned issuer includes a legend notifying the recipient that a registration statement has been filed, the web address or hyperlink to the SEC website, and a toll-free number for requesting a statutory prospectus. *Id.*

9.40 17 C.F.R. § 230.433(d). An immaterial inadvertent failure to file the free writing prospectus with the SEC will not automatically render the communication in violation of section 5(b) of the Act. 17 C.F.R. § 230.164(b).

10. *See* § 1.8 *supra* and chapters 7 and 12 *infra.*

11. Use of Electronic Media, Sec. Act Rel. No. 33–7856, 2000 WL 502290 (SEC April 28, 2000). As explained by the Commission, "Information on a web site would be part of a Section 10 prospectus only if an issuer (or person acting on behalf of the issuer, including an intermediary with delivery obligations) acts to make it part of the prospectus." *Id.*

effective date,[12] the prospectus must continue to be accurate.[13] For example, where there has been a change of events, a change in earnings, or a revaluation of projected performance, the prospectus must be updated lest it be in violation of section 10(a).[14] This is so even if there is no need to update the registration statement.[15]

Frequently, changes in the prospectus will be made by affixing stickers that contain the updated or corrected information. Rule 424(c) explicitly allows for prospectus supplements, commonly referred to as "stickers," to be filed with the Commission when it becomes necessary to update the prospectus.[17] In the usual case,[18] it is not necessary to attach them to a full prospectus before filing, although a full prospectus will usually be required to be given to investors. Stickering saves the registrant the expense of reprinting the entire prospectus. When a prospectus has been updated by post-effective amendments, before it can be used, ten copies of the updated prospectus must be filed with the Commission.[19]

Although the SEC provides for the use of stickers as an alternative to the filing of a post-effective amendment, there is no clear guide concerning the point at which information becomes so significant that stickering alone will not be sufficient. Most reported discussions of stickering do not clearly distinguish between the types of updating that require a post-effective amendment as opposed to just a sticker. Materiality is the point at which either will be required.[20] Some information is important enough to require an amendment.[21] For example, in the shelf-offering context, one release suggested that changes qualifying as "fundamental" in the meaning of Item 512(a)(1)(ii) of Regulation S–K seem to require an amendment as opposed to a sticker.[22]

§ 2.5[4] Effect of Prospectus Delivery Requirements

Sections 5(b)(1) and 5(b)(2) operate together in an attempt to assure that absent an exemption, any purchaser of a security in registration will receive a complete section 10(a) statutory prospectus at some point during the transaction. During the waiting period for any given offering there may be a number of offerees who receive only limited summary prospectuses, or no prospectus

---

12. *See* Funeral Directors Mfg. & Supply Co., 39 S.E.C. 33, 34 (SEC 1959).

13. *See* SEC v. Manor Nursing Centers, Inc., 458 F.2d 1082 (2d Cir.1972); Note, Prospectus Liability for Failure to Disclose Post–Effective Developments: A New Duty and Its Implications, 48 Ind.L.J. 464 (1973).

14. SEC v. Manor Nursing Centers, Inc., 458 F.2d 1082 (2d Cir.1972).

15. SEC v. Manor Nursing Centers, Inc., 458 F.2d 1082, 1099 (2d Cir.1972).

17. 17 C.F.R. § 230.424(c).

18. There is an exception in some employee benefit plan contexts. Sec. Act Rel. No. 33–6714, 1987 WL 113872 (May 27, 1987), p. 41.

19. 17 C.F.R. § 230.424(c).

20. *See, e.g.,* In the Matter of Blinder, Robinson & Co., Inc., Admin. Proc. File No. 3–6380, 1990 WL 321585 (SEC Initial Dec. April 27, 1990) ("whether ... purchase ... was a material development which should be disclosed by a ... 'sticker.' ").

21. Except for scattered references, it would appear that materiality is the only threshold of importance. A 1993 release suggests, or implies, that the distinction between information meriting a sticker and that requiring an amendment is one of kind, not degree. Sec. Act Rel. No. 33–7015, 1993 WL 370960 (Sept. 21, 1993) ("Stickers ... are used to update certain types of information (but not year-end financial statements)."). There is no comprehensive list of what other types of information fall in each class.

22. Examples given of "fundamental" updates include changes in interest rates, redemption prices, maturities, final method of distribution, or underwriters. Multijurisdictional Disclosure, Sec. Act Rel. No. 33–6841, 1989 WL 1000327 (August 4, 1989).

at all if their interest is solicited orally or over the telephone.[32] Ordinarily, these offerees will have to receive a section 10(a) prospectus prior to any sale to them. In addition, Securities Exchange Act Rule 10b–10[33] requires that all transactions for a customer's account be confirmed in writing. Since section 2(a)(10) of the 1933 Act includes such a written confirmation in the definition of prospectus, if sent through the mails the terms of the statute contemplate that the sales confirmation must be accompanied by a section 10 prospectus to avoid a violation of section 5(b)(1). However, as part of the public offering reforms introduced in 2005,[33.5] the SEC adopted 1933 Act Rule 172(a)(10) which provides that the prospectus delivery requirements of section 5(b)(1) do not apply to sales confirmations conforming to 1934 Act Rule 10b–10.[33.10] In Rule 173, adopted as part of the 2005 offering reform rules, the SEC now takes an "access equals delivery" approach to the prospectus requirement with respect to sales confirmations.[33.11] Beyond Rule 173's "access equals delivery" provisions, many dealer transactions after the effective date will be exempt from the prospectus delivery requirements by virtue of section 4(3) of the Act and Rule 174.[33.12]

Allocation notices do not trigger section 5(b)(1)'s prospectus deliver requirements.[33.15] In addition, before a security in registration can be delivered for sale under section 5(b)(2) it must be accompanied or preceded by a section 10(a) prospectus.[34] As noted above, under Rule 172(b), which was adopted as part of the 2005 offering reform, a final prospectus is deemed to precede or accompany a security for sale for purposes of section 5(b)(2) of the Act so long as the final prospectus meeting the requirements of Securities Act section 10(a) is filed or the issuer makes a good faith and reasonable effort to file it with us as part of the registration statement within the required Rule 424 prospectus filing timeframe.[34.5]

In summary, absent an exemption, sections 5(b)(1) and 5(b)(2) require furnishing or providing most offerees and virtually all purchasers access to a statutory prospectus.

---

32. *See* § 2.4 *supra.*

33. 17 C.F.R. § 240.10b–10.

Rule 15c2–8(b) provides that unless the issuer was previously subject to the Exchange Act's reporting requirements (or exempted from such reports under section 12(a)(1)), a broker-dealer must deliver a preliminary prospectus to any person expected to receive a confirmation of sale at least forty-eight hours prior to the mailing of the confirmation. 17 C.F.R. § 240.15c2–8(b).

33.5 *See* Securities Offering Reform, Sec. Act Rel. No. 33–8591, Sec. Exch. Act Rel. No. 34–52056, Inv. Co. Act Rel. No. IC–26993 70 Fed. Reg. 44722–01, 2005 WL 1692642 (SEC August 3, 2005).

33.10 17 C.F.R. § 230.172(a)(1) ("Written confirmations of sales of securities in an offering pursuant to a registration statement that contain information limited to that called for in Rule 10b–10 under the Securities Exchange Act of 1934 (§ 240.10b–10 of this chapter) and other information customarily included in written confirmations of sales of securities, which may include notices provided pursuant to Rule 173").

33.11 17C.F.R. § 230.273.

33.12 *See* 15 U.S.C.A. § 77d(3); 17 C.F.R. § 230.174 which are discussed in § 4.31 *infra*

33.15 17 C.F.R. § 230.172(a)(2) ("Notices of allocation of securities sold or to be sold in an offering pursuant to the registration statement that may include information identifying the securities (including the CUSIP number) and otherwise may include only information regarding pricing, allocation and settlement, and information incidental thereto.").

34. 15 U.S.C.A. § 77e(b)(2). *See* Annot. What Constitutes Violation of § 5(b)(2) of Securities Act of 1933 (15 USCS § 77e(b)(2)), Requiring Security to be Accompanied or Preceded by Prospectus, 28 A.L.R.Fed. 811 (1976).

34.5 17 C.F.R. § 230.172(b). *See* 17 C.F.R. § 230.424.

The seller of a security, delivering a security for sale, who does not himself or herself send the prospectus bears the burden of proving that one has been received by the purchaser.[35] It has been held, however, that under appropriate circumstances the seller may justifiably assume that a statutory prospectus has been received.[36] Although the seller can rely on a prospectus having been sent by someone else,[37] the risks are great since failure to meet the burden of proving that one was in fact received will result in strict liability under section 12(a)(1)[38] as well as possible exposure to SEC, civil, or criminal sanctions.[39]

Use of a section 10(b) prospectus for section 5(b)(1) purposes will not satisfy the prior receipt requirement of section 5(b)(2). This is the case since the language of section 5(b)(1) speaks in terms of making a prospectus conform to a section 10 prospectus, which can be either a section (a) or section 10(b) prospectus. In contrast section 5(b)(2)'s requirement of prospectus delivery at or before delivery of the security can be satisfied only by a section 10(a) prospectus. Section 5 is violated regardless of whether there is reason to believe that the prospectus delivery requirements have been satisfied. As pointed out above, prior receipt of a section 10(b) prospectus will not satisfy section 5(b)(2)'s prospectus delivery requirement. Accordingly, prudent practice would dictate delivery of a prospectus with the security, even where the sender reasonably believes that a section 10(a) prospectus has already been sent.

§ 2.5[6] Exemption From Prospectus Delivery Requirements for Dealer Transactions

The prospectus requirements do not apply if an appropriate exemption from 1933 Act registration can be established. In addition to the more general securities exemptions contained in section 3 and transaction exemptions contained in section 4 of the 1933 Act,[48] there are certain circumstances under which section 5(b)'s prospectus delivery requirements do not apply. Thus, for example, section 4(3) of the Act[49] exempts transactions by a dealer, including an underwriter no longer acting as such, for securities not constituting part of an unsold allotment provided that the transaction has not taken place prior to the expiration of forty days after the registration statement's effective date or the first date that the security was "bona fide offered" to the public, whichever is later. The statutory forty-day period for registered offerings is extended to ninety days if the issuer has not previously sold securities pursuant to an effective registration statement, unless a shorter period has been specified by the SEC.[50] This forty- or ninety-day period sometimes has been referred to as the quiet period.

---

35. *See* In re Jaffe & Co., [1969–70 Transfer Binder] Fed.Sec.L.Rep. (CCH) ¶ 77,805 (SEC, April 20, 1970).

36. Competitive Associates, Inc. v. Advest Co., 1975 WL 419, [1975–76 Transfer Binder] Fed.Sec.L.Rep. (CCH) ¶ 95,302 (S.D.N.Y.1975) (purchaser was mutual fund represented by an agent of its portfolio manager who is under a fiduciary duty with regard to its investment decisions).

37. *See* Sec. Act Rel. No. 33–2623 (SEC Gen'l Counsel July 25, 1941); Sec. Act Rel. No. 33–628 (SEC Gen'l Counsel, June 4, 1936).

38. 15 U.S.C.A. § 77*l* (a)(1).

39. *See* chapter 7 *infra.*

48. 15 U.S.C.A. §§ 77c, 77d. *See* chapter 4 *infra.*

49. 15 U.S.C.A. § 77d(3).

50. *Id.*

As pointed out above, section 4(3) expressly authorizes the SEC to shorten the period after the effective date of the registration statement during which nonparticipating dealers must comply with the prospectus delivery requirements. The Commission has exercised this authority in Rule 174 which dispenses with the prospectus requirements prior to the expiration of the forty- or ninety-day period for dealers who are neither underwriters nor members of the selling group.[51] Rule 174 dispenses with the prospectus delivery requirements if immediately prior to the filing of the registration statement the issuer was subject to the 1934 Act periodic reporting requirements,[52] or if the registration statement of a private foreign issuer using American Depositary Receipts is on Form F–6, provided that the deposited securities need not be registered under the 1933 Act.[53] Rule 174(c)[54] further dispenses with the delivery requirements where the registration statement relates to offerings to be made from time to time,[55] and the forty- or ninety-day period specified in section 4(3) has expired.

Rule 174's exemption for nonparticipating dealers from the post-effective prospectus delivery period is limited to securities of issuers which, immediately prior to the filing of the registration statement, were subject to the 1934 Act's periodic reporting requirements.[56] Thus, the exemption does not apply to first-time issuers or issuers whose securities were not widely held prior to the filing of the registration statement.[57] In 1988, Rule 174 was amended to provide more limited relief for many of those registrants who have not previously been subject to the 1934 Act's reporting requirements.[58] Under Rule 174(d), the prospectus delivery period applicable to dealers not otherwise participating in the offering (as opposed to underwriters or participating dealers) is shortened to twenty-five days for dealers (including underwriters no longer acting as such) with regard to securities which, as of the offering date, are listed on a national securities exchange or authorized for inclusion in an automated quotation system sponsored by a registered securities association (*i.e.*, NASDAQ).[59] As in the case for the statutory post: effective delivery requirement period for registered offerings, Rule 174's twenty-five-day period begins to run from the later of (1) the registration statement's effective date or (2) the first date upon which the security was "bona fide offered to the public."[60] In light of Rule 174(d), the full statutory prospectus delivery period for nonparticipating dealers applies primarily to securities which are traded through the NASD's bulletin board system or in the pink sheets.[61] It must be remembered, that, as is the case with the other exemptions provided by Rule

---

51. 17 C.F.R. § 230.174.

52. 17 C.F.R. § 230.174(b).

53. 17 C.F.R. § 230.174(a).

54. 17 C.F.R. § 230.174(c).

55. *See* 17 C.F.R. § 230.415 which is discussed in § 3.11 *infra*.

56. 17 C.F.R. § 230.174(b).

57. The 1934 Act period reporting requirements are discussed in § 9.2 *infra*.

58. *See* Sec. Act Rel. No. 33–6763, [1987–88 Transfer Binder] Fed.Sec.L.Rep. (CCH) ¶ 84,226 (SEC April 4, 1988).

59. 17 C.F.R. § 230.174(d). *See* § 14.3 *infra* for a description of NASDAQ.

60. 17 C.F.R. § 230.174(d).

61. Quotations for securities not listed on a national exchange or traded through NASDAQ are available from pink sheets which are circulated by the market maker. *See* § 10.3 *infra*.

174, the shorter twenty-five-day prospectus delivery period does not apply to a dealer who is acting as an underwriter.[62]

Once an underwriter has completed his underwriting commitment and the public offering is complete, the underwriter is under no duty to make continuing disclosures about the issuer.[63] Rule 174 also imposes an additional requirement for penny stock offerings.[64] In the case of a blank check penny stock offering, the ninety-day period does not begin to run until the securities are released from escrow pursuant to Rule 419.[65]

Another exemption from the prospectus delivery requirements is found in Rule 153 which deals with sales to be "preceded by a prospectus" as used in section 5(b)(2); this does not apply to the delivery requirements of section 5(b)(1).[66] Where a transaction involving a security in registration has been carried out on a national securities exchange,[67] Rule 153 provides that a sale is preceded by a prospectus to a member of the exchange where section 10(a) prospectuses have been delivered to the exchange for redelivery to its members upon request. Rule 153 applies to sales to members of a national exchange occurring prior to forty days after the effective date or the first date upon which the security was "bona fide offered to the public," whichever is later, provided that (a) the exchange has requested sufficient copies of the prospectus appearing reasonably necessary to comply with its members' requests and (b) the issuer or an underwriter has complied with all such requests.[68] Additionally, under Rule 153a,[69] when securities are issued pursuant to a reclassification, merger, consolidation, or acquisition of assets in a transaction subject to Rule 145,[70] section 5(b)(2)'s prospectus delivery requirement is satisfied by delivery of a qualifying proxy statement to shareholders entitled to vote or whose consent is required for the transaction.

§ 2.5[7] Broker–Dealer Compliance With Prospectus Delivery Requirements

Beyond the prospectus delivery requirements and exemptions that are discussed above, the Commission has established standards of conduct for brokers or dealers participating in the distribution of securities covered by a 1933 Act registration statement. 1934 Act Rule 15c2–8[71] requires that each participating broker or dealer take reasonable steps to comply with all written requests for a final section 10(a) prospectus after the effective date and until the termination of the distribution or expiration of the forty- or ninety-day period provided in section 4(3). Participating brokers and dealers must also take reasonable steps to assure that all associated persons who are expected to solicit customers after the effective date shall have sufficient copies of the

---

62.   17 C.F.R. § 230.174(f).

63.   In re Chaus Securities Litigation, 1990 WL 188921 (S.D.N.Y.1990).

64.   The SEC's penny stock rules are discussed in § 14.19 *infra.*

65.   17 C.F.R. § 230.174(g). *See* 17 C.F.R. § 230.419.

66.   17 C.F.R. § 230.153.

67.   *See* section 6 of the Exchange Act, 15 U.S.C.A. § 78f which is discussed in § 14.3 *infra.*

68.   17 C.F.R. § 230.153(a)(1).

69.   17 C.F.R. § 230.153a.

70.   17 C.F.R. § 230.145. *See* § 5.2 *infra.*

71.   17 C.F.R. § 240.15c2–8(c). The rule has similar proscriptions with regard to the waiting period. *See* § 2.4 *supra.*

final section 10(a) prospectus.[72] Additionally, managing underwriters must take reasonable steps to assure that all participating brokers and dealers have, pursuant to their requests, sufficient copies of the final prospectus.[73]

§ 2.5[8] Broker–Dealer Recommendations

As discussed in a previous section,[74] broker-dealer buy recommendations might well ordinarily qualify as offers to sell and thus would be subject to the prospectus requirements if disseminated in writing during the waiting or post-effective periods.[75] SEC Rules 137, 138, and 139 exclude certain broker-dealer recommendations from the prospectus requirements.[76]

By 2000, there was increasing concern over the independence of securities analysts.[77] In 2002, the NASD proposed and adopted new rules imposing a quiet period for analysts' recommendations when the analyst's firm participates as an underwriter.[78] The NASD rules require quiet periods during which a firm acting as manager or co-manager of a securities offering may not issue a report on a company within forty days after an initial public offering or within ten days after a secondary offering.[79]

---

72. 17 C.F.R. § 240.15c2–8(e).

73. 17 C.F.R. § 240.15c2–8(g).

74. *See* discussion in § 2.3 *supra*.

75. *See* discussion in § 2.3[6] *supra*.

76. 17 C.F.R. §§ 230.137, 230.138, 230.139. *See* discussion in § 2.3 *supra*.

77. *See* § 14.16[6] *infra*.

78. *See* Sec. Exch. Act Rel. No. 34–45526, 2002 WL 389246 (SEC March 14, 2002) (similar rules were also put forth by the New York Stock Exchange); NASD Announces New Rules Governing Recommendations Made by Research Analysts, http://www.nasdr.com/news/pr2002/release_02_009.html (NASDR Feb. 7, 2002). *See* National Association of Securities Dealers, Inc., Sec. Exch. Act Rel. No. 34–45526, 2002 WL 373104 (SEC March 8, 2002).

79. The rules also prohibit a firm from offering or threatening to withhold favorable research to induce business.

Chapter 3

THE 1933 ACT REGISTRATION PROCESS AND DISCLOSURE

Table of Sections

---

§ 3.1   The Decision to Go Public

§ 3.1[1] Process of Going Public—Overview

Unless it is structured to fall within one of the 1933 Act's exemptions,[1] any time a company plans for financing other than through a bank loan, the financing through the issuance of securities will implicate the 1933 Act's registration provisions.[2] Of course, many capital raising plans are accomplished through exempt offerings. However, when an exemption is not available, or when a company decides to go public for other reasons, it is necessary to register the offering under the Securities Act of 1933.

The registration statement that is to be filed with the SEC[3] is the result of a joint effort by, among others, the issuer, the issuer's attorneys (both inside house counsel and outside general counsel), the underwriter, the underwriter's attorneys, and the accountants who serve as auditors for the financial statements. In many cases there will also be special securities counsel whose responsibilities are to help draft and supervise the preparation of the registration statement and to be watchful for SEC disclosure problems.

---

§ 3.1

1. 15 U.S.C.A. §§ 77c, 77d; 77z–3. *See* chapter 4 *infra.*

2. 15 U.S.C.A. §§ 77f, g. *See* William Barker, SEC Registration of Public Offerings Under the Securities Act of 1933, 52 Bus. Law. 65 (1996).

3. There are various alternative forms for the registration statement. *See* § 3.4 *infra.*

The registration statement generally will be printed professionally and in many instances technical experts will need to be retained to prepare reports about the issuer's business. The substantial expense involved in this process means that issuers will frequently prefer alternative means of financing. In addition to the substantial expense, a registered offering requires strict compliance with the applicable disclosure provisions, lest there be substantial liability exposure of the key participants in the registration and offering process.[4] Additionally, particular aspects of the issuer's business or past operations may create especially problematic disclosure issues.[5]

The initial step in the registration process is the decision to embark upon public financing. Thus, the first question to be answered is whether or not the needed capital should be procured by way of a registered public offering or, alternatively, through a private placement[6] or some other exempt method of financing. As a general matter, exempt offerings entail less cost, both in terms of the actual marketing expenses as well as professional fees, printing, and other indirect costs of preparing the registration statement. Exempt offerings may also involve less exposure under the Act's civil liability provisions than registered public offerings.

In deciding whether or not to embark upon a registered offering, there are a number of advantages and disadvantages that need to be considered. The potential advantages and disadvantages must be weighed carefully in order to determine whether a public offering is the most appropriate means of financing.

In addition to the factors discussed below, there is a consequence that occurs in the event that a company, after raising money, invests the funds in securities of other companies.[10] Investing funds in securities of other companies can result in becoming an inadvertent investment company[11] and thereby implicate the provisions of the Investment Company Act of 1940.[12]

§ 3.1[2] Advantages of Going Public

The advantages include creating a public market that will allow for future public financing to provide for company expansion, diversification, increase in working capital, or retirement of preexisting debt. In many instances the company may be in need of large capital infusions and such substantial sums may not feasibly be available through bank loans or other means of private financing. The issuer may want the potential for additional equity rather than debt financing. Furthermore, the presence of a favorable climate in the public market may make a registered public offering the most efficient fundraising device. The creation of a public market for an issuer's securities will result in increased liquidity of the holdings of the principal owners, as well as the holdings of the minority shareholders.

---

4. *See* chapter 7 *infra.*

5. *See, e.g.,* Daniel I. Winnike & Christopher E. Nordquist, Federal Securities Law Issues for the Sticky Offering, 48 Bus.Law. 869 (1993).

6. 15 U.S.C.A. § 77d(2); 17 C.F.R. § 240.506. *See* § 4.22–4.24 *infra.*

10. Companies sometimes do this to put the investors' money to work prior to investing those funds in the business itself.

11. Inadvertent investment companies are discussed in § 20.3 *infra.*

12. 15 U.S.C.A. §§ 80a–1 through 80a–52. *See* chapter 20 *infra.*

Frequently, an issuer's offering of its securities will be accompanied or followed by a secondary offering. In a secondary offering, insiders or others who have received the issuer's securities (generally as part of a previous nonpublic transaction) decide to sell their shares to the public.[13] In such a situation, the selling shareholders may be able to ride "piggy back" on a registered primary offering. Even in the absence of a registered secondary offering, with the public market created by the primary offering, existing shareholders may be able to sell their shares in the aftermarket.[14] An issuer's public financing thus may help selling shareholders who want to liquidate their holdings in whole or in part and thereby take advantage of the liquidity and favorable market conditions created by the primary offering of the issuer.[15]

Another frequent beneficial by-product of going public is that the process gives the company increasing prestige and publicity among the general public, thus providing the issuer with a more favorable image and putting it in a better competitive position for its products or services. Additionally, the fact that a corporation has a public market for its securities may create an air of financial success. In some cases, a public offering will improve the company's net worth and enhance its ability to raise additional funds in the future. There are also collateral benefits of going public such as the company's ability to adopt attractive employee stock option and/or stock purchase plans in order to attract good key employees. A further advantage to going public is that the company whose stock is publicly traded may be in a better position to acquire other companies through the means of an exchange offer using the shares of the acquiring company as consideration for the shares of the target company.[16]

§ 3.1[3] Consequences, Disadvantages, and "Costs" of Going Public

There are a variety of consequences, many of them potential disadvantages, to public financing. Thus, it is necessary for a company to carefully consider all aspects of the alternative means of financing. For example, notwithstanding the above-mentioned favorable aspects of public financing, it must be kept in mind that economic and market conditions may not be ripe for taking advantage of this method. A number of other potential pitfalls can be identified.

A direct consequence of going public through a 1933 Act registered offering is that the company becomes subject to the periodic reporting obligations of the Securities Exchange Act of 1934.[17] As noted above, among other things, this means that the company's shares can now be freely traded

---

13. See §§ 4.27, 4.28 infra.

14. Such shares may remain restricted after the public offering. That is, the preexisting shareholders may not be able to sell their securities without registration or an applicable exemption. See §§ 4.23–4.26.1. SEC Rule 144 sets forth a safe harbor for selling these shares without registration. 17 C.F.R. § 230.144 which is discussed in § 4.29 infra.

15. Tag-along, or piggy-back, secondary distributions frequently create disclosure problems concerning dilution of the public's investment and use of the proceeds. See, e.g., In the Matter of Universal Camera Corp., 19 S.E.C. 648 (1945); §§ 3.9, 4.28 infra.

16. The converse may also be true. A public company with diluted ownership may be an easier target, albeit an expensive one for takeover by others than a company with a closely-knit ownership.

17. Section 15(d) of the 1934 Act, 15 U.S.C.A. § 78o(d) requires periodic reports for all companies issuing securities under a 1933 Act registration statement.

in the public markets. On the other hand, it also means that there are compliance costs and liability exposure that goes with public ownership.

In addition to the substantial cost of a registered offering, there is the high expense of maintaining a public company, not the least of which is the increased expense and potential liability exposure created by the registration and periodic reporting provisions of the Securities Exchange Act of 1934.[18] Public ownership, especially when it involves common stock, frequently results in loss of control over many management matters. Dividend policy is very likely to be affected, since in order to maintain a marketable security, depending upon the industry and the practices of competing companies, the directors frequently have to be willing to declare dividends—so as to make the security marketable in competition with other securities of a similar type as well as with the higher yielding bond market. In operating the enterprise, management of a publicly held company has to pay heed to the day-to-day market activity in the stock, and thus may focus more closely on the short term, as opposed to the long term, goals of the business. Just as a publicly traded company may be in a better position to acquire other companies, the fact that a company is publicly held may make it an easier target as a takeover candidate.[19]

Perhaps the most serious potential economic disadvantage of going public, from a financial point of view, is that contrary to the best plans and intentions of the underwriter and financial analyst, the issuer might not find a receptive market for its securities. When a public offering falls upon an unreceptive market, the result is that the stock will sell at a discount substantially below the anticipated price that was probably based on past earnings (if any) and the company's book value.[20] This will in turn decrease public and investor confidence in the issuer's business. Whenever the market provides such a soft reception, the issuer and selling shareholders may find themselves with less capital than had been anticipated.

Another factor which frequently is determinative in selecting the form and method of corporate financing is the actual cost of the registration statement itself. A public offering can easily cost more than several hundred thousand dollars when one includes the printing costs, underwriters commissions, directly resulting legal fees and auditing fees, as well as indirect costs that may be necessary to put the company in a position to withstand the public disclosures required in the registration statement. Finally, as mentioned above, the potential liabilities that may result from a problematic public offering may mitigate in favor of an exempt offering.

In 2002, Congress significantly increased the burdens on public companies when it enacted the Sarbanes–Oxley Act.[21] The Sarbanes–Oxley Act, which is discussed throughout this treatise where applicable,[22] adopted comprehensive amendments to the federal securities laws including heightened

18. 15 U.S.C.A. §§ 78*l*, 78m. *See* chapter 9. *See generally,* Carl W. Schneider & Jason M. Schergel, "Now That You Are Publicly Owned," 36 Bus.Law. 1631 (1981).

19. Takeovers and the tender offer provisions of the federal securities laws are discussed in chapter 11 *infra*.

20. One way to account for some of the hazards of an unreceptive offering is to embark on a contingent offering, if the circumstances so warrant.

21. Sarbanes–Oxley Act of 2002, Pub. Law 107–204 (July 30, 2002). *See* Senate Report No. 107–205 (July 3, 2002).

22. For a brief summary of the coverage of Sarbanes–Oxley, *see* § 1.2[3][D][3] *supra*.

disclosure and corporate governance obligations. These reforms placed significant new compliance obligations on public companies, thus resulting in increased compliance costs.[23] For example, the Sarbanes–Oxley Act imposed heightened periodic disclosure requirements[24] as well as accounting and auditing reforms.[25]

It often asserted that increasingly onerous SEC disclosure requirements have made public financing so expensive that a number of businesses are in fact deprived of access to the public market. One response was simplification of the disclosure requirements, especially with regard to relatively small issues.[26] These developments in disclosure eased a number of the negative aspects of public financing for many comparatively small issuers. However, the increased burdens on public companies imposed by the Sarbanes–Oxley Act of 2002 have significantly increased the cost of SEC compliance. These increased burdens and costs are likely to weigh heavily against a smaller company going public.

§ 3.1[4] Contingent Public Offerings

Issuers who frequently embark on public offerings do so in response to general financing needs, including, for example, expansion of the business. It is not uncommon for an issuer to envision a project that requires a minimum capitalization from the offering. This type of specifically targeted financing does not cause a problem where the issuer has an established track record or there are other reasons to believe that the securities will be sold at the offering price. However, sometimes an issuer will want to take precautions when a minimum amount of funds is needed. In such a case, the securities may be offered on an "all or none" basis.[27] In an "all or none" offering, if within a specified period there is not a full subscription to all shares being offered, the offering is cancelled. A variation on the "all or none" offering is a "part or none" offering in which a refund offer will be made if less than a specified portion of the offering has been subscribed to. In both "all or none" and "part or none" offerings, the subscribers' funds typically will be placed in an escrow account and are not made available to the issuer unless the terms of the offering have been fulfilled.[28]

The issuer's financing needs may not be the only cause of "all or none" or "part or none" clauses in the terms of the offering. The "part or none" offering, like "all or none" offerings, can have the effect of assuring potential investors that there is sufficient investment interest to make the offering worthwhile. Both "all or none" and "part or none" offerings put a great deal of pressure on those marketing the securities,[29] and thus these offerings may

---

23. *See, e.g.* Dan Roberts, GE Says it Faces $30m Bill for Governance, Financial Times 1B (April 29, 2004).

24. *See* §§ 9.3 *infra.*

25. *See* § 9.6 *infra.*

26. The SEC adopted two 1933 Act registration forms (Forms SB–1 and SB–2) which are available to small business issuers. *See* § 3.4 *infra.* Additionally, there are simplified 1934 Act disclosures for these issuers as well. *See* § 9.3 *infra.* In fact, the Commission has adopted a simplified set of disclosure instructions generally applicable to small business issues. Reg. S–B.

27. *See* Robert B. Robbins, All-or-None Offerings: An Update, 19 Rev.Sec. & Commod. Reg. 181 (1986); Robert B. Robbins, All-or-None Offerings, 19 Rev.Sec. & Commod. Reg. 59 (1986).

28. *See* Richard W. Jennings & Harold Marsh, Jr., Securities Regulation: Cases and Materials 30 (6th ed. 1987).

29. SEC v. Blinder, Robinson & Co., 542 F.Supp. 468, 476 (D.Colo.1982), *affirmed* 1983 WL 20181, [1984–85 Transfer Binder] Fed.Sec.L.Rep. (CCH) ¶ 99,491 (10th Cir.1983), *cert. denied* 469

be susceptible to manipulation.[30] Issuers embarking on "all or none" and "part or none" offerings must be specific as to the offering price, the duration of the offering, and the amount of securities that must be sold to make the offering effective.[31] Also, the possibility of a refund in an offering that is not fully subscribed cannot be offered on a selective basis but must be offered to all would-be purchasers.[32] It is actionable when an issuer erroneously gives the impression that a contingent offering has been sufficiently subscribed to.[33] Issuers undertaking a contingent offering have a continuing obligation of full disclosure until the contingency is met.[34]

§ 3.2 Preparation of the Registration Statement

Once an issuer has elected to embark upon a public offering and has decided upon the type of security (*i.e.* debt or preferred stock or common stock) to be offered, the issuer in consultation with its financial advisers will fix the relative rights and preferences. The next step frequently is to meet with financial advisers, potential underwriters and counsel in order to hammer out the basic terms of the offering including the anticipated price and, if applicable, yield. After this has been accomplished, each of the participants in the registration statement—*i.e.*, the issuer, counsel, auditors, and the underwriter—will embark on its respective role in the joint preparation process. The underwriters will not only be engaged in the preliminary steps in forming the underwriting syndicate but will also be enmeshed in substantial factual investigation of the issuer's condition; this investigation is to ensure that the offering will be marketable and also to make certain that all disclosures are accurate. Taking reasonable steps to assure the accuracy of the registration statement is necessary to protect the underwriter from potential liability under the 1933 Act.

Each of the participants in the preparation of the registration statement has a duty of reasonable investigation.[3] The highly factual nature of the due diligence standard precludes a one-size-fits-all template for formulating a due diligence program so as to guarantee success in establishing that the requisite reasonable investigation has been made. Risks that may be peculiar to the

U.S. 1108, 105 S.Ct. 783, 83 L.Ed.2d 777 (1985) ("in an 'all or none' offering of securities by a new company, whether all the securities have been sold to the public in bona fide market transactions is of particular importance because the 'all or none' contingency is the investors' principal protection. Each investor is comforted by the knowledge that unless his judgment to take the risk is shared by enough others to sell out the issue, his money will be returned"). It has been suggested, however, that the applicable SEC regulations were not imposed in response to this concern. Robert B. Robbins, All-or-None Offerings, 19 Rev.Sec. & Commod. Reg. 59, 62 (1986).

30. *See, e.g.,* C.E. Carlson, Inc. v. SEC, 859 F.2d 1429 (10th Cir.1988).

31. 17 C.F.R. § 240.10b–9. Manipulation in connection with offerings is discussed in chapter 6 *infra. See* in particular § 6.3 *infra.*

32. SEC Rule 10b–9 declares it to be a manipulative or deceptive act or contrivance to offer a refund unless all the securities are offered pursuant to an "all or none" or "part or none" offering. 17 C.F.R. § 240.10b–9(a). *See* §§ 6.3, 12.1 *infra.*

33. See, e.g., SEC v. Sands, 902 F.Supp. 1149 (C.D.Cal.1995) (mini-max offering whereby there was a part-or-none contingency with the remaining securities to be offered on a best efforts basis).

34. Banc One Capital Partners Corp. v. Kneipper, 67 F.3d 1187 (5th Cir.1995) (misrepresentations made after the initial subscription are actionable).

§ 3.2

3. *See, e.g.,* 17 C.F.R. § 230.176. *See* § 7.4 *infra.*

issuer's business may trigger more specific duties of reasonable investigation. Notwithstanding the variable nature of the reasonable investigation requirement, a number of generalizations may be made. The following activities are examples of the steps to be taken by the lawyers involved in the registration process.

First, it is necessary to amass information concerning the issuer's operations. This entails a thorough factual investigation of all aspects of the business, including an examination of the past dealings of insiders and affiliated companies. This complete factual investigation should include both personal interviews of the issuer's key personnel and careful document reviews of the issuer's files. The inquiry should extend to conferences with the head of each division of the issuer as well as the company's principal officers and managers.

The document reviews should be used to establish a complete history of the company. Corporate minute books frequently provide a good starting point for historical investigation. There should be a comprehensive review of the shareholder and director minutes of the company as well as those of all subsidiaries and affiliates. The review of past minutes not only will help uncover factual information, but it also serves as a "legal check-up"; any past illegalities or significant improprieties will most likely have to be disclosed in the registration statement. The initial document review will help establish a precise view of the issuer's capitalization. Accounting expertise will be necessary at this stage. A review of the charter and bylaws as well as all loans and guarantees and other financing agreements (including long-term leases) will shed light upon any applicable limitations and restrictions on current and future financing. In addition, a complete review of the company's dividend policy may reveal restrictions on financing.

The registration statement's detailed disclosure requirements mandate a thorough analysis of the company's business including a detailed description of all divisions, departments and lines of business, and accounting practices. There should thus be inquiry into all major customers and suppliers, including a determination of the issuer's dependency on one or more of them, as well as of the existence of alternative major customers and suppliers. The investigation should involve a complete examination of the issuer's marketing, merchandising, and pricing methods and policies, and a description of past practices. There should be a survey of the physical plant, including an examination of all leases (copies may be necessary for the registration statement), as well as title searches, where applicable. The survey should also encompass equipment including its condition, as well as anticipated maintenance and replacement requirements.

Counsel will have to obtain copies of all significant labor agreements. Are any due to expire? Are strikes or substantially higher labor expenses likely to result? If so, these are issues that may have to be discussed in the registration statement.

The registration statement must identify and describe security arrangements including pledges, assignments, and accounts receivable. If the issuer has a parent, subsidiary, or other affiliated corporations, careful attention must be given to intra-corporate, inter-subsidiary, and parent-subsidiary transactions. Counsel has to keep a watchful eye for potential conflicts of interest that may appear in mark-ups, supply and requirements contracts, loans, salaries, and stock ownership.

There must be a thorough investigation with regard to the issuer's management structure. It is necessary to obtain detailed resumes of each officer and director encompassing the past five years. Corporate minutes may be helpful in gathering information about management. In many cases personal interviews will be advisable. There should be a detailed description of all direct and indirect management compensation, as well as any insider transactions which have occurred within the past two years.[7] Relevant insider transactions include borrowings, loans, transactions in the issuer's shares, as well as contracts between the issuer and companies controlled by the insiders. Counsel should compile a list of the issuer's securities held by its officers and directors, including all shares beneficially owned, such as those held by family members, trusts, or corporations. There should be close scrutiny of all fringe benefits. Restricted and qualified stock option plans and stock or cash bonus incentive plans should be scrutinized closely. A careful review should be made of all employment and employment-related agreements.

The pre-registration review should also encompass a study of the issuer's research and development activities—both in the past and whatever may be contemplated for the immediate future. This should include an explanation of the accounting methods, percentage and completion method, and the stage of development.

In preparing for the registration statement, the issuer should compile its operating statistics including relevant trends and ratios. There should be a description of production backlog with respect to all firm orders. There must be a complete inventory, including a breakdown by lines of business and product lines. Counsel should review past tax returns to determine whether all taxes have been paid and whether future taxes have been properly estimated and withheld. Counsel should be fully aware of all competitors' activities including industry trends, reports (if available), and the price range and relative strength of comparable products. Counsel should also inquire as to whether the issuer has been in compliance with all applicable state and federal regulatory, environmental, health and safety, and labor laws.

The team preparing the registration statement must thoroughly understand all of the issuer's financial relationships. Banking relationships must be fully examined and described in detail (including lines of credit, and revolving credit agreements). A comprehensive review of the issuer's cash flow, including the source of funds, should be undertaken. Counsel with the aid of accountants should determine all contingent liabilities, including an evaluation of all pending litigation—at a minimum all pleadings should be reviewed. Current financial statements must be prepared. Most registration forms require a balance sheet at least as current as ninety days prior to filing and audited profit and loss statements for three years (or two years unaudited for an offering pursuant to Regulation A's qualified exemption for small issues).[9]

Counsel should examine all significant contracts to which the issuer is a party; this includes insurance coverage. There should also be a review of all

---

7. *See* item 404 of Regulation S–K which sets forth the types of transactions and relationships with management. Transactions with officers, directors, and affiliates draw particular attention in the registration materials. *See* § 3.9 *infra.*

9. 17 C.F.R. § 240.251 *et seq. See* § 4.17 *infra.*

patents and trademarks. All special risk factors with regard to the issuer generally, industry-wide conditions, and the particular securities to be offered must be analyzed and described in detail in the registration statement. There should be a review of all prior offerings, both private and public. Copies of all prior registration statements and underwriting agreements should be obtained and analyzed, as should be the case with 1934 Act filings such as Forms 8–K, 10–K, 10–Q, and proxy statements.[10]

It is important that the pre-filing investigation focus not only on the issuer's business generally, but also on the specific disclosure issues that may arise from the terms of the securities to be covered by the registration statement. Counsel must ensure proper documentation of resolutions and corporate minutes authorizing the offering. It may be necessary to increase capitalization and, in some cases, a formal shareholder vote may be required. All undesired stock transfer and issuing restrictions should be eliminated from the charter and/or bylaws. It may be necessary to secure the consent of creditors or other third parties before issuing the shares in question.

There must be compliance with all corporate law requirements of the state of incorporation, as well as any state in which the issuer is qualified to do business as a foreign corporation. There must also be compliance with the blue sky laws of all states in which securities are to be offered. Finally, depending upon the nature of issuer's business, there may be state or federal administrative approval that must be obtained prior to the offering.

After the foregoing factual inquiries and document preparation have taken place, there are a number of legal tasks that must be attended to as part of the underwriting process. These will generally be performed by issuer's counsel or in some cases by underwriters' counsel. It is often necessary to hire special securities counsel to coordinate the offering and supervise preparation of the registration statement. Such special counsel should then be present at preliminary discussions between the issuer and underwriters concerning the terms of the offering. Both issuer's and underwriters' counsel will be involved in the preparation of a letter of intent between the company and managing underwriter. The letter of intent generally will set forth the number of shares to be offered, the offering price, and basic underwriting terms and will provide for pre-clearance with the National Association of Securities Dealers (NASD).[12]

Counsel will then meet with the accountants to review the financial information required for SEC filing; a timetable should be established. The issuer must select a stock transfer agent and a financial printer. It will be necessary to estimate the number of copies of both the registration statement and prospectus needed for the SEC, blue sky law compliance, broker-dealers, securities exchanges, and customers. At this point counsel should be making the factual inquiries outlined above as well as gathering all of the information necessary for the registration statement.

Underwriters' counsel will be preparing the underwriters' agreement with the issuer, agreement among underwriters, and agreements for the selling group. They must also prepare a questionnaire for underwriters to

---

10. *See* chapter 9 *infra.* If the issuer is using Form S–2 or S–3, which integrate 1933 Act and 1934 Exchange Act disclosures, due diligence requirements may be affected. *See* §§ 3.4, 3.5, 7.4 *infra.*

12. *See* NASD Manual (CCH) ¶ 2151.02. The NASD is discussed in § 14.3 *infra.*

establish, among other things, sufficient financial responsibility to bear the underwriting risk. Counsel should also assist in drafting a letter inviting participation in the underwriting group. Formerly issuer's and underwriters' counsel needed to make a survey of all applicable blue sky laws, prepare a blue sky list, and draft a tentative timetable for compliance with those laws. However, the National Securities Markets Improvement Act of 1996[13] preempted state registration requirements with respect to offerings registered under the Securities Act of 1933. As a result of this development, the only blue sky requirements that remain involve the filing of notification of the federal registration.

When ready, proofs of the registration materials should be distributed to all counsel, the issuer's principal officers, the accountants and the managing underwriters, all of whom should conduct a thorough review. The issuer's directors should also receive and review copies of the registration materials. Sometime prior to sending the mock-ups to the printer, a first stage of the "due diligence" meeting[14] should be held and may need to be reconvened after thorough review and receipt of all comments. The next step is to file the registration statement along with the payment of applicable fees.[15] If certain summary or preliminary prospectuses are to be used,[16] additional SEC filings may be necessary. At this time, blue sky filings may also be necessary, as will filings with the NASD.[17] In the event that the securities are to be listed on an exchange, listing applications must be prepared and filed.[18]

Counsel's job does not end with the filing of the registration statement. There are a number of post-filing activities that must be completed, in addition to work on any amendments that must be filed. The issuer may want to prepare and distribute press releases; this may also take place prior to filing provided there are no gun jumping violations as spelled out by SEC Rule 135.[19] Provisions will have to be made for stock certificates including obtaining CUSIP (Committee on Uniform Security Identification Procedures) numbers (unless the shares will be uncertificated). Special securities counsel, along with the issuer's and underwriters' counsel will have to review the accountant's comfort[20] letter. Underwriters' counsel will have to prepare a distribution list and transmit letters to other underwriters and members of the selling group.

Once the registration materials are filed, the relevant administrative agencies (including the SEC and applicable state securities administrators) may respond with letters of comment.[21] All counsel must review SEC, NASD, and blue sky letters of comment. Counsel will then prepare replies and applicable amendments to be filed with the SEC, NASD and state securities administrators. It will often be necessary to file "delaying" amendments in

---

13. Pub. L. No. 104–290, 110 Stat. 3416 (1996).

14. The due diligence requirement is discussed directly below and in § 7.4 *infra*.

15. *See* § 3.5 *infra*.

16. Summary and preliminary prospectuses are discussed in § 2.4 *supra*.

17. *See* NASD Manual (CCH).

18. *See* American Stock Exchange Manual (CCH); New York Stock Exchange Manual (CCH).

19. 17 C.F.R. § 230.135. *See* § 2.3 *supra*.

20. A comfort letter states that the audit is materially accurate. *See* footnote 30 *infra*.

21. As is explained more fully in § 3.7 *infra*, the SEC employs an informal review process through letters of comment rather than resorting to formal refusal order proceedings under section 8 of the Act. 15 U.S.C.A. § 77h.

order to give the registrant sufficient time to respond to the letters of comment.[22] At this point, it is time to arrange for the due diligence meeting of counsel, management, and underwriters, where all of the filings as amended will be scrutinized. All initial prospectuses must be updated, a process which includes sending of amendments to all who received initial prospectuses. If applicable, underwriters' counsel will have to supervise preparation for newspaper and NASD quotations. It is at this stage that tombstone ads[23] will generally be prepared. It is also necessary to prepare for NASD and SEC clearance and draft notifying telegrams to blue sky commissioners. The final underwriting agreement will not generally be signed until coordination of SEC clearance time and date and all last-minute amendments such as the price amendment have been filed.

Frequently, the final step in the registration process is the pricing of the issue. In most instances, the price will be determined jointly by the underwriters and issuer. Because of their firm commitment obligations, underwriters will generally be conservative in pricing an issue. In the case of additional offerings of securities that are already publicly traded, the price ordinarily will be determined by the closing price on the day before the offering. As an alternative to a fixed price for an offering, securities may be offered "at the market" (or "at market") which means that the proceeds will be based on a fluctuating market price.[24] While an "at market" offering may find a warmer reception in a thin market, a primary drawback is that the issuer (or selling shareholders in a secondary distribution) cannot predict exactly how much money will be raised until the distribution has been completed. "At market" offerings are particularly susceptible to manipulation.[25] Accordingly, the SEC does not permit stabilizing activity during "at market" offerings.[26] When a minimum amount of capital is needed by the issuer and there is some concern that the offering may not be fully subscribed, the shares can be offered on an "all or none" or "part or none" basis.[27] In such a case, the terms of the offering will specify the minimum number of shares that must taken by investors in order for the sale to proceed. If within a specified period there is not a full subscription to all shares being offered, the offering is canceled and any monies refunded. Alternatively, the offering may take place, provided the subscribers will be offered a refund. This latter option cannot be offered selectively but must be offered to all would-be purchasers.[28] Issuers embarking on "all or none" and "part or none" offerings must be specific as to the

22. The delay may be necessary since it takes time for the SEC staff (or other regulator) to review the registration statement and prepare the letter of comment. Absent such a delaying amendment, the registration would become effective twenty days after it was filed. 15 U.S.C.A. § 77h. Delaying amendments, which are expressly permitted by SEC Rule 473 (17 C.F.R. § 230.473) are typically accomplished by placing code words on the face of the registration statement. *See* Charles C. Cohen, Book Review, 7 J.L. & Comm. 119, 120 n. 4 (1987).

23. 17 C.F.R. § 230.134. *See* section 2(10) of the 1933 Act; 15 U.S.C.A. § 77b(10) and § 2.4 *supra.*

24. "At market" offerings are discussed in § 6.3 *infra.*

25. *See, e.g.,* In re Hazel Bishop Inc., 40 S.E.C. 718 (SEC 1961).

26. *See* Regulation M which is discussed in § 6.2 *infra.*

27. *See* § 6.3 *infra.*

28. 17 C.F.R. § 240.10b–9. For an analogous equal opportunity Rule, *see* Rule 14d–10, 17 C.F.R. § 240.14d–10 which mandates equal treatment for all holders of shares subject to a tender offer, which is discussed in § 11.5 *infra.*

offering price, the duration of the offering, and the amount of securities that must be sold to make the offering effective.[29]

After filing the final amendments and the application for acceleration with the SEC, counsel should prepare a closing memorandum. A number of *[handwritten: Closing memo]* tasks remain. Notification telegrams and copies of the final prospectus must be sent to appropriate blue sky authorities. Transfer agent instructions must be distributed as must payment instructions.

There should then be one final review of all documents and the current status of the issuer. Generally, there will be a cold comfort letter[30] prior to closing. The stock certificates must be checked and counted. All payments must be made in accordance with the prospectus's description. It may be necessary to coordinate market making activities or even stabilizing activities[31] or any planned stabilizing activities which can be carried out only if in full compliance with the SEC's Regulation M.[32] Circumstances may require post effective amendments to registration statements and the prospectus. For first time registrants, it will be necessary to file with the SEC a "Report of Sales."[33]

The foregoing steps are merely illustrative of a typical registration and may vary according to the nature of the issuer and the offering. Variations may also result from use of one of the alternative registration forms that are described briefly in the next section. Many of the steps described above will also be necessary in a registration pursuant to Regulation A's qualified exemption for small offerings[34] or in preparing offering circulars for other exempt offerings.[35] Also, much of the attorney's factual investigation will have to be made for private placements, especially those in reliance upon SEC Regulation D.[36]

Compilation of a checklist of the necessary steps can be helpful in fulfilling due diligence obligations while preparing registration materials.[37] It has also been suggested that selecting one person as a "due diligence officer" to oversee the registration process will help assure compliance.[38]

The sections that follow provide an overview of the disclosure process. The discussion is not intended to provide a step-by-step "how-to" guide. The

---

29. 17 C.F.R. § 240.10b–9.

30. An accountant's comfort letter generally states that it is not aware of any material changes since the most recent audit. It is frequently referred to as a cold comfort letter because the accountant does not state positively that the information is correct, only that nothing has come to his or her attention to indicate that the information is incorrect.

Joel Krieger and Dorothy Walker, Earnings Per Share, Getting the Most from Comfort Letters, 10 Insights 27 (Oct. 1993).

31. Market makers are discussed in § 14.10 *infra.*

32. Where an offering of securities faces a soft market, SEC rules permit bids designed to stabilize the market price but only if in compliance with Rule 104 of Regulation M, 17 C.F.R. § 242.104. Regulation M is discussed in § 6.1 *infra.*

33. 17 C.F.R. § 230.463.

34. *See* section 3(b) of the 1933 Act; 15 U.S.C.A. § 77c(b) and § 4.16 *infra.*

35. *See, e.g.,* the informational requirements for offerings under Regulation D. 17 C.F.R. § 230.502(b). Regulation D is discussed in §§ 4.20–4.22, 4.25 *infra.*

36. 17 C.F.R. §§ 230.501–230.508, discussed in §§ 4.19–4.25 *infra.*

37. *See, e.g.,* Carlos L. Israels, Checklist for Underwriters' Investigations, 18 Bus. Law. 90 (1962), as updated in ABA, Selected Articles in Securities Law 71 (1968); Robert A. Spanner, Limiting Exposure in the Offering Process, 20 Rev. Sec. & Commod. Reg. 59 (1987).

38. *Id.*

most helpful source for framing disclosures are the Commission's Regulation S–K[39] (or Regulation S–B, for small business issuers[40]) for descriptive disclosure items and Regulation S–X[41] for accounting matters. Violations of the disclosure requirements set forth in Regulation S–K (or Regulation S–B which is applicable to small business issuers) are not *per se* actionable as securities fraud,[42] but can be used to support a claim based on one of the express or implied liability provisions.[43]

§ 3.3 Information Required in the Registration Statement and the Statutory Prospectus; Schedule A

The registration statement is the basic disclosure document that must be filed with the SEC for 1933 Act registration.[1] There are a number of alternative disclosure forms which may be available to issuers for registration.[2] The availability of the various forms depends upon the nature of the issuer and/or the circumstances surrounding the offering, as well as the types of securities offered. Regardless of the registration form to be filed, it is a document that is divided into two principal sections. The information contained in the first portion of the registration statement is the same as that which will be found in the prospectus as required by section 10(a) of the 1933 Act and Schedule A.[3] The statutory prospectus must be delivered before the consummation of any sale pursuant to a registered offering.[4] Schedule A provides only a bare-bones outline of the types of disclosures which are required. Detailed disclosure requirements are found in the SEC's registration forms and in Regulation S–K (and Regulation S–B, for small business issuers).

Schedule A merely provides a skeletal description of the types of information that must be disclosed. The specific items that need be disclosed are listed in the instructions and individualized line item disclosures called for by the SEC registration form.[8] The forms provide the skeletal description of what needs to be disclosed. More detailed guidance and explanation of what is required for disclosure is contained in Regulation S–K,[9] and for small business issuers in Regulation S–B.[10] Guidelines for disclosures relating to accounting matters are found in Regulation S–X.[11]

---

39. 17 C.F.R. § 229.10 *et seq.*, 7 Fed. Sec. L. Rep. (CCH) ¶ 71,001 *et seq.*

40. 17 C.F.R. § 228.10 *et seq.*, 7 Fed. Sec. L. Rep. (CCH) ¶ 70,701 *et seq.*

41. 17 C.F.R. § 210.1–01 *et seq.*, 6 Fed. Sec. L. Rep. (CCH) ¶ 69,101 *et seq.*

42. Securities Fraud is discussed in chapters 7, 12 *infra.*

43. *See* Feldman v. Motorola, Inc., 1994 WL 160115, [1993–1994 Transfer Binder] Fed. Sec. L. Rep. (CCH) ¶ 98,133 (N.D.Ill.1994) (private suit involving SEC Rule 10b–5).

§ 3.3

1. *See* 15 U.S.C.A. §§ 77f, 77g.

2. The various forms for registration are discussed in § 3.4 *infra.*

3. *See* 15 U.S.C.A. §§ 77g, 77j(a), 77aa.

4. 15 U.S.C.A. § 77e(b)(2).

8. *See* § 3.4 *infra* for a description of the various registration forms.

9. 17 C.F.R. § 229.10 *et seq.*, 7 Fed. Sec. L. Rep. (CCH) ¶ 71,001 *et seq.*

10. 17 C.F.R. § 228.10 *et seq.*, 7 Fed. Sec. L. Rep. (CCH) ¶ 70,701 *et seq.* A small business issuer is a United States or Canadian company with annual revenues of less than $25,000,000. If the company is a majority owned subsidiary, then the parent must also be a small business issuer in order to qualify. Investment companies do not qualify as small business issuers. Reg. S–B, Item 10(a)(1).

11. 17 C.F.R. § 210.10–1 *et seq.*, 6 Fed. Sec. L. Rep. (CCH) ¶ 69,101 *et seq.*

The second part of the registration statement consists of additional information which is not sent out in the prospectus but which is available in the SEC files for public inspection. As noted at the outset of this section, Schedule A is only the starting point. It is necessary to look to the applicable registration form which will supply the bare-bones description of what has to be disclosed. It is then necessary to turn to Regulation S–K or, in the case of small business issuers, to Regulation S–B for a detailed description of the ways in which the information must be presented. In addition, Regulation S–X sets forth the disclosure guide and presentation requirements for financial information.

The 1933 Act forms and rules set forth the disclosures required for 1933 Act registration. In drafting disclosures for 1933 Act forms, additional disclosures that may be required for an analogous 1934 Act disclosure item need not be consulted.[12]

In January 1997, the SEC proposed amendments to Rule 421 to require the use of clear, concise, and understandable language in prospectuses.[13] The rule proposal was part of the SEC's larger initiative to require the use of "plain English" in SEC filings and reports to shareholders and investors. The plain English initiative, which began in the mid 1990s as a pilot program, involves amendments to various provisions of Regulation S–K and Regulation S–B. In a lengthy official release, the Commission describes what it means by plain English and also provides several examples of appropriate disclosure styles. The plain English requirements include: use of the active rather than passive voice, short sentences, use of definite, concrete everyday words, presentation of information in tabular form or with bullet lists, the avoidance of legal jargon and highly technical business terminology, as well as the avoidance of multiple negatives.[14]

The SEC began the implementation of the plain English requirement for 1933 Act prospectuses. In 1998, the Commission added Rule 421(d)[15] which requires the use of plain English with respect to several parts of the prospectus. The rule applies to the cover page as well as to the summary and risk factors sections of the prospectus. The SEC explained that in addition to mandating the foregoing for the specified portions of the prospectus, the rule gives "issuers more specific guidance on how to make the entire prospectus clear, concise, and understandable."[16] The Commission has affirmed its commitment to plain English by trying to follow the guidelines in its own rulemaking. Most notably, when revising its shareholder proposal rule, the SEC used a plain English format.[17] Notwithstanding its original commitment

---

12. *See, e.g.,* In re N2K, Inc. Securities Litigation, 82 F.Supp.2d 204, 207–208 (S.D.N.Y.2000) (1934 Act Rule 12b–20 did not apply to 1933 Act disclosures).

13. Plain English Disclosure, Sec. Act Rel. No. 33–7380, 62 Fed. Reg. 3152, 1997 WL 17695 (F.R.) (SEC Jan. 21, 1997). For a more detailed discussion of the plain English initiatives, *see* § 3.10[2] *infra.*

14. Plain English Disclosure, Sec. Act Rel. No. 33–7380, 62 Fed. Reg. 3152, 1997 WL 17695 (F.R.) (SEC Jan. 21, 1997). *See also, e.g.,* Note, Plain English: A Reappraisal of the Intended Audience of Disclosure Under the Securities Act of 1933, 72 So. Cal. L. Rev. 851 (1999).

15. 17 C.F.R. § 230.421. *See* Plain English Disclosure, Sec. Act Rel. No. 33–7497, 63 Fed. Reg. 6370–01, 1998 WL 44199 (F.R.) (SEC Feb. 6, 1998).

16. Sec. Act Rel. No. 33–7497, 63 Fed. Reg. 6370–01, 1998 WL 44199 (F.R.) (SEC Feb. 6, 1998).

17. Rule 14a–8, 17 C.F.R. § 14a–8(c). *See* Peter J. Romeo & Richard J. Parrino, The New Shareholder Proposal Rules, 31 Rev. Sec. & Commodities Reg. 203 (1998). *See* § 11.7 *infra.*

to adhere more closely to the plain English requirements in its own rulemaking, aside from the shareholder proposal rule, the SEC rules have not been rewritten to conform to the plain English requirements that are applicable to SEC filers.

§ 3.4 Registration Forms and Integrated Disclosure

§ 3.4[1] Overview of 1933 Disclosure Requirements

For more than fifty-five years, the SEC has administered two parallel disclosure systems: one for the registration of public offerings under the Securities Act of 1933 and the other for the periodic reporting requirements of the Securities Exchange Act of 1934.[1] The parallel systems resulted in a great deal of duplicative filings and unnecessary paperwork. In 1982, the Securities and Exchange Commission adopted an integrated disclosure system for registration of securities under the 1933 Act.[2] While some duplication remains, the institution of integrated disclosure has made great strides in easing the disclosure burden. The current system integrates and simplifies the disclosure requirements under the 1933 and 1934 securities acts.[3] The Commission has explained that its goal in adopting the integrated system was "to revise or eliminate overlapping or unnecessary disclosure and dissemination requirements wherever possible, thereby reducing burdens on registrants while at the same time ensuring that security holders, investors and the marketplace have been provided with meaningful, non-duplicative information upon which to base investment decisions."[4]

In 1996, the Commission issued a concept release, seeking comments on the elimination of transaction specific registration in favor of a system of company registration.[5] Under the proposed system, specific transactions would not have to be registered so long as the company supplies enhanced disclosure on a continuing basis. The proposed system reportedly received favorable comment.[6]

In 1998, the Commission issued a proposal to totally revise its registration process.[7] The magnitude of these proposals let the Commission to dub the proposals "the aircraft carrier." The proposals were initially met with signifi-

---

§ 3.4

1. See § 9.2 infra for a discussion of the Exchange Act's periodic reporting requirements for issuers.

2. See Sec.Act Rel. No. 33–6383, Acc.Rel. No. 306, [1937–82 Acc't'g Rel. Transfer Binder] Fed.Sec.L.Rep. (CCH) ¶ 72,328 (March 3, 1982). The concept of integrated disclosure is based in large part on the American Law Institute's Proposed Federal Securities Code.

3. Unlike the 1933 Act which is directed towards securities distributions, the 1934 Exchange Act deals with day-to-day trading and the securities markets in general. See § 1.2 supra, chapters 9, 14 infra.

4. Special Report, 1982 Integrated Disclosure Adoptions, Fed.Sec.L.Rep. (CCH) No. 956 at p. 15 (March 11, 1982).

5. See Sec. Act Rel. No. 33–7314 (SEC July 30, 1996). See Stephen J. Choi, Company Registration: Toward a Status–Based Antifraud Regime, 64 U. Chi. L. Rev. 567 (1997); Michael McDonough, Comment, Death in One Act: The Case for Company Registration, 24 Pepp. L. Rev. 563 (1997). See also, e.g., Dale Arthur Osterle, The Inexorable March Toward a Continuous Disclosure Requirement for Publicly Traded Corporations: "Are We There Yet?", 20 Cardozo L. Rev. 135 (1998).

6. Special Report, 29 Sec. Reg. & L. Rep. (BNA) 66 (January 17, 1997).

7. Sec. Act Rel. No. 33–7606 (SEC Nov. 3, 1998). The "aircraft carrier" proposals were followed by a series of proposals that would overhaul the regulation of tender offers and other corporate acquisitions. See Exch. Act Rel. No. 34–40633 (SEC Nov. 3, 1998).

cant opposition from various sources. Only time will tell whether the proposals will be implemented in whole or in part. Among other things, theses proposals would overhaul the disclosures required in registered offerings, revise the current prospectus delivery rules, eliminate many of the restrictions on pre-offering communications, amend the rules dealing with integration of private and public offerings, and also significantly revise the periodic disclosure requirements. Under these proposals, new Forms A, B, and C would have replaced the existing 1933 Act registrations forms. Large seasoned companies would be permitted to use Form B and be able to make an offering immediately upon filing. The prospectus delivery requirements would be revised to require delivery of a prospectus during the time that the investor truly needs the information in Form B before the investment decision is made. The proposals would also accelerate the timing for disclosure of quarterly results on other disclosures to expand the items that would need to be disclosed promptly on 1934 Act Form 8–K. The foregoing is but a summary of some of the widespread reforms that would be implemented by the SEC's "aircraft carrier" proposals. The proposals have sparked considerable controversy and it remains to be seen whether they will be adopted in whole or in part.

As discussed in the preceding section, Schedule A provides a skeletal outline of the types of information to be made available in connection with a registered offering of securities. Each of the registration forms provided by the SEC go into slightly more detail in describing the types of disclosures that must be made. The applicable forms frequently refer to Regulation S–K, or Regulation S–B, for small issuers, which set forth in detail the ways in which the relevant information should be set forth.

As part of its small business initiatives of 1992, the SEC adopted Regulation S–B which qualifies and with respect to many items replaces Regulation S–K as the applicable disclosure guide for small business issuers.[8] Domestic issuers having revenues of less than 25 million dollars for their most recent fiscal year qualify for use of Regulation S–B's simplified disclosures that are applicable for both 1933 and 1934 Act filings. A company having more than 25 million dollars worth of its voting stock held by nonaffiliates does not qualify as a small business issuer.

§ 3.4[2] Materiality

'Materiality'

The basic dividing line between what has to be disclosed and what information may be withheld is determined by the Concept of materiality which is discussed in various sections throughout this treatise.[10] problems in the context of an expanding definition of the concept of "materiality."[11] Materiality consists of those facts with a reasonable investor would consider

---

8. *See* Sec. Act Rel. No. 33–6949, 6 Fed.Sec.L.Rep. (CCH) ¶ 72,439 (SEC July 30, 1992); Sec. Act Rel. No. 33–6924, [1991–1992 Transfer Binder] Fed.Sec.L.Rep. (CCH) ¶ 84,931 (March 11, 1992).

10. *See, e.g.,* § 7.3[1] *infra* (section 11 of the 1933 Act), § 10.3[4] *infra* (1934 Act proxy rules), § 12.9 *infra* (SEC Rule 10b–5).

11. *See,* James O. Hewitt, Developing Concepts of Materiality and Disclosure, 32 Bus.Law. 887 (1977); Lewis D. Lowenfels, Questionable Corporate Payments and the Federal Securities Laws, 51 N.Y.U.L.Rev. 1 (1976); A.A. Sommer, Jr. Therapeutic Disclosure, 4 Sec.Reg.L.J. 263 (1976). *See also, e.g.,* Donald Langevoort, Half–Truths: Protecting Mistaken Inferences by Investors and Others, 52 Stan. L. Rev. 87 (1999).

significant in making an investment decision.[12] Since the hallmark of disclosure for both the 1933 Act registration statement and all 1934 Act filings is embodied in the concept of "materiality," the problems relating to disclosure in registration statements and other required filings are quite similar. Because the primary purpose of 1933 Act registration statements is to provide full and adequate information regarding the distribution of securities, certain types of disclosures may be more sensitive and thus of more concern with regard to public offerings than to other required filings.[13]

§ 3.4[3] Integrating 1933 Act Disclosure With the 1934 Act

Many observers believed that the repetitive nature of the dual filing systems of the Securities Act of 1933 and the Securities Exchange Act of 1934 resulted in needless duplicative filings and that this needed to be remedied by a thoughtful and measured approach. The proposed cure was first recommended in a seminal law review article.[15] The author suggested emphasizing the 1934 Act reporting requirements and at the same time eliminate many of the duplicative disclosures formerly required by the 1933 Act.[16] Periodic reporting rather than emphasizing one-time disclosures in connection with public offerings seemed to be in the best interest of investor protection.[17]

This idea of an integrated disclosure system subsequently received the support of the American Law Institute ("ALI"), which constructed a model securities code "which would unify the disparate federal securities laws into a fully integrated disclosure system."[18] The proposed securities code containing a fully integrated system was completed and had garnered the approval of the Commission; however, Congress opted not to incorporate the proposed system after all and left the issue unresolved.[19] Congress was not willing to replace the familiarity of the 1933 and 1934 Acts with a new and unproven system.[20]

Despite the failure of the ALI securities code, an integrated disclosure system was partially realized. And, in 1982, the Commission adopted an integrated disclosure system in Regulation S–K.[21]

In addition to its specialized registration forms and small business initiatives, the Commission has established a three-tiered system of registration and prospectus disclosure of registrant-oriented information based upon the registrant's reporting history and market following. The integrated disclosure system recognizes that transaction-specific information, that is, information specific to the securities issuance, should always be disclosed in the registration statement and prospectus. The more general registrant-oriented information, however, may already be available in reports by the registrant

---

12. *See, e.g.,* Basic Inc. v. Levinson, 485 U.S. 224, 108 S.Ct. 978, 99 L.Ed.2d 194 (1988); TSC Industries, Inc. v. Northway, Inc., 426 U.S. 438, 96 S.Ct. 2126, 48 L.Ed.2d 757 (1976).

13. For a good discussion of materiality in the 1933 Act offering process *see* Feit v. Leasco Data Processing Equipment Corp., 332 F.Supp. 544 (E.D.N.Y.1971).

15. Milton H. Cohen, "Truth in Securities" Revisited, 79 Harv.L.Rev. 1340 (1966).

16. *See also, e.g.,* Michael McDonough, *Death in One Act: The Case for Company Registration,* 24 PEPP. L. REV. 563, 585 (1997).

17. *See Id.* at 587.

18. *Id.* This commissioned group was led by scholars in the securities field, most notably Harvard University Professor Louis Loss. *See id.*

19. *See id.*

20. *See id.*

21. *See* 17 C.F.R. §§ 229.10–229.915. Regulation S–K is discussed in § 9.4 *infra.*

under the Exchange Act and need not be duplicated unnecessarily. Exchange Act reporting companies include all issuers whose securities are traded on a national exchange as well as those with ten million dollars or more in assets and having a class of equity securities held by more than five hundred persons.[22] The framework for the two-level system is provided by two alternative registration forms: S–1 and S–3.[22.5]

Due Diligence and Integrated Disclosure

A collateral issue related to integrated disclosure is the extent to which it affects the due diligence of participants in the registration process. As is discussed elsewhere,[24] the issuers, officers and directors, signers of the registration statement, underwriters, accountants, and certain experts each have due diligence obligations with regard to the accuracy of the registration materials. In many instances, the due diligence obligation includes a duty to investigate the accuracy of statements made in the registration materials. When a registration statement incorporates by reference information from other filings made with the SEC, the extent of this due diligence obligation may be affected. For example, does the auditing CPA or underwriter have equal responsibility for the information that is derived from other SEC filings? The efficiency to be achieved by integrated disclosure would appear to be undercut by requiring due diligence examination of all previous 1934 Act filings that become a part of the registration materials by virtue of Form S–3.

§ 3.4[4] 1933 Act Registration Forms[25]

§ 3.4[4][A] One Size Fits All Long–Form Disclosure—Form S–1

Form S–1 remains the basic, long-form registration statement that is generally available to issuers unless they qualify for one of the other forms. It requires complete registrant and transaction information to be provided in the prospectus.[26] As a practical matter, Form S–1 is to be used primarily by first-time issuers, non-reporting companies,[26.5] and unseasoned public companies[26.10]

---

22. 15 U.S.C.A. § 78*l*; 17 C.F.R. § 240.12g–1. *See* § 9.2 *infra*.

22.5 Form S–2 was rescinded in 2005.

24. *See* § 3.2 *supra* and § 7.4 *infra*.

25. The discussion that follows focuses on the registration of offerings under the 1933 Act. Companies that have publicly traded securities are also subject to periodic reporting and disclosure requirements under the Securities Exchange Act of 1934. The 1934 Act's registration, reporting and disclosure requirements are discussed in chapter 9 *infra*.

26. *See* Special Report, Integrated Disclosure Adoptions *supra* footnote 2 at 19–20. *See* the description of Schedule A in § 3.3 *supra*.

26.5 "A non-reporting issuer is an issuer that is not required to file reports pursuant to Section 13 or Section 15(d) of the Exchange Act, regardless of whether it is filing such reports voluntarily." Securities Offering Reform, Sec. Act Rel. No. 33–8591, Sec. Exch. Act Rel. No. 34–52056, Inv. Co. Act Rel. No. IC–26993 70 Fed. Reg. 44722–01, 2005 WL 1692642 (SEC August 3, 2005).

26.10 "An unseasoned issuer is an issuer that is required to file reports pursuant to Section 13 or Section 15(d) of the Exchange Act, but does not satisfy the requirements of Form S–3 or Form F–3 for a primary offering of its securities." Securities Offering Reform, Sec. Act Rel. No. 33–8591, Sec. Exch. Act Rel. No. 34–52056, Inv. Co. Act Rel. No. IC–26993 70 Fed. Reg. 44722–01, 2005 WL 1692642 (SEC August 3, 2005).

Until the public offering reforms of 2005,[26.15] Form S–1 required that all disclosures be included within the registration statement. This resulted in duplicative disclosures for those companies already subject to the 1934 Act periodic reporting requirements.[26.20] In 2005, Form S–1 was amended so as to permit companies that have filed at least one annual report and who are current in their 1934 Act filings to incorporate by reference information in previously filed SEC reports, provided that the information incorporated by reference is readily available on a web site maintained by the company.[26.25] As of December, 2005, the types of information that may be incorporated from current 1934 Act reports include summary information, risk factors, use of proceeds, plan of distribution, descriptions of the company's business, property and legal proceedings, financial statements, selected financial data and rations of earnings to fixed charges, and management's discussion and analysis (MD & A). Companies that within the preceding three years have been blank check companies, shell companies, or penny stock issuers may not take advantage of incorporation by reference.

§ 3.4[4][B]   Former Form S–2 for Public Companies

Until December 2005, the SEC offered issuers the option of former Form S–2 which required a lesser degree of detail in disclosure that Form S–1. Former Form S–2, which was rescinded as part of the SEC's offering reforms in 2005,[26.30] was available for registrants which have reported for three years or more under the Exchange Act. Information which the issuer provided on Form 10–K of the Exchange Act was incorporated by reference into the prospectus. Along with the description of the offering in the prospectus, the registrant using former Form S–2 had to provide either an annual report or comparable information in the prospectus itself. The more common practice was to use a unitary prospectus rather than to attach the annual report. Since, as discussed above, Form S–1 was amended to permit incorporation by reference for most 1934 Act reporting companies, Former Form S–2 became superfluous and thus was rescinded.

§ 3.4[4][C]   Form S–3 for Seasoned Issuers

Form S–3 is available for seasoned issuers[29.5]—those companies that meet the form's qualifications with respect to a history of public trading and 1934 Act reporting. Form S–3[30] requires the least detailed level of disclosure to

---

26.15 *See* Securities Offering Reform, Sec. Act Rel. No. 33–8591, Sec. Exch. Act Rel. No. 34–52056, Inv. Co. Act Rel. No. IC–26993 70 Fed. Reg. 44722–01, 2005 WL 1692642 (SEC August 3, 2005).

26.20 The avoidance of this duplicative disclosure was the creation of an integrated disclosure system that was substantially implemented in the 1970s.

26.25 The requirement of ready access may be satisfied by a hyperlink from the issuer's web site to the reports on the SEC web site.

26.30 *See* Securities Offering Reform, Sec. Act Rel. No. 33–8591, Sec. Exch. Act Rel. No. 34–52056, Inv. Co. Act Rel. No. IC–26993 70 Fed. Reg. 44722–01, 2005 WL 1692642 (SEC August 3, 2005). The offering reforms are discussed throughout chapter 2 *supra* where appropriate.

29.5 A seasoned issuer is a company that qualifies for S–3 registration. In contrast, "An unseasoned issuer is an issuer that is required to file reports pursuant to Section 13 or Section 15(d) of the Exchange Act, but does not satisfy the requirements of Form S–3 or Form F–3 for a primary offering of its securities." Securities Offering Reform, Sec. Act Rel. No. 33–8591, Sec. Exch. Act Rel. No. 34–52056, Inv. Co. Act Rel. No. IC–26993 70 Fed. Reg. 44722–01, 2005 WL 1692642 (SEC August 3, 2005).

30. Form S–3 is among those for which delaying amendments are not expressly authorized for postponing the effective date.

investors by allowing for the fullest possible incorporation by reference from Exchange Act reporting. Unless there has been a material change in the issuer's affairs, no registrant-oriented information will be required to be disclosed to investors. Only the transaction-specific description of the offering need be specified in the prospectus.

When promulgated, Form S–3 required the registrant to meet the three year reporting requirement of former Form S–2 in addition to a "market following" test. In 1992, the SEC reduced the thirty-six month reporting requirement to a twelve month reporting requirement. As originally adopted, Form S–3's "market following" test contained alternative standards of one hundred and fifty million dollar minimum value of voting stock held by non-affiliates ("the float"); or a one hundred million dollar float and an annual trading volume of at least three million shares.[31] In 1992, the Commission reduced this market float requirement to an aggregate market value of seventy-five million dollars regardless of the annual trading volume. The theory behind the market following test is that such widely-held securities have a sufficiently large informed market following so that more detailed disclosure is not necessary. Another of the reforms in 1993 was to expand Form S–3 to permit registration of investment-grade asset-backed securities irrespective of any previous reporting history.

§ 3.4[4][D] Forms for Small Businesses

Registration of securities under the 1933 Act is an expensive and otherwise burdensome process. Accordingly, the securities laws present barriers to small business's access to the U.S. capital markets. There is a widely recognized public policy to support small businesses as an important part of the U.S. economy. This public policy is furthered by encouraging small business to get started and to have the best possible chance for success. The policy of encouraging small business is reflected in a number of initiatives at both the federal and state levels. The existence of the Small Business Administration[33] is but one example. The policy of encouraging small business formation and capitalization thus comes into conflict with the regulatory philosophy underlying the securities laws. Mindful of these two potentially conflicted policies— investor protection and easing the barriers faced by small businesses, the federal securities laws have provided some incentives to small businesses. These incentives are designed to provide easier access to the capital markets but at the same time not forgetting about the investor protection thrust of the federal securities laws. It follows that some barriers have been lifted both through relaxed registration requirements and special exemptions from registration for securities offerings by small businesses. These streamlined registration forms, which are discussed below, should be considered as an alternative to the small issue exemptions from 1933 Act registration.[34]

In addition to the basic framework for registration established by Forms S–1 and S–3, there are some additional and more specialized forms which have been promulgated by the Commission. These forms, which are discussed below, are geared to special situations. All registration statements are to be

---

31. *See* Special Report, Integrated Disclosure, *supra* footnote 2 at 23–30.

33. *See, e.g.,* http://www.sba.gov/ (the Small Business Administration's web page).

34. These exemptions are discussed in §§ 4.15–4.25 *infra*.

filed with the SEC's central office in Washington, D.C. Form SB–1 and Form SB–2 filings may be made either in the central Commission office.

Beginning in the mid 1970s, the SEC has made great strides to facilitate small issues and offerings by small issuers.[36] The Commission created Form S–18 as a short form registration statement to be used for small issues and could be used for offerings when the aggregate offering price did not exceed seven and one half million dollars and the securities are to be sold for cash; Form S–18 was a major step in the continuing effort to make public offerings more economically feasible for small businesses and other less established enterprises. In many instances registration under Form S–18 was preferable to qualifying for an exemption from registration since there were no restrictions on resales of the securities;[37] the same is true of the successor forms SB–1 and SB–2 which are discussed below. Form S–18 was available only if the issuer was not subject to 1934 Act reporting requirements; nor was it available to a majority-owned subsidiary of a 1934 Act reporting company. Thus, as a practical matter, Form S–18 was available essentially only for a first-time public offering.

In 1992, the SEC proposed and adopted a new registration form, Form SB–2, which replaced Form S–18. Unlike its predecessor, Form S–18, the availability of Form SB–2 is premised upon the size of the issuer rather than on the dollar amount of securities to be offered. Form SB–2 thus is made available to small business issuers for an unlimited amount of securities. The streamlined form is available to a "small business issuer" which is defined as an issuer with revenues of less than twenty-five million dollars for its most recent fiscal year, provided that the issuer is not a foreign private issuer, a foreign government, an investment company, or a majority-owned subsidiary of a non-"small business issuer." As noted above, the simplified disclosure requirements for Form SB–2 appear in Regulation S–B, which sets forth small business issuer disclosure requirements under both the 1933 and 1934 Acts; formerly small business issuers were governed by Regulation S–K. The streamlined disclosure provisions for small business issuers were adopted in conjunction with an expansion of some of the exemptions from registration. In 1993, the Commission continued its small business initiatives by adopting Form SB–1 for use by small business issuers.[40] Form SB–1 is available to small business issuers for up to ten million dollars worth of securities in any twelve month period. However, offerings to employees made under Form S–8 are not included in the ten million dollar ceiling. Furthermore, a small business issuer may use Form SB–1 until the dollar ceiling has been reached, at which time the issuer must look to another form; in such a case, Form SB–2 would usually be the most appropriate (unless, of course, the issuer no longer qualifies as a small business issuer). Form SB–1 is a streamlined disclosure document, designed to facilitate the registration process. In adopting Form SB–1, the Commission gives the registrant the alternative of using the question and answer format that is also permitted for Regulation A offerings.

---

36. Regulation D is the prime example. *See* §§ 4.17–4.22 *infra. See also, e.g.,* Sections 3(b) and 4 of the 1933 Act 15 U.S.C.A. §§ 77c(b), (d) as well as Regulations A and D, 17 C.F.R. Pts. 251 *et seq.,* 501 *et seq.,* which are discussed in chapter 4 *infra.*

37. For example, SEC Rule 144 limits resales of securities purchased in transactions governed by Regulation D. 17 C.F.R. § 230.144. Rule 144 is discussed in § 4.26 *infra.*

40. *See* Sec.Act Rel. No. 33–6996, [1992–1993 Transfer Binder] Fed.Sec.L.Rep. (CCH) ¶ 85,134 (SEC April 29, 1993).

§ 3.4[4][E] Offerings to Employees

Form S–8 is available to 1934 Act reporting companies with regard to securities offered to employees, including the employees of subsidiaries who are offered the parent's securities, pursuant to any benefit plan. Registration for an offering to employees, advisors, and consultants under Form S–8 is much more simple and inexpensive than other registration forms. The information about the issuer that must be disclosed in an offering under Form S–8 is minimal[42] and does not provide the type of disclosures that are required by other registration forms. Additionally, unlike most other registration forms, a form S–8 registration is effective immediately and thus there is no waiting period that exists with registered offerings generally. Unlike most other registered offerings, securities offered in a Form S–8 registration may be subject to resale restrictions.[44] Registration under Form S–8 applies only to the issuance to employees and does not protect resales by employees which must either qualify for their own exemption or be registered under the 1933 Act.[45] Absent such an exemption, the employees' resales of securities will be in violation of section 5 of the Act.[46] Rule 701 sets forth an exemption from registration for securities offered to employees of nonpublic companies.[47]

§ 3.4[4][F] Securities Issued in Connection with a Merger or Other Corporate Reorganization—Form S–4

Form S–4 (and Form F–4 for foreign issuers)[50] may be used for registration of securities issued in mergers, combinations, consolidations, acquisitions of assets, recapitalizations, and other transactions governed by SEC Rule 145.[51] Form S–15 formerly was available, subject to compliance with the specified conditions, in certain mergers in which a vote of the acquired corporation's securities holders is not required; and in an exchange offer for securities of another issuer which would result in ownership of more than fifty percent of that class of the other issuer's securities. However, Form S–15 was rescinded, leaving Form S–4 as the appropriate form for mergers and other business combinations.

---

42. *See* Form S–8 Part II.

44. *See, e.g.,* SEC v. Cavanagh, 155 F.3d 129, 133–34 (2d Cir.1998) (shares registered pursuant to Form S–8 registration statement when issued to management were not still registered when resold to third parties).

45. *E.g.,* SEC v. Cavanagh, 155 F.3d 129 (2d Cir.1998) (shares registered on Form S–8 should have been reregistered before being resold by the defendants). *See also* Form S–8 Instruction C.

46. SEC v. Cavanagh, 155 F.3d 129 (2d Cir.1998); SEC v. DCI Telecommunications, Inc., 122 F.Supp.2d 495, 501 (S.D.N.Y.2000); In the Matter of Sky Scientific, Inc., Admin. Proc. File No. 3–9201, 69 S.E.C. Docket 763, 1999 WL 114405 (SEC March 5, 1999); In the Matter of Hollywood Trenz, Inc., Sec. Act Rel. No. 33–7533, 1998 WL 214285 (SEC 1998) (settlement of administrative action).

47. 17 C.F.R. § 230.701. The Rule 701 exemption has a maximum amount of either $1 million or a higher number based on the outstanding securities of the class being offered to employees. *See* § 4.18 *infra.*

50. Forms S–4 and F–4 are among those forms which do not have express authorization for use of delaying amendments to postpone the effective date.

51. 17 C.F.R. § 230.145. *See* § 5.2 *infra.* Form S–4 is coordinated with disclosures in connection with shareholder votes, which are governed by the proxy regulation under the 1934 Act. 15 U.S.C.A. § 78n. *See* chapter 11 *infra.*

Form S–4 replaced former Form S–14. For other SEC steps towards increased integration of the 1933 Act disclosures and those mandated by the Exchange Act's proxy Rules, *see* Exch.Act Rel. No. 34–23788, [1986–87 Transfer Binder] Fed.Sec.L.Rep. (CCH) ¶ 84,043 (Nov. 10, 1986).

§ 3.4[5] Disclosure Guides and Procedures—Regulations S–K, S–B, S–X

§ 3.4[5][A] Regulations S–K, S–B, and S–X Distinguished

In order to facilitate understanding of the registration process, the SEC has divided the applicable disclosure rules into three categories. Regulations S–K and S–B spell out in detail what must be disclosed and the manner in which it is to be presented. Regulation C[67] sets forth the relevant procedures. Regulation S–X[68] provides accounting rules and requirements for the form and contents of financial statements. Regulation S–X applies to financial statements required by any of the securities acts.

The disclosure provisions of Regulation S–K are discussed in more detail in subsequent sections of this treatise.[69] Also, as discussed more fully in a later section,[70] in January 1997, the SEC proposed amendments to various items of Regulations S–K and S–B in order to encourage more readable disclosures.[71] This "plain English" initiative for SEC filings was designed to make disclosures more meaningful to investors. In a lengthy and helpful official release, the Commission describes what it means by plain English and also provides several examples of appropriate disclosure styles.[72] The plain English requirements include: use of the active rather than passive voice, short sentences, use of definite, concrete everyday words, presentation of information in tabular form or with bullet lists, the avoidance of legal jargon and highly technical business terminology, as well as the avoidance of multiple negatives.

§ 3.4[6] EDGAR

The SEC has entered the electronic age through the use of its computerized system known as "EDGAR" (Electronic Data Gathering And Retrieval Project); under the program the SEC can receive electronically transmitted computerized filings. The computerized filings can be transmitted by telephone or can be sent to the Commission on diskette or magnetic tape. After a pilot program, EDGAR was used for 1933 and 1934 Act registration statements as well as selected 1934 Act filings and for some filings under the Investment Company Act of 1940.[97] Since its inception as a pilot program, the Commission has been expanding the EDGAR program and has adopted rules that, subject to exceptions, *require* electronic filings for most SEC filings.[98]

§ 3.6   SEC Statutory Procedures—Section 8

§ 3.6[1] Statutory Waiting Period

Section 8 of the 1933 Act[1] sets forth the SEC machinery for dealing with a registration statement once it has been filed. As discussed in the previous

---

67.   17 C.F.R. §§ 230.400–230.494.

68.   17 C.F.R. §§ 210.1–01–210.12–17, 6 Fed. Sec. L. Rep. (CCH) ¶ 69,101 *et seq.*

69.   *See* § 9.4 *infra.*

70.   For a more detailed discussion of the plain English initiatives, *see* § 3.8 *infra.*

71.   Plain English Disclosure, Sec. Act Rel. No. 33–7380, 62 Fed. Reg. 3152, 1997 WL 17695 (F.R.) (SEC Jan. 21, 1997).

72.   Plain English Disclosure, Sec. Act Rel. No. 33–7380, 62 Fed. Reg. 3152, 1997 WL 17695 (F.R.) (SEC Jan. 21, 1997).

97.   *See* Survey, Federal Securities Regulation, 41 Bus.Law. 925, 966–67 (1986).

98.   Sec.Act Rel.No. 33–6651 (June 26, 1986).

§ 3.6

1.   15 U.S.C.A. § 77h.

section,[2] the Securities and Exchange Commission relies heavily on an informal comment policy rather than invoking the formal procedures of section 8. Section 8(a) establishes the basic statutory rule that a registration statement becomes effective[3] twenty days after the later of the filing of the initial registration statement or the most recent amendment to the registration statement.[4] The exigencies of the offering process (or of disclosure requirements) may result in the issuer requiring more than the statutory twenty days to prepare additional material before the registration statement is in proper condition for the effective date. In such cases, there is a procedure, which is available for most registration forms[5] that will allow for further postponement of the effective date by filing what is known as a delaying amendment. Delaying amendments are generally invoked by issuers requiring more time. Conversely, issuers not needing the twenty-day waiting period may shorten the statutory period by filing with the Commission a request for acceleration of the effective date.[6] In addition to the acceleration procedure, the SEC may consent to having the amendment relate back to the filing of the registration statement so as not to cause the twenty-day period to start anew.[7] Beyond setting forth the statutory time schedule for the waiting period, Section 8 also contains the formal SEC procedures available for delaying or suspending the effectiveness of a registration statement. Section 8(b)[8] authorizes the Commission, after notice and opportunity for a hearing, to issue an order refusing to permit the registration statement to become effective until there have been such corrective amendments as the order may require. In addition to section 8(b) refusal orders, section 8(d)[9] empowers the Commission, again after notice and opportunity for a hearing,[10] to issue a stop order suspending the effectiveness of a registration statement. In addition, section 8(e) expressly authorizes Commission investigations to determine whether a

---

2. *See* § 3.5 *supra.*

3. Recall that it is only after the effective date that sales of the securities in registration can be made. *See* section 5(a), 15 U.S.C.A. § 77e(a). The significance of the effective date is discussed in §§ 2.1, 2.5 *supra.*

4. 15 U.S.C.A. § 77h(a).

5. Delaying amendments are not expressly permitted for Forms S–3, S–4, F–4, S–8, F–1, F–2, F–3, F–7, F–8, F–9, and F–10. The different registration forms are described in § 3.4 *supra.*

6. Section 8(a). 15 U.S.C.A. § 77h(a). Rule 461 provides the procedures for acceleration requests.

7. 15 U.S.C.A. § 77h(a). Thus, for example, it is common for an issuer not to set the price until the eve of the offering and to file a price amendment without triggering another twenty-day waiting period.

8. 15 U.S.C.A. § 77h(b).

9. 15 U.S.C.A. § 77h(d).

10. The procedures are not parallel as the section 8(b) refusal order may be issued ten days after notice since the statute sets forth the requirement that notice of hearing must be given within ten days. In contrast, there is a fifteen-day period applicable to section 8(d) stop orders.

Notwithstanding the foregoing notice periods, the hearing may be delayed upon the request of the Commission or the registrant. Thus, there may be considerable delay between the statutory notice period and the eventual hearing.

Stop and refusal orders therefore have different notice requirements. The trade-off is that the shorter refusal order procedure may be used only if the Commission sends the required notice within ten days of the filing of the registration statement. This very short time fuse has resulted in the relatively infrequent use of the refusal order. In fact, as of 1990, there were only two reported instances of the SEC invoking the refusal order procedure rather than relying on the more flexible stop order procedure.

stop order should be issued.[11] The instigation of formal section 8 proceedings has consequences beyond the adverse publicity and impact on the pending offering. Rule 262[12] provides that such formal proceedings may disqualify an issuer, underwriter or affiliate from eligibility for certain exemptions from registration.[13]

§ 3.6[2] Acceleration of the Effective Date

Section 8(a) of the Act[15] sets forth general guidelines that the Commission should consider in determining whether to grant acceleration of the effective date. Specifically, the SEC is directed to consider: the adequacy of information made available to the public, the ease with which the terms and features of the securities to be issued can be understood, the ease of understanding the relationship of the securities to be issued to the capital structure, and the ease of understanding the rights of securities holders.[17] In addition, the Act requires that the Commission more generally consider the public interest and investor protection.[18] It would appear that Congress did not contemplate that requests for acceleration would be considered "casually" nor be granted "as a matter of course."[19] Rather, the discretion to grant acceleration was designed to be exercised "only with full regard for the Act's purpose to provide investors with the information they need to be able to protect themselves against fraud and misrepresentation."[20]

SEC Rule 461[21] supplements the foregoing statutory criteria and also sets forth the procedures and requirements for requests for acceleration of the effective date.[22] There are seven stated reasons for the denial of acceleration: (1) failure to make a genuine effort to keep the prospectus reasonably readable and concise, so as to make the information readily understandable by the investing public;[23] (2) if the preliminary prospectus that has been distributed is found to have been inadequate or inaccurate in any material respect;[24] (3) if the issuer, a person controlling the issuer, or an underwriter is under current SEC investigation;[25] (4) if, in a firm commitment underwriting, the underwriter is not in compliance with the SEC's financial responsibility and net capital requirements;[26] (5) if there have been manipulative transactions by

---

11. 15 U.S.C.A. § 77h(e).

12. 17 C.F.R. § 230.262.

13. Specifically, the disqualification applies to Regulation A (offerings up to $5 million), and Rule 505 (offerings up to $5 million). *See* §§ 4.17 (Regulation A), 4.21 (Rule 505), 4.22 (Rule 504) *infra.*

15. 15 U.S.C.A. § 77h(a).

17. 15 U.S.C.A. § 77h(a).

18. *Id.*

19. In the Matter of Universal Camera Corp., 19 S.E.C. 648, 657 (SEC 1945).

20. *Id.*

21. 17 C.F.R. § 230.461.

22. *See also* the discussion in § 3.7[3] *infra.*

23. Rule 461(b)(1), 17 C.F.R. § 230.461(b)(1).

24. Rule 461(b)(2), 17 C.F.R. § 230.461(b)(2). In such a case, acceleration may not be granted until the Commission has received adequate assurance that appropriate corrections have been made and distributed to all underwriters and dealers who received the deficient preliminary prospectus. *Id.*

25. Rule 461(b)(3), 17 C.F.R. § 230.461(b)(3).

26. Rule 461(b)(4), 17 C.F.R. § 230.461(b)(4). The SEC net capital requirements are found in Rule 15c3–1 of the Exchange Act. 17 C.F.R. § 240.15c3–1. *See* chapter 14 *infra* for discussion of broker-dealers.

anyone proposed to be associated with the offering where those transactions have artificially affected the price of the securities to be offered;[27] (6) in the case of a secondary offering, if the issuer has failed to take adequate steps to assure compliance with Regulation M's prohibitions[28] on purchases by participants during a distribution;[29] and (7) if the underwriter's compensation is subject to NASD review, and the NASD has not issued a "no objection" statement.[30] In addition, failure to comply with the undertaking required by SEC Regulations S–K and S–B[31] if there are provisions for indemnification of participants who violate the 1933 Act will render acceleration unavailable. Compliance with the SEC's plain English requirements is also a factor in deciding whether to grant a request for acceleration of the effective date.[32]

§ 3.6[3] SEC Refusal Orders

As already pointed out, section 8(b) of the Act provides for refusal orders in the event that the Commission decides to prevent the registration statement from becoming effective. As discussed earlier, the more common practice is for the Commission to rely on the less formal practice of comment letters and delaying amendments until the registrant can correct any deficiencies identified by the Commission.[33] However, there are occasions when the SEC will resort to the more formal section 8 procedures—either a refusal order or a stop order—especially when it is believed that the issuer has not been making a good faith effort to comply with the Act's requirements.[34]

§ 3.6[4] SEC Investigations and Stop Orders

As mentioned above, section 8(e) empowers the Commission to commence an "examination" to determine whether a stop order should be issued.[38] In the course of a section 8(e) examination, the Commission has the power to take testimony and examine documents. It may make inquiries of the issuer, the underwriter, "or any other person" respecting any matter that pertains to the question of whether a stop order should be issued.[39] In addition, the SEC may require production and certification of a balance sheet or other financial

---

27. Rule 461(b)(5), 17 C.F.R. § 230.461(b)(5).

28. *See* § 6.1 *infra.*

29. Rule 461(b)(7), 17 C.F.R. § 230.461(b)(7). Failure to take such precautions may also provide the basis for refusal order or stop order proceedings. *See, e.g.,* In the Matter of Hazel Bishop, Inc., 40 S.E.C. 718 (SEC 1961) which is discussed in §§ 4.28, 6.1 *infra. See also, e.g.,* Rickard Ramore Gold Mines, Ltd., 2 S.E.C. 377, 385–86, 1937 WL 1511 (SEC 1937) (registration statement should disclose options and directors' and officers' agreements which took stock off market; investors are entitled to know of "any artificial restraints" on the market).

30. Rule 461(b)(6), 17 C.F.R. § 230.461(b)(6).

In its Rules of Fair Practice, the National Association of Securities Dealers sets forth requirements to assure that broker dealers not participate in underwriting ventures unless the underwriter's compensation or other terms of the distribution process are neither unfair nor unreasonable.

31. Regulation S–K Item 512(h); Regulation S–B Item 512(e). Indemnification is discussed in § 7.14 *infra.*

32. The plain English requirements are discussed in § 3.10[2] *infra.*

33. *See* discussion in § 3.7 *supra.*

34. *See, e.g.,* Doman Helicopters, Inc., 41 S.E.C. 431 (SEC 1963).

38. 15 U.S.C.A. § 77h(e).

39. *Id.*

statements.[40] A registrant's failure to cooperate in the course of a section 8(e) examination can lead to the issuance of a stop order.[41]

§ 3.6[5] Withdrawal of the Registration Statement

Once the registration statement has been filed, the registrant may not withdraw from registration without the Commission's permission.[53] In 2001, SEC Rule 477 was amended to provide for automatic withdrawal of the registration statement unless within fifteen days after the application to withdraw the registration statement, the Commission objects to the request for withdrawal.[54]

Ordinarily, the Commission will accede to requests to withdraw the registration statement. It is the Commission's stated policy to permit withdrawal of the registration statement if "consistent with the public interest and protection of investors."[55] Denying permission to withdraw the registration statement and the SEC's decision to institute formal proceedings under section 8 can have significant consequences. For example, the imposition of a stop order or refusal order may disable the participants from participating in certain exempt offerings over the next five years.[56]

§ 3.7 Processing the Registration Statement After Filing

§ 3.7[1] Law versus Lore: What Really Happens—Informal Procedures

Under the terms of section 8(a) of the Act, once the registration statement has been filed, it becomes effective on the twentieth day after filing, with the twenty-day period beginning to run anew on the date that each amendment is filed.[1] As is explained more fully below, the formal statutory time periods and procedures are rarely invoked. Section 8(b) of the 1933 Act[2] empowers the SEC to issue a refusal order for deficiencies that are apparent on the face of the registration statement, provided that the Commission acts within ten days after the filing. Section 8(d)[3] permits the SEC to issue a stop order to prevent the effective date of a registration statement, and section 8(e)[4] permits the Commission to institute investigations as to whether a stop order should be issued.

The procedures spelled out in section 8 of the Act do not provide an accurate picture of the SEC registration review process as it generally proceeds. Although Congress may have contemplated that the Commission would initiate formal section 8 proceedings whenever defective registration statements are filed, such formal proceedings are the exception rather than

---

40. *Id.*

41. *See* In the Matter of Augion–Unipolar Corp., Admin. Proc. File No. 3–2079, [1969–1970 Transfer Binder] Fed. Sec. L. Rep. (CCH) ¶ 77,836 (SEC 1970), *affirmed* 44 S.E.C. 613 (SEC 1971). *See also* In the Matter of Blimpie Corp., 44 S.E.C. 558 (SEC 1971).

53. 17 C.F.R. § 230.477; Peoples Securities Co. v. SEC, 289 F.2d 268 (5th Cir.1961) (registrant does not have an absolute right to withdraw registration statement).

54. 17 C.F.R. § 230.477.

55. 17 C.F.R. § 230.477.

56. *See e.g.,* 17 C.F.R. §§ 230.252; 230.505(b)(2)(iii). *See* §§ 4.15, 4.18, *infra.*

§ 3.7

1. Section 8(a); 15 U.S.C.A. § 77h(a).

2. 15 U.S.C.A. § 77h(b). For discussion of the other SEC enforcement powers *see* § 9.5 *infra.*

3. 15 U.S.C.A. § 77h(d).

4. 15 U.S.C.A. § 77h(e).

the rule. Instead, registration review is accomplished through the less formal means of written correspondence and telephone conversations between the SEC staff and the registrant's counsel.[5]

The Commission's reliance on the informal review process dates back to its earliest years.[6] As previously explained, the formal procedures set out in section 8 are used infrequently. For example, in 1970, only 28 such examinations were initiated out of 4,314 registration statements filed, while only six resulted in the initiation of stop order proceedings.[7] There has been no significant increase in the use of section 8 proceedings. Although the scarcity of formal review proceedings has been described as "a tribute to the administrative flexibility of the Commission,"[8] some might also attribute it to undue pressures exerted by the Commission during its informal discussions and negotiations with registrants.[9] Another, more plausible explanation for the lack of more detailed review is the fact that the SEC is both understaffed and overworked.[10]

Rather than relying on the stop order and the refusal order proceedings, the Commission staff generally responds to the initial filing with a detailed "letter of comment" or "deficiency letter," advising the issuer of changes that the Commission would like to see in the registration statement. These comments are not limited to specific disclosure items but also refer to readability and the ease with which the disclosures can be understood.[11] As a practical matter, virtually all registration statements filed with the Commission require at least one amendment.[12] Failure to respond to the letter of comment (or deficiency letter), in and of itself, has no legal consequences, except that it carries with it the implied threat of the Commission's initiating a formal stop order proceeding. Accordingly, rather than risk public disclosure and adverse publicity of the deficiencies that would result from formal SEC action, most registrants will readily comply with the Commission's requests. In the event that the registration statement is about to become effective as a result of the expiration of the twenty-day period, the SEC will generally suggest that the issuer file a "delaying amendment" in order to avoid the more drastic initiation of formal administrative proceedings. Since an amendment starts a new twenty-day waiting period, even the most trivial change will operate as a delaying amendment.

Sometimes either the Commission or the need for last-minute additions will require minor amendments to the registration statement after all other deficiencies have been corrected. A common procedure to prevent delaying the effectiveness of the registration due amendment is to apply to the Commission

---

5. Although not a formal process, the SEC Rules do provide a basis for the giving of informal advice. *See* 17 C.F.R. § 202.2 (prefiling assistance and interpretive advice) and 17 C.F.R. § 202.3 (processing of filings).

6. *See, e.g.* In the Matter of Universal Camera Corp., 19 S.E.C. 648, 659, [1945–1947 Transfer Binder] Fed. Sec. L. Rep. (CCH) ¶ 75,560 (SEC 1945).

7. 36 S.E.C. Ann.Rep. 29, 34, 35 (1970). *See also, e.g.,* 46 S.E.C.Ann.Rep. 141 (1980).

8. Richard W. Jennings & Harold Marsh, Jr., Securities Regulation 183 (5th ed.1982).

9. *See, e.g.* Orel Sebring, Log Jam on the Potomac—The Current Delay Problem of the SEC, 15 Bus.Law. 921 (1960).

10. *Cf.* John Mulford, "Acceleration" Under the Securities Act of 1933—A Reply to the Securities and Exchange Commission, 14 Bus.Law. 156 (1958).

11. 17 C.F.R. § 230.421. *See* § 3.10 *infra.*

12. *See, e.g.,* Richard W. Jennings & Harold Marsh, Jr., Securities Regulation 174–175 (5th ed.1982). *See also* Louis Loss, Fundamentals of Securities Regulation 128–30 (1983).

for acceleration of the effective date pursuant to section 8(a).[13] For example, it is frequently very difficult to arrive at a firm price for a new issue prior to the eve of the offering. Accordingly, it is common practice for the issuer or registrant to omit the offering price from the preliminary SEC filing. After the correction of all other deficiencies the issuer or other registrant will then file a "price amendment" followed by a request for acceleration to allow the offering to proceed as contemplated.[14]

In addition to the requirements of full disclosure and accuracy that can prevent a registration statement from becoming effective, the statute and rules provide that the prospectus must constantly be kept current, even after the effective date. A prospectus containing misleading information, even though it becomes misleading after the effective date, is not in compliance with section 10 of the Act.[15] This is true even if it would not be necessary to the registration statement and prospectus to update the full registration statement.[16] Post effective amendments are frequently made by affixing stickers that contain the updated or corrected information. Stickering saves the registrant the expense of reprinting the entire prospectus. There may be some instances, however, when the changes are so significant that stickering will not be sufficient.

§ 3.7[2] SEC Review Practices

The SEC does not review the merits of the registration statement and the offering. Rather, in reviewing 1933 Act registration statements, as is the case with SEC review of filings generally, the focus is on the adequacy and clarity of the disclosure. Specifically, the SEC will consider whether the applicable disclosure items are explained in sufficient detail and with sufficient clarity. In addition to the review of the adequacy of the disclosures, the SEC will examine clarity and, in particular, will conduct a "plain English" review of those portions of the registration statement that are subject to the SEC's plain English disclosure requirements.[20]

§ 3.7[3] SEC Policies On Acceleration Requests

In the event that the issuer desires an effective date prior to the expiration of twenty days after the filing of the last amendment to the registration statement, it can file with the Commission a request for an acceleration of the effective date pursuant to Rule 461.[25] The rule provides that the issuer should advise the Commission of the request for acceleration not later than the second business day before the desired effective date. The Commission has a wide range of discretion in deciding whether or not to grant the request for acceleration. There are no express statutory guidelines for acceleration and the few guides that have been prepared by the Commission are exceedingly vague. When the SEC denies a request for acceleration of the registration statement, the denial is usually based upon incomplete or inade-

---

13. 15 U.S.C.A. § 77h(a).

14. *See* L. Loss *supra* footnote 12 at 130–31.

15. SEC v. Manor Nursing Centers, 458 F.2d 1082 (2d Cir.1972). *See* § 2.5 *supra*.

16. SEC v. Manor Nursing Centers, 458 F.2d 1082 (2d Cir.1972).

20. Plain English is discussed in § 3.10[2] *infra*.

25. 17 C.F.R. § 230.461.

quate disclosure.[26] The Commission in one of its seminal decisions,[27] relied on the statutory criteria that were added to the Act in 1940 and which set forth four basic but quite generalized criteria that it will consider in deciding whether or not to grant a request for acceleration:

> (1) the adequacy of the information about the issuer that was available to the public before the registration,

> (2) the ease with which the nature of the securities can be understood,

> (3) the ease with which the relationship of the securities to the capital structure of the issuer can be understood, and,

> (4) the ease with which the rights of holders of the securities can be understood.[29]

Compliance with the plain English requirements[30] is a significant factor in granting requests for acceleration of the effective date.

The lack of definite guidelines is but one of the criticisms that has led to objections to the Commission's use of acceleration.[31] As explained by the Commission, the acceleration procedure was enacted by Congress in order to give added flexibility to the SEC and at the same time reduce the harshness that otherwise resulted from a rigid twenty-day waiting period:

> This provision for acceleration was added to the Act in 1940 to relax the rigidity of the previous requirements. Its terms make plainly evident the persistent concern of Congress for the protection of investors and emphasize the intention of Congress to require that before permitting a registration to become effective the Commission must be satisfied that the information in the statement itself, together with any information previously available to the public about the issuer, will enable prospective investors to understand clearly what it is they are asked to buy.

> Consistently with these provisions the Act authorizes the Commission to take steps that may be necessary to defer the public sale of any security subject to registration until the statement is cleared of material inaccuracies or omissions and contains a complete and correct statement of the information requisite to a clear understanding of the security's character and quality.[32]

In addition to the four criteria discussed above, the Commission has set forth a number of factors that it will weigh in considering the request for acceleration. The SEC has announced that it may refuse to grant acceleration

---

26. *See* 17 C.F.R. § 230.460.

27. In the Matter of Universal Camera Corp., 19 S.E.C. 648, 658, [1945–1947 Transfer Binder] Fed. Sec. L. Rep. (CCH) ¶ 75,560 (SEC 1945).

29. In the Matter of Universal Camera Corp., 19 S.E.C. 648, 657–58, [1945–1947 Transfer Binder] Fed. Sec. L. Rep. (CCH) ¶ 75,560 (SEC 1945). The Commission also noted that Congress did not draft the Act so that the SEC would grant acceleration "casually" or "as a matter of course." *Id.* At 657. Rather, the SEC is directed to exercise its discretion only if the public interest will thus be served. *Id.*

30. The plain English requirements are discussed in §§ 3.8[2], 3.10[2] *infra*.

31. *See, e.g.,* Edward N. Gadsby & Ray Garrett, Jr., Acceleration Under the Securities Act of 1933—A Comment on the A.B.A.'s Legislative Proposal, 13 Bus.Law. 718 (1958); John Mulford, "Acceleration" Under the Securities Act of 1933—A Reply to the Securities and Exchange Commission, 14 Bus.Law. 156 (1958).

32. Universal Camera, 19 S.E.C. 648, 658 (SEC 1945).

in the following situations: (a) when the issuer has an indemnification agreements with its officers, directors or underwriters that transcends or is inconsistent with SEC policy on indemnification agreement unless there is a waiver or a compliance with SEC policies; (b) when there is a pending SEC investigation under any provision of the acts administered by the SEC of the issuer, a person controlling the issuer, or one of the underwriters; (c) when one or more of the underwriters, due to the underwriting commitment, may put at risk its financial responsibility as established by Rule 15c3–1[33] of the Exchange Act; or (d) when there is or has been market manipulation by any person "connected" with the offering.[34] These are just some of the grounds for denial of acceleration that are listed in Rule 461.

On occasion, the SEC has been harshly criticized for using denial of acceleration as an ad hoc sanction for these events which, standing alone, would not provide a sufficient basis for the issuance of either a refusal order or a stop order.[36]

Indemnification agreements are not the only issue that has led the Commission to deny requests for acceleration of the effective date. In 1989, the Commission staff refused to grant acceleration as not in the public interest because of a clause in the issuer's charter requiring shareholders to submit to arbitration any claim asserted against or on behalf of the issuer.[37]

Due to the wide latitude that the Commission allows itself for the denial of acceleration, requests for acceleration should not be made lightly. This is especially so where the registrant is concerned about the marketability of the securities being offered. News of SEC denial of an acceleration request may alert the investment community to potential problems (both real and unreal) with the securities. Except with price amendments or relatively minor amendments which start the twenty day period running anew, because of the customary review procedures for new issuers and the more speculative ventures, acceleration may as a practical matter be limited to more established companies.

§ 3.8   Frequent Deficiencies in Registration Statements and Other Disclosures; The Plain English Requirement

§ 3.8[1] Frequent Deficiencies

Registration statement disclosures cover a wide range of topics, including the company's business generally, the terms of the offering, as well as identification and discussion of significant risk factors. There are a number of areas that are particularly susceptible to inadequate or misleading disclosures.[1] First, the registration statement may fail to adequately explain the issuer's prior adverse trends in sales and in income. For example, the

---

33. 17 C.F.R. § 240.15c3–1.

34. Rule 461(b), 17 C.F.R. § 230.461(b).

36. *See, e.g.,* John Mulford, "Acceleration" Under the Securities Act of 1933—A Reply to the Securities and Exchange Commission, 14 Bus.Law. 156 (1958).

37. When issuer's counsel objected, he was informed that the Commission had informally approved the staff's position. A FOIA request for the staff's submission to the Commission was denied. *See* Carl W. Schneider, Arbitration in Corporate Governance Documents: An Idea the SEC Refuses to Accelerate, 4 Insights, no. 5 at p. 21 (May 1990).

§ 3.8

1. *See* Regulation S–K. 17 C.F.R. §§ 229.10–229.802.

Commission has taken the position that it is not sufficient merely to state that the issuer's income declined due to increased expenses. The 1933 Act demands, and the SEC requires, full disclosure as to precisely which expenses were increased and the reasons for their increase. Further, the issuer should explain whether such increased costs are reasonably expected to continue and, if so, whether past performance is a reasonable guide to the future. A second common deficiency in registration statements is the failure to include information concerning the relative contribution to sales and/or income of the issuer's various products, product lines, lines of business, divisions, and subsidiaries. The Commission requires identification of the sources of income and/or losses according to division and lines of business. The allocation according to lines of business does not depend upon whether or not the issuer operates its divisions on a parent-subsidiary basis. A third frequently occurring problem is the registration statement's failure to give a full, fair, and detailed description of the use of the proceeds to be raised by the offering. The Commission requires specific identification of the use of the proceeds from the offering. A fourth common disclosure problem arises out of the registration statement's treatment of transactions between the issuer and management or principal shareholders. Because of the obvious sensitivity of insider transactions, especially when there is an actual or potential conflict of interest situation, disclosure problems frequently arise.

A fifth common deficiency in 1933 Act disclosure documents is the registrant's failure to make the prospectus readable and understandable by the general investing public. The SEC has stated its belief that these problems are exacerbated by the failure to use simple language, tables, charts, and other pictorial visual devices.[6] A sixth common deficiency is that the 1933 Act prospectus may have either an insufficient or overly verbose introductory statement. According to the Commission, an introductory statement, when required, should include identification of all of the factors that make the particular offering speculative and also of those aspects that are unique to that offering, as opposed to the industry or type of offering in general.[7] It is the SEC's position that overly verbose statements are obscure and therefore contrary to full disclosure requirements. Lack of readability can be just as harmful as a failure to disclose enough since the material information may well get lost in the issuer's verbosity, thus negating the intended impact of the cautionary introductory statement. This concern is reflected in the "buried facts" doctrine which holds that disclosures can be obscured by burying them in footnotes or appendices.[8] The SEC has pointed out, however, that a company's failure to include everything in the summary portion of a prospectus or other disclosure document will not automatically trigger the "buried facts" doctrine.[9]

---

6. *See* Sec. Act Rel. No. 33–6276 (Dec. 23, 1980); Sec. Act Rel. No. 33–6235 (Sept. 2, 1980).

7. *See e.g.,* In the Matter of Universal Camera Corp., 19 S.E.C. 648 (1945); Regulation S–K, items 502–503, 17 C.F.R. §§ 229.501–502.

8. *See* Plain English Disclosure, Sec. Act Rel. No. 33–7497, 63 Fed. Reg. 6370–01, 1998 WL 44199 (F.R.) (SEC Feb. 6, 1998) ("Under the buried facts doctrine, a court would consider disclosure to be false and misleading only if its overall significance is obscured because material information is 'buried,' for example, in footnotes or appendices").

9. Plain English Disclosure, Sec. Act Rel. No. 33–7497, 63 Fed. Reg. 6370–01, 1998 WL 44199 (F.R.) (SEC Feb. 6, 1998).

A Seventh Circuit decision raises significant questions concerning the appropriate audience for registration statements.[10] Whereas the SEC has taken the position that the registration statement should be written with the ordinary investor in mind, Judge Easterbrook in Wielgos v. Commonwealth Edison Co.[11] took the position that, at least in the case of widely-followed securities, the adequacy of disclosures should be judged by the needs of sophisticated analysts. In *Wielgos,* the registrant had a sufficiently wide market following that it used registration Form S–3. The court held that disclosure should therefore be geared to the professional investors who in effect set the price for the stock. Thus, according to Judge Easterbrook:

> Descriptions in Forms 10–K and registration statements are almost useless to individual investors. They require absorption by professional traders and investors. What these professionals need is new information specific to the issuer. Telling them over and again how the NRC works, or that costs are rising in the nuclear power industry, or even that Commonwealth Edison had run into trouble with its welds (which became known a few months before this stock was sold), has nothing to do with the accuracy of prices in the market. Investors who buy 500 shares of stock rely on the market price....[12]

Judge Easterbrook is most certainly correct in his assertion that registration statements should not be cluttered with useless detail.[13] In fact, the SEC has long taken this position. On the other hand, Judge Easterbrook's elitist description of the market and the inefficiency of catering to the small investor ignores the basic disclosure thrust of the securities laws and portends unfortunately narrow tests of materiality.

Another disclosure problem that has emerged, both with regard to 1933 Act registration statements and to SEC filings in general, is the issuer's failure to disclose improper transactions involving domestic political activity, including campaign contributions, or foreign involvement.[14] A number of problems have also arisen in the context of the so-called "new disclosure" concerning social issues with which the issuer has a controversial relationship. Similarly, ethical investors may want to know where their invested funds are going. The courts and the Commission have dealt with these problems in the context of an expanding definition of the concept of "materiality."[15] Since the hallmark of disclosure for both the 1933 Act registration statement and all 1934 Act filings is embodied in the concept of "materiality," the problems relating to disclosure in registration statements and other required filings are quite similar. Because the primary purpose of 1933 Act registration statements is to provide full and adequate information regarding the distribution

---

10. *See also, e.g.,* Note, Plain English: A Reappraisal of the Intended Audience of Disclosure Under the Securities Act of 1933, 72 So. Cal. L. Rev. 851 (1999).

11. 892 F.2d 509 (7th Cir.1989). *See also* the discussion in § 3.3 *supra.*

12. 892 F.2d at 518.

13. Thus, for example, it was not actionable to fail to explain in detail the elementary economic principle that increased competition could have an adverse effect on the company's profits. O'Sullivan v. Trident Microsystems, Inc., 1994 WL 124453, [1993–1994 Transfer Binder] Fed. Sec. L. Rep. (CCH) ¶ 98,116 (N.D.Cal.1994).

14. *See, e.g.,* SEC v. Jos. Schlitz Brewing Co., 452 F.Supp. 824 (E.D.Wis.1978).

15. *See,* James O. Hewitt, Developing Concepts of Materiality and Disclosure, 32 Bus.Law. 887 (1977); Lewis D. Lowenfels, Questionable Corporate Payments and the Federal Securities Laws, 51 N.Y.U.L.Rev. 1 (1976); A.A. Sommer, Jr. Therapeutic Disclosure, 4 Sec.Reg.L.J. 263 (1976). *See also* §§ 11.14, 13.5 *infra.*

of securities, certain types of disclosures may be more sensitive and thus of more concern with regard to public offerings than to other required filings.[16]

§ 3.8[2] Plain English Requirements—Overview

As discussed more fully in a subsequent section of this treatise,[20] in January 1997, the SEC proposed amendments to Rule 421 to require the use of clear, concise and understandable language in prospectuses.[21] The rule proposal was part of SEC's larger initiative to require the use of "plain English" in SEC filings and reports to shareholders and investors.[22] The plain English initiative, which started out as a pilot program, is now embodied in Rule 421.[23] In a lengthy official release,[24] the Commission describes what it means by plain English and also provides several examples of appropriate disclosure styles. The plain English requirements include: use of the active rather than passive voice, short sentences, use of definite, concrete everyday words, presentation of information in tabular form or with bullet lists, the avoidance of legal jargon and highly technical business terminology, as well as the avoidance of multiple negatives.[25] The plain English requirements also call for increased white space in prospectuses in order to make the information more readable.

§ 3.9 Common Disclosure Problems—Dilution of the Public's Investment, Business Risks, Transactions With Controlling Persons, and Projections

§ 3.9[1] Overview

Because of both the potential for self-dealing and the access to inside information, transactions by the issuer's insiders frequently require detailed disclosure in the 1933 Act registration statement. The Commission shows particular concern where a significant portion of the proceeds will not be going into the issuer's business. Whenever an investment is a speculative one, the prospectus must provide the potential investor with notice and give detailed disclosures as to the reasons therefor. The prospectus must also contain an explanation of risks peculiar to the issuer or the issuer's industry.

§ 3.9[2] Dilution of the Public's Investment, Business Risks

A vintage case which, nevertheless, still accurately reflects the Commission's disclosure policy is In the Matter of Universal Camera Corp.[1] In that

---

16. For a good discussion of materiality in the 1933 Act offering process *see* Feit v. Leasco Data Processing Equipment Corp., 332 F.Supp. 544 (E.D.N.Y.1971).

20. *See* § 3.10[2] *infra.*

21. Plain English Disclosure, Sec. Act Rel. No. 33–7380, 62 Fed. Reg. 3152, 1997 WL 17695 (F.R.) (SEC Jan. 21, 1997). For a more detailed discussion of the plain English initiatives, *see* § 3.6 *supra.*

22. For examples of plain English, *see* § 3.10[2] *infra.*

23. 17 C.F.R. § 230.421.

24. Plain English Disclosure, Sec. Act Rel. No. 33–7497, 63 Fed. Reg. 6370–01, 1998 WL 44199 (F.R.) (SEC Feb. 6, 1998).

25. The SEC in its own rulemaking, however, has not been true to the plain English requirements. Consider, for example, the SEC rules for lawyer conduct which use a double negative to describe when lawyers must report up the corporate ladder suspected material misconduct. 17 C.F.R. § 205.2(e)(2) ("Evidence of a material violation means credible evidence, based upon which it would be unreasonable, under the circumstances, for a prudent and competent attorney not to conclude that it is reasonably likely that a material violation has occurred, is ongoing, or is about to occur.").

§ 3.9

1 19 S.E.C. 648 (SEC 1945).

case, the issuer embarked upon an offering of securities that would have resulted in the rearrangement of control in an existing corporation. The issuer was to receive just under twenty percent of the aggregate offering proceeds,[2] a figure which could possibly have increased to just under forty percent upon exercise of certain warrants.[3] The registration statement that was filed came under sharp criticism in the administrative stop order proceedings initiated by the Commission. To begin with, the SEC objected that the issuer's registration statement was deficient due to an inadequate introductory statement. Although the registrant included the required legend on the first page to the effect that the investment was a speculative one, it failed to clearly "describe the speculative aspects" so as to be "plainly evident to the ordinary investor."[4] It is certain that today the Commission would require an equally explicit introductory statement explaining the speculative nature of such an investment. Under current law, any prospectus covering a speculative offering must explain why the issue is speculative by giving all pertinent details without obscuring any of the key facts or burying them in a lengthy narrative.[5]

Perhaps the most serious disclosure problem in Universal Camera's registration statement was the failure to adequately describe the intended use of the proceeds from the offering. This was a particularly sensitive issue on the facts before the Commission since the bulk of the securities in registration represented a secondary offering and, thus, none of the proceeds from these sales was to flow to the issuer. Specifically, the Commission pointed to the registration statement's failure to explain to the investor the significance of the low percentage of proceeds the issuer was to receive and its failure to reveal that the shareholders, who were to make a huge profit on their secondary sales, would nonetheless have retained both voting control in the corporation and a forty-three percent participation in earnings by virtue of the Class B stock which they would continue to hold.[6] Thirdly, the registration statement failed to contrast plainly the offering price with the book value of the securities offered. Finally, the registration materials discussed inadequately the potential impact of the warrants and their eventual exercise.

As is discussed more fully in a subsequent section,[7] particularly difficult disclosure problems can arise in connection with an initial public offering of a

---

2. The registration statement covered a public offering of 663,500 shares of class A stock, of which 530,500 shares were being sold by existing shareholders as a secondary distribution. The selling shareholders had acquired the shares covered in the secondary offering for a total of $30,000 but they were to receive $2,100,865 from reselling them through the registered offering. The remaining 133,000 Class A shares represented a primary offering by the issuer which was to receive $524,985 in net proceeds.

3. The registration statement also covered warrants which if fully exercised would cause the issuer to receive an additional $863,500.

4. 19 S.E.C. at 652.

5. See Regulation S–K items 502–503, 17 C.F.R. §§ 224.502–503. See generally 17 C.F.R. § 231.4936 (1982) (rescinded March 3, 1982). In Sec.Act Rel. No. 33–6332 (August 6, 1981) the SEC proposed to eliminate the Guides for the Preparation and Filing of Registration Statements and Reports, with limited exceptions. These guides have been replaced by Regulation S–K. Sec.Act Rel. No. 33–6384 (March 3, 1982).

6. 19 S.E.C. at 653.

7. See § 4.25 infra.

company with substantial preexisting shareholders even where those shares are not to be offered in connection with the registered offering. By virtue of Rule 144,[8] it is possible that there will be a substantial influx of these shares into the market upon the expiration of ninety days following the public offering.[9] In such a case, the 1933 Act registration statement must adequately disclose the possibility of these sales and the downward price pressure that could result.[10]

In the course of the *Universal Camera* opinion, the Commission explicitly called for plainly phrased statements as opposed to elaborate, and hence more technical, prose. This 1948 opinion marked the beginning of an SEC impetus for readable prospectuses in order to make them understandable to less sophisticated investors.[11] The Commission is not alone in this concern as courts have also recognized the necessity to use simple language.[12]

In the late 1990s, the Commission formalized these requirements in its plain English initiatives.[13] The Commission's plain English requirements include: use of the active rather than passive voice, short sentences, use of definite, concrete everyday words, presentation of information in tabular form or with bullet lists, the avoidance of legal jargon and highly technical business terminology, as well as the avoidance of multiple negatives.[14]

In addition to the misstatements and omissions relating to the issuer's financial structure and the impact of the offering upon the issuer's capital structure, Universal Camera's registration statement was further woefully deficient with regard to the description of the corporation's business. In the period immediately preceding the filing of Universal Camera's registration statement, the issuer had received the bulk of its profits from government war-related contracts for the sale of binoculars. Clearly, this enterprise was not likely to continue after the war and the registration statement did not sufficiently disclose the company's pre-war activities nor its post-war plans. The registration statement simply talked in terms of "designing and preparing improved and additional photographic products which would find a ready sale" without discussing or describing in detail the nature of such products. The Commission held that this was a significant deficiency in the registration statement, especially in light of the express requirements of the registration form that was used for the filing and which called for detailed disclosure.[15] In the course of the proceedings, the issuer agreed to amend the registration statement so as to cure its deficiencies, and accordingly the SEC, in the

---

8.   17 C.F.R. § 230.144. *See* § 4.26 *infra*.

9.   After there has been a registered public offering, the issuer becomes subject to the 1934 Act periodic reporting requirements. Section 15(d) of the 1934 Act, 15 U.S.C.A. § 78o(d). *See* § 9.3 *infra*. Once this information has been available for ninety days, unregistered securities may be sold. Rule 144(e) permits, within a three month period, public sales of unregistered securities of up to the greater of one percent of the outstanding securities or the average weekly reported trading volume. Rule 144(c) contains the informational requirements.

10.   Furthermore, it is conceivable that if there is a substantial volume of these unregistered secondary sales, they might be integrated into the initial offering even though they fall within Rule 144(e)'s volume limitations. The integration doctrine is discussed in § 4.29 *infra*.

11.   *See generally* Regulation S–K, 17 C.F.R. §§ 229.01 *et seq.*

12.   *See, e.g.,* Feit v. Leasco Data Processing Equipment Corp., 332 F.Supp. 544, 549 (E.D.N.Y. 1971).

13.   *See* § 3.10[2] *infra*.

14.   Rule 421, 17 C.F.R. § 230.421.

15.   19 S.E.C. at 655.

exercise of its power to award relief in the public interest, dismissed the Commission proceedings.

The *Universal Camera* decision is instructive on a number of sensitive disclosure problems. It highlights the importance of describing the specific use to be made of the proceeds, especially with regard to a secondary offering that accompanies a primary one. The opinion further stresses the necessity to use identifying statements, such as the legend required for speculative issues to alert the reader to risky aspects of the offering. Finally, the issuer must clearly disclose the nature of its business, both in terms of the past and also with regard to future plans. The registration materials must be especially descriptive where the issuer's business is cyclical or unusually dependent upon external events. Similarly, effects of costs of compliance with regulatory requirements of environmental protection laws must also be adequately disclosed.[16]

One further noteworthy aspect of the *Universal Camera* decision is the fact that, in the course of its opinion, the SEC emphasized that "it is not this Commission's function under the Securities Act to approve or disapprove securities * * *. The Act leaves it to the investor, on the basis of the facts disclosed, to weigh the earning prospects of a registered security against the risks involved and to judge for himself whether he wishes to invest his money in it."[17] This accurately sets forth the direct impact of the 1933 Act. However, the indirect effects of full disclosure cannot be ignored. Detailed disclosures may make a particular offering so unmarketable as to have the effect of precluding a public sale. This type of merit scrutiny can be achieved directly under the state securities laws that permit a merit analysis of the securities in registration.[18]

§ 3.9[3] Transactions of Controlling Persons, Management Stability and Integrity, Secondary Sales

Another instructive opinion is found in the 1964 SEC decision of In the Matter of Franchard Corp.[19] The issuer was a real estate development syndication managed by Mr. Glickman, who was the principal owner and manager of the development project. The issuer undertook a series of public offerings. All prospectuses properly showed that Glickman owned most of the Class B and a major portion of the Class A stock. However, they failed to disclose that during the period of these offerings, all of his Class B and most of his Class A stock had been pledged to banks for loans totaling four and one-quarter million dollars at interest rates up to twenty-four percent. Notwithstanding the pledges, Glickman retained his voting rights in the stock. The issue before the Commission was whether these loans to the major shareholder and manager of the enterprise ought to have been disclosed. The applicable forms for filing of the registration statement expressly provide for the disclosure of

---

16. *See, e.g.,* Levine v. NL Industries, Inc., 926 F.2d 199 (2d Cir.1991) (disclosure of environmental compliance costs; action under Exchange Act Rule 10b–5). *Compare* the SEC's treatment of the misleading statements in *Universal Camera* concerning new products *with* Gart v. Electroscope, Inc., 24 F.Supp.2d 969 (D.Minn.1998) (adequate explanation in risk factors relating to new products).

17. *Id.* at 656, 657.

18. *See, e.g.,* Uniform Securities Act § 304; chapter 8 *infra.*

19. 42 S.E.C. 163 (SEC 1964).

all material transactions between the issuer, its affiliates, and management.[20] It was at least arguable that the pledges of stock in question were not subject to such provisions since these were not transactions between Glickman and the issuer, but rather were between Glickman and a bank that was not affiliated with the issuer.[21] However, the Commission pointed out that an investor's evaluation of management is an important part of any investment decision, especially in a business such as real estate syndication, in which the management's know-how is the primary asset of the enterprise. Thus, any facts which would be likely to indicate a possible change of management would be material to the reasonable investor. The Commission concluded that disclosure of the secured loans was necessary because it would put the investor on notice that Glickman's interest in the company might be foreclosed upon, and that the corporation's management would change as a result. In the course of its opinion in *Franchard*, the Commission also highlighted the importance of adequately disclosing questionable activities by management. Questionable dealings by management can bear upon the issue of management integrity generally, which, of course, may be a valid investor concern.[23] Item 401 of Regulation S–K requires certain disclosures relating to management and control persons.[24] For example, members of management and control persons must disclose certain legal proceedings which have occurred in the preceding five years and are "material to an evaluation of the ability or integrity of any director, person nominated to become a director or executive officer of the registrant."[25] The disclosure obligation applied to sanctions against a controlled person's corporation even if he or she was not a named party in the underlying proceeding.[26]

The precise limits of the *Franchard* decision's rationale are not self-evident. The decision raises questions as to the materiality of disclosures relating to the personal aspects of the lives and dealings of key personnel. It is relatively evident that Glickman's crucial position in running the enterprise

---

20.   *See* Schedule A item (14); Form S–1 item 17; Form S–2 item 12.

21.   Glickman, who was president of the company, had also taken personal loans from the issuer and its affiliates. These loans clearly should have been disclosed as transactions with the issuer. *Id.*

23.   SEC v. Joseph Schlitz Brewing Co., 452 F.Supp. 824 (E.D.Wis.1978) (nondisclosure of commercial kickback payments was material because it related to management integrity); In the Matter of Franchard Corp., 42 S.E.C. 163 (SEC 1964) (nondisclosures of off-book loans to C.E.O. related to management integrity and were material). *Compare, e.g.,* Gaines v. Haughton, 645 F.2d 761 (9th Cir.1981) (drawing distinction between director breaches of trust which are presumptively material and allegations of waste of corporate assets). *But cf.* Darby v. Century Business Services, Inc., 96 Fed. Appx. 277 (6th Cir. 2004) (allegations that chairman of the board was described as having a sterling business record with other companies, without disclosing that he had paid largest insider trading fine in history of Canada and was "shady operator through offshore accounts," did not satisfy heightened pleading requirements for securities fraud claim under Private Securities Litigation Reform Act (PSLRA), given failure to identify any statement made that allegedly was misleading, and thus to plead misstatements about chairman's business record with requisite particularity).

Not every potential problem involving high ranking officials will necessarily rise to the level of material facts that need to be disclosed. *Cf.* State of New Jersey v. Sprint Corp., 314 F.Supp.2d 1119 (D. Kan. 2004) (no duty to disclose possibility that two high level executives might have to leave the company because of tax problems relating to tax shelter investments).

24.   17 C.F.R. § 229.401.

25.   Reg. S–K item 401(f), 17 C.F.R. § 229.401(f).

26.   *See* United States v. Yeaman, 194 F.3d 442 (3d Cir.1999) (officer director and controlling shareholder of corporation subject to SEC sanctions had to disclose those proceedings pursuant to item 401(f)).

made his high risk personal financial transactions material to prospective investors. On the other hand, there are many companies which are dependent upon one or a few key executives who may be undergoing changes or pressures in their personal lives that might bear upon their management ability. At what point do these factors become material? For example, must it be disclosed that a corporate chief executive officer is in ill health? Is it a material fact that a major corporate executive is under psychiatric care and potentially suicidal? Is it relevant that a corporate executive is in the midst of a harrowing divorce and suffering severe depression which might interfere with his or her management ability? Clearly, at some point such information becomes more personal to the executive than useful to the investing public. But it is equally clear that an attorney preparing a registration statement has no bright line tests regarding which aspects of a key executive's personal life will be deemed material for disclosure purposes. When an executive's personal dealings affect the issuer's business or at least present a strong potential for doing so, the materiality threshold may be reached and therefore disclosure will probably be necessary.

There are two other decisions that deserve mention in this discussion of transactions by controlling persons. In one case,[29] the registration statement was claimed to have been materially misleading because it failed to disclose that two major shareholders intended to dispose of their holdings shortly after the public offering. These transactions amounted to twenty-five percent of the number of shares covered by the registration statement but only four percent of the total stock that was outstanding after the offering. The federal district court held that there was a triable issue of fact as to the materiality of the alleged omission and accordingly refused to dismiss the complaint. In another case,[30] the registration statement disclosed the sale of one hundred and twenty thousand shares in a private placement that had taken place two years earlier. It was further stated that those private placement purchasers had agreed not to dispose of their shares in a transaction that would constitute a public distribution unless a registration statement covering such sales had become effective. Shortly after an unrelated registered offering, these private placement purchasers sold a total of seven thousand shares without filing a registration statement and in reliance upon the exemption provided in SEC Rule 144.[31] The plaintiff alleged that these sales were contrary to the disclosures in the registration statement, and, since they had been intended all along, rendered the registration statement materially misleading. The plaintiff further claimed that although the unregistered sales may have been in compliance with Rule 144, they depressed the market price of the plaintiff's stock that had been purchased during the primary offering and thus that failure to have described this predictable impact was a material omission. The court, agreeing with the plaintiff, held that the registration statement was misleading in failing to adequately describe Rule 144 and its exemption from the registration requirements of section 5. A fair description of the effects under Rule 144 would have put the investor on notice of the possibility of insider sales that would not need to be registered and might also have an adverse effect on the market price.

29.   Birdman v. Electro–Catheter Corp., 352 F.Supp. 1271 (E.D.Pa.1973).

30.   Langert v. Q–1 Corp., 1974 WL 377, [1973–1974 Transfer Binder] Fed.Sec.L.Rep. 94,445 (S.D.N.Y.1974).

31.   17 C.F.R. § 230.144. See § 4.29 infra.

The foregoing cases are illustrative of sensitive disclosure problems that may arise in connection with a registered offering. Counsel must be particularly mindful of these problems in making the pre-filing investigation into the issuer and the circumstances surrounding the offering.

§ 3.9[4] Projections and Soft Information

At one time, the SEC objected to the use of favorable projections and other "soft" information in disclosure documents on the grounds that investors would likely be misled.[36] This policy of discouraging projections came under much criticism from many constituencies.[37] It was contended, among other things, that projections by management can provide useful information to the investing public. In response to the criticism of its former policy, the Commission reconsidered its approach to soft information[38] and now not only permits but in fact encourages,[39] and in some cases mandates, the use of non-misleading projections by certain issuers.

SEC Rule 175[41] (applicable to 1933 Act disclosures) and Rule 3b-6[42] (applicable to 1934 Act disclosures) provide a safe harbor for projections by 1934 Act reporting companies[43] and for similar disclosures made in the 1933 Act registration statements. These rules provide that there is no liability for "forward-looking statements" unless the issuer made or reaffirmed such a statement without a reasonable basis or unless the disclosure was not made in good faith. Thus, a good faith statement of present intent does not become actionable simply because of a change of intent;[47] however, the change of intent which makes the previous statement no longer accurate will give rise to an obligation to give timely notice of that change by making a corrective disclosure.[48] While a good faith statement of intent will not be actionable, a statement made without any reasonable basis may be.[49]

The fact that a projection turns out not to be realized does not, standing alone, give rise to a cause of action under the securities laws.[50] The complaint must therefore be based on something more than the fact that the projections

36. *See* Carl W. Schneider, Nits, Grits, and Soft Information in SEC Filings, 121 U.Pa.L.Rev. 254 (1972). *Cf.* Goldman v. Belden, 580 F.Supp. 1373 (W.D.N.Y.1984), *judgment vacated* 754 F.2d 1059 (2d Cir.1985) ("faulty economic prognostication" did not violate antifraud provisions).

The Commission took the view that material unfavorable projections need be disclosed while favorable projections should not be contained in disclosure documents. This asymmetrical view was changed in Rule 175. 17 C.F.R. § 230.175.

37. *E.g.*, Bruce A. Mann, Prospectuses: Unreadable or Just Unread?—A Proposal to Reexamine Policies Against Permitting Projections, 40 Geo.Wash.L.Rev. 222 (1971).

38. *See* Sec.Act Rel. No. 33–5992 (Nov. 7, 1978; rescinded in Sec.Act Rel. No. 33–6384 (March 3, 1982)). (Guides for disclosure of future economic performance). *See also* Note, Disclosure of Future–Oriented Information Under Securities Laws, 88 Yale L.J. 338 (1978).

39. *See, e.g.*, Instruction 7 to Regulation S–K Item 303(a) which provides that "forward-looking information" is "encouraged, but not required." 17 C.F.R. § 229.303(a), Instruction 7.

41. 17 C.F.R. § 230.175.

42. 17 C.F.R. § 240.3b–6.

43. *See* 15 U.S.C.A. §§ 78g, 78m(a), 78o(d) which are discussed in §§ 9.2, 9.3 *infra*.

47. In re Phillips Petroleum Securities Litigation, 881 F.2d 1236, 1245 (3d Cir.1989), *on remand* 738 F.Supp. 825 (D.Del.1990).

48. *Id.*

49. Snap–On Inc. v. Ortiz, 1999 WL 592194, [1999–2000 Transfer Binder] Fed. Sec. L. Rep. (CCH) ¶¶ 90,633 (N.D. Ill. 1999) (corporate officer's statement that he intended to remain with company would be actionable if made without reasonable basis).

50. *See, e.g.*, Hillson Partners Limited Partnership v. Adage, Inc., 42 F.3d 204 (4th Cir.1994).

did not come to fruition.[51] Projections by their very nature may or may not prove to be accurate. Therefore, the issue is not whether a projection turns out not to come to fruition. The critical question is whether the projection was fraudulent when made. There must be some material misstatement or omission from the projection. The fact that the method used for projections has been accurate in the past will act against finding a projection to be actionable.[55] As discussed below, adequate cautionary language can prevent a projection from being fraudulent. As is the case with projections, a statement of opinion that turns out not to be an accurate reflection of future events is not actionable under the securities laws.[57]

Many courts have indicated that they will tolerate a certain amount of sales puffery to the extent that reliance on such statements would not be reasonable.[58] However, nondisclosure that in the past there had been a repeated failure to meet projected performance may be actionable.[59] Similarly, a projection that is inconsistent with undisclosed facts will be actionable.[60] However, when the forecast is consistent with past performance, no action will lie.[61] Nor will a projection turn out to be actionable when the alleged undisclosed facts are not material.

Overly optimistic projections can, of course, form the basis of a private civil action by purchasers injured by materially misleading statements.[63] Similarly, forward-looking statements which fail to include projected losses may be materially misleading.[64] However, following the rules established under the common law of fraud, a mere projection,[65] forecast,[66] or prediction of future events is not actionable.[67] Nevertheless, when the incorrect prediction implies the presence of facts which do not exist, then an action will lie for

---

51. *See, e.g.,* In re Seagate Technology II Securities Litigation, 1995 WL 66841, [1994–1995 Transfer Binder] Fed. Sec. L.Rep. (CCH) ¶ 98,530 (N.D.Cal.1995) (executive's optimism was consistent with independent industry analysts and thus was not actionable).

55. *See, e.g.,* In re Sybase, Inc. Securities Litigation, 48 F.Supp.2d 958 (N.D.Cal.1999).

57. *See, e.g.,* Eisenstadt v. Centel Corp., 113 F.3d 738 (7th Cir.1997) (repeated statements that auction process was going smoothly was not actionable).

58. *E.g.,* In re Advanta Corp. Securities Litigation, 180 F.3d 525, 538–539 (3d Cir.1999) (optimistic statements about the future were "mere puffery").

59. *See* Schwartz v. Michaels, 1992 WL 382394, [1992–1993 Transfer Binder] Fed.Sec.L.Rep. (CCH) ¶ 97,259 (S.D.N.Y.1992).

60. *E.g.,* Malone v. Microdyne Corp., 26 F.3d 471 (4th Cir.1994).

61. *E.g.,* Bentley v. Legent Corp., 849 F.Supp. 429 (E.D.Va.1994) (statements that operations were "on plan" or "on target" were not actionable).

63. *See, e.g.,* Goldman v. Belden, 754 F.2d 1059 (2d Cir.1985); Eisenberg v. Gagnon, 766 F.2d 770 (3d Cir.1985), *cert. denied* 474 U.S. 946, 106 S.Ct. 342, 88 L.Ed.2d 290 (1985).

64. C.E. Carlson, Inc. v. SEC, 859 F.2d 1429 (10th Cir.1988) (affirming denial of summary judgment for defendant).

65. According to the American Institute of Certified Public Accountants, financial projections deal with financial position, results of operations, and changes in financial position that are based on "knowledge and belief, given one or more hypothetical assumptions." AICPA Financial Forecasts and Projections Task Force, Guide For Prospective Financial Statements 12. Projections, thus, set forth one or more possible scenarios of future performance.

66. In contrast to financial projections, financial forecasts are based on actual expectations rather than upon hypothetical assumptions but reflect "to the best of the responsible party's knowledge and belief, an entity's expected financial position, results of operations, and changes in financial position" based on "assumptions reflecting conditions it expects to exist and the course of action it expects to take." *Id.* at 11.

67. *E.g.,* Hillson Partners L.P. v. Adage, Inc., 42 F.3d 204 (4th Cir.1994) (Chief executive officer's statements in press release that the year would produce "excellent" results were merely predictions and thus not actionable misrepresentations of fact).

misrepresentation.[68] The materiality of contingent events is judged in light of the magnitude of the event and its probability.[69] Possibilities that are extremely contingent or speculative are not material.[70]

Absent a specific line item disclosure requirement or the impetus of the Management Discussion and Analysis,[71] there is no requirement that management make projections or predictions.[72] The fact that management has made internal projections and even has made confidential projections to entities outside the corporation does not in itself trigger a duty of public disclosure.[73] A company is thus not subject to a public disclosure requirement simply because it has made some private projections.[74] The court went on to point out that the nondisclosure to the public of projections might have been actionable had the projections been "based upon existing negative factors that were known only to the company."[75]

§ 3.9[5] Statutory Safe Harbor for Forward–Looking Statements

Section 27A of the 1933 Act,[77] which was part of the Private Securities Litigation Reform Act of 1995, provides a safe harbor for forward-looking statements and protects issuers from private litigation based on good faith projections. As described in a number of decisions, "[i]n order to be eligible for safe harbor, the forward-looking statements must either (1) be identified as forward-looking and be accompanied by meaningful cautionary language; (2) be immaterial; or (3) not be made with actual knowledge that the

---

68. *E.g.* Rodney v. KPMG Peat Marwick, 143 F.3d 1140 (8th Cir.1998) (question of fact whether prospectus for mortgage-related securities fund contained material misrepresentations of risk).

69. *E.g.*, Basic Inc. v. Levinson, 485 U.S. 224, 238, 108 S.Ct. 978, 987, 99 L.Ed.2d 194 (1988); United States v. Mylett, 97 F.3d 663, 667 (2d Cir.1996). See § 12.9 *infra.*

70. Klein v. General Nutrition Cos., 186 F.3d 338 (3d Cir.1999).

71. Item 303 of Regulation S–K requires management to give certain projections with regard to known material adverse or favorable trends in operations and financial condition. *See, e.g.,* Mark S. Croft, MD & A: The Tightrope of disclosure, 45 S.C. L. Rev. 477 (1994). *See also* Appendix A (Practitioner's Edition only).

72. *See, e.g.,* Proxima Corp. Securities Litigation, 1994 WL 374306, [1993–1994 Transfer Binder] Fed. Sec. L. Rep. (CCH) ¶ 98,236 (S.D.Cal.1994).

73. Levit v. Lyondell Petrochemical Co., 984 F.2d 1050 (9th Cir.1993); Glassman v. Computervision Corp., 90 F.3d 617 (1st Cir.1996) (fact that quarter's results lagged behind internal projections did not trigger a duty of disclosure); Saddle Rock Partners, Ltd. v. Hiatt, 1996 WL 859986, [1997 Transfer Binder] Fed. Sec. L. Rep. (CCH) ¶¶ 99,413 (W.D. Tenn. 1996) (failure to disclose internal projections was not actionable); In re Cirrus Logic Securities Litigation, 946 F.Supp. 1446 (N.D.Cal.1996) (failure to disclose internal projections while making earnings estimates was not actionable); Sheppard v. TCW/DW Term Trust 2000, 938 F.Supp. 171 (S.D.N.Y.1996) (internal projections were not material facts that had to be disclosed in prospectus). *See also, e.g.,* In re Convergent Technologies Securities Litigation, 948 F.2d 507 (9th Cir.1991) (failure to give detailed internal projections about new product line was not actionable); In re Compaq Securities Litigation, 848 F.Supp. 1307 (S.D.Tex.1993) (no duty to disclose management's internal consideration of effects of general economic conditions).

74. Levit v. Lyondell Petrochemical Co., 984 F.2d 1050 (9th Cir.1993). *Accord* Walter v. Holiday Inns, Inc., 985 F.2d 1232 (3d Cir.1993). *But cf.* Schwartz v. System Software Associates, Inc., 813 F.Supp. 1364 (N.D.Ill.1993) (undisclosed internal written forecasts could demonstrate that public disclosures were materially misleading).

75. 984 F.2d at 1053.

77. 15 U.S.C.A. § 77z–2. A parallel section was added to the 1934 Act. 15 U.S.C.A. § 78u–5(c). *See* § 129 *infra.*

statement was false or misleading."[79] Once established, the statutory safe harbor will protect the defendant from liability in a private suit. However, to ensure protection from SEC actions, an issuer must satisfy the safe harbor requirements for soft information set forth in 1933 Act Rule 175.[80] The section 27A safe harbor allows corporate management to disclose forward-looking information[81] and projections to investors while retaining protection under the safe harbor. Section 27A applies to 1934 Act reporting companies, persons acting on behalf of such companies, outside reviewers retained by such companies, and underwriters deriving or obtaining forward-looking information from such companies. Additionally, the statute explicitly does not impose a duty to update forward-looking statements.[82] The statutory safe harbor applies only to forward-looking statements. It is not always easy to distinguish forward-looking statements that will get the protection of the safe harbor from statements of fact that will not. For example, a statement that a company was "on target" to meet expectations was held not to be a forward-looking statement and thus the protections of the safe harbor did not apply.[85]

In order to comply with the safe harbor, an issuer must satisfy at least one of its two prongs. Under the first prong, an issuer must identify all written or oral forward-looking statements as forward-looking and provide "meaningful cautionary statements" that identify important factors that could cause actual results to differ materially from those in the forward-looking statement. This prong of the safe harbor incorporates the judicially created "bespeaks caution" doctrine and elements of Rule 175. Boilerplate language will not satisfy the requirement of "meaningful cautionary" language; instead, substantive information about the factors that could affect the reliability of the forward-looking statement must be provided.[88] Issuers seeking to invoke the section 27A safe harbor must identify important factors in the statements that could materially affect the projection. This does not mean an issuer must identify all factors or that if an issuer fails to identify the factor which ultimately changes the forward-looking projection, it will fall outside the safe harbor. The use of the language "meaningful" and "important factors" in section 27A is meant to provide a standard for courts in deciding what constitutes a cautionary statement. However, on appropriate facts, courts may continue to find that a forward-looking statement is immaterial and therefore, not actionable under the 1933 and 1934 Acts.

The second prong of the safe harbor provision requires a plaintiff in a private action to establish that the individual or business entity made the forward-looking statement with actual knowledge that it was false or misleading.[89] This requirement focuses on the state of mind of the person or entity making the projection rather than the content of the cautionary statements. The essence of this prong is that the intent of the speaker is more important

79. In re Sun Healthcare Group Securities Litigation, 181 F.Supp.2d 1283, 1288 (D.N.M.2002) (decided under the 1934 Act counterpart).

80. 17 C.F.R. § 230.175.

81. *See, e.g.,* Ehlert v. Singer, 245 F.3d 1313 (11th Cir.2001) (section of prospectus concerning risks of technological change was forward-looking despite inclusion of some statements of present conditions).

A similar safe harbor applies to 1934 Act disclosures. *See, e.g.,* In re Pacific Gateway Exchange, Inc., Securities Litigation, 2002 WL 851066, Fed.Sec.L. Rep. ¶ 91906 (N.D.Cal.2002) (applying safe arbor to protect forward-looking statements in Form 10–K filing).

82. 1933 Act section 27A(d), 15 U.S.C.A. § 77z–2(d) ("Nothing in this section shall impose upon any person a duty to update a forward-looking statement").

85. In re Secure Computing Corp. Securities Litigation, 120 F.Supp.2d 810 (N.D.Cal.2000).

88. H.R. Conf. Rep. No. 104–369, 104th Cong., 1st Sess. at 43 (1995).

89. *See, e.g.,* Helwig v. Vencor, Inc., 251 F.3d 540 (6th Cir.2001).

than the misleading impact of the statement on the plaintiff. Even if the plaintiff can establish the requisite intent, his or her claim will fail if the bespeaks caution doctrine has been properly satisfied. This is so because the language of the statute also indicates that even if a statement is identified as knowingly false under the second prong of the safe harbor test, if it satisfies the first prong the forward-looking statement, it will nevertheless remain not actionable.

§ 3.9[6] The Bespeaks Caution Doctrine

As discussed above, the essence of liability for materially misleading projections is not that the prediction did not prove accurate but rather that the investor has been misled as to the reliability of the projections.[94] Thus, it is beyond question that under appropriate circumstances, warnings and disclaimers can limit investors' ability to reasonably rely on projections of future earnings.[95] A number of courts have adopted what is sometimes referred to as the "bespeaks caution" doctrine.[96] In 1995, Congress codified the bespeaks caution doctrine,[97] holds that sufficient cautionary language may preclude misstatements from being actionable.[98] The doctrine relates to materiality since it addresses the question of whether the misstatements are materially misleading when judged in light of the total mix of information available to the investor.[99] The bespeaks caution doctrine, which applies both to material misstatements and omissions in connection with projections and predictions,[100] should not be applied too quickly.[101] Properly viewed, the bespeaks caution doctrine applies only to projections, predictions, and other "soft information"; it will not be applicable to negate material misstatements of present or historical facts.[102] Thus, a defendant must first establish that the alleged misstatement is, in fact, forward-looking. Even with regard to projections and predictions, cautionary language will not always be adequate to prevent an antifraud claim,[103] especially if it is generalized and boiler-plate. Nor should the doctrine be applied if the falsity of the statements was known

---

94. *See, e.g.,* In re Infonet Services Corp. Securities Litigation, 310 F.Supp.2d 1080, 1103 (C.D. Cal. 2003) (citing this treatise).

95. Harris v. Ivax Corp., 182 F.3d 799 (11th Cir.1999) (projections of future losses were protected by safe harbor and cautionary language); Eizenga v. Stewart Enterprises, Inc., 124 F.Supp.2d 967 (E.D.La.2000) (forward-looking statements were not actionable); Friedman v. Arizona World Nurseries Ltd. Partnership, 730 F.Supp. 521 (S.D.N.Y.1990).

96. For a discussion of the evolution of the doctrine, *see* In re Donald J. Trump Casino Securities Litigation, 793 F.Supp. 543 (D.N.J.1992), *affirmed* 7 F.3d 357 (3d Cir.1993).

97. 1933 Act § 27A(c)(2), 15 U.S.C.A. § 77z–2(c)(2); 1934 Act § 21E(c)(2), 15 U.S.C.A. § 78u–5(c)(2). See §§ 7.17, 12.15 *infra.*

98. *E.g.,* In re Syntex Corp. Securities Litigation, 95 F.3d 922 (9th Cir.1996) (statement that FDA settlement would not have a material adverse effect was not actionable, the statement adequately bespoke caution that the outcome could not be predicted with certainty).

99. *See, e.g.,* Asher v. Baxter International, Inc., 377 F.3d 727 (7th Cir. 2004) (discovery was necessary to determine if bespeaks caution doctrine applied); In re Donald J. Trump Casino Securities Litigation, 7 F.3d 357, 371 (3d Cir.1993).

100. *See, e.g.,* In re Donald J. Trump Casino Securities Litigation, 7 F.3d 357, 371 (3d Cir.1993).

101. *See, e.g.,* In re ValueVision International Inc. Securities Litigation, 896 F.Supp. 434, 443 (E.D.Pa.1995) ("in order to conclude that cautionary statements render the misrepresentations and omissions immaterial, a defendant must prove that the cautionary statements 'discredit the other one so obviously that the risk of deception drops to nil' ").

102. Shaw v. Digital Equipment Corp., 82 F.3d 1194 (1st Cir.1996).

103. *E.g.,* Asher v. Baxter International, Inc., 377 F.3d 727 (7th Cir. 2004) (discovery was necessary to determine if bespeaks caution doctrine applied).

to the defendants at the time of the cautionary warnings.[105] In order for the bespeaks caution doctrine to justify the dismissal of fraud claims, the cautionary language must be sufficient to negate any reasonable reliance on predictions that may appear optimistic. The bespeaks caution doctrine may not be invoked when the warnings are given while the speaker is in possession of nonpublic facts inconsistent with the projections being made.[107] In such a case, the cautionary language itself may be a materially misleading statement.

§ 3.9[7] Management Discussion and Analysis

In addition to these voluntary projections, an issuer must disclose in the registration statement material changes in financial condition and operations that are expected to take place as a result of the financing to be raised by the offering covered by the 1933 Act registration.[126] Similarly, soft information relating to asset valuations may be mandated material disclosures under the Securities Exchange Act of 1934.[127] Even more striking is the soft information required by item 303 of Regulation S–K in the course of its Management Discussion and Analysis (MD&A) of financial condition and report of operations, requiring management to disclose and discuss both adverse and favorable trends and uncertainties.[128] The MD&A disclosures focus not only on current operations but also on management's plans for the future.

The SEC Release that introduced the MD&A disclosure requirements is very instructive as to their purpose and operation. The SEC Release appears as Appendix B at the end of this treatise.

The purpose of the MD&A disclosures is to provide one portion of the prospectus or other disclosure document that is devoted to a narrative analysis of the company's financial condition.[129] Most of the discussion and disclosures in a registration statement are limited to historical facts. Factual disclosures alone cannot provide a basis for forecasting the future.[130] The MD&A disclosures are designed to give investors a better basis for assessing the future prospects of the company in making their decision to invest in the securities covered by the registration statement.[131]

Although item 303 requires disclosure of "known trends or uncertainties," it does not alter the basic rule that projections are not required.[132] Thus,

---

105. *See* In re Grand Casinos, Inc., Securities Litigation, 988 F.Supp. 1273 (D.Minn.1997).

107. Voit v. Wonderware Corp., 977 F.Supp. 363 (E.D.Pa.1997) (bespeaks caution doctrine could not be raised as defense to presently known facts).

126. Regulation S–K, item 303, 17 C.F.R. § 229.303.

127. *E.g.,* Flynn v. Bass Brothers Enterprises, Inc., 744 F.2d 978 (3d Cir.1984) (section 14(e) of the Williams Act requires disclosure of material asset valuations given in the course of a tender offer).

128. *E.g.,* Form S–1, Item 11(h); Form SB–2, Item 17. *See* Management Discussion and Analysis of Financial Condition, Sec. Act Rel. No. 33–6835 (SEC May 18, 1989).

129. *See* Management's Discussion and Analysis of Financial Condition and Results of Operations, Sec. Act Rel. No. 33–6835, 1989 WL 258977 (SEC May 18, 1989).

130. *See, e.g.* In re Convergent Technologies Securities Litigation, 948 F.2d 507, 512–514 (9th Cir.1991).

131. *See* Concept Release on Management's Discussion and Analysis of Financial Condition and Operations, Sec. Act Rel. No. 33–6711, 1987 WL 112322 (SEC Apr. 24, 1987).

132. Instruction 7 to Regulation S–K Item 303(a) which provides that "forward-looking information" is "encouraged, but not required." 17 C.F.R. § 229.303(a), Instruction 7.

a failure to make a projection is not actionable unless there is a nondisclosure of facts or known trends that were "known only to the company."[133] Similarly, in contrast to the MD&A mandate that management make timely disclosure of known trends, it is clear that standing alone there is no duty to disclose internal projections of future performance.[134]

Failure to disclose uncertainties resulting from volatile economic and political conditions can also violate the MD&A disclosure mandate.[138] Failure to discuss a known trend of decreasing sales will violate the MD&A requirements.[139] Similarly, it was a violation to fail to discuss the impact that a trend of decreasing sales would have on net sales, revenues, and earnings.[140]

MD&A disclosures require management to disclose their current evaluation of trends[140.5] and uncertainties, but they do not require management to foresee the future. The adequacy of the disclosures should not be judged by hindsight. Accordingly, a failure to foresee a slow down and disclose it as a trend in the MD&A was held not actionable.[144] However, a failure to discuss the impact of a production delay that the company was experiencing did violate MD&A.[145] Also, a failure to discuss the impact of accounting practices can violate the MD&A requirements.[146]

The MD&A disclosures are part of the periodic reporting requirements and thus do not depend upon whether the information has already been disseminated into the market. Thus, the fact that information has already been disclosed in a press release does not alleviate the necessity of making appropriate MD&A disclosures.[147]

The MD&A disclosure requirements of Item 303(a) or Regulation S–K do not by themselves provide a basis for a private right of action.[152] On appropriate facts, however, inadequate MD&A disclosures can give rise to liability under SEC Rule 10b–5 or section 11 of the 1933 Act.

133. Levit v. Lyondell Petrochemical Co., 984 F.2d 1050, 1053 (9th Cir.1993), relying in part on In re Convergent Technologies Securities Litigation, 948 F.2d 507, 516 (9th Cir.1991).

134. In re VeriFone Securities Litigation, 11 F.3d 865 (9th Cir.1993).

138. In re Caterpillar Inc., Exch. Act Rel. No. 34–30532, 6 Fed.Sec.L.Rep. (CCH) ¶ 73,829 (SEC March 31, 1992) (settlement order).

139. Shared Medical Systems, Inc., Administrative Proceeding File No. 3–8295, Sec. Exch. Act Rel. No. 34–33632, 56 S.E.C. Docket 199, 1994 WL 49960 (SEC Feb. 17, 1994).

140. *Id.*

140.5 A trend is something more than a one time occurrence and thus refers to "persistent conditions" with respect to the company's business environment. Kapps v. Torch Offshore, Inc., 379 F.3d 207 (5th Cir. 2004) (60% decline in price of natural gas was not a "trend"); Oxford Asset Management, Ltd. v. Jaharis, 297 F.3d 1182, 1191 (11th Cir.2002).

144. Steckman v. Hart Brewing, Inc., 143 F.3d 1293 (9th Cir.1998).

145. In re Presstek, Inc., Administrative Proceeding File No. 3–9515, Sec. Exch. Act Rel. No. 34–39472, 66 S.E.C. Docket 328, Release No. AE–997, 1997 WL 784548 (SEC Dec. 15, 1997).

146. *See, e.g.,* In re Skaff, Administrative Proceeding File No. 3–9878, Sec. Exch. Act Rel. No. 34–41313, 69 S.E.C. Docket 1415, Release No. AE–112, 1999 WL 228426 (SEC April 20, 1999).

147. In re Shared Medical Systems Corp., Sec. Exch. Act Rel. No. 34–33632 (SEC Feb. 17, 1994) (failure to disclose slower than anticipated sales activity even though there had been public disclosure of those difficulties).

152. Oran v. Stafford, 226 F.3d 275 (3d Cir.2000); In Re Rasterops Corp. Securities Litigation, 1993 WL 183510, [1992–1993 Transfer Binder] CCH Fed. Sec. L. Rep. & 97,445, at 96,488 (N.D. Cal.1993).

§ 3.9[8] Duties to Correct and Update

As discussed in a later section of this treatise,[158] there is no duty to disclose material information absent a line-item disclosure requirement.[159] However, once the issuer has made a statement on a topic, there may be a duty to update or correct the information should it become stale or inaccurate. Accordingly, once a company has made statements of fact, there is a duty to correct if it is later determined that the information was in fact materially inaccurate. The issue is more difficult with regard to earnings (or other) projections and when the issuer has an obligation to make corrective disclosures when it becomes evident that the projections are inadequate. The proper distinction is between correction of inaccurate factual statements—where there is a duty to correct and situations where the projections simply turn out not to come to pass. Since projections are by their nature likely not to be completely predictive of the future, the trend is to find no duty to update a projection that was proper at the time simply because as time progresses, the projection appears more likely to prove inaccurate.

§ 3.10 Presentation of Disclosure; Plain English

Regulation S–K provides detailed guidance for compliance with the line-item disclosure that is required by the various forms and schedules that have to be filed with the SEC under both the Securities Act of 1933 and the Securities Exchange Act of 1934.[1] However, those disclosure guides do not directly address drafting issues and writing style. Over the years, the Commission has been concerned with the readability of prospectuses and other disclosures.[2] It is important that disclosure filings explain rather than obscure the pertinent issues. The discussion that follows examines issues of readability and the SEC's plain English requirements.[3]

§ 3.10[2] The Plain English Requirements

As pointed out in an earlier section of this treatise,[15] in January 1997, the SEC proposed various amendments to require the use of clear, concise and understandable language in prospectuses.[16] The proposal was part of the SEC's larger initiative to require the use of "plain English" in SEC filings and reports to shareholders and investors. The purpose of the plain English disclosures is to make it easy for the ordinary investor to understand the disclosures.

---

158. *See* § 12.19 *infra.*

159. *E.g.*, Gallagher v. Abbott Laboratories, 269 F.3d 806 (7th Cir.2001).

§ 3.10

1. Regulation S–K (17 C.F.R. §§ 229.10 *et seq.*) and the parallel disclosure guides for small business issuers in Regulation S–B (17 C.F.R. §§ 228.10 *et seq.*) are discussed in § 3.4[4][A] *supra* and § 9.4 *infra.*

2. *See, e.g.*, Report to the SEC on Disclosure to Investors ("The Wheat Report") 54 (1969). *See also, e.g.*, Milton Cohen, "Truth in Securities" Revisited, 79 Harv. L. Rev. 1340, 1351–1352 (1966); Robert Knauss, A Reappraisal of the Role of Disclosure, 62 Mich. L. Re. 607 (1964).

3. For examples of plain English, *see* § 3.10 [2] *infra.*

15. *See* § 3.8[2] *supra.*

16. Plain English Disclosure, Sec. Act Rel. No. 33–7380, 62 Fed. Reg. 3152, 1997 WL 17695 (F.R.) (SEC Jan. 27, 1997). *See also, e.g.*, Note, Eschew Obfuscation—The Merits of the SEC's Plain English Doctrine, 31 U. Mem. L. Rev. 135 (2000); Note, Plain English: A Reappraisal of the Intended Audience of Disclosure Under the Securities Act of 1933, 72 So. Cal. L. Rev. 851 (1999).

The plain English initiative, which evolved from a pilot program into a permanent one, involves amendments to various provisions of Regulations S–K and Regulation S–B. In a lengthy and helpful official release,[18] the Commission describes what it means by plain English and also provides several examples of appropriate disclosure styles.[19] The SEC plain English manual along with some SEC staff interpretations are reproduced as Appendix A of this treatise.

The SEC implemented its plain English initiative and now requires that in drafting disclosure documents, registrants should be aware of the readership of the disclosures and, of course, should also familiarize themselves with the substantive requirements that determine which information needs to be disclosed. In preparing the disclosures, registrants should employ "clear writing techniques" in order provide for more effective communication of the information subject to disclosure. The Commission further explains what it means by plain English. Disclosures should be made in the active rather than passive voice. Drafters of disclosure documents should use short sentences using definite, concrete, everyday language. Drafters of disclosure documents can make the disclosures more readable by using tabular presentations and bullet lists where appropriate. The plain English release cautions against the use of legal jargon and highly technical business terminology. Finally, the SEC encourages the avoidance of multiple negatives. In addition to the foregoing stylistic lessons, the plain English release emphasizes that registrants should design and organize their disclosure documents so they are "easy and inviting to read." The plain English guidelines thus call for the increased use of white space in order to make the prospectus more readable. The Commission showed its commitment to the plain English program by following it in its own rulemaking, most notably with its revisions to the shareholder proposal rule.[20]

§ 3.11   Delayed and Continuous Offerings—Shelf Registrations

It is generally contemplated that the entire allotment of securities covered by a registered offering will be made available for purchase on the effective date. This is not always the case, however. For example, insiders, promoters or underwriters might receive securities directly from the issuer with an intent to resell at a later date.[1] Delayed offerings may also arise in connection with corporate acquisitions.[2] Also, in light of fluctuating interest rates, it may be desirable to get a debt offering all ready to go by filing the applicable registration statement, but then wait for a propitious moment to finalize it and offer the securities for sale. These and other delayed offerings

---

18. Plain English Disclosure, Sec. Act Rel. No. 33–7497, 63 Fed. Reg. 6370–01, 1988 WL 44199 (F.R.) (SEC Feb. 6, 1998).

19. *See* Appendix A.

20. Rule 14a–8, 17 C.F.R. § 14a–8(c). *See* Peter J. Romeo & Richard J. Parrino, The New Shareholder Proposal Rules, 31 Rev. Sec. & Commodities Reg. 203 (1998). *See* § 10.8 *infra.*

§ 3.11

1. *See generally* Symposium, Current Problems of Securities Underwriters and Dealers, 18 Bus.Law. 27, 44–55 (1962).

2. This may arise in a transaction when controlling persons of the acquired company receive securities of the acquiring corporation. Rule 145 governs such transactions and Form S–14 allows for delayed offerings under limited circumstances. *See* 17 C.F.R. § 230.145 which is discussed in § 5.2 *infra.*

have led to what is known as shelf registration. In a shelf registration the registration statement is filed but the securities are put on the shelf until the manner and date of the offering are determined.

For a long time the SEC took a dim view of shelf registrations, primarily because of the potential for misleading the investing public. Section 6(a) of the 1933 Act provides that a registration statement's effectiveness is limited to securities to be offered.[4] The Commission formerly adhered to the position that "it is misleading to include in a registration statement 'more securities than are presently intended to be offered, and thus give securities offered at some remote future date at least the appearance of a registered status.' "[5] Furthermore, there was concern that permitting delayed offerings would conflict with the thrust of the Securities Act; it, thus, had been observed that "[t]he fact that the time and manner of distribution is not presently determinable clashes with the theory that the registration statement must speak as of the date of its effectiveness."[6]

Over time, much of the weight behind the foregoing objections has yielded to market realities coming from various constituents of the financial community; there was an increased call for the additional flexibility in financing that would result from allowing more shelf registrations. One reason that has been advanced is that shelf registrations will promote more competitive rates among underwriters, as shelf registrations give issuers more negotiating room.[7] Additionally, shelf registrations have proved very helpful with debt offerings during periods of fluctuating interest rates.

Through the early 1980s, the Commission allowed shelf registrations only in a limited number of cases in which the offering plan was relatively definite and part of a larger offering.[9] In 1982, the Commission promulgated a shelf registration rule which was effective on an experimental basis until December, 1983.[10] In November 1983, the Commission decided that the experiment had been a success and adopted Rule 415, with some modification, on a permanent basis.[11] Except in certain circumstances (such as dividend reinvestment plans), shelf registration is not available to issuers who must use the long-form registration Form S–1 or even the abbreviated Form S–2 as opposed to the registration forms available for the most seasoned issuers. Additional circumstances under which the less seasoned issuers may take advantage of shelf registration are set forth below. Shelf registration is available, without restriction on the circumstances surrounding the offering, to those more established issuers which qualify for short form registration on Form S–3 or Form F–3 (for foreign issuers). Additionally, in order to qualify for any shelf registration, it must reasonably be expected that the securities so offered will be sold within two years of the effective date.

---

4. 15 U.S.C.A. § 77f(a) ("A registration statement shall be deemed effective only as to the securities specified therein as proposed to be offered.").

5. Shawnee Chiles Syndicate, 10 S.E.C. 109, 113 (SEC 1941).

6. Richard W. Jennings & Harold Marsh, Jr., Securities Regulation: Cases and Materials 390 (5th ed. 1982).

7. For a detailed discussion of the pros and cons, *see* Sec. Act Rel. No. 33–6423 (Sept. 2, 1982).

9. Sec. Act Rel. No. 33–4936, Guides 4, 10, 36, 53 (Dec. 9, 1968) (rescinded).

10. 17 C.F.R. § 230.415 (1982). *See* Sec. Act Rel. No. 33–6423 (Sept. 2, 1982).

11. Sec.Act Rel. No. 33–6499 (Nov. 17, 1983).

As part of its public offering reforms that were adopted in 2005,[13.5] the SEC eased its shelf offering rule as generally applied and also adopted a system of automatic shelf registration for well-known seasoned issuers (WKSIs).[13.10]

With respect to shelf registrations generally, the revised shelf registration rule expanded from two years to three years the time horizon for the aggregate amount of securities anticipated to be offered and thus to be put on the shelf. Restriction on "at market" offerings were also eliminated. The revisions codified and clarified the information to be included (as well as that to be excluded) from the base shelf registration statement; the rule also specifies the manner of including information in the registration statement. In addition the revised rule permits immediate takedowns of securities and also allows prospectus supplements (rather than the former requirement of post-effective amendments) for material changes in the plan of distribution that was described in the base prospectus.

The revised shelf registration rule is even more permissive for WKSIs. "Automatic shelf registration" means that when a WKSI files a shelf registration, its effectiveness is automatic. There is a pay-as-you-go structure for registration fees. WKSIs are allowed to file skeletal base registration statements and add the details later. For example, after the effective date, WKSIs can add to their shelf registrations both additional classes of securities and eligible majority-owned subsidiaries. WKSIs do not have to specify the amount of securities to be offered pursuant to the shelf registration. Furthermore, WKSIs are allowed to omit from the shelf registration more information than is allowed for other issuers. For example, WKSIs may omit whether it is a primary or secondary offering. A description of the securities (other than identification of the class of securities) may be omitted as may the names of any selling shareholders and disclosures regarding the plan of distribution. All of this information is then to be disclosed in the prospectus supplement when the securities are to actually be taken off the shelf.

13.5 Securities Offering Reform, Sec. Act Rel. No. 33–8591, Sec. Exch. Act Rel. No. 34–52056, Inv. Co. Act Rel. No. IC–26993 70 Fed. Reg. 44722–01, 2005 WL 1692642 (SEC July 19, 2005).

13.10 *See* 17 C.F.R. § 230.405 for the definition of WKSIs and the description in § 2.3[1] *supra*.

Chapter 4

EXEMPTIONS FROM 1933
ACT REGISTRATION

Table of Sections

Sec.

4.36 Integration of Transactions

---

§ 4.1 Securities and Transactions Exempt From the 1933 Act's Registration Requirements—Sections 3 and 4 of the 1933 Act

§ 4.1[1] Overview of Exemptions

As discussed in an earlier section,[1] section 5 of the 1933 Act, which contains that Act's basic prohibition against offers and sales without registration, explicitly applies on its face to all offers and all sales of *any* security.[2] This broadly drafted prohibition thus is presumptively applicable to all securities transactions. Of course, most transactions that take place on a daily basis are not subject to section 5's prohibitions and the 1933 Act's registration requirements. This is because the Act provides a number of exemptions from the operation of section 5 and, hence, from the 1933 Act's registration requirements. These exemptions from 1933 Act registration in turn provide a mechanism for rebutting the presumption that registration is necessary before any person offers or sells a security. As discussed more fully below, this means that in order for a transaction to be exempt, the burden of establishing the exemption falls on the person offering or selling securities without complying with the 1933 Act's registration and prospectus delivery requirements.

The Securities Act of 1933 provides three statutory bases for exemption from the Act's registration provisions. It is imperative to keep in mind that, to a large extent, the 1933 exemptions provide only an exemption from the Act's registration requirements and thus do not affect the Act's antifraud provisions. Section 3 of the 1933 Act lists various categories of securities that are exempt from registration.[4] Section 4 of the act describes a variety of transactions that qualify for an exemption for registration.[5] Section 28 of the Act gives the SEC broad exemptive rulemaking power beyond that granted by the statutory exemptions that are found in sections 3 and 4 of the Act.[6] Notwithstanding the broad exemptive authority granted by section 28, the overwhelming majority of exemptions are grounded in section 3 or 4 of the Act. Many exemptions are based on rules or regulations explaining or implementing the terms section 3 and section 4 of the Act. In applying and interpreting the rules, it is crucial to keep in mind that the rule can be no broader than the statute enabling the rule. Accordingly, an exemptive rule under section 3 or 4 of the Act must be read in conjunction with the terms of the statute to assure that the rule is within the bounds authorized by the statute. This is not a problem, however, when the SEC exercises its authority under section 28 of the Act since the statute there does not provide restrictions on the scope or size of the exemption.

---

§ 4.1

1. See § 2.2 *supra.*

2. 15 U.S.C.A. § 77e.

4. 15 U.S.C.A. § 77c.

5. 15 U.S.C.A. § 77d.

6. 15 U.S.C.A. § 77z–3. *See* § 4.35 *infra.* There is parallel general exemptive authority from the provisions of the 1934 Act. 15 U.S.C.A. § 78mm. *See* § 9.2[5] *infra.*

The statutory exemptions from registration and the applicable SEC rules are discussed in the remainder of this chapter. First, the sections that follow provide a discussion of considerations that apply to registration exemptions generally. Understanding these general consideration help put issues in context when interpreting the specific exemptions under the Act and applicable SEC rules. The discussion of general considerations is then followed in subsequent sections by a more detailed analysis of each of the 1933 Act exemptions and applicable SEC rules.

§ 4.1[3] Establishing an Exemption; Consequences of Failure to Do So

The burden of proof for establishing any of the exemptions lies with the person claiming an exemption. A corollary to the burdens of proof and persuasion resting with the person seeking to establish the availability of the exemption is the fact that exemptions are to be strictly construed. Because of the strict construction and burden of proof, transactions must be carefully structured and documented in order to be sure of securing an exemption. A high degree of care is necessary in structuring transactions because an exemption is easily lost. For example, one nonqualifying offeree or purchaser can destroy the exemption with regard to all who purchased securities in the would-be exempt offering.[20] Another hurdle in successfully establishing an exemption from registration under the 1933 Act is the integration doctrine.[21] Under the integration doctrine, multiple transactions that may be separate in form will be scrutinized as one transaction in order to determine whether an exemption exists.[22] Thus, for example, two transactions that appear to be exempt may be combined and, as a consequence of integration, have both exemptions destroyed. The integration is not limited to successive exempt transactions and can also be used to integrate an exempt transaction with a registered offering.[23]

Once an exemption is destroyed or made unavailable, all offers and sales that purportedly were made under the failed exemption will then be in violation of section 5 of the 1933 Act[24] unless some other exemption can be found. Furthermore, someone who has purchased a security that has been sold in violation of section 5 has a one-year right of rescission under section 12(a)(1) of the Act.[25]

§ 4.1[4] Exempt Securities: Section 3 of the 1933 Act

Section 3 of the Securities Act of 1933[26] exempts various types of securities, most of which are dependent upon the nature of the issuer and/or

---

20. *E.g.,* Doran v. Petroleum Management Corp., 545 F.2d 893 (5th Cir.1977), *appeal after remand* 576 F.2d 91 (5th Cir.1978). Thus, for example, in an intrastate offering, an offer to an out-of-state resident can destroy the exemption with regards to all in-staters who participated in the offering. The intrastate exemption is discussed in § 4.12 *infra.*

21. *See* § 4.36 *infra.*

22. *See* § 4.36 *infra.*

23. *See, e.g.,* 17 C.F.R. §§ 230.152, 230.155.

24. 15 U.S.C.A. § 77e.

25. 15 U.S.C.A. 77*l*(a)(1). *See* § 7.2 *infra.*

26. 15 U.S.C.A. § 77c. *See generally* J. William Hicks, Exempted Transactions Under the Securities Act of 1933 (1980); I, IV Louis Loss, Securities Regulation 559–715, 2586–2682 (2d ed. 1961, 1969 Supp.).

terms of the security. Section 3(a) exemptions are self-executing and are not dependent upon SEC rules for their implementation.[27] In contrast, section 3(b) is not self-implementing.[28] Section 3(b)[29] empowers the SEC to exempt securities which, in the Commission's discretion and by virtue of either the "small amount involved" or limited character of the public offering, do not need the registration protection of the Act. The subsection (b) exemptions which are limited to five million dollars for any one issue of securities are found in Regulation A (up to $5 million dollars),[30] SEC Rule 505 (up to $5,000,000)[31] and Rule 504 (up to $1,000,000).[32] The Commission also exercised its exemptive power under section 3(b) to exempt from registration employee stock compensation plans, provided that the issuer is not subject to the Securities Exchange Act's periodic reporting requirements. Section 3(c) of the Act[35] gives the Commission similar exemptive power with regard to investment companies that are registered under the Small Business Investment Act of 1958; the Commission has exercised this power in Regulation E[36] which covers offerings up to five million dollars.

§ 4.1[5] Exempt Transactions: Section 4 of the 1933 Act

Transaction Exemptions Under Section 4

As is the case with section 3(a), section 4 sets forth a series of exemptions and is not dependent upon SEC rulemaking for their implementation. On the other hand, an understanding of the SEC rules that have been adopted is crucial to understanding of the section 4 exemptions. In contrast to the section 3 exemptions, which are expressly designated as exempt securities, section 4 of the Act contains a number of exemptions that apply to specific transactions. These include the exemption for nonpublic offerings by issuers,[37] transactions by persons other than issuers, underwriters and dealers,[38] unsolicited brokers' transactions,[39] certain dealer transactions occurring after the effective date,[40] transactions involving certain mortgage notes secured by real property,[41] and transactions up to five million dollars that are offered and sold

---

27. There are a number of SEC interpretative and safe harbor rules that help explain the scope of these exemptions. Section 4 of the Act is the same in that SEC rules are not necessary to implement the exemptions, but there are a number of SEC rules that are crucial to understanding the scope of the exemptions.

28. Also, as pointed out in the subsection that follows, section 3(b), like some of the section 3(a) exemptions, although denominated as exempt securities, in fact operate like transaction exemptions.

29. 15 U.S.C.A. § 77c(b). *See* § 4.16 *infra.* Although not couched in terms of an exemption, registration Form S–18 is a short form for use in offerings of no more than 7.5 million dollars. Thus, for example, although they are subject to the antifraud provisions of both the 1933 and 1934 Acts, Treasury securities are exempt from 1933 Act registration. *See, e.g.,* Kahn v. Salomon Brothers Inc., 813 F.Supp. 191 (E.D.N.Y.1993).

30. 17 C.F.R. §§ 230.251–.264. *See* § 4.17 *infra.*

31. 17 C.F.R. § 230.505. *See* § 4.22 *infra.*

32. 17 C.F.R. § 230.504. *See* § 4.21 *infra.*

35. 15 U.S.C.A. § 77c(c).

36. 17 C.F.R. §§ 230.601–.610a.

37. Section 4(2), 15 U.S.C.A. § 77d(2). *See* § 4.23 *infra.*

38. Section 4(1), 15 U.S.C.A. § 77d(1). *See* § 4.26 *infra.*

39. Section 4(4), 15 U.S.C.A. § 77d(4). *See* § 4.26 *infra.*

40. Section 4(3), 15 U.S.C.A. § 77d(3). *See* § 4.31 *infra.*

41. Section 4(5), 15 U.S.C.A. § 77d(5). *See* § 4.32 *infra.*

only to "accredited investors."[42] In working with transaction exemptions, it must be remembered that the exemption extends to the transaction, not to individuals. Thus, for example, someone who himself or herself is neither an issuer, underwriter, nor dealer may be involved in a transaction that would preclude reliance on the section 4(1) exemption.[43]

Section 3 Exemptions That Operate Like Transaction Exemptions

In addition to the foregoing exemptions that are aptly denominated as transaction exemptions, a number of the so-called exempt securities are in essence transaction exemptions. This is the case with the exemption for exchanges between an issuer and its security holders,[44] the intrastate exemption for purely local offerings,[45] and the exemptions provided by SEC rules promulgated under sections 3(b) and (c).[46] These exemptions expire at the termination of the qualifying transaction. Most of the security exemptions in section 3 are couched in terms of the nature of the security and/or its issuer, and will attach so long as the security maintains the required attributes, rights, and obligations.

§ 4.1[6] General Exemptive Authority: Section 28 of the 1933 Act: Exemption by SEC Rule or Regulation

In 1996, Congress departed from the more limited exemptive authority that had traditionally been a part of the 1933 Act when it enacted a broader exemptive authority, not linked to the nature of the securities nor the nature of the transaction. In 1996, section 28 of the 1933 Act was added and now provides that the Commission may exempt transactions, securities, and persons if in the public interest and consistent with investor protection.[47] The Commission's Exemptive authority under section 28 applies to any person, security, or transaction but is limited to an exemption by SEC rule or regulation. In contrast, the parallel general Exemptive power under the Securities Exchange Act of 1934[48] not only permits exemption by rule or regulation but also by administrative order.[49]

The virtually unlimited power of the SEC to provide exemptions from the Act by rule or regulation frees the Commission from the more rigid parameters of the specific exemptions set forth in sections 3 and 4 of the Act. While this greater flexibility is desirable, it is hoped that the Commission will not exercise this power to gut many of the valuable investor protection requirements of the securities laws. The SEC has been proceeding cautiously. In

---

42. Section 4(6), 15 U.S.C.A. § 77d(6). *See* § 4.20 *infra. Compare* 15 U.S.C.A. § 77b(a)(15) (definition of accredited investor). *See also, e.g.,* C. Steven Bradford, Transaction Exemptions in the Securities Act of 1933: An Economic Analysis, 45 Emory L.J. 591 (1996).

43. *E.g.,* SEC v. Softpoint, Inc., 958 F.Supp. 846 (S.D.N.Y.1997). *See also, e.g.,* SEC v. Holschuh, 694 F.2d 130, 137–38 (7th Cir.1982); United States v. Wolfson, 405 F.2d 779 (2d Cir.1968), *cert. denied* 394 U.S. 946, 89 S.Ct. 1275, 22 L.Ed.2d 479 (1969).

44. Section 3(a)(9), 15 U.S.C.A. § 77c(a)(9). *See* Thompson Ross Securities, 6 S.E.C. 1111 (SEC 1940); § 4.10 *infra.*

45. Section 3(a)(11), 15 U.S.C.A. § 77c(a)(11). *See* § 4.12 *infra.*

46. 15 U.S.C.A. §§ 77(b), (c). *See* § 4.4 *infra.*

47. 15 U.S.C.A. § 77z–3. *See* § 4.34 *infra.*

48. Securities Exchange Act section 36, 15 U.S.C.A. § 78mm(a). *See* § 9.2[5] *infra.*

49. *Ibid.*

1998, it proposed eliminating the five-million-dollar ceiling on Rule 701 benefit plan offerings.[50] This change was made in 1999.[51]

§ 4.1[7] Applicability of State Securities Laws

Until 1996, an exemption from registration under the 1933 Act did not affect the need for an exemption or registration under any applicable state securities laws.[52] However, in 1996, Congress changed this overlapping coverage when it enacted the National Securities Markets Improvement Act of 1996.[53] Section 18(b) of the 1933 Act[54] provides a preemption of, and thus an exemption from, state securities registration requirements. The preemption extends to most publicly offered securities which are registered with the SEC[55] and to many transactions that are exempt from SEC registration by virtue of section 3 or 4 of the 1933 Act.[56] Most of the federal exemptions set forth in section 3 of the 1933 Act trigger the preemptive provisions. The primary federal exemptions that are not preempted by the 1996 legislation are offerings subject to the intrastate exemption, the section 3(b) exemptions (most notably, Regulation A and Rules 504 and 505 of Regulation D).[57] Many transactions that are exempt under section 4 of the 1933 Act also qualify for the federally mandated exemption from state law registration requirements.[58]

The logic behind the preemptive pattern as adopted by Congress appears to be that federally exempt transactions can be subject to state securities law registration requirements only when the securities are offered to unsophisticated purchasers or offered solely to residents of a single state. Although the legislative purpose was to preempt a great deal of state law involvement in federally exempt transactions, many federally exempt transactions will still need registration or an independent exemption under state law.[59]

§ 4.3 Securities of Governments, Banks, Insurance Companies, and Qualified Pension Plans—Section 3(a)(2)

Section 3(a)(2) of the 1933 Act[1] exempts qualified securities which are either issued or guaranteed by governmental organizations or federal reserve banks. Section 3(a)(2) also provides an exemption from 1933 Act registration for securities of certain insurance companies. This portion of the exemption

50. Sec. Act Rel. No. 33–7511, 63 Fed. Reg. 10785, 30 Sec. Reg. & L. Rep. (BNA) 368 (SEC March 5, 1998). Rule 701 is discussed in § 4.18 *infra*.

51. *See* Sec. Act Rel. No. 33–7645 (SEC Feb. 25, 1999).

52. State securities laws, commonly referred to as "Blue Sky" laws, are considered in chapter 8 *infra*.

53. Pub. L. No. 104–290, 110 Stat. 3416 (1996).

54. 15 U.S.C.A. § 77r.

55. 15 U.S.C.A. § 77r(b)(1).

56. 15 U.S.C.A. § 77r(b)(4).

57. These exemptions are discussed in §§ 4.16–4.18, 4.21–4.22 *infra*.

58. Curiously, a transaction exempt under section 4(2)'s nonpublic offering exemption are not preempted unless they are in compliance with an SEC rule or regulation.

59. *See* Rutherford B. Campbell, Jr., Blue Sky Laws and the Recent Congressional Preemption Failure, 22 J. Corp. L. 175 (1997).

§ 4.3

1. 15 U.S.C.A. § 77c(a).

applies to securities issued by state, local and federal governments, including their subdivisions and administrative bodies.[2]

§ 4.3[1] Government and Municipal Securities

§ 4.3[1][A] Scope of Exemption

Section 3(a)(2) exempts securities issued by the federal government, federal agencies, states, and qualifying state government agencies (including municipalities). In addition to straight-forward direct government financing, the section 3(a)(2) exemption also covers qualifying joint efforts of government and industry. Accordingly, the exemption covers government-guaranteed obligations. Thus, securities issued by Government National Mortgage Association (GNMA or "Ginnie Mae") or Federal National Mortgage Association (FNMA or "Fannie Mae") would qualify for the exemption, but derivative securities[3] based on these obligations, such as futures contracts, would not.[4]

Just as state and local government guarantees can qualify a security for exemption from 1933 Act registration, so can a federal guarantee. However, the fact that there is a federal guarantee will not assure the exemption when the investment involves risks not ordinarily associated with instruments issued or guaranteed by the government.[11]

§ 4.3[2] Bank Securities

Section 3(a)(2) also exempts from 1933 Act registration securities issued by Federal Reserve Banks, including certificates of deposit.[18] Section 3(a)(2) does not cover securities issued by industrial loan companies or their subsidiaries, as those are dealt with under section 3(a)(5).[19] However, Federal Land Bank stock is covered by section 3(a)(2)'s exemption.[20] Not every investment involving bank accounts will be exempt from the securities laws. Thus, when an investment program involving bank accounts possesses all the characteristics of a security, the securities laws will apply.[21]

---

2. Most of the governmental securities issued under section 3(a)(2) are not traded on exchanges or through the National Association of Securities Dealers. In order to fill this regulatory gap, Congress created The Municipal Securities Rule–Making Board to cover broker-dealers who are not registered under the 1934 Exchange Act. *See* 15 U.S.C.A. §§ 78o, 78o–4. Municipal securities regulation is discussed in § 14.6 *infra*.

3. For example, stripped a government obligation of the interest payments and marketing the "zero coupon" portion (some of which have been marketed as "TIGRs" or "GATORs"), which are sold through stock brokers will not qualify for the exemption. The exemption is not available since in these instances the government is not the issuer of the security, the broker acting as the issuer of this derivative instrument. *Cf., e.g.*, Small Business Admin. Guaranteed Loans, [1975–1976 Transfer Binder] Fed. Sec. L. Rep. (CCH) ¶ 80,243 (SEC No Action Letter Nov. 8, 1974).

4. This is because the derivative security is not protected by a government guarantee. *Ibid.*

11. *See, e.g.*, J.P. Morgan Structures Obligations Corp., [1994–1995 Transfer Binder] Fed. Sec. L. Rep. (CCH) ¶ 76,906 (SEC No Action Letter July 27, 1994) (interests in swap transactions involved different risks).

18. 15 U.S.C.A. § 77c(a)(2). Sears v. Likens, 912 F.2d 889 (7th Cir.1990) (securities issued or guaranteed by state bank are exempt from 1933 Act registration requirements).

19. 15 U.S.C.A. § 77c(a)(5) (1976). *See* § 4.6 *infra*.

20. Dau v. Federal Land Bank of Omaha, 627 F.Supp. 346 (N.D.Iowa 1985).

21. *See also, e.g.*, SEC v. Deyon, 977 F.Supp. 510 (D.Me.1997) (bank account investment program was a security). The definition of security is discussed in § 1.6 *supra*.

The exemption for bank securities is designed to exempt bank deposits and the like. The exemption does not purport to exclude investment securities in the bank or bank holding company.

§ 4.3[3] Pension Plans

In addition to government securities and bank securities, section 3(a)(2) further exempts from 1933 Act registration certain qualifying employee pension plans which are set up in the form of a trust or a collective trust maintained by a bank or an insurance company.[23] In order to qualify for the exemption under the terms of the statute, the plan must be a qualified plan under section 401 or 402(a)(2) of the Internal Revenue Code.[24] The section 3(a)(2) exemption applies to all such employee plans, regardless of whether they are pension, profit sharing, or stock plans.[25]

§ 4.4　Short Term Commercial Paper—Section 3(a)(3)

Section 3(a)(3) of the Securities Act of 1933[1] provides an exemption from registration for notes, drafts, notes of exchange, or bankers' acceptances arising "out of a current transaction" with a maturity at the time of issue of not more than nine months. The nine-month limitation does not include grace periods or any renewal of the security that is limited in the same manner as the original obligation. Short term commercial paper is thus granted an exemption from 1933 Act registration although it is, nevertheless, subject to the Act's antifraud provisions. In contrast to the 1933 Act's approach of providing an exemption from registration, short term commercial paper is expressly excluded from the definition of "security" under the Securities Exchange Act of 1934[4] and thus is not subject to that Act's antifraud provisions.[5] As discussed more fully in an earlier section of this treatise,[6] in *Reves v. Ernst & Young*,[7] the Supreme Court applied the "family resemblance" test in holding that certain demand notes were securities.

§ 4.5　Securities of Eleemosynary Organizations—Section 3(a)(4)

Section 3(a)(4) of the Act[1] exempts from registration all securities issued by a not-for-profit issuer that is organized and operated exclusively for

---

23. *See* Rule 132, 17 C.F.R. § 230.132. *Cf.* Rule 701's exemption for certain compensation plans of issuers not subject to Exchange Act reporting requirements. 17 C.F.R. § 230.701. *See* § 4.18 *infra*.

24. I.R.C. §§ 401, 402(a)(2). Also exempted are plans of governmental employers qualifying under I.R.C. § 414(d).

25. There are parallel exemptions from the 1934 Exchange Act. 15 U.S.C.A. §§ 78c(A)(12), 78l(g)(2)(H).

§ 4.4

1. 15 U.S.C.A. § 77c(a)(3).

4. 15 U.S.C.A. § 78c(a)(10).

5. *Id.*

6. *See* § 1.6 *supra*.

7. 494 U.S. 56, 110 S.Ct. 945, 108 L.Ed.2d 47 (1990), *rehearing denied* 494 U.S. 1092, 110 S.Ct. 1840, 108 L.Ed.2d 968 (1990).

§ 4.5

1. 15 U.S.C.A. § 77c(a)(4). *Cf.,* Timothy L. Horner & Hugh H. Makens, Securities Regulation of Fundraising Activities of Religious and Other Nonprofit Organizations, 27 Stetson L. Rev. 473 (1997).

religious, educational, benevolent, fraternal, charitable, or reformatory purposes. Somewhat related to the section 3(a)(4) exemption is section 3(a)(13) which was adopted in 1996 to provide an exemption for securities "issued by or any interest or participation in any church plan, company or account" that is excluded from the definition of investment company as a church plan.[2]

In order to qualify for section 3(a)(4)'s exemption for securities of not-for-profit issuers, no part of the issuer's net earnings may inure to the benefit of "any person, private stockholder, or individual."[4] With regard to nonprofit organizations, the availability of this exemption has generally been treated as coextensive with the issuer's federal tax status.

§ 4.6 Securities of Building and Loan Associations, Farmers Cooperatives and the Like—Section 3(a)(5)

Section 3(a)(5) of the 1933 Act[1] provides an exemption from registration for securities issued by savings and loan associations, building and loan associations, cooperative banks, homestead associations, and similar institutions, provided that the issuer is subject to supervision by state or federal governmental authorities. The exemption does not apply, however, where the issuer takes for itself more than three percent of the offering's face value in the form of a fee or other remuneration, either at the time of investment or termination.[2] Section 3(a)(5) further exempts securities issued by farmers cooperatives and certain corporations that qualify for the federal taxation exemption.[3]

§ 4.8 Certificates Issued Under the Bankruptcy Act by Receivers and Trustees—Section 3(a)(7)

Section 3(a)(7) exempts from registration certificates issued by trustees, receivers, or debtors in possession under the Federal Bankruptcy Act, provided that the certificates are issued pursuant to court approval.[1] Even though the exemption may apply to securities sold as part of the original issue, it does not extend to downstream sales, in which case the person selling to secondary recipients of the certificates must register unless some other independent exemption is available. The statute expressly requires court approval of the issue in order to render the exemption available.

The section 3(a)(7) exemption supplements the exemptions for bankruptcy reorganizations that are included in section 3(a)(10)'s exemption for

---

2. Section 3(c)(14) of the Investment Company Act of 1940 exempts church plans described in § 414(e) of the Internal Revenue Code and "no part of the assets may be used for ... other than the Exclusive Benefit Plan Participants." 15 U.S.C.A. § 80a–3(c)(14). The exemption provided by section 3(a)(13) is discussed in § 4.14 *infra*. The Investment Company Act of 11940 is discussed in chapter 20 *infra*.

4. 15 U.S.C.A. §77(c)(4). Section 3(a)(4) was amended by the Philanthropy Protection Act of 1995, 104th Cong., 1st Sess., (1995) to add what is now the last phrase of the section: "or any security of a fund is excluded from the definition of an investment company under Section 3(c)(10)(B) of the Investment Company Act of 1940." The Investment Company Act of 11940 is discussed in Chapter 20 *infra*.

§ 4.6

1. 15 U.S.C.A. § 77c(a)(5).

2. *Id.*

3. *See* I.R.C. §§ 501(a), 501(c)(2), (16), 521.

§ 4.8

1. 15 U.S.C.A. § 77c(a)(7).

securities issued pursuant to certain administratively or judicially approved reorganizations.[3] The section 3(a)(7) exemption which applies to trustee certificates has its counterpart in the Bankruptcy Act,[4] which not only provides an exemption from section 5 of the 1933 Act but also from the Trust Indenture Act of 1939,[5] as well as from state and local laws. Section 1145(a) of the Bankruptcy Act[6] exempts from 1933 Act registration, as well as provides an exemption from state securities laws, securities of the bankrupt if they are (1) offered under a reorganization plan and are (2) exchanged for claims or interests in the debtor. As is the case with the exemptions under sections 3(a)(9)[7] (exchanges of securities exclusively between the issuer and its existing securities holders) and 3(a)(10)[8] of the 1933 Act (securities issued in certain administratively or judicially approved exchanges), the exemption from 1933 Act registration that is provided by the Bankruptcy Act does not apply to resales of the securities so issued. However, an exemption for the resales may be secured independently including, for example, SEC Rule 144.[10]

§ 4.9 Insurance Policies and Annuity Contracts—Section 3(a)(8)

Section 3(a)(8)[1] exempts from 1933 Act registration insurance policies and annuity contracts issued by corporations that are subject to the supervision of a state insurance commissioner, bank commissioner, or agency or officer performing a similar regulatory function. The Commission has pointed out that if the insurance or annuity contract does not place upon the issuer a "meaningful mortality risk" the policy cannot be regarded as "life insurance" or an exempt "annuity."[2] Furthermore, simply taking on a "meaningful mortality risk" does not assure the issuer an exemption from registration under the securities laws, where the annuity or other insurance contract is in essence an investment contract.[3] For example, the Supreme Court has held that when analyzing a variable annuity under which the entire investment risk rests with the purchaser, the section 3(a)(8) exemption does not apply.[4]

---

3. 15 U.S.C.A. § 77c(a)(10). *See* § 4.11 *infra*.

4. 11 U.S.C.A. § 364(f). These certificates can be issued by either a trustee or a debtor in possession (*see* 11 U.S.C.A. §§ 1107(a), 1108) while section 3(a)(7) also exempts certificates issued by a receiver. The exemption provided by section 364(f) of the Bankruptcy Act does not apply to downstream sales or to sales by certain underwriters. *See* 11 U.S.C.A. § 1145(b)(1).

5. 15 U.S.C.A. § 77aaa–77bbbb. *See* chapter 19 *infra*.

6. 11 U.S.C.A. § 1145(a). Section, 1145(a)(2), allows the "offer" or "sale" of securities via warrants, options, rights, and conversion privileges, if two general requirements are met. Section 1145(a)(1) allows the exchange to include partial cash payment. Section 1145(a)(3) governs sale of a debtor's portfolio securities (limited exemption).

7. 15 U.S.C.A. § 77c(a)(9). *See* § 4.10 *infra*.

8. 15 U.S.C.A. § 77c(a)(10). *See* § 4.11 *infra*.

10. 17 C.F.R. § 230.144 which is discussed in § 4.29 *infra*.

§ 4.9

1. 15 U.S.C.A. § 77c(a)(8).

2. Sec. Act Rel. No. 33–6051 (April 5, 1979). *See* SEC v. United Benefit Life Insurance Co., 387 U.S. 202, 211, 87 S.Ct. 1557, 1562, 18 L.Ed.2d 673 (1967).

3. Sec. Act Rel. No. 33–6051 (April 5, 1979). *See* Liner v. DiCresce, 905 F.Supp. 280 (M.D.N.C.1994) (financial security plans sold by bankrupt dairy company were securities even though they included insurance-like benefits in the event of death or forced retirement).

4. SEC v. Variable Annuity Life Insurance Co., 359 U.S. 65, 79 S.Ct. 618, 3 L.Ed.2d 640 (1959); Malone v. Addison Insurance Marketing, Inc., 225 F.Supp.2d 743 (W.D. Ky. 2002) (but indexed or fixed annuities are not securities).

As is the case with any question of whether an investment contract exists,[5] the expectations of the policyholder must be viewed in light of an "economic reality" test, and the court's inquiry thus is not limited to the policy on its face. Ordinarily, a fixed annuity will qualify for section 3(a)(8)'s exemption.[7]

§ 4.10 Securities Exchanged Exclusively With Existing Security Holders—Section 3(a)(9)

Section 3(a)(9) provides an exemption from 1933 Act registration for securities exchanged by the issuer exclusively with its existing security holders, so long as no commission or other remuneration is paid for promotional activities in soliciting the exchange.[1] The exemption is not available for securities exchanged in the course of Bankruptcy Act proceedings that would be governed by 11 U.S.C.A. § 1145.[2] Section 1145 provides its own exemption from state securities laws, securities of the bankrupt if they are (1) offered under a reorganization plan and are (2) exchanged for claims or interests in the debtor. The Bankruptcy Act exemption is supplement by section 3(a)(7) of the 1933 Act.[3]

The exemption provided by section 3(a)(9) is limited to exchanges taking place solely between the issuing company and its existing securities holders. The requirement that the exchange be exclusively with existing holders does not, however, mean that all securities holders must be included.[4] It is only required that persons who are not shareholders cannot participate in the exchange.

§ 4.11 Securities Issued in Judicially or Administratively Approved Reorganizations—Section 3(a)(10)

Section 3(a)(10)[1] of the 1933 Act exempts from registration securities issued in exchange for other securities, where the issuance has been approved by a court or an appropriate administrative body. The section 3(a)(10) exemption is used primarily with respect to securities issued in an exchange pursuant to business combinations and reorganizations that are subject to regulatory approval,[3] securities exchanged pursuant to settlement of litiga-

---

5. *See* § 1.6 *supra.*

7. *E.g.,* Otto v. Variable Annuity Life Insurance Co., 611 F.Supp. 83 (N.D.Ill.1985).

§ 4.10

1. 15 U.S.C.A. § 77c(a)(9). *See, e.g.,* International Controls Corp., [1990–1991 Transfer Binder] Fed. Sec. L. Rep. (CCH) ¶ 79,604 (SEC No Action Letter Aug. 6, 1990) (no action would be recommended for issuer's exchange offer to registered debenture holders).

2. 11 U.S.C.A. § 1145. *See generally,* J. *William* Hicks, Recapitalizations Under Section 3(a)(9) of the Securities Act of 1933, 61 Va. L.Rev. 1057 (1975). *See also* § 4.8 *supra*; 4.11 *infra.*

3. 15 U.S.C.A. § 77c(a)(7). *See* § 4.8 *supra.*

4. *See.* Letter of General Counsel relating to sections 3(a)(9) and 4(1), Sec. Act Release No. 33–2029, 1939 WL 1053, 1 Fed. Sec. L. Rep. (CCH) ¶ 2140 (SEC No Action Letter Aug. 8, 1939). Carolina Wholesale Florists, Inc., SEC No–Action Letter, 1976 WL 12584 (Aug. 17, 1976); Systemedics, Inc., 1976 WL 12578 (SEC No Action Letter Jan. 19, 1976); Frier Indus., Inc., 1975 WL 11274 (SEC No Action Letter Oct. 16, 1975).

§ 4.11

1. 15 U.S.C.A. § 77c(a)(10).

3. This can include approval by a foreign governmental body. *See, e.g.,* Gilat Satellite Networks Ltd., 2002 WL 31863756 (SEC No Action Letter Dec. 19, 2002) (approval by Israeli court under the Israeli Corporations Code).

tion,[4] and exchanges of securities in connection with bankruptcy proceedings that are not subject to Chapter 11 of the Federal Bankruptcy Code.[5] The exchange of securities need not be limited to securities—it may partly involve cash.[6]

In order for the exemption to apply, the administrative or judicial approval must be after a "hearing * * * at which all persons to whom it is proposed to issue securities * * * shall have the right to appear."[7] Absent another exemption, all downstream public sales of securities acquired under the exemption must be registered under the 1933 Act. The section 3(a)(10) exemption is a relatively narrow one, as not all approved reorganizations are covered.

§ 4.12   The Exemption for Purely Intrastate Offerings—Section 3(a)(11); SEC Rule 147

§ 4.12[1]   Intrastate Offerings—The Statutory Exemption—Section 3(a)(9)

An issuer may embark upon a public offering of its securities and avoid the federal registration requirements under the intrastate exemption provided that all aspects of the offering are within the confines of a single state and are purely local in nature.[1] The intrastate exemption from 1933 Act registration is found in section 3(a)(11) which exempts "[a]ny security which is part of an issue offered and sold only to persons resident within a single State or Territory, where the issuer of such security is a person resident and doing business within, or, if a corporation, incorporated by and doing business within, such State or Territory."[2] Both the courts and the SEC have narrowly interpreted the scope of the intrastate offering exemption, thus making it a feasible alternative only in a relatively few situations. The statutory exemption speaks in terms of "part of an issue" which seems to imply that the exemption may be available only for primary offerings. There is authority supporting the interpretation that the intrastate exemption does not apply to secondary offerings.[3] However, other exemptions which utilize the "part of an issue" concept may apply to secondary offerings.[4] To the extent that an exempt intrastate offering is a public one, it will be subject to the state's blue sky registration requirements.[5]

---

4. See, e.g., The AES Corporation, SEC No–Action Letter, 1995 WL 242363 (Apr. 26, 1995).

5. Securities issued in federal bankruptcy proceedings can qualify for the exemption under section 3(a)(7) of the 1933 Act. 15 U.S.C.A. § 77c(a)(7). See § 4.8 supra.

6. See, e.g., UBO Bancorp., 1982 WL 30461 (SEC No Action Letter July 8, 1982) Bayswater Realty & Inv. Trust, 1981 WL 26640 (SEC No Action Letter Aug. 13, 1981).

7. 15 U.S.C.A. § 77c(a)(10).

§ 4.12

1. 15 U.S.C.A. § 77c(a)(11).

2. Id.

3. E.g., SEC v. Tuchinsky, 1992 WL 226302, [1992 Transfer Binder] Fed. Sec. L. Rep. (CCH) ¶ 96,917 (S.D.Fla.1992), relying on III Louis Loss & Joel Seligman, Securities Regulation 1142–44 & fns. 5–6 (3d ed. 1989) and cases cited therein.

4. See Regulation A, a section 3(b) exemption, which utilizes the "part of the issue" language, but is expressly applicable to secondary offerings. 17 C.F.R. § 230.251(b).

5. Smaller offerings may find an exemption under state law as well. State securities laws are considered in chapter 8 infra.

The intrastate offering exemption is found in section 3 of the Act, and thus couched in terms of exempt securities as compared with the language of section 4's transaction exemptions.[6] However, in actuality, the intrastate exemption operates more like a transaction exemption since it is tied to the particular transaction in question and therefore is not limited to the security itself in regard to the nature of the issuer's rights and obligations thereunder. Unlike most of the other section 3(a) exemptions for certain types of securities, such as those for securities issued or guaranteed by a governmental subdivision, bank deposits, short term commercial paper, and securities of non-profit, charitable organizations, the section 3(a)(11) intrastate exemption will attach only as long as the transaction meets certain transactional requirements, although there is no change in the terms of the underlying security. While the exemption is dependent upon the premise that all securities which form a part of the offering will come to rest in the hands of local residents, an out-of-state resale seven months after the primary offering to residents may not void the intrastate exemption for the original offering.[7]

The title "intrastate" exemption may be misleading to the extent that it may indicate a lack of sufficient interstate contact so as to deprive the SEC of jurisdiction. The exemption is aimed at offerings that are local in character and for which all interested parties including the issuer, and all offerees reside in that locality. The exemption is not in any way dependent upon the absence of the 1933 Act's jurisdictional requirement that the sale of a security be conducted through a means or instrumentality of interstate commerce.

The choice of a state's boundaries is a somewhat arbitrary line for the limits of the locality, considering the exemption's purpose. However, it is one of convenience, as it eliminates what otherwise might be difficult factual questions in determining the scope of the local offering exemption. Despite the purpose of the exemption as evidenced by the legislative history, a corporation located in the heart of New York City may not rely on the local "intrastate" exemption for issuance of stock to a New Jersey resident directly across the river, while an issuer in Amarillo, Texas may rely on the exemption for sale to a resident of the southernmost tip of Texas. Because of its geographical contours, the intrastate exemption has proven to be more useful in the Western portion of the United States where there are fewer intrastate metropolitan areas.

Section 3(a)(11) is not a detailed statutory provision that would provide a great deal guidance as to how to ensure compliance with the exemption's requirements. Persons deciding to rely on the exemption have to draw from the relatively scant judicial precedent and SEC interpretive releases and rules available. Prior to SEC Rule 147[10] most precedential guidance was found in SEC no action letters. Because of the close factual questions involved, it became common practice for issuers deciding to rely on the intrastate exemption to request a no action letter[11] from the Commission before proceeding. However, the no action letter is a very inefficient method of administrative lawmaking. Furthermore, reliance upon no action letters, which by their very

---

6. *See* § 4.1 *supra.*

7. Busch v. Carpenter, 598 F.Supp. 519 (D.Utah 1984), judgment affirmed in part, reversed in part 827 F.2d 653 (10th Cir.1987).

10. 17 C.F.R. § 230.147.

11. The no action letter process for informal SEC advice is discussed in § 1.4[4] *supra* and § 16.32 *infra.*

nature are expressly confined to the facts as given, provides little precedential value and thus little comfort to the corporate planner trying to tailor the transaction to the exemption. In response to the uncertainty surrounding the scope of the exemption, the SEC promulgated Rule 147 as a "safe harbor rule." Full compliance with the rule will give the issuer and anyone else relying on it safety from claims that the transaction in question has gone beyond the bounds of section 3(a)(11). However, like the other safe harbor rules,[12] Rule 147 is not exclusive and failure to comply with the rule does not even raise a presumption that the statutory exemption is not available. Accordingly, the pre-Rule 147 case law and SEC interpretations continue to be relevant today.

From the face of the statute, it is apparent that in order to qualify for a section 3(a)(11) exemption, not only all purchasers but also all offerees of the securities in question must be residents within a single state.[13] Furthermore, the issuer must be a resident of the same state and be doing business there. In the case of a corporation, in addition to the requirement that its principal place of business be within the state, it is also necessary that the state be the corporation's place of incorporation. This last requirement necessarily eliminates the vast number of corporations which, while doing business in one state, select some other jurisdiction such as Delaware to be the state of incorporation in order to take advantage of that state's more attractive corporation laws. Section 3(a)(11) does not expressly address whether other business entities such as limited partnerships, limited liability companies, and business trusts must be organized in the state in order to qualify as an issuer under the intrastate exemption. However, the rule of domestic incorporation for corporate issuers should apply by analogy to other forms of doing business. In its safe harbor rule, the SEC expressly extends the requirement of in-state organization to a "limited partnership, trust or other form of business organization."[15] A limited partnership with in-state investors and in-state business will not be disqualified from relying on the intrastate exemption solely because the corporate general partner is a wholly-owned subsidiary of a corporation incorporated outside of the state.[16]

Even where the above-mentioned statutory requirements have been satisfied, the issuer still is not perfectly safe under the intrastate exemption. For example, it has been held that where an offering was made only to Minnesota residents and the issuer, a Minnesota corporation, had its only office in Minnesota, the fact that the proceeds would be used outside of the state was sufficient in and of itself to make the intrastate exemption unavailable.[17] The decision raises significant questions about the exemption's application to any issuer with out-of-state operations and if the offering proceeds may be even

---

12. *E.g.,* Rules 506 and 144 which are discussed in §§ 4.25, 4.29 *infra. See e.g.,* Tom A. Alberg & Martin E. Lybecker, New SEC Rules 146 and 147: The Nonpublic and Intrastate Offering Exemptions from Registration for Sale of Securities, 74 Colum.L.Rev. 622 (1974).

13. All offerees in the offering in question must be residents. However, the existence of preexisting non resident shareholders in the company will not prevent the use of the intrastate exemption.

15. Rule 147(c)(1)(i); 17 C.F.R. § 230. 147(c)(1)(i).

16. GHM/Massachusetts Health Care PartnersCI Limited Partnership, 1988 WL 234449, [1988 Transfer Binder] Fed. Sec. L. Rep. ¶ 78,808, (SEC No Action Letter May 31, 1988).

17. SEC v. McDonald Investment Co., 343 F.Supp. 343 (D.Minn.1972). Compare Rule 147 which imposes an eighty percent minimum on the proceeds to be used within the state. 17 C.F.R. § 230.147(c)(2)(iii).

indirectly attributed to that portion of the business.[18] This use of the proceeds requirement is not as troubling if it is viewed in terms of the overall business operations,[19] but it seems to be overreaching if it will void the exemption for securities of an issuer who derives substantial income from in-state operations. For example, an issuer using the proceeds of the offering to purchase wine outside the state for resale within the state can still satisfy the in-state business requirement.[20]

Similarly, a local issuer that planned to use eighty-five percent of the proceeds from an intrastate offering to pay off a loan to an out-of-state bank that was used to finance purchase of an in-state bank dealing primarily with in-state customers was allowed to rely on the exemption.[21] Use of a subsidiary or other device to segregate independent out-of-state operations by a subsidiary may also avoid running afoul of the requirement that the principal business be within the state of the offering.[22] In contrast, it is clear that where the issuer's income-producing operations are located outside of the state, the intrastate exemption will not be available.[23]

As is the case with other exemptions, where two or more purportedly separate transitions are in fact part of a single issue, the two transactions will be integrated.[24] In such cases, all offers made for the transactions to be integrated must qualify for the exemption.

§ 4.12[2] Intrastate Offerings—The SEC's "Safe Harbor"—Rule 147

As is the case with SEC policy and court decisions on issuer residence, in order to qualify for the safe harbor of Rule 147, both the issuer's place of incorporation or organization and its "principal office" must be located within the same state; and, if an individual, his or her principal residence must be located within that state.[26] Rule 147 further requires that in order for an issuer to be deemed doing business within the state, it must have derived at least eighty percent of its gross revenues per annum as well as eighty percent of its assets (including those of its subsidiary on a consolidated basis) from

---

18. The issuer planned to use the proceeds for loans secured by real property outside of the state. Although the loan contracts were to be governed by Minnesota law and despite the fact that the issuer had in-state income as well, the court denied the exemption. In its broadest reading, the decision can be seen as adding to the statutory doing-business requirement a rule that the proceeds from the particular offering be used in the state. *Compare, e.g.,* Master Financial, Inc., 1999 WL 343087 (SEC No Action Letter May 27, 1999) (intrastate exemption was available where offering was used to fund company's in-state lending operations, the fact more than 20 percent of the Company's gross revenues is interest and other payments received on a portfolio of loans made to out-of state borrowers).

19. *See* SEC v. Truckee Showboat, Inc., 157 F.Supp. 824 (S.D.Cal.1957); 17 C.F.R. § 230.147(c)(2).

20. Adventures in Wine, [1976–1977 Transfer Binder] Fed. Sec. L. Rep. (CCH) ¶ 80,952 (SEC 1977).

21. Fina Bancorp., Inc., 19 Sec.Reg. & L.Rep. (BNA) 961 (SEC No Action Letter June 15, 1987).

22. Fidelity Credit Corp., 1988 WL 234463 (SEC No Action Letter June 23, 1988) (transferring out-of-state assets to a subsidiary operating outside of the state and not integrated with the operations of the parent company may enable the in-state parent to continue to have intrastate offerings without having the exemption jeopardized by the out-of-state subsidiary's operations).

23. *See, e.g.,* Busch v. Carpenter, 827 F.2d 653, 658 (10th Cir.1987); Chapman v. Dunn, 414 F.2d 153, 158–59 (6th Cir.1969); SEC v. Truckee Showboat, Inc., 157 F.Supp. 824 (S.D.Cal.1957).

24. *See* § 4.36 *infra* for discussion of integration generally.

26. 17 C.F.R. § 230.147(c)(1).

activities and/or real property located within the state over the past fiscal year.[27] This eighty percent requirement is not included within the statute but indicates the Commission's position that the statutory concept of "doing business" means that something more than having the state as the location of the principal office and the place of incorporation or organization is necessary.

Rule 147 imposes a condition that eighty percent of the net proceeds of the offering be used in the state.[28] When taking a look at the face of the statute, there is at least a question as to whether either of the rule's eighty percent requirements is an overreaching interpretation. Nevertheless, they are interpretations which have not yet met successful challenges either at the administrative or judicial level. Since Rule 147 is a safe harbor rule, such challenges are unlikely. The eighty percent test nevertheless is evidence of the SEC's position that something more than the principal office requirement is necessary. Thus, it is fair to assume that issuers falling significantly below the eighty percent threshold may have difficulty establishing the statutory exemption.

Both under the statutory exemption and pursuant to Rule 147, downstream sales of part of an intrastate issue to nonresidents can destroy the availability of the intrastate exemption. Obviously, an issuer cannot select an in-state resident to operate as a conduit or underwriter[29] and thereby avoid the limitations of the exemption. However, even inadvertent downstream sales to nonresidents, at least those taking place within a reasonably short period after the distribution for which the exemption is claimed, will destroy the exemption for all sales made pursuant to the exemption. The safe harbor guidelines for limitation on resales is found in Rule 147(e)[30] which prohibits all resales to nonresident purchasers within nine months "from the date of the last sale by the issuer of such securities." Even outside of the safe harbor rule, it is clear that a limited number of nonresident resales will render the exemption inapplicable to the entire offering.[31] In such a case, even the resident purchasers will be placed in a position of being able to claim that the securities they purchased were sold in violation of section 5, thus giving them a right of rescission under section 12(a)(1).[32] It has long been the Commission's position, however, that once securities sold pursuant to the intrastate exemption have finally come to rest in the hands of residents, subsequent isolated resales to nonresidents will not destroy the prior exemptions.[33] In terms of planning such transactions, the nine-month safe harbor guidelines of Rule 147 provide a good rule of thumb.

Notwithstanding Rule 147's detail as to the requirements of residency so far as the issuer is concerned, the rule is much more open with regard to

---

27. 17 C.F.R. § 230.147(c)(2)(i), (ii).

28. 17 C.F.R. § 230.147(c)(2)(iii).

29. Underwriter is defined in section 2(a)(11), 15 U.S.C.A. § 77b(a)(11). *See* § 4.27 *infra.*

30. 17 C.F.R. § 230.147(e). A shorter period might still be permitted under the case law interpreting the scope of the statutory exemption.

31. *See* Hillsborough Investment Corp. v. SEC, 276 F.2d 665 (1st Cir.1960), *s.c.* 173 F.Supp. 86 (D.N.H.1958).

32. Section 3(a)(11) Exemption for Local Offerings, Sec. Act Rel. No 33–4434, 1961 WL 3670, 1 Fed. Sec. L. Rep. (CCH) ¶ 2270–2277 (SEC Dec. 6, 1961). *See* 15 U.S.C.A. § 77l (a)(1) which is discussed in § 7.2 *infra.*

33. Section 3(a)(11) Exemption for Local Offerings, Sec. Act Rel. No 33–4434, 1961 WL 3670, 1 Fed. Sec. L. Rep. (CCH) ¶¶ 2270–2277 (SEC Dec. 6, 1961). *See also* Busch v. Carpenter, 827 F.2d 653 (10th Cir.1987), *affirming in part* 598 F.Supp. 519 (D.Utah 1984); Commonwealth Equity Trust, 19 Sec.Reg. & L.Rep. (BNA) 355 (SEC No Action Letter Feb. 20, 1987); First National Bank & Trust Co. (SEC No Action Letter Dec. 19, 1985); Scientific Manufacturing, Inc. (SEC No Action Letter June 13, 1983).

purchasers' and offerees' residence. The test applicable to an individual is "his principal residence,"[34] which seems to limit each individual to one state, thus eliminating vacation homes and the like. A similar test has been adopted under the statute.[35] Business entities including corporations, trusts, and partnerships qualify as resident offerees and purchasers if they have their principal office in the state.[36] There is no requirement that the offeree be organized under the laws of that state, although it would have to be so organized in order to qualify as an issuer. Furthermore, the rule's eighty percent revenue and asset tests do not apply to offerees and purchasers as they apply only to issuers. The rule also provides that where a corporation, partnership, or trust is formed *for the purpose* of purchasing the securities in question, *all* of its beneficial owners must be residents.[37] It thus appears that a bona fide preexisting entity may qualify as a purchaser although it has nonresident owners. As to such entities, the SEC has opined that a nonresident trustee of a resident's individual retirement account will not disqualify the trust as a resident purchaser.[38] Similarly, with regard to partnerships, it has been held that the fact that one partner resided in another state was not in itself sufficient to prevent the partnership from being a resident for purposes of section 3(a)(11).[39] The SEC has indicated that Rule 147 would be available for limited partnership interests to be offered solely to residents of the partnership's state of organization even though the general partner was wholly owned by an out-of-state corporation.[40]

Another key factor in an intrastate offering and in deciding whether or not reliance is to be placed upon Rule 147 is the integration doctrine which operates to telescope two or more transactions into one and also applies to other exemptions under the Act.[41] The integration doctrine is the Commission's counterpart of the IRS' step-transaction analysis under which transactions that appear to be separate in form will be scrutinized closely as to substance in order to determine whether or not in fact they should be treated as two distinct transactions. Specifically, with regard to the intrastate exemption contained in section 3(a)(11), the question of the exemption's availability arises in the context of determining whether a given security transaction is "part of an issue" within the meaning of the statute. The determination of which transactions constitute an "issue" or "part of an issue" is a matter of federal rather than state law.[42] In determining whether the integration doctrine will apply and whether the transaction is to be considered part of a

---

34. 17 C.F.R. § 230.147(d)(2).

35. *See generally* J. William Hicks, Exempted Transactions Under the Securities Act of 1933 ch. 4 (1980 rev. ed.).

36. 17 C.F.R. § 230.147(d)(3).

37. 17 C.F.R. § 230.147(d)(3).

38. Fair Valley Properties No. 2, [1981–1982 Transfer Binder] Fed. Sec. L. Rep. (CCH) ¶ 77,003 (SEC No Action Letter 1981).

39. Grenader v. Spitz, 390 F.Supp. 1112 (S.D.N.Y.1975), *reversed on other grounds* 537 F.2d 612 (2d Cir.1976), *cert. denied* 429 U.S. 1009, 97 S.Ct. 541, 50 L.Ed.2d 619 (1976).

40. GHM/Massachusetts Health Care Partners–I Limited Partnership, 20 Sec.Reg. & L.Rep. (BNA) 936 (SEC No Action Letter available May 31, 1988).

41. *See, e.g.,* Sidney Sosin, The Intrastate Exemptions, Public Offering and the Issue Concept, 16 W.Res.L.Rev. 110 (1974). The integration doctrine has particular impact with regard to Regulation A offerings (*see* § 4.17 *infra*) and Regulation D's exemptions (*see* §§ 4.19–4.25 *infra*). *See also* § 4.36 *infra*.

42. Section 3(a)(11) Exemption for Local Offerings, Sec. Act Rel. No 33–4434, 1961 WL 3670, 1 Fed. Sec. L. Rep. (CCH) ¶¶ 2270–2277 (SEC Dec. 6, 1961).

certain issue, the Commission will consider a number of factors: "(1) are the offerings part of a single plan of financing; (2) do the offerings involve issuance of the same class of security; (3) are the offerings made at or about the same time; (4) is the same type of consideration to be received; and (5) are the offerings made for the same general purpose."[43] Rule 147 in its preliminary notes expressly adopts this five factor test and points out that "any one or more of the * * * factors may be determinative."[44] The rule establishes a six-month safe harbor for avoiding integration with out-of-state sales.[45]

In 1996, Congress preempted state Blue Sky registration requirements[46] with respect to many transactions.[47] Intrastate transactions that qualify for the section 3(a)(11) exemption are not exempt from state registration requirements.[48] The entire premise of the intrastate exemption from federal registration is that the states are more appropriate regulators for transactions occurring solely within the borders of a single state. Accordingly, the transactions must be registered under state law unless an exemption can be found.

§ 4.15   The Small Issue Exemptions

Congress and the Commission over time have developed a number of exemptions for small issues. The small issue exemptions were adopted in recognition of the economics involved, and more importantly because of the SEC's view that due to their size or scope, or the nature of the purchasers, certain transactions do not call for the expansive disclosure required by a full-fledged 1933 Act registration.

The applicable rules, which are discussed in the succeeding sections, are based upon section 4(2)'s exemption for transactions not involving a public offering,[9] section 3(b)'s exemptions for certain offerings not in excess of five million dollars,[10] or section 4(6)'s exemption for sales exclusively to accredited investors.[11] Small issues that are *purely* local in nature may qualify for section 3(a)(11)'s intrastate exemption,[12] which is not dependent on the size of the offering.

In 1982, the Commission adopted Regulation D[13] in an effort to simplify the overlapping rough edges of the most frequently relied upon small issue

43. *Id.*

44. Preliminary note to Rule 147; 17 C.F.R. § 230.147.

45. 17 C.F.R. § 230.147(b)(2). *See* the nine-month limit on resales in Rule 147(e). *See also* Busch v. Carpenter, 598 F.Supp. 519 (D.Utah 1984), *affirmed in part and reversed in part* 827 F.2d 653 (10th Cir.1987) (out-of-state resale occurring seven months after intrastate offering did not destroy the exemption for the intrastate sales).

46. State securities laws are discussed in chapter 8 *infra.*

47. Pub. L. No. 104–290, 110 Stat. 3416 (1996). *See, e.g.,* Symposium, The National Securities Markets Improvements Act—One Year Later, 53 Bus. Law. 507 (1998); Comment, The National Securities Market Improvement Act: How Improved is the Securities Market?, 36 Duq. L. Rev. 365 (1998).

48. 15 U.S.C.A. § 77r(b)(4)(C).

§ 4.15

9. 15 U.S.C.A. § 77d(2). *See* § 4.24 *infra.* The section 4(2) exemption is not limited to small issues. It can be used, and frequently is used for large nonpublic offerings. *Id.*

10. 15 U.S.C.A. § 77c(b). *See* §§ 4.16–4.17, 4.21–4.22 *infra.*

11. 15 U.S.C.A. § 77d(6). *See* § 4.23 *infra.*

12. 15 U.S.C.A. § 77c(a)(11). *See* § 4.12 *supra.*

13. 17 C.F.R. §§ 230.501–506. *See* §§ 4.19–4.25 *infra. See generally* Marvin H. Mahoney, Regulation D: Coherent Exemptions for Small Business Under the Securities Act of 1933, 24 Wm.

exemptions. Regulation A[14] is another exemption for offerings by an issuer of up to five million dollars per year, of which no more than $1.5 million can be attributed to a secondary offering by existing shareholders.[15]

The chart on pages 171–172 summarizes some of the most frequently used exemptions.[16]

& Mary L.Rev. 121 (1982); Theodore Parnall, Bruce R. Kohle & Curtis W. Huff, Private and Limited Offerings After a Decade of Experimentation: The Evolution of Regulation D, 12 N.M.L.Rev. 633 (1982).

14. 17 C.F.R. §§ 230.251–252. *See* § 4.17 *infra. See generally* Harvey Frank, The Processing of Small Issues Under Regulation A, 1962 Duke L.J. 507 (1962).

15. *See* Sec. Act Rel. No. 33–6949, 6 Fed. Sec. L. Rep. (CCH) ¶ 72,439 (SEC July 30, 1992); Sec. Act Rel. No. 33–6924, [1991–1992 Transfer Binder] Fed. Sec. L. Rep. (CCH) ¶ 84,931 (March 11, 1992). The exemption was limited to issues up to $1.5 million prior to the 1992 amendment.

16. This chart is derived from Sec. Act Rel. No. 33–6389 (March 8, 1982). The chart does not include section 3(a)(11)'s intrastate exemption which is not limited either in the number of offerees, nor in the dollar amount of the offering. Nevertheless the intrastate exemption may prove to be an effective exemption by offerings by local small business issuers. *See* § 4.12 *infra.*

Comparison Item	Reg. A	Rule 504	Rule 505	4(2) Rule 506	Sec. 4(6)
Aggregate Offering Price Limitation	$5 million by issuer (every 12 months) ($1.5 million/person other than the issuer).	$1.0 million (every 12 months).	$5.0 million (every 12 months).	Unlimited.	$5.0 million.
Number of Investors	Unlimited	Unlimited	35 + unlimited accredited investors.	35 + unlimited accredited investors.	Unlimited accredited.
Investor Qualification	None.	None.	Accredited or none required.	All purchasers must be sophisticated and wealthy (alone or with purchaser representative) "Accredited" purchaser is presumed to be qualified. [Query whether § 4(2)'s offeree qualifications must also be read into rule 506).	ONLY Accredited.
Limitations on Manner of Offering	Offering Circular. Some limited advertising or announcement.	None.	*General solicitation*: there cannot be a general solicitation unless either (1) the issuer has registered under state law that requires the public filing and distribution of a substantive disclosure document or (2) the offering is exempt under state law that permits a general solicitation.	General solicitation not permitted.	General solicitation not permitted.
Limits on Resale	None.	Securities issued in a Rule 504 offering are subject to the resale restrictions of Rule 144 (17 C.F.R. § 230.144) unless either (1) the issuer has registered under state law that requires the public filing and distribution of a substantive disclosure document or (2) the offering is exempt under state law that permits a general solicitation.	Restricted.	Restricted.	Restricted.
Issuer Qualifications	Only U.S. and Canadian issuers. No investment companies or "development stage" companies. No issuers or underwriters which are disqualified by Reg. A wrongdoing rules.	No investment companies. Not available to 1934 Act reporting companies. No blank check companies. But see rule 504s.	No investment companies or issuers which are disqualified under Reg. A's wrongdoing rules.	None.	None.
Notice of Sales to SEC	Form 1–A: 7 copies to National or Regional Office. Sales material —7 copies—to Regional Office 5 days before use. Form 2–A to report sales.	Form D: 5 copies filed within 15 days of first sale, every 6 months after first sale and 30 days after last sale.	Form D: 5 copies filed within 15 days of first sale, every 6 months after 1st sale, and 30 days after last sale.	Form D: 5 copies filed within 15 days of first sale, every 6 months after 1st sale, and 30 days after last sale.	Form D (Form 4(6) was rescinded 4/15/82).

Comparison Item	Reg. A	Rule 504	Rule 505	4(2) Rule 506	Sec. 4(6)

Information Requirements	Offering Circular—See rule 253.	No information.	1. If purchased solely by accredited, no information specified.
			2. If purchased by non-accredited:
			a. *Non-reporting companies must furnish:*
			  i. Offerings up to $2.0 million: the same kind of information required in a Regulation A offering.
			  ii. Offerings up to $7.5 million: information in part 1 of Form S–18 or available registration, 2 year financials, 1 year audited—if undue effort or expense, issuers other than limited partnerships only balance sheet as of 120 days before offering must be audited. If limited partnership and undue effort or expense, financials may be tax basis.
			  iii. Offerings over $7.5 million [not applicable to rule 505].
			
			b. *Reporting Companies:*
			  i. Rule 14a–3 annual report to shareholders, definitive proxy statement and 10–K, if requested, plus subsequent reports and other updating information or
			  ii. Information in most recent Form S–1 or Forms 10 or Form 10–K plus subsequent reports and other updating information.
			c. *Issuers must make avail. prior to sale:*
			  1. Exhibits
			  ii. Written information given to accredited investors
			  iii. Opportunity to ask questions & receive answers
				1. If purchased solely by accredited, no information specified.
				2. If purchased by non-accredited:
				a. *Non-reporting companies must furnish:*
				  i. Offerings up to $2.0 million: the same kind of information required in a Regulation A offering.
				  ii. Offerings up to $7.5 million: information in part 1 of Form S–18 or available registration, 2 year financials, 1 year audited—if undue effort or expense, issuers other than limited partnerships only balance sheet as of 120 days before offering must be audited. If limited partnership and undue effort or expense, financials may be tax basis.
				  iii. Offerings over $7.5 million: information in part 1 of available registration—if undue efforts or expenses, issuers other than limited partnerships only balance sheet as of 120 days before offering must be audited—if limited partnership and undue effort or expense, financials may be tax basis.
				
				b. *Reporting Companies:*
				  i. Rule 14a–3 annual report to shareholders, definitive proxy statement and 10–K, if requested, plus subsequent reports and other updating information or
				  ii. Information in most recent Form S–1 or Forms 10 or Form 10–K plus subsequent reports and other updating information.
				c. *Issuers must make avail. prior to sale:*
				  1. Exhibits
				  ii. Written information given to accredited investors
				  iii. Opportunity to ask questions & receive answers
					No information specified.

§ 4.16   Qualified Exemptions for Small Issues; Sections 3(b), 4(6), and 3(c)

§ 4.16[1]   Limited Offerings—Section 3(b)

Section 3(b) of the 1933 Act[1] empowers the SEC to promulgate rules and regulations exempting issues of securities where the aggregate per issue offering price to the public does not exceed five million dollars.[2] The only statutory limitation on the creation of the exemption is that the Commission

---

§ 4.16

1.   15 U.S.C.A. § 77c(b).

2.   In 1992, the SEC recommended to Congress that the section 3(b) limit be increased from $5 million to $10 million.

must find "that the enforcement of [the Act] with respect to such securities is not necessary in the public interest and for the protection of investors by reason of the small amount involved or the limited character of public offering."[3] Over the years, section 3(b), which when enacted in 1933 had a $100,000 cap, has to some extent kept up with inflation.[4] The statutory limit was increased in 1980 to the current five million dollars. In the 1990's, the SEC was engaged in a number of small issues initiatives which were designed to make offerings of small issues and by small issuers more efficient without sacrificing the goal of investor protection. With this in mind, in 1992, the Commission recommended that Congress increase section 3(b)'s ceiling to ten million dollars. This proposal was never adopted and has since been rendered moot. Notwithstanding the inflation that has taken place over the nearly twenty-five years since the current five million dollar ceiling was adopted, Congress has not acted to raise it. However, in 1996, Congress granted the SEC the authority to effectively raise the limit. As a general proposition, the SEC was granted expanded rulemaking discretion in 1996 when Congress enacted section 28 of the 1933 Act, discussed below, which allows the SEC to exempt any person, security, or transaction when it believes that it is in the public interest to do so.[5]

Section 3(b) is significantly different from the other major exemptions from registration as it is not self-executing. It is dependent upon SEC rules for implementation. It is not simply the size of the offering that leads to the exemption; it is compliance with the guidelines established by the applicable SEC rules.

The section 3(b) exemptions include the qualified exemptions for offerings up to five million dollars sanctioned by Regulation A,[6] and Rule 504's exemption for offerings not exceeding one million dollars.[7] Section 3(b) also empowers Rule 505's exemption for certain offerings up to five million dollars, sold to no more than thirty-five "unaccredited investors," but which may also include an unlimited number of "accredited investors."[8] Additionally, the section 3(b) exemptions for small issues should be read in conjunction with Rule 506's non-exclusive safe harbor for exempt transactions that do not involve a public offering.[9] The Commission has also exercised its exemptive power under section 3(b) to exempt from registration employee and consultant stock compensation plans (ranging from $500,000 to $5,000,000 annually), provided that the issuer is not subject to the Securities and Exchange Act's periodic reporting requirements.[10]

---

3. 15 U.S.C.A. § 77c(b).

4. The maximum amount was increased from $100,000 in 1933 to $300,000 in 1945, and to $500,000 in 1970. Notwithstanding the increases, there was a clamoring for additional exemptions from federal registration for small issues. Accordingly, in recent years, the upward limits of the exemption have been significantly expanded: from $500,000 to 1.5 million-dollars in 1978 and then again to two million dollars within the same year.

5. 15 U.S.C.A. § 77z–3. *See* § 4.35 *infra*. The exemption must be by rule or regulation. This is in contrast to the 1934 Act's general exemptive authority which may also be implemented by SEC order. 15 U.S.C.A. § 78mm.

6. 17 C.F.R. §§ 230.251–263. *See* § 4.17 *infra*.

7. 17 C.F.R. § 230.504. *See* § 4.21 *infra*.

8. 17 C.F.R. § 230.505. *See* § 4.22 *infra*.

9. 17 C.F.R. § 230.506. *See* § 4.25 *infra*.

10. 17 C.F.R. § 230.701, adopted in Sec. Act Rel. No. 33–6768, [1987–1988 Transfer Binder] Fed. Sec. L. Rep. (CCH) ¶ 84,231 (April 14, 1988). *See* § 4.18 *infra*.

§ 4.16[2] Limited Offerings Solely to Accredited Investors— Section 4(6)

In conjunction with the 1980 amendments that increased the dollar amount in section 3(b) to the current five million dollar ceiling, Congress enacted section 4(6)[20] to further expand the exemptions available for small issues. Section 4(6) exempts all security sales made to "accredited investors" where the aggregate amount sold does not exceed the dollar limit of section 3(b) (*i.e.*, five million dollars). The only conditions to a section 4(6) exemption are that there be no public advertising or solicitation for the offering, and that an appropriate notice of reliance on the exemption be filed with the SEC. SEC Form 4(6), which was the appropriate document for filing a section 4(6) notice, was rescinded in 1982 and has been replaced by Form D.

The section 4(6) exemption is available only for sales of securities that have been offered only to "accredited investors" as defined in section 2(a)(15) of the Act.[21] The statutory definition of this term expressly includes a number of institutional investors, including banks, insurance companies, and investment companies that are registered under the Investment Company Act of 1940, small business investment companies licensed by the Small Business Administration, and employee benefit plans that are subject to ERISA. Additionally, the definition of an accredited investor states that "any person who, on the basis of such factors as financial sophistication, net worth, knowledge, and experience in financial matters, or amount of assets under management qualifies as an accredited investor under rules and regulations which the Commission shall prescribe."[22]

Section 2(a)(15)'s concept of an accredited investor[30] is incorporated into Regulation D's small issue exemptions.[31] Section 4(6) was designed as a companion to the exemptions available under section 3(b). This has been accomplished through the Commission's inclusion of the accredited investor concept into Regulation D.

§ 4.17 Regulation A—Qualified Exemption for Offerings Up to $5,000,000 Per Year

§ 4.17[1] Overview of Regulation A

The oldest, and at one time most widely used of the section 3(b) exemptions for small issues, is the qualified exemption from registration established pursuant to Regulation A, which is embodied in SEC Rules 251 through 263.[1] The exemption provided in Regulation A is dependent upon the securities being offered through the use of an offering circular, in a manner similar to the use of a prospectus in a registered offering. In order to use the Regulation A exemption, an issuer may not offer securities that exceed an

---

20. 15 U.S.C.A. § 77(d)(6).

21. 15 U.S.C.A. § 77b(a)(15).

22. 15 U.S.C.A. § 77b(a)(15)(ii). *See* 17 C.F.R. § 230.215.

30. 15 U.S.C.A. § 77b(a)(15). *See also* 17 C.F.R. § 230.215.

31. *See* Rule 501(a), 17 C.F.R. § 230.501(a). Regulation D is discussed in §§ 4.19–4.22, 4.25 *infra.*

§ 4.17

1. 17 C.F.R. §§ 230.251 thru 230.263.

aggregate amount of five million dollars in any one year.[2] As has been the case with section 3(b),[3] the dollar ceiling for a Regulation A offering has increased over time.

In order to qualify for the Regulation A exemption, the issuer (and selling shareholders in the case of a secondary distribution) must comply with the Regulation's notification and disclosure requirements, including the offering circular delivery requirements that, in essence, have the same effect as a "mini registration." The Regulation A disclosure statements contain much of the information that would be included in a full-blown registration statement, and Rule 253's provisions for an offering circular are analogous to the section 5(b) prospectus delivery requirements.[5] Similarly, Rule 255 provides for the use of a preliminary offering circular prior to the date on which the offering becomes qualified for Regulation A sales.[6] As compared with a registered offering, Regulation A has broader provisions for prefiling gun-jumping sales solicitations. In particular, Rule 254 permits a solicitation of investor interest prior to the use of an offering statement.[7] This procedure is colloquially referred to as testing the waters. It is to be recalled that any comparable testing in the context of a registered offering would constitute an illegal offer to sell in violation of section 5 of the Act.[8]

As outlined above, and discussed more fully below, in order to comply with Regulation A, the qualifying issuer must follow steps similar to those required in a full-fledged registration.[15] Nevertheless, the Regulation A offering will prove to be significantly less expensive than registration, especially in terms of legal, printing, underwriting and accounting fees.

There are a number of advantages to relying upon a Regulation A offering rather than one of the other exemptions or, alternatively going through a full-fledged 1933 Act registration. Unlike a registered public offering, securities issued in a Regulation A offering are not automatically subject to the periodic reporting requirements of the Securities Exchange Act of 1934.[16] Unlike a 1933 Act registration, Regulation A does not require that the financial statements be audited (unless the company already has audited financials). Regulation A offerings are far less expensive than registered offerings. For example, in 1997, the average cost of a Regulation A offering was $40,000 to $60,000 as opposed to the $400,000 to $1 million cost for a registered offering using SEC Form S–1. Unlike a registered offering[17] (and other exemptions

---

2.   17 C.F.R. § 230.254.

3.   The maximum amount was increased from $100,000 in 1933 to $300,000 in 1945, and to $500,000 in 1970. Notwithstanding the increases, there was a clamoring for additional exemptions from federal registration for small issues. Accordingly, over the years, the upward limits of the exemption have been significantly expanded: from $500,000 to 1.5 million dollars in 1978 and then again to two million dollars within the same year. In 1980, the ceiling was raised to the current $5 million, and in 1992 the SEC proposed that Congress raise it again to $10 million.

5.   17 C.F.R. § 230.253. The prospectus requirements are discussed in §§ 2.4, 2.5 *supra.*

6.   17 C.F.R. § 230.255.

7.   17 C.F.R. § 230.254.

8.   15 U.S.C.A. § 77e. *See* § 2.3 *supra.*

15.   *See* chapter 3 *supra.*

16.   Section 15(d) of the 1934 Act provides that the periodic reporting requirements apply to issuers who have registered an offering under the Securities Act of 1933. 15 U.S.C.A. § 78o(d). *See* § 9.3 *infra.*

17.   Another advantage is the "test the waters" process for Regulation A offerings. At one point the SEC said it was considering regulations that would permit a testing of the waters

from registration), the issuer may test the waters to see if there is sufficient investor interest in the offering before embarking on the process.[18] An issuer under Regulation A has three choices of format for the required disclosures.

Regulation A also offers a number of advantages over other exemptions. Unlike most of the other transaction exemptions, general solicitations and advertising is permissible. Unlike most of the other transaction exemptions, there are no restrictions on the resale of securities initially sold under regulation A.[19] Additionally, unlike many of the other exemptions, Regulation A imposes no offeree or purchaser qualification requirements; in other words, anyone can be an offeree or purchaser in a Regulation A offering.

Regulation A is not simply a safe harbor from 1933 Act registration; it is an exclusive harbor, as there is no self-executing statutory exemption. Accordingly, deviations from the rules' requirements will result in loss of the exemption. The SEC has provided, however, that trivial deviations do not necessarily result in loss of the Regulation A exemption. As is also the case with Regulation D,[20] insignificant deviations from Regulation A will not result in a loss of the exemption, provided that there has been a good faith attempt to comply and the deviation does not involve "a condition or requirement directly intended to protect the individual or entity" challenging the transaction.[21] The exception for insignificant deviations does not apply in an SEC administrative proceeding under Rule 258 to suspend the Regulation A qualification.[22]

Many issuers who might otherwise rely on a Regulation A exemption may avail themselves of the streamlined registration for issuers qualifying to use Form SB–1.[23] Form SB–1 is available for offerings not in excess of seven-and-one-half million dollars. Although registration under Form SB–2 may be more onerous than a Regulation A exemption, the registered offering provides more certainty as to compliance with the Act, but also will automatically trigger the periodic reporting obligations of the 1934 Act.[24] Form SB–1 is not the only short form 1933 Act registration for small businesses. Form SB–2 provides another alternative registration form for small business issuers.[25]

§ 4.17[2] Issuers Eligible for Regulation A

The Regulation A exemption is not available to every issuer. Regulation A may be used only by an issuer which is organized under the laws of the United States or Canada and which has its principal place of business in the

---

process for planned registered public offerings but no such rule was ever adopted. *See* Note, Note "Testing the Waters"—The SEC's Feet Go From Wet to Cold, 83 Cornell L. Rev. 464 (1998).

18. Rule 254, 17 C.F.R. § 230.254.

19. However, in order to assure true liquidity for Regulation A securities, issuers may need to voluntarily subject themselves to the 1934 Act's periodic reporting requirements. *See* chapter 9 *infra.* Alternatively, the issuer can provide adequate public information to enable registered broker-dealers to trade in the securities. *See* 1934 Act Rule 15c2–11, 17 C.F.R. § 230.15c2–11.

20. *See* Rule 508, 17 C.F.R. § 230.508. *See* Carl W. Schneider, A Substantial Compliance Defense ("I and I") Defense and Other Changes Are Added to SEC Regulation D, 44 Bus. Law. 1207 (1989).

21. Rule 260, 17 C.F.R. § 230.260.

22. Rule 260(c), 17 C.F.R. § 230.260(c). *See* 17 C.F.R. § 230.258.

23. *See* § 3.4 *supra.*

24. *See* chapter 9 *infra.*

25. *See* § 3.4 *supra.*

United States or Canada.[26] Furthermore, the issuer must not have been subject to the 1934 Act's periodic reporting requirements immediately before the Regulation A offering.[27] The issuer's business may also be a disqualification from the Regulation exemption. The exemption is unavailable for the offer or sale of: (1) fractional undivided interests in oil, gas, or mineral rights,[28] or (2) for securities issued by registered investment companies.[29] Additionally, Regulation A may not be used by "development stage" companies, which are those issuers that have no specific business plan.[30] It is further provided that a plan to merge with unidentified companies does not qualify as a specific business plan.[31] The rationale behind the business plan requirement is to make Regulation A unavailable for "blank check" companies and other common vehicles for initial offerings in the penny stock markets.[32]

Regulation A contains so-called "bad boy" provisions which deny the availability of the exemption where the issuer, its predecessors, or any affiliated issuer has been subject to proceedings stemming from violations of the federal securities laws.[33]

§ 4.17[3] Regulation A—Disqualification Provisions

By virtue of Rule 262,[34] Regulation A is not available where there have been disclosure or other SEC related problems in the past. Specifically, the exemption presumptively is inapplicable where the issuer, its predecessors or affiliated issuers: (1) have filed a registration statement which is currently subject to examination pursuant to section 8 of the 1933 Act,[35] (2) were subject to a refusal order or stop order within the past five years,[36] or (3) were subject to any proceeding pursuant to Rule 258 (which empowers the SEC to issue sanctions similar to those under section 8 with regard to Regulation A)[37] within five years prior to the filing of the Regulation A notification.[38] The rule also disqualifies an issuer from using Regulation A where any of the issuer's predecessors or affiliated issuers have been convicted within the previous five years of any felony or misdemeanor in connection with any security transaction.[39] Thus, for example, an issuer will be disqualified from using Regulation

26. Rule 251(a)(1), 17 C.F.R. § 230.251(a)(1).

27. Rule 251(a)(2), 17 C.F.R. § 230.251(a)(2).

28. Rule 251(a)(5), 17 C.F.R. § 230.251(a)(5). There is a separate exemption for these interests. *See* Regulation B and SEC Rule 300, 17 C.F.R. § 230.300.

29. Rule 251(a)(4), 17 C.F.R. § 230.252(a)(4). The Investment Company Act is discussed in chapter 20 *infra*.

30. Rule 251(a)(3), 17 C.F.R. § 230.251(a)(3).

31. *Id.*

32. Penny stocks and the SEC's initiatives to regulate the penny stock markets is discussed in § 14.19 *infra*.

33. Rule 262, 17 C.F.R. § 230.262, which is discussed *infra* in this section. These "bad boy" provisions are also incorporated into Rule 505's section 3(b) exemption. Rule 505, 17 C.F.R. § 230.505; *see* § 4.21 *infra*.

34. 17 C.F.R. § 230.262.

35. Rule 262(a)(1), 17 C.F.R. § 230.262(a)(1). Section 8 is the provision that empowers the Commission to prevent the effectiveness of a 1933 Act registration. 15 U.S.C.A. § 77h. *See* § 7.1 *infra*; § 3.6 *supra*.

36. Rule 262(a)(1), 17 C.F.R. § 230.262(a)(1).

37. 17 C.F.R. § 230.258.

38. Rule 262(a)(2), 17 C.F.R. § 230.262(a)(2).

39. Rule 262(a)(3), 17 C.F.R. § 230.262(a)(3).

A if its predecessors or any affiliated issuer has been convicted within five years of any crime involving the making of any false filing with the SEC. Similarly, court orders entered within the previous five years, permanently or temporarily restraining or enjoining the issuer from violating the securities laws or from engaging in any act in connection with the purchase or sale of any security involving false filings with the Commission, will disqualify the issuer from using Regulation A. Rule 262's issuer disqualification is not limited to violations of the federal securities laws and thus applies if state blue sky laws or other relevant statutes such as the Federal Mail Fraud Act[40] have been violated. Rule 262 will also disqualify an issuer subject to any order issued by the United States Postal Service against the issuer for false representation.[41]

The disqualifications are not limited to the issuer and its affiliated entities. Similar "bad boy" prohibitions are supplied by Rule 262(b)[42] if the issuer's officers, directors, general partners, or ten-percent beneficial owners have been subject to similar SEC sanctions or court orders. Rule 262(c)[43] creates a comparable disability if the Regulation A issuer uses an underwriter who has been subject to similar proceedings within the past five years.[44] The prohibition relating to underwriters also will render the exemption unavailable if the SEC finds that the issuer used a disqualified *de facto* underwriter.[45]

Rule 262's disqualifications by their terms apply to offerings exempt under Regulation A. However, the SEC has extended them to other exemption transactions. Thus, Rule 505's exemption[46] for certain offerings up to five million dollars also is subject to Rule 262's disqualification provisions.[47]

Rule 262's disqualifications are not absolute. Application may be made to the Commission to waive the bad boy disqualification provisions. The Commission may lift any of the foregoing "bad boy" disqualifications "upon a showing of a good cause, that it is not necessary under the circumstances that the exemption be denied."[48] The SEC has used its no action letter process for granting exemptions from Rule 262's Regulation A disqualifications.

§ 4.17[4] Regulation A—Limitations on Dollar Amount of the Offering

An issuer which is not subject to any of the disqualifications listed in Rule 262 may then qualify for Regulation A, provided that the aggregate offering price of all securities so offered, including any other securities sold under Regulation A,[51] does not exceed five million dollars. In addition, there is a

---

40. Mail and wire fraud are discussed in § 22.4 *infra*.

41. Rule 262(a)(5), 17 C.F.R. § 230.262(b).

42. 17 C.F.R. § 230.262(b).

43. 17 C.F.R. § 230.262(c).

44. *But cf.* Stephens, Inc., 30 Sec. Reg. & L. Rep. (BNA) 1795 (SEC No Action Letter Nov. 23, 1998) (broker-dealer's settlement of civil "play to pay" charges would not be disqualifying).

45. In the Matter of Shearson, Hammill & Co., Sec. Act Rel. No. 7743 (Nov. 12, 1965).

46. 17 C.F.R. § 230.505. The Rule 505 exemption is discussed in § 4.21 *infra*.

47. 17 C.F.R. § 230.505(a).

48. 17 C.F.R. § 230.262.

51. For purposes of the rule the distribution is not completed until each of the securities offered "ultimately comes to rest in the hands of the investing public." R.A. Holman & Co., Inc. v. SEC, 366 F.2d 446, 449–50 (2d Cir.1966), *amended on rehearing,* 377 F.2d 665 (2d Cir.1967), *cert.*

further limit with regard to secondary offerings; no more than one and one-half million dollars may be attributable to the offering price of securities offered by all selling shareholders. However, there can be no resales by affiliates if the issuer has not had a net income from continuing operations in at least one of its last two fiscal years.[52]

§ 4.17[5] Integration With Other Offerings

Formerly, the Regulation A dollar ceiling would be decreased by any other section 3(b) securities sold within the past year, as well as any securities sold in violation of section 5(a). This was of particular importance because any Regulation A offering which occurs within a year of an offering made in reliance upon another exemption is subject to being overturned if the exemption relied upon for the earlier offering is somehow destroyed or otherwise unavailable. In such a case, all securities sold in reliance on Regulation A would also have been sold in violation of section 5(a), since the sales will not have been exempt from registration. Although this method of calculation continues under two other section 3(b) exemptions—Rules 504 and 505[54]—it is no longer the case under Regulation A. As of the 1992 amendments, Regulation A's five million dollar ceiling includes other securities offered within the past twelve months under Regulation A, but there is no aggregation for securities sold under the other section 3(b) exemptions or in violation of section 5. Beyond the dollar computation question, Regulation A provides a safe harbor from integration for prior offers and sales of securities and for subsequent offers or sales where the subsequent transactions involve: (1) securities sold under a registration statement,[55] (2) securities offered as part of an incentive plan pursuant to the exemption provided in Rule 701,[56] (3) securities sold pursuant to an employee benefit plan,[57] (4) sales of securities outside the United States that are exempt under Regulation S,[58] or (5) any sales made more than six months after the Regulation A offering is completed.[59] Even if transactions do not qualify for the safe harbor from integration, integration may be avoided if the transactions satisfy the test for integration generally.[60]

§ 4.17[6] Regulation A—Filing and Notification Requirements

Rules 252, 256, and 257[61] contain Regulation A's filing and notification requirements. Seven copies of notification, now known as an offering statement, must be filed on Form 1–A at the Commission's national office in Washington, DC. Formerly, Regulation A filings could be made in SEC

---

denied 389 U.S. 991, 88 S.Ct. 473, 19 L.Ed.2d 482 (1967), *rehearing denied* 389 U.S. 1060, 88 S.Ct. 767, 19 L.Ed.2d 867 (1968).

52. Rule 251(b), 17 C.F.R. §§ 230.251(b).

54. 17 C.F.R. §§ 230.504, 505. *See* §§ 4.21, 4.22 *infra*.

55. Rule 251(c)(2)(i), 17 C.F.R. § 230.251(c)(2)(i).

56. Rule 251(c)(2)(ii), 17 C.F.R. § 230.251(c)(2)(ii). The Rule 701 exemption is discussed in § 4.18 *infra*.

57. Rule 251(c)(2)(iii), 17 C.F.R. § 230.251(c)(2)(iii).

58. Rule 251(c)(2)(iv), 17 C.F.R. § 230.251(c)(2)(iv). Regulation S (Rules 901 *et seq.*) is discussed in § 17.4 *infra*.

59. Rule 251(c)(2)(v), 17 C.F.R. § 230.251(c)(2)(v).

60. *See* Non–Public Offering Exemption Sec. Act Rel. No. 33–4552, 1962 WL 3573, 1 Fed.Sec.L. Rep. (CCH) ¶ 2781 (Nov. 6, 1962). Integration is discussed in § 4.36 *infra*.

61. 17 C.F.R. §§ 230.252, 256, 257.

Regional offices, but as of October 1, 1996, the Regional Offices ceased accepting these filings. Instead, they must be made with the small business office at the Commission's national headquarters in Washington.[62] The Commission has provided two alternative formats for Form 1–A. First, there is a narrative format that parallels the traditional registration form under the Act. In an attempt to make the process easier for many issuers, the Commission has also established an alternative form in question and answer format. Regardless of which format is used, the offering statement must be signed by the issuer, its chief executive and financial officers, a majority of its board of directors,[63] and all persons for whose account any of the securities are to be offered.[64] There is a nonrefundable five hundred dollar initial filing fee, with no subsequent fees for amendments.[65] All amendments to the initial notification must be filed together with three additional copies and must be signed in the same manner as the original filing. Paralleling the procedure for 1933 Act registrations, absent a delaying notation, the offering statement becomes effective on the twentieth calendar day following its filing.[66] Filing of amendments begins the twenty-day period anew.[67]

§ 4.17[7] Regulation A—Testing the Waters

Rule 254 expressly permits the issuer, prior to the filing of the offering statement, to test the waters in order to obtain indications of interest from potential investors.[82] Solicitations that would otherwise be illegal offers to sell may be made prior to the filing of the offering circular so long as the solicitation does no more than solicit indications of investor interest and makes clear that offers and sales can only be made after filing of the offering statement pursuant to an offering circular. Although it is not a condition of the exemption, Rule 254(b) provides that such solicitations of investor interest be on file with the SEC on or before its use. The rule further sets forth specific warnings and disclaimers that should be in the prefiling solicitation. Specifically, it must be explained that no money is being solicited or will be accepted, and that sales will be made only by use of an offering circular.[83] The solicitation of interest must also make it clear that an indication of interest does not result in an obligation of any kind.[84] The solicitation should also identify the issuer's business and also must name its chief executive officer.[85] In order to take advantage of the testing the waters procedure, the materials used for testing the waters should be submitted to the SEC for review on or before the first day they are used.[86]

---

62. *See* Sec. Act Rel. No. 33–7373, 1996 SEC LEXIS 3423 (SEC Dec. 16, 1996).

63. This parallels the requirements for a registration statement. *See* chapter 3 *supra*.

64. Rule 252(d), 17 C.F.R. §§ 230.252(d).

65. Rule 252(f), 17 C.F.R. § 230.252(f).

66. Rule 252(g)(1), 17 C.F.R. § 230.252(g)(1).

67. Rules 252(g)(3), 252(h)(1), 17 C.F.R. §§ 230.252(g)(3), (h)(1).

82. 17 C.F.R. § 230.254. At one point the SEC said it was considering regulations that would permit a testing of the waters process for planned registered public offerings but no such rule was ever adopted. *See* Note, Note "Testing the Waters"—The SEC's Feet Go From Wet to Cold, 83 Cornell L. Rev. 464 (1998).

83. Rule 254(b)(2)(iii), 17 C.F.R. §§ 230.254(b)(2)(iii).

84. Rule 254(b)(2)(i), (ii), 17 C.F.R. §§ 230.254(b)(2)(i), (ii).

85. Rule 254(b)(2)(iv), 17 C.F.R. §§ 230.254(b)(2)(iv).

86. Rule 254(b)(1), 17 C.F.R. § 230.254(b)(1). The rule provides that while it is "not a condition to any exemption pursuant to this rule ... the issuer shall submit a copy ..." to the SEC's national office in Washington, D.C. (attention to: the Office of Small Business Review).

As noted above, these solicitations can take place only prior to the filing of the offering statement. Accordingly, no sales can take place for at least twenty days from the date of the last such testing of the waters. Presumably, this minimum twenty calendar day cooling-off period, which generally will be longer, will give investors sufficient opportunity to receive, read, and evaluate the materials in the Regulation A disclosure documents which are discussed below.

§ 4.18 Rule 701—Exemption for Employee Compensation Plans of Issuers Not Subject to Exchange Act Periodic Reporting Requirements

§ 4.18[1] Overview of Rule 701

In 1988, the Commission exercised its exemptive power under section 3(b) to exempt from registration employee stock compensation plans (ranging from five hundred thousand dollars to five million dollars annually), provided that the issuer is neither subject to the Securities Exchange Act's periodic reporting requirements nor an investment company which is (or is required to be) registered under the Investment Company Act of 1940.[1] In 1999, the Commission eliminated the five million dollar annual ceiling so that the exemption is now available for offerings that do not exceed the greater of one million dollars (rather than the former $500,000 limit) or fifteen percent of the issuer's total assets, or fifteen percent of the outstanding securities of that class.[2] Issuers relying on Rule 701's exemption are not precluded from also relying on other exemptions.[3]

§ 4.18[2] Issuer Qualification for Rule 701

Since the Rule 701 exemption is limited to securities of non-reporting companies, it is not available to issuers whose securities are traded on a national exchange or on the more active over-the-counter markets.[4] A subsidiary of a public company may rely on Rule 701 for issuing its securities to its employees, at least when the nonpublic subsidiary's securities are issued to consultants and advisers who are not insiders of the parent.[5] Rule 701 is limited to offerings by issuers and thus does not apply to secondary offerings by resellers. Accordingly, since the exemption is available only to issuers, it cannot be relied upon by affiliates or anyone else reselling securities on the issuer's behalf.[6]

---

§ 4.18

1. 17 C.F.R. § 230.701, adopted in Sec. Act Rel. No. 33–6768, [1987–1988 Transfer Binder] Fed. Sec. L. Rep. (CCH) ¶ 84,231 (April 14, 1988). The Investment Company Act is discussed in chapter 20 *infra*.

2. Rule 701(d)(2), 17 C.F.R. § 230.701(d)(2). *See* Sec. Act Rel. No. 33–7645 (SEC Feb. 25, 1999). The Commission was able to raise Rule 701's dollar limit by amending the rule in reliance on section 28's general exemptive authority. 15 U.S.C. § 77z–3.

3. "Attempted compliance with the rule does not act as an exclusive election; the issuer can also claim the availability of any other applicable exemption." 17 C.F.R. § 230.701, preliminary note 3.

4. The Exchange Act's periodic reporting requirements are discussed in §§ 9.2, 9.3 *infra*.

5. American Bar Association, 1999 WL 592214, 31 Sec. Reg. & L. Rep. (BNA) 1186 (SEC No Action Letter Aug. 3, 1999).

6. 17 C.F.R. § 230.701 preliminary note 4.

§ 4.18[3] Rule 701—Qualifying Compensation Plans

The exemption set out in Rule 701 applies to a wide variety of compensation plans. It applies to purchase plans, option plans, bonus plans, stock appreciation rights, profit sharing, thrift, incentive, or similar plans.[7] Rule 701 permits an issuer to offer securities pursuant to a written contract or written compensation plan to its employees, directors, general partners, trustees, officers, consultants, or advisers.[8] The securities can be issued only in return for bona fide services but not in return for services rendered in connection with a capital raising transaction involving securities.[9] Thus, the exemption is not available for compensation of underwriters or most promoters.

In its preliminary notes to Rule 701, the Commission observes that "[t]he exemption provided by the rule is not available to any issuer for any transaction which, while in technical compliance with such rule, is part of a plan or scheme to evade the registration requirements of the Act."[10] Thus, issuers must be careful to document the bona fide nature of any compensation plan which they seek to bring within the exemption.

§ 4.18[4] Limitation on Dollar Amount of Rule 701 Offering

The maximum amount of securities that can be offered within a twelve-month period pursuant to a compensation plan varies from one million dollars to a larger amount, depending upon the size of the company and number of shares already outstanding. The rule formerly established a five hundred thousand dollar limit, with two alternative means of raising that limit up to five million dollars.[12] However, in 1999, the Commission changed the five hundred thousand dollar limit to one million dollars and also eliminated the five million dollar ceiling.[13] An offering under Rule 701 may exceed the one million dollar limit based on either the issuer's net assets or previously outstanding securities of the same class. The issuer may rely on Rule 701 for an amount up to the greater of (1) fifteen percent of the total assets of the issuer,[14] measured at the issuer's most recent balance sheet date, if no older than its last fiscal year end[15] or (2) fifteen percent of the outstanding amount of the class of securities being offered and sold in reliance on this section, measured at the issuer's most recent balance sheet date, if no older than its last fiscal year end.[16] Although the Commission has lifted the former five million dollar ceiling, offerings under Rule 701 in excess of five million dollars must be made with the use of a disclosure document.[17]

---

7. 17 C.F.R. § 230.701(b)(2).

8. 17 C.F.R. § 230.701(b)(1).

9. 17 C.F.R. § 230.701(b)(1).

10. 17 C.F.R. § 230.701, preliminary note 6. In such a case registration would be required. *Id.*

12. Former Rule 701(b)(5), 17 C.F.R. § 230.701(b)(5) (1998).

13. Rule 701(d)(2), 17 C.F.R. § 230.701(d)(2). *See* Sec. Act Rel. No. 33–7645 (SEC Feb. 25, 1999).

14. Or of the issuer's parent if the issuer is a wholly-owned subsidiary and the securities represent obligations that the parent fully and unconditionally guarantees.

15. Rule 701(d)(2)(ii), 17 C.F.R. § 230.701(d)(2)(ii).

16. Rule 701(d)(2)(iii), 17 C.F.R. § 230.701(d)(2)(iii).

17. Rule 701(e), 17 C.F.R. § 230.701(e).

§ 4.18[5] Integration Doctrine Not Applicable to Rule 701 Offerings

When successive offerings are part of a single plan of financing, ordinarily the Commission may invoke the integration doctrine in order to integrate the multiple transactions into one.[18] Unlike the other exemptions, there is an express exclusion[19] from the integration doctrine. Additionally, unlike the other section 3(b) exemptions,[20] securities sold pursuant to other section 3(b) exemptions need not be counted in the five million dollar ceiling.

§ 4.18[6] Restrictions on Resale Following Rule 701 Offerings

Securities acquired pursuant to a Rule 701 offering are deemed to be restricted securities within the meaning of Rule 144.[21] The securities may not be resold unless in compliance with the Act's registration requirements or pursuant to an exemption.[22] In the event that the issuer becomes an Exchange Act reporting company, after ninety days of reporting company status, nonaffiliates of the issuer are permitted to resell the securities acquired in a Rule 701 offering by following the guidelines set forth in Rule 144, but without having to comply with Rule 144's informational requirements, one-year holding period, limitations on amount of securities to be sold, or notification requirements.[23] In such a case, affiliates may also resell their stock under Rule 144 but must comply with all of the rule's limitations except for the holding period.

§ 4.19 Coordination of the Small Issue and Limited Offering Exemptions: Regulation D—An Overview

§ 4.19[1] Regulation D in Context

In promulgating Regulation D,[1] the SEC adopted a comprehensive scheme for exemptions relating to small issues and small issuers. Regulation D is "designed to simplify and clarify existing exemptions, to expand their availability, and to achieve uniformity between federal and state exemptions."[2] The exemptions of Regulation D combine many of the elements of section 3(b)'s qualified exemptions for small issues,[3] section 4(6)'s exemption for

---

18. Integration is discussed in § 4.36 *infra*.

19. "Offers and sales exempt pursuant to this '230.701 are deemed to be part of a single, discrete offering and are not subject to integration with any other offering or sale whether registered under the Act or otherwise exempt from the registration requirements of the Act." Rule 701(f), 17 C.F.R. § 230.701(f).

20. Regulation A, which is discussed in § 4.17 *supra;* Rule 504, which is discussed in § 4.21 *infra;* and Rule 505, which is discussed in § 4.22 *infra*.

21. Rule 701(g)(1), 17 C.F.R. § 230.701(g)(1). *See* Rule 144, 17 C.F.R. § 230.144.

22. Rule 701(g)(2), 17 C.F.R. § 230.701(g)(2).

23. Rule 701(g)(3), 17 C.F.R. § 230.701(g)(3).

§ 4.19

1. 17 C.F.R. §§ 230.501–230.506.

2. Sec. Act Rel. No. 33–6389, [1981–1982 Transfer Binder] Fed. Sec. L. Rep. (CCH) ¶ 83,106 (March 8, 1982).

3. 15 U.S.C.A. § 77c(b). *See* § 4.16 *supra*.

offerings to "accredited investors,"[4] and section 4(2)'s exemption for issuer transactions not involving a public offering.[5]

Although embodied in one regulation, it is imperative to keep in mind that Regulation D is not a single integrated exemption but rather consists of three separate but interrelated exemptions.[6] Rule 504, promulgated under section 3(b), provides an exemption for certain offerings not exceeding one million dollars within a twelve-month period.[7] Rule 505, which similarly is a section 3(b) exemption, exempts certain offerings not exceeding five million dollars within a twelve-month period.[8] The third exemption, Rule 506, promulgated under section 4(2), permits nonpublic offerings to qualified purchasers without any limitation on dollar amount.[9] Although Regulation D contains a number of common definitions and requirements for the three exemptions set forth in Rules 504, 505, and 506, it is best to consider each exemption on its own terms rather than attempting to define a common thread that runs throughout. This is because the three rules are aimed at three different types of transactions. For example, although Rules 504 and 505 are both section 3(b), exemptions, Rule 504 contemplates that there may be a public offering within the confines of an exempt Rule 504 offering within the one million dollar limit. On the other hand, general solicitations are prohibited by both rules 505 and Rule 506. Since Rule 505 is a section 3(b) exemption, it is subject to the five million dollar ceiling while Rule 506 is not. Finally, to the extent that the Rule 506 is derived from the section 4(2) exemption, it is dependent upon the offering limitations imposed on that exemption by the Supreme Court.[10]

§ 4.20 Regulation D: Definitions, Conditions, and Filing Requirements—SEC Rules 501, 502, and 503

§ 4.20[1] Overview of Regulation D

Regulation D is a series of eight rules establishing three small issue or limited offering exemptions from the registration requirements of the 1933 Securities Act.[1] Rules 501 through 503 set forth the definitions, terms, and conditions that apply to the three exemptions provided in Rules 504, 505, and 506.[2] The rules provide exemptions for offerings that are limited in the type and number of offerees as well as for those limited in dollar amount. The definitions in Rules 501 through 503 consolidate, clarify, and expand terms

---

4. 15 U.S.C.A. § 77d(6). *See* § 4.23 *infra.*

5. 15 U.S.C.A. § 77d(2). *See* § 4.24 *infra.* Rule 506 provides a safe harbor for the section 4(2) exemption. 17 C.F.R. § 230.506. For a chart depicting the basic coverage of Regulation D *see* § 4.15 *supra.*

6. Regulation D consists of three basic exemptions as set out in Rules 504, 505 and 506. 17 C.F.R. §§ 230.504–230.506. *See* §§ 4.19–4.22, 4.25 *infra.*

7. 17 C.F.R. § 230.504. In a rule 504 offering, no more than $500,000 of the aggregate offering price may be attributable to securities sold without registration under state law. 17 C.F.R. § 230.504(b)(2)(i). *See* § 4.21 *infra.*

8. 17 C.F.R. § 230.505. *See* § 4.23 *infra.*

9. 17 C.F.R. § 230.506. *See* § 4.25 *infra.*

10. SEC v. Ralston Purina Co., 346 U.S. 119, 73 S.Ct. 981, 97 L.Ed. 1494 (1953). *See* § 4.24[1] *infra.*

§ 4.20

1. 17 C.F.R. §§ 230.501–230.506. *See* Sec. Act Rel. No. 33–6389 (March 8, 1982).

2. These exemptions are discussed in §§ 4.21, 4.22, 4.25 *infra.*

that had been used in former SEC Rules 146, 240, and 242, all of which were rescinded effective June 30, 1982.[3]

§ 4.20[2] Regulation D—Definitions

Rule 501 sets forth eight definitions applicable throughout Regulation D. Briefly, they are as follows.

An "accredited investor,"[12] a term which is also defined in section 2(a)(15) of the Act,[13] is any person who in fact comes within, or whom the issuer reasonably believes comes within, any of eight categories of investors at the time securities are sold to him or her. Generally, these categories include wealthy and/or financially sophisticated investors such as banks, insurance companies, tax-exempt organizations, directors and executive officers of the issuer, and natural persons who have considerable net worth or large annual incomes. The Regulation D exemptions either limit or exclude offerings made to any nonaccredited persons. The concept of accredited investor is also relevant to the amount and type of information the issuer must furnish to purchasers during a Regulation D offering.[14] Additionally, section 4(6) of the Act[15] exempts offerings of up to five million dollars where all offerees and purchasers are accredited investors. Failure to take adequate precautions to screen accredited investors is likely to result in the loss of an exemption.[16]

An "affiliate"[17] is a person who controls, is controlled by, or is under common control with the person with whom he or she is affiliated.[18] This definition captures the same concept that is found in the definition of control person under SEC Rule 405.[19]

"Aggregate offering price"[20] is defined to include all consideration, including non-cash items, received by an issuer for the issuance of its securities. The definition includes a comment regarding how to determine the price of securities sold in whole or in part for non-cash consideration. Determination of the aggregate offering price is important for Rules 504 and 505,[21] which have dollar ceilings of one million and five million dollars, respectively.[22]

---

3. *See* Sec. Act Rel. No. 33–6389 (March 8, 1982).

12. 17 C.F.R. § 230.501(a).

See Howard Friedman, On Being Rich, Accredited, and Undiversified: The Lacunae in Contemporary Securities Regulation, 47 Okla. L. Rev. 291 (1994).

13. 15 U.S.C.A. § 77b(a)(15); 17 C.F.R. § 230.215. *See* § 4.23 *infra*.

14. *See* 17 C.F.R. § 230.502(b).

15. 15 U.S.C.A. § 77d(6). *See* § 4.23 *infra*.

16. *See, e.g.,* SEC v. Interlink Data Network of Los Angeles, Inc., 1993 WL 603274, [1993–1994 Transfer Binder] Fed. Sec. L. Rep. (CCH) ¶ 98,049 (C.D.Cal.1993).

17. 17 C.F.R. § 230.501(b).

18. 17 C.F.R. § 230.501(c).

19. 17 C.F.R. § 230.405.

20. 17 C.F.R. § 230.501(c). As explained more fully elsewhere, the aggregate offering price includes all securities sold within the preceding twelve months under section 3(b) or in violation of section 5. *See* § 4.17 *supra* and §§ 4.21, 4.22 *infra*.

21. 17 C.F.R. §§ 230.504, 230.505. *See* §§ 4.21, 4.22 *infra*.

22. Rules 505 and 506 are not available if there has been a general solicitation of offerees. Rule 504 offerings can be made with a general solicitation only if made pursuant to a state law mandated disclosure document. A general solicitation can also be used in a Rule 504 offering only to accredited investors (as that term is defined in Rule 501(a) under a state law exemption that permits a general solicitation. The concept of general solicitation is discussed *infra*.

Rule 501 defines "business combination"[23] as any transaction defined in Rule 145[24] of the 1933 Act. This includes mergers and consolidations of more than one organization.

Rule 501 further provides the method for calculating the number of purchasers involved in an exempt offering.[25] This computation is relevant to the exemptions provided by Rules 505 and 506,[26] which are limited to thirty-five purchasers. However, in making the thirty-five purchaser computation, accredited investors[27] are not included.[28] Accordingly, there can be more than 35 actual purchasers if there are accredited investors in the group of purchasers.

Rule 501(f)[29] defines "executive officer" to include the president, and certain vice presidents as well as other policy makers of the issuer.

"Issuer" under Regulation D[30] follows the definition in section 2(a)(4) of the 1933 Act,[31] with the exception that in certain offerings during reorganizations under the Bankruptcy Act, the trustee or debtor in possession may be considered an issuer under Rule 501(g).

A "purchaser representative"[32] is defined, broadly, to be a person unaffiliated with the issuer who has such knowledge and experience in financial and business matters that he is capable of evaluating the risks and merits of a proposed offering. A purchaser representative can be used to qualify purchasers for Rule 506's safe harbor for private placements.[33]

§ 4.20[3] Conditions of Regulation D Offerings

Rule 502[34] establishes four conditions that are applicable to all Regulation D offerings. Those conditions relate to: (1) the integration doctrine, (2) the information to be supplied to offerees, (3) the manner of soliciting purchasers, and (4) limitations on resales.

The first condition sets forth a safe harbor to avoid the integration of more than one exempt offering; it also provides a five-factor test to be considered for offerings that may not be protected by the safe harbor.[35] In short, there is a window that will last for at least twelve months during which the question of whether to integrate transactions will be answered according to the highly factual five-factor test.[36] There is a safe harbor from integration for transactions taking place outside of that period. As discussed more fully in a subsequent section, Rule 502(a) provides that offers and sales taking place

---

23. 17 C.F.R. § 230.501(d).

24. 17 C.F.R. § 230.145. *See* § 5.2 *infra*.

25. 17 C.F.R. § 230.501(e).

26. 17 C.F.R. §§ 230.505(b), 230.506(b). *See* §§ 4.21, 4.25 *infra*.

27. *See* § 4.20[2][A] *supra*.

28. 17 C.F.R. § 230.501(e).

29. 17 C.F.R. § 230.501(f).

30. 17 C.F.R. § 230.501(g).

31. 15 U.S.C.A. § 77b(a)(4).

32. 17 C.F.R. § 230.501(h).

33. 17 C.F.R. § 230.502.

34. 17 C.F.R. § 230.506. *See* § 4.25 *infra*.

35. 17 C.F.R. § 230.502(a).

36. *See* § 4.36 *infra*.

more than six months before the beginning for the Regulation D offering and those taking place more than six months after the completion of the offering will not be integrated into the Regulation D offering.[37] Transactions that are not integrated under either the safe harbor or the five-factor test will not destroy the exemption.

The second condition establishes the type of information that an issuer is required to supply to purchasers for an offering exempted by Regulation D.[38] If all of the purchasers are accredited investors as defined in Rule 501, then Rule 502 does not require that any specific information be furnished to them by the issuer. Formerly, the SEC required that if there was at least one unaccredited purchaser, all purchasers (including those who are accredited) had to be provided with the specified information. The SEC deleted this requirement and has replaced it with a *recommendation* that all purchasers be given this information. The amount and format of information required will depend on the size of the offering and whether the issuer is a reporting company under the Securities Exchange Act of 1934.[39]

Issuers subject to the 1934 Act's periodic reporting requirements are required to make available information contained in the most recent annual and quarterly reports as well as any disclosures made pursuant to the proxy rules.[40] With regard to issuers that are not subject to the 1934 Act reporting requirements, the mandated disclosures depend on the size of the offering. With regard to nonfinancial information, Rule 502(b)(2)(i)(A)[41] calls for disclosures that are comparable to the information that would be required in Part I of the registration statement that the issuer would be required to file in a public offering,[42] or, if the issuer is eligible to use Regulation A,[43] the types of information that would be required on Part II of Form 1–A. With regard to information relating to the financial statement, the degree of disclosure varies with the size of the offering. For offerings of up to two million dollars, the financial disclosures should generally conform to the requirements of Item 310 of Regulation S–B.[44] Financial disclosures in offerings up to seven and one-half million dollars must contain the same type of information that would be required in Part I of Registration Form SB–2, whether or not the issuer would qualify for use of that form; except that only the issuer's balance sheet (which must be dated within one hundred and twenty days of the offering) need be certified.[45] For offerings up to seven and one-half million dollars, if

---

37. 17 C.F.R. § 230.502(a).

38. 17 C.F.R. § 230.502(b). *See* SEC Rules 215 and 501, 17 C.F.R. §§ 230.215, 230.501 for the definition of accredited investor.

39. The 1934 Act registration and reporting requirements are discussed in §§ 9.2, 9.3 *infra*.

40. 17 C.F.R. § 230.502(b)(2)(ii).

41. 17 C.F.R. § 230.502(b)(2)(i)(A). The disclosures must contain the types of information required by Part II of Form 1–A.

42. The degree of disclosure may vary with the size of the issuer and the size of the offering. The alternative registration forms are discussed in § 3.4 *supra*.

43. Regulation A is available to issuers not subject to the 1934 Act's reporting requirements and may be used for offerings of up to five million dollars. Regulation A is discussed in § 4.17 *supra*.

44. 17 C.F.R. § 230.502(b)(2)(i)(B)(2). However, only the issuer's balance sheet need be audited; that balance sheet must be dated within 120 days of the offering. Regulation S–B is the disclosure guide for small business issuers. *See* § 3.4 *supra*.

45. 17 C.F.R. § 230.502(b)(2)(i)(B)(2). Form SB–2 and its eligibility requirements are discussed in § 3.4 *supra*.

the issuer is not a limited partnership and is unable to obtain audited financial statements without unreasonable effort or expense, then only the issuer's balance sheet must be audited and dated within 120 days of the offering.[46] In the case of a limited partnership that cannot obtain audited statements without an undue burden, it is sufficient to furnish financial statements prepared in accordance with federal income tax standards and generally accepted accounting principles.[47]

For offerings over seven and one-half million dollars, the issuer must make disclosures as would be required by the applicable 1933 Act registration form. Where the issuer is not a 1934 Act reporting company and cannot obtain audited financial statements without unreasonable delay and expense, it may elect to provide an audited balance sheet dated within one hundred and twenty days of the beginning of the offering.[48] With regard to limited partnership offerings by nonreporting companies, if an audited financial statement cannot be obtained without unreasonable effort or expense, then the issuer may provide a balance sheet, dated within one hundred and twenty days of the start of the offering, provided that the balance sheet has been prepared in accordance with federal income tax requirements and the balance sheet has been examined and reported on by an independent or certified public accountant.[49] Failure to comply with any applicable informational requirements will generally be fatal to a Regulation D offering.[50]

Rule 502(b)(1) provides that the foregoing informational requirements do not apply to offerings of up to one million dollars that are made pursuant to Rule 504. As pointed out above, the information requirements do not apply to Rule 505 or Rule 506 offerings in which all purchasers are accredited investors. However, if there are any nonaccredited investors, then each nonaccredited purchaser must receive the required information. Formerly, the Commission required that the offering circular go to *all* investors if there were any unaccredited investors. Although the SEC no longer imposes the affirmative disclosure requirements for all investors, it recommends that even accredited investors be supplied with the offering circular.

The third condition of Rule 502 prohibits the offer or sale of securities by a general solicitation or general advertising.[51] The concept of general solicitation is more concerned with the types of potential investors that are contacted rather than the number of potential investors contacted. Thus, for example, a general solicitation may exist even if relatively few potential investors are contacted if those persons contacted do no satisfy the necessary sophistication, wealth, and/or experience requirements for the offering. Similarly, contacting a large number of qualified potential investors will not constitute a general solicitation.[52] One of the benchmarks of a general solicitation is contacting potential investors with no previous relationship to the issuer or persons promoting the offering. Accordingly, one way to avoid a general solicitation is

---

46.   17 C.F.R. § 230.502(b)(2)(i)(B)(2).

47.   *Id.*

48.   17 C.F.R. § 230.502(b)(2)(i)(B)(3).

49.   *Id.*

50.   *See, e.g.,* SEC v. Interlink Data Network of Los Angeles, Inc., 1993 WL 603274, [1993–1994 Transfer Binder] Fed. Sec. L. Rep. (CCH) ¶ 98,049 (C.D.Cal.1993).

51.   17 C.F.R. § 230.502(c).

52.   *See, e.g.,* Iponet, 1996 WL 431821 (SEC No Action Letter July 26, 2000) (permitting use of the Internet to contact accredited investors).

to use an underwriter or other promoter who has a ready list of qualified potential investors with whom they have dealt previously.[54] Mass mailings will constitute a general solicitation,[55] as will mailings to a group of unrelated investors whose names were obtained through purchase of a mailing list.[56] Similarly, mailing lists, however compiled, will constitute a general solicitation, unless the potential investors have been properly screened as qualified for the offering.

This prohibition applies in both Rule 505 and Rule 506 offerings.[58] The prohibition against general solutions also applies to offerings under Rule 504 unless made in compliance with applicable state laws.[59] As discussed more fully in a later section, the existence of unqualified offerees in a Rule 505 or Rule 506 offering may be sufficient to establish that a general solicitation has occurred.[60] The existence of a general solicitation will be a significant factor in finding the exemption unavailable.[61]

Advertisements and other generally directed offers to sell clearly constitute a general solicitation. Similarly, contacting a wide variety of potential purchasers without regard to their wealth, sophistication, or investment sophistication will be a general solicitation. In order to avoid having a general solicitation, persons to whom inquiries are sent must be prescreened in such a way so as to assure that they do not represent a cross section of the investing public. Thus, for example, assuring that only accredited investors will receive offering materials will preclude a finding that a general solicitation has taken place, even if a large number of investors are contacted.[63] Safeguards can be imposed on online offerings to assure, through the use of passwords, that only qualified investors have access to the offering information.[64]

Finally, Rule 502(d)[68] sets forth limits on the resale of securities acquired in a Regulation D transaction. Formerly, these restrictions did not apply to offerings under Rule 504. However, in 1999, the Commission amended Rule 504 to require resale restrictions except in two situations.[69] Resale restrictions thus now apply in most Regulation D offerings.[70] As a safeguard against illegal

---

54. This was done successfully, for example, in Mary S. Krech Trust v. Lakes Apartments, 642 F.2d 98 (5th Cir.1981).

55. *See* Pennsylvania Securities Commission, 1990 WL 285794 (SEC No Action Letter January 16, 1990)

56. In the Matter of Kenman Corp., Administrative Proceeding File No. 3–6505 Release No. 34–21962, 32 S.E.C. Docket 1352, 1985 WL 548507 n. 6 (SEC April 19, 1985).

58. *See* §§ 4.21, 4.25 *infra.*

59. *See* § 4.21 *infra.*

60. *See* § 4.26 *infra.*

61. *See, e.g.,* SEC v. Interlink Data Network of Los Angeles, Inc., 1993 WL 603274, [1993–1994 Transfer Binder] Fed. Sec. L. Rep. (CCH) ¶ 98,049 (C.D.Cal.1993).

63. *See, e.g.,* Lamp Technologies, Inc., 1997 WL 282988 (SEC No Action Letter May 29, 1997).

64. *See* Use of Electronic Media, Sec. Act Rel. No. 33–7856, 2000 WL 502290 (SEC April 28, 2000).

68. 17 C.F.R. § 230.502(d).

69. Resale restrictions must be imposed unless either (1) the securities are registered under state law that requires the filing and distribution of a substantive disclosure document, or (2) the securities are offered only to accredited investors under a state law exemption from registration that permits a general solicitation. Rule 504(b)(1).

70. Even without resale restrictions under Regulation D, securities acquired in any exempt transaction cannot be resold without an applicable exemption. Section 4(1)'s exemption ordinarily will apply unless the seller is an affiliate of the issuer. *See, e.g.,* Hawkins, 1997 SEC No–Act. LEXIS 700 (SEC No Action Letter June 26, 1997). Section 4(1), 15 U.S.C.A. § 77d(1) is discussed in §§ 4.26, 4.27 *infra.*

resales, the issuer relying upon a Regulation D exemption, based on either a Rule 505 or Rule 506 offering (or a Rule 504 offering unless the resale restriction has been lifted) is required to exercise reasonable care to assure that purchasers are not underwriters as defined by section 2(a)(11) of the 1933 Act.[71] It is common for issuers to require all purchasers in a nonpublic offering to sign letters of investment intent.[72] Rule 502(d) requires the issuer to take precautions against resales, including issuing appropriate transfer instructions to the transfer agent and placing a legend indicating the transfer restriction on the share certificate. Section 8–204 of the Uniform Commercial Code provides that any such restrictions must appear in a prominent restrictive legend on the share certificates.[73] Failure to comply with the UCC's provisions can result in liability to transferees who acquire the securities without knowledge of the restrictions.[74]

In light of the resale restrictions that apply to securities offered under Regulation D, it is common for purchasers of significant amounts of Regulation D securities to be concerned about liquidity. Any registered secondary offering requires the issuer's cooperation. Accordingly, one way to achieve liquidity is for purchasers of Regulation D securities to bargain with the issuer for registration rights. These registration rights can be couched in a variety of ways. For example, the purchaser might exact a contractual right to participate in any public offerings by the issuer.[75] Understandably, issuers of non-public securities are reluctant to grant the purchasers the right to insist on a registration on demand. But such demand rights do appear in rare instances. Registration rights are also found in merger agreements involving merger of a nonpublic company into a public company since in many such transactions, the shares issued in the merger will be subject to Rule 144 resale restrictions absent a registration statement covering those shares.[76]

Rule 503 sets forth requirements for maintaining a record of exempt sales. Under Rule 503, the Commission requires an initial filing within fifteen days after the first sale of securities pursuant to a Regulation D offering; subsequent notices of sales are due every six months after the first sale and thirty days after the final sale.[77] In May 1996, the SEC voted to eliminate the

---

71. 15 U.S.C.A. § 77b(a)(11). *See* §§ 4.28–4.29 *infra.* There are no restrictions on resale in a Rule 504 transaction under certain circumstances. 17 C.F.R. § 230.504(b)(1). Since any security acquired in a Rule 504 transaction, absent an exemption for that resale, cannot be resold without registration, the purchaser may well be subject to resale limitations. *See* § 4.27 *infra.* Accordingly, although not required by Rule 504, the issuer may nevertheless want to take precautions against such resales taking place. *See* § 4.22 *infra.*

72. *See* § 4.24 *infra.*

73. *See* § 23.5 *infra.*

74. *See, e.g.,* Dean Witter Reynolds, Inc. v. Selectronics, Inc., 188 A.D.2d 117, 594 N.Y.S.2d 174 (1993) (company was liable to a transferee who acquired shares that had been issued in a private placement and thus were subject to resale restrictions which were not revealed in a restrictive legend as required by UCC § 8–204; the transferee who took thus acquired the stock without notice or knowledge of the restrictions and was entitled to recover damages associated with its attempts to sell the stock).

75. This is often referred to as "piggyback" rights as it enables the secondary sellers to piggyback on the primary registered offering by the issuer. *Cf.* Moffat v. Harcourt Brace & Co., 892 F.Supp. 1431 (M.D.Fla.1994) (issuer's delay in applying for registration did not violate agreement with holder of "piggyback" registration rights).

76. *See, e.g.,* Herrmann Holdings Ltd. v. Lucent Technologies Inc., 302 F.3d 552 (5th Cir. 2002) (upholding breach of contract claim to cause an S–3 registration to become effective as soon as practicable).

77. 17 C.F.R. § 230.503 (1995).

filing requirement for Form D that previously applied to Rules 504, 505, 506, and section 4(6) of the Act.[78] However, the next year, the Commission did an about face and decided to retain Regulation D's filing requirement.[79] In addition to the Form D filing requirement, as of November 1996, public companies required to file reports under the Exchange Act must disclose unregistered sales of securities in their periodic reports filed with the Commission.[80]

§ 4.21 Regulation D's Exemption for Small Issues of $1,000,000 or Less—SEC Rule 504

Rule 504[1] provides an exemption from registration for offerings by small issuers not to exceed one million dollars in any twelve-month period.[2] It was formerly the rule that no more than five hundred thousand dollars of the aggregate offering price in a Rule 504 offering could be attributable to securities that are sold without registration under state law.[3] The SEC amended Rule 504 so as to eliminate many of the limitations that formerly existed. Thus, Rule 504 now permits offerings of up to $1 million worth of securities regardless of registration under state law.[4] The ban on general solicitations and the requirement that the securities be restricted that were formerly applicable in all Rule 504 offerings have been eliminated for those offerings made solely to accredited investors and for offerings where delivery of a disclosure document is delivered to purchasers pursuant to state securities law registration requirements or pursuant to an exemption under applicable state securities laws.[5] Similarly, while there are no longer across-the-board restrictions on resale of securities purchased in a Rule 504 offering, resale restrictions will apply unless delivery of a disclosure document is required under state law.

In addition to the one million dollar limit on each offering, the Rule 504 exemption is available only to an issuer that is neither an investment company nor subject to the reporting requirements of the Securities Exchange Act of 1934.[7] In order to take advantage of the rule, offers and sales must conform to some of the terms and conditions for Regulation D offerings that are set forth in Rules 501 through 503. Rule 502(a)'s safe harbor from

78. *See* SEC Eliminates Rules, Forms; Proposes Additional Streamlining, 28 Sec. Reg. & L. Rep. (BNA) 696 (May 31, 1996). Under the proposal, the Form D would still need to have been filled out and retained by the issuer but would not have had to be filed. *Id.*

79. *See* Phase Two Recommendations of Task Force on Disclosure Simplification, Sec. Act Rel. No. 33–7431, 62 Fed. Reg. 39755, 1997 WL 401054 (SEC July 18, 1997).

80. *See* Periodic Reporting of Unregistered Equity Sales, Sec. Exch. Act Rel. No. 34–37801, [1996–1997 Transfer Binder] Fed. Sec. L. Rep. (CCH) ¶ 85,852 (SEC Oct. 10, 1996). The Exchange Act's periodic reporting requirements are discussed in § 9.3 *infra.*

§ 4.21

1. 17 C.F.R. § 230.504. Prior to 1988, rule 504 exempted offerings not exceeding $500,000. *See* Sec. Act Rel.No. 33–6758, [1987–1988 Transfer Binder] Fed. Sec. L. Rep. (CCH) ¶ 84,221 (March 3, 1988).

2. 17 C.F.R. § 230.504(b)(2)(i).

3. 17 C.F.R. § 230.504 (1990).

4. 17 C.F.R. § 230.504.

5. Rule 504(b), 17 C.F.R. § 230.504(b).

7. Securities Exchange Act of 1934, Pub.L. 291, 48 Stat. 881 (codified in 15 U.S.C.A. §§ 78a *et seq.*). *See* §§ 9.2–9.3 *infra.*

integration[8] applies to Rule 504 offerings.[9] As discussed in an earlier section of this treatise,[10] these general conditions include a prohibition on general solicitations of purchasers,[11] and restrictions on resales of the securities by purchasers in the exempt offering.[12] Rule 504 does not provide an across-the-board prohibition on a general solicitation of purchasers. Additionally, the resale restrictions applicable to other Regulation D offerings are not imposed on all Rule 504 transactions.[13] Furthermore, Rule 502(b)(1) expressly excludes[14] Rule 504 offerings from Regulations D's informational requirements. Moreover, to the extent that a Rule 504 offering involves a general solicitation of purchasers, registration will presumably be required under applicable state blue sky laws.[15]

As mentioned above, Rule 504 does not impose restrictions on resale for those offerings requiring disclosure documents under state law as well as for those made only to accredited investors. However, even with regard to those offerings where the restrictions on resale do not apply, purchasers in a Rule 504 transaction who subsequently decide to sell their shares will need to secure their own exemption from registration under federal law. Accordingly, at least in those instances in which the Rule 504 offering is not registered under a state blue sky law, the securities so acquired may be de facto restricted since, for example, a downstream sale by an accredited investor does not ordinarily carry with it an exemption from registration. Moreover, since Rule 504 is a transaction exemption and securities acquired under it cannot be resold without registration or an independent exemption, the issuer using Regulation D may want to take reasonable care to assure that purchasers do not intend to dispose of securities they buy in such a way as to make those purchasers statutory underwriters.[16] Specifically, in many Rule 504 offerings, the issuer must at least (1) make reasonable inquiry to determine whether the purchaser is acquiring the securities for himself or for other persons, (2) disclose in writing before the sale to each purchaser that the securities have not been registered and, therefore, cannot be resold unless they are registered under the Act or unless an exemption from registration is available, and (3) place a legend on the securities stating that they have not been registered and reciting restrictions on their transferability and sale.[17] As noted above, these restrictions on resale are not expressly imposed in some Rule 504 transactions and, thus, for example, do not apply if the securities are registered in states requiring delivery of a disclosure document.

---

8. Rule 502(a), 17 C.F.R. § 230.502(a). *See* § 4.20[3][A] *supra* for discussion of Regulation D's integration provision and § 4.36 *infra* for discussion of integration generally.

9. Rule 504(b)(1), 17 C.F.R. § 230.502(1).

10. *See* § 4.19 *supra*.

11. Rule 502(c), 17 C.F.R. § 230.502(c).

12. Rule 502(d), 17 C.F.R. § 230.502(d).

13. Rule 504(b)(1), 17 C.F.R. § 230.504(b)(1).

14. Rule 504(b)(1) subjects Rule 504 offerings to the requirements of Rule 502(a) (integration), Rule 502(c) (ban on general solicitation), and Rule 502(d) (restrictions on resale). However, Rule 504(b)(1) does not make reference to Rule 502(b)'s (informational requirements).

15. Rule 502(b)(1), 17 C.F.R. § 230.502(b)(1).

16. 17 C.F.R. § 230.502(d).

17. *Id.* Former Rule 504(b)(ii) required that unless there are no restrictions on resale because of registration under state law, the restrictions must be disclosed. 17 C.F.R. § 230.504(b)(ii) (1988).

There is no mandatory disclosure as a precondition to the Rule 504 exemption. This is in contrast to the informational requirements of Regulation A's qualified exemption for small issues,[18] Rule 506's safe harbor for private placements,[19] as well as Rule 505's exemption for offerings of up to five million dollars.[20]

In 1996, the Commission amended Rule 504 to make it explicit that there are no informational requirements.[21] However, the Commission reconsidered this position in light of increased concern over the use of the Internet for unregistered offerings of microcap securities.[22] In particular, the Commission was concerned with so-called "pump and dump" offerings where Rule 504 was used for internet offerings (to "pump" the securities into the market) and then creating a secondary market (so that the securities could be "dumped" by the initial purchasers). In 1999, the Commission amended Rule 504 to provide that a general solicitation can be used in a Rule 504 offering only if one of two conditions is met. A general solicitation can be used for a Rule 504 offering if the transaction is registered under a state securities law that requires public filing and delivery of a substantive disclosure document.[23] Alternatively, a general solicitation can be used for an offering only to accredited investors (as that term is defined in Regulation D)[24] under a state law exemption that permits a general solicitation.[25]

Rule 502 establishes a six-month safe harbor for the integration of Regulation D offerings and a five-factor test for determining whether offerings that fall outside the safe harbor will be integrated.[26] As noted above, Rule 502 expressly provides that if the issuer sells securities pursuant to Rule 504, no specific information is required to be furnished to purchasers.[27]

Rule 501[28] provides definitions of certain terms used in Rules 502–506. Rule 503 sets forth the requirement that the issuer record the Rule 504 transaction on Form D which must be filed with the Commission within fifteen days after the offering begins.[29] Additionally, 1934 Act reporting companies making sales of securities under the section 4(6) exemption must disclose those transactions in their periodic reports filed with the SEC.[30]

---

18. 17 C.F.R. §§ 230.251–.260. *See* § 4.17 *supra.*

19. 17 C.F.R. § 230.506. *See* § 4.25 *infra.*

20. Rule 505 requires that information be furnished to investors unless all investors are accredited. 17 C.F.R. §§ 230.502(b), 230.505. *See* § 4.22 *supra.*

21. *See* Sec. Act Rel. No. 33–7300 (May 31, 1996).

22. *See* Sec. Act Rel. No. 33–7644 (SEC Feb. 25, 1999).

23. Rule 504(b)(1)(i),(ii), 17 C.F.R. § 230.504(b)(1)(i), (ii).

24. Rule 501(a), 17 C.F.R. § 230.501(a).

25. Rule 504(b)(1)(iii), 17 C.F.R. § 230.504 (b)(1)(iii).

26. 17 C.F.R. § 230.502(a).

27. 17 C.F.R. § 230.502(b)(1)(i).

28. 17 C.F.R. § 230.501. *See* § 4.20 *supra.*

29. 17 C.F.R. § 230.503.

30. *See* Periodic Reporting of Unregistered Equity Sales, Sec. Exch. Act Rel. No. 34–37801, [1996–1997 Transfer Binder] Fed. Sec. L. Rep. (CCH) ¶ 85,852 (SEC Oct. 10, 1996). The Exchange Act's periodic reporting requirements are discussed in § 9.3 *infra.*

§ 4.22 Regulation D's Exemption for Limited Offerings Not Exceeding $5,000,000—SEC Rule 505

SEC Rule 505[1] combines elements of the private placement exemption under section 4(2),[2] the safe harbor of Rule 506[3] and section 4(6)'s[4] exemption for offerings to "accredited investors" not exceeding five million dollars. Whereas Rule 506 has no limit on the dollar amount of an offering, Rule 505 exempts offerings only where the aggregate offering price of an issue, together with all securities previously offered pursuant to a section 3(b) exemption or in violation of section 5(a), does not exceed five million dollars within a twelve-month period.[5]

A Rule 505 offering may be made to an unlimited number of "accredited investors" and no more than thirty-five other "purchasers."[6] Unlike the safe harbor for non-public offerings under Rule 506,[7] there is no requirement that the unaccredited investors be sophisticated in order to participate in a Rule 505 offering. Furthermore, if an issuer takes reasonable steps to assure that the thirty-five unaccredited investor limit is not exceeded, the presence of an inadvertent extra unaccredited but otherwise qualified purchaser should not destroy the exemption.[8]

"Accredited investor" is defined in Rule 501 as any person who in fact comes within or whom the issuer reasonably believes comes within any of eight categories of investors at the time securities are sold to him or her.[9] Generally, these categories include wealthy and/or financially sophisticated investors such as banks, insurance companies, tax-exempt organizations, directors and executive officers of the issuer, and natural persons who have a large net worth or very sizeable annual incomes.[10] When calculating the number of purchasers for purposes of Rule 505, one must exclude all accredited investors and certain relatives of a purchaser, and trusts, estates and corporations in which a purchaser has more than a fifty percent beneficial ownership.[11] In other instances, a corporation or other business entity will generally be counted as one purchaser,[12] as is each client of an investment adviser or broker.[13]

---

§ 4.22

1. 17 C.F.R. § 230.505. For a case holding that rule 501 was satisfied by an offering of less than $5,000,000 to an accredited investor, *see* Wright v. National Warranty Co., 953 F.2d 256, 259–60 (6th Cir.1992).

2. 15 U.S.C.A. § 77d(2). *See* § 4.24 *infra*.

3. 17 C.F.R. § 230.506. *See* § 4.25 *infra*.

4. 15 U.S.C.A. § 77d(6). *See* § 4.23 *infra*.

5. 17 C.F.R. § 230.505(a), (b)(2)(i).

6. 17 C.F.R. § 230.505(b)(2)(ii).

7. 17 C.F.R. § 230.506. *See* § 4.25 *infra*.

8. 17 C.F.R. § 230.505(b)(2)(ii) ("there are no more than or the issuer reasonably believes that there are no more than 35 purchasers of securities....."). In 1989 the Commission amended Rule 505 to include the language referring to the that the issuer's must reasonable belief that the purchaser limitations are met.

9. 17 C.F.R. § 230.501(a). *See* §§ 4.20 *supra* and 4.23 *infra*. *See also* section 2(a)(15) and Rule 215; 15 U.S.C.A. § 77b(a)(15); 17 C.F.R. § 230.215 which are discussed in § 4.20 *infra*.

10. *See* § 4.23 *infra*.

11. 17 C.F.R. § 230.501(e)(1).

12. 17 C.F.R. § 230.501(e)(2).

13. 17 C.F.R. § 230.501(e) note.

In order to be eligible to take advantage of the Rule 505 exemption the issuer must be neither an investment company nor be subject to any of the "bad boy" disqualification provisions contained in Rule 262(b) and(c) of Regulation A.[14] Further, all offers and sales made under Rule 505 must satisfy the terms and conditions of Rules 501 through 503 of Regulation D.[15]

In addition to defining "accredited investor," Rule 501 defines other terms used in Regulation D.[16] Rule 502 prohibits the use of general advertising or soliciting during an offering exempt under Rule 505. Further, Rule 502(b)[18] also requires the disclosure of certain information to purchasers who do not qualify as "accredited purchasers" as defined in Rule 501.[19] The SEC recommends, however, that if there are any nonaccredited investors, that all purchasers, including those who are accredited, receive the private placement memorandum. If all purchasers are accredited investors, then neither Rule 502 nor Rule 505 requires specific information to be disclosed to any purchasers. Rule 502 also provides a six-month safe harbor for the integration of Regulation D offerings and a five-factor test for determining whether offerings that fall outside the safe harbors will be integrated.[20] In addition, the SEC places limits on resales of securities acquired in a transaction under Regulation D, and, as a preventive measure, requires that issuers exercise reasonable care to determine that they are not selling to section 2(a)(11) underwriters.[21] Rule 503 requires that the issuer record the Regulation D transaction on Form D which must be filed with the Commission within 15 days of the commencement of the offering.[22] In addition, sales of unregistered securities by a 1934 Act reporting company must be disclosed in the periodic reports filed with the SEC.[23]

In 1989, the Commission amended Regulation D by adding Rule 508[24] to provide that minor variations from an exemption's requirements will not destroy the availability of the exemption.[25] Rule 508 provides a savings clause for an insignificant failure to comply with a condition of the exemption that is not "directly intended to protect" the investor,[26] provided that the issuer made a good faith and reasonable attempt to comply.[27]

---

14. 17 C.F.R. § 230.505(a).

15. 17 C.F.R. § 230.505(b)(1). *See* 17 C.F.R. §§ 230.501–.503.

16. *See* § 4.19 *supra.*

18. 17 C.F.R. § 230.502(b).

19. 17 C.F.R. § 230.502(b), (c).

20. 17 C.F.R. § 230.502(a). *See* § 4.19 *supra.* Integration is discussed in § 4.36 *infra.*

21. 17 C.F.R. § 230.502(d). *Compare, e.g.,* Note, Regulation A: Direct Public Offerings and the Internet, 79 Denver U.L. Rev. 229 (2001).

22. 17 C.F.R. § 230.503.

23. *See* Periodic Reporting of Unregistered Equity Sales, Sec. Exch. Act Rel. No. 34–37801, [1996–1997 Transfer Binder] Fed. Sec. L. Rep. (CCH) ¶ 85,852 (SEC Oct. 10, 1996). The Exchange Act's periodic reporting requirements are discussed in § 9.3 *infra.*

24. 17 C.F.R. § 230.508.

25. *See* Carl W. Schneider, A Substantial Compliance Defense ("I and I") Defense and Other Changes Are Added to SEC Regulation D, 44 Bus. Law. 1207 (1989).

26. Rule 508's safe harbor for certain noncompliance with Regulation D only affects claims by private parties. Rule 508 does not preclude SEC actions in such instances. Rule 508(b), 17 C.F.R. § 230.508(b) ("Where an exemption is established only through reliance on [this rule], the failure to comply shall nonetheless be actionable by the Commission under section 20 of the Act").

27. 17 C.F.R. § 230.508.

§ 4.23 The Statutory Exemption for Limited Offerings to "Accredited Investors"—Section 4(6)

§ 4.23[1] Scope of Section 4(6)

Section 4(6)[1] exempts from the 1933 Act's registration requirements transactions in which the aggregate sales price does not exceed the maximum amount permitted by section 3(b)[2]—currently five million dollars—provided that all offers and sales are made only to "accredited investors."[3] The section 4(6) exemption is preconditioned upon the absence of general advertising or public solicitation in the offering process. The statute also requires that appropriate notice of sales made in reliance on section 4(6) be filed with the SEC. Form 4(6) was repealed in 1982 and replaced by Form D.

The term "accredited investor" is defined in section 2(a)(15)(i)[4] to include institutional investors such as banks, registered investment companies, employee benefit plans subject to ERISA, and insurance companies. An alternative method for falling within the category of accredited investor under section 2(a)(15)(ii) is to be someone who on the basis of factors such as financial sophistication, net worth, and knowledge and experience in financial matters, qualifies as an "accredited investor" as defined by the Commission's rules.[5] Specifically, SEC Rule 215[6] defines "accredited investor" as used in section 2(a)(15)(ii) to include eight categories of offerees and purchasers.[7]

<hr>

§ 4.23

1. 15 U.S.C.A. § 77(d)(6).

2. 15 U.S.C.A. § 77c(b). *See* § 4.16 *supra.*

3. *See* 15 U.S.C.A. § 77b(15). *See also* 17 C.F.R. § 230.215.

4. 15 U.S.C.A. § 77b(a)(15)(i).

5. 15 U.S.C.A. § 77b(a)(15)(ii). *See* 17 C.F.R. § 230.215.

6. 17 C.F.R. § 230.215. The definition appears to be an expanding one. In 1988 the Commission enlarged the definition of accredited investor and also proposed still additional expansion. *See* Sec. Act Rel. No. 33–6758, [1987–1988 Transfer Binder] Fed. Sec. L. Rep. (CCH) ¶ 84,221 (March 3, 1988) (adopting new definition); Sec. Act Rel.No. 33–6759, [1987–1988 Transfer Binder] Fed. Sec. L. Rep. (CCH) ¶ 84,221 (March 3, 1988) (proposing additional expansion).

7. Rule 215 includes:

(a) Any savings and loan association or other institution specified in section 3(a)(5)(A) of the Act whether acting in its individual or fiduciary capacity; any broker or dealer registered pursuant to section 15 of the Securities Exchange Act of 1934; an employee benefit plan within the meaning of Title I of the Employee Retirement Income Security Act of 1974, if the investment decision is made by a plan fiduciary, as defined in section 3(21) of such Act, which is a savings and loan association, or if the employee benefit plan has total assets in excess of $5,000,000 or, if a self-directed plan, with investment decisions made solely by persons that are accredited investors;

(b) Any private business development company as defined in section 202(a)(22) of the Investment Advisers Act of 1940;

(c) Any organization described in section 501(c)(3) of the Internal Revenue Code, corporation, Massachusetts or similar business trust, or partnership, not formed for the specific purpose of acquiring the securities offered, with total assets in excess of $5,000,000;

(d) Any director, executive officer, or general partner of the issuer of the securities being offered or sold, or any director, executive officer, or general partner of a general partner of that issuer;

(e) Any natural person whose individual net worth, or joint net worth with that person's spouse at the time of his purchase exceeds $1,000,000;

(f) Any natural person who had an individual income in excess of $200,000 in each of the two most recent years or joint income with that person's spouse in excess of $300,000 in each of those years and has a reasonable expectation of reaching the same income level in the current year;

The significance of the concept of accredited investor is not limited to the section 4(6) exemption. As discussed elsewhere in this treatise,[8] accredited investors are not counted when computing Rule 505's or Rule 506's thirty-five purchaser limitation.[9] Additionally, offerings made solely to accredited investors are not subject to the offering circular requirements of Rules 505 and 506.[10]

The full effect of the section 4(6) exemption for sales to accredited investors is that it combines many of the features of a private placement[11] and that of the qualified exemption available under section 3(b).[12] The exemption also complements the private placement exemption provided by section 4(2) and Rule 506.[13]

§ 4.24 Exemption for Issuer Transactions Not Involving a Public Offering ("The Private Placement Exemption")—Section 4(2)

§ 4.24[1] Scope of the Section 4(2) Exemption

Section 4(2) of the 1933 Act[1] exempts "transactions not involving any public offering." The exemption for transactions not involving a public offering is limited to issuers and thus cannot be relied upon by persons other than the issuer. However, non-issuers may be able to take advantage of the so-called section 4(1½) exemption, which is discussed in a later section of this treatise.[2] The section 4(2) exemption, which is also commonly referred to as the private placement exemption, can be useful for both closely held and public issue corporations.

The exemption for nonpublic offerings can be used by small firms, as well as by publicly held companies.[4] Public companies issuing unregistered securities, including those issued under the section 4(2) exemption, must disclose those transactions in their periodic reports filed with the SEC.[5]

The exemption for non-public offerings applies to offerings to institutional investors that are sufficiently sophisticated and have sufficiently strong

---

(g) Any trust, with total assets in excess of $5,000,000, not formed for the specific purpose of acquiring the securities offered, whose purchase is directed by a sophisticated person as described in § 230.506(b)(2)(ii); and

(h) Any entity in which all of the equity owners are accredited investors.

8. *See* §§ 4.20, 4.22 *supra* and 4.25 *infra*.

9. 17 C.F.R. § 230.501(e)(1)(iv).

10. 17 C.F.R. § 230.502(b)(1)(i).

11. 15 U.S.C.A. § 77d(2); 17 C.F.R. § 230.506. *See* § 4.25 *infra*.

12. 15 U.S.C.A. § 77c(b). *See* § 4.16 *supra*. The same combination is found in Rule 505, 17 C.F.R. § 230.505 which is discussed in § 4.22 *supra*.

13. 15 U.S.C.A. § 77d(2); 17 C.F.R. § 230.506.

§ 4.24

1. 15 U.S.C.A. § 77d(2).

2. *See* § 4.30 *infra*.

4. In contrast, the exemptions provided by Rule 504 and Regulation A can be used only by nonpublic companies. *See* §§ 4.17, 4.21 *supra*. The same is true of offerings to employees and consultants under Rule 701. *See* § 4.18 *supra*.

5. *See* Periodic Reporting of Unregistered Equity Sales, Sec. Exch. Act Rel. No. 34–37801, [1996–1997 Transfer Binder] Fed. Sec. L. Rep. (CCH) ¶ 85,852 (SEC Oct. 10, 1996). The Exchange Act's periodic reporting requirements are discussed in § 9.3 *infra*.

bargaining positions that they do not need the protections of federal registration. Secondly, the exemption also applies to an offering that is made to a limited number of qualified private individuals who, like institutional investors, are sufficiently sophisticated and are able to bear the investment's risk so as not to need the Act's registration protections. In addition to the administrative and judicial interpretations relating to the scope of this broadly drafted statutory exemption, SEC Rule 506[7] provides a safe harbor for any issuer who is able to meet the rule's requirements.

The nonpublic offering exemption was enacted for a number of reasons. Congress was concerned with avoiding the cumbersome registration requirements when the benefits to the public were too remote and thus when there was no practical need for the Act's application. The section 4(2) exemption was designed to apply to specific or isolated sales as well as offerings to a very small number of securities holders so that the public interest is not involved. As will be seen from the discussion of the case law that has developed, as well as from the parameters of the safe-harbor rule, even today very small offerings to a limited number of purchasers will not be exempt if the offerees and purchasers do not qualify as sufficiently sophisticated (and/or wealthy) investors.[10]

In order to provide more certainty in planning transactions, the SEC adopted the safe harbor rule contained in Rule 506. Compliance with the rule will provide an exemption, but according to the SEC, noncompliance does not raise even an inference that the exemption is unavailable.[11] Since Rule 506 is only a safe harbor rule, the pre-existing judicial and administrative interpretations remain an important part of the law today as they are still available to issuers who do not choose or are not able to comply with each and every provision of Rule 506.

In SEC v. Ralston Purina Co.,[13] the Supreme Court rejected the defendant's contention that an offering of stock that was limited to its own employees was necessarily exempt as not involving a public offering. The defendant, relying on a literal reading of the statute, maintained that an offering to a limited group could not properly be characterized as a public offering. The Court ruled that since the stock being offered was made available to all employees regardless of connection with the issuer and knowledge of the business, the offerees and purchasers represented a sufficiently large and representative slice of the investing public so as to render the exemption unavailable. In discussing the scope of the exemption, the Court announced the guidelines that have continued to form the basis for all private placement exemptions. In the first instance, all offerees must have access to the types of information that would be contained in a full-fledged 1933 Act registration statement. Secondly, the offerees must be capable of

---

7. 17 C.F.R. § 230.506. *See* § 4.25 *infra.*

10. *See, e.g.,* Lawler v. Gilliam, 569 F.2d 1283 (4th Cir.1978); G. Eugene England Foundation v. First Federal Corp., 663 F.2d 988 (10th Cir.1973); Butler v. Phlo Corp., 2001 WL 863426, [2001–2002 Transfer Binder] Fed. Sec. L. Rep. (CCH) ¶ 91,499 (S.D.N.Y.2001) (2 purchasers who did not meet sophistication requirements).

11. Rule 506 (17 C.F.R. § 230.506) is discussed in § 4.25 *infra.* As a result of 1989 amendments to Regulation D, de minimis departures from the exemption's requirements will not render the exemption unavailable. 17 C.F.R. § 230.508. *See* § 4.20 *supra* and § 4.25 *infra.*

13. 346 U.S. 119, 73 S.Ct. 981, 97 L.Ed. 1494 (1953). *See also, e.g.,* United States v. Custer Channel Wing Corp., 376 F.2d 675 (4th Cir.1967), *cert. denied,* 389 U.S. 850, 88 S.Ct. 38, 19 L.Ed.2d 119 (1967) (section 4(2) was unavailable; criminal contempt affirmed).

fending for themselves; in more recent cases, this has been interpreted to mean that the offerees must be sufficiently sophisticated to demand and understand the information that is available to them. Both offeree sophistication and access to information must be shown in order for the section 4(2) exemption to be established.[15] The ability to fend for oneself is thus dependent upon access to information. It has therefore been held that the exemption will not be available even though the offerees are sufficiently sophisticated where they did not have access to the types of information that would otherwise have to be disclosed in the registration statement.[16] Conversely, the Commission has made it clear that a brochure containing desired information by itself is not sufficient since the nature and/or sophistication of the offerees is an equally important factor.[17] In addition, the offering brochure, even if disseminated only to qualified purchasers, may be deemed insufficient unless the offerees have an opportunity to meet with representatives of the issuer and to inspect relevant corporate books and records.[18]

The Supreme Court in *Ralston Purina* pointed out that even though the number of purchasers involved will not necessarily be the determinative factor, it is a significant one in considering the scope of the exemption. Accordingly, the fact that there were as many as five hundred employee offerees in the *Ralston Purina* case helped tip the balance against a section 4(2) exemption from registration. In addition to (1) the number of offerees, (2) the offerees' need for information and (3) the offerees' access to information, the courts will consider a fourth factor: the size of the offering, both in terms of the number of securities offered and the aggregate offering price. The number of offerees and size of the offering, as measured by the number of units offered, are significant because the larger the numbers of each, the more difficult it is to control downstream sales that would eventually filter the securities into the hands of the general investing public. As it becomes more likely that the securities sold pursuant to the private placement exemption will filter down to the investing public without a subsequent 1933 Act registration, the less likely it is that the section 4(2) exemption will be available.

In addition to the foregoing factors, the SEC has indicated that any "public advertising is inconsistent with a claim of private offering."[21] In light of the ban on public advertising, issuers frequently have to turn to investment bankers and other promoters in order to find an existing pool of potential customers. It is clearly permissible for a brokerage firm that is handling the private placement to contact its customers provided they meet the offering's suitability standard.[22] This was a common method of promoting tax shelters and is still widely used for other ventures that require a substantial invest-

---

15. SEC v. Kenton Capital, Ltd., 69 F.Supp.2d 1, 11–12 (D.D.C.1998) (sophistication will not substitute for access to information).

16. Gilligan, Will & Co. v. SEC, 267 F.2d 461 (2d Cir.1959), *cert. denied* 361 U.S. 896, 80 S.Ct. 200, 4 L.Ed.2d 152 (1959). *See also, e.g.,* Van Dyke v. Coburn Enterprises, Inc., 873 F.2d 1094 (8th Cir.1989).

17. Sec. Act Rel. No. 33–5487 (Jan. 23, 1974).

18. *Cf.* Rule 502(b)(2)(v), 17 C.F.R. § 230.502(b)(2)(v).

21. Non-Public Offering Exemption, Sec. Act Rel. No. 33–4552, 1962 WL 69540, 1 Fed.Sec.L. Rep. (CCH) ¶ 2781 (Nov. 6, 1962).

22. Mary S. Krech Trust v. Lakes Apartments, 642 F.2d 98 (5th Cir.1981), *rehearing denied* 645 F.2d 72 (5th Cir.1981). The court there noted that the burden is on the issuer to establish the identity of all offerees and purchasers and to prove their suitability.

ment. In such a case it is necessary to determine from the terms and risks of the offering the minimum offeree suitability standards. Where a private placement is not handled by a conduit with a ready list of potential offerees, all activities directed toward contacting the offerees will be closely scrutinized, lest the issuer run afoul of the general solicitation prohibition. The use of investment seminars and other promotional meetings have been a significant factor in denying the availability of the exemption for non-public offerings.[23] Investment seminars (or "road shows") that are limited to qualified offerees who have been prescreened presumably would not violate the prohibition on a general solicitation. In general, where the issuer is unable to prove that there were a limited number of offerees, the uncertainty concerning the number of offerees can preclude reliance on the section 4(2) exemption.

A common practice of private placement issuers has been to require all purchasers to sign an "investment letter" attesting to their lack of intent to resell the securities to the public. Although this may still be a necessary precaution,[25] and is required under Rule 506,[26] the fact that the issuer requires such investment letters is self-serving and thus will not in and of itself have any probative value as to the existence of the exemption or the issuer's reasonable efforts to assure that no downstream sales would occur without registration.[27]

The burden of proof for establishing the availability of the exemption falls on the person claiming the protection of the exemption. The exemption may be denied because of the issuer's failure to demonstrate that all offerees "received both written and oral information concerning [the issuer], that all offerees of its securities had access to any additional information which they might have required or requested and that all offerees of its securities had personal contacts with the officers of [the issuer]."[29] Although offerees need not have personal contact or a relationship with the issuers in all cases, following the lead of the Fifth Circuit, there have been a number of judicial decisions that have given the section 4(2) exemption a very limited scope, at least with regard to offerees who do not qualify as institutional investors.[30] It is fair to say that in light of all factors the courts have developed, the ultimate question in proving a section 4(2) exemption boils down to questions of fact.

A literal reading of a number of cases interpreting the scope of the section 4(2) exemption would lead to the following requirements for private placements not involving institutional investor purchasers, arguably regardless of reliance on the safe harbor provided by Rule 506. Each offeree must have access to the types of information which would be disclosed should the issuer be required to undertake a full-fledged registration under the Act.[33] This

---

23. *See* Koehler v. Pulvers, 614 F.Supp. 829 (S.D.Cal.1985).

25. *E.g.,* United States v. Hill, 298 F.Supp. 1221, 1231 (D.Conn.1969) (failure to sign investment letter was a factor in denying section 4(2) exemption).

26. *See* 17 C.F.R. § 230.502(d).

27. SEC v. Continental Tobacco Co., 463 F.2d 137 (5th Cir.1972).

29. SEC v. Continental Tobacco Co., 463 F.2d 137, 160 (5th Cir.1972).

30. Van Dyke v. Coburn Enterprises, 873 F.2d 1094 (8th Cir.1989) (section 4(2) exemption upheld; inside offerees had full access to information, outside offerees had the economic bargaining power to obtain any information); *See* Lawler v. Gilliam, 569 F.2d 1283 (4th Cir.1978); Doran v. Petroleum Management Corp., 545 F.2d 893 (5th Cir.1977), *appeal after remand* 576 F.2d 91 (5th Cir.1978); SEC v. Continental Tobacco Co., 463 F.2d 137 (5th Cir.1972); Hill York Corp. v. American International Franchises, Inc., 448 F.2d 680 (5th Cir.1971).

33. The Fifth Circuit has indicated that disclosure by the issuer and access by the offeree are to be interpreted as disjunctive requirements. Doran v. Petroleum Management Corp., 545 F.2d

requirement has been held not to have been satisfied if access was not given to each offeree, even though such an offeree without access did not become an eventual purchaser. As one court put it, "[e]ven the offeree-plaintiff's 20–20 vision with respect to the facts underlying the security would not save the exemption if any one of his fellow offerees was blind."[34] It has quite properly been suggested, however, that the statute does not justify denying the exemption to an issuer who, although taking reasonable precautions, makes an isolated offer or offers to nonqualifying offerees.[35] The cases further require that offerees must also be sophisticated with respect to business and financial matters generally. Additionally, an offeree's knowledge of the particular business may be a factor. Knowledgeable investors with generalized investment experience will qualify as purchasers in a non-public offering when the nature of the enterprise does not require that there be a special level of sophistication.[36] Often, the nature of the investment will require more specific experience on the part of the purchasers.[37]

Questions can be raised as to the propriety of an investor sophistication requirement as a precondition to a section 4(2) exemption. It is evident that the Supreme Court's primary concern in the *Ralston Purina* case was that offerees in a nonpublic offering have access to the types of information that would be available with a registered public offering.[39] However, as discussed directly above, the courts have since required that the offerees possess a certain degree of sophistication. It has been suggested by some observers that these cases took their lead from Rule 506's predecessor and that investor sophistication may not properly be an element of the section 4(2) nonpublic offering exemption.[40] While offeree access to information is a necessary element of any transaction exempted under section 4(2), it clearly cannot be sufficient. The offerees as a class must somehow represent something other than a slice of the investing public.[41]

As noted above, it is clear that access to information is a precondition to any section 4(2) exemption. As the foregoing discussion points out, informational access alone may not be sufficient if the investors are not able to fend for themselves. As a safety precaution, each offeree should receive an offering circular containing full disclosure. The cases interpreting the section 4(2) exemption do not expressly require the use of an offering circular.[46] However,

---

893 (5th Cir.1977), *appeal after remand* 576 F.2d 91 (5th Cir.1978). *See, e.g.,* SEC v. Kenton Capital Ltd., 69 F.Supp.2d 1, 11–12 (D.D.C.1998) (sophistication will not substitute for access to information).

34.   545 F.2d at 902.

35.   The issuer has the burden of making a *reasonable* inquiry into each purchaser's background. Anastasi v. American Petroleum, Inc., 579 F.Supp. 273, 275 (D.Colo.1984).

36.   Cowles v. Dow Keith Oil & Gas, Inc., 752 F.2d 508, 512 (10th Cir.1985), *cert. denied* 479 U.S. 816, 107 S.Ct. 74, 93 L.Ed.2d 30 (1986).

37.   *See, e.g.,* Parker v. Broom, 820 F.2d 966 (8th Cir.1987) (purchaser was familiar with seller and the history of the investment).

39.   SEC v. Ralston Purina Co., 346 U.S. 119, 73 S.Ct. 981, 97 L.Ed. 1494 (1953).

40.   Carl W. Schneider Section 4(1½) Private Resales of Restricted or Control Securities, 49 Ohio St. L.J. 501, 509, n. 41 (1988).

41.   To take an extreme example, consider an offering of securities to 10 individuals with red hair, when all offerees were given information comparable to that which would appear in a registration statement. Even assuming that all purchasers would be purchasing for investment rather than for resale, the section 4(2) exemption should not be available. *Cf.* SEC v. Sunbeam Gold Mines Co., 95 F.2d 699, 701 (9th Cir.1938).

46.   Van Dyke v. Coburn Enterprises, Inc., 873 F.2d 1094, 1098 (8th Cir.1989) (the exemption was available even though "[w]hile reasonable minds may disagree as to whether the appellants

offering circulars, or private placement memorandums have become increasingly common. The use of an offering circular is a good way for planners of private placement transactions to assure that the initial access to information requirements are satisfied.

Each offeree must be provided with an opportunity to ask questions of the issuer and verify information through access to the issuer's books and face-to-face meetings. Beyond the foregoing limitations on the offerees and the prohibition against general solicitation of buying interest, there are added requirements that the cases and SEC releases have established with regard to restrictions on resales. As pointed out above, although it is not sufficient to assure the exemption, investment letters from all purchasers may well be a necessary precondition to the offering. The issuer should place appropriate legends of the restrictions on stock transfer on the stock certificates or other evidence of the security and similar instructions should be given to the stock transfer agent who should be told to issue a stop transfer order for any transfers in violation of the restrictions. Because of the resale restrictions, persons taking a substantial amount of shares in a private placement who anticipate a possible subsequent resale should consider the advisability of a contractual agreement obligating the issuer to cooperate in a registered offering of those shares. These general guidelines that have developed from the case law closely parallel Rule 506's safe harbor requirements.

Beyond the above-mentioned limitations on the structure of the offering, the section 4(2) exemption must be read in light of the exemptions provided by section 4(1)[52] (exempting transactions not involving an issuer, underwriter, or dealer), section 4(4)[53] (exempting unsolicited brokers' transactions), section 4(6)[54] (exempting offerings up to five million dollars to accredited investors), and Rule 144[55] (dealing with downstream resales of securities issued under one of the aforementioned exemptions). Even if a qualified offeree purchases a security offered pursuant to a private placement, his or her subsequent downstream sale may well destroy the exemption. Further, through the doctrine of integration, downstream sales may relate back and destroy the original section 4(2) exemption.[58]

In summary, a review of the relevant cases reveals that an issuer relying on the statutory section 4(2) exemption, rather than upon Rule 506's safe-harbor provisions, may be subjecting itself to a great deal of uncertainty. In addition to the guidelines that appear from the judicial decisions, the planner must not lose sight of the original factors established by the *Ralston Purina* decision.[62] In evaluating the availability of the exemption, the courts and the SEC will look not only to the number and nature of the offerees and their access to the types of information that would be contained in the registration statement but also to the relationship of the offerees to the issuer, the

had been furnished the necessary information to make an informed investment decision, it is without dispute that they had access to the necessary information'').

52. 15 U.S.C.A. § 77d(1). *See* § 4.26 *infra.*

53. 15 U.S.C.A. § 77d(4). *See* § 4.26 *infra.*

54. 15 U.S.C.A. § 77d(6). *See* § 4.20 *supra.*

55. 17 C.F.R. § 230.144. *See* § 4.26 *infra.*

58. *See, e.g.,* 17 C.F.R. § 230.502(a).

62. *See* SEC v. Ralston Purina Co., 346 U.S. 119, 73 S.Ct. 981, 97 L.Ed. 1494 (1953).

relationship of the offerees to each other, the manner of the offering, and the number of shares to be offered.

§ 4.25   Safe Harbor for Private Placements Under Section 4(2)—SEC Rule 506

SEC Rule 506[1] provides an exemption for the offer and sale of securities to no more than thirty-five purchasers;[2] as is the case under the Rule 505[3] exemption, "accredited investors"[4] are not counted toward that limit.[5] Thus, for example, there could be one hundred accredited investors in addition to the thirty-five unaccredited purchasers. Even with regard to the thirty-five unaccredited investors, if an issuer takes reasonable steps to assure that the number is not exceeded, the presence of an inadvertent extra unaccredited but otherwise qualified purchaser should not destroy the exemption.[6]

Rule 506 further places qualifications on permissible purchasers. Each purchaser who is not an accredited investor himself, herself, or through a purchaser representative, must have such knowledge and experience in financial and business matters that the purchaser or qualifying representative is capable of evaluating the merits and risks of the prospective investment.[7] As was the case with its predecessor (former Rule 146), Rule 506 is a "safe harbor" rule. If an offering of securities fails to meet the requirements of Rule 506, the issuer may still qualify for a 4(2) exemption if it conforms to requirements developed through cases and SEC releases.

Rule 506 is available to any issuer, whether or not it is an investment company, a non-reporting company, or subject to any of the disqualification provisions contained in Rule 252(c), (d), (e), or (f) of Regulation A.[10] However, all offers and sales made under Rule 506 must satisfy the terms and conditions of Rules 501, 502, and 503 of Regulation D.[11]

An unsophisticated purchaser may still qualify as a Rule 506 investor through the use of an appropriate purchaser representative. "Purchaser representative" is defined by Rule 501 to be any person who satisfies or whom the issuer reasonably believes satisfies the following four conditions: (1) is not an insider of the issuer (*i.e.,* affiliate, director, officer, or beneficial owner of ten percent of a class of the issuer's equity securities), (2) has such knowledge and experience in financial and business matters that he is capable of

---

§ 4.25

1.   17 C.F.R. § 230.506(b)(2)(i); 17 C.F.R. § 230.501(a), (e).

2.   The following individuals and entities are not to be counted in the thirty-five purchaser ceiling: (1) any relative, spouse, or relative of the spouse of a purchaser who has the same principal residence as the purchaser, (2) any trust or estate in which a purchaser and any of the relatives just mentioned collectively have more than fifty percent of the beneficial interest, (3) any corporation or other organization which a purchaser together with his relatives and trusts and estates owns more than fifty percent of the equity securities or equity interests and (4) any accredited investor. 17 C.F.R. § 230.501(e).

3.   17 C.F.R. § 230.505.

4.   Accredited investor is defined in 17 C.F.R. § 230.501(a). *See also* 15 U.S.C.A. § 77b(a)(15).

5.   17 C.F.R. § 230.501(e)(1)(iv).

6.   17 C.F.R. § 230.506(b)(2)(i) ("there are no more than or the issuer reasonably believes that there are no more than 35 purchasers of securities . . . .").

7.   17 C.F.R. § 230.506(b)(2)(ii).

10.   17 C.F.R. § 230.506(a).

11.   17 C.F.R. § 230.506(b)(1). *See* 17 C.F.R. §§ 230.501–.503.

evaluating, alone, or together with other purchaser representatives or with the purchaser, the merits and risks of the prospective investment, (3) is acknowledged by the purchaser in writing to be his purchaser representative with reference to each prospective investment considered, and (4) discloses to the purchaser before the purchaser's acknowledgment just mentioned any material relationship between the purchaser representative or his affiliates and the issuer or its affiliates that exists, is contemplated, or has existed within the previous two years, including any compensation received or to be received as a result.[12] Insiders of the issuer, however, are allowed to serve as purchaser representatives for certain relatives, trusts, and estates, as well as for corporations in which they have fifty percent beneficial interest.[13] The concept of purchaser representative allows the issuer to reach unsophisticated wealthy investors who do not satisfy the "nature of purchaser requirements" of Rule 506.

Rule 501 also provides the method for calculating the number of purchasers under Rule 506. The following individuals and entities are not to be counted in the thirty-five purchaser ceiling: (1) any relative, spouse, or relative of the spouse of a purchaser who has the same principal residence as the purchaser, (2) any trust or estate in which a purchaser and any of the relatives just mentioned collectively have more than fifty percent of the beneficial interest, (3) any corporation or other organization which a purchaser together with his relatives and trusts and estates owns more than fifty percent of the equity securities or equity interests and (4) any accredited investor.[16]

Regulation D places limits on the manner of the offering and solicitation methods. Rule 502 prohibits the use of general advertising or soliciting during an offering exempt under Rule 506.[17] Rule 502 also recommends the disclosure of certain information to all purchasers if any one purchaser is not an "accredited investor" as defined in Rule 501.[18] If all purchasers are accredited investors, then neither Rule 502 nor Rule 506 requires specific information to be disclosed to any purchaser.[19]

Rule 502 sets forth a six-month safe harbor for the integration of Regulation D offerings and a five-factor test for determining whether offerings that fall outside the safe harbor will be integrated.[20] Rule 502 also places limits on resales of securities acquired in a transaction under Regulation D and, as a preventive measure, requires that issuers exercise reasonable care to determine that they are not selling exempt securities to section 2(a)(11) underwriters.[21] Additionally, Rule 503 requires that the issuer record the Regulation D transaction on Form D, which must be filed with the Commis-

---

12. 17 C.F.R. § 230.501(h).

13. 17 C.F.R. § 230.501(h)(1)(i), (ii), (iii).

16. 17 C.F.R. § 230.501(e).

17. 17 C.F.R. § 230.502(c). A suitability questionnaire sent to customers along with customer account applications, which if sufficiently detailed may create a "substantive relationship" between the customer and the broker so that if sufficient sophistication is established, there will not be a general solicitation in violation of Rule 502. In re E.F. Hutton & Co., 18 Sec.Reg. & L.Rep. (BNA) 171 (SEC No Action Letter Dec. 3, 1985).

18. 17 C.F.R. § 230.502(b)(1).

19. 17 C.F.R. §§ 230.502(b)(1)(i), 230.506(b)(1).

20. 17 C.F.R. § 230.502(a). See § 4.20 supra.

21. 17 C.F.R. § 230.502(d). See 15 U.S.C.A. § 77b(11); § 4.27 infra.

sion within fifteen days after the commencement of the offering.[22] Furthermore, public companies that sell unregistered securities, including those sold in reliance upon the Rule 506 exemption must make appropriate disclosures in their periodic reports filed with the Commission.[23]

As is the case with the section 4(2) exemption,[24] Rule 506 is limited to transactions by an issuer. Therefore, persons other than the issuer who seek an exemption from registration for their sales must look elsewhere.[25] The Commission has tried to present the issuer seeking a private placement exemption with a reasonable safe harbor rule. However, the Commission's efforts under Rule 506's predecessor have not gone without strong criticism on the grounds that the requirements are very difficult to comply with and, hence, the rule does not provide a sufficiently safe predictor for planners of securities transactions.[26]

Rule 506 does not include any offeree qualification requirements such as those found in its predecessor or the cases interpreting the section 4(2) nonpublic offering exemption.[29] To the extent that Rule 506 is based on section 4(2), rather than section 3(b) or 4(6)—each of which has a five million dollar ceiling,[30] it is arguable that the statute requires the offeree qualifications to be read into the rule. The SEC in adopting Rule 506 wanted to ease the problems associated with offeree qualification under its predecessor— former Rule 146—but there is no indication of the SEC's statutory basis for ignoring the judicially imposed offeree requirements. In fact, the SEC has indicated that the nature and number of offerees remain relevant in determining whether there has been a general solicitation so as to render Rule 506 and section 4(2) unavailable.[31] The safe harbor protection, thus, is no longer dependent upon the issuer being able to prove that *each* offeree was qualified.[32] On the other hand, if the issuer cannot show that it took adequate precautions against the solicitation of nonqualified offerees, it may lose the section 4(2) exemption because of the inability to show that a general solicitation did not take place. Accordingly, the effect of the deletion of the offeree qualification requirement in Rule 506 is that when an issuer takes reasonable precautions but somehow an unqualified offeree is given an offer, the safe harbor may still be available. It is important to recall that not all preliminary contacts with prospective offerees will constitute an offer. Thus, it is permissible to make preliminary inquiries to determine if prospective offerees are in fact qualified so long as these preliminary contacts do not give detail as to the nature and terms of the planned offering.

22. 17 C.F.R. § 230.503.

23. *See* Periodic Reporting of Unregistered Equity Sales, Sec. Exch. Act Rel. No. 34–37801, [1996–1997 Transfer Binder] Fed. Sec. L. Rep. (CCH) ¶ 85,852 (SEC Oct. 10, 1996). The Exchange Act's periodic reporting requirements are discussed in § 9.3 *infra*.

24. *See* § 4.24 *supra*.

25. *See* § 4.30 *infra* for discussion of the so-called "4(1½)" exemption.

26. *See, e.g.,* Robert A. Kessler, Private Placement Rules 146 and 240–Safe Harbor?, 44 Fordham L.Rev. 37 (1975).

29. *E.g.* SEC v. Ralston Purina Co., 346 U.S. 119, 73 S.Ct. 981, 97 L.Ed. 1494 (1953); Doran v. Petroleum Management Corp., 545 F.2d 893 (5th Cir.1977), *appeal after remand* 576 F.2d 91 (5th Cir.1978); SEC v. Continental Tobacco Co., 463 F.2d 137 (5th Cir.1972); Hill York Corp. v. American International Franchises, Inc., 448 F.2d 680 (5th Cir.1971). *See* § 4.24 *supra*

30. 15 U.S.C.A. §§ 77c(b), 77(d)(6). *See* § 4.16 *supra*.

31. Interpretive Release on Regulation D, Sec. Act Rel. No. 33–6455, 27 S.E.C. Docket 347, 1983 WL 409415, 1 Fed. Sec. L. Rep. (CCH) ¶ 2380 (SEC March 3, 1983) (answer to question 73).

32. Compare former Rule 146.

As pointed out above, Rule 506(b)(2)(ii) provides that a purchaser must either be knowledgeable, act through a purchaser representative, or be qualified as an accredited investor. In addition to institutional investors, the definition of accredited investor includes individuals with a net worth of more than one million dollars or an annual income in excess of two hundred thousand dollars, as well as married couples with a combined net worth of one million dollars, or a combined annual income of more than three hundred thousand dollars.[36] In so defining qualified purchasers, Rule 506 substitutes wealth as a criterion in lieu of investor knowledge and sophistication. Rule 502(b)(1)[37] provides that where all Rule 506 purchasers are accredited, the issuer is not under the affirmative disclosure obligations set forth in Rule 502(b)(2).[38] Formerly, the rule required that if there was one unaccredited purchaser, *all* purchasers had to receive a private placement memorandum containing the specified information. Under the current version of the rule, there is no such mandate as the informational requirement applies only to unaccredited investors. However, the SEC recommends that in light of anti-fraud considerations *all purchasers* receive this information.[39] Accordingly, the failure to deliver an offering memorandum to accredited investors will not destroy the safe harbor exemption. Nevertheless, there seems little reason not to follow the Commission's advice and supply the offering circular to accredited investors if one has been prepared for unaccredited investors.

Rules 502 and 506 on their face give the reader the impression that for a private placement made solely to accredited investors there are no informational requirements. Rule 502 only addresses the issuer's need to provide a disclosure statement and does not address the additional requirement (derived from the courts' interpretation of the statute) that all purchasers in a non-public offering have access to current information about the issuer. In the *SEC v. Ralston Purina* decision,[40] the Supreme Court announced *two* prerequisites for the section 4(2) non public offering exemption. First, the offerees must have access to the same type of current information about the issuer that would be required in a registered offering. Second, the purchasers must be sufficiently sophisticated and knowledgeable to evaluate the information. Rule 506(b) permits the offeree qualification to be established if the purchaser is an accredited investor.[41] This goes to only the first part of the *Ralston Purina* test. As a section 4(2) exemption, Rule 506 cannot go beyond the parameters of the statute.[42] Since the statute, as interpreted by the Supreme Court, requires access to current issuer information, such a requirement should be read into Rule 506.[43] Accordingly, Rule 502 should not be read as

36. 17 C.F.R. § 230.501(a).

37. 17 C.F.R. § 230.502(b)(1).

38. 17 C.F.R. § 230.502(b)(2). The same affirmative disclosure obligations apply to Rule 505 offerings. *See* § 4.22 *supra.*

39. *Ibid.*

40. 346 U.S. 119, 73 S.Ct. 981, 97 L.Ed. 1494 (1953). *See* § 4.24 *supra.*

41. 17 C.F.R. § 230.506(b)(2)(ii). Alternatively, an unsophisticated unaccredited investor may qualify through the use of a purchaser representative. *Id.*

42. At least in theory, the SEC could invoke the general exemptive authority set forth in section 28 of the Act (15 U.S.C.A. § 77z–3) to depart from section 4(2)'s limitations. However, there has not been any indication of a movement in this direction.

43. In contrast, since Rule 505 is a section 3(b) exemption, a Rule 505 offering which is sold only to accredited investors does not have the same access to information requirement. The trade-off is that, unlike Rule 506, Rule 505 is limited to offerings of no more than $5,000,000.

dispensing with the access to information requirement; its sole purpose is to relieve the issuer of the burden of preparing a disclosure memorandum in offerings where all purchasers are accredited.

Minor variations from an exemption's requirements will not destroy the availability of the exemption.[44] Specifically, Rule 508 provides that an insignificant failure to comply with a condition that is not "directly intended to protect" the investor[45] will not destroy the exemption, provided that the issuer made a good faith and reasonable attempt to comply.[46]

Applicability of State Securities Laws

In 1996, Congress preempted the states' ability to apply their Blue Sky registration requirements[47] to many transactions.[48] Some exempt transactions carry with them the state law preemption but section 4(2) does not except for those transactions exempt pursuant to an SEC rule or regulation.[49] This means that when the transaction qualifies for Rule 506's safe harbor, there is an exemption from state law registration requirements.[50] However, if the safe harbor or rule 506 is unavailable or lost, then the state registration requirements are not preempted and the issuer must either register under state law or find an applicable state law exemption.

§ 4.26   An Overview of Transactions by Persons Other Than Issuers, Underwriters, and Dealers: Section 4(1); Unsolicited Brokers' Transactions—Section 4(4)

The registration requirements of the 1933 Act are not limited to offerings by the issuer. Secondary transactions—that, is sales by existing shareholders—may also trigger section 5's registration and prospectus obligations. Because of the proscription of section 5, the burden is on a seller of securities, including existing shareholders, to establish an exemption from registration.[1] Section sections 4(1),[2] 4(3),[3] and 4(4)[4] of the 1933 Act provide the most common exemptions available for secondary transactions.

---

44. *See* Carl W. Schneider, A Substantial Compliance Defense ("I and I") Defense and Other Changes Are Added to SEC Regulation D, 44 Bus. Law. 1207 (1989).

45. Rule 508's safe harbor for certain noncompliance with Regulation D only affects claims by private parties. Rule 508 does not preclude SEC actions in such instances. Rule 508(b), 17 C.F.R. § 230.508(b) ("Where an exemption is established only through reliance on [this rule], the failure to comply shall nonetheless be actionable by the Commission under section 20 of the Act").

46. 17 C.F.R. § 230.508. The adopting release points out that a failure to comply with the prohibition against a general solicitation does not fall within Rule 508's exemptive reach. Sec. Act Rel. No. 33–6825, [1989 Transfer Binder] Fed. Sec. L. Rep. (CCH) ¶ 84,404 (March 14, 1989).

47. State securities laws are discussed in chapter 8 *infra.*

48. Pub. L. No. 104–290, 110 Stat. 3416 (1996). *See, e.g.,* Symposium, The National Securities Markets Improvements Act—One Year Later, 53 Bus. Law. 507 (1998); Comment, The National Securities Market Improvement Act: How Improved is the Securities Market?, 36 Duq. L. Rev. 365 (1998).

49. 15 U.S.C.A. § 77r(b)(4)(D).

50. *See, e.g.,* Lillard v. Stockton, 267 F.Supp.2d 1081, 1116 (N.D. Okla. 2003) (state registration claim for Rule 506 offering was preempted by NSMIA).

§ 4.26

1. *E.g.,* SEC v. Ralston Purina Co., 346 U.S. 119, 126, 73 S.Ct. 981, 985, 97 L.Ed. 1494 (1953) (the burden of establishing an exemption falls on the person claiming the exemption). *See* § 4.1[3] *supra.*

2. 15 U.S.C.A. § 77d(1). *See* § 4.26[1] *infra.*

3. 15 U.S.C.A. § 77d(3). *See* § 4.31 *infra.*

4. 15 U.S.C.A. § 77d(4). *See* § 4.26[2] *infra.*

Section 4(1) of the 1933 Act[6] provides a registration exemption for "transactions by any person other than an issuer, underwriter or dealer." Section 4(1), especially when read in connection with the dealers' and unsolicited brokers' transaction exemptions in sections 4(3) and 4(4),[7] exempts most day-to-day transactions that are effected on an exchange or in the over-the-counter markets.[8] Since section 4(2)'s private placement exemption[9] is limited to issuer transactions, it has no application to the millions of shares that are traded daily on the national exchanges and NASDAQ where, although not involving a public offering, the transactions are not effected by issuers. The section 4(1) exemption helps fill this void. Section 4(1), which is also known as the exemption for nonprofessionals, exempts transactions rather than people and thus may not be available to someone who is not an issuer, underwriter or dealer but is involved in a transaction with one.[10] However, the mere involvement by a broker in a secondary transaction will not render the exemption unavailable.[11] Furthermore, unsolicited brokers' transactions are exempt under section 4(4).

The section 4(1) transaction exemption is limited to bona fide non-underwriter transactions. It is not available for sales that constitute an attempt to evade the Act's registration requirements.[12] Thus, for example, share of stock in a blank check company through a market maker will not qualify for the exemption.[13]

§ 4.26[1] Section 4(1)—The Exemption for Nonprofessionals— Basic Definitions

Issuers, underwriters, and dealers are persons or entities who are engaged in securities transactions by virtue of their professions. Thus, one way to look at the section 4(1) exemption is an exemption for ordinary transactions by ordinary, nonprofessional investors. A better understanding of the scope of the exemption flows from the definition of the terms "issuer," "underwriter," and "dealer."

Issuers. By its terms, section 4(1) exempts all transactions by persons who are not issuers, underwriters or dealers. Section 2(a)(4) of the Act[14] defines "issuer" to include every person who issues or proposes to issue a security. In addition, in the case of a voting trust or other trust certificates, "issuer" refers to the person or persons performing the acts and assuming the duties of depositor or manager under the provisions of the trust or other

---

6. 15 U.S.C.A. § 77d(1). *See* Report, The Section "4(1½)" Phenomenon: Private Resales of "Restricted" Securities, 34 Bus.Law. 1961 (1979).

7. 15 U.S.C.A. §§ 77d(3), 77d(4).

8. Section 4(3) exempts transactions by nonparticipating dealers and underwriters no longer acting as underwriters after more than forty or ninety days after the registration statement's effective date. 15 U.S.C.A. § 77d(3).

9. 15 U.S.C.A. § 77d(2). *See* § 4.24 *supra.*

10. SEC v. Holschuh, 694 F.2d 130, 137–38 (7th Cir.1982); United States v. Wolfson, 405 F.2d 779 (2d Cir.1968), *cert. denied* 394 U.S. 946, 89 S.Ct. 1275, 22 L.Ed.2d 479 (1969).

11. Ackerberg v. Johnson, 892 F.2d 1328, 1334 n. 4 (8th Cir.1989).

12. *E.g.,* NASD Regulation, Inc., 32 Sec. Reg. & L. Rep. (BNA) 207 (SEC No Action Letter Jan. 21, 2000).

13. NASD Regulation, Inc., 32 Sec. Reg. & L. Rep. (BNA) 207 (SEC No Action Letter Jan. 21, 2000) (neither section 4(1) nor Rule 144's safe harbor was available).

14. 15 U.S.C.A. § 77b(a)(4).

agreement.[15] The definition of issuer is not limited to initial distributions. For example, it has been held that a transaction is not exempt and the issuer concept applies to reissue of stock that had previously been reacquired by the issuing corporation.[16] It has also been held that the concept of issuer applies to a corporation acting as a promoter by setting up a number of limited partnerships for syndication.[17] The statutory definition of issuer does not generally raise any significant problem of judicial interpretation since it is usually easy to identify the issuer for a particular security.

Underwriters. The question of who is an underwriter, which is taken up in more detail in the next section of this treatise,[18] is not nearly as simple as defining "issuer." Section 2(a)(11)[19] provides that an "underwriter" is anyone who purchases a security from the issuer with a view toward distribution of the security, as well as anyone who offers to sell or offers for sale for an issuer in connection with a distribution, including anyone involved in any indirect participation in such undertaking or the underwriting of the distribution. The most troubling problems of the definition in operation arise in the context of persons who, although not denominated as underwriters in the generic sense of the term, act as conduits for placing the securities in the hands of members of the investing public. In addition to the general definition of underwriter, section 2(a)(11) further provides that anyone who sells securities on behalf of a controlling person of the issuer is deemed an underwriter.[20] There are thus three ways to qualify for underwriter status: (1) purchasing from the issuer with a view towards distribution, (2) direct or indirect participation in an underwriting effort, and (3) selling securities on behalf of a control person. Underwriter status not only renders the section 4(1) exemption unavailable, but it also provides the basis for liability for misstatements in connection with a registered offering.[21]

Dealers. Section 2(a)(12) of the Act[22] defines "dealer" to include any person who for all or part of his or her time is in the business of offering, buying, selling, or otherwise dealing or trading in securities issued by others. It does not matter whether such sales activity is direct or indirect and the statutory definition of dealer further applies whether one is acting as agent, broker, or principal with regard to the securities transactions in question. Since virtually all day-to-day transactions are effected through the means of a registered broker-dealer, the section 4(1) exemption standing alone would not exclude the transactions from coverage of the Act's registration provisions. However, as noted above, section 4(1) must be read in tandem with section 4(3)'s exemption for most dealers' transactions and section 4(4)'s exemption for unsolicited brokers' transactions.

15. *Id.*

16. SEC v. Stanwood Oil Corp., 516 F.Supp. 1181, 1184 (W.D.Pa.1981).

17. SEC v. Holschuh, 694 F.2d 130, 138–39 (7th Cir.1982); SEC v. Murphy, 626 F.2d 633, 644 (9th Cir.1980).

18. *See* § 4.27 *infra.*

19. 15 U.S.C.A. § 77b(a)(11).

20. *See, e.g.,* United States v. Wolfson, 405 F.2d 779 (2d Cir.1968), *cert. denied* 394 U.S. 946, 89 S.Ct. 1275, 22 L.Ed.2d 479 (1969); SEC v. Netelkos, 592 F.Supp. 906 (S.D.N.Y.1984); § 4.27 *infra.*

21. Section 11(a) imposes civil liability upon underwriters for damages resulting from reliance on material misstatements or omissions in the registration statement. 15 U.S.C.A. § 77k(a). *See* § 7.4 *infra.*

22. 15 U.S.C.A. § 77b(a)(12).

§ 4.26[2] Section 4(4)—Unsolicited Brokers' Transactions

One of the key provisions for dealing with many day-to-day securities transactions is found in section 4(4)'s exemption for unsolicited brokers' transactions.[24] Section 4(4) exempts "brokers' transactions executed upon customers' orders on any exchange or in the over-the-counter market but not the solicitation of such orders." Neither the 1933 Act nor the SEC rules promulgated thereunder contain a definition of "broker," but it is clear that the concept cannot be coextensive with that of a "dealer" under section 2(a)(12). Additional learning on the meaning of the term "broker" can be gathered by reference to the Securities Exchange Act of 1934. Section 3(a)(4) of the 1934 Act[25] defines "broker" as anyone, other than a bank, engaged in the business of effecting securities transactions for the account of others. The 1934 Act definition of broker comports with the generic meaning of the term and thus would seem to be equally applicable to the 1933 Act. As such, brokers form a subclass of dealers and include anyone who is in the business of effecting securities transactions as agent for others. Accordingly, persons who only execute transactions on their own behalf or as principals may still be categorized as "dealers" but do not fall within the concept of "broker" within the statutory exemption from registration provided in section 4(4). The section 4(4) exemption only applies to transactions in which the broker acts as the purchaser's agent, rather than as an agent for someone else such as the issuer or underwriter.

Another significant aspect of the section 4(4) exemption is that it extends to "brokers' *transactions.*" Both the courts and SEC have pointed out the distinction in terminology between "transactions" and the concept of a "distribution."[26] It has accordingly been held that although a particular securities sale may be at the behest of the customer and thus executed through a broker without his or her solicitation, it may nevertheless be subject to the Act's registration requirements. The brokers' transaction exemption has thus been held inapplicable if the amount of securities sold is so large as to constitute a "distribution"—as compared with the day-to-day "transaction" that the section 4(4) exemption was designed to cover.[27] The concept of distribution sufficient to confer underwriter status does not depend on a certain percentage of the market float but rather on the fact that a significant amount of shares are involved.[28] In addition to the magnitude of the sales in question, a distribution may be found to exist based on the types of selling efforts that are employed. The term "distribution" is used to describe "the entire process in a public offering through which a block of securities is dispersed and ultimately comes to rest in the hands of the investing public."[30] The existence of a distribution will depend on a number of

24. 15 U.S.C.A. § 77d(4). *See also* section 4(3) of the Act, 15 U.S.C.A. § 77d(3) which is discussed in § 4.31 *infra.*

25. 15 U.S.C.A. § 77c(a)(4).

26. *E.g.,* Gilligan, Will & Co. v. SEC, 267 F.2d 461, 466 (2d Cir.1959), *cert. denied* 361 U.S. 896, 80 S.Ct. 200, 4 L.Ed.2d 152 (1959), citing H.R.Rep. No. 1838, 73d Cong.2d Sess. 41 (1934).

27. *See, e.g.,* United States v. Wolfson, 405 F.2d 779, (2d Cir.1968), *cert. denied* 394 U.S. 946, 89 S.Ct. 1275, 22 L.Ed.2d 479 (1969); In the Matter of Ira Haupt & Co., 23 S.E.C. 589 (SEC 1946); SEC Rule 144, 17 C.F.R. § 230.144. *See* §§ 4.28–4.29 *infra.*

28. *See* Quinn & Co. v. SEC, 452 F.2d 943, 946 (10th Cir.1971).

30. In the Matter of Wonsover, Administrative Proceeding File No. 3–8584, Sec. Exch. Act Rel. No. 34–41123, 69 S.E.C. Docket 608, 1999 WL 100935 n. 25 (SEC March 1, 1999), petition denied 205 F.3d 408 (D.C.Cir.2000).

factors relating to the magnitude of the transaction including the number of shares for sale, the trading volume that those shares represent, the percentage of outstanding shares, and the public float. The amount of the shares being sold is not as significant as the percentage of the public float that those shares represent.[32]

The section 4(4) exemption is unavailable to a broker who has reasonable grounds to believe that the customer is a statutory underwriter.[33] The Commission has indicated that brokers receiving restricted stock have a duty of reasonable inquiry as to whether the customer entering a sell order is a statutory underwriter.[34] Furthermore, a broker or dealer who is asked to sell a substantial block of securities is under an obligation to investigate whether the transaction involves a control person and/or underwriter; and reliance on the customer's assertions alone may not satisfy the obligation of reasonable investigation.[35]

The SEC does not have any rules relating specifically to brokers' transactions themselves. However, Rule 144(g)'s provision relating to brokers' transactions may give some guidance as to the scope of the section 4(4) exemption.[36]

§ 4.27   Who Is an Underwriter?—Section 2(a)(11)

Section 2(a)(11) of the Act[1] sets forth a broad-based statutory definition of "underwriter" which includes (1) persons who acquire securities of the issuer with a view towards distribution, (2) all persons who directly or indirectly participate in the offering, selling or underwriting process, as well as (3) persons selling on behalf of a control person of the issuer. The definition's significance goes beyond the section 4(1) exemption from registration.[2] For example, section 2(a)(11) also helps determine the scope of the class of persons liable for material misstatements and omissions made in connection with registered offerings.[3]

§ 4.27[1]   The Underwriter Concept—Section 2(a)(11) and Applicable SEC Rules

The statutory definition of "underwriter" sets forth three ways in which a someone may fall within the definition of underwriter: (1) by purchasing from the issuer with a view towards distribution, (2) by direct or indirect participation in an underwriting effort, and (3) by selling securities on behalf of a control person. As is discussed more fully below, underwriter status

---

32. *See* Examination of the Registration of Securities To Be Offered and Sold on a Delayed or Continuous Basis in the Future, Sec. Act Rel. No. 33–6391, 24 S.E.C. Docket 1502, 1982 WL 529089 (SEC March 12, 1982).

33. In re Robert G. Leigh, 50 S.E.C. 189, 1990 WL 309872 [1990 Transfer Binder] Fed. Sec. L. Rep. (CCH) ¶ 84,700 (Feb. 1, 1990) (broker had reason to know that customer selling unregistered securities had acquired the shares from the issuer with a view to selling them).

34. *Id.*

35. In the Matter of Transactions in Securities of Laser Arms Corporation by Certain Broker–Dealers, 1991 WL 292009, Sec.Exch.Act Rel. No. 34–28878 (SEC Feb. 14, 1991).

36. 17 C.F.R. § 230.144(g).

§ 4.27

1. 15 U.S.C.A. § 77b(a)(11).

2. *See* 15 U.S.C.A. § 77d(1), which is discussed in § 4.29 *supra*; § 4.32 *infra*.

3. *See* 15 U.S.C.A. § 77k(a), which is discussed in § 7.3 *infra*.

requires the existence of a "distribution,"[5] which is generally interpreted to involve a large amount of securities.

Whether a transaction falls within the section 4(1) exemption by involving an "underwriter" often boils down to a question of fact as to the would-be underwriter's state of mind in acquiring the security.

One key aspect of the part of the statutory definition is that in order to be classified as a statutory underwriter, the participant must have been acting on behalf of or purchasing from an issuer. In this context, however, the statute provides that a control person is considered to be an issuer. Willfully acting as a conduit for distributing shares without registration is sufficient to create underwriter status, even though the person acting as an underwriter did not intend act as an underwriter.[7] Underwriter status thus can follow from playing an essential role in the distribution even though the underwriter was not the actual seller. The general approach to underwriter status may be summarized as follows: when a substantial amount of securities are sold on behalf of an issuer (or control person) or are purchased from an issuer (or control person) and subsequently resold within a short period of time, underwriter status may attach. On the other hand, the mere fact that a dealer sells a large amount of securities will not necessarily create underwriter status. The essence of underwriter status is establishing that the securities were acquired with from the issuer or control person with an intent to resell.

The legislative history of section 2(a)(11) reveals that the congressional intent was to include as underwriters all persons who might operate as conduits for securities being placed into the hands of the investing public.[12] So long as the ultimate purchasers are members of the general public, as opposed to qualified private placement purchasers,[14] the transaction calls for the protection of the Securities Act's registration provisions.[15] The exemption thus places great emphasis on the ultimate purchasers of the securities, rather than the nature of the person acting as a conduit for the sale of securities to the members of the public.[16]

The concept of distribution refers to the process by which a block of privately held securities is dispersed to the investing public.[17] Although distributions normally involve a large amount of stock, that is not necessarily the case.[18]

The statutory definition excludes members of the selling group from the definition of underwriter. Although certainly involved in the distribution process, those dealers who receive nothing more than their ordinary sales commissions are not classified as section 2(a)(11) underwriters. The exclusion

---

5. *See, e.g.,* United States v. Wolfson, 405 F.2d 779 (2d Cir.1968), *cert. denied* 394 U.S. 946, 89 S.Ct. 1275, 22 L.Ed.2d 479 (1969); In the Matter of Ira Haupt & Co., 23 S.E.C. 589, Sec. Exch. Act Rel. No. 34–3845, 1946 WL 24150 (SEC 1946).

7. *See, e.g.,* Geiger v. SEC, 363 F.3d 481 (9th Cir. 2004).

12. *See* S.E.C. v. Lybrand, 200 F.Supp.2d 384, 2002 WL 987284 at *7 (S.D.N.Y.2002) (relying on this treatise).

14. *See* 15 U.S.C.A. § 77d(2); 17 C.F.R. § 230.506; §§ 4.24, 4.25 *supra.*

15. H.R.Rep. No. 85, 73d Cong., 1st Sess. 13–14 (1933).

16. *See, e.g.,* In the Matter of Kirby, 2000 WL 1787908 (SEC Initial Dec. Dec. 7, 2000) (relying on this treatise).

17. Geiger v. SEC, 363 F.3d 481 (9th Cir. 2004) (relying on this treatise).

18. Geiger v. SEC, 363 F.3d 481 (9th Cir. 2004); Pennaluna & Co. v. SEC, 410 F.2d 861, 865 (9th Cir.1969) (.025% of the outstanding shares constituted a distribution).

of transactions in which the only remuneration is "the usual and customary distributors' or sellers' commission"[19] is designed to protect members of the selling group and nonparticipating brokers from being included in the concept of underwriter. SEC Rule 141[20] provides that a dealer's commission includes the normal spread between the offering price and the dealer's cost, whether the dealer was purchasing the security prior to reselling it or acting merely as a broker executing a customer's order.[21]

Rule 142[22] excludes from the definition of underwriter persons who are not affiliated with either the underwriter or the issuer and who purchase or make a commitment to purchase all or part of any unsold allotment, so long as the securities are acquired for "investment" rather than for "distribution." The purpose of Rule 142 has been explained as recognition of "the value of secondary capital in facilitating the flow of investment funds into industry, and of the fact that the owners of such secondary capital cannot practicably perform the duty of thorough investigation and analysis imposed by the Act on the underwriter proper."[23] Accordingly, "a person who does no more than agree with an underwriter to take over some or all of the undistributed portion of the issue, and who purchases for investment any securities which his commitment thus obliges him to take up, does not thereby subject himself to liability as an underwriter of the securities of the issue actually distributed to the public."[24]

In contrast to Rules 141 and 142's exclusions of certain transactions from the concept of underwriter, SEC Rule 140[25] expressly includes within the definition one type of indirect participation in the distribution process. Rule 140 confers underwriter status on any entity whose chief business is the purchase of securities of one issuer (or of two or more affiliated issuers) and where that entity utilizes the sale of its own securities to finance the purchases. Under Rule 140, where such holding company or investment company acquires the issuer's securities, those securities will be deemed to have been acquired by an underwriter within the meaning of section 2(a)(11).[26] Beyond the above-mentioned Commission rules, the task of defining "underwriter" has for the most part been left to judicial interpretation and SEC decision-making. For example, just as ordinary brokerage transactions will not classify a broker-dealer as an underwriter, engaging in routine market-making activities, by simply acting as a conduit between broker-dealers, will not result in underwriter status.[27]

It is very common for institutional investors, as well as wealthy individuals, to purchase large blocks of both registered and unregistered offerings. When these investors subsequently sell their securities, there frequently may

---

19. 15 U.S.C.A. § 77b(a)(11).

20. 17 C.F.R. § 230.141.

21. *Id.*

22. 17 C.F.R. § 230.142.

23. Opinion of SEC General Counsel, Sec. Act Rel. No. 1862 (Dec. 14, 1938).

24. *Id.*

25. 17 C.F.R. § 230.140.

26. *See id.*

27. In re Laser Arms Corp. Securities Litigation, 794 F.Supp. 475 (S.D.N.Y.1989), *affirmed* 969 F.2d 15 (2d Cir.1992).

be a question as to the necessity for registration under the Act.[28] The problem is most likely to arise where the initial offering was not registered under the Act. Downstream sales are dealt with in Rule 144, which is not the exclusive method of compliance for either affiliates or nonaffiliates of the issuer.[29] Rule 144 requires a one-year holding period before the securities can be resold under the safe harbor.[30] The rule further imposes limitations on the volume of sales after the one-year period has expired.[31] The Commission has recognized that the inherent dangers of such large block purchases filtering down to the investing public (even when in connection with a public offering) may call for additional protection under the Act. Accordingly, the SEC formulated the "presumptive underwriter doctrine," under which anyone who purchased at least ten percent of a registered offering could be considered an underwriter, unless the purchaser was able to prove that he or she had sufficient investment intent. The ten percent threshold is not a hard and fast rule but certainly remains a significant factor in determining underwriting status under the Act. The presumptive underwriter rule has continued vitality in a "modified form" as it will still be considered in addition to other factors.[33]

§ 4.27[2] Case Law Developments—Inadvertent Underwriters

In one of the earliest judicial pronouncements on point, the Second Circuit made it clear that any substantial involvement in the distribution process would confer underwriter status, thus rendering unavailable the section 4(1) exemption from 1933 Act registration. In SEC v. Chinese Consolidated Benevolent Association,[34] a not-for-profit association helped solicit investment in foreign government bonds.[35] The defendants maintained that they were not acting as securities promoters in the traditional sense, and that in promoting a worthy cause they should be exempt from the Act's coverage. Although their arguments swayed Judge Swan who wrote a vigorous dissent, the court held that the voluntary association's sales efforts were sufficient participation in the distribution and underwriting process so as to render the defendants "underwriters" within the meaning of section 2(a)(11).[36] In his dissent, Judge Swan maintained that a logical extension of the court's opinion would make a newspaper an underwriter if a column or editorial recommends a bond in order to help a struggling government, or merely announces an

---

28. *See, e.g.,* United States v. Wolfson, 405 F.2d 779 (2d Cir.1968), *cert. denied* 394 U.S. 946, 89 S.Ct. 1275, 22 L.Ed.2d 479 (1969).

29. 17 C.F.R. § 230.144. *See also* 17 C.F.R. § 230.144(d)(1).

30. Rule 144(e), 17 C.F.R. § 230.144(e).

31. 17 C.F.R. § 230.144(e).

33. Robert J. Ahrenholz & William E. Van Valkenberg, The Presumptive Underwriter Doctrine: Statutory Underwriter Status for Investors Purchasing a Specified Portion of a Registered Offering, 1973 Utah L.Rev. 773, 775.

34. 120 F.2d 738 (2d Cir.1941), *cert. denied* 314 U.S. 618, 62 S.Ct. 106, 86 L.Ed. 497 (1941). *See also, e.g.,* In the Matter of State Bank of Pakistan, 1992 WL 102234, [1991–1992 Transfer Binder] Fed. Sec. L. Rep. (CCH) ¶ 89,946 (SEC 1992).

35. The Republic of China authorized the issuance of bonds in the aggregate of fifty million dollars. The defendant, a voluntary association organized in New York, created a committee to solicit funds for China through the sale of these bonds. The committee acted merely as a conduit, receiving no remuneration either directly or indirectly as it was participating in what it viewed to be a worthy cause. The only activity of the association was to forward the $600,000 it received to China and to distribute the bonds to the individual purchasers here in the United States.

36. *See* 120 F.2d at 741.

impending offering.[37] The short answer to Judge Swan's contention is that it is a matter of degree. It is most certainly correct that incidental or collateral selling efforts or recommendations should not be sufficient to render someone potentially liable for violations of the Securities Act. Absent some other exemption, however, when an organization acts as a conduit for the sale of securities, such activity should be sufficient not only to confer jurisdiction but also to trigger the registration requirements, whether or not remuneration is received. This method of analysis makes each decision extremely factual, and relatively little firm footing is provided for counselors and corporate planners in relying on the available precedent.

The problems created by the "inadvertent underwriter" cases can create a nightmare for the corporate planner. The difficulty in planning was highlighted by the celebrated decision in SEC v. Guild Films Co.[40] which involved the foreclosure sale of pledged securities.

In *Guild Films,* the inadvertent underwriters were banks engaging in a foreclosure sale of a substantial block of securities in Guild Films Company; the securities had been held as collateral for loans to a major shareholder of the company.[41] The Second Circuit accepted the Commission's argument that the banks were acting as an underwriters under section 2(a)(11) even though the banks may have accepted the stock as collateral in good faith and had not dealt directly with the corporation that was the issuer of the securities.[42] The court reasoned that "the banks knew that they had been given unregistered stock and that the issuer had specifically forbidden that the stock be sold. * * *"[43] In the court's view, this was sufficient to put the bank in a position in which it must have either held on to the stock, found some other independent exemption, or registered its sales upon foreclosure. The issue was not the bank's culpability in facilitating downstream sales, but rather whether the sales were made in such a manner as to trigger the need for the protection provided by registration.[45] In contrast, when a bona fide pledge is made and there is no substantial likelihood that the pledgee will have to foreclose, it is unlikely that the pledgee will be found to be a statutory underwriter in the event that there is a foreclosure and the securities are sold.

The Commission has adhered to the rule that sales of pledged securities can, under certain circumstances, create underwriter status. Specifically, under Rule 144(d)(4)(D),[47] [*144 (d) (3) (iv)*] all securities sold by a bona fide pledgee are

---

37. *Id.* at 742 (Swan, J., dissenting): "Hence, a single newspaper editorial, published without instigation by the Chinese Government and merely urging the purchase of the bonds in the name of patriotism, would make the newspaper an 'underwriter.' I cannot believe the statute should be so interpreted."

40. 279 F.2d 485 (2d Cir.1960), *cert. denied* 364 U.S. 819, 81 S.Ct. 52, 5 L.Ed.2d 49 (1960).

41. The shareholder was Hollywood personality Hal Roach. The shares that were used as collateral had been issued pursuant to a private placement, with the purchaser signing the necessary investment letter. The lower court found that notwithstanding the investment letter, Roach's intent was to resell the security at a later date. The bank had obtained the stock as collateral after negotiations to renew Roach's note. When it became necessary for the bank to foreclose on the note, the stock transfer agent refused to enter the sale and suit was brought to compel the transfer. At the same time the SEC brought suit to enjoin the sale on the ground that it would violate the Act's registration provisions.

42. 279 F.2d at 489–90.

43. 279 F.2d at 490.

45. For a more recent decision requiring registration for sale of pledged securities, *see* United States v. Lindo, 18 F.3d 353 (6th Cir.1994).

47. 17 C.F.R. § 230.144(d)(4)(D).

deemed to be acquired when they were acquired by the pledgor, and are aggregated with any sales by the pledgor for the purpose of calculating the rule's ceiling on resales. The rule further provides that where there is a pledge without any recourse against the pledgor, the acquisition date of the security for purposes of creating downstream selling liability is the date of the pledge rather than the date of acquisition by the pledgor.[48] In 1991, the Commission instituted enforcement proceedings in connection with a broker's sale of control securities to satisfy a margin account.[49] The broker knew that the customer was a control person and apparently ignored the volume limitations applicable to such sales. The initiation of proceedings was especially significant in that the broker in question had relied on no action letters that had been given to others in the past. These proceedings highlight the precarious nature of trying to distill general principles from specific no action responses.[50]

§ 4.27[3] Investment Intent—The Holding Period

In determining whether or not a person is a statutory underwriter, one of the key questions is whether the would-be underwriter had sufficient investment intent at the time of purchase. The issue is raised in the context of whether the securities were purchased with a view toward distribution. One of the primary questions then becomes: how does one determine the seller's original intent at the time the securities were acquired? The period that the securities were held in between the purchase and subsequent sale is a significant factor in determining whether they were originally purchased with the requisite investment intent. A sale closely following the acquisition of the securities is strong circumstantial evidence that an investment intent did not exist.[56] In a leading case it was held within the context of a criminal prosecution that "[t]he passage of two years before the commencement of distribution of any of these shares is an insuperable obstacle to my finding that [defendant] took these shares with a view to distribution thereof, in the absence of any relevant evidence from which I could conclude that he did not take the shares for investment."[57] The decisions in the Second Circuit thus formed the basis of a two-year rule of thumb for the holding period. Since this initially arose in the context of a criminal prosecution, which carries a higher standard of proof, a more rigid rule, or even a longer holding period, arguably could be applied in a civil action or SEC enforcement proceeding. However, the trend has not been in this direction. In fact, in 1997, the SEC shortened the holding period for resales of restricted securities under the safe harbor

48. *Id.* Cf. Shearson Lehman Hutton Holdings Inc. v. Coated Sales, Inc., 697 F.Supp. 639 (S.D.N.Y.1988) (stock transfer agent had no lawful basis to refuse to transfer stock to pledgee on default).

49. Morgan Stanley & Co., Sec.Exch.Act Rel. No. 34–28,990, Admin.Proc. File No. 3–7473 (March 20, 1991).

50. *See* § 1.4[4] *supra*.

56. *See, e.g.,* In the Matter of DG Bank (Schweiz) AG [1991–1992 Transfer Binder] 1992 WL 45901, Fed. Sec. L. Rep. (CCH) ¶ 84,945 (SEC March 5, 1992) (a bank selling restricted securities within two months of their acquisition from the issuer could not establish the availability of the section 4(1) exemption).

57. United States v. Sherwood, 175 F.Supp. 480, 483 (S.D.N.Y.1959) (defendant had purchased shares of the issuer's stock in a private placement and held it for two years). *Compare, e.g.,* Gilligan, Will & Co. v. SEC, 267 F.2d 461 (2d Cir.1959), *cert. denied* 361 U.S. 896, 80 S.Ct. 200, 4 L.Ed.2d 152 (1959) (ten-month holding period held insufficient).

provisions of Rule 144 from two years to one.[58] Interestingly, as early as 1935, this same one year period had been suggested as creating a strong inference of investment intent.[59]

The Commission adopted the holding period as a general rule of thumb for determining investment intent and also incorporated a holding period into Rule 144 (now one year) which presents a safe harbor for persons selling securities that have been acquired in a private placement or pursuant to a Regulation D exemption.[60] Rule 144 places limitations on the amount of securities that may be sold even after the holding period has expired.[62]

Courts and the Commission will also look to the circumstances surrounding the downstream sale as well as to the initial purchase. It is clear that when properly viewed, the holding period for securities acquired in a private placement or other nonpublic offerings is merely a very rough guideline and thus is not the be-all and end-all of the "underwriter" issue. In the last analysis, whether or not the purchaser had an intent to distribute is a question of fact to be answered by looking to all of the particular circumstances.[64]

The "Change in Circumstances" Exception

In the pre-Rule 144 case law, sales made prior to the expiration of the two-year holding period from the date of acquisition were permitted if the seller was able to demonstrate that he or she had the sufficient investment intent.[65] As a result, it became common for sellers to claim that although they had the requisite investment intent at the time of purchase, subsequent changes in their personal situations necessitated the resale of the securities.[66] Sellers of securities often took the position that since they had not purchased the securities with a view toward distribution, they should be relieved from the Act's registration requirements. Although the Commission often refused to issue no-action letters based on this "change of circumstances" defense, it was frequently relied upon by planners in permitting transactions without registration and also was acknowledged by the Commission as a legitimate way of avoiding underwriter status.[68] The change in circumstances defense was highly factual and not easy to predict when it might be applied.

The change in circumstances defense was not available where the changed circumstances were reasonably foreseeable at the time of purchase, nor where the only change was that the issuer failed to meet the investor's

58. 17 C.F.R. § 230.144 which is discussed in § 4.29 *infra*.

59. Opinion of General Counsel relating to Rule 142, Sec. Act Rel. No. 33–1862, 1938 WL 31127 (SEC Dec. 14, 1938).

60. *See* Notice of Adoption of Rule 144 Relating to the Definition of the Terms § Underwriter' in Sections 4(1) and 2(11) and § Brokers' Transactions' in Section 4(4) of the Securities Act of 1933, Sec. Act Rel. No. 33–5223, 1972 WL 18134 (Jan. 11, 1972).

62. 17 C.F.R. § 230.144(e).

64. Gilligan, Will & Co. v. SEC, 267 F.2d 461 (2d Cir.1959), *cert. denied* 361 U.S. 896, 80 S.Ct. 200, 4 L.Ed.2d 152 (1959).

65. *See, e.g.*, Vohs v. Dickson, 495 F.2d 607, 620–621 (5th Cir.1974) (considering change in circumstances as one factor in concluding that purchaser made purchase with the necessary investment intent).

66. *See* SEC, "Disclosure to Investors"—Report and Recommendations to The Securities and Exchange Commission From the Disclosure Policy Study, "The Wheat Report," 160–77 (1969).

68. *E.g.*, Radiation Materials Co., Publicly Available September 18, 1972 1933 Act § 4(1) 1972 WL 8103 (SEC No Action Letter available Sept. 18, 1972).

expectations of success.[70] Additionally, the availability of the change in circumstances defense was directly related to the period of time for which the securities had been held; the shorter the holding period, the more compelling the evidence required.[71] The change in circumstances defense only added to the uncertainty in structuring transactions and resulted in "troublesome inconsistency."[72] Accordingly, in adopting Rule 144, the Commission purported to rescind the change in circumstances defense.[73] There is, however, a question as to the Commission's authority to make such a pronouncement beyond the context of a safe harbor rule. To the extent that the change in circumstances defense is a valid interpretation in terms of the section 2(a)(11) statutory definition of one who purchases with an intent to redistribute, the SEC cannot by administrative fiat change the meaning of the statute.[74] However, if the change in circumstances defense was merely an administrative interpretation rather than a part of the statutory definition, the SEC can effectively eliminate the defense by changing its interpretation. In any event, since Rule 144 is non-exclusive, the change in circumstances defense arguably survives even if it is abolished for those relying upon the rule. Nevertheless, the SEC has taken the position that it has been abolished in all cases.[75]

§ 4.27[4] Sales on Behalf of Controlling Persons

The last sentence of section 2(a)(11)'s statutory definition of underwriter provides that anyone who sells a security on behalf of a controlling person is an underwriter.[76] Thus, a control person of the company frequently will not be in a position to rely on the section 4(1) exemption from registration. Although there is no statutory definition of "control" in Rule 405[78] the Commission defines control as "the possession, direct or indirect, of the power to direct or cause the direction of the management and policies of a person, whether through the ownership of voting securities, by contract, or otherwise."[79] Accordingly, the question of who is a control person is highly factual and is not dependent upon ownership of any specific percentage. For example, it has been held that someone owning eight percent of a company's stock was not a control person; if he had been a control person this would have rendered anyone handling sales on his behalf an automatic statutory underwriter.[81] A state court held that three individuals owning thirty-eight percent of the issuer's stock did not exercise control and thus were not control persons.[82]

---

70. *See* Gilligan, Will & Co. v. SEC, 267 F.2d 461, 462–68 (2d Cir.1959), *cert. denied* 361 U.S. 896, 80 S.Ct. 200, 4 L.Ed.2d 152 (1959).

71. SEC, "Disclosure to Investors"—Report and Recommendations to The Securities and Exchange Commission From the Disclosure Policy Study, "The Wheat Report," 167 (1969).

72. *Id.* at 176.

73. Notice of Adoption of Rule 144 Relating to the Definition of the Terms 'Underwriter' in Sections 4(1) and 2(11) and 'Brokers' Transactions' in Section 4(4) of the Securities Act of 1933, Sec. Act Rel. No. 33–5223, 1972 WL 18134 (Jan. 11, 1972).

74. *Cf.* Vohs v. Dickson, 495 F.2d 607, 620–621 (5th Cir.1974) (considering change in circumstances as one factor in concluding that purchaser made purchase with the necessary investment intent).

75. *Id.*

76. 15 U.S.C.A. § 77b(a)(11).

78. 17 C.F.R. § 230.405.

79. 17 C.F.R. § 230.405(f).

81. United States v. Sherwood, 175 F.Supp. 480 (S.D.N.Y.1959).

82. WNH Investments, LLC v. Batzel, 1995 WL 262248, [1995 Transfer Binder] Fed. Sec. L. Rep. (CCH) ¶ 98,764 (Del.Ch.1995) (section 4(1) exemption held applicable).

Control is not limited to voting control and can be found to exist where it is exercised other than through stock ownership.[83] Thus, any policy-making officer falls within Rule 405's definition and thus would be deemed a controlling person. The SEC has indicated that in the context of a sizable secondary distribution, the burden of proving the absence of control may be allocated to the person claiming the exemption.[84]

Where a series of coordinated secondary offerings resulted in a corporation's publicly held shares shifting from nine percent of those outstanding to forty-six percent of those outstanding, the broker/dealer handling such sales on behalf of controlling persons was held to have been a statutory underwriter.[85] The Commission rejected the contention that since the transactions were executed upon the selling customer's orders they should be exempt under section 4(4)[86] as unsolicited broker's transactions.[87] The Commission reasoned that such a large infusion of privately held stock into the public market constituted a "distribution," as opposed to the type of day-to-day transaction or "trading" that section 4(4) was designed to exempt.[88] Thus, it is clear that any large block sales of securities by insiders (i.e., control persons or affiliates) that have not been registered will be subject to the Act's registration requirements, absent some independent exemption.

An interesting question arises as to whether insiders or control persons must register securities purchased on the open market when, after a significant period of time, they decide to sell. In a somewhat analogous situation, the Commission held that even though securities issued prior to 1933 were exempt under former section 3(a)(1) of the Act,[90] a subsequent sale by controlling persons was a new distribution which went beyond the scope of the former section 3(a)(1) exemption.[91] The rationale for requiring registration of such large sales is that a large volume of sales will cause a disruption of an otherwise orderly public market and thus the disclosure protections of the registration requirements are needed. Disclosure informs the market of who is selling and why they are selling. Also, registration will inform the market of the issuer's current condition. This rationale for disclosure through registration can be extended to certain large block transactions by controlling persons. Furthermore, although once public, if the securities have been privately held for a sufficiently long period of time, the impact on the market is the same as if they had never been publicly issued. Unless dealing with restricted stock, large block transactions by institutional investors are not

83. 17 C.F.R. § 230.405(f).

84. In the Matter of Wittow, File No. 3–2182, 44 S.E.C. 666, Release No. 34–9303, 1971 WL 11265 *4 (SEC Aug. 24, 1971).

85. In the Matter of Ira Haupt & Co., 23 S.E.C. 589, Sec. Exch. Act Rel. No. 34–3845, 1946 WL 24150 (SEC 1946), noted 14 U.Chi.L.Rev. 307 (1947).

86. 15 U.S.C.A. § 77d(4). The SEC decision in *Ira Haupt* was based on section 4(4)'s predecessor, an earlier version of section 4(2).

87. In the Matter of Ira Haupt & Co., 23 S.E.C. 589, 600–06, Sec. Exch. Act Rel. No. 34–3845, 1946 WL 24150 (SEC 1946). *Accord* United States v. Wolfson, 405 F.2d 779 (2d Cir.1968), *cert. denied* 394 U.S. 946, 89 S.Ct. 1275, 22 L.Ed.2d 479 (1969).

88. In the Matter of Ira Haupt & Co., 23 S.E.C. 589 at 600–06, Sec. Exch. Act Rel. No. 34–3845, 1946 WL 24150 (SEC 1946). *Accord* Gilligan, Will & Co. v. SEC, 267 F.2d 461, 466 (2d Cir.1959), *cert. denied* 361 U.S. 896, 80 S.Ct. 200, 4 L.Ed.2d 152 (1959), citing H.R.Rep. No. 1838, 73d Cong. 2d Sess. 41 (1934). *See also, e.g.,* Ackerberg v. Johnson, 892 F.2d 1328, 1335 n. 6 (8th Cir.1989).

90. 15 U.S.C.A. § 77c(a)(1). *See* § 4.2 *supra*.

91. 23 S.E.C. at 599–600.

generally registered, but in these instances the sellers presumably do not qualify as control persons and thus are not "issuers" for the purposes of section 2(a)(11)'s definition of underwriter. It arguably does not make sense to require registration solely because such a large block of unrestricted stock had been sold by a control person of the issuer. However, the insider's access to nonpublic information, which would have to be disclosed in a registration statement, can be used to distinguish insider large block sales from other large transactions in a company's shares.

In United States v. Wolfson,[92] the Second Circuit alarmed the brokerage industry when it noted that brokers were potentially liable as underwriters for selling a controlling person's securities.[93] The court held that defendant Wolfson, the control person who had siphoned his securities to the public by making sales through a number of brokers, was not exempt since such transactions were through an underwriter as defined in section 2(a)(11).[94] The court noted that section 4(1) exempts "transactions" and not classes of people. Citing the section 2(a)(11) definition of underwriter, the court pointed out that the brokers had supplied outlets for the stock of appellants who were "issuers" within the section 2(a)(11) definition of that term even if they were not "issuers" as defined by section 2(a)(4)[95] for purposes of the Act in general.[96] Thus, the brokers were "underwriters" within the meaning of section 2(a)(11), and according to the court, "the stock was sold in 'transactions by underwriters' which are not within the exception of section 4(1). * * * "[97]

It is clear that a broker is under a duty to be aware of facts surrounding a transaction and "red flags" that he or she is participating in a distribution may lead to a finding that the broker was in fact an underwriter.[99] When a broker-dealer receives an order to sell a substantial amount of stock, he or she must investigate to determine if the sale will be in compliance with the securities laws.[101] Underwriter status thus can thus be found on the basis of knowingly assisting in the sales even without actual intent to act as an underwriter.[102]

The section 4(1) exemption, and hence the definition of underwriter, was not the only issue involved in the *Wolfson* case. The appellants in *Wolfson* also argued that the brokers could not be underwriters because the sales in question fell within the section 4(4) exemption for brokers' orders executed upon customers' orders on any exchange or in the over-the-counter market.

---

92. 405 F.2d 779 (2d Cir.1968), *cert. denied* 394 U.S. 946, 89 S.Ct. 1275, 22 L.Ed.2d 479 (1969).

93. *Id.* at 782–83.

94. *Id.* Wolfson, together with members of his immediate family and his right-hand man, owned 1,149,775 shares, or over forty percent of the outstanding stock of Continental Enterprises, Inc.; the remainder being spread among some 5,000 outside shareholders. In the eighteen month period between August 1, 1960 and January 31, 1962, 633,825 unregistered shares of the forty percent block were sold through a variety of brokerage houses.

95. 15 U.S.C.A. § 77b(a)(4).

96. Wolfson, 405 F.2d at 782.

97. *Id.*

99. *See, e.g.,* In the Matter of Wonsover, Administrative Proceeding File No. 3–8584, Sec. Exch. Act Rel. No. 34–41123, 69 S.E.C. Docket 608, 1999 WL 100935 *7 (SEC March 1, 1999), petition denied 205 F.3d 408 (D.C.Cir.2000).

101. *See, e.g.,* Wonsover v. SEC, 205 F.3d 408, 415 (D.C.Cir.2001).

102. Geiger v. SEC, 363 F.3d 481 (9th Cir. 2004).

The court agreed that section 4(4) exempted the brokers for their parts in the transaction, since the brokers had not solicited the orders, and were unaware at the time that the transactions were part of a distribution of securities by appellants.[103] Wolfson and his associates, on the other hand, were "control persons [who] must find their own exemptions."[104] Otherwise, the court reasoned, appellants would gain from having kept the true facts from the brokers.[105] In a situation in which the broker is not an unwitting participant, the size of the total secondary distribution may well preclude the application of section 4(4) to shield the brokers.

§ 4.29   The Safe Harbor Exemption for Secondary Transactions—SEC Rule 144

As noted in preceding sections of this treatise,[1] the case law and SEC interpretations of section 2(a)(11)[2] underwriter status and the scope of the exemptions under sections 4(1)[3] and 4(4)[4] have not provided much firm practical guidance to the planner of corporate for transactions involving the sale of restricted securities nor for transactions involving the sale of any securities held by control persons. Since many of the questions concerned with the need to register downstream securities sales essentially depend upon the resolution of factual issues, the decisions on point are frequently confusing and often may even appear to be inconsistent with one another. The resulting uncertainty was widely perceived by the practicing bar and documented by the "Wheat Report" recommendations which were transmitted in 1969 to the SEC.[6] In response to this and other issues identified in the Wheat Report, the Commission promulgated a number of additional regulations, including Rule 144.[7] The Commission thus recognized the need for more helpful guidelines for the securities bar in planning unregistered secondary transactions. Rule 144 was adopted to provide more guidance to the planner and other participants by clarifying the answers to the question of who is an underwriter and thereby defining the scope of the statutory exemptions under sections 4(1) and 4(4).

The Commission explained that section 4(1) "was intended to exempt only trading transactions between individual investors with respect to securities already issued and not to exempt distributions by issuers or acts of other individuals who engage in steps necessary to such distributions."[9] The SEC

---

103.   Wolfson, 405 F.2d at 782–83.

104.   *Id.* at 782.

105.   *Id.*

§ 4.29

1.   *See* §§ 4.26–4.27 *supra.*

2.   15 U.S.C.A. § 77b(a)(11).

3.   15 U.S.C.A. § 77d(1).

4.   15 U.S.C.A. § 77d(4).

6.   *See* "Disclosure to Investors": Report and Recommendation to the Securities and Exchange Commission from the Disclosure Policy Study, "The Wheat Report," 160–77 (1969).

7.   17 C.F.R. § 230.144.

9.   Notice of Adoption of Rule 144 Relating to the Definition of the Terms 'Underwriter' in Sections 4(1) and 2(11) and 'Brokers' Transactions' in Section 4(4) of the Securities Act of 1933, Sec. Act Rel. No. 33–5223, 1972 WL 18134 (Jan. 11, 1972) (citing SEC v. Chinese Consolidated Benevolent Association, 120 F.2d 738 (2d Cir.1941), *cert. denied* 314 U.S. 618, 62 S.Ct. 106, 86 L.Ed. 497 (1941).

further pointed out that the language of section 2(a)(11)'s definition of underwriter[10] is disjunctive, and thus the mere absence of a view toward subsequent distribution when making the initial purchase from the issuer would not preclude a finding that the purchaser had underwriter status.[11] The Commission therefore reaffirmed the absence of any strict intent requirement as an element of inadvertent underwriter status.[12]

Rule 144 operates as a safe harbor and as such is not the exclusive method by which an affiliate of the issuer may sell restricted securities in reliance upon an exemption.[13] The rule also applies to both sales of restricted securities by all persons and to sales of any securities by affiliates of the issuer.[14] The rule is thus a safe harbor for both affiliates and nonaffiliates. However, reliance on non-Rule 144 precedent will impose "a strong burden" on the person claiming the exemption.[16] As is the case with any safe harbor rule, Rule 144 will not protect a transaction that although in technical compliance with the rule, is part of a scheme to evade the 1933 Act's registration requirements.

"Restricted securities" are defined in Rule 144 as including those acquired directly or indirectly from an issuer in a non-public offering,[18] as well as securities subject to the resale restrictions imposed by the exemptions provided by Regulation D.[19] Rule 144 also is available with regard to securities issued under section 3(a)(9)'s exemption[20] for securities issued exclusively in exchange with existing securities holders. In 1998, securities issued in off-shore offerings under Regulation S were added to the list of restricted securities.[22] Due to the safe harbor nature of the rule, there is the alternative of relying upon the pre-Rule 144 case law and SEC interpretations when selling restricted stock.[23] The Commission has emphasized, however, that persons who offer or sell restricted securities without relying on Rule 144 will have a "substantial burden of proof in establishing that an exemption * * * is available," and that "brokers * * * who participate in the transactions do so at their risk."[24]

A significant exception to the vitality of pre-Rule 144 case law and interpretations is the Commission's position that the "change of circumstances" defense no longer applies to downstream sales by persons purchasing from an issuer that had not registered the securities.[25] Furthermore, although

---

10.   15 U.S.C.A. § 77b(a)(11).

11.   Notice of Adoption of Rule 144 Relating to the Definition of the Terms 'Underwriter' in Sections 4(1) and 2(11) and 'Brokers' Transactions' in Section 4(4) of the Securities Act of 1933, Sec. Act Rel. No. 33–5223, 1972 WL 18134 (Jan. 11, 1972).

12.   The problems of the inadvertent underwriter are discussed in § 4.27 *supra*.

13.   17 C.F.R. § 230.144(j).

14.   As discussed *infra*, formerly the Commission treated restricted and unrestricted securities as fungible.

16.   Notice of Adoption of Rule 144 Relating to the Definition of the Terms 'Underwriter' in Sections 4(1) and 2(11) and § Brokers' Transactions' in Section 4(4) of the Securities Act of 1933, Sec. Act Rel. No. 33–5223, 1972 WL 18134 (Jan. 11, 1972).

18.   This includes securities sold in reliance upon Rule 506's safe harbor. 17 C.F.R. § 230.506.

19.   17 C.F.R. § 230.144(a)(3).

20.   15 U.S.C.A. § 77c(a)(9). *See* § 4.10 *supra*.

22.   *See* Sec. Act Rel. No. 33–7505 (SEC Feb. 18,1998).

23.   *See* §§ 4.26–4.28 *supra*.

24.   Notice of Adoption of Rule 144 Relating to the Definition of the Terms 'Underwriter' in Sections 4(1) and 2(11) and 'Brokers' Transactions' in Section 4(4) of the Securities Act of 1933, Sec. Act Rel. No. 33–5223, 1972 WL 18134 (Jan. 11, 1972).

25.   *Id.*

the downstream seller's holding period prior to sale is a significant factor, in the Commission's view, "the fact that securities have been held for a particular period of time does not by itself establish the availability of an exemption from registration."[26] Thus, Rule 144's one year provision (which formerly was two years) is not determinative under the case law in deciding what the holding period should be under the statutory section 4(1) exemption.[27] The former two-year period was certainly useful by analogy, especially in light of its derivation from the early case law.[28] However, it remains to be seen whether the SEC's shortening of the period under Rule 144 will lead to a parallel relaxing of the requirements by the courts dealing with transactions not governed by the rule's safe harbor provisions.

Since Rule 144 applies differently to affiliates and non-affiliates, it is imperative to know who is an affiliate. Under the terms of the rule, affiliate status attaches to persons who directly or indirectly control, are similarly controlled by, or are under common control with the issuer.[31] Rule 405 defines "control" as the ability to influence, directly or indirectly, management decisions.[32] It follows that affiliate status is not limited to those who own stock but would certainly seem to apply to high level executives who are making decisions on behalf of management.[33] Questions relating to Rule 144 can be highly factual depending on the facts of each transaction. Although the SEC has continued to issue no action letters on general interpretations of Rule 144, it will not issue no-action letters with regard to particular transactions[34]

Compliance with Rule 144 requires dissemination of sufficient current public information concerning the issuer. There are only two ways to satisfy the rule's information requirements. A company that is subject to the reporting requirements of the 1934 Exchange Act satisfies the rule, provided, of course, that all reports are accurate and up to date.[35] For companies that are not subject to the 1934 Act, the issuers must make similar information publicly available in order to qualify for Rule 144—specifically, most of the information required by paragraph (a)(4) of SEC Rule 15c2–11 relating to the publication of quotations by broker-dealers must be disclosed.[36] It is to be

---

26. Notice of Adoption of Rule 144 Relating to the Definition of the Terms 'Underwriter' in Sections 4(1) and 2(11) and § Brokers' Transactions' in Section 4(4) of the Securities Act of 1933, Sec. Act Rel. No. 33–5223, 1972 WL 18134 (Jan. 11, 1972).

27. Martin Lipton, James H. Fogelson & Wayne L. Warnken, Rule 144–A Summary Review After Two Years, 29 Bus.Law. 1183, 1197 (1974), citing Notice of Adoption of Rule 144 Relating to the Definition of the Terms 'Underwriter' in Sections 4(1) and 2(11) and § Brokers' Transactions' in Section 4(4) of the Securities Act of 1933, Sec. Act Rel. No. 33–5223, 1972 WL 18134 (Jan. 11, 1972). See § 4.27 supra.

28. See United States v. Sherwood, 175 F.Supp. 480, 483 (S.D.N.Y.1959) and the discussion in § 4.27 supra.

31. 17 C.F.R. § 230.144(a)(1).

32. 17 C.F.R. § 230.405(f). See generally A.A. Sommer, Jr., Who's "In Control"?—SEC, 21 Bus.Law. 559 (1966). See also, e.g., Campbell, "Defining Control in Secondary Distributions," 18 B.C. Ind. & Com. L. Rev. 37 (1977)

33. See, e.g., United States v. Sprecher, 783 F.Supp. 133, 159 (S.D.N.Y.1992).

34. See Notice of Adoption of Rule 144 Relating to the Definition of the Terms 'Underwriter' in Sections 4(1) and 2(11) and 'Brokers' Transactions' in Section 4(4) of the Securities Act of 1933, Sec. Act Rel. No. 33–5223, 1972 WL 121583 (Jan. 11, 1972).

35. 17 C.F.R. § 230.144(c)(1). The 1934 Act registration and periodic reporting requirements are discussed in §§ 9.2–9.3 infra.

36. 17 C.F.R. § 230.144(c)(2). See 17 C.F.R. § 240.15c2–11. Insurance companies that do not file periodic reports under the 1934 Act must make publicly available all of the information required by 15 U.S.C.A. § 78l(g)(2)(G)(i). 17 C.F.R. § 230.144(c)(2).

noted that unlike the Rule 506 safe harbor exemption for nonpublic offerings by an issuer,[37] Rule 144's information requirements concern information that is publicly available, and does not mandate that this (or any other) information be made specifically available to offerees and purchasers of the restricted securities.

In addition to Rule 144's public information requirement, the rule imposes a one-year holding period for resales of restricted securities. Rule 144 thus applies to both affiliates of the issuer as well as to nonaffiliates who have purchased restricted securities from the issuer (or other seller) and who elect to resell those securities without filing a registration statement.[38] The one-year holding period shortened the previous two-year holding period that had been borrowed from the rule of thumb established in the *Sherwood* case[39] and is designed to help determine whether the person purchasing the security from the issuer had an investment intent, as opposed to having purchased the securities with a view towards distribution. In determining the one-year holding period, any securities obtained by way of stock dividends, splits, recapitalization, or conversions are deemed to have been acquired when the original security was purchased from the issuer.[40] Similarly, securities which have been deposited with a pledgee in the course of a bona fide pledge are deemed to have been acquired by the pledgee on the date that they were originally acquired by the pledgor unless there is no recourse against the pledgor, in which case the pledgee's date of acquisition starts the two-year holding period running anew.[41] When the securities in question have been purchased with a promissory note or pursuant to an installment contract, the one-year holding period does not begin to run until full payment has been made.[42] The rule further provides that securities acquired by gift (from persons other than the issuer) are treated as having been acquired by the donee on the date that the donor acquired them.[44] Once the donor ceases to be an affiliate, however, so do the non-affiliate donees.[45] Additionally, securities acquired from the settlor of a trust or held by a deceased's estate are considered to have been acquired by the trust or estate on the date that they were first acquired by the settlor or the deceased.[46]

Even beyond the expiration of the one-year holding period for restricted securities, Rule 144 places restrictions on all sales of securities by affiliates relying on the rule. These restrictions thus apply to affiliates' sales of both restricted and unrestricted securities. Rule 144(e)(1) permits sales by affiliates provided that the aggregate amount sold, combined with all sales of other securities of the same class (whether restricted or not) sold by the affiliate

---

37. 17 C.F.R. § 230.506. *See* § 4.25 *supra.*

38. *See* 17 C.F.R. § 230.144(d)(1). Until February, 1997, the holding period was two years.

39. United States v. Sherwood, 175 F.Supp. 480 (S.D.N.Y.1959). *See* § 4.27 *supra.*

40. 17 C.F.R. § 230.144(d)(4)(A), (B).

41. 17 C.F.R. § 230.144(d)(4)(D). *Compare* SEC v. Guild Films Co., 279 F.2d 485 (2d Cir.1960), *cert. denied* 364 U.S. 819, 81 S.Ct. 52, 5 L.Ed.2d 49 (1960) which is discussed in § 4.27 *supra.*

42. 17 C.F.R. § 230.144(d)(2). *But cf.* Fountain Oil, Inc., 28 Sec. Reg. & L. Rep. (BNA) 514 (SEC No Action Letter available April 5, 1996).

44. 17 C.F.R. § 230.144(d)(4)(E).

45. *See* Resales of Restricted and Other Securities, Sec. Act Rel. No. 33–6099, 17 S.E.C. Docket 1422, 1979 WL 174360 (SEC Aug. 2, 1979).

46. 17 C.F.R. § 230.144(d)(4)(F), (G).

within the preceding three months, does not exceed the specified volume limit. The rule places a limit of (i) one percent of the shares of that class outstanding as shown by the most recent report of the issuer, or (ii) the average weekly reported volume of trading in such securities on national exchanges and/or reported through the consolidated transaction reporting system, or any automated quotation system of a registered securities association such as NASDAQ.[55] As a result of this provision, a substantial amount of secondary sales may take place following ninety days after an initial public offering.[56] As is discussed more fully in the preceding section of this treatise,[57] the likelihood of a large amount of such secondary sales can lead to disclosure issues in connection with the registered offering and conceivably even an integration problem, unless there are contractual restrictions against such secondary sales.[58]

These "dribble out" provisions also apply to nonaffiliates' sales of restricted securities after the initial one-year holding period has expired. Once the one-year holding period for restricted securities has expired, the dribble-out provisions apply to nonaffiliates' sales of restricted securities for an additional year. Rule 144(k) thus eliminates these resale restrictions when the securities have been beneficially owned by the nonaffiliate for at least two years prior to their sale.[59] Furthermore, under subsection (f),[60] all transactions by either affiliates or nonaffiliates made in reliance upon the rule must be made in "brokers' transactions" as defined in section 4(4) of the Act,[61] or in transactions directly with a "market maker."[62] The person selling the security under Rule 144 may not solicit or arrange for solicitations of offers to buy securities in anticipation of the transaction, nor may he or she make any payment in connection with the offer or sale to any person other than the broker executing the transaction.[63]

Rule 144(g)[64] further defines the scope of section 4(4)'s brokers' transaction exemption for the purposes of the rule. The broker's activity must be limited to the execution of the order or orders to sell as agent for the person selling. In order for Rule 144 to apply, the broker may receive no more than the usual and customary broker's commission, and may neither solicit nor arrange for customers' orders to buy the securities that would be sold in a transaction.[65] There are three exceptions to Rule 144(g)'s ban on solicitation:

55. 17 C.F.R. § 230.144(e)(1). NASDAQ (the National Association of Securities Dealers' Automated Quotation system) is discussed in 14.3 *infra.*

56. Once it has completed a registered public offering, the issuer becomes subject to the 1934 Act periodic reporting requirements. Section 15(d) of the 1934 Act, 15 U.S.C.A. § 78o(d). *See* § 9.3 *infra.*

57. *See* § 4.28 *supra.*

58. If there is a substantial volume of these unregistered secondary sales, they might be integrated into the initial offering even though they fall within Rule 144(e)'s volume limitations. The integration doctrine is discussed in § 4.36 *infra.*

59. 17 C.F.R. § 230.144(k).

60. 17 C.F.R. § 230.144(f).

61. 15 U.S.C.A. § 77d(4). *See* § 4.26 *supra.*

62. Market makers are dealers who qualify to maintain a trading market for over-the-counter securities. They will frequently be placing orders for their own account. *See* § 14.10 *infra.* The term is defined in section 3(a)(38) of the 1934 Exchange Act, 15 U.S.C.A. § 78c(a)(38).

63. 17 C.F.R. § 230.144(f).

64. 17 C.F.R. § 230.144(g).

65. *Id.*

(1) the broker may contact other dealers who have indicated interest in the securities within the past sixty days, (2) he or she may make inquiries to other customers who have shown an "unsolicited bona fide interest" in the securities within the past ten business days, and (3) the broker may publish bid and asked quotations in an inter-dealer quotation system "provided that such quotations are incident to the maintenance of a bona fide inter-dealer market for the security for the broker's own account. * * *"[66] The final prerequisite under subsection (g) is that the broker must make a reasonable inquiry as to whether the person for whose account the securities are being sold is an underwriter or whether the transaction is part of a distribution. Although subsection (g) was adopted solely pursuant to Rule 144, its terms are certainly helpful by way of analogy to anyone planning a transaction in reliance upon a section 4(4) exemption.[68]

In addition to compliance with all of the foregoing requirements of the rule, subsection (h)[69] requires filing of notice of most Rule 144 sales. Form 144 must be completed whenever the amount of securities sold in reliance on the rule within any three-month period is more than five hundred shares, or the aggregate sales price is more than ten thousand dollars.

It is, of course, possible for an issuer to restrict resales beyond the time periods set out in Rule 144. The enforceability of such a provision, like any other contractual limitations, will be determined by the applicable state law of contracts and stock transfers.[71] It can be actionable to sell restricted securities without adequately informing the purchaser of the restrictions on resale.[72]

As discussed more fully in the next section, in 1990, the SEC adopted an exemption for downstream sales to qualified institutional investors. As is the case with Rule 144, Rule 144A[73] classifies certain offers and sales as not involving a distribution, so that persons participating in such offers and sales are not considered "underwriters."

§ 4.30 The Section "4(1½)" Exemption for Downstream Sales; Rule 144A

As discussed in previous sections of this treatise,[1] section 4(1)'s exemption for transactions not involving an issuer, underwriter, or a dealer,[2] and section 4(4)'s exemption for unsolicited brokers' transactions[3] both provide avenues to exempt transactions made by persons other than an issuer. In contrast, section 4(2)'s nonpublic offering exemption[4] is limited by its terms to "trans-

---

66. 17 C.F.R. § 230.144(g).

68. 15 U.S.C.A. § 77d(4). The section 4(4) exemption is discussed in § 4.26 *supra*.

69. 17 C.F.R. § 230.144(h).

71. *See* Catherines v. Copytele, Inc. 602 F.Supp. 1019 (E.D.N.Y.1985).

72. *See, e.g.,* Sliter v. Cruttenden Roth, Inc., 2000 WL 1745184 (N.D.Ill.2000) (failure to disclose Rule 144 resale restrictions could be material).

73. 17 C.F.R. § 230.144A. *See, e.g.,* Jeffrey B. Tevis, Asset-Backed Securities: Secondary Market Implications of SEC Rule 144A and Regulation S, 23 Pac.L.J. 135 (1991).

§ 4.30

1. *See* §§ 4.26–4.29 *supra*.

2. 15 U.S.C.A. § 77d(1).

3. 15 U.S.C.A. § 77d(4).

4. 15 U.S.C.A. § 77d(2). *See* § 4.24 *supra*.

actions by an issuer"[5] and thus is not available for downstream sales. The rationale underlying the section 4(2) exemption seems to support a comparable exemption for downstream sales by nonissuers.

As explained previously, two primary elements of the section 4(2) exemption are: (1) the purchaser's access to current information about the issuer and (2) the purchaser's ability to evaluate that information.[7] In addition, in order to qualify for the section 4(2) exemption, the issuer is not permitted to engage in a general solicitation, but rather must target the offers to a discrete group of offerees.[8]

§ 4.30[1]   Basis for the Section 4(1½) Exemption

The rationale underlying the nonpublic offering exemption for issues would appear to apply equally to secondary transactions. Conceptually, a sale by a person other than the issuer that meets the informational, purchaser qualification and other requirements of section 4(2) should similarly be exempt.

Consider, for example, a private placement by Issuer Co. where S and B both would qualify as purchasers for a section 4(2)[10] offering. Assume further that at the time of the offering S had adequate funds but B did not, and S purchased stock pursuant to the section 4(2) exemption. Two months later, S decides to sell her stock and learns that B now has sufficient cash on hand. Since the presumptive one-year holding period has not yet passed, S cannot take advantage of section 4(1)'s safe harbor Rule 144.[11] Similarly, she cannot be certain that she has satisfied the requirements of the section 4(1) exemption. Assuming that the issuer is willing to make current information available to B, there would seem no reason to require registration of S's sale to B as the only alternative to waiting until Rule 144's one-year holding period has elapsed.[12]

Since, in the foregoing example, the issuer could validly issue shares directly to B as a qualified private placement purchaser, why should S not be able to take advantage of a similar exemption? The answer to this question is that, as discussed above, the statutory language of section 4(2) is limited to transactions by an issuer. It can be argued, however, that section 4(1) would support such an exemption. In the above example, S clearly is not an issuer or a dealer, so in order to qualify for the exemption, she must be able to

---

5. 15 U.S.C.A. § 77d(2). *See also* section 4(6) (15 U.S.C.A. § 77d(6)) which exempts issuer transactions not exceeding $5,000,000, provided that the offering is made only to accredited investors. *See* 4.23 *supra*.

7. *See, e.g.,* SEC v. Ralston Purina Co., 346 U.S. 119, 73 S.Ct. 981, 97 L.Ed. 1494 (1953).

8. The *Ralston Purina* decision (SEC v. Ralston Purina Co., 346 U.S. 119, 73 S.Ct. 981, 97 L.Ed. 1494 (1953)) talks in terms of offeree access to information and offeree ability to evaluate the investment. *See* the authorities discussed in § 4.24 *supra. Cf.* SEC Rule 506's safe harbor which requires that there not have been a general solicitation of purchasers. 17 C.F.R. § 230.506. *See* 17 C.F.R. § 230.502(c) and the discussion in §§ 4.20, 4.25 *supra*.

10. *See, e.g.,* SEC v. Ralston Purina Co., 346 U.S. 119, 73 S.Ct. 981, 97 L.Ed. 1494 (1953) and the other authorities discussed in § 4.24 *supra*.

11. 17 C.F.R. § 230.144. *See* § 4.29 *supra*.

12. Even after the expiration of the one-year holding period, there may be volume limitations on S's resales. Thus, for example Rule 144(e) limits resales to a certain percentage of the outstanding shares or average trading volume. 17 C.F.R. § 230.144(e). *See* § 4.29 *supra*. These resale restrictions do not apply to nonaffiliates of the issuer who have held their shares for at least three years. 17 C.F.R. § 230.144(k). However, the volume limitations on resales remain applicable so long as the seller is an affiliate.

demonstrate that she is not an underwriter. As discussed in an earlier section, an underwriter is someone who assists an issuer during a distribution or someone who has purchased securities from an issuer with a view towards distribution. It would appear that a downstream sale which complies with the requirements of section 4(2) is not properly classified as a distribution and, as such, the seller is not properly qualified as an underwriter under section 2(a)(11)'s definition. Accordingly, the proper basis of any exemption for the downstream seller in the foregoing example is section 4(1); while the requirements that must be satisfied may be derived from the parameters of the section 4(2) exemption for issuers. Unfortunately, the SEC no action letters that have been cited as the basis for the section 4(1½) exemption do not provide a consistent statement of what is necessary to satisfy the exemption.[16]

In the situation presented by the example above, there is considerable support for what has become known as the section 4(1½) exemption. Although not expressly contained in the statute nor formally adopted by the Commission, support for the so-called section 4(1½) exemption can be found in SEC no action letters, SEC interpretative releases, the courts' decisions, and the commentators' writings.[21] The absence of a formal SEC rule or interpretative release explaining the exemption means that it is difficult to ascertain the precise scope of the exemption. To a large extent, the parameters of exemption have developed through no action letters and commentators' analysis.

The SEC has recognized that the section 4(1½) exemption is available to affiliates of the issuer[23] and should equally apply to nonaffiliates.[24] There are, of course, some limitations on the use of the exemption. Thus, for example, too many sales in reliance on the exemption within a short period of time might well result in the finding of a distribution.[25] Although the section 4(1½) exemption does not appear to be as restrictive as Rule 144's volume limitations on resales of restricted securities,[26] the magnitude of the transaction and the number of downstream purchasers are factors in considering the availability of the section 4(1½) exemption. A general solicitation of purchasers that is not permitted under section 4(2)[28] will render the section 4(1½) exemption unavailable. Similarly, the absence of qualified purchasers or available adequate current information about the issuer would preclude application of the exemption.[29]

---

16. ABA Committee on Federal Regulation of Securities, The Section "4(1½)" Phenomenon: Private Resales of Restricted Securities, 34 Bus.Law.1961 (1979).

21. *See* ABA Committee on Federal Regulation of Securities, The Section "4(1½)" Phenomenon: Private Resales of Restricted Securities, 34 Bus.Law.1961 (1979); Christopher D. Olander & Margaret S. Jacks, The Section 4(1½) Exemption—Reading Between the Lines of the Securities Act of 1933, 15 Sec.Reg.L.J. 339 (1988); Carl W. Schneider, Section 4(1½): Private Resales of Restricted or Control Securities, 49 Ohio St.L.J. 501 (1988); Robert B. Titus, Secondary Trading Stepchild of the Securities Laws, 20 Conn.L.Rev. 595 (1988); Comment, Reinterpreting the "Section 4(1½)" Exemption From Securities Registration: The Investor Protection Requirement, 6 U.S.F.L.Rev. 681 (1982).

23. Sec. Act Rel.No. 33–6188 n. 178, 1980 WL 29482, 1 Fed. Sec. L. Rep. (CCH) ¶ 1051 (SEC Feb. 1, 1980).

24. *See* Christopher D. Olander & Margaret S. Jacks, The Section 4(1½) Exemption—Reading Between the Lines of the Securities Act of 1933, 15 Sec.Reg.L.J. 339, 361–363 (1988).

25. *See* ABA Committee on Federal Regulation of Securities, The Section "4(1½)" Phenomenon: Private Resales of Restricted Securities, 34 Bus.Law.1961, 1972 (1979). *See also* § 4.23, *supra.*

26. 17 C.F.R. § 230.144(e); *see* § 4.29 *supra.*

28. *See* § 4.27 *supra.*

29. *See* § 4.27 *supra.*

The Eighth Circuit explained that the section 4(1½) exemption is merely an application of the section 4(1) exemption for transactions not involving an issuer, underwriter, or dealer.[30] The court explained that the section 4(1) exemption for private resales depends upon a finding that distribution has taken place and that the definition of distribution is coextensive with section 4(2)'s non-public offering exemption.[31]

§ 4.30[2] Elements of the Section 4(1½) Exemption

The section 4(1½) exemption is most useful for purchasers of securities sold in a private placement who cannot rely on section 4(1)[32] or SEC Rule 144.[33] There are a number of reasons that these exemptions may not be available. The most likely reason for not being able to rely on these exemptions is that the seller has not held the securities for a sufficiently long period so as to preclude a finding that he or she purchased the securities with a view towards distribution. Another possibility is that the seller is a control person who cannot meet Rule 144 volume limitations on resale.

What, then, are the elements of the section 4(1½) exemption? The elements of the section 4(1½) exemption are as follows. First, the purchaser must have access to the current information about the issuer similar to the types of information that would be made available through a registration statement.[34] This requirement emanates from section 4(2), and, in fact has been characterized as the most important of the section 4(2) requirements.[35] As discussed in an earlier section, while accredited investor status may eliminate the need for offeree and purchaser qualification, it does not eliminate the access to information requirement.[36] Thus, although the issuer is not involved in the transaction directly, the issuer's willingness to make current information available is of the utmost importance in a section 4(1½) transaction.

Second, in addition to the requirement that a purchaser have access to current information about the issuer, the purchaser must meet section 4(2) qualifications. Hence, the purchaser must be sufficiently sophisticated to qualify for the section 4(2) exemption. The applicable case law under section 4(2) has described the purchaser's qualifications in terms of sophistication, ability to understand the risks of the investment, and the suitability of the investment for that particular investor.[38] This definition would include institutional investors as well as experienced individuals.[39] Additionally, Regulation D provides that an unsophisticated investor can qualify as a section 4(2)

---

30. Ackerberg v. Johnson, 892 F.2d 1328 (8th Cir.1989).

31. 892 F.2d at 1335 n. 6.

32. 15 U.S.C.A. § 77d(1). *See* § 4.26 *supra.*

33. 17 C.F.R. § 230.144.

34. *See, e.g.,* SEC v. Ralston Purina Co., 346 U.S. 119, 73 S.Ct. 981, 97 L.Ed. 1494 (1953); Doran v. Petroleum Management Corp., 545 F.2d 893 (5th Cir.1977), *appeal after remand* 576 F.2d 91 (5th Cir.1978).

35. *See* Carl W. Schneider, Section 4(1½): Private Resales of Restricted or Control Securities, 49 Ohio St.L.J. 501, 506, 511 (1988).

36. *See* the discussion in § 4.25 *supra.*

38. *E.g.,* SEC v. Ralston Purina Co., 346 U.S. 119, 73 S.Ct. 981, 97 L.Ed. 1494 (1953).

39. Presumably, section 2(a)(15)'s concept of an accredited investor (15 U.S.C.A. § 77b(a)(15)) which is incorporated into Regulation D as well, would operate as an alternative basis for purchaser qualification for the section 4(1½) exemption.

purchaser through a purchaser representative having the requisite sophistication and expertise.[40] Rule 506 further provides that where the purchasers are accredited investors, the knowledge and sophistication requirements need not be satisfied.[41] It would appear that the same tests should carry over to the section 4(1½) exemption.[42]

Third, any general solicitation of purchasers will destroy the section 4(2) exemption[43] and thus would be equally fatal to the section 4(1½) exemption. Fourth, if too many section 4(1½) sales take place within a given time frame, there is the possibility that a distribution will be found to exist.[45] In such a case, the seller could be said to have been participating in a distribution, thus rendering the exemption unavailable.[46]

One other aspect of the section 4(1½) exemption deserves mention. While a transaction made in reliance on the section 4(1½) exemption must bear all the indicia of a section 4(2) offering by an issuer, a significant difference is the fact that the proceeds from a section 4(1½) transaction do not go to the issuer but rather to the selling shareholder(s). As discussed in an earlier section,[47] when engaging in registered secondary distributions, drafters of applicable disclosures must make it clear that the proceeds do not inure to the issuer's benefit. Accordingly, it follows that in any transaction based upon the section 4(1½) exemption, it should be clearly explained that the proceeds go to the selling shareholders. It has also been suggested that a selling shareholder who is an insider or control person may have certain additional disclosure obligations.[48]

There is a general consensus that the above-mentioned criteria are relevant in determining the availability of the section 4(1½) exemption. Since the exemption is not based on either a specific statutory provision or SEC rule, it does not provide the degree of certainty generally sought when planning an exempt transaction. However, in absence of authority denying the existence of the exemption, it seems safe to rely on its existence in light of the consensus among the commentators, practicing bar, and the Commission.

§ 4.30[4] The Safe Harbor for Certain Sales to Qualified Institutional Buyers—SEC Rule 144A

Rule 144A permits downstream resales of restricted securities to institutional investors.[50] Rule 144A, like Rule 144, classifies certain offers and sales as not involving a distribution, so that persons participating in such offers and sales are not considered "underwriters" under section 2(a)(11). Essentially,

---

40. Rule 506 recognizes that the sophistication requirement can be satisfied through a purchaser representative. 17 C.F.R. § 230.506(b)(ii). *See also* 17 C.F.R. § 230.501(h) (definition of purchaser representative).

41. 17 C.F.R. § 230.506(b)(2)(ii).

42. *See, e.g.,* SEC v. Cavanagh, 1 F.Supp.2d 337, 368 (S.D.N.Y.1998) (seller's failure to investigate the nature of his proposed purchasers, and failure to attempt to limit transferability precluded application of the section 4 (1½) exemption)

43. *See* the discussion in § 4.25 *supra.*

45. *See, e.g.,* In re Oklahoma–Texas Trust, 2 S.E.C. 764, 769 (1937), *affirmed* 100 F.2d 888 (10th Cir.1939).

46. *See* § 4.26 *supra.*

47. *See* § 3.9 *supra.*

48. The extent of the seller's disclosure obligations "should depend upon [his] status as an insider and also upon his access to information that is unavailable to the purchaser." Carl W. Schneider, Section 4(1½): Private Resales of Restricted or Control Securities, 49 Ohio St. L.J. 501, 507 (1988).

50. Sec. Act Rel.No. 33–6806, [1988–1989 Transfer Binder] Fed. Sec. L. Rep. (CCH) ¶ 84,335 (SEC Oct. 25, 1988).

the exemption covers any sale to a "qualified institutional buyer," which is defined as any institution (including insurance companies, investment companies, employee benefit plans, banks, and savings and loan associations) that owns more than $100 million worth of securities of unaffiliated issuers and, in the case of banks and savings and loans, has a net worth of at least $25 million.

In addition to direct transactions among these classes of institutions, the rule also permits securities dealers to participate in transactions, either as purchasers for their own account, provided they themselves own at least $10 million worth of securities of unaffiliated issuers, or as agents for qualified institutions. Indeed, the rule contemplates the formation of an active trading market in Rule 144A securities, in which qualified institutions and dealers can enter bids and offers.

Rule 144A only applies to sales of securities of a class that is *not* listed on a national securities exchange nor traded in the NASDAQ system. In order to avoid minimizing or diluting this requirement, the rule specifies that convertible securities do not constitute a separate class of securities unless they are issued with at least a ten percent conversion premium.[56]

With respect to securities issued by companies subject to the 1934 Act reporting requirements, or by foreign issuers, use of the rule is not conditioned on the availability of any additional information about the issuer. With respect to securities of other issuers, however, the rule is only available if the prospective purchaser has received from the issuer a brief statement of the nature of the issuer's business and certain specified financial statements.[57]

Simultaneously with the adoption of Rule 144A, the SEC approved the establishment by the National Association of Securities Dealers (NASD) of a screen-based computer and communication system called PORTAL (Private Offerings, Resales and Trading through Automated Linkages) to facilitate secondary trading of Rule 144A securities. The adoption of Rule 144A and the establishment of the PORTAL system create the potential for an active trading market in foreign securities and in unregistered debt and equity issues of domestic issuers, limited to a designated class of large institutions and dealers. Qualifying offerings of foreign securities to institutional investors may now take advantage of a conditional exemption from Regulation M (formerly Rules 10b–6, 10b–7, and 10b–8), which limits sales by participants during a distribution.[58]

§ 4.31 The Exemption for Certain Dealers' Transactions— Section 4(3)

Although dealers' transactions are not exempt from registration by virtue of section 4(1),[2] many will be exempt as unsolicited brokers' transactions

---

56. 17 C.F.R. § 230.144A(d)(3)(i).

57. 17 C.F.R. § 230.144A(d)(4)(i). The rule further provides that the requirement of reasonably current information will be presumed to be satisfied if there is a balance sheet as of no more than 16 months prior to the date of resale and the balance sheet depicts profit, loss, and retained earnings for the twelve months preceding the date of the balance sheet. To qualify for the presumption, the balance sheet must either be of a date not more than six months prior to the date of resale or, alternatively, be accompanied by a statement of profit, loss, and retained earnings for the period ending no more than six months prior to the resale date. 17 C.F.R. § 230.144A(d)(4)(ii)(A).

58. Securities Industry Association, [1990–1991 Transfer Binder] Fed. Sec. L. Rep. (CCH) ¶ 79,669 (SEC No Action Letter April 25, 1991).

§ 4.31

2. 15 U.S.C.A § 77d(1). Section 2(a)(12) defines "dealer" very broadly to cover anyone in the business of making securities transactions. 15 U.S.C.A. § 77b(a)(12).

within the meaning of section 4(4).[3] Section 4(3) of the Act[4] exempts additional dealer transactions from the Act's registration and prospectus delivery requirements. In terms of the number of transactions covered, section 4(3) is probably the most significant of the transaction exemptions. Section 4(3) dispenses with the registration and delivery requirements for all dealers' transactions taking place more than forty days, or in some cases ninety days, after the first date on which the security was offered to the public or after the effective date of the registration statement, whichever is later.[5] This forty-or ninety-day period is known as the "quiet period." Section 4(3)'s exemption applies both to dealers and to underwriters[6] who are no longer acting as underwriters.

The forty- (or ninety-) day time period during which a dealer's transactions are *not* exempt under section 4(3)(B) is tolled for any time during which a stop order pursuant to section 8 of the Act[7] is in effect with regard to the registration statement. The forty-day period does not apply to first-time issuers who have not previously sold securities pursuant to an effective registration statement; for them, the applicable period is ninety rather than forty days after the first sale or effective date of the registration statement. The section also provides that a shorter time period may be established by the Commission as it "may specify by rules and regulations or order."[8]

Since section 4(3)'s dealers' transaction exemption is limited to the prospectus delivery requirements and comes into existence only after the effective date (or bona fide offering date), it has no bearing on prefiling gun-jumping violations of section 5(c)[9] nor upon section 5(a)'s prohibitions against sales prior to the effective date.[10] Similarly, section 4(3) has no bearing upon section 5(b)(1)'s prospectus delivery requirements during the waiting period after filing of the registration statement but prior to the effective date.[11] Accordingly, the dealer's exemption operates only to excuse compliance with section 5(b)(1) and 5(b)(2)'s prospectus delivery requirements[12] during the post-effective period upon expiration of the forty- or ninety-day period. The vast majority of day-to-day transactions occur more than forty (or ninety) days after the securities were offered to the public. Hence, section 4(3) covers most transactions taking place in the U.S. securities markets.

Section 4(3)(C)[13] further provides that the exemption for dealer transactions does not apply to sales of securities that are either part or all of an

3. 15 U.S.C.A. § 77d(4). *See* § 4.26 *supra.*

4. 15 U.S.C.A. § 77d(3).

5. 15 U.S.C.A. § 77d(3)(A), (B).

6. The definition of underwriter is discussed in § 4.27 *supra. See* 15 U.S.C.A. § 77b(a)(11).

7. 15 U.S.C.A. § 77h. *See* §§ 2.5 *supra*, 7.1 *infra.*

8. 15 U.S.C.A. § 77d(3)(B). Rule 174 is such a rule. 17 C.F.R. § 230.174.

9. 15 U.S.C.A. § 77e(c). *See* § 2.3 *supra.*

10. 15 U.S.C.A. § 77e(a). *See* Rule 174, 17 C.F.R. § 230.174, which is discussed below.

11. 15 U.S.C.A. § 77b(i). *See* § 2.4 *supra.*

12. Section 5(b)(1) requires that any prospectus comply with section 10's statutory prospectus requirements while section 5(b)(2) requires delivery of a section 10(a) prospectus when the securities are delivered for sale. 15 U.S.C.A. § 77e(b)(1), (2), 77j. *See* §§ 2.5, 3.3 *supra.*

13. 15 U.S.C.A. § 77d(3)(C).

unsold allotment to that dealer. This means that regardless of the amount of time that has elapsed since the beginning of the offering, any underwriting activity by a dealer will implicate the prospectus delivery requirements. It is to be noted, however, that once the forty- or ninety-day period has expired, a dealer, including an underwriter no longer acting as such, can take advantage of the exemption even if another dealer has an unsold allotment.

SEC Rule 174[14] expands upon the exemption provided in section 4(3) and thereby provides an additional exemption from the prospectus delivery requirements for certain dealer transactions. The rule dispenses with the delivery requirements during the forty-day period following the effective date, and during the ninety-day period for first time issuers. Rule 174 applies to securities of issuers which prior to the offering are subject to the 1934 Act reporting requirements,[15] as well as to foreign issuers whose securities are traded using American Depositary Receipts that have been registered on Form F-6.[16] Additionally, under Rule 174 the prospectus requirements do not apply to dealers' transactions for all registered offerings that are to be made from "time to time."[17] A general matter for issuers that are subject to and current in their 1934 Act periodic reports[18] immediately prior to the public offering, there is no prospectus delivery requirement during the post effective period for non participating dealers (including participating dealers whose participation has been completed).[19] For first-time issuers (and other issuers who were not subject to and current in their 1934 Act reports immediately prior to the offering) whose securities are listed on a national exchange or NASDAQ, the ninety-day period that otherwise would apply for the prospectus delivery requirements for nonparticipating dealers under section 4(3) is shortened to twenty-five days.[20]

As summarized directly above, Rule 174's exemption for nonparticipating dealers from the post-effective prospectus delivery period is limited to securities of issuers which, immediately prior to the filing of the registration statement were subject to the 1934 Act's periodic reporting requirements.[21] Thus, the exemption does not apply to first-time issuers or issuers whose securities were not widely held prior to the filing of the registration statement.[22] In 1988, Rule 174 was amended to provide relief for many of these registrants who have not previously been subject to the 1934 Act's reporting requirements.[23] Under Rule 174(d), the prospectus delivery period for nonparticipating dealers is shortened to twenty-five days for dealers (including underwriters no longer acting as such) with regard to securities which, as of the offering date, are listed on a national securities exchange or authorized for inclusion in an automated quotation system sponsored by a registered securi-

---

14. 17 C.F.R. § 230.174.

15. The 1934 Act registration and reporting requirements are discussed in §§ 9.2, 9.3 *infra*.

16. Private foreign issuers are discussed in § 17.4 *infra*.

17. 17 C.F.R. § 230.174(c). *See* § 3.11 *supra* for a discussion of shelf registration.

18. 1934 Act §§ 13, 15(d), 15 U.S.C.A. §§ 78m, 78o. *See* chapter 9 *infra*.

19. Rule 174(b), 17 C.F.R. § 230.174(b).

20. 17 C.F.R. § 230.174(d).

21. 17 C.F.R. § 230.174(b).

22. The 1934 Act periodic reporting requirements are discussed in §§ 9.2, 9.3 *infra*.

23. *See* Sec. Act Rel.No. 33-6763, [1987–1988 Transfer Binder] Fed. Sec. L. Rep. (CCH) ¶ 84,226 (SEC April 4, 1986).

ties association (*i.e.,* NASDAQ).[24] As in the case for the statutory prospectus delivery period for registered offerings,[25] Rule 174's twenty-five day period begins to run from the later of (1) the registration statement's effective date or (2) the first date upon which the security was "bona fide offered to the public."[26] In light of Rule 174(d), the full statutory prospectus delivery period for nonparticipating dealers applies only to securities which are traded through listings in the pink sheets or the NASD electronic bulletin board.[27] It must be remembered, that, as is the case with the other exemptions provided by Rule 174, the shorter twenty-five day prospectus delivery period does not apply to a dealer who is acting as an underwriter.[28]

Rule 174(e) provides that none of its exemptions from the prospectus delivery requirements apply if the registration statement was subject to a section 8 stop order;[29] nor is an exemption available if so ordered by the SEC upon application or its own motion in a particular case.[30] The rule, as is the case with the section 4(3) exemption, explicitly does not affect the obligation of an underwriter to deliver the prospectus, although it applies to dealers who, though underwriters for the offering, have sold or otherwise disposed of their allotment and thus are no longer acting as underwriters.

Rule 174(g) imposes an additional requirement for penny stock offerings.[31] In the case of a blank check penny stock offering, the ninety-day period does not begin to run until the securities are released from escrow pursuant to Rule 419.[32]

§ 4.33 Exemption[1] for Certain Offshore Transactions in Securities of United States Issuers—Regulation S

With the growing globalization of the securities markets, there have been an increasing number of questions concerning the applicability of the United States securities laws to transactions taking place outside of the United States.[2] To the extent that a United States issuer offers securities exclusively to non United States citizens in offshore transactions, there is substantial question as to the propriety of requiring registration under the 1933 Act, even though there would be jurisdiction to do so.

---

24. 17 C.F.R. § 230.174(d). *See* §§ 14.3, 14.10 *infra* for a description of NASDAQ and the operation of the over-the-counter markets.

25. 15 U.S.C.A. § 77d(3)(B).

26. 17 C.F.R. § 230.174(d).

27. Quotations for securities not listed on a national exchange or traded through NASDAQ used to be available from pink sheets which are circulated by the market maker. The pink sheets have been replaced by the NASD's electronic bulletin board. *See* § 14.10 *infra.*

28. 17 C.F.R. § 230.174(f).

29. 15 U.S.C.A. § 77h. *See* § 7.1 *infra.*

30. 17 C.F.R. § 230.174(e).

31. The penny stock rules are discussed in § 14.19 *infra.*

32. 17 C.F.R. § 230.174(g). *See* 17 C.F.R. § 230.419.

§ 4.33

1. Strictly speaking, Regulation S (17 C.F.R. §§ 230.901 *et seq.*) is not an "exemption" from the 1933 Act's registration requirements but rather creates a safe harbor for offshore offerings respect to which the SEC will decline to exercise jurisdiction. Nevertheless, the impact of Regulation S is much the same as an exemption from registration.

2. *See* § 17.3 *infra* for discussion of the jurisdictional issues; including a discussion of the treatment of foreign securities traded in the United States.

Regulation S[9] sets forth two safe harbors:

One safe harbor applies to offers and sales by issuers, securities professionals involved in the distribution process pursuant to contract, their respective affiliates, and persons acting on behalf of any of the foregoing (the "issuer safe harbor"), and the other applies to resales by persons other than the issuer, securities professionals involved in the distribution process pursuant to contract, their respective affiliates (except certain officers and directors), and persons acting on behalf of any of the foregoing (the "resale safe harbor"). An offer, sale or resale of securities that satisfies all conditions of the applicable safe harbor is deemed to be outside the United States within the meaning of the General Statement and thus not subject to the registration requirements of Section 5.[10]

The safe harbors are premised on two general conditions:

First, any offer or sale of securities must be made in an "offshore transaction," which requires that no offers be made to persons in the United States and that either: (i) the buyer is (or the seller reasonably believes that the buyer is) offshore at the time of the origination of the buy order, or (ii) for purposes of the issuer safe harbor, the sale is made in, on or through a physical trading floor of an established foreign securities exchange, or (iii) for purposes of the resale safe harbor, the sale is made in, on or through the facilities of a designated offshore securities market, and the transaction is not pre-arranged with a buyer in the United States. Second, in no event could "directed selling efforts" be made in the United States in connection with an offer or sale of securities made under a safe harbor. "Directed selling efforts" are activities undertaken for the purpose of, or that could reasonably be expected to result in, conditioning of the market in the United States for the securities being offered.[11] Exceptions to the general conditions are made with respect to offers and sales to specified institutions not deemed U.S. persons, notwithstanding their presence in the United States.[12]

The safe harbor for issuers has three categories of securities offerings, which are based on various factors including the nationality and reporting status of the issuer and the degree of U.S. market interest in the issuer's securities.[13] The first category consists of securities of foreign issuers with no substantial United States market interest,[14] provided that the securities are offered and sold in offerings that are directed overseas,[15] as well as securities backed by the full faith and credit of a foreign government,[16] and securities issued pursuant to certain employee benefit plans. The second category includes securities of 1934 Act reporting issuers, non-reporting foreign is-

---

9. 17 C.F.R. § 240.901 *et seq*.

10. Sec. Act Rel. No. 33–6863, [1989–1990 Transfer Binder] Fed. Sec. L. Rep. 84,524 (SEC April 24, 1990).

11. *See, e.g.,* Skadden, Arps, Meagher & Flom, [1993 Transfer Binder] Fed. Sec. L. Rep. (CCH) ¶ 76,677 (SEC No Action Letter May 18, 1993) (foreign security's quotation on Stock Exchange Automated Quotations system ("SEAQ") was not a directed selling effort).

12. Sec. Act Rel. No. 33–6863, [1989–1990 Transfer Binder] Fed. Sec. L. Rep. (CCH) ¶ 84,524 (SEC April 24, 1990).

13. *Id.*

14. 17 C.F.R. § 240.902(n).

15. 17 C.F.R. § 240.902(j).

16. *See* 17 C.F.R. § 240.902(e).

suers' debt securities, non-reporting foreign issuers' non-participating preferred stock, and asset-backed securities. The third category consists of securities of non-reporting United States issuers and equity offerings by non-reporting foreign issuers with a substantial United States market interest.[18]

In order to qualify for Regulation S, the securities must be traded on a qualified foreign market.[19] In contrast, the current version of the rule lists qualifying foreign exchanges by name as well as listing the required characteristics of qualifying off-shore markets.[20] The SEC has been willing to waive the exchange requirement for securities traded on the European Association of Securities Dealers Automated Quotation System[21] as well as for other off-shore securities exchanges.[22] The SEC staff using a no action letter has listed the steps that must be taken in order for an off-shore market to qualify for the trading of Regulation S securities.[23]

§ 4.35   The SEC's General Exemptive Authority

Until 1996, all exempt securities and transactions had to fit within the guidelines established by section 3 and 4 of the 1933 Act.[1] However, that changed when Congress gave the SEC general exemptive authority. Added in 1966, Section 28 of the 1933 Act provides that the Commission may exempt transactions, securities, and persons if in the public interest and consistent with investor protection.[2] The SEC now has a choice of working within the statutory limitations of the exemptions set forth in sections 3 and 4 of the 1933 Act or in expanding those parameters through rulemaking deemed to be in the public interest.

Unlike the exemptions set forth in sections 3 and 4 of the Act, the exemptive authority established by section 28 is not constrained by the terms of the securities being offered, the amount of the offering, or the nature of the offering. The only meaningful limitation of the SEC's exemptive authority is that it be consistent with investor protection and in furtherance of the public interest.

This broad exemptive power permits the SEC to adopt exemptive rules and regulations and thereby frees the Commission from the more rigid parameters of the specific exemptions set forth in sections 3 and 4 of the 1933 Act. While this greater flexibility is desirable, it is to be hoped that the Commission will not exercise this power to gut many of the valuable investor protection requirements of the securities laws. To date, the Commission has used the general exemptive power sparingly. In 1999, the Commission utilized this authority to eliminate the five million dollar limit that formerly applied

---

18.   The third, is the residual category which was adopted substantially as reproposed.

19.   17 C.F.R. § 230.902(a).

20.   17 C.F.R. § 230.902(a).

21.   Regulation S: Initial Public Offerings of Domestic Companies on European Association of Securities Dealers Automated Quotation, 31 Sec. Reg. & L. Rep. (BNA) 1059 (SEC No Action Letter July 27, 1999).

22.   *E.g.,* OM Stockholm Exchange, [2000–2001 Transfer Binder] Fed. Sec. L. Rep. (CCH) ¶ 78,010, 2000 WL 1526340 (SEC No Action Letter Sept. 27, 2000).

23.   OM Stockholm Exchange, [2000–2001 Transfer Binder] Fed. Sec. L. Rep. (CCH) ¶ 78,010, 2000 WL 1526340 (SEC No Action Letter Sept. 27, 2000).

§ 4.35

1.   15 U.S.C.A. §§ 77c, 77d. *See* §§ 4.1–4.34 *supra.*

2.   15 U.S.C.A. § 77z–3.

to certain offerings made pursuant to a compensatory benefit plan for employees and others.[4] At the time of this writing, the SEC has not, however, used this authority to lift other dollar ceilings such as the one found in Regulation A.[5]

The SEC's exemptive power under Section 28 of the 1933 Act is limited to rules and regulations. There is a parallel exemptive authority in section 36 of the Securities Exchange Act of 1934.[6] In contrast to the 1933 Act formulation for the Commission's general exemptive authority, the parallel exemptive power under the Securities Exchange of 1934 is broader in that it permits an exemption by order in addition to one granted by a rule or regulation.[7]

§ 4.36 Integration of Transactions

§ 4.36[1] Overview of the Integration Doctrine

As discussed throughout this chapter, it is necessary to structure transactions carefully in order to assure that they qualify for exemption from the 1933 Act's registration requirements. It is imperative to consider not only each step in a particular offering, but also to be mindful of past and possible future transactions. Whenever there is a series of securities transactions, it may not be sufficient to ensure the exemption that each transaction can stand on its own. In addition to each transaction being able to qualify for an exemption, it must also be clear that when viewed as a whole, the series of transactions does not run afoul of the Act's registration provisions and prospectus requirements.

Under the "integration" doctrine, the SEC will examine multiple offerings to determine whether they should be treated as a single, unitary transaction. Frequently, an issuer will embark on two (or more) separate exempt transactions within a relatively short period. In such a case the Commission may give close scrutiny in order to determine whether all offers and sales from the two (or more) securities offerings should be telescoped and integrated into one transaction. When the integration doctrine is employed it is possible that the two (or more) offerings combined will lose the attributes that entitled them to protection. The integration doctrine is not limited to multiple exempt transactions; it can also be used to integrate a would-be exempt offering with a registered offering where some of the offers or sales in the registered offering would destroy the availability of the exemption.

The integration doctrine is based on highly factual components and, as such does not provide much bright-line guidance outside of the few safe harbor rules that exist.[4] This section will discuss the various applications of the integration doctrine.

---

4. Rule 701(d)(2); 17 C.F.R. § 230.701(d)(2). *See* § 4.18 *supra*.

5. Regulation A is discussed in § 4.17 *supra*.

6. 15 U.S.C.A. § 78mm.

7. 1934 Act § 36, 15 U.S.C.A. § 78mm. There thus is no grant of power to individualize exemptions on an ad hoc basis under the 1933 Act. *Compare* SEC Rule 0–12, 17 C.F.R. § 240.0–12, setting forth the procedures to apply for an exemptive order under the 1934 Act.

§ 4.36

4. *See, e.g.,* Rule 502(a) which provides a safe harbor from integration in connection with Regulation D offerings. 17 C.F.R. § 230.502(a).

Illustrative Examples

A few examples will help illustrate the ways in which the integration doctrine can operate. Consider an intrastate offering made by a local issuer offered only to residents of the state of incorporation and principal place of business. Assume further that some of the purchasers in the intrastate offering are relatively unsophisticated; the offering would nevertheless qualify for the intrastate exemption.[5] Two weeks later, the issuer offers the same class of stock to several wealthy and sophisticated out-of-state investors in a manner that would satisfy section 4(2)'s nonpublic offering exemption.[6] If the integration doctrine were applied to these transactions, no exemption would be available because the sophisticated out-of-state purchasers would destroy the intrastate exemption while the unsophisticated in-state purchasers would render the non-public offering exemption unavailable.

Similarly, assume that a private placement is followed within two weeks by a registered public offering. If the two transactions are integrated, the private placement sales would be considered part of the registered offering and in violation of section 5.[7] Although the integration doctrine will not be applied every time two offerings take place within close proximity, the possibility must be taken into account. By taking the possibility of integration into account, the transactions can be structured in such a way to minimize or even eliminate the possibility of the doctrine being applied.

Outside the context of the safe harbor rules, the integration doctrine is based on a multifaceted subjective test and depends on the facts of the particular transactions in question. Accordingly, the precise parameters of the integration doctrine are uncertain. This lack of certainty is problematic for the planner of exempt transactions who must plan cautiously in order to guard against the risk of integration. This lack of certainty is still one more reason to try to stay within the confines of the SEC's safe harbor rules.[9]

§ 4.36[2] The Integration Doctrine Explained and Defined

§ 4.36[2][A] Explanation of the Integration Doctrine

The integration doctrine first emerged with regard to the intrastate offering exemption[10] in the context of determining which transactions constitute "part of an *issue*" which is offered in accordance with the intrastate limitations.[11] The "part of an issue" concept (and hence integration) applies to section 3(b) exemptions such as Regulation A.[12] Similarly, the issue concept has been carried over to section 3(a)(9)'s exemption[13] for exchanges of securi-

---

5. 15 U.S.C.A. § 77c(a)(11). *See* § 4.12 *supra.*

6. 15 U.S.C.A. § 77d(2). *See* §§ 4.24–4.25 *supra.*

7. This assumes that the would-be private placement sales took place prior to the registered offering's effective date or that there was noncompliance with the prospectus delivery requirements. *See* §§ 2.4, 2.5 *supra.*

9. *E.g.,* 17 C.F.R. § 230.506 (nonpublic offerings by issuers); 17 C.F.R. § 230.147 (intrastate exemption). *See also* 17 C.F.R. §§ 230.504, 230.505, 230.701.

10. 15 U.S.C.A. § 77c(a)(11). *See* § 4.12 *infra.*

11. *See* Non–Public Offering Exemption, Sec. Act Rel. No. 33–4552, 1962 WL 69540, 1 Fed.Sec.L. Rep. (CCH) ¶ 2781 (Nov. 6, 1962); Sec. Act Rel. No. 33–97, 11 Fed.Reg. 10,949 (Dec. 28, 1933).

12. 15 U.S.C.A. § 77c(b); 17 C.F.R. §§ 230.251 *et seq. See* §§ 4.16, 4.17 *supra.*

13. 15 U.S.C.A. § 77c(a)(9). *See* § 4.10 *supra.*

ties exclusively with existing securities holders.[14] The integration doctrine has also been applied to section 3(a)(10)'s exemption for administratively approved reorganizations.[15] The SEC has made it clear that integration applies equally to the transaction exemptions under section 4 and, in particular, section 4(2)'s exemption for transactions not involving a public offering.[16] Unless specifically excluded by the exemption,[17] integration could potentially be applied to several other exemptions.

The SEC has developed a five-factor test to determine whether the integration doctrine should be applied to two or more transactions:

1. whether the sales are part of a single plan of financing;

2. whether the sales involve issuance of the same class of securities;

3. whether the sales have been made at or about the same time;

4. whether the same type of consideration is received; and

5. whether the sales are made for the same general purpose.[20]

The Commission has not given any guidance on how these factors should be weighted. Accordingly, it would appear that in a particular case any one or more of the five factors could be determinative. For example, the absence of a prearranged single plan of financing has been held to preclude integration.[22]

§ 4.36[2][B] The Highly Factual Nature of Integration Questions

The foregoing guidelines with respect to the integration doctrine do not provide much certainty in planning transactions. Furthermore, because the integration doctrine's availability is essentially dependent upon questions of fact[24] varying with the nuances of each situation, it is often difficult to glean any learning from the relatively sparse precedent that exists. Much of the relevant precedent is based on no action letters, which by their nature are of limited precedential value.[26]

Although the integration doctrine is subjective and, as discussed above, the precedent is not very helpful, a few generalizations can be made. It would seem unlikely that a bona fide employee compensation plan would be integrated with a capital-raising offering.[29] Similarly, there would ordinarily not be

14. *See* Richard W. Jennings & Harold Marsh, Jr., Securities Regulation: Case and Materials 442 (6th ed. 1987) ("This is accomplished by reading the word 'exclusively' as modifying both 'exchanged' and 'security holders.' ").

15. *See* ABA Committee on Federal Regulation of Securities, Integration of Offerings: Report of Task Force on Integration of Securities Offerings, 41 Bus.Law. 595, 600–02 (1986).

16. *See* Sec. Act Rel. No. 33–4552, 1 Fed. Sec. L. Rep. (CCH) ¶¶ 2770–2783 (Nov. 6, 1962).

17. *See, e.g.,* 17 C.F.R. § 230.701(b)(6).

20. *See* Sec. Act Rel. No. 33–4552, 1 Fed.Sec.L. Rep. (CCH) ¶¶ 2770–2783 (Nov. 6, 1962); Section 3(a)(11).

22. *E.g.,* Barrett v. Triangle Mining Corp., 1976 WL 760, [1975–1976 Transfer Binder] Fed.Sec.L. Rep. (CCH) ¶ 95,438 (S.D.N.Y.1976); Livens v. William D. Witter, Inc., 374 F.Supp. 1104 (D.Mass.1974).

24. *See, e.g.,* Non–Public Offering Exemption, Sec. Act Rel. No. 33–4552, 1962 WL 69540, 1 Fed.Sec.L. Rep. (CCH) ¶ 2781 (Nov. 6, 1962) (the integration doctrine "depends on the particular facts or circumstances").

26. The questionable reliability of no action letters' precedential value is discussed in § 1.4[4] *supra.*

29. *E.g.* Pacific Physician Services, Inc. (SEC No Action Letter available August 20, 1985) ("the primary purpose of the offering to key employees [is] to provide such persons with an

any reason to integrate stock issued in connection with a merger or other share exchange and stock issued for cash.

§ 4.36[2][C] Issuer Integration

The integration doctrine is not limited to successive offerings by the same issuer—sometimes referred to as "offering integration."[30] Successive offerings by issuers having separate forms but economic interdependence may also be integrated;[31] this has been referred to as "issuer integration."[32] Additionally, offerings of different issuers are integrated because they are part of a single enterprise—this has been dubbed "venture integration."[33]

§ 4.36[3] Safe Harbors for Avoiding Integration

As noted earlier in this section, the Commission has provided safe harbors for avoiding integration. Thus, for example, Rule 502(a)[34] of Regulation D provides that offers and sales made more than six months before the start or six months after the completion of the Regulation D offering will not be integrated.[35] The six-month safe harbor is dependent upon there not being any non Regulation D offers or sales of the same class of securities within both six-month periods, except that sales pursuant to an employee benefit plan are permitted.[36] In some Regulation D offerings, the issuer may not be able to rely on the safe harbor from integration because of other offers or sales within either of the six-month periods. In such situations, the Commission's normal integration rules, including the five-factor integration test, are applicable for determining whether the Regulation D exemption is available.[40] Thus, for example, where following a private placement complying with Regulation D, the issuer decides to embark on a public offering, the issuer may still rely on Rule 152[41] to avoid integration.[42]

As is the case with Regulation D, Rule 147's safe harbor for intrastate offerings establishes a safe harbor from integration, provided there are no non-Rule 147 offers or sales within six months before the beginning of the offering or six-months after its completion.[43] However, the Rule 147 safe

---

opportunity to acquire proprietary interests in the Company and to encourage them to remain in its service while the primary purpose of the public offering [is] to raise capital for the Company's business operations, this Division is of the view that the offerings would not be integrated since they are not intended for the same purpose and are not part of a single plan of financing").

30. *See* ABA Committee on Federal Regulation of Securities, Integration of Offerings: Report of Task Force on Integration of Securities Offerings, 41 Bus.Law. 595, 617–20 (1986).

31. *See, e.g.,* SEC v. Holschuh, 694 F.2d 130 (7th Cir.1982) (integrating offerings by separate coal exploration limited partnerships which acquired their leasehold rights from the same company); SEC v. Murphy, 626 F.2d 633 (9th Cir.1980). *See also, e.g.,* Botto & Associates, 1989 WL 245530 (SEC No Action Letter Jan. 25, 1989) (refusing to concur that company was a separate issuer for integration purposes with regard to intrastate exemption).

32. *See* ABA Committee on Federal Regulation of Securities, Integration of Offerings: Report of Task Force on Integration of Securities Offerings, 41 Bus.Law. 595, 621–23 (1986).

33. *Id.* at 620–21.

34. 17 C.F.R. § 230.502(a).

35. *Id.*

36. *Id.*

40. 17 C.F.R. § 230.502(a) NOTE.

41. 17 C.F.R. § 230.152 which is discussed *infra.*

42. Vintage Group, Incorporated (SEC No Action Letter April 11, 1988).

43. 17 C.F.R. § 230.147(b)(2).

harbor does not exclude from the integration doctrine sales within those six-month periods made in connection with employee benefit plans, unless those plans are exempt under section 3 or 4 of the Act.[44] Following the same pattern as Regulation D, where a transaction fails to meet the safe harbor requirements, the Commission's subjective five-factor test will apply.[45] In contrast to the safe harbors described above, Rule 701, which provides an exemption for certain employee compensation plans,[46] states that the integration doctrine does not apply to transactions covered by the Rule 701 exemption for certain offerings to employees and consultants of nonpublic companies.[47]

§ 4.36[4] Integrating Nonpublic and Public Offerings

§ 4.36[4][A] Successive Offerings

As pointed out at the outset of this section, integration is not limited to multiple exemptions, but can also be applied to integrate a transaction made in reliance on an exemption together with a registered offering. Thus, for example, an issuer planning a public offering, under many circumstances, may not be able to engage in an offering of the same class of stock in reliance on the section 4(2) nonpublic offering exemption.[54] This is especially true when the proceeds from the private placement offering are to be used as seed money for an upcoming public offering.[55]

However, Rule 152 makes it clear that a decision to have a public offering made *after* the nonpublic offering will not destroy the exemption.[57] The protection provided by Rule 152 is quite narrow. The rule does not provide any protection to an issuer that first has planned a public offering and also embarks on a private one. Furthermore, the burden of proving an exemption rests with the person claiming the exemption. Accordingly, the person following a nonpublic offering with a public one must carry the difficult burden of proving a negative—i.e., the lack of a prior intent to go public. Thus, when a public offering follows a private one, it is wise to limit integration problems by, *inter alia,* issuing a different class of securities, being able to identify distinct purposes for the two offerings, or using a different type of consideration. However, if the separate class of securities are convertible into the securities to be publicly offered, integration is still possible.[62] However, the fact that there are conversion rights will not preclude the avoidance of integration.[63]

---

44. *Id.* Compare 17 C.F.R. § 230.502(a).

45. 17 C.F.R. § 230.147(b)(2) NOTE.

46. 17 C.F.R. § 230.701. *See* § 4.18 *supra.*

47. 17 C.F.R. § 230.701(b)(6).

54. *See, e.g.,* LaserFax, Inc., [1985–1986 Transfer Binder] Fed. Sec. L. Rep. (CCH) ¶ 78,136 (SEC No Action Letter Aug. 15, 1985).

55. *Id.*

57. 17 C.F.R. § 230.152.

62. LaserFax, Inc., [1985–1986 Transfer Binder] Fed. Sec. L. Rep. (CCH) ¶ 78,136 (SEC No Action Letter Aug. 15, 1985) (indicating a good case for integration existed; Regulation D offering was to be used as seed money for upcoming public offering).

63. Barry's Jewelers, Inc., 1998 WL 425887 (SEC No Action Letter July 20, 1998) (initial public offering following bankruptcy reorganization); Black Box, Inc., 1990 WL 286633 (SEC No Action Letter June 26, 1990) (securities issued pursuant to a reorganization followed by an initial public offering of the new company).

§ 4.36[4][B] Discontinued Offerings

Under Regulation D, six months after the withdrawal of a registration statement, the issuer could commence a private offering without worrying about the integration doctrine.[81] Similarly, six months after the termination of a private offering under Regulation D, a company can file a registration statement without invoking the integration doctrine.[82] It has been longstanding SEC policy that if an issuer waits less than six months following withdrawal of a registration statement before starting a private offering (or less than six months after the termination of a private offering before filing a registration statement), the traditional five-factor test applies to the question of whether the registered and private offerings should be integrated.[83]

In 2001, the SEC adopted Rule 155[84] to provide a safe harbor from integration for a discontinued or abandoned private offering followed by a registered public offering, and also for an abandoned public offering followed by a private offering. The integration safe harbors contained in Rule 155 were designed to provide clarity and certainty regarding two common situations involving abandoned offering. The SEC made it clear that the safe harbors of Rule 155 do not otherwise affect traditional integration analyses.[85] Rule 155 sets forth conditions under which an issuer that begins a private offering but sells no securities is able to abandon the private offering and begin a registered offering without having the abandoned private offering and subsequent public offering subjected to the integration doctrine. The SEC cautions that any private offering relying on safe harbor from integration must satisfy the conditions of a private offering exemption,[86] so that the private offering is in fact bona fide.[87] In order to effectively terminate the abandoned private offering, the issuer and all persons acting on the issuer's behalf must terminate all offering activity with respect to the private offering. Any prospectus filed as part of the subsequent registration statement must include disclosures regarding abandonment of the private offering. The issuer further is required to wait thirty days after abandoning the private offering before filing the registration statement, unless the securities were offered in the private offering only to persons who were (or who the issuer reasonably believed to be) accredited investors[88] or sophisticated.[89]

81. Rule 502(d), 17 C.F.R. § 230.502(d) which is discussed in § 4.20[3][A] *supra.*

82. *Id.*

83. *See* Integration of Abandoned Offerings, Sec. Act Rel. No. 33–7943, 2001 WL 68771 (SEC Jan. 26, 2001).

84. 17 C.F.R. § 230.155, Integration of Abandoned Offerings, Sec. Act Rel. No. 33–7943, 2001 WL 68771 (SEC Jan. 26, 2001). The amendments were originally proposed as amendments to Rule 152. *See* Sec. Act Rel. No. 33–7606A, 63 Fed. Reg. 67174 (SEC Nov. 13, 1998). Rule 152 is discussed in § 4.36[4][A] *supra.*

85. Integration of Abandoned Offerings, Sec. Act Rel. No. 33–7943, 2001 WL 68771 (SEC Jan. 26, 2001).

86. For purposes of the Rule 155, a "private offering" is defined as an unregistered offering of securities that is exempt from registration under Section 4(2) or 4(6) of the Securities Act or Rule 506 of Regulation D which provides a safe harbor for qualifying for the purposes of Section 4(2) non public offering exemption. The section 4(2) non public offering exemption is discussed in § 4.24 *supra.* The section 4(6) exemption for offerings not in excess of five million dollars made solely to accredited investors is discussed in § 4.23 *supra.* Rule 506 is discussed in § 4.25 *supra.*

87. Integration of Abandoned Offerings, Sec. Act Rel. No. 33–7943, 2001 WL 68771 (SEC Jan. 26, 2001).

88. Accredited investor is defined in section 2(a)(15) of the Act and Rules 215 and 501(a). 15 U.S.C.A. § 77b(a)(15); 17 C.F.R. §§ 230.215, 230.501(a).

89. Under Rule 155 an investor is sophisticated if the investor, either alone or with his or her representative, has such knowledge and experience in financial and business matters to be

In addition, Rule 155 provides safe harbor from integration that permits an issuer that started a registered offering to withdraw the registration statement before any securities are sold,[91] and then begin a private offering. In order to rely on Rule 155's safe harbor from integration, the issuer and any person acting on its behalf is required to wait thirty days after the effective date of withdrawal of the registration statement before the issuer can begin the private offering. Rule 155's safe harbor further requires the issuer to provide each offeree in the private offering with information concerning withdrawal of the registration statement, the fact that the private offering is unregistered, and the legal implications of the private offering's unregistered status. Additionally, any disclosure document that is used in the private offering must disclose any changes in the issuer's business or financial condition that occurred after the issuer filed the registration statement that are material to the investment decision in the private offering.[92]

---

capable of evaluating the merits and risks of the prospective investment. 17 C.F.R. § 230.155. *See* Rule 506(b)(2)(ii) of Regulation D; 17 C.F.R. § 230. 506(b)(2)(ii).

91. *See* Rule 477, 17 C.F.R. § 230.477.

92. 17 C.F.R. § 230.155.

Chapter 5

THE THEORY OF SALE: CORPORATE RECAPITALIZATIONS, REORGANIZATIONS AND MERGERS UNDER THE 1933 ACT

Table of Sections

---

§ 5.0   Overview of Chapter—Definition of Sale in Context

As discussed in previous sections of this treatise, the registration requirements are triggered by offers to sell and sales of securities.[1] The concept of offer to sell is not as simple as it might first appear since it is not limited to offers as defined by traditional contract law principles.

§ 5.1 1933 Act Application to Unconventional Transactions— Section 2(a)(3)'s Definition of Sale; Gifts, Bonus Plans, and Pledges; Effect of State Law

§ 5.1[1]   Statutory Definition of Sale

Section 2(a)(3) of the 1933 Act[1] defines "sale" as including "every contract of sale or disposition of a security or interest in a security, for value."[2] The definition under the Securities Exchange Act of 1934[3] is far less detailed than its 1933 Act counterpart but has been interpreted in a similar

---

§ 5.0

1. Section 2(a)(3) of the 1933 Act defines "sale" and "offer to sell." 15 U.S.C.A. § 772(a)(3). *See* § 5.1 *infra.*

§ 5.1

1. 15 U.S.C.A. § 77b(a)(3).

2. 15 U.S.C.A. § 77b(a)(3).

3. Section 3(a)(14) of the Exchange Act simply provides: "[t]he terms 'sale' and 'sell' each include any contract to sell or otherwise dispose of." 15 U.S.C.A. § 78c(a)(14).

fashion even though it does not expressly speak in terms of a disposition for value.

The statutory definition of sale obviously encompasses the exchange of securities for cash, but what about less conventional transactions such as the exercise of options, mergers, exercise of conversion rights, pledges, and the like? The courts have frequently been asked to address whether these exchanges of securities for something other than cash fall within the statutory definition of sale.[5] Under the 1933 Act definition, [the definition of] a sale is implicated to the extent that there is a disposition for value.

Exchanges of securities ordinarily would implicate the definition of sale. This is because when an investor parts with one security in exchange for another, he or she is giving up value in exchange for the security to be acquired. Some exchanges of securities are exempt from the 1933 Act's registration provisions, but these exemptions[9] clearly demonstrate a Congressional intent to treat exchanges of securities as sales. However, when an exchange of securities is involuntary and does not significantly alter the rights of the securities holders, the exchange will not be treated as a sale.[10]

For many years, the SEC took the view that shares issued in connection with mergers and other qualifying corporate reorganizations did not constitute sales that would trigger the 1933 Act's registration requirements.[11] The Commission has since abandoned its former "no sale" approach to mergers and other forms of combinations in favor of 1933 Act coverage.[12]

Additional definitional questions have arisen when attempting to decide whether stock dividends and corporate spin-offs constitute purchases and sales of securities.[13] These topics, which are discussed in the succeeding sections, have not been the only ones relating to the definition of sale. For example, questions may arise as to whether various other types of dispositions of securities qualify as sales under the statutory definition.

§ 5.1[2] Gifts and Bonus Plans

Even beyond exchanges of securities and the exercise of options or conversion rights, other definitional issues with regard to what constitutes a "sale." Ordinarily, a gift of securities will not constitute a sale under the securities laws. Gifts of securities have on occasion been scrutinized in order to determine whether they are in fact sales so as to trigger the application of the securities laws.

A bona fide gift will not be a sale even though some intangible or even indirect tangible benefit (such as a consequential tax deduction) inures to the donor's benefit. For example, when a charitable donor receives a tax deduc-

---

5. Similar problems have arisen under the 1934 Act's provision regarding the reporting of insider transactions and the disgorgement of insider short-swing profits. Section 16 of the 1934 Act, 15 U.S.C.A. § 78p. *See* §§ 13.1–13.4 *infra*.

9. Section 3(a)(7) (receivers' certificates), section 3(a)(9) (exchanges exclusively between an issuer and existing securities holders), section 3(a)(10) (certain administratively or judicially approved exchanges). 15 U.S.C.A. § 77c(a)(7), 77c(a)(9), and 77c(a)(10). *See* §§ 4.8, 4.10, 4.11 *supra*.

10. *See, e.g.,* In the Matter of Penn Central Securities Litigation, 494 F.2d 528, 534 n. 6a (3d Cir.1974).

11. Former Rule 133, 17 C.F.R. § 230.133 (1971) (rescinded by Sec.Act Rel.No. 33–5316 (Oct. 6, 1972)).

12. *See* § 5.2 *infra*.

13. *See* § 5.3 *infra*.

tion for his or her gift of securities, has there been a disposition for value? Presumably, ordinarily there is no sale in the case of a charitable contribution,[20] even though the donor receives a tax benefit as a result of the gift. The receipt of such a tax benefit in exchange for the donation of a security is not sufficient to classify the gift as a disposition for value. There may nevertheless be securities law consequences that flow from a gift of securities. Thus, for example, after the gift has been made, if the donee sells the securities that he or she was given, that sale, as is the case with any sale of securities, will require either registration under the 1933 Act or an exemption from registration before the securities can fall into the hands of the investing public.

The fact that a gift ordinarily is not a sale under the securities laws will not protect someone who is trying to evade the 1933 Act's registration provisions by trying to disguise a transaction as a gift. Accordingly, in those instances when the donor's "gifts" of securities are followed by widespread downstream sales of those securities, these would-be gifts may be characterized as a subterfuge to evade registration[24] and thus viewed as sales requiring either 1933 Act registration or an exemption from registration.[25] The SEC has accordingly taken the position that "value" for the disposition may be deemed received when the gift results in the creation of a public market for the issuer's securities—especially where that public market did not previously exist.[26] In such a case, registration of the would-be gift will be required unless, of course, an appropriate exemption can be found.[27]

In one case, the court found that a "gift" which forms part of a distribution of securities can be viewed as a sale in violation of section 5 of the 1933 Act.[28] This is true because, as pointed out above, a gift cannot be used as a ruse to disguise a transaction that truly is a sale. Thus, a calculated plan to "give" stock away as part of a sales promotion for a company's products will be viewed as a sale of the stock since the customer is paying for the product, and hence, for the securities that are part of the return consideration.[29] The Commission has gone further and has indicated that even without tying the "free" stock to a product purchase, a corporate promotion of "free" stock can

20. According to Professor Loss, it "seems clear * * * that a *bona fide* gift or loan of a security does not normally involve an offer or sale." 1 Louis Loss, Securities Regulation 576 (2d ed. 1961), relying in part on Shaw v. Dreyfus, 172 F.2d 140 (2d Cir.1949), *cert. denied* 337 U.S. 907, 69 S.Ct. 1048, 93 L.Ed. 1719 (1949) which was decided under the short-swing profit provisions of section 16(b), 15 U.S.C.A. § 78p(b), which is discussed in § 13.4 *infra*.

24. *See* In re H & B Carriers, Inc., 20 Sec.Reg. & L.Rep. (BNA) 742 (Utah Sec.Div. April 26, 1988).

25. This reasoning is analogous to that used in connection with corporate spin-off transactions. *See, e.g.,* SEC v. Datronics Engineers, Inc., 490 F.2d 250 (4th Cir.1973), *cert. denied* 416 U.S. 937, 94 S.Ct. 1936, 40 L.Ed.2d 287 (1974); SEC v. Harwyn Industries Corp., 326 F.Supp. 943 (S.D.N.Y.1971), both of which are discussed in § 5.3 *infra*.

26. *See, e.g.,* American Brewing Co., 31 Sec. Reg. & L. Rep. (BNA) 194 (SEC No Action Letter Jan. 27, 1999) (stock "give away" was really a sale); In the Matter of Capital General Corp., Sec. Act Rel. No. 33–7008, [1993 Transfer Binder] Fed. Sec. L. Rep. (CCH) ¶ 85,223 (SEC July 23, 1993).

27. *See* In re H & B Carriers, Inc., 20 Sec.Reg. & L.Rep. (BNA) 742 (Utah Sec.Div. April 26, 1988) (applying Utah blue sky law). A gift of assessable stock may properly be characterized as a sale. *Cf.* In re H & B Carriers, Inc., 20 Sec.Reg. & L.Rep. (BNA) 742 (Utah Sec.Div. April 26, 1988).

28. *See* SEC v. Cavanagh, 1998 WL 440029, [1998 Transfer Binder] Fed. Sec. L. Rep. (CCH) ¶ 90,271 (S.D.N.Y. 1998).

29. American Brewing Co., 31 Sec. Reg. & L. Rep. (BNA) 194 (SEC No Action Letter Jan. 27, 1999) (offering a "free" share of a brewery's voting stock with each case of beer purchased at retail).

be a sale. For example, the practice of offering "free" stock in exchange for visiting a company's website and registering to receive the stock has been viewed as a sale.[30] In no action letters, the SEC has thus taken the position that "a person's registration on or visit to an issuer's internet site" is sufficient consideration (or value) to be a sale under section 2(a)(3) of the 1993 Act.[31] Similarly, requiring the mailing of a self-addressed stamped envelope in exchange for "free" stock is a sale of the stock since the issuer receives value in terms of the name and address of the recipient who thus "registers" with the issuer.[32] In all of the foregoing instances involving promotions with "gifts" of stock, the company is clearly receiving value—i.e., the potential customer's name and a way to contact him or her—in exchange for the "free" stock.

§ 5.1[3] Employee Compensation Plans

A variation on the rule that a bona fide gift is not a sale arises in the context of bonus compensation plans. Following the rationale applicable to gifts, an employee bonus plan that is a true bonus—that is, over and above the employee's bargained-for consideration—is a gift and hence not a sale. On the other hand, when a so-called bonus plan is in fact a type of compensation for services, then there has been a disposition for value, and a "sale" will have taken place. Along these lines, the SEC has opined that the giving of shares to employees upon their retirement in exchange for "extraordinary services" was in fact a gift rather than a sale and thus did not require registration under the 1933 Act.[34] Thus, a stock bonus that is not bargained for and is given in appreciation of past services can be said to be without consideration and hence not a sale.[35] However, when a so-called bonus or bonus plan is in fact part of an employee's expected compensation, the stock is issued in exchange for value and thus, the "bonus" will be viewed as a sale.[36] Other forms of employee compensation plans will clearly be sales as the shares are issued in exchange for the employee's services. The SEC has created an exemption for many such plans.[37] And, for those employee stock and option plans that are not exempt, there is a specially tailored registration form.[38]

---

30. Andrew Jones, 31 Sec. Reg. & L. Rep. (BNA) 839 (SEC No Action Letter June 8, 1999); Vanderkam & Sanders, 31 Sec. Reg. & L. Rep. (BNA) 230 (SEC No Action Letter Jan. 27, 1999). *See also, e.g.,* Internet "Free Stock" Offerings Mostly Illegal, SEC's Walker Says, 31 Sec. Reg. & L. Rep. (BNA) 458 (April 9, 1999). *Cf.,* Gregory Zuckerman, SEC Clears Web Firms' Stock Giveaway, Wall St. J. C1 (Nov. 16, 1999) (shares to be given away were registered with the SEC).

31. Vanderkam & Sanders, 31 Sec. Reg. & L. Rep. (BNA) 230 (SEC No Action Letter Jan. 27, 1999). *Accord, e.g.,* Andrew Jones, 31 Sec. Reg. & L. Rep. (BNA) 839 (SEC No Action Letter June 8, 1999); SimplyStocks.com, 1999 SEC No–Act. Lexis 131 (SEC No Action Letter Feb. 4, 1999).

32. Jones & Rutten, 1999 SEC No–Act. Lexis 555 (SEC No Action Letter June 8, 1999).

34. New Jersey Resources Corp., 17 Sec.Reg. & L.Rep. (BNA) 282 (SEC No Action Letter Jan. 28, 1985) (the Commission response noted that since (1) this was a publicly traded company, (2) the bonus was involuntary from the employees' perspective, and (3) the employees did not part with value, there was no need to invoke the protections of the Act's registration requirements).

35. Knoll Int'l, Inc., 18 Sec.Reg. & L.Rep. (BNA) 1763 (SEC No Action Letter Oct. 20, 1986). *See also, e.g.,* Ocean Express Seafood Restaurants, Inc., 19 Sec.Reg. & L.Rep. (BNA) 537 (SEC No Action Letter March 26, 1987).

36. *See, e.g.,* Harris v. Republic Airlines, Inc., 1988 WL 56256, [1987–88 Transfer Binder] Fed.Sec.L.Rep. (CCH) ¶ 93,772 (D.D.C.1988). *See* § 5.3 *infra* for a discussion of employee stock plans. *See also* § 4.18 *supra* for a discussion of the exemption for certain compensation plans of issuers which are not subject to the Exchange Act's periodic reporting requirements. *Cf.* SEC v. Ralston Purina Co., 346 U.S. 119, 73 S.Ct. 981, 97 L.Ed. 1494 (1953) (offering to employees was not exempt from registration).

37. Rule 701, 17 C.F.R. § 230.701. *See* § 4.18 *supra.* Stock and option plans that are limited to key employees may be exempt as transactions not involving a public offering. Section 4(2), 15 U.S.C.A. § 77d(2), which is discussed in § 4.24 *supra.*

38. 1933 Act Form S–8 is available to 1934 Act reporting companies with regard to securities offered to employees—including the employees of subsidiaries who are offered the parent's

§ 5.1[4] Convertible Securities

Section 2(a)(1)'s definition of security[44] expressly includes conversion rights which themselves constitute securities separate and distinct from the underlying common stock or other security and, thus, must be registered for sale, absent an applicable exemption. The question arises, however, whether an exercise of conversion rights is itself a sale of the convertible security and a purchase of the underlying security. Section 2(a)(3)'s definition of sale requires that there be a disposition for "value" in order for a sale to take place.[45] When a conversion right is exercised, the holder of the security merely is receiving something he or she had a right to all along—the underlying security. Hence, it would seem to follow that a conversion ordinarily will not be a disposition "for value" since the owner already had those rights prior to exercising the right of conversion.[46] The SEC's safe harbor exemption from 1933 Act registration for resales of restricted securities takes the position that an exercise of a conversion right is not a sale and thus does not require registration.[47] Analogously, the Commission takes the position that an exercise of conversion rights is not a sale or purchase of securities within the meaning of the insider trading provisions of section 16(b) of the Securities Exchange Act of 1934.[48]

§ 5.1[5] Pledges

The Supreme Court, in Rubin v. United States, held that a pledge of securities is a sale for purposes of the 1933 Act's antifraud provisions.[50] Although there would seem to be no reason to expect a different result under the 1934 Act, the courts have been sharply divided. The Second and Sixth Circuits have ruled that a pledge is a sale for purposes of SEC Rule 10b–5.[52] However, prior to the Supreme Court's decision in *Rubin,* the Fifth and Seventh Circuits had ruled that a pledge is not a sale under the 1934 Act.[53] These cases arose out of transactions that were viewed as commercial loans not involving traditional investment risks and thus were held not to be within the purview of the securities laws.

---

securities—pursuant to any benefit plan. The simplified 1933 Act registration process that is available for offerings qualifying to use Form S–8 is discussed in § 3.4[4][E] *supra.*

44. 15 U.S.C.A. § 77b(a)(1). *See* Sec.Act Rel.No. 33–3210 (April 9, 1947).

45. 15 U.S.C.A. § 77b(3).

46. Gilligan, Will & Co. v. SEC, 267 F.2d 461 (2d Cir.1959) (the court did not question the conversion as a sale although sale of the underlying common stock after conversion was held to require registration), *cert. denied,* 361 U.S. 896, 80 S.Ct. 200, 4 L.Ed.2d 152 (1959)

47. Rule 144(d)(4), 17 C.F.R. § 230.144(d)(4).

48. Rule 16b–6(a), 17 C.F.R. § 240.16b–6(a) (dealing with derivative securities). Earlier cases had been in conflict on the issue.

50. 449 U.S. 424, 101 S.Ct. 698, 66 L.Ed.2d 633 (1981).

52. Chemical Bank v. Arthur Andersen & Co., 726 F.2d 930, 939–45 (2d Cir.1984), *cert. denied* 469 U.S. 884, 105 S.Ct. 253, 83 L.Ed.2d 190 (1984), relying in part on dictum from Marine Bank v. Weaver, 455 U.S. 551, 554 n. 2, 102 S.Ct. 1220, 1222 n. 2, 71 L.Ed.2d 409, 414 n. 2 (1982), *on remand* 683 F.2d 744 (3d Cir.1982). *See also* Mansbach v. Prescott, Ball & Turben, 598 F.2d 1017 (6th Cir.1979).

53. Alley v. Miramon, 614 F.2d 1372 (5th Cir.1980); Lincoln National Bank v. Herber, 604 F.2d 1038 (7th Cir.1979); National Bank of Commerce of Dallas v. All American Assurance Co., 583 F.2d 1295 (5th Cir.1978).

In the aftermath of *Rubin,* most pledges of securities will qualify as sales under the securities laws. However, this does not mean that someone collaterally affected by the transaction will be considered a party to it. Accordingly, it has been held that a pledge of stock by a major shareholder to secure the margin loans of other investors did not constitute an unregistered sale of the pledgor's securities with respect to those investors.[55]

§ 5.1[6] Installment Sales

In most instances, installment payments under an installment sale of securities will not be new "sales" of the securities. However, where each payment involves a new investment decision, each payment may properly be treated as a new sale.[62] Also, a stated policy of not enforcing unpaid subscriptions or installments may lead to the conclusion that calls for additional payments will be treated as new sales.[63] Similarly, calls for assessments on assessable stock will be offers of sale under the 1933 Act.[64]

§ 5.2 Corporate Recapitalizations, Reorganizations, and Mergers Under the 1933 Act: Rule 145

§ 5.2[1] Reorganizations Exempt From 1933 Act Registration

As pointed out in the preceding chapter, section 3(a)(9) of the 1933 Act provides an exemption from registration for securities that are exchanged by the issuer exclusively with its existing security holders, provided that no sales commission or other remuneration is paid in connection with solicitation for the exchange.[1] The section 3(a)(9) exemption does not extend to downstream sales by the securities holders or in cases in which the exchange was made to persons who were likely to act as statutory underwriters.[2] The exemption further is limited to 1933 Act registration and thus does not address the 1934 Securities Exchange Act's applicability to solicitation of shareholders' votes needed to approve certain exchanges.[3] Also, section 3(a)(9) is limited to exchanges of securities by the same issuer and therefore has no application to mergers or other reorganizations in which the security holders receive securities of another issuer.[4]

Section 3(a)(9) is not the only 1933 Act exemption applicable to corporate reorganizations. Section 3(a)(7)[5] exempts certain certificates of interest issued in connection with bankruptcy reorganizations. Further, section 3(a)(10)[6]

---

55. Silva Run Worldwide Ltd. v. Gaming Lottery Corp., 1998 WL 167330, [1998 Transfer Binder] Fed. Sec. L. Rep. (CCH) ¶ 90,196 (S.D.N.Y.1998).

62. *See* § 5.4 *infra.*

63. *See, e.g.,* Goodman v. Epstein, 582 F.2d 388, 409–414 (7th Cir.1978), *cert. denied* 440 U.S. 939, 99 S.Ct. 1289, 59 L.Ed.2d 499 (1979); Troyer v. Karcagi, 476 F.Supp. 1142, 1148 (S.D.N.Y. 1979).

64. 1933 Act Rule 136, 17 C.F.R. § 230.136.

§ 5.2

1. 15 U.S.C.A. § 77c(a)(9). *See* § 4.10 *supra. See generally* J. William Hicks, Recapitalizations under Section 3(a)(9) of the Securities Act of 1933, 61 Va.L.Rev. 1057 (1975).

2. *See* Sec.Act Rels. Nos. 33–646, 33–2029 (Feb. 3, 1937; Aug. 8, 1939).

3. In such a case the exchange is not exclusively with existing security holders of the issuer.

4. Where the issuer is a 1934 Act reporting company, the federal proxy rules would govern such solicitations. 15 U.S.C.A. § 78n(a). *See* chapter 10 *infra.*

5. 15 U.S.C.A. § 77c(a)(7). *See* § 4.8 *supra.*

6. 15 U.S.C.A. § 77c(a)(10). *See* § 4.11 *supra.*

exempts judicially or administratively approved reorganizations where the approval is issued after a public hearing and considers the fairness of the transaction.[7] In addition, under appropriate circumstances, issuers involved in corporate reorganizations may also be able to avoid registration because the transaction qualifies for an exemption, such as the exemptions for intrastate,[8] nonpublic,[9] Regulation A,[10] or Regulation D[11] offerings. Absent an available exemption, securities issued in connection with corporate reorganizations will have to be registered under the 1933 Act.

§ 5.2[2] Rule 145

A corporation's shareholders' participation in a plan of reorganization or a merger will generally result in the corporation's exchange or issuance of new securities.[12] To the extent that such a reorganization or merger would involve the disposition of shares for value, the solicitation of shareholder consent would seem to fall within section 2(a)(3)'s definition of "offer to sell"[13] with regard to the securities to be issued in the recapitalization, merger, or plan of exchange. Nevertheless, for a long time, the Commission took the position that whenever securities were issued as part of an exchange pursuant to a statutory merger, consolidation, or sale of corporate assets, their issuance did not involve a sale of securities within the meaning of section 2(a)(3) of the Act.[14] The "no sale" doctrine had become the focus of frequent and severe criticism[15] and was discarded in 1972 with the Commission's adoption of Rule 145, which treats exchanges pursuant to mergers and reorganizations as sales.[16]

In adopting Rule 145, the Commission declared these share exchanges to involve sales of securities and thus in need of registration under the 1933 Act absent an exemption. Rule 145 therefore imposed registration requirements

---

7. Stock acquired in a merger where the fairness has been passed upon by a state agency is exempt under section 3(a)(10) and the stock received by the shareholders is not restricted stock under Rule 144. Borland Finance Co., 19 Sec.Reg. & L.Rep. (BNA) 1769 (SEC No Action Letter Oct. 10, 1987). The shareholders' holding period is to be determined by Rule 145(d)(2) and the shareholders are not permitted to tack on the Rule 144 holding period of the disappearing corporation's stock. *Id.*

8. 15 U.S.C.A. § 77c(a)(11); 17 C.F.R. § 230.147. *See* § 4.12 *supra.*

9. 15 U.S.C.A. § 77d(2). *See* § 4.24 *supra.*

10. 17 C.F.R. §§ 230.251 *et seq. See* § 4.17 *supra.*

11. 17 C.F.R. §§ 230.501 *et seq. See* §§ 4.19–4.22, 4.25 *supra.*

12. The prominent exception is where the shareholders are cashed out. Redeemable preferred shares issued in a cash-out merger need not be registered so long as they are redeemed immediately. Cambior, Inc., 19 Sec.Reg. & L.Rep. (BNA) 240 (SEC No Action Letter Jan. 22, 1987).

13. 15 U.S.C.A. § 77b(a)(3). *See* § 5.1 *supra.*

14. 17 C.F.R. § 230.133 (1971) (rescinded by Sec.Act Rel.No. 33–5316 (Oct. 6, 1972)).

15. Rule 133 and its "no sale" theory was attacked not only on the basis of being "unforgiveably formalistic" but also because it excluded from the Act's registration requirements transactions which created the need for the type of public disclosures required to be contained in 1933 Act registration statements. 1 L. Loss, Securities Regulation 552 (2d ed. 1961). One justification for the no sale rule was that many of these transactions result in sufficient public information, since for 1934 Act reporting companies the plan of recapitalization, merger, or other reorganization would be submitted to a shareholder vote and thus be subject to the proxy disclosure requirements imposed by the 1934 Act. *See* "Disclosure to Investors": Report and Recommendations to the Securities and Exchange Commissions from the Disclosure Policy Study, "The Wheat Report," 251–78 (1964).

16. 17 C.F.R. § 230.145. *See* Sec.Act Rels. Nos. 33–5136, 33–5463 (Oct. 6, 1972, Feb. 28, 1974).

on all otherwise non-exempt business combinations involving a shareholder vote and the issuance of shares to the voting shareholders.[17] Rule 145 transactions may be registered on Form S–4 which is designed specifically for corporate combinations. The SEC was mindful of the overlapping Exchange Act coverage and thus further provided for coordination between the 1933 Act prospectus requirements and the proxy rules of the 1934 Act.[18] This type of coordination between the 1933 and 1934 Act is consistent with the 1970s initiative to implement an integrated disclosure system.[19]

The rule does not apply, however, to tender offers or open-market share acquisitions because these are not corporate reorganizations but rather involve transactions with the shareholders directly. When such a tender offer involves the issuance of securities, registration may be required but Rule 145 is not available. Also, the 1934 Act's tender offer provisions may come into play.[20]

Rule 145(a)[21] provides that there is an "offer," "offer to sell," "offer for sale," or "sale" within the meaning of section 2(a)(3) of the 1933 Act when a plan for reclassification, merger, consolidation, or transfer of corporate assets in exchange for securities of another issuer is submitted to securities holders for a vote or otherwise for their consent. An exception to Rule 145 involves a reorganization when the sole effect of the reorganization is a change of the issuer's domicile or state of incorporation.[22] In such a case, 1933 Act registration is not required.[23] However, any additional corporate restructuring beyond the change of domicile will implicate Rule 145 and, absent an exemption, will bring the 1933 Act's registration requirements into play.[24]

Rule 145 thus includes in section 2(a)(3)'s definition of sale and offer for sale most corporate combinations. Formerly, unless an exemption could be found, any communication, written or oral, designed to influence the shareholder's vote or consent would have run afoul of the 1933 Act's gun-jumping prohibitions unless a registration statement has been filed.[25] The only types of pre-filing publicity that are permitted are those that would comply with Rule 135.[26] As discussed below, Rule 135(a)(2)(D) permits limited prefiling communications with shareholders. The prospectus requirements[27] apply to solicita-

---

17. *Id.* The rule thus covers mergers, consolidations, sales of corporate assets, and share exchanges involving shareholder votes and to which the corporations are parties.

18. 15 U.S.C.A. § 78n(a). *See* Chapter 10 *infra.*

19. *See* § 3.4 *supra.*

20. Tender offers are discussed in Chapter 11 *infra.*

21. Sec.Act Rel.No. 33–5316 (Oct. 6, 1972). *See* 17 C.F.R. §§ 240.14a–2, 14a–6, 14c–5.

22. *See, e.g.,* General Electric Capital Corp., [1999–2000 Transfer Binder] Fed. Sec. L. Rep. (CCH) ¶ 77,890, 2000 WL 1119236 (SEC No Action Letter July 26, 2000) (merger for sole purpose of reorganization in another state would not result in sales under section 2(a)(3) of the 1933 Act).

23. 17 C.F.R. § 230.145(a)(2). *See, e.g.,* C. Brewer Homes, Inc., 26 Sec. Reg. & L. Rep. (BNA) 1268 (SEC No Action Letter avail. Aug. 26, 1994).

24. *See, e.g.,* In the Matter of Carolina Pipeline, Inc., 419 Sec.Reg.L.Rep. (BNA) C–1 (SEC Sept. 2, 1977). *But cf.* America West Airlines, Inc., 28 Sec. Reg. & L. Rep. (BNA) 650 (SEC No Action Letter available April 25, 1996) (reorganization of business into holding company structure did not require registration).

25. 15 U.S.C.A. § 77e(c). *See* § 2.3 *supra.*

26. 17 C.F.R. § 230.135.

27. 15 U.S.C.A. § 77e(b). *See* 15 U.S.C.A. § 77b(a)(10). A 1934 Act proxy statement will not violate the prospectus requirements. 17 C.F.R. § 230.145(b)(2). The prospectus requirements are discussed in § 2.4 *supra.*

tions regarding the shareholder's vote or consent for Rule 145 transactions. In 1999, the SEC liberalized the types of announcements that can be made once there has been a public announcement[28] of the proposed business combination.[29]

In addition to the general exceptions or exemptions from the prospectus requirements under the 1933 Act, Rule 135(a)(2)(D) states that certain communications do not constitute a "prospectus" as defined in section 2(a)(10)[30] of the Act.[31] The rule further provides that these permissible communications do not come within the concept of the "offer to sell" within the meaning of section 5 of the Act.[32]

Rule 135 excludes from the definition of prospectus communications which contain no more than (1) the issuer's name, (2) the name of the persons whose assets are to be sold or whose securities are to be exchanged or who are otherwise parties to the transaction, (3) a brief description of the business of the parties to the transaction, (4) the date, time and place of the meeting at which the security holders will be voting or giving their consent to the transaction, (5) a brief description of the transaction, (6) the basis upon which the transaction will be made, (7) and any legend or other statement required by state or federal laws or administrative body.[33] Rule 135 thus provides an exemption from the gun-jumping prohibitions by permitting dissemination of the foregoing information prior to the filing of a registration statement. In addition to the foregoing limited communications which may be sent out during the pre-filing and waiting periods, any written communication that meets the requirements of the 1934 Act's proxy disclosure and filing requirements is not deemed either a "prospectus" or "offer to sell" so as to require a statutory prospectus or filing of the registration statement prior to its dissemination.[34] The rule thus coordinates the 1934 Act's proxy rules with the 1933 Act's registration requirements.

§ 5.2[3] Rule 145 and Downstream Sales

SEC Rule 145 addresses the problem of downstream sales after the corporate combination has been approved and consummated and the new securities have been issued. Rule 145(c)[35] imposes 1933 Act obligations upon any party to a transaction covered by Rule 145(a), other than the issuer, including any person who is an affiliate of such party, at the time it is submitted for the security holders' vote or consent. Parties to a Rule 145 transaction, including affiliates of the issuer, who offer for sale or sell the

---

28. "Public announcement" encompasses all communications that put the market on notice of a proposed transaction. "Public announcement" means any communication by a party to the transaction, or any person authorized to act on a party's behalf, that is reasonably designed to, or has the effect of, informing the public or security holders in general about the transaction. 1933 Act Rule 165(f)(3), 17 C.F.R. § 230.165(f)(3).

29. Rule 145(b)(1), 17 C.F.R. § 230.145(b)(1). Regulation of Takeovers and Security Holder Communications, Sec. Act Rel. No. 33–7760, 1999 WL 969596 (SEC Oct. 22, 1999).

30. 15 U.S.C.A. § 77b(10).

31. 17 C.F.R. § 230.135(a)(2)(D).

32. 15 U.S.C.A. § 77e.

33. 17 C.F.R. § 230.135.

34. *Id.*

35. 17 C.F.R. § 230.145(c).

securities issued in the Rule 145 transaction, are deemed to be engaged in a distribution and therefore are underwriters under section 2(11) of the Act.[36]

Rule 145(d)[37] excludes certain downstream sales from those which create underwriter status under subsection (c) of the rule. Any person selling securities acquired in a Rule 145 transaction who would otherwise be deemed an underwriter under Rule 145(c) is excluded from the definition provided that the sales are in compliance with Rule 144(d)'s volume limitations[38] and are executed in unsolicited brokers transactions.[39] In order to take advantage of this exclusion, it is further required that the issuer be a 1934 Act reporting company that has made all current reports publicly available or, alternatively, has made publicly available similar information.[40] Rule 145 was amended in 1984 to expand the scope of permissible downstream sales of securities acquired in a business combination. Nonaffiliates receiving securities registered under the 1933 Act in a business combination may sell the securities without registration if they have owned the securities for one year provided that Rule 144's informational requirements have been satisfied,[41] or after two years if such current information is not publicly available.[42] Stock acquired in a Rule 145 transaction that is not registered but was issued in reliance on section 3(a)(10)'s exemption for administratively approved mergers is not restricted stock under Rule 144.[43] One way to minimize the impact of the resale restrictions that may apply in Rule 145 transactions is to provide for registration rights to the shareholders of the target company with respect to the shares they receive in the merger exchange.[44]

With regard to computing the holding period generally, the shareholders' holding period is to be determined by Rule 145(d)(2), and shareholders are not permitted to tack on the Rule 144 holding period of the disappearing corporation's stock.[45] The Rule 144 tacking would presumably have been permissible if the merger had been exempt under section 4(2)'s nonpublic offering exemption.[46]

When securities issued in a corporate combination are not registered under the 1933 Act because of reliance on an exemption, downstream sales may trigger the Act's registration requirements, unless the downstream sales are themselves exempt.[47] Just as Rule 144(d) imposes a one year holding

---

36. *Id. See* 15 U.S.C.A. § 77b(11).

37. 17 C.F.R. § 230.145(d).

38. 17 C.F.R. § 230.144(e). *See* § 4.29 *supra.*

39. 17 C.F.R. § 230.144(f), (g). *See* 15 U.S.C.A. § 77d(4); § 4.26 *supra.*

40. 17 C.F.R. § 230.144(c).

41. Rule 145(d)(2), 17 C.F.R. § 230.145(d)(2).

42. Rule 145(d)(3), 17 C.F.R. § 230.145(d)(3). The exemption is conditional upon compliance with Rule 144(c)'s holding period computation. *Id. See* Rule 144(c), 17 C.F.R. § 230.144(c); § 4.29 *supra.*

43. Borland Finance Co., 19 Sec.Reg. & L.Rep. (BNA) 1769 (SEC No Action Letter Oct. 10, 1987).

44. *See, e.g.,* Herrmann Holdings Ltd. v. Lucent Technologies, Inc., 302 F.3d 552 (5th Cir. 2002) (upholding breach of contract claim to cause an S–3 registration to become effective as soon as practicable).

45. *See* Borland Finance Co., 19 Sec.Reg. & L.Rep. (BNA) 1769 (SEC No Action Letter Oct. 10, 1987).

46. Rule 144 is discussed in § 4.29 *supra.*

47. 15 U.S.C.A. § 77d(1), (4). *See* § 4.26 *supra.*

period on restricted securities,[48] any Rule 145 transaction must be registered on Form S–4 or on a more general registration form where the securities so issued are to be traded by the recipients in such a large amount as to constitute a distribution.[49] Otherwise, a merger or other form of business combination would be a convenient device for avoiding the Act's registration requirements and getting securities into the hands of the general investing public without a full-fledged registration statement.[50]

§ 5.3   Section 2(a)(3)'s Definition of Sale: Warrants, Employee Stock Plans, Stock Dividends, and Spin–Offs Under the 1933 Act

As pointed out earlier,[1] Section 2(a)(3) of the 1933 Act provides that "sale" includes "every contract of sale or disposition of a security or interest in a security, for value."[2] This definition of sale ordinarily includes the requirement that before there has been a sale, there must have been an investment decision by the purchaser.

§ 5.3[1] Warrants, Conversion Rights, Options, and Security Futures Products

Section 2(a)(1)'s definition of security[5] makes it clear that options, warrants, and conversion rights themselves constitute securities separate and distinct from the underlying common stock or other security. The question arises, however, whether an exercise of conversion rights is itself a sale of the convertible security and a purchase of the underlying security. Section 2(a)(3)'s definition of sale requires that there be a disposition for "value" in order for a sale to take place.[6] As pointed out earlier,[7] when the owner of a convertible security exercises a conversion right, the holder of the convertible security is receiving something he or she had a right to all along—the underlying security. Hence, it would seem to follow that the conversion was not "for value" since the owner already had those rights prior to conversion.[8] This view is supported both by the case law and by SEC rulemaking.[9]

When options or warrants are issued to security holders without consideration or in conjunction with the sale of some other security, there is no sale of the options or warrants unless they are immediately exercisable.[10] However,

---

48. 17 C.F.R. § 230.144(d)(1). *See* § 4.29 *supra.*

49. Form S–4.

50. *See* SEC v. Datronics Engineers, Inc., 490 F.2d 250 (4th Cir.1973), *cert. denied* 416 U.S. 937, 94 S.Ct. 1936, 40 L.Ed.2d 287 (1974); Sec.Act Rel.No. 33–4982 (SEC July 2, 1979); § 5.3 *infra.*

1. *See* § 5.1 *supra.*

2. 15 U.S.C.A. § 77b(a)(3). *See* § 5.1 *supra.*

5. 15 U.S.C.A. § 77b(a)(1). *See* Sec.Act Rel.No. 33–3210 (April 9, 1947).

6. 15 U.S.C.A. § 77b(3).

7. *See* § 5.1[3] *supra.*

8. In Gilligan, Will & Co. v. SEC, 267 F.2d 461 (2d Cir.1959), *cert. denied,* 361 U.S. 896, 80 S.Ct. 200, 4 L.Ed.2d 152 (1959), the court did not question the conversion as a sale although sale of the underlying common stock after conversion was held to require registration. *Accord,* Rule 144(d)(4). 17 C.F.R. § 230.144(d)(4)

9. *Ibid.*

10. The last sentence of section 2(a)(3) provides the same rule for conversion rights. 15 U.S.C.A. § 77b(a)(3). *See* H.R.Rep. No. 85, 73d Cong. 1st Sess. 11 (1933).

options, warrants, or conversion rights that are immediately exercisable will be viewed as the issuer's "offer to sell" the underlying security, which in turn will have to be registered unless an exemption can be found.[11] Additionally, options or warrants, although not immediately exercisable, if transferred for consideration, will constitute a sale since they have been disposed of for value.[12] Furthermore, even after the option has been acquired, the exercise of the option may constitute a distinct purchase.

§ 5.3[2] Stock Dividends

The original version of the 1933 Act as it appeared in the House of Representatives would have exempted stock dividends paid in the company's own shares (or shares of another company[20]) from the registration requirements. The congressional conference committee that considered the House and Senate versions of the 1933 Act deleted the exemption as unnecessary, reasoning that stock dividends "are exempt without expressed provision as they do not constitute a sale, not being given for value."[21] It follows that the declaration and issuance of stock dividends where the shareholders do not have an election to obtain cash in lieu of the stock do not constitute sales of securities. Similarly, stock splits do not constitute sales under the 1933 Act.[22] This does not mean, however, that downstream sales following a stock dividend or stock split may be made with impunity, since these resales of shares received as a stock dividend or stock split will raise potential statutory underwriter questions, especially if there are so many shares sold as to constitute a "distribution."[23]

The SEC has taken the position that when, as the result of director action, the shareholders have no election to receive the dividend in cash, or when the stock is issued in lieu of a cash dividend pursuant to an election prior to declaration of the dividend, there is no value and hence no sale.[24] This latter situation rarely arises; however, the use of a no-sale approach here is highly debatable since the shareholder is making an investment decision when the election is made.[25] In the more common situation, when a cash dividend is declared and the shareholder purchases additional shares, as is the case with a dividend reinvestment plan ("DRIP"), the shareholder is clearly parting with value in exchange for receiving the stock and such distributions of shares will

---

11. *See* Sec.Act Rel.No. 33–97 (Dec. 28, 1933); 1 Louis Loss, Securities Regulation 579 (2d ed. 1961); Allen E. Throop & Chester T. Lane, Some Problems of Exemption under the Securities Act of 1933, 4 Law & Contemp.Prob. 89 (1937).

12. "Warrant" generally refers to an option to purchase the issuer's stock. Other stock options which are contracts between the prospective purchaser and seller can also require registration. There are several national exchanges which trade options in publicly traded stock. These exchanges are supervised by the SEC. *See* § 14.3 *infra*.

20. This type of transaction frequently is referred to as a "spin-off". *See* § 5.3[3] *infra*.

21. H.R.Rep. No. 152, 73d Cong. 1st Sess. 25 (1933).

22. *See* Gurvitz v. Bregman & Co., 379 F.Supp. 1283 (S.D.N.Y.1974).

23. *See* Hafner v. Forest Laboratories, Inc., 345 F.2d 167, 168 (2d Cir.1965).

24. Sec.Act Rel.No. 33–929 (July 29, 1936).

25. In order for the shareholder's opportunity to elect cash or stock as a dividend not to lead to a sale, the dividend must be declared in stock rather than cash by the directors. In making such an election, the corporation can still be seen as receiving value: the savings of the cash dividend. Nevertheless the SEC's position has been that no sale occurs presumably because it is only when the dividend is declared that it assumes the status of a debt. Sec.Act Rel.No. 33–929 (July 29, 1936)..

be considered sales and thus subject to the 1933 Act registration requirements absent an applicable exemption.[26]

§ 5.3[3] Exchanges of Securities

As noted in a previous section,[27] there are exemptions from registration for certain exchanges of securities such as those exchanges exclusively with existing security holders,[28] or exchanges which are pursuant to certain judicial or administratively approved transactions.[29] But these exemptions, although denominated as "security exemptions" under section 3 of the 1933 Act, are nevertheless treated as transaction exemptions and thus will not apply to insulate down-stream sales of the securities issued in an exempt exchange.[30] Accordingly, absent a separate exemption, downstream sales of securities issued in an exempt exchange transaction will have to be registered under the 1933 Act.

Absent an exemption, an exchange, other than one pursuant to preexisting conversion rights,[31] of one class of securities for another will constitute a sale under the securities laws. In such a case, there is a disposition for value (the value being the receipt of the securities received in the exchange). In the case of non-exempt exchanges of securities, any change in the rights and obligations of the issuer or securities holders or amendment to the security constitutes both a sale and a new issue, regardless of whether such amendatory action is permissible under state corporation law.[32] Thus, for example, the SEC staff has taken the position that registration will be required if a corporation that has issued tracking stock with respect to some of its operations decides to exchange common stock in a subsidiary with holders of the tracking stock.[33] The SEC also gave no action relief to demutualization plans where the company would be filing 1932 Act reports prior to the demutualization.[34]

§ 5.3[4] Spin–Off Transactions

Just as a corporation's dividends in its own shares do not constitute sales under the Securities Act of 1933,[35] the same rule applies to dividends paid in shares of other corporations, such as in the case of a split-up or spin-off transaction, since the corporation is not receiving value in return. It has been held, for example, that a shareholder who receives stock of another issuer as a dividend may not sue under the antifraud provisions since no sale has taken

26. *Id. But cf.* Sec.Act Rel.No. 33–5515 (SEC Aug. 8, 1974). Dividend reinvestment plans frequently are registered for sale under the SEC's shelf registration rule. Rule 415, 17 C.F.R. § 230.415; *see* § 3.11 *supra.*

27. *See* §§ 4.10, 5.2[1] *supra.*

28. 15 U.S.C.A. § 77c(a)(9).

29. 15 U.S.C.A. §§ 77c(a)(6), (a)(7), (a)(10). *See* §§ 4.7–4.8, 4.11 *supra.*

30. *See, e.g., In the Matter of Thompson Ross Securities Co.,* 6 S.E.C. 1111 (SEC 1940).

31. *See* § 5.3[1] *supra.*

32. *See, e.g.,* United States v. New York, New Haven & Hartford Railroad Co., 276 F.2d 525 (2d Cir.1960), *cert. denied,* 362 U.S. 961, 80 S.Ct. 877, 4 L.Ed.2d 876 (1960); SEC v. Associated Gas & Electric Co., 99 F.2d 795 (2d Cir.1938).

33. *See* Liberty Media Corp., 2001 WL 109542 (SEC No Action Letter Feb. 7, 2001).

34. Nationwide Financial Services, Inc., 2002 WL 1856163 (SEC No Action Letter Aug. 9, 2002).

35. 15 U.S.C.A. § 77b(a)(3). *See* § 5.3[2] *supra.*

place where there is no aftermarket for the securities so distributed.[36] However, the Commission has made it clear that a spin-off may not be used as a scheme to avoid registration[37] and that in such a case "value" may be found from the creation of a public market for shares that prior to the spin-off were privately held and illiquid.[38] As discussed below, registration is likely to be required when the shares will be distributed by resales after the spin-off.[39] However, when the spun-off shares are properly restricted against resale, registration will not be required.[40] Shell corporations have also been used to attempt to evade the 1933 Act's registration requirements.[41]

On occasion, corporations with a large number of shareholders have made use of their existing shareholders to effectuate distributions of shares in corporations that formerly were closely held. For example, in SEC v. Harwyn Industries Corp.,[42] a company with a large number of shareholders actively sought privately-held companies desiring to go public. After acquiring the shares of these privately-held companies for valid consideration, these shares would be distributed to the public company's shareholders as a stock dividend or spin-off, with the conduit company retaining some of the privately held company's shares. It was then a matter of time before the shares of the once privately held company became traded publicly. The Commission successfully sought an injunction against such transactions without registration or an exemption notwithstanding the defendants' argument that no value was received by the corporation and that hence there was no sale. The court found that not only did the transactions violate the spirit of the Act,[43] but since the transactions created a public market for the securities of the once privately-held corporation, value could be said to have accrued to that corporation.[44] Additionally, when reselling the shares so received via the stock dividend, the spun-off company's shareholders' distribution of shares constituted a disposition for value. The court further noted that the defendants in *Harwyn* acted in good faith, believing that there was a valid basis for not registering the transaction under the 1933 Act.[45] The spin-off is not always used in good faith, and has also been utilized as an intentional attempt to evade 1933 Act registration. This device has also been used to attempt to create a public

---

36. Rathborne v. Rathborne, 508 F.Supp. 515 (E.D.La.1980), *judgment affirmed,* 683 F.2d 914 (5th Cir.1982).

37. *See* Sec.Act Rel.No. 33–4982 (July 2, 1969).

38. *See, e.g.,* SEC v. Datronics Engineers, Inc., 490 F.2d 250 (4th Cir.1973), *cert. denied,* 416 U.S. 937, 94 S.Ct. 1936, 40 L.Ed.2d 287 (1974); SEC v. Harwyn Industries Corp., 326 F.Supp. 943 (S.D.N.Y.1971).

39. *Cf.* Chronimid, Inc., 26 Sec. Reg. & L. Rep. (BNA) 1646 (SEC No Action Letter available Nov. 17, 1994) (registration not required where securities issued in spin-off would be subject to resale restrictions of SEC Rule 144); MB Communications, Inc., 26 Sec. Reg. & L. Rep. (BNA) 821 (SEC No Action Letter available May 23, 1994) (permitting use of Form S–8 for registration of transactions following a spin-off).

40. *E.g.,* Digital Commerce Corp., [1999–2000 Transfer Binder] Fed. Sec. L. Rep. (CCH) ¶ 77,873 (SEC No Action Letter 2000); Chronimid, Inc., 26 Sec. Reg. & L. Rep. (BNA) 1646 (SEC No Action Letter available Nov. 17, 1994) (registration not required where securities issued in spin-off would be subject to resale restrictions of SEC Rule 144).

41. *E.g.,* SEC v. Lybrand, 200 F.Supp.2d 384 (S.D.N.Y.2002) (founders of shell corporation were underwriters and thus transactions were not entitled to section 4(1) exemption from registration).

42. 326 F.Supp. 943 (S.D.N.Y.1971).

43. *Id.* at 953.

44. *Id.*

45. 326 F.Supp. at 954.

market for shares without the required registration. In such instances the violation of the 1933 Act's registration requirement is even clearer than in the case of a good faith attempt to secure an exemption from registration.[46]

The foregoing decisions dealing with spin-offs and shell corporations arose in the limited context of transactions in which there was no other bona fide business purpose; in other words, the spun-off corporation was acquired solely for the purpose of spinning it off. However, the impact of these rulings is broad, as they also have a bearing on more legitimate spin-off transactions.[47] Consider, for example, a publicly held company that decides to spin-off a portion of its business. Such a spin-off may be motivated, for example, by a managerial decision that the spun-off portion of the business is no longer desired, or in order to achieve compliance with the antitrust laws. Alternatively, the spin-off may be a final step in the acquisition of a company with some undesired assets that the acquiring company decides to dispose of. In any of these cases, the spin-off transaction, although not the result of a scheme to evade registration, will nevertheless require registration under the 1933 Act or an applicable exemption from registration. The rationale underlying the 1933 Act's registration requirement is that the transaction places in the hands of the investing public shares that previously were privately held. Although the transaction by which the securities are transferred from the spinning-off corporation to its shareholders may not include value even in the sense of *Harwyn* and its progeny, the transaction is clearly part of a distribution. It is to be anticipated that the securities so distributed to the shareholders may be sold, unless resales are restricted subject to Rule 144 and related law.[48] In such cases, the spin-off transaction and subsequent resales may place the corporation in a position of participating in a distribution within the meaning of section 2(a)(11)'s definition of underwriter.[49] The value requirement of the sale definition is satisfied since the publicly held corporation's shareholders clearly receive value when they sell their spun-off shares. When such downstream sales are of sufficiently substantial magnitude so as to constitute a "distribution," the spin-off transaction would constitute a type of indirect participation in the distribution that in turn would trigger section 2(11)'s definition.[50] However, when it is not reasonably anticipated that there will be downstream resales following the spin-off transaction, registration will not be required.[51]

The discussion above addresses the 1933 Act registration issues relating to spin-off transactions. Even if a spin-off transaction can successfully be accomplished without 1933 Act registration, the 1934 Act may still need to be considered. Thus, for example, another limitation on securities issued in

46. SEC v. Datronics Engineers, Inc., 490 F.2d 250 (4th Cir.1973), *cert. denied* 416 U.S. 937, 94 S.Ct. 1936, 40 L.Ed.2d 287 (1974).

47. *See generally,* Simon M. Lorne, The Portfolio Spin-off and Securities Registration, 52 Tex.L.Rev. 918 (1974).

48. 17 C.F.R. § 230.144. *Cf.* 17 C.F.R. § 230.145(d) (1982). *See* §§ 4.29, 5.2 *supra.*

49. 15 U.S.C.A. § 77b(11) which is discussed in § 4.27 *supra.* See, e.g., S.E.C. v. Lybrand, 200 F.Supp.2d 384, 393 (S.D.N.Y.2002) (sales of shares in spin-off transaction were neither protected by the § 4(1) exemption nor by Rule 144).

50. *Cf.* SEC v. Chinese Consolidated Benevolent Association, 120 F.2d 738 (2d Cir.1941), *cert. denied,* 314 U.S. 618, 62 S.Ct. 106, 86 L.Ed. 497 (1941).

51. *See* Consolidated Silver Standard Mines Ltd., 17 Sec.Reg. & L.Rep. (BNA) 2034 (SEC No Action Letter Oct. 30, 1985) (spin-off by Canadian corporation with only 3.2 percent of its shares held by 148 shareholders in the United States).

unregistered spin-off transactions is found in 1934 Act Rule 15c2–11, which makes it illegal for a broker to either initiate or continue to give price quotes for a security in the absence of adequate publicly available information.[52] This rule has the effect of preventing the creation of an informed public market with regard to any security.[53] Thus, for example, market makers cannot make a market in unregistered securities without adequate public information.[54]

The SEC's ability to require 1933 Act registration of spin-off transactions depends in large part upon whether the transaction results in the creation of a secondary market for shares that formerly did not exist. The distribution of a subsidiary's shares from the parent corporation to the shareholders of the parent corporation, standing alone, is not a sale. Accordingly, the corporation has not sold its shares to one of its shareholders who receives the shares directly in a spin-off transaction.[55] Since the shareholders of the parent corporation have no choice in the matter when they received the shares of the spun-off subsidiary, there is no investment decision to be made and, hence, no sale.[56] However, as pointed out above, when the spin-off transaction brings with it the likelihood of unregistered downstream sales by the shareholders receiving the shares that are spun off, it may well be necessary to register the transaction under the Securities Act of 1933, lest the transaction as a whole be considered an improper unregistered sale of securities.[57]

The SEC has eliminated the burden of registration for certain bona fide spin-offs so long as adequate information is provided to the public markets. In 1997, the SEC clarified its position on the applicability of the registration requirements to certain spin-off transactions.[58] The SEC staff has taken the position that 1933 Act registration will not be required for spin-off transactions that meet the following five conditions: (1) the stockholders of the parent corporation do not provide consideration for the shares being spun off, (2) the shares are spun off on a pro rata basis to the parent corporation's shareholders, (3) the parent corporation provides adequate information both to its shareholders and to the trading markets,[59] (4) the parent corporation has a valid business purpose for the spin-off transaction, and (5) in the event

---

52. *See* Evans & Sutherland Computer Corp., 26 Sec. Reg. & L. Rep. (BNA) 822 (SEC No Action Letter available May 23, 1994). *Accord* Pacific Telsis Group, 26 Sec. Reg. & L. Rep. (BNA) 267 (SEC No Action Letter available Feb. 14, 1994); ITT Corp., 26 Sec. Reg. & L. Rep. (BNA) 241 (SEC No Action Letter available February 3, 1994). *Cf.* Pacific Telesis Group, 26 Sec. Reg. & L. Rep. (BNA) 570 (SEC No Action Letter available April 1, 1994) (no action request granted as to odd lot purchase programs in connection with spin-off).

53. *E.g.,* Evans & Sutherland Computer Corp., 26 Sec. Reg. & L. Rep. (BNA) 822 (SEC No Action Letter available May 23, 1994); Ralston Purina Corp., 26 Sec. Reg. & L. Rep. (BNA) 527 (SEC No Action Letter available March 25, 1994).

54. *See* NASD Regulation, Inc., 32 Sec. Reg. & L. Rep. (BNA) 207 (SEC No Action Letter Jan. 21, 2000) (neither section 4(1) nor Rule 144's safe harbor was available to allow market makers to give quotes for unregistered "blank check" company).

55. *See* Isquith v. Caremark International, Inc., 136 F.3d 531 (7th Cir.1998).

56. 136 F.3d at 533.

57. Chugai Pharmaceutical Co., Ltd., 2002 WL 826918 (SEC No Action Letter April 30, 2002).

58. Legal Bulletin No. 4, Sec. L. Daily (BNA) (SEC Div. Corp. Fin. Sept. 17, 1997).

59. If the parent corporation is a 1934 Act reporting company, it can satisfy the informational requirement by providing essentially the same information that is required by Regulation 14A or Regulation 14C of the proxy rules. The proxy rules are discussed in Chapter 10 *infra*. In the event that the subsidiary being spun off has already been a reporting company for at least ninety days, then the information requirement is satisfied by providing stockholders with information regarding the distribution ratio, the treatment of fractional shares, and the spin-off transaction's expected tax consequences.

that the parent corporation is spinning off securities that are restricted within the context of SEC Rule 144, it must have held those securities for at least one year.[60] Under these circumstances, the Commission will thus permit the infusion of adequate information into the market without a formal 1933 Act registration.[61]

In the past, through its no-action letters, the SEC staff has taken the position that a spin-off requiring a shareholder vote to transfer assets to the subsidiary would require registration under 1933 Act Rule 145(a)(3). Where the parent corporation is the sole shareholder of a wholly owned subsidiary whose shares are to be spun off to the parent corporation's shareholders, the Commission no longer requires 1933 Act registration of the spin-off simply because a shareholder vote may be required for the transfer of assets to the subsidiary which is the first step of the planned transaction.

Another limitation on unregistered spin-offs is found in 1934 Act Rule 15c2–11, which makes it illegal for a broker to either initiate or continue giving price quotes for a security in the absence of adequate publicly available information.[62] This rule has the effect of preventing the creation of an uninformed public market with regard to any security.[63]

As the foregoing discussion makes clear, the problem created by unregistered spin-off transactions is the ability to effectuate a public distribution without adequate information being made available. Where adequate information is available, registration may not be required. Thus, the SEC staff has taken the position that registration of a spin-off is not necessary when the spin-off is accompanied by an information statement meeting the requirements of Regulation 14C of the Exchange Act,[64] provided that the spun-off shares are registered under section 12 of the Exchange Act.[65] The Exchange Act registration satisfies the public information requirement, as it subjects the issuer to that Act's periodic reporting requirements.[66]

The antifraud rules may also apply to spin-off transactions. However, the Seventh Circuit has held that a stockholder of a parent company who receives shares in a company that is spun off as a pro rata dividend cannot maintain an antifraud suit.[67] The court reasoned that, since the stockholders do not purchase the shares they receive as a dividend, they cannot satisfy Rule 10b–5's[68] purchaser/seller standing requirement.[69]

---

60. Rule 144, 17 C.F.R. § 230.144. Formerly there was a two-year holding period, but the Commission reduced this to one year. *See* § 4.29 *supra.*

61. *See, e.g.,* Isquith v. Caremark International, Inc., 136 F.3d 531, 533 (7th Cir.1998) (no action letter was issued permitting a spin-off without registration if the issuer filed an "information statement").

62. 17 C.F.R. § 240.15c2–11.

63. Regulation of broker-dealers is discussed in chapter 14 *infra.*

64. Regulation 14C is discussed in § 10.8 *infra.*

65. *See* Crane Co., 20 Sec.Reg. & L.Rep. (BNA) 1429 (SEC No Action Letter avail. Aug. 31 1988); Lydall, Inc., 20 Sec.Reg. & L.Rep. (BNA) 1427 (SEC No Action Letter avail. Aug. 25, 1988).

66. *See* §§ 9.2, 9.3 *infra.*

67. Isquith v. Caremark International, Inc., 136 F.3d 531 (7th Cir.1998).

68. 17 C.F.R. § 240.10b–5. *See* chapter 12 *infra.*

69. Isquith v. Caremark International, Inc., 136 F.3d 531 (7th Cir.1998). *See* § 12.7 *infra* for discussion of Rule 10b–5 standing.

§ 5.4   Periodic Payments; The Investment Decision Doctrine

Investments in securities typically require that the investor pay the consideration prior to receiving the securities. On occasion, however, payments are scheduled to be made on an installment basis.[1] In such instances, the question may arise as to when the sale takes place: at the time of the contract, or is there a new sale at the time of each payment? Determining whether an installment payment is a sale can implicate the 1933 Act's registration provisions. The identification of the sale date(s) has been significant primarily for statute of limitations purposes.[2] Determining whether an installment payment constitutes a sale depends on the definitions of purchase and sale. Ordinarily, installment payments will not involve multiple sales.[3]

---

§ 5.4

1. At times, this has been particularly common in the sale of certain limited partnership interests.

2. *See* § 7.10 *infra.*

3. However, a stated policy of not enforcing unpaid subscriptions or installments may lead to the conclusion that calls for additional payments will be treated as new sales. See, e.g., Goodman v. Epstein, 582 F.2d 388, 409–414 (7th Cir.1978), *cert. denied,* 440 U.S. 939, 99 S.Ct. 1289, 59 L.Ed.2d 499 (1979); Troyer v. Karcagi, 476 F.Supp. 1142, 1148 (S.D.N.Y.1979).

Chapter 6

IPO PRACTICES: MANIPULATION, STABILIZATION AND HOT ISSUES

Table of Sections

---

§ 6.1 Manipulation: An Overview

Securities that are offered to the public are sometimes subject to manipulation. The Securities Act of 1933 contains registration, disclosure, and antifraud provisions. That Act does not address aftermarket activities of securities offered under a 1933 Act registration statement. Market regulation generally is the province of the Securities Exchange Act of 1934.[1]

As discussed more fully in subsequent sections of this treatise,[2] there are a number of provisions of the Securities Exchange Act of 1934 which prohibit manipulative conduct in connection with securities trading. Section 9 of the Exchange Act[3] prohibits manipulative activity in connection with securities that are traded on a national securities exchange. Section 9(e) of the Exchange Act contains an express remedy[5] to redress damages incurred by investors who have been injured by illegal manipulative conduct with regard to those exchange-listed securities. Since it is limited by its terms to securities traded on a national exchange, section 9 does not apply to the vast number of securities traded in the over-the-counter markets. Nevertheless, there are parallel provisions that prohibit manipulation of over-the-counter securities.[6] However, unlike section 9(e), there is no express private remedy for such manipulative conduct.

---

§ 6.1

1. 15 U.S.C.A. §§ 78a *et. Seq.*

2. *See* §§ 6.1–6.3, 12.1, chapter 14 *infra.*

3. 15 U.S.C.A. § 78i. *See* § 12.1 *infra.*

5. 15 U.S.C.A. § 78i(e). *See* § 12.1 *infra.*

6. *See, e.g.,* Securities and Exchange Commission v. Resch–Cassin & Co., Inc., 362 F.Supp. 964, 975 (S.D.N.Y.1973) ("It is well settled that the manipulative activities expressly prohibited by § 9(a)(2) of the Exchange Act with respect to a listed security are also violations of § 17(a) of the Securities Act and § 10(b) of the Exchange Act when the same activities are conducted with respect to an over-the-counter security"). *See also* § 12.1[3][C] *infra.*

In contrast to section 9's narrower reach, section 10(b) of the Exchange Act[7] empowers the SEC to promulgate rules prohibiting manipulative and deceptive devices and contrivances in connection with purchases and sales of securities.[8] The only stated jurisdictional limitation on the section 10(b) rules is that the prohibited activity must occur "directly, or indirectly, by the use of any instrumentality of interstate commerce."[9] Under the terms of section 15(c)(1) of the Exchange Act,[10] the Commission is given the power to promulgate rules prohibiting brokers and dealers from engaging in "manipulative, deceptive, or otherwise fraudulent" devices and contrivances.[11]

The essence of securities manipulation is engaging in a transaction for the sole purpose of changing the market price of the stock or other security being manipulated. The Exchange Act's prohibitions against manipulation are designed to preclude artificial interferences with the operation of a free and open market. It is irrelevant that the conduct may be designed to help the market reflect the true value of the security. The fact that the alleged manipulator believes the stock is undervalued and is merely trying to correct market inaccuracies is neither an excuse for nor a defense to a charge of improper manipulative activity.[12] Thus, a successful government prosecution for manipulation does not depend on a showing that the price was actually driven above or below the security's fair value.[13] On the other hand, an investor who does not suffer a loss as a result of the manipulative conduct cannot maintain a private remedy, even though market manipulation has taken place.[14]

§ 6.2   Manipulation and Price Stabilization Involving Public Offerings

§ 6.2[1] Manipulation in Public Offerings

Both during and immediately after a public offering, the market is trying to digest the securities that are part of the new issue. In the after-market following an initial offering of securities, price fluctuations are common and there is the potential for price manipulation. As will be discussed in this section, under limited circumstances the issuer may artificially stabilize the price of the security being offered publicly. All other stabilizing activities that are not protected by SEC rules fall within the category of illegal manipulation.

Section 9 of the Securities Exchange Act of 1934[1] prohibits manipulative conduct relating to the trading of securities listed on a national exchange. Also, section 9(e) provides an express remedy in the hands of investors who are injured as a consequence of the illegal manipulation of the price of an

---

7.   15 U.S.C.A. § 78j(b).

8.   The section 10(b) rules are described in § 12.1[3][B] *infra*.

9.   15 U.S.C.A. § 78j(b).

10.   15 U.S.C.A. § 78*o*(c)(1).

11.   *See* § 12.1 *infra*.

12.   *See* United States v. Hall, 48 F.Supp.2d 386 (S.D.N.Y.1999).

13.   *See Id.*

14.   Gurary v. Winehouse, 190 F.3d 37 (2d Cir.1999), *affirmed in part, vacated in part on other grounds,* 235 F.3d 792 (2d Cir.2000).

§ 6.2

1.   15 U.S.C.A. § 78i.

exchange-traded security.[2] Furthermore, section 10(b) of the 1934 Act[3] specifically empowers the Commission to promulgate rules defining the scope of prohibited manipulative conduct with regard to any security. Problems of secondary distributions,[4] as well as primary offerings with a soft or unreceptive market, create a climate conducive to manipulative activity aimed at keeping the security's price at an artificially high level. Often a new issue will arrive and will be welcomed with a significantly higher demand than supply. This is known as a "hot issue." Hot issues are not necessarily the result of manipulation, although manipulative and deceptive sales practices can create the appearance of a bona fide hot issue. Hot issues occur when the demand for a new offering exceeds the supply of securities being offered for sale. Offerings that are legitimately hot issues present an environment conducive to manipulation.[6] Furthermore, manipulation can result in giving the appearance of a hot issue (or artificially heating up a bona fide hot issue) by artificially stimulating demand for the offering or by artificially restricting the supply of securities.

Section 9(a)(6) of the Exchange Act[8] specifically prohibits any transaction that is entered into for the purpose of "pegging, fixing, or stabilizing" the price of securities unless said transactions are in accordance with the procedures set out by applicable SEC rules.[9] In 1940, the Commission issued a Securities Act release[10] in which the Commission discussed the possible approaches to the stabilization problem. The SEC saw that it had three choices in approaching securities price stabilization: (1) the Commission could outlaw all stabilization activities by insiders; (2) it could take the other extreme and permit stabilizing transactions without any limitations; or (3) it could issue piecemeal regulation that would have the effect of prohibiting only detrimental stabilizing activity. The Commission opted for the third alternative and has continued to operate under a system of piecemeal regulation ever since.

Initial Public Offerings (or IPO's) are not the only public offerings that may present an environment that is conducive to manipulation. Frequently, issuers decide to raise new capital by selling additional securities of a class that is already publicly traded. The Commission has recognized that the natural effect of the influx of new stock on the market, unless a comparable demand is created, would necessarily be to deflate the market price, at least in the short term. Stabilizing activity is arguably necessary for some offerings in order to make the offering a viable one and to assure a greater degree of certainty in the amount of money that an issuer can expect to raise as a result of such a distribution. The Securities and Exchange Commission thus allows limited stabilizing activity in this type of situation. The stabilizing rules are highly complex in their attempt to permit only necessary activity without providing an avenue for otherwise illegal artificial price manipulation. A brief

---

2. 15 U.S.C.A. § 78i(e). *See* § 12.1[4][A] *infra.*

3. 15 U.S.C.A. § 78j(b). Section 10(b) also relates to antifraud protections and is the governing section for Rule 10b–5. *See* chapter 12 *infra.*

4. *See, e.g., In the Matter of Hazel Bishop Inc.,* 40 S.E.C. 718 (SEC 1961) which is discussed in § 4.28 *supra.*

6. Hot issues are discussed in § 6.2 *infra.*

8. 15 U.S.C.A. § 78k(a)(6).

9. For such a rule *see* Regulation M which is discussed in §§ 6.2[2]–6.2[8] *infra.*

10. Sec. Act Rel. No. 33–2446 (March 18, 1940).

description of the anti-manipulation rules is contained in the sections that follow.

In 1994, the Commission decided to undertake a review of the trading practices rules that had been in force for years.[11] The Commission thus solicited comments on what type of anti-manipulative trading rules are appropriate in the current state of the markets. The reexamination was prompted by recognition of differences in market structures and trading practices that have developed since the former regulatory scheme was adopted.[12]

§ 6.2[3] Regulation M—Scope of Rule 101

In general, Rule 101 prohibits distribution participants and their affiliated purchasers from bidding for purchasing—or attempting to induce any person to bid for or purchase—a covered security during a specified period (restricted period).[22] Rule 101 applies only to distribution participants[23] and their affiliated purchasers[24] in connection with a distribution of securities.

A distribution of securities under Regulation M is distinguished from ordinary trading transactions by the "magnitude of the offering" and the presence of "special selling efforts and selling methods."[29] The current rule thus is not limited to the types of distributions generally covered by the 1933 Act registration requirements. In exploring the magnitude of the purported distribution, the SEC looks at a number of factors, including the number of shares for sale, the trading volume that those shares represent, the percentage of outstanding shares, and the public float.[30] The amount of the shares being sold is not as significant as the percentage of the public float that the sales represent.[31] The concept of distribution is to be interpreted flexibly in order to permit the anti-manipulation rules "to evolve with changes in the practices and methods of offering securities."[32]

Under Regulation M, public offerings, private placements, shelf offerings, mergers and acquisitions, exchange offers, forced conversions of securities, warrant solicitations, and at-the-market offerings are distributions.[33] With respect to shelf offerings, the Commission has taken the view that each takedown off a shelf is to be individually examined to determine whether that particular offering constitutes a distribution.[34]

11. Review of Antimanipulation Regulation of Securities Offerings, Sec. Exch. Act Rel. No. 34–33924, 59 Fed. Reg. 21681, [1993–1994 Transfer Binder] Fed. Sec. L. Rep. (CCH) ¶ 85,335 (SEC April 26, 1994).

12. *Id.*

22. 17 C.F.R. § 242.101.

23. 17 C.F.R. § 242.100.

24. 17 C.F.R. § 242.100.

29. 17 C.F.R. § 242.100.

30. *See* Review of Antimanipulation Regulation of Securities Offerings, Sec. Act Rel. No. 33–7057, 56 S.E.C. Docket 1302, Release No. IS–657, 1994 WL 138672 (SEC April 19, 1994).

31. *See* Examination of the Registration of Securities To Be Offered and Sold on a Delayed or Continuous Basis in the Future, Sec. Act Rel. No. 33–6391, 24 S.E.C. Docket 1502, 1982 WL 35908 (SEC March 12, 1982).

32. *See* Review of Antimanipulation Regulation of Securities Offerings, Sec. Act Rel. No. 33–7057, 56 S.E.C. Docket 1302, Release No. IS–657, 1994 WL 138672 (SEC April 19, 1994).

33. Anti–Manipulation Rules Concerning Securities Offerings, SEC Rel. Nos. 33–7375; 34–38067; IC–22412, 62 Fed. Reg. 520, 526 (1997).

34. *See* Sec. Exch. Rel. No. 19565, 48 Fed. Reg. 10631.

The trading restrictions of Rule 101 cover securities which are either the subject of a distribution or reference securities.[35] Rule 100 sets forth the definitions that apply throughout Regulation M. Under Rule 100's definition, the term "reference security" is a security into which a subject security may be converted, exchanged, or exercised, or which, under the terms of the subject security, may in whole or in significant part determine the value of the subject security.[36] The anti-manipulative restrictions are effective only during the specifically defined restrictive period.[37] Depending on the average daily trading volume value[38] of the offered security and the public float value[39] of the issuer, the restricted period commences either one or five business days before the day of the pricing of the offering security and continues until the distribution is over.[40]

The Commodity Futures Modernization Act of 2000[41] permitted for the first time trading in security future products. The purchase of a security futures product when the underlying security is in distribution is covered by Regulation M.[42]

§ 6.2[4] Regulation M—Exclusions and Exemptions From Rule 101's Prohibitions

Rule 101 excludes from its coverage actively-traded securities.[43] The Commission believes that actively-traded securities are widely followed by the investment community, and thus aberrations in price are more likely to be discovered and quickly corrected. Moreover, actively-traded securities are generally traded on exchanges or other organized markets with high levels of transparency and surveillance.[44] The rule also excludes investment rated

---

35. 17 C.F.R. § 242.101.

36. 17 C.F.R. § 242.100.

37. 17 C.F.R. § 242.101(a).

38. The average daily trade volume (ADTV) of a covered security is defined on the basis of reported worldwide average daily trading volume during a specified period prior to the filing of the registration statement or prior to the pricing of the offering, depending on the circumstances. *See* Anti-manipulation Rules Concerning Securities Offerings, SEC Rel. Nos. 33–7375; 34–38067; IC–22412 (Dec. 20, 1996), 62 Fed. Reg. 520, 546 (1997).

39. As for public float value, the Commission adopted a definition that reflects its usage in Form 10–K (i.e., the aggregate amount of common equity securities held by non-affiliates). 17 C.F.R. § 249.310. *See also* Sec. Act Rel. No. 7326 (Aug. 30, 1996), 61 Fed. Reg. 47706 (1996).

40. 17 C.F.R. § 242.100. The restricted period means: (1) for any security with an ADTV value of $100,000 or more of an issuer whose common equity securities have a public float value of $25 million or more, the period begins on the later of one business day prior to the determination of the offering price or such time that a person becomes a distribution participant, and ends upon such person's completion of participation in the distribution; and (2) for all other securities, the period begins on the later of five business days prior to the determination of the offering price or such time that a person becomes a distribution participant and ends upon such person's participation of the distribution. In case of a distribution involving a merger, acquisition, or exchange offer, the period begins on the day proxy solicitation or offering materials are first disseminated to security holders and till the completion of the distribution.

41. Pub. Law No. 106–554, 114 Stat. 2763 (Dec. 21, 2000).

42. *See* Commission Guidance on the Application of Certain Provisions of the Securities Act of 1933, the Security Exchange Act of 1934, and Rules Thereunder to Trading in Security Futures Products, Sec. Act Rel. No. 33–8107, Sec. Exch. Act Rel. No. 34–46101, 67 Fed. Reg. 43233, 2002 WL 1377488 (SEC June 27, 2002).

43. Actively-traded securities are those with an ADTV value of at least $1 million that are issued by an issuer whose common equity securities have a public float value of at least $150 million. 17 C.F.R. § 242.101(c)(1).

44. *See* Anti-Manipulation Rules Concerning Securities Offering, SEC Rel. Nos. 33–7375; 34–38067; IC–22412 (Dec. 20, 1996), 62 Fed. Reg. 520, 527 (1997).

nonconvertible and asset backed securities;[45] "exempted securities" as defined in Section 3(a)(12) of the Exchange Act;[46] and face-amount certificates of securities issued by an open-end management investment company or unit investment trust.[47]

In addition to allowing permissible stabilizing activity under certain circumstances, which is discussed below,[48] Rule 101 provides a list of transactions to which the rule's prohibitions do not apply.[49]

§ 6.2[5] Regulation M—Scope of Rule 102

Rule 102 is similar in format to Rule 101: issuers and selling security holders, and their affiliated purchasers,[65] must refrain from bidding for, purchasing, or attempting to induce any person to bid for or purchase a covered security during the applicable restrictive period, unless an exception permits the activity.[66] The restrictive period is subject to the same definition that is applicable to Rule 101 as proscribed by the definition section of Regulation M. The Commission affords fewer exceptions in Rule 102 than in Rule 101 because issuers and selling security holders have the greatest interest in an offering's outcome, and generally do not have the same market access needs as underwriters.[67] The underwriters have the responsibility of bringing the securities public and also may be involved in other securities transactions which requires them to purchase securities while the offering is taking place. In contrast, the issuer and selling shareholders can simply refrain from purchasing securities until the distribution is complete.

§ 6.2[7] Regulation M—Scope of Permissible Stabilizing Activity

Rule 104 of Regulation M[84] sets forth the parameters of permissible stabilizing activity to prevent or retard a decline in the market price of a security and thus to facilitate an offering.[86] To begin with, both the possibility and existence of stabilizing activity must be disclosed to any purchaser prior to completion of each transaction.[87] An issuer may satisfy the notice to the purchaser requirement by placing a legend on the inside front cover of the prospectus.[88] Furthermore, any person who enters a bid for the purpose of stabilizing the price of any security shall notify the market on which the bid is placed and disclose the purpose of such bid to the person with whom the bid is entered.[89] Also, any person effecting a syndicate covering transaction,[90] or

---

45. 17 C.F.R. § 242.101(c)(2).

46. 17 C.F.R. § 242.101(c)(3).

47. 17 C.F.R. § 242.101(c)(4).

48. 17 C.F.R. § 242.104.

49. 17 C.F.R. § 242.101(b).

65. 17 C.F.R. § 242.100.

66. 17 C.F.R. § 242.102(a).

67. *See* Anti–Manipulation Rules Concerning Securities Offerings, SEC Rel. Nos. 33–7375; 34–38067; IC–22412 (Dec. 20, 1996), 62 Fed. Reg. 520, 530 (1997).

84. 17 C.F.R. § 242.104.

86. 17 C.F.R. § 242.104.

87. 17 C.F.R. § 242.104(h).

88. 17 C.F.R. § 242.104(h)(3).

89. 17 C.F.R. § 242.104(h)(1).

90. 17 C.F.R. § 242.100. A syndicate covering transaction is the placing of any bid or the effecting of any purchase on behalf of the sole distributor or the underwriting syndicate or group to reduce a syndicate short position.

placing a penalty bid[91] shall disclose that fact to the self-regulatory organization that has direct oversight authority over the principal market in the United States.[92] Additionally, anyone subject to Rule 104 is required to keep the information of stabilizing activity for a period of three years.[93]

In addition to the above disclosure requirement, the SEC regulates the mechanics of all legitimate stabilizing activity. Participants in a distribution may engage in stabilizing activity only to the extent the stabilizing activity complies with Rule 104. Under the rule, no stabilizing bid may be higher than the lower of the offering price or the stabilizing bid for the security in the principal market.[94] The rule strictly regulates the first stabilizing bid made in connection with the offering.[95] Once a stabilizing bid has been initiated,[96] it may be increased, maintained, reduced, or adjusted in accordance with the provisions of the rule.[97]

In adopting the anti-manipulation rules, the Commission was aware of the additional risks of price manipulation that can be associated with "at market" offerings.[98] Most securities offerings are marketed through a fixed price that is fixed before the offering commences. In contrast, in an at market offering, rather than the issuer setting a predetermined offering price prior to the commencement of the offering, the securities are offered with a fluctuating price to be determined by the market price for securities of the same class that are already traded. Thus, each sale in an at market offering will be the then prevailing market price rather than at a price fixed before the offering commenced. As was the case with the former Rule 10b–7, Regulation M's Rule 104 expressly prohibits all stabilizing activity with regard to any offering of securities at the market[99] as opposed to a fixed price offering.

§ 6.2[8] Regulation M—Manipulative Short Sales, Rule 105

Rule 105 is intended to prevent manipulative short selling prior to a public offering by short sellers who cover their short positions by purchasing securities in the offering, thus largely avoiding exposure to market risk.[107]

91. 17 C.F.R. § 242.100. Rule 100 defines penalty bid to mean an arrangement that permits the managing underwriter to reclaim a selling concession otherwise accruing to a syndicate member in connection with an offering when the securities originally sold by the syndicate member are purchased in syndicate covering transactions.

92. 17 C.F.R. § 242.104(h)(2).

93. 17 C.F.R. § 242.104(i). Rule 17a–2(c)(1) sets forth the three-year period. Amendments to Rule 17a–2 under the Exchange Act require managing underwriters to keep records of syndicate covering transactions and penalty bids, in addition to stabilizing information. 17 C.F.R. § 240.17a–2.

94. 17 C.F.R. § 242.104(f).

95. *Id.*

96. Rule 104 also includes a provision for initiating a stabilizing bid in any market immediately before the opening of quotations. In this case, stabilizing may be initiated with reference to the lower of: the price at which stabilizing could have been initiated in the principal market at its previous close; or the most recent price at which an independent transaction in the offered security has been effected in any market after the close of the principal market, if the person stabilizing knows or has reason to know of such transaction. 17 C.F.R. § 242.104(f)(2)(ii)(A).

97. 17 C.F.R. § 242.104(f)(3), (4), (5), (6).

98. *See, e.g.,* In the Matter of Hazel Bishop Inc., 40 S.E.C. 718 (SEC 1961).

99. 17 C.F.R. § 242.104(e).

107. 17 C.F.R. § 242.105.

Such short sale could result in a lower offering price and reduce an issuer's proceeds.[108] Under the rule, certain short sales are prohibited from being covered with securities offered by an underwriter, broker, or dealer participating in the offering. Rule 105 covers those short sales effected in the period commencing five business days prior to the offering's pricing and ending with such pricing.[109]

Rule 105 does not apply to short sales of derivative securities in accordance with the general approach of Regulation M.[110] The Commission may, either upon request or upon its own motion, grant an exemption from Rule 105's prohibitions.[113] Such an exemption from the short sale prohibition may be granted either unconditionally or pursuant to specified terms and conditions.[114] In 2004, the SEC adopted a comprehensive regulation of short sales in Regulation SHO.[115] At the same time, the SEC issued interpretive guidance on the application of Regulation M's Rule 105 to short sales.[116] It also amended Rule 105 to eliminate the exemption for shelf offerings.[117]

§ 6.3   Aftermarket Activities, IPO Practices, Hot Issues, Workout Markets, and Controlled Markets

Setting the initial offering price for securities in a public offering can be a difficult task. If the securities are overpriced, the offering will not succeed, since there will be no demand for the supply offered at the excessive price. As discussed in the preceding section[1] of this treatise, even well-priced offerings can be met with a soft reception if the market cannot absorb all of the securities offered at once. In such a case, some of the offering will be sold but part of the initial allotment will remain unsold. Frequently in such a case, the securities will then trade in the after market at a price below the offering price because of the excess supply from the unsold initial allotment that is hanging over the market. In such an environment, it may take time for the entire initial allotment to be sold. Also, as discussed in the preceding section[2] of this treatise, under certain circumstances and subject to specified safeguards, price stabilization may be permitted in order to facilitate a smoother initial offering.[3]

The desire to raise the capital targeted by an initial public offering creates an incentive to not overprice the securities being offered lest there be

---

108. *See* the discussion on short sales in § 14.22 *infra*.

109. 17 C.F.R. § 242.105(a).

110. The Commission is satisfied that any manipulative short sales involving derivative transactions continue to be addressed by the general anti-manipulation provisions, including Section 9(a)(2) of and Rule 10b–5 under the Exchange Act. *See* Anti-manipulation Rules Concerning Securities Offerings, SEC Rel. Nos. 33–7375; 34–38067; IC–22412 (Dec. 20, 1996), 62 Fed. Reg. 520, 538 (1997).

113. 17 C.F.R. § 242.105(c).

114. *Id.*

115. *See* Short Sales, Sec. Exch. Act Rel. No. 34–50103, 2004 WL 1697019 (SEC 2004) (adoption of Regulation SHO).

116. *See id.*

117. *See id.* Shelf offerings are discussed in § 3.11 *supra*.

§ 6.3

1. *See* § 6.2 *supra*.

2. *See* 6.2[7] *supra*.

3. *See* Rule 104 of Regulation M, 17 C.F.R. § 242.104.

a cool reception in the market. As discussed in a subsequent section[4] of this treatise, one possible response to the fear of not raising sufficient funds is to condition the offering on a certain number of shares being sold. In these part-or-none or all-or-none offerings, the offering will be cancelled unless the issuer and underwriters are able to sell the minimum number of shares specified. These conditional offerings present special disclosure problems as well as the increased temptation for manipulation.[5]

The incentive not to overprice the securities being offered will often result in an offering where the initial demand exceeds the supply of shares covered by the initial offering. In such a case, the trading in the aftermarket will be at a price that exceeds the initial offering price. The benefit of the increased aftermarket price does not inure directly to the issuer but rather results in profits for the selling shareholders.

Pricing of offerings is thus a very difficult task. Overpricing will result in a poor reception or even a failed offering. Underpricing will not only result in a hot issue, it will create questions as to whether the company's management could have raised more capital. In an extreme case, significant underpricing could lead to a claim by preexisting shareholders that management breached their duty of care in pricing the shares. Thus, there is pressure not to underprice the securities being offered. At the same time, there are pressures in the other direction. The fear of a failed or unsuccessful offering is so strong that it pushes management in the direction of conservative pricing. Further-more, even if the market takes the securities at a high initial price, declines in the aftermarket can lead to suits by investors claiming that the initial offering was overpriced and that the offering materials were materially misleading in violation of the securities laws. The mechanics of pricing go beyond the scope of this treatise but the reader should keep in mind that this is as much an art as a science.

Just as stabilization can become a problem in securities offerings that appear in a soft market,[7] there are manipulation temptations that can arise in a bull market for the securities in distribution. When the offering is oversub-scribed, there is frequently little doubt that once the stock begins to trade publicly in the aftermarket it will exceed the original offering price. In the case of such a "hot issue" there is great potential for abuse. There may also be the temptation to create the appearance of a hot issue in order to create additional buying demand and upward price pressure.

In 1959, the Commission conducted and issued a study dealing with price increases that were found to have occurred immediately following certain public registered offerings.[9] The Commission's study found that a number of undesirable practices were taking place. In many cases, the underwriter would allot a portion of the registered offering to active trading firms which were not members of the selling group. These firms would in turn make a market for the securities contemporaneously with the public offering. In one case cited by the SEC study, a security that was initially offered at three dollars per share was selling for as much as five to seven dollars by the end of the first day following the offer.

---

4. *See* § 6.4 *infra.*

5. *See Id.*

7. *See* § 6.2[7] *supra.*

9. Sec. Act. Rel. No. 33–4150 (Oct. 23, 1959).

Not all abusive activities during a hot issue are based on price manipulation. For example, another practice identified by the Commission was for underwriters to allot portions of the securities in registration to their partners, officers, employees, and relatives in anticipation of a "hot issue" and quick profit in the stock.

The Commission went on to point out a number of the legal consequences of such activities. In the first instance, any arrangements regarding workouts, special allotments of securities or the creation of trading firms to be used as market makers must be disclosed in detail on the registration statement. Second, any trading firms would clearly fall within the category of "underwriter" within the meaning of section 2(a)(11).[10] Third, also involved would be violations of the Act's antifraud provisions. Specifically, Rule 10b–5 of the Exchange Act[11] and section 17(a) of the 1933 Act[12] would be violated in that the activities would be giving the public the impression that the entire offering has been subscribed to by the public when, in fact, a substantial portion has gone either to insiders or to trading firms.[13] Fourth, these types of workout activities would also violate Regulation M's prohibitions on manipulation which expressly forbid an underwriter or participant in a distribution from bidding for or purchasing securities being distributed. Fifth, the SEC has pointed out that a broker/dealer acting as a trading firm would in all likelihood be in violation of Rule 15c1–8[15] which prohibits sales on the market of securities in distribution. A sixth consequence is that any participating broker/dealer would be subject to possible sanctions imposed by the Commission, a stock exchange, or National Association of Securities Dealers.[16] The SEC has expressed the opinion that current regulation is adequate to curb abuses in connection with hot issues.[17]

Another problem associated with hot issues is the practice of "free riding" whereby a subscriber to the offering hopes to resell at a premium but plans to withdraw the order if the "temperature seems to go down before allotment."[18] Free riding clearly falls within the purview of manipulative conduct.[19] Free riding as manipulative and deceptive conduct is not limited to new offerings. Illegal free riding takes place any time a purchaser of securities does not have the funds to pay for the purchase but rather intends to take a "free ride" on the securities purchased.[20] For example, investors who open

---

10. 15 U.S.C.A. § 77b(a)(11).

11. 17 C.F.R. § 240.10b–5. *See* chapter 12 *infra*.

12. 15 U.S.C.A. § 77(a). *See* §§ 7.11, 12.22 *infra*.

13. Sec. Act Rel. No. 33–4150 (Oct. 23, 1959).

15. 17 C.F.R. § 240.15c1–8.

16. *See* NASD Interpretation with Respect to "Free–Riding and Withholding," NASD Manual (CCH) ¶ 2151.06. *See also, e.g.,* SEC Approves Proposed Changes to NASD Rule Relating to "Hot Issues," 26 Sec. Reg. & L. Rep. (BNA) 1709 (Dec. 23, 1994).

17. No Need for Hot Issues Market Rules, SEC Tells Congress, 16 Sec.Reg. & L.Rep. (BNA) 1446 (Aug. 28, 1984).

18. " 'Free riding' is the practice whereby a stock is purchased without sufficient funds available to pay for it, the stock is sold prior to the settlement date of the purchase, and the proceeds of the sale are used to pay for the original purchase." In the Matter of Account Management Corp., Admin. Proc. File No. 3–8857; Sec. Exch. Act Rel. No. 34–36314, 60 S.E.C. Docket 962, 1995 WL 579449 footnote 6 (SEC Sept. 29, 1995), relying on United States v. Tager, 788 F.2d 349, 350 (6th Cir.1986).

19. *See, e.g.,* L.H. Alton v. SEC, 229 F.3d 1156 (9th Cir.2000) (table, text in Westlaw) (upholding SEC sanctions for free riding and hot issue violations).

20. *See, e.g.,* A.T. Brod & Co. v. Perlow, 375 F.2d 393 (2d Cir.1967).

accounts and misrepresent their net worth to a number of brokerage firms and then purchase securities without sufficient funds for payment have engaged in illegal free riding.[21] It is not uncommon to use nominee accounts to hide the true identity of the securities owners in order to facilitate a free riding scheme.[22]

Complicity by a brokerage firm in a free riding scheme is a violation of the securities laws. Thus, for example, criminal prosecutions have resulted from a brokerage firm's policy of selling IPOs to friends and celebrities and then buying those shares at a premium before reselling them to members of the public at an inflated price.[23] There have been numerous regulatory concerns over IPO allocation policies generally. Investigations have been launched into the allocation policies of many major investment banks and rulemaking is likely to follow. In fact, the NASD proposed new rules to define improper IPO practices. Following the NASD rule proposals, the SEC chairman called upon the NASD and the stock exchanges to undertake a comprehensive review of IPO practices including allocation practices as well as the roles of issuers and underwriters in price setting and the offering process in general. Although the NASD rules explicitly list types of improper IPO conduct, the conduct so described was already impermissible under the antifraud and anti-manipulation provisions.[27]

In its free riding and withholding interpretation, the NASD identifies several categories of "restricted person" who cannot receive securities during a hot issue.[28] The list of restricted persons includes, among others, any officer, director, general partner, employee, or agent of a broker-dealer or their family members, or a senior officer or certain specified employees of certain institutional investors.[29] The NASD disqualification of restricted persons "ensures that NASD members and their associated persons make bona-fide distributions to the public of securities that are part of a public offering."[30] The NASD interpretation is meant to prevent artificial restrictions on the supply of hot issue offerings.[31]

The NASD free riding and withholding interpretation is prophylactic in nature and has been held not to require a showing of scienter.[32] The NASD

21. *E.g.*, SEC v. Teyibo, 1993 WL 144859, [1992–1993 Transfer Binder] Fed.Sec.L.Rep. (CCH) & 97,405 (D.Md.1993) (illegal free-riding in U.S. Treasury bonds).

22. *See, e.g.*, In the Matter of H.J. Meyers & Co., Administrative Proceeding File No. 3–9754, Sec. Act Rel. No. 33–7694, 70 S.E.C. Docket 74, 1999 WL 436513 (SEC June 30, 1999).

23. People v. Schwartz, 34 Sec.Reg. & L.Rep. 532 (N.Y.Sup.Ct. March 8, 2002) (guilty pleas entered; $21 million in restitution ordered).

27. The North Americana Securities Administrators Association issued a comment that the NASD's proposals on IPO practices did not do much more than restate existing law. NASAA Letter of Comment, http://www.nasaa.org/nasaa/Files/ File_Uploads/NASDIPO.37523–63215.pdf (Sept. 23, 2002).

28. NASD Rule Interpretation IM–2110–1.

29. Id.

30. In the Matter of Crute, Admin. Proc. File No. 3–9428, Sec. Exch. Act Rel. No. 34–40474, 68 S.E.C. Docket 118, 68 S.E.C. Docket 123, 1998 WL 652110 (SEC Sept. 24, 1998), relying on Sherman, Fitzpatrick & Co. Inc., 51 S.E.C. 1048, 1054 (1994).

31. In the Matter of Crute, Admin. Proc. File No. 3–9428, Sec. Exch. Act Rel. No. 34–40474, 68 S.E.C. Docket 118, 68 S.E.C. Docket 123, 1998 WL 652110 (SEC Sept. 24, 1998), relying on First Philadelphia Corp., 50 S.E.C. 360, 361 (1990).

32. In the Matter of Crute, Admin. Proc. File No. 3–9428, Sec. Exch. Act Rel. No. 34–40474, 68 S.E.C. Docket 118, 68 S.E.C. Docket 123, 1998 WL 652110 (SEC Sept. 24, 1998), relying on First Philadelphia Corp., 50 S.E.C. 360, 361 (1990).

interpretation also is designed to prevent withholding. Withholding securities from the market restricts supply and thus places upward pressure on the price of the new issue.[33] Preventing withholding of securities from the market is designed to ensure "that public customers who want to purchase them will not be forced to acquire them in the aftermarket at a higher price."[34]

Although firms are given considerable leeway in how they allocate IPO's, there are limits. Thus, for example, requiring the customer turn over a share of their trading profits in exchange for the allocation clearly is illegal.[39] Nor is it permissible to repurchase the securities of selected customers receiving shares from an IPO at a predetermined price before reselling those shares to members of the public.[40]

There are other prohibited manipulative practices that can occur in connection with hot issues. For example, a brokerage firm might unduly encourage its registered representatives to encourage customer purchases by giving sales people a higher commission for transactions where the customer purchases rather than sells the securities in question. Especially if undisclosed to the customer, this type of compensation for trades encourages the creation of more purchases than sales. Another practice is to pre-sell the offering in the after-market.[42] Under this manipulation, registered representatives (and in some cases unregistered sales personnel) require or encourage customers to commit to purchasing shares in the after market in order to get part of the allotment out of the original issue. This, of course, generates additional aftermarket buying activity that is manipulative, in that it is designed to push the price higher once the security comes to market. Thus, soliciting offers before the offering takes place can be part of such a manipulation[44] as can taking aftermarket orders before the offering takes place.[45] In addition, combining a public offering with "boiler room" or other improper high pressure sales tactics[46] are manipulative, as they precondition the aftermarket following an initial offering.[47] For example, generating bids during a distribution is manipulative.[48] A somewhat related aftermarket practice that has been challenged is requiring "tie-in" purchases by institutional investors and thereby conditioning their participating in the IPO on an agreement to

---

33. Withholding is manipulative in any market since it keeps the securities at an artificially high price by arterially restricting supply.

34. In the Matter of Sherman, Fitzpatrick & Co., Admin. Proc. File No. 3–7878, 51 S.E.C. 1048, Sec. Exch. Act Rel. No. 34–33923, 56 S.E.C. Docket 1356, 1994 WL 148475 (SEC. April 19, 1994).

39. *See, e.g.,* SEC Charges CSFB with Abusive IPO Allocation Practices; CSFB Will PAY $100 Million TO Settle SEC and NASD Actions; Millions in IPO Profits Extracted From Customers in Exchange for Allocations in "Hot" Deals SEC News Digest 2002–14, 2002 WL 77626 (Jan. 22, 2002).

40. *See* People v. Wood (N.Y.Sup.Ct. March 8, 2002) (guilty pleas entered).

42. *See, e.g.,* NASDR, Disciplinary Actions Reported for April, 1999 WL 33176514 * 16 (NASDR April 1999).

44. *See, e.g.,* SEC v. Bouchy, Civ–96–2629–phx-srb, Litigation Release No. 16943, 2001 WL 286253 (D. ARIZ. March 23, 2001).

45. *See, e.g.,* In the Matter of A.S. Goldmen & Co., 2001 WL 588039 *8, Sec. Exch. Act Rel. No. 34–44328 (SEC May 21, 2001).

46. Boiler rooms and high pressure sales tactics are discussed in § 14.18 *infra*.

47. *See, e.g.,* SEC v. Madden, CV 00 3632, Litigation Release No. 16600, 72 S.E.C. Docket 1801, 2000 WL 781334 (E.D.N.Y. June 20, 2000).

48. *See, e.g.,* In re Schatzer, 1995 WL 560153 (SEC initiation of proceedings Sept. 22, 1995).

purchase in the aftermarket at higher prices.[49] These types of tie-in agreements violate Regulation M's prohibitions against manipulation during public offerings.[50]

Another IPO-related manipulation is for participants in the offering to repurchase in the aftermarket at a premium in order to drive the market price up further.[51] Also, parking[52] part of the public offering[53] with nominees in order to take advantage of the hot issue aftermarket is a manipulative practice.[55]

Yet another improper sales practice associated with hot issues is offering sales personnel extra commissions for generating customer purchases of the securities being offered.[56] Along similar lines, offering high compensation to underwriters can be indicative of improper IPO selling efforts.[57] Manipulative activity in connection with IPOs is a serious matter and can run result in significant criminal consequences.[58]

Although the Commission prohibits withholding securities from the market as well as channeling securities to relatives of the issuer, underwriters and participating dealers, there is no express limitation on dealers' showing favoritism towards certain customers. For example, although a brokerage firm's method of allocating securities during a hot issue might be "unfair" in terms of parity among its customers, so long as the stock does not go to a select group of insiders, there is no violation of the securities laws' hot issue prohibitions.[66] As a result of these and other ways in which firms favor their larger customers, most investors do not have access to hot issues in the new issues market. Requiring customers to give a quid pro quo for IPO allocations violates the antifraud provisions.[67] This includes tie-in or "laddering" arrangements that require IPO purchasers to commit to purchasing additional

---

49. *See* Billing v. Credit Suisse First Boston Corp., 33 Sec. Reg. & L. Rep. (BNA) 309 (S.D.N.Y. 2001) (antitrust suit charging illegal tie-in arrangements in connection with IPOs).

50. Prohibited Solicitations and "Tie-in" Agreements for Aftermarket Purchases, Staff Legal Bull. No. 10, http://www.sec.gov/interps/legal/slbmr10.htm (SEC Div. Market Reg. Aug. 25, 2001).

51. *See, e.g.,* In the Matter of Ackerly, S.E.C. 95–163, 1995 WL 471111 (SEC Aug. 10, 1995) (order instituting proceedings); In the Matter R.B. Webster Investments, Inc., Admin. Proc. File No. 3–8113, 51 S.E.C. 1269, Sec. Exch. Act Rel. No. 34–34659, 57 S.E.C. Docket 1494, 1994 WL 512475 (SEC Sept. 13, 1994).

52. Parking is discussed in § 14.23 *infra*.

53. *See, e.g.,* In the Matter of Salloum, Administrative Proceeding File No. 3–7402, Sec. Exch. Act Rel. No. 34–35563, 59 S.E.C. Docket 39, 1995 WL 215268 (SEC April 5, 1995).

55. *See, e.g.,* SEC v. Lavigne, 00–CV–6024, Litigation Release No. LR–16788, 2000 WL 1643954 (E.D.N.Y. Nov. 2, 2000).

56. Offering such specials violates NASD rules even outside of the context of a public offering. *See* In the Matter of Josephthal & Co., 33 Sec. Reg. & L. Rep. (BNA) 799 (NASDR May 22, 2001).

57. In the Matter of A.S. Goldmen & Co., 2001 WL 588039 *6, Sec. Exch. Act Rel. No. 34–44328 (SEC May 21, 2001) ("Providing greater than normal sales compensation arrangements pertaining to the distribution of a security is indicative of special selling efforts and selling methods").

58. For example, in one instance manipulations which included artificial hot issues resulted in convictions under state racketeering laws. *See* A.S. Goldmen Trial Brings Guilty Verdicts For Firm and Officials, Wall. St. J. , 2001 WLBWSJ 2870494 (July 24, 2001); Gina Edwards, A.S. Goldmen Trial: Jury Finds Marchianos, Firm Guilty of Racketeering, Other Crimes, Naples Daily News, *http://www.naplesnews.com/01/07/naples/d649382a.htm* (July 24, 2001).

66. *See, e.g.,* In the Matter of Institutional Securities of Colorado, SEC Admin. Proc. File No. 3–5104 (March 8, 1977).

67. *See* Lincolnshire L.P. v. Essex, LLC, 244 F.Supp.2d 912 (N.D.Ill. 2002).

shares in the after market.[68] The existing rules and regulations thus clearly prohibit this practice. Any additional rules that may be adopted to directly address tying or laddering would simply be clarifying existing law rather than introducing some new prohibitions.

At times when the new issues markets are active, some brokerage firms have opted to allocate scarce issues only to those customers who commit to a certain amount of IPO purchases each year. Another development has been underwriters setting aside stock from new issues for the accounts of customers who can direct additional new issue business to the underwriters.[69] The NASD has advised its members that this practice, referred to as "spinning"[70] or "flipping,"[71] may violate NASD rules.[72]

The Commission has held it to be unlawful for a participating dealer or underwriter to turn away subscribers to a new issue while at the same time soliciting purchasers for the unsold allotment.[104] This practice of turning away bona fide offers to purchase gives the appearance of a receptive market or even a "hot issue" since it leads the investor to believe that the offering is oversubscribed when, in fact, securities that represented part of the original allotment are still being peddled.[105] This improper withholding of securities to be offered is known as a "workout" market in which the underwriter and/or

---

68. *See, e.g.*, In re Initial Public Offering Securities Litigation, 241 F.Supp.2d 281 (S.D.N.Y. 2003) (upholding complaint challenging this practice). This is also known as pre-selling the aftermarket. In addition to the antifraud and anti-manipulation implications, pre-selling the aftermarket violates section 5 of the 1933 Act insofar as the customer is asked to commit to purchase the securities prior to the date on which the offering becomes effective. The operation of section 5 is discussed in chapter 2 *supra*.

69. *See* Michael Siconofoli, Underwriters Set Aside IPO Stock for Officials of Potential Customers, Wall St. J. p. A1, col. 6 (Tues. Nov. 12, 1997). *Cf.* In re Monetta Financial Services, Inc., Admin. Proc. File No. 3–9546, 32 Sec. Reg. & L. Rep. (BNA) 434, 2000 WL 320457 (SEC 2000) (investment adviser fined for allocating shares of hot IPOs to directors of a mutual fund client; the SEC alleged that the shares were allocated in exchange for future brokerage business that might be generated by the investment adviser's clients).

70. Therese H. Maynard, Spinning in a Hot IPO—Breach Of Fiduciary Duty or Business as Usual?, 43 Wm and Mary L. Rev. 2023 (2002).

71. " 'Flipping' is the practice of buying a 'hot issue' and then selling it within a short period of time into a rising market, earning a quick profit on the transactions." In the Matter of Account Management Corp., Admin. Proc. File No. 3–885; Sec. Exch. Act Rel. No. 34–36314, 60 S.E.C. Docket 962, 1995 WL 579449 footnote 3 (SEC Sept. 29, 1995). *See also, e.g.,* Royce de R Barondes, Adequacy of Disclosure on Restrictions on Flipping IPO Securities, 74 Tulane L. Rev. 883 (2000). *Cf.* Sanders v. Gardner, 7 F.Supp.2d 151 (E.D.N.Y. 1998) (affirming arbitration award based in part on manipulative flipping in connection with IPO).

72. *See* NASD Sends Members Warning Concerning Allocation of Hot IPO's, 29 Sec. Reg. & L. Rep. (BNA) 1667 (Dec. 5, 1997). Spinning involves diverting hot issues to venture capitalists and/or executives of companies who have the potential of directing their company's future offerings to the underwriters. Flipping occurs when it is anticipated that the purchasers of the shares so allocated will be taking a free ride on the hot issue. *Id.* The NASD announced that diversion of hot issues to venture capitalists may be justified only if the underwriter can establish: (1) "that the securities were sold to such persons in accordance with their normal investment practice," (2) "that the aggregate of the securities so sold is insubstantial and not disproportionate in amount as compared to sales to members of the public," and (3) "that the amount sold to any such persons is insubstantial in amount." *Id.*

104. In the Matter of Shearson, Hammill & Co., 42 S.E.C. 811 (SEC 1965). *Cf.* Eichler v. SEC, 757 F.2d 1066 (9th Cir.1985) (sanctioning brokers for failing to fill orders from aftermarket in issue that broker had underwritten).

105. *Cf.* Brogren v. Pohlad, 960 F.Supp. 1401 (D.Minn.1997) (giving the appearance of a more active market than exists can be actionable under rule 10b–5).

the issuer as a result of manipulative transactions are giving the appearance of a market that does not conform to reality. Workout tactics involve not only violations of the anti-manipulation provisions,[106] but also give rise to violations of the antifraud provisions.

All or none offerings, present an environment that is particularly conducive to manipulative activity.[110] For example, it is improper for a broker participating in an "all or none" or "part or none" offering to accept customer funds unless it promptly transmits those funds to an escrow agent or other entity.[111] The prompt transmission requirement is designed to safeguard the customer's right to a quick refund in the event that the offering contingency is not met. Manipulation is not the only issue, as disclosure problems can also occur in connection with "part or none," or "mini max" offerings as they are sometimes called.[112] In such offerings, the offering materials must accurately disclose the material aspects of any "all or none" or "part or none" conditions.

Other manipulative practices, that are not limited to new issues, occur in the context of controlled markets. This happens when a security has only one active market maker or multiple market makers[113] act in collusion to artificially control the market. Generically referred to as "house stocks,"[114] securities in controlled markets are particularly susceptible to manipulation.[115] Whether or not the market for a particular security is in actuality a controlled market is a question of fact.[116] An underwriter's control over the market is not in itself a violation of the Act.[117] However, it violates the antifraud provisions to fail to disclose control over the market for securities handled by the market-maker and broker-dealer in question.[118] Another manipulative practice is to

106. Sections 9, 10(b) and 15(c), 15 U.S.C.A. §§ 78i, 78j(b), 78o(c). *See* § 12.1 *infra. Cf.* SEC v. Sayegh, 906 F.Supp. 939 (S.D.N.Y.1995) (trader whose firm was market maker violated Rule 10b–5 by consistently posting high bids and entering into cross trades for the purpose of creating the illusion of an active market).

110. *See* Rule 10b–9, 17 C.F.R. § 240.10b–9; Rooney, Pace, Sec. Exch.Act.Rel. No. 34–23763 (Admin.Proc.File No. 3–6332 Oct. 31, 1986), [1986–87 Transfer Binder] Fed.Sec.L.Rep. (CCH) ¶ 84,048. *See generally* Robert B. Robbins, All-or-None Offerings, 19 Rev.Sec. & Commodities Reg. 59 (1986); §§ 6.3, 12.1 *infra.*

111. 17 C.F.R. § 240.15c2–4. *See* In re Lowell H. Listrom & Co., Exch.Act. Rel. No. 34–22689, [1985–86 Transfer Binder] Fed.Sec.L.Rep. (CCH) ¶ 83,946 (SEC Dec. 5, 1985).

112. *See, e.g.,* SEC v. First Pacific Bancorp, 142 F.3d 1186 (9th Cir.1998) (CEO held accountable for profits made in mini max offering where minimum offering amount had not in fact been met).

113. Regulation of market makers and manipulative activities relating to market makers are discussed in § 14.10[5] *infra.*

114. *See, e.g.,* United States v. DiStefano, 129 F.Supp.2d 342 (S.D.N.Y.2001).

115. *See, e.g.,* Eichler v. SEC, 757 F.2d 1066 (9th Cir.1985).

116. *See, e.g.,* In the Matter of Hibbard, Brown & Co. Admin. Proc. File No. 3–8418 March 13, 1995 Release No. 34–35476, 58 S.E.C. Docket 2561, 1995 WL 116488 n. 20 (SEC March 13, 1995).

117. Pagel, Inc, 48 S.E.C. 223, 226 (1985), aff'd sub nom. Pagel, Inc. v. SEC, 803 F.2d 942 (8th Cir.1986).

118. SEC v. First Jersey Securities, 101 F.3d 1450, 1467–1468 (2d Cir.1996) (violation of 1933 Act § 17(a) and 1934 Act § 10(b)). *See also, e.g.* Norris & Hirshberg, Inc. v. SEC, 177 F.2d 228, 232–233 (D.C.Cir.1949).

compensate brokers for encouraging customer purchases[119] or discouraging customers' sales[120] and thereby push the market price higher.[121]

The goal of the various statutes and rules prohibiting market manipulation is to prohibit activities that rig the market and thereby would inhibit the operation of the "natural law" of supply and demand.[123] In this way, the market price of securities will reflect—as much as is possible—a fair and just price for each security.[124] When a brokerage firm acts as an underwriter for an IPO and then acts as a market maker in the aftermarket there are delicate conflict of interest problems. Failure to adequately separate the underwriting and market making functions can result in violations of market making obligations.

---

119. *See, e.g.,* In the Matter of Olde Discount Corp., Administrative Proceeding File No. 3–9699, Sec. Act Rel. No. 33–7577, 67 S.E.C. Docket 2045, 1998 WL 575171 (SEC September 10, 1998)*amended*, 1999 WL 149774 (S.E.C. 1999).

120. *See, e.g,* In the Matter of DeMaio, Administrative Proceeding File No. 3–7912, 54 S.E.C. Docket 1509, Release No. ID–37, 1993 WL 300297 (SEC Aug. 4, 1993).

121. *See, e.g.,* In the Matter of A.S. Goldmen & Co., 2001 WL 588039, Sec. Exch. Act Rel. No. 34–44328 (SEC May 21, 2001).

123. *See, e.g.,* SEC v. First Jersey Securities, 101 F.3d 1450, 1466 (2d Cir.1996), cert. denied 522 U.S. 812, 118 S.Ct. 57, 139 L.Ed.2d 21 (1997); Varljen v. H.J. Meyers, Inc., 1998 WL 395266 (S.D.N.Y.1998).

124. *Id.*

Chapter 7

LIABILITY UNDER THE SECURITIES ACT OF 1933

Table of Sections

---

§ 7.1 Consequences of Deficient Registration Statements— Administrative Action, Criminal Sanctions, SEC Injunctive Relief, and Private Remedies

Violations of the 1933 Act registration, disclosure, and prospectus requirements can have a number of consequences. Many of them can be devastating. Deficiencies in the registration materials can result in administrative proceedings by the SEC, criminal sanctions brought by the Department of Justice, and injunctive relief in judicial proceedings instated by the SEC. This is supplemented by private remedies that may exist in favor of investors who purchased securities subject to the defective registration.[1] These deficiencies may take various forms. For example, the deficiency can be the result of incomplete or misleading disclosures.[2] Failure to comply with the prospectus delivery requirements[3] can have serious consequences, as can

---

§ 7.1

1. *See* §§ 7.2–7.9 *infra.*

2. *See* §§ 3.4, 3.9–3.10 *supra* for discussion of the 1933 Act disclosure requirements.

3. *See* §§ 2.4–2.5 *supra* for discussion of the prospectus delivery requirements that apply after a 1933 Act registration has been filed, through both the waiting and post-effective periods.

dissemination of information in violation of the 1933 Act's gun-jumping provisions.[4] The 1933 Act's remedial and enforcement provisions must be viewed in the context of the Act's registration process. Recall, for example, that the 1933 Act's registration process consists of the preparation of the registration statement with its detailed disclosures, followed by the filing of the registration statement, and then a waiting period before the registration statement becomes effective and the securities may be sold to the public.

In order to prevent a deficient registration statement from becoming effective, the SEC can institute formal administrative proceedings for the purpose of issuing a refusal order.[5] Refusal order proceedings must be instituted within ten days of the registration statement's filing.[6] The refusal order can be issued only after the registrant has been given notice and has had an opportunity for a hearing.[7] Alternatively, when faced with material deficiencies in the registration statement, the Commission may commence formal stop order proceedings at any time.[8] But again, the order can be issued only after formal notice and opportunity for a hearing.[9] As is pointed out in an earlier section,[10] most such deficiencies are dealt with informally through the use of deficiency letters and delaying amendments. Accordingly, the formal proceedings established by section 8 provide a statutory framework that does not reflect the normal process that is used for dealing with deficient registration materials. Instead, section 8 reflects the formal process that is used only when the registrant fails to comply with the SEC's less formal procedures for processing registration statements.

Anti–Fraud Provisions

Beyond the foregoing remedies for violation of the prospectus and registration requirements, the 1933 Act imposes sanctions for fraudulent conduct in connection with securities sales. Under the general antifraud provision contained in section 17(a),[11] material misstatements and omissions may result in both criminal sanctions and an SEC civil suit. Additionally, there is sparse authority in support of an implied private remedy for violations of section 17(a).[12]

Private Remedies

Any material deficiencies in the registration statement that carry over to the prospectus will result in violations of section 5(b)'s prospectus delivery requirements,[13] which call for an accurate and up-to-date prospectus.[14] Any

---

4. *See* § 2.3 *supra* for discussion of the pre-filing or quiet period that exists before a registration statement has been filed.

5. Section 8(b), 15 U.S.C.A. § 77h(b). *See* §§ 3.6, 3.9 *supra*.

6. Section 8(b), 15 U.S.C.A. § 77h(b).

7. *Id.*

8. Section 8(d), 15 U.S.C.A. § 77h(d). *See* William R. McLucas, Stop Order Proceedings Under the Securities Act of 1933: A Current Assessment, 40 Bus.Law. 515 (1985).

9. Section 8(d), 15 U.S.C.A. § 77h(d).

10. *See* § 3.7 *supra*.

11. 15 U.S.C.A. § 77q(a). *See* § 7.11 *infra*.

12. *See* § 12.22 *infra*.

13. 15 U.S.C.A. § 77e(b). *See* Sections 2(a)(10), 10, 15 U.S.C.A. §§ 77b(a)(10), 77j.

14. *E.g.,* SEC v. Manor Nursing Centers, Inc., 458 F.2d 1082 (2d Cir.1972). *See* §§ 2.4, 2.6 *supra*.

violation of section 5 gives rise to possible criminal sanctions[15] as well as to judicially secured SEC equitable sanctions.[16] Purchasers of securities that were sold in violation of section 5 have an express civil remedy for rescission pursuant to section 12(a)(1), which permits suit against a violator who is a seller[17] of the securities in privity with the purchaser.[19] Section 12(a)(2) gives a rescission remedy against sellers who make material misstatements or omissions in connection with a sale.[20] In addition, section 11 of Act imposes express civil liability upon persons preparing and signing materially misleading registration statements.[21]

Irrespective of any such implied remedy, section 12(a)(2) of the Act[22] creates an express right of action in the hands of defrauded purchasers. There is good authority[23] to support the proposition that all of these private remedies are cumulative and further, do not preclude a parallel implied remedy under Rule 10b–5 of the Exchange Act.[24] Although, of course, double recovery will not be permitted for a single injury.

Section 13 of the Act[25] sets out the applicable statute of limitations for private remedies under the Securities Act of 1933.[26] Actions under sections 11 and 12(a)(2) must be brought within one year of the date of the actionable misstatement or omission.[27] An action under section 12(a)(1) for violation of section 5's registration and prospectus delivery requirements must be brought within one year of the date of the registration violation.[28] Notwithstanding a longer delay in discovery, actions under sections 11 and 12(a)(1) must in all instances be brought within three years after the security was first offered to the public. All section 12(a)(2) actions are similarly subject to a three year repose period so that in no event may suit be brought more than three years of the sale.[29]

In the 1990s, Congress enacted legislation to curtail suspected abuses in connection with securities class actions. In particular, the Private Securities Litigation Reform Act of 1995[34] imposed procedural requirements and additional protection for projections and other forward-looking statements. The

---

15. 15 U.S.C.A. §§ 77e, 77x.

16. 15 U.S.C.A. § 77t.

17. *See, e.g.,* Pinter v. Dahl, 486 U.S. 622, 108 S.Ct. 2063, 100 L.Ed.2d 658 (1988) (discussing what is meant by the requirement that the defendant sold the securities to the plaintiff).

19. 15 U.S.C.A. § 77*l*(a)(1).

20. 15 U.S.C.A. § 77*l*(a)(2).

21. 15 U.S.C.A. § 77k. *See* §§ 7.3–7.4 *infra.*

22. 15 U.S.C.A. § 77l(a)(2). *See* § 7.6 *infra.*

23. Herman & MacLean v. Huddleston, 459 U.S. 375, 103 S.Ct. 683, 74 L.Ed.2d 548 (1983), *on remand* 705 F.2d 775 (5th Cir.1983). *See* chapters 10, 11, 12 *infra.*

24. 17 C.F.R. § 240.10b–5. *See* chapter 12.

25. 15 U.S.C.A. § 77m. *See* § 7.10 *infra.* The statute of limitations for implied remedies is discussed in § 12.16 *infra.*

26. In contrast, a longer statute of limitations applies to fraud claims brought under Rule 10b–5 and other antifraud provisions of the Securities Exchange Act of 1934. *See* § 12.16 *infra.*

27. 15 U.S.C.A. § 77m.

28. *Id.*

29. *Id.*

34. Pub. Law No. 104–67, , 109 Stat. 737 (104th Cong. 1st Sess. December 22, 1995) (HR 1058). *See* § 7.17[1], 12.15[1] *infra.*

Securities Litigation Uniform Standards Act of 1998[35] significantly preempted the role of the states in securities litigation by precluding most securities fraud class actions from being brought in state court or under state law.

§ 7.2 Civil Liability for Failure to Comply With Section 5's Requirements—Section 12(a)(1)'s Private Remedy

§ 7.2[1] Overview of Section 12(a)(1)

Section 12(a)(1) of the 1933 Act[1] provides that anyone who offers or sells a security in violation of section 5[2] is liable in a civil action to the person purchasing such security "from him."[3] Section 12(a)(1) is not limited to violations of Section 5's prospectus requirements;[4] any violation of section 5 can form the basis of a section 12(a)(1) cause of action.[5] This includes sales made before the registration statement's effective date[6] as well as offers to buy or offers to sell made prior to the filing of the registration statement.[7]

Agency principles apply in determining who is a purchaser for purposes of section 12. Thus, when an agent purchases securities for the account of the principal, the principal as the true party in interest should be able to bring suit under section 12. In contrast, when someone who purchases securities on behalf of another has sufficient indicia of ownership, that person qualifies as a purchaser under section 12 and thus can bring suit thereunder.[8] A violation of section 5 gives the purchaser a right of rescission (or rescissory damages) under section 12(a)(1).[9] Notwithstanding the statutory right of rescission, section 12(a)(1) does not interfere with the passage of title to the securities that have been sold in violation of section 5 of the Act.[10]

An action under section 12(a)(1) may be brought in either law or equity. As is the case with the other express civil actions under the 1933 Act, a section 12(a)(1) action may be brought either in state or federal court, but there is no right of removal to federal court for actions initiated in a state tribunal.[11] As a result of the Securities Litigation Uniform Standards Act of 1998, private class actions with more than fifty class members in fraud-based actions under the securities laws must be brought in federal court.[12]

---

35. Pub. Law No. 105–353, 112 Stat. 3227 (105th Cong. 2d sess. November 3, 1998) (S 1260). *See* § 7.17[2], 12.15[2] *infra.*

§ 7.2

1. 15 U.S.C.A. § 77*l*(a)(1).

2. 15 U.S.C.A. § 77e. *See* §§ 2.2–2.5 *supra.*

3. 15 U.S.C.A. § 77*l*(a)(1). The same language that limits permissible defendants to sellers in privity with the plaintiff applies to actions under section 12(a)(2) as well.

4. The prospectus delivery requirements are discussed in §§ 2.4, 2.5.

5. *See, e.g.,* Baldwin v. Kulch Associates, Inc., 39 F.Supp.2d 111, 115 (D.N.H.1998).

6. Sales prior to the effective date violate section 5(a). 15 U.S.C.A. § 77e(a). *See* §§ 2.4, 2.5 *supra.*

7. 15 U.S.C.A. § 77e(c). *See* § 2.3 *supra.*

8. *See* Monetary Management Group v. Kidder, Peabody & Co., 604 F.Supp. 764, 767 (E.D.Mo.1985) (investment adviser had standing).

9. 15 U.S.C.A. § 77*l*(a)(1).

10. Allison v. Ticor Title Insurance Co., 907 F.2d 645, 648 (7th Cir.1990), *appeal after remand* 979 F.2d 1187 (7th Cir.1992).

11. Section 22(a), 15 U.S.C.A. § 77v(a). *See* § 17.1 *infra.*

12. 1933 Act § 16, 15 U.S.C.A. § 77p. *See* § 7.17[2] *infra.*

Damages under section 12(a)(1) are limited to the return of purchase price of the security with interest, upon tender of the security. If the securities are no longer owned by the purchaser, the defendant is liable for damages based on the loss comprising the difference between the plaintiff's purchase price and sale price.[13] By virtue of section 13,[14] the section 12(a)(1) action must be brought within one year of the violation upon which it is based, but in no event may suit be commenced more than three years after the security was *bona fide* offered to the public.[15] For statute of limitations purposes, the sale occurs, and the statute generally begins to run, on the date the parties entered into a binding contract of sale.[16] It has been held that a showing of plaintiff's due diligence and reliance on the defendant's representations will be sufficient to extend the limitations period up to the three-year limit at least where the basis of the action sounds in fraud.[17] The doctrine of equitable tolling does not apply to actions governed by section 13 and thus will not extend the three-year period.[18]

The objective of section 12(a)(1) is a prophylactic one rather than merely compensatory. It has thus been held that since the action is designed to enforce registration requirements, the defense of estoppel will not bar a rescission action for a violation of section 5.[25] The Fifth Circuit thus held that only if plaintiff had refused an unconditional tender of a refund would the defendant have been able to raise the defense of estoppel.[26] However, not all courts have agreed.[27] The better view is that estoppel, as that term is ordinarily understood, is not a defense to a section 12(a)(1) action. Similarly, the fact that the plaintiff is a sophisticated investor who can fend for himself or herself will not preclude recovery under section 12(a)(1).[29] Nevertheless,

---

13. 15 U.S.C.A. § 77*l*. *See* Kilmartin v. H.C. Wainwright & Co., 580 F.Supp. 604, 607–08 (D.Mass.1984) for discussion of the tender requirement of section 12.

14. 15 U.S.C.A. § 77m.

15. The concept of being bona fide offered to the public is a question of fact as to whether the securities were in fact offered. The concept of a bona fide offer does not mean that the offering was in fact registered. Otherwise unregistered offerings would never have a limitations period since they would not fall under this strained interpretation of "bona fide." *See* Slagell v. Bontrager, 616 F.Supp. 634 (W.D.Pa.1985), affirmed 791 F.2d 921 (3d Cir.1986).

16. *E.g.* Amoroso v. Southwestern Drilling Multi–Rig, 646 F.Supp. 141 (N.D.Cal.1986). *See* § 7.10 *infra*. *See also* § 5.4 *supra*.

17. *E.g.*, Finne v. Dain Bosworth Inc., 648 F.Supp. 337 (D.Minn.1986); Prawer v. Dean Witter Reynolds, Inc., 626 F.Supp. 642 (D.Mass.1985) (section 12(a)(2) claim); Boyd v. Merrill Lynch, Pierce, Fenner & Smith, Inc., 611 F.Supp. 218 (S.D.Fla.1985), *on rehearing* 614 F.Supp. 940 (S.D.Fla.1985) (action under section 12(a)(2)). *See* Intre Sport Ltd. v. Kidder, Peabody & Co., 625 F.Supp. 1303 (S.D.N.Y.1985), *modified* 1986 WL 4906, Fed.Sec.L.Rep. (CCH) ¶ 92,714 (1986) (plaintiff failed to meet burden of proving due diligence; lapse of one-year period barred section 12 and section 11 claims). *But see* LeCroy v. Dean Witter Reynolds, Inc., 585 F.Supp. 753 (E.D.Ark. 1984) (tolling does not apply where section 12(a)(1) violation is based on failure to comply with prospectus delivery requirements and does not sound in fraud). *See* § 7.10 *infra*.

The burden of establishing due diligence rests with plaintiff. *E.g.* Krome v. Merrill Lynch & Co., 637 F.Supp. 910 (S.D.N.Y.1986), *vacated in part on other grounds* 110 F.R.D. 693 (D.N.Y. 1986) (decided under section 12(a)(2)).

18. *E.g.* Gutfreund v. Christoph, 658 F.Supp. 1378 (N.D.Ill.1987).

25. *See* Henderson v. Hayden, Stone Inc., 461 F.2d 1069 (5th Cir.1972).

26. 476 F.2d at 429–430. The fact that the defendant imposed a ten-day limit on the refund offer was sufficient to eliminate any such defense to the section 12(a)(1) action.

27. *See* Murken v. Barrow, 1989 WL 168062, [1989–1990 Transfer Binder] Fed.Sec.L.Rep. ¶ 94,815 at p. 94,413 (C.D.Cal.1989).

29. Byrnes v. Faulkner, Dawkins & Sullivan, 550 F.2d 1303 (2d Cir.1977) (Market maker may claim the protection of section 12(a)(1)).

the Supreme Court in Pinter v. Dahl[30] ruled that on appropriate facts, although they may be rare, the *in pari delicto* (or equal fault) defense will be available in an action under section 12(a)(1). The Court held that the law applicable in Rule 10b–5 cases[31] carried over to section 12(a)(1) cases as well. Specifically, the *in pari delicto* defense will bar a claim under section 12(a)(1) only when the plaintiff's fault in causing the section 5 violation can be said to be equal to the defendant's. The Court further noted that this test of relative responsibility of the plaintiff and defendant is dependent on a factual inquiry, and thus its application may vary from case to case.[32] The Court additionally observed that in order for a section 12(a)(1) plaintiff's claim to be defeated by the equal fault defense, the plaintiff's role in the transaction must have been one of a promoter rather than simply of an investor.[33] As such, the *in pari delicto* defense is quite narrow and will not be applicable in most section 12(a)(1) actions.

Section 12(a)(1) on its face imposes a strict privity requirement since the violator of section 5 is liable only to the person purchasing the security from him. The fact that section 12(a)(1) does not require a causal connection between the violation and any drop in price resulting in injury to the purchaser is further evidence of the prophylactic intent of Congress.[36] Accordingly, a purchaser will be granted rescission when the price of the security drops due to a change in the issuer's circumstances or market factors wholly unrelated to the section 5 action. Also, it has been held that where there has been a violation of the section 5(b)(1) prospectus delivery requirement followed by the purchaser's receipt of a complete statutory prospectus prior to the delivery of the security, the legal sale does not cure the illegal offer and the purchaser is entitled to maintain an action under section 12(a)(1).[37]

§ 7.2[2]   Who is Liable Under Section 12(a)(1)?[38]

One problem that arises with respect to both section 12(a)(1) as well as with section 12(a)(2), which imposes liability on the seller for the material misstatements or omissions in connection with any sale of securities whether or not registered under the 1933 Act,[39] is that of identifying permissible defendants. The question is defined in terms of who is a "seller" within the meaning of section 12. The courts have applied common law principles to identify persons other than the actual seller/violator. It has been held that absent some special relationship between the issuer and the seller, a purchaser not in privity with the issuer has no claim under section 12(a)(1) or

30. 486 U.S. 622, 108 S.Ct. 2063, 100 L.Ed.2d 658 (1988). *See* Mark S. Klock, Promoter Liability and In Pari Delicto Under Section 12(a)(1), 17 Sec.Reg.L.J. 53 (1989).

31. *See* Bateman Eichler, Hill Richards, Inc. v. Berner, 472 U.S. 299, 105 S.Ct. 2622, 86 L.Ed.2d 215 (1985). *See* § 12.21 *infra*.

32. 486 U.S. at 639, 108 S.Ct. at 2074, 100 L.Ed.2d at 677.

33. *Id.* at 638–39, 108 S.Ct. at 2074, 100 L.Ed.2d at 677.

36. *See, e.g.,* Diskin v. Lomasney & Co., 452 F.2d 871 (2d Cir.1971); In re NBW Commercial Paper Litigation, 813 F.Supp. 7, 20 (D.D.C.1992) (section 12(a)(1) does not have a causation requirement).

37. Diskin v. Lomasney & Co., 452 F.2d 871 (2d Cir.1971). *See also, e.g.,* 3 Louis Loss, Securities Regulation 1695–96 (2d ed. 1961).

38. For a more detailed discussion of who is a seller under section 12, *see* § 7.7 *infra*.

39. 15 U.S.C.A. § 77l(a)(2) which is discussed in § 7.6 *infra*. Section 12(a)(2) expressly applies to most exempted securities. However, the Supreme Court has limited the section 12(a)(2) remedy to sales that are part of an offering by prospectus. Gustafson v. Alloyd Co., 513 U.S. 561, 115 S.Ct. 1061, 131 L.Ed.2d 1 (1995). See § 7.6 *infra*.

12(a)(2).[40] However, it is clear that traditional agency principles that would give rise to a finding of privity in a normal contract situation apply with equal force in the securities context.[41] In applying this general agency rationale in the securities context, the courts require *active* participation in the negotiations leading to the sale in question.[42] It has been held that a broker who actively touts a particular stock to a customer may be found to have been a "substantial factor," and therefore subject to section 12(a)(2) liability as a seller although he may not have been the actual person transacting the final sale.[43] The continued validity of the substantial factor test was put to rest in light of the Supreme Court's decision in *Pinter v. Dahl.*

The Court in *Pinter* indicated that a section 12 defendant must have been both an immediate and direct seller of the securities to the plaintiff.[44] The Court stressed that section 12 liability depends on the defendant having been more than a remote participant in the sale.[45] Thus, merely participating in the preparation of the registration statement does not satisfy the active participation requirement so as to render such participants in privity with a purchaser.[46] Even substantial involvement in the preparation of registration and offering materials will not create liability unless there is also active involvement in the negotiations leading to the sale in question.[47] Similarly, an indirect connection with the selling process will not be sufficient to render the defendant liable in an action under section 12.[48]

Aiding and abetting liability applies to the securities acts generally for purposes of criminal prosecutions and at least certain SEC enforcement actions.[51] However, it is clear that aiding and abetting liability will not be found to exist in actions under section 12. As a result of a 1994 Supreme Court decision, it is now clear that aiding and abetting cannot support recovery in any private right of action under the securities laws.[53]

Vicarious liability principles carry over to section 12 actions.[55] Also, section 15 of the 1933 Act[56] calls for joint and several liability of controlling

---

40. Pinter v. Dahl, 486 U.S. 622, 108 S.Ct. 2063, 100 L.Ed.2d 658 (1988), *on remand* 857 F.2d 262 (5th Cir.1988).

41. *See* Buchholtz v. Renard, 188 F.Supp. 888 (S.D.N.Y.1960).

42. *See* Wasson v. SEC, 558 F.2d 879 (8th Cir.1977); Lennerth v. Mendenhall, 234 F.Supp. 59 (N.D.Ohio 1964).

43. Hill York Corp. v. American International Franchises, Inc., 448 F.2d 680 (5th Cir.1971).

44. 486 U.S. at 650, 108 S.Ct. at 2080, 100 L.Ed.2d at 684. *See* § 7.7 *infra. See also, e.g.,* DeMaria v. Andersen, 153 F.Supp.2d 300, 307–308 (S.D.N.Y.2001) (remote purchasers cannot sue remote sellers under section 12(a)(1)).

45. 486 U.S. at 654, 108 S.Ct. at 2082, 100 L.Ed.2d at 686.

46. Collins v. Signetics Corp., 443 F.Supp. 552 (E.D.Pa.1977), *affirmed* 605 F.2d 110 (3d Cir.1979).

47. *See* In re Infonet Services Corp. Securities Litigation, 310 F.Supp.2d 1080, 1101 (C.D. Cal. 2003) (citing this treatise).

48. *E.g.,* Stokes v. Lokken, 644 F.2d 779 (8th Cir.1981) (lawyer not liable under section 12); Wright v. Schock, 571 F.Supp. 642, 657–659 (N.D.Cal.1983), *affirmed* 742 F.2d 541 (9th Cir.1984) (bank and title company not liable).

51. Notwithstanding a long line of circuit and district court cases to the contrary, in 1994, the Supreme Court ruled that there is no implied right of action for aiding and abetting violations of the Securities Exchange Act's general antifraud provisions. Central Bank of Denver, N.A. v. First Interstate Bank of Denver, 511 U.S. 164, 114 S.Ct. 1439, 128 L.Ed.2d 119 (1994). *See* §§ 7.13, 12.25 *infra.*

53. Central Bank of Denver, N.A. v. First Interstate Bank of Denver, 511 U.S. 164, 114 S.Ct. 1439, 128 L.Ed.2d 119 (1994).

55. *See, e.g.* Underhill v. Royal, 769 F.2d 1426 (9th Cir.1985).

56. 15 U.S.C.A. § 77*o*.

persons with regard to violations of either section 11 or section 12 of the Act. Along these lines it has been held that section 15 creates merely secondary rather than primary liability for someone who is not a seller under section 12.

§ 7.3   Liability for Misstatements and Omissions in the Registration Statement—The Private Remedy Under Section 11 of the 1933 Act

The prospectus and 1933 Act registration statement can provide the basis of liability to purchasers of the securities covered by the registration statement. Section 11(a) of the Securities Act of 1933[1] creates an express right of action for damages[2] by securities purchasers when a registration statement contains untrue statements of material fact or omissions of material[3] fact. A section 11 claim cannot be brought on the basis of oral statements since the statute speaks in terms of misstatements and omissions in the registration statement.[4]

§ 7.3[2]   Who Can Sue; Nature of Suit Under Section 11

An action under section 11 may be brought by "any person acquiring such security" unless it can be shown that at the time of purchase the purchaser knew of the misstatement or omission. This language has been interpreted to mean that the plaintiff must be able to trace the securities to those covered by the registration statement.[18] This is true regardless of whether the plaintiff purchased in the after market or as part of the original offering.[19] Nevertheless, the courts construe the tracing requirement strictly.

Section 11 permits the plaintiff to bring suit either in law or equity in any court of competent jurisdiction. By virtue of section 22(a) of the Act[21] the plaintiff has an absolute choice of forum since actions under the 1933 Act may be brought either in federal or state court, and there is no right of removal from a state tribunal to a federal one.[22] However, as a result of the Securities

---

§ 7.3

1.   15 U.S.C.A. § 77k.

2.   The section 11 remedy is limited to damages; injunctive relief is not available. K/A & Co. v. Hallwood Energy Partners, L.P., 1990 WL 37866, [1990–1991 Transfer Binder] Fed.Sec.L.Rep. (CCH) ¶ 95,758 (S.D.N.Y.1990).

3.   Normal concepts of materiality apply in section 11 actions. Materiality is discussed in § 12.9 *infra.* Thus, for example, the bespeaks caution doctrine, relating to soft information and projections is applicable in actions under section 11. In re Worlds of Wonder Securities Litigation, 35 F.3d 1407 (9th Cir.1994). Soft information is discussed in § 3.9 *supra* and § 12.9 *infra.*

4.   In re Sterling Foster & Co. Securities Litigation, 222 F.Supp.2d 216, 267 (E.D.N.Y. 2002).

18.   *E.g.,* Salomon Smith Barney v. Asset Securitization Corp., 1999 WL 1095605, [1999–2000 Transfer Binder] Fed. Sec. L. Rep. (CCH) ¶ 90,723 (S.D.N.Y. 1999).

19.   The Supreme Court in Gustafson v. Alloyd Co., 513 U.S. 561, 115 S.Ct. 1061, 131 L.Ed.2d 1 (1995) held that section 12(a)(2) actions can only be brought by plaintiffs who purchased as part of a public offering as opposed to purchasing in the aftermarket. *See* § 7.6 *infra.* This limitation does not carry over to section 11 actions where the only requirement is that the plaintiff can trace the securities to the public offering. Joseph v. Wiles, 223 F.3d 1155 (10th Cir.2000).

21.   15 U.S.C.A. § 77v(a).

22.   *See generally* Thomas L. Hazen, Allocation of Jurisdiction Between the State and Federal Courts for Private Remedies Under the Federal Securities Laws, 60 N.C.L.Rev. 707 (1982). *See* § 17.1 *infra.*

Litigation Uniform Standards Act of 1998, private class actions with more than fifty class members in fraud-based actions under the securities laws must be brought in federal court.[23] Since section 11 is based on materially misleading disclosures, the mandatory federal forum would apply to all such class actions. In the aftermath of the Litigation Reform Act, plaintiffs still have a choice between a federal and state court forum with respect to individual actions, including section 11 claim as well as class actions involving fifty or fewer plaintiffs.[24]

§ 7.3[3] Permissible Defendants in a Section 11 Suit

Section 11(a) lists the categories of persons and entities in addition to the issuer which may be liable for misstatements or omissions in the registration statement:[27] (1) all signers of the registration statement;[28] (2) every director, person performing a similar function, or partner at the time of the filing of the registration statement; (3) all persons named with their consent in the registration statement as about to become a director, person performing similar functions, or partner; (4) every accountant, engineer, or appraiser, or any person whose profession gives authority to statements made by him or her, who has with consent been named in the registration statement as having prepared or certified any part of the filing, or any report or evaluation used in connection with the registration statement; and (5) every underwriter with respect to the security in registration.[29] Individuals and entities that do not fall within one of these categories do not incur liability under section 11. Primary liability under section 11 is supplemented by controlling person liability.[31]

§ 7.3[4] Absence of Reliance Requirement in Section 11

When a section 11(a) plaintiff has acquired the securities more than twelve months after the effective date of the registration statement, and if the issuer has distributed an "earnings statement" for that period, the plaintiff must prove reliance on the material misstatement or omission.[37] However, the purchaser need not prove that he or she actually read the registration statement in order to establish such reliance.[38] Without proof of plaintiff's actual knowledge of the misstatement or omission at time of purchase, there is a conclusive presumption of reliance for any person purchasing the security prior to the expiration of twelve months.[39]

§ 7.3[5] Tracing Securities to the Registration Statement

In order for a purchaser of the security to succeed in an action under section 11, he or she must prove that the shares purchased are traceable to

---

23. 1933 Act § 16, 15 U.S.C.A. § 77p. *See* § 7.17[2] *infra.*

24. Kelly v. McKesson HBOC, Inc., 2002 WL 88939 (Del.Super.2002) (permitting section 11 claim to proceed in state court).

27. *See* Hagert v. Glickman, Lurie, Eiger & Co., 520 F.Supp. 1028, 1033 (D.Minn.1981).

28. Section 6 sets forth who must sign. 15 U.S.C.A. § 77f(a) (1976). The required signers include the issuer, the issuer's principal executive, financial and accounting officers and a majority of the issuer's board of directors or persons performing similar functions. *See* §§ 3.4–3.5 *supra.*

29. 15 U.S.C.A. § 77k(a).

31. 1933 Act § 15, 15 U.S.C.A. § 77o.

37. 15 U.S.C.A. § 77k(a), last paragraph.

38. 15 U.S.C.A. § 77k(a).

39. *See, e.g.,* Barnes v. Osofsky, 373 F.2d 269 (2d Cir.1967).

the offering covered by the registration statement.[40] In light of the statutory language, the courts have rigidly enforced the tracing requirement.

Remote secondary and market transactions are not subject to section 11 claims, and thus tracing the securities back to the initial offering will not always satisfy a section 11 claim.[42] This does not mean, however, that section 11 actions are limited only to initial purchasers of shares covered by the registration statement. An investor who purchases his or her shares shortly after the offering can satisfy the section 11 tracing requirement.[43] This rule may have been brought into question by the Supreme Court's ruling in Gustafson v. Alloyd Co.,[44] which severely limited the scope of the private remedy under section 12(a)(2)[45] of the Act by ruling that the section 12(a)(2) remedy does not apply to transactions which do not occur in connection with a public offering or offering by prospectus. The policy underlying the *Gustafson* decision cannot justifiably limit an action under section 11 to plaintiffs who were initial purchasers.[47]

§ 7.3[8]　Measure of Damages Under Section 11

Another key difference between section 11 and the express remedies provided by section 12 is the measure of damages. With regard to both actions authorized by section 12, the appropriate measure of damages is rescission and the return of the purchase price paid by the plaintiff.[82] Section 11(e)[83] sets forth three alternative methods of computing the damages in an action under section 11 for material misrepresentations or omissions in a registration statement. Under section 11(e) a plaintiff is entitled to recover the difference between the amount paid for the securities (not to exceed the public offering price) and (1) the value at of time of suit, (2) the price at which plaintiff sold the securities prior to suit, or (3) the price at which the security was sold after suit was brought but before judgment so long as the damages so computed under this third alternative would be less than those based on the difference between the price paid for the security (not to exceed the offering price) and the value at the time suit was brought.

As the statutory damage formulations present something other than a bright line approach, problems of proof abound in damage cases under section 11. Proof problems are further exacerbated by the express provision in section 11(e) that the statutory damages shall be reduced to the extent that the defendant is able to prove that any portion of (or all of) said damages "represents other than the depreciation in value of each security resulting from" the misstatement or omission. Since the burden of proving the absence of a causal connection falls on the defendant, loss causation need not be

---

40. *E.g.*, Krim v. pcOrder.com, 2003 WL 21076787, Fed.Sec.L.Rep. ¶ 92415 (W.D. Tex. 2003).

42. Gould v. Harris, 929 F.Supp. 353 (C.D.Cal.1996). *See also, e.g.*, Harden v. Raffensperger, Hughes & Co., 933 F.Supp. 763 (S.D.Ind.1996) (section 11 standing is limited to those plaintiffs who purchase securities that are the "direct subject" of the registration statement).

43. *See* Lee v. Ernst & Young, LLP, 294 F.3d 969 (8th Cir.2002) (plaintiffs who were aftermarket purchasers could trace securities to the registration statement); Joseph v. Wiles, 223 F.3d 1155 (10th Cir.2000).

44. 513 U.S. 561, 115 S.Ct. 1061, 131 L.Ed.2d 1 (1995).

45. 15 U.S.C.A. § 77l(a)(2).

47. *See, e.g.*, Joseph v. Wiles, 223 F.3d 1155 (10th Cir.2000).

82. 15 U.S.C.A. § 77l.

83. 15 U.S.C.A. § 77k(e).

shown in order for plaintiff to establish a prima facie case under section 11.[87] However, to the extent that the defendant is able to establish this negative causation defense, damages will not be recoverable under section 11.

Thus, when the entire decline in the price of the stock is attributable to external market forces, there will be no damages under section 11.[88] It has been held by one court that upon a showing that the misrepresentation was material, there is a presumption that the market decline was related to the nondisclosure or misstatement.[89] Accordingly, to the extent that the defendant is able to prove the price decrease was due to external market forces or intervening events relating to the issuer's fundamental position, section 11 damages will be reduced. In contrast, section 12 provides for a return of the purchase price regardless of the cause of the decline in market value. In addition to the statutory measure of damages under section 11(e), a court may in its discretion award costs and attorneys fees to the successful party.[90]

§ 7.3[9] Statute of Limitations

Section 13 of the 1933 Act[91] provides for a statutory limitations period of one year after discovery of the misstatement or omission, or after discovery should have been made by the exercise of reasonable diligence, but in no event can a section 11 action be brought more than three years after the security was "bona fide offered to the public." The statute of limitations is the same for actions brought under section 11 or section 12(a)(2). In contrast, the one year statute begins to run from the date of violation for suits based on section 12(a)(1) of the Act to redress violations of section 5. Also, the three-year maximum limit for an action for fraud under section 12(a)(2) begins to run from the sale rather than offering date.

In 2002, Congress enacted an all purpose limitations period applicable to "a private right of action that involves a claim of fraud, deceit, manipulation, or contrivance in contravention of a regulatory requirement concerning the securities laws."[92] The limitations period runs two years from the date of discovery, with a five-year repose period running from the date of the violation.[93] Section 13 of the 1933 Act which is applicable to section 11 and 12 of that act was not repealed and it would seem that the newer two-year/five-year limitations/repose period was not designed to supercede section 13 of the 1933 Act.[94] The better view is that the longer limitations period added by the

---

87. *See, e.g.,* Garbini v. Protection One, Inc., 49 Fed.Appx. 169 (9th Cir. 2002).

88. Akerman v. Oryx Communications, Inc., 609 F.Supp. 363 (S.D.N.Y.1984), *affirmed and remanded* 810 F.2d 336 (2d Cir.1987).

89. *Id.*

90. 15 U.S.C.A. § 77k(e).

91. 15 U.S.C.A. § 77m.

92. 28 U.S.C.A. § 1658(b). *See* Sarbanes–Oxley Act of 2002, Pub. Law 107–204 (July 30, 2002).

93. *Ibid.*

94. The new limitations period speaks in terms of fraud and deceit. Neither section 11 nor section 12 of the 1933 Act require a showing of fraud or scienter. Many courts have held that the specificity requirements in pleading applicable to fraud actions do not apply to sections 11 or 12 of the 1933 Act since those sanctions are not fraud based. *See* § 12.13 *infra.* For the same reason, it can be argued that the shorter limitations period in 1933 Act section 13 should be applied to actions under sections 11 and 12 of that Act.

Sarbanes–Oxley Act does not extend the one-year/three-year period imposed by section 13 of the 1933 Act.[95]

§ 7.3[10] Defenses to Section 11 Claims

The statutory list of all potential section 11 defendants is exclusive.[96] There is generally no problem in identifying at least the potential defendants for any particular section 11 action. Room for interpretation is to be found, however, in connection with the reference to "every underwriter" in section 11(a)(5). Section 2(a)(11) of the 1933 Act[97] gives a broad statutory definition to the term underwriter, which goes far beyond the generic meaning of the term as used in connection with registered public offerings. This statutory definition of underwriter includes persons purchasing the securities from an issuer with a view to distribution, all those who offer or sell securities on behalf of an issuer in connection with a distribution, in addition to anyone who "participates or has a direct or indirect participation in any such undertaking."[98] Although it has been indicated that "underwriter" under section 11 tracks the full scope of the statutory definition under section 2(a)(11); in order to prevail, the plaintiff must still prove the defendant's actual participation in the distribution.[99] An underwriter's liability under section 11 is limited to the extent of the aggregate price of the securities underwritten by him or her. This limitation on damages does not apply, however, if the underwriter received from the issuer some benefit that was not available to similarly situated underwriters.

As mentioned above, section 11(a)(4) creates liability for professionals who lend their services to deficient registration statements. It has been held that an accountant may not be held liable unless the misleading information is expressly attributable to that accountant.[100] Further, it has been held that "as a matter of law," an independent accountant's liability under section 11 is limited to those figures which he or she certifies.[101] Thus, unless the accountant is an auditor or otherwise lends his or her name to a statement, there is no section 11 liability. Similarly, an attorney who prepares the registration statement is not a proper section 11 defendant unless he or she is also a director or signer of the registration statement.[102] Aside from such cases, the attorney will only be liable under section 11 pursuant to a subsection (a)(4) expert opinion.[103] An attorney's activities in preparing and reviewing the

---

95. In re Worldcom, Inc. Securities Litigation, 308 F.Supp.2d 214, 225 (S.D.N.Y. 2004); In re WorldCom, Inc. Securities Litigation, 294 F.Supp.2d 431 (S.D.N.Y. 2003).

96. *E.g.,* In re ZZZZ Best Securities Litigation, 1989 WL 90284, [1989 Transfer Binder] Fed.Sec.L.Rep. ¶ 94,485 (C.D.Cal.1989).

97. 15 U.S.C.A. § 77b(11).

98. *Id.* The section explicitly excludes from the definition of underwriter members of the selling group whose only remuneration is equivalent to a regular broker's commission.

99. *Id. See* § 4.26 *supra.*

100. McFarland v. Memorex Corp., 493 F.Supp. 631, 644–47 (N.D.Cal.1980), *reconsideration granted* 581 F.Supp. 878 (N.D.Cal.1984). *See also, e.g.,* Steiner v. Southmark Corp., 734 F.Supp. 269 (N.D.Tex.1990) (sufficiently alleging liability of accountants).

101. McFarland v. Memorex Corp., 493 F.Supp. 631, 643 (N.D.Cal.1980), *reconsideration granted* 581 F.Supp. 878 (N.D.Cal.1984), citing Grimm v. Whitney–Fidalgo Seafoods, Inc., 1973 WL 495, [1977–1978 Transfer Binder], Fed.Sec.L.Rep. (CCH) ¶ 96,029 (S.D.N.Y.1973).

102. *E.g.* Kitchens v. United States Shelter, 1988 WL 108598, [1988–89 Transfer Binder] Fed.Sec.L.Rep. (CCH) ¶ 93,920 (D.S.C.1988).

103. *See* Austin v. Baer, Marks & Upham, 1986 WL 10098, [1986–87 Transfer Binder] Fed.Sec.L.Rep. (CCH) ¶ 92,881 (D.Or.1986).

registration statement do not mean that the entire registration statement has been "expertised" so as to render the attorney liable under section 11.[104] However, an attorney, whether representing the issuer or underwriter, may be liable under section 17(a), which provides the basis for SEC injunctive relief and may, according to some decisions, even give rise to civil liability based on negligence.[105] Similarly, attorneys have been held liable as "sellers" under section 12.[106] After identifying the proper defendants, the key issues under section 11 are the appropriate standard of care and the defenses that may be asserted under section 11(b) by all defendants other than the issuer, who is strictly liable.[107] These topics are taken up in the succeeding section.

In 1995, as part of the Securities Litigation Reform Act, section 11 of the 1933 Act was amended to use fault as a basis for determining the relative liability of some defendants. Under the new regime, where fraud is involved, only those defendants who are guilty of fraud are jointly and severally liable. If none of the defendants has acted fraudulently, then all defendants, other than outside directors, are held jointly and severally liable. Outside directors who have not knowingly engaged in the violation are liable only according to their relative fault regardless of whether any of the other defendants acted fraudulently. Section 11(f)(1)[108] provides that all persons who are covered by subsection (a) and not excepted in section 11(f)(2) shall be jointly and severally liable unless one or more defendants are guilty of fraudulent misrepresentation and others are not; in such a case only the more culpable defendants are jointly and severally liable.[109] The section further expressly provides for a defendant's right of contribution against joint defendants, as would be the case in an action on a contract. Unlike the general rule for tort cases, such joint and several liability may not exceed the amount that the individual would be held accountable for were he or she sued separately. Since section 11(b) includes a due diligence defense for non-issuers, joint and several liability requires a showing of fault on the part of each non-issuer defendant.[110] Outside directors, however, are specifically excepted from joint and several liability for non-knowing violations even if none of the defendants were guilty of fraud.[111] Instead, a system of proportionate liability is implemented for non-knowing outside directors. The driving force behind this amendment was a concern over the possibility that under the former joint and several liability regime, peripheral defendants could be held liable for the entire loss caused by the principal wrongdoers.[113]

104. *See* Ahern v. Gaussoin, 611 F.Supp. 1465, 1482 (D.Or.1985); In re Flight Transportation Corp. Securities Litigation, 593 F.Supp. 612, 616 (D.Minn.1984), relying on Escott v. BarChris Constr. Corp., 283 F.Supp. 643, 683 (S.D.N.Y.1968).

105. *See* §§ 7.11, 12.22 *infra.*

106. Junker v. Crory, 650 F.2d 1349, 1360 (5th Cir.1981). *See* § 7.2 *supra.*

107. With regard to the strict liability of issuers, *see, e.g.,* In re NationsMart Corp. Securities Litigation, 130 F.3d 309 (8th Cir.1997) (referring to section 11 liability as virtually absolute).

108. 15 U.S.C.A. § 77k(f).

109. A broader limitation on joint and several liability was adopted under the 1934 Act. See § 12.26 infra.

110. *Id.*

111. 15 U.S.C.A. § 77k(f)(2). The proportionate liability of outside directors was added by the Private Securities Litigation Reform Act of 1995.

113. *See* H.R. Conf. Rep. No. 104–369, 104th Cong., 1st Sess. at 37–38 (1995).

§ 7.4   Defenses Under § 11(b)—Due Diligence, Reliance on Experts, and Reasonable Investigation

Section 11(b)[1] contains three types of defenses for persons other than the issuer to an action under section 11(a)[2] for material misstatements or omissions in the registration statement. The issuer is strictly liable, and no degree of prudence will absolve the issuer of a section 11 claim for damages. The only defenses available to the issuer are the purchaser's knowledge of the inaccuracies, lack of materiality, or expiration of the statute of limitations.

§ 7.4[1] "Whistle–Blowing" Defense

The first two defenses contained in section 11(b) relate to one who discovers the material misstatement or omission and takes appropriate steps to prevent the violation. A person other than the issuer who would otherwise be liable under section 11 is relieved of liability if, prior to the effective date, he or she resigns from the position that connects him or her with the registration statement (or takes all legal steps toward resignation, or ceases to act in that capacity) *and* if he or she has given written notice to the issuer and the SEC of such action and further disclaims all responsibility for the applicable parts of the registration statement.[3] If the registration statement becomes effective without the knowledge of a potential section 11 defendant, he or she may avoid liability by taking appropriate steps toward resignation and advising the SEC, in addition to giving "reasonable public notice that such part of the registration statement had become effective without his knowledge."[4] All the parties to a registration statement are thus put in a position where self-policing is required.

A potential section 11 defendant can thus avoid liability if he or she "blew the whistle" and brought the violations to the attention of the issuer and the SEC. These whistle blowing requirements present particularly sensitive problems for the attorney who becomes aware of potential violations. Anyone would agree that the attorney in such a position should advise the client (who will generally be the issuer) not to proceed with the offering, and also he or she should resign from the representation if the issuer refuses the advice. The statute on its face, however, goes even further and requires that the attorney who would otherwise be liable under section 11 (as a signer, director or section 11(a)(4) expert) blow the whistle on his or her client.

§ 7.4[2] Due Diligence Defenses

Section 11(b)(3) contains the most frequently used defense. It provides that any person other than the issuer who is a potential section 11(a) defendant is absolved of liability with regard to any part of the registration statement not made under the authority of an expert, provided that the defendant "had, after reasonable investigation, reasonable ground to believe and did believe, at the time such part of the registration statement became effective, that the statements therein were true and that there was no

---

§ 7.4

1. 15 U.S.C.A. § 77k(b).

2. 15 U.S.C.A. § 77k(a). *See* § 7.3 *supra.*

3. 15 U.S.C.A. § 77k(b)(1).

4. 15 U.S.C.A. § 77k(b)(2).

omission to state a material fact * * *."[6] A person who is named in the registration statement as an expert is not liable under section 11(a) for misstatements as an expert if, after reasonable investigation, there was reasonable ground to believe, combined with an actual belief, that there was no material misstatement or omission.[7] Furthermore, the expert is not liable if the statement in the registration materials "did not fairly represent his statements as an expert or was not a fair copy of or extract" of his or her report or valuation as an expert.[8] As for persons who would otherwise be liable for statements made in reliance upon experts, there is no liability if there was reasonable ground to believe, plus an actual belief that the statement did not contain any material misstatements or omissions. Finally, as for any part of the registration statement that purports to be made by a public official or "a copy of or extract from a public official document," there is no liability for anyone who had reasonable grounds to believe and did actually believe that there were no material misstatements or omissions.[9]

Section 11(c) expressly establishes the appropriate standard of care: "the standard of reasonableness shall be that required of a prudent man in the management of his own property."[10] This is a significant departure from the traditional state law standard that applies to officers and directors, which is generally articulated in terms of that conduct which would be befitting of a reasonable officer or director or person under like circumstances.[11] By speaking in terms of the degree of care that one would use in handling one's own affairs, the 1933 Act apparently provides for a higher standard,[12] at least to the extent that it does not seem to include the shield of the business judgment rule. The due diligence defense involves mixed questions of law and fact. When the facts are not disputed, summary judgment will be appropriate, because leaving such decisions to judges rather than juries will result in more predictability and uniformity of result.[13] However, where there is a material dispute as to the facts, summary judgment will not be appropriate.[14]

To date, the most definitive word on the scope of section 11(b)(3) defenses of due diligence and reasonable investigation has emanated from the New York federal district court decision in Escott v. BarChris Construction Corp.[15]

---

6. 15 U.S.C.A. § 77k(b)(3)(A).

7. 15 U.S.C.A. § 77k(b)(3)(B).

8. *Id.*

9. 15 U.S.C.A. § 77k(b)(3)(D).

10. 15 U.S.C.A. § 77k(c). *See* 17 C.F.R. § 230.176.

11. *See, e.g.,* Revised Model Business Corp. Act § 8.30(a)(2)(1984); Model Business Corp. Act § 35 par. 2 (1977 Supp.).

12. *See* James D. Cox & Thomas L. Hazen, Cox & Hazen on Corporations ch. 10 (2d ed. 2003).

13. *See* In re Software Toolworks, Inc. Securities Litigation, 789 F.Supp. 1489 (N.D.Cal.1992), *affirmed in part and reversed in part,* 38 F.3d 1078 (9th Cir.1994).

14. *See, e.g.,* In re Software Toolworks, Inc. Securities Litigation, 50 F.3d 615 (9th Cir.1994) (but holding that underwriter had sufficiently established due diligence defense).

15. 283 F.Supp. 643 (S.D.N.Y.1968). *See also, e.g.,* In re Worldcom, Inc. Securities Litigation, 346 F.Supp.2d 628, 672 (S.D.N.Y. 2004). The issuer, BarChris, was in the business of building bowling alleys for contracted customers on a highly leveraged basis. The company had two methods of financing. The primary method involved entering into a contract with a customer for construction and equipment of a bowling alley with the customer making a comparatively small down payment. Upon completion of the facility, the customer would pay the balance of the contract price in notes payable, which BarChris would discount. The alternative method of financing consisted of a sale and leaseback arrangement. After completing the interior of the bowling alley, the facility would then be sold to a factor for the full construction price. The factor

The registration statement in *BarChris* contained a number of misstatements. In the first instance, there were over-statements regarding the comparison of the fiscal year 1960 to past performance, but the court found that such misstatements were not material, since the correct figures would have shown a growth potential which was virtually equivalent to that presented in the registration statement. These misstatements thus failed to cross the materiality threshold as they were not of the magnitude likely to be significant to the reasonable investor.[16] The most substantial misstatements concerned failure to accurately disclose the increases in customer defaults in payment of the notes held by BarChris and the possibility that the issuer would have to repossess certain leased assets which would necessarily injure its cash position.[17] There were additional omissions regarding loans to certain officers of the corporation. The section 11(b) defenses also focused on the registration statement's signers' and participants' failure to ascertain and disclose the inaccuracies regarding the likelihood that the issuer would be foreclosing on several of its notes, as well as their failure to disclose that BarChris was already engaged and about to be further engaged in the actual operation of bowling alleys.

In the course of its opinion, the court in *BarChris* treated each of the classes of defendants separately, thus creating a sliding scale of liability. The decision makes it clear that the highest standard of care attaches to an insider who signed the registration statement, especially if the insider is one of the designated principal officers who must sign prior to SEC filing.[18] Similarly, as to directors, the majority of whom must also sign, the court was careful to draw a distinction between insiders and outsiders. The court further made clear that any expertise brought by a signer, such as a legal or accounting background, will be factored into the formula of the standard of care under the circumstances. This sliding scale of liability as elevated by expert knowledge is arguably contrary to what would appear on the face of section 11(c) to be a unitary standard of conduct, that of the "prudent man" with no mention of any special knowledge that he may possess.[19] Nevertheless, there has been neither judicial nor SEC authority that has questioned the *BarChris* sliding scale of liability.

Beyond the appropriate standard of care, the court in *BarChris* also looked at the defense of reliance upon experts and specifically disclaimed any reading of the statute that would entitle signers to point to reliance on an attorney who had read the entire registration statement, even if the attorney is a securities expert reading the papers as a check against possible disclosure

would then lease the interior to a customer or to a BarChris subsidiary, which in turn would lease the facility to the customer.

Under either method of financing BarChris received very little up-front money for construction. It was thus necessary for the company to seek public financing on a number of occasions to provide the necessary cash to cover its operations. The prospectus and registration statement in question were filed in connection with a public offering of debentures.

16. Materiality is considered in §§ 10.4, 12.9 *infra*.

17. The failure to disclose customer delinquencies standing alone was a 1.35-million dollar inflation of the balance sheet. *See* 283 F.Supp. at 680.

18. Section 6 requires that the registration statement be signed by the issuer's principal executive officers, principal financial officer, comptroller or principal accounting officer and the majority of the board of directors or persons performing similar functions. 15 U.S.C.A. § 77f(a). *See* §§ 3.2, 3.5 *supra*.

19. "The standard of reasonableness shall be that required of a prudent man in the management of his own property." 15 U.S.C.A. § 77k(c).

problems. Specifically, the court held that the only *expertised* portion of the prospectus and registration statement were audited figures prepared by the independent accountant. It was reasoned that section 11(b)(3) is explicit in its requirement that the portion provided by an expert giving rise to justifiable reliance is limited to statements that were "parts of the registration statement which purported to be made upon the authority of an expert."[20] In so ruling, the court held that even as to other financial data that the accountants may have looked at, the prospectus and registration statement were not expertised. The same rule was applied to portions of the registration statement that were prepared by attorneys. Thus, registration materials are not expertised merely because they are examined or even prepared by attorneys, accountants, or other experts.[21]

Although the decision imposed liability on attorneys and accountants, it was based on their role as signers or as experts named in the registration materials. The *BarChris* court thus did not impose liability upon a professional who renders advice in connection with portions of the registration statement, but does not provide a statement which purports to be made upon his or her expertise. There does not seem to be any basis for holding professionals not named as experts to be liable for any misstatement under section 11 unless they were signers, directors, or underwriters, as required by section 11(a). It is clear, however, that any participant in the registration statement's preparation is subject to other potential liabilities. Negligence will clearly be grounds for an SEC injunction under section 17(a) and may create civil liability.[22] Conduct approaching fraud will create liability under SEC Rule 10b–5.[23] Additionally, active participation in any sale as a "seller" creates the potential for liability under sections 12(a)(1) and 12(a)(2).[24] Another significant aspect of the *BarChris* ruling is that neither attorneys nor accountants who are covered by section 11(a) are justified in relying upon the client; they must make their own independent "due diligence" investigation. Unfortunately, there is not a bright line test for determining when the required due diligence has been met. Since due diligence arises as an affirmative defense, the burden of establishing it falls on the defendant.

Even in a situation where a defendant may attempt to avail himself or herself on the reliance on experts defense, the courts are not satisfied by blind reliance. Borrowing from the standard in criminal cases generally, the appropriate requirements for a reliance on experts defense are as follows: (1) *full disclosure* of pertinent facts known by the person claiming reliance, and (2) *good faith* reliance on the opinion given.[25] With regard to portions of the registration statement that have been prepared by experts, those section 11 defendants who can reasonably rely are relieved of their reasonable investigation and due diligence obligations for the expertised portions.[26]

20. Escott v. BarChris Construction Corp., 283 F.Supp. at 683.

21. *E.g.,* In re Flight Transportation Corporation Securities Litigation, 593 F.Supp. 612, 616 (D.Minn.1984) (relying on *Escott v. BarChris Construction Corp.*).

22. *See* Aaron v. SEC, 446 U.S. 680, 100 S.Ct. 1945, 64 L.Ed.2d 611 (1980), *on remand* 666 F.2d 5 (2d Cir.1981); §§ 7.11, 12.22 *infra.*

23. 17 C.F.R. § 240.10b–5. *See* chapter 12 *infra.*

24. 15 U.S.C.A. §§ 77*l*(a)(1), (2). *See* §§ 7.2 *supra,* 7.6 *infra.*

25. *See, e.g.,* United States v. Lindo, 18 F.3d 353, 356 (6th Cir.1994); United States v. Duncan, 850 F.2d 1104, 1117 (6th Cir.1988); United States v. Phillips, 217 F.2d 435, 442 (7th Cir.1954).

26. *E.g.,* In re Software Toolworks, Inc. Securities Litigation, 50 F.3d 615 (9th Cir.1994).

Although there have been a number of decisions since *BarChris*, that decision remains the leading authority on the appropriate standard of conduct under section 11. The best way to appreciate the full thrust of the *BarChris* opinion (and its progeny) is to examine the court's treatment of each defendant.

Officers' and Directors' Liability

Although not having the title of president, the functional chief executive officer, who was also a member of the corporation's executive committee, was a signer of the registration statement. The court noted that this chief executive officer and member of the executive committee was totally familiar with all aspects of the issuer's business and was "personally in charge" of all dealing with the factors, as well as handling negotiations that included discussion of customer delinquencies. The court found that he "knew all the relevant facts" and "could not have believed that there were no untrue statements" and thus could not assert a valid due diligence defense.[27] The two founders of the business, its titular president and vice-president, had less actual involvement than the chief executive officer and were "men of limited education." The court conceded that "it is not hard to believe that for them the prospectus was difficult reading, if indeed they read it at all."[28] However, the court viewed their limited expertise as irrelevant since a signing officer's liability is dependent upon neither whether he or she has read the registration statement nor if having read it, he or she understood it at all. The test is whether the signing officer acted with due diligence under the circumstances. The court found a lack of due diligence in signing without having read or understood the registration statement. People who do not possess the minimum necessary knowledge should not be serving as officers or directors. In addition, the two signing founding officers had been beneficiaries of loans from the corporation that were not disclosed in the prospectus. On the basis of all of the foregoing facts, the court held that these two signers had failed to meet their defenses of due diligence.

The treasurer and chief financial officer, "a certified public accountant and an intelligent man," was, as his job required, "thoroughly familiar" with the company's finances, including the problem of customer delinquency.[29] He was also a member of the executive committee which gave him access to information as to operations of the business that he might otherwise not be informed of by virtue of his corporate office. In addition, the treasurer worked on the actual preparation of the registration statement, including having met with the company's attorneys. The essence of his defense was that since all the facts and figures appeared in the company's books, the treasurer was justified in relying upon the auditor's expertise. After noting that this created "an issue of credibility" the court ruled that in any event he failed to prove his defense.[30]

Outside Directors' Liability

Another controversial aspect of the *BarChris* court's decision arose with respect to an outside director who was neither an officer nor employee but

---

27. Escott v. BarChris Construction Corp., 283 F.Supp. at 684.

28. *Id.* at 684.

29. *Id.* at 685.

30. *Id.* at 685.

signed the registration statement. The outside director testified that he did not know that he was signing a registration statement but he vaguely understood that it was something "for the SEC." The court further conceded that the outside director believed all representations as to the company's business made by the insiders. Although he became a director "on the eve of the financing" and "had little opportunity to familiarize himself with the company's affairs," the court nonetheless held him liable for failing to make any investigation whatsoever before having signed the registration statement.[31] This might seem to be an extremely high burden to put upon a newly elected outside director; however, he did sign the registration statement. The court would have been much harder pressed to find liability under section 11(a)(2) of an outside director who had not signed the registration statement. The *BarChris* decision thus provides a good lesson for unwary outside directors who are asked to sign the registration statement.

Attorneys' Liabilities

One of the most controversial aspects of the *BarChris* ruling arose out of the court's holding liable a young attorney who was only four years out of law school at the time of the registration statement. He had previously been house counsel and assistant secretary and was then secretary to the corporation and a member of the board of directors. Although he was not a director at the time of the initial filing, he was fully liable under section 11. The court was willing to agree that as corporate secretary and house counsel he was not a principal officer; however, by being keeper of corporate minutes, he certainly had access to inside information.[32] Furthermore, he had examined the contracts in question and had advised the issuer that certain contracts may not have been legally enforceable, a fact not recorded in the registration statement. The court conceded that this young attorney "did not know of many inaccuracies in the prospectus," but that he had sufficient knowledge of the business that he was at least put on inquiry notice of potential problems, and thus should have investigated "the truth of all the statements in the unexpertised portion of the document, which he signed."[33] Since the young attorney made no independent investigation whatsoever, he was held not to have met the burden of proving his due diligence defense. The court did not indicate how much investigation would have been sufficient to let him off the hook.

Another attorney who was hit with liability in the course of the *BarChris* decision was outside counsel who sat on the board of directors. He not only signed this and other registration statements for the issuer, but also took primary responsibility for preparing the initial drafts of one of the registration statements that formed the basis of the suit. Section 11 does not provide any bases for suing someone who simply prepares or drafts a registration statement,[34] yet since this attorney was both a director of the issuer and a signer of the registration statement, he was properly viewed as a section 11 defendant.

31. *Id.* at 688. *See also, e.g.,* In re Worldcom, Inc. Securities Litigation, 346 F.Supp.2d 628, 672 (S.D.N.Y. 2004). *Compare, e.g.,* Weinberger v. Jackson, 1990 WL 260676, [1990–1991 Transfer Binder] Fed.Sec.L.Rep. (CCH) ¶ 95,693 (N.D.Cal.1990) (outside director met his standard of due diligence and reasonable inquiry).

32. Escott v. BarChris Construction Corp., 283 F.Supp. at 687.

33. *Id.* at 687.

34. Nevertheless, liability may exist under other sections. *See* chapter 12 *infra. See also* § 7.15 *infra.*

The court made note of the fact that this was not a legal malpractice action, but "in considering Grant's [outside counsel's] due diligence defenses, the unique position he occupied cannot be disregarded."[35] This defendant as outside counsel, director and signer, claimed that he was justified in relying upon the statements of his clients, but the court held that under the statute he had a duty to make an independent investigation. The obvious lesson of this aspect of the ruling is that counsel should be hesitant to sign any registration statement since their expertise and access to inside information by virtue of their attorney-client relationship may impose an especially high standard of conduct. Furthermore, since section 11(a)(2) renders all directors liable, an attorney who sits as a director but does not sign the registration statement is equally open for potential liability, especially if he or she worked on the registration statement in any capacity. However, an attorney who helps prepare the registration statement cannot be held liable under section 11 unless he or she is an officer, director, signer of the registration statement, or expert within the meaning of section 11.[36]

Underwriters' Liabilities

In the *BarChris* opinion and elsewhere the courts have made it clear that the underwriter plays a special role in the due diligence process since investors rely on the underwriter's investigation of the issuer. The underwriter's presence in the offering can act as an implied representation that the underwriter has investigated the issuer.[38] Thus, for example, an underwriter cannot rely blindly on an auditor's comfort letter, when there were red flags that should have put the underwriter on notice of the alleged improprieties.[38.5] The underwriter is obligated to look behind the financial statements and seek verification as to their accuracy and/or currency.[38.10] In its decision involving the WorldCom fraud, the district court applied traditional principles that were established in the *Barchris* decision for the underwriters' due diligence obligations.[38.15]

Much of the court's opinion in *BarChris* is devoted to the liability of the underwriters[39] and the accountants who performed the 1960 audit.[40] As for the

---

35. Escott v. BarChris Construction Corp., 283 F.Supp. at 690. *See* Donald B. Hilliker, Target Defendants for the 1980's: Securities Lawyers' Malpractice Insurance, 1980 Ins.L.J. 563 (1980); Symposium, Responsibilities and Liabilities of Lawyers and Accountants, 30 Bus.Law. 227 (1975); Comment, Due Diligence and the Expert in Corporate Securities Registration, 42 S.Cal.L.Rev. 293 (1969).

36. *E.g.,* In re Flight Transportation Corporation Securities Litigation, 593 F.Supp. 612, 613 (D.Minn.1984) (fact that attorney worked on registration statement did not make the registration expertised by him).

38. Sanders v. John Nuveen & Co., 524 F.2d 1064, 1069–1070 (7th Cir.1975), *vacated and remanded on other grounds,* 425 U.S. 929, 96 S.Ct. 1659, 48 L.Ed.2d 172 (1976).

38.5 In re Worldcom, Inc. Securities Litigation, 346 F.Supp.2d 628, 672 (S.D.N.Y. 2004) ("underwriters' reliance on audited financial statements may not be blind. Rather, where 'red flags' regarding the reliability of an audited financial statement emerge, mere reliance on an audit will not be sufficient to ward off liability").

38.10 *See, e.g., Glassman v. Computervision Corp.,* 90 F.3d 617, 629 (1st Cir. 1996)("[A] failure by the underwriters either to verify a company's statements as to its financial state or to consider new information up to the effective date of an offering would almost certainly constitute a lack of due diligence."); In re Worldcom, Inc. Securities Litigation, 346 F.Supp.2d 628, 677 (S.D.N.Y. 2004).

38.15 *See* In re Worldcom, Inc. Securities Litigation, 346 F.Supp.2d 628 (S.D.N.Y. 2004).

39. Escott v. BarChris Construction Corp., 283 F.Supp. at 692–697.

40. *See* § 7.4[2][D] *infra.*

underwriters, the facts were extremely damaging and thus justified a finding of liability. The partner in the underwriting firm who had primary responsibility for investigating the issuer was also a director of the issuer. Not only does this position with the issuer create a potential conflict of interest, it also gives access to certain types of inside information that might otherwise not be available to an underwriter, as the issuer and underwriter can no longer be viewed as dealing on a purely arms-length basis. Furthermore, the court noted that the only investigation made by the underwriter about the issuer was directed toward the decision whether or not to participate in the offering and was *not* directed toward compliance with the requirements of the statute's registration provisions. The court acknowledged that after the underwriter's partner was made a director of the issuer, he did make an independent investigation of the prospectus' accuracy, but as was the case with the other defendants, he failed to follow up on a number of questionable disclosures. The court further pointed out that although there was a "due diligence meeting" one week before the offering date, the underwriters failed to make any independent investigation after the meeting. The court thus held the managing underwriter liable because of its failure to meet the defense of due diligence. In contrast, where underwriters make a reasonable investigation, the defense will be available.[41]

In the course of its opinion in *BarChris*, the court chided the underwriters for failing to have looked beyond the contracts represented by the backlog figures.[42] The court in *BarChris* pointed out that "the other underwriters, who did nothing and relied solely on directors and on the lawyers" did not establish a due diligence defense except as to the 1960 audit.[44] The court also went on to question whether the other underwriters can ever rely upon due diligence of the managing underwriter.[45] In analyzing the significance of the *BarChris* decision with regard to the underwriters, it must be remembered that the underwriter's investigation there was supervised by a partner who also was a director of the issuer. As such, the underwriter's investigation was not a truly independent one.

The *BarChris* decision raises questions as to the underwriter's outside counsel's standard of responsibility. In the course of its ruling that the managing underwriter failed to meet the due diligence standard, the court rejected the underwriter's reliance on counsel. The underwriter's outside counsel sent a young associate to check *BarChris'* corporate records. The associate did not check the issuer's contracts nor did he locate several executive committee minutes. The court held that this was an insufficient investigation and thus precluded reliance by the underwriter. Underwriter's counsel did not fit within the list of section 11 defendants and thus was not held liable. The court did not inquire, however, into the law firm's potential liability to its client for malpractice or any common law right of indemnity by a principal against its agent.

In order to establish their due diligence, underwriters must show that they engaged in reasonable independent investigation of the issuer and of the offering. An example of an underwriter's successful due diligence defense

---

41. *See, e.g.,* In re Software Toolworks Inc. Securities Litigation, 50 F.3d 615 (9th Cir.1994).

42. Escott v. BarChris Construction Corp., 283 F.Supp. at 697.

44. Escott v. BarChris Construction Corp., 283 F.Supp. at 697.

45. *Id.* n. 26.

arose in In re International Rectifier Securities Litigation.[47] There, the underwriters: (1) reviewed the issuer's internal financial forecasts, contracts, and other documents, (2) made a physical inspection of the issuer's major facilities, (3) employed analysts having expertise in the issuer's business, (4) conducted extensive interviews with eleven of the issuer's senior and middle management, (5) interviewed the issuer's major customers, outside quality consultants, auditors, and legal counsel, and (6) obtained written verification of the prospectus' accuracy and a "cold comfort" letter from the auditors that there were not material changes in the financial position since the last audit.

Accountants' Liabilities

The court in *BarChris* found that the auditors failed to establish their standard of due diligence. As is the case with other section 11 defendants, the accountants have the burden of establishing their due diligence. The court in *BarChris* found that the auditors failed to establish their standard of due diligence. The field survey for the audit was performed by an individual who was not yet a CPA and had no prior knowledge of the bowling alley industry. This was his first major assignment as a senior accountant. The court conceded that although the investigator may have asked the right questions and received what he considered satisfactory answers, he failed to verify them. Further, it was apparent that there had been an increase in notes payable but nonetheless the auditor's investigator had "no conception how tight the cash position was."[49] Since the auditor's investigator had met with only one officer and had various other bases of inquiry notice, the court found that the burden of establishing due diligence had not been met and that the auditors were liable for all mistakes in the 1960 audited figures.

As part of the Private Securities Litigation Reform Act of 1995,[50] Congress codified many existing auditing requirements.[51] Among other things, the legislation requires procedures designed to detect illegal activities, procedures designed to identify material related-party transactions.

Aftermath of BarChris

The *BarChris* decision raises many questions concerning the extent of independent investigation that must be made. Specifically, how much of a factual inquiry must be made? Must attorneys, accountants, and underwriters make trips all over the country to inspect the physical plant of the issuer? Must there be at least a spot-check of company inventories? Must there be title searches of property claimed to be owned by the issuer? Must there be an eyeball review of all substantial contracts of the issuer? Must there be a complete opening of the company's files to outsiders such as the underwriters? These are just some of the questions that arise from the decision. The safe answer to each of these questions is clearly "yes." One effective way to help assure compliance with section 11's due diligence requirement is to appoint a due diligence officer to supervise the preparation of the registration statement.[52]

---

47. 1997 WL 529600, [1997 Transfer Binder] Fed. Sec. L. Rep. (CCH) ¶ 99,469 (C.D.Cal.1997).

49. Escott v. BarChris Construction Corp., 283 F.Supp. at 702.

50. Pub. Law No. 104–67, , 109 Stat 737 (104th Cong. 1st Sess. December 22, 1995) (HR 1058).

51. Section 10A of the 1934 Act, U.S.C.A. § 78j–1. *See* the discussion in § 9.6 *infra*.

52. *See* Robert A. Spanner, Limiting Exposure in the Offering Process, 20 Rev.Sec. & Commod.Reg. 59 (1987) (also containing a helpful checklist of due diligence steps).

A second instructive decision on the scope of section 11(b) defenses arose in the context of an exchange offer in Feit v. Leasco Data Processing Equipment Corp.[53] Unlike the underwriters in the *BarChris* case, there was no interlocking directorate or relationship between the issuer and the underwriter. Accordingly, the underwriters were truly outsiders who were dealing at arms length with the issuer. Thus, the court noted that "dealer-managers cannot, of course, be expected to possess the intimate knowledge of corporate affairs of inside directors, and their duty to investigate should be considered in light of their more limited access."[54] The same clearly could not have been said of the underwriters in *BarChris* because of their interlocking management. The court noted that the underwriters in *Feit* did comply with industry standards and made somewhat of an independent investigation. The court concluded that they "have just barely established * * * that they had reasonable ground to believe that the omission of a specific figure was justified."[55] In so ruling, the court found that unlike the underwriters in the *BarChris* case, in the *Feit* case Leasco's underwriters were justified in relying on the client's representations.

It is evident from the foregoing discussion that the courts have not been able to articulate a bright-line test as to the requisite standard of care under section 11. What has emerged, however, is the fact that courts will impose a sliding scale depending upon the defendant's knowledge, expertise, status with regard to the issuer, its affiliates or underwriters, and the degree of the defendant's actual participation in the registration process and in preparing the registration materials.

In an effort to clarify its position, the SEC promulgated Rule 176[57] which reinforces the judicial sliding scale of culpability and further provides for the necessity of a case-by-case, highly factual analysis, as is done with common law negligence.

§ 7.5 Damages in Actions Under Section 11

§ 7.5[1] The Statutory Formula

Section 11 permits damages awards to injured purchasers of securities sold pursuant to a 1933 Act registration statement where the registration materials contain material misstatements or omissions of fact.[1] This remedy is in addition to the action provided by section 12(a)(2) which is not limited to registered offerings and provides the purchaser with a cause of action against a seller of securities where the seller is responsible for material misstatements or omissions.[2] Although both section 11 and section 12(a)(2) are directed at

---

53. 332 F.Supp. 544 (E.D.N.Y.1971). *See* Note, Section 11 in the Exchange Offer Setting: An Analysis of Feit v. Leasco Data Processing Equipment Corp., 1972 Duke L.J. 1023.

54. 332 F.Supp. at 582. Compare Kitchens v. U.S. Shelter, 1988 WL 108598, [1988–89 Transfer Binder] Fed.Sec.L.Rep. (CCH) ¶ 93,920 (D.S.C.1988) (appraisal firm satisfied burden of proving due diligence).

55. *Id.* at 582.

57. 17 C.F.R. § 230.176.

§ 7.5

1. 5 U.S.C.A. § 77k. *See* §§ 7.3, 7.4 *supra*. *Cf.* In re Websecure, Inc. Securities Litigation, 1997 WL 770414, [1998 Transfer Binder] Fed. Sec. L. Rep. (CCH) ¶ 90,112 (D. Mass. 1997) (refusing to order asset freeze in section 11 action since there was not showing that defendants were dissipating assets).

2. 15 U.S.C.A. § 77l(a)(2). *See* §§ 7.6, 7.7 *infra*.

materially misleading information in connection with sales of securities, they provide for a different measure of damages. Damages under section 11 are based on a complex formula, which in essence is designed to award the difference between the purchase price and the true value of the securities, thereby reflecting the extent to which the purchase price was inflated by the material misstatements or omissions.[3] This figure is then reduced by that portion of the loss that defendant can show was attributable to factors other than the misstatements in question.[4]

Section 12(a)(2), as is the case with private actions under section 12(a)(1),[5] permits the purchaser to rescind the transaction or recover rescissory damages; this means that damages under section 12(a)(1) are not limited to those caused by the violation.[6] In contrast to the measure of damages set forth in section 12(a)(1), in an action under section 12(a)(2) there now is an affirmative defense if the defendant can establish that the plaintiff's loss was caused by factors other than the section 12(a)(2) misstatement.[7] This is similar to the negative causation defense available in section 11 actions. Section 11 damages, as is the case with those available in an action under 1934 Act Rule 10b–5, are limited to those caused by the misrepresentation or omission. In a Rule 10b–5 action, loss causation is part of the plaintiff's prima facie case.[8] In contrast, under section 11, loss causation is not an element of the plaintiff's claim, but rather its absence is a defense with the burden of proof falling on the defendant.[9]

§ 7.5[2] The Section 11Damage Calculus

Damages under section 11(e) consist of the difference between the purchase price (but not in excess of the offering price) and the value of the security at the time of suit (if the plaintiff still owns the security) or, if the plaintiff has sold the security prior to bringing suit, the sale price.[10] In the event that the plaintiff owns the security at the time of suit[11] but sells the security prior to judgment, then damages are based on the difference between the purchase price and the sales price if that figure is less than the difference between the purchase price and the value at the time suit is brought.[12]

---

3. 15 U.S.C.A. § 77k(e). *See, e.g.,* Paul Grier, A Methodology for the Calculation of Section 11 Damages, 5 Stan. J.L. Bus. & Fin. 99 (1999).

4. 15 U.S.C.A. § 77k(e). *See also, e.g.,* McMahan & Co. v. Wherehouse Entertainment, Inc., 65 F.3d 1044 (2d Cir.1995) (benefit of the bargain damages are not available in section 11 action but are available under Rule 10b–5).

5. 15 U.S.C.A. § 77*l*(a)(1). Section 12(a)(1) which permits actions by purchasers against sellers who violate section 5's registration requirements is discussed in § 7.2 *supra.*

6. Aaron v. Empresas La Moderna, S.A. De C.V., 46 Fed.Appx. 452 (9th Cir.2002) (causation is not an element of a prima facie case under section 11 or 12 of the 1933 Act, but it is necessary to establish a prima facie case of a 1934 Act Rule 10b–5 violation).

7. Section 12(b), 15 U.S.C.A. § 77*l*(b). *See* §§ 7.6, 7.8 *infra. See also, e.g.,* Goldkrantz v. Griffin, 1999 WL 191540, [1999 Transfer Binder] Fed. Sec. L. Rep. (CCH) ¶ 90,462 (S.D.N.Y. 1999) (no evidence that market decline was due to misrepresentation in offering materials).

8. *See* § 12.11 *infra.*

9. *See, e.g.,* Lyne v. Arthur Andersen & Co., 772 F.Supp. 1064 (N.D.Ill.1991).

10. 15 U.S.C.A. § 77k(e).

11. *See* Alpern v. UtiliCorp United, Inc., 84 F.3d 1525 (8th Cir.1996) (damage date for claim added by amended complaint related back to the date of filing the original complaint).

12. *Id.*

A section 11 plaintiff does not have the obligation to mitigate his or her damages.[13] The formula set forth in section 11(e) presents the plaintiff who has not yet sold his or her securities with a strategic decision: whether or not to sell. Under the statutory formula, a plaintiff who has not sold prior to judgment will have damages calculated based on the "value"[14] at the time of suit. If the plaintiff does not sell prior to bringing suit, and the price of the securities declines, such decline is not part of the section 11 damages, even if plaintiff sells prior to judgment. Similarly, if the price climbs after the date of suit and the plaintiff holds the securities through the judgment, damages are based on the value on the date of suit without taking account of the subsequent market rise.[15] However, if the price rises after the date that suit is brought and plaintiff sells the securities prior to judgment, damages will be limited to the lesser of the difference between the purchase price and the value on the date of suit, or the difference between the purchase price and the sale price. Accordingly, the section 11 plaintiff who continues to hold the securities can gain by a subsequent price rise (providing there is no sale prior to judgment) but will not be protected against a price decline.

§ 7.5[2][A] Determination of "Value"

In a section 11 action, a plaintiff who has not sold the security at the time suit is brought presumably carries the burden of initially proving a decline in value of the shares between the time the security was purchased and the time of sale or suit.[16] From the terms of the statute, it would seem that the "value" of the security does not necessarily equal market price on the date of suit.[17] However, the use of "value" in section 11(e)(1) rather than "price" should not be taken as an open invitation to disregard or look too far beyond the market price. Courts should not look beyond market price on the date of suit without a compelling reason for doing so. Thus, for example, if trading has been halted, market price cannot be used as a yardstick. Similarly, if the market price had significant fluctuation on the date of suit, a court will have to determine whether the "value" is best represented by the closing price, the mean price, or some other price on that day. Where, however, the market price on the date of suit is both reliable and readily ascertainable, the price should be the court's focal point. In a questionable decision, one court found that the value of the security was in fact higher than the market price since there was sufficient documentation of "panic selling" prior to the date of original sale which had artificially lowered market price.[18] However, the better approach would have been to hold the defendant accountable for the panic selling which resulted from the misrepresentations and subsequent corrective disclosure.

13. *See* Voege v. Ackerman, 364 F.Supp. 72, 73 (S.D.N.Y.1973).

14. While market price may be the best evidence of value, other factors may be considered as well.

15. This was the case for example in Beecher v. Able, 435 F.Supp. 397 (S.D.N.Y.1975), *affirmed* 575 F.2d 1010 (2d Cir.1978) where the market price continued to rise and eventually the securities climbed back to their original offering price.

16. *See* Grossman v. Waste Management, 589 F.Supp. 395, 415 (N.D.Ill.1984).

17. Beecher v. Able, 435 F.Supp. 397 (S.D.N.Y.1975), *affirmed on other grounds* 575 F.2d 1010 (2d Cir.1978).

18. *Id.*

§ 7.5[2][B] The Negative Causation Defense

While the damages set forth in section 11(e) subsections (1) through (3) would appear to be analogous to the rescissory damages available under section 12,[20] the statute provides further that a defendant in a section 11 action may limit his or her liability to the extent that the decline in value of the security was attributable to the misstatements or omissions which formed the basis of the suit.[21] By virtue of section 12(b) of the Act,[22] a similar negative causation defense is now available in actions under section 12(a)(2), but not for suits brought under section 12(a)(1).

Significantly, under section 11, and under section 12(a)(2) as well, the burden is on the defendant to prove the absence of causation rather than the more traditional approach of requiring the plaintiff to prove that his or her damages were both in fact and proximately caused by the defendant's misconduct.[23] It has been observed that section 11(e) "does not focus on the causal relationship between the misstatement and the original purchase, but rather on the relationship between the misstatement and any subsequent decline in value."[24]

§ 7.6   Section 12(a)(2)—Liability for Material Misstatements or Omissions by Sellers of Securities

§ 7.6[1] Elements of Section 12(a)(2) Claim

Section 12(a)(2) of the 1933 Act[1] creates an express private remedy for material[2] misstatements or omissions in connection with the sale or offer for sale of a security; the offeror and seller[3] of the security is liable to the purchaser of the security. Section 12(a)(2) supplements liability under section 11 and 12(a)(1), as it is not dependent upon the Act's registration requirements.[5] The remedies under the securities laws are cumulative. Section 12(a)(2) applies to both written and oral communications.[7] The use of prospectus and oral communications are stated in the alternative. Accordingly, it is inappropriate to give undue weight to the prospectus and thereby give short shrift to the impact of the oral representations.[8] On the other hand, oral

---

20. *See* § 7.9 *infra.*

21. 15 U.S.C.A. § 77k(e) explains that the damages computed under subsections (1) through (3) are to be reduced.

22. 15 U.S.C.A. § 77*l*(b).

23. *See, e.g.,* McMahan & Co. v. Wherehouse Entertainment, Inc., 65 F.3d 1044, 1048–1049 (2d Cir. 1995).

24. Akerman v. Oryx Communications, Inc., 609 F.Supp. 363, 368 (S.D.N.Y.1984), *affirmed* 810 F.2d 336 (2d Cir.1987).

§ 7.6

1. 15 U.S.C.A. § 77l(a)(2).

2. *See, e.g.,* In re Donald J. Trump Casino Securities Litigation, 7 F.3d 357, 369 (3d Cir.1993) (materiality is the same under sections 11 and 12(a)(2) of the 1933 Act).

3. Section 12(a)(2) liability may only be imposed on "sellers" of securities as that term has been defined by the Supreme Court. Pinter v. Dahl, 486 U.S. 622, 108 S.Ct. 2063, 100 L.Ed.2d 658 (1988). *See* § 7.2[2] *supra* and § 7.7 *infra.*

5. 15 U.S.C.A. §§ 77k, 77*l*(a)(1). *See* §§ 7.2, 7.3–7.4 *supra.*

7. *See, e.g.,* McMahan & Co. v. Wherehouse Entertainment, Inc., 900 F.2d 576, 581 (2d Cir.1990), (phone conversation).

8. MidAmerica Federal Savings & Loan Association v. Shearson/American Express, Inc., 886 F.2d 1249 (10th Cir.1989).

statements will not be actionable if they do not materially affect the total mix of information available to the investor. Furthermore, accurate disclosure in the prospectus likely control over any alleged misstatements made orally or otherwise outside of the prospectus.[10] Although the 1933 Act provides for concurrent jurisdiction in the state courts, class actions brought on behalf of more than fifty plaintiffs must be brought in federal court.[11] In the aftermath of the Litigation Reform Act, plaintiffs still have a choice between a federal and state court forum with respect to individual actions, including as section 12 claim, as well as class actions involving fifty or fewer plaintiffs.[12]

Like section 12(a)(1), section 12(a)(2) is limited to liability of sellers and thus imposes a strict privity requirement.[13] In a rather surprising and highly questionable decision, one court has indicated that an offeree who did not actually purchase the stock may bring an action under section 12(a)(2).[14] Nevertheless, it seems clear that the plaintiff must be a purchaser since section 12(a)(2) in stating its privity requirement speaks in terms of securities *purchased* from the defendant.[15] The privity requirement has been strictly construed. It has thus been held that limited partners did not have standing under section 12(a)(2) to assert claims that allegedly arose in connection with their partnership's purchases of securities.[16] Accordingly, purchaser status must be established as a result of a direct rather than derivative relationship to the purchase of securities covered by the registration statement. The court indicated, however, that the result might have been different had the limited partners brought a derivative action rather than suing in their individual capacities.

As is the case with section 12(a)(1), difficult questions arise under section 12(a)(2) as to what degree of active participation in the transaction is necessary to classify someone as a section 12 "seller."[17] Generally, issuers and underwriters are not sellers within the meaning of section 12 unless they actively participate in the negotiations with the plaintiff/purchaser.[18] Similarly, an attorney's having worked on the offering circular will not make him or her a seller.[19] On the other hand, a broker who deals directly with the plaintiff is a section 12 seller.[20] In order to be a seller under section 12, the defendant must not only have a direct relationship with the plaintiff; he or she must also have been directly involved in the sale.[21]

---

10.   Ambrosino v. Rodman & Renshaw, Inc., 972 F.2d 776 (7th Cir.1992) (written disclosures precluded reliance on oral misrepresentations that were at variance with the writing).

11.   1933 Act § 22(a), 15 U.S.C.A. § 77v(a). *See* § 1933 Act § 16, 15 U.S.C.A. § 77p, which is discussed in § 7.17 *infra*.

12.   Kelly v. McKesson HBOC, Inc., 2002 WL 88939 (Del.Super.2002) (permitting section 12 claim to proceed in state court).

13.   Qualifications for a section 12 seller are discussed in § 7.2 *supra*.

14.   Doll v. James Martin Associates (Holdings) Ltd., 600 F.Supp. 510 (E.D.Mich.1984).

15.   *See, e.g.,* Shaw v. Digital Equipment Corp., 82 F.3d 1194 (1st Cir.1996) (dismissing section 12(a)(2) claims against all defendants except underwriters).

16.   Davis v. Coopers & Lybrand, 787 F.Supp. 787 (N.D.Ill.1992).

17.   *See, e.g.,* Junker v. Crory, 650 F.2d 1349 (5th Cir.1981).

18.   *See* Foster v. Jesup & Lamont Securities Co., 759 F.2d 838 (11th Cir.1985).

19.   *E.g.,* Moore v. Kayport Package Express, Inc., 885 F.2d 531 (9th Cir.1989).

20.   *E.g.,* Quincy Co–Operative Bank v. A.G. Edwards & Sons, Inc., 655 F.Supp. 78 (D.Mass. 1986).

21.   Pinter v. Dahl, 486 U.S. 622, 108 S.Ct. 2063, 100 L.Ed.2d 658 (1988).

Section 12(a)(2) liability is narrower than section 11 insofar as privity is required for the former.[22] However, section 12(a)(2) is also broader than section 11 since it applies to all sellers and is not limited to the types of persons specified in section 11(a). Section 12(a)(2) is not limited to written statements and, unlike section 11, applies to oral misrepresentations.[24] Furthermore, as compared with Rule 10b–5 which would give the injured purchaser an implied right of action under the 1934 Act,[25] section 12(a)(2) liability does not require scienter.

Section 12(a)(2) renders the seller liable if he or she "shall not sustain the burden of proof that he did not know, and in the exercise of reasonable care could not have known, of such untruth or omission."[26] The imposition of a "reasonable care" standard is different language than the "due diligence" rubric of section 11.[27] It is clear that section 12(a)(2)'s requirement of "reasonable care" imparts some sort of negligence standard and that it is not necessary for the purchaser to show any type of scienter on the seller's part.[28] Although there is not a *per se* affirmative investigation requirement, it has been held that the section 12(a)(2) standard of reasonable care may impose a duty to investigate depending upon the circumstances.[29] Reasonable care imparts a sliding scale of standards of conduct and has been held to impose a duty of *continuing investigation* in the case of the exclusive dealer of the security in question.[30] On the other hand, two justices of the Supreme Court have taken the position that any imposition of an affirmative investigation requirement is a misapplication of the "reasonable care" standard since the "investigation" language of section 11 is said to call for a greater undertaking than the "care" requirement of section 12(a)(2).[31]

Reliance is generally an element of a fraud claim.[45] However, it is generally held that once the plaintiff has proved a material omission, it is not necessary for plaintiff to establish reliance in a section 12(a)(2) action.[46] A plaintiff with knowledge of the fraud cannot claim reliance and thus in such a case the section 12(a)(2) claim should be dismissed.[47]

In 1995, Congress introduced section 12(b) to the 1933 Act[51] that provides an affirmative defense to a 12(a)(2) action where there is an absence of loss

22. *See, e.g.,* In re Ultrafem, Inc. Securities Litigation, 91 F.Supp.2d 678 (S.D.N.Y. 2000) (section 12(a)(2) claim dismissed but section 11 claim was stated).

24. *E.g.,* Metromedia Co. v. Fugazy, 983 F.2d 350, 361–62 (2d Cir.1992), *affirming* 753 F.Supp. 93 (S.D.N.Y.1990).

25. *See* chapter 12 *infra.*

26. 15 U.S.C.A. § 77*l*(a)(2).

27. *See* § 7.4 *supra.*

28. *See, e.g.,* Wigand v. Flo–Tek, Inc., 609 F.2d 1028 (2d Cir.1979).

29. Sanders v. John Nuveen & Co., 619 F.2d 1222, 1228 (7th Cir.1980), *cert. denied* 450 U.S. 1005, 101 S.Ct. 1719, 68 L.Ed.2d 210 (1981).

30. *See* Franklin Savings Bank v. Levy, 551 F.2d 521, 527 (2d Cir.1977) (commercial paper).

31. John Nuveen & Co. v. Sanders, 450 U.S. 1005, 101 S.Ct. 1719, 68 L.Ed.2d 210 (1981) (Powell, J., joined by Rehnquist, J.; dissenting from a denial of certiorari).

45. *See, e.g.,* Pell v. Weinstein, 759 F.Supp. 1107 (M.D.Pa.1991), *judgment affirmed* 961 F.2d 1568 (3d Cir.1992) (no section 12(a)(2) claim where plaintiff committed to transaction in question prior to seeing allegedly misleading statements).

46. Wright v. National Warranty Co., 953 F.2d 256 (6th Cir.1992) (reliance is not an element of a section 12(a)(2) claim; the fact that plaintiff was an insider did not by itself bar a section 12(a)(2) action).

47. *E.g.,* Mayer v. Oil Field Systems Corp., 803 F.2d 749 (2d Cir.1986).

51. 15 U.S.C.A. § 77*l*(b).

causation. Analogous to the negative causation defense under section 11 of the Act,[52] if a defendant proves that a portion or all of the decline in value of a security was caused by factors unrelated to the material misstatement or omission that is the subject of the 12(a)(2) action, the plaintiff is disallowed that portion of corresponding loss. The burden of proof is on the defendant to prove the absence of loss causation, and in some situations this defense will allow a defendant to avoid an action for recession.

The section 12(a)(2) action may be brought in either law or equity.[53] Additionally, like section 12(a)(1) but unlike section 11 or the implied remedy under Rule 10b–5 of the Exchange Act,[54] damages are limited to either rescission and return of the purchase price or damages based on that amount if the purchaser no longer owns the security. Borrowing from general principles from the law of equity, it has been held that in order to qualify for relief under section 12(a)(2), the plaintiff must make a demand for rescission promptly upon learning of the misrepresentation.[56]

The Supreme Court has held that in computing damages under section 12, tax benefits are not to be considered as income received by the plaintiff and therefore are not to be deducted from the damage award.[57] Thus, the fact that the plaintiffs received tax benefits does not affect their rescissory damages. Unlike an action under section 11,[58] there is no provision in section 12 for the award of costs or attorneys fees. However, where the claim or defense is without merit costs and fees may be awarded as a sanction under Rule 11 of the Federal Rules of Civil Procedure.[59] Additionally, where the section 12 claims are brought with pendent state claims, state law may permit the award of costs and attorneys fees.[60] By virtue of section 13 of the 1933 Act[61] the purchaser must bring suit within one year after discovery of the misstatement or omission, or within one year after the date upon which such discovery should have been made through the exercise of reasonable diligence, but in no event may an action be brought more than three years after the sale.

52. 15 U.S.C.A. § 77k(e). *See* § 7.5 *supra.*

53. Section 22(a) of the 1933 Act provides that suit can be brought in state or federal court and there is no right of removal to federal court for suits brought in state court. 15 U.S.C.A. § 77v(a). *See* § 17.1 *infra.* However, as a result of the Securities Litigation Uniform Standards Act of 1998, private class actions with more than fifty class members in fraud or disclosure based actions under the securities laws must be brought in federal court. 1933 Act § 16, 15 U.S.C.A. § 77p. *See* § 7.17[2] *infra.* Since a section 12(a)(2) action is premised on materially misleading disclosures, the mandatory federal forum applies to such class actions. *See id.*

54. 17 C.F.R. § 240.10b–5.

56. Westinghouse Electric Corp. v. "21" International Holdings, Inc., 821 F.Supp. 212 (S.D.N.Y.1993), relying on Gannett Co. v. Register Publishing Co., 428 F.Supp. 818, 827–28 (D.Conn.1977) (the necessity of a prompt demand for rescission in an action under Rule 10b–5 also applies to section 12(a)(2) actions).

57. Randall v. Loftsgaarden, 478 U.S. 647, 106 S.Ct. 3143, 92 L.Ed.2d 525 (1986).

58. 15 U.S.C.A. § 77k(e). Section 11 costs and attorneys fees are discussed in § 7.16 *infra.*

59. Fed.R.Civ.P. 11. Rule 11 sanctions are discussed in § 12.14 *infra.*

60. Austin v. Loftsgaarden, 768 F.2d 949 (8th Cir.1985), *reversed on other grounds* 478 U.S. 647, 106 S.Ct. 3143, 92 L.Ed.2d 525 (1986); Monetary Management Group v. Kidder, Peabody & Co., 615 F.Supp. 1217 (E.D.Mo.1985).

61. 15 U.S.C.A. § 77m.

§ 7.6[2] Judicially Imposed Limits on Section 12(a)(2)—The Public Offering or Batch Offering Limitation

§ 7.6[2][A] Evolution of the Public Offering Limitation

Section 12(a)(2) has no express limits on its application except for those discussed earlier in this section. However, beginning in the 1990s, many decisions have held that section 12(a)(2) applies only to distributions of securities and not to isolated after-market transactions that are not part of a "batch offering."[62] Although not all courts concurred, subsequently the Supreme Court in a five-to-four decision concurred by imposing a public offering limitation on the scope of the section 12(a)(2) remedy.[63] The impact of the public offering limitation is twofold. In the first instance, it means that section 12(a)(2) is not available for misstatements made in connection with a small, limited, or private offering of securities. Secondly, the section 12(a)(2) remedy is no longer available for transactions occurring in the after-market regardless of whether those transactions are privately negotiated or take place in the public markets.

Those courts reaching this unfortunate and erroneous conclusion that section 12(a)(2) should be interpreted as limited to public offerings cannot find this limitation in the express language of the statute. Instead, the courts have implied the limitation by relying on the statutory language of section 12(a)(2), which refers to misstatements and omissions made by "*prospectus or oral communication.*"[64] The courts have extrapolated from the words of the statute that the use of the term "prospectus" shows a legislative intent to limit the section's operation to the offering process. The error in this approach is due in part to the fact that the statutory definition of prospectus[65] does not have any such restriction and thus, on its face, applies to *all* written, television, or radio offers to sell securities, including a sales confirmation, and a contract to sell.[66]

§ 7.6[2][B] Criticism of the Public Offering Limitation

Such a limiting view of section 12(a)(2) is not only unwise as a matter of policy, it does not comport with the Act's legislative history.[68] The cases which limit the scope of section 12(a)(2) are inconsistent with the Supreme Court's earlier pronouncement that overlap between multiple remedies under the securities laws "is neither unusual nor unfortunate."[69] Furthermore, Congress took great care in drafting the provisions of the 1933 Act and it is difficult to imagine that they would have intended a severe limitation on the scope of section 12(a)(2) and not make it an explicit one.[70] It has aptly been

---

62. *E.g.,* Ballay v. Legg Mason Wood Walker, Inc., 925 F.2d 682 (3d Cir.1991), *cert. denied* 502 U.S. 820, 112 S.Ct. 79, 116 L.Ed.2d 52 (1991).

63. Gustafson v. Alloyd Co., 513 U.S. 561, 115 S.Ct. 1061, 131 L.Ed.2d 1 (1995).

64. 15 U.S.C.A. § 77l(a)(2).

65. 15 U.S.C.A. § 77b(a)(10).

66. *See* § 2.5 *supra.*

68. *See, e.g.,* Louis Loss, Securities Act Section 12(a)(2): A Rebuttal, 48 Bus. Law. 47 (1992). *But see* Elliot J. Weiss, The Courts Have it Right: Securities Act § 12(a)(2) Applies only to Public Offerings, 48 Bus. Law. 1 (1992).

69. Herman & MacLean v. Huddleston, 459 U.S. 375, 383, 103 S.Ct. 683, 688, 74 L.Ed.2d 548, 556 (1983).

70. *See* Louis Loss, The Assault on Securities Act Section 12(a)(2), 105 Harv.L.Rev. 908, 916–17 (1992); Therese Maynard, The Future of Securities Act Section 12(a)(2), 45 Ala. L. Rev. 817 (1994).

observed that "it is almost inconceivable that [the 1933 and 1934 Acts]—which repeatedly have been treated as *in pari materia*—were meant to afford no civil remedy whatsoever to the great bulk of investors who do not participate in distributions."[71] It thus should be clear that section 12(a)(2) has application to private transactions as well as to public offerings. Therefore, for example, although not dealing directly with the specific issue involved in the batch offering cases, the Second Circuit stated unequivocally that section 12(a)(2) "consistently has been applied to private as well as to public offerings of securities."[72]

§ 7.6[2][C] The *Gustafson* Decision

Notwithstanding the above-described difficulties in arriving at a limiting interpretation of section 12(a)(2), in a sharply divided five-to-four decision in Gustafson v. Alloyd Co.,[84] the Supreme Court reached just such a result. As had been the case in the previous lower court decisions, the Supreme Court focused on the use of the term "prospectus" in section 12(a)(2). Unlike what the lower courts had done in many instances, the Supreme Court did not base its decision on the concept of a "batch offering." Nevertheless, the Court did seem to equate the use of a prospectus with a public offering. As is discussed more fully below, in all likelihood, however, section 12(a)(2) will remain applicable to some exempt offerings.

The Court in *Gustafson* acknowledged that section 2(a)(10) broadly defines prospectus to include any written offer to sell.[85] The Court then looked to section 10 of the Act,[86] which sets forth the statutory prospectus requirements; the Court concluded that the term, as it is used in section 12(a)(2), should be read as coextensive with the concept of prospectus in section 10. Accordingly, the Court rejected the plaintiff's contention that the contract for sale qualified as a "prospectus" under section 12(a)(2) and thereby limited section 12 to offerings by prospectus. The Court concluded, "the word 'prospectus' is a term of art referring to a document that describes a public offering of securities by an issuer or controlling shareholder."[90] The majority opinion in *Gustafson* explained: "[t]he contract of sale, and its recitations, were not held out to the public and were not a prospectus as the term is used in the 1933 Act."[91] The *Gustafson* decision has not put the matter completely to rest. A number of questions survive the Court's rather strained reading of the 1933 Act.[92]

---

71. Louis Loss, The Assault on Securities Act Section 12(a)(2), 105 Harv.L.Rev. 908, 916 (1992) (footnote omitted). *See also* Louis Loss, Securities Act Section 12(a)(2): A Rebuttal, 48 Bus. Law. 47 (1992)

72. Metromedia Co. v. Fugazy, 983 F.2d 350, 361 (2d Cir.1992), *cert. denied* 508 U.S. 952, 113 S.Ct. 2445, 124 L.Ed.2d 662 (1993); Cewnick Fund v. Castle, 1993 WL 88243, [1992–1993 Transfer Binder] Fed.Sec.L.Rep. (CCH) ¶ 97,392 (S.D.N.Y.1993).

84. 513 U.S. 561, 115 S.Ct. 1061, 131 L.Ed.2d 1 (1995).

85. 15 U.S.C.A. § 77b(a)(10). *See* § 2.4 *supra.* This is supplemented by a broadly interpreted definition of "offer to sell" in section 2(a)(3), 15 U.S.C.A. § 77b(a)(3). *See* § 2.3 *supra.*

86. 15 U.S.C.A. § 77j. *See* § 2.4 *supra.*

90. 513 U.S. at 584, 115 S.Ct. at 1073–74.

91. *Id.*

92. *See, e.g.,* In re Transkaryotic Therapies, Inc. Securities Litigation, 319 F.Supp.2d 152 (D.Mass.2004) (upholding section 12(a)(2) complaint as to plaintiff who purchased out of the public offering but not those who purchased in the open market).

§ 7.6[2][D] Remaining Questions on the Public Offering Limitation

In a public offering, are section 12(a)(2) plaintiffs limited to direct purchasers? Section 11 of the 1933 Act,[93] which creates liability for material misstatements and omissions in a registration statement, has a strict tracing requirement. The plaintiff must be able to trace the securities purchased to the registration statement. Under this requirement, purchasers in the immediate aftermarket are eligible to bring section 11 claims.[94] Similarly, immediate aftermarket purchasers are proper plaintiffs in a section 12(a)(2) action.[95] At least one court has allowed a section 12(a)(2) claim for a purchaser who was too remote for a section 11 claim.[96]

Is the section 12(a)(2) remedy now limited only to statements in the prospectus? The answer is clearly "no" so long as the offering was made through the use of a prospectus.[97] An interesting twist on the public offering requirement occurred in a 1999 district court decision.[98] The court there equated the section 12(a)(2) with a public offering regardless of whether a prospectus was used; the court reasoned that section 12(a)(2) applies to public offerings where registration was required even if there was no registration.[99] The significance of such an approach must be tempered against the fact that in an offering in which registration was required but there was a failure to register or to comply with the prospectus delivery requirements, the plaintiff would have a claim for recession under section 12(a)(1) of the Act without having to show either misrepresentation or causation.[100]

§ 7.11 The Securities Act's General Prohibition on Material Misstatements and Omissions—Section 17

Section 17 of the 1933 Act,[1] which is drafted in terms of defining a violation of the Act, contains general antifraud proscriptions that supplement section 5[2] and the express civil liability provisions.[3] Section 17(a) prohibits fraud, material misstatements, and omissions of fact in connection with[4] the

---

93. 15 U.S.C.A. § 77k. *See* § 7.3 *supra.*

94. *See* Hertzberg v. Dignity Partners, Inc., 191 F.3d 1076 (9th Cir.1999).

95. *E.g.,* Feiner v. SS & C Technologies, Inc., 47 F.Supp.2d 250, 253 (D.Conn.1999) (aftermarket plaintiff).

96. Brosious v. Children's Place Retail Stores, 189 F.R.D. 138 (D.N.J.1999) (secondary purchasers were too remote for section 11 claim but were proper plaintiffs in section 12(a)(2) claim).

97. *See, e.g.,* Feiner v. SS & C Technologies, Inc., 47 F.Supp.2d 250, 253 (D.Conn.1999) (it is not necessary that a prospectus was delivered to the plaintiff).

98. Flake v. Hoskins, 55 F.Supp.2d 1196 1228–1229 (D.Kan.1999).

99. *Id.*

100. 15 U.S.C.A. § 77l(a)(2) which provides a right of rescission against a section 12 seller of securities if the sale was made in violation of section 5 of the Act. Section 12(a)(1) is discussed in § 7.2 *supra.*

§ 7.11

1. 15 U.S.C.A. § 77q. One of the major contributions of section 17(a) of the 1933 Act is that it was the model for Rule 10b–5 of the 1934 Act which has become the broadest of the antifraud proscriptions under the securities laws. *See* § 12.3 *infra.*

2. 15 U.S.C.A. § 77e. *See* §§ 2.1–2.5 *supra.*

3. Sections 11 and 12 are discussed in §§ 7.2–7.5 *supra.*

4. *See, e.g.,* SEC v. Zandford, 535 U.S. 813, 122 S.Ct. 1899, 153 L.Ed.2d 1 (200), *reversing* 238 F.3d 559 (4th Cir.2001) (broker's conversion was fraud in connection with a securities transaction and thus did not violate section 17(a)).

sale[5] of securities.[6] Section 17(a) applies regardless of whether the securities are registered or whether they are exempt from registration under section 3 of the Act.[7] In 2000, section 17(a) was amended to extend its antifraud reach to security-based swap agreements even though those agreements are exempted from the definition of security.[8]

As is the case with Exchange Act Rule 10b–5,[9] section 17(a) does not impose an affirmative duty to disclose. Instead it imposes liability for omissions that make the statements made materially misleading.[10] However unlike its Exchange Act counterpart, section 17(a) applies only to sales of and *offers to sell* securities and thus to activities of the offeror or seller but not to fraud by the purchaser. Section 17(a) covers negligent material misstatements and omissions.[11]

The early decisions were divided on the question of whether section 17(a) will support an implied private remedy. The overwhelming majority of recent decisions have not been at all receptive to the private right of action.[21] The trend against implying a remedy has been so strong that the Eighth Circuit affirmed the imposition of Rule 11 sanctions against counsel signing a complaint alleging a remedy under section 17(a).[22] Accordingly, prior to filing a section 17 claim, counsel should make a careful investigation and be confident that the issue has not been resolved clearly to the contrary in that circuit.

Notwithstanding the growing support for the absence of an implied private remedy, violations of section 17 can lead to SEC actions resulting in disgorgement of improper profits.[23] Also, the absence of a private damage remedy does not necessarily preclude the possibility of injunctive relief in a private action.

In addition to section 17(a)'s antifraud prohibitions, section 17(b)[25] prohibits disseminating information about a security without disclosing any consideration received or to be received, directly or indirectly, in connection with sales of the security. Section 17(b) is not limited to formal offers to sell. Also, like section 17(a), 17(b) applies to securities whether or not in registra-

---

5. Section 17(a) focuses on sellers (as opposed to Rule 10b–5 which address fraud by either sellers or purchasers). In Pinter v. Dahl, 486 U.S. 622, n. 9, 108 S.Ct. 2063, 100 L.Ed.2d 658 (1988), the Supreme Court held that the private damage remedy under section 12 of the Act (15 U.S.C.A. § 77*l*) can only be brought against someone who actually sold the security to the plaintiff. At least one court has held that section 17(a) applies to sellers in much the same way as section 12(a).

6. 15 U.S.C.A. § 77q(a).

7. 15 U.S.C.A. § 77q(c). Section 3's exemptions are discussed in chapter 4 *supra*.

8. 15 U.S.C.A. § 77q(a) as amended by Pub. Law 106–554, 114 Stat. 2763 (December 21, 2000).

9. 17 C.F.R. § 240.10b–5. *See* chapter 12 *infra*.

10. United States v. Crop Growers Corp., 954 F.Supp. 335, 349–350 (D.D.C.1997).

11. Aaron v. SEC, 446 U.S. 680, 100 S.Ct. 1945, 64 L.Ed.2d 611 (1980), *on remand* 666 F.2d 5 (2d Cir.1981).

21. *E.g.*, Bath v. Bushkin, Gaims, Gaines & Jonas, 913 F.2d 817 (10th Cir.1990). *See also* the authorities in § 12.22 *infra*.

22. Crookham v. Crookham, 914 F.2d 1027 (8th Cir.1990) ($10,000 sanction).

23. SEC v. Mesa Limited Partnership, [1990 Transfer Binder] Fed.Sec.L.Rep. (CCH) ¶ 95,492 (N.D.Tex.1990). SEC remedies are discussed in § 16.2 *infra*.

25. 15 U.S.C.A. § 77q(b).

tion or exempt under section 3.[28] Section 17(b) was designed to prevent the misleading impression of impartiality in certain recommendations.[29] As explained in the House Report, section 17(b)'s prohibitions were "particularly designed to meet the evils of the 'tipster sheet,' as well as articles in newspapers or periodicals that purport to give an unbiased opinion but which in reality are bought and paid for."[30] Section 17(b) has been held applicable to periodicals receiving compensation for favorable recommendations notwithstanding a challenge that such regulation violates First Amendment rights of free speech.[31] As a general proposition section 17(b) withstands a First Amendment attack since the prohibition is addressed to commercial speech.[32] Among other things, the anti-touting provisions of section 17(b) are reasonably related to governmental interests in protecting the deception of investors.[33]

§ 7.12　Multiple Defendants—Joint and Several Liability; Liability of Controlling Persons

Section 11(f) of the 1933 Act[1] provides that multiple defendants in section 11 actions are jointly and severally liable for the damages awarded with the exception of outside directors who did not have knowledge of the misstatements or omissions. Those outside directors are held to be accountable according to proportionate liability.

Consistent with the trend in common law negligence cases, the federal courts have recognized a right of contribution among joint tortfeasors.[3] The extent of this right to contribution is a matter of federal law. In addition to section 11(f), section 18(b) of the 1934 Act[5] also provides for contribution among defendants in an action for false filings under section 18(a).[6] But what about liabilities arising under other sections of the securities acts? Although both the 1933 and 1934 Acts recognize joint and several liability of controlling persons,[7] there is silence on whether this liability is coupled with a right of contribution. Similarly, the Acts are silent as to the existence of a right to contribution in the event of joint and several liability arising out of joint activity. The right to contribution is distinct from any contractual agreement for indemnification.

28.　15 U.S.C.A. § 77q(c).

29.　*See, e.g.,* SEC v. Liberty Capital Group, Inc., 75 F.Supp.2d 1160 (W.D.Wash.1999).

30.　H.R.Rep. No. 85, 73d Cong., 1st Sess. 24 (1933).

31.　SEC v. Wall Street Publishing Institute, Inc., 851 F.2d 365 (D.C.Cir.1988). The First Amendment argument was based on the Supreme Court's decision in Lowe v. SEC, 472 U.S. 181, 105 S.Ct. 2557, 86 L.Ed.2d 130 (1985) which held that the Investment Advisers Act does not require registration of newsletters rendering investment advice. Although not decided directly on constitutional grounds, the Court's decision in *Lowe* was premised on finding an interpretation of the Investment Advisers Act that would not be unconstitutional.

32.　United States v. Wenger, 292 F.Supp.2d 1296, 1303–1307 (D. Utah 2003).

33.　*Id. See also* SEC v. Wall Street Publishing, 851 F.2d 365 (D.C. Cir. 1988).

§ 7.12

1.　15 U.S.C.A. § 77k(f).

3.　Globus, Inc. v. Law Research Service, Inc., 318 F.Supp. 955 (S.D.N.Y.1970), *judgment affirmed* 442 F.2d 1346 (2d Cir.1971), *cert. denied* 404 U.S. 941, 92 S.Ct. 286, 30 L.Ed.2d 254 (1971).

5.　15 U.S.C.A. § 78r(b).

6.　15 U.S.C.A. § 78r(a). *See* § 12.19 *infra*.

7.　15 U.S.C.A. §§ 77*o*, 78r.

At one time, the universal common law rule was that there was no right to contribution among joint tortfeasors.[10] The reason for this rule was the law's reluctance to aid wrongdoers. Many states have modified the rule to allow contribution in negligence actions, but many still do not allow contribution among intentional tortfeasors.[11] Some state corporate statutes provide a right of contribution for directors who are liable for mismanagement.[12]

The general rule that has developed in federal securities cases is that there is a right of contribution. In the absence of a statutory provision requiring contribution under the federal securities laws, some courts look to the law of the forum state.[14] Where one party is considerably more culpable than others, there may not be a claim for equal contribution.[15] The Supreme Court ruled that there is an implied right of contribution in actions under SEC Rule 10b–5 of the 1934 Act.[19] In so ruling, the Court distinguished cases decided under other federal statutes containing an express right of action but no right of contribution. The case against an implied right of contribution is stronger where Congress created a right of action but said nothing about a right to contribution. Although a number of decisions caution against the implication of additional federal remedies,[20] once the courts have recognized an implied right of action, then it is appropriate to flesh it out so as to render it a reasonable remedy.[21] Implying a right of contribution is consistent with this goal. The Court pointed out that sections 9(e) and 18(a) of the 1934 Act,[22] both of which contain an express right of action, provide for a right of contribution. The Court concluded that the similarities between sections 9(e), 18(a), and 10(b) justify the recognition of an implied right of contribution under Rule 10b–5.

A number of courts have held that non-settling defendants may not pursue their right of contribution against settling defendants.[25] However, not all courts agreed that the policy favoring settlements overrides the right of contribution. The Private Securities Litigation Reform Act put the issue to rest by precluding actions for contribution following a settlement.

---

10. *E.g.* Merryweather v. Nixan, 1799, 8 Term.Rep. 186, 101 Eng.Rep. 1337. *See generally* W. Prosser *supra* note 7 § 50. This no contribution rule has been the subject of much debate and is continually being eroded by the courts.

11. *E.g.* Uniform Contribution Among Joint Tortfeasor Act. The trend both in the courts and legislatures had been to expand the situations in which contribution applies. *See* W. Prosser *supra* note 7 § 50.

12. *See* 8 Del.Code § 174(b). Although there are some older cases recognizing a right to contribution in the absence of statute, "their continued authority is uncertain." W. Cary & M. Eisenberg, Corporations: Cases and Materials 1402 (5th unab. ed. 1980).

14. First Federal Savings & Loan Assoc. v. Oppenheim, Appel, Dixon & Co., 631 F.Supp. 1029 (S.D.N.Y.1986).

15. Smith v. Mulvaney, 1985 WL 29953, [1984–85 Transfer Binder] Fed.Sec.L.Rep. (CCH) ¶ 92,084 (S.D.Cal.1985); Adalman v. Baker, Watts & Co., 599 F.Supp. 752 (D.Md.1984).

19. Musick, Peeler & Garrett v. Employers Insurance of Wausau, 508 U.S. 286, 113 S.Ct. 2085, 124 L.Ed.2d 194 (1993).

20. *See* § 12.2 *infra.*

21. *See* 508 U.S. at 292–293, 113 S.Ct. at 2088–89, relying on Virginia Bankshares, Inc. v. Sandberg, 501 U.S. 1083, 111 S.Ct. 2749, 115 L.Ed.2d 929 (1991) and Blue Chip Stamps v. Manor Drug Stores, 421 U.S. 723, 95 S.Ct. 1917, 44 L.Ed.2d 539 (1975).

22. 15 U.S.C.A. §§ 78i(e), 78r(a). *See* §§ 12.1, 12.19 *infra.*

25. Nelson v. Bennett, 662 F.Supp. 1324, 1332 (E.D.Cal.1987) (quoting In re Nucorp Energy Securities Litigation, 661 F.Supp. 1403, 1408 (S.D.Cal.1987)).

Section 21D(f)(7) of the 1934 Act[27] establishes a settlement bar rule for pretrial settlements. If a defendant settles a claim prior to trial, the court is directed to enter a bar order which will preclude all future claims for contribution against the settling defendant arising out of the action.[28] The bar order is bilateral in that it prohibits not only contribution claims against the settling defendant, but also any contribution claims the settling defendant might have except against someone whose liability was extinguished by the settlement.[29] The rule barring contribution against settling defendants applies to actions brought under section 11 of the 1933 Act.[30] The Reform Act further provides that any judgment subsequently obtained against non-settling defendants shall be reduced by the greater of (1) an amount corresponding to the settling defendant's percentage responsibility or (2) the dollar amount paid by the settling defendant to the plaintiff.[31] The specific prohibitions of the Reform Act bar contribution for liability arising out of settlements even with regard to claims where a right of contribution might be found other under provisions of the securities laws.[32] Statutory controlling person liability adds a basis for secondary liability that is unavailable to plaintiffs in fraud actions that are not based on the securities laws.[33]

Liability of Controlling Persons

Section 15 of the Act[34] imposes joint and several liability upon controlling persons for the acts of persons under their control. Section 20 of the 1934 Act has a comparable provision.[36] Notwithstanding a slight difference in language, these two provisions have been interpreted similarly.[37]

Controlling person liability, which is highly factual, will not be imposed if "the controlling person had no knowledge of or reasonable grounds to believe in the existence of the facts by reason of which the liability of the controlled person is alleged to exist."[39] This defense would not be available under common law principles of vicarious liability under the doctrine of respondeat superior. The "lack of knowledge" defense to controlling person liability has been held to relate to the basic facts underlying the course of business; therefore, standing alone, lack of knowledge of the particular transaction does not preclude controlling person liability.[40] The burden of establishing the lack of knowledge defense falls on those persons charged with controlling person

27.   15 U.S.C.A. § 78u–4(f)(7).

28.   *Id.*

29.   15 U.S.C.A. § 78u–4(f)(7).

30.   *See* In re Cendant Corp. Securities Litigation, 139 F.Supp.2d 585 (D. N.J. 2001).

31.   15 U.S.C.A. § 78u–4(f)(7).

32.   *See, e.g.,* In re Cendant Corp. Securities Litigation, 139 F.Supp.2d 585 (D.N.J. 2001) (Litigation Reform Act precludes contribution after settlement even though contribution might otherwise be permitted under section 11 of the 1933 Act).

33.   In re Miller, 276 F.3d 424, 429 (8th Cir.2002).

34.   *See* 15 U.S.C.A. § 77o.

36.   15 U.S.C.A. § 78t(a).

37.   *E.g.,* Farley v. Henson, 11 F.3d 827 (8th Cir.1993); Hollinger v. Titan Capital Corp., 914 F.2d 1564, 1578 (9th Cir.1990), *cert. denied* 499 U.S. 976, 111 S.Ct. 1621, 113 L.Ed.2d 719 (1991).

39.   15 U.S.C.A. § 77o.

40.   San Francisco–Oklahoma Petroleum Exploration Corp. v. Carstan Oil Co., 765 F.2d 962 (10th Cir.1985). *But see* Durham v. Kelly, 810 F.2d 1500 (9th Cir.1987) (corporate president's wife exercised some control but not held liable since she did not induce the misstatements in question).

liability.[41] Although controlling person liability under the 1933 and 1934 Acts is generally the same, controlling person liability under the 1933 Act has been held not to require knowledge of the misstatements in question although such knowledge is required for controlling person liability under the 1934 Act.[42] A number of courts further require specific allegations of the controlling person's participation in the wrongful conduct.[43]

§ 7.13   Multiple Defendants—Aiding and Abetting

§ 7.13[1][A]   Aiding and Abetting's Demise

As discussed in the preceding section, when multiple defendants have violated the securities laws, their activities will frequently result in joint and several liability.[2] Similarly, the federal securities laws impose liability upon persons in control of the actual violators.[3] However, neither the Securities Act of 1933 nor the Securities Exchange Act of 1934 expressly imposes liability on secondary participants in securities violations. The district and circuit courts, nevertheless, applied common law principles of aiding and abetting to reach such offenders. However, in 1994, the Supreme Court held that there is no private right of action for aiding and abetting violations of the Securities Exchange Act's general antifraud provisions.[4] The Court reasoned that in the absence of express statutory authority, there could be no private right of action for aiding and abetting. In so ruling, the Court refused to imply such a remedy from the general criminal statute that makes it a crime to aid and abet any primary federal crime.[5] The Court pointed to the absence of aiding and abetting language in Rule 10b–5 or in any of the securities laws' general remedial provisions.[6]

Congress, in the Private Securities Litigation Reform Act of 1995, declined to overrule the Supreme Court's decision in *Central Bank*.[19] However, at the same time, the 1995 legislation gave the SEC the power to bring enforcement actions against persons who knowingly provide substantial assistance to primary violators of the securities laws.[20] Therefore, aiders and abettors may be held liable to the same extent as controlling persons[21] in SEC actions so long as the requisite element of knowledge is shown. Even beyond the SEC's enforcement authority, to the extent that a primary violation can be alleged, liability may still be established for participating in the transaction.

---

41. *See, e.g.,* Mecca v. Gibraltar Corp., 746 F.Supp. 338 (S.D.N.Y.1990).

42. In re Twinlab Corp. Securities Litigation 103 F.Supp.2d 193 (E.D.N.Y.2000); Degulis v. LXR Biotechnology, Inc., 928 F.Supp. 1301, 1315 (S.D.N.Y.1996).

43. *See, e.g.,* Rosen v. Cascade International, 21 F.3d 1520, 1525 (11th Cir.1994).

§ 7.13

2. *See* § 7.12 *supra.*

3. *See id.*

4. Central Bank of Denver, N.A. v. First Interstate Bank of Denver, 511 U.S. 164, 114 S.Ct. 1439, 128 L.Ed.2d 119 (1994). *See* § 12.25 *infra.*

5. 18 U.S.C.A. § 2.

6. 511 U.S. at 180–181, 114 S.Ct. at 1449–50.

19. *See* S. Rep. No. 104–98, 104th Cong., XX Sess. at (1995).

20. Section 20(f) of the 1934 Act, 15 U.S.C.A. § 78t.

21. Controlling person liability is considered in § 7.12 *supra* and § 12.24 *infra.*

§ 7.14 Multiple Defendants—Indemnification Agreements

Virtually all state corporation statutes have provisions that authorize the corporation to indemnify officers and directors against liabilities incurred by them in the scope of carrying out the business of their office.[1] Under these statutes, officers or directors who have been successful in any action against them in their corporate capacity have an absolute right to indemnification for all expenses in defending the suit, including their attorneys fees.[2] Where an action is brought by a third party, a defendant—although unsuccessful on the merits of the suit—may nevertheless be reimbursed by the corporation acting through a resolution of the board of directors for any judgment and settlement payments in addition to all expenses that were "actually and reasonably incurred" in the litigation, provided that in committing the acts resulting in liability, the defendant "acted in good faith and in a manner he reasonably believed to be in or not opposed to the best interest of the corporation."[3] Many of these state statutes further provide that their indemnification provisions are not exclusive of any other rights that may be conferred by corporate bylaw, charter, agreement, or other stockholder or director action.[4] It would seem to follow that expenses that would not be subject to indemnification under the terms of the statute may not properly be the subject of a preexisting contractual arrangement.

While the foregoing indemnification rules provide a great deal of controversy in general, they are of particular interest with regard to liabilities incurred for violations of the federal securities law. Because of their federal impact, indemnification agreements have been subjected to scrutiny and limited under the securities laws.

In 1944, the Securities and Exchange Commission molded its initial policy on indemnification agreements, in connection with a registered offering by Johnson & Johnson Company. This since became known as the *"Johnson & Johnson* formula," and has been followed consistently by the Commission. Under the formula, in order to qualify for acceleration of the effective date unless all of officers', directors', or controlling persons' rights of indemnification arising out of the offering are waived, the registrant must state in the registration statement that the Commission adheres to the position that such indemnification arrangements are against the public policy embodied in the Securities Act and are therefore unenforceable.[6] In order to qualify for acceleration when the indemnification agreements are not waived, the issuer must make the additional undertaking that unless any lawsuit arising out of the offering is settled by controlling precedent, all claims for indemnification arising out of securities liabilities will be submitted for court approval.[7] The requirement of court approval does not apply, however, to expenses of a successful defense to such an action. The *Johnson & Johnson* formula has

---

§ 7.14

1. *See, e.g.,* 8 Del.Code § 145; Revised Model Bus.Corp. Act §§ 8.50–8.58.

2. *See, e.g.,* 8 Del.Code § 145(c).

3. *See, e.g.,* 8 Del.Code §§ 145(a), (b).

4. *See, e.g.,* 8 Del.Code § 145(f).

6. *See* Regulation S-K, Items 510, 512, 17 C.F.R. §§ 229.510, 229.512. This was formerly contained in Note to SEC Rule 460. 17 C.F.R. § 230.460 (1982). Acceleration of the effective date is discussed in § 2.2 *supra. See* 17 C.F.R. § 230.461.

7. *See* Sec. Act Rel. No. 33–4936 guide 46 (Dec. 9, 1968) (rescinded and replaced by 17 C.F.R. § 290.702.)

been criticized on several grounds, including its limitation to indemnification agreements and the fact that it does not extend to company-paid insurance policies.[8]

The Commission's policy on indemnification is bolstered by the several court decisions in the case of Globus v. Law Research Service, Inc.[9] In that case, it was held that regardless of whether the individual involved is an officer, director, or an underwriter, the policy underlying the Securities Act renders void an indemnification agreement to the extent that as applied it would cover fraudulent misconduct. The court's rationale was that invalidating all such indemnification agreements would "encourage diligence, investigation and compliance with the requirements of the statute by exposing issuers and underwriters to the substantial hazard of liability for compensatory damages."[10] The obvious concern was that permitting any participant in the registration process to contract away his or her potential liabilities would necessarily result in a less wholehearted fulfilling of one's obligations. Although the same rationale would arguably apply to issuer-paid liability insurance policies, the Globus decision has not been so extended. In Eichenholtz v. Brennan,[12] the Third Circuit followed the rule that has been established in a number of cases: that even where the underwriter was merely negligent, it would contravene the policy of the securities laws to permit indemnification. However, indemnification for litigation defenses may be permitted when the defendant establishes his or her due diligence defense.[13] Another court has upheld an indemnification agreement between an investor and the limited partnership which he sued where the litigation that triggered the agreement was frivolous.[14]

Some underwriters have tried to avoid the Globus ruling by entering into contribution agreements which do not purport to give across-the-board indemnity.[15] It is questionable whether the Globus rule can (or should) be so easily circumvented. Courts have continued to show their dislike for indemnification agreements in the securities context. Strict construction of the extent of any contractual right to indemnification may prevent a court from having to reach the public policy issue. Thus, for example, an indemnification clause between an underwriter and broker-dealer was held to apply only to representations by the issuer in the offering materials and not to oral misrepresentations made by the brokerage firm seeking indemnification.[16]

8. *See, e.g.,* Raychem Corp. v. Federal Insurance Co., 853 F.Supp. 1170 (N.D.Cal.1994) (permitting insurance to cover indemnification of Rule 10b-5 settlement). *See also* Milton P. Kroll, Reflections on Indemnification Provisions and SEC Liability Insurance in the Light of BarChris and Globus, 24 Bus.Law. 681, 689 (1969).

9. 418 F.2d 1276 (2d Cir.1969), *cert. denied* 397 U.S. 913, 90 S.Ct. 913, 25 L.Ed.2d 93 (1970).

10. 418 F.2d at 1289.

12. 52 F.3d 478 (3d Cir.1995).

13. *See* Goldstein v. Alodex Corp., 409 F.Supp. 1201 (E.D.Pa.1976) (permitting indemnification of directors pursuant to settlement where the evidence showed that they had established their due diligence and therefore would not have been held liable under section 11).

14. Zissu v. Bear, Stearns & Co., 627 F.Supp. 687 (S.D.N.Y.1986), *affirmed* 805 F.2d 75 (2d Cir.1986).

15. *See* Helen S. Scott, Resurrecting Indemnification: Contribution Clauses in Underwriting Agreements, 61 N.Y.U.L.Rev. 223 (1986). *See also,* Note, Contractual Shifting of Defense Costs in Private Offering Securities Litigation, 136 U.Pa.L.Rev. 971 (1988).

16. McCoy v. Goldberg, 1992 WL 237327, [1992–1993 Transfer Binder] Fed.Sec.L.Rep. (CCH) ¶ 97,009 (S.D.N.Y.1992).

Another aspect of the *Globus* opinions is that they do not go so far as to expressly or even impliedly approve of the broader SEC policy as stated in the acceleration requirements. *Globus* is limited to agreements as applied to indemnify individuals and entities for fraudulent misconduct, whereas the Commission's policy apparently is directed toward all indemnification agreements, including those that would cover liability for merely negligent conduct such as where the defendant fails to meet his burden of proof of due diligence and reasonable investigation. Arguably, the *Globus* rationale is not limited to liabilities arising out of 1933 Act registration, and therefore, may carry over to all potential liability under the securities acts including those arising under the 1934 Exchange Act and implied liabilities thereunder for fraudulent misconduct. Since actions under Rule 10b–5 require a showing of scienter,[17] it would appear that according to the court's analysis, any such liability would not be susceptible to coverage by an indemnification agreement.[18] However, a defendant may nevertheless seek contribution from others who are jointly and severally liable.

The Commission extended its policy against indemnification agreements when it advised three mutual funds that they cannot lawfully indemnify their investment advisers for legal expenses incurred in SEC administrative proceedings wherein the investment advisers were found to have violated the securities laws.[20] The Commission reasoned that the indemnification agreements were not only in violation of the acts' policies, but also contravened the fiduciary duties imposed on investment company directors.[21]

§ 7.17   Special Rules and Procedures for Securities Class Actions

In 1995 and 1998, Congress amended the securities laws to implement additional requirements for securities class actions. There are parallel provisions applicable to litigation under the 1933 and 1934 Act. The discussion that follows discusses the procedures generally and the provisions that apply to actions under sections 11 and 12 of the 1933 Act.[1]

In the 1990s, there was increasing concern with the supposed abuses of class actions involving securities law violations. As a result, Congress responded with two sets of amendments to the securities laws which are designed to curb these abuses. First, Congress enacted the Private Securities Litigation Reform Act of 1995, which addresses many areas of private litigation, including procedural reforms, enhanced pleading standards, and increased protection for disclosures involving soft information and projections. These changes are discussed in this section and throughout this Treatise as appropriate. Many of the Reform Act provisions could be avoided by bringing suit in state court. Congress responded with the Securities Litigation Uniform Standards

---

17. Ernst & Ernst v. Hochfelder, 425 U.S. 185, 96 S.Ct. 1375, 47 L.Ed.2d 668 (1976), *rehearing denied* 425 U.S. 986, 96 S.Ct. 2194, 48 L.Ed.2d 811 (1976). *See* § 12.8 *infra.*

18. *E.g.* Globus v. Law Research Service, Inc., 442 F.2d 1346 (2d Cir.1971), *cert. denied* 404 U.S. 941, 92 S.Ct. 286, 30 L.Ed.2d 254 (1971).

20. Sec. Act Rel. No. 33–6463 (April 21, 1983).

21. *Id. See* 15 U.S.C.A. §§ 80a–17(h), (i), 36(a).

§ 7.17

1. 15 U.S.C.A. §§ 77k, 77*l* which are discussed elsewhere in chapter 7. The impact of the amendments on 1934 Act class actions under rule 10b–5, the proxy rules, and the Williams Act are discussed in § 12.15 *infra.*

Act of 1998 which prevents most securities fraud based class actions from being brought in state court. The Uniform Standards Act is also discussed in this section.

§ 7.17[1] Private Securities Litigation Reform Act of 1995

As part of the Private Securities Litigation Reform Act of 1995,[3] Congress imposed some significant limitations on class actions brought under the securities laws. Section 27 of the 1933 Act[4] establishes special procedures necessary for instituting private actions under the securities laws and in the process purports to discourage frivolous lawsuits. The 1995 legislation was designed to curtail suspected abuses including the use of class actions to bring strike suits for the purpose of coercing a settlement of baseless claims. The Congressional reforms contained in the 1995 Reform Act cover a number of areas, such as restrictions on the class representative, limits on attorneys fees, pretrial discovery, and the burden of proof on some issues. A parallel provision was adopted for claims arising under the Securities Exchange Act of 1934.[6]

Section 27 of the 1933 Act[7] requires that a "lead plaintiff" be appointed as the representative party in all class action suits, presumably to encourage substantial investors[8] to gain control of suits and discourage lawyer-driven suits.[9] The lead plaintiff and lead counsel provisions are part and parcel of the Reform Act's intent to prevent the "race to the courthouse" phenomenon sometimes associated with class actions which generally determine the lead plaintiff under the first to file rule. Not all aggressive attorney conduct in forming a class action will be improper.[11] However, the clear message of the act is to limit lawyer-driven suits.[12] The Reform Act's lead plaintiff requirements supplement the rules that apply to class actions generally.[13] Thus, for example, the class representative must establish that the representative adequately represents the class.[14] The adequacy of representation includes an

---

3. Pub. Law No. 104–67, 109 Stat. 737 (104th Cong. 1st Sess. December 22, 1995) (HR 1058).

4. 15 U.S.C.A. § 77z–1.

6. Section 21D, 15 U.S.C.A. § 78u–4. *See* § 12.25 *infra.*

7. 15 U.S.C.A. § 77z–1. *See also* 15 U.S.C.A. § 78u–4.

8. *See, e.g.,* Newby v. Enron Corp., 188 F.Supp.2d 684 (S.D.Tex.2002) (appointing the University of California the as lead plaintiff).

9. *See* 104 H.R. Conf. Rep. No–369, 104th Cong., 1st Sess. at 33 (1995) (stating that the rules were intended to "effectively discourage the use of professional plaintiffs"); S. Rep. No. 104–98, 104th Cong., 1st Sess. at 10 (1995) (" 'One way of addressing this problem is to restore lawyers and clients to their traditional roles by making it harder for lawyers to invent a suit and then attach a plaintiff.' "(quoting testimony of Mark E. Lackritz)).

11. Knisley v. Network Associates, Inc., 77 F.Supp.2d 1111 (N.D.Cal.1999) (offering to reimburse brokerage firms for sending notice of class action to customers was neither a violation of the Reform Act nor improper attorney conduct).

12. *See, e.g.,* In re Network Associates, Inc. Securities Litigation, 31 Sec. Reg. & L. Rep. (BNA) 1574 (N.D. Cal. 1999) (condemning lawyer's conduct in defining group of lead plaintiffs).

13. The adequacy of the plaintiff as a class representative can be raised sua sponte by the court on its own motion and also will be taken into consideration into account when considering plaintiff's motion for class certification. *See, e.g.,* Fields v. Biomatrix, Inc., 198 F.R.D. 451 (D.N.J.2000); In re The First Union Corp. Securities Litigation, 157 F.Supp.2d 638 (W.D.N.C. 2000); Takeda v. Turbodyne Technologies, Inc., 67 F.Supp.2d 1129, 1138 (C.D.Cal.1999).

14. *See, e.g.,* Baffa v. Donaldson, Lufkin & Jenrette Securities Corp., 222 F.3d 52 (2d Cir.2000); In re Drexel Burnham Lambert Group, Inc., 960 F.2d 285 (2d Cir.1992). Lack of complete knowledge concerning the detailed facts underlying a securities law claim is not a bar to a finding of adequate representation.

inquiry into whether the representative's interest comports with those of the class and also whether the attorneys have the experience and ability to conduct the litigation. The burden of establishing the adequacy of representation falls on the plaintiff.

Section 27(b)(4) of the 1933 Act[75] provides that all discovery be stayed during the pendency of a motion to dismiss or motion for summary judgment in order to alleviate discovery expenses on defendants.[76] The discovery stay is mandatory, but may be avoided in instances where undue prejudice[78] would otherwise result.

In order to discourage abusive litigation, the Act requires that courts perform a mandatory review once there is a final adjudication[84] of the action in order to determine whether any party or attorney violated Rule 11(b) of the Federal Rules of Civil Procedure.[85] If a court finds that an attorney or party has engaged in improper conduct in violation of Rule 11(b), the statute directs the court to impose sanctions on the attorney or party pursuant to the rule unless convinced otherwise by the violator. Prior to the imposition of sanctions, the court must give the attorney or party notice and an opportunity to respond. A presumption in favor of awarding all attorney fees and costs incurred in the action arises when a party files a complaint in violation of Rule 11(b) and a presumption in favor of awarding the prevailing party attorney fees and costs incurred as a direct result of the violation arises when a party's responsive pleading or dispositive motion violates Rule 11(b). However, rebuttal evidence may be offered that an award of attorneys' fees and costs is unreasonable or that the Rule 11 violation was de minimis. If this defense fails, sanctions are to be imposed pursuant to requirements of Rule 11.

§ 7.17[2] Securities Litigation Uniform Standards Act of 1998—Preemption

The class action procedural reforms of the 1995 Reform Act applied only to class actions brought in federal court. Under the 1933 Act's general jurisdiction provision,[90] private actions under sections 11 and 12 of the Securities Act can be brought in either federal or state court. Additionally, state securities law and common law fraud were able to provide alternative state court forums for class action plaintiffs who could thereby avoid the

75. 15 U.S.C.A. § 77z–1(b)(4). *See* 1934 Act § 21D(b)(3)(B), 15 U.S.C.A. § 78u–4(b)(3).

76. S. Rep. No. 104–98, 104th Cong., 1st Sess. at 14 (1995) (finding that discovery costs often force defendants to settle securities class action claims). The discovery stay is subject to two statutory exceptions. Discovery need not be stayed if particularized discovery is necessary to either preserve evidence or to prevent undue prejudice to the moving party. *See, e.g.,* Medical Imaging Centers of America, Inc. v. Lichtenstein, 917 F.Supp. 717, 721 (S.D.Cal.1996) (there was no showing undue prejudice). The discovery stay has been held to not extend to the mandatory disclosures required by Rule 26(a)(1) of the Federal Rules of Civil Procedure. Medhekar v. United States District Court for the Northern District of California, 99 F.3d 325 (9th Cir.1996), *reversing* Hockey v. Medhekar, 932 F.Supp. 249 (N.D.Cal.1996).

78. Vacold LLC v. Cerami, 2001 WL 167704 *6 (S.D.N.Y.2001); Global Intellicom, Inc. v. Thomson Kernaghan & Co., 1999 WL 223158 *2 (S.D.N.Y.1999).

84. The statutory command for a mandatory Rule 11 review at the end of the proceedings means at the end of the district court's adjudication of the matter; it does not include exhaustion of appellate remedies. *See* DeMarco v. Depotech Corp., 131 F.Supp.2d 1185 (S.D.Cal.2001).

85. Section 27 of the 1933 Act, 15 U.S.C.A. § 77z–1; Section 21D of the 1934 Act, 15 U.S.C.A. § 78u–4. Rule 11 sanctions are discussed in § 12.4[4] *infra.*

90. 1933 Act § 22(a), 15 U.S.C.A. § 77v(a) which is discussed in § 17.1 *infra.*

provisions of the 1995 Reform Act. Congress largely eliminated these alternatives in the Securities Litigation Uniform Standards Act of 1998 (SLUSA).[91]

In short, SLUSA mandates that most class actions involving publicly traded securities be brought in federal court. SLUSA applies not only to actions under the federal securities laws, but also to most fraud-based[93] class action suits brought under state securities law as well.[94] Although SLUSA requires dismissal of covered state court suits, the bringing of a claim in state court is not such an abuse of courts as to *per se* require a federal court under the All Writs and Anti–Injunction Act[95] to enjoin future state court claims.[96] On the author hand, a district court has the discretion to issue an injunction under the All Writs Act enjoining filing of future state court claims.[97] In addition, common law class actions based on fraud with regard to covered securities are preempted. SLUSA is not complete in its elimination of state court class actions, however. Class actions involving securities that are not publicly traded may still remain in state court.[98] Also, SLUSA applies only to class actions and thus not to individual or derivative suits[99] and there is an exception for certain claims involving corporate transactions that are brought in the state of incorporation. Furthermore, suits that are based on state law other than fraud, such as breach of contract[100] or conversion,[101] are not preempted.

The fact that a complaint is based on federal securities fraud does not preclude a plaintiff from amending the complaint to drop the federal claims and proceed only with state claims that are not preempted by SLUSA.[102] In contrast, where the amended complaint is merely an attempt to disguise a securities fraud claim as something else, SLUSA's preemptive provisions apply.[103]

---

91.   Pub. Law No. 105–353, 112 Stat. 3227 (105th Cong.–2d Sess. November 3, 1998) (S 1260).

93.   The Uniform Standards Act does not preempt all state claims. Thus, for example, conversion is not fraud based and thus is not preempted. Burns v. Prudential Securities, 116 F.Supp.2d 917 (N.D.Ohio 2000). *See also, e.g.,* Falkowski v. Imation Corp., 309 F.3d 1123 (9th Cir. 2002), opinion amended by 320 F.3d 905 (9th Cir.2003) (action by employees claiming fraud in connection with stock options involved covered securities and thus were preempted by SLUSA and had to be brought in federal court).

94.   15 U.S.C.A. § 77p(b). *But cf.* Desmond v. BankAmerica Corp., 120 F.Supp.2d 1201 (N.D. Cal. 2000) (removal to federal court was improper since state class action was filed prior to Uniform Standards Act).

95.   28 U.S.C.A. §§ 1651(a), 2283.

96.   Newby v. Enron Corp., 302 F.3d 295 (5th Cir.2002).

97.   *Id.*

98.   *See, e.g.,* Comment, Uncharted Waters: Securities Class Actions in Texas After the Securities Litigation Uniform Standards Act of 1998, 31 St. Mary's L.J. 143 (1999).

99.   *E.g.,* Central Laborers' Pension Fund v. Chellgren, 2004 WL 1348880 (E.D. Ky. 2004).

100.   *E.g.,* Green v. Ameritrade, Inc., 279 F.3d 590 (8th Cir.2002).

101.   Burns v. Prudential Securities, 116 F.Supp.2d 917 (N.D.Ohio 2000).

102.   *See, e.g.,* Schuster v. Gardner, 319 F.Supp.2d 1159 (S.D. Cal. 2003) (remanding state claims to state court).

103.   *See, e.,g.,* Sparta Surgical Corp. v. NASD, Inc., 159 F.3d 1209 (9th Cir. 1998). *Cf.* Merrill Lynch, Pierce, Fenner & Smith v. Dabit, ___ U.S. ___, 126 S.Ct. 1503, 164 L.Ed.2d 179 (2006) (SLUSA preempts state law claims that could be brought by someone who held rather than sold securities).

Chapter 8

STATE BLUE SKY LAWS

Table of Sections

§ 8.1   State Blue Sky Laws: Their Origins, Purpose, and Basic Coverage

§ 8.1[1]   State Blue Sky Laws

This treatise is addressed primarily to the federal law of securities regulation. The emphasis on federal law should not be taken to indicate, however, that the states do not play a significant role in regulating securities transactions. In fact, state law represents the genesis of U.S. securities regulation. Securities regulation in this country began as a matter of state law, and it was not until twenty-two years after the first state securities law that Congress enacted federal securities regulation.[1]

As noted above, the state legislatures entered the arena of securities regulation more than twenty years before Congress. In 1911, Kansas enacted the first American legislation regulating the distribution and sale of securities.[2] A number of states followed suit, and today every state has enacted a securities act. As noted above, the statutes, which vary widely in their terms and scope, are commonly referred to as "blue sky" laws, an appellation with several suggested origins. It has been said, for example, that the Kansas legislature was spurred by the fear of fast-talking eastern industrialists selling everything including the blue sky.[6] The discussion that follows is limited to a

---

§ 8.1

1. Kansas adopted the first state securities law in 1911 (Kans.Laws 1911, c. 133) which was twenty-two years before the enactment of the Securities Act of 1933.

2. Kans.Laws 1911, c. 133. Selective regulation predated the Kansas enactment. Some more limited securities regulation existed before the Kansas statute. For example, in 1852 Massachusetts was regulating securities issued by common carriers. *See* Harry G. Henn & John R. Alexander, Laws of Corporations 843 (3d ed. 1983).

Blue sky laws had been challenged but were subsequently held to be constitutional as a valid use of police power of the states to protect the public against "speculative schemes." Hall v. Geiger–Jones Co., 242 U.S. 539, 550, 37 S.Ct. 217, 220, 61 L.Ed. 480 (1917).

6. *See, e.g.,* Hall v. Geiger–Jones, 242 U.S. 539, 550, 37 S.Ct. 217, 220, 61 L.Ed. 480 (1917) (the statute was aimed at "speculative schemes that have no more basis than so many feet of 'blue sky' * * * ").

For a discussion of the origins of the term "blue sky law," *see* 1 Louis Loss & Joel Seligman, Securities Regulation 34 (1989); Jonathan R. Macey & Geoffrey P. Miller, Origin of the Blue Sky Laws, 70 Tex. L. Rev. 347, 359 n.59 (1991). *See also, e.g.,* Louis Loss & Edward M. Cowett, Blue Sky Law 7 n.22 (1958) (to prevent unscrupulous securities sales of "building lots in the blue sky.")

general overview of the widely varying state blue sky regimes. Most states have adopted either the Uniform Securities Act or the Revised Uniform Securities Act. Traditionally, researching state securities regulation has been difficult. There is relatively little case law, and the administrative rules and regulations are not as readily available as are the federal regulations. However, online research has made the process easier. In addition to Westlaw and Lexis, is an increasing number of sources on the Internet.[8]

Although federal legislation in 1996 significantly narrowed the influence of state securities laws with respect to the state registration of public offerings of securities,[9] state securities laws remain robust in many other areas may still be invoked with respect to various securities transactions. For example, even with respect to the offer and sale of securities, state law can still have significant impact in regulating fraudulent transactions.[10] The state laws also remain important in regulating broker-dealers[11] and investment advisers.[12]

Unlike the federal securities regulation, the state securities acts generally permit a merit analysis of the investment before certain securities can be offered for sale within that state's borders. The states thus have what is known as a merit approach (at least with regard to some offerings of securities), which is in contrast to federal securities law's exclusive focus on full disclosure. State law merit regulation imposes a substantive scrutiny that goes further than the full disclosure approach of the federal laws. Under the registration by qualification, state securities administrators are empowered to look into the merits of the investment being offered.[13] The state acts also generally provide for a short form registration for securities of more established issuers[14] and for an even simpler registration by coordination where the issue is being registered at the federal level with the SEC.[15] As is the case with the federal registration provisions, the state securities acts provide numerous exemptions.[16] Although many of the state securities acts do not cover broker-dealer regulation in detail, most of the state statutes at least require state registration or, at least, notification of federal registration as a broker-dealer. State securities law, in addition to requiring registration of broker-dealers,[17] generally prohibits fraudulent practices in connection with distributions and other securities transactions.[18] Under merit regulation, the states may impose

---

8. *See, e.g.,* Mary E. Cornaby, Blue Sky in Deep Cyberspace: New Internet Research for State Securities Law Practice, 52 Bus. Law. 379 (1996).

9. Pub. L. No. 104–290, 110 Stat. 3416 (1996). *See* § 8.1[2] *infra.*

10. The New York Attorney General, Elliot Spitzer has been especially vigilant in this regard but he has not been alone.

11. Broker-dealer regulation is discussed in chapter 14 *infra.*

12. Investment adviser regulation is discussed in chapter 21 *infra.*

13. Uniform State Securities Act § 304 (hereinafter cited as "Uniform Act"). Revised Uniform State Securities Act § 304 (hereinafter cited as "Revised Act"). *See* § 8.2 *infra.* For a criticism of the merit approach *see, e.g.,* Note, At What Cost Paternalism? A Call to State Legislatures, 22 Ariz.St.L.J. 963 (1990).

14. This is known as registration by notification.

15. Uniform Act § 303; Revised Act § 303.

16. Uniform Act § 402, discussed in §§ 8.3–8.5 *infra.* Revised Act §§ 401–402. The federal exemptions from registration are discussed in chapter 4 *supra.*

17. As noted below, the 1996 Congressional legislation, significantly preempted the role of the states with regard to broker dealers that are regulated under federal law.

18. Uniform Act §§ 201–204. *See id.* § 409 (criminal penalties); *id.* § 410 (civil liabilities). Many states also regulate investment advisers. *See* Bruce H. Saul, Registration of Investment Advisers Under State Law, 25 Rev.Sec. & Commod.Reg. 41 (1992); chapter 14 *infra.*

standards that are stricter than their federal counterpart. The Uniform Standards Act preempts only registration requirements; it does not affect the ability of the states to pursue fraud in the sale of securities.

[handwritten margin note: Uniform Standards Act preempts registration requirements]

Each state has its own statutory law governing securities offerings. These state statutes are often referred to as "blue sky" laws. The state securities laws regulate securities distributions as well as broker-dealer activities. Many states also regulate tender offers. A large number of states regulate the activities of investment advisers. The various state securities laws differ significantly from one another. The discussion that follows is designed to give an overview of state securities regulation. Readers desiring more details as to specific state securities laws should consult state-specific sources.

In the 1990s, state securities administrators in most states increased their enforcement of broker-dealer registration. In order to increase efficiency by eliminating duplicative efforts, most states have required broker-dealer registration that parallels that of federal Form B–D.[21] Currently, renewal of federal broker-dealer registration is transmitted electronically by the SEC to the states; before long, initial applications will be similarly transmitted. In 1996, Congress preempted the ability of the states to impose certain regulatory burdens on broker-dealers. Specifically, the amendments prohibit the states from regulating the extension of credit by broker dealers as well as imposing capital or recordkeeping requirements.[22]

In 1996 Congress delegated to the states regulation of investment advisers managing less than twenty-five million dollars in assets.[25] One reason for the increased concern of state regulators is the growing financial planning industry. The fact that many financial planners do not qualify as investment advisers under federal law has spurred many state administrators to consider the need for regulation.

Under most blue sky laws, there is a designated state official or administrator who performs functions parallel to those performed by the SEC at the federal level.[28] The administrator may deny a registration and thus prohibit offerings until a proper registration statement has been filed and has become effective.[29] Again, as is the case with the SEC, the state administrator is vested with rulemaking authority.[30]

There is relatively little case law under the state acts, thus leaving the attorney to rely upon whatever administrative rules a state may adopt. There has been a major effort toward uniformity, promoted by the American Law Institute's Uniform Securities Act, from which there are significant departures in many states.[31] In addition, there is a national association of state administrators (the North American Securities Administrators Associations: NASAA) as well as several regional associations. Periodically these groups issue proposed rules, position papers, and draft legislation or policy state-

---

21. *See* §§ 14.3–14.5 *infra.*

22. Pub. L. No. 104–290, 110 Stat. 3416 (1996). *See* section 15(h) of the Securities Exchange Act of 1934, 15 U.S.C.A. § 78*o*.

25. 15 U.S.C.A. § 80b–203A.

28. *See* §§ 1.3–1.4 *supra.*

29. Uniform Act § 306; Revised Act § 306.

30. Uniform Act § 412; Revised Act § 705.

31. Notable variations are found in California and in New York's Martin Act. West's Ann.Cal. Corporations Code §§ 25000–25804; N.Y. McKinney's Gen.Bus.Law §§ 352–359–h.

ments that can aid the lawyer in attempting to comply with the state securities regulations. A major push for uniformity occurred in connection with a Uniform Limited Offering Exemption for small issues to be coordinated with Regulation D under the 1933 Act.[32]

What is the proper relationship between the federal securities laws and state blue sky laws? The federal securities acts expressly allow for concurrent state regulation under the blue sky laws.[48] The state securities acts have traditionally been limited to disclosure and qualification with regard to securities distributions. Typically, the state securities acts have general antifraud provisions to further these ends—especially since, beginning in the 1980s, many states have become involved in the regulation of tender offers. These states' tender offer statutes, many of which have been federally preempted, are taken up in another section of this treatise.[49] Even aside from the tender offer context, state blue sky laws can come into conflict with the federal securities laws.

[handwritten margin note: 1996 amendments NSMIA]

In 1996, Congress significantly limited the role of state law in securities regulation. By enacting the National Securities Markets Improvement Act of 1996 (NSMIA),[59] Congress reversed the pattern established under the first sixty-three years of federal securities regulation which had embodied concurrent state and federal regulation. The 1996 amendments explicitly preempted state law in many areas of securities regulation. Particularly affected are the registration and reporting requirements applicable to securities transactions.

Section 18(b) of the 1933 Act, as enacted by the 1996 legislation, provides that a number of securities offerings will be exempted from state law regulation in terms of registration and reporting requirements.[60] Notwithstanding the curtailing of state law regulatory jurisdiction, state antifraud provisions are preserved. Section 18(b) precludes state regulation requiring registration or qualification of several categories of covered securities: securities listed on the New York Stock Exchange securities exempted from state registration and reporting requirements; parallel preemption exists with respect to securities traded on the American Stock Exchange or through the NASD's National Market.[61] Although precluding substantive registration and reporting requirements by the states, the Act expressly preserves the states' right to require filing of documents solely for notice purposes.[62] This preservation of the states' authority to require notice filings has the effect of preserving state registration by coordination of the federal registration.[63]

[handwritten margin note: but still allows state's notice requirements ... + coordination ...]

The preemption of state registration requirements is not limited to the above-mentioned publicly traded securities. Under NSMIA, a large number of

---

32.   17 C.F.R. §§ 230.501–230.506.

48.   15 U.S.C.A. §§ 77r, 78bb.

49.   *See* §§ 11.12–11.13 *infra*.

59.   Pub. L. No. 104–290, 110 Stat. 3416 (104th Cong., 2d Sess. 1996).

60.   15 U.S.C.A. § 77r.

61.   Section 18(b)(1)(A), 15 U.S.C.A. § 77r(b)(1)(A). The Act also gives the SEC rulemaking power to expand the exemption to other listed securities on a securities exchange that has listing standards similar to those identified in subsection (b)(1)(A). Section 18(b)(1)(B), 15 U.S.C.A. § 77r(b)(1)(B). Also exempted are securities of the same issuer with equal seniority, or that are senior to the securities exempted from state regulation under subsections (1)(A) and (1)(B). Section 18(b)(1)(C), 15 U.S.C.A. § 77r(b)(1)(C).

62.   Section 18(c)(2), 15 U.S.C.A. § 77r(c)(2).

63.   Registration by coordination is discussed in § 8.2[3] *infra*.

federally exempt securities and transactions are now also exempted from state regulation.[64] Additionally, even for those securities and transactions not otherwise exempted from state regulation, sales to "qualified purchasers," as defined by the SEC, are exempted from state imposed registration and reporting requirements that go beyond the federal filings.[65]

The preemptive effect of NSMIA can be summarized as follows. Most publicly offered securities which are registered federally cannot be regulated by the states beyond notice and/or coordinated filings. Many federally exempt transactions and securities are also preempted. The primary federal exemptions that are not preempted by the 1996 legislation are offerings subject to the intrastate exemption, and the section 3(b) exemptions (most notably, Regulation A and Rules 504 and 505 of Regulation D).[66] Also, transactions exempt under section 4(2)'s nonpublic offering exemption are not preempted unless they are in compliance with an SEC rule or regulation.[67] The logic behind the preemptive pattern seems to be that federally exempt transactions can result in state registration requirements only when the securities are offered to unsophisticated purchasers.[68] Although the legislative purpose was to preempt a great deal of state law regarding exempt transactions, it has been observed that most federally exempt transactions may still need registration or an independent exemption under state law.[69]

NSMIA is not limited to state regulation of securities offerings and aftermarket transactions. For example, the amendments severely limit state regulation of broker-dealers.[70] NSMIA provides for exclusive federal jurisdiction over investment companies registered under the Investment Company Act of 1940.[71] NSMIA's 1996 amendments do not completely eliminate state law impact with regard to securities transactions insofar as the Act further preserves the states' ability to bring enforcement actions with regard to fraudulent practices in connection with securities.[72] The 1996 amendments also create a division of regulatory responsibility between the states and the

---

64. Section 18(b)(4), 15 U.S.C.A. § 77r(b)(4).

65. Section 18(b)(3), 15 U.S.C.A. § 77r(b)(3). The SEC is empowered to define categories of qualified purchaser "consistent with the public interest and the protection of investors." *Id.*

66. The section 3(b) exemption and Regulations A and D are discussed in § 4.17, 4.19–4.22 *supra*. The section 3(a)(11) exemption is discussed in § 4.12 *supra*.

67. SEC Rule 506 is the safe harbor for the section 4(2) exemption. As a result of the statute's curious wording, a transaction exempt under Rule 506 is subject to state law preemption but other section 4(2) exemptions are not. *See, e.g.,* Lillard v. Stockton, 267 F.Supp.2d 1081, 1116 (N.D. Okla. 2003) (state registration claim for Rule 506 offering was preempted by NSMIA).

Although the language of the statute clearly limits covered securities exempt under section 4(2) of the 1933 Act to be one that is recognized by an SEC rule, at least one court has disregarded the express language of the statute. In Temple v. Gorman, 201 F.Supp.2d 1238 (S.D.Fla.2002), the court held that the intent of Congress was to include as a covered security, all transactions exempt under section 4(2) even if not in compliance with Rule 506 of Regulation D. Although there may not be any good reason for distinguishing between section 4(2) and Rule 506 transactions, the court's ruling is highly suspect in terms of the clear language of the statute.

68. *Id.*

69. Rutherford B. Campbell, Jr., Blue Sky Laws and the Recent Congressional Preemption Failure, 22 J. Corp. L. 175 (1997).

70. Specifically, the amendments prohibit the states from regulating the extension of credit by broker dealers as well as imposing capital or recordkeeping requirements. This is found in section 15(h) of the 1934 Act, 15 U.S.C.A. § 78*o*.

71. Section 18(b)(2), 15 U.S.C.A. § 77r(b)(2). The Investment Company Act is considered in Chapter 20 *infra*.

72. Section 18(c)(1), 15 U.S.C.A. § 77r(c)(1).

SEC regarding the regulation of investment advisers depending upon the amount of investment assets under the adviser's management.[73]

NSMIA also required the SEC to study the role of state securities regulation. Specifically, the Commission was directed, after consulting with the states, issuers, and broker-dealers, to study and report on the uniformity of the state securities regulatory requirements for securities not exempted from state regulation by the 1996 amendments. The results of the study were to be reported no later than October 11, 1997.

Congress took further preemptive action a few years later. As part of the Securities Litigation Uniform Standards Act of 1998 (SLUSA), most securities class actions involving publicly traded securities were banned from state court, making federal jurisdiction exclusive.[74] The preemption of state court actions includes state common law and securities law fraud-based claims involving covered securities, which are defined to include most publicly traded securities registered with the SEC. SLUSA does not completely eliminate state court class actions, however.[75] Class actions involving securities that are not publicly traded may still remain in state court. SLUSA does not apply to claims brought by states, their political subdivisions, or pension plans; nor does it apply to investigations and enforcement actions by state securities administrators. Further, SLUSA applies only to class actions and thus not to individual or derivative suits, and there is an exception for certain claims involving corporate transactions that are brought in the state of incorporation.[76]

---

73. Section 203A of the Investment Advisers Act of 1940, 15 U.S.C.A. § 80b–203A. Effective, April 10, 1997, investment advisers managing more than $25 million in assets and advisers to registered investment companies fall under the exclusive jurisdiction of the SEC. Investment advisers and the Investment Advisers Act of 1940 are considered in Chapter 21 *infra.* For those advisers still subject to state regulation, the Act limits the amount of regulation by states other than the adviser's principal place of business.

Investment Advisers not subject to exclusive federal jurisdiction are to be regulated solely by the states; and in particular, the state of the adviser's principal place of business. *See* Mari–Anne Pisarri, The Investment Advisers Supervision Coordination Act, 30 Rev. Sec. & Commod. Reg. 185 (1997).

74. 1933 Act § 16, 15 U.S.C. § 77; 1934 Act § 28, 15 U.S.C.A. § 78pp. *See* § 7.17[2] *supra,* § 12.15[2] *infra. See also, e.g.,* Richard W. Painter, Responding to a False Alarm: Federal Preemption of State Securities Fraud Causes of Action, 84 Cornell L. Rev. 1 (1998).

75. *See, e.g.,* Comment, Uncharted Waters: Securities Class Actions in Texas After the Securities Litigation Uniform Standards Act of 1998, 31 St. Mary's L.J. 143 (1999).

76. 1933 Act § 16(d)(1), 15 U.S.C.A. § 77p(d)(1); 1934 Act § 28(f)(3)(A), 15 U.S.C.A. § 78pp(f)(3)(A).

Chapter 9

SECURITIES EXCHANGE ACT OF 1934—REGISTRATION AND REPORTING REQUIREMENTS FOR PUBLICLY TRADED COMPANIES

Table of Sections

§ 9.1 The Securities Exchange Act of 1934—Overview

The Securities Exchange Act of 1934[1] is addressed to virtually all aspects of securities transactions and the securities markets generally. This broad scope of the Securities Exchange Act of 1934 is in contrast to the Securities Act of 1933, which is focused on distributions of securities. The Securities Act deals with securities distributions and imposes registration and disclosure requirements for those transactions in addition to providing exemptions from the registration requirements. The Securities Exchange Act has a much broader focus both with regard to transactions in securities and also with respect to regulation of the markets and the securities industry.

The Securities Exchange Act of 1934 governs day-to-day securities transactions as compared with simply initial and secondary distributions. The Exchange Act imposes registration and reporting requirements upon issuers of certain securities.[2] The Exchange Act also regulates securities dealers and other market professionals,[3] national securities exchanges,[4] and self-regulatory organizations such as the NASD,[5] as well as municipal securities, municipal securities dealers,[6] and government securities dealers.[7]

---

§ 9.1

1. 15 U.S.C.A. §§ 78a *et seq.*

2. 15 U.S.C.A. § 78*l*(g)(1). *See* 15 U.S.C.A. §§ 78n, 78*o*(d). *See* §§ 9.2–9.3 *infra.*

3. 15 U.S.C.A. §§ 78*o*, 78*o*–1. *See* § 14.3 *infra.*

4. 15 U.S.C.A. §§ 78f, 78q, 78s. *See* § 14.3 *infra.*

5. 15 U.S.C.A. § 78*o*–3. *See* § 14.3 *infra.* The NASD is currently the only non-exchange self-regulatory organization. From time to time consideration has been given to the formation of a municipal securities dealers' association.

6. 15 U.S.C.A. § 78*o*–4. *See* § 14.6 *infra.*

7. 15 U.S.C.A. § 78*o*–5. *See* § 14.7 *infra.*

The Securities Exchange Act's registration and periodic reporting provisions with regard to securities and issuers in turn trigger other reporting and remedial provisions of the Act. For example, the Exchange Act regulates the proxy machinery of reporting companies,[8] tender offers for securities of publicly traded companies,[9] insider short-swing profits,[10] manipulative practices regarding publicly traded securities,[11] and prohibitions against fraud in connection with the purchase or sale of a security.[12] In addition, the Act imposes annual and periodic reporting requirements upon securities required to be registered.[13] In addition to the foregoing regulation of publicly traded securities, the Exchange Act, through SEC Rule 10b–5,[14] prohibits fraud in connection with all securities transactions, regardless of whether they are publicly traded.

The Exchange Act is not limited to the regulation of issuers and their securities; the Act also focuses on the structure and operation of the securities markets.[15] This market regulation encompasses regulation of the markets themselves, as well as of the broker-dealers who participate in those markets. With regard to the market system and the broker-dealer industry, the Exchange Act requires registration of all national exchanges, as well as all professional traders, dealers and brokerage firms that are members of these exchanges.[16]

The Securities Exchange Act created Securities and Exchange Commission (the "SEC") and is the organic statute governing the wide panoply of the SEC's administrative authority. Pursuant to the SEC's oversight responsibilities for exchanges and self-regulatory organizations,[17] the Commission operates as a licensing authority for broker-dealers and is empowered to prohibit unprofessional conduct.[18] It also sets minimum capital requirements for licensed brokers and dealers.[19] The SEC's rulemaking power is, however, limited to the those areas set out in the statute. The securities laws provide an "intelligible conceptual line excluding the Commission from corporate governance."[20] Accordingly, the Circuit Court of Appeals for the District of Columbia invalidated the Commission's attempt to regulate substantive voting rights of shareholders.[21] Such regulation goes beyond full disclosure and encroaches upon the traditional province of state corporate law.

8. 15 U.S.C.A. § 78n. *See* §§ 10.1–10.9 *infra.*

9. 15 U.S.C.A. §§ 78m(d), (e), 78n(d), (e), (f). *See* §§ 11.1–11.12 *infra.*

10. 15 U.S.C.A. § 78p. *See* §§ 13.1–13.4 *infra.*

11. 15 U.S.C.A. §§ 78k, 78j. *See* chapter 5 *supra* and §§ 12.1, 14.3[6] *infra.*

12. 15 U.S.C.A. § 78j(b); 17 C.F.R. § 240.10b–5. *See* chapter 12 *infra.*

13. 15 U.S.C.A. §§ 78n, 78o. *See* § 9.3 *infra.* *Cf.* Edmund Kitch, The Theory and Practice of Securities Disclosure, 61 Brook. L. Rev. 509 (1995).

14. 17 C.F.R. § 240.10b–5. *See* chapter 12 *infra.*

15. *See* Chapter 14 *infra.*

16. 15 U.S.C.A. §§ 78f, 78q, 78s. *See* § 14.3 *infra.*

17. 15 U.S.C.A. § 78o–3. *See* § 14.3 *infra.*

18. *See* chapter 14 *infra.*

19. 17 C.F.R. § 240.15c3–1.

20. Business Roundtable v. SEC, 905 F.2d 406 (D.C.Cir.1990).

21. *Id. See* the discussion in § 10.1 *infra.*

SEC rulemaking is limited not only by the statutory mandate of the organic legislation that grants the rulemaking power; it is also limited by the requirement that the rulemaking bear a reasonable relationship to the purposes underlying the statutory mandate.[22] The SEC rulemaking is not the only vehicle for the agency's impact on the law, as the SEC frequently makes law in its role as prosecutor by bringing cases that the Commission believes are likely to establish helpful precedent.[23]

§ 9.2 Registration of Securities Under the Securities Exchange Act of 1934

§ 9.2[1] Registration Requirements

Section 12(a) of the Exchange Act[1] makes it unlawful for any broker or dealer to effect any transaction in a security on a national exchange unless a 1934 Act registration has been effected for the security. Accordingly, all securities traded on a national exchange must be registered with the Commission.[2] Registration under the 1934 Act in turn triggers the Act's periodic reporting requirements,[3] proxy regulation,[4] insider trading[5] and antimanipulation[6] prohibitions, as well as the regulation of tender offers.[7]

In addition to the above-mentioned registration and disclosure requirements for exchange listed securities, the Securities Exchange Act of 1934 also imposes registration requirements on certain over-the-counter securities. By virtue of section 12(g)(1) of the Exchange Act and Rule 12g–1, 1934 Act registration must be filed by issuers which have both a class of equity securities having more than five hundred shareholders of record and more than ten million dollars in total assets.[8] Section 12 registration in turn subjects the company to the 1934 Act's periodic reporting and among other requirements proxy regulation,[9] tender offer and other takeover regulation,[10]

22. *See, e.g.,* Timpinaro v. SEC, 2 F.3d 453 (D.C.Cir.1993) (remanding SEC rule regarding large traders' utilization of the Small Order Execution System since the Commission failed to establish that the assertions underlying the rule's prohibition were supported in fact). Although the court remanded for further agency proceedings, it let the rule stand pending remand.

23. *See* Roberta S. Karmel, Creating Law at the Securities and Exchange Commission: The Lawyer as Prosecutor, 61 Law & Contemp. Probs. 33 (Winter 1998).

1. 15 U.S.C.A. § 78*l*(a) (1976). The registration requirement is set forth in section 12(g). 15 U.S.C.A. § 78*l*(g). *See* Checklist for Registration of Securities Under Section 12(g) of the Securities Exchange Act of 1934, 25 Bus.Law. 1631 (1970).

2. For discussion of securities trading on other than the listed exchange, *see* Yakov Amihud & Haim Mendelson, A New Approach to the Regulation of Trading Across Securities Markets, 71 N.Y.U.L. Rev. 1411 (1996).

3. *See* § 9.3 *infra. See generally* Carl W. Schneider & Jason M. Shargel, "Now That You Are Publicly Owned * * *," 36 Bus.Law. 1631 (1981).

4. 15 U.S.C.A. §§ 78n(a)-(c). *See* chapter 10 *infra.*

5. 15 U.S.C.A. § 78p. *See* chapter 13 *infra.*

6. 15 U.S.C.A. § 78i. Section 9 applies only to those securities listed on a national exchange. *Id. See also* section 10 and section 18's express antifraud remedies for false SEC filings. 15 U.S.C.A. §§ 78j, 78r. *See* §§ 12.1, 12.19 *infra.*

7. 15 U.S.C.A. §§ 78m(d)-(e), 78n(d)-(f).

8. The statute requires registration for companies with assets of more than one million dollars but Rule 12g–1 exempts issuers with assets under ten million dollars. 15 U.S.C.A. § 78*l*(g)(1); 17 C.F.R. § 240.12g–1. The ceiling was raised from five to ten million in the Spring of 1996. *See* Sec. Exch. Act Rel. No. 34–37157, Relief From Reporting by Small Issuers (SEC May 9, 1996).

9. *See* 1934 Act §§ 14(a), 14(b), 14(c), 15 U.S.C.A. §§ 78n(a), 78n(b), 78n(c). Proxy regulation is discussed in chapter 10 *infra.*

10. See 1934 Act §§ 13(d), 13(e), 14(d), 14(e), 14(f), 1 15 U.S.C.A. §§ 78m(d), 78m(e),m 78n(d), 78n(e), 78n(f). For discussion of takeover regulation under the 1934 Act, *see* chapter 11 *infra.*

and reporting of insider transactions in the company shares.[11] Section 12 registration requirements cease when the registered securities have fewer than three hundred shareholders of record or when there are fewer than five hundred shareholders on the last day of each of the past three years.[12] In today's environment, it is somewhat curious that section 12(g)(1) focuses on shareholders of record. With many shares being held by brokerage houses in street name,[13] and also depositories such as Cede Corporation, the number of beneficial owners (each of whom makes there own investment decisions) far exceeds the number of shareholders of record. Under current ownership patterns, It would appear that beneficial ownership is a better barometer of how widely held a company truly is.

Section 12(f) of the Exchange Act permits unlisted trading privileges through the medium of an exchange for securities listed on another exchange or traded in the over-the-counter markets.[14] Additionally under Rule 19c–3,[15] the SEC permits off-exchange trading of exchange-listed securities.

The issuer's disclosure and reporting obligations do not end with the filing of the Exchange Act registration statements. Exchange-listed securities, as well as those over-the-counter equity securities subject to section 12(g)(1)'s registration requirements,[33] incur periodic reporting obligations as established by section 13(a).[34] These periodic reports include the 10–K annual report[35] and the 10–Q quarterly report.[36] Also required on Form 8–K[37] are filings of certain specified material changes in the issuer's condition or operations.[38] Supplementing the interim disclosures required by Form 8–K are the requirements of the Sarbanes–Oxley Act[39] that there be disclosure on "a rapid and current basis" of information regarding material changes in financial condition or operations, which may include trend and qualitative information and graphic presentations, as the SEC determines is necessary or useful to investors and in the public interest.[40] Regulation FD,[41] adopted by the SEC in 2000, prohibits registered issuers from making selective disclosures to securities

11. Section 16 of the 1934 Act (15 U.S.C.A. § 78p is discussed in chapter 13 *infra*.

12. 17 C.F.R. § 240.12g–4(a).

13. In 1999, between 70 and 80 percent of publicly held securities were held in street name. *See* 23A Jerry W. Markham & Thomas Lee Hazen, Broker–Dealer Operations Under Securities and Commodities Law § 8.11[2] (2d ed. 2003).

14. 1934 Act § 12 (f)(1)(A), 15 U.S.C.A. § 78*l*(f)(1)(A).

15. 17 C.F.R. § 240.19c–3.

33. Over-the-counter equity securities that have more than 500 shareholders of record and whose issuers have more than $10 million in assets must be registered under the Exchange Act. 15 U.S.C.A. § 78*l*(g), 17 C.F.R. § 240.12g–1.

34. 15 U.S.C.A. § 78m(a); § 9.3 *infra*.

35. 17 C.F.R. § 249.10–K. *See also* Form 10–KSB for small business issuers. 17 C.F.R. § 249.10–KSB.

36. 17 C.F.R. § 249.10–Q. *See also* Form 10–QSB for small business issuers. 17 C.F.R. § 249.10–QSB.

37. 17 C.F.R. § 249.8–K.

38. *See* 17 C.F.R. § 240.13a–11.

39. Sarbanes–Oxley Act of 2002, Pub. Law 107–204 (July 30, 2002).

40. 15 U.S.C.A. § 78m(*l*).

41. 17 C.F.R. §§ 243.100–243.103.

analysts. Regulation FD thus requires that any disclosures to analysts also promptly be made public and may be done through a Form 8–K[42] filing.

Beyond setting forth the periodic reporting requirements, 1934 Act registration triggers other disclosure provisions. By virtue of section 14(a),[47] all proxy material for registered securities must be filed with the Commission. Section 14(d) requires SEC filings of almost all tender offers to purchase equity securities subject to the registration and reporting requirements.[48] Anyone who purchases five percent of any class of any 1934 Act registered equity security must file a full disclosure as to the purpose of such acquisition pursuant to section 13(d).[49] The section 13(d) filing requirement applies to transactions that put the purchaser beyond the five percent threshold. Additionally, all purchases or sales of equity securities by officers, directors, and beneficial owners of ten percent of any registered class of equity security must be recorded in filed reports of such transactions pursuant to section 16(a).[50] Beyond any implied remedies that may exist under the Exchange Act,[51] investors who are injured in reliance upon materially misleading statements in filed documents may bring suit under section 18(a).[52] Liability also exists for those engaging in manipulative conduct with regard to exchange-listed securities[53] and for insider short-swing profits in connection with the purchase and sale of securities registered under the 1934 Act.[54]

§ 9.2[2] Exemptions From 1934 Act Registration Requirements

Section 12(g)(2)[66] of the Exchange Act sets forth exemptions from the Act's over-the-counter equity security registration requirements. Section 12(g)(1) does not apply to: (a) securities listed and registered on national securities exchanges as those securities must be registered under section 12(a); (b) securities of issuers that are registered under the Investment Company Act of 1940;[67] (c) securities of savings and loans, building and loans associations, and similar institutions subject to state or federal authority that represent other than non-withdrawable capital issued; (d) securities of not-for-profit, charitable issuers; (e) securities issued by "cooperative associations" as defined in the Agricultural Marketing Act;[68] (f) securities issued by certain other mutual or cooperative associations; (g) certain insurance company securities; and (h) certain employee stock-bonus, pension or profit-sharing plans.[69]

---

42. Item 5 or 9 of Form 8–K provides the appropriate forum for disclosures required by Regulation FD. 17 C.F.R. § 249.8–K, items 5, 9.

47. 15 U.S.C.A. § 78n(a). *See* Rule 14a–6, 17 C.F.R. § 240.14a–6(j); chapter 10 *infra*.

48. 15 U.S.C.A. § 78n(d). Issuer tender offers for its own shares are covered by section 13(e). 15 U.S.C.A. § 78m(e). *See* chapter 11 *infra*.

49. 15 U.S.C.A. § 78m(d). *See* §§ 11.1, 11. 8 *infra*.

50. 15 U.S.C.A. § 78p(a). *See* § 13.2 *infra*.

51. *See* chapter 13 *infra*.

52. 15 U.S.C.A. § 78r(a). *See* § 12.19 *infra*. This may be true more in theory than in practice as liability is generally promised under Rule 10b–5 rather than section 18(a).

53. 15 U.S.C.A. § 78i(e). *See* § 12.1 *infra*.

54. 15 U.S.C.A. § 78p(b). *See* chapter 13 *infra*.

66. 15 U.S.C.A. § 78*l*(g)(2).

67. *See* section 8 of the Investment Company Act of 1940, 15 U.S.C.A. § 80a–8; chapter 20 *infra*.

68. 12 U.S.C.A. §§ 1141 *et seq.*

69. 15 U.S.C.A. § 78*l*(g)(2).

§ 9.2[5] SEC's General Exemptive Authority

In 1996, Congress gave the SEC broad exemptive authority under the Securities Exchange Act of 1934. In 1996 Congress added section 36 of the Act, which provides that the Commission may exempt persons, transactions, or securities if in the public interest and consistent with investor protection.[90] The exemption may be granted by rule regulation or order.[91] In 1998, the Securities and Exchange Commission adopted Rule 0–12[92] of its rules of general application to set forth the procedures for processing requests for exemptive orders under section 36 of the 1934 Act. The procedure, which follows a parallel process under the Trust Indenture Act of 1939, leaves the SEC with the sole discretion whether or not to consider the application.[93] In addition, the Commission may decide to publish in the Federal Register the fact that the application for an exemption has been made. The notice will also indicate the earliest date that the application will be acted upon, which will be at least twenty-five days following the publication of the notice.

§ 9.3 Annual, Periodic, and Continuous Reporting Requirements for Public Companies

The Exchange Act's periodic disclosure and reporting obligations are found in section 13(a) of the Act.[1] SEC Rule 10b–5[2] is the Exchange Act's general antifraud prohibition.[3] That rule prohibits fraud and material misstatements in connection with the purchase or sale of a security.[4] Rule 10b–5 does not by itself impose affirmative disclosure requirements absent some independent duty to disclose, such as one imposed by a line-item disclosure requirement of an applicable SEC required filing.[5] Mere nondisclosure, absent an independent duty such as a line-item disclosure mandate, contemporaneous insider trading,[6] or some other collateral activity, is insufficient to establish a violation of Rule 10b–5.

Section 13(a)(2) of the Exchange Act[8] requires all issuers of equity securities subject to section 12's registration requirements[9] to file annual and quarterly reports and copies thereof as provided by the applicable SEC rules.

---

90. 15 U.S.C.A. § 78mm(a). The exemptive power does not extend to government securities dealer regulation (section 15C) of the Act. 15 U.S.C.A. § 78o–5(b).

91. This is in contrast to the parallel exemptive power under the 1933 Act, which is limited to exemptions by rule or regulations and does not include individualized orders. 1933 Act § 28, 15 U.S.C.A. § 77z–3. *See* § 4.35 *supra.*

92. 17 C.F.R. § 240.0–12.

93. *Id. See* Sec. Exch. Act Rel. No. 34–39624 (SEC 1998).

§ 9.3

1. 15 U.S.C.A. § 78m(a).

2. 17 C.F.R. § 240.10b–5.

3. *See* chapter 12 *infra.*

4. 17 C.F.R. § 240.10b–5. *See* § 12.3 *infra.*

5. *See, e.g.,* Blanchard v. Edgemark Financial Corp., 2001 WL 587861, Fed. Sec. L. Rep. ¶ 91349 (N.D.Ill.2001) ("it is highly doubtful that Rule 10b–5 alone is sufficient to trigger a similar duty of disclosure ... the language of the rule does not provide any basis for such an affirmative disclosure requirement. Mere nondisclosure, absent insider trading or some other collateral activity, will not establish a violation under Rule 10b–5"), quoting James D. Cox & Thomas Lee Hazen, Cox and Hazen on Corporations § 12.11 (2d ed. 2003).

6. *See* § 12.17 *infra.*

8. 15 U.S.C.A. § 78m(a).

9. 15 U.S.C.A. § 78d(a), (g)(1). *See* § 9.2 *supra.*

When dealing with section 12(a) registrations (for securities traded on a national securities exchange), duplicate originals of the annual and quarterly reports must be filed with the securities exchanges on which the securities are listed. For all section 12 registrations, the issuer's first annual report must be filed for the fiscal year following the last full fiscal year reported in the section 12 registration statement.[10] Most issuers must pay a nonrefundable fee upon filing of the annual report.[11]

The Sarbanes–Oxley Act of 2002[12] accelerated the deadline for filing periodic reports under the 1934 Act.[13] The accelerated filing dates are being phased in. For the first year following these new rules, the annual report on Form 10–K must still be filed within 90 days of the end of the fiscal year. The due date for the Form 10–K filing is reduced to seventy-five days in the second year and to sixty days in the third and subsequent years. Quarterly reports on Form 10–Q continue to be due forty-five days after the end of the quarter for the first year, but this is reduced to forty days in the second year and to thirty-five days for the third and subsequent years following the new rules. Additionally, effective without any phase-in periods are the new rules for reporting of insider transactions under section 16 of the Act.[14] Formerly, insider transactions had to be filed within ten days following the month in which the insider had a change in share ownership, but now those reports reflecting changes in beneficial ownership must be filed with the SEC by the end of the second business day after the day of execution of the transaction.[15]

The general form for annual reports of issuers subject to the Exchange Act's registration and reporting requirements is Form 10–K.[16] The Commission provides alternative forms for special situation issuers. Employee stock purchase, savings, and similar plans must use Form 11–K.[17] Form 18–K[18] is for securities issued by foreign governments and political subdivisions. Registered management investment companies use Form N–1R,[19] while small business investment companies are to file their annual reports on Form N–5R.[20]

SEC Rule 13a–13[21] sets out the Exchange Act's quarterly reporting requirements for issuers of registered securities, which are generally to be filed on Form 10–Q.[22] By virtue of Rules 13a–13(b) and (c),[23] the quarterly

---

10.   17 C.F.R. § 240.13a–1.

11.   *Id.*

12.   Sarbanes–Oxley Act of 2002, Pub. Law 107–204 (July 30, 2002).

13.   *See* http://www.sec.gov/news/press/2002–128.htm. *See also* SEC Approves Rules Advancing Deadlines for Quarterly, Annual, and Insider Reports, 34 Sec. Reg. & L. Rep. (BNA) 1451 (Sept. 2, 2002).

14.   15 U.S.C.A. § 78p. Section 16 is discussed in chapter 13 *infra.*

15.   15 U.S.C.A. § 78p(a)(4). *See* Ownership Reports, Sec. Exch. Act Rel. No. 34–46313, 2002 WL 1792168 (SEC Aug. 6, 2002).

16.   17 C.F.R. § 249.10–K; 4 Fed.Sec.Law Rep. (CCH) ¶ 31,101. *See also* Form 10–KSB for small business issuers. 17 C.F.R. § 249.10–KSB.

17.   17 C.F.R. § 249.11–K. *See* 4 Fed. Sec. L. Rep. (CCH) ¶ 31,151.

18.   *See id.* 32,001–32,004.

19.   *See* 5 Fed.Sec. Law Rep. (CCH) ¶ 52,301.

20.   *See id.* ¶ 51,481.

21.   17 C.F.R. § 240.13a–13.

22.   17 C.F.R. § 129.10–K, 4 Fed.Sec.Law Rep. (CCH) ¶ 31,031. *See* also Form 10–QSB for small business issuers. 17 C.F.R. § 249.10–QSB.

23.   17 C.F.R. § 240.13a–13(b), (c).

reporting requirements do not apply to either (1) investment companies filing quarterly reports under Rule 13a–12[24] or (2) foreign private issuers filing reports under Rule 13a–16[25] on Form 6K. Furthermore, certain life insurance companies need not complete Part I of Form 10–Q.[26]

In 1992, the SEC introduced a number of small business initiatives that were designed to facilitate registration and reporting from small business issuers.[27] A small business issuer is defined as a company with revenues of less than twenty-five million dollars, provided that the aggregate market value of the issuer's voting stock held by non-affiliates does not exceed twenty-five million dollars.[28] Regulation S–B replaces Regulation S–K as the basic disclosure guide for small business issuers. In addition, simplified forms 10–SB (registration of securities), 10–KSB (annual report), and 10–QSB (quarterly report) are now available for 1934 Act periodic filings by small business issuers.

In the 1990s, the SEC began experimenting with an electronic data gathering analysis and retrieval project known as EDGAR, under which the SEC accepts selected filings such as 10–Ks, 10–Qs, and 8–Ks. These filings can be made through telephone transmission of data, magnetic tape, or diskettes. The Commission has continued to expand the scope of the EDGAR program and implemented the operational phase. The phase-in has been completed with exceptions in the case of hardship.

In March 2004, the SEC adopted several new items for Form 8–K's mandatory disclosure.[48] As a result of these additions, the required 8–K disclosures now include the following additional items:

- entry into a material non-ordinary course agreement;
- termination of a material non-ordinary course agreement;
- creation of a material direct financial obligation or a material obligation under an off-balance sheet arrangement;
- triggering events that accelerate or increase a material direct financial obligation or a material obligation under an off-balance sheet arrangement;
- material costs associated with exit or disposal activities;
- material impairments;
- notice of delisting or failure to satisfy a continued listing rule or standard; transfer of listing; and
- non-reliance on previously issued financial statements or a related audit report or completed interim review (restatements).

24. 17 C.F.R. § 240.13a–12.

25. 17 C.F.R. § 240.13a–16.

26. 17 C.F.R. § 240.13a–13(c).

27. *See* Sec. Act Rel. No. 33–6949, 6 Fed.Sec.L.Rep. (CCH) ¶ 72,439 (SEC July 30, 1992). *See* § 3.4[3][D] *supra*.

28. 17 C.F.R. § 240.12b–2.

48. *See* SEC Votes to Adopt Additional 8–K Requirements and to Propose Amendments to Form 20–F and Fund Manager Disclosure Requirements, SEC 04–31 (SEC news release March 11, 2004), available on Westlaw.

In addition to the foregoing new items, the SEC transferred two disclosure items in part from the periodic reporting requirements. Specifically, a Form 8–K disclosure must now be made for unregistered sales of equity securities and material modifications to rights of security holders.[49] Also, the SEC expanded existing required Form 8–K disclosure with respect to departure of directors or principal officers, election of directors, or appointment of principal officers, and amendments to Articles of Incorporation or Bylaws and change in fiscal year.[50]

The amendments to Form 8–K were accompanied by a limited safe harbor under 1934 Act section 10(b)[51] and Rule 10b–5[52] for failure to timely file seven of the new items on Form 8–K. The safe harbor will not apply to, or impact, any other duty to disclose a company may have and extends only until the due date of the company's periodic report for the relevant period.[53]

An issuer whose securities are not registered, nevertheless, will have to file the same periodic reports pursuant to section 15(d)[54] if it issued the securities under a 1933 Act registration. Section 15(d) reporting requirements are suspended when the number of securities holders falls below three hundred.[55] Successor corporations must continue the periodic reporting obligations of their predecessors.[56]

In addition to section 13's periodic reporting requirements, further disclosures are required by the Foreign Corrupt Practices Act amendments,[57] which have a very broad reach. The Foreign Corrupt Practices Act was designed to combat international corruption and bribery and contains substantive provisions aimed directly at this conduct. The Act also introduced related disclosure obligations under the Securities Exchange Act of 1934. The amendments to the Securities Exchange Act were so broadly drafted as to require neither foreign involvement nor corrupt practices.[59] Section 13(b)(2)[60] requires all issuers subject to section 12 or section 15(d) to:

(A) make and keep books, records, and accounts, which, in reasonable detail, accurately and fairly reflect the transactions and dispositions of the assets of the issuer; and

(B) devise and maintain a system of internal accounting controls sufficient to provide reasonable assurances that:

(i) transactions are executed in accordance with management's general or specific authorization;

---

49. *Id.*

50. *Id.*

51. 15 U.S.C.A. § 78j(b).

52. 17 C.F.R. § 240.10b–5. Rule 10b–5 is discussed in chapter 12 *infra.*

53. *See* SEC Votes to Adopt Additional 8–K Requirements and to Propose Amendments to Form 20–F and Fund Manager Disclosure Requirements, SEC 04–31 (SEC news release March 11, 2004), available on Westlaw.

54. 15 U.S.C.A. § 78o(d).

55. *Id.*

56. *See* SEC v. Research Resources, Inc., 1986 WL 11446 (S.D.N.Y.1986) (Unpublished Case).

57. Pub.L. No. 95–213, 91 Stat. 1494 (Dec. 19, 1977). *See* § 22.2 *infra.*

59. *See generally* Program, Practical Implications of the Foreign Corrupt Practices Act of 1977, and Recent Developments, 35 Bus.Law. 1713 (1980).

60. 15 U.S.C.A. § 78m(b)(2).

(ii) transactions are recorded as necessary (I) to permit preparation of financial statements in conformity with generally accepted accounting principles or any other criteria applicable to such statement, and (II) to maintain accountability for assets;

(iii) access to assets is permitted only in accordance with management's general or specific authorization; and

(iv) the recorded accountability for assets is compared with the existing assets at reasonable intervals and appropriate action is taken with respect to any difference.

When initially adopted, these internal controls requirements were the subject of considerable controversy.[61] There have been several proposals for repeal or sharp reduction in scope. Failure to keep an adequate system of internal controls can result in significant SEC sanctions. In 2001, the SEC pumped new life into the significance of the internal controls requirements when the Commission announced a program to encourage 1934 Act reporting companies self-policing of their reporting obligations.[63]

There are a number of especially sensitive disclosure problems under the 1934 Act. These include disclosure of executive compensation,[64] projections of future performance,[65] and disclosures related to corporate takeovers.[66] In 2001, the SEC expanded the disclosures required for employee compensation plans. In particular, the SEC now requires detailed disclosures of equity-based compensation plans, including those not requiring shareholder approval, for all employees and not just for executive compensation.[67] Thus, all equity-based compensation, including stock options, for any employee must be disclosed unless immaterial.[68]

Issuers subject to the periodic reporting requirements may take advantage of the SEC's integrated disclosure program. Reporting companies now qualify for short-form registration of public offerings under the 1933 Act.[69]

Issuers that are subject to the 1934 Act periodic reporting requirements but not the registration requirements of section 12 of the Act[70] are not subject to many of the 1934 Act provisions for issuers. Unregistered 1934 Act reporting companies are not required to comply with the SEC's proxy regulations under section 14(a) of the Act[71] which, among other things, requires that all proxy material for registered securities must be filed with the Commission. Unregistered reporting companies are not subject to section 14(d)'s filing requirements for most tender offers to purchase the issuer's equity securi-

61. *See, e.g.,* Mehren, Introduction to the Foreign Corrupt Practices Act of 1970 Law Procedures and Practices, 10 Inst.Sec.Reg. 65 (1979).

63. *See* Report of Investigation Pursuant to Section 21(a) of the Securities Exchange Act of 1934 and Commission Statement of the Relationship of Cooperation to Agency Enforcement Decisions, Sec. Exch. Act Rel. No. 34–44969, 2001 WL 1301408 (SEC Oct. 23, 2001).

64. *See* § 10.6 *infra.*

65. *See* § 3.9 *supra.*

66. *See* chapter 11 *infra.*

67. *See* Disclosure of Equity Compensation Plan Information, Sec. Act Rel. No. 33–8048, Sec. Exch. Act Rel. No. 34–45189, 2001 WL 1646708 (Dec. 21, 2001).

68. *Id.*

69. 1933 Act Forms S–2, S–3 and integrated disclosure are discussed in § 3.4 *supra.*

70. 15 U.S.C.A. § 78*l. See* § 9.2 *supra.*

71. 15 U.S.C.A. § 78n(a). *See* Rule 14a–6, 17 C.F.R. § 240.14a–6(j); chapter 10 *infra.*

ties.[72] Additionally, unregistered reporting companies are not subject to section 13(d)'s filing requirements. Section 13(d) is triggered when someone purchases five percent of any class of any 1934 Act registered equity security and thus must file a full disclosure as to the purpose of such acquisition pursuant to section 13(d).[73] Also, all purchases or sales of equity securities by officers, directors, and beneficial owners of ten percent of any registered class of equity security must be recorded in filed reports of such transactions pursuant to section 16(a),[74] but these rules do not apply to unregistered reporting companies. With regard to the 1934 Act's express liability provisions, securities of unregistered issuers subject to the periodic reporting requirements do not qualify for the liability provision relating manipulation of exchange-listed securities.[75] Similarly, equity securities of unregistered periodic reporting issuers are not subject to liability for ill-gotten insider short-swing profits in connection with the purchase and sale of securities registered under the 1934 Act.[76]

Management Discussion and Analysis

As discussed earlier,[76.1] Item 303 of Regulation SBK requires periodic reports (as well as 1933 Act registration statements to contain a section setting forth management discussion and analysis (MD & A) of the company's operations by, among other things, to disclose and discuss both adverse and favorable trends and uncertainties. Factual disclosures alone do not provide a basis for forecasting the future. The MD & A disclosures are designed to give investors a better basis for assessing the future prospects of the company.[76.2]

§ 9.3[2][A] CEO and CFO Certification of SEC Filings

In the wake of the massive disclosure problems involving Enron and WorldCom, there was mounting pressure to hold corporate executives accountable for misleading disclosures. For example, the Senate unanimously passed a corporate fraud bill to enhance criminal penalties for corporate fraud;[77] that bill was enacted into law.[78] The SEC proposed accelerating the due date for periodic reports.[79] The SEC also proposed quicker disclosures of certain insider transactions via Form 8–K.[80] While these proposals were pending, the SEC issued an order requiring that CEOs and CFOs of over 900

---

72. 15 U.S.C.A. § 78n(d). Issuer tender offers for its own shares are covered by section 13(e). 15 U.S.C.A. § 78m(e). *See* chapter 11 *infra.*

73. 15 U.S.C.A. § 78m(d). *See* §§ 11.1, 11.8 *infra.*

74. 15 U.S.C.A. § 78p(a). *See* § 13.1 *infra.*

75. 15 U.S.C.A. § 78i(e). *See* § 12.1 *infra.*

76. 15 U.S.C.A. § 78p(b). *See* chapter 13 *infra.*

76.1 *See* § 3.9[7] *supra.*

76.2 The SEC Release that introduced the MD & A disclosure requirements is very instructive as to their purpose and operation. See Sec. Act Rel. No. 33–6835, 1989 WL 1092885 (SEC 1989).

77. Public Company Accounting Reform and Investor Protection Act of 2002, S. 2673, 107th Congress. *See* Public Company Accounting Reform and Investor Protection Act of 2002, Sen. Rep. No. 107–205 (July 3, 2002).

78. Sarbanes–Oxley Act of 2002, Pub. Law 107–204 (July 30, 2002).

79. *See* Acceleration of Periodic Report Filing Dates and Disclosure Concerning Website Access to Reports, Sec. Exch. Act Rel. No. 34–8089 (SEC April 12, 2002).

80. *See* Form 8–K Disclosure of Certain Management Transactions, Sec. Exch. Act Rel. No. 34–8090 (SEC April 12, 2002).

public companies[81] make personal certifications under oath as to the accuracy of past Exchange Act filings.[82] The certification requirement increases CEO and CFO accountability by allowing for criminal sanctions in the event that there are false affirmations of accuracy. In essence, the certification requirement deprives these high ranking officers of a deniability defense to false filings. It is noteworthy that the certification requirement was imposed by order rather than by formal SEC rulemaking. Among other things, the SEC order was effective immediately which would not have been the case had the Commission resorted to the formal rulemaking procedures.[83] The imposition of the certification requirement without resort to formal rulemaking procedures did not occur without objection.[84] However, the certification requirement was implemented and subsequently codified into far-reaching amendments to the securities laws that occurred in the summer of 2002.[85]

Specific criminal penalties are imposed for CEOs and CFOs who knowingly file false certifications.[90] In addition to criminal penalties, the Act requires disgorgement of executive compensation that was not properly reported. Specifically, if a company is required to restate its financials due to "material noncompliance of the issuer, as a result of misconduct" with reporting requirements, the CEO and CFO must reimburse the company for (1) any bonus or other incentive-or equity-based compensation received during the 12 months following the first public release of the document containing the financials which were later restated and (2) any profits from the sale of securities during those 12 months.[91]

§ 9.3[2][B] Periodic Review of Company Filings

The Sarbanes–Oxley Act also requires the SEC to review periodic company disclosures systematically and at least once every three years.[92] The factors the SEC must consider in determining the frequency of review include whether the company has made a material restatement, significant stock price volatility, companies with the largest market capitalization, being an emerging company with "disparities in price-earnings ratios" or having operations which significantly affect material sectors of the economy.[93]

§ 9.3[2][C] Executive Officer Loans Prohibited

Another requirement imposed by the 2002 legislation is the prohibition of most loans to corporate officials. The Act prohibits loans by a company to directors and executive officers, but there are exceptions for limited categories

---

81. The Order applies to public companies with revenues of at least $1.2 billion in their last fiscal year.

82. *See* Order Requiring the Filing of Sworn Statements Pursuant to Section 21(a)(1) of the Securities Exchange Act of 1934, SEC Order File No. 4–460, http://www.sec.gov/rules/other/4–460.htm (SEC June 27, 2002).

83. SEC Rulemaking is discussed in § 16.36 *infra*.

84. *See* Lawyers question SEC's Use of § 21(a) to Impose CEO Certification Requirement, 34 Sec. Reg. & L. Rep. (BNA) 1185 (July 22, 2002).

85. Sarbanes–Oxley Act of 2002, Pub. Law 107–204 (July 30, 2002).

90. 18 U.S.C.A. § 1350 (up to $1 million and ten years in prison for a false certification; up to $5 million and twenty years in prison for "willfully" making a false certification).

91. 15 USCA § 7243. The Act does not specify the applicable standard of culpability–namely whether negligence is sufficient or alternatively whether knowing misconduct is required.

92. 15 U.S.C.A. § 7266.

93. *Id.*

of loans issued in the ordinary course of the company's business for existing loans so long as they are not renewed or materially modified.[94] This provision created considerable concern because of its broad reach. The SEC implemented exemptions when deemed appropriate.[95]

Also, questions have been raised as to the extent to which the loan prohibition will have possible unintended consequences. For example, the provision may come into play with respect to cashless stock option exercises and in many other situations,[96] such as when a company makes an advance payment of indemnification for its officers and directors to pending litigation. Since in many cases the payment is contingent on a successful resolution of the underlying litigation, the advance could be viewed as a loan in violation of section 13(k) of the Exchange Act.

§ 9.3[2][E] Forfeiture of Certain Bonuses and Profits

Section 304 of the Sarbanes–Oxley Act[104] requires disgorgement of certain payments to the CEO or CFO. Specifically, when a company issues an accounting restatement as a result of material noncompliance with the disclosure and accounting requirements, the company's CEO and CFO must disgorge any bonuses or incentive-based compensation during the twelve-month period following the filing of the disclosures that were subsequently restated.[105] In addition the CEO and CFO must disgorge any profits realized from the sale of company securities during that twelve-month period.[106] On their face, these disgorgement provisions do not require that either the CEO or CFO have culpability for the noncompliance in question.[107] The SEC is given the authority to provide exemptions from these disgorgement provisions.[108]

§ 9.4 Disclosure Guidelines—Regulations S–K and S–B

§ 9.4[1] Background of Regulation S–K

As discussed throughout this treatise, the SEC administers and oversees two parallel disclosure systems.[1] The Securities Act of 1933 (the "1933 Act"), which focuses on the registration of public offerings and the Securities Exchange Act of 1934 (the "1934 Act"), which imposes registration and periodic reporting requirements on mostly publicly held companies,[2] are two

---

94. 15 U.S.C.A. § 78m(k).

95. Thus, for example, the SEC exempted foreign banks from the prohibitions on loans to officers. 17 C.F.R. § 240.13k–1. *See* Final Rule: Foreign Bank Exemption from the Insider Lending Prohibition of Exchange Act Section 13(K), Sec. Exch. Act Rel. No. 34–49616, 2004 WL 892236 (SEC 2004).

96. *See* § 9.7[4] *infra.*

104. Sarbanes–Oxley Act of 2002, Pub. Law 107–204 § 304 (July 30, 2002), codified in 15 U.S.C.A. § 7243.

105. 15 U.S.C.A. § 7243(a)(1).

106. 15 U.S.C.A. § 7243(a)(2).

107. It has been suggested, however, that culpability should be a prerequisite of the disgorgement obligation. *See* John Patrick Kelsh, Section 304 of the Sarbanes–Oxley Act of 2002: The Case for a Personal Culpability Requirement, 59 Bus. Law. 1005 (2004).

108. 15 U.S.C.A. § 7243(b).

§ 9.4

1. *See, e.g.,* § 3.4 *supra.*

2. *See* §§ 9.2, 9.3 *supra.*

parallel systems that when followed, often created duplicative filings and superfluous paperwork. Although the duplicative disclosures were often "provided at different times and under different circumstances, disclosure under both Acts flowed from a common core of information."[3] Accordingly, many observers believed that the repetitive nature of the dual filing system was a thorn in the side of corporate activity, and one that needed to be remedied by a thoughtful and measured approach.[4]

The idea of integrated and hence more efficient disclosure was first noted in 1966, by Milton H. Cohen, when he wrote the article, *Truth in Securities Revisited*,[5] wherein he suggested emphasizing the 1934 Act reporting requirements and at the same time eliminating many of the duplicative disclosures formerly required by the 1933 Act.[6] Focusing on periodic reporting rather than emphasizing one-time disclosures in connection with public offerings appeared to be in the best interest of investor protection.[7]

This idea of an integrated disclosure system subsequently received the support of the American Law Institute ("ALI"), which constructed a model securities code "which would unify the disparate federal securities laws into a fully integrated disclosure system."[8] However, once the securities code containing a fully integrated system was completed and had garnered the approval of the Commission, Congress opted not to incorporate the proposed new system after all and left the issue unresolved.[9] The legislators were unwilling to replace the familiarity of the 1933 and 1934 Acts with a new and unproven system; and without a strong lobbying presence the ALI model securities code was defeated.[10] However, as noted in an earlier section of this treatise,[11] the proposed securities code has left its mark on federal securities regulation.

Despite the failure of the ALI securities code, an integrated disclosure system was partially realized. And in 1982, the Commission adopted an integrated disclosure system in Regulation S–K.[12]

In adopting Regulation S–K,[13] the Commission was trying to ease the burden of duplicative disclosures and "sought to define (1) what information is material in securities transactions, and (2) when and how such information should be disclosed to investors and the market."[14] It was determined that

---

3. Michael McDonough, Death in One Act: The Case for Company Registration, 24 Pepp. L. Rev. 563, 585 (1997) (quoting Harold S. Bloomenthal et al., Securities Law Handbook 23, 60–61 (1995)).

4. *See generally id.*

5. Milton H. Cohen, "Truth in Securities" Revisited, 79 Harv.L.Rev. 1340 (1966).

6. *See also, e.g.,* Michael McDonough, Death in One Act: The Case for Company Registration, 24 Pepp. L. Rev. 563, 585 (1997).

7. *See id.* at 587.

8. *Id.* This commissioned group was led by scholars in the securities field, most notably Harvard University Professor Louis Loss. *See id.*

9. *See id.*

10. *See id.*

11. *See* § 1.2[2][D][2] *supra.*

12. *See generally* Michael McDonough, Death in One Act: The Case for Company Registration, 24 Pepp. L. Rev. 563 (1997).

13. 17 C.F.R. §§ 229.10–229.915.

14. Gerald S. Backman & Stephen E. Kim, A Cure For Securities Act Metaphysics: Integrated Registration, Insights, May 1995, at 18, 19.

much of the same information that was material under one Act was going to also be material under the other.[15] Further, the Commission concluded that the amount and nature of the disclosure required was inextricably tied to the investors' pre-existing knowledge and familiarity with the security involved.[16] It was with this backdrop that the Commission adopted Regulation S–K.[17]

§ 9.4[2]　Overview of Regulation S–K and Regulation S–B

Regulation S–K, which contains the informational disclosure requirements for both the 1933 Act and the 1934 Act, organizes these disclosure requirements in a uniform manner. These uniform disclosure requirements, or Basic Information Package, cover Forms 10–Q, 10–K, the annual shareholder report under the 1934 Act, and Forms S–1, S–2, S–3, S–4, S–8, S–11, and formerly S–18 under the 1933 Act. Former Form S–18 was replaced by Form SB–2 as part of the SEC's small business initiative. Qualifying small business issuers can take advantage of a reduced level of disclosure, which is governed by Regulation S–B.[18] The reduced disclosure obligations of Regulation S–B for small business issuers largely parallels the general disclosure requirements established in Regulation S–K. Regulation S–K provides for a detailed description of the ways in which the disclosed information must be presented.[19] And in doing so, the Commission hoped that Regulation S–K would provide investors with the same disclosure enjoyed in the 1933 Act prospectus to the Exchange Act reports, while also affording certain issuers the ability to incorporate by reference their 1934 Act reports into the prospectus during a public offering.[20] As discussed earlier in this treatise,[21] Regulation S–K also creates a three-tiered system of 1933 Act registration of public offerings through the Commission's adoption of Forms S–1, S–2, and S–3.

§ 9.4[3]　Structure of Regulation S–K

Regulation S–K is divided into ten subparts (Subpart 1—Subpart 1000). Subpart 1 sets out the Commission's procedures on two volitional disclosure issues—projections or forward looking statements and security ratings. Subpart 100 itemizes disclosures regarding the business of the registrant, while Subpart 200 sets forth disclosure requirements for the registrant's securities. Subpart 300 provides guidance for disclosing information regarding the registrant's financial information, and Subpart 400 deals with management and certain security holders. Subpart 500 requires disclosure concerning the issuer's registration statement and prospectus, while Subpart 600 lists required exhibits to various filings. Subpart 700 provides for "miscellaneous" disclosures regarding unregistered securities and indemnification of directors and officers. Subpart 800 speaks to the industries guide for the 1933 Act and 1934 Act Filings, and Subpart 900 articulates disclosure responsibilities

---

15. *See id.*

16. *See id.*

17. *See* 17 C.F.R. §§ 229.10–229.915.

18. 17 C.F.R. § 228.10 *et seq. See* § 3.4[3][D] *supra.*

19. *See* § 3.4 *supra.*

20. *See, e.g.,* John C. Coffee, Jr., Is the Securities Act of 1933 Obsolete? The SEC Increasingly Appears to Believe so But Has Not Yet Adopted a Consistent Policy to Replace It, Nat'l L.J., Sept. 4, 1995, at B4, 1158.

21. *See* chapter 3 *supra.*

concerning roll-up transactions. Subpart 1000, which was adopted as Regulation M–A, applies to mergers and acquisitions.

§ 9.6 Accounting and Auditing Requirements

§ 9.6[1] Accounting Requirements

§ 9.6[1][A] Financial Matters Generally

In addition to its disclosure requirements, the Exchange Act imposes numerous financial reporting and accounting requirements. Regulation S–X[2] sets forth the SEC's accounting rules for the preparation of SEC filings and the audited financial statements required by the 1933 and 1934 Acts. The Commission's general approach to financial reporting has been to rely upon generally accepted accounting principles (GAAP) and Generally Accepted Auditing Standards (GAAS). Generally Accepted Accounting Principles are adopted by the Federal Accounting Standards Board (FASB). Generally Accepted Auditing Standards are adopted by the American Institute of Certified Public Accountants (AICPA). It has been observed that General Accounting Practice does not consist of a rigid set of rules, but rather encompasses a range of reasonable alternative treatments.

As a result of the Sarbanes–Oxley Act of 2002,[5] a company's CEO and CFO must make personal certifications with respect to the company's financial information. Specifically, the Act requires that company CEOs and CFOs personally certify that the financial statements "fairly present" the company's financial condition, results of operations, and cash flows.[6] It is likely that this is simply a reaffirmation of the statements' accuracy rather than a standard to be applied in addition to GAAP and GAAS, since the "fairly presents" language that is found in the Sarbanes–Oxley Act is consistent with that generally found in accounting firms' audit letters.

The Commission believes that departures from GAAP can be harmful to investors. The SEC has cautioned against the use of pro forma financial information that varies from Generally Accepted Accounting Practices. The SEC explained that although pro forma financial information can be useful to investors, it can be misleading and therefore harmful if it differs from the results that would be announced under GAAP accounting.[7] There have been a number of massive investigations resulting from accounting irregularities in recent years. One consequence has been the proposal that there be more regulatory oversight of the accounting profession.[9] In 2002, this became law as part of the Sarbanes–Oxley Act,[10] which created the Public Company Accounting Oversight Board.[11] The five-member Public Company Accounting Oversight Board is charged with the obligation of overseeing the auditing of public

2. 17 C.F.R. §§ 210.1–01–210.12–29.

5. Sarbanes–Oxley Act of 2002, Pub. Law 107–204 (July 30, 2002). *See also* the discussion below.

6. 15 U.S.C.A. § 7241. *See* § 9.3[2] *supra.*

7. Sec. Act Rel. No. 33–8039, Sec. Exch. Act Rel. No. 34–45124, Rel. No. FR–59, 2001 WL 1545743 (SEC Dec. 4, 2001).

9. *See* Public Statement by SEC Chairman: Regulation of the Accounting Profession, http://www.sec.gov/news/speech/spch535.htm (Jan. 17, 2002).

10. Sarbanes–Oxley Act of 2002, Pub. Law 107–204 (July 30, 2002).

11. 15 U.S.C.A. § 7211.

companies and adopting auditing, quality control, ethics, independence, and other standards regarding auditing. The Act further requires the Oversight Board to adopt rules relating to work paper retention, second audit partner review and approval of audit reports, and testing by auditors of companies' internal control systems (with a report to be contained in the audit report on the auditors' findings and evaluation of these systems). One hundred and eighty days after the establishment of the Board, it is illegal for an accounting firm to audit public companies unless the accounting firm is registered with the Board.

The Sarbanes–Oxley Act directed the SEC to adopt rules providing that 10–Ks and 10–Qs are to disclose all material off-balance sheet transactions, arrangements, obligations (including contingent obligations) and other relationships with unconsolidated entities and others that may have a material current or future effect on the financial condition, changes in financial condition, results of operation, liquidity, capital expenditures, capital resources or significant components of revenues or expenses.[12]

The Sarbanes–Oxley Act also mandates that the SEC promulgate rules requiring that pro forma financial information included in SEC reports or press releases be presented so as to (1) not be misleading and (2) reconcile the pro forma information with the financial condition and results of operations of the company under GAAP.[13]

In addition to the foregoing legislative changes, the SEC has pursued more vigorously the auditor independence requirements.[14] At the same time, shareholders have taken an increased interest in the independence of their company's auditors.[15]

The Sarbanes–Oxley Act[16] called for SEC rulemaking requiring a company's annual report to address (1) management's responsibility for establishing and maintaining an adequate system of internal controls for financial reporting, and (2) management's year-end assessment of the internal control system's effectiveness. Also, the auditors must attest to and report on management's assessment of the internal controls' effectiveness in accordance with standards established by the Public Company Accounting Oversight Board. The SEC rules as adopted specify the details of the required statement and auditor certification.[19]

On occasion, the SEC will adopt different standards for use in its disclosure documents.[20] The extent of an auditor's compliance with GAAS and GAAP is relevant in determining the scope of liability for material[21] misstate-

---

12. 15 U.S.C.A. § 78m(j). The Sarbanes–Oxley Act mandates a study to improve the transparency of reporting of off-balance sheet items.

13. Sarbanes–Oxley Act of 2002, Pub. Law 107–204 § 401(July 30, 2002).

14. *See, e.g.,* In the Matter of Horton & Co., Rel. No. ID—208, 2002 WL 1430201 (SEC Initial Decision (July 2, 2002).

15. *E.g.,* Liz Claiborne, Inc., 2002 WL 562180 (SEC No Action Letter March 13, 2002) (management could not exclude proposal requesting auditors not perform non-audit services).

16. Sarbanes–Oxley Act section 404, Pub. L. 107–204, 116 Stat. 745 (2002). 15 U.S.C.A. § 7262.

19. *See* SEC News Digest 2003–101, 2003 WL 21223853 (SEC May 28, 2003).

20. *Cf.* Checkosky v. SEC, 23 F.3d 452 (D.C.Cir.1994) (the SEC appeared to give its own interpretation of GAAS and GAAP, but the court remanded for further explanation).

21. Materiality is not simply a matter of the numbers, it depends on the surrounding facts and circumstances. *See, e.g.,* Staff Accounting Bulletin No. 99–Materiality, Release No. SAB 99, 64 Fed. Reg. 451250–01 (Aug. 12, 1999).

ments or omissions. Failure to comply with applicable accounting standards can result in significant liability.[23] However, not every variation from GAAP will result in liability under the securities laws.[24]

In 1999, the SEC amended rule 102(e) of its Rules of Practice to make it clear that the Commission can suspend or bar accountants from practicing before the Commission if they engage in "improper professional conduct."[32] Under the rule as amended, accountants and other professionals can be disciplined for intentional, reckless, and in some cases, negligent conduct. The Commission explained that it will issue Rule 102(e) sanctions against an accountant or other professional who has demonstrated that he or she is not competent to practice before the SEC. Specifically, the amended rule provides that "improper professional conduct" means intentional or reckless conduct that violates applicable professional accounting standards.[33] Additionally, improper conduct includes negligent conduct when such conduct is either a single instance of highly unreasonable conduct or repeated instances of unreasonable conduct.[34]

§ 9.6[1][B] Non–GAAP Financial Measures

Section 401 of the Sarbanes–Oxley Act[61] directed the SEC to adopt rules addressing public companies' disclosure or release of certain financial information that is calculated and presented on the basis of methodologies other than in accordance with generally accepted accounting principles. In response, the SEC adopted a new disclosure regulation, Regulation G to require public companies that disclose or release such non-GAAP financial measures to include a presentation of the most directly comparable GAAP financial measure and a reconciliation of the disclosed non-GAAP financial measure to the most directly comparable GAAP financial measure.[62] The SEC also amended Item 10 of Regulation S–K and Item 10 of Regulation S–B to provide additional guidance to those registrants that include non-GAAP financial measures in Commission filings.[63] The SEC further amended Form 8–K[64] so as to require registrants to furnish to the Commission earnings releases or similar announcements.[65]

The SEC defines non-GAAP financial measures as numerical measures of either historical or future financial performance, financial position, or cash

---

23. *See, e.g.,* In re Matter of Microstrategy, Inc., Sec. Exch. Act Rel. No. 34–43724, Admin. Proc. File No. 3–10388 (SEC Dec. 14, 2000) (awarding $10 million disgorgement plus $350,000 in penalties related to overstatement of revenues and earnings).

24. *See, e.g.,* In re Carter–Wallace, Inc. Securities Litigation, 150 F.3d 153 (2d Cir.1998).

32. Rule 102(e)(1)(ii), 17 C.F.R. § 210.102(e)(1)(ii). *See* Sec. Act Rel. No. 33–7593, 1998 WL 7201 (SEC Oct. 19, 1998). Rule 102(e) is discussed in §§ 16.3, 16.4 *infra*.

33. Rule 102(e)(1)(iv)(A), 17 C.F.R. § 201.102(e)(1)(iv)(A).

34. Rule 102(e)(1)(iv)(B), 17 C.F.R. § 201.102(e)(iv)(B).

61. Sarbanes–Oxley Act of 2002, Pub. Law 107–204 (July 30, 2002) § 401, amending section 13 of the Exchange Act, 15 U.S.C.A. § 78m.

62. 17 C.F.R. §§ 244.100 *et seq. See* Conditions for use of Non–GAPP Financial Measures, Sec. Act Rel. No. 33–8176, Sec. Exch. Act Rel. No. 34–47226, 2003 WL 161117 (SEC Jan. 22, 2003).

63. *Id.*

64. Form 8–K is the form used by the SEC for items that are subject to continuous (or real time) disclosure as compared to the quarterly disclosure requirements of Forms 10Q and 10K. *see* § 9.3 *supra*.

65. *See* Conditions for Use of Non–GAPP Financial Measures, Sec. Act Rel. No. 33–8176, Sec. Exch. Act Rel. No. 34–47226, 2003 WL 161117 (SEC Jan. 22, 2003).

flow that either: (1) effectively excludes amounts that would be included in the most directly comparable GAAP accounting measure or (2) effectively includes amounts that would be excluded in the comparable GAAP measure.[66]

Another Sarbanes–Oxley provision that arose out of the Enron and related scandals is the requirement in section 401 that the SEC adopt rules to require disclosure of off-balance sheet arrangements.[67] The SEC implemented this requirement in 2003.[68] The amendments require a public company to provide an explanation of its off-balance sheet arrangements in a separately captioned subsection of the "Management's Discussion and Analysis" ("MD&A") section of required SEC filings. The amendments also require public companies (but not small business issuers) to provide an overview of certain known contractual obligations in a tabular format.[69]

§ 9.6[2] Audit Requirements

Section 10A of the 1934 Act[70] details the audit requirements of issuer financial statements by independent public accountants.[71] Section 10A(a) requires that audits be conducted within generally accepted auditing standards and that procedures be designed to uncover illegal acts having direct and material effects on financial statements. The SEC does not have to prove scienter in order to establish a violation of section 10A's requirements for the auditor to take action if certain irregularities are discovered.[72]

In addition, section 10A(b) requires independent public accountants who become aware of any information suggesting that illegal acts have or may have occurred to perform an investigation and inform the management of the issuer. If an auditor determines that a detected illegal action is material and management has taken no action to remedy it, the auditor is required to report the illegal act to the board of directors. Issuers receiving such reports from auditors must, not later than one business day after receipt of the report, inform the Commission and provide the auditor with a copy of the report submitted to the Commission. If an auditor does not receive notice from the issuer within one business day, the auditor must either resign or provide the Commission with a copy of the report not later than one business day after the failure to receive notice. Auditors electing to resign must also furnish the Commission with a copy of the report not later than one business day after the failure to receive notice. Section 10A(c) provides that independent public accountants will not be held liable in a private action for any statement, findings, or conclusions made in the report. However, section 10A(d) allows civil penalties to be imposed for the willful conduct of auditors

---

66. *Id.*

67. Sarbanes–Oxley Act of 2002, Pub. Law 107–204 (July 30, 2002) § 401, amending section 13 of the Exchange Act, 15 U.S.C.A. § 78m by adding a new subsection (j).

68. Disclosure in Management's Discussion and Analysis About Off–Balance Sheet Arrangements and Aggregate Contractual Obligations, Sec. Act Rel. No. 33–8182, Sec. Exch. Act Rel. No. 34–47264, 2003 WL 175446 (SEC Jan. 28, 2003).

69. *See id.*

70. 15 U.S.C.A. § 78j–1. *See, e.g.,* Andrew W. Reiss, Note, Powered by More Than GAAS: Section 10A of the Securities Litigation Reform Act Takes the Accounting Progression for a New Ride, 25 Hofstra L. Rev. 1261 (1997).

71. *See, e.g.,* Paul R. Brown, Jeanne A. Calderon & Baruch Lev, Administrative and Judicial Approaches to Auditor Independence, 30 Seton Hall L. Rev. 443 (2000).

72. SEC v. Solucorp Industries, Ltd., 197 F.Supp.2d 4 (S.D.N.Y.2002).

in failing to provide the Commission with reports under sections 10A(c) and (d).

The statutory auditing requirements focus primarily on three aspects of the audit. First, as is the case under generally accepted auditing standards, the auditor must have in place procedures that are reasonably designed to detect illegal activities that have a direct and material effect on the figures in the financial statements. If the auditor becomes aware that an illegal act may have occurred, the auditor is required to make several determinations. The auditor must determine the likelihood that the illegal act occurred, as well as the potential effect of the illegal act on the issuer's financial statements.[74] Unless it is determined that the illegal activity is clearly immaterial, the auditor must inform appropriate members of management and assure that the audit committee is also informed.

A second focus of the statutory auditing requirements deals with related party transactions.[75] The auditors must have procedures reasonably designed to detect related party transactions that are material to the issuer's financial statements or that otherwise would require disclosure in the financial statements. Third, the auditor must make an evaluation of whether there is substantial doubt concerning the issuer's ability to continue operating as a going concern during the upcoming fiscal year.

Auditor Independence

Whenever the SEC imposes requirements that financial information be audited, the SEC applies its own definition of auditor independence in order to determine whether the audit is in fact an independent audit. The issue has become increasingly complex over time as the services that accounting firms provide have expanded, thus creating additional possibilities for relationships that could compromise auditor independence.[76] After considerable controversy, in 2000, the Commission adopted its revised rules on auditor independence.[77] Many observers believed that accounting firms had previously been permitted too much leeway in determining whether they in fact satisfied the independence requirements, while other observers feared SEC rules that would be too stringent. Under the current auditor independence rules as amended in 2000, the SEC identifies four situations in which an accountant lacks sufficient independence to act as an auditor for financial statements. First, an accountant does not have sufficient independence to act as an auditor if the accountant has either a mutual or conflicting interest with the client. Second, the necessary independence is lacking if the accounting firm audits the client's work (as opposed to merely performing financial audits). Third, the accounting firm lacks independence if it (or its employees) acts as an employee or manager of the client, such as would be the case if the accountant assumes outsourced management responsibilities. Fourth, an accounting firm lacks

---

74. This includes contingent effects such as fines, penalties, and damages resulting from the illegal activity.

75. Related party transactions have come under heightened focus in the wake of scandals such as Tyco's, which involved massive loan forgiveness, huge bonuses, and use of corporate funds for personal purposes. The prohibition of executive loans in the Sarbanes–Oxley Act of 2002, Pub. Law 107–204 (July 30, 2002) is but one example of this concern. *See* § 9.7[4] *infra*.

76. *See, e.g.,* KMPG LLP, [2000–2001 Transfer Binder] Fed. Sec. L. Rep. (CCH) ¶ 91,252 (SEC No Action Letter 2000).

77. *See* Revision of the Commission's Auditor Independence Requirements, Sec. Exch. Act Rel. No. 34–43602, 2000 WL 1726933 (SEC Nov. 21, 2000) (adopting release).

sufficient independence to act as an SEC auditor if the accounting firm acts as an advocate for the client.

The SEC's auditor independence requirements are based on both fact and appearance. The SEC's auditor independence requirements establish a general standard of auditor independence based on whether the accountant is not, or if a reasonable investor knowing all relevant facts and circumstances would conclude that the accountant is not capable of exercising objective and impartial judgment on all of the issues encompassed within the accountant's engagement.[79] Independence may depend in large part on the non-audit services that are provided by the company's principal accountant. The SEC has approved of the following factors[80] that the company's audit committee should consider in determining whether the SEC independence requirements are satisfied:

- Whether the non-audit service facilitates the performance of the audit, improves the company's financial reporting process, or otherwise is in the public interest;

- Whether the non-audit service is being performed for the audit committee;

- The effects of the non-audit service on audit effectiveness and on the timeliness and quality of the company's financial reporting process;

- Whether the non-audit service is performed by the audit personnel and specialists who routinely provide recurring audit support and whether such activity enhances the audit personnel's knowledge of the company's business and operations;

- Whether the audit personnel's role in [performing the non-audit service is inconsistent with the auditor's role];

- Whether the audit firm's personnel would be assuming a management role or have a mutuality of interest with the company's management;

- Whether in effect the auditors would be in the position of auditing their own figures and numbers;

- Whether the non-audit project must be started and completed quickly;

- Whether the audit firm has unique expertise with regard to the non-audit service; and

- The size of the fee charged for the non-audit service.

The Sarbanes–Oxley Act of 2002 mandated reforms that have a significant impact on audit committees. This legislation supplements the existing SEC rules of the SEC as well as the rules of the stock exchanges. With respect to committee composition, the Act requires that the audit committee must be composed solely of independent directors.[89] Subject to exemptions that may be granted by SEC rulemaking, independence under the Act requires that the audit committee member not receive any consulting or other fees other than

---

79. *See* Revision of the Commission's Auditor Independence Requirements, Sec. Exch. Act Rel. No. 34–43602, 2000 WL 1726933 (SEC Nov. 21, 2000) (adopting release); Revision of the Commission's Auditor Independence Requirements, Sec. Exch. Act Rel. No. 34–42994, 65 FR 43148–01, 2000 WL 950197 (SEC July 12, 2000) (proposing release).

80. *See* Revision of the Commission's Auditor Independence Requirements, Sec. Exch. Act Rel. No. 34–43602, 2000 WL 1726933 (SEC Nov. 21, 2000) (adopting release). These factors were adopted from the Blue Ribbon Committee on Improving the Effectiveness of Corporate Audit Committees.

89. 15 U.S.C. 78j–1(m).

board or committee fees.[90] Nor can an audit committee member be "an affiliated person" of the company or its subsidiaries.[91] Section 303 prohibits "any officer or director of an issuer, or any other person acting under the direction thereof, to take any action to fraudulently influence, coerce, manipulate, or mislead any independent public or certified accountant engaged in the performance of an audit of the financial statements of that issuer for the purpose of rendering such financial statements materially misleading."[92]

The Sarbanes–Oxley Act also mandates that the SEC issue rules requiring companies to disclose in their periodic reports whether or not (and if not, why not) the audit committee has at least one member who is a "financial expert."[93] In defining "financial expert," the SEC must consider whether a person has, through education and experience as an auditor or a principal financial officer, comptroller or principal accounting officer of a company, an understanding of generally accepted accounting principles and financial statements, experience in the preparation of financial statements of generally comparable companies, experience with internal accounting controls, and an understanding of audit committee functions.[94]

The audit committee is to be "directly responsible for the appointment, compensation and oversight" of the auditor.[95] This includes the resolution of disagreements between management and the auditor regarding financial reporting. The Act makes it explicit that the auditor must report directly to the audit committee.[96]

Members of a corporation's audit committee are thus subject to high standards of oversight of the company's financial situation. Accordingly, when there are accounting irregularities, audit committee members may be exposed to controlling person liability.[97] Audit committee members will not easily escape liability simply by claiming that they relied on the audit firm.[98]

The Sarbanes–Oxley Act requires that all auditing services must be approved in advance by the audit committee.[99] This includes comfort letters and statutory audits. There are nine specified categories of non-audit services that auditors may not provide audit clients. These include financial information systems design and implementation, internal audit outsourcing, and any other service that the Public Company Accounting Oversight Board determines is impermissible. In addition, permitted non-audit services must be approved in advance by the audit committee,[100] although there is a limited de minimis exception to this preapproval requirement.

90. *Id.*

91. Accordingly, audit committee membership cannot include a director who owns a controlling stock interest in the company and may also exclude officers or directors of controlling shareholders.

92. Sarbanes–Oxley Act § 303, codified at 15 U.S.C.A. § 7242.

93. 15 USCA § 7265.

94. The SEC's implementation of the financial expert requirement are discussed in § 9.7[3] *infra.*

95. 15 U.S.C. 78j–1(m).

96. *Id.*

97. In re Lernout & Hauspie Securities Litigation, 286 B.R. 33 (D. Mass. 2002). Controlling person liability is discussed in § 12.24 *infra.*

98. In re Lernout & Hauspie Securities Litigation, 286 B.R. 33 (D. Mass. 2002).

99. 15 U.S.C. 78j–1(m).

100. The audit committee may delegate the authority to grant preapprovals to one or more members, whose decisions must be presented to the full committee at its scheduled meetings.

The Act also imposes whistle-blower protections by requiring that audit committees establish procedures for the receipt, retention and treatment of complaints received by the company regarding accounting; internal accounting controls, or auditing matters; and the confidential, anonymous submissions by employees of concerns regarding questionable accounting or auditing matters.[101]

Audit committees must be granted the authority to engage independent counsel and other advisors as they determine necessary to carry out their duties, and appropriate funding, as determined by the audit committee, for compensating such advisors, as well as the accounting firm for its audit services.

§ 9.7 Corporate Governance and the Federal Securities Laws; Codes of Ethics, Compensation Limitations, and Listing Standards

§ 9.7[1] Overview of Corporate Governance Provisions

As a general proposition, the federal securities laws are focused on disclosure, while matters relating to corporate governance are relegated to state corporate law.[1] Over the years, however, there have been various provisions of the securities laws that have at least an indirect impact on corporate governance. In 2002, the Sarbanes–Oxley Act[3] introduced major corporate governance reforms that now are a matter of federal law. For example, the securities laws now require disclosures with respect to corporate codes of ethics.[4] There are new independence requirements for auditors and members of the audit committee.[5] There are also controls on executive compensation.[6] Additionally, the listing standards of the stock exchanges and the NASD also impose corporate governance limits on publicly held corporations.[7] The Sarbanes–Oxley provisions imposed significant new compliance obligations on public companies.[8] The subsections that follow address these provisions.

§ 9.7[2] Codes of Ethics

Section 406 of the Sarbanes–Oxley Act directed the SEC to develop rules requiring disclosures relating to public companies' codes of ethics.[9] Neither the statute nor the SEC rules expressly mandate that a public company has a

---

101. *Id.*

§ 9.7

1. *See generally* James D. Cox & Thomas Lee Hazen, Cox and Hazen on Corporations (2d ed. 2003).

3. Sarbanes–Oxley Act of 2002, Pub. Law 107–204 (July 30, 2002).

4. Sarbanes–Oxley Act of 2002, Pub. Law 107–204 (July 30, 2002) §§ 406, 407, codified in 15 U.S.C.A. §§ 7264, 7265. *See* § 9.7[2] *infra.*

5. Sarbanes–Oxley Act of 2002, Pub. Law 107–204 (July 30, 2002) § 301, amending section 10A of the 1934 Act, 15 U.S.C.A. § 78j–1. *See* § 9.7[3] *infra. See also* § 9.6 *supra.*

6. *See* § 9.7[4] *infra.*

7. NYSE Corporate Governance Rule Proposals, http://www.nyse.com/pdfs/corp_gov_pro_b.pdf. *See* § 9.7[3] *infra.*

8. *See, e.g.* Dan Roberts, GE Says it Faces $30m Bill for Governance, Financial Times 1B (April 29, 2004).

9. 15 U.S.C.A. § 1764; Sarbanes–Oxley Act of 2002, Pub. Law 107–204 (July 30, 2002) § 406.

code of ethics, but the disclosure requirements clearly provide a strong incentive since companies that do not adopt a code of ethics will have to make that disclosure and will appear out of line with the companies that have adopted such a code.[10] As such this is an indirect intervention in corporate governance rather than a mandate on any particular structure.

In adopting the code of ethics disclosure requirements,[11] the SEC requires companies to disclose whether they have adopted a corporate "code of ethics" that covers the conduct of the company's principal executive and senior financial officers.[12] If the company has not adopted a code of ethics, it must explain why it has not done so.[13] It is very likely that this will have the effect of shaming companies into adopting a code of ethics. If a company has adopted a code of ethics, it must make the code available to the public. In addition, the company must make disclosures when it amends its code of ethics or when it grants specific waivers from the code's requirements.

In order to qualify as a "code of ethics," the code must include "written standards that are reasonably designed to deter wrongdoing."[14] In addition, the code of ethics must be designed to promote honest and ethical conduct. Honest and ethical conduct includes how the company handles actual and apparent conflicts of interest between personal and professional relationships. The code of ethics must also be designed to promote full, fair, accurate, and timely disclosures in the company's SEC filings as well as in the company's public communications generally. The code of ethics must be designed to promote compliance with laws, rules, and regulations applicable to the company's business. The code of ethics must identify appropriate reporting procedures within the organization with respect to code violations. In particular, the code must identify "appropriate person or persons" to whom reports of violations should be made. It is also essential that the a code of ethics adequately provides a system of accountability to assure compliance with the code's substantive provisions. As noted above, the company is not required to have a code of ethics with each of these attributes. However, the New York Stock Exchange and NASDAQ Stock Market have both proposed rules that would require listed companies to have these codes of ethics. In any event, if a public company either has no code of ethics or has one that lacks any of these components, then the Item 406 of Regulation S–K company must disclose that it does not have a code of ethics.

In adopting its rules dealing with corporate codes of ethics, the SEC also adopted rules addressing the composition of audit committees. Section 407 of the Sarbanes–Oxley Act[15] imposes disclosures with respect to the audit committee and "financial experts" serving on that committee.[16]

---

10. Corporate codes of conduct existed before Sarbanes–Oxley. *See, e.g.,* Harvey L. Pitt & Karl A. Groskaufmanis, Minimizing Corporate Civil and Criminal Liability: A Second Look at Corporate Codes of Conduct, 78 Geo. L.J. 1559 (1990).

11. *See* Disclosure Required by Sections 406 and 407 of the Sarbanes–Oxley Act of 2002, Sec. Act Rel. No. 33–8177, Sec. Exch. Act Rel. No. 34–47235, 2003 WL 164269 (SEC Jan. 23, 2003).

12. Regulation S–K, Item 406.

13. *Id.*

14. Reg. S–K Item 406.

15. 15 U.S.C.A. § 1765; Sarbanes–Oxley Act of 2002, Pub. Law 107–204 (July 30, 2002) § 407.

16. *See* Disclosure Required by Sections 406 and 407 of the Sarbanes–Oxley Act of 2002, Sec. Act Rel. No. 33–8177, Sec. Exch. Act Rel. No. 34–47235, 2003 WL 164269 (SEC Jan. 23, 2003); § 9.7[3] *infra.*

§ 9.7[3] Audit Committees; Financial Experts

As discussed in a previous section,[17] the SEC places particular emphasis on public companies' audit committees. Amendments to section 10A of the 1934 Act strengthened the requirement that audit committee members be independent.[18] Those provisions are discussed in an earlier section of this treatise.[19] In addition, section 407 of the Sarbanes–Oxley Act[20] mandated that the SEC require disclosures relating to the presence of a financial expert on the audit committee.[21] In particular, the company must disclose whether it has an "audit committee financial expert"[22] in the audit committee and if not, why it does not.[23] As is the case with the code of ethics requirement discussed above,[24] this is likely to shame most companies into having a financial expert on the audit committee. Companies having a financial expert on the audit committee must disclose the name of the financial expert and whether he or she is independent of management.[25]

The SEC sets forth various criteria for determining whether someone qualifies as an "audit committee financial expert" as that term is used with respect to the audit committee disclosure requirements. The SEC describes a financial expert as someone who has an understanding of financial statements and generally accepted accounting principles and is able to assess the general application of these principles.[26] The financial expert must also have an understanding of internal controls and financial reporting procedures as well as an understanding of the functions and role of an audit committee. In addition to the foregoing qualifications relating to understanding and knowledge, the SEC specifies the types of experience that a financial expert should have. This experience includes preparing, auditing, analyzing, or evaluating financial statements presenting accounting issues that are "generally comparable"[27] in terms of depth and complexity to those that can reasonably be expected to arise in connection with the company's financial statements.[28] This experience requirement may also be satisfied by having actively super-

17. See § 9.6[2] supra.

18. Section 301 of the Sarbanes–Oxley Act prohibits audit committee members from receiving any compensation from the company other than their director fees. Sarbanes–Oxley Act of 2002, Pub. Law 107–204 (July 30, 2002) § 301, codified as amendments to 15 U.S.C.A. § 78j–1.

19. See § 9.6[2] supra.

20. 15 U.S.C.A. § 1765; Sarbanes–Oxley Act of 2002, Pub. Law 107–204 (July 30, 2002) § 407.

21. See Disclosure Required by Sections 406 and 407 of the Sarbanes–Oxley Act of 2002, Sec. Act Rel. No. 33–8177, Sec. Exch. Act Rel. No. 34–47235, 2003 WL 164269 (SEC Jan. 23, 2003).

22. The rules as originally proposed referred to this person as a "financial expert," but the SEC modified the term to an "audit committee financial expert." See Disclosure Required by Sections 406 and 407 of the Sarbanes–Oxley Act of 2002, Sec. Act Rel. No. 33–8177, Sec. Exch. Act Rel. No. 34–47235, 2003 WL 164269 (SEC Jan. 23, 2003).

23. Reg. S–K Item 401.

24. See § 9.7[2] supra.

25. Reg. S–K Item 401.

26. This understanding must extend to accounting for estimates, accruals, and reserves.

27. This was not in the requirements as originally proposed but was added to make the requirements more flexible. See Disclosure Required by Sections 406 and 407 of the Sarbanes–Oxley Act of 2002, Sec. Act Rel. No. 33–8177, Sec. Exch. Act Rel. No. 34–47235, 2003 WL 164269 (SEC Jan. 23, 2003).

28. See Disclosure Required by Sections 406 and 407 of the Sarbanes–Oxley Act of 2002, Sec. Act Rel. No. 33–8177, Sec. Exch. Act Rel. No. 34–47235, 2003 WL 164269 (SEC Jan. 23, 2003).

vised[29] anyone performing those functions.[30] The SEC further provides the ways in which the audit committee financial expert may acquire the required attributes described above.[31] For example, in addition to qualifications acquired through education, experience as a senior financial officer, accountant or auditor, as well as experience in similar positions will help qualify someone as an audit committee financial expert.[32] This also includes experience "actively supervising" a senior financial officer, accountant or auditor, or persons performing similar functions.[33] These are simply examples of ways to acquire the necessary attributes, the SEC also permits the company to look to "other relevant experience." In the event that the company is relying on "other relevant experience" to qualify someone as an audit committee financial expert, Instruction 2 to Item 401 of Regulations S–K and S–B require a brief listing of that relevant experience.

As discussed in an earlier section,[34] a director's liability under the securities laws will be heightened by any special expertise that he or she has. Item 401 to Regulations S–K and S–B provides a safe harbor to clarify that an audit committee financial expert is not deemed an "expert" for any purpose.[35] The SEC also explains that designation as an audit committee expert does not impose any duties, obligations, or liabilities beyond those already imposed on audit committee members.[36]

§ 9.7[4] Executive and Director Compensation; Prohibition on Certain Loans to Executives; Extraordinary Payments

The federal securities laws require that directors of public companies who serve on audit committees be independent.[49] Thus, section 301 of the Sarbanes–Oxley[50] Act prohibits directors who serve on audit committees from receiving any payments from the company except for director fees.[51]

Section 402 of the Sarbanes–Oxley Act[52] prohibits certain loans made by companies to their directors and executive officers. Section 13(k) of the Securities Exchange Act of 1934 expressly prohibits most loans by a company to its directors and executive officers or its subsidiary's directors and executive officers.[53] The prohibition applies not only to the initiation of loans but also to the extension of loans already in existence at the time of the 2002

---

29. The ability to acquire the necessary attributes by actively supervising rather than actually performing the activities in question was added to the requirements as proposed before the new provisions were adopted. *Id.*

30. *Id.*

31. *Id.*

32. *Id.*

33. *Id.*

34. *See* § 7.2 *supra.*

35. Consider, for example, section 11 of the 1933 Act (15 U.S.C.A. § 77k) which places heightened liability on "experts" for material misstatements and omissions in a registration statement.

36. *See* Disclosure Required by Sections 406 and 407 of the Sarbanes–Oxley Act of 2002, Sec. Act Rel. No. 33–8177, Sec. Exch. Act Rel. No. 34–47235, 2003 WL 164269 (SEC Jan. 23, 2003).

49. *See* NYSE Corporate Governance Rule Proposals, http://www.nyse.com/pdfs/corp_gov_pro_b.pdf.

50. Sarbanes–Oxley Act of 2002, Pub. Law 107–204 (July 30, 2002) § 301.

51. Sarbanes–Oxley Act of 2002, Pub. Law 107–204 (July 30, 2002) § 301. One highly publicized set of egregious loan programs that led to this prohibition involved Tyco Corporation whose executives were indicted and tried under pre-Sarbanes–Oxley Act law.

52. Sarbanes–Oxley Act of 2002, Pub. Law 107–204 (July 30, 2002) § 402, amending section 13 of the 1934 Act, 15 U.S.C.A. § 78m.

53. 15 U.S.C.A. § 78m(k)(1).

amendment to the Act.[54] The prohibition on loans does not extend to loans made in the ordinary course of the company's business.[55] Thus, for example, a bank may make mortgage loans to its directors and executives and a brokerage firm may make margin loans to its directors and executives.[56] Also, the SEC implemented exemptions when deemed appropriate.[57]

§ 9.8   Controls on Attorney Practice[1]

§ 9.8[1]   Regulating Administrative Practice of Attorneys; The Sarbanes–Oxley Lawyer Conduct Rules

When representing clients of regulated industries, lawyers play various roles in dealing with the applicable administrative agencies. Administrative agencies frequently function as tribunals and as such may implement rules regulating the practice of law before the agency. Since 1935,[2] the Securities and Exchange Commission has regulated the conduct of lawyers who practice before it.[3] The SEC adopted the predecessor to its current Rule 102(e) of its Rules of Practice[4] "in order to protect the integrity of its processes from incompetent, unethical, or dishonest professionals, including attorneys."[5] The SEC has explained that the rule is premised not only on its "inherent authority"[6] but also on its statutory authority to adopt rules "as may be necessary or appropriate to implement the [securities laws]."[7]

Rule 102(e) and its predecessors have had a controversial history. In 2002, in response to the corporate governance crisis unearthed by high profile investigations such as the one involving Enron Corporation, Congress enacted numerous amendments to the federal securities laws under the aegis of the Sarbanes–Oxley Act of 2002.[9] Section 307 of that Act directed the SEC to adopt rules defining proper client representation in SEC matters.[10]

---

54. *Id.*

55. 15 U.S.C.A. § 78m(k)(2).

56. *Id.*

57. Thus, for example, the SEC exempted foreign banks from the insider lending prohibitions. *See* Rule 13k–1, 17 C.F.R. § 240.13k–1. *See* Foreign Bank Exemption from the Insider Lending Prohibition of Exchange Act Section 13(k), Sec. Exch. Act Rel. No. 34–49616, 2004 WL 910901 (SEC 2004).

§ 9.8

1. This section is adapted from Thomas Lee Hazen, Administrative Law Controls on Attorney Practice–A Look at the Securities and Exchange Commission's Lawyer Conduct Rules, 55 Admin. Law. Rev. 323 (2003).

2. 1 Fed.Reg. 1753 (1936) (Rule II(k)). See also 1 SEC Ann.Rep. 45 (1935).

3. The current Rule is Rule 102 of the SEC's Rules of Practice. 17 C.F.R. § 201.102. Rule 102(e) is discussed in §§ 9.8[3], 16.2[18], 16.4[3] *infra.*

4. 17 C.F.R. § 201.102(e). In 1995, Rule 102(e) appeared as a recodification for former Rule 2(e). The first regulation was found in Rule II(1). *See* In re Keating, Muething & Klekamp, Sec. Exch. Act Rel. No. 34–15982, 1979 WL 186370 *17 note 15 (SEC July 2, 1979).

5. *Id.* *17

6. *Id.*

7. Section 23(a)(1) of the Securities Exchange Act of 1934, 15 U.S.C. § 78w (2000).

9. Sarbanes–Oxley Act of 2002, Pub. Law 107–204 (July 30, 2002), codified in 15 U.S.C. § 7245 (2002 supp.). *See* Senate Report No. 107–205 (July 3, 2002). Sarbanes–Oxley Act of 2002, Pub. Law 107–204 sec. 307 (July 30, 2002).

10. Sarbanes–Oxley Act of 2002, Pub. Law 107–204 (July 30, 2002), codified in 15 U.S.C. § 7245 (2002 supp.).

§ 9.8[3] SEC Rule 102[34]

The SEC Rules of Practice contain a broad definition of what constitutes practice before the Commission.[35] Rule 102 applies not only to lawyers and accountants but also to other professionals who practice before the Commission.[36] The rule has been used primarily against lawyers and accountants. A key difference between the role of lawyers and accountants is that accountants act as certifiers of financial statements and thus are specifically subject to independence requirements.[37]

The concept of practice before the Commission is a broad one. SEC practice is not limited to administrative hearings or representation in connection with SEC investigations, but rather also extends to transacting any business with the Commission, including preparation of documents for filing with the SEC.[38]

§ 9.8[4] Role of Lawyers in SEC Practice

Although administrative agencies' regulation of lawyer conduct is not new, in the 1990s, in response to the lawyers' role in various financial frauds, there was an expansion of the rules regarding attorney conduct when practicing before certain administrative agencies.[74]

The federal securities laws' primary concern is with full disclosure in the securities markets. The Securities and Exchange Commission is the agency charged with administering the securities laws.[75] Lawyers play a crucial role in advising clients and in drafting disclosures. Since 1935, the SEC has regulated the standards of professionals who practice before the Commission.[76] Section 307 of the Sarbanes–Oxley Act[77] mandated that the SEC specify standards of conduct for attorneys practicing before the Commission. In November 2002, the SEC announced its rule proposals relating to attorney conduct.[78]

The role lawyers play in facilitating securities frauds, albeit unwittingly in many cases, should not be ignored. There has been recent concern of the roles lawyers play as a result of failures such as Enron, Worldcom, and Tyco.[79]

---

34. *See also* § 16.4 *infra.*

35. 17 C.F.R. § 201.102(f). *See* § 9.8[5] *infra.*

36. This includes engineers and other experts who may be acting on the behalf of a company or other person involved in SEC proceedings. *Id.*

37. 15 U.S.C. § 78j–1 (2000).

38. *Id.*

74. *E.g.,* 12 C.F.R. § 513.4. See Jonathan R. Macey & Geoffrey P. Miller, Reflections on Professional Responsibility in a Regulatory State, 63 Geo. Wash. L. Rev. 1105, 1106–1107 (1995); In the Matter of Kaye, Scholer, Fierman, Hays & Handler: A Symposium on Government Regulation, Lawyers' Ethics, and the Rule of Law, 66 S. Cal. L. Rev. 977, 977–78 (1993).

75. *See generally* chapter 16 *infra.*

76. 1 Fed.Reg. 1753 (1936) (Rule II(k)). See also 1 SEC Ann.Rep. 45 (1935). *See* In re Keating, Muething & Klekamp, Sec. Exch. Act Rel. No. 34–15982, 1979 WL 186370 note 15 (SEC July 2, 1979). *See also, e.g.,* Simon M. Lorne & W. Hardy Callcott, Administrative Actions Against Lawyers Before the SEC, 50 Bus. Law. 1293 (1995).

77. Sarbanes–Oxley Act of 2002, Pub. Law 107–204 (July 30, 2002). *See* Senate Report No. 107–205 (July 3, 2002).

78. *See* Implementation of Standards of Professional Conduct For Attorneys, File No. S7–45–02, Sec. Act Rel. No. 33–8150, Sec. Exch. Act Rel. No. 34–46868, 2002 WL 31627090 (SEC Nov. 21, 2002).

79. Testimony of Susan P. Koniak, Professor of Law, Boston University School of Law Before the Senate Judiciary Committee February 6, 2002 ("Where were the Lawyers? Behind the

However, this is not a new concern. For example, as was explained long ago,

> [J]ust as a fine, natural football player needs coaching in the fundamentals and schooling in the wiles of the sport, so, too, it takes a corporation lawyer with a heart for the game to organize a great stock swindle or income tax dodge and drill the financiers in all the precise details of their play.
>
> Otherwise, in their natural enthusiasm to rush in and grab everything that happens not to be nailed down and guarded with shotguns, they would soon be caught offside and penalized, and some of the noted financiers who are now immortalized as all-time all-America larcenists never would have risen beyond the level of the petty thief or short-change man.[80]

Similarly, Judge Friendly wrote: "In our complex society the accountant's certificate and the lawyer's opinion can be instruments for inflicting pecuniary loss more potent than the chisel or the crowbar."[81]

In writing about the lawyers' role in the savings and loan scandals of the 1980s, Judge Stanley Sporkin[82] asked:

> Where were these professionals, a number of whom are now asserting their rights under the Fifth Amendment, when these clearly improper transactions were being consummated?
>
> Why didn't any of them speak up or disassociate themselves from the transactions?[83]

Quite properly, the SEC for a long time has held the view that lawyers should be held accountable for failing to prevent the client from complying with the securities laws' disclosure requirements.[84] For example, in the *National Student Marketing* case,[85] the SEC took the position that lawyers participated in a fraudulent scheme when they "failed to refuse to issue their opinions * * * and failed to insist that the financial statements be revised and shareholders be resolicited, and failing that, to cease representing their respective clients and, under the circumstances, notify the plaintiff Commission concerning the misleading nature of the nine month financial statements."[86] The court agreed that the lawyers had an obligation to do something.[87]

Curtain Wearing their Magic Caps Hearing on Accountability Issues: Lessons Learned From Enron's Fall").

80.   Westbrook Pegler, New York World Telegram Jan. 19, 1923 at p. 19, quoted in William O. Douglas, Directors Who Do Not Direct, 47 Harv. L. Rev. 1305, 1329 n.65 (1934).

81.   United States v. Benjamin, 328 F.2d 854, 863 (2d Cir.), *cert. denied* 377 U.S. 953, 84 S.Ct. 1631, 12 L.Ed.2d 497 (1964).

82.   Prior to serving on the federal bench, Judge Sporkin was Director of the SEC Division of Enforcement. It was under his watch that the SEC became especially vigilant over the roles of lawyer.

83.   Lincoln Savings and Loan Ass'n v. Wall, 743 F.Supp. 901, 920 (D.D.C. 1990).

84.   In re Carter and Johnson, Sec. Exch. Act Rel. No. 34–17597, 1981 WL 36552, 36553 (SEC Feb. 28, 1981).

85.   SEC v. National Student Marketing Corp., 457 F.Supp. 682 (D.D.C.1978).

86.   SEC v. National Student Marketing Corp., 360 F.Supp. 284, 290 (D.D.C. 1973).

87.   SEC v. National Student Marketing Corp., 457 F.Supp. 682, 713 (D.D.C.1978).

§ 9.8[6] Increasing Attorney Accountability—Sarbanes–Oxley Section 307 and its Background

On March 7, 2002, a group of law professors sent a letter to SEC Chairman Harvey Pitt urging the SEC to amend its Rules of Practice to better define what constitutes proper representation of public companies.[117] In particular, the letter asked that the Commission adopt a rule to conform to Rule 1.13 of the American Bar Association's Model Rules of Professional Conduct.[118] In relevant part, Rule 1.13 requires that when an attorney who is representing a corporation is made aware of serious wrongdoing, the attorney must take steps to correct the problem. Those steps include what is sometimes referred to as "climbing the corporate ladder"—reporting the violation to someone within the corporation in a position of authority to take corrective action. The Model Rule requires the attorney to continue to climb the ladder, even to the Board of Directors, until the attorney is satisfied that the matter will be attended to properly. The letter to Chairman Pitt asked that the SEC adopt a rule indicating that a lawyer who does not take this action can be suspended from practice before the SEC. On March 28, David Becker, the SEC's General Counsel responded on Chairman Pitt's behalf that since 1981, the SEC "has not brought Rule 102(e) proceedings against on allegations of professional conduct, or otherwise used the Rule to establish professional responsibilities of lawyers."[119] Mr. Becker's letter further stated that "[t]here is a strong view among the bar that these matters are more appropriately addressed by state bar rules ..." Later in the spring of 2002, Senator John Edwards' office submitted a proposed provision that was made part of the Sarbanes-Oxley Act as section 307 of that Act.[120] The Act thus requires the SEC to impose the obligations to report the wrongdoing within the corporation.[122] The Act does not require the attorney to blow the whistle outside of the corporate entity. However, in the late 1970s, the SEC took the position that reporting violations to the SEC might be required at some point. This was a controversial position that was opposed by the American Bar Association because of its perceived conflict with the attorney's obligation of confidentiality and was never implemented.

§ 9.8[7] The SEC Rules—Climbing the Corporate Ladder

Section 307 of Sarbanes–Oxley mandates only a climbing the ladder requirement within the corporate entity and thus does not implicate the attorney client privilege. However, in its proposed rules, the SEC went even further in calling for a noisy withdrawal from representation and notification

---

117. March 7, 2002 letter to Chairman Pitt from Richard Painter, *et al.*, at http://www.abanet.org/buslaw/corporateresponsibility/responsibility_relatedmat.html

118. ABA Model Rules of Professional Conduct Rule 1.13. *See also, e.g.,* Lawrence A. Hamermesh, The ABA Task Force on Corporate Responsibility and the 2003 Changes to the Model Rules of Professional Conduct, 17 Geo. J. Leg. Ethics35 (2003).

119. March 28 letter from David Becker to Painter, *et al.*, at http://www/abanet.org/buslaw/corporateresponsibility/responsibility_relatedmat.html.

120. Sarbanes–Oxley Act of 2002, Pub. Law 107–204 sec. 307 (July 30, 2002), codified at 15 U.S.C.A. § 7245.

122. For discussion of the Act, *see, e.g.,* John C. Coffee, Jr., Gatekeeper Failure and Reform: The Challenge of Fashioning Relevant Reforms, 84 B.U.L. Rev. 301 (2004); Thomas Lee Hazen, Administrative Law Controls on Attorney Practice–A Look at the Securities and Exchange Commission's Lawyer Conduct Rules, 55 Admin. Law. Rev. 323 (2003); M. Peter Moser Stanley Keller, Sarbanes–Oxley 307: Trusted Counselors or Informers? 49 Vill. L. Rev. R 833 (2004); Mark A. Sargent, Lawyers in the Moral Maze, 49 Vill. L. Rev. 869 (2004).

to the SEC if the attorney is not satisfied that the course taken by the client would correct the wrongful conduct. The SEC recognized that this proposal went beyond the mandate of the statute and in light of the anticipated controversy, specifically solicited comments on this expansion. As expected, the noisy withdrawal requirement met with opposition from large portions of the securities bar.[125]

On January 23, 2003, the SEC adopted a modified version of the proposed rules.[133] In the first instance, the Commission deferred for further consideration the most controversial aspect of the rule proposal—the noisy withdrawal requirement. In doing so, the SEC solicited additional comments on the noisy withdrawal requirement. It has been suggested that the SEC is likely at some point to implement a noisy withdrawal requirement in some form.[134]

The SEC rules as adopted contain the up the ladder requirement mandated by section 307 of Sarbanes–Oxley, but at the same time the rules diluted the threshold for triggering the internal reporting requirement. In particular, the original rules spoke in terms of requiring the lawyer to begin climbing the ladder, if the attorney "reasonably believes" that a material violation might have occurred. In place of this "reasonably believes" trigger, the SEC substituted a threshold formulated as a double negative:[135] the internal reporting requirement is triggered by "credible evidence based upon which it would be *unreasonable*, under the circumstances, for a prudent and competent attorney *not to conclude* that a material violation has occurred, is ongoing, or is about to occur."[136] This is a difficult standard to prove in an enforcement action. A more troublesome problem with this high threshold of proof is that it may actually operate to discourage communication of information to attorneys so as to create deniability. In other words, as one commentator has suggested, under the rules as adopted, ignorance may be bliss.[137]

The "up the ladder" reporting operates as follows. Under Rule 205.3(b), an attorney who is practicing before the SEC in representation of a public company who becomes aware of a material violation must "report such evidence to the issuer's chief legal officer (or the equivalent thereof) or to both the issuer's chief legal officer and its chief executive officer (or the equivalents

---

125. *See, e.g.*, Letter from Edward H. Fleischman et al to the Securities Exchange Commission (Nov. 25, 2002); Tamara Loomis, 75 Law Firms Weigh In With Letter to SEC on Disclosures, N.Y.L.J. p.1 (Dec. 18, 2002); Attorneys Call for Delay, More Discussion of SEC Rule Proposals on Noisy Withdrawal, 34 Sec. Reg. & L. Rep. (BNA) 2045 (Dec. 23, 2002).

133. SEC Press Release, SEC Adopts Attorney Conduct Rule Under Sarbanes–Oxley Acthttp://www.sec.gov/news/press/2003–13.htm (Jan. 23, 2003).

134. *See, e.g.*, Otis Bilodeau, SEC Signals Lawyers Still in Crosshairs, Legal Times 1, 13 (Jan. 27, 2003).

135. It is ironic that in drafting this standard, the SEC violated one of its own drafting principles. Specifically, in its plain English requirements that apply to many SEC filings by public companies, the SEC admonishes against the use of double negatives. *See, e.g.*, Plain English Disclosure, Sec. Act Rel. No. 33–7380, 62 Fed. Reg. 3152, 1997 WL 17695 (F.R.) (SEC Jan. 27, 1997). *See also, e.g.*, Note, Eschew Obfuscation–The Merits of the SEC's Plain English Doctrine, 31 U. Mem. L. Rev. 135 (2000); Note, Plain English: A Reappraisal of the Intended Audience of Disclosure Under the Securities Act of 1933, 72 So. Cal. L. Rev. 851 (1999).

136. 17 C.F.R. § 205.2(e).

137. See, e.g., John C. Coffee, Corporate Securities, Myth & Reality: SEC's Proposed Attorney Standards, N.Y.L.J. p. 5, col. (Jan. 15, 2003).

thereof) forthwith."[140] Since the reporting is within the corporation, the attorney-client privilege is in no way diminished.[141]

The first step of the ladder thus is the report to the company's chief legal officer or equivalent officer.[143] The chief legal officer (or equivalent) must then investigate the situation[144] (or turn the matter over to a Qualified Legal Compliance Committee (QLCC)[145] within the corporation). If the chief legal officer (CLO) concludes that a material violation "has occurred, is ongoing, or is about to occur, he or she shall take all reasonable steps to cause the issuer to adopt an appropriate response, and shall advise the reporting attorney thereof."[146]

If the attorney making the original report is satisfied that the CLO has taken appropriate action, then nothing further needs to be done by the reporting attorney. If however, the reporting attorney is not satisfied that appropriate action has been taken, the reporting attorney must climb the next rung of the corporate ladder.

---

140. 17 C.F.R. § 205.3(b).

141. *See* Implementation of Standards of Professional Conduct for Attorneys, Sec. Act Rel. No. 33–8186, Sec. Exch. Act Rel. No. 34–48282, 2003 WL 203262 (SEC Jan. 29, 2003) ("Section 205.3(b) clarifies an attorney's duty to protect the interests of the issuer the attorney represents by reporting within the issuer evidence of a material violation by any officer, director, employee, or agent of the issuer. The section was broadly approved by commenters").

143. If the reporting attorney believes that it would be futile to report to the CLO, then the reporting attorney should proceed directly to the second step of the ladder as set forth in Rule 205.3(b)(3) (17 C.F.R. § 205.3(b)(3)). This bypass is found in Rule 205.3(b)(4), 17 C.F.R. § 205.3(b)(4).

144. 17 C.F.R. § 205.3(b)(2).

145. Rule 205.3(c) permits, but does not require, a corporation to establish a reporting system as an alternative to reporting to the chief legal officer or equivalent.

146. 17 C.F.R. § 205.3(b)(2).

Chapter 10

SHAREHOLDER SUFFRAGE—
PROXY REGULATION

Table of Sections

---

§ 10.1   The Regulation of Shareholder Suffrage Under the Exchange Act—Section 14 and the Proxy Rules: Introduction; Regulation of Voting Rights

With the passage of the Securities Exchange Act in 1934, Congress took note that a number of the great corporate frauds had been perpetrated through management solicitation of proxies that did not indicate to the shareholders the nature of any matters to be voted upon. Accordingly, section 14 of the Act[1] was included in the legislation in order to regulate the shareholder voting machinery for companies that are subject to both the registration requirements of section 12 of the Act[2] and the reporting requirements of section 13.[3] Although focusing on the voting process, the federal proxy rules do not address substantive voting rights, which remain a matter of state law and are generally determined by the law of the state of incorporation.

There are four primary aspects of SEC proxy regulation. First, by virtue of section 14(a) there must be full and fair disclosure of all material facts with regard to any management submitted proposals that will be subject to a shareholder vote. Secondly, material misstatements, omissions, and fraud in

---

§ 10.1

1. 15 U.S.C.A. § 78n.
2. 15 U.S.C.A. § 78*l. See* § 9.2 *supra.*
3. 15 U.S.C.A. § 78m. *See* § 9.3 *supra.*

connection with the solicitation of proxies are prohibited,[6] and the courts have recognized implied private remedies in the hands of injured investors.[7] Thirdly, the federal proxy regulation facilitates shareholder solicitation of proxies as management is not only required to submit relevant shareholders proposals in its own proxy statements,[8] but also to allow the proponents to explain their position in the face of any management opposition.[9] Fourthly, the proxy rules mandate full disclosure in non-management proxy materials[10] and thus are significant in corporate control struggles and contested take-over attempts.[11]

In contrast to the Exchange Act's disclosure approach, the securities exchanges have traditionally imposed rules affecting voting rights of listed companies' shares.[17] In 1988, the SEC broke with tradition and introduced its voting rights rule to protect against the dilution of shareholder rights,[18] a matter previously regulated only by virtue of exchange rules. As discussed more fully below, the SEC's rule was struck down as not supported by the Commission's statutory grant of power. The exchange and NASD shareholder voting rules were not affected and thus continue to apply.

The applicable exchange and NASD rules not only govern the dilution of voting rights but also mandate a shareholder vote under certain circumstances. Thus, for example, under the New York Stock Exchange's so-called twenty percent rule,[19] a shareholder vote is required for any action by an issuer which would result in the issuance of additional shares having a significant diluting effect. If the issuance of shares would increase the outstanding shares of a class of exchange listed securities by more than twenty percent, the issuer must seek formal shareholder approval even though no approval would otherwise be required under the law of the state of incorporation or any other state law.[20] The American Stock Exchange has a similar rule[21] as does the National Association of Securities Dealers for securities traded through its NASDAQ automated quotation system.[22]

Under the New York Stock Exchange's one share/one vote rule, all New York Stock Exchange listed shares had to be given voting rights, and they must be equal voting rights.[23] The American Stock Exchange required that

---

6. 17 C.F.R. § 240.14a–9.

7. J.I. Case Co. v. Borak, 377 U.S. 426, 84 S.Ct. 1555, 12 L.Ed.2d 423 (1964). *See* § 10.3 *infra.*

8. 17 C.F.R. § 240.14a–8. *See* § 10.8 *infra.*

9. 17 C.F.R. § 240.14a–8(b).

10. *See* 17 C.F.R. § 240.14a–2.

11. *See generally* Edward R. Aranow & Herbert A. Einhorn, Proxy Contests for Corporate Control (2d ed. 1968).

17. *See,* N.Y.S.E. Company Manual §§ 312.00, 313.00; American Stock Exchange Listing Standards, Policies and Requirements § 122, Am. Stock Exch. Guide (CCH) ¶ 10,022.

18. 17 C.F.R. § 240.19c–4.

19. N.Y.S.E. Company Manual § 312.00.

20. N.Y.S.E. Company Manual § 312.00.

21. American Stock Exchange Listing Standards, Policies and Requirements § 122, Am. Stock Exch. Guide (CCH) ¶ 10,022 ("The Exchange will not approve an application for the listing of a non-voting common stock issue. The Exchange may approve the listing of a common stock which has the right to elect only a minority of directors").

22. NASDAQ Marketplace Rules 4310(c)(25)(G)(i)(d), 4320(e)(21)(G)(i)(d), and 4460(i)(1)(D).

23. The one share/one vote rule prohibits the listing of shares with less than full voting rights. N.Y.S.E. Listed Company Manual § 313.00(C), (D).

common stock be voting stock but did not limit dual class voting.[24] Traditionally, the NASD and the over-the-counter markets did not have limitations on nonvoting or dual class voting stock. However, the NASD has since agreed with the New York and American exchanges upon a uniform voting rights rule.

This issuance of weighted voting stock has become a common anti-takeover maneuver.[25] Such unequal voting rights violate the New York Stock Exchange's one share/one vote rule. However, in light of the increasing use of this defensive tactic, the exchange undertook a reevaluation of its one share/one vote rule and suspended enforcement of the rule.[26] Under a compromise solution drafted by the New York Stock Exchange, which required SEC approval, listed companies could have created a class of shares with unequal voting rights provided that the recapitalization be approved by both a majority of independent directors and a majority of the shareholders.[27] Previously, the NASD had postponed consideration of its proposed voting rights rule.[28]

The SEC was concerned that some action be taken and urged the exchanges and the NASD to adopt a uniform voting rights rule that would limit dual class voting that is instituted as a defensive anti-takeover maneuver. Despite this attempt to resolve the problem through self regulation, the exchanges and the NASD were unable to reach an accord. The SEC then responded by proposing its own rule. Rule 19c–4 became effective in 1988. However, just two years after the adoption of the SEC's rule, it was ruled invalid.[32]

The D.C. Circuit Court of Appeals in Business Roundtable v. SEC ruled that the Commission lacked statutory authority to promulgate a rule regulating substantive voting rights.[40] Accordingly, Rule 19c–4 was declared invalid. The court noted that shareholder voting rights traditionally have been a matter of state corporate law, but that they could be regulated by the Commission upon an appropriate grant of statutory authority. The court reviewed the various statutory provisions put forth by the Commission as a basis for the regulation. Section 19(c)[41] set forth three bases for regulation: (1) assurance of fair administration of self regulatory organizations, (2) conformity to the requirements of the Exchange Act, and (3) promulgation of rules "otherwise in furtherance of the" Act's purpose. The SEC relied on the third basis. Section 14 of the Act[42] expressly states that the regulation of the proxy process is to ensure "fair shareholder suffrage." The court noted, however, that the legislative purpose must be defined in terms of the *means* of regulation selected and section 14 regulates the proxy process, *not* substantive

---

24. American Stock Exchange Listing Standards, Policies and Requirements § 122, Am. Stock Exch. Guide (CCH) ¶ 10,022 ("The Exchange will not approve an application for the listing of a non-voting common stock issue. The Exchange may approve the listing of a common stock which has the right to elect only a minority of the board of directors").

25. Defensive tactics to takeovers are discussed in § 11.10 *infra.*

26. *See* New York Stock Exchange Initial Report of the subcommittee on Shareholder Participation and Qualitative Listing Standards, "Dual Class Capitalization" (Jan. 3, 1985); Roberta S. Karmel, Is One Share, One Vote Archaic? N.Y.L.J. p. 1 (Feb. 26, 1986).

27. *See* NYSE "Reluctantly" Adopts Dual Share Classification: SEC Approval Needed, 18 Sec.Reg. & L.Rep. (BNA) 998 (July 11, 1986).

28. *See* Stall on One Share/One Vote Accord Seen Likely to Spur Congressional Action, 17 Sec.Reg. & L.Rep. (BNA) 1707 (Sept. 27, 1985).

32. Business Roundtable v. SEC, 905 F.2d 406 (D.C.Cir.1990).

40. Business Roundtable v. SEC, 905 F.2d 406 (D.C.Cir.1990).

41. 15 U.S.C.A. § 78s(c).

42. 15 U.S.C.A. § 78n.

voting rights. The court further pointed out that reading section 19(c) as broadly as the Commission suggested could give the SEC power to regulate many matters of corporate management traditionally left to state law.[43] This simply would be too broad an interpretation of section 19(c)'s residual power. The court thus reasoned that if Rule 19c–4 is to survive, the SEC's power to regulate the substantive voting rights must be distinguished from other matters of corporate governance. The court concluded that there was no support for a "special and anomalous exception to the Act's otherwise intelligible conceptual line excluding the Commission from corporate governance."[44]

The long history of the New York Stock Exchange's one share/one vote rule was held not to constitute a sufficient basis for reading SEC regulatory authority into the Act. In December of 1994, a uniform rule that had been agreed upon by these three self regulatory organizations was approved by the SEC.[51]

Notwithstanding the development of exchange and NASD voting rights rules, the primary source of shareholder voting rights remains the law of the state of incorporation. Many state statutes permit shareholders to have disparate voting rights.[52]

§ 10.2 Full Disclosure in the Solicitation of Proxies

§ 10.2[1] Overview of Proxy Disclosure Requirements

Subject to limited exceptions and exemptions,[2] section 14(a) of the Exchange Act[3] makes it unlawful to solicit proxies with respect to any non-exempt security registered under section 12 of the Exchange Act[4] in contravention of such rules and regulations as the SEC shall establish. The proxy rules are concerned with assuring full disclosure to investors of matters likely to be considered at shareholder meetings. In addition, as discussed more fully below, in the event that proxies will not be solicited, shareholders must nevertheless receive a management information statement that will provide the disclosures that would have been contained in the proxy statement had proxies been solicited. Also, as discussed more fully below, the proxy rules impose disclosure obligations not only on management but on any shareholder or third party that decides to solicit proxies or otherwise influence shareholder votes.[5] In addition to proxy solicitation materials, Rule 14a–3(b) requires the sending of an annual report of the company's operations to shareholders.[6]

---

43. For example, could the SEC properly require independent directors or set shareholder quorum and vote requirements?

44. 905 F.2d at 413.

51. *See* SEC Approves New Voting Rights Rule, Adopts Rule Streamlining SRO Regulation, 26 Sec. Reg. & L. Rep. (BNA) 1708 (Dec. 23, 1994).

52. *See, e.g.,* Jeffrey N. Gordon, Ties that Bond: Dual Class Common Stock and the Problem of Shareholder Choice, 76 Calif.L.Rev. 1 (1988).

§ 10.2

2. Many foreign private issuers are exempt from the proxy rules. *See* Rule 3a12–3, 17 C.F.R. § 240.3a12–3. The exemption does not, however, extend to the Williams Act tender offer and share acquisition disclosure requirements.

3. 15 U.S.C.A. § 78n(a).

4. 15 U.S.C.A. § 78k.

5. Third parties do not, however, have an obligation to disclose in advance their intent to utilize the proxy machinery. *See* Azurite Corp. v. Amster & Co., 844 F.Supp. 929 (S.D.N.Y.1994).

6. 17 C.F.R. § 240.14a–3(b). *See* § 10.6[2] *infra.*

§ 10.2[2] Proxy Solicitations: Nature of the Regulation

Regulation 14A consists of a series of SEC rules that set forth the applicable disclosure requirements. In Rules 14a–3 through 14a–15[10] the Commission sets forth the types of information that must be contained in public companies' proxy solicitations subject to the Act. These requirements are discussed in the sections that follow. The discussion directly below provides an overview of regulatory concerns.

The regulation of proxy disclosure has been a major item on the SEC's agenda over the past two decades. In 1990, Congress enacted the Shareholder Communication Act, which extends the applicability of the proxy rules that apply to reporting companies generally to mutual funds and other investment companies that are registered under the Investment Company Act of 1940.[12] In 1992, the Commission enacted major revisions to the proxy solicitation rules in order to facilitate communications by and between institutional holders of shares of 1934 Act reporting companies.[13] The rules adopted in 1992 included the relaxation of the definition of proxy solicitation, the elimination of a prefiling requirement for proxy materials, permitting preliminary proxy materials to be used before the filing of the definitive proxy statement, and other changes to facilitate institutional shareholder involvement in corporate governance.

The Securities and Exchange Commission makes a distinction between the proxy itself and solicitation materials. The proxy is any shareholder consent or authorization regarding the casting of that shareholder's vote.[16]

The applicable Securities and Exchange Commission rule takes a broad view of the terms "solicit" and "solicitation" so as to include in the definition "any request for a proxy whether or not accompanied by or included in a form of any request to execute or not to execute, or to revoke, a proxy; [and] the furnishing of any communication to security holders under circumstances reasonably calculated to result in the procurement, withholding or revocation of a proxy."[17] This definition has been liberally interpreted by the courts to include materials such as open letters to regulatory bodies, which although not directed toward shareholders, are reasonably calculated to affect a reasonable shareholder's voting decision.[18] Along the same lines, a press release challenging the integrity of a limited partnership's managers and urging holders of limited partnership interests to vote in a certain way met the basic definition of proxy solicitation.[19] A company's newsletter urging shareholders

---

10. 17 C.F.R. §§ 240.14a–3C240.14a–15.

12. 15 U.S.C.A. § 78n(b).

13. Exch. Act Rel. 34–31326 (SEC Oct. 22, 1992).

16. The Commission also explains that "[T]he consent or authorization may take the form of failure to object or dissent." 17 C.F.R. § 240.14a–1.

17. 17 C.F.R. § 240.14a–1(f).

18. Long Island Lighting Co. v. Barbash, 779 F.2d 793 (2d Cir.1985) (proxy rules can cover advertisement indirectly addressed to shareholders that appears in publications having a general circulation).

19. Capital Real Estate Investors Tax Exempt Fund Limited Partnership v. Schwartzberg, 929 F.Supp. 105 (S.D.N.Y.1996) (the press release failed to fall within the safe harbor of Rule 14a–1 since the proxy solicitation had begun prior to the press release in question).

not to vote until they received revised proxy materials was quite properly held to have been a proxy solicitation.[20] Similarly, a newsletter urging shareholders to reject a shareholder proposal was a solicitation subject to the SEC filing requirements.[21] Communications which clearly serve another function, even when occurring around the same time as a shareholder vote, will not be subject to the proxy rules simply because of their timing and possible tangential effect on a voting decision. Thus, for example, research recommendations by brokerage firms may not implicate the proxy rules even though they contain reference to issues that may be relevant to any upcoming vote by the shareholders of a company mentioned in the research report.[22]

As part of an effort to increase shareholder participation in corporate governance, in 1992, the Commission amended the proxy rules to provide that a shareholder may announce how it intends to vote on a matter and explain the reasons for the vote without having to comply with the proxy rules.[23]

The proxy rules provide an exemption for shareholders desiring to communicate with one another so long as proxies are not actually being solicited.[25] The purpose of this exemption was to permit institutional shareholders to communicate with one another without having to comply with the filing requirements. There also is an exemption from the proxy rules for solicitations by persons other than the issuer where no more than ten persons are solicited.[26] Owners of more than five million dollars of the issuer's securities must give public notice of their intent to engage in this type of soliciting activity.[27]

§ 10.2[3] Proxy Solicitations: Required Disclosures

Required Disclosures

SEC Rule 14a–3[33] sets forth the types of information that must be included in materials used for proxy solicitations.[34] All nonexempt proxy solicitations must be accompanied or preceded by the information required in

---

20. Krauth v. Executive Telecard, Ltd., 870 F.Supp. 543 (S.D.N.Y.1994), s.c. 890 F.Supp. 269 (S.D.N.Y.1995).

21. Shoen v. AMERCO, 885 F.Supp. 1332 (D.Nev.1994).

22. Merrill Lynch, Pierce, Fenner & Smith, Inc., 1997 WL 720940 (SEC No Action Letter Oct. 24, 1997) (indicating that the proxy rules would not apply to research reports complying with either Rule 138 or 139 of the 1933 Act).

23. Rule 14a–1; 17 C.F.R. § 240.14a–1. *See* Regulation of Communications Among Shareholders, Sec. Exch. Act Rel. No. 34–31326, 52 S.E.C. Docket 2028, 1992 WL 301258 (SEC Oct. 16, 1992).

25. Rule 14a–2(b)(1), 17 C.F.R. § 240.14a–2(b)(1). *See* Regulation of Communications Among Shareholders, Sec. Exch. Act Rel. No. 34–31326, 52 S.E.C. Docket 2028, 1992 WL 301258 (SEC Oct. 16, 1992).

26. Rule 14a–2(b)(2), 17 C.F.R. § 240.14a–2(b)(2).

27. Rule 14a–2(b)(1), 17 C.F.R. § 240.14a–2(b)(1).

33. 17 C.F.R. § 240.14a–3.

34. In 2000, Rule 14a–3 was amended to permit avoiding multiple mailings by sending a single set of materials to household, provided that the shareholders consent to this practice, known as "householding." After obtaining the shareholder's consent, the delivery requirements can be met by sending a single proxy statement and annual report to one address for all consenting shareholders that reside at that address as part of a single household. 17 C.F.R. § 240.14a–3. *See* Delivery of Proxy Statements and Information Statements to Households, Sec. Exch. Act Rel. No. 34–43487, 2000 WL 1608837, [2000–2001 Transfer Binder] Fed. Sec. L. Rep. (CCH) ¶ 86,404 (SEC Oct. 27, 2000).

Schedule 14A.[35] Schedule 14A requires the following information, in addition to the date, time, and place of the meeting.[36] The first page of the proxy statement must disclose the approximate date on which the proxy statement and the form of proxy were first given to securities holders.[37] The proxy statement must include the deadline for submitting shareholder proposals for inclusion in the proxy statement and form of proxy for the next annual meeting.[38] In addition, the proxy statement must state the last date for submission of shareholder proposals for the next annual meeting irrespective of their inclusion in management's proxy statement.[39] The proxy statement must also disclose whether the proxies solicited are revocable and if so, the manner in which it may be revoked.[41] The proxy statement must identify and explain the availability of statutory dissenters rights of appraisal for any proposals to be voted upon.[42] This includes an explanation of whether the failure to vote against the proposal will result in a waiver of statutory appraisal rights.[43] The proxy statement must contain a description of the person making the solicitation, including identifying who is bearing the cost of the solicitation.[44] The proxy statement must contain disclosures relating to interests of directors, officers, and "participants" in matters to be voted upon.[46]

The proxy statement must also list all of the company's voting securities and principal holders thereof.[47] The record date for determining which shareholders are entitled to vote and explanation of cumulative voting rights, if any, must also be disclosed in the proxy statement.[48] If any action is to be taken with respect to election of directors, the proxy statement must disclose and explain the nominees' relationship to affiliated companies and interest in issuer's activities.[49]

Management's proxy statement must disclose the compensation of the company's executive officers and directors.[50] Each year the shareholders of a publicly held company are entitled to disclosure of the following: (1) the direct and indirect compensation paid to the top executives; (2) a comparison chart, comparing the company's executive compensation stock price performance with that of comparable companies over the past five years; and (3) the compensation committee's report of policies and criteria used in fixing executive compensation.[51] In addition, in a reversal of its past policy, the SEC staff now takes the position that shareholder proposals relating to executive

35. 17 C.F.R. § 240.14a–101.

36. Schedule 14A, item 1(a).

37. Schedule 14A, item 1(b).

38. Schedule 14A, item 1(c).

39. Schedule 14A, item 1(c). *See* Rule 14a–5(e)(2), 17 C.F.R. § 240.14a–5(e)(2).

41. Schedule 14A, item 2.

42. Schedule 14A, item 3.

43. Schedule 14A, item 3, instruction 1.

44. Schedule 14A, item 4.

46. Schedule 14A, item 5.

47. Schedule 14A, item 6.

48. *Id.*

49. Schedule 14A, item 7 is quite complex in requiring detailed disclosures. 17 C.F.R. § 240.14a–101 item 7.

50. Schedule 14A, item 8.

51. Schedule 14A, item 8.

compensation may not automatically be excluded from management's proxy statement on the grounds that they relate to the ordinary business of the issuer.[52]

The proxy statement must also disclose relationships with any independent public accountant providing services in connection with the solicitation or matters to be acted upon, including shareholder approval of independent auditors. The proxy statement must disclose the aggregate fees that the auditor billed the company for each of the following types of services: (a) audit and review of the company's financial statements, (b) financial information systems design and implementation services performed by the company's principal accounts, and (c) all other services provided by the company's principal accountants.[54]

The proxy statement must describe in detail any bonus, profit sharing, and other benefit plans to be voted upon.[55] Similar information is required with regard to any pension or retirement plans to be acted upon.[56] The disclosures relating to compensation and pension plans must include detailed descriptions of any options, warrants, or rights to be voted upon.[57]

The proxy statement must describe in detail any securities to be authorized for issuance.[58] In the case of any modification or exchange of securities, the proxy statement must contain detailed disclosures.[59] If the proxy statement is seeking authorization for the issuance of securities or for the modification or exchange of securities, the proxy statement must provide financial statements relating to any such transactions.[60]

The proxy statement must describe extraordinary transactions that are up for shareholder consideration. In the case of mergers, consolidations, and acquisitions, the proxy statement must provide detailed disclosures relating to any mergers, consolidations, or acquisitions to be voted upon.[61]

If property is to be acquired or disposed of as a result of a shareholder vote, there must be a description of any property to be acquired or disposed of upon a shareholder vote.[62] There must also be a description of the terms of the transaction.[63]

The proxy statement must contain a restatement of any accounts that would be made necessary by the actions to be voted upon.[64] If applicable, the proxy statement must identify and describe any reports to be acted upon.[65]

52. *See* § 10.8 *infra* which discusses the shareholder proposal rule (Rule 14a–8, 17 C.F.R. § 240.14a–8).

54. Schedule 14A, item 9.

55. Schedule 14A, item 10.

56. *Id.*

57. *Id.*

58. Schedule 14A, item 11.

59. Schedule 14A, item 12.

60. Schedule 14A, item 13.

61. Schedule 14A, item 14. *See also* Regulation M–A, 17 C.F.R. §§ 229.1001 et seq.

62. Schedule 14A, item 15.

63. *Id.*

64. Schedule 14A, item 16.

65. Schedule 14A, item 17.

If shareholder action is to be taken with respect to any matters that are not required to be submitted to the shareholders, the proxy statement must contain an explanation of why shareholder approval is being sought.[66] If the proxy solicitation involves amendments to the articles of incorporation, charter, or other documents requiring shareholder approval, the proxy statement must provide the reasons for any such proposed amendments.[67]

In the event that any matters not specified above are being submitted to the shareholders for a vote, the proxy statement must contain disclosures in the same degree of detail as would be required by the enumerated disclosure requirements.[68]

When many items are to be submitted for shareholder consideration, they must be clearly identified so that shareholders can make informed decisions on how to vote. With respect to all matters to be voted upon, the proxy statement must set forth the vote required for approval for each matter submitted to the shareholders.[70]

Schedule 14A's disclosure requirements apply both to management's proxy statement and proxy solicitations by others.[71] When the proxy solicitation relates to the annual meeting of security holders, where directors are to be elected, an annual report must accompany or precede a proxy solicitation on behalf of the issuer.[72] The proxy rules permit presentation of a "short slate" of directors.[73] The SEC's decision to permit short slates of directors was designed to encourage shareholder participation in the election process by providing a more likely opportunity for minority representation on the board.

Proxy solicitation materials must clearly discuss each item for which shareholder votes are solicited. Combining (or "bundling") two or more items together can be materially misleading and will interfere with the proper exercise of shareholder suffrage.[75]

Rule 14a–4[76] sets forth the appropriate form for the proxy itself as opposed to solicitation materials. For example, boldface type must indicate whether or not the proxy is solicited on behalf of the issuer's management. The proxy must also provide the person solicited with an opportunity to vote for or against proposals (management may indicate which proposals it supports) as well as the ability to abstain or withhold authority from voting as to any matters. In the case of a shareholder election of directors, the proxy must leave room for write-in candidates.[78] In addition to seeking proxies on specific issues, the proxy rules permit the solicitation of discretionary proxies.[79]

---

66. Schedule 14A, item 18.

67. Schedule 14A, item 19.

68. Schedule 14A, item 20.

70. Schedule 14A, item 21.

71. *See, e.g.,* IBS Financial Corp. v. Seidman & Associates, L.L.C., 954 F.Supp. 980 (D.N.J. 1997), *affirmed in part, reversed in part,* 136 F.3d 940 (3d Cir.1998) (Schedule 14A by group of dissident shareholders contained adequate disclosures).

72. 17 C.F.R. § 240.14a–3(b). *See* § 10.6[2] *infra.*

73. Rule 14a–4(b)(2), 17 C.F.R. § 240.14a–4(b)(2).

75. Koppel v. 4987 Corp., 167 F.3d 125 (2d Cir.1999). *But cf., e.g.,* Koppel v. 4987 Corp., 2001 WL 47000, [2000–2001 Transfer Binder] Fed. Sec. L. Rep. (CCH) ¶ 91,306 (S.D.N.Y. 2001).

76. 17 C.F.R. § 240.14a–4.

78. 17 C.F.R. § 240.14a–4(b)(2)(iii).

79. *See, e.g.,* Union of Needletrades v. May Department Stores Co., 26 F.Supp.2d 577 (S.D.N.Y.1997).

Technological advancements have continuing significant impact on proxy solicitations. For example, it is now technologically possible for the corporation to receive proxies by telephone. However, most states require a writing, and questions have arisen concerning whether these datagram proxies provide the necessary "fundamental indicia of authenticity and genuineness needed to accord them a presumption of validity."[80] It may nevertheless be possible to formulate a telephonic system that will satisfy such state law requirements.[81] In addition to the mechanics of voting, which is a matter of the applicable state corporate law, technology has affected the delivery of the disclosure documents under federal law. The SEC permits electronic delivery of documents that need to be delivered to investors.[82] In order for the electronic delivery to satisfy the securities laws' disclosure obligations, the investor must previously have consented to electronic rather than hard copy delivery.[83]

Rule 14a–5[84] provides guidance as to the presentation of information in a proxy statement, including the size and form of printed material. In many cases, five preliminary copies of each proxy statement and the form of the proxy to be used must be filed with the SEC at least ten business days prior to the first date on which they are to be sent; however, the preliminary copies need not be filed if the proxy solicitation pertains to the regular annual meeting (or a special meeting held in lieu of the annual meeting) and the only matters to be considered are the election of directors, or approval or ratification of auditors and/or shareholder proposals.[85] Once the initial proxy statement is actually sent to the shareholders, eight definitive copies must be filed with the Commission, and three additional copies must at the same time be filed with each national securities exchange listing the issuer's security.[86]

The advance filing requirements of Rule 14a–6 for the proxy statement were designed to promote full disclosure and complete dissemination of information in order to achieve the desired result of informed shareholder voting. It has been held that a violation of this rule can result in an implied private right of action.[90]

Rule 14a–10 prohibits the solicitation of undated, predated, or postdated proxies.[97] Rule 14a–12, permits proxy solicitation subject to certain conditions and prior to the furnishing of a proxy statement. Under Rule 14a–12 either there must be a description of the participants in the solicitation[98] or,

---

80. Parshalle v. Roy, 567 A.2d 19 (Del.Ch.1989) (invalidating the particular datagram method used in that case).

81. *See* David M. Doret, Arthur B. Crozier & Alan M. Miller, Datagram Proxies, 23 Rev.Sec. & Commod.Reg. 45 (1990).

82. Use of Electronic Media, Sec. Act Rel. No. 33–7856, 2000 WL 502290 (SEC April 28, 2000). *See also, e.g.,* Use of Electronic Media for Delivery Purposes, Sec. Act Rel. No. 33–7233, 60 Fed. Reg. 53458, 1995 WL 600083 (SEC Oct. 6, 1995).

83. Use of Electronic Media, Sec. Act Rel. No. 33–7856, 2000 WL 502290 (SEC April 28, 2000). *See* § 9.5[2] *supra.*

84. 17 C.F.R. § 240.14a–5.

85. 17 C.F.R. § 240.14a–6(a).

86. 17 C.F.R. § 240.14a–6(c). *See* §§ 14.1, 14.3–14.5 *infra* for discussion of the regulation of national exchanges and member broker-dealers.

90. Morris v. Bush, 1999 WL 58857, [1999 Transfer Binder] Fed. Sec. L. Rep. (CCH) ¶ 90,430 (N.D. Tex. 1999).

97. 17 C.F.R. § 240.14a–10.

98. 17 C.F.R. § 240.14a–12(a)(1)(i). *See* Instruction 3 to Item 4 of Schedule 14A, 17 C.F.R. § 240.14a–101.

alternatively, there must be a prominent legend in clear, plain language advising security holders where they can obtain information about the participants.[99] All sources of financing behind the solicitation must also be disclosed. Former Rule 14a–11[100] set forth special requirements relating to the solicitation of shareholders' votes in connection with the election of directors; however, that rule was made unnecessary by many of the provisions of Rule 14a–12.[101]

§ 10.3 Rule 14a–9 and the Implied Remedy for Material Misstatements and Omissions in Proxy Materials; Standing to Sue; Scienter vs. Negligence; Attorneys' Fees

§ 10.3[1] The Implied Private Remedy for Material Misstatements in the Solicitation of Proxies

Rule 14a–9 prohibits material misstatements and omissions in connection with the solicitation of proxies.[1] Rule 14a–9's prohibitions against material misstatements and omissions in proxy solicitations apply to all proxy solicitations and thus are not limited to management's proxy materials.

The Supreme Court has repeatedly recognized an implied remedy for violation of Rule 14a–9's antifraud provisions.[2] In fact, the Rule 14a–9 private remedy was the first Exchange Act implied right of action to be recognized by the Court.[3] Although the Court has not been generous in granting additional implied rights of action,[4] there have been indications that the Rule 14a–9 remedy continues to be relatively expansive.[5] In contrast, it has been held that there is no private remedy for violation of SEC Rule 14b–1[6] which imposes on brokerage firms the duty to transmit proxy materials to their customers.[7]

§ 10.3[2] Standing to Sue Under Rule 14a–9

Since it is an implied remedy, there is no express provision regarding appropriate plaintiffs in private actions under the proxy rules. Presumably, all a private plaintiff need show in a Rule 14a–9 action is that he or she was injured in connection with a proxy solicitation covered by the Exchange Act's regulation, regardless of whether there was either a purchase or sale of securities[8] involved.[9]

99. 17 C.F.R. § 240.14a–12(a)(1)(i).

100. 17 C.F.R. § 240.14a–11. (1999) (rescinded)

101. *See* Regulation of Takeovers and Security Holder Communications, Sec. Exch. Act Rel. No. 34–42055, 1999 WL 969596 (SEC Oct. 22, 1999).

§ 10.3

1. 17 C.F.R. § 240.14a–9.

2. TSC Industries, Inc. v. Northway, Inc., 426 U.S. 438, 96 S.Ct. 2126, 48 L.Ed.2d 757 (1976); Mills v. Electric Auto–Lite Co., 396 U.S. 375, 90 S.Ct. 616, 24 L.Ed.2d 593 (1970); J.I. Case Co. v. Borak, 377 U.S. 426, 84 S.Ct. 1555, 12 L.Ed.2d 423 (1964).

3. J.I. Case Co. v. Borak, 377 U.S. 426, 84 S.Ct. 1555, 12 L.Ed.2d 423 (1964).

4. *See* § 12.2 *infra.*

5. *See* §§ 10.4–10.5 *infra.*

6. 17 C.F.R. § 240.14b–1. *See* § 10.10 *infra.*

7. Pundaleeka v. Fidelity Brokerage Services, Inc., [1999–2000 Transfer Binder] Fed. Sec. L. Rep. (CCH) ¶ 90,905, 1999 WL 412615 (N.D.Ill.1999).

8. The courts have imposed a purchaser/seller standing requirement in private damage actions under SEC Rule 10b–5. *E.g.,* Blue Chip Stamps v. Manor Drug Stores, 421 U.S. 723, 95 S.Ct. 1917, 44 L.Ed.2d 539 (1975), *rehearing denied* 423 U.S. 884, 96 S.Ct. 157, 46 L.Ed.2d 114 (1975). *See* § 12.7[1] *infra.*

9. *See, e.g.,* Capital Real Estate Investors Tax Exempt Fund Limited Partnership v. Schwartzberg, 929 F.Supp. 105 (S.D.N.Y.1996).

Thus, for example, a corporation or a shareholder has standing to complain of a proxy rule violation so long as it can show injury and a causal connection between the violation and the injury.[10] The federal proxy rules were designed to protect the right of a shareholder to a fully-informed vote on matters with regard to which proxies have been solicited. Even in the case of management misstatements in connection with a shareholder proposal, standing is not limited to the shareholder whose proposal was the subject of the alleged violations. Any shareholder entitled to vote on the proposal has a right to full disclosure and thus may sue to redress such a violation of the proxy rules.[11]

However, since the proxy regulations are designed to protect shareholder voting rights, standing should be limited to shareholders who had a right to vote.[12] Making an analogy to cases decided under the Williams Act antifraud provisions[13] applicable to tender offers,[14] it has been held that someone whose interest in the proxy solicitation is merely as a defeated proxy contestant is not within that "especial" class of persons for whom a section 14(a) remedy will be implied.[15] Courts should be careful in giving too broad a reading to this limitation on standing to sue under the proxy rules. It is one thing to say that a proxy contestant whose only interest is in gaining control of a corporation should not be given standing under the proxy rules, since federal proxy regulation was designed to protect full disclosure in the exercise of shareholder suffrage and not to guarantee rights to would-be control acquirers. It would be quite another, however, to deny standing to shareholders seeking to protect their interest through a proxy battle simply because they are proxy contestants with regard to the vote in question.

While courts should strive to protect the rights of shareholders whose interest in the corporation is likely to be affected by proxy rule violations, the courts should be mindful of potential misuse and abuse of proxy litigation. Accordingly, a shareholder challenging a vote for ulterior reasons should not be granted standing.[16]

A shareholder who did not have shareholder status at the time of the alleged proxy violations does not have standing to sue as a shareholder under Rule 14a–9.[17] In contrast, although it was argued that standing in proxy cases

10. *See* Stahl v. Gibraltar Financial Corp., 967 F.2d 335 (9th Cir.1992).

11. United Paperworkers International Union v. International Paper Co., 985 F.2d 1190 (2d Cir.1993); Krauth v. Executive Telecard, Ltd., 890 F.Supp. 269, 286 (S.D.N.Y.1995).

12. *E.g.,* Royal Business Group v. Realist, Inc., 933 F.2d 1056 (1st Cir.1991), affirming 751 F.Supp. 311 (D.Mass.1990) (section 14(a) action dismissed since plaintiff was not a shareholder and thus any injury that may have been due to alleged proxy rule violations could not be challenged under the Act).

13. Section 14(e) of the 1934 Act, 15 U.S.C.A. § 77n(e).

14. *See, e.g.,* Piper v. Chris–Craft Industries, Inc., 430 U.S. 1, 97 S.Ct. 926, 51 L.Ed.2d 124 (1977). *See* § 11.19 *infra.*

15. Royal Business Group, Inc. v. Realist, Inc., 933 F.2d 1056, 1060 (1st Cir.1991), affirming 751 F.Supp. 311 (D.Mass.1990). *Cf.* Bolton v. Gramlich, 540 F.Supp. 822 (S.D.N.Y.1982) (refusing demand for reimbursement of proxy expenses by unsuccessful tender offerors).

16. *See* AMR Corp. v. UAL Corp., 781 F.Supp. 292 (S.D.N.Y.1992).

17. Murray v. Hospital Corp. of America, 682 F.Supp. 343 (M.D.Tenn.1988). *See also* Gabrielsen v. BancTexas Group, Inc., 675 F.Supp. 367, 373–74 (N.D.Tex.1987).

should be limited to shareholders, it has been held that a director had standing to bring suit challenging an election based on alleged misstatements in the proxy materials.[18] The court reasoned that "[s]tanding depends on injury, and we believe that one who alleges that he has been wrongfully ousted from a Board of Directors because management improperly persuaded other shareholders not to vote for him, has articulated an injury cognizable under section 14(a)."[19] While the court's decision granting proxy rule standing to directors certainly furthers the integrity of the voting process, it may seem to be at odds with Supreme Court cases holding that implied remedies are limited to members of an especial class which the legislation is designed to protect.[20] In response to criticism of granting directors standing to sue, it can be argued that shareholders' interests are furthered by allowing directors to challenge alleged misstatements. Nevertheless, this extension of proxy rule standing to directors seems to be contrary to the current direction of implied remedies.[21]

Ordinarily, a candidate for a director position will not have standing to challenge proxy solicitations under the proxy rules. Nevertheless, when the defeated director candidate is also a shareholder, he or she may be able to state a federal proxy claim.[22] However, it would seem that for such standing to exist, the claim must be couched in terms of the plaintiff's rights as a shareholder to full disclosure rather than in terms of the would-be director's rights to a fair election.

§ 10.3[3] Is Scienter Required Under Rule 14a–9?

It is an elementary principle of common law fraud that the defendant committing the fraud must have acted with a state of mind amounting to scienter.[26] Scienter also is required to prove a violation of SEC Rule 10b–5.[27] However, scienter is not required to establish a violation of Rule 14a–9's prohibitions against material misstatements and omissions in connection with a proxy solicitation. For example, a number of federal courts of appeals and district courts have upheld private 14a–9 claims based on negligence, thus not requiring scienter.[28] The reasoning underlying the Supreme Court's ruling in Aaron v. SEC[30] mandates that a showing of negligent conduct will suffice.

18. Palumbo v. Deposit Bank, 758 F.2d 113 (3d Cir.1985).

19. Id. at 116.

20. E.g. Piper v. Chris–Craft Industries, Inc., 430 U.S. 1, 97 S.Ct. 926, 51 L.Ed.2d 124 (1977), rehearing denied 430 U.S. 976, 97 S.Ct. 1668, 52 L.Ed.2d 371 (1977) (competing tender offeror does not have standing under the Williams Act; if there is such an especial class, it is the target company and its shareholders). See §§ 11.10, 12.2 infra.

21. See id. It can be argued that persons who stand for election in a regulated proxy contest have a more direct interest than the defeated tender offeror who was denied standing in the Piper case.

22. Morris v. Bush, 1999 WL 417928, [1999 Transfer Binder] Fed. Sec. L. Rep. (CCH) ¶ 90,521 (N.D. Tex. 1999) (sustaining § 124(a)(9) claim by former board members against ousted chairman of the board).

26. E.g., Derry v. Peek, 14 App.Cas. 337 (House of Lords 1889). See generally W. Page Keeton, Dan B. Dobbs, Robert E. Keeton & David G. Owen, Prosser and Keeton on Torts § 107 (5th ed. 1984).

27. Aaron v. SEC, 446 U.S. 680, 100 S.Ct. 1945, 64 L.Ed.2d 611 (1980); Ernst & Ernst v. Hochfelder, 425 U.S. 185, 96 S.Ct. 1375, 47 L.Ed.2d 668 (1976).

28. E.g., In re Rockefeller Center Properties, Inc. Securities Litigation, 311 F.3d 198, 211 (3d Cir. 2002).

30. 446 U.S. 680, 100 S.Ct. 1945, 64 L.Ed.2d 611 (1980).

§ 10.3[4] Materiality Under Rule 14a–9–A Preview

In order to be actionable under Rule 14a–9, the misstatement or omission must have been a material one. The concept of materiality under the proxy rules is much the same as under the securities laws generally.[37] This means that the misstatement or omission must be of a character that there is "a substantial likelihood that a reasonable shareholder *would* consider it important in deciding how to vote."[38] Ordinarily determinations of materiality involves a highly factual inquiry and thus summary judgment rarely is appropriate.[39]

§ 10.3[5] Causation Under Rule 14a–9

As discussed more fully in a later section of this treatise,[40] the Supreme Court in Virginia Bankshares, Inc. v. Sandberg[41] has narrowed the type of causation that will suffice for a private plaintiff to establish a claim under the proxy rules. The Court in *Virginia Bankshares* held, in a five-to-four decision, that a private right of action did not lie for alleged deficiencies in proxies related to a shareholder vote that was not required to effectuate the transaction in question. *Virginia Bankshares* involved a vote taken under a state corporate law conflict of interest statute that applies to transactions between a corporation and interested directors. In an earlier decision, the Supreme Court had indicated by way of dictum that something less than but-for causation might support a claim for violation of the proxy rules.[42] The Court's subsequent decision in *Virginia Bankshares* indicates that but-for causation is in fact required.

Following the decision in *Virginia Bankshares,* it is clear that a shareholder cannot complain of alleged violations in connection with a proxy solicitation when the state law does not require the shareholder vote as a necessary step in the consummation of the transaction.[43] But what about the situation where a shareholder vote is required but the management soliciting the proxies controls sufficient votes to assure the success of the vote? As discussed more fully in a subsequent section of this treatise,[44] there is considerable authority for the proposition that even in such a case a plaintiff can sue if it can be shown that the transaction would have taken a different form had it not been for the misstatements or omissions in question.[45] Thus,

---

37. *E.g.,* In re DNAP Securities Litigation, 2000 WL 1358619, [2000–2001 Transfer Binder] Fed. Sec. L. Rep. (CCH) ¶ 91,215 (N.D.Cal. 2000) (proxy statement for merger was not materially misleading).

38. TSC Industries, Inc. v. Northway, Inc., 426 U.S. 438, 449, 96 S.Ct. 2126, 2132, 48 L.Ed.2d 757 (1976) (emphasis added). *Accord* Basic Inc. v. Levinson, 485 U.S. 224, 108 S.Ct. 978, 99 L.Ed.2d 194 (1988).

39. *E.g.,* Marks v. CDW Computer Centers, Inc., 122 F.3d 363, 369–70 (7th Cir.1997).

40. *See* § 10.5 *infra.*

41. 501 U.S. 1083, 111 S.Ct. 2749, 115 L.Ed.2d 929 (1991), *appeal after remand* 979 F.2d 332 (4th Cir.1992), *opinion vacated* 1993 WL 524680 (4th Cir.1993).

42. Mills v. Electric Auto–Lite Co., 396 U.S. 375, 90 S.Ct. 616, 24 L.Ed.2d 593 (1970).

43. *See, e.g.,* Dominick v. Marcove, 809 F.Supp. 805 (D.Colo.1992).

44. *See* § 10.5 *infra. See also, e.g.,* Stahl v. Gibraltar Financial Corp., 967 F.2d 335 (9th Cir.1992).

45. Wilson v. Great American Industries, Inc., 979 F.2d 924 (2d Cir.1992); Cowin v. Bresler, 741 F.2d 410 (D.C.Cir.1984) (election of directors); Schlick v. Penn–Dixie Cement Corp., 507 F.2d 374, 384 (2d Cir.1974), *cert. denied* 421 U.S. 976, 95 S.Ct. 1976, 44 L.Ed.2d 467 (1975). *See also, e.g.,* Howing Co. v. Nationwide Corp., 972 F.2d 700 (6th Cir.1992), *cert. denied* 507 U.S. 1004, 113

for example, it has been held that a shareholder who claimed interference with a statutory right of appraisal was able to maintain a claim under the proxy rules.[46] However, where the defendants had sufficient votes to assure the consummation of the transaction in question, Rule 10b–5 could not be used to provide a remedy for the alleged unfairness of the merger.[47] Also, there is language in the *Virginia Bankshares* decision that could support the conclusion that proof that the required number of votes were assured may be sufficient to defeat a claim for violation of the proxy rules.[48] For example, in Grace v. Rosenstock[49] the Second Circuit held that minority shareholders were unable to establish that material misstatements in the proxy materials caused the freeze-out transaction that they challenged.[50] In that case, the plaintiff minority shareholders had voted against the merger and thus were entitled to dissenters' appraisal rights under state law as their exclusive remedy.[51]

In any event, the causal connection between the alleged violations and the ultimate transaction and/or injury must be direct.[52] It follows, for example, that a claim for misstatements made in connection with the directors' election was too remote from the injury that resulted from alleged director misconduct after the election in question.[53]

Courts have broken down causation into two separate but related concepts. Causation consists of both: (1) *loss causation,*[53.1] which is a connection between the misstatements and the actual economic harm resulting from the transaction, and (2) *transaction causation,* which is designed to demonstrate that the misstatements or omissions were causally related to the occurrence of the transaction.[55]

S.Ct. 1645, 123 L.Ed.2d 266 (1993) (decided under section 13(e)'s going private rules). *But see* Boone v. Carlsbad Bancorporation, 972 F.2d 1545 (10th Cir.1992).

46.   Wilson v. Great American Industries, Inc., 979 F.2d 924 (2d Cir.1992).

47.   Boone v. Carlsbad Bancorporation, Inc., 972 F.2d 1545 (10th Cir.1992). This is consistent with a long line of cases holding that the federal securities laws are not to be used as a back-door remedy for corporate law concerns. For discussion of the inapplicability of the federal securities laws as a remedy for unfairness, *see* § 12.20 *infra.*

48.   Thouret v. Hudner, 1996 WL 38824, [1995–1996 Transfer Binder] Fed. Sec. L. Rep. (CCH) ¶ 99,037 (S.D.N.Y.1996) (no private right of action since the minority shareholder's and others' votes were totally irrelevant to the passage of the company's slate of directors).

49.   228 F.3d 40 (2d Cir.2000).

50.   *Id.*

51.   *Id. See* § 12.20 *infra.*

52.   General Electric Co. v. Cathcart, 980 F.2d 927 (3d Cir.1992) (too attenuated a connection between misstatements concerning directors' election and subsequent misconduct in office). *See also, e.g.,* Integrated Technology & Development, Inc. v. Rosenfield, 103 F.Supp.2d 574 (E.D.N.Y. 2000) (where alleged misrepresentations took place after the transactions in question, causation could not be established); Heil v. Lebow, 1993 WL 15032, [1992–1993 Transfer Binder] Fed.Sec. L.Rep. (CCH) ¶ 97,324 (S.D.N.Y.1993) (alleged failure to disclose secret plan was not actionable when the alleged plan was never implemented); Diamond v. ML–Lee Acquisition Fund II, L.P., 1992 WL 420922, [1992–1993 Transfer Binder] Fed.Sec.L.Rep. (CCH) ¶ 97,275 (S.D.N.Y.1992) (failure to establish loss causation).

53.   General Electric Co. v. Cathcart, 980 F.2d 927 (3d Cir.1992).

53.1   The plaintiff must also establish loss causation—a connection between misrepresentation and resulting damages. See Dura Pharmaceuticals, Inc. v. Broudo, 544 U.S. 336, 125 S.Ct. 1627, 161 L.Ed.2d 577 (2005) (decided under 1934 Act Rule 10b–5). *See also* the discussion in § 12.11 *infra.*

55.   Schlick v. Penn–Dixie Cement Corp., 507 F.2d 374, 380–381 (2d Cir.1974), *cert. denied* 421 U.S. 976, 95 S.Ct. 1976, 44 L.Ed.2d 467 (1975).

§ 10.3[6] Relief Other Than Damages in Actions Under Rule 14a–9

In addition to an action for damages, Rule 14a–9 will support a claim for injunctive relief in actions by private parties or the SEC. For example, courts have been willing to order that a new meeting be held in the face of proxy violations that have tainted shareholder votes.[57] This enables both sides to resolicit proxies, albeit at considerable expense.[58] On appropriate facts, a court may issue an injunction that restores the status quo prior to the tainted shareholder vote.[59] On the other hand, once a transaction has been implemented, courts are understandably reluctant to try to unscramble the eggs and put the parties back where they were before the tainted proxy solicitation and ensuing shareholder vote.

If suit is brought in advance of the meeting where the shareholder vote is to take place, a court may require corrective disclosures prior to any vote taking place.[60] When such corrective disclosures are possible, this is a far less expensive route than requiring a new vote. Accordingly, corrective disclosures should be favored in cases where the shareholders can be given adequate time to digest and evaluate the new information before casting their votes.

§ 10.7 Security Holders' Access to the Proxy System: Right to Information; Shareholder List

An issuer subject to the Securities Exchange Act's registration and reporting requirements[1] and thus to the SEC proxy rules, must comply with written shareholder requests for information with regard to matters to be voted on at a shareholder meeting.[2] Specifically, Rule 14a–7(a) requires the issuer to provide the following information upon request by a shareholder: (1) a statement of the approximate number of security holders who have been or are to be solicited on behalf of the issuer; and (2) an estimate of the cost of mailing a specified proxy statement including cost of bankers, brokers or other persons acting on the issuer's, behalf.[3] Also, if a security holder so requests, the issuer must mail, at the security holder's expense, any material relating to matters to be voted upon at the meeting to all holders that were solicited by the issuer or someone acting on the issuer's behalf.[4] If the issuer so desires, in lieu of complying with the securities holder's request it may provide the security holder with a mailing list of all persons entitled to vote

---

57. *E.g.* Fradkin v. Ernst, 571 F.Supp. 829 (N.D.Ohio 1983); GAF Corp. v. Heyman, 559 F.Supp. 748 (S.D.N.Y.1983), *reversed on other grounds* 724 F.2d 727 (2d Cir.1983) (no violation found); Bertoglio v. Texas International Co., 488 F.Supp. 630 (D.Del.1980).

58. *E.g.* SEC v. May, 134 F.Supp. 247 (S.D.N.Y.1955), *affirmed* 229 F.2d 123 (2d Cir.1956) (preliminary injunction). *But cf.* Citizens First Bancorp., Inc. v. Harreld, 559 F.Supp. 867 (W.D.Ky.1982).

59. *See, e.g.,* Crouch v. Prior, 905 F.Supp. 248 (D.Vi.1995) (restoring management as it existed prior to vote).

60. *See, e.g.,* Morris v. Bush, 1999 WL 58857, [1999 Transfer Binder] Fed. Sec. L. Rep. (CCH) ¶ 90,430 (N.D. Tex. 1999) (enjoining individual who failed to file preliminary voting statement with the SEC and who allegedly made materially false proxy solicitation).

§ 10.7

1. 15 U.S.C.A. §§ 78*l*, 78m. *See* §§ 9.2, 9.3 *supra*.

2. 17 C.F.R. § 240.14a–7.

3. 17 C.F.R. § 240.14a–7(a).

4. 17 C.F.R. § 240.14a–7(b).

on the relevant proposals.[5] In the case of roll-up reorganizations[6] and going private transactions subject to SEC Rule 13e–3,[7] the requesting shareholder can make an election to receive a mailing list or to have the issuer make the mailing at the shareholder's expense.[8]

The federal proxy rules' guarantee of security holders' access to the proxy machinery is supplemented by shareholders' common law and statutory inspection rights that are provided by state corporate law. Put in its most general terms, corporate shareholders have a right to inspect relevant corporate books and records pursuant to a request stating a proper purpose therefor.[12] Although in most cases much of this information will already be available because of the 1934 Act's registration and periodic reporting requirements, these state law inspection rights can give security holders access to more detailed information and to the documents and other corporate records forming the basis of publicly reported information.

§ 10.8   Security Holders' Access to the Proxy System: Shareholder Proposals and the Shareholder Proposal Rule

Scope of the Shareholder Proposal Rule

One of the more critical aspects of proxy rules' impact on corporate governance and shareholder input is found in the shareholder proposal rule, which is embodied in SEC Rule 14a–8.[2] Over the years, there has been a continuing controversy as to the proper role for the federal securities laws in corporate governance. Shareholder access to the proxy process in general, and in particular to management's proxy statement, has been a major focus of the struggle to define the appropriate line of demarcation between corporate governance issues that properly fall within the purview of state law and investor-protection concerns that more appropriately fit with the federal regulatory scheme for transactions in securities. The SEC and the courts have struggled with these issues, as has Congress.

The thrust of the shareholder proposal rule has not been a significant change in the success of shareholder proposals. Nevertheless, the SEC and the courts for a long time have recognized the importance of shareholder access to management's proxy statement, even though shareholder proposals typically fail miserably. Corporate governance has been significantly affected by the shareholder proposal rule, notwithstanding the continued lack of success of shareholder proposals. For example, the Second Circuit has awarded attorneys fees under the "common benefit" rule where a shareholder action resulted in requiring inclusion of a shareholder proposal (relating to the company's employment practices), even though approximately ninety percent of the

---

5.   17 C.F.R. § 240.14a–7(c).

6.   A roll-up reorganization is a transaction in which the issuer changes the form of doing business such as by rolling up a limited partnership into a corporation. *See* Item 901 of Reg. S–K.

7.   17 C.F.R. § 240.13e–3. The SEC's going private rules are discussed in § 11.8[2] *infra.*

8.   Rule 14a–7, 17 C.F.R. § 240.14a–7 as amended in Exch. Act Rel. No. 34–31326 (SEC October 22, 1992).

12.   *E.g.* ALI–ABA, Revised Model Business Corporation Act § 16.02 (1984).

§ 10.8

2.   17 C.F.R. § 240.14a–8.

shares voted against the proposal.[4] The court reasoned that the failure of the proposal was insignificant because, standing alone, the right of a shareholder to cast an informed vote is a substantial interest worthy of vindication.[5]

If a shareholder proposal is not a proper matter for consideration under the state of incorporation's corporate governance rules, then the federal law permits management to exclude the proposal from management's proxy statement.[6] In reading the discussion that follows, the reader should keep in mind that while a shareholder proposal that may be valid under state law is properly excludable, it must nevertheless be described in the issuer's proxy statement.[7] The basic thrust of Rule 14a–8 is that a shareholder proposal which is proper for consideration under state law must be included in the management's proxy statement along with a brief statement explaining the shareholder's reason for supporting the proposal's adoption, provided that it is submitted to the issuer in a timely fashion.

The number of shareholder proposals have been increasing. For example, the spring 2003 voting season reached record proportions.[9] This, in turn, resulted in increased use of the SEC no-action letter process by management seeking to exclude shareholder proposals from management's proxy statement.

There are relatively few judicial decisions dealing with the shareholder proposal rule. Interpretations of the shareholder proposal rule have constantly been refined through the SEC's no action letter process.[11] These no action letters are publicly available[12] and generally are not subject to judicial review.[13]

Each year, the Commission is faced with hundreds of requests for no action letters. In addition to giving initial responses through the no action letter process, in appropriate instances, the SEC staff will reconsider its position after receiving additional information.[14] Although the case-by-case approach of no action letters may not be the most efficient lawmaking process, it does provide a good source of insight into the SEC's current views.

---

4. Amalgamated Clothing & Textile Workers Union v. Wal–Mart Stores, Inc., 54 F.3d 69 (2d Cir.1995).

5. *Id.*

6. Rule 14a–8(i)(1), 17 C.F.R. § 240.14a–8(i)(1), which is discussed in § 10.8[2] *infra.*

7. Schedule 14A, item 21.

9. *See* 2003 Proxy Resolutions Set to be Highest in Terms of Number, Ability to Get a Vote, 35 Sec. Reg. & L. Rep. (BNA) 280 (Feb. 17, 2003) (referring to a report issued by several shareholder advocacy groups).

11. No action letters provide a vehicle for seeking SEC advice on particular securities law issues. The interpretations are issued by staff members in response to specific requests. The no action letters and SEC responses are publicly available. The no action letter process is discussed generally in § 1.4[4] *supra* and § 16.32[2] *infra.*

12. No action letter requests are on file with the SEC and are available on Westlaw, among other sources.

13. *See* Amalgamated Clothing & Textile Workers Union v. SEC, 15 F.3d 254 (2d Cir.1994) (shareholder could not obtain judicial review of SEC no action letter permitting management to exclude shareholder proposal as the SEC letter did not represent a "final order"); Kixmiller v. SEC, 492 F.2d 641 (D.C.Cir.1974) (judicial review of SEC action is confined to orders issued by the Commission and does not extend to no action letter responses).

14. *See, e.g.,* UAL Corp., 2001 WL 111453 (SEC No Action Letter Feb. 6, 2001) (granting request to reconsider position in initial no action response).

The Second Circuit has recognized the existence of a private right of action by shareholders to enforce their rights under Rule 14a–8.[15] If management wrongfully refuses to disclose a shareholder proposal, a court may enjoin the upcoming meeting.[16] In addition, material misstatements in management's opposition to a shareholder proposal can result in a voiding of the vote and an order that the proposal be resubmitted to the shareholders at the next annual meeting.[17] Management's ability to exclude shareholder proposals regarding social issues is limited. In *Amalgamated Clothing & Textile Workers Union v. Wal–Mart Stores*,[18] the court overturned the SEC's permitting management to exclude shareholder proposals relating to the company's equal employment and affirmative action programs. The court reasoned that the SEC's formal guidelines for the ordinary business basis for exclusion superseded inconsistent no action responses.

SEC Staff Legal Bulletin Number 14[20] provides useful guidance to both companies and their shareholders dealing with the SEC's shareholder proposal rule.

Shareholder Eligibility Requirements

Management's proxy statement for the annual meeting must disclose the deadline for submitting shareholder proposals for inclusion in the proxy statement and form of proxy for the next annual meeting.[21] In addition, management's proxy statement must state the last date for submission of shareholder proposals for the next annual meeting irrespective of the process set forth in the shareholder proposal rule.[22]

In order to preclude the proposal from being subject to exclusion from management's proxy materials, the shareholder submitting the proposal must meet certain eligibility requirements. In order to qualify for protection under the shareholder proposal rule, the proponent of the proposal must be a beneficial owner of a class of security that would be entitled to vote on the proposal at the shareholder meeting.[23] Additionally, Rule 14a–8 applies only if the proponent has owned the securities for at least one year and meets or exceeds the rule's minimum ownership requirement (the lesser of one percent or one thousand dollars in market value of such securities).[24] In addition to the minimum ownership and holding period requirements, the proponent of a shareholder proposal must continue to be a security holder through the date on which the meeting is held.[25] If the proponent dies prior to the meeting, the eligibility requirements have not been met and management can exclude the

---

15.   Roosevelt v. E.I. Du Pont de Nemours & Co., 958 F.2d 416 (D.C.Cir.1992).

16.   New York City Employees' Retirement System v. Dole Food Co., 795 F.Supp. 95 (S.D.N.Y. 1992), *appeal dismissed, opinion vacated* 969 F.2d 1430 (2d Cir.1992) (preliminary injunction).

17.   United Paperworkers International Union v. International Paper Co., 801 F.Supp. 1134 (S.D.N.Y.1992), *affirmed and modified* 985 F.2d 1190 (2d Cir.1993).

18.   821 F.Supp. 877 (S.D.N.Y.1993).

20.   Staff Legal Bulletin No. 14 (CF) (SEC Div. of Corp. Fin. July 13, 2001).

21.   Schedule 14A item 1(c). *See* Rule 14a–5(e)(1), 17 C.F.R. § 240.14a–5(e)(1).

22.   Schedule 14A item 1(c). *See* Rule 14a–5(e)(2), 17 C.F.R. § 240.14a–5(e)(2).

23.   17 C.F.R. § 240.14a–8(a)(1). *Cf.* Randall S. Thomas & Kenneth J. Martin, Should Labor be Allowed to Make Shareholder Proposals?, 73 Wash. L. Rev. 41 (1998).

24.   17 C.F.R. § 240.14a–8(a)(1).

25.   17 C.F.R. § 240.14a–8(a)(1).

proposal from its proxy statement.[26] The same would of course be true if the proponent ceases to be a shareholder for any other reason prior to the meeting.

Even if the shareholder continues to meet the eligibility requirements, nonattendance at the meeting (either in person or through a representative) will render the proposal excludible from management's proxy statement.[27] Nonattendance by the proponent at meetings where he or she submitted a proposal in the past will also justify management in excluding a proposal from management's proxy statement.[28] Additionally, management may exclude a shareholder proposal introduced by a shareholder who would not be entitled to vote on the proposal.[29] Even if the proposal shareholder owns a class of shares that would be entitled to vote on the proposal, management may exclude a shareholder proposal if the shareholder submitting it turns out only to be a nominal proponent for someone else's proposal.[30]

If management makes a request, the proponent of a shareholder proposal for inclusion in management's proxy statement must provide documentary evidence that the minimum ownership requirements have been satisfied.[31] The proponent's refusal to document sufficient ownership to satisfy the eligibility criteria may justify management in excluding the proposal from the proxy statement.[32] In addition, a shareholder's failure to respond with a statement that the one-year holding period for eligibility has been met provides sufficient basis for management's exclusion of the shareholder's proposal from management's proxy statement.[33]

A shareholder formerly could submit up to two proposals, but this has been reduced to one proposal per year.[48]

§ 10.8[2] Grounds for Exclusion—Impropriety Under the Law of the State of Incorporation

§ 10.8[2][A] State Law Generally

The corporate law of the state of incorporation is the ultimate source for the answer to the question of whether a proposal is a proper matter for shareholder consideration. Under the SEC's shareholder proposal rule, management may exclude a proposal which is not proper under the law of the issuer's state of incorporation if a corporation (or state of organization for some other form of business entity). The state law's allocation of governing power within the company may thus determine whether the proposal relates to a proper exercise of that power.

---

26. Oregon Trail Financial Corp., [1999–2000 Transfer Binder] Fed. Sec. L. Rep. (CCH) ¶ 77,874, 2000 WL 821710 (SEC No Action Letter June 26, 2000) (management could exclude the proposal under Rule 14a–8(f)).

27. Rule 14a–8(h)(1), 17 C.F.R. § 240.14a–8(h)(1).

28. *E.g.,* Eastman Chemical Co., 2001 WL 223401 (SEC No Action Letter Feb. 27, 2001).

29. Media General, Inc., 2001 WL 138964 (SEC No Action Letter Feb. 10, 2001) (shareholder proponent held a class of stock not entitled to vote on the proposal).

30. *E.g.,* PG & E Corp., 2002 WL 471701 (SEC No Action Letter March 1, 2002) (management could exclude proposal since shareholder was just a nominal proponent).

31. Rule 14a–8(f), 17 C.F.R. § 240.14a–8(f).

32. Rule 14a–8(f), 17 C.F.R. § 240.14a–8(f).

33. *E.g.,* AT & T Corp., 2001 WL 70431 (SEC No Action Letter Jan. 24, 2001).

48. Rules 14a–8(d), (f), 17 CF.R. §§ 240.14a–(8)(d), (f).

Whether the shareholder meeting in question is an annual or special meeting may bear upon whether a particular shareholder proposal is a proper matter for consideration under state law. For example, under Delaware law, where a shareholder meeting is called to conduct specific business, shareholders' proposals regarding unrelated matters are not proper proposals under state law and thus may be excluded from management's proxy statement.[65] If a proposal is proper under state law, then Rule 14a–8(i)(1) cannot be relied upon as a basis for excluding the proposal from management's proxy statement.[66] It is to be remembered that state law may give a broad definition of proper matters for shareholders. In deciding whether a proposal is excludible as relating to a matter that would violate of state law, the Commission staff may decide to rely on opinion of counsel contained in the no action letter request.[68]

Mandatory Versus Recommended Action

State law defines the respective roles of shareholders and directors in corporate governance. In its notes to the shareholder proposal rule, the SEC points out that the wording of the proposal may determine whether it is a proper matter under state law. Under the law of most states, only the board of directors may initiate amendments to the articles of incorporation,[71] and it follows that a shareholder proposal to amend the articles, as opposed to a proposal recommending amendment to the articles, is not proper and thus may be excluded from management's proxy statement.[72] A similar result follows for other corporate action.

Bylaw Amendments; Shareholder Rights Plans

Many state laws permit shareholder initiative on bylaw amendments.[81] Under such a regime, proposals for amendment rather than merely recommending that the board make such amendments will be permissible shareholder proposals.[82] The SEC indicated that in the absence of clear Delaware law on point, it was unable to conclude that the mandatory bylaw amendment was excludible under rule 14a–8(i)(1).[83] This was an apparent reversal of the Commission's previous position as to the propriety of mandatory bylaw amendments under Delaware law. The Delaware Chancery Court refused to consider the issue on procedural grounds.[84] In contrast to Delaware, the Oklahoma Supreme Court has upheld under Oklahoma law the propriety of a shareholder initiated bylaw limiting the use of poison pills or other shareholder rights plans.[85] In addition, even under Delaware law, framing the share-

---

65. *See, e.g.,* J.P. Morgan & Co., 2000 WL 1877573 (SEC No Action Letter Dec. 22, 2000).

66. *See, e.g.,* The Boeing Co., 2001 WL 128120 (SEC No Action Letter Feb. 8, 2001).

68. *See, e.g.,* General Dynamics Corp., 2001 WL 246749 (SEC No Action Letter March 5, 2001).

71. *E.g.* Del Code § 242(b)(1); Model Bus. Corp. Act § 10.03.

72. *E.g.,* PSB Holdings, Inc., 2002 WL 201870 (SEC No Action Letter Jan. 23, 2002).

81. *E.g.,* Del. § 109; Model Bus. Corp. Act § 10.20.

82. *See, e.g.,* Post Properties, Inc., 2004 WL 615143 (SEC No Action Letter March 26, 2004).

83. Honeywell International Inc., 2002 WL 1052001 (SEC No Action Letter April 19, 2002).

84. General Datacomm Industries, Inc. v. State of Wisconsin Investment Board, 1999 WL 66533 (Del.Ch.1999).

85. International Brotherhood of Teamsters General Fund v. Fleming, 975 P.2d 907 (Okla. 1999).

holder proposal regarding limitations on poison pills and shareholder rights plans in terms of a recommendation should eliminate management's grounds for excluding the proposal.[86] However, in one no action response, a proposal recommending that no rights plans be adopted without shareholder approval was deemed to be excludible as violative of Delaware law.[87]

§ 10.8[3] Grounds for Exclusion—Impropriety Under Law Generally

Management may exclude a shareholder proposal from the proxy statement if the proposal would violate any state, federal, or foreign law to which the company is subject.[91] Thus, if the substance of the proposal would violate state or federal law, such as requiring the company to breach existing contracts, the proposal may be excluded.[92] Similarly, a proposal calling for improper discrimination may be excluded.[93] The Commission notes, however, that exclusion from management's proxy statement on the grounds that the shareholder proposal involves a violation of foreign law is not appropriate if compliance with the foreign law in question would result in a violation of domestic state or federal law.[94] Also, management desiring to exclude the shareholder proposal has the burden of establishing that the proposal would involve a violation of state law.[95] If management does not establish that the proposal would violate other law, the proposal may not be excluded on the basis of Rule 14a–8(i)(2).[96]

§ 10.8[4] Grounds For Exclusion—Materially Misleading Proposals, Proposals in Violation of The Proxy Rules, and Overly Vague Proposals

A shareholder proposal is excludible if it violates the federal proxy rules.[100] Most commonly, this basis for exclusion is invoked when the shareholder proposal is materially misleading in violation of Rule 14a–9.[101] If the alleged misstatement is cured, then the proposal will not be excludable.[102] In a number of no action responses, the Commission has indicated that if the

---

86. Sears, Roebuck and Co., 2004 WL 224471 (SEC No Action Letter Jan. 27, 2004) (management could not exclude a proposal that would amend the company's bylaws to provide for the creation of a shareholder committee to communicate with the Board regarding the subject matter of shareholder proposals that are approved and not acted upon).

87. General Dynamics Corp., 2001 WL 246749 (SEC No Action Letter March 5, 2001).

91. 17 C.F.R. § 240.14a–8(i)(2).

92. *E.g.*, Cendant Corp., 2004 WL 187657 (SEC No Action Letter Jan. 16, 2004).

93. *See, e.g.*, Churchill Downs Inc., 2004 WL 1637290 (SEC No Action Letter March 2, 2004) (management could exclude proposal seeking to impose a ten–year ban upon any and all Japanese horse owners attempting to enter their horse in a Churchill Downs Incorporated facility for a Kentucky Derby/Triple Crown race event).

94. Note to Rule 14a–8(i)(2), 17 C.F.R. § 240.14a–8(i)(2).

95. *E.g.*, Liz Claiborne, Inc., 2002 WL 571646 (SEC No Action Letter March 18, 2002).

96. *See, e.g.*, SBC Communications Inc., 2001 WL 125054 (SEC No Action Letter Jan. 31, 2001).

100. Rule 14a–8(i)(3), 17 C.F.R. § 240.14a–8(i)(3).

101. *Compare, e.g.,* Bank One Corp., 2000 WL 287861 (SEC No Action Letter March 8, 2000) (management could exclude proposal on basis that it was too vague and indefinite) *with, e.g.,* Emerson Electric Co., 2000 WL 1469731 (SEC No Action Letter Oct. 3, 2000) (management could not exclude shareholder proposal on grounds that it was materially misleading).

102. *See, e.g.,* Bristol–Meyers Squibb Co., 2002 WL 464044 (SEC No Action Letter March 4, 2002).

proposal itself is not materially misleading but the shareholder's statement supporting the proposal contains materially misleading statements, management may exclude the materially misleading statements,[103] but must include the proposal and the non-misleading portions of the supporting statement.[104] In addition to materially misleading statements, management may exclude a shareholder proposal under Rule 14a–8(i)(3) if the proposal is too vague or indefinite.[105]

§ 10.8[5] Grounds for Exclusion—Personal Grievance

A shareholder proposal is excludible if it relates to a personal claim or grievance of the shareholder.[106] This basis for exclusion applies whether the personal claim or grievance is against the issuer or against any other person.[107] The burden is on management desiring to exclude the proposal to establish that it is based on a personal grievance rather than proper shareholder concerns about corporate matters.[108] The use of a nominee to sponsor the proposal to mask the identity of the true proponent will not limit management's ability to omit the proposal as relating to a personal grievance.[109]

§ 10.8[6] Grounds for Exclusion—Not Significantly Related to the Issuer's Business

Rule 14a–8(i)(5) permits management to exclude a shareholder proposal if the proposal is not significantly related to the issuer's business.[118] This basis for exclusion has both an objective and subjective test.

A shareholder proposal is not excludible from management's proxy statement if it relates to more than five percent of the company's business.[120] The shareholder proposal rule permits exclusion of a proposal if it "relates to operations which account for less than 5 percent of the company's total assets at the end of its most recent fiscal year, and for less than 5 percent of its net earnings and gross sales for its most recent fiscal year, and *is not otherwise related to the company's business.*"[121] By virtue of this last clause, the five-percent threshold operates as a safe harbor for management seeking to exclude a shareholder proposal from the proxy statement only if the proposal is not otherwise significant to the company's business.

A shareholder proposal must be included if it relates to operations above the five-percent threshold, but it must also be included if it is significantly related to the issuer's business even if the quantitative threshold is not met. Thus, for example, activities which relate to social responsibility may be the subject of shareholder proposals even if they fall below the five percent

---

103. *See, e.g.,* Raytheon Co., 2001 WL 204745 (SEC No Action Letter Feb. 26, 2001).

104. *E.g.,* UnitedHealth Group Inc., 2001 WL 25785 (SEC Jan. 8, 2001).

105. *See* Smithfield Foods, Inc., 2003 WL 21693599 (SEC No Action Letter July 18, 2003).

106. Rule 14a–8(i)(4), 17 C.F.R. § 240.14a–8(i)(4).

107. Rule 14a–8(i)(4), 17 C.F.R. § 240.14a–8(i)(4).

108. *See, e.g.,* International Business Machines Corp., 2002 WL 31863762 (SEC No Action Letter Dec. 18, 2002).

109. *E.g.,* MGM Mirage, 2001 WL 294174 (SEC No Action Letter March 19, 2001).

118. 17 C.F.R. § 240.14a–8(i)(5).

120. 17 C.F.R. § 240.14a–8(i)(5).

121. *Id.*

threshold.[122] Proposals relating to socially relevant issues may be excluded, however, if they do not relate to significant issues concerning the company's business.

§ 10.8[7] Grounds for Exclusion—Beyond the Issuer's Power

A shareholder proposal is excludible from management's proxy statement if the proposal relates to matters beyond the issuer's control. Thus, "[i]f the company would lack the power or authority to implement the proposal," it is excludible.[135] This includes situations where an attempt to implement the proposal would violate the law.[136] This basis for exclusion permits a company's management to exclude shareholder proposals that relate to issues other than corporate governance. Rule 14a–8(i)(6) also permits exclusions of proposals that cannot be accomplished within traditional strictures of corporate governance.

§ 10.8[8] Grounds for Exclusion—Ordinary Business

A shareholder proposal may be excluded by management if it relates to the ordinary business of the issuer,[144] but of course not all business operations of the company relate to "ordinary business." The ordinary business basis for exclusion has had a long and checkered history. As the following discussion indicates it is not always easy to identify a clear demarcation between which proposals are excludible from management's proxy statement and which are not. Furthermore, there are a number of topics for which the SEC has changed its position over time.

Rule 14a–8(i)(7)'s ordinary business basis for exclusion has been the most utilized basis for exclusion in recent years. The SEC's approach to shareholder proposals is extremely fact specific. Subtle variations in wording can determine whether management may exclude the proposal or not.

Although shareholders have enjoyed considerable success in having their proposals included over management's objection, the vast majority of no action responses under Rule 14a–8(i)(7) uphold management's ability to exclude the proposal.

In deciding whether a shareholder proposal is excludable, it must be determined whether in fact the proposal focuses on day-to-day business matters so as to qualify as ordinary business operations or whether the proposal involves significant policy issues.[152] It may not be sufficient that the proposal have some relation to matters of social policy if it is really focusing on the company's ordinary day-to-day operations.

In the past, the Commission permitted management to exclude the shareholder proposal from its proxy statement if the proposal was not proper-

---

122. *E.g.*, Lovenheim v. Iroquois Brands, Ltd., 618 F.Supp. 554 (D.D.C.1985) (proposal relating to production of pate de fois gras was not excludible even though it related to less than five percent of the company's business).

135. 17 C.F.R. § 14a–8(i)(6).

136. Sensar Corp., 2001 WL 506141 (SEC No Action Letter May 14, 2001) (proposal that executive options be rescinded and reissued under new terms could be excluded as implementation of the proposal would result in breaching existing contract rights).

144. 17 C.F.R. § 14a–8(i)(7).

152. *See, e.g.,* General DataComm Industries, Inc., SEC No–Act LEXIS 1037 (SEC No Action Letter Dec. 9, 1998) (bylaw amendment to reprice employee stock options raises significant policy issues and thus in not excludible under rule 14a–8(i)(7)).

ly prepared and submitted in terms of form. Currently, the SEC will comment on the substance of the proposal even if there are some problems as to form.[174] Under this approach, the SEC provides the proposing shareholder with an opportunity to redraft the proposal so as to make it proper under the shareholder proposal rule.

A shareholder proposal addressing the date[194] or location[195] of the annual meeting relates to the ordinary business operations and thus may be excluded by management. Shareholder proposals concerning procedures for conducting the meeting relate to the ordinary business and may be excluded from management's proxy statement.

Proposals directed to the company's method of raising capital have been excluded as concerning the ordinary business operations of the issuer.[215] Proposals relating to the administration of company stock purchase programs have been considered excludible as relating to the company's ordinary business.[216] Proposals focused on the company's issuance of stock options and other derivative securities have also been considered excludible as relating to the company's ordinary business.[217] However, management may not be able to exclude proposals relating to stock option policy rather than day-to-day administration of stock option programs.[218]

As the foregoing discussion indicates, the gist of the balance struck by the SEC is that shareholder proposals relating to day-to-day management or administration issues will be excludible,[224] while proposals relating to matters of corporate policy will not.[225] It follows, for example, that although proposals relating to the time and amount of dividends may be excludible as relating to the company's ordinary business,[226] the decision whether to declare dividends can be framed as a policy matter, and proposals to that effect may not be excluded from management's proxy statement.[227] In contrast, a proposal

---

174. *E.g.,* Johnson Controls, Inc., [1999–2000 Transfer Binder] Fed. Sec. L. Rep. (CCH) ¶ 77,642 (SEC No Action Letter Oct. 26, 1999).

194. Verizon Communications Inc., 2001 WL 125043 (SEC No Action Letter Jan. 30, 2001) (management could exclude shareholder proposal relating to the date of the annual meeting).

195. The Gillette Co., 2004 WL 260353 (SEC No Action Letter Feb. 4, 2004) (management could exclude proposal relating to the location of the annual meeting).

215. Irvine Sensors Corp., 2001 WL 8319 (SEC No Action Letter Jan. 2, 2001) (proposal requesting that company raise future capital primarily through offerings to existing shareholders instead of relying on private placements).

216. Medstone International, Inc., 2003 WL 2013182 (SEC No Action Letter May 1, 2003).

217. *See, e.g.,* Sempra Energy, 2001 WL 109541 (SEC No Action Letter Jan. 30, 2001).

218. *See, e.g.,* Cintas Corp., 2004 WL 1846205 (SEC No Action Letter Aug. 13, 2004) (management could not exclude a shareholder proposal urging the board to adopt a policy that the cost of employee and director stock options be recognized in the company's income statement).

224. *E.g.,* Tyco International Ltd., 2000 WL 1874063 (SEC No Action Letter Dec. 21, 2000) (management could exclude shareholder proposal relating to pension benefits of employees of companies acquired by the issuer).

225. *E.g.,* Kmart Corp., 2001 WL 286894 (SEC No Action Letter March 16, 2001) (management could not rely on "ordinary business" grounds to exclude shareholder proposal relating to principles defined by the International Labor Organization).

226. *E.g.,* Synovus Financial Corp., 2004 WL 414579 (SEC No Action Letter March 1, 2004) (management could rely on Rule 14a–8(i)(7) to exclude a proposal requesting that the company's dividend reinvestment plan be revised to provide for quarterly optional cash investments and the elimination of investment fees on reinvested dividends or optional cash payments and further requesting that the plan be administered by the company through its own operating unit and not outsourced).

227. Sonoma West Holdings, Inc., 2000 WL 1182875 (SEC No Action Letter Aug. 17, 2000).

recommending that the company adopt a dividend reinvestment plan may be excluded from management's proxy statement on the grounds that it relates to the company's ordinary business operations.[228] Management may exclude a shareholder proposal suggesting a formula that would determine the size of a dividend.[229] However, management could not exclude a proposal calling for a report on the company's dividend policies.[230]

The SEC generally takes the position that proposals relating to employment practices, including the termination, hiring, or promotion of employees may be excluded as relating to ordinary business operations.[231] The SEC staff generally considers proposals relating to the evaluation of employees to be within the company's ordinary business.[232] This is true even with respect to proposals relating to senior management.[233]

However, when employment practices significantly implicate broader social issues, then there may be an argument that management may not exclude the shareholder proposal from management's proxy statement.[234] Over the years, the SEC has had difficulty in dealing with these questions. In fact, the Commission has changed its general position on at least two occasions.

In 1992, the SEC, in its controversial *Cracker Barrel* no action letter, permitted exclusion of a shareholder proposal regarding the company's hiring practices on the basis that the proposal related to the company's ordinary business.[235] The *Cracker Barrel* no action letter favoring exclusion of shareholder proposals dealing with discriminatory employment policies sparked controversy both within and outside the SEC. In 1997, the Commission proposed reversing the *Cracker Barrel* policy.[236] Shortly thereafter, the *Cracker Barrel* approach was repudiated by the SEC.[237] The Commission decided to

228. Prudential Financial, Inc., 2003 WL 942650 (SEC No Action Letter March 5, 2003). CoBiz Inc., 2002 WL 834243 (SEC No Action Letter March 25, 2002) (management could exclude proposal asking company to establish a dividend reinvestment plan).

229. Microsoft Corp., 2002 WL 1979399 (SEC No Action Letter Aug. 26, 2002) (management could exclude proposal calling for directors to declare dividends to provide 3% annual yield on share value); DPL Inc., 2002 WL 126571 (SEC No Action Letter Jan. 11, 2002) (relying on Rule 14a–8(i)(13)).

230. Potlatch Corporation, 2002 WL 448471 (SEC No Action Letter March 6, 2002) (management could not rely on Rule 14a–8(i)(7) to exclude a shareholder proposal calling for a report explaining the company's past and current dividend policy and alternative plans for future dividends, as well as addressing the ownership of the company's shares by members of a group named in the proposal).

231. *See, e.g.,* Merrill Lynch & Co., Inc., 2002 WL 356739 (SEC No Action Letter Feb. 8, 2002).

232. *See, e.g.,* The MONY Group Inc., 2004 WL 434374 (SEC No Action Letter March 1, 2004).

233. The MONY Group Inc., 2004 WL 434374 (SEC No Action Letter March 1, 2004) (management could exclude a proposal recommending the board promptly conduct an investigation into and a possible replacement of the company's chief executive officer and its president and chief operating officer).

234. *E.g.,* Marriott International, Inc., 2002 WL 597336 (SEC No Action Letter March 19, 2002) (management could not exclude shareholder proposal urging the board of directors to adopt, implement and enforce a workplace code of conduct based upon International Labor Organization conventions, including principles that relate to the right to join unions and bargain collectively and a prohibition on discrimination against workers' representatives).

235. Cracker Barrel Old Country Store, Inc., [1992–1993 Transfer Binder] Fed. Sec. L. Rep. ¶ 76,418 (SEC No Action Letter October 13, 1992).

236. Amendments to Rules on Shareholder Proposals, Sec. Exch. Act Rel. No. 34–39093, 62 Fed. Reg. 50682–01 (SEC Sept. 26, 1997).

237. *See, e.g.,* Note, Roll Out the Barrel: the SEC Reverses its Stance on Employment–Related Shareholder Proposals Under SEC Rule 14a–8–Again, 25 Del. J. Corp. L. 277 (2000).

revert to its former practice and explained that shareholder proposals relating to employment practices would no longer automatically be eligible for inclusion.[238] Thus, the SEC once again follows its pre-*Cracker Barrel* practice of reviewing each proposal relating to employment practices to determine if it relates to the ordinary business as opposed to more far-reaching social issues.[239] Under current practice, the Commission will review each shareholder proposal in order to determine whether it relates to ordinary business or significant social issues.[240]

The SEC staff also reversed its position on precisely the type of proposal that had been involved in *Cracker Barrel* by opining that management could not exclude a shareholder proposal relating to the banning of discrimination based on sexual orientation in the company's employment practices.[246] Since certain types of discriminatory employment practices clearly are matters of significant social concern, shareholder proposals relating to these discriminatory hiring practices may not properly be excluded from management's proxy statement.[247] Similarly, management may not be able to exclude a proposal questioning the company's discriminatory promotion policies.[248]

Management may exclude from its proxy statement shareholder proposals relating to the specifics of employee compensation.[249] The SEC staff has concurred for example in excluding some proposals relating to specific and details of executive compensation, under the ordinary business rationale.[251]

In contrast to the approach taken for specific compensation issues, some shareholder recommendations relating to compensation policies generally may not be excluded by management as relating to the ordinary business of the company.[265]

---

238. *Id.*

239. Sec. Exch. Act Rel. No. 34–40019 (SEC May 28, 1998).

240. For the SEC position under the revised approach, *see* Exxon Corp., 31 Sec. Reg. & L. Rep. (BNA) 478 (SEC No Action Letter March 9, 1999) (management could not exclude proposal asking company to develop a written policy prohibiting discrimination based on sexual orientation).

246. *E.g.*, AT & T Corp., 2001 WL 121991 (SEC No Action Letter Jan. 31, 2001) (management could not exclude shareholder proposal requesting that the board of directors amend the company's Equal Opportunity Statement to eliminate the words "sexual preference or orientation"); Emerson Electric Co., 2000 WL 1634117, 32 Sec. Reg. & L. Rep. (BNA) 1603 (SEC No Action Letter Oct. 27, 2000).

247. *E.g.*, The Coca–Cola Co., 2003 WL 122319 (SEC No Action Letter SEC Jan. 7, 2003) (management could not rely on either 14a–8(i)(3) nor 14a–8(i)(7) to exclude proposal requesting that the board of directors amend the company's "corporate, diversity, and equal employment policies to exclude reference to sexual orientation" and "cease support of homosexual lifestyle and other deviant lifestyle behaviors opposed by the majority of people.").

248. Newell Rubbermaid Inc., 2001 WL 203956 (SEC No Action Letter Feb. 21, 2001) (management could not exclude shareholder proposal requesting that the board prepare a report on Newell's "glass ceiling" progress, including a review of specified topics).

249. *See, e.g.*, General Electric Co., 2004 WL 187659 (SEC No Action Letter Jan. 15, 2004) (management could exclude proposal requesting that the company initiate a review and report on certain pension plan-related matters).

251. *See, e.g.*, Huntington Bancshares Inc., 2001 WL 46821 (SEC No Action Letter Jan. 11, 2001) (management could exclude shareholder proposal recommending that cash incentive awards be based not only on return on average shareholders equity, but also return on average assets and customer satisfaction surveys).

265. *E.g.*, ConAgra Foods, Inc., 2003 WL 21697390 (SEC No Action Letter July 18, 2003) (management could not exclude a proposal requesting that the board of directors modify all current and all future stock option plans for all senior executives and corporate directors).

§ 10.8[9] Grounds for Exclusion—Proposals Relating to Election to Office

A shareholder proposal may be excluded if it relates to election to a corporate office.[369] A proposal may be excluded if it "relates to an election for membership on the company's board of directors or analogous governing body."[370] The purpose of this basis for exclusion is to recognize the adversary nature of contested elections. The proxy rules generally provide the ground rules for disclosures relating to contested elections but do not guarantee the insurgents access to management's proxy statement. Management can thus exclude a shareholder proposal calling for the removal of a corporate officer or director.[374]

It is clear, however, that a proposal is not excludible simply because it relates to the election process.[413] Thus, for example, a proposal recommending mandatory retirement for directors could not be excluded.[414] For the same reason, proposals relating to qualifications of future directors may not be excluded.[415] Shareholder proposals geared to requiring independent directors relate to the process and corporate governance generally, rather than specific elections and thus may not be excluded from management's proxy statement.[416]

§ 10.8[10] Grounds for Exclusion—Shareholder Proposals Contradicting Management Proposals

Management may exclude a shareholder proposal that contradicts a proposal submitted by management.[423] The rationale here is that the matter is already before the shareholders and the appropriate response of shareholders who disagree with management is to vote against the proposal. The SEC notes that in seeking a no action letter, management should specify the points of conflict between the shareholder proposal and management's proposal.[424]

§ 10.8[11] Grounds for Exclusion—Mootness

Management may omit a shareholder proposal from management's proxy statement if the subject of the proposal has become moot.[425] Management can exclude a shareholder proposal if it has already substantially been implemented.[426]

---

369. 17 C.F.R. § 240.14a–8(i)(8).

370. 17 C.F.R. § 240.14a–8(i)(8).

374. *E.g.,* NetCurrents, Inc., 2001 WL 435670 (SEC No Action Letter April 25, 2001).

413. *See, e.g.,* Peoples Energy Corp., 2002 WL 31520070 (SEC No Action Letter Nov. 3, 2002) (management could not exclude a shareholder proposal urging the board to take the necessary steps to nominate at least two candidates for each directorship to be filled by voting of shareholders at the annual meeting).

414. Technology Research Corp., 31 Sec. Reg. & L. Rep. (BNA) 695 (SEC No Action Letter May 12, 1999).

415. *E.g.,* The Boeing Co., 2002 WL 356723 (SEC No Action Letter Feb. 7, 2002).

416. *E.g.,* General Dynamics Corp., 28 Sec. Reg. & L. Rep. (BNA) 233 (SEC No Action Letter available Feb. 5, 1996) (management could not exclude proposal recommending independent board of directors so long as shareholder-amended proposal to eliminate requirement that non qualifying candidates for director be disqualified at the upcoming meeting).

423. Rule 14a–8(i)(9). 17 C.F.R. § 240.14a–8(i)(9).

424. Note to Rule 14a–8(i)(9). 17 C.F.R. § 240.14a–8(i)(9).

425. 17 C.F.R. § 240.14a–8(i)(10).

426. *Id.*

§ 10.8[12] Grounds for Exclusion—Duplicative Proposals

Management may exclude a shareholder proposal that substantially duplicates another proposal submitted for the same shareholder meeting.[429] This basis for exclusion is designed to prevent shareholders from harassing management through the use of repetitive proposals.[430] The fact that the matter is already before the shareholders is sufficient to satisfy the proxy rules basis for exclusion.

§ 10.8[13] Grounds for Exclusion—Resubmissions

Management may exclude a shareholder proposal if it is substantially the same as one that was submitted in the past year and did not receive a significant number of votes.[433] This is designed to permit management to exclude proposals that the shareholders have recently resoundingly defeated.[434] The proposal may be excluded if it is substantially the same; it is not necessary that the proposal be identical to a previous one.[435] However, a significant difference from a previous proposal will preclude management's ability to exclude it from its proxy statement.[436] Furthermore, if the prior year's proposal was not formally submitted to the shareholders, the fact that it garnered less than three percent of the vote cannot be used as a basis for exclusion from management's proxy statement.[437]

The rule looks to the preceding five years and permits the exclusion of the proposal if it did not cross a specified threshold of shareholder support the last time it was submitted for shareholder consideration.[438] A proposal is not excludible simply because the business activity in question was addressed in a prior proposal if the second proposal is requesting that different action be taken.[439]

In addition to Rule 14a–8(i)(12)'s permission to exclude proposals that were unsuccessful in the past, Rule 14a–8(h) permits a company to exclude a shareholder proposal that was previously submitted if the proponent failed to appear at the meeting to present the proposal.[440]

§ 10.8[14] Grounds for Exclusion—Relating to Dividends

Management may exclude a shareholder proposal if it relates to a specific amount of dividends.[441] Since stock splits are essentially dividends paid in stock rather than cash, the rationale for permitting exclusion of shareholder

---

429. 17 C.F.R. § 240.14a–8(i)(11).

430. *See, e.g.*, Airborne Freight Corp. 2000 WL 217938 (SEC No Action Letter Feb. 14, 2000) (management could exclude duplicative proposal).

433. 17 C.F.R. § 240.14a–8(i)(12).

434. *See, e.g.* General Motors Corp., 2001 WL 267688 (SEC No Action Letter March 11, 2001).

435. Chevron Corp., 31 Sec. Reg. & L. Rep. (BNA) 415 (SEC No Action letter March 4, 1999).

436. In re Emerson Electric Co., 16 Sec.Reg. & L.Rep. (BNA) 1982 (SEC No Action Letter Nov. 21, 1984) (shareholder proposal that issuer report on military sales is different from prior proposal for formulation of "ethical criteria" for defense contracts).

437. Baldwin Piano & Organ Co., 32 Sec. Reg. & L. Rep. (BNA) 723, 2000 WL 520641 (SEC No Action Letter May 1, 2000).

438. 17 C.F.R. § 14a–8(i)(12):

439. *See, e.g.*, Chevron Corp. (refusing to permit exclusion of proposal requesting an environmental impact study on the results of gas drilling operations in national wildlife refuge where previous proposal asked for immediate cessation of such operations).

440. Rule 14a–8(h), 17 C.F.R. § 240. 14a–8(h).

441. 17 C.F.R. § 14a–8(i)(13).

proposals relating to the specific amount of dividends extends to proposals relating to recommendations regarding stock splits.[442] Similarly, management may exclude a proposal relating to the administration of a dividend reinvestment plan since it relates to the company's ordinary business operations.[443] The ordinary business[444] basis for exclusion thus supplements Rule 14a–8(i)(13)'s reference to dividend proposals that focus on the amount of the dividend. However, a proposal that relates to a change in capital structure involves more than a stock dividend and thus may not be excluded as a proposal relating to a specific dividend payment.[445]

§ 10.8[15] Consequences of Excluding Shareholder Proposals; Practical Considerations

Notwithstanding the shareholder proposal rule's permission to management to exclude proposals under certain circumstances, in close cases, the proposals should be included since, practically speaking, management in most instances will nevertheless have to make reference to the shareholder proposal in its proxy statement. The management has little to lose by including most shareholder proposals, as they have virtually no chance of success and generally receive less than three percent of the vote.

Even if the issuer properly excludes the proposal and supporting statement, it must nevertheless describe the proposal, assuming that under state law it is a proper matter for shareholder action. Item 20 of schedule 14A requires the proxy statement to include identification of any action to be taken at the shareholder meeting that is not otherwise described in the proxy statement.[455] Furthermore, if the issuer's management decides to solicit proxies that will be voted against a shareholder proposal, the antifraud proscriptions will require disclosure of the proposal and intention to vote against it.[456] Management violates the proxy rules if it fails to disclose in its proxy

---

442. *E.g.,* NVR, Inc., 2001 WL 40393 (SEC No Action Letter Jan. 11, 2001).

443. *See* Synovus Financial Corp., 2004 WL 414579 (SEC No Action Letter March 1, 2004) (management could rely on Rule 14a–8(i)(7) to exclude a proposal requesting that the company's dividend reinvestment plan be revised to provide for quarterly optional cash investments and the elimination of investment fees on reinvested dividends or optional cash payments and further requesting that the plan be administered by the company through its own operating unit and not outsourced).

444. Rule 14a–8(i)(7)'s ordinary business provision is discussed in § 10.8[8] *supra.*

445. *See, e.g.,* Urstadt Biddle Properties Inc., 1998 WL 886893 (SEC No Action Letter Dec. 17, 1998).

455. "If any action is to be taken with respect to any matter not specifically referred to above, describe briefly the substance of each such matter in substantially the same degree of detail as is required by Items 5 to 20, inclusive * * *."

456. Even if the proxy does not contain a specific reference to the proposal, there is generally a request to give a proxy for "such other matters" as may come up for a shareholder vote. If the proxy is sought in this manner, full disclosure should require a description of any such matter known to the persons soliciting the proxy and how they intend to vote thereon. *See* Idaho Power Co., [1996–1997 Transfer Binder] Fed. Sec. L. Rep. (CCH) ¶ 77,224 (SEC No Action Letter March 13, 1996) (management could not vote against shareholder proposal without adequate disclosures in management's proxy statement as to its reason for opposition and its intent to vote against; also the proposal must appear on the proxy card). *Cf.* Medical Committee for Human Rights v. SEC, 432 F.2d 659, 677 (D.C.Cir.1970) "the rationale underlying [the shareholder proposal rule] was the Commission's belief that the corporate practice of circulating proxy materials which failed to make reference to the fact that a shareholder intended to present a proposal at the annual meeting rendered the solicitation inherently misleading. *See* Hearings on Security and Exchange Commission Proxy Rules Before the House Comm. on Interstate and Foreign Commerce, 78th Cong., 1st Sess., pt. 1, at 169–170 (1943)". *Cf.* Shoen v. AMERCO, 885 F.Supp. 1332 (D.Nev.1994) (issuer must disclose that other shareholder proposals may be brought up at the meeting and that the proxy will be voted on such matters as the proxy holder sees fit).

statement that a shareholder plans to submit proposals at the upcoming shareholder meeting.[457]

§ 10.9   Disclosure in Lieu of Proxy Solicitation—Section 14(c)

If an issuer subject to the registration requirements of section 12 of the Exchange Act does not solicit proxies, its security holders are still guaranteed information by virtue of section 14(c).[1] The issuer must file with the SEC and send to its security holders information similar to that which is required for a proxy solicitation. These informational requirements are set out in Regulation 14C[2] and Schedule 14C.[3]

§ 10.10   Securities Held in Street Name; Broker–Dealers and Federal Proxy Regulation—Section 14(b)

Increasingly large numbers of securities are being held in the name of broker-dealers for their customers' accounts.[1] In 1999, between seventy and eighty percent of publicly held securities were held in street name.[2] Holding the customer's stock or other securities in street name is not only a matter of convenience, but also may be necessary for the extension of credit pursuant to the margin requirements.[3] Additionally, with the time for settlement of transactions moving from five to three business days, it is becoming increasingly cumbersome for customers to hold their share certificates since there is less time to deliver them for sale.

Section 14(b) of the Exchange Act[4] requires all broker-dealers who are members of a national exchange or national security association[5] to forward proxy solicitation materials to their customers in whose account the securities are held. The statute makes it unlawful to fail to comply with such rules as the commission may promulgate.[6] The Commission has exercised the rulemaking power delegated by section 14(b).[7] The rules relating to shareholder communications have been extended to banks and other entities holding securities in their names as fiduciaries for the beneficial owners.[8]

---

457. *See* Shoen v. AMERCO, 885 F.Supp. 1332 (D.Nev.1994). *See also, e.g.* United Mine Workers of America v. Pittson Co., 1989 WL 201060, [1989–1990 Transfer Binder] Fed.Sec.L.Rep. 94,946 (D.D.C.1989).

§ 10.9

1. 15 U.S.C.A. § 78n(c).

2. 17 C.F.R. §§ 240.14c–1 through 14c–7.

3. 17 C.F.R. § 240.14c–101.

§ 10.10

1. SEC, Street Name Study (1976).

2. *See* 23A Jerry W. Markham & Thomas Lee Hazen, Broker–Dealer Operations Under Securities and Commodities Law § 8.11[2] (2d ed. 2003).

3. 15 U.S.C.A. § 78g. Margin requirements are discussed in § 14.9 *infra*.

4. 15 U.S.C.A. § 78n(b).

5. The rule also applied to broker-dealers regulated directly by the SEC, a category abolished effective December, 1983. In other words section 14(b) applies to all broker-dealers who are subject to Exchange Act regulation and oversight by the SEC. *See* chapter 14 *infra*.

6. 15 U.S.C.A. § 78n(b).

7. *See* 17 C.F.R. § 240.14b–1 *et seq.* For an early view of the problem *see* Edward R. Aranow & Herbert A. Einhorn, Corporate Proxy Contests: Solicitation and Validity of Brokers' Proxies, 23 U.Chi.L.Rev. 640 (1956).

8. Pub.L. No. 99–222, 99 Stat. 1737 (1985), amending 15 U.S.C.A. § 78n(b). *See* 17 C.F.R. § 240.14b–2.

All participants in a proxy solicitation[9] are generally subject to Regulation 14A.[10] However, specific exemptions apply to broker-dealers who are merely complying with section 14(b). Rule 14a–2(a)(1) provides that a broker-dealer who transmits such proxy material to his or her customer is not considered a participant in the proxy solicitation provided the broker-dealer: (1) does not receive a commission or other remuneration other than reimbursement of reasonable expenses; (2) furnishes promptly to the customers so solicited copies of all material; and (3) does no more than give impartial instructions to the customer as to how to forward the proxies to the appropriate depository.[11] However, if a broker-dealer sends along its own literature concerning the issuer, the exemption from the proxy regulations is extinguished.[12] Any attempt by the broker-dealer to exert any influence over the customer's voting or other participation in the proxy solicitation similarly renders the broker-dealer subject to Regulation 14A and the regular proxy rules.[13]

---

9. "Participant" is defined in Instruction 3 to Item 4 of Schedule 14A to include directors, nominees, persons sponsoring the solicitation, persons financing the solicitation, anyone extending credit for the solicitor, and anyone taking an active role in any of the above. 17 C.F.R. § 240.14a–101.

10. 15 U.S.C.A. § 78n(a). *See* § 10.2 *supra.*

11. 17 C.F.R. § 240.14a–2(a)(1).

12. Sec. Exch. Act Rel. No. 34–7208 (SEC Jan. 7, 1964).

13. *Id.*

Chapter 11

TENDER OFFER AND TAKEOVER REGULATION

Table of Sections

---

§ 11.1 Federal Control of Tender Offers—The Williams Act; The Terminology of Takeovers

During the 1960s, the securities markets witnessed a substantial increase in the use of tender offers—publicly announced offers to purchase the shares of a target company—as a means of effecting corporate combinations. The tender offer was used to replace or supplement the then more conventional statutory merger route. The increased use of tender offers was due in part to the fact that target companies subject to the Exchange Act's reporting requirements were required to hold a shareholder vote and to comply with the Act's proxy rules[2] when participating in a statutory merger.[3] The competitive

---

§ 11.1

2. 15 U.S.C.A. § 78n(a); 17 C.F.R. §§ 240.14a–9 *et seq.* The proxy rules mandate full disclosure and provide for implied private remedies for material misrepresentations in connection with the solicitation of shareholder votes for issuers that are subject to the Exchange Act's reporting requirements.

3. *See* chapter 10 *supra.*

atmosphere and vociferousness with which such takeover battles were waged became extreme both in terms of public and private ramifications. The terminology used to describe takeover tactics reflects the intensity of takeover battles.[4]

The securities laws contained a regulatory gap. By and large, there were no disclosure provisions applicable to tender offers. As such, shareholders of target companies were frequently given very little information about outsiders desiring to take control of their company. Investment decisions surrounding pending takeovers thus had to be made without the types of information that Congress intended investors to generally have available.

The war-like nature of corporate takeovers and the regulatory gap for tender offers led to Congressional action. In 1968, Congress adopted the tender offer and takeover provisions of the Williams Act amendments[5] to the Exchange Act.

§ 11.1[1] The Terminology of Takeovers

The intensity with which corporate takeover battles are waged is illustrated by the jargon that has developed to describe various takeover tactics—both offensive and defensive maneuvers. For example, aggressors may use the surprise element through a quickly assembled offer known as a "midnight special."[6] A "bear hug" involves an initial "friendly" approach to management of the target company with an express or implied choice of coming quietly now or being dragged along later. "Smoking gun" refers to a mistake that impedes the progress of the tender offer or defensive tactic.[7] A "show stopper" is a mistake so drastic that it results in the offer's failure. "White knights" may be brought in by the target company to fend off an unwanted suitor; "gray knights" are competing suitors who are not solicited by the target company but are viewed as preferable to the initial aggressor, and "black knights" are competing suitors who are less attractive. "Shark repellent" refers to preventive measures by companies viewed as potential targets in order to fend off unwanted suitors.[8] "Shark repellent" may also be used to refer to state tender offer statutes that may present additional impediments to takeovers.[9] Many of these state laws have been held preempted by the federal legislation.[10] The "wounded list" refers to executives who have lost their jobs or their health during the course of a takeover campaign. Takeovers can also involve "shootouts" and eventually some resolution through "hired guns" (the attorneys). Also important in the world of takeovers are the "arbs" or arbitrageurs whose predictions of a tender offer's success may become a self-fulfilling prophecy.

---

4. *See* § 11.1[1] *infra.*

5. Pub.L. No. 90–439, 82 Stat. 454 (1968) (codified at 15 U.S.C. §§ 78m(d)–(e), n(d)–(f)).

6. For a vivid example of a midnight special, *see* Wellman v. Dickinson, 475 F.Supp. 783 (S.D.N.Y.1979).

7. Defensive tactics are discussed in § 11.10 *infra.*

8. A common device has been the use of protective charter provisions such as high vote requirements for a merger.

9. *See* § 11.11 *infra.*

10. *See* § 11.13 *infra.*

A relatively novel financing development in the 1980s, frequently referred to as "junk bonds" (euphemistically described solely as "high yield" bonds), were low quality, non-investment grade corporate debt obligations. These highly speculative debt instruments often were used to finance leveraged buyouts (also known as "LBOs") of target companies. A variation of the LBO is the MBO, or management buyout, where existing management takes over the company by taking it private.[13]

Another common takeover device is the two-tiered offer. Under the prototypical front-end loaded, two-tiered offer, the offeror makes an offer for a limited number of target company shares with notice that a second step of the acquisition will follow at a lower price.[14] This second step is frequently referred to as the "cram down." It has fairly been said that a front-end loaded offer followed by a cram down places the shareholders in a "prisoner's dilemma," while the acquiring corporation is able to purchase control at a "blended price."[15]

Additionally, as defensive tactics[16] to thwart hostile takeovers continue to abound, new and colorful names are devised. A number of these terms have developed over the years. Consider, for example, the Pac–Man defense, which consists of the target company's attempt to acquire the predator would-be acquirer. A number of companies have authorized or adopted "poison pills," which involve the issuance of preferred stock, debt securities, or rights to acquire such securities that have a high buy-back price, which is triggered by a hostile acquisition of the target company. A variation on the poison pill is the "poison put," which entitles shareholders of the target company to "put" their shares to the acquirer at a high price. As discussed in a later section, many of these poison pills and poison puts have come under attack but have frequently been upheld.[17] "Greenmail" is the term that has come to be used for premiums paid out of the corporate treasury to buy back the hostile bidder's shares at a premium above the price that he or she paid. "Golden parachutes" are compensation agreements with the target company's top management, which provide for high severance payments in the event of a change in control. "Tin parachutes" are similar arrangements that may be made available to less senior executives. Under the "scorched earth" defense of its turf, a target company makes itself so unattractive for acquisition that the acquirer becomes uninterested.

§ 11.1[2] Overview of the Regulation Imposed by the Williams Act

The Williams Act amendments to the Securities Exchange Act of 1934 introduced sections 13(d), 13(e), 14(d), 14(e), and 14(f) to the Exchange Act.[18]

---

13. The SEC's going private rules are discussed in § 11.8 *infra.*

14. Several states, following the lead of Maryland, have enacted "fair price" statutes that prohibit the use of unfriendly front-end loaded two-tiered offers. Md. Corp's & Ass'ns Code §§ 3–602, 3–603. *See* §§ 11.12–11.13 *infra.*

15. *See generally* Two–Tier Tender Offer Pricing, Sec.Exch. Act Rel. No. 34–21,079, [1984 Transfer Binder] Fed.Sec.L.Rep. (CCH) ¶ 83,637 (SEC June 21, 1984).

16. *See* § 11.20 *infra.*

17. *See, e.g.,* Minstar Acquiring Corp. v. AMF Inc., 621 F.Supp. 1252 (S.D.N.Y.1985) (holding nontransferrable dividend right to be violative of New Jersey law).

18. 15 U.S.C.A. §§ 78m(d), 78m(e), 78m(d), 78n(e), 78n(f).

As is the case with federal proxy regulation,[19] the filing requirements of the Williams Act are limited to securities registered under section 12 of the Act.[20] Both section 13(d)[21] and section 13(e),[22] as is the case with section 14(d)[23] and 14(f),[24] apply only to securities subject to the Exchange Act registration requirements and accompanying reporting requirements.[25] Registered reporting companies are those issuers having a class of securities traded on a national securities exchange, as well as those issuers having assets of at least $10,000,000 and also having a class of equity securities with more than 500 shareholders of record.[26] The filing and reporting provisions of the Williams Act do not apply to those issuers who, although not having to register under section 12 of the Exchange Act, nevertheless are required to file periodic reports under section 15(d).[27] In contrast to the other provisions of the Williams Act, section 14(e)[28] applies to *any* tender offer utilizing an instrumentality of interstate commerce, even if the target company is not subject to the Exchange Act's registration and reporting requirements.

Section 13(d) of the Act[29] focuses on creeping, open market, and privately negotiated acquisitions of equity securities subject to the 1934 Act's registration[30] and reporting requirements. Any person who acquires, directly or indirectly, more than a five percent beneficial ownership interest in any class of equity security subject to the Exchange Act's registration requirements must file a statement of ownership with the Commission within ten days after reaching the five percent threshold.[31] The purpose of section 13(d)'s notice requirement is to put both investors and the target company's management on notice of a possible impending takeover attempt. However, the purchaser has ten days between the crossing of the five percent threshold and the disclosure date. This provides a ten day window for additional undisclosed acquisitions of the target company's stock. This permits the acquisition of considerably more stock than the five percent threshold before any disclosure need be made. As such, this early warning mechanism has its defects. Despite numerous attempts to close it, the ten day window remains open.[32]

The Schedule 13D is the appropriate form for section 13(d) filings, and the person (or group) filing must disclose information about itself, its officers, directors, and principal business, as well as any financing arrangements that

---

19. *See* §§ 10.1–10.2 *supra.*

20. 15 U.S.C.A. § 78*l*. *See* § 9.2 *supra.*

21. 15 U.S.C.A. § 78m(d).

22. 15 U.S.C.A. § 78m(e).

23. 15 U.S.C.A. § 78n(d).

24. 15 U.S.C.A. § 78n(f).

25. *See* §§ 9.2, 9.3 *supra.*

26. 15 U.S.C.A. § 78*l*; 17 C.F.R. § 240.12g–1.

27. 15 U.S.C.A. § 78o(d). Section 15(d) reporting companies include issuers that have issued securities pursuant to a 1933 Act registration statement and have at least 300 security holders of that class of securities. *Id. See* § 9.3 *supra.*

28. 15 U.S.C.A. § 78m(e).

29. 15 U.S.C.A. § 78m(d). *See, e.g.,* William Robinson & J. Daniel Mahoney, Schedule 13D: Wild Card in a Takeover Bid, 27 Bus.Law. 1107 (1972). *See* § 11.2 *infra.*

30. *See* § 9.2 *supra.*

31. The filing requirements are triggered not only by purchases of securities, but also by the formation of a group to exercise control in common. *See* § 11.1 *infra.*

32. *See, e.g.,* D'Amato Introduces Comprehensive Proposal for Tender Offer Reform, 19 Sec.Reg. & L.Rep. (BNA) 84 (Jan. 24, 1987).

have been entered into to finance the purchase.[33] Furthermore, the Schedule 13D must contain a statement of the purchaser's future intentions with regard to the target company. For example, the purchaser must disclose whether a public tender offer, statutory merger, consolidation or other form of corporate fusion or combination is possible or likely to take place. As an alternative, the purchaser may merely state that its purchase was for purely investment purposes, if that is in fact the case.

Section 13(e) of the Act[34] makes it unlawful for issuers subject to the Exchange Act's registration requirements to purchase their own shares in contravention of SEC rules which, as discussed in a later section of this Chapter,[35] require SEC filings. Furthermore, since the Schedule 13D and Schedule 13E–1 are filed documents, any material misstatement or omission will give rise to a private cause of action under 18(a) of the Exchange Act to an investor who purchases or sells the security and actually relies on that information.[36]

The SEC has promulgated its going private rules[37] pursuant to section 13(e).[38] These going private rules are designed to protect security holders of issuers engaging in transactions that will result in cessation of 1934 Act reporting requirements.[39] The rules assure adequate disclosures in connection with going private transactions regardless of the form that the transaction may take.

In contrast to section 13(d)'s focus on open-market and privately negotiated acquisitions, sections 14(d), (e), and (f) are directed at "tender offers." The term "tender offer" is not defined anywhere in the Act nor in the SEC rules and regulations, however, and the absence of a statutory definition gave rise to much litigation and proposed administrative or statutory amendment.

Section 14(d) of the Act[41] requires that any person planning a "tender offer" for any class of equity security subject to the registration and reporting requirements of the Exchange Act must file with the Commission all solicitations, advertisements, and any other material to be used in connection with the tender offer. This filing must take place prior to the distribution of the tender offer material. In addition, the tender offeror must file a long form Schedule TO[42] with the Commission disclosing information similar to that required in the Schedule 13D. Also, anyone who is opposing or supporting the tender offer for securities subject to the Act's registration requirements must file any material related to the tender offer prior to its distribution.

Section 14(e)[44] prohibits fraud, deceit, and material misrepresentation or omissions "in connection with any tender offer or request or invitation for tenders, or any solicitation of security holders in opposition to or in favor of

---

33. 17 C.F.R. § 240.13d–101.

34. 15 U.S.C.A. § 78m(e). *See* § 11.7 *infra*.

35. *See* § 11.8 *infra*.

36. 15 U.S.C.A. § 78r(a). *See* § 12.8 *infra*.

37. 17 C.F.R. §§ 240.13e–1–13e–4.

38. 15 U.S.C.A. § 78m(e).

39. *See* § 11.17 *infra*.

41. 15 U.S.C.A. § 78n(d). *See* § 11.14 *infra*.

42. 17 C.F.R. § 17 C.F.R. § 240.14d–100.

44. 15 U.S.C.A. § 78n(e). *See* § 11.15 *infra*.

any such offer, request or invitation." Section 14(e) is the only provision of the Williams Act that applies across the board and is not limited to tender offers directed at the securities of 1934 Act registered reporting companies. Furthermore, although the Supreme Court has held that section 14(e) will not support a private right of action in the hands of a competing tender offeror,[45] it remains open whether a shareholder of the target company or the target company itself retains an implied private right of action.[46] Similarly, it is unclear whether a private remedy can be implied for violations of sections 13(d), 13(e), and 14(d), although most courts recognize at least a potential for injunctive relief.[47]

The final provision of the Williams Act, section 14(f),[48] requires a tender offeror to publicly disclose, on appropriate SEC filing forms, the names and descriptions of persons to be elected directors or any agreements affecting directors during the transfer of management control that are connected with a tender offer for equity securities subject to the Act's reporting requirements.

§ 11.2 Filing Requirements for Acquisition of More Than Five Percent of Equity Securities of an Exchange Act Reporting Company—Section 13(d)

§ 11.2[1] Section 13(d) Filing Requirements

Any person, other than the issuer, who directly or indirectly acquires beneficial ownership of more than five percent of a class of equity security registered pursuant to section 12 of the 1934 Act,[1] must file appropriate disclosures with the SEC pursuant to section 13(d).[2] An issuer's purchases of its own shares, directly or through an affiliate, are subject to similar disclosure requirements by virtue of section 13(e).[3]

Any person acquiring five percent of a class of voting equity securities must, within ten days after reaching the five percent threshold, file with the Commission six copies of a statement reflecting the information required by section 13(d)(1).[12] The purchaser thus has a ten-day window between the crossing of the five percent threshold and the disclosure date. This ten-day period provides a window of opportunity for acquiring considerably more than the five percent threshold before section 13(d)'s early warning disclosures must be made. An SEC advisory group recommended amending the rules to require filing in advance of the five percent purchase[13] but no such change has taken place. Accordingly, there frequently will be a flurry of purchases after the five percent threshold has been crossed.

---

45. Piper v. Chris–Craft Indus., Inc., 430 U.S. 1, 97 S.Ct. 926, 51 L.Ed.2d 124 (1977), *rehearing denied* 430 U.S. 976, 97 S.Ct. 1668, 52 L.Ed.2d 371 (1977).

46. *See* § 11.19 *infra.*

47. *See* § 11.18 *infra.*

48. 15 U.S.C.A. § 78n(f). *See* § 11.16 *infra. See generally* David L. Ratner, Section 14(f): A New Approach to Transfers of Corporate Control, 54 Cornell L.Rev. 65 (1968).

§ 11.2

1. 15 U.S.C.A. § 78*l.*

2. 15 U.S.C.A. § 78m(d)(*l*). Section 12, 15 U.S.C.A. § 78*l*, is discussed in § 9.2 *supra.*

3. 15 U.S.C.A. § 78m(e); 17 C.F.R. § 240.13e–3. *See* § 11.17 *infra.*

12. 17 C.F.R. § 240.13d–1. *See* 15 U.S.C.A. § 78m(d)(1).

13. *See* 15 Sec.Reg. & L.Rep. (BNA) 156 (June 17, 1983).

The normal filing required by section 13(d) is embodied in Schedule 13D.[14] However, some large investors who would otherwise be required to make a Schedule 13D filing may qualify for a shorter form Schedule 13G.[15] By virtue of Rule 13d–1(b),[16] qualifying institutional investors, and other "passive investors" whose intent is not to acquire or influence the control of the target company. This passive investor rule permits the acquisition of up to twenty percent of the target company's securities without having to comply with the more detailed disclosure requirements of Schedule 13D. If the passive investor decides to exert control,[18] then he or she must make a Schedule 13D filing and there is a ten-day cooling off period before he or she can act in accordance with the new disclosure regarding control. Filing a Schedule 13G and withholding the intent to acquire control is a violation of the Act.[19] Certain institutional investors that are able to file Schedule 13G may also have to make annual filings under section 13(f).[20]

Schedule 13D disclosures are designed to alert the investing public to significant acquisitions of securities and the intentions of the person making the acquisitions. Specifically, Schedule 13D requires disclosure of the identity and background[21] of the person acquiring the target company securities. The Schedule 13D must reveal the source and amount of funds or other consideration being used to acquire the target securities.[22] The filing must also describe the purpose of the transaction[23] that triggers the Schedule 13D filing obligation. The Schedule 13D must reveal the interest of all persons making the filing in the target securities of the issuer.[24] Disclosures also must be made with respect to contracts and other arrangements between the persons making the Schedule 13D filing and any other persons concerning the target securities of the issuer, including voting agreements, options, and distributions of profits.[25]

§ 11.2[2] Who Must File Under Section 13(d); Formation of a "Group"

By virtue of section 13(d)(3),[31] when two or more people or entities get together to act as a partnership, limited partnership, syndicate, or other group for the purpose of acquiring, holding, or disposing of a target company's securities, the syndicate or group is deemed to be a "person" for the purposes of section 13(d).[32] Accordingly, a Schedule 13D must be filed when members of

---

14. 17 C.F.R. § 240.13d–1. Schedule 13D is found in 17 C.F.R. § 240.13d–101.

15. 17 C.F.R. § 240.13d–102. *See* 15 U.S.C.A. §§ 78m(d)(5), 78m(g); 17 C.F.R. § 240.13d–5.

16. 17 C.F.R. § 240.13d–1(b).

18. *See, e.g.,* Hallwood Realty Partners, L.P. v. Gotham Partners, 95 F.Supp.2d 169 (S.D.N.Y. 2000) (failure to disclose intent to exercise control and liquidate company).

19. *See id.*

20. 15 U.S.C.A. § 78m(f). *See* § 11.3 *infra.*

21. Schedule 13D, item 2. This includes disclosure of criminal convictions and of suits involving securities law violations within the preceding 5 years. Schedule 13D, item 2(c), (d)

22. Schedule 13D, item 3.

23. Schedule 13D, item 4.

24. Schedule 13D, item 5.

25. Schedule 13D, item 6.

31. 15 U.S.C.A. § 78m(d)(3).

32. *See, e.g.,* Global Intellicom, Inc. v. Thomson Kernaghan & Co., 1999 WL 544708, [1999 Transfer Binder] Fed. Sec. L. Rep. (CCH) ¶ 90,534 (S.D.N.Y.1999).

such a "group" in the aggregate acquire five percent of a class of equity securities subject to the Act's reporting requirements.[33] The Second Circuit has held that the members' agreement to acquire control may be established by the pattern of purchases leading up to the five percent threshold.[37] Thus, hovering just hundredths of percentage point below the five percent threshold can be evidence of a conscious decision to act together prior to the group crossing the five percent threshold.[38]

§ 11.2[4] Exemptions From Section 13(d) Filing Requirements

Section 13(d)(6) of the 1934 Act exempts certain acquisitions from section 13(d)'s and 13(g)'s filing requirements.[65] These filing requirements do not apply to an offer to acquire securities in consideration for securities to be issued under a 1933 Act registration statement. Also exempt are all acquisitions of beneficial interest which, considered with all other acquisitions by the same person over the preceding twelve months, do not exceed two percent of that class of equity securities. Section 13(d)(6) further exempts any acquisition of an equity security by the issuer of that security and any other acquisition or proposed acquisition that the commission shall exempt by its rules. The purchase of securities by the issuer is governed by section 13(e) and rules promulgated thereunder.[66]

§ 11.3 Reports of Institutional Investment Managers—Section 13(f)

Section 13(f)(1)[1] requires disclosure by institutional investment managers which exercise control over accounts containing significant portfolio holdings of equity securities, subject to the Exchange Act's filing requirements. These institutional investors must file Form 13F upon acquiring equity securities, subject to the registration requirements of section 12 of the 1934 Act[2] or the Investment Company Act[3] when the aggregate fair market value of all such equity securities exceeds one hundred million dollars.[4]

§ 11.4 Definition of Tender Offer

Section 13(d)'s early warning filing requirements are aimed at creeping acquisitions of substantial amounts of stock using open market or privately negotiated large block purchases.[1] In contrast, section 14's Williams Act filing

---

The Second Circuit extended the group concept to the definition of person to section 16 of the Act which governs reporting of insider trades and disgorgement of short-swing profits. Morales v. Quintel Entertainment, Inc., 249 F.3d 115 (2d Cir.2001); Morales v. Freund, 163 F.3d 763 (2d Cir.1999). *See* § 13.3 *infra*.

33. *See* IBS Financial Corp. v. Seidman & Associates, LLC, 136 F.3d 940 (3d Cir.1998) (inadequate disclosures concerning the formation of a group).

37. Corenco Corp. v. Schiavone & Sons, Inc., 488 F.2d 207, 215 (2d Cir.1973).

38. *Id.*

65. 15 U.S.C.A. § 78m(d)(6).

66. 15 U.S.C.A. § 78m(e). *See* § 11.8 *infra*.

§ 11.3

1. 15 U.S.C.A. § 78m(f)(1).

2. 15 U.S.C.A. § 78l. *See* § 9.2 *supra*.

3. *See* § 20.3 *infra*.

4. *See* 17 C.F.R. § 240.13f–1:

§ 11.4

1. 15 U.S.C.A. § 78m(d). *See* §§ 11.1, 11.2 *supra*, § 11.8 *infra*.

and disclosure provisions are called into play when there is a "tender offer." "Tender offer" is not defined in the Williams Act. Both the courts and the SEC have broadly construed the term, providing a flexible definition. The statutory meaning of "tender offer" is important in that it determines the applicability of section 14(d)'s[2] filing requirements, section 14(e)'s[3] general antifraud proscriptions, and section 14(f)'s[4] disclosure requirements relating to new directors.

On more than one occasion, Congress has considered and rejected[5] express objective definitions of tender offer, such as the one embodied in the proposed Federal Securities Code.[6] The federal legislative pattern indicates either indecision or a congressional intent to retain a flexible definition and to leave the resolution of the issue to the SEC and the federal judiciary. The SEC has seized upon this flexibility (intended or not). In contrast, most state tender offer statutes contain objective definitions.[7]

In the past, the SEC declined to set objective standards[8] to determine the existence of tender offers. This position was "premised upon the dynamic nature of [the] transactions [involved] and the need for the Williams Act to be interpreted flexibly."[9] Needless to say, what the SEC views as needed flexibility is viewed by corporate planners as resulting in unnecessary lack of predictability.

The SEC's long-standing position is that the definition of tender offer "is not limited to the classical 'tender offer' where the person desiring to acquire shares makes a public invitation or a written offer to the shareholders to tender their shares. Nor is there a requirement that the shares be tendered through a depository. The change in control may be effected by direct purchase from shareholders without a public or a written invitation for tenders having been made."[14] This still reflects the Commission's position even though the proposed definition was not adopted. The essence of the SEC's position is that "tender offer" covers more than traditional takeover attempts involving public solicitation and may, under appropriate circumstances, include privately negotiated and open market purchases.

The Eight Factor Test

Even in the absence of a formal rule expressly defining the term, the SEC has developed an eight-factor test to determine whether a tender offer exists. The eight factors can be summarized as follows:

(1) active and widespread solicitation of public shareholders;

2. 15 U.S.C.A. § 78n(d). *See* § 11.5 *infra.*

3. 15 U.S.C.A. § 78n(e). *See* §§ 11.6, 11.10 *infra.*

4. 15 U.S.C.A. § 78n(f). *See* § 11.7 *infra.*

5. *See, e.g.,* Full Disclosure of Corporate Equity Ownership and in Corporate Takeover Bids, Hearings on S.510 Before the Subcomm. on Securities of the Senate Comm. on Banking and Currency, 90th Cong., 1st Sess. 131 (1967).

6. The proposed Code would have required an offer or solicitation directed towards more than thirty-five persons. *See* A.L.I.Fed.Sec.Code § 292 (1979); *Id.* § 299.9(a) (Tent.Draft No. 1 1972).

7. *See, e.g.,* 8 Del.Code § 203(c)(2).

8. *See, e.g.,* Sec.Act Rel. No. 33–5731 (Aug. 2, 1976).

9. *Id.*

14. *E.g.,* Cattlemen's Investment Co., [1971–72 Transfer Binder] Fed.Sec.L.Rep. (CCH) ¶ 78,-775 (SEC Staff Reply April 24, 1972).

(2) solicitation for a substantial percentage of the issuer's stock;

(3) whether the offer to purchase is made at a premium over prevailing market price;

(4) whether the terms of the offer are firm rather than negotiable;

(5) whether the offer is contingent on the tender of a fixed minimum number of shares;

(6) whether the offer is open only for a limited period of time;

(7) whether the offerees are subject to pressure to sell their stock; and

(8) the existence of public announcements of a purchasing program that precede or accompany a rapid accumulation of stock.[15]

These factors are simply broad guidelines. They are factors to be weighed not simply counted numerically. Hence, whatever predictability does exist must be gleaned not from the factors alone but from the cases and SEC rulings that are discussed below.

The Developing Interpretation and Case Law

In an early release, the Commission took the position that a "special bid"—the placement of a fixed-price bid on an exchange for a specified large number of shares—constitutes a tender offer.[17] Thus, although ordinary open market purchases are not to be classified as tender offers, use of the facilities of an exchange will not automatically preclude the finding of a "tender offer."[19] Ordinarily, open market purchases will not constitute a tender offer. In fact, as discussed below, there are no federal cases finding a tender offer on the basis of open-market purchases. An early federal district court decision held that a large block purchase of shares made without the intent to obtain control is not a tender offer under the Williams Act. The court looked to the legislative history, which "made clear that the type of activity intended to be regulated ... is the acquisition of control of a corporation by outsiders through the purchase of its shares."[20] According to the legislative history, a tender offer occurs when a target company shareholder must decide whether or not to sell shares in connection with a transfer of control.[21]

Arguably, a series of control-related open market purchases would fall within the tender offer definition as well. The cases, however, have taken a contrary view. Notwithstanding the weight of current case law to the contrary, purchasers engaged in a series of open market transactions as a first step in acquiring control should be aware of the risk, albeit a small one, that courts may find against them on the "tender offer" issue. Open market

---

15. The eight-factor test which is not contained in an official SEC release has evolved over a period of time and is discussed in Wellman v. Dickinson, 475 F.Supp. 783 (S.D.N.Y.1979); Hoover Co. v. Fuqua Industries, Inc., 1979 WL 1244, [1979–1980 Transfer Binder] Fed.Sec.L.Rep. (CCH) ¶ 97,107 (N.D.Ohio 1979).

17. Sec.Exch.Act Rel. No. 34–8392 (Aug. 30, 1968).

19. *Id.*

20. Dyer v. Eastern Trust & Banking Co., 336 F.Supp. 890, 907 (D.Me.1971). *See* Smallwood v. Pearl Brewing Co., 489 F.2d 579 (5th Cir.1974), *cert. denied* 419 U.S. 873, 95 S.Ct. 134, 42 L.Ed.2d 113 (1974).

21. *See* S.Rep. No. 550, 90th Cong., 1st Sess. 2 (1967); H.R.Rep. No. 1711, 90th Cong., 2d Sess. 2 (1968).

purchases combined with secretive, high pressure private transactions could well fall within the Act's purview.

Under section 13(d), open market purchases will trigger disclosure obligations within ten days of the acquisition of five percent or more of a company's securities.[23] In contrast, section 14(d)'s filing requirements begin with the commencement of the offer.[24] Therefore, if a series of open-market purchases constitutes a tender offer, full disclosure must be made simultaneously with the first purchase. There have been many proposals before the SEC to require advance filing under section 13(d) as well. Adoption of this position would, in large part, eliminate the significance of the open market purchase controversy with the very important exception that a "tender offer" triggers potential liability under section 14(e)'s antifraud proscriptions.[26]

A plan of successive open market purchases has been held not to be a tender offer where the aggregate amount of shares so purchased fell short of the five percent threshold.[27] Even where the five percent threshold was exceeded, an attempt to exercise voting control after a series of open market purchases has been held insufficient to make the acquisition a tender offer.[28] Similarly, the purchase of twenty-five percent of a company's stock in a two-day period was held not to be a tender offer where only one of the SEC's eight factors was present.[29] A "street sweep" for a target's own shares, consisting of large block purchases within a short period of time,[30] was not a tender offer even though it was designed to defeat a hostile third-party offer.[31] The most compelling case to date for characterizing a series of open-market purchases as a tender offer was Hanson Trust PLC v. SCM Corp.,[32] which held that a street sweep and a group of privately negotiated purchases for twenty-five percent of the target company's outstanding stock was not a tender offer, even though these purchases occurred on the heels of the withdrawal of a publicly announced tender offer. The court refused to find these transactions to constitute a tender offer because, among other things, the price of the purchases was at the market price and the privately negotiated purchases were accomplished without any pressure or secrecy.[34] The result also might have been different had the withdrawal of the tender offer been part of a plan designed to evade the protections of the Williams Act.[35]

23. 15 U.S.C.A. § 78m(d). See § 11.1 *supra*.

24. 15 U.S.C.A. § 78n(d).

26. 15 U.S.C.A. § 78n(e). See §§ 11.6, 11.10 *infra*.

27. Gulf & Western Industries, Inc. v. Great Atlantic & Pacific Tea Co., 356 F.Supp. 1066 (S.D.N.Y.1973), *affirmed* 476 F.2d 687 (2d Cir.1973).

28. Water & Wall Associates, Inc. v. American Consumer Industries, Inc., 1973 WL 383, [1973 Transfer Binder] Fed.Sec.L.Rep. (CCH) ¶ 93,943 (D.N.J.1973). *Accord* SEC v. Carter Hawley Hale Stores, Inc., 760 F.2d 945 (9th Cir.1985).

29. Brascan Ltd. v. Edper Equities Ltd., 477 F.Supp. 773 (S.D.N.Y.1979).

30. For example, within a two-hour trading period, the target company purchased 6.5 million of its own shares (approximately 18%); this was part of a defensive repurchase program that would have resulted in acquisition of 18.5 million shares (more than half of the company's outstanding stock).

31. SEC v. Carter Hawley Hale Stores, Inc., 760 F.2d 945 (9th Cir.1985).

32. 774 F.2d 47 (2d Cir.1985).

34. *Id.*

35. *Cf.* Field v. Trump, 850 F.2d 938 (2d Cir.1988), *cert. denied* 489 U.S. 1012, 109 S.Ct. 1122, 103 L.Ed.2d 185 (1989), wherein the court found that a privately negotiated purchase sandwiched between the withdrawal of one tender offer and the initiation of a second, both at a lower price, was part of a single tender offer.

The courts finding that these open market purchase programs are not tender offers have relied on the legislative history in distinguishing large scale stock acquisitions from tender offers. For example, it has been observed that the Williams Act was not intended to "subject any ... extensive market acquisition program to immediate characterization as a tender offer."[36] For similar reasons, courts have found that open market purchases are not tender offers under analogous state statutes.[37]

The cases involving both open market and privately negotiated stock purchases seem to turn on whether or not the "pressure-creating characteristics of a tender offer"[38] accompany the transactions. Thus, where a publicly announced intention to acquire a substantial block of stock was followed by rapid acquisition of shares, the court held that a tender offer had occurred.[39] In contrast, where acquisition proceeded more slowly and none of the SEC's eight factors were present, the court found no more than "a particularly aggressive and successful open market [and privately negotiated] stock buying program."[40]

A number of decisions have discussed whether privately negotiated transfers of a controlling block of shares can constitute a tender offer. The cases conflict, but most hold that privately negotiated transactions are susceptible of being categorized as tender offers even though most privately negotiated purchases will not fall within the definition of tender offer. Any privately negotiated purchase that interferes with a shareholder's "unhurried investment decision" and "fair treatment of ... investors"[41] defeats the protections of the Williams Act and is, most likely, a tender offer. In Wellman v. Dickinson,[42] a company formed a subsidiary, LHIW [Let's Hope It Works], through which it made simultaneous secret offers to twenty-eight of the target company's largest shareholders. These shareholders represented a total of thirty-five percent of the company's outstanding shares. The identity of the actual tender offeror was not disclosed. Further, the target shareholders were given a short period of time—from one-half hour to overnight—in which to make a decision. The court held that a tender offer had taken place.[43] In a subsequent case, a firm agreement to purchase fifty-one percent (majority control) of a company was held to be a privately negotiated sale of stock outside the scope of section 14's tender offer provisions because of the absence of most of the SEC's eight factors.[44] In addition, the Second Circuit has held

---

36. Ludlow Corp. v. Tyco Laboratories, Inc., 529 F.Supp. 62, 69 (D.Mass.1981). *Cf.* SEC v. Carter Hawley Hale Stores, Inc., 760 F.2d 945 (9th Cir.1985) (issuer's open market repurchase program in response to a tender offer was not a tender offer).

37. *E.g.,* Condec Corp. v. Farley, 578 F.Supp. 85 (S.D.N.Y.1983) (purchase of 8.7% of the target company's stock was not a tender offer under the New York Takeover Disclosure Act).

38. Ludlow Corp. v. Tyco Laboratories, Inc., 529 F.Supp. 62, 68 (D.Mass.1981).

Subsequently it was held that a highly publicized cash merger proposal at a premium above the market price constituted a tender offer. Zuckerman v. Franz, 573 F.Supp. 351 (S.D.Fla.1983).

39. S–G Securities, Inc. v. Fuqua Investment Co., 466 F.Supp. 1114 (D.Mass.1978) (twenty-eight percent of target company). *Compare, e.g.,* SEC v. Carter Hawley Hale Stores, Inc., 760 F.2d 945 (9th Cir.1985).

40. Ludlow Corp. v. Tyco Laboratories, Inc., 529 F.Supp. 62, 67 (D.Mass.1981). *See also, e.g.,* Hanson Trust PLC v. SCM Corp., 774 F.2d 47 (2d Cir.1985).

41. Cattlemen's Investment Co. v. Fears, 343 F.Supp. 1248 (W.D.Okl.1972) (finding a tender offer to have occurred).

42. Wellman v. Dickinson, 475 F.Supp. 783 (S.D.N.Y.1979).

43. *Id.*

44. Astronics Corp. v. Protective Closures Co., Inc., 561 F.Supp. 329 (W.D.N.Y.1983).

that where the tender offeror and the solicited shareholder agree on secrecy and the private nature of the transaction, the acquisition of nearly ten percent of a target company's outstanding shares does not constitute a tender offer.[45] Unlike the *Wellman* decision discussed above, this case did not involve a hostile, high pressure move to take control such that the interests of investor protection called for section 14(d)'s advance notice and filing requirements. Similarly, the Second Circuit has held that absent special facts, five privately negotiated purchases which, combined with one open market purchase, totaled twenty-five percent of an issuer's outstanding stock did not constitute a tender offer.[46]

The theme that emerges from the foregoing cases is that when a privately negotiated attempt to take control of a company raises problems that the Williams Act was designed to ameliorate (such as secrecy and high pressure), a tender offer may exist. This is a significant broadening of the tender offer definition, especially since it brings many transactions that are not subject to the filing requirements of section 13(d) within the reach of section 14(e)'s antifraud provisions. Among the key factors to look for in privately negotiated transactions are high pressure tactics, such as the "midnight special" and "bear hug" tactics used in the *Wellman* case.

Clearly, a tender offer need not be hostile in order to be subject to section 14(d)'s requirements. Where the target company's management supports the shift in control, abuses may arise that will necessitate the application of the tender offer definition.[48] It has been opined that a tender offeror's decision to extend an existing tender offer to an additional number of shares does not create a new tender offer so as to start the filing requirements of section 14(d) anew.[49] Along similar lines, shares purchased prior to the commencement of a tender offer will not be integrated into that tender offer.[50]

As the foregoing discussion illustrates, in the absence of an SEC rule or statutory amendment, the definition of tender offer remains elusive. The cases have established some limits to the flexible definition. The inquiry, however, is highly factual and is handled on an ad hoc basis.

§ 11.5 Filings, Disclosures and Procedures for Tender Offers—Section 14(d) and Regulation 14D

§ 11.5[1] Overview of Filing and Disclosure Requirements

Section 14(d) of the Exchange Act[1] and applicable SEC rules require the filing of tender offers along with certain mandated disclosures. Filing requirements are not limited to the tender offeror but apply to anyone who is recommending in favor of or against a tender offer covered by the Act. In addition, there are certain substantive requirements for any tender offer

---

45. Kennecott Copper Corp. v. Curtiss–Wright Corp., 584 F.2d 1195 (2d Cir.1978).

46. Hanson Trust PLC v. SCM Corp., 774 F.2d 47 (2d Cir.1985).

48. Smallwood v. Pearl Brewing Co., 489 F.2d 579 (5th Cir.1974), *cert. denied* 419 U.S. 873, 95 S.Ct. 134, 42 L.Ed.2d 113 (1974).

49. American General Insurance Co., [1971–1972 Transfer Binder] Fed.Sec.L.Rep. (CCH) ¶ 78,588 (SEC Staff Reply Dec. 22, 1971).

50. Lerro v. Quaker Oats Co., 84 F.3d 239 (7th Cir.1996).

§ 11.5

1. 15 U.S.C.A. § 78n(d).

subject to section 14(d), but those do not extend to the fairness of the tender offer.[2] The basic thrust of section 14(d) is disclosure. Section 14(d) requires that the tender offer be fairly and fully described, but it does not require that the price offered be a fair one.[3]

Section 14(d)(1) of the Exchange Act[4] requires that all "tender offer material" for equity securities subject to the registration requirements of section 12 must be filed with the Commission and accompanied by the appropriate disclosures.[5] The filing requirements do not apply to issuers whose periodic reporting obligations arise under section 15(d).[6] Section 14(d) requires disclosures of the type specified in Schedule 13D under section 13(d)[7] in addition to such other information as the SEC may require. As is the case with a Schedule 13D filing for acquisition of five percent or more of a class of a target company's stock,[8] the section 14(d) filings must be updated to reflect material changes and developments.[9] Section 14(d) does not apply to an issuer's acquisition of its own shares,[10] as those transactions are covered by section 13(e), which by virtue of SEC rulemaking imposes regulations for issuer tender offers that are comparable to Regulation 14D's rules for third party offers.[11]

Regulation 14D sets out the Commission's filing and disclosure requirements under section 14(d). Rule 14d-1[12] provides the basic definitions for covered tender offers and further incorporates by reference all general definitions applicable under other provisions of the Exchange Act. In addition to the long-form filing set out in Schedule TO[13] the tender offeror must file ten copies of all additional tender offer material with the Commission no later than the date upon which it is first published or disseminated.[15] These constitute filed documents within the context of section 18(a)'s imposition of liability[16] upon those responsible therefor to injured purchasers or sellers relying on materially misleading information contained therein.

The filing requirements apply to the formal tender offer. Bidders are permitted to make a pre-commencement announcement of the offer. However, it is fraudulent to make such an announcement without an intent to commence the tender offer within a reasonable time.[17]

2. *Cf.* Santa Fe Industries, Inc. v. Green, 430 U.S. 462, 97 S.Ct. 1292, 51 L.Ed.2d 480 (1977) (the federal securities laws were not designed to regulate fairness; the focus is on disclosure). *See* § 12.20 *infra*.

3. Wardrop v. Amway Asia Pacific Ltd., 2001 WL 274067, [2000–2001 Transfer Binder] Fed. Sec. L. Rep. (CCH) ¶ 91,346 (S.D.N.Y. 2001).

4. 15 U.S.C.A. § 78n(d)(1).

5. 15 U.S.C.A. § 78n(d)(1).

6. 15 U.S.C.A. § 78o(d).

7. 15 U.S.C.A. § 78m(d) which is discussed in § 11.2 *supra*.

8. 15 U.S.C.A. § 78n(d). *Compare* 15 U.S.C.A. § 78m(d) which is discussed in § 11.2 *supra*.

9. 15 U.S.C.A. § 78n(d).

10. 15 U.S.C.A. § 78n(d)(1).

11. 15 U.S.C.A. § 78m(e).

12. 17 C.F.R. § 240.14d-1.

13. 17 C.F.R. § 240.14d-100.

15. 17 C.F.R. § 240.14d-3(b).

16. 15 U.S.C.A. § 78r(a) which is discussed in § 12.19 *infra*.

17. Rule 14e-8, 17 C.F.R. § 240.14e-8.

As is the case with the proxy rules,[18] the filing requirements are not limited to the first formal filing of the initial offer. All other documents used in the tender offer and solicitation must thus be on file with the commission prior to their use.[19]

§ 11.5[2][B] Schedule TO

The information that a tender offeror must disclose at the time of the commencement of the offer depends to some extent upon the terms of the offer that is being made. All "bidders" must file the Schedule TO. "Bidder" is defined as any person who makes a tender offer or on whose behalf a tender offer is made, except that an issuer seeking to acquire its own securities is not within the definition. Further, for the purpose of determining whether or not a tender offer has been made, two or more persons who act as a partnership, limited partnership, syndicate, or other "group" for the purpose of acquiring, holding, or disposing of the target company[31] must file eight copies of the Schedule TO,[32] including exhibits, with the Commission prior to the commencement of the tender offer. The information required by the Schedule TO for third party bidders is the same as required for issuer self-tenders.[33] In addition to prescribing the form of the tender offer statement, Regulation 14D imposes certain substantive procedures on the mechanics and terms of the tender offer.[34]

The Schedule TO begins with a summary term sheet, as required by item 1001 of Regulation M–A.[35] The summary term sheet is not required if the information is contained in a prospectus pursuant to a 1933 Act registration statement for the securities to be issued pursuant to the tender offer.[36] Schedule TO requires disclosure of the name of the bidder, name of the target company, and the title of class of securities being sought.[37] It also requires that all "persons" reporting under the Schedule provide their names and addresses, as well as disclosing whether or not they belong to a "group" within the meaning of section 14(d)(2).[38] Further, it is necessary to disclose the source of funds to be used in connection with the tender offer[39] and the identity and background of the person filing the document, including the disclosure of any criminal conviction within the past five years of the person presenting the tender offer.[40] The Schedule TO must describe the terms of the

---

18. *See* 17 C.F.R. § 240.14a–3 and Schedule 14A which is discussed in § 10.2 *supra.*

19. 17 C.F.R. § 240.14d–3.

31. 15 U.S.C.A. § 78n(d)(2). A similar provision is found in section 13(d)(3), 15 U.S.C.A. § 78m(d)(3).

32. 17 C.F.R. § 240.14d–100.

33. Additionally, the concept of what constitutes a "group" with regard to section 13(d) filings has its parallel here. *See* the discussion of what constitutes a "group" in § 11.1 *supra.*

34. *See* § 11.6 *infra.*

35. Schedule TO item 1. *See* Regulation M–A item 1001, 17 C.F.R. § 229.1001.

36. Schedule TO, item 1. The 1933 Act prospectus requirements are discussed in chapter 2 *supra.*

37. Schedule TO item 2. *See* Item 1002(a) through (c) of Regulation M–A. 17 C.F.R. §§ 229.1002(a)–1002(c).

38. *See* 15 U.S.C.A. § 78n(d)(2). A similar provision is found in section 13(d)(3), 15 U.S.C.A. § 78m(d)(3). *See* § 11.2[2] *supra.*

39. Schedule TO item 7. *See* Items 1007(a), (b) and (d) of Regulation M–A, 17 C.F.R. §§ 229.1007(a), 229.1007(b), 229.1007(d).

40. *Id.*

tender offer.[41] The tender offer document must also disclose all past contracts, transactions, or negotiations between the tender offeror and the target company, the purpose of the tender offer and the bidder's plans and proposals for the future with regard to the target company.[42] The Schedule TO must divulge the bidder's current interest and holdings of securities of the target company.[43] The Schedule TO filing must identify all persons retained, employed, or compensated in connection with the tender offer,[44] as well as the bidder's financial statements[45] when the bidder's financial structure is material to an investor's decision whether or not to tender shares in the target company. For example, any tender offer involving an exchange of the target company's securities for the tender offeror's shares would necessarily trigger the financial statement requirement.[47] Additionally, if financing conditions are involved in the tender offer, the bidder's financial statements will be material.[48] In addition to the disclosure items specified in Schedule TO, additional disclosures may be required if necessary to make the statements made not materially misleading.[50]

In addition to the disclosures above, the Schedule TO filing must list any present or proposed material contracts, arrangements, understandings, or relationships between the bidder, its officers, directors, controlling persons, or subsidiaries and the target company or any of its officers, directors, controlling persons, or subsidiaries that would bear upon the target company shareholders' decision whether or not to tender his or her shares. Further, steps toward compliance with necessary administrative approval for the offer must be disclosed, as must the applicability of the antitrust laws, or the margin requirements[51] as well as the pendency of material legal proceedings. When there have been material misstatements in a Schedule TO filing, they can be cured by subsequent correction, provided that adequate prominence is given to the curative changes.[53]

§ 11.5[3] Other Requirements Imposed by Regulation 14D

Section 14(d)(3) of the Act[66] provides that in determining the applicable percentage of outstanding shares of any class of equity securities, securities held by the issuer or its subsidiary must be excluded from the computation.

41. Schedule TO item 4. *See* Items 1004(a) through (b) of Regulation M–A, 17 C.F.R. §§ 229.1004(a)–229.1004(b).

42. Schedule TO item 5. *See* Items 1005(a) (b) and (e) of Regulation M–A. 17 C.F.R. §§ 229.1005(a), 229.1005(b), 229.1005(e).

43. Schedule TO item 8. *See* Item 1008 of Regulation M–A, 17 C.F.R. § 229.1008.

44. Schedule TO item 9. *See* Item 1009(a) of Regulation M–A, 17 C.F.R. § 229.1009(a).

45. Schedule TO item 10. *See* Items 1010(a) and (b) of Regulation M–A, 17 C.F.R. §§ 229.1010(a), 229.1010(b).

47. See Instructions 1 and 2 to Schedule TO item 10.

48. *Id.*

50. *See* Schedule TO item 11, Regulation M–A item 1011, 17 C.F.R. § 229.1011.

51. *See, e.g.,* Irving Bank Corp. v. Bank of New York Co., 692 F.Supp. 163 (S.D.N.Y.1988) (tender offer must accurately disclose status of Federal Reserve Board approval for proposed acquisition of target company).

53. *See, e.g.,* American Insured Mortgage Investors v. CRI, Inc., 1990 WL 192561, [1990–1991 Transfer Binder] Fed.Sec.L.Rep. (CCH) ¶ 95,730 (S.D.N.Y.1990) (material changes had to be highlighted through the use of boldface and italic typeface).

66. 15 U.S.C.A. § 78n(d)(3).

Also, section 14(d)(4)[67] requires full disclosure according to such rules as the Commission may promulgate with regard to any solicitation or recommendation to a target company's securities holders either to accept or reject a tender offer or request for tender made by someone else. These disclosure requirements are set out in Schedule 14D–9.[68] Schedule 14D–9 is the disclosure document that must be filed in connection with any other solicitation or recommendation for or against tender offers. The Schedule 14D–9 is in essence a short form of the Schedule TO requiring similar disclosures with regard to anyone making recommendations concerning a bidder's offer.[69] As is the case with an offeror's Schedule TO, material changes must be reflected by "prompt" amendment to the Schedule 14D–9.

§ 11.5[3][A] Bidders' Right of Access to Target Company's Shareholders

SEC Rule 14d–5 spells out the target company's obligation to respond to requests for a shareholder list in connection with tender offers.[71] Briefly, if the bidder or other person presents the request according to the rule's requirements, the target company's management must comply, but the reasonable cost of compliance is to be charged to the bidder. Faced with such a request, the target company has the option of mailing the bidder's materials, within three business days of receipt, to the target company's holders.[72] Alternatively, the target company may, within three business days, deliver the stockholder lists to the bidder making the request.[73] The SEC dictates the proper form for the bidder's written request.[74] Also, a bidder's request for such shareholder lists subjects the bidder to certain requirements, including the return of any lists furnished by the target company.[75]

§ 11.5[3][B] Shareholders' Withdrawal of Tendered Securities

Section 14(d)(5) of the Act[76] provides that all securities deposited pursuant to a tender offer may be withdrawn by or on behalf of the depositor at any time until the expiration of seven days after the first publication of the formal tender offer (or request or invitation) and at any time after sixty days from the date of the original tender offer or request for invitation unless a different period is provided for by SEC rules. Rule 14d–7,[77] which formerly limited withdrawal rights to fifteen days after the commencement of the tender offer or ten days after the commencement of a competing offer, has been amended

---

67. 15 U.S.C.A. § 78n(d)(4).

68. 17 C.F.R. § 240.14d–101.

69. *Cf.* Gerber v. Computer Associates International, Inc., 860 F.Supp. 27 (E.D.N.Y.1994) (allegedly misleading Schedule 14D–9 can form the basis of a private suit under Rule 10b–5).

71. 17 C.F.R. § 240.14d–5.

72. 17 C.F.R. § 240.14d–5(b). The bidder is to be informed of the progress of any such mailing undertaken by the target company.

73. 17 C.F.R. § 240.14d–5(c). These rights are in addition to the right to shareholder lists under the proxy rules as well as inspection rights under state law. *See* § 10.7 *supra*. *See generally* James D. Cox, Thomas L. Hazen & F. Hodge O'Neal, Corporations §§ 13.2–13.11 (1995).

74. 17 C.F.R. § 240.14d–5(e).

75. 17 C.F.R. § 240.14d–5(f).

76. 15 U.S.C.A. § 78n(d)(5).

77. 17 C.F.R. § 240.14d–7.

to provide that withdrawal rights may be exercised throughout the period that the tender offer remains open, which must be for at least twenty business days.[78] Any increase or decrease in the consideration offered under the tender offer triggers the requirement that the tender offer be open for ten business days from the date of change in consideration.[79] The rule also sets out the appropriate form of the notice of withdrawal. Shareholders who tendered shares prior to receiving notice of offeror's Schedule 14D–1 (the predecessor of the current Schedule TO[80]) amendment relating to the source of funds being used for the offer were held entitled, under the former version of Rule 14d–7, to withdrawal rights for fifteen days from the notice.[81] Under the current rule, the duration of the tender offer is the appropriate extension of time for withdrawal rights.[82] By virtue of Rule 14e–1(a),[83] all tender offers by persons other than the issuer must remain open for twenty business days.[84] The same twenty-day period is applicable to issuer self-tenders.[85]

§ 11.5[3][C] Pro Rata Acceptance of Tendered Shares; Extensions of the Tender Offer

Section 14(d)(6) of the Act[86] requires pro rata acceptance of shares tendered where the tender offer by its terms does not obligate the tender offeror to accept all shares tendered. This takes pressure off the target company's shareholders who would otherwise have to make a quick decision were acceptance to be on a first come basis. Rule 14d–8[87] extends the pro rata requirements to the entire period of the tender offer. A tender offeror may not extend the proration period after expiration of the offer where the effect would be to alter the pro rata acceptance of the shares tendered.[88]

Section 14(d)(7) of the Act[89] provides that whenever a person varies the terms of a tender offer or request before the expiration thereof by increasing the consideration offered to the holders of the securities sought, the person making such an increase in consideration must pay to all persons tendering securities pursuant to their requests that same price whether or not the securities were tendered prior to the variation of the tender offer's terms.[90] This can be especially important if a series of transactions are integrated and held to be parts of a single tender offer. Thus, for example, it has been held that a privately negotiated purchase entered into on the heels of the purported withdrawal of a tender offer was part of the same control-related transac-

---

78. 17 C.F.R. § 240.14e–1.

79. 17 C.F.R. §§ 240.13e–4(f)(1)(ii), 240.14e–1(b).

80. 17 C.F.R. § 240.14d–100.

81. Cardiff Acquisitions, Inc. v. Hatch, 751 F.2d 917 (8th Cir.1984).

82. 17 C.F.R. § 240.14d–7.

83. 17 C.F.R. § 240.14e–1(a).

84. *Id.*

85. 17 C.F.R. § 240.13e–4(f)(1)(i). As is the case with third party offers, any increase or decrease in the consideration offered requires that the offer remain open at least ten business days from the notice thereof. 17 C.F.R. § 240.13e–4(f)(1)(ii).

86. 15 U.S.C.A. § 78n(d)(6).

87. 17 C.F.R. 240.14d–8.

88. Pryor v. United States Steel Corp., 794 F.2d 52 (2d Cir.1986).

89. 15 U.S.C.A. § 78n(d)(7).

90. *See, e.g.,* Field v. Trump, 850 F.2d 938 (2d Cir.1988) (recognizing private remedy for violations of section 14(d)(7)).

tion and thus violated the prohibition on discriminatory pricing of purchases in the course of a single tender offer.[92]

§ 11.5[3][D] The "All Holders" Requirement

The SEC rules under the Williams Act are designed to ensure that shareholders of the target company are treated equally during the pendency of a tender offer. A 1985 Delaware Supreme Court decision upheld a tender offer by an issuer that excluded a hostile tender offeror.[93] However, under equal treatment rules adopted by the SEC, such exclusion is prohibited; at the same time that the Commission adopted these equal treatment rules, the SEC adopted "best price" requirements.[94] Although the equal treatment and best price rules are based on different sections, the validity of these requirements may be questionable in light of the Supreme Court ruling that section 14(e) can regulate manipulative conduct only to the extent of protecting against deception.[95]

There is an explicit exception in the "all holders" requirement for tender offers that exclude one or more shareholders in compliance with a constitutionally valid state statute.[101] In addition to reserving general exemptive power under the "all holders" rules,[102] the SEC has promulgated a specific but limited exemption for "odd-lot tender offers" by issuers—an odd-lot offer is one that is limited to security holders owning less than a specified number of shares under one hundred.[103]

The "all holders" rule will support a private right of action.[107]

§ 11.5[3][E] The Equal Treatment and "Best Price" Requirements

As noted above, the Commission has also adopted a "best price" rule that requires equal treatment[109] for all securities holders, and thus entitles anyone receiving payment under the tender offer to the highest consideration paid to any other security holder at any time during such tender offer.[110] Rule 14d–10's best price requirements have been held to support an implied private right of action.[111]

---

92. *Id.*

93. Unocal Corp. v. Mesa Petroleum Co., 493 A.2d 946 (Del.1985).

94. 17 C.F.R. §§ 240.13e–4(f), 240.14d–10.

95. Schreiber v. Burlington Northern, Inc., 472 U.S. 1, 105 S.Ct. 2458, 86 L.Ed.2d 1 (1985). *See* § 11.6 *infra.*

101. 17 C.F.R. §§ 240.13e–4(f)(9)(ii), 240.14d–10(b)(2). The SEC questions, however, whether such state statutes are in fact constitutional. *See* Exch.Act Rel. No. 34–23421 (July 11, 1986). For a discussion of the constitutionality of state statutes affecting tender offers, *see* 11.13 *infra.*

102. 17 C.F.R. §§ 240.13e–4(h)(8), 240.14d–10(e).

103. 17 C.F.R. § 240.13e–4(h)(5). However, both the all holders and best price requirements will apply to the terms of the odd-lot tender offer.

107. *See, e.g.,* In re Digital Island Securities Litigation, 357 F.3d 322 (3d Cir. 2004); Polaroid Corp. v. Disney, 862 F.2d 987 (3d Cir.1988) (also upholding validity of "all holders" rule).

109. *See* 15 U.S.C.A. § 78n(d)(7).

110. 17 C.F.R. §§ 240.13e–4(f)(8)(ii), 240.14d–10(a)(2). *See, e.g.,* Field v. Trump, 850 F.2d 938 (2d Cir.1988) (purchase of dissident director's shares during brief purported withdrawal of tender offer violated SEC best price requirement since same premium was not offered to all tendering shareholders).

111. Epstein v. MCA, Inc., 50 F.3d 644 (9th Cir.1995) (suit by shareholders who were treated less favorably than others).

The SEC best price requirement applies only to shares purchased during a single tender offer.[112] A press release announcing an impending tender offer is not necessarily the commencement of the offer for purposes of the best price rule; accordingly the price paid for shares purchased after the press release but prior to the commencement of the tender offer did not affect the price at which the tender offer could be made.[113] As such, unlike state "fair price" statutes,[114] the SEC best price rule does not regulate two-tiered offers consummated in two distinct steps. On appropriate facts, two transactions that are distinct in form only may be integrated into a single transaction for the purpose of enforcing the best price and equal treatment requirements. The best price requirement cannot be avoided, for example, by delaying additional payments to selected insiders until after the close of the tender offer.[115] Thus, the equal treatment rule has been applied even beyond the bidder's self-proclaimed expiration date.[116]

The SEC best price requirements do not prohibit different types of consideration, and the different consideration need not be substantially equivalent in value so long as the tender offer permits the security holders to elect among the types of consideration offered.[119] However, offering tax favored preferred shares to some shareholders but not others can violate the equal treatment requirement.[120] Not all payments in connection with a tender offer will implicate the best price rule. Thus, for example payments to target company executives will not automatically be considered as part of the consideration for the executives' tendering their shares.[121]

When different types of consideration are offered to all shareholders, the tender offeror may limit the availability and offer it to tendering shareholders on a pro rata basis.[122] As is the case with the "all holders" requirements, the Commission has reserved for itself the power to grant exemptions from the operation of the "best price" requirement.[123]

The integration doctrine was developed under the 1933 Act to address multiple transactions that appear to be separate in form but in substance are part of a single transaction.[124] The same approach could be applied to integrat-

---

112. *See, e.g.,* Lerro v. Quaker Oats Co., 84 F.3d 239 (7th Cir.1996).

113. Kahn v. Virginia Retirement System, 783 F.Supp. 266 (E.D.Va.1992). As observed in § 11.5[2][A] *supra,* the press release announcing the tender offer will be considered the commencement of the tender offer for many purposes. *See also, e.g.,* Gerber v. Computer Associates International, Inc., 303 F.3d 126 (2d Cir.2002) (looking to the date of the press release as the commencement of the tender offer).

114. *E.g.,* M.D. Corps. & Ass'ns Code §§ 3–602, 3–603. *See* § 11.12 *infra. Compare, e.g.,* Field v. Trump, 850 F.2d 938 (2d Cir.1988), *cert. denied* 489 U.S. 1012, 109 S.Ct. 1122, 103 L.Ed.2d 185 (1989).

115. Millionerrors Investment Club v. General Electric Co. PLC, 2000 WL 1288333, [1999–2000 Transfer Binder] Fed. Sec. L. Rep. (CCH) ¶ 90,994 (W.D.Pa.2000).

116. Gerber v. Computer Associates International, Inc., 303 F.3d 126 (2d Cir.2002).

119. 17 C.F.R. §§ 240.13e–4(f)(10), 240.14d–10(c).

120. Epstein v. MCA, Inc., 50 F.3d 644 (9th Cir.1995).

121. Harris v. Intel Corp., 2002 WL 1759817 (N.D.Cal.2002), order vacated by 2002 WL 31548118 (N.D.Cal.2002) (bonuses to target company's executives did not violate best price rule; not did they violate the all holders rule).

122. 17 C.F.R. §§ 240.13e–4(f)(10), 240.14d–10(c).

123. 17 C.F.R. §§ 240.13e–4(h)(8), 240.14d–10(e).

124. *See* § 4.36 *supra.*

ing two successive tender offers. For example, it might be argued that successive tender offers by the same bidder, although distinct in form, are part of a single transaction and thus should be subject to the best price requirement. However, the Seventh Circuit has given a narrow reading to Rule 14d–10(a)(2)'s best price requirement and permitted a higher price to be paid to controlling shareholders immediately before the commencement of the tender offer to other shareholders.[125] The court reached this conclusion notwithstanding the fact that a higher price to the controlling shareholder was integral to the entire transaction when viewed as a whole. The court's opinion, written by Judge Easterbrook, reasoned that the language of the SEC best price rule calls for a bright line test for determining what constitutes the pendency of a tender offer for the purposes of the rule. Judge Easterbrook believed that the rule of equal treatment for all shareholders should yield to what he viewed as the practicalities of the situation. It is arguable, however, that the purpose of the best price rule and other equal treatment rules during the pendency of the offer were designed to assure that all shareholders be treated the same in what is in essence a single transaction. Should the rule of the Seventh Circuit be sustained, it will then be necessary that the ensuing tender offer adequately describe the terms of the transaction to the controlling group. In contrast to the Seventh Circuit's approach, other courts have taken a broad view of the integration concept. For example, it has been held that compensation incentives could be so inexorably entwined with a tender offer that they would be subject to the Williams Act's best price and equal treatment requirements.[128]

Violations of the best price equal treatment rule can result in civil liability.[129]

§ 11.5[3][F] Prompt Payment for Shares Tendered

SEC Rule 14e–1(c), which is not a part of Regulation 14D and therefore applies to all tender offers, requires that the bidder pay the consideration offered or return the tendered securities "promptly" after the termination or withdrawal of the tender offer. The rule does not define "promptly." Nevertheless, the SEC has explained that the standard for promptness may be determined by the practices of the financial community, including current settlement practices.[132] In most instances, the current settlement practice is for the payment of funds and delivery of securities no later than the third business day after the date of the transaction.[133] The Commission considers payment within these time periods as "prompt" under Rule 14e–1(c).[134] The Commission has indicated that waiting as long as thirty days does not satisfy the prompt payment requirement.[135]

---

125. Lerro v. Quaker Oats Co., 84 F.3d 239 (7th Cir.1996).

128. Katt v. Titan Acquisitions, Ltd., 133 F.Supp.2d 632 (M.D.Tenn.2000).

129. *See Id.,* Maxick v. Cadence Design Systems, Inc., 2000 WL 33174386, [2000–2001 Transfer Binder] Fed. Sec. L. Rep. (CCH) ¶ 91,214 (N.D.Cal.2000).

132. *See* Sec. Exch. Act Rel. No. 34–16384, 44 Fed. Reg. 70326 (SEC Nov. 29, 1979).

133. *See* 1934 Act Rule 15c6–1(a), 17 CFR 240.15c6–1(a).

134. *See* Commission Guidance on Mini–Tender Offers and Limited Partnership Tender Offers, Release No. 34–43069, 2000 WL 1050530 (SEC July 24, 2000).

135. *Id.*

§ 11.5[3][G] Post Tender Offer Extensions of Time for Tendering

Rule 14d–11,[136] which was adopted in 1999, permits the tender offeror to extend the offer for shareholders who did not tender their shares during the original offer.[137] Pursuant to Rule 14d–11, a tender offeror has the option of allowing non tendering shareholders to tender their shares for a period of at least three business days and not more than twenty business days following the closing of the offer.[138] Unlike target company shareholders tendering during the original term of the tender offer, target company shareholders tendering during this post-offer period have the right to withdraw their shares once they are tendered.[139]

§ 11.5[3][I] Exemptions From Regulation 14D

Section 14(d)(8) of the Act[157] exempts certain tender offers or request for tenders from the scope of section 14(d)'s requirements. When the acquisition of the securities sought together with all other acquisitions by the same person of securities of the same class within the preceding twelve months does not exceed two percent of the outstanding securities of the class, section 14(d) does not apply.[158] Similarly, section 14(d) does not apply where the tender offeror is the issuer of the security.[159] The Act also gives the SEC exemptive power by rule, regulation or order from transactions "not entered into for the purpose of, and not having the effect of, changing or influencing the control of the issuer or otherwise as not comprehended within the purposes of this subsection."[160]

§ 11.5[3][J] Unregulated Mini-Tender Offers

Section 14(d) of the 1934 Act by its terms[161] does not apply its filing and other requirements to third party tender offers where after the completion of the offer, the tender offeror does not wind up with more than five percent of the class of equity securities that are the subject of the tender offer. Not only does this mean that such mini-tender offers are not also subject to the Schedule TO filing, they are not subject to the proration[162] and equal treatment requirements[163] of section 14(d), nor are they subject to the "all holders" rule,[164] which means that bidders making unregulated mini-tender offers can

---

136. Rule 14d–11, 17 C.F.R. § 240.14d–11.

137. Under the terms of SEC Rule 14e–1, 17 C.F.R.' 240.14e–1, a tender offer must remain open for at least twenty business days. *See* § 11.6 *infra.*

138. Rule 14d–11, 17 C.F.R. § 240.14d–11. *See* Regulation of Takeovers and Security Holder Communications Exch. Act Rel. No. 34–42055, 1999 WL 969596 (SEC Oct. 22, 1999).

139. Rule 14d–11, 17 C.F.R. § 240.14d–11. *Compare* the withdrawal rights that tendering shareholders get pursuant to section 14(d)(5) and Rule 14d–7. 15 U.S.C.A. § 78n(d)(5), 17 C.F.R. § 240.14d–7.

157. 15 U.S.C.A. § 78n(d)(8).

158. 15 U.S.C.A. § 78n(d)(8)(A).

159. 15 U.S.C.A. § 78n(d)(8)(B). *See* § 11.9 *infra.*

160. 15 U.S.C.A. § 78n(d)(8)(C).

161. 15 U.S.C.A. § 78n(d).

162. As discussed above, section 14(d)(6) requires that if more than the solicited shares are tendered, the tenders must be accepted on a prorated basis. 15 U.S.C.A. § 78n(d)(6). *See* § 11.5[3][C] *supra.*

163. *See* 15 U.S.C.A. § 78n(d)(7).

164. 17 C.F.R. § 240.14d–10(a)(2). *See* § 11.5[3][E] *supra.*

selective target a group of shareholders. Furthermore, in the course of a mini-tender offer, tendering shareholders granted the right to withdraw any shares so tendered.[165]

In the 1990s, an unscrupulous practice developed whereby some people tried to take advantage of this absence of regulation by making mini-tender offers to shareholders at a price below the then current market price. The hope in these offers was to lure unsophisticated shareholders into thinking that this was a takeover attempt and thereby lure them into tendering their shares below the market price for the securities. In a number of cases, the SEC instituted administrative proceedings, which resulted in finding that since targeted shareholders were denied material information, such as the below market price nature of the offer and the absence of withdrawal rights once the shares were tendered, these mini-tender offers violated the antifraud prohibitions.[170]

In addition to instituting administrative enforcement actions, the SEC has issued a set of guidelines to be followed in mini-tender offers. These guidelines in essence provide that in mini-tender offers the bidder should act in accordance with the rules that would apply if the offer were subjected to section 14(d) regulation.[171] A bidder making a mini-tender offer should give an adequate description of itself,[172] including disclosures relating to its financing of the offer.[173]

§ 11.6 Unlawful Tender Offer Practices—Section 14(e) and Regulation 14E

§ 11.6[1] Section 14(e)—Antifraud and SEC Rulemaking

The foregoing provisions of the Williams Act are limited to transactions with respect to equity securities that are subject to the Securities Exchange Act's both registration and reporting requirements. In sharp contrast, section 14(e) of the Exchange Act[1] prohibits material misstatements, omissions, and fraudulent practices in connection with tender offers regardless of whether the target company is subject to the Exchange Act's reporting requirements. Thus, for example, section 14(e) and SEC rules promulgated thereunder will apply to an unregistered tender offer; it is not necessary that the target company be a public company.[3] Although there may be policy reasons not to include tender offers for the shares of companies that are not registered under the Exchange Act, the language of section 14(e) justifies federal regulation so long as the transaction in question involves a tender offer. Section 14(e)

---

165. As discussed above, section 14(d)(5) grants withdrawal rights with respect to covered tender offers. 15 U.S.C.A. § 78n(d)(5). *See* § 11.5[3][B] *supra.*

170. *E.g.,* In the Matter of City Investment Group, LLC, 2000 WL 745333 (SEC 2000).

171. Commission Guidance on Mini–Tender Offers and Limited Partnership Tender Offers, Release No. 34–43069, 2000 WL 1050530 (SEC July 24, 2000).

172. *Id.*

173. *Id.*

§ 11.6

1. 15 U.S.C.A. § 78n(e).

3. Clearfield Bank & Trust v. Omega Financial Corp., 65 F.Supp.2d 325, 336 (W.D.Pa.1999). Section 14(e)'s jurisdictional reach thus parallels SEC Rule 10b–5 which similarly is not limited to publicly traded securities. 17 C.F.R. § 240.10b–5. *See* § 12.3 *infra.*

requires full and fair disclosure of the tender offer's terms; it does not require that the price be substantively fair.[4]

Materiality issues under the Williams Act are to be decided in much the same way as under the other disclosure provisions of the securities laws. Courts are not inclined to engage in judicial "nit-picking" by requiring such stringent materiality scrutiny that would eventually work against shareholder interests.[5] Accordingly, subjective motivation behind fully disclosed transactions need not be spelled out.[6]

Another issue is the standard of culpability necessary to establish a violation of section 14(e). Rule 10b–5 requires a showing of scienter;[24] section 17(a) of the 1933 Act[25] and the proxy antifraud provision of section 14a(9) of the Exchange Act[26] do not.[27] Most courts have held that in order to establish a violation of section 14(e), and therefore the rules promulgated thereunder, it must be established that the defendant acted with scienter.[29]

In what could be a very far-reaching decision, the Supreme Court in Schreiber v. Burlington Northern, Inc.,[30] limited the scope of section 14(e). *Schreiber* involved a claim that the defendant target company's renegotiation of the terms of a tender offer was manipulative and hence in violation of section 14(e).[31] Rather than directly face the issue of defining manipulative conduct,[32] the Court held that "[w]ithout misrepresentation or nondisclosure section 14(e) has not been violated."[33]

The Supreme Court has held that there is no private remedy in the hands of a competing tender offeror.[37] However, most lower courts have recognized a

---

4. Wardrop v. Amway Asia Pacific Ltd., 2001 WL 274067, [2000–2001 Transfer Binder] Fed. Sec. L. Rep. (CCH) ¶ 91,346 (S.D.N.Y. 2001), relying on Santa Fe Industries, Inc. v. Green, 430 U.S. 462, 97 S.Ct. 1292, 51 L.Ed.2d 480 (1977) (the federal securities laws were not designed to regulate fairness; the focus is on disclosure). *See* § 12.20 *infra.*

5. Macfadden Holdings, Inc. v. JB Acquisition Corp., 802 F.2d 62, 71 (2d Cir.1986), relying on Data Probe Acquisition Corp. v. Datatab, Inc., 722 F.2d 1, 5 (2d Cir.1983), *cert. denied,* 465 U.S. 1052, 104 S.Ct. 1326, 79 L.Ed.2d 722 (1984).

6. Diamond v. Arend, 649 F.Supp. 408, 415–16 (S.D.N.Y.1986).

24. 17 C.F.R. § 240.10b–5. *See* § 12.8 *supra.*

25. 15 U.S.C.A. § 77q(a). *See* § 7.11 *supra.*

26. 15 U.S.C.A. § 78n(a)(9). *See* §§ 10.3–10.4 *supra.*

27. *E.g.,* Aaron v. SEC, 446 U.S. 680, 100 S.Ct. 1945, 64 L.Ed.2d 611 (1980) (section 17(a)(2),(3) of the 1933 Act does not require a showing of scienter). *See* § 12.8 *infra.*

29. Clearfield Bank & Trust v. Omega Financial Corp., 65 F.Supp.2d 325, 342–344 (W.D.Pa. 1999) (and authorities cited therein). *See* § 11.10 *infra.*

30. 472 U.S. 1, 105 S.Ct. 2458, 86 L.Ed.2d 1 (1985).

31. Burlington Northern had made a hostile tender offer to purchase 25.1 million shares of El Paso Gas for $24 per share. After negotiations with El Paso management, the original offer was withdrawn, El Paso management was given "golden parachute" severance payments, and a new tender offer was made for 21 million shares from the public and 4.1 million shares from El Paso at $24 per share. It was claimed that a combination of El Paso management's golden parachutes and a decision to reduce the size of the offer to the public in order to infuse more cash into El Paso (presumably to pay for the golden parachutes) artificially affected the price of the El Paso stock and thus constituted manipulation.

See also, e.g., Sullivan & Long v. Scattered Corp., 47 F.3d 857, 864 (7th Cir.1995) (section 14(e) is violated only by deceptive conduct).

32. *See* discussion in § 11.11 *infra.*

33. 472 U.S. at 12, 105 S.Ct. at 2465, 86 L.Ed.2d at 10.

37. Piper v. Chris–Craft Industries, Inc., 430 U.S. 1, 97 S.Ct. 926, 51 L.Ed.2d 124 (1977). The Court held that recognized principles of implying federal rights of action did not warrant the remedy sought by the *Piper* plaintiff. *Id.* at 33, 97 S.Ct. at 944.

remedy in the hands of the target company or one of its shareholders,[38] as well as the right of a competing tender offeror to seek injunctive relief.[39] The question of the availability of private remedies under the Williams Act is taken up in detail in a subsequent section of this treatise.[40]

§ 11.6[2]　Regulation 14 and Other Tender Offer Regulations

§ 11.6[2][A]　Duration of Tender Offer

Rule 14e–1[42] requires that any person making a tender offer hold the offer open for at least twenty business days from the date upon which it is first published. The twenty-day waiting period formerly did not apply, however, where the tender offer was by the issuer and was not made in anticipation of, or in response to, another person's takeover attempt.[43] As a result of amendments that became effective on March 1, 1986, Rule 14e–1's time periods apply to all issuer self-tenders.[44] Once the period during which a tender offer closes, the tender offeror now has the option of extending the offering period from between three and twenty business days for those shareholders of the target company who did not tender their shares during the tender offer.[45] However, shareholders who tender during this optional post tender offer period do not have withdrawal rights.[46] In 1991, the Commission amended Rule 14e–1 to provide for a sixty-calendar day (instead of twenty business day) period during which a tender offer is part of a roll-up transaction.[47]

Rule 14e–1(b) further provides that the tender offeror may not increase or decrease the terms of the offer, the type of consideration, or the dealer's soliciting fee unless the tender offer remains open for at least ten business days from the publication of the notice of such increase.[48] It is also declared to be an unlawful practice for a tender offeror to fail to pay the consideration offered or return the securities tendered promptly after either the withdrawal or termination of the tender offer.[49] Rule 14e–1(d)[50] makes it unlawful to extend the length of the tender offer without issuing a notice of such extension by press release or other public announcement, and a notice must give sufficient detail of the time period of the tender offer and its extension.

---

38. *See, e.g.,* Seaboard World Airlines, Inc. v. Tiger International, Inc., 600 F.2d 355 (2d Cir.1979) (recognizing the 14(e) remedy but finding no substantive violation).

39. *See, e.g.,* Humana, Inc. v. American Medicorp, Inc., 445 F.Supp. 613 (S.D.N.Y.1977). *Cf.* Rondeau v. Mosinee Paper Corp., 422 U.S. 49, 95 S.Ct. 2069, 45 L.Ed.2d 12 (1975).

40. *See* §§ 11.9, 11.10 *infra.*

42. 17 C.F.R. § 240.14e–1(a).

43. 17 C.F.R. § 240.14e–1 (1985).

44. *See* Sec. Exch. Act Rel. No. 34–22788 (Jan. 14, 1986). These amendments were part of a more generalized scheme to subject issuer self-tenders to the same requirements as third-party tender offers. *See* § 11.8 *infra.*

45. Rule 14d–11, 17 C.F.R. § 240.14d–11. *See* Regulation of Takeovers and Security Holder Communications, Exch. Act Rel. No. 34–42055, 1999 WL 969596 (SEC Oct. 22, 1999).

46. Rule 14d–11, 17 C.F.R. § 240.14d–11. In contrast shareholders who tender their shares during the pendency of a tender offer may withdraw their shares prior to the closing of the tender offer.

47. A roll-up transaction is defined in Item 901(c) of Regulation S–K as any transaction involving the reorganization of one or more partnerships into another entity.

48. 17 C.F.R. § 240.14e–1(b). *See also* 17 C.F.R. § 240.13e–4(f)(1)(ii) (imposing the same requirement for tender offers by issuers).

49. 17 C.F.R. § 240.14e–1(c).

50. 17 C.F.R. § 240.14e–1(d).

Prior to 1999, there was uneven treatment for exchange offers as compared with cash tender offers. This was because, in an exchange offer, there is a twenty-day waiting period from the filing of the 1933 Act registration statement until the effective date of the registration statement.[51] Under the 1933 Act, sales cannot be made until after the effective date; section 5(a)(1) of the 1933 Act[52] could be violated if tenders were solicited prior to the effective date of an exchange offer. This resulted in a disparity of treatment since with a cash tender offer, Exchange Act Rule 14e–1(a)'s twenty business day period begins to run from the filing of the tender offer. However, an exchange offer requires a 1933 Act filing as well, which generally takes considerably more time to prepare than the Schedule TO that must be filed under the 1934 Act. Under the tender offer rules as amended in 1999, an exchange offer can commence on the date that the 1933 Act registration statement is filed with the SEC.[53]

The *Schreiber* decision,[54] discussed above, requires deception as an element of any section 14(e) violation. To the extent that the reasoning carries over to the SEC rulemaking power, that decisions casts a cloud over the validity of Rule 14e–1 because the rule regulates the duration of the offer and thus goes beyond mandating full disclosure.[55] For example, what is it about a tender offer that remains open for only nineteen business days that makes it more deceptive than one which is open for the twenty business day period mandated by Rule 14e–1? It can, of course, be argued that the SEC's power to mandate a period during which the tender offer must remain open is justified, since it gives investors and the market the time necessary to digest the information mandated by the Williams Act's affirmative disclosure requirements.[56]

§ 11.6[2][B] Target Company's Management Response to a Third–Party Tender Offer

Whenever a tender offer is made for a target company's shares, the target company has ten business days from the first date upon which the tender offer is published to respond.[57] Rule 14e–2[58] requires that the target company's management make one of the following responses within the ten-day period: (1) a recommendation of acceptance or rejection of the tender offer; (2) an expression of no opinion with a decision to remain neutral towards the offer; or (3) that it is not able to take a position with respect to bidder's offer. The Rule 14e–2 statement must also include all reasons for the position taken, or the stance of neutrality, as well as any explanation of the inability to take a position. In setting forth its reasons, the target company's management is, of

51. *See* 1933 Act § 8(a), 15 U.S.C.A. § 77h(a). The 1933 Act registration requirements are discussed in chapter 2 *supra*.

52. 15 U.S.C.A. § 77e(a)(1).

53. *See* Regulation of Takeovers and Security Holder Communications, Exch. Act Rel. No. 34–42055, 1999 WL 969596 (SEC Oct. 22, 1999).

54. Schreiber v. Burlington Northern, Inc., 472 U.S. 1, 105 S.Ct. 2458, 86 L.Ed.2d 1 (1985).

55. *But see* Polaroid Corp. v. Disney, 862 F.2d 987 (3d Cir.1988), which upheld the SEC's "all holders" rule (Rule 14d–10, 17 C.F.R. § 240.14d–10), reasoning that requiring the offer be made to all shareholders furthers the disclosure goals of the Williams Act.

56. *Cf.* Polaroid Corp. v. Disney, 862 F.2d 987 (3d Cir.1988).

57. 17 C.F.R. § 240.14e–2.

58. *Id.*

course, subject to all of the rules concerning materiality as well as the potential civil and criminal liabilities for material misstatements.

§ 11.6[2][C] Insider Trading Prohibited

Rule 14e–3[62] prohibits insider trading during a tender offer.[63] The Rule 14e–3 prohibitions expressly apply not only to insiders of the target company but also to anyone else:

> who is in possession of material information relating to such tender offer which information he knows or has reason to know is nonpublic and which he knows or has reason to know has been acquired directly or indirectly from (1) the offering person, (2) the issuer of the securities sought or to be sought by such tender offer, or (3) any officer, director, partner or employee or any other person acting on behalf of the offering person or such issuer....[64]

The rule goes on to state that there is no violation if the transaction was an independent investment decision rather than based on knowledge of material non-public information. Rule 14e–3 supplements the insider trading prohibitions that are found in Rule 10b–5,[65] as well as in the insider trading legislation enacted by Congress in 1984 and in 1988.[66]

It has been held that Rule 14e–3 will support a private remedy in the hands of the target company.[67] A preliminary injunction was issued against a tender offer where the tender offer was based upon the alleged misappropriation of information by a former target company officer.[68] The Ninth Circuit held that a private remedy seeking disgorgement of illegal profits made in violation of Rule 14e–3 can be brought only by contemporaneous traders[69] as provided in section 20A's remedy for insider trading.[70] A number of courts, including the Supreme Court, have upheld the validity of Rule 14e–3.[71]

§ 11.6[2][D] Prohibition of Contemporary Purchases During Tender Offer

Rule 14e–5 prohibits tender offerors from purchasing shares subject to a tender offer and related securities[72] during the term of a tender offer.[73] As

---

62. 17 C.F.R. § 240.14e–3.

63. *See* § 12.17 *infra* for a discussion of insider trading generally. *See also* chapter 13 *infra* for treatment of the Act's short-swing profit provisions.

64. 17 C.F.R. § 240.14e–3(b). Rule 14e–3 was promulgated to fill a gap in the law created by the Supreme Court in Chiarella v. United States, 445 U.S. 222, 100 S.Ct. 1108, 63 L.Ed.2d 348 (1980). *See* § 12.17 *infra*.

65. 17 C.F.R. § 240.10b–5.

66. The Insider Trading Sanctions Act of 1984 (ITSA), among other things, allows the SEC to recoup three times the insider's profits. *See* § 12.17 *infra*. The Insider Trading and Securities Fraud Enforcement Act of 1988 is discussed in § 12.17 *infra*.

67. Burlington Industries, Inc. v. Edelman, 1987 WL 91498, [1987 Transfer Binder] Fed.Sec. L.Rep. (CCH) ¶ 93,339 (4th Cir.1987), *affirming on the opinion below* 666 F.Supp. 799 (M.D.N.C. 1987).

68. Private remedies under section 14(e) are discussed in § 11.10 *infra*.

69. Brody v. Transitional Hospitals Corp., 280 F.3d 997 (9th Cir.2002).

70. 15 U.S.C.A. § 78t–1(a). *See* § 12.17[7][B] *infra*.

71. *E.g.,* United States v. O'Hagan, 521 U.S. 642, 117 S.Ct. 2199, 138 L.Ed.2d 724 (1997).

72. *See, e.g.,* Pearson PLC, [2000–2001 Transfer Binder] Fed. Sec. L. Rep. (CCH) ¶ 78,019 (SEC No Action Letter Aug. 3, 2000) (treating stock options as related securities for Rule 14e–5 purposes).

73. 17 C.F.R. § 240.14e–5.

discussed in a previous section of this treatise,[74] the tender offer commences once the Schedule TO is filed with the SEC[75] Rule 14e–5's prohibition against trading along side of a tender offers depends upon the existence of a tender offer.[76] On appropriate facts, the Commission has been willing to recognize exemptions from 14e–5's prohibitions on purchases outside of the tender offer.[77] It has been held that violations of Rule 14e–5's predecessor supported a private damage action,[79] but not all courts seem to agree that such a private remedy exists.[80]

Rule 14e–5 prohibits not only purchases of the securities subject to a tender offer, but also of any securities immediately convertible into such security. In contrast, the purchase of an option or security futures product is allowed, since it is not immediately convertible into the underlying security.[86] However, if the futures contract expires before the termination of the tender offer then the purchase of a security futures product will be precluded under Rule 14e–5.[87]

§ 11.6[2][E] Short Tendering and Hedged Tendering Prohibited

Short tendering of securities during a tender offer is the practice of tendering or guaranteeing securities not owned by the person making the tender or guarantee.[88] Rule 14e–4 prohibits short tendering.[90] The SEC amended Rule 14e–4's predecessor to not only outlaw short tendering but also to prohibit "hedged tendering" by market professionals in tender offers for less than all of the target company's outstanding stock.[91]

The prohibition against short tendering means that during a tender offer, it is illegal to tender shares that you do not own. Thus, it is necessary that anyone tendering shares during a tender offer either actually be the owner or be a bona fide beneficial owner of the shares being tendered. Hedged tender-

---

74. *See* § 11.5[2] *supra*.

75. *See, e.g.,* Lerro v. Quaker Oats Co., 84 F.3d 239 (7th Cir.1996).

76. Simon DeBartolo Group, L.P. v. Richard E. Jacobs Group, Inc., 186 F.3d 157, 175 (2d Cir.1999) (no tender offer where the proposal did not include the acquisition of an equity interest; hence Rule 10b–13 did not apply).

77. *E.g.,* Pearson PLC, [2000–2001 Transfer Binder] Fed. Sec. L. Rep. (CCH) ¶ 78,019 (SEC No Action Letter Aug. 3, 2000) (exemption for purchases of stock options during tender offer for common stock where optionholders who were not eligible for the tender offer would receive consideration comparable to that offered for the common stock under the tender offer).

79. City National Bank v. American Commonwealth Financial Corp., 801 F.2d 714 (4th Cir.1986), *cert. denied* 479 U.S. 1091, 107 S.Ct. 1301, 94 L.Ed.2d 157 (1987).

80. *See, e.g.,* Beaumont v. American Can Co., 797 F.2d 79 (2d Cir.1986) (questioning the existence of a private remedy).

86. *See* In re Commission Guidance on Application of Certain Provisions of Securities Act of 1933, Securities Act of 1934, Rules Thereunder to Trading in Security Futures Products, Sec. Act Rel. No. 33–8107, Sec. Exch. Act Rel. No. 34–46101, 2002 WL 1357820 (SEC June 21, 2002).

87. *Id.*

88. *See* Merrill Lynch, Pierce, Fenner & Smith, Inc. v. Bobker, 636 F.Supp. 444 (S.D.N.Y. 1986), *reversed* 808 F.2d 930 (2d Cir.1986) (denying proration to shareholder who sold short while tendering).

90. 17 C.F.R. § 240.14e–4.

91. *See* 16 Sec.Reg. & L.Rep. (BNA) 575–576 (March 30, 1984) (amending former Rule 10b–4, 17 C.F.R. § 240.10b–4). In 1989, the SEC asked for comment on the deregulation of hedged tendering. Sec.Exch.Act Rel. No. 34–26609, [1989 Transfer Binder] Fed.Sec.L.Rep. (CCH) ¶ 84,401 (March 8, 1989).

ing consists of tendering shares that are encumbered by a call option or some other obligation to sell the shares to someone other than the tender offeror. The prohibitions against short tendering and hedged tendering are designed to eliminate related manipulative practices in connection with a tender offer.

Hedged tendering occurs when market professionals sell on the open market that portion of their target company holdings that they estimate will not be accepted by the tender offeror. Rule 14e–4 is designed to prevent tendering shares that are not actually owned. Where a shareholder responded to a tender offer for less than all of the target's shares by tendering his entire holdings coupled with a short sale, the rule was not violated.[92] The court reasoned that since he tendered only his actual holdings, the tendering shareholder did not improve his proration position, but rather was taking "a separate gamble" that the stock price would decline after the proration date.[93] Also, it has been held that, at least where shareholders could not allege that their offers of tender were diluted, there is no implied private remedy for short tenders in violation of Rule 14e–4.[94] Security futures products will be counted in someone's long position for purposes of Rule 14e–4 only upon the contract settlement, when the futures product ceases trading and the owner in essence owns the underlying security.[95]

§ 11.6[2][F] Two–Tiered Tender Offers Permitted

Sometimes a tender offer decides to make a tender offer for control of a company and then follows the tender offer by a merger of the target company into the acquiring company at a price below that which was paid in the tender offer. This is commonly referred to as a two-tiered front-end loaded offer. There is nothing under federal law to prohibit such offers so long as the first step adequately discloses any plans for a second step merger. In contrast, a number of states have adopted fair price statutes that place insurmountable barriers on these front-end loaded offers.[96] The SEC, for some time, has been considering taking action that would curtail suspected unfairness and abuses in connection with the pricing of two-step or two-tiered tender offers.[97] Such substantive limitations on the scope and terms of tender offers would be difficult to support under section 14(e) in light of the *Schreiber* decision. However, section 14(d) might support some limitations.[98]

§ 11.6[2][G] Exemption for Closed–End Investment Companies

SEC Rule 14e–6[99] provides an exemption for closed-end registered investment companies.[100] A closed-end investment company repurchases its own

---

92. Merrill Lynch, Pierce, Fenner & Smith, Inc. v. Bobker, 808 F.2d 930 (2d Cir.1986).

93. *Id.* at 935.

94. John Olagues Trading Co. v. First Options of Chicago, Inc., 588 F.Supp. 1194 (N.D.Ill. 1984).

95. *See* In re Commission Guidance on Application of Certain Provisions of Securities Act of 1933, Securities Act of 1934, Rules Thereunder to Trading in Security Futures Products, Sec. Act Rel. No. 33–8107, Sec. Exch. Act Rel. No. 34–46101, 2002 WL 1357820 (SEC June 27, 2002).

96. *See* the discussion in § 11.4 *infra.*

97. Sec.Exch. Act Rel. No. 34–21079 (June 21, 1984).

98. 15 U.S.C.A. § 78n(d)(1), which empowers the Commission to require "such additional information as the Commission may by rules and regulations [prescribe] as necessary or appropriate in the public interest or for the protection of investors." *See* § 11.5 *supra.*

99. 17 C.F.R. § 240.14e–6.

100. Investment company regulation is discussed in chapter 20 *infra.*

shares from investors wanting to sell their investment company shares. This option ordinarily is constantly open to closed-end company shareholders. In order to avoid unnecessary entanglement with the tender offer laws, Rule 14e–6 exempts most closed-end investment companies from the requirements of Rules 14e–2 and 14e–3.[101]

§ 11.6[2][H] Roll–Up Transactions

SEC Rule 14e–7 imposes special rules for tender offers in connection with roll-up transactions.[102] This was promulgated in response to section 14(h) of the Exchange Act.[103]

§ 11.6[2][I] Prohibition Against False Statements of Intent to Make Tender Offer

SEC Rule 14e–8 prohibits anyone from announcing a planned tender offer if the tender offeror does not have the intention to announce and complete the offer within a reasonable time.[104] This rule was adopted in 1999 when the SEC eliminated its gun jumping provisions prior to the commencement of a tender offer.[105] Rule 14e–8 does not require the tender offeror to have financing in place, but the would-be tender offeror's ability to finance the proposed tender offer will be considered in determining whether any pre-tender announcement is in compliance with the rule.[106]

§ 11.6[2][J] Target's Defensive Tactics Not Prohibited

As discussed in a later section of this treatise,[107] frequently management will want to oppose a third-party tender offer and will do so by engaging in defensive tactics. State law may place significant restrictions on the target company's management's ability to fend off a hostile offer. For a while, there was some question as to whether federal law would have an impact in curtailing these defensive tactics. It is now clear that this is entirely within the purview of state law. A significant judicial development under section 14(e) was the Sixth Circuit's ruling that a defensive lock-up arrangement may be struck down as a manipulative arrangement.[108] This controversially expansive holding had the potential of opening new frontiers for the federal regulation of tender offers, although it represented a minority view.[109] The

---

101. 17 C.F.R. §§ 240.14e–1, 240.14e–2.

102. 17 C.F.R. § 240.14e–7.

103. 15 U.S.C.A. § 78n(h).

104. 17 C.F.R. § 240.14e–8.

105. *See* Regulation of Takeovers and Security Holder Communications Exch. Act Rel. No. 34–42055, 1999 WL 969596 (SEC Oct. 22, 1999). *See also, e.g.,* § 11.5 *supra.*

106. *See* Regulation of Takeovers and Security Holder Communications Exch. Act Rel. No. 34–42055, 1999 WL 969596 (SEC Oct. 22, 1999).

107. *See* § 11.4 *infra.*

108. Mobil Corp. v. Marathon Oil Co., 669 F.2d 366 (6th Cir.1981). *See, e.g.,* Elliot J. Weiss, Defensive Responses to Tender Offers and the Williams Act's Prohibition Against Manipulation, 35 Vand.L.Rev. 1087 (1982).

109. *See, e.g.,* Radol v. Thomas, 772 F.2d 244 (6th Cir.1985), *cert. denied,* 475 U.S. 1086, 106 S.Ct. 1469, 89 L.Ed.2d 724 (1986) (two-tiered, front-end loaded tender offer is not manipulative under either the Williams Act or Rule 10b–5); Gearhart Industries, Inc. v. Smith International, Inc., 741 F.2d 707 (5th Cir.1984) (poison pill in the form of "springing warrants" that gave

Schreiber decision[110] now makes it clear that defensive tactics cannot violate section 14(e), even if manipulative, unless there has been a material misrepresentation or omission.

§ 11.7   Arrangements Affecting Director Turnover in Connection With a Tender Offer—Section 14(f)

As is the case with any transfer of corporate control, tender offers will frequently result in a shift in corporate management. Accordingly, it is not uncommon to find tender offers containing agreements relating to management turnover and the election of new directors. These control transfers can raise problems under state law relating to invalid control premiums and other breaches of fiduciary duty. The Williams Act superimposes certain disclosure obligations. Under section 14(f) of the Exchange Act,[3] when a tender offer for equity securities subject to the Act's reporting requirements contains agreements concerning the designation of new directors otherwise than through a formal vote at a meeting of securities holders, there must be full disclosure. Contemplated management turnover, including any arrangement regarding the make-up of the majority of directors, also must be disclosed.[4] Thus, for example, where a stock purchase agreement permits the purchaser to designate a majority of the issuer's directors, section 14(f)'s disclosure obligation is triggered.[5] When the agreed-upon shift in control occurs, a second filing obligation arises.[6]

§ 11.8   Issuer Purchases of Its Own Stock—Section 13(e) and the Going Private Rule; Issuer Self–Tender Offers

§ 11.8[1]   Issuer's Share Repurchases

§ 11.8[1][A]   Issuer Share Repurchases in Response to Someone Else's Tender Offer

Rule 13e–1[7] applies to an issuer's purchases of its own stock after a third party has filed a tender offer for its securities. An issuer of securities subject to the Exchange Act's registration and reporting requirements may not purchase its own securities once a third party tender offer has been made unless the issuer files with the Commission eight copies of a statement containing the following information: (1) a description of the securities to be purchased; (2) the names and classes of persons from whom the securities are

---

holders right to purchase shares at low price in the event of a takeover was not manipulative under section 14(e)); Feldbaum v. Avon Products, Inc., 741 F.2d 234 (8th Cir.1984) (lock-up option was not manipulative and could not give rise to section 14(e) claims in the absence of materially distorted disclosures); Schreiber v. Burlington Northern, Inc. 731 F.2d 163 (3d Cir.1984), *affirmed* 472 U.S. 1, 105 S.Ct. 2458, 86 L.Ed.2d 1 (1985).

110. Schreiber v. Burlington Northern, Inc., 472 U.S. 1, 105 S.Ct. 2458, 86 L.Ed.2d 1 (1985). *See, e.g.,* Norman S. Poser, Stock Market Manipulation and Corporate Control Transactions, 40 U.Miami L.Rev. 671 (1986).

§ 11.7

3. 15 U.S.C.A. § 78n(f).

4. 15 U.S.C.A. § 78n(f). *See* 17 C.F.R. § 240.14f–1.

5. Drobbin v. Nicolet Instrument Corp., 631 F.Supp. 860 (S.D.N.Y.1986).

6. *Id.*

§ 11.8

7. 17 C.F.R. § 240.13e–1.

to be purchased; (3) the purposes for which they are being purchased; and (4) the source of all funds used to finance the purchases.[8] This filing is supplemented by Schedule 14D–9[9] which requires a statement to be filed by an issuer making a solicitation or recommendation to security holders to accept or reject the tender offer and Rule 14e–2's[10] provisions requiring the issuer to send to the security holders a statement recommending acceptance or rejection of the tender offer or expressing no opinion toward it. Issuer purchase of its own shares is just one of the possible responses to a tender offer.[11] An issuer's filings under Rule 13e–1 with regard to defensive share repurchases do not alleviate the need for making filings under Rule 13e–3 or Rule 13e–4 if the transaction is likely to result in the cessation of 1934 Act reporting obligations or constitute a tender offer.[12]

§ 11.8[1][B] Manipulation in Connection With Issuer Repurchases

Purchases by an issuer or affiliate of its own securities, if not properly handled, can raise questions of manipulation.[13] Rule 14e–5[14] prohibits purchases by persons making a tender offer other than pursuant to the terms of the tender offer.

Rule 10b–18 provides a safe harbor from the antimanipulation rules for qualifying purchases by the issuer and affiliates.[20] Purchases pursuant to issuer purchases or tender offers governed by either Rule 13e–1 or 13e–4 are excluded from Rule 10b–18's safe harbor.[21] There also are exclusions from the safe harbor for merger-related transactions. Among other things, Rule 10b–18's safe harbor depends upon both the trading volume and the price at which the issuer's bids are placed.[23]

Rule 10b–18 covers purchases by an issuer, or affiliated purchaser of an issuer,[29] of the issuer's common stock.[30] The applicability of the safe harbor is computed on the basis of all open market repurchases of an issuer's common stock computed on a daily basis based on the volume during the four previous weeks. Certain enumerated transactions are not considered to be Rule 10b–18

---

8. *Id.*

9. 17 C.F.R. § 240.14d–101. *See* § 11.5 *supra.*

10. 17 C.F.R. § 240.14e–2. *See* § 11.6 *supra.*

11. Defensive tactics are discussed in § 11.11 *infra.*

12. Maynard Oil Co. v. Deltec Panamerica S.A., 630 F.Supp. 502 (S.D.N.Y.1985).

13. Sections 9 and 10 of the Exchange Act prohibit manipulation. 15 U.S.C.A. §§ 78i, 78j.

14. 17 C.F.R. § 240.14e–5. *See* 11.6[2][D] *supra.*

20. 17 C.F.R. § 240.10b–18. *See* § 12.1 *infra.*

21. 17 C.F.R. § 240.10b–18(a)(3).

23. The rule is quite complex. 17 C.F.R. § 10b–18. *See* Sec.Exch.Act Rel. No. 34–17222 (Nov. 4, 1980). The volume computation is made on a daily basis. *See, e.g.,* Answers to Frequently Asked Questions Concerning Rule 10b–18 ("Safe Harbor" for Issuer Repurchases), answer to question 5, *http://www.sec.gov/divisions/marketreg/r10b18faq0504.htm* (SEC 2004).

29. Affiliated purchaser includes anyone acting in concert with an issuer to effect such a purchase as well as an affiliate who directly or indirectly controls the issuer's purchases or whose purchases are directly or indirectly controlled by the issuer. 17 C.F.R. § 240.10b–18(a)(2). It is further provided, however, officers and directors who have participated in the decision to undertake a Rule 10b–18 purchase are not for that reason alone affiliated purchasers. *Id.* Similarly, broker-dealers executing Rule 10b–18 purchases on the issuer's behalf are not affiliated purchasers. *Id.*

30. 17 C.F.R. § 240.10b–18.

purchases and thus are not subject to the rule's limitations.[34] The rule then goes on to set out the rather elaborate conditions for Rule 10b–18 purchases that are not deemed to be in violation of the anti-manipulation rules.[35] As is the case with any safe harbor, failure to satisfy Rule 10b–18's conditions does not raise a presumption that the purchases were made in violation of the anti-manipulation rules.[36] Also, it must be remembered that as a safe harbor, failure to comply with each of Rule 10b–18's requirements with respect to any one purchase may disqualify other purchases from the safe harbor's protection.[37]

Rule 10b–18, as amended, requires companies to make disclosures in their quarterly and annual reports that will list all repurchases of their equity securities. This disclosure obligation exists with respect to repurchases in open market transactions as well as to privately negotiated purchases. However, privately negotiated purchases are not subject to Rule 10b–18's more substantive provisions.[39] Disclosure is required irrespective of whether the repurchases were made pursuant to Rule 10b–18's safe harbor. Rule 10b–18 is only a safe harbor from manipulation charges and compliance with the rule does not insulate the company from exposure for other securities law violations in connection with the repurchase of shares.[40]

§ 11.8[2] The Going Private Rule

In its so-called "going private" rules, the Commission regulates an issuer's purchases of its own shares outside of the contested tender offer milieu. The SEC's going private rules supplement the state law remedies that exist for breaches of fiduciary duties in connection with freeze-out and going private transactions.

§ 11.8[2][A] Rule 13e–3 Filings

Rule 13e–3,[45] which applies primarily to issuers subject to section 12's registration requirements,[46] defines the types of transactions covered. A Rule 13e–3 transaction is one of a series of transactions that involves either (1) the purchase or tender offer by an issuer or its affiliates of any equity security subject to the Act's reporting requirements, or (2) a proxy solicitation subject to Regulation 14A,[47] or a distribution of information subject to Regulation 14C,[48] to the holders of equity securities subject to the Act's reporting requirements that is sent out by the issuer or affiliate in connection with a merger, consolidation, reclassification, recapitalization, reverse stock split, or

---

34.   17 C.F.R. § 240.10b–18(a)(3).

35.   17 C.F.R. § 240.10b–18(b).

36.   17 C.F.R. § 240.10b–18(c).

37.   *See, e.g.,* Answers to Frequently Asked Questions Concerning Rule 10b–18 ("Safe Harbor" for Issuer Repurchases), answer to question 5, *http://www.sec.gov/divisions/marketreg/r10b18faq0504.htm* (SEC 2004).

39.   *See, e.g.,* Answers to Frequently Asked Questions Concerning Rule 10b–18 ("Safe Harbor" for Issuer Repurchases), answer to question 8, *http://www.sec.gov/divisions/marketreg/r10b18faq0504.htm* (SEC 2004).

40.   *Id.*

45.   17 C.F.R. § 240.13e–3.

46.   There is limited application to section 15(d) reporting companies.

47.   17 C.F.R. §§ 240.14a–1–14a–103. *See* §§ 10.1–10.2 *supra.*

48.   17 C.F.R. §§ 240.14c–1–14c–101. *See* § 10.9 *supra.*

similar transaction. Any of the foregoing Rule 13e–3 transactions are covered by the Schedule 13E–3 disclosure and filing requirements if the effect of the transaction or transactions is the cessation of the reporting obligations under the Exchange Act. A difficult problem is judging the point at which the issuer should be able to predict a reasonable likelihood of such a result.[49] It is not always easy to determine at what point a transaction or series of transactions is likely to result in the issuer having fewer than three hundred shareholders. It has been held that an open market purchase program in response to a hostile takeover did not trigger Rule 13e–3's filing requirements because crossing the three hundred shareholder threshold was primarily dependent upon the success of plaintiff's hostile tender offer.[50] The going private rules require that the issuer must file a Schedule 13E–3,[51] which requires disclosures similar to those required under Schedule 13D[52] and Schedule TO.[53]

§ 11.8[2][C] Can the SEC Require Substantive Fairness?

Prior to the Supreme Court decision in Santa Fe Industries, Inc. v. Green,[84] the Commission proposed a series of going private rules, one of which would have given the SEC power to prohibit such transactions merely on the basis of unfairness to the shareholders.[85] Although it would appear that the *Santa Fe* decision precludes scrutiny of transactional fairness,[86] the SEC continued to take the position that it has the power to regulate the fairness of going private transactions.[87] In 1977, the Commission included the fairness requirement in its post-*Santa Fe* version of its going private rules. However, when the going private rules were adopted, and as currently enforced, the SEC deleted the fairness requirement, noting that it "believes the question of regulation should be deferred until there is an opportunity to determine the efficacy of [the rules as adopted]."[88]

§ 11.8[3] Issuer Self–Tender Offers

Issuers on occasion will make a tender offer for their own shares. These are commonly known as issuer self-tender offers. Third party tender offers most frequently arise in the context of an attempt to gain control of the target company. In contrast, issuer self-tender offers are frequently used for other reasons as well. For example, issuers may want to offer its shareholders the convenience and savings of being able to sell back to the corporation odd-lot shareholdings.[90]

---

49. *See* Sec.Exch.Act Rel. No. 34–16075 (Aug. 2, 1979).

50. Maynard Oil Co. v. Deltec Panamerica S.A., 630 F.Supp. 502 (S.D.N.Y.1985).

51. 17 C.F.R. § 240.13e–100.

52. 17 C.F.R. § 240.13d–101. *See* § 11.2 *supra*.

53. 17 C.F.R. § 240.14d–100. *See* § 11.5 *supra*.

84. 430 U.S. 462, 97 S.Ct. 1292, 51 L.Ed.2d 480 (1977). *See* § 12.20 *infra*.

85. Sec.Act Rel. No. 33–5567 (Feb. 6, 1975).

86. 430 U.S. at 474–77, 97 S.Ct. at 1301–03.

87. *See, e.g.,* Sec.Act. Rel. No. 33–5884 (Nov. 17, 1977).

88. Sec.Act. Rel.No. 33–6100 (Aug. 2, 1979).

90. In 1996, the SEC relaxed some of its rules relating to such odd-lot tender offers. *See* Odd-Lot Tender Offers by Issuers, Sec. Exch. Act Rel. No. 34–38068, 1996 SEC LEXIS 3452 (SEC Dec. 20, 1996).

Rule 13e–4[91] sets out the filing and disclosure requirements for tender offers by a reporting company for its own shares. Schedule 13E–4's[92] disclosure requirements are the same as those which apply to third party tender offers.[93] Thus, issuer self-tender offers that are covered by Rule 13e–4[94] are subject to the same rules that apply to third parties under Regulations 14D[95] and 14E.[96] The issuer making a self-tender offer must file a Schedule TO.[97]

The filing requirements and other rules set forth in SEC Rule 13e–4 apply to defensive tender offers, as well as to other issuer tender offers. A target company that responds with a self-tender without responding to the third-party offer in good faith may run afoul of state law, and the self-tender may be enjoined.[99]

§ 11.9 Private Remedies Under the Williams Act—Remedies for Violations of Sections 13(d), 13(e), 14(d)

Sections 13(d),[1] 13(e),[2] and 14(d)[3] of the Securities Exchange Act create various obligations in connection with covered corporate control transactions. This section addresses the extent to which they can support an implied private right of action. Most of the litigation concerning the question of the existence of implied private rights of action under the Williams Act has arisen in the context of section 14(e)'s general antifraud proscriptions.[4] The courts seem to be consistent in favoring the existence of at least a limited implied remedy under section 14(e), at least when the suit is brought by a target company shareholder in furtherance of the interests of target company shareholders generally.[5] However, that remedy, as is the case with any remedy that would exist under sections 13(d), 13(e), and 14(d), must be considered more questionable in light of the decline in federal implied remedies generally.[6]

Since sections 13(d), 13(e), and 14(d) all apply to issuers subject to the Exchange Act's registration and reporting requirements,[7] and involve mandatory filings with the Commission, there are a number of other remedies for material misstatements. For example, any investor who is injured by reliance

---

91. 17 C.F.R. § 240.13e–4.

92. 17 C.F.R. § 240.13e–101.

93. *See* § 11.5 *supra.*

94. 17 C.F.R. § 240.13e–4.

95. 17 C.F.R. §§ 240.14d–1–14d–101.

96. 17 C.F.R. §§ 240.14e–1–14e–3.

97. 17 C.F.R. § 240.14d–100.

99. Plaza Securities Co. v. Fruehauf Corp., 643 F.Supp. 1535 (E.D.Mich.1986) (Michigan law); AC Acquisitions Corp. v. Anderson, Clayton & Co., 519 A.2d 103 (Del.Ch.1986) (self-tender was not reasonable nor supportable by the business judgment rule) (opinion withdrawn).

§ 11.9

1. 15 U.S.C.A. § 78m(d). *See* § 11.8 *supra.*

2. 15 U.S.C.A. § 78m(e). *See* § 11.8 *supra.*

3. 15 U.S.C.A. § 78n(d). *See* § 11.5 *supra.*

4. 15 U.S.C.A. § 78n(e). *See* §§ 11.6 *supra,* 11.10 *infra.*

5. *See* § 11.10 *infra. Cf.* Piper v. Chris–Craft Industries, Inc., 430 U.S. 1, 97 S.Ct. 926, 51 L.Ed.2d 124 (1977) (competing tender offeror did not have standing to bring suit under section 14(e)).

6. *See* § 12.2 *infra. See* § 1.8 *supra* for an overview of the private remedies available under the 1933 and 1934 Acts.

7. 15 U.S.C.A. §§ 78*l,* 78m(a). *See* §§ 9.2, 9.3 *supra.*

upon material misstatements in the Schedule 13D,[8] Schedule 13E–3,[9] Schedule TO[10] (the successor to Schedule 14D–1[11]), or Schedule 14D–9,[12] may sue for damages under the express remedy provided in section 18(a) of the Act.[13] It is to be noted, however, that the section 18(a) remedy is an extremely limited one insofar as it requires the investor to have actually relied upon the documents filed with the Commission.[14] In addition to the express liability provisions of section 18(a), any material misstatements or omissions that give rise to an injury in connection with the purchase or sale of a security will state a cause of action under SEC Rule 10b–5.[15] Furthermore, material misstatements and omissions in documents required by sections 13(d), 13(e), and 14(d) will give rise to the potential for criminal penalties as well as for SEC enforcement actions.[16] These remedial and criminal penalties also apply to failures to file or delays in filing. However, no private remedy would appear to exist under Rule 10b–5 for mere delay.[17] The question of an independent implied remedy under the Williams Act's filing requirements thus becomes significant. The cases are in conflict, but there have been a number of decisions that have held that the relevant provisions of sections 13 and 14 in and of themselves provide a basis for at least limited private relief. One pattern that has been emerging is the availability of injunctive relief[18] as opposed to damages. However, some courts have recognized the availability of an action for damages.[19] In 2002, the Second Circuit ruled that there is no private damage remedy to be implied under section 13(d).[20] At the same time that the court denied the existence of a damage remedy, the court stressed that it continued to adhere to its earlier view that injunctive relief may be had on appropriate facts.

In Rondeau v. Mosinee Paper Corp.,[22] the Supreme Court indicated that a target company may have standing to complain of delays by a purchaser in filing a Schedule 13D where it can show a resultant injury. The Court held that due to the absence of substantial share acquisitions by the purchaser after the date upon which the Schedule 13D was due, the target company had failed to show an injury sufficient to support a cause of action for the

---

8.   17 C.F.R. § 240.13d–101. *See* § 11.5 *supra.*

9.   17 C.F.R. § 240.13e–100. *See* § 11.8 *supra.*

10.   17 C.F.R. § 240.14d–100.

11.   17 C.F.R. § 240.14d–100 (1998). *See* § 11.5 *supra.*

12.   17 C.F.R. § 240.14d–101. *See* § 11.5 *supra.*

13.   15 U.S.C.A. § 78r(a).

14.   *See* § 12.18 *infra* for discussion of the section 18(a) remedy.

15.   17 C.F.R. § 240.10b–5 which is discussed in chapter 12 *infra. See, e.g.,* Gerber v. Computer Associates International, Inc., 860 F.Supp. 27 (S.D.N.Y.1994) (allegedly misleading Schedule 14D–9 can form the basis of a private suit under Rule 10b–5).

16.   15 U.S.C.A. § 78aa.

17.   The only possible way to state a Rule 10b–5 violation would be the claim that a delay in filing constituted a material omission, but this would be an uphill battle. Further, only purchasers and sellers can bring a private suit under Rule 10b–5. Blue Chip Stamps v. Manor Drug Stores, 421 U.S. 723, 95 S.Ct. 1917, 44 L.Ed.2d 539 (1975). *See* § 12.7 *infra.*

18.   *E.g.,* International Broadcasting Corp. v. Turner, 734 F.Supp. 383 (D.Minn.1990) (injunctive relief is available under appropriate circumstances).

19.   *E.g.,* Field v. Trump, 850 F.2d 938 (2d Cir.1988).

20.   Hallwood Realty Partners, L.P. v. Gotham Partners, L.P., 286 F.3d 613 (2d Cir.2002). *Accord, e.g.,* Edelson v. Ch'ien, 2004 WL 422674 (N.D. Ill. 2004).

22.   422 U.S. 49, 95 S.Ct. 2069, 45 L.Ed.2d 12 (1975).

defendant's delay. Following the opening that was left by this Supreme Court decision, many subsequent cases have held that a target company has standing to seek injunctive relief to bar additional purchases until the Schedule 13D has been filed.[23] However, there have also been some decisions to the contrary, holding that no private remedy exists even for injunctive relief.[24] While the shareholders of the target company may be able to bring suit, the shareholders of the acquiring company may not base a claim under section 13(d).[25]

Even in the cases recognizing an implied right to private injunctive relief, not every violation will support such relief. It has been held, for example, that in determining whether to issue a preliminary injunction for violation of section 13(d)'s filing requirements, the court should consider whether there has been injury to the shareholders and the investing public as well as to the target company.[26] Quite properly, the courts are reluctant to interfere with highly contested takeover attempts where any relief will have a substantial impact on the market,[27] but in an appropriate case a preliminary injunction will be issued.[28] Additionally, curative amendments to the Schedule 13D filing will warrant the lifting of any injunctive relief that had previously been granted.[29]

A number of courts have held that not only does a section 13(d) remedy extend to failure to file, but also to filings that contain material misstatements and\or omissions.[30]

Since time is of the essence in takeover battles, frequently the relief sought in an action under 13(d), 13(e), or 14(d) will be one for preliminary injunctive relief. Plaintiffs in such actions bear an especially high burden in light of the dual requirement that they prove both a substantial likelihood of success on the merits and irreparable injury if the preliminary injunction is not issued. Failure to meet either a substantial likelihood of success or irreparable injury will result in a denial of preliminary relief.[34] However, serious violations will warrant preliminary relief, since waiting until a full trial on the merits will usually mean that the challenged transaction will take place years before the case is resolved. As one court has put it, "[e]ffectively the only relief available to an issuer, under the prevailing view, is an order

---

23. *E.g.,* CNW Corp. v. Japonica Partners, L.P., 874 F.2d 193 (3d Cir.1989).

24. *E.g.,* Kalmanovitz v. G. Heileman Brewing Co., 769 F.2d 152 (3d Cir.1985) (competing tender offeror lacked standing for claims under sections 13(e), 14(d), and 14(e)).

25. In re Dow Chemical Securities Bhopal Litigation, 2000 WL 1886612, [2000–2001 Transfer Binder] Fed. Sec. L. Rep. (CCH) ¶ 91,282 (S.D.N.Y. 2000).

26. *See* Mid–Continent Bancshares, Inc. v. O'Brien, 1981 WL 1404, [1982 Transfer Binder] Fed.Sec.L.Rep. (CCH) ¶ 98,734 (E.D.Mo.1981).

27. *See, e.g.,* CNW Corp. v. Japonica Partners, L.P., 776 F.Supp. 864 (D.Del.1990) (preliminary injunction denied due to failure to establish irreparable harm).

28. *See* Life Investors, Inc. v. Ago Holding, N.V., 1981 WL 15483, [1981–1982 Transfer Binder] Fed.Sec.L.Rep. (CCH) ¶ 98,356 (8th Cir.1981) (decided under section 14(d)).

29. Chromalloy American Corp. v. Sun Chemical Corp., 474 F.Supp. 1341 (E.D.Mo.1979).

30. *E.g.,* Indiana National Corp. v. Rich, 712 F.2d 1180 (7th Cir.1983) (injunction action brought by target company).

34. *See, e.g.,* Cardiff Acquisitions, Inc. v. Hatch, 751 F.2d 917 (8th Cir.1984). (section 14(d) claim; although Williams Act may have been violated, district court did not abuse its discretion in denying preliminary injunction).

requiring the five percent owner to file a corrected 13D and perhaps enjoining further acquisitions pending the corrections."[35]

It has been held that a tender offeror has standing to bring an injunction on behalf of the target company's shareholders against the target company management for violations of Rule 13e–4[36] with regard to an issuer's defensive purchases of its shares in response to a tender offer.[37] In contrast, a former president was held not to have standing to sue for damages flowing from alleged 13D violations that resulted in his loss of economic advantage due to a drop in target's stock resulting from a blocking of a proposed sale of the company.[38] This ruling is consistent with the fact that the Williams Act was designed to protect investors, not defeated tender offerors[39] or others who may be adversely affected.

On appropriate facts, some courts have recognized the potential for an implied remedy for damages for violations of section 14(d). Thus, for example, shareholders denied a tender offer premium because of the tender offeror's wrongful interference with their proration rights could recover in an action under section 14(d)(6).[46] The courts have recognized an implied right of action under Rule 14a–10's[47] all holders requirement.[48] Additionally, the Sixth Circuit recognized a private remedy for violation of section 13(e)'s going private provisions which allegedly resulted in the loss of plaintiff's state law appraisal remedy due to material misstatements or omissions.[49] With the foregoing exceptions, the law seems clear that private damage remedies will not be implied solely on the basis of section 13 or 14's filing requirements. To the extent that a plaintiff can establish that the filing contained material misstatements or omissions, then an action may lie either under section 18(a) of the Exchange Act[50] or under SEC Rule 10b–5.[51]

§ 11.10 Private Remedies Under the Williams Act—Is There an Implied Remedy Under Section 14(e)?

Congress, in enacting the Williams Act's tender offer provisions, did not provide any express remedy for injured investors. Any investor injured by reliance upon a materially misleading required SEC filing has an express

---

35. Hubco, Inc. v. Rappaport, 628 F.Supp. 345, 354 (D.N.J.1985).

36. 17 C.F.R. § 240.13e–4. *See* § 11.8 *supra*.

37. Crane Co. v. Harsco Corp., 511 F.Supp. 294 (D.Del.1981). *But cf.* Polaroid Corp. v. Disney, 862 F.2d 987 (3d Cir.1988) (indicating standing under all holders rule is limited to target company shareholders and does not extend to target company itself).

38. Nowling v. Aero Services International, Inc., 752 F.Supp. 1304 (E.D.La.1990). *Accord*, Mates v. North American Vaccine, Inc., 53 F.Supp.2d 814 (D.Md.1999) (president/director lacked standing under section 13(d)).

39. *See, e.g.,* Piper v. Chris–Craft Industries, Inc., 430 U.S. 1, 97 S.Ct. 926, 51 L.Ed.2d 124 (1977), which is discussed in § 11.10 *infra*.

46. Pryor v. USX Corp., 1991 WL 346368, [1991–1992 Transfer Binder] Fed.Sec.L.Rep. (CCH) ¶ 96,630 (S.D.N.Y.1991) (unpublished case). Section 14(d)(6) and proration rights are discussed in § 11.5 *supra*.

47. 17 C.F.R. § 240.14a–10.

48. *See, e.g.,* In re Digital Island Securities Litigation, 357 F.3d 322 (3d Cir. 2004); Polaroid Corp. v. Disney, 862 F.2d 987 (3d Cir.1988).

49. Howing Co. v. Nationwide Corp., 972 F.2d 700 (6th Cir.1992), *cert. denied* 507 U.S. 1004, 113 S.Ct. 1645, 123 L.Ed.2d 266 (1993) (decided under section 13(e)'s going private rules).

50. 15 U.S.C.A. § 78r(a). As noted elsewhere, the section 18(a) remedy is a relatively limited one. *See* § 12.18 *infra*.

51. 17 C.F.R. § 240.10b–5. *See* §§ 12.2–12.13 *infra*.

remedy under section 18(a).[1] Anyone so injured as a purchaser or seller of a security may also have a remedy implied under Rule 10b–5.[2] Whether the Williams Act provides its own antifraud remedy for damages is somewhat questionable,[3] especially in light of the decline of implied remedies generally.[4] However, most courts that have considered the issue have recognized an implied remedy under section 14(e) in the hands of the target company or a target company shareholder.[5] For example, it has been held that a nontendering target shareholder has standing to sue both the target and acquiring corporations.[6]

In Piper v. Chris–Craft Industries, Inc.,[7] the Supreme Court held that a competing offeror cannot maintain a private right of action under section 14(e)'s general antifraud proscriptions. In so deciding, the Court did not rule out any private remedy; in fact, the opinion held out much hope for the recognition of a section 14(e) private right of action in the hands of the target company or its shareholders. The Court in *Piper* reasoned that the purpose of the Williams Act was to further investor protection by serving the shareholders of the target company, not competing tender offerors who, at best, were collateral beneficiaries of the tender offer provisions.[8] Even if the legislation was directed at a special class of persons so as to warrant the implication of a private remedy,[9] a competing tender offeror was not a member of that group. The Court pointed out that section 14(e) was directed toward "full and fair disclosure for the benefit of investors,"[10] and thus "Congress was seeking to broaden the scope of protection afforded to shareholders confronted with competing claims."[11] The precise scope of the *Piper* ruling is far from clear. Justice Blackmun in his concurrence took the position that the *Piper* decision

---

§ 11.10

1. 15 U.S.C.A. § 78r(a). However, this remedy is relatively narrow in scope. *See* § 12.18 *infra*.

2. 17 C.F.R. § 240.10b–5. *See* chapter 12 *infra*.

3. *See* § 11.6 *supra* for a discussion of implied remedies under sections 13(d), (e) and 14(d). *See* § 1.8 *supra* for an overview of the private remedies available under the 1933 and 1934 Acts.

4. *See* § 12.2 *infra*.

5. *E.g.,* Clearfield Bank & Trust v. Omega Financial Corp., 65 F.Supp.2d 325 (W.D.Pa.1999); (section 14(e) supports a private right of action in connection with a tender offer for the shares of a company not subject to the 1934 Act's reporting requirements).

6. Plaine v. McCabe, 797 F.2d 713 (9th Cir.1986). *But cf.* Priddy v. Edelman, 679 F.Supp. 1425 (E.D.Mich.1988) (nontendering shareholder lacked standing to sue for violation of Rule 10b–13's prohibition against a bidder's purchases outside of the tender offer).

7. 430 U.S. 1, 97 S.Ct. 926, 51 L.Ed.2d 124 (1977). The 14(e) claim was but one facet of the voluminous litigation which emerged out of this bitterly waged tender offer battle. In the initial go-round, Chris–Craft, although being denied the requested injunctive relief, secured a determination that Bangor Punta's May 8, 1969 press release announcing its upcoming exchange offer violated the gun jumping prohibitions of section 5(a) of the 1933 Act. Chris–Craft Industries, Inc. v. Bangor Punta Corp. 426 F.2d 569 (2d Cir.1970) (en banc); 15 U.S.C.A. § 77e(a) (1970). *See also* SEC Rule 135, 17 C.F.R. § 230.135. Both the earlier stage of the litigation as well as the case at the Supreme Court level involved the claim that Bangor Punta's open market purchases of Piper stock during the pendency of the registered exchange offer constituted a violation of Rule 10b–6. 17 C.F.R. § 240.10b–6. The 10b–6 claim and discussion of 10b–13 are contained in the Court's opinion in 430 U.S. at 42–46, 97 S.Ct. at 949–52.

8. 430 U.S. at 31–34, 97 S.Ct. at 944–46.

9. This is one of the tests the Court has stressed with regard to implied remedies generally. Implied remedies are discussed in § 12.2 *infra*.

10. 430 U.S. at 31, 97 S.Ct. at 944 (quoting 113 Cong.Rec. 24664 (Aug. 30, 1967) (remarks of Sen. Williams)). *See* Rondeau v. Mosinee Paper Corp., 422 U.S. 49, 58, 95 S.Ct. 2069, 2075, 45 L.Ed.2d 12 (1975).

11. 430 U.S. at 34, 97 S.Ct. at 945.

would have been better placed on the grounds of lack of standing rather than the absence of an implied remedy.[13] Justice Stevens in his dissent pointed out that since the plaintiff had already acquired the target company's shares, it could be viewed as a shareholder with standing to sue under the Act.[14]

There are a number of federal circuit court decisions recognizing a target shareholder's right to sue for violation of section 14(e), at least where the injury is not premised on the loss of an opportunity to control the target company.[15] In order to challenge misstatements or omissions, must the plaintiff show actual reliance? A number of decisions under the proxy rules indicate that actual reliance would not be required so long as a causally-related injury could be shown.[16] Thus a shareholder who did not tender his or her shares should not be precluded from challenging the tender offer. Reliance remains an element of the claim even in those cases that a plaintiff is not put to the test of actual reliance. This means that there must have been a material misstatement on which a reasonable investor could have relied in making an erroneous decision of whether to tender shares.[17]

Additionally, a target company's management may seek private injunctive relief for violations of section 14(e).[18] And, it has further been held that, although unable to claim damages in light of the *Piper* decision, a competing offeror may sue for injunctive relief.[19] The plaintiff's dual burden of proving a substantial likelihood of success on the merits as well as irreparable injury makes it very difficult to secure preliminary injunctive relief; courts are mindful of the time premiums involved in tender offers and are thus reluctant to interfere.

Although tender offers necessarily involve the purchase or sale of securities, a Rule 10b–5 claim in connection with a tender offer will fail if it does not further investor protection. Accordingly, a competing tender offeror generally cannot state a 10b–5 claim when section 14(e) has not been violated.[26] Furthermore, even in suits brought by the target company or its shareholders, where there could be an overlap between the section 14(e) and Rule 10b–5 claims, there are advantages to pressing the 14(e) claim, if it exists. Rather

---

13.   430 U.S. at 48–53, 97 S.Ct. at 952–55.

14.   *Id.* at 56–59, 97 S.Ct. at 956–58. The majority's response was that even if standing were to be found, the plaintiff's claim lacked the requisite causation since the injury complained of was the loss of an opportunity to gain control rather than any typical investor-oriented injury. *Id.* at 36, 97 S.Ct. at 946.

15.   *See, e.g.,* Schlesinger Investment Partnership v. Fluor Corp., 671 F.2d 739 (2d Cir.1982); Osofsky v. Zipf, 645 F.2d 107 (2d Cir.1981); Seaboard World Airlines, Inc. v. Tiger International Inc., 600 F.2d 355 (2d Cir.1979); Smallwood v. Pearl Brewing Co., 489 F.2d 579, 596 (5th Cir.1974).

16.   *E.g.,* Western District Council of Lumber Production and Industrial Workers v. Louisiana Pacific Corp., 892 F.2d 1412 (9th Cir.1989) (upholding standing of nonrelying shareholder).

17.   *See, e.g.,* Salsitz v. Peltz, 227 F.Supp.2d 222 (S.D.N.Y. 2002) (failure to establish detrimental reliance; court refused to presume reliance).

18.   *E.g.,* Polaroid Corp. v. Disney, 862 F.2d 987 (3d Cir.1988) (granting target company's request for preliminary relief but limiting standing under Rule 14d–10's all holders rule to target company shareholders); Florida Commercial Banks v. Culverhouse, 772 F.2d 1513 (11th Cir. 1985); Prudent Real Estate Trust v. Johncamp Realty, 599 F.2d 1140 (2d Cir.1979).

19.   *E.g.,* Mobil Corp. v. Marathon Oil Co., 669 F.2d 366 (6th Cir.1981).

26.   *See* Luptak v. Central Cartage, 1979 WL 1280, [1981 Transfer Binder] Fed.Sec.L.Rep. (CCH) ¶ 98,034 (E.D.Mich.1979), construing Piper v. Chris–Craft Industries, Inc., 430 U.S. 1, 42–46, 97 S.Ct. 926, 949–52, 51 L.Ed.2d 124 (1977).

than Rule 10b–5's purchaser/seller standing limitation,[27] a section 14(e) claim would seem to depend upon whether the plaintiff was the target of a tender offer solicitation or opposition to a tender offer, rather than whether he or she was an actual purchaser or seller.[28] Also, it is arguable that since section 14(e) does not have the "deceptive device" language that is present in Rule 10b–5 by virtue of section 10(b),[29] section 14(e)—as is the case with section 17(a)(2) and (3) of the 1933 Act[30]—may not require a showing of scienter.[31] Although section 14(e) does prohibit manipulative, fraudulent, and deceptive acts, that prohibition is in addition to its prohibition of material misstatements and omissions. However, some courts have nonetheless found that scienter is required for a violation of section 14(e).[32] The Supreme Court's ruling in Schreiber v. Burlington Northern, Inc.,[33] emphasizes that disclosure is not only the primary but probably the sole focus of section 14(e). Since section 17(a) of the 1933 Act, another disclosure-oriented provision, has been held to be violated upon a showing of negligence,[34] it is arguable that the *Schreiber* decision permits a no scienter approach to section 14(e). However, the Supreme Court's narrow reading of section 14(e) in *Schreiber* strongly favors a scienter requirement.[36] In addition to the federal remedy, nondisclosures in connection with a tender offer may be actionable under state law.[38] The Uniform Standards Act of 1998 preempted most state claims based on fraud in any class action on behalf of more than fifty persons.[39] Those suits would thus have to be brought under federal law in federal court.[40]

§ 11.11   Responses to Tender Offers: Anti–Takeover Moves and Defensive Tactics

§ 11.11[1] Responding to a Tender Offer or Other Takeover Attempt

When faced with an uninvited or hostile takeover attempt, management of the target company will frequently decide to oppose the offer. Defensive tactics can raise questions under both state and federal law. When a target's management decides to fight off a contender for control, there is always the possibility of being charged with wasting of corporate assets or other forms of

---

27.   Blue Chip Stamps v. Manor Drug Stores, 421 U.S. 723, 95 S.Ct. 1917, 44 L.Ed.2d 539 (1975), *rehearing denied* 423 U.S. 884, 96 S.Ct. 157, 46 L.Ed.2d 114 (1975). *See* § 12.7 *infra.*

28.   Western District Council of Lumber Production and Industrial Workers v. Louisiana Pacific Corp., 892 F.2d 1412 (9th Cir.1989).

29.   15 U.S.C.A. § 78j(b). *See* § 12.20 *infra.*

30.   15 U.S.C.A. § 77q(a)(2) and (3).

31.   Caleb & Co. v. E.I. DuPont de Nemours & Co., 599 F.Supp. 1468 (S.D.N.Y.1984) (scienter is not required in suit for violation of Rule 14e–1(c)'s prompt payment requirement).

32.   Pryor v. United States Steel Corp., 591 F.Supp. 942 (S.D.N.Y.1984), *affirmed in part, reversed in part* 794 F.2d 52 (2d Cir.1986).

33.   472 U.S. 1, 105 S.Ct. 2458, 86 L.Ed.2d 1 (1985).

34.   Aaron v. SEC, 446 U.S. 680, 100 S.Ct. 1945, 64 L.Ed.2d 611 (1980), *on remand* 666 F.2d 5 (2d Cir.1981).

36.   *See, e.g.,* Orlett v. Cincinnati Microwave, Inc., 953 F.2d 224 (6th Cir.1990) (claim failed since scienter not shown).

38.   *See* Eisenberg v. Chicago Milwaukee Corp., 537 A.2d 1051 (Del.Ch.1987); Kahn v. United States Sugar Corp., 1985 WL 4449 (Del.Ch.1985).

39.   Pub. Law No. 105–353, 112 Stat. 3227 (105th Cong., 2d Sess. November 3, 1998) (S 1260). *See* § 12.15[2] *infra.*

40.   15 U.S.C.A. § 78bb(f).

mismanagement.[1] In some instances, as a matter of state law, management's defensive tactics will be upheld under the business judgment rule, although there are limits in the context of defensive maneuvers.[3] In the first instance, courts recognize that in fending off challengers, incumbent management represents existing corporate policies, and management is entitled to use reasonable expenditures of corporate funds in order to defend its policies, so long as the control contest reflects a battle of policies rather than personalities.[4] For example, management may buy out a corporate raider with corporate funds at a premium without breaching a duty to the shareholders where the raider has threatened liquidation.[5] The practice of purchasing the raider's shares at a premium has come to be known as "greenmail." Another common tactic is the issuance of additional shares to dilute the aggressor's interest; this will succeed if management can show a valid business purpose[6] but may not if it is merely to defeat a takeover attempt.[7] The same is true with a corporation's repurchase of its shares, even if not from the aggressor.[8]

The illustrative corporate law cases discussed above focus on concepts of self-dealing and the fiduciary duties of corporate officers and directors. Some of the same concepts may come into play under the federal securities acts. Although aimed primarily at disclosure, the antifraud and antimanipulation provisions[9] have provided protection at the federal level. As will be seen directly below, the courts have been in conflict as to how far the federal protection should go.[10] The Supreme Court's ruling that section 14(e) does not

---

§ 11.11

1. *See generally* 3 James D. Cox & Thomas L. Hazen, Cox and Hazen on Corporations, ch. 23 (2d ed. 2003).

3. *See, e.g.,* Revlon, Inc. v. MacAndrews & Forbes Holdings, Inc., 506 A.2d 173 (Del.1985) (once a target is for sale, management's only obligation is to assure the best price). The Delaware Supreme Court has had a difficult time explaining exactly when the *Revlon* auction duty will be triggered as opposed to those instances in which target management is permitted to act. *Compare* Paramount Communications, Inc. v. Time Inc., 571 A.2d 1140 (Del.1989) (*Revlon* duty did not apply to merger consistent with target's long-term business plan) *with* Paramount Communications Inc. v. QVC Network, 637 A.2d 34 (Del.1994) (*Revlon* auction duty prevented target management from taking sides in takeover battle). For discussion of the Delaware and other state law developments, *see* 3 Cox & Hazen *supra* footnote 1 at ch. 23.

4. *E.g.,* Cheff v. Mathes, 41 Del.Ch. 494, 199 A.2d 548 (Del.1964); Kaplan v. Goldsamt, 380 A.2d 556 (Del.Ch.1977); Campbell v. Loew's, Inc., 36 Del.Ch. 563, 134 A.2d 852 (1957) (proxy battle); Rosenfeld v. Fairchild Engine & Airplane Corp., 309 N.Y. 168, 128 N.E.2d 291 (1955) (proxy battle).

5. Cheff v. Mathes, 41 Del.Ch. 494, 199 A.2d 548 (1964). However, the SEC proposed legislation that would have prohibited the paying of such "greenmail" to a holder of more than three percent of the stock who has held the stock for less than three years. *See* 16 Sec.Reg. & L.Rep. (BNA) 793 (May 11, 1984).

6. *Cf.* Tallant v. Executive Equities, Inc., 232 Ga. 807, 209 S.E.2d 159 (1974) (issuance of shares to raise capital upheld although as a result the current principal owner lost control).

7. Norlin Corp. v. Rooney, Pace Inc., 744 F.2d 255 (2d Cir.1984) (preliminary injunction against voting shares issued to newly created ESOP); Chicago Stadium v. Scallen, 530 F.2d 204 (8th Cir.1976) (preliminary injunction against issuance of shares to corporate president); Klaus v. Hi–Shear Corp., 528 F.2d 225 (9th Cir.1975) (shares issued to newly created employees stock plan held to be a breach of duty but preliminary injunction denied); Condec Corp. v. Lunkenheimer Co., 43 Del.Ch. 353, 230 A.2d 769 (1967).

8. *E.g.,* Ivanhoe Partners v. Newmont Mining Corp., 535 A.2d 1334 (Del.1987) (upholding independent directors' decision to aid "street sweep" by the target company's largest shareholder). *Compare, e.g.,* Herald Co. v. Seawell, 472 F.2d 1081 (10th Cir.1972) (upholding purchase of shares to fund employee stock plan) *with* Petty v. Penntech Papers, Inc., 347 A.2d 140 (Del.Ch.1975) (preliminary injunction issued against redemption of one class of voting stock). *Cf.* SEC v. Carter Hawley Hale Stores, Inc., 760 F.2d 945 (9th Cir.1985) (issuer's defensive repurchase program held not to be a tender offer).

9. *E.g.,* Rule 10b–5 and section 14(e), 15 U.S.C.A. § 78n(e), 17 C.F.R. § 240.10b–5. *See* § 11.10 *supra* and chapter 12 *infra*.

10. *Compare e.g.,* Mobil Corp. v. Marathon Oil Co., 669 F.2d 366 (6th Cir.1981) *with* Panter v. Marshall Field & Co., 646 F.2d 271 (7th Cir.1981), *cert. denied* 454 U.S. 1092, 102 S.Ct. 658, 70

prohibit manipulation unless there has been a material misstatement or omission[11] is a major impediment to the federal control of defensive tactics under the current statutory framework.

The Williams Act's disclosure requirements are designed to make sure that whatever defensive tactics may be taken are open and above-board. When faced with the time pressures of a takeover attempt, the target company's management is put in a most difficult position. By virtue of SEC Rule 14e–2,[12] the target company's management has ten business days from the date the tender offer is first published to provide its security holders with its position on the merits of the offer. Under the rule, which is not limited to reporting companies, target management has limited alternatives. It may recommend acceptance or rejection of the offer, or it may simply issue a statement to the effect that management either is standing neutral or is presently unable to take a position on the merits of the tender offer. In opposing or recommending the acceptance of an offer, the target company's management is required to set forth its reasons; and, of course, such statements are subject to the anti-fraud provisions of section 14(e).[13]

§ 11.11[2] Varieties of Defensive Tactics and State Law Regulation

When faced with an outsider's attempt to take over the company, target management will frequently respond with a defensive tactic, such as seeking a friendly suitor or "white knight."[14] For example, the white knight may be granted a "lock-up" option, which gives it an advantage in acquiring the target over other bidders, or the target may arrange to sell its "crown jewel," or most desirable asset, to the white knight, thereby diminishing the target's attractiveness to others. The successful use of defensive tactics may perpetuate the target company's incumbent management in the successor or surviving corporation, presenting a potential conflict of interest between management's desire to stay in office and the company's best interests. Defensive tactics are thus subject to state corporate law prohibitions on self-dealing,[16] although as noted above, the target management's actions will often have at least the protection of the business judgment rule.[17]

L.Ed.2d 631 (1981) and Buffalo Forge Co. v. Ogden Corp., 717 F.2d 757 (2d Cir.1983), *cert. denied* 464 U.S. 1018, 104 S.Ct. 550, 78 L.Ed.2d 724 (1983).

11.   Schreiber v. Burlington Northern, Inc., 472 U.S. 1, 105 S.Ct. 2458, 86 L.Ed.2d 1 (1985).

12.   17 C.F.R. § 240.14e–2.

13.   15 U.S.C.A. § 78n(e). *See* §§ 11.15, 11.19 *supra.*

For a case finding nondisclosures in management's Schedule 14D–9 opposition not to be material, *see* Gulf Corp. v. Mesa Petroleum Co., 582 F.Supp. 1110 (D.Del.1984). *Cf.* Horowitz v. Pownall, 582 F.Supp. 665 (D.Md.1984) (question of fact existed as to materiality of omissions from Schedule 14D–9 filed by an opponent of a tender offer).

14.   *See, e.g.,* Kern County Land Co. v. Occidental Petroleum Corp., 411 U.S. 582, 93 S.Ct. 1736, 36 L.Ed.2d 503 (1973); Buffalo Forge Co. v. Ogden Corp., 717 F.2d 757 (2d Cir.1983), *cert. denied* 464 U.S. 1018, 104 S.Ct. 550, 78 L.Ed.2d 724 (1983). *See also, e.g.,* Dynamics Corp. of America v. CTS Corp., 635 F.Supp. 1174 (N.D.Ill.1986) *affirmed* 794 F.2d 250 (7th Cir.1986) *reversed on other grounds* 481 U.S. 69, 107 S.Ct. 1637, 95 L.Ed.2d 67 (1987) (upholding white knight defense as reasonable although it may not have been "most reasonable").

16.   Detailed discussion of the state corporate law ramifications goes beyond the scope of this book. *See* generally 3 Cox & Hazen *supra* footnote 1, ch. 23.

17.   *See* Buffalo Forge Co. v. Ogden Corp., 555 F.Supp. 892, 903 (W.D.N.Y.1983), *affirmed* 717 F.2d 757 (2d Cir.1983) ("[T]he business judgment rule is applicable to actions undertaken within

There have been a number of cases in Delaware and elsewhere that indicate the states are taking a firmer role in regulating tender offer practices of target company directors. As a starting point, the protection of the business judgment rule has been severely limited by two Delaware Supreme Court decisions. First, in Smith v. Van Gorkom,[18] the court invalidated the directors' acceptance of an offer recommended by the president where the board acted in only two hours and without ever having obtained an appraisal or even having seen the offer. Second, in Revlon, Inc. v. MacAndrews & Forbes Holdings, Inc.,[19] the Delaware court ruled that in agreeing to a lock-up arrangement with a white knight, the target company's directors breached their fiduciary duty to their shareholders. However, in another case, the Delaware Supreme Court validated the use of a poison pill.[21] The Delaware court has also permitted the use of a discriminatory issuer self-tender which excluded the hostile bidder.[23] However, the Delaware court has further held that a target company's directors' funding an ESOP after control had passed to another company were not protected by the business judgment rule.[24] The Delaware court has severely limited management entrenchment tactics by identifying target management's primary duty once a company is for sale, as "maximization of the company's value at a sale for the stockholders' benefit."[25] Subsequent decisions have somewhat clouded the issue of when this duty to maximize value is triggered.[26]

A by-product of the creation of state law remedies against such tactics is that failure to disclose facts in the course of a transaction that would have alerted shareholders of such a remedy may well give rise to an action for material misrepresentation under Rule 10b–5 or section 14(e).[27] However, a breach of a state law fiduciary duty will not be actionable under the federal securities laws.[28]

Other common alternatives to finding a "white knight" as a defensive tactic include: the issuance of additional shares to dilute any holdings of the

---

the context of bidding wars and other contests for control of a corporation.") (citing Treadway Companies v. Care Corp., 638 F.2d 357 (2d Cir.1980)).

18.   488 A.2d 858 (Del.1985).

19.   506 A.2d 173 (Del.1985). *See, e.g.*, Note, Outside Directors and the Modified Business Judgment Rule in Hostile Takeovers: A New Test for Director Liability, 62 S.Cal.L.Rev. 645 (1989).

21.   Moran v. Household International, Inc., 500 A.2d 1346 (Del.1985).

23.   Unocal Corp. v. Mesa Petroleum Co., 493 A.2d 946 (Del.1985). The SEC has since adopted rules prohibiting exclusionary tender offers both by issuers and third parties. 17 C.F.R. §§ 240.13e–4(f)(8)(i), 240.14d–10(a)(1). These rules may be subject to challenge in light of the Supreme Court's ruling that the thrust of the Williams Act's antifraud provisions is deception, and that manipulative conduct alone will not suffice. *See* Schreiber v. Burlington Northern, Inc., 472 U.S. 1, 105 S.Ct. 2458, 86 L.Ed.2d 1 (1985) which is discussed in § 11.6 *supra*. The "all holders" rules are discussed in § 11.5 *supra*.

24.   Frantz Mfg. Co. v. EAC Industries, Inc., 501 A.2d 401 (Del.1985).

25.   Revlon, Inc. v. MacAndrews & Forbes Holdings, Inc., 506 A.2d 173, 182 (Del.1985). *Accord* Plaza Securities Co. v. Fruehauf Corp., 643 F.Supp. 1535, 1543 (E.D.Mich.1986) (applying Michigan law).

26.   *See, e.g.*, Paramount Communications, Inc. v. Time Inc., 571 A.2d 1140 (Del.1989) (*Revlon* auction duty not triggered where target company had preexisting business plan involving corporate combination with another company).

27.   *See* § 12.20 *infra*.

28.   *E.g.*, In re United States Shoe Corp. Litigation, 718 F.Supp. 643 (S.D.Ohio 1989).

would-be acquiring company;[29] stock repurchase programs to strengthen the control of "inside" or "friendly" shareholders;[30] restrictive by-law and charter provisions, (sometimes referred to as "porcupine provisions" or "shark repellent") such as extraordinarily high voting requirements for mergers with other corporations;[31] staggering of directors' terms of office which necessarily increases the time it will take to effect a turnover in management; obligating the corporation to long-term salary or bonus contracts (known as "golden parachutes" or "silver wheelchairs") for top management in the event of a change in control; and using state tender offer statutes to introduce additional delays into the tender offer process.[34] Golden parachutes generally take the form of contractual rights to high severance payments. Large parachute payments have been referred to as platinum parachutes, while plans that cover lower-level employees are known as tin parachutes. One supposed justification of the golden parachute is that it takes away any conflict of interest when management evaluates a third party offer since the incentive of managers' retaining their jobs by opposing the offer is counterbalanced by the high severance payments they would receive if the offer is successful. The federal tax code provide that excessive parachute payments are not deductible to the payor corporation, and further, an excise tax is imposed upon the recipient.[36] Assuming there is full disclosure, golden parachute arrangements do not present problems under the federal securities laws.[37] A similar move is for the target company to reincorporate in a state with more onerous antitakeover laws.[38] Other defensive and preventive tactics used over the years include: the acquisition of another business by the target company, creating a potential antitrust threat to impending tender offers;[39] the purchase of a radio station or some other heavily regulated business to tie up the takeover attempt in administrative proceedings which may be needed to approve any change of ownership in the regulated business;[40] and the "Pac–Man" defense, where the target company makes a tender offer for control of the original aggressor.[41]

---

29. *See, e.g.,* Unilever Acquisition Corp. v. Richardson–Vicks, Inc., 618 F.Supp. 407 (S.D.N.Y. 1985).

30. *See, e.g.,* LTV v. Grumman Corp., 526 F.Supp. 106 (E.D.N.Y.1981) (corporation and pension plan made market purchases of more than 1 million shares of corporation's own stock in a single day to prevent tender offeror from acquiring majority control).

31. *See, e.g.,* Young v. Valhi, Inc., 382 A.2d 1372 (Del.Ch.1978) (charter provision required approval of eighty percent of the issued and outstanding common shares in order to accomplish a merger with any offeror holding at least five percent of the corporation's stock).

34. State tender offer statutes are discussed in § 11.12 *infra.* Their constitutionality is discussed in § 11.13 *infra.*

36. I.R.C. §§ 280G(b), (c), 4999. *See* Comment, Golden Parachutes and Draconian Measures Aimed at Control: Is Internal Revenue Code Section 280G the Proper Regulatory Mode of Shareholder Protection?, 54 U.Cin.L.Rev. 1293 (1986).

37. *See* Brill v. Burlington Northern, Inc., 590 F.Supp. 893 (D.Del.1984). There have been some attempts to amend the federal law to prohibit parachute arrangements.

38. One limitation on the efficacy of state law in thwarting a tender offer is the line of cases striking down many of those statutes in the face of federal preemption or the Constitution's commerce clause. *E.g.,* Edgar v. MITE Corp., 457 U.S. 624, 102 S.Ct. 2629, 73 L.Ed.2d 269 (1982); § 11.13 *infra.*

39. *See* Consolidated Gold Fields PLC v. Minorco, S.A., 871 F.2d 252 (2d Cir.1989) (affirming the issuance of a preliminary injunction against tender offer on antitrust grounds); Panter v. Marshall Field & Co., 646 F.2d 271, 290–91 (7th Cir.1981), *cert. denied* 454 U.S. 1092, 102 S.Ct. 658, 70 L.Ed.2d 631 (1981) (target department store chain acquired stores in areas where tender offeror national retail chain was already operating).

40. *See* Stephen A. Hochman & Oscar D. Folger, Deflecting Takeovers; Charter and By-law Techniques, 34 Bus.Law. 537, 558 (1979).

41. *See* Martin Marietta Corp. v. Bendix Corp., 549 F.Supp. 623 (D.Md.1982).

Another defensive tactic is the "poison pill," which is a conditional stock right that is triggered by a hostile takeover and makes the takeover prohibitively expensive.[43] The poison pill is a variation of the scorched earth[44] defense whereby the target company prepares itself for self-destruction in the event of a hostile takeover. Another variation on the poison pill is the so-called "flipover" provisions in corporate charters, which prohibit combinations with persons who have acquired more than a stated percentage of the issuer's stock without prior approval of the target company's directors. Under such flipover provisions, the shareholders receive rights in the acquiring company's shares for any takeover occurring within a predetermined period.[45] Another device which has survived judicial challenge,[46] but is now prohibited by an SEC rule[47] is the discriminatory issuer self-tender that excludes the hostile bidder from the offer's terms. Greenmail, which consists of target's management buying back the hostile bidder's shares at a premium, has also been a widely used tactic.[48] A common charter amendment has been the so-called "fair price" amendment under which all shareholders are guaranteed the best price paid to any one shareholder.[49] Many states have adopted fair price statutes which are to the same effect.[50] Still another approach has been the issuance of preferred shares with extraordinary voting power. Such unequal voting rights have been held to violate state law[51] and also violate the New York Stock Exchange's and NASD's voting rights rules.

§ 11.12   State Regulation of Tender Offers

§ 11.12[1] State Tender Offer Regulation—Overview

Prior to the adoption of the Williams Act[1] in 1968, there was virtually no specialized regulation of tender offers at either the federal or state level.[2] In less than twenty years, the states went through three generations of takeover

---

43. *See, e.g.,* Comprehensive Care Corp. v. RehabCare Corp., 98 F.3d 1063 (8th Cir.1996) (adoption of poison pill did not violate federal securities law).

44. *See* Minstar Acquiring Corp. v. AMF Inc., 621 F.Supp. 1252 (S.D.N.Y.1985) (scorched earth tactics raised a strong presumption that directors were acting only to enrich themselves).

45. The new New York takeover law has a similar provision barring takeovers for five years where the acquiring company has acquired twenty percent of the target company's stock without prior target director approval. N.Y.Bus.Corp.L. § 912.

46. Unocal Corp. v. Mesa Petroleum Co., 493 A.2d 946 (Del.1985).

47. 17 C.F.R. §§ 240.13e–4(f)(8)(i), 240.14d–10(a)(1).

48. *E.g.,* Fry v. Trump, 681 F.Supp. 252 (D.N.J.1988) (receipt of greenmail is not a breach of fiduciary duty; but upholding securities claims based on statements that defendant was not a greenmailer); Cheff v. Mathes, 41 Del.Ch. 494, 199 A.2d 548 (1964) (payment of greenmail held not a breach of fiduciary duty).

49. Fair price amendments are in response to front end loaded, two tier tender offers.

50. *E.g.,* Md.Corps. & Ass'ns Code §§ 3–602, 3–603. *See* § 11.12 *infra.*

51. *See* Asarco Inc. v. Court, 611 F.Supp. 468 (D.N.J.1985). *See also* Packer v. Yampol, 1986 WL 4748 (Del.Ch.1986) (unpublished case).

§ 11.12

1. Pub.L.No. 90–439, 82 Stat. 454 (1968) (codified at 15 U.S.C.A. §§ 78m(d)–(e), 78n(d)–(f)).

2. To the extent that a tender offer triggered other securities provisions, there would be an impact. For example, an exchange offer would implicate the registration provisions with regard to the tender offeror's securities being issued, unless, of course, an applicable exemption could be found. Similarly, if a shareholder vote were for some reason required, the proxy regulations would be implicated.

statutes.[4] To paraphrase Oliver Wendell Holmes,[5] it may fairly be said that three generations of takeover statutes is enough.[6] Investor protection has not been the motivating factor behind these statutes. In most instances, state tender offer acts have been passed at least in part to protect incumbent management and other employees of local companies that were potential takeover targets. As a result, rather than merely supplementing the federal legislation, most state statutes impose more impediments to the takeover, thus inhibiting or at least slowing down any transaction.[7] In tender offer jargon, these acts are often referred to as "shark repellent" because of their deterrent effect.

The federal legislation embodied in the Williams Act attempts to strike a balance between the need for disclosure and investor protection on the one hand, and, on the other, the fear of eliminating too many potential tender offerors from the market place. Much of the state legislation to date has probably gone too far in the direction of deterring bidders from participating in the tender offer market. The Supreme Court has held that when the state law limitations on tender offers prove too restrictive and conflict with the basic policy of the Williams Act, these laws are invalid because they impose an unconstitutional burden on interstate commerce.[8] Other federal courts have used the preemption doctrine to invalidate state tender offer statutes under appropriate circumstances.[9] Both the preemption and Commerce Clause issues are discussed in the next section of this treatise.[10] The discussion that follows is designed to present an overview of existing legislation.

Although there are some basic and general similarities between many of the state tender offer statutes, their lack of uniformity is far greater than that of state blue sky laws.[11] Accordingly, compliance with multiple statutes is a significant hurdle and can be a nightmare for the tender offeror. Because there is such a wide variance in statutory terms and provisions, the discussion that follows is merely a broad overview. The applicable statutes must be carefully scrutinized in order to master their individual regulatory provisions. In the words of one commentator, "State takeover acts are similar to snowflakes—if you think you have found identical ones, you are probably not looking closely enough."[12]

§ 11.12[2] Scope of State Tender Offer Regulation

The various state statutes employ a wide range of jurisdictional provisions. It is thus possible that more than one state act will apply to any particular tender offer. The majority of the state acts base jurisdiction on the target company's incorporation within the state, or on the location within the

---

4. *See* Thomas L. Hazen, State Antitakeover Legislation—The Second and Third Generations, 23 Wake Forest U.L.Rev. 77 (1988).

5. Buck v. Bell, 274 U.S. 200, 207, 47 S.Ct. 584, 71 L.Ed. 1000 (1927) ("Three generations of imbeciles are enough").

6. *Id.* at 80 (paraphrasing Justice Holmes).

7. The most prominent example is the imposition of waiting periods between the filing and effective date of the tender offer. *See, e.g.,* 8 Del.Code § 203(a)(1); Ohio Rev.Code § 1707.041(B)(1).

8. *See* Edgar v. MITE, 457 U.S. 624, 102 S.Ct. 2629, 73 L.Ed.2d 269 (1982). *See* § 11.13 *infra.*

9. *See, e.g.,* Great Western United Corp. v. Kidwell, 577 F.2d 1256 (5th Cir.1978), *vacated on other grounds sub nom.* Leroy v. Great Western United Corp., 443 U.S. 173, 99 S.Ct. 2710, 61 L.Ed.2d 464 (1979).

10. *See* § 11.13 *infra.*

11. *See* chapter 8 *supra.*

12. Note, State Regulation of Tender Offers, 3 J.Corp.Law 603, 603 (1982) (footnote omitted).

state of the target company's principal place of business and/or substantial target company assets.[13] Some statutes take a less well-defined approach by looking to substantial contacts with the state.[14] Another variation among the states arises in the context of subject matter jurisdiction by virtue of the elusive definition of "tender offer." There is no universally accepted definition of tender offer, although most acts are brought into play by virtue of securities transactions that fall within that category under federal law. While the federal act contains no statutory definition, the state statutes generally include precise but diverse statutory definitions including the number of solicited target company shareholders required before the act applies.[16] For example, many states define a qualifying transaction in terms of the number of persons solicited. Some of the state statutes raise questions analogous to those raised under the Williams Act. For example, one state court has held that a series of open market purchases does not constitute a tender offer.[17]

§ 11.12[3] First Generation State Tender Offer Statutes

§ 11.12[3][A] Types of First Generation Statutes

Major variations among the state tender offer statutes are found in the qualification requirements. Following the pattern of the state blue sky laws, many of the state tender offer statutes go beyond the disclosure philosophy of the Williams Act by giving the state administrator the power to review the merits of the tender offer[18] or the adequacy of the disclosure.[19] The state administrator is often empowered to hold hearings which may be initiated by the administrator,[20] the target company,[21] or a certain percentage of the target company's shareholders.[22] Thus, even where merit analysis is not permitted, the tender offer could be tied up in administrative hearings. The procedures vary among the statutes as to who may or must appear at such hearings and the extent of allowable pre-hearing discovery.[23] Under most statutes, administrative orders with respect to tender offers are self-executing,[24] but under some acts the administrator must first seek judicial enforcement.[25] The cost and delay involved in these enforcement procedures led many states to employ

---

13. *See, e.g.,* Conn.Gen.Stat.Ann. § 36–457(a); Ohio Rev.Code § 1707.041(A)(1); S.D.Codified Laws Ann. 47–32–3.

14. *See, e.g.,* LSA–Rev.Stat. 51:1500.1(13).

16. *See, e.g.,* N.H.Rev.Stat.Ann. 421–A:2(VI)(a) (" 'Takeover bid' does not include: (3) Any . . . offer to acquire an equity security, or the acquisition of such equity security pursuant to such offer . . . from not more than 25 persons . . .").

17. Sheffield v. Consolidated Foods Corp., 302 N.C. 403, 276 S.E.2d 422 (1981).

18. *See, e.g.,* N.J.Stat.Ann. 49:5–4(a); S.C.Code § 35–2–70(1). *See also* Kennecott Corp. v. Smith, 507 F.Supp. 1206 (D.N.J.1981) (New Jersey Takeover Law frustrates the purpose of the Williams Act by substituting Bureau Chief's view of the offer for the informed judgment of shareholders).

19. *E.g.,* LSA–Rev.Stat. 51:1501(E); 70 Pa.Stat. § 74(d).

20. *E.g.,* Vernon's Ann.Mo.Stat. § 409.530.

21. *E.g.,* 70 Pa.Stat. § 74(d).

22. *E.g.,* Conn.Gen.Stat.Ann. § 36–460(a) (aggregate owners of ten percent of the outstanding equity securities of the class involved in the tender offer may petition the commissioner to schedule a hearing).

23. *See, e.g.,* LSA–Rev.Stat. 51:1501(E).

24. *E.g.,* Neb.Rev.Stat. § 21–2406; N.J.Stat.Ann. 49.5–12(a); 71 Okl.Stat. § 437; S.C.Code § 35–2–70(2).

25. *See* Vernon's Ann.Mo.Stat. § 409.535; Wis.Stat.Ann. 552.17.

a so-called "fiduciary approach" to review. Under this approach, the administrator may waive compliance with the qualification requirements if the target company's management endorses the tender offer.[26]

Even state regulation that is limited to full disclosure, as opposed to a merit or substantive review of the terms of the offer, may impose burdens beyond those created by the federal legislation. The most prominent example is the commonly found state-imposed waiting period of ten,[27] twenty,[28] or thirty days[29] between the filing of the tender offer and the date on which it becomes effective. Not only are such waiting periods not a part of the federal statute, but, in 1979, the SEC, by promulgating Rule 14d–2(b),[30] purported to preempt all such waiting periods.[31] Although the preemptive effect of Rule 14d–2(b) has not specifically been decided, the Supreme Court has held that waiting periods may contribute to a state statute's invalidity as an undue burden on interstate commerce.[32]

The filing requirements imposed by the various state tender offer statutes generally require more detailed disclosures than the federal Williams Act.[33] These additional disclosures have been challenged as not providing relevant information to the target's shareholders.[34] Nevertheless, the courts have tended to view the disclosure requirements as enhancing and thus not in conflict with the federal scheme.[35]

§ 11.12[3][B] The Highly Dubious Vitality of First Generation State Tender Offer Statutes

As noted at the outset of this section, in some instances more than one state's tender offer act may purport to apply to any particular tender offer. The lack of uniformity among state statutes can create considerable problems for the tender offeror in addition to the burden of compliance with the substantive requirements of each state's act. As a result of challenges, several state tender offer statutes have been declared unconstitutional.[43] Thus, despite attempts to retain some state control by amending offensive provisions, the first generation of state tender offer statutes have been deprived of much of their intended effectiveness as takeover deterrents.

---

26. *See, e.g.,* Idaho Code § 30–1501(5)(e); Ohio Rev.Code § 1707.041(A)(1)(d); 71 Okl.Stat. § 414(1)(d).

27. *E.g.,* Conn.Gen.Stat.Ann. § 36–460.

28. *E.g.,* 8 Del.Code § 203(a)(1); 70 Pa.Stat. § 74(a).

29. *E.g.,* N.C.Gen.Stat. § 78B–4(a).

30. 17 C.F.R. § 240.14d–2(b).

31. *See* Sec.Act Rel.No. 33–6158 (SEC Nov. 29, 1979).

32. Edgar v. MITE Corp., 457 U.S. 624, 102 S.Ct. 2629, 73 L.Ed.2d 269 (1982). *See* § 11.13 *infra.*

33. *See, e.g.,* Ohio Rev.Code § 1707.041(–)(3)(d) (planned changes in employment policies); 70 Pa.Stat. § 75(4) (probable effect of takeover on labor relations).

34. Donald C. Langevoort, State Tender–Offer Legislation: Interests, Effects, and Political Competency, 62 Cornell L.Rev. 213, 230 (1977).

35. *See, e.g.,* Great Western United Corp. v. Kidwell, 577 F.2d 1256 (5th Cir.1978), *vacated on other grounds sub nom.* Leroy v. Great Western United Corp., 443 U.S. 173, 99 S.Ct. 2710, 61 L.Ed.2d 464 (1979).

43. *See, e.g.,* Kennecott Corp. v. Smith, 507 F.Supp. 1206 (D.N.J.1981) (New Jersey takeover statute preempted by Williams Act); Hi–Shear Industries, Inc. v. Campbell, 1980 WL 1476, [1981 Transfer Binder] Fed.Sec.L.Rep. (CCH) ¶ 97,804 (D.S.C.1980) (South Carolina Tender Offer Disclosure Act preempted by Williams Act).

§ 11.12[4] Second Generation State Takeover Statutes

Following the Supreme Court's ruling in Edgar v. MITE Corp.,[44] a number of states enacted "second generation" takeover statutes that were designed to overcome the constitutional infirmities of the Illinois statute that was struck down in *MITE*. The basic thrust of these statutes is to regulate tender offers through state law rules relating to corporate governance rather than through state securities laws and administrative regulations.[45] The basic approach of such statutes is substantive regulation of tender offers. Ohio was the first state to adopt second generation legislation.[46] Ohio was followed by Minnesota, Missouri, and Michigan.[47] Other states have since enacted second generation statutes.[48]

The Ohio Act, which governs all forms of takeovers and is not limited to tender offers, applies to Ohio corporations having fifty or more shareholders and a principal place of business, principal offices, or substantial assets within the state.[49] The act then classifies takeover transactions by the percentage of shares owned by the acquiring person, with each control zone triggering the act's substantive requirements. Acquiring persons must deliver to the target company a disclosure statement describing the proposed acquisition. The target company's board then has ten days to call a special shareholders' meeting which must take place within fifty days. At that meeting, the transaction requires approval of a majority of the disinterested shares not owned or controlled by the acquiring person or any affiliate. In addition to the disinterested majority approval requirements, the Ohio legislation enables corporations to adopt charter amendments with even higher voting require- ments or, alternatively, vest the corporation's directors with the sole power to approve the transaction, thus disenfranchising the shareholders.[50] Prior to the Supreme Court decision upholding the Indiana Control Share Act,[51] the Ohio statute had been struck down as violative of the Commerce Clause.[52] Similar- ly, Indiana's and Hawaii's versions of this control share approach to tender offer legislation had been struck down under the Supremacy Clause of the Constitution because of their conflict with the Williams Act.[53] But, as noted

---

44. 457 U.S. 624, 102 S.Ct. 2629, 73 L.Ed.2d 269 (1982). *See* § 11.13 *infra*.

45. *See generally,* Dennis I. Block, Nancy E. Barton & Andrea J. Roth, State Takeover Statutes: The "Second Generation", 13 Sec.Reg.L.J. 332 (1986); Stephen Bainbridge, State Takeover and Tender Offer Regulations Post–MITE: The Maryland, Ohio and Pennsylvania Attempts, 90 Dick.L.Rev. 731 (1986); Thomas L. Hazen, State Antitakeover Legislation—The Second and Third Generations, 23 Wake Forest U.L.Rev. 77 (1988); Arthur R. Pinto, The Constitution and the Market for Corporate Control: State Takeover Statutes After CTS Corp., 29 Wm. & Mary L.Rev. 699 (1988).

46. Ohio Rev.Code § 1701.83.2. *See* Gary P. Kreider, Fortress Without Foundation? Ohio Takeover Act II, 52 U. Cin.L.Rev. 108 (1983); Note, Has Ohio Avoided the Wake of MITE? An Analysis of the Constitutionality of the Ohio Control Share Acquisition Act, 46 Ohio St.L.J. 203 (1985).

47. Minn.Stat.Ann. §§ 302A.011, 302A.671; Vernon's Ann.Mo.Stat. §§ 351.015, 351.407.

48. For example, Idaho, New York, and Oklahoma have enacted various forms of second generation statutes. Idaho Code §§ 30–1501–30–1510; Okl.Stats.Ann.tit. 71 §§ 451–462; N.Y.Bus. Corp.L. § 902.

49. Ohio Rev.Code § 1701.83.1.

50. *Id.* §§ 1701.52, 1701.59.

51. CTS Corp. v. Dynamics Corp. of America, 481 U.S. 69, 107 S.Ct. 1637, 95 L.Ed.2d 67 (1987).

52. Fleet Aerospace Corp. v. Holderman, 796 F.2d 135 (6th Cir.1986), *vacated* 481 U.S. 1026, 107 S.Ct. 1949, 95 L.Ed.2d 521 (1987).

53. Dynamics Corp. of America v. CTS Corp., 794 F.2d 250 (7th Cir.1986), *on remand* 638 F.Supp. 802 (N.D.Ill.1986), *reversed* 481 U.S. 69, 107 S.Ct. 1637, 95 L.Ed.2d 67 (1987); Terry v. Yamashita, 643 F.Supp. 161 (D.Hawai'i 1986).

above, the Supreme Court has since upheld the Indiana Control Share Act.[54] Other states have adopted control share statutes.

In contrast to the Ohio approach, Maryland takes a more structural approach in regulating share acquisitions. The Maryland statute requires any takeover be approved by at least eighty percent of the shares and two-thirds of the disinterested shares unless all shareholders receive the "best price" paid by the acquiring person within a two-year period.[56] The best price approach, patterned after fair price charter amendments adopted by many corporations in other states as a defensive anticipatory tactic, is to fend off two-tiered offers. The Maryland Act excludes "friendly" offers from its coverage. A number of states have adopted fair price statutes, some of which vary the terms of the Maryland Act.

The New York, Tennessee, Minnesota, Oklahoma, Utah, and Idaho second generation statutes basically take a disclosure approach.[58] The chief feature of the disclosure approach is that many of the statutes include open market purchases and require disclosure in such a way as to close the ten-day window that currently exists under section 13(d) of the Williams Act.[59]

Ohio, Indiana, Maine, and Pennsylvania have expanded the factors directors may consider in opposing takeovers.[60] Many other states have adopted similar "constituency" or "stakeholder" statutes, which permit management to consider interests other than those of the shareholders in making decisions. Target management in these states thus may rely on interests other than shareholder wealth maximization as a basis for resisting a takeover. These statutes generally make it clear that although management may consider other interests, it does not have to. Still another approach taken in some of the second generation statutes is to give dissenters' rights to a wide variety of control transactions.

§ 11.12[5] Third Generation Takeover Statutes

Once one of the second generation state takeover statutes—the Indiana Control Share Act—had passed constitutional scrutiny in the Supreme Court,[65] the third generation of tender offer statutes began to appear.[66] One form that such statutes are taking is to apply the law of the host state to corporations incorporated elsewhere. Such statutes, in regulating what has been called pseudo-foreign corporations, raise additional constitutional and policy questions. North Carolina was the first state to adopt a third genera-

---

54. CTS Corp. v. Dynamics Corp. of America, 481 U.S. 69, 107 S.Ct. 1637, 95 L.Ed.2d 67 (1987). *See* § 11.13 *infra.*

56. Md. Corp's & Ass'ns Code §§ 3–602, 3–603.

58. Idaho Code § 30–1502 *et seq.* (Supp.1986); Minn.Stat.Ann. § 80–.01 *et seq.* (West 1986); N.Y.–McKinney's Bus.Corp.Law §§ 1601–1613 (1986); Okl.Stat.Ann. 71 § 451 (1986); Utah Code Ann. 1986, § 16–10–76.5.

59. *See* § 11.11 *supra. See also* Cardiff Acquisitions, Inc. v. Hatch, 751 F.2d 906 (8th Cir.1984), *appeal after remand* 751 F.2d 917 (8th Cir.1984) (upholding the disclosure provisions of the Minnesota statute). *But see* APL Limited Partnership v. Van Dusen Air, Inc., 622 F.Supp. 1216 (D.Minn.1985).

60. West's Ann.Ind.Code § 23–1–35–1(d) (Burns Supp.1986); 13–A Me.Rev.Stat.Ann. § 716 (Supp.1986); Ohio Rev.Code § 1701.59 (Baldwin Supp.1986); 42 Pa.Stat. § 8363 (Purdon Supp. 1986). An SEC study found that stock prices of 36 Ohio companies declined after the adoption of the 1986 amendments. 19 Sec.Reg. & L.Rep. (BNA) 741 (May 22, 1987); Fed.Sec.L.Rep. (CCH) Report Bull. no. 1233 (May 27, 1987).

65. CTS Corp. v. Dynamics Corp. of America, 481 U.S. 69, 107 S.Ct. 1637, 95 L.Ed.2d 67 (1987). *See* § 11.13 *infra.*

66. For yet another suggested approach for state legislation, *see* Stephen M. Bainbridge, Redirecting State Takeover Laws at Proxy Contests, 1992 Wis.L.Rev. 1071.

tion statute aimed at regulating foreign corporations,[67] and a number of other states followed suit.[68] North Carolina has since repealed the extraterritorial reach of its antitakeover laws.[69] The New Hampshire legislature adopted a statute that applies to foreign target companies[70] The New Hampshire Supreme Court upheld that statute's application to a New Hampshire company and did not reach the issue of whether it would be constitutional if applied to corporations not incorporated in New Hampshire.[71]

Although the third generation statutes purporting to regulate foreign corporations are generally based upon substantial contacts within the state, the rationale of the *CTS* decision strongly indicates that such statutes may not withstand constitutional scrutiny.[72] In fact, the Oklahoma statute was struck down by a federal district court on the grounds that it was unconstitutional to the extent that it applied to non-Oklahoma corporations.[73]

Another variety of third generation takeover statute is modeled on the New York "freeze" statute,[74] also known as a business combination statute. The idea behind such statutes is to delay any transaction that would complete the second step of a two-step acquisition, in those instances in which the first step was not agreed to by target company's management. Thus, for example, the New York statute prohibits a merger or other business acquisition within five years of the control acquisition date unless the transaction was approved by the target company's directors *prior* to the control acquisition date. Other states have followed the New York lead,[75] including Delaware, which has adopted a three-year-freeze statute.[76] Based on earlier Supreme Court doc-

---

67. In adopting both a best price and control share statutes, North Carolina purported to apply its law not only to corporations incorporated in the state, but also to corporations incorporated elsewhere having more than forty percent of its domestic assets in the state and more than four percent of its domestic employees in the state. N.C.Gen.Stat. § 55–9–01 *et seq.* ("Shareholder Protection Act"); *Id.* § 55–9A–01 *et seq.* ("Control Share Acquisitions Act"). It is further provided that neither the North Carolina best price nor control share statutes apply to corporations if in express conflict with the laws of the state of incorporation. *Id.*

In 1990, the North Carolina legislature eliminated the application of these acts to corporations not incorporated in the state.

68. Ariz.H.R.Res. 2002, 38th Leg., 3d Sess., 1987 Ariz.Legis.Serv. 32–45; 1987 Fla.Laws 87–257; Idaho Code § 30–5002(9); Mass.Gen.Laws Ann. ch. 110D, 110E.

69. N.C.Gen.Stat. §§ 55–9–01 *et seq.*, 55–9A–01 *et seq.*

70. N.H. Rev. Stat. § 421–A:2 (applying takeover statute to target companies having more than 100 shareholders and its principal office or substantial assets in the state and having either (1) more than 10 percent of its shareholders resident in the state; (2) more than 10 percent of its shares owned by New Hampshire residents; or (3) ten thousand shareholders resident in New Hampshire).

71. New England Dragway, Inc. v. M–O–H Enterprises, Inc., 149 N.H. 188, 817 A.2d 288 (2003).

72. For example, the Court in *CTS* expressly noted that the state of incorporation has a special interest in regulating the internal affairs of its corporations:

The Indiana statute imposes no such problem [presenting an undue burden on interstate commerce]. So long as each state regulates voting rights *only in the corporations it has created,* each corporation will be subject to the law of only one state.

107 S.Ct. at 1649, 95 L.Ed.2d at 85 (emphasis supplied).

73. TLX Acquisition Corp. v. Telex Corp., 679 F.Supp. 1022 (W.D.Okl.1987). *Cf.* Veere, Inc. v. Firestone Tire & Rubber Co., 685 F.Supp. 1027 (N.D.Ohio 1988) (indicating that there was no problem with constitutionality of Ohio statute since it applied only to target companies incorporated in Ohio).

74. N.Y.Bus.Corp.Law § 912.

75. Ariz.Rev.Stat. §§ 10–1221–10–1222 (three-year delay); Minn.Stat.Ann. § 302A.673 (five-year delay); Vernon's Ann.Mo.Stat. § 351.459(3)(b) (five-year delay); N.J.Stat.Ann. § 49.5–1 (five-year delay); Wash.S.B. No. 6084, 1987 Wash.Leg.Serv. (No. 10) 11 (five year delay); Wis.Stat.Ann. § 180.725 (three year delay).

76. Del.Corp.Code § 203.

trine, there would appear to be considerable question whether such statutes can withstand constitutional scrutiny.[77] Nevertheless, the Delaware statute has withstood challenges at the preliminary injunction stage because of the failure to show a likelihood of success on the merits of the constitutional challenge, but the court noted that although the statute was probably constitutional, the constitutionality issue is not an easy one.[78] The Wisconsin freeze statute has been upheld by the Seventh Circuit.[79] There thus is mounting authority in support of these questionable freeze statutes.

Other third generation statutes have taken still different approaches. For example, the Ohio Foreign Business Acquisition Act imposed stricter burdens on foreign bidders, but that statute has been invalidated by at least one court.[80] Pennsylvania has taken yet another approach by expressly sanctioning use of poison pills as a defensive measure.[81] This addition to the defensive weapon arsenal has not been successfully challenged.

The varieties of third generation statutes have continued to proliferate. In the spring of 1990, Pennsylvania adopted the most ambitious antitakeover statute to date. In addition to adopting a control share statute,[82] the Pennsylvania legislature enacted a provision requiring any person owning more than twenty percent of a company's voting shares to disgorge any profit realized from a subsequent sale of the shares within an eighteen-month period.[83] The impact of this provision is to discourage suitors by locking them in as shareholders in the event that their takeover attempt is unsuccessful. It is arguable that this provision conflicts with the policy of section 16(b) of the Exchange Act which requires disgorgement of profits on short-swing transactions over a six-month period.[84] Also in 1990, Massachusetts enacted a statute that mandates dividing the directors into groups and staggering the election of directors.[85] A corporation's board by a majority vote may choose to opt out

---

77. *Cf.* Hyde Park Partners, L.P. v. Connolly, 839 F.2d 837 (1st Cir.1988) (Massachusetts statute imposing one-year moratorium on takeover attempts as a sanction for violation of the statute's disclosure provisions held likely to be preempted by Williams Act).

78. *E.g.,* RP Acquisition Corp. v. Staley Continental, Inc., 686 F.Supp. 476 (D.Del.1988); BNS Inc. v. Koppers Co., 683 F.Supp. 454 (D.Del.1988).

79. Amanda Acquisition Corp. v. Universal Foods Corp., 877 F.2d 496 (7th Cir.1989). *See also* West Point–Pepperell, Inc. v. Farley Inc., 711 F.Supp. 1096 (N.D.Ga.1989) (upholding the Georgia business combination statute); Realty Acquisition Corp. v. Property Trust, 1989 WL 214477, [1990 Transfer Binder] Fed.Sec.L.Rep. ¶ 95,245 (D.Md.1989) (unpublished case) (Maryland business combination statute was not preempted by Williams Act). *See also, e.g.,* Note, Delaware's Section 203 Antitakeover Statute Survives Constitutional Attack, 68 Tex.L.Rev. 235 (1990).

80. Campeau Corp. v. Federated Department Stores, 679 F.Supp. 735 (S.D.Ohio 1988).

81. *See* Pennsylvania Enacts Law Against Hostile Takeovers, 20 Sec.Reg. & L.Rep. (BNA) 502 (April 1, 1988).

82. *Cf.* Committee for New Management of Guaranty Bancshares Corp. v. Dimeling, 772 F.Supp. 230 (E.D.Pa.1991) (Pennsylvania Control Share Act applied to revocable proxies granting discretionary authority even though proxy was not part of takeover attempt).

83. 15 Pa.Cons.Stat.Ann. § 2571.

84. 15 U.S.C.A. § 78p(b) which is discussed in chapter 13 *infra. Cf., e.g.,* Kern County Land Co. v. Occidental Petroleum Corp., 411 U.S. 582, 93 S.Ct. 1736, 36 L.Ed.2d 503 (1973) (interpreting section 16(b) so as not to conflict with the Williams Act policy of not unduly deterring tender offers).

85. Mass.Gen.Laws.Ann. c. 149, § 184. *See, e.g.,* David B. Hilder & Lawrence Ingrassia, Norton Wins a Round Against BTR Bid as Massachusetts Lawmakers Clear Bill, Wall St.J. A12 (April 18, 1990).

of the law should the directors decide to have all directors elected annually. Shareholders can opt out of staggered elections only upon a two–thirds vote.[86] As has been the case with other state antitakeover legislation, the Massachusetts statute was designed to suit the needs of a particular company in responding to a hostile approach by a would-be acquirer.[87]

§ 11.12[6] Evaluation of State Takeover Legislation

Even beyond the constitutional issues that are discussed in the next section,[88] state tender offer statutes are problematic. The proliferation of stronger state regulation is likely to provide wide variations in regulatory approaches. While many aspects of state statutes may have some merit, the state to state variation is highly undesirable in light of the national scope of the problem. Piecemeal state regulation is also troublesome when one considers the factors that have motivated state legislatures. The primary interest of the states has been to support managements of target companies located in the state as well as economic development and jobs within the state. While economic development and state employment issues are certainly valid considerations, they are only part of the takeover picture. The interests of shareholders who may be scattered throughout the country may not adequately be addressed by state legislation. Similarly, state legislation views the economic interests as ending with the borders of the state and thus does not consider the overall impact on the national economy. For example, it is not difficult to conceive of takeovers that will not only leave shareholders better off, but also would relocate some or all aspects of the business to locations where they could be run more efficiently. It is a truism that one state's economic loss may be another's economic gain. In light of these issues, the new generations of tender offer statutes appear to make it even more incumbent that Congress enter the field in order to preserve the uniformity and even handed treatment for takeovers of public companies that was initiated with the passage of the Williams Act amendments.

§ 11.13 Validity of State Tender Offer Statutes—The Commerce Clause and the Preemption Problem; SEC Rule 14d–2(b)

State tender offer legislation has frequently been challenged under the Supremacy[1] and Commerce[2] Clauses of the Constitution. Under the Suprema-

---

86. Since the board of directors can opt out (as is the case with business combination statutes), the Massachusetts law does not adversely impact a company's ability to pursue a friendly suitor. The effect of the Massachusetts law, as is the case with the business combination statutes, is to delay the effective transfer of control. The business combination statutes merely alter the timing of a second-step merger but do not otherwise affect the ability of the acquirer to assume control of the acquired company. In contrast, the Massachusetts law postpones the ability to elect a majority of the directors.

87. *See* David B. Hilder & Lawrence Ingrassia, Norton Wins a Round Against BTR Bid as Massachusetts Lawmakers Clear Bill, Wall St.J. A12 (April 18, 1990). For a similar occurrence in North Carolina, *see* Thomas L. Hazen, State Anti–Takeover Legislation: The Second and Third Generations, 23 Wake Forest U.L.Rev. 77 (1988).

88. *See* § 11.13 *infra.*

§ 11.13

1. "This Constitution, and the Laws of the United States . . . shall be the Supreme Law of the Land." U.S. Const. art. VI, cl. 2. *See* John E. Nowak, Ronald D. Rotunda & J. Nelson Young, Constitutional Law 18–20 (2d ed. 1983).

2. "The Congress shall have the power . . . [t]o regulate commerce . . . among the several States." U.S. Const. art. I, § 8, cl. 3.

cy Clause, to the extent Congress has exercised its legislative power, a state may not enact inconsistent legislation.[3] Hence, state laws are preempted when either explicitly prohibited by,[4] or directly in conflict with,[5] federal legislation. Not every challenge to a takeover statute will be ripe. For example, shareholders of a potential target company did not have standing to challenge a state's takeover statute prior to the commencement of a tender offer or other takeover attempt.[6]

§ 11.13[1] Preemption Challenges to State Takeover Statutes

Preemption is largely a matter of congressional intent.[7] State legislation may be implicitly preempted when there is an overriding federal interest in the subject of the legislation,[8] or when the federal regulations are so pervasive as to create an inference that Congress intended to "occupy the field" completely.[9] Similarly, state law may be invalid if it conflicts indirectly with the federal law by standing as an obstacle to the full accomplishment of federal regulatory objectives.[10] In any case, a balancing of state and federal interests is required.[11]

The Williams Act does not expressly prohibit state regulation of tender offers. Furthermore, because corporate law regulation has not generally been considered to be a matter of overriding federal concern,[12] and because the Williams Act is not a detailed comprehensive regulatory scheme, but rather a minimum standard,[13] there is no inference that Congress intended to preempt all state tender offer regulation.[14] In the absence of an explicit or implicit

---

3. Swift & Co. v. Wickham, 382 U.S. 111, 86 S.Ct. 258, 15 L.Ed.2d 194 (1965).

4. *See, e.g.,* Rice v. Santa Fe Elevator, 331 U.S. 218, 236, 67 S.Ct. 1146, 1155, 91 L.Ed. 1447 (1947) (Federal Warehouse Act expressly preempts all concurrent state regulation).

5. Florida Lime and Avocado Growers, Inc. v. Paul, 373 U.S. 132, 142–43, 83 S.Ct. 1210, 1217, 10 L.Ed.2d 248 (1963), *rehearing denied* 374 U.S. 858, 83 S.Ct. 1861, 10 L.Ed.2d 1082 (1963) ("A holding of federal exclusion of state law is inescapable ... where compliance with both federal and state regulation is a physical impossibility....").

6. Armstrong World Industries, Inc. v. Adams, 961 F.2d 405 (3d Cir.1992).

7. California v. Zook, 336 U.S. 725, 69 S.Ct. 841, 93 L.Ed. 1005 (1949); Head v. New Mexico Board of Examiners, 374 U.S. 424, 83 S.Ct. 1759, 10 L.Ed.2d 983 (1963).

8. *See, e.g.,* Pennsylvania v. Nelson, 350 U.S. 497, 76 S.Ct. 477, 100 L.Ed. 640 (1956) (Congressional enactment of internal security laws to safeguard against overthrow of the government by force reflected overriding federal interest requiring preemption of supplementary state anti-communist legislation).

9. Rice v. Santa Fe Elevator, 331 U.S. 218, 230, 67 S.Ct. 1146, 1152, 91 L.Ed. 1447 (1947); City of Burbank v. Lockheed Air Terminal Inc., 411 U.S. 624, 93 S.Ct. 1854, 36 L.Ed.2d 547 (1973).

10. Hines v. Davidowitz, 312 U.S. 52, 67, 61 S.Ct. 399, 404, 85 L.Ed. 581 (1941).

11. *See id.* at 73–74, 61 S.Ct. at 407–08. *See generally* Note, The Preemption Doctrine: Shifting Perspectives on Federalism and the Burger Court, 75 Colum.L.Rev. 623 (1975).

12. Corporation law has traditionally been primarily state law but largely because of the federal securities statutes a "Federal Corporations Law" has been developing. *See generally* William L. Cary & Melvin A. Eisenberg, Cases and Materials on Corporations, 13–14 (5th ed.1980).

13. *See* Note, Securities Law and the Constitution: State Tender Offer Statutes Reconsidered, 88 Yale L.J. 510, 519–20 (1979).

14. In fact, it has been argued that Congress implicitly accepted the prospect of state regulation by adding the Williams Act to the 1934 Act without also amending section 28(a) of the Act, 15 U.S.C.A. § 78bb(a), which provides that "Nothing in this chapter shall affect the jurisdiction of the securities commission ... of any state over any security or any person insofar as it does not conflict with provisions of this chapter or the rules and regulations thereunder." But the applicability of this provision to state tender offer legislation is questionable. *See* Donald

prohibition of state regulation, supremacy clause questions focus on whether state takeover laws conflict either directly or indirectly with the operation of the Williams Act.

§ 11.13[2] Commerce Clause Challenges to State Takeover Legislation

A state statute which survives preemption analysis may nonetheless be unenforceable under the Commerce Clause. State legislation is valid only if it regulates even-handedly to effectuate a legitimate local public interest, affects interstate commerce only incidentally, and imposes burdens on such commerce not clearly excessive in relation to the putative local benefits.[15] The protection of local incumbent management from foreign "raiders" is not a legitimate local interest in itself; however, regulation of the internal affairs of domestic corporations and the protection of local target corporations and shareholders from fraud and overreaching in the course of tender offers are clearly bona fide state concerns.[16] Thus, the vulnerability of state tender offer acts under the commerce clause is due largely to their extraterritorial coverage and the resulting cumulative burden on interstate commerce.[17]

§ 11.13[2][A] The Early Cases

In Great Western United Corp. v. Kidwell,[18] the Fifth Circuit became the first federal appellate court to consider the constitutionality of a state tender offer act. In *Kidwell,* the tender offeror was a Delaware corporation with its principal offices in Dallas, Texas. The target was organized under the laws of the state of Washington with shareholders across the United States. The Idaho takeover statute required that a registration statement be declared effective by the director of the state's Department of Finance prior to the commencement of any tender offer for an Idaho target company.[19] The offeror was required to mail a copy of the statement to the target, and the material terms of the offer had to be publicly disclosed no later than the filing date. Within twenty days of the filing, the director could hold a discretionary hearing if he thought it necessary to ensure full disclosure and equal treatment of all shareholders.[20] A hearing was required if the target company requested it, and the director's determination as to the adequacy of the registration statement had to be announced within thirty days of filing unless more time was needed.[21] The Act's jurisdictional provisions were triggered by target companies having substantial assets located in Idaho or that were

---

C. Langevoort, State Tender–Offer Legislation: Interests, Effects, and Political Competency, 62 Cornell L.Rev. 213, 247 (1977).

15. Pike v. Bruce Church, Inc., 397 U.S. 137, 90 S.Ct. 844, 25 L.Ed.2d 174 (1970).

16. *See* Donald C. Langevoort, State Tender–Offer Legislation: Interests, Effects, and Political Competency, 62 Cornell L.Rev. 213, 242 (1977).

17. *E.g.,* CTS Corp. v. Dynamics Corp. of America, 481 U.S. 69, 107 S.Ct. 1637, 95 L.Ed.2d 67 (1987). *See* Diane S. Wilner & Craig A. Landy, The Tender Trap: State Takeover Statutes and Their Constitutionality, 45 Fordham L.Rev. 1, 22–23 (1976).

18. 577 F.2d 1256 (5th Cir.1978), *reversed on other grounds sub nom.* Leroy v. Great Western United Corp., 443 U.S. 173, 99 S.Ct. 2710, 61 L.Ed.2d 464 (1979), *on remand* 602 F.2d 1246 (5th Cir.1979).

19. Idaho Code § 30–1503(1).

20. Idaho Code § 30–1503(4)–(5). The statute did not authorize the director to review the merits of the offer.

21. Idaho Code § 30–1503(4), (5).

either incorporated or had principal offices in the state and had securities registered under the Idaho Code or the 1934 Act.[22] Although its disclosure requirements were more stringent than those of the Williams Act, Idaho's provisions for withdrawal rights, pro rata acceptance, and price increases merely duplicated the corresponding federal provisions.[23]

The Fifth Circuit found it unnecessary to determine whether the true purpose of the takeover law was to protect investors as Idaho contended, or to protect incumbent management as the district court had found.[24] In either case Congress had rejected Idaho's "fiduciary approach" to investor protection, which relied upon the business judgment of corporate directors with a fiduciary duty to their shareholders. Instead, recognizing that investors often benefit from tender offers, Congress had chosen the "market approach" wherein the function of federal regulation was to let the investor, on a fully informed basis, decide for himself or herself after allowing both the offeror and incumbent management to fully present their arguments.[25] The court found that the Idaho law benefited target companies by giving them advance notice of tender offers and the power to postpone offers indefinitely by insisting on a hearing. Moreover, Idaho gave preferential treatment to target companies by not regulating target defensive tactics as stringently as the offeror's activities. Indeed, the target board could exclude the offer from state regulation completely by simply approving the offer.[26] The court reasoned that the state law clearly "disrupted the neutrality indispensable for the proper operation of the federal approach to tender offer regulation,"[27] and thus stood as "an obstacle to the accomplishment and execution of the full purposes and objectives of the Williams Act" and was necessarily preempted.[28]

Following the Fifth Circuit's opinion in *Kidwell*, state and federal district court rulings on the constitutionality of state tender offer statutes remained contradictory.[29] Most courts, however, agreed with the Fifth Circuit's conclusion that the Williams Act was intended both to protect shareholders and to maintain a neutral balance between incumbent management and offeror.[30] Hence, following the *Kidwell* reasoning, to the extent that state statutes provided management with the weapon of delay, they were most often found to disrupt the neutral balance and hinder achievement of the objectives of the

---

22. Idaho Code § 30–1501(6).

23. *Compare* Idaho Code §§ 30–1503(2)(C), 30–1506(2)–(4) *with* 15 U.S.C.A. §§ 78m(d), 78n(d)(5)–(7).

24. 577 F.2d at 1278–79 (citing Appellants Brief at 39–42 and the district court's opinion, 439 F.Supp. at 437.)

25. 577 F.2d at 1279. *But cf.* North Star International v. Arizona Corporation Commission, 720 F.2d 578 (9th Cir.1983).

26. 577 F.2d at 1278.

27. *Id.* at 1279–80.

28. *Id.* at 1280, 1281. The court pointed out that by requiring more extensive disclosure than the Williams Act, Idaho might actually be harming investors. Too much data could hide relevant disclosures and create unnecessary confusion, thus inhibiting the offeror's efforts to communicate material information.

29. *Compare, e.g.,* Dart Industries, Inc. v. Conrad, 462 F.Supp. 1 (S.D.Ind.1978) (Delaware statute preempted by the Williams Act) *with* AMCA International Corp. v. Krouse, 482 F.Supp. 929 (S.D.Ohio 1979) (Ohio takeover law not preempted).

30. *See* MITE Corp. v. Dixon, 633 F.2d 486, 495 (7th Cir.1980), *affirmed sub nom.* Edgar v. MITE Corp., 457 U.S. 624, 102 S.Ct. 2629, 73 L.Ed.2d 269 (1982). The neutrality principle was reaffirmed by the Supreme Court in CTS Corp. v. Dynamics Corp. of America, 481 U.S. 69, 107 S.Ct. 1637, 95 L.Ed.2d 67 (1987).

Williams Act. On the other hand, a minority of courts held that the sole purpose of the Williams Act was to protect investors, and that Congress had no intention to legislate neutrality into tender offers. Neutrality, they concluded, was simply one characteristic of the legislation.

In response to the mounting confusion and the increasing number of tender offers, the SEC adopted tender offer rules which were intended to preempt state regulation by creating a direct conflict with most state statutes.[31] Before those new rules could be tested, however, the Fourth and Seventh Circuits reached opposite results in controversies involving the takeover statutes of Virginia[32] and Illinois[33] respectively. The Supreme Court decided to review the Illinois case, and in Edgar v. MITE Corp.,[34] the constitutionality of state tender offer legislation was squarely before the Court for the first time.

§ 11.13[2][B] The MITE Decision

MITE Corporation, organized under the laws of Delaware with its principal office in Connecticut, initiated a tender offer for all outstanding shares of an Illinois corporation. MITE complied with the requirements of the Williams Act but did not comply with the Illinois Act,[35] electing instead to file suit in district court in Illinois, seeking declaratory and injunctive relief from the statute's enforcement.

Under the Illinois Business Takeover Act, an offer became effective twenty days after filing with the Secretary of State and notifying the target of the terms of the offer, unless the Secretary of State called a hearing to determine the fairness of the offer.[36] During the waiting period, the offeror could not communicate with the target shareholders, although the target was free to contact shareholders as it pleased.[37] Target companies were defined by the Act as any corporation of which ten percent of the class of securities subject to the tender offer was owned by Illinois residents, or for which any two of the following conditions were met: the corporation had its principal place of business located in Illinois, was organized under Illinois law, or had at

---

31. *See* Sec.Act Rel. No. 33–6022 (SEC Feb. 5, 1979); Sec.Act Rel. No. 33–6158 (SEC Nov. 29, 1979); Sec.Act Rel. No. 33–6159 (SEC Nov. 29, 1979).

32. In Telvest v. Bradshaw, 618 F.2d 1029 (4th Cir.1980), *on remand* 547 F.Supp. 791 (E.D.Va.1982), the Fourth Circuit appeared to adopt the minority view that the sole purpose of the Williams Act was to protect investors, and not necessarily to maintain neutrality between offerors and incumbent management. Although the constitutionality of Virginia's takeover statute was not directly at issue, in the court's view, the statute's stated purpose ("to protect the interests of offerees, investors, and the public by requiring that an offeror make fair, full and effective disclosure to offerees . . .", Va.Code § 13.1–528(B)) "seem[ed] consistent with rather than antagonistic to the purpose of the Williams Act." *Id.* at 1034.

33. In MITE Corp. v. Dixon, 633 F.2d 486 (7th Cir.1980), *affirmed sub nom.* Edgar v. MITE Corp., 457 U.S. 624, 102 S.Ct. 2629, 73 L.Ed.2d 269 (1982), the Seventh Circuit followed the *Kidwell* "neutrality" rationale and concluded that the Illinois Business Take–Over Act was preempted by the Williams Act because it substituted regulatory control for investor autonomy and provided for hearings and other delays greatly in excess of those mandated by Congress. *Id.* at 498. Moreover, the Illinois Act violated the commerce clause because its substantial obstruction of interstate commerce could not be justified by the state's "tenuous interest in protecting resident shareholders and regulating control transfers." *Id.* at 502.

34. 457 U.S. 624, 102 S.Ct. 2629, 73 L.Ed.2d 269 (1982).

35. Under the Illinois Act any takeover offer for the shares of a target company had to be registered with the Secretary of State. Ill.–S.H.A. ch. 121½, § 137.54.A (repealed).

36. Ill.–S.H.A. ch. 121½, § 137.54.E (repealed).

37. Ill.–S.H.A. ch. 121½, § 137.58.1 (repealed).

least ten percent of its stated capital and paid-in surplus represented within the state.[38]

The Supreme Court agreed with the Seventh Circuit that the Illinois law was invalid under the Commerce Clause because it imposed an excessive indirect burden on interstate commerce.[39] Illinois derived no benefit from protecting non-resident investors, and the state's asserted interest in investor protection was seriously undermined by the fact that the target company's competing offer for its own shares was completely exempt from the coverage of the Act.[40] The substantive protections provided by the Illinois Act were essentially equivalent to those provided by the Williams Act. The Court noted that the additional disclosure requirements of the Illinois Act might not substantially enhance the shareholders' ability to make a decision and concluded that the protections the Illinois Act afforded resident shareholders were for the most part "speculative."[41]

A plurality of the Court would also have invalidated the Illinois Act as an impermissible direct regulation of interstate commerce.[42] The plurality found a substantial difference between state blue sky laws which regulate transactions taking place within the state, and the Illinois law which could conceivably apply to tender offers involving no Illinois shareholders at all.[43] The Commerce Clause precluded the application of a state statute to commerce occurring entirely outside the state's borders whether or not the commerce had effects within the state.[44] Three of the six Justices reaching the merits in *MITE* would have affirmed the Seventh Circuit on supremacy clause grounds as well.[45] The Justices agreed with the lower court that in imposing the requirements of the Williams Act, Congress had adopted a "policy of even-handedness."[46]

The SEC's then-recently adopted tender offer rules were not at issue in *MITE*.[47] Nevertheless, the Seventh Circuit observed that one rule in particular, Rule 14d–2(b),[48] conflicted directly with the Illinois Act.[49] Under Rule 14d–2(b), an offeror's public announcement of certain material terms of a tender offer causes the offer to commence for the purposes of section 14(d) of the 1934 Act,[50] despite the fact that a state statute might not allow offers to begin

---

38. Ill.–S.H.A. ch. 121½, § 137.52.10 (repealed).

39. Edgar v. MITE Corp., 457 U.S. 624, 642, 102 S.Ct. 2629, 2641, 73 L.Ed.2d 269 (1982). *Accord e.g.,* Mesa Petroleum Co. v. Cities Service Co., 715 F.2d 1425 (10th Cir.1983) (Oklahoma takeover statute ruled unconstitutional); Batus, Inc. v. McKay, 684 F.Supp. 637 (D.Nev.1988) (invalidating Nevada statute).

40. 457 U.S. at 645, 102 S.Ct. at 2642.

41. *Id.* at 645, 102 S.Ct. at 2642.

42. *Id.* at 641–644, 102 S.Ct. at 2640–41.

43. *Id.* at 643, 102 S.Ct. at 2641. The plurality noted that while blue sky laws affect interstate commerce in securities only incidentally, the Illinois Act directly regulated transactions taking place across state lines. *Id.* at 641–644, 102 S.Ct. at 2640–41.

44. *Id.* at 643, 102 S.Ct. at 2641.

45. *Id.* at 632–42, 102 S.Ct. at 2635–40.

46. *Id.* at 633, 102 S.Ct. at 2636 (citing Piper v. Chris–Craft Industries, 430 U.S. 1, 97 S.Ct. 926, 51 L.Ed.2d 124 (1977)).

47. *Id.* at 637 n. 11, 102 S.Ct. at 2638 n. 11.

48. 17 C.F.R. § 240.14d–2(b).

49. MITE Corp. v. Dixon, 633 F.2d 486, 499 n. 25 (7th Cir.1980), *affirmed sub nom.* Edgar v. MITE Corp., 457 U.S. 624, 102 S.Ct. 2629, 73 L.Ed.2d 269 (1982).

50. A public announcement by a bidder which includes the identity of the bidder, the identity of the subject company, and the amount and class of securities being sought and the price or

until after any applicable waiting period and hearing process.[51] The SEC recognized that the conflict between Rule 14d–2(b) and the state statutes made compliance with both sets of requirements impossible, but despite its long history of cooperation with the states in securities regulation, the Commission concluded that the rule was necessary for the protection of investors and that the state takeover statutes then in effect frustrated the operation and purposes of the Williams Act.[52] The overwhelming majority of state and federal courts considering the enforceability of state statutes after the effective date of Rule 14d–2(b) have reached the same conclusion.[53]

In the wake of *Kidwell, MITE,* and Rule 14d–2(b), the provisions which add the most to the value of state statutes as takeover deterrents had been rendered largely unenforceable.[54] Pre-commencement notification provisions and waiting periods, for example, have almost certainly been preempted by Rule 14d–2(b).[55] In addition, state provisions for administrative hearings,[56] more extensive disclosure requirements,[57] and withdrawal and proration rights,[58] other than those established by the Williams Act, have been held invalid, as have state efforts to regulate creeping tender offers.[59] Friendly offer

---

range of prices being offered therefor with respect to a tender offer in which cash or exempt securities are the only consideration shall be deemed to constitute the commencement of a tender offer. Rule 14d–2(b)–(c).

51. Sec.Act Rel. No. 33–6158 (SEC Nov. 29, 1979).

52. *Id.* (citing brief for SEC as *amicus curiae* in Leroy v. Great Western United Corp., 443 U.S. 173, 99 S.Ct. 2710, 61 L.Ed.2d 464 (1979)).

53. *See, e.g.,* Kennecott Corp. v. Smith, 507 F.Supp. 1206 (1981); Crane Co. v. Lam, 509 F.Supp. 782 (E.D.Pa.1981); Canadian Pacific Enterprises v. Krouse, 506 F.Supp. 1192 (S.D.Ohio 1981); Kelly v. Beta–X Corp., 103 Mich.App. 51, 302 N.W.2d 596 (1981); some courts have conceded such preemption, however, only with respect to the waiting period provisions.

54. *See, e.g.,* Newell Co. v. Connolly, 624 F.Supp. 126 (D.Mass.1985) (Massachusetts statute probably in conflict with Williams Act, placing an undue burden on interstate commerce); Missouri Public Service Co. v. Amen, 1983 WL 1503, [1985–1986 Transfer Binder] Fed.Sec.L.Rep. (CCH) ¶ 92,488 (D.Neb.1983) (Nebraska act was undue burden on interstate commerce). *Cf.* Mesa Partners II v. Unocal Corp., 607 F.Supp. 624 (W.D.Okl.1985) (Oklahoma Energy Resource Conservation Act was an undue burden on interstate commerce); Sharon Steel Corp. v. Whaland, 124 N.H. 1, 466 A.2d 919 (1983). *See* C.M.A. McCauliff, Federalism and the Constitutionality of State Takeover Statutes, 67 Va.L.Rev. 295 (1981); Robert A. Profusek & Henry L. Gompf, State Tender Offer Legislation After MITE: Standing Pat, Blue Sky or Corporation Law Concepts: 7 J.Corp.L. 3 (1984). *See also, e.g.* Harold S. Bloomenthal, The New Tender Offer Regimen, State Regulation and Preemption, 30 Emory L.J. 35 (1981); Theodore R. Boehm, State Interests and Interstate Commerce: A Look at the Theoretical Underpinnings of Takeover Legislation, 36 Wash. & Lee L.Rev. 733 (1979).

55. No decision reported to date has sustained a state precommencement waiting period in the face of Rule 14d–2(b).

56. Either as an embodiment of the "benevolent bureaucracy" approach, Hi–Shear Industries, Inc. v. Campbell, 1980 WL 1476, [1981 Transfer Binder] Fed.Sec.L.Rep. (CCH) ¶ 97,804 (D.S.C. 1980), or as a mechanism for delay, Batus, Inc. v. McKay, 684 F.Supp. 637 (D.Nev.1988); Hi–Shear Industries, Inc. v. Neiditz, 1980 WL 1477, [1981 Transfer Binder] Fed.Sec.L.Rep. (CCH) ¶ 97,805 (D.Conn.1980). *See* Mark A. Sargent, On the Validity of State Takeover Regulation: State Responses to *MITE* and *Kidwell,* 42 Ohio St.L.J. 689, 697–98 (1981).

57. These have been held invalid when used as a tool for harassment by target management, (Dart Industries v. Conrad, 462 F.Supp. 1 (S.D.Ind.1978)), or as ancillary to a proceeding incompatible with the Williams Act, (Kennecott Corp. v. Smith, 507 F.Supp. 1206 (D.N.J.1981)).

58. It was so held primarily on the ground that the state provisions create delays which benefit target management. *See, e.g.,* Kennecott Corp. v. Smith, 507 F.Supp. 1206 (D.N.J.1981). *But cf.* Wylain, Inc. v. TRE Corp., 412 A.2d 338 (Del.Ch.1979) (Delaware provision permitting stockholders to withdraw shares any time during offer was merely one of the "greater protections" which states are entitled to provide). *Id.* at 348.

59. *See* Telvest v. Bradshaw, 618 F.2d 1029 (4th Cir.1980), *on remand* 547 F.Supp. 791 (E.D.Va.1982).

exemptions are also clearly vulnerable in light of the Supreme Court's apparent acceptance of *Kidwell's* "regulatory neutrality" approach.[60]

The susceptibility of "traditional" first generation state tender offer statutes has led many states to overhaul their regulatory schemes, purging those aspects that have been found either to conflict with the Williams Act or to impose excessive burdens on interstate commerce. Furthermore, to meet the threshold requirement that the statute "effectuate a legitimate local public interest," some states have narrowed the definition of "target company" to include only those entities in which the state has a more substantial interest.[63] It has been argued that by imposing only minor delays essential to ensure the type of full and fair disclosure contemplated by the Williams Act, and by limiting application to domestic corporations with a substantial presence in the state, the revised statutes complement federal legislation, expressing a bona fide state interest in investor protection and corporate control without obstructing the effectuation of any Congressional purpose.[64]

It has also been argued, however, that state takeover laws should be preempted by Congress because state laws inherently favor target management.[66] The American Law Institute's proposed Federal Securities Code adopted this line of thinking, providing for preemption of state law in any federally regulated takeover bid.[67]

As is discussed more fully in the preceding section,[68] following the Supreme Court decision in *MITE,* a number of states adopted second generation takeover statutes in an attempt to continue to regulate tender offers without imposing the undue burden identified by the *MITE* Court. Two major varieties of statutes have arisen: the control share statutes and the so-called fair price statutes.

Under control share acquisition acts, modeled on legislation that was originally enacted in Ohio,[70] limits are imposed upon a control person's voting rights. In essence, the control person is, at least temporarily, disenfranchised.

---

60. *See* Edgar v. MITE Corp., 457 U.S. 624, 635, 102 S.Ct. 2629, 2637, 73 L.Ed.2d 269 (1982).

63. *See, e.g.,* Conn.Gen.Stat.Ann. § 36–457(a) (" 'Target Company' means any stock corporation which is organized under the laws of this state, has its principal executive office in this state and has, on a consolidated basis, five hundred or more employees and fifty million dollars of tangible assets in this state . . ."); West's Ann.Ind.Code 23–2–3.1–1(j) (" 'Target Company' means an issuer . . . which is organized under the laws of this state, has its principal place of business in this state, and has substantial assets in this state."); Md.Code, Corp. & Assn's Code, §§ 11–902(h)(2)(iv), (i)(1)–(2) (the target must be organized in Maryland, doing business in the state, and have at least thirty five shareholders in the state).

64. *See, e.g.,* Mark A. Sargent, On the Validity of State Takeover Regulation: State Responses to *MITE* and *Kidwell,* 42 Ohio St.L.J. 689, 729–30 (1981).

66. *See* L.P. Acquisition Co. v. Tyson, 772 F.2d 201 (6th Cir.1985) (Michigan statute is preempted by Williams Act). *But cf.* NUI Corp. v. Kimmelman, 765 F.2d 399 (3d Cir.1985) (federal proxy regulation did not preempt New Jersey statute regulating public utility proxy contests).

67. ALI Fed.Sec.Code Proposed Official Draft § 1603(c)(1) (1980).

68. *See* § 10.21 *supra.*

70. Ohio Rev.Code § 1701.83.2. The constitutionality of the Ohio statute was upheld on a motion for preliminary injunctive relief in Veere, Inc. v. Firestone Tire & Rubber Co., 685 F.Supp. 1027 (N.D.Ohio 1988). The Ohio statute was held to be in conflict with the Williams Act and therefore was preempted by federal law. Luxottica Group v. United States Shoe Corp., 919 F.Supp. 1085 (S.D.Ohio 1995). However, a subsequent district court decision upheld the Ohio statute. United Dominion Industries Ltd. v. Commercial Intertech Corp., 943 F.Supp. 857 (S.D.Ohio 1996).

Once the control threshold[72] is crossed, the person in control cannot vote the control shares unless there has been a favorable vote by a majority of the disinterested shares.[73] The concept of disinterested shares excludes not only those held by the person seeking control, but also shares controlled by the target company's management. The Supreme Court, in upholding the Indiana statute, pointed to this feature as preserving neutrality between the control contestants and thus leaving the decision to the target company's shareholders.

The other variety of second generation statutes, known as "fair price," or more accurately, "best price" statutes, provide that any person acquiring a covered corporation must pay the "best price" paid to any one shareholder to all shareholders.[74] The best price requirement can be waived by a shareholder vote.[75] Also, most best price statutes do not apply to friendly takeovers as they may be waived, or otherwise avoided by the target company's board of directors,[76] while a few statutes are not waivable by the directors.

§ 11.13[2][C] The CTS Decision

In CTS Corp. v. Dynamics Corp. of America,[78] the Supreme Court upheld the Indiana control share statute, pointing out that, unlike the Illinois statute which was struck down in *MITE*, the Indiana statute was not balanced in favor of incumbent management.[79] It is thus significant that state takeover statutes maintain a position of neutrality, rather than favoring target management.[80] The Supreme Court's decision in *CTS* has far-reaching implications in permitting states to control the takeover arena by regulating corporate internal affairs.

Although the *CTS* decision does not address the issue, there is a strong argument that best price statutes will withstand constitutional scrutiny. On the other hand, since most best price statutes are waivable by the board of directors, it is arguable that they do not protect the independent shareholder against incumbent management. Giving incumbent management the power to block the hostile takeover by waiving the statute's barrier to permit a friendly defensive arrangement can be viewed as violating the *CTS* neutrality require-

---

72. Control under the Indiana statute is defined in terms of acquiring twenty percent of the voting stock or crossing the threshold above ⅓ or ½ voting control. Ind.Bus.Corp.Law § 23–1–42–1.

73. Disinterested shares are shares not owned by any person seeking to acquire control of the corporation, or by the corporation's officers or directors. Ind.Bus.Corp.Law § 23–1–42–3 (Sup. 1986); N.C.Gen.Stats. § 55–9A–01(b)(4) (1987).

74. *E.g.,* Md. Corp.'s & Ass'ns Code §§ 3–602, 3–603 (defining best price to include the price paid during the past two years); N.C.Gen.Stats. §§ 55–9–01 *et seq.* (best price not defined).

In addition to its best price requirement, the Hawaii statute requires a bidder offer to purchase all of the target company's shares. Haw.Rev.Stat. § 417E–2(3).

75. Md. Corp.'s & Ass'ns Code §§ 3–601 *et seq.* (⅔ shareholder vote); N.C.Gen.Stats. § 55–9–01 (95% vote).

76. Md. Corp.'s & Ass'ns Code §§ 3–601 *et seq.*

78. 481 U.S. 69, 107 S.Ct. 1637, 95 L.Ed.2d 67 (1987).

79. *Id.* at 81–82, 107 S.Ct. at 1645, 95 L.Ed.2d at 80.

80. The Indiana statute, if anything may be seen as favoring the outside bidder because the statute's provisions are triggered by the announcement of an intent to acquire twenty percent of the stock. Once the potential acquirer has made the announcement, he or she can then mandate the shareholder meeting for the vote of disinterested shares. This enables the acquirer to force a shareholder vote prior to acquiring the shares. Ind.Code Ann. § 23–1–42. In contrast, the North Carolina Statute does not permit the acquirer to call the meeting until the shares have been acquired or until there is a legal commitment to acquire them. N.C.Gen.Stat. §§ 55–9A–01 *et seq.*

ment. As the Court pointed out in the *CTS* decision, the control share acquisition statute disenfranchises both the person seeking control and target company management, and thus preserves the neutrality mandated by the Williams Act.

With regard to the Commerce Clause issue, the teaching of the Supreme Court in *CTS* seems to be contained in a three-factor analysis. First, antitakeover legislation enacted by the states must preserve the neutrality of the Williams Act and thus cannot favor target management in its defense of hostile takeovers. Second, the state legislation must leave to the shareholders the decision whether to accept the offer. Third, the Court seems to be more receptive to burdens on interstate commerce arising out of the regulation of internal corporate affairs, at least when the law in question is from the state of incorporation.

As discussed in the preceding section,[83] the third generation of state takeover statutes includes statutes that apply to corporations incorporated outside the state,[84] while other states have adopted freeze statutes,[85] which delay the second step of any two-step merger or other business combination unless the transaction was approved by the target company's directors *prior* to the acquisition of a designated amount of shares by the would-be acquirer.

Although the third generation statutes purporting to regulate foreign corporations are generally based upon substantial contacts within the state, the rationale of the *CTS* decision strongly indicates that such statutes may not withstand constitutional scrutiny.[86] Thus, federal courts have invalidated the Oklahoma and Tennessee statutes on the grounds that they were unconstitutional to the extent that they applied to corporations incorporated outside the state.[87] With regard to the freeze statutes found in Delaware, New York, and elsewhere, there is considerable question whether such statutes can withstand constitutional scrutiny.[88] It can be argued, for example, that the

---

83. *See* § 11.12 *supra.*

84. Ariz.H.R.Res. 2002, 38th Leg., 3d Sess., 1987 Ariz.Legis.Serv. 32–45; 1987 Fla.Laws 87–257; Idaho Code § 30–5002(9); Mass.Ann.Laws Chs. 110D, 110E; former N.C.Gen.Stat. §§ 55–9A–01 *et seq.* (1989).

85. Ariz.Rev.Stat. §§ 10–1221–10–1222 (three year delay); Del.Corp.Code § 203 (three year delay); Minn.Stat.Ann. § 302A.673 (five year delay); Mo.Ann.Stat. § 351.459(3)(b) (five year delay); N.J.Rev.Stat. § 49.5–1 (five year delay); N.Y.Bus.Corp.Law § 912 (five year delay); Wash S.B. No. 6084, 1987 Wash.Leg.Serv. (No. 10) 11 (five year delay); Wis.Stat.Ann. § 180.725 (three year delay).

86. For example, the Court in *CTS* expressly noted that the state of incorporation has a special interest in regulating the internal affairs of its corporations:

The Indiana statute imposes no such problem [presenting an undue burden on interstate commerce]. So long as each state regulates voting rights *only in the corporations it has created,* each corporation will be subject to the law of only one state.

481 U.S. at 89, 107 S.Ct. at 1649, 95 L.Ed.2d 85 (emphasis supplied). *See* Thomas L. Hazen, State Anti–Takeover Legislation: The Second and Third Generations, 23 Wake Forest U.L.Rev. 77 (1988).

87. Tyson Foods, Inc. v. McReynolds, 865 F.2d 99 (6th Cir.1989), *affirming* 700 F.Supp. 906 (M.D.Tenn.1988) (Tennessee statute); TLX Acquisition Corp. v. Telex Corp., 679 F.Supp. 1022 (W.D.Okl.1987) (Oklahoma statute). *Cf.* Veere, Inc. v. Firestone Tire & Rubber Co., 685 F.Supp. 1027 (N.D.Ohio 1988) (indicating that there was no problem with constitutionality of Ohio statute since it applied only to target companies incorporated in Ohio). *See also* P. John Kozyris, Some Observations on State Regulation of Multistate Takeovers—Controlling Choice of Law Through the Commerce Clause, 14 Del.J.Corp.L. 499 (1989).

88. *Cf.* Hyde Park Partners, L.P. v. Connolly, 839 F.2d 837 (1st Cir.1988) (Massachusetts statute imposing one-year moratorium on takeover attempts as a sanction for violation of the statute's disclosure provisions held likely to be preempted by Williams Act).

imposition of a multi-year delay before a merger can be consummated imposes an undue burden on interstate commerce. Nevertheless, the Delaware and New York statutes have withstood challenges at the preliminary injunction stage because of the failure to show a likelihood of success on the merits or the failure to show irreparable injury.

The Seventh Circuit has upheld the Wisconsin version of the freeze statute.[90] The court acknowledged that the three-year waiting period between the purchase of shares by an acquirer not supported by target management and a subsequent merger between the acquirer and target company might well make Wisconsin companies less attractive as takeover targets. However, the court said that the Williams Act did not create a federal right to receive tender offers and thus, the state law was not preempted by the federal statute. The court also ruled that the Wisconsin statute did not violate the Commerce Clause. According to the court, there was no unconstitutional burden on interstate commerce since the law of the state of incorporation properly governs a company's internal affairs and the statute in question was "neutral" in that it does not discriminate according to residence alone. The Seventh Circuit's decision, when combined with the cases decided under the Delaware law, gives growing support to these highly questionable freeze statutes.

The permissible scope of state tender offer legislation is still in the process of being narrowed and defined, and the future of "revised" state statutes remains uncertain. Some degree of uniformity has already been achieved with respect to state takeover legislation. It would seem that some uniformity is clearly desirable in light of the potential impact of tender offers on the national economy.[91] However, disagreement remains as to how much uniformity is necessary and how it should be achieved. Whatever the outcome, state statutes will have played an important role in shaping federal policy and in defining the scope of the Congressional purpose of investor protection.

---

90. Amanda Acquisition Corp. v. Universal Foods Corp., 877 F.2d 496 (7th Cir.1989).

91. *See, e.g.,* brief for SEC as amicus curiae, Great Western United Corp. v. Kidwell, 577 F.2d 1256 (5th Cir.1978), *reversed on other grounds sub nom.* Leroy v. Great Western United Corp., 443 U.S. 173, 99 S.Ct. 2710, 61 L.Ed.2d 464 (1979).

Chapter 12

Manipulation and Fraud—Civil Liability; Implied Private Remedies; SEC Rule 10b–5; Fraud in Connection With the Purchase or Sale of Securities; Improper Trading on Nonpublic Material Information

Table of Sections

---

§ 12.1 Market Manipulation and Deceptive Practices—Sections 9, 10, 14(e), 15(c)

The overwhelming majority of the securities laws' liability provisions (both civil and criminal) focus on disclosure and registration requirements. In addition, there is a group of provisions geared to preventing artificial market activity and practices designed to have the effect of setting manipulated—and hence, artificial—security prices. These provisions are those directed specifically to address market manipulation. The purpose of the various statutes and rules prohibiting market manipulation is to prevent activities that rig the market and thereby to permit the operation of the "natural law" of supply and demand.[1] In this way the market price of securities will reflect as much as is possible a fair and just price for each security.[2] Although it can take many forms, manipulation consists of any intentional interference with supply and demand.[3]

What Constitutes Manipulative Conduct?

Section 9 of the Exchange Act outlaws manipulative practices in connection with the trading of exchange-listed securities and also provides a private remedy for investors injured by the prohibited manipulative conduct.[8] In 2000, section 9(a)'s anti-manipulation provisions (but not section 9(e)'s private right of action) were extended to securities-based swap agreements even though those agreements are not securities under the Act.[9]

Section 9's prohibitions are supplemented by section 10(b),[10] which empowers the SEC to promulgate rules barring manipulative as well as deceptive conduct, and also by section 15(c),[11] which prohibits fraudulent and manipulative conduct by broker-dealers. The language of section 9 limits its application to manipulation of securities that are subject to the Exchange Act's

---

§ 12.1

1. *See, e.g.,* SEC v. First Jersey Securities, 101 F.3d 1450, 1466 (2d Cir.1996), *cert. denied*, 522 U.S. 812, 118 S.Ct. 57, 139 L.Ed.2d 21 (1997); Varljen v. H.J. Meyers, Inc., 1998 WL 395266 (S.D.N.Y.1998).

2. *Id.*

3. Brooklyn Capital & Securities Trading, Inc., 52 S.E.C. 1286, Sec. Exch. Rel. No. 34–38454, 64 S.E.C. Docket 483, 1997 WL 144843 *3 (SEC 1997) (manipulation is the "intentional interference with the forces of supply and demand") (quoting Pagel, Inc., 48 S.E.C. 223, 226 (1985), aff'd, 803 F.2d 942 (5th Cir. 1986)).

8. 15 U.S.C.A. § 78i.

Sections 10 and 15 of the Securities Exchange Act cover manipulation with regard to NASDAQ listed securities or others in the over-the-counter markets. Cowen & Co. v. Merriam, 745 F.Supp. 925 (S.D.N.Y.1990).

Some commentators have questioned the efficiency of prohibiting manipulative activities. *See, e.g.,* Daniel R. Fischel & David J. Ross, Should the Law Prohibit "Manipulation" in Financial Markets?, 105 Harv.L.Rev. 503 (1991). However, these prohibitions are necessary in order to maintain accurate pricing by the markets.

9. 15 U.S.C.A. § 78i(a) as amended by Pub. Law 106–554, 114 Stat. 2763 (December 21, 2000); 15 U.S.C.A. §§ 77b–1(b)(1), 78c–1(b)(1) (both of which exclude "security-based swap agreements" from the definition of "security").

10. 15 U.S.C.A. § 78j(b).

11. 15 U.S.C.A. § 78o(c). Broker-dealer regulation and selected fraudulent and manipulative practices including churning, scalping, and boiler room operations are discussed in chapter 14 *infra.*

registration and reporting requirements[13] by virtue of being listed on a national exchange,[14] whereas section 10(b) is not so limited and applies to all securities transactions utilizing an instrumentality of interstate commerce. Unlike most other provisions of the 1934 Act, section 9 is limited to securities on a national exchange and does not apply to the securities of the many registered reporting companies that are traded in the over-the-counter markets.[16] Section 15(c) of the Act—in prohibiting fraudulent broker-dealer practices—covers securities traded in the over-the-counter markets, in addition to municipal securities.[17]

In interpreting the Exchange Act provisions, the courts have recognized the concept of manipulation as a narrow one. In the first instance, there is a specific intent requirement.[18] Manipulation, as that term is used in the securities laws, does not extend to many acts and practices that have the effect of manipulating the price of a security but are not so specifically intended. Presumably, manipulation has the same meaning under each of the Exchange Act provisions. In order to prevail in a suit charging manipulation, it must be proven that the defendant's primary intent in entering the transaction was price manipulation.[19] It is not sufficient that the challenged conduct simply had the effect of artificially affecting the price of the security. The Supreme Court has repeatedly stated that manipulation is "a term of art" limited to certain types of transactions specifically designed to artificially affect the price of a security.[20] Therefore, the fact that the conduct in question affects the price of a security will not by itself mean that it was an illegal manipulative act. Once the manipulative intent is present, however, conduct that affects the price is manipulative.[22]

Common examples of manipulation include wash sales and matched orders.[28] A wash sale is a fictitious sale where there is no change in beneficial ownership and thus no true economic consequence.[29] A matched order occurs when orders are entered simultaneously to buy and sell the same security.[30]

---

13.   15 U.S.C.A. §§ 78*l*, 78m(a). *See* §§ 9.2, 9.3 *supra.*

14.   The National Exchanges are the formal securities exchanges registered under section 6 of the 1934 Act. 15 U.S.C.A. § 78f.

16.   15 U.S.C.A. § 78i(a).

17.   15 U.S.C.A. § 78n(c)(1).

18.   *See, e.g.,* Schreiber v. Burlington Northern, Inc., 472 U.S. 1, 105 S.Ct. 2458, 86 L.Ed.2d 1 (1985); Santa Fe Industries, Inc. v. Green, 430 U.S. 462, 476, 97 S.Ct. 1292, 1302, 51 L.Ed.2d 480 (1977); Ernst & Ernst v. Hochfelder, 425 U.S. 185, 199, 96 S.Ct. 1375, 1383, 47 L.Ed.2d 668 (1976).

19.   *E.g.,* S.E.C. v. U.S. Environmental, Inc., 155 F.3d 107 (2d Cir.1998); United States v. Minuse, 142 F.2d 388, 389 (2d Cir.1944), *cert. denied,* 323 U.S. 716, 65 S.Ct. 43, 89 L.Ed. 576 (1944).

20.   Santa Fe Industries, Inc. v. Green, 430 U.S. 462, 476, 97 S.Ct. 1292, 1302, 51 L.Ed.2d 480 (1977); Ernst & Ernst v. Hochfelder, 425 U.S. 185, 199, 96 S.Ct. 1375, 1383, 47 L.Ed.2d 668 (1976). *See* Schreiber v. Burlington Northern, Inc., 472 U.S. 1, 105 S.Ct. 2458, 86 L.Ed.2d 1 (1985).

22.   *E.g.,* Markowski v. SEC, 274 F.3d 525 (D.C.Cir. 2001). *See also, e.g.,* GFL Advantage Fund, Ltd. v. Colkitt, 272 F.3d 189, 205 (3d Cir. 2001); Nanopierce Technologies, Inc. v. Southridge Capital Management LLC., 2002 WL 31819207 *8, Fed. Sec. L. Rep. ¶ 92253 (S.D.N.Y. 2002); Internet Law Library v. Southridge Capital Mgmt., 223 F.Supp.2d 474 (S.D.N.Y. 2002).

28.   *See, e.g.,* Edward J. Mawod & Co. v. SEC, 591 F.2d 588 (10th Cir.1979).

29.   *See, e.g.,* Ernst & Ernst v. Hochfelder, 425 U.S. 185, 205, n. 25, 96 S.Ct. 1375, 47 L.Ed.2d 668 (1976); Dietrich v. Bauer, 76 F.Supp.2d 312, 339 (S.D.N.Y.1999).

30.   Dietrich v. Bauer, 76 F.Supp.2d 312, 340 (S.D.N.Y.1999) ("A market manipulation claim can also be based on matched orders—'orders for the purchase/sale of a security that are entered

Another manipulative practice is known as "parking," which consists of transferring record ownership of securities in order to hide the true identity of the beneficial owner.[31] A planned series of purchases of securities that is specifically designed to artificially restrict the supply and thereby raise prices is a manipulation.[32]

Manipulation can take many forms. Manipulations often have a number of common characteristics. For example, the following factors are "classic elements" of a market manipulation: (i) restriction of the "float" or floating supply of the securities in the public market; (ii) price leadership by the manipulator; (iii) dominating and controlling the market for the security; and (iv) a collapse of the market for the security after the manipulative activity has ceased.[33] The foregoing factors are indicia of market manipulation, but are not necessarily present in every manipulation case.[34]

Subjective intent combined with deceptive conduct can establish manipulation.[40] Manipulative conduct is not limited to conduct that actually causes a rise (or fall) in the stock price. It includes conduct that retards a decline in price that would otherwise result from supply and demand forces.[41]

The Deception Requirement

The impact of the Supreme Court's decision in Schreiber v. Burlington Northern, Inc.[78] could arguably be carried over to section 10(b). The Court in *Schreiber* held that "[w]ithout misrepresentation or non-disclosure, '14(e) has not been violated.'"[79] The Court reached this conclusion by a rather unusual view of the section's legislative history.[80] When enacted in 1968, section 14(e) prohibited material misrepresentations and omissions of material fact as well as "fraudulent, deceptive, or manipulative acts or practices" in connection with a tender offer.

---

with the knowledge that orders of substantially the same size, at substantially the same time and price, have been or will be entered by the same or different persons for the sale/purchase of such security'"), *quoting from* Ernst & Ernst v. Hochfelder, 425 U.S. 185, 205, n. 25, 96 S.Ct. 1375, 47 L.Ed.2d 668 (1976).

31. *See, e.g.,* Yoshikawa v. SEC, 192 F.3d 1209 (9th Cir.1999); SIPC v. Vigman, 74 F.3d 932, 933 n. 3 (9th Cir.1996).

32. *See, e.g.,* SEC v. National Bankers Life Ins. Co., 334 F.Supp. 444, 446 (N.D.Tex.1971), *affirmed,* 477 F.2d 920 (5th Cir.1973).

33. *See, e.g.,* SEC v. Resch–Cassin & Co., 362 F.Supp. 964, 976 (S.D.N.Y.1973).

34. In the Matter of Swartwood, Hesse, Inc., 50 S.E.C. 1301, 1307, Admin. Proc. No. 3–6985 Sec. Act Rel. No. 34–31212, 52 S.E.C. Docket 1557, 1992 WL 252184 (SEC 1992).

40. *See, e.g.,* Nanopierce Technologies, Inc. v. Southridge Capital Management LLC., 2002 WL 31819207 *8, Fed. Sec. L. Rep. ¶ 92253 (S.D.N.Y. 2002), relying on Internet Law Library v. Southridge Capital Mgmt., 223 F.Supp.2d 474 (S.D.N.Y. 2002).

41. In the Matter of Faherty, 2003 WL 1125247 (SEC 2003).

78. 472 U.S. 1, 105 S.Ct. 2458, 86 L.Ed.2d 1 (1985).

79. *Id.* at 12, 105 S.Ct. at 2464–65, 86 L.Ed.2d at 10. The Court further noted, "[n]owhere in the legislative history is there the slightest suggestion that section 14(e) serves any purpose other than disclosure * * *" *Id.* at 11, 105 S.Ct. at 2464, 86 L.Ed.2d at 9. *See also, e.g.,* Metzner v. D.H. Blair & Co., 689 F.Supp. 262 (S.D.N.Y.1988) (nondisclosure of market manipulation violates Rule 10b–5).

In 1988, the Third Circuit gave a narrow reading to the scope of the *Schreiber* decision in upholding the validity of SEC Rule 14d–10 (17 C.F.R. § 240.14d–10). Polaroid Corp. v. Disney, 862 F.2d 987, 994–95 (3d Cir.1988); *see* § 11.5 *supra.*

80. 472 U.S. at 13, 105 S.Ct. at 2465, 86 L.Ed.2d at 10. *See also* the discussion in § 11.6 *supra.*

§ 12.1[3] Manipulative and Deceptive Acts and Practices—Section 10; Section 15(c)

§ 12.1[3][A] Overview of Anti–Manipulation Provisions

A later chapter of this treatise[87] discusses in more detail the various SEC and NASD prohibitions that address fraudulent and deceptive practices generally as well as particular types of misconduct by broker-dealers. Broker-dealers and their employees are, of course, subject to Rule 10b–5's general anti-fraud proscriptions that prohibit any person from engaging in deceptive conduct in connection with a purchase or sale of a security.[88] SEC Rule 15c1–2[89] is a rule specifically tailored to broker-dealers and generally prohibits fraudulent, manipulative and deceptive practices in connection with securities brokerage transactions. The types of specific conduct that are addressed in other broker-dealer rules include market manipulation,[90] high pressure sales tactics,[91] deceptive recommendations,[92] generation of excessive commissions,[93] unauthorized trading,[94] improper order executions,[95] improper extension of credit for securities transactions,[96] and misuse of customer funds or securities.[97] Manipulation can arise in many respects in connection with a public offering of securities.[98] For example, SEC Regulation M[99] severely regulates purchases of publicly offered securities by participants in a public offering.

Beyond the above-mentioned specific manipulative broker-dealer activities and the general anti-manipulation and deception rules, the SEC makes it clear that violation of its rules is not limited to violation of any specified SEC rules, but rather covers all conduct that operates as a deceptive or manipulative device.[100] In addition to the applicable statutes and SEC rules, the rules of the various self-regulatory organizations (the stock exchanges and the National Association of Securities Dealers) impose standards of conduct on broker dealers.[101] Finally, these requirements may be supplemented in appropriate cases by fiduciary duty principles.[102] Because they result from artificial activity, manipulated prices are in and of themselves unfair.[103]

---

87. *See* §§ 14.3[6], 14.10[5], 14.14–14.23 *infra.*

88. 17 C.F.R. § 240.10b–5. *See* §§ 12.3–12.12 *infra.*

89. 17 C.F.R. § 240.15c1–2.

90. *See* §§ 6.2–6.3 *supra* (manipulation in connection with public offerings), § 12.1 *supra* (manipulation generally), and § 14.10[5] *infra* (manipulation by market makers).

91. *See* § 14.18 *infra.*

92. *See* §§ 14.15–14.18 *infra.*

93. *See* § 14.20 *infra.*

94. *See* § 14.21 *infra.*

95. *See* § 14.13 *infra.*

96. *See* § 14.9 *infra.*

97. *See* § 14.8[2] *infra.*

98. *See* § 6.2 *supra* (discussing Regulation M and manipulation and stabilization during a distribution) and § 6.3 *supra* (discussing hot issues and work-out markets).

99. 17 C.F.R. §§ 242.101 *et seq.*; *See* Anti–Manipulation Rules Concerning Securities Offerings, Sec. Rel. Nos. 33–7375; 34–38076; IC–22412 (Dec. 20, 1996), 62 Fed. Reg. 520 (1997). *See* § 6.2 *supra.*

100. Rule 15c1–2(c), 17 C.F.R. § 240.15c1–2(c).

101. NASD Manual Conduct Rule 2110 (available on Westlaw) ("a member in the conduct of its business, shall observe high standards of commercial honor and just and equitable principles of trade").

102. *See* § 14.15 *infra.*

103. *See, e.g.,* Universal Heritage Investments Corporation, 47 S.E.C. 839, 843 (1982).

Section 10(a) of the 1934 Act[104] prohibits "short sales" and "stop loss" orders in violation of SEC rules.[105] Section 10(b), which is much broader, provides that it is unlawful "to use or employ [utilizing any means or instrumentality of interstate commerce], in connection with the purchase or sale of any security * * * any manipulative or deceptive device or contrivance in contravention of such rules and regulations as the Commission may prescribe as necessary or appropriate in the public interest or for the protection of investors."[106] The SEC, following the legislative mandate, has invoked its rulemaking authority to prohibit a wide variety of conduct that is outlined here and discussed more fully in other sections of this book.

§ 12.1[3][B][2] The Section 10(b) Rules

Rule 10b–1[107] applies the prohibitions against market manipulation contained in section 9(a)[108] to securities exempt from section 12's registration requirements.[109]

Rule 10b–3 prohibits broker-dealers from engaging in manipulative or deceptive acts and practices with regard to securities not traded on a national exchange[114] and with regard to municipal securities.[115] Rule 10b–3 thus closes a large part of the gap left by section 9, which applies only to transactions effected through a national exchange.

Former Rule 10b–4 addressed short tendering in connection with tender offers and has been replaced by Rule 14e–4.[116]

Rule 10b–5[120] is the broadest of the section 10(b) rules. Rule 10b–5 prohibits material misstatements and omissions as well as fraudulent acts in connection with purchases and sales of securities; it supports a broad implied private right of action.[121] Rule 10b–5 is considered throughout this chapter.

Former Rule 10b–6,[122] which is now part of Regulation M, prohibited purchases during a distribution of securities by persons interested in the distribution, except for stabilizing bids in compliance with former Rule 10b–7 which is now Rule 104 of Regulation M.[123] Former Rule 10b–8,[124] which is now a part of Regulation M, prohibited manipulative and deceptive devices in

---

104. 15 U.S.C.A. § 78j(a).

105. Rule 10a–1, 17 C.F.R. § 240.10a–1 sets out the SEC's position. Rule 10a–1 was amended when the SEC adopted Regulation SHO governing short sales. *See, e.g.,* Short Sales, Sec. Exch. Act Rel. No. 34–50103, 2004 WL 1697019 (SEC 2004).

106. 15 U.S.C.A. § 78j(b).

107. 17 C.F.R. § 240.10b–1.

108. 15 U.S.C.A. § 78i(a).

109. 15 U.S.C.A. § 78*l*.

114. 17 C.F.R. § 240.10b–3(a).

115. 17 C.F.R. § 240.10b–3(b). Municipal securities are discussed in § 14.6 *infra.*

116. 17 C.F.R. § 240.14e–4. *See* 17 C.F.R. § 240.10b–4 (1990). *See* Chapter 11 *supra.*

120. 17 C.F.R. § 240.10b–5.

121. *See* §§ 12.3–12.4 *infra.*

122. 17 C.F.R. § 240.10b–6 (1996). *See, e.g.,* Fred N. Gerard & Michael L. Hirschfeld, The Scienter Requirement Under Rule 10b–6, 46 Bus.Law. 777 (1991).

123. 17 C.F.R. § 240.10b–7 (1996). *See* § 6.1 *supra.*

124. 17 C.F.R. § 240.10b–8 (1998).

connection with a securities distribution through rights held by security holders.

Rule 10b–9 prohibits "all or none" offerings of securities unless all such securities are "sold at a specified price within a specified time, and * * * the total amount due to the seller is received by him by a specified date."[125] A private right of action for violation of Rule 10b–9 has been recognized by at least one court.[128]

Rule 10b–10 requires that brokers confirm all transactions in writing.[129] Among other things, the confirmation must disclose the broker's commission and whether he or she is acting as principal or as an agent for someone other than the customer.[130]

Former Rule 10b–13[133] which prohibited a tender offeror from purchasing securities targeted by the tender offer once the tender offer has commenced has been carried forward in Rule 14e–5,[135] which is now a part of Regulation 14E governing manipulative and deceptive tender offer practices.

Rule 10b–16[137] requires disclosure of credit terms in connection with margin transactions.[138] Rule 10b–17 prohibits untimely announcements of dividends, stock splits, reverse stock splits, and rights or subscription offerings.[139] Rule 10b–18 sets out a safe harbor rule for issuer purchases of its own shares.[142]

§ 12.1[3][C] Manipulation Rules Under Section 15 of the Exchange Act

Section 15(c) prohibits brokers and dealers from participating in manipulative, deceptive or fraudulent acts and practices in connection with sales, or attempts to induce purchases or sales, of securities.[174] This prohibition extends to dealings in municipal securities[175] and transactions in connection with the procedures set up to facilitate a national market system.[176] As is the case with section 10(b), the rules promulgated under section 15(c) span a wide variety of conduct.[180]

---

125. 17 C.F.R. § 240.10b–9(a)(1).

128. Bormann v. Applied Vision Systems, Inc., 800 F.Supp. 800 (D.Minn.1992) (describing the decision as a case of first impression).

129. 17 C.F.R. § 240.10b–10.

130. *Id.*

133. 17 C.F.R. § 240.10b–13 (1998). *See* Lewis D. Lowenfels, Rule 10b–13, Rule 10b–6 and Purchases of Target Company Securities During an Exchange Offer, 69 Colum.L.Rev. 1392 (1969). *See also* §§ 6.1, 11.6 *supra.*

135. 17 C.F.R. § 240.14e–5.

137. 17 C.F.R. § 240.10b–16.

138. *See* § 14.9 *infra.*

139. 17 C.F.R. § 240.10b–17.

142. 17 C.F.R. § 240.10b–18. *See* § 11.6 *supra.*

174. 15 U.S.C.A. §§ 78*o*(c)(1), (c)(2).

175. 15 U.S.C.A. § 78*o*(c)(2).

176. 15 U.S.C.A. § 78*o*(c)(6). *See* § 14.2 *infra.*

180. Many of these rules are discussed in other sections of this book. *See* especially chapter 14 *infra.*

Rule 15c1–2 prohibits fraud and misrepresentation by securities brokers and dealers and also prohibits conduct that operates as a fraud[182] and material misstatements and omissions[183] within section 15(c)'s purview. Rule 15c1–3 prohibits brokers and dealers from implying that the SEC has reviewed their financial standing and/or business practices.[184] Under Rule 15c1–5,[185] broker-dealers including municipal securities dealers who control or are controlled by the issuer of a security, cannot enter a customer's transaction without disclosing the control relationship.[186]

Rule 15c1–6[187] requires brokers and dealers participating or interested in a distribution to fully disclose such participation or interest. Rule 15c1–7 prohibits churning or the charging of excessive fees[188] in connection with discretionary accounts, and requires prompt disclosure of all transactions made on behalf of discretionary accounts.[189] Rule 15c1–8[190] prohibits sales "at the market" unless the broker or dealer has a reasonable belief that a market exists. Rule 15c1–9 prohibits brokers and dealers from disseminating pro forma financial statements with regard to issuers and their securities unless the assumptions underlying the pro forma figures are explicitly disclosed and explained.[191] Rule 15c2–1 prohibits brokers and dealers from hypothecating customers' securities and certain commingling of securities held by the broker-dealer for the customer.[192]

Rule 15c2–4 requires prompt transmission by brokers and dealers of all funds or other consideration received in connection with underwriting activities.[193] Rule 15c2–5 requires disclosures of the terms of and risks associated with securities transactions on credit;[194] compliance with Regulation T's margin procedures[195] will satisfy the rule.[196]

In 1992, the Commission adopted more comprehensive penny stock regulation in Rules 15g–1 through 15g–6[200]; these rules replaced the former Rule 15c2–6.

182. 17 C.F.R. § 240.15c1–2(a). This language parallels Rule 10b–5(c) and section 17(a)(3) of the 1933 Act. 15 U.S.C.A. § 77q(a)(3); 17 C.F.R. § 240.10b–5.

183. 17 C.F.R. § 240.15c1–2(b).

184. 17 C.F.R. § 240.15c1–3.

185. 17 C.F.R. § 240.15c1–5.

186. *See* Rule 12b–2 for the Exchange Act's broad definition of control, which includes the power to directly or indirectly influence management. 17 C.F.R. § 240.12b–2. *Accord* 17 C.F.R. § 230.405.

187. 17 C.F.R. § 240.15c1–6.

188. 17 C.F.R. § 240.15c1–7(a). *See* § 14.14 *infra*.

189. 17 C.F.R. § 240.15c1–7(b).

190. 17 C.F.R. § 240.15c1–8. *See* § 6.2 *supra*.

191. 17 C.F.R. § 240.15c1–9. Compare Rule 175's safe harbor for projections by issuers. 17 C.F.R. § 230.175. *See* § 3.9 *supra*.

192. 17 C.F.R. § 240.15c2–1.

193. 17 C.F.R. § 240.15c2–4. The funds can be held in a separate account with a bank if received in connection with an "all or none" or other conditional offering. 17 C.F.R. § 240.15c2–4(b).

194. 17 C.F.R. § 240.15c2–5.

195. *See* § 14.9 *infra*.

196. 17 C.F.R. § 240.15c2–5(b). The rule does not apply to municipal securities. 17 C.F.R. § 240.15c2–5(c). *See* § 14.6 *infra*.

200. 17 C.F.R. §§ 240.15g–1 to 240.15g–6.

Rule 15c2–7[201] generally requires all market quotations to be properly identified, including the identity of the broker or dealer placing the quotation. The rule thus prohibits "fictitious" quotations without disclosure to the applicable inter-dealer quotation system that any such quotation is properly being entered on behalf of another broker-dealer or is entered pursuant to an arrangement with other broker-dealers.

Rule 15c2–8[202] establishes what constitutes proper conduct relating to brokers' and dealers' prospectus delivery obligations under the Securities Act of 1933.[203] Rule 15c2–11 prohibits brokers or dealers from entering or resuming quotations in securities unless there is adequate available current public information concerning the security and issuer.[204] There is a safe harbor for determining whether the public information is reasonably current.[205]

§ 12.1[4] Manipulation: Private Remedies

§ 12.1[4][A] Manipulation of Exchange Listed Securities— Section 9(e)'s Express Remedy

Section 9(e) gives a private remedy in damages to any investor who is injured by conduct in violation of section 9,[215] which is limited to securities on a national exchange.[216] Section 9 requires that the plaintiff's injury arise out of the purchase or sale of a manipulated security; it is not sufficient that the plaintiff retained the security that was the subject of the alleged manipulation.[217] In addition to costs and reasonable attorneys' fees, the plaintiff is entitled to damages based on the difference between the actual value and the price as affected by the manipulative conduct.[218] Liability under section 9(e) is expressly limited to persons "willfully" participating in the manipulative conduct; willfulness would seem to be an even stricter requirement than scienter, which is required generally in suits under Rule 10b–5.[219] It must be remembered that, in addition to the defendant's willful participation, the

---

201. 17 C.F.R. § 240.15c2–7.

202. 17 C.F.R. § 240.15c2–8.

203. *See* 15 U.S.C.A. §§ 77e(b) and 77j, which are discussed in §§ 2.4, 2.5 *supra.*

204. 17 C.F.R. § 240.15c2–11. The types of information required are tied into the 1933 and 1934 Acts' disclosure requirements for issuers. Among other things, the rule operates to preclude widespread distribution of securities without registration. *See* § 5.3 *supra.*

205. Unless the broker or dealer has information to the contrary, a timely balance sheet will suffice. 17 C.F.R. § 240.15c2–11(g). This is defined as a balance sheet reflecting the past twelve months and which is no more than sixteen months old. *Id.*

215. 15 U.S.C.A. § 78i(e). As discussed *infra,* section 9(e)'s express remedy is limited to exchange-listed securities. At least one court has indicated, however, that manipulative conduct may be challenged by way of an implied action under section 9(a). *See* Matthey v. KDI Corp., 699 F.Supp. 135 (S.D.Ohio 1988).

216. *E.g.,* Cowen & Co. v. Merriam, 745 F.Supp. 925 (S.D.N.Y.1990) (section 9 action could not be brought for alleged manipulation in stock traded through the NASD Automated System since NASDAQ is not a "national securities exchange"). Conduct that violates section 9 cannot successfully be attacked under the antitrust laws because of the antitrust immunity that flows from SEC regulation of the securities markets. *See, e.g.,* Friedman v. Salomon/Smith Barney, Inc., 2000 WL 1804719, [2000–2001 Transfer Binder] Fed. Sec. L. Rep. (CCH) ¶ 91,273, 2000–2 (S.D.N.Y. 2000), *rehearing denied,* 2001 WL 64774 (S.D.N.Y.2001). *See also, e.g.,* United States v. NASD, 422 U.S. 694, 95 S.Ct. 2427, 45 L.Ed.2d 486 (1975); Finnegan v. Campeau Corp., 915 F.2d 824 (2d Cir.1990).

217. Lowe v. Salomon Smith Barney, Inc., 206 F.Supp.2d 442 (W.D.N.Y.2002) (dismissing plaintiff's manipulation claim).

218. 15 U.S.C.A. § 78i(e).

219. *See* § 12.8 *infra.*

substantive violation requires proof of manipulative intent. In addition, in order to recover for manipulative conduct, the plaintiff must show that his or her injury was a direct, rather than remote, consequence of the prohibited activity. All of the foregoing factors combine to make the section 9(e) remedy a very limited one.

§ 12.1[4][B] Manipulation: Implied Remedies

The Fifth Circuit initially held that manipulative activity that comes within the scope of section 9 cannot give rise to a Rule 10b–5 action independently; plaintiff had to establish that all of section 9's elements had been met.[223] Quite properly, however, that decision was vacated and remanded[224] for further consideration in light of Herman & MacLean v. Huddleston,[225] which held that the remedies under Rule 10b–5 and section 11 of the 1933 Act[226] are cumulative. In light of that Supreme Court ruling, it seems implausible that the section 9 and Rule 10b–5 remedies are mutually exclusive.[227] In other words, a plaintiff injured by the defendant's manipulative conduct may sue under either or both sections.[228] Accordingly, it is clear that manipulation can form the basis of a Rule 10b–5 claim, provided that all of the elements of a 10b–5 claim can be established.[229] Those principal elements include showing that the defendant acted with scienter,[230] that the plaintiff was deceived by relying on the deceptive conduct,[231] and that the injury[232] was caused by the defendant's conduct.[233] Additionally, when a claim is based on violation of any of the SEC rules promulgated under section 15,[234] a private remedy will exist.

§ 12.2 Implied Remedies in the Federal Courts

§ 12.2[1] The Trend Limiting Implied Remedies

Although the securities laws provide a wide variety of express statutory remedies for injured investors,[1] powerful private enforcement weapons have arisen out of implied rights of action. However, the Supreme Court has been

---

223. Chemetron Corp. v. Business Funds, Inc., 682 F.2d 1149 (5th Cir.1982), *vacated and remanded*, 460 U.S. 1007, 103 S.Ct. 1245, 75 L.Ed.2d 476 (1983), *on remand*, 718 F.2d 725 (5th Cir.1983).

224. *Id.*

225. 459 U.S. 375, 103 S.Ct. 683, 74 L.Ed.2d 548 (1983).

226. 15 U.S.C.A. § 77k. *See* §§ 7.3, 7.4 *supra*.

227. *See also, e.g.,* Marc I. Steinberg, The Propriety and Scope of Cumulative Remedies Under the Federal Securities Laws, 67 Cornell L.Rev. 557 (1982).

228. *See, e.g.,* Chemetron Corp. v. Business Funds, Inc., 718 F.2d 725 (5th Cir.1983).

229. For an overview of the elements of a Rule 10b–5 claim, *see* § 12.4 *infra*.

230. Scienter is discussed in § 12.8 *infra*.

231. Reliance is discussed in § 12.10 *infra*.

232. Damages are discussed in § 12.12 *infra*.

233. Causation is discussed in § 12.11 *infra*.

234. 15 U.S.C.A. § 78o; *see* § 12.1[3][C] *supra*.

§ 12.2

1. Sections 11, 12(a)(1), and 12(a)(2) of the 1933 Act, 15 U.S.C.A. §§ 77k, 77*l*(a)(1), (2); *see* §§ 7.2–7.6 *supra* (dealing with, respectively, misleading registration materials, failure to comply with that Act's prospectus requirements, and material misstatements by sellers of securities); Sections 9(e), 16(b), and 18(a) of the Exchange Act, 15 U.S.C.A. §§ 78i(e), 78p(b), 78r(a) (dealing with manipulation of exchange-listed securities, disgorgement of insider short-swing profits, and material misstatements and omissions in SEC filings).

See § 1.8 *supra* for an overview of the private remedies available under the 1933 and 1934 Acts.

narrowing the number of implied remedies available under federal statutes. This narrowing trend has resulted in limiting the remedies that have been recognized. Since it is clear that private remedies will not lightly be read into the statutes, it is questionable whether additional new remedies will be recognized. On the other hand, there are some firmly entrenched implied rights of action for securities law violations; however, even they have been significantly narrowed since the mid 1970s.

The restrictive trend of the implication cases generally has not bypassed the securities laws. The Supreme Court has reaffirmed its past recognition of implied private rights of action for violations of Rule 10b–5 and section 10(b) of the Securities Exchange Act of 1934[2] and the proxy disclosure requirements of section 14(a) of the Act.[3] At the same time, there has been a narrowing of the scope of these remedies.[4] The lower courts are in conflict as to the existence of implied remedies under section 17(a) of the 1933 Act and section 14(e) of the Exchange Act,[5] while other remedies have been denied.[6] At the Supreme Court level there have been a number of decisions denying or limiting private rights of action in the securities area. The Court has denied the existence of an implied remedy for damages under the anti-fraud provision of the Investment Advisers Act of 1940,[7] and found no remedy under section 17(a) of the Securities Exchange Act of 1934.[8] Also, the Court held that a competing tender offeror does not have an implied remedy for violation of the Exchange Act's anti-fraud provisions with regard to tender offers, but nevertheless indicated that a private remedy may exist in the hands of a more appropriate plaintiff.[9]

---

2. 15 U.S.C.A. § 78j(b); 17 C.F.R. § 240.10b–5. *See, e.g.,* Herman & MacLean v. Huddleston, 459 U.S. 375, 103 S.Ct. 683, 74 L.Ed.2d 548 (1983); Affiliated Ute Citizens v. United States, 406 U.S. 128, 92 S.Ct. 1456, 31 L.Ed.2d 741 (1972).

3. 15 U.S.C.A. § 78n(a); 17 C.F.R. § 240.14a–9. *See* J.I. Case Co. v. Borak, 377 U.S. 426, 84 S.Ct. 1555, 12 L.Ed.2d 423 (1964). *See also, e.g.,* TSC Indus., Inc. v. Northway, Inc., 426 U.S. 438, 96 S.Ct. 2126, 48 L.Ed.2d 757 (1976).

4. *See, e.g.,* Central Bank of Denver v. First Interstate Bank of Denver, 511 U.S. 164, 114 S.Ct. 1439, 128 L.Ed.2d 119 (1994) (there is no implied remedy against aiders and abettors); Santa Fe Industries, Inc. v. Green, 430 U.S. 462, 97 S.Ct. 1292, 51 L.Ed.2d 480 (1977) (Rule 10b–5 covers only deceptive conduct), *on remand,* 562 F.2d 4 (2d Cir.1977); Ernst & Ernst v. Hochfelder, 425 U.S. 185, 96 S.Ct. 1375, 47 L.Ed.2d 668 (1976), *rehearing denied,* 425 U.S. 986, 96 S.Ct. 2194, 48 L.Ed.2d 811 (1976) (a violation of Rule 10b–5 requires a showing of scienter); Blue Chip Stamps v. Manor Drug Stores, 421 U.S. 723, 95 S.Ct. 1917, 44 L.Ed.2d 539 (1975), *rehearing denied,* 423 U.S. 884, 96 S.Ct. 157, 46 L.Ed.2d 114 (1975) (plaintiff must have been a purchaser or seller).

See also Lewis D. Lowenfels, Recent Supreme Court Decisions Under the Federal Securities Laws: The Pendulum Swings, 65 Geo. L.J. 891 (1977). *Compare* Thomas L. Hazen, The Supreme Court and the Securities Laws: Has the Pendulum Slowed? 30 Emory L.J. 3 (1981).

5. 15 U.S.C.A. §§ 77q(a), 78n(e). *See* §§ 11.6, 11.10 *supra,* § 12.22 *infra.*

6. These include violation of exchange and NASD rules, *see* §§ 10.6–10.10, 10.14 *supra,* and violation of the Exchange Act's margin requirements, *see* § 14.9 *infra. But cf.* In the matter of the Arbitration Between Offerman & Co. v. Hamilton Investments, Inc., [1993–1994 Transfer Binder] Fed. Sec. L. Rep. (CCH) ¶ 98,233 (E.D.Wis.1994) (absence of private right for investors does not mean that an NASD member may not be able to bring an action for violation of NASD rules).

7. Transamerica Mortgage Advisors, Inc. v. Lewis, 444 U.S. 11, 100 S.Ct. 242, 62 L.Ed.2d 146 (1979). The Court there did, however, recognize an implied right of rescission. The Investment Advisers Act is discussed in chapter 21 *infra.*

8. Touche Ross & Co. v. Redington, 442 U.S. 560, 99 S.Ct. 2479, 61 L.Ed.2d 82 (1979), *on remand,* 612 F.2d 68 (2d Cir.1979). Section 17(a) contains reporting requirements for members of exchanges and broker-dealers under the Municipal Securities Rule–Making Board or the NASD. *See* §§ 14.3, 14.6 *infra.*

9. Piper v. Chris–Craft Industries, Inc., 430 U.S. 1, 97 S.Ct. 926, 51 L.Ed.2d 124 (1977), *rehearing denied,* 430 U.S. 976, 97 S.Ct. 1668, 52 L.Ed.2d 371 (1977).

The Supreme Court ruled that there is no implied right of action against aiders and abettors of securities law violations.[10] Notwithstanding these and other narrowing decisions, the Court has held that the Rule 10b–5 remedy is cumulative and applies even though there may be express remedies covering the transaction in question.[11] Additionally, at the same time that it was limiting securities remedies, the Court recognized an implied remedy under the Commodity Exchange Act[12] in a decision that may also have some lessons for actions under the securities laws.[13]

§ 12.3 Section 10(b) and the Evolution of the Implied Remedy Under SEC Rule 10b–5

§ 12.3[1] The Statutory Context

The primary private remedy for fraud available under the Securities Exchange Act has been the one implied SEC Rule 10b–5,[1] which prohibits fraudulent conduct in connection with a purchase or sale of securities. Although several Supreme Court cases have limited the scope of the 10b–5 private right of action, it continues to be a significant weapon against securities fraud. To put the Rule 10b–5 remedy in its proper perspective, it must be viewed in conjunction with the other modes of private relief provided by the securities laws. Some of the concurrent antifraud provisions are found in the Securities Act of 1933.

The 1933 Act contains two sections providing for express private damage remedies for misrepresentation in connection with the sale of a security.[4] These supplement the 1933 Act's general antifraud provision embodied in section 17(a).[5] Section 17(a) does not create an express right of action and, although there is considerable authority to the contrary, it has been held by some courts to support an implied private remedy.[6] In contrast to these provisions in the 1933 Act, the express remedies available under the Securities Exchange Act of 1934 are much more limited in scope. Section 9(e) of the Exchange Act[7] confers a private right of action upon an injured investor against one who has willfully engaged in market manipulation of securities

---

Section 14(e) is discussed in §§ 11.6, 11.10 *supra*.

10. Central Bank of Denver v. First Interstate Bank of Denver, 511 U.S. 164, 114 S.Ct. 1439, 128 L.Ed.2d 119 (1994), which is discussed in § 12.25 *infra*. *See also, e.g.,* Gustafson v. Alloyd Co., 513 U.S. 561, 115 S.Ct. 1061, 131 L.Ed.2d 1 (1995) (giving a tortured and narrow reading to the express remedy under section 12(2) of the 1933 Act); the *Gustafson* case is discussed in § 7.6 *supra*.

11. Herman & MacLean v. Huddleston, 459 U.S. 375, 103 S.Ct. 683, 74 L.Ed.2d 548 (1983), *on remand*, 705 F.2d 775 (5th Cir.1983). *See* §§ 7.3, 7.4, *supra* and 12.18 *infra*.

12. Merrill Lynch, Pierce, Fenner & Smith, Inc. v. Curran, 456 U.S. 353, 102 S.Ct. 1825, 72 L.Ed.2d 182 (1982). *See* §§ 14.25, 22.7 *infra*.

13. *See* §§ 14.25, 22.7 *infra*.

§ 12.3

1. 17 C.F.R. § 240.10b–5. *See, e.g.,* Symposium, Happy Birthday 10b–5: 50 Years of Antifraud Regulation, 61 Fordham L.Rev. S1 (1993).

4. Sections 11 and 12(a)(2). 15 U.S.C.A. §§ 77k, 77l(a)(2). *See* §§ 7.2–7.6 *supra*. This is in addition to section 12(a)(1), which provides a right of rescission for all securities sold in violation of the Act's registration provisions. 15 U.S.C.A. § 77l(a)(1). *See* § 7.2 *supra*.

5. 15 U.S.C.A. § 77q(a).

6. *See* Thomas L. Hazen, A Look Beyond The Pruning of Rule 10b–5: Implied Remedies and Section 17(a) of The Securities Act of 1933, 64 Va.L.Rev. 641 (1978); § 12.22 *infra*.

7. 15 U.S.C.A. § 78i(e). *See* § 12.1 *supra*.

subject to the 1934 Act's registration and reporting requirements[8] by virtue of being listed on a national exchange.[9] Section 18(a) of the Act[10] sets out a private right of action for an investor who has been injured due to reliance on materially misleading statements or omissions of material facts in documents required to be filed with the Commission. Section 16(b)'s disgorgement of insider short-swing profits[11] is the third express private remedy contained in the 1934 Act. A fourth private remedy was created by The Insider Trading and Securities Fraud Enforcement Act of 1988.[12]

The express remedies under the 1933 Act apply only to fraud in connection with the sale of securities, thus providing protection only to injured purchasers and not to injured sellers. The 1934 Act's express remedies do not distinguish between purchasers and sellers. The 1934 Act's express remedies are restricted, however, to securities subject to the Act's reporting requirements.[13] These express remedies are also subject to a number of other limiting factors that are discussed in earlier sections of this book. Section 10(b)[14] and Rule 10b–5[15] do not have many of these limiting factors. Although arguments have been made to the contrary, the overwhelming majority of decisions agree that the Rule 10b–5 remedy is cumulative with the express remedies noted above.[16]

§ 12.3[2] History of Rule 10b–5

A proper perspective on Rule 10b–5 also requires an examination of the rule's history and development. The general antifraud provision of the 1934 Act is contained in section 10(b), which provides that it is unlawful "to use or employ [utilizing any means or instrumentality of interstate commerce], in connection with the purchase or sale of any security * * * any manipulative or deceptive device or contrivance in contravention of such rules and regulations as the Commission may prescribe as necessary or appropriate in the public interest or for the protection of investors."[18] In Rule 10b–5 the SEC fashioned its most encompassing antifraud prohibition.

Promulgated in 1942, Rule 10b–5 was patterned directly upon section 17(a) of the 1933 Act, except that 10b–5 further extends to misstatements and

---

8. The scope of the Exchange Act's issuer registration and reporting requirements is discussed in §§ 9.2–9.3 *supra.*

9. *See* section 6 of the 1934 Act, 15 U.S.C.A. § 78f. Section 9 is thus more limited than most of the 1934 Act's liability and reporting provisions, which apply equally to many over-the-counter securities. 15 U.S.C.A. § 78*l. See* §§ 9.2, 9.3 *supra.*

10. 15 U.S.C.A. § 78r(a). *See* § 12.18 *infra.*

11. 15 U.S.C.A. § 78p(b). *See* chapter 13 *infra.*

12. Section 20A, 15 U.S.C.A. § 78t–1. *See* § 12.17 *infra.*

13. The same is also true of some implied remedies. For example, the implied remedy under proxy Rule 14a–9 protects shareholders injured in connection with shareholder votes and does not necessarily involve either a purchase or sale. 17 C.F.R. § 240.14a–9. *See, e.g.,* J.I. Case Co. v. Borak, 377 U.S. 426, 84 S.Ct. 1555, 12 L.Ed.2d 423 (1964).

14. 15 U.S.C.A. § 78j(b).

15. 17 C.F.R. §§ 240.10b–5.

16. *See, e.g.,* Herman & MacLean v. Huddleston, 459 U.S. 375, 103 S.Ct. 683, 74 L.Ed.2d 548 (1983), *on remand,* 705 F.2d 775 (5th Cir.1983). *See generally* Marc I. Steinberg, The Propriety and Scope of Cumulative Remedies Under the Federal Securities Laws, 67 Cornell L.Rev. 557 (1982).

18. 15 U.S.C.A. § 78j(b). *See generally* Steve Thel, The Original Conception of Section 10(b) of the Securities Exchange Act, 42 Stan.L.Rev. 385 (1990); Symposium, Happy Birthday 10b–5: 50 Years of Antifraud Regulation, 61 Fordham L.Rev. S1 (1993).

omissions occurring in connection with either a *purchase or sale* of securities, while the parent section is limited to fraudulent sales and offers to sell. The rule prohibits: (1) fraudulent devices and schemes, (2) misstatements and omissions of material facts, and (3) acts and practices which operate as a fraud or deceit. When it adopted Rule 10b–5, the Commission, without even realizing its eventual reach, created a powerful antifraud weapon.[23] According to one account, the decision to adopt the rule and model it on section 17(a) was arrived at without any deliberation, with the only official discussion consisting of one SEC Commissioner reportedly observing, "we are against fraud, aren't we?"[24] Given this background, it is clear that not much can be gleaned from the history of the rule, although the courts frequently refer to the legislative history behind the statute. The clear purpose of Rule 10b–5 is to provide protection against investors being duped into purchasing or selling securities.

§ 12.3[3] The Development of the Implied Rule 10b–5 Remedy

In 1946, a federal district court held that, notwithstanding the absence of an express private right of action, Rule 10b–5 gives rise to a private remedy in the hands of injured investors.[26] The implied remedy started to grow and flourish in the district and circuit courts but did not receive formal Supreme Court approval until twenty-four years later.[27] Over the years there seems to have been a general demise of implied remedies in the federal courts.[28] Nevertheless, the Rule 10b–5 remedy remains firmly entrenched. The Rule 10b–5 action has, however, been cut down in scope in many respects.

In the 1970s and 1980s, a series of Supreme Court cases limited the scope of the private right of action under Rule 10b–5; this trend carried through the end of the century. First, the Court ruled that, in order to maintain an action, the plaintiff must be either a purchaser or seller of the securities in question.[31] Second, a showing of negligent conduct will not suffice; the defendant must have acted with scienter.[32] Third, the conduct complained of must be "deceptive."[33] Notwithstanding these limiting decisions, which are discussed in later sections, the Rule 10b–5 implied remedy remains an important one in appropriate cases for a number of reasons.

It is quite easy to establish federal jurisdiction to support a Rule 10b–5 claim. All that is required is for some aspect of the securities transaction

---

23. *See* Sec.Exch. Act Rel. No. 34–3230 (May 21, 1942) ("The new rule closes a loophole in the protections against fraud administered by the commission by prohibiting individuals or companies from buying securities if they engage in fraud in their purchase").

24. *See* Conference on Codification of the Federal Securities Laws, 22 Bus.Law. 793, 922 (1967).

26. Kardon v. National Gypsum Co., 69 F.Supp. 512 (E.D.Pa.1946).

27. Superintendent of Insurance v. Bankers Life & Casualty Co., 404 U.S. 6, 92 S.Ct. 165, 30 L.Ed.2d 128 (1971), *on remand*, 401 F.Supp. 640 (S.D.N.Y.1975). In the course of one of its subsequent limiting 10b–5 decisions, the Court observed that 10b–5 represented a legislative acorn that had grown into a judicial oak badly in need of pruning. Blue Chip Stamps v. Manor Drug Stores, 421 U.S. 723, 737, 95 S.Ct. 1917, 1926, 44 L.Ed.2d 539 (1975), *rehearing denied*, 423 U.S. 884, 96 S.Ct. 157, 46 L.Ed.2d 114 (1975).

28. *See* § 12.2 *supra.*

31. Blue Chip Stamps v. Manor Drug Stores, 421 U.S. 723, 95 S.Ct. 1917, 44 L.Ed.2d 539 (1975). *See* § 12.7 *infra.*

32. Ernst & Ernst v. Hochfelder, 425 U.S. 185, 96 S.Ct. 1375, 47 L.Ed.2d 668 (1976).

33. Santa Fe Industries, Inc. v. Green, 430 U.S. 462, 97 S.Ct. 1292, 51 L.Ed.2d 480 (1977).

under attack to have been carried out through the use of an instrumentality of interstate commerce. For example, even an intrastate telephone call has been held sufficient to satisfy the jurisdictional requirements of Rule 10b–5.[35] While a face-to-face conversation itself will not satisfy the jurisdictional requirements, there may be 10b–5 jurisdiction if the conversations are part of a transaction that utilizes an instrumentality of interstate commerce.[36] Also, although it might be argued that the language of section 10(b) and Rule 10b–5 require otherwise, it seems to be the majority rule that it is not necessary that the misrepresentation be communicated through an instrumentality of interstate commerce, so long as there is a connection between the use of the jurisdictional means and the fraud.

Additionally, through the doctrine of supplemental or pendent jurisdiction,[38] a plaintiff with a Rule 10b–5 claim may bring related state statutory or common law claims into the federal court. The significance of pendent jurisdiction has diminished because of the Securities Litigation Uniform Standards Act of 1998, which preempted state law with regard to class actions of fifty persons or more involving securities fraud.[41] Individual actions, class actions on behalf of fewer than fifty persons, and derivative actions may still have parallel state law claims.

The Rule 10b–5 remedy may be used in a wide variety of factual contexts. The 10b–5 action has been used to address the problems of material corporate misstatements or nondisclosures,[43] insider trading,[44] and corporate mismanagement problems that arise in the context of transactions in shares or other securities.[45] Furthermore, a parallel antifraud remedy has been implied under proxy Rule 14a–9.[46] There will frequently be cumulative Rule 10b–5 and 14a–9 remedies available in the case of mergers and corporate reorganizations, which involve both a shareholder vote and securities transactions.[47] Similarly, Rule 10b–5 has a role to play in the tender offer context, which necessarily

---

35. Loveridge v. Dreagoux, 678 F.2d 870 (10th Cir.1982); Dupuy v. Dupuy, 511 F.2d 641 (5th Cir.1975).

36. Leiter v. Kuntz, 655 F.Supp. 725 (D.Utah 1987) (mailing of financial statement by defendant's attorney plus use of telephone to change face-to-face meeting held sufficient to support Rule 10b–5 jurisdiction).

It is very difficult to imagine a securities transaction that does not in some respect involve an instrumentality of interstate commerce. For example, if the share certificates or any communications concerning the transaction are sent through the mail, then there is the use of an instrumentality of interstate commerce. If the securities transfer is cleared through an instrumentality of interstate commerce there presumably would be a sufficient connection with interstate commerce even if the share certificates were hand delivered. A reading of many thousand cases has not revealed one single decision in which the absence of an instrumentality of interstate commerce was by itself sufficient to preclude jurisdiction.

38. *See* United Mine Workers of America v. Gibbs, 383 U.S. 715, 86 S.Ct. 1130, 16 L.Ed.2d 218 (1966). *See* § 17.1[4] *infra.*

41. 1934 Act § 28(f), 15 U.S.C.A. § 78bb(f); 1933 Act § 16(f), 15 U.S.C.A. § 77p(f). *See* § 12.15[2] *infra.*

43. *See* § 12.9 *infra.*

44. *See* § 12.17 *infra.*

45. *See* § 12.20 *infra.*

The private remedy under Rule 10b–5 also has been used to seek redress against various pernicious broker-dealer practices. *See, e.g.,* § 14.20 *infra* for a discussion of churning.

46. 17 C.F.R. § 240.14a–9. *See* J.I. Case Co. v. Borak, 377 U.S. 426, 84 S.Ct. 1555, 12 L.Ed.2d 423 (1964).

47. *See, e.g.,* SEC v. National Securities, Inc., 393 U.S. 453, 468, 89 S.Ct. 564, 573, 21 L.Ed.2d 668 (1969) (The overlap is "neither unusual nor unfortunate").

involves the sale of target company stock.[48] In addition, the fact that securities may be exempt from registration under the Securities Act of 1933[49] will not preclude an action under Rule 10b–5. Thus, for example, a 10b–5 action may be brought for fraud in connection with United States Treasury securities,[50] or with regard to municipal securities.[51] One exception is that since short term commercial paper is expressly excluded from the 1934 Act's definition of a security,[52] Rule 10b–5 will not apply to transactions involving short term commercial paper falling within the statutory exclusion.

§ 12.4   Rule 10b–5 Overview; Summary of the Principal Elements

There are five principal elements for stating a claim under Rule 10b–5. The plaintiff must show: (1) fraud or deceit (2) by any person (3) in connection with (4) the purchase or sale (5) of any security. Furthermore, since Rule 10b–5, like its parent section, requires deceit or fraud, the elements of common law fraud—materiality, reliance, causation, and damages—thus must be part of any Rule 10b–5 claim.

Purchase or Sale

An important corollary to the "purchase or sale" requirement is that, in order to have standing to sue, a 10b–5 plaintiff in a private damages action must have been either a purchaser or seller of the securities that form the basis of the material omission, misstatement, or deceptive conduct.[16] Most courts allow a remedy for a corporation (or in a shareholder derivative suit) for certain transactions in its own shares, including corporate repurchases of its own shares at an inflated price, or an additional issuance of corporate shares on an unfavorable basis.[17]

By Any Person

As pointed out directly above and as discussed in a subsequent section of this treatise,[18] a plaintiff in a private damage action under Rule 10b–5 must have been a purchaser or seller of the security forming the basis of the complaint.[19] There is no parallel requirement for defendants in Rule 10b–5 actions.

The courts generally have assumed that it is not necessary for the defendant to have been a purchaser or seller of securities in order to be held

---

48.   *See also* section 14(e) of the Williams Act, 15 U.S.C.A. § 78n(e); §§ 11.6, 11.10 *supra*.

49.   *See* § 4.1 *supra*.

50.   *E.g.,* Kahn v. Salomon Brothers, Inc., 813 F.Supp. 191 (E.D.N.Y.1993). The regulation of government securities dealers is discussed in § 14.7 *infra*.

51.   The regulation of municipal securities dealers is discussed in § 14.6 *infra*.

52.   15 U.S.C.A. § 78c(a)(10). *See* § 4.4 *supra*.

§ 12.4

16.   Blue Chip Stamps v. Manor Drug Stores, 421 U.S. 723, 95 S.Ct. 1917, 44 L.Ed.2d 539 (1975), *rehearing denied*, 423 U.S. 884, 96 S.Ct. 157, 46 L.Ed.2d 114 (1975). The purchaser/seller standing requirement is discussed in § 12.7 *infra*.

17.   *E.g.,* Alabama Farm Bureau Mutual Casualty Co. v. American Fidelity Life Ins. Co., 606 F.2d 602 (5th Cir.1979), *cert. denied*, 449 U.S. 820, 101 S.Ct. 77, 66 L.Ed.2d 22 (1980) (repurchase of shares).

18.   *See* § 12.7 *infra*.

19.   *E.g.,* Blue Chip Stamps v. Manor Drug Stores, 421 U.S. 723, 95 S.Ct. 1917, 44 L.Ed.2d 539 (1975), *rehearing denied*, 423 U.S. 884, 96 S.Ct. 157, 46 L.Ed.2d 114 (1975).

to have violated Rule 10b–5.[20] Any statement reasonably calculated to affect the investment decision of a reasonable investor will satisfy the "in connection with" requirement even if the defendant was not a purchaser or seller.[21] Thus, for example, a non-seller who makes statements that induce the sale in question may be liable even though not an actual seller of the securities in question.[22] This does not mean, however, that liability for Rule 10b–5 violations will extend to all collateral participants. Although aiders and abettors can be held liable in criminal[23] and SEC enforcement actions,[24] aiders and abettors are not subject to liability in private damage actions.[25] Thus, in private suits, only primary violators can be held liable.[26]

Of Any Security

Rule 10b–5 applies to any purchase or sale by any person of *any* security. The fact that a security is exempt from 1933 or 1934 Act registration does not affect the applicability of Rule 10b–5's proscriptions.[27] The rule applies regardless of whether the security is registered under the 1934 Act, and regardless of whether the company is publicly-held or closely-held. Rule 10b–5 applies even to government and municipal securities, and in fact, to any kind of entity that issues something which can be called a "security." Because of this broad scope, the rule may be invoked in many situations. As a result of the Commodity Futures Modernization Act of 2000,[28] section 10(b) now applies to security-based swap agreements even though those instruments are not securities.[29]

Scienter

One of the essential elements of a fraud claim is demonstrating that the defendant acted with scienter. In its strictest sense, scienter means an intent to deceive, but there is substantial authority under common law that making statements in reckless disregard of the truth will suffice to establish scienter.[31] In 1976, the Supreme Court held that a valid claim for damages under Rule 10b–5 must establish that the defendant acted with scienter.[32] The Court,

---

20. *See, e.g.*, Basic Inc. v. Levinson, 485 U.S. 224, 108 S.Ct. 978, 99 L.Ed.2d 194 (1988), *on remand*, 871 F.2d 562 (6th Cir.1989) (upholding liability for misleading statement but not directly addressing whether defendant's not being a purchaser or seller precluded liability).

21. *E.g.*, SEC v. Texas Gulf Sulphur, 401 F.2d 833 (2d Cir.1968), *cert. denied*, 394 U.S. 976, 89 S.Ct. 1454, 22 L.Ed.2d 756 (1969) (misstatements in a corporate press release were made "in connection with" purchases and sales made by shareholders in the open market and violated rule 10b–5, even though corporation itself was not buying nor selling shares).

22. Keeling v. Telehub Communications Corp., 2001 WL 688495, [2000–2001 Transfer Binder] Fed. Sec. L. Rep. (CCH) ¶ 91,330 (N.D. Ill. 2001).

23. 18 U.S.C.A. § 2. *See, e.g.*, United States v. Bradstreet, 135 F.3d 46 (1st Cir.1998) (upholding criminal conviction for aiding and abetting).

24. 15 U.S.C.A. § 78t(e).

25. Central Bank of Denver, N.A. v. First Interstate Bank of Denver, 511 U.S. 164, 114 S.Ct. 1439, 128 L.Ed.2d 119 (1994). *see* § 12.25 *infra*.

26. *See* § 12.25[3] *infra*.

27. Ontario Public Service Employees Union Pension Trust Funds v. Nortel Networks Corp., 369 F.3d 27 (2d Cir. 2004) (citing this treatise).

28. Pub. Law 106–554, 114 Stat. 2763 (December 21, 2000).

29. 15 U.S.C.A. § 78j(b).

31. *See* the authorities in § 12.18 *infra*.

32. Ernst & Ernst v. Hochfelder, 425 U.S. 185, 96 S.Ct. 1375, 47 L.Ed.2d 668 (1976), *rehearing denied*, 425 U.S. 986, 96 S.Ct. 2194, 48 L.Ed.2d 811 (1976). In 1980, the Court held that the scienter standard applies under Rule 10b–5 regardless of whether the action is a private

however, did not decide whether a showing of reckless conduct would satisfy the scienter requirement.[33] Nevertheless, the majority of lower court decisions has found that recklessness is sufficient to state a claim under Rule 10b–5.[34]

Materiality

In order for a misstatement or omission to be actionable under Rule 10b–5, it must be a material one. The Supreme Court has defined materiality in terms of the type of information that a reasonable investor would consider significant in making an investment decision.[35] The materiality of a particular item is based on a highly factual inquiry and is to be determined within the total mix of information that is publicly available.[36]

Reliance

Following the basic requirements for proving common law fraud, reliance is an element of any Rule 10b–5 claim.[37] In a sharply divided decision, the Supreme Court has recognized the fraud-on-the-market presumption of reliance[38] under which a showing that a material misstatement or omission adversely affected the market price creates a presumption of reliance. Defendant may rebut the presumption of reliance or show that reliance was unreasonable.[40]

Causation

Again, as is the case with common law fraud, in addition to scienter, materiality, and reliance, causation is an element of a Rule 10b–5 action. Many courts have divided causation into two subparts: transaction causation and loss causation. Transaction causation requires a showing that, but-for the violations in question, the transaction would not have occurred (at least in the form that it took). Loss causation requires a showing of a causal nexus between the transaction and the plaintiff's loss.[41]

Damages

Also, as is the case with any fraud claim, the plaintiff must be able to establish damages. In most Rule 10b–5 litigation, the appropriate measure of damages is the out-of-pocket loss proximately caused by the material misstatement or omission.[42]

---

damage action or an enforcement action brought by the Commission. Aaron v. SEC, 446 U.S. 680, 100 S.Ct. 1945, 64 L.Ed.2d 611 (1980), *on remand*, 666 F.2d 5 (2d Cir.1981). *See* § 12.8 *infra* for a discussion of the scienter requirement.

33. *Hochfelder*, 425 U.S. at 193–94 n.12, 96 S.Ct. at 1381–1382 n. 12; *Aaron*, 446 U.S. at 690–91, 100 S.Ct. at 1952, 1953. The Court had the opportunity to decide this question in Central Bank of Denver, N.A. v. First Interstate Bank of Denver, 511 U.S. 164, 114 S.Ct. 1439, 128 L.Ed.2d 119 (1994), but disposed of the case on other grounds. *See* § 12.8, 12.25 *infra*.

34. *See* § 12.8 *infra*.

35. Basic Inc. v. Levinson, 485 U.S. 224, 108 S.Ct. 978, 99 L.Ed.2d 194 (1988) (decided under Rule 10b–5); TSC Industries, Inc. v. Northway, Inc., 426 U.S. 438, 96 S.Ct. 2126, 48 L.Ed.2d 757 (1976) (decided under the proxy rules).

36. As materiality questions are highly fact-specific, summary judgment will rarely be appropriate. Materiality is discussed in § 12.9 *infra*.

37. Reliance is discussed in § 12.10 *infra*.

38. Basic Inc. v. Levinson, 485 U.S. 224, 108 S.Ct. 978, 99 L.Ed.2d 194 (1988).

40. *See* § 12.10 *infra*.

41. See Dura Pharmaceuticals, Inc. v. Broudo, 544 U.S. 336, 125 S.Ct. 1627, 161 L.Ed.2d 577 (2005). Causation is discussed in § 12.11 *infra*.

42. *E.g.*, Wool v. Tandem Computers Inc., 818 F.2d 1433 (9th Cir.1987); Harris v. Union Electric Co., 787 F.2d 355, 367 (8th Cir.1986), *cert. denied*, 479 U.S. 823, 107 S.Ct. 94, 93 L.Ed.2d

Statute of Limitations

As part of the Sarbanes–Oxley Act[45] Congress enacted a statute of limitations (two years from discovery but not more than five years after the violation) for "a claim of fraud, deceit, manipulation, or contrivance in contravention of a regulatory requirement concerning the securities laws."[46]

Cumulative Remedies

In Herman & MacLean v. Huddleston,[47] the Supreme Court held that the remedies under Section 11 of the 1933 Act, for misstatements in registration materials, and Rule 10b–5 are cumulative. Presumably, Rule 10b–5 remedies are cumulative with other express remedies as well.[48]

§ 12.5   "In Connection With" the Purchase or Sale of Any Security

The courts have generally assumed it is not necessary that the defendant have been a purchaser or seller of securities in order to be held to have violated Rule 10b–5.[1] It is sufficient that the material misstatement, omission, or fraudulent act, in the words of both the statute and the rule, be "in connection with the purchase or sale of any security * * *."[2] This means that there must be some connection between the misstatements or conduct in question and a transaction in securities. The courts have interpreted this language broadly. However broadly this may be interpreted, there are limits and, as discussed below, there must be a significant connection between the fraud and a purchase or sale of securities.

Any statement that is reasonably calculated to affect the investment decision of a reasonable investor will satisfy the "in connection with" requirement.[6]

As a general proposition, dissemination to the public through a medium of communication upon which the reasonable investor would rely will satisfy the "in connection with" requirement.[11] Even a technical advertisement in a specialized journal could be said to be in connection with a purchase or sale of a security if it is likely to affect the readers' investment decisions about the company's securities. Thus, for example, advertisements in a medical journal

---

45 (1986). On occasion, disgorgement of ill-gotten profits or benefit-of-the-bargain might be a more appropriate measure of damages. Damages are discussed in § 12.12 *infra*.

45. Sarbanes–Oxley Act of 2002, Pub. Law 107–204 (July 30, 2002).

46. 28 U.S.C.A. § 1658(b).

47. 459 U.S. 375, 103 S.Ct. 683, 74 L.Ed.2d 548 (1983).

48. This includes the express remedies under §§ 12(a)(1) and 12(a)(2) of the 1933 Act. The measure of damages under § 12 of the 1933 Act is based on rescission. *See also* the remedy under § 18(a) of the 1934 Act (misstatements in false filings). The new remedies under the Insider Trading and Securities Fraud Sanctions Act of 1988, codified in § 21A of the 1934 Act (disgorgement of profits in an action by contemporaneous traders), are expressly in addition to any other express or implied remedies.

§ 12.5

1. *See e.g.,* Basic Inc. v. Levinson, 485 U.S. 224, 108 S.Ct. 978, 99 L.Ed.2d 194 (1988), (upholding liability for misleading statement but not directly addressing the question of whether defendant's not being a purchaser or seller precluded liability).

2. 15 U.S.C.A. § 78j(b); 17 C.F.R. § 240.10b–5.

6. *E.g.,* Pelletier v. Stuart–James Co., 863 F.2d 1550 (11th Cir.1989).

11. *See, e.g.,* Semerenko v. Cendant Corp., 223 F.3d 165 (3d Cir.2000).

concerning a new drug could form the basis of a securities fraud claim.[12] This result is not without controversy.

Public announcements and other dissemination of information can be in connection with the purchase or sale even if the speaker or disseminator is not a purchaser or seller. Although the existence of a public market at the time of any news release is not by itself sufficient to satisfy the "in connection with" requirement,[15] if the news release relates to matters likely to affect the price of the stock significantly, the requirement is satisfied.[16] Similarly, information contained in periodic SEC filings such as the annual or quarterly report will be considered to have been in connection with the purchase or sale of a security where the material disclosed relates to the types of information that an investor would use in deciding to purchase or sell a security.[17] Press releases and other statements directed to issues that investors deem important in making investment decisions are likely to be considered to have been made in connection with the purchase or sale of a security.

The "in connection with" requirement will not support a Rule 10b–5 action for simply any wrongdoing that just happens to involve securities.[20] It has thus been held that a *de minimus* "touch" test is not sufficient to satisfy the "in connection with" requirement.[21]

A 1987 Supreme Court decision under the federal mail fraud statute[49] supports a broad reading of Rule 10b–5's "in connection with" requirement. The mail fraud statute covers any person who causes the mail to be used to further the wrongful conduct. The Supreme Court in Carpenter v. United States[50] held that a scheme by a reporter to give advance notice to his friends concerning upcoming columns in the Wall Street Journal depended upon the dissemination of the Wall Street Journal and that this was a sufficient connection to invoke the mail fraud statute.[51] This is a surprising rationale, since the defendants did not utilize the mail themselves but rather the newspaper when published utilized the mails. The Court's expansive reading of the Mail Fraud Act's jurisdictional requirement may be used to support an equally broad reading of Rule 10b–5's "in connection with" requirement. The connection to the mails in *Carpenter* was at best tangential in comparison with the more substantial "in connection with" requirement that traditionally has been required under Rule 10b–5.

In *United States v. O'Hagan*,[52] the Supreme Court held that a Rule 10b–5 violation does not require that the fraud be linked to identifiable purchasers

---

12. In re Carter–Wallace, Inc. Securities Litigation, 150 F.3d 153 (2d Cir.1998) (refusing to dismiss claim).

15. SEC v. Texas Gulf Sulphur, 401 F.2d 833 (2d Cir.1968) (Hayes, J., concurring in part and dissenting in part), *cert. denied*, 394 U.S. 976, 89 S.Ct. 1454, 22 L.Ed.2d 756 (1969).

16. 401 F.2d 833.

17. *See, e.g.,* Semerenko v. Cendant Corp., 223 F.3d 165 (3d Cir.2000).

20. *See* Levitin v. PaineWebber, Inc., 159 F.3d 698 (2d Cir.1998), *affirming*, 933 F.Supp. 325 (S.D.N.Y.1996) (failure to disclose that broker earned interest on customer's collateral for short sale transaction did not come within Rule 10b–5's "in connection with" requirement).

21. Head v. Head, 759 F.2d 1172, 1175 (4th Cir.1985).

49. 18 U.S.C.A. § 1341.

50. 484 U.S. 19, 108 S.Ct. 316, 98 L.Ed.2d 275 (1987).

51. 484 U.S. at 28, 108 S.Ct. at 322, 98 L.Ed.2d at 285. *See* § 12.11, 12.17 *infra*.

52. United States v. O'Hagan, 521 U.S. 642, 117 S.Ct. 2199, 138 L.Ed.2d 724 (1997).

or sellers of securities.[53] A breach of duty to the source of confidential information will support a Rule 10b–5 violation so long as the confidential information is misused in connection with securities trading. It thus is not necessary that the source of the information to whom the duty was owed have been a purchaser, seller or issuer of the securities in question.

The broad interpretation of the "in connection with" requirement in *O'Hagan* was reaffirmed by the Supreme Court in SEC v. Zandford.[54] In *Zandford*, the SEC sued a stock broker who emptied his client's account and converted the proceeds. The defendant contended that since there was no fraud in connection with specific securities transactions, Rule 10b–5 could not be used to challenge the broker's actions. The Supreme Court rejected this argument, reasoning that the purpose of the federal securities laws was to assure the existence of honest securities markets and to promote investor confidence. The court explained that there was the requisite deception insofar as the broker failed to disclosed the challenged embezzlement out of a securities account to his customer and that this was sufficient connection to establish securities fraud.[55] The *Zandford* decision is significant in that it establishes a broad test for the reach of the securities laws. Rather than simply focus on a specific transaction, if the fraud involves securities in any meaningful way, then the securities laws are implicated.[56] It is also noteworthy that the Justices who are generally divided in securities decisions were unanimous in the *Zandford* holding.

The Supreme Court's decision in *Zandford* makes it clear that Rule 10b–5 is violated when there has been a failure to adequately disclose past misconduct even though the misconduct itself did not involve a purchase or sale of securities. Thus, the failure to disclose the embezzlement of cash from a securities brokerage account was sufficient to satisfy the "in connection with" requirement on the facts before the Court in *Zandford*. Similarly, a Rule 10b–5 violation was stated on the basis of a securities brokerage firm's alleged failure to disclose that it engaged in a pay-for-play scheme under which it offered investment services in exchange for cash payments and campaign donations.[57]

§ 12.6 "Purchase or Sale"—Identifying Purchases and Sales Under Rule 10b–5

§ 12.6[1] Definitions of Purchase and Sale

Rule 10b–5 applies to fraud and misstatements or omissions in connection with the *purchase* or *sale* of any security.[1] The definitions of purchase and sale go far beyond garden-variety cash for stock transactions.[2] However, not every transfer of securities will constitute a sale.

53. *Id.* The *O'Hagan* decision is discussed in § 12.17 *infra*.

54. 535 U.S. 813, 823–824, 122 S.Ct. 1899, 1905–1906, 153 L.Ed.2d 1 (2002).

55. 535 U.S. 813, 823–824, 122 S.Ct. 1899, 1905–1906, 153 L.Ed.2d 1 (2002).

56. *See, e.g.,* Shaw v. Charles Schwab & Co., Inc., 2003 WL 1463842, Fed. Sec. L. Rep. ¶ 92413 (Cal. Super. 2003) (the "in connection with" requirement is satisfied even if the misstatement does not directly relate to the value of the security).

57. SEC v. Santos, 292 F.Supp.2d 1046 (N.D. Ill. 2003).

§ 12.6

1. 17 C.F.R. § 240.10b–5.

2. *See, e.g.,* § 12.5 *supra*.

The securities laws contain various formulations of the definitions for purchase and sale but each is designed to identify a transaction in which the securities are acquired or disposed of for value. Thus, for example, section 2(a)(3) of the 1933 Act[4] defines "sale" as including "every contract of sale or disposition of a security or interest in a security, for value." In most situations, this definition will encompass transactions such as exercise of options, mergers, exercise of conversion rights, pledges, and the like.[5] On its face, the 1934 Act definition may be even broader, as there is no explicit requirement that the security be disposed of for value. Thus, for example, it is not necessary to show that there is consideration in the traditional sense.[6] As one court explained, "[t]he fact that no 'value' was paid is not necessarily dispositive."[7] Section 3(a)(14) provides: "[t]he terms 'sale' and 'sell' each include any contract to sell or otherwise dispose of."[8] It is noteworthy that the definition "includes" contracts to sell but does not purport to be exclusive and thus limited by the express examples of what is a sale that are given in the statute. The Exchange Act contains a parallel definition of "purchase."[9] The definition of purchase or sale includes a "contract of sale" even though the sale does not take place and no securities are transferred.[10] Furthermore, the "in connection with" requirement does not require identification of the specific security, or a demonstration that money was actually invested in securities, to qualify plaintiff as a purchaser of the securities within the meaning of Rule 10b–5.[11]

Concepts of purchase and sale are to be construed flexibly in order to accomplish the purpose of the securities laws.[12] The courts will consider the economic reality of the transaction and whether it lends itself to fraud in the making of an investment decision. As one court explained, "several factors have so far emerged in this inquiry: (1) whether a transfer of ownership or control of the security occurred; (2) whether consideration or value was given; (3) whether, in appropriate contexts, there was a change in the fundamental nature of the security; and (4) whether the transaction had a direct effect on the conduct of the securities market."[15]

Whether or not a contract of sale is binding will ordinarily depend on state law.[17] Thus an oral contract of sale, including an oral option contract, is a sale of a security subject to the federal securities laws.[18]

---

4. 15 U.S.C.A. § 77b(a)(3).

5. *See* § 5.1 *supra.*

6. Seolas v. Bilzerian, 951 F.Supp. 978, 986–87 (D.Utah 1997), relying in part on Rathborne v. Rathborne, 683 F.2d 914, 920 (5th Cir.1982).

7. Seolas v. Bilzerian, 951 F.Supp. 978, 986–87 (D.Utah 1997), relying in part on Rathborne v. Rathborne, 683 F.2d 914, 920 (5th Cir.1982).

8. 15 U.S.C.A. § 78c(a)(14).

9. Section 3(a)(13), 15 U.S.C.A. § 78c(a)(13) ("The terms 'buy' and 'purchase' each include any contract to buy, purchase, or otherwise acquire . . .").

10. *E.g.*, Falkowski v. Imation Corp., 320 F.3d 905 (9th Cir. 2003).

11. Grippo v. Perazzo, 357 F.3d 1218 (11th Cir. 2004).

12. *See, e.g.*, In re American Continental Corp., 49 F.3d 541 (9th Cir.1995).

15. Seolas v. Bilzerian, 951 F.Supp. 978, 987 (D.Utah 1997).

17. *See* § 5.1[7] *supra.*

18. The Wharf (Holdings) Ltd. v. United International Holdings, 532 U.S. 588, 121 S.Ct. 1776, 149 L.Ed.2d 845 (2001).

§ 12.6[2] Rights to Purchase or Sell

An agreement that falls short of a binding contract to purchase securities will not support a plaintiff's standing as a purchaser.[20] Thus, for example, it has been held that a share subscription agreement which binds the purchaser but not the seller is not a sale unless and until the seller becomes bound.[21]

§ 12.6[4] Convertible Securities

A voluntary conversion of convertible securities can satisfy Rule 10b–5's purchase or sale requirement.[28] Rule 10b–5 is not limited, however, to voluntary exchanges.

§ 12.6[6] Pledges of Securities

Although there appear to be some decisions to the contrary, ordinarily a pledge of securities will constitute a sale. The Supreme Court in Rubin v. United States ruled that a pledge of securities is a sale for purposes of the 1933 Act's antifraud provisions.[39] Since Rule 10b–5 was modeled on section 17(a) of the 1933 Act,[40] there would seem to be no reason to expect a different result under the 1934 Act, but the courts appear to be divided. The Second and Sixth Circuits have ruled that a pledge is a sale for purposes of SEC Rule 10b–5.[41] However, prior to the Supreme Court's decision in *Rubin*, the Fifth and Seventh Circuits had ruled that a pledge is not a sale under the 1934 Act.[42]

§ 12.6[7] Gifts

Ordinarily, a gift will not be a sale under the securities laws.[50] However, there may be a basis on appropriate facts for characterizing a gift as a sale under the Act. In one case, the complaint was that the plaintiff made a gift of securities that the defendant fraudulently led him to believe were worth much less than their true value. The court ruled that since such misrepresentations might need the protections of the securities laws, it would not dismiss the claim.[51]

There are cases that have held gifts to be sales under the 1933 Act. However, these have arisen in connection with claims that there was a failure to register the sale, rather than in the context of the antifraud provisions. The court found that a gift which forms part of a distribution of securities can be

---

20. Return on Equity Group, Inc. v. MPM Technologies, Inc., 66 Fed.Appx. 400 (3d Cir. 2003) (fact that contract could have been paid in shares rather than cash was not sufficient to invoke Rule 10b–5); Cohen v. Stratosphere Corp., 115 F.3d 695 (9th Cir.1997) (plaintiffs did not have binding contracts to purchase securities and thus lacked standing under Rule 10b–5).

21. Keith v. Lighthouse Securities, Ltd., 1997 WL 380430 [1997 Transfer Binder] Fed. Sec. L. Rep. (CCH) ¶ 99,547 (D.Conn.1997).

28. FS Photo, Inc. v. PictureVision, Inc., 61 F.Supp.2d 473 (E.D.Va.1999).

39. Rubin v. United States, 449 U.S. 424, 101 S.Ct. 698, 66 L.Ed.2d 633 (1981).

40. 15 U.S.C.A. § 77q(a), which is discussed in § 7.11 *supra* and § 12.22 *infra*. *See* § 12.3 *supra* for discussion of the origins of Rule 10(b)–5.

41. Chemical Bank v. Arthur Andersen & Co., 726 F.2d 930, 939–45 (2d Cir.1984), *cert. denied*, 469 U.S. 884, 105 S.Ct. 253, 83 L.Ed.2d 190 (1984); Mansbach v. Prescott, Ball & Turben, 598 F.2d 1017 (6th Cir.1979).

42. Alley v. Miramon, 614 F.2d 1372 (5th Cir.1980); Lincoln National Bank v. Herber, 604 F.2d 1038 (7th Cir.1979).

50. *See, e.g.,* Sanderson v. H.I.G. P–XI Holding, Inc., 2000 WL 1042813, [1999–2000 Transfer Binder] Fed. Sec. L. Rep. (CCH) ¶ 91,047 (E.D.La. 2000).

51. Berk v. Maryland Publick Banks, Inc., 6 F.Supp.2d 472 (D.Md.1998).

viewed as sale in violation of section 5 of the 1933 Act.[52] However, classifying the foregoing "gifts" as sales for 1933 Act purposes does not mean that there will be liability for fraud, since an investor who pays nothing has nothing to lose and thus will have difficulty showing damages caused by any misrepresentation in connection with the gift.

§ 12.6[8] Periodic Payments; The Investment Decision Doctrine

Ordinarily, securities transactions require that the investor pay the consideration prior to or at the time he or she is to receive the securities. On occasion, however, payments may be set up on an installment basis. In such instances, does the sale occur at the time of the contract's making or is there a new sale at the time of each payment? The answer to this question may, of course, be significant for statute of limitations purposes. It is generally said that a purchase and sale do not take place until "the parties to the transaction are committed to each other."[55] Under what is known as the "investment decision" doctrine,[56] when every payment involves a new investment decision, each payment will be treated as a sale.[57] In contrast, when the contract involves a single decision with subsequent periodic payments, there is only one sale.

§ 12.7 Standing to Sue Under SEC Rule 10b–5

§ 12.7[1] The Purchaser/Seller Requirement

Rule 10b–5's applicability is premised upon a transaction that is "in connection with" a "purchase or sale" of a security. Six years after the initial recognition of an implied private 10b–5 remedy,[5] the Second Circuit held in Birnbaum v. Newport Steel Corp.[6] that a 10b–5 plaintiff in a private damages action must have been either a purchaser or seller of the securities that form the basis of the material omission, misstatement, or deceptive conduct. The *Birnbaum* decision, which was adopted by the Supreme Court nearly twenty years later, in Blue Chip Stamps v. Manor Drug Stores,[7] has been followed by a number of inroads in the purchaser/seller standing requirement.

---

52. In SEC v. Cavanagh, 1998 WL 440029, [1998 Transfer Binder] Fed. Sec. L. Rep. (CCH) ¶ 90,271 (S.D.N.Y. 1998) the court held that a gift cannot be used as a ruse to disguise what truly is a sale; Thus, a plan to "give" stock away as part of a sales promotion for a company's products would constitute a sale since the customer would be paying for the product; American Brewing Co., 31 Sec. Reg. & L. Rep. (BNA) 194 (SEC No Action Letter Jan. 27, 1999) (offering a "free" share of a brewery's voting stock with each case of beer purchased at retail); Vanderkam & Sanders, 31 Sec. Reg. & L. Rep. (BNA) 230 (SEC No Action Letter Jan. 27, 1999) ("a person's registration on or visit to an issuer's internet site" is sufficient consideration (or value) to be a sale under section 2(a)(3) of the 1993 Act).

55. *E.g.,* Kahn v. Kohlberg, Kravis, Roberts & Co., 970 F.2d 1030, 1040 (2d Cir.1992), *cert. denied*, 506 U.S. 986, 113 S.Ct. 494, 121 L.Ed.2d 432 (1992).

56. *See* §§ 5.4, 7.10 *supra. See generally* Note, Defenses to the Statute of Limitations in Federal Securities Cases. The Fraudulent Concealment Doctrine and the Investment Decision Doctrine, 38 S.C.L.Rev. 789 (1987).

57. *E.g.,* Department of Economic Development v. Arthur Andersen & Co., 683 F.Supp. 1463, 1475 (S.D.N.Y.1988).

§ 12.7

5. Kardon v. National Gypsum Co., 69 F.Supp. 512 (E.D.Pa.1946).

6. 193 F.2d 461 (2d Cir.1952), *cert. denied*, 343 U.S. 956, 72 S.Ct. 1051, 96 L.Ed. 1356 (1952).

7. 421 U.S. 723, 95 S.Ct. 1917, 44 L.Ed.2d 539 (1975), *rehearing denied*, 423 U.S. 884, 96 S.Ct. 157, 46 L.Ed.2d 114 (1975).

After the purchaser/seller standing rule was developed, it soon became clear that a plaintiff shareholder satisfies the purchaser/seller standing requirement in a shareholder derivative suit brought on behalf of a corporation defrauded in connection with its purchase or sale of securities.[36] While a shareholder can bring a derivative suit in a representative capacity for the corporation, other members of the corporate community cannot. Thus, for example, a corporate director cannot bring a claim based on a transaction by the corporation.[37] Similarly, Rule 10b–5 standing does not extend to non-shareholder officers.[38] Even being a shareholder will not assure standing to sue. In order to state a 10b–5 claim based on the corporation's purchase or sale of a security, the shareholder must be suing in a derivative rather than individual capacity.[39] The plaintiff must be able to establish the type of claim which can be brought derivatively.

Share exchanges or cash-out transactions pursuant to a corporate merger or other business combination will ordinarily constitute purchases and sales for Rule 10b–5 purposes.[50] However, when the merger is in fact a matter of form rather than substance, a purchase and sale will not result from the share exchange.[51] Where a corporation ceases to exist due to a merger or other form of corporate reorganization, it has been held that the successor corporation, although not itself a purchaser or seller of the securities in question, may maintain a Rule 10b–5 action for securities sold or purchased by the disappearing corporation.[52] In contrast, an exchange of shares or merger with a shell company that is undertaken merely for "corporate restructuring" has been held not to constitute a purchase or sale under Rule 10b–5.[53] This result finds some support both in "corporate law theory"[54] and SEC Rule 145 under the 1933 Act, which takes the position that there is no sale where the sole purpose of the merger is to change the issuer's domicile.[55]

When shareholders receive stock as a dividend, can they maintain a suit for alleged fraud under Rule 10b–5? The Seventh Circuit has held that they cannot.[61] The court held that shares issued pro rata to shareholders in a spin-off transaction[62] are not "purchased" since no consideration is paid by the

---

36. *E.g.,* Frankel v. Slotkin, 984 F.2d 1328 (2d Cir.1993). For discussion of derivative suits generally, *see* 2 James D. Cox & Thomas L. Hazen Cox and Hazen on Corporations, ch. 15 (2d ed. 2003).

37. Brannan v. Eisenstein, 804 F.2d 1041 (8th Cir.1986). *Cf., e.g.,* Linsey v. E.F. Hutton & Co., 675 F.Supp. 1 (D.D.C.1987) (bishop could not maintain suit against broker for alleged fraud against his church).

38. Powers v. British Vita, P.L.C., 842 F.Supp. 1573 (S.D.N.Y.1994).

39. *See, e.g.,* Smith v. Ayres, 845 F.2d 1360 (5th Cir.1988).

50. *See, e.g.,* Realmonte v. Reeves, 169 F.3d 1280 (10th Cir.1999)(investors who received shares in stock-for-stock exchange could not be excluded from class action on grounds that other investors engaged in cash-for-stock transactions).

51. Goldberg v. Hankin, 835 F.Supp. 815 (E.D.Pa.1993) (shareholder of bank that was transformed into bank holding company was not a purchaser as a result of the exchange of shares pursuant to the bank holding company's formation).

52. Nanfito v. Tekseed Hybrid Co., 341 F.Supp. 240 (D.Neb.1972), *affirmed,* 473 F.2d 537 (8th Cir.1973).

53. In re Penn Central Securities Litigation, 494 F.2d 528 (3d Cir.1974).

54. *See* Richard W. Jennings & Harold Marsh, Jr., Securities Regulation: Cases and Materials 1123 (6th ed. 1987).

55. 17 C.F.R. § 230.145. *See* § 5.2 *supra.*

61. Isquith v. Caremark International, Inc., 136 F.3d 531 (7th Cir.1998).

62. Spin-off transactions are discussed in § 5.3 *supra.*

shareholders.[63] The court, per Chief Judge Posner, rejected the argument that the shareholders receiving the dividend purchased the spun-off shares, since the value of the parent corporation's stock was reduced as a result of the spin-off.[64]

A pledge of securities generally is held to be a sale under the Exchange Act, and accordingly, the pledgees are "purchasers" and able to maintain a Rule 10b–5 cause of action—although there is some conflict on this point.[65]

§ 12.7[2] Standing to Seek Injunctive Relief

There is authority to the effect that a person need be neither a purchaser nor a seller of the securities in order to maintain an action for injunctive relief under Rule 10b–5.[79] There is also some authority to the contrary.[80] Some courts take the position that the equitable relief exception to the purchaser/seller requirement applies only where the relief sought is prophylactic.[81] Furthermore, even among those courts that do not require the plaintiff in an injunction action to have been a purchaser or seller, the plaintiff must still be able to show some direct injury resulting from the alleged Rule 10b–5 violation.[82]

§ 12.7[3] Variations on the Purchaser/Seller Requirement

§ 12.7[3][A] Forced Sellers

Following the Second Circuit's decision in Birnbaum v. Newport Steel Corp.,[85] the courts created a number of doctrines (or exceptions) to give 10b–5 standing to persons who would not otherwise directly qualify as purchasers or sellers. Under the "aborted seller" rule, where the defendant enters into a contract to purchase securities without any intention of paying for them, the plaintiff would-be seller has been held to have a 10b–5 cause of action.[86] Other courts applying the "aborted seller" doctrine required either that the plaintiff demonstrate a clear "investment decision" or that granting standing would be "in the public interest."[87] Fraudulently inducing shareholders not to part with their shares will not by itself support a Rule 10b–5 damage action.[88] Even with additional compelling factors, it is highly doubtful that the "aborted seller" doctrine survives the Supreme Court decision in Blue Chip Stamps v. Manor

---

63. Isquith v. Caremark International, Inc., 136 F.3d 531 (7th Cir.1998).

64. *Id.*

65. *E.g.*, Madison Consultants v. FDIC, 710 F.2d 57 (2d Cir.1983).

79. Mutual Shares Corp. v. Genesco, Inc., 384 F.2d 540 (2d Cir.1967); Tully v. Mott Supermarkets, Inc., 540 F.2d 187, 194 (3d Cir.1976) (dictum).

80. Cowin v. Bresler, 741 F.2d 410 (D.C.Cir.1984); Packer v. Yampol, 630 F.Supp. 1237 (S.D.N.Y.1986) (plaintiff cannot sue on behalf of investing public generally); Atlantic Federal Savings & Loan Ass'n v. Dade Savings & Loan Ass'n, 592 F.Supp. 1089 (S.D.Fla.1984).

81. Doll v. James Martin Associates (Holdings) Ltd., 600 F.Supp. 510, 522–23 (E.D.Mich. 1984).

82. Advanced Resources International, Inc. v. Tri–Star Petroleum Co., 4 F.3d 327 (4th Cir.1993).

85. 193 F.2d 461 (2d Cir.1952), *cert. denied*, 343 U.S. 956, 72 S.Ct. 1051, 96 L.Ed. 1356 (1952).

86. *E.g.*, Richardson v. MacArthur, 451 F.2d 35 (10th Cir.1971).

87. Abrahamson v. Fleschner, 568 F.2d 862, 868 (2d Cir.1977), *cert. denied*, 436 U.S. 905, 98 S.Ct. 2236, 56 L.Ed.2d 403 (1978).

88. *See, e.g.*, Chanoff v. U.S. Surgical Corp., 857 F.Supp. 1011 (D.Conn.1994).

Drug Stores.[89] However, as noted above, when there is a binding contract of sale, a would-be purchaser or seller can bring suit since the contract itself is a security.

When a shareholder is frozen out of a corporation or otherwise put in the position of a "forced seller," Rule 10b–5 standing ordinarily will exist even though there was no voluntary investment decision.[90] It has been said that the forced-seller doctrine should be interpreted narrowly in light of *Blue Chip Stamps*.[91] Forced purchasers also have standing under Rule 10b–5.[92]

§ 12.7[3][B] Would-be Purchasers and Sellers; Deferred Sellers

Most of the inroads on the purchaser/seller doctrine seem to survive the Supreme Court's adoption of the purchaser/seller standing requirement in Blue Chip Stamps v. Manor Drug Stores.[93] In that case the Court held that the plaintiffs had a right to purchase the securities in question under an antitrust consent decree. The plaintiffs refrained from purchasing the securities, allegedly relying on misleading statements made by the defendants designed to deter the planned purchase; the Court held that these would-be purchasers could not state a 10b–5 cause of action.[94] For the same reasons, the holder of an unexercised right of first refusal to purchase securities does not have standing under Rule 10b–5.[95] A binding contract right to purchase securities will support Rule 10b–5 standing even if the right to purchase is contingent.[96] However, the absence of a binding contract will preclude Rule 10b–5 standing.[97] A decision to release a claim to purchase securities does not support Rule 10b–5 standing[98] since the plaintiff is nothing more than a frustrated or would-be purchaser. A necessary corollary to these holdings would seem to be that mere "would-be" sellers cannot raise 10b–5 claims.[99] *Blue Chip Stamps* is best described as a case of the frustrated purchaser since the plaintiff had a right to purchase the securities under the terms of a consent decree. It would seem that, for similar reasons, the former exception to the *Birnbaum* doctrine for the "frustrated seller" does not survive *Blue*

---

89. 421 U.S. 723, 95 S.Ct. 1917, 44 L.Ed.2d 539 (1975).

90. *See, e.g.*, Alley v. Miramon, 614 F.2d 1372 (5th Cir.1980). Greenstein v. Paul, 400 F.2d 580 (2d Cir.1968); Vine v. Beneficial Finance Co., 374 F.2d 627 (2d Cir.1967), *cert. denied*, 389 U.S. 970, 88 S.Ct. 463, 19 L.Ed.2d 460 (1967).

91. *See* Jacobson v. AEG Capital Corp., 50 F.3d 1493, 1499 (9th Cir.1995) ("forced sale doctrine does not cut a wide swath"; shareholder who participated in bankruptcy reorganization could not qualify as a forced-seller).

92. *E.g.*, Zweig v. Hearst Corp., 594 F.2d 1261 (9th Cir.1979).

93. 421 U.S. 723, 95 S.Ct. 1917, 44 L.Ed.2d 539 (1975), *rehearing denied*, 423 U.S. 884, 96 S.Ct. 157, 46 L.Ed.2d 114 (1975). *See* Note, Standing Under Rule 10b–5 after *Blue Chip*, 75 Mich.L.Rev. 413 (1976).

94. *See also, e.g.*, Cohen v. Stratosphere Corp., 115 F.3d 695 (9th Cir.1997) (plaintiffs did not have binding contracts to purchase securities and thus lacked standing under Rule 10b–5).

95. Union Pacific Resources Group, Inc. v. Rhone–Poulenc, Inc., 45 F.Supp.2d 544 (N.D.Tex. 1999), *affirmed in part, reversed in part*, 247 F.3d 574 (5th Cir.2001) (right of first refusal that was not exercised did not constitute a purchase or sale of a security).

96. Griggs v. Pace American Group, Inc., 170 F.3d 877 (9th Cir.1999).

97. Cohen v. Stratosphere Corp., 115 F.3d 695 (9th Cir.1997).

98. Lawrence v. Cohn, 325 F.3d 141 (2d Cir. 2003).

99. *E.g.*, Calenti v. Boto, 24 F.3d 335 (1st Cir.1994).

Chip Stamps.[101] *In fact, in Merrill Lynch, Pierce, Fenner & Smith v. Dabit,*[101.1] the Supreme Court held that Securities Litigation Uniform Standards Act (SLUSA)[101.2] preempts state law claims that could be brought by someone who held rather than sold securities. The Court noted that the absence of a Rule 10b–5 remedy reinforced the application n of SLUSA's preemptive effect.

§ 12.7[4] Rights and Options

Contract rights to purchase (or sell) securities can classify the holder as a purchaser or seller of the underlying security, or may themselves be securities.[116] Thus, for example, a preemptive right to purchase shares is a contract to purchase and can provide the basis for Rule 10b–5 standing.[117] Similarly, an executory contract to acquire shares pursuant to an employment agreement can form the basis of a Rule 10b–5 claim.[118] A contract creating a conditional right to purchase securities has been held to confer standing even though the would-be purchaser received cash in lieu of securities in connection with a merger.[119]

§ 12.8 Rule 10b–5 and the Scienter Requirement; Section 17(a) and Rule 14a–9 Compared

§ 12.8[1] Rule 10b–5's Scienter Requirement; Section 17(a) Compared

Rule 10b–5 describes the type of conduct proscribed but it does not set out the appropriate standard of culpability. The question has thus arisen as to whether the securities laws reach negligent misconduct or are limited to intentional misstatements and omissions. After twenty years of conflicting cases, in 1976 the Supreme Court held in Ernst & Ernst v. Hochfelder[2] that, in order to establish a valid claim for damages under Rule 10b–5, it must be proven that the defendant acted with scienter. The Supreme Court subsequently held in Aaron v. SEC[3] that the scienter standard applies under Rule 10b–5 regardless of whether the action is one for damages or an enforcement

---

101. The aborted or frustrated-seller basis for standing was rejected in Weiner v. Rooney, Pace Inc., 1987 WL 11281 [1987 Transfer Binder] Fed.Sec.L.Rep. (CCH) ¶ 93,174 (S.D.N.Y.1987). *See also* Nevitsky v. Manufacturers Hanover Brokerage Services, 654 F.Supp. 116 (S.D.N.Y.1987) (broker's refusal to consummate sale could not support a 10b–5 claim due to failure to satisfy the purchaser/seller standing requirement). *Cf.* Riley v. Merrill Lynch, Pierce, Fenner & Smith, Inc., 292 F.3d 1334 (11th Cir.2002) (indicating that the Securities Litigation Uniform Standards Act of 1998 would not preempt state law claims that plaintiffs held securities and thus were deterred from selling; but finding that the claims involved a purchase of covered securities and thus were preempted).

101.1 ___ U.S. ___, 126 S.Ct. 1503, 164 L.Ed.2d 179 (2006).

101.2 *See* § 12.15[2] *infra.*

116. *E.g.,* Wharf (Holdings) Ltd. v. United International Holdings, Inc., 532 U.S. 588, 121 S.Ct. 1776, 149 L.Ed.2d 845 (2001).

117. Brennan v. EMDE Medical Research, Inc., 652 F.Supp. 255 (D.Nev.1986). *See also* Zlotnick v. TIE Communications, 836 F.2d 818 (3d Cir.1988) (short seller has Rule 10b–5 standing).

118. Technology Exchange Corp. of America, Inc. v. Grant County State Bank, 646 F.Supp. 179 (D.Colo.1986).

119. *See, e.g.,* Griggs v. Pace American Group, Inc., 170 F.3d 877 (9th Cir.1999).

§ 12.8

2. 425 U.S. 185, 96 S.Ct. 1375, 47 L.Ed.2d 668 (1976).

3. 446 U.S. 680, 100 S.Ct. 1945, 64 L.Ed.2d 611 (1980).

For a pre-*Aaron* discussion of the issue, *see* Lewis Lowenfels, Scienter or Negligence Required for SEC Injunctions Under Section 10(b) and Rule 10b–5: A Fascinating Paradox, 33 Bus.Law. 789 (1978).

action brought by the Commission. In the context of a criminal case, in addition to scienter, the prosecution must establish that the defendant acted willfully, which means that he or she acted with a realization that the acts were wrongful.[5]

The Supreme Court in *Aaron v. SEC* also held that scienter is not an element of an SEC claim for injunctive relief under sections 17(a)(2) and (a)(3) of the 1933 Act.[6] The Court reasoned that, although the language of Rule 10b–5 is identical in all relevant parts to that of section 17(a) of the 1933 Act, section 10(b)'s overall scope is statutorily limited to manipulative or deceptive conduct.[7] "Manipulation" is a term of art that is limited to certain specific types of trading practices and thus is not applicable in most antifraud cases.[8] In fact, there is a considerable question of whether the concept of manipulation can validly play any role with regard to Rule 10b–5.[9] The statutory deception requirement has been held to mandate a showing of scienter in order to state a 10b–5 claim because deception connotes common law fraud and common law fraud requires scienter.[10] As discussed more fully below, one corollary of Rule 10b–5's deception and scienter requirements is that, as is the case with fraud generally, the complaint must be pleaded with sufficient particularity.[11]

§ 12.8[2] Rule 10b–5's Scienter Requirement; The Proxy Rules Compared

Section 14(a) of the Exchange Act and Rule 14a–9 promulgated thereunder give rise to an implied antifraud remedy in connection with a proxy solicitation.[12] Section 14(a) does not expressly impose the limitation that SEC rules address conduct that is manipulative or deceptive. A number of courts have held that the absence of a similar deception requirement in the language of section 14(a)[13] results in a finding that negligence is sufficient to state a claim under the proxy rule's antifraud provisions.[14] The reasoning of the

5. United States v. Stewart, 305 F.Supp.2d 368 (S.D.N.Y. 2004) ("In a criminal prosecution, the government must also prove that the defendant acted 'willfully,' that is, with a realization that she was acting wrongfully"). *See also, e.g.,* United States v. Dixon, 536 F.2d 1388, 1395 (2d Cir. 1976). *But cf.* United States v. Tarallo, 380 F.3d 1174, 1179 (9th Cir.2004) ("A defendant may commit securities fraud 'wilfully' by intentionally acting with reckless disregard of the truth").

6. *See* 15 U.S.C.A. § 77q(a)(2), (3). The Court also held that scienter must be shown in an action under section 17(a)(1).

7. 15 U.S.C.A. § 78j(b).

8. *See, e.g.,* Santa Fe Industries, Inc. v. Green, 430 U.S. 462, 476, 97 S.Ct. 1292, 1302, 51 L.Ed.2d 480 (1977).

9. Schreiber v. Burlington Northern, Inc., 472 U.S. 1, 105 S.Ct. 2458, 86 L.Ed.2d 1 (1985), held that manipulative conduct does not violate section 14(e) unless there has been deception in terms of a material misstatement or omission. *See* §§ 11.15, 12.1 *supra.*

10. Ernst & Ernst v. Hochfelder, 425 U.S. 185, 197, 96 S.Ct. 1375, 1382, 47 L.Ed.2d 668 (1976). *See, e.g.,* Aaron v. SEC, 446 U.S. 680, 695, 100 S.Ct. 1945, 1954, 64 L.Ed.2d 611 (1980).

11. *E.g.,* Serabian v. Amoskeag Bank Shares, Inc., 24 F.3d 357 (1st Cir.1994) (scienter sufficiently alleged).

12. 15 U.S.C.A. § 78n(a); 17 C.F.R. § 240.14a–9. *E.g.,* J.I. Case & Co. v. Borak, 377 U.S. 426, 84 S.Ct. 1555, 12 L.Ed.2d 423 (1964). *See* § 10.3 *supra.*

13. Section 14(a), like section 17(a) of the 1933 Act, is not limited to deceptive and manipulative acts and practices. Section 14(a) provides that it is unlawful to solicit proxies with regard to securities registered under section 12 (15 U.S.C.A. § 78l; *see* § 9.2 *supra*) "in contravention of such rules and regulations as the Commission may prescribe as necessary or appropriate in the public interest or for the protection of investors." 15 U.S.C.A. § 78n(a).

14. *See, e.g.,* In re Rockefeller Center Properties, Inc. Securities Litigation, 311 F.3d 198, 211 (3d Cir. 2002); In re NAHC, Inc. Securities Litigation, 306 F.3d 1314, 1329 (3d Cir. 2002).

Supreme Court in *Aaron* seems to compel a finding that scienter is not required in an action under the proxy rules. Accordingly, it is appropriate that a majority of the decisions conclude that negligence is sufficient to establish a violation of section 14(a) and Rule 14a–9's prohibitions on material misrepresentations and omissions in connection with proxy solicitations.

§ 12.8[3] Recklessness as Scienter

It is clear that the scienter requirement is satisfied by a showing of intentional misrepresentation made with the intent to deceive. But what about conduct that falls short of willful misrepresentation? In reaching its decisions in *Hochfelder* and *Aaron* the Court did not decide whether a showing of reckless conduct would satisfy the scienter requirement.[15] It has long been the rule at common law that, at least under certain circumstances, the showing of reckless disregard of the truth or the making of a statement with no belief in its truth constitutes scienter in an action for deceit.[16] While the recklessness question remains unsettled at the Supreme Court level, the vast majority of the circuit and district court decisions have found that recklessness is sufficient to state a claim under 10b–5. The Supreme Court granted certiorari on the issue of whether recklessness can form the basis of aider and abettor liability under Rule 10b–5.[18] However, the Court never reached the scienter issue since it disposed of that case by ruling that there is no implied remedy against aiders and abettors.[19] Accordingly, the circuit and district court cases recognizing recklessness as sufficient to satisfy the scienter requirement have not been disturbed and remain the overwhelming majority view.[20] It seems equally clear that the Private Securities Litigation Reform Act of 1995[21] did not alter the recklessness standard.[22]

Since the *Hochfelder* and *Aaron* scienter requirements are borrowed from common law fraud, there is every reason to believe that the common law definition, including reckless disregard of the truth, should also apply in the Rule 10b–5 context. One problem raised by the recklessness standard, howev-

---

15. 425 U.S. at 193–94 n. 12, 96 S.Ct. at 1381 n. 12; 446 U.S. at 690–691, 100 S.Ct. at 1952.

16. *E.g.,* Derry v. Peek, 14 App.Cas. 337 (House of Lords 1889). *See generally* W. Page Keeton, Dan B. Dobbs, Robert E. Keeton & David G. Owen, Prosser and Keeton on Torts § 107 (5th ed. 1984). *See also, e.g.,* SEC v. Bremont, 954 F.Supp. 726 (S.D.N.Y.1997) (representations made in reckless disregard of the truth establish scienter).

In Brophy v. Redivo, 725 F.2d 1218 (9th Cir.1984), the court held that volitional conduct is not sufficient, as there must be an intent to defraud. A broker's voluntarily entering into unauthorized transactions did not satisfy the scienter requirement since there was no evidence of an intent to defraud the customer.

18. Central Bank of Denver v. First Interstate Bank of Denver, 508 U.S. 959, 113 S.Ct. 2927, 124 L.Ed.2d 678 (1993), *opinion below* 969 F.2d 891 (10th Cir.1992). Certiorari had been sought on the question of whether a showing of recklessness could support aiding and abetting liability and, in granting certiorari on this issue, the Court also asked the parties to brief the question of whether there is an implied action against aiders and abettors. This became the eventual ground for the Court's decision.

19. Central Bank of Denver v. First Interstate Bank of Denver, 511 U.S. 164, 114 S.Ct. 1439, 128 L.Ed.2d 119 (1994). *See* § 12.25 *infra.*

20. *See, e.g.,* Howard v. SEC, 376 F.3d 1136 (D.C. Cir. 2004); In re Advanta Corp. Securities Litigation, 180 F.3d 525, 539 (3d Cir.1999); SEC v. U.S. Environmental, Inc., 155 F.3d 107 (2d Cir.1998).

21. *See* § 12.15 *infra.*

22. *E.g.,* Novak v. Kasaks, 216 F.3d 300, 316 (2d Cir.2000) (the Litigation Reform Act did not heighten the scienter requirement, it only added a particularity requirement); Gelfer v. Pegasystems, Inc., 96 F.Supp.2d 10 (D.Mass.2000).

er, is that it does not provide as easy a test in application as would one requiring a showing of actual intent. The concept of recklessness belies the existence of a bright line test for when the scienter threshold has been crossed. Recklessness is obviously a matter of degree and requires something considerably more than negligent conduct, but it still falls short of actual intentional action.[23] It is clear that, in order to establish scienter, the defendant must have had more than a tangential connection to both the transactions and statements under scrutiny.[24]

Some courts have spoken in terms of a "barely reckless" standard,[25] whereas a number of courts seem to be leaning more toward a "highly reckless" standard.[26] It has also been suggested that the *Hochfelder* decision does not preclude the applicability of a flexible duty[27] standard depending upon the relationship between the plaintiff and the defendant and all the surrounding facts of the particular case.[28] The Ninth Circuit in an *en banc* ruling rejected the flexible duty standard that it had followed in earlier cases.[29]

The stringent recklessness standard adopted by the Ninth Circuit has been phrased in terms of deliberate or conscious recklessness.[31] As other courts have put it: "[a]n egregious refusal to see the obvious, or to investigate the doubtful, may in some cases give rise to an inference of ... recklessness."[32]

The recklessness standard has also been articulated in terms of whether the defendants "had reasonable grounds to believe material facts existed that were misstated or omitted, but nonetheless failed to obtain and disclose such facts although they could have done so without extraordinary effort."[33] Borrowing from the common law, the formulation of the test for recklessness is properly articulated in terms of whether or not the defendants made the

23. *See, e.g.,* AUSA Life Insurance Co. v. Ernst & Young, 206 F.3d 202 (2d Cir.2000) (sufficient allegations of scienter; scienter depends on what defendants should reasonably have expected to happen, not simply what they wanted to happen). *See also, e.g.,* Allan Horwich, The Neglected Relationship of Materiality and Recklessness in Actions Under Rule 10b–5, 55 Bus. Law. 1023 (2000). Materiality is discussed in § 12.9 *infra.*

24. *See, e.g.,* National Union Fire Insurance Co. v. Wilkins–Lowe & Co., 29 F.3d 337 (7th Cir.1994) (principal's tangential connection to activities of agent who converted customer funds was too indirect to satisfy the scienter requirement).

25. *See* Stern v. American Bankshares Corp., 429 F.Supp. 818 (E.D.Wis.1977).

26. *E.g.,* In re Silicon Graphics Inc. Securities Litigation, 183 F.3d 970, 988 (9th Cir.1999) (requiring "deliberate recklessness"); Meadows v. SEC, 119 F.3d 1219 (5th Cir.1997) (liability under Rule 10b–5 requires at least severe reckless conduct); Newton v. Merrill Lynch, Pierce, Fenner & Smith, 115 F.3d 1127 (3d Cir.1997), *reversed on other grounds,* 135 F.3d 266 (3d Cir.1998) (en banc) (scienter involves an extreme departure from standards of ordinary care).

27. *See* White v. Abrams, 495 F.2d 724 (9th Cir.1974).

28. Broad v. Rockwell International Corp., 614 F.2d 418 (5th Cir.1980), *modified,* 642 F.2d 929 (5th Cir.1981), *cert. denied,* 454 U.S. 965, 102 S.Ct. 506, 70 L.Ed.2d 380 (1981); Healey v. Catalyst Recovery of Pennsylvania, Inc., 616 F.2d 641 (3d Cir.1980).

29. Hollinger v. Titan Capital Corp., 914 F.2d 1564 (9th Cir.1990), *cert. denied,* 499 U.S. 976, 111 S.Ct. 1621, 113 L.Ed.2d 719 (1991). *Compare, e.g.,* the pre-*Hochfelder* decision in White v. Abrams, 495 F.2d 724, 735–36 (9th Cir.1974).

31. *See, e.g.,* Employers Teamsters Local Nos. 175 and 505 Pension Trust Fund v. Clorox Co., 353 F.3d 1125, 1134 (9th Cir. 2004).

32. MBI Acquisition Partners v. Chronical Publishing Co., 301 F.Supp.2d 873 (W.D. Wis. 2002), quoting Rehm v. Eagle Fin. Corp., 954 F.Supp. 1246, 1255 (N.D.Ill.1997) and Goldman v. McMahan, Brafman, Morgan & Co., 706 F.Supp. 256, 259 (S.D.N.Y.1989).

33. Keirnan v. Homeland, Inc., 611 F.2d 785, 788 (9th Cir.1980).

Scienter may be inferred from circumstantial evidence. *E.g.,* Wechsler v. Steinberg, 733 F.2d 1054 (2d Cir.1984).

statements in question with no belief in the truth or the falsity of the assertion or with reckless disregard to the truth or the falsity.[34] This test has been historically valid under common law.

§ 12.8[4] Pleading and Proving Scienter

Scienter is based on the defendant's state of mind and, as is the case in many cases, may be difficult to prove with direct evidence. On appropriate facts, a court may be willing to permit an inference that the defendant acted with the requisite scienter. However, such an inference should not be made lightly.[40] In making the determination of culpability, the court should consider all inferences and weigh them together in determining whether the defendant acted with scienter.[41] Thus, the presence of some facts that could lead to an inference of scienter may be negated by other inferences.[42] Scienter should be inferred only when the fact pattern indicates that the defendants must have been acting with the requisite state of mind.[43] In order to withstand the scrutiny imposed by the Private Securities Litigation Reform Act of 1995,[44] the inference of scienter must be both reasonable and strong.[45]

Although the Private Securities Litigation Reform Act reinforced that specificity requirement with respect to pleading scienter, that Act did not provide specific statutory guidance as to what constitutes a strong inference of scienter so as to withstand a motion to dismiss. As developed more fully below, the various circuits have struggled to provide guidelines, with some apparent disagreements as to some of the factors to be considered, such as the relevance of motive and opportunity in establishing scienter. The absence of specific statutory guidelines has left the courts to determine the sufficiency of pleadings involving scienter on a case-by-case basis.[48] A review of the cases indicates the factors that the courts consider, but it is difficult to make generalizations since it is a quantitative rather than a qualitative analysis in determining whether a strong inference has been established.[49]

---

34. Derry v. Peek, 14 App.Cas. 337 (House of Lords 1889).

While constructive knowledge alone arguably would not satisfy scienter, at least one court has allowed the alternative pleading of actual or constructive knowledge of fraud to withstand a motion to dismiss, Chisholm v. St. Pierre, 1981 WL 1695 [1981–1982 Transfer Binder] Fed.Sec. L.Rep. (CCH) ¶ 98,337 (D.Mass.1981).

40. *See* Rothman v. Gregor, 220 F.3d 81, 94–95 (2d Cir.2000).

41. Gompper v. VISX, Inc., 298 F.3d 893 (9th Cir.2002) (affirming finding of no scienter).

42. *Id.*

43. *See, e.g.,* Miller v. Champion Enterprises Inc., 346 F.3d 660 (6th Cir. 2003) (insufficient allegations of recklessness).

44. Pub. Law No. 104–67, 109 Stat. 737 (104th Cong. 1st Sess. December 22, 1995) (HR 1058).

45. *See, e.g.,* Aldridge v. A.T. Cross Corp., 284 F.3d 72 (1st Cir.2002) (sufficiently alleging scienter).

48. Ottmann v. Hanger Orthopedic Group, Inc., 353 F.3d 338, 345 (4th Cir. 2003) ("a flexible, case-specific analysis is appropriate in examining scienter pleadings. Both the absence of any statutory language addressing particular methods of pleading and the inconclusive legislative history regarding the adoption of Second Circuit pleading standards indicate that Congress ultimately chose not to specify particular types of facts that would or would not show a strong inference of scienter.").

49. Ottmann v. Hanger Orthopedic Group, Inc., 353 F.3d 338, 345–346 (4th Cir. 2003) ("courts should not restrict their scienter inquiry by focusing on specific categories of facts, such as those relating to motive and opportunity, but instead should examine all of the allegations in each case to determine whether they collectively establish a strong inference of scienter. And, while particular facts demonstrating a motive and opportunity to commit fraud (or lack of such facts) may be relevant to the scienter inquiry, the weight accorded to those facts should depend

As is the case with the other elements of fraud, scienter is subject to Federal Rule of Civil Procedure Rule 9(b)'s requirement that fraud be pleaded with particularity.[50]

§ 12.9 Materiality in Rule 10b–5 Actions

§ 12.9[1] Materiality in Context

In a common law action for fraud or deceit, in addition to proving the requisite degree of culpability (*i.e.,* scienter),[1] the successful plaintiff must prove a material[2] misstatement or omission and reliance[3] upon the misstatement or omission in question. As is the case with scienter, the materiality[5] and reliance requirements carry over to 10b–5 actions. As explained below, in order to be materially misleading, there must be a significant element of inaccuracy[7] or obfuscation. Technically accurate information can still be materially misleading if the significant facts are buried in the disclosure document and thus not readily apparent to the average reader. Thus, under the "buried facts" doctrine, disclosures can be obscured by burying them in footnotes or appendices.[8]

The test of materiality depends not upon the literal truth of statements, but upon the ability of reasonable investors to become accurately informed.[9] This is sometimes referred to as the mosaic misrepresentation thesis.[10] Courts should not focus on a particular sentence that is part of a larger statement or disclosure without considering the entirety the statements in question.[11] Accordingly, when there is adequate cautionary language warning investors as to certain risks, optimistic statements are not materially misleading.[12] As discussed more fully below, a finding of materiality is based on the total mix

---

on the circumstances of each case."); Helwig v. Vencor, Inc., 251 F.3d 540, 551 (6th Cir. 2001) ("Congress was concerned with the quantum, not type, of proof.").

50. Fed.R.Civ.P. 9. *See, e.g.,* Gompper v. VISX, Inc., 298 F.3d 893 (9th Cir.2002) (allegations did not satisfy the Reform Act's standards for pleading scienter).

§ 12.9

1. *See* § 12.8 *supra.*

2. As developed more fully in this section, a term is material if it is sufficiently important to a reasonable investor to have a substantial impact on his or her decision to invest.

3. The reliance requirement, which is closely related to the concept of materiality, is discussed in § 12.10 *infra.*

5. It has been observed that "[f]or the securities lawyer 'materiality' is the name of the game." Richard W. Jennings & Harold Marsh, Jr., Securities Regulation: Cases and Materials 1023 (5th ed. 1982).

7. *See, e.g.,* Karacand v. Edwards, 53 F.Supp.2d 1236, 1252 (D.Utah 1999).

8. *See* Plain English Disclosure, Sec. Act Rel. No. 33–7497, 63 Fed. Reg. 6370–01, 1998 WL 44199 (F.R.) (SEC Feb. 6, 1998) ("Under the buried facts doctrine, a court would consider disclosure to be false and misleading only if its overall significance is obscured because material information is 'buried,' for example, in footnotes or appendices"). *See also, e.g.,* Gould v. American Hawaiian Steamship Company, 331 F.Supp. 981 (D.Del.1971); Kohn v. American Metal Climax, Inc., 322 F.Supp. 1331 (E.D.Pa.1970), modified, 458 F.2d 255 (3d Cir.1972).

9. *E.g.,* McMahan & Co. v. Wherehouse Entertainment, Inc., 900 F.2d 576, 579 (2d Cir.1990), *cert. denied,* 501 U.S. 1249, 111 S.Ct. 2887, 115 L.Ed.2d 1052 (1991).

10. In re Genentech, Inc., Securities Litigation, 1989 WL 137189 [1989–1990 Transfer Binder] Fed.Sec.L.Rep. 94,813 (N.D.Cal.1989), s.c. 1989 WL 106834 [1989 Transfer Binder] Fed.Sec. L.Rep. 94,544 (N.D.Cal.1989).

11. *See, e.g.,* Kapps v. Torch Offshore, Inc., 379 F.3d 207 (5th Cir. 2004).

12. *See, e.g.,* Kapps v. Torch Offshore, Inc., 379 F.3d 207 (5th Cir. 2004); In re Worlds of Wonder Securities Litigation, 35 F.3d 1407 (9th Cir.1994).

of information available.[13] However, the mere fact that information may be publicly available does not mean that it is necessarily incorporated into every statement made.[14] Thus, for example, it was held that even though information in a company's Form 10K filing and annual report to shareholders might have clarified alleged misstatements in a proxy solicitation, the alleged misstatements in the company's proxy statement might nevertheless be actionable.[15] The Second Circuit reasoned that for shareholders making their determination of how to vote based on the proxy statement, the information contained in the 10K and annual report were not part of the total mix reasonably available to the shareholders who would be voting.[16]

§ 12.9[2] Factual Nature of Materiality

It has repeatedly been held that the concept of materiality cannot be distilled into a bright-line test.[24] Thus, summary judgment based on a finding of no materiality ordinarily will not be appropriate.[25] Determinations of materiality relating to accounting matters are not determined on a mathematical basis alone; misstatements may otherwise be important to shareholders.[26]

§ 12.9[3] Materiality Defined

Materiality depends on whether the plaintiff can establish "a substantial likelihood that a reasonable shareholder *would* consider it important."[34] The test of materiality is whether a reasonable investor would have considered the matter significant;[35] it is not necessary to show that the investor *would* have acted differently.[36] It is not sufficient to show that a shareholder might have found the information to be of interest.[37] Once materiality is established, however, the investor still has to show a causal connection between the

---

13. *See, e.g.,* Ieradi v. Mylan Laboratories, Inc. 230 F.3d 594 (3d Cir.2000); Longman v. Food Lion, Inc., 197 F.3d 675 (4th Cir.1999).

14. *See, e.g.,* Berry v. Valence Technology, Inc., 175 F.3d 699, 706 (9th Cir.1999) (statement in a magazine article criticizing a company and its stock did not demonstrate that the market already knew of the company's fraud).

15. United Paperworkers International Union v. International Paper Co., 985 F.2d 1190 (2d Cir.1993).

16. *Id.*

24. *E.g.,* Basic Inc. v. Levinson, 485 U.S. 224, 108 S.Ct. 978, 99 L.Ed.2d 194 (1988); Ganino v. Citizens Utilities Co., 228 F.3d 154 (2d Cir.2000).

25. *E.g.,* Castellano v. Young & Rubicam, Inc., 257 F.3d 171 (2d Cir.2001); Marks v. CDW Computer Centers, Inc., 122 F.3d 363, 369–70 (7th Cir.1997).

26. In re Unisys Corp. Securities Litigation, 2000 WL 1367951, [2000–2001] [Transfer Binder] Fed. Sec. L. Rep. (CCH) ¶ 91,218, (E.D. Pa. 2000) (misstatements relating to less than 1% of income could be material), *relying on* In re Westinghouse Securities Litigation, 90 F.3d 696, 714–715 (3d Cir.1996) (misstatement of loan reserves amounting to .54% of total income could have been material but was not, since it was not demonstrated that this was otherwise important to investors); SEC v. Jos. Schlitz Brewing Co., 452 F.Supp. 824 (E.D.Wis.1978) (nondisclosure of kickback scheme was material because, inter alia, it reflected on the lack of management integrity).

34. TSC Industries, Inc. v. Northway, Inc., 426 U.S. 438, 449, 96 S.Ct. 2126, 2132, 48 L.Ed.2d 757 (1976) (emphasis added). *Accord* Basic Inc. v. Levinson, 485 U.S. 224, 108 S.Ct. 978, 99 L.Ed.2d 194 (1988).

35. *See, e.g.,* United States v. Peterson, 101 F.3d 375 (5th Cir.1996).

36. Folger Adam Co. v. PMI Industries, Inc., 938 F.2d 1529 (2d Cir.1991), *cert. denied,* 502 U.S. 983, 112 S.Ct. 587, 116 L.Ed.2d 612 (1991).

37. Milton v. Van Dorn Co., 961 F.2d 965 (1st Cir.1992). *See also, e.g.,* United States v. Bingham, 992 F.2d 975 (9th Cir.1993) (defendant's use of false identity and hiding the fact that he was an officer and director, in connection with sale of security was not a Rule 10b–5 violation).

violation, the transaction, and any loss which he or she suffered.[38] It has been said that "materiality" encompasses those facts "which in reasonable and objective contemplation might affect the value of the corporation's stock or securities."[39]

In an early leading case involving Rule 10b–5, the Second Circuit looked to the Restatement of Torts in defining materiality in terms of whether a reasonable person "would attach importance [to the fact misrepresented] in determining his choice of action in the transaction in question."[40] When a defendant targets unreasonably naive or careless investors, the more objective reasonable person standard will not preclude a finding of materiality.[41] Such misstatements can thus be the subject of SEC or criminal action.[42]

As noted earlier, the materiality determination is to be made in light of the total mix of information available.[44] Thus, for example, oral statements will be considered in light of available written information.[45] Focusing on the total mix of information available means that plaintiffs may not base a claim on nondisclosure of publicly-known information.[46]

The fact that materiality is to be determined in context means that a purchaser or seller is not necessarily entitled to all information relating to each of the circumstances surrounding the transaction.[47]

An increasing number of SEC filings are made electronically—to the point that most filings are electronic.[78] Additionally, investors can view the filings online through the SEC website and also frequently through the company's own website. The materiality of misleading or omitted information will be based on an examination of both the hard copy and the electronic version in order to determine whether the misleading or omitted information is material in light of the "total mix" of information available.[79] The electronic filing process cannot reproduce graphic images contained in the hard copy but instead must include "a fair and accurate narrative description, tabular representation or transcript of the omitted material."[80] A good-faith attempt to provide an accurate narrative or tabular description satisfies the antifraud rules.[81]

---

38. *See* § 12.11 *infra.*

39. Kohler v. Kohler Co., 319 F.2d 634, 642 (7th Cir.1963).

40. List v. Fashion Park, Inc., 340 F.2d 457, 462 (2d Cir.1965), *cert. denied,* 382 U.S. 811, 86 S.Ct. 23, 15 L.Ed.2d 60 (1965).

41. United States v. Davis, 226 F.3d 346, 358 (5th Cir.2000) ("the naivety, carelessness, negligence, or stupidity of a victim" does not preclude criminal liability for fraud).

42. *See* United States v. Davis, 226 F.3d 346, 358 (5th Cir.2000).

44. *See, e.g.,* Shawmut Bank, N.A. v. Kress Associates, 33 F.3d 1477 (9th Cir.1994).

45. Ambrosino v. Rodman & Renshaw, Inc., 972 F.2d 776 (7th Cir.1992) (written disclosures precluded action based on oral statements at variance with the writing); Casella v. Webb, 883 F.2d 805, 808 (9th Cir.1989) ("Statements made in the course of an oral presentation 'cannot be considered in isolation,' but must be viewed 'in the context of the total presentation' ").

46. Sailors v. Northern States Power Co., 4 F.3d 610 (8th Cir.1993).

47. Acito v. IMCERA Group, Inc., 47 F.3d 47 (2d Cir.1995) (deficiencies found by FDA inspectors at one of over thirty business locations was not material). *See also, e.g.,* Wilensky v. Digital Equipment Corp., 903 F.Supp. 173 (D.Mass.1995), *affirmed in part, reversed in part,* 82 F.3d 1194 (1st Cir.1996) (failure to disclose details of new marketing strategy was not actionable).

78. *See* § 3.4[6] *supra* for discussion of EDGAR, the SEC's electronic filing system.

79. Demaria v. Andersen, 318 F.3d 170 (2d Cir. 2003).

80. EDGAR Rule 304(a), 17 C.F.R. § 232.304(a).

81. 17 C.F.R. § 232.304(b)(2) ("to the extent such descriptions, representations or transcripts represent a good faith effort to fairly and accurately describe omitted graphic, image, audio or

Not every miniscule inaccuracy will be actionable.[82] Thus, for example, the mere fact that a company's disclosures are not consistent with generally accepted accounting practices does not mean that they are actionable under the securities laws.[83] However, reckless departures from accepted accounting practices can be material[84] and made with scienter.[85]

In the context of an insider trading case, the time at which insiders begin to trade is strong circumstantial evidence of materiality.[86]

Management's motives frequently will not be material and therefore need not be disclosed.[94] Information tending to show conflicts of interest of directors, officers, or other major participants is likely to be material.[95] Similarly, facts pertaining to management integrity are likely to be material.[96] Disputes within management are likely to be material.[97] However, it has been held that a description of the company's business plan was accurate and not materially misleading despite a failure to disclose that the board of directors and CEO were divided as to the wisdom of the strategy.[98]

§ 12.9[4] Immateriality of Vague Statements; Sales Talk and "Puffing"; Statements of Opinion and Intent

Summary judgment or dismissal of the complaint is appropriate when the statements are too vague to be actionable.[100] Similarly, nondisclosure of extremely contingent or speculative possibilities will be immaterial as a matter of law.[101] Additionally if there are adequate cautionary warnings, claims based on projections and other forward looking statements[102] may be subject to dismissal or summary judgment.[103]

video material, they are not subject to the civil liability and anti-fraud provisions of the federal securities laws."). *See* Demaria v. Andersen, 318 F.3d 170 (2d Cir. 2003).

82. *See, e.g.,* ABC Arbitrage Plaintiffs Group v. Tchuruk, 291 F.3d 336 (5th Cir.2002) (the misstatements concerned amounts of money that were too small to have been material); Press v. Quick & Reilly, Inc., 218 F.3d 121 (2d Cir.2000) (broker-dealer's alleged nondisclosure of conflict of interest did not violate Rule 10b–5 or Rule 10b–10).

83. *See, e.g.,* In re Carter–Wallace, Inc. Securities Litigation, 150 F.3d 153 (2d Cir.1998) (company's departure from GAAP was not securities fraud).

84. *E.g.,* In re Datastream Systems, Inc. Securities Litigation, 2000 WL 33176025, [1999–2000 Transfer Binder] Sec. Reg. L. Rep. (CCH) ¶ 90,907 (D.S.C. 2000).

85. *E.g.,* In re Sunbeam Securities Litigation, 89 F.Supp.2d 1326 (S.D. Fla. 1999) (sufficient allegations of accountant's scienter in reviewing company's books); Chalverus v. Pegasystems, Inc., 59 F.Supp.2d 226 (D.Mass.1999) (sufficient allegations in addition to GAAP violations to establish scienter).

86. *See* SEC v. Texas Gulf Sulphur Co., 401 F.3d 833 (2d Cir.1968), *cert. denied*, 394 U.S. 976, 89 S.Ct. 1454, 22 L.Ed.2d 756 (1969).

94. *See, e.g.,* Ward v. Succession of Freeman, 854 F.2d 780 (5th Cir.1988).

95. *See, e.g.,* Kahn v. Wien, 842 F.Supp. 667 (E.D.N.Y.1994) (proxy solicitation).

96. *E.g.,* SEC v. Enterprise Solutions, 142 F.Supp.2d 561 (S.D.N.Y. 2001) (concealment of founder/consultant's criminal past was material).

97. Cooperman v. Individual, Inc., 171 F.3d 43 (1st Cir.1999).

98. *Id.*

100. *See, e.g.,* Werbowsky v. American Waste Services, Inc., 172 F.3d 51 (6th Cir.1998).

101. *E.g.,* Klein v. General Nutrition Cos., 186 F.3d 338 (3d Cir.1999); In re John Alden Financial Corporation Securities Litigation, 249 F.Supp.2d 1273, 1283–1284 (S.D. Fla. 2003) (statement that company was "on track" for an excellent year was not actionable; summary judgment granted in defendant's favor).

102. *See, e.g.,* In re Copper Mountain Securities Litigation, 311 F.Supp.2d 857 (N.D. Cal. 2004) (forward looking statements in press release were not actionable).

103. Parnes v. Gateway 2000, Inc., 122 F.3d 539 (8th Cir.1997); Olkey v. Hyperion 1999 Term Trust, Inc., 98 F.3d 2 (2d Cir.1996).

As a general proposition, statements of opinion are not actionable[104] unless they relate to management's assessment of the company[105] or to other material facts. Thus, for example, general statements of optimism are not actionable.[106]

Borrowing from the common law of misrepresentation in certain cases the courts have tolerated some degree of "puffing" or "sales talk."[108] However, given the importance of full candor, courts should be reluctant to permit misrepresentation under the guise of puffing. Misrepresentation by implying the existence of certain facts cannot be disguised as mere puffing.[110] Similarly, use of percentages may imply a factual basis and if so, cannot be protected as mere puffing.[111] Reading the relevant securities cases yields the following general rule: while a good faith opinion (or even "puffing") is not material, a statement of opinion made with no belief in its truth is actionable. This is consistent with the general rule that merely because statements are couched as opinion does not preclude a finding that there is an express or implied misrepresentation of fact. Similar results follow with regard to statements of intent. It is clear that a good faith statement of present intent does not become actionable simply because of a change of intent.[114]

§ 12.9[5] Materiality of Contingent Events

As discussed elsewhere in this treatise, disclosures relating to contingent events may be actionable.[119] In such cases, materiality is judged in light of the magnitude of the event in question and the probability of its occurrence.[120] The greater the magnitude and the greater the probability of the event, the more likely it is that it will be material. Thus, for example, relatively uncertain contingencies that would have a great impact on the company may be material. Conversely, a virtually certain event with substantially less significance may also be material. However, too much uncertainty will result in a finding of immateriality.[121]

---

104. *See, e.g.,* Marsh Group v. Graff, 46 Fed.Appx. 140, 2002 WL 1997949 (4th Cir. 2002) (statements that dividend were "sacred" or "sacrosanct" were immaterial).

105. *See, e.g.,* the discussion of management discussion and analysis in § 12.9[7][B] *infra.*

106. *See, e.g.,* Fishbaum v. Liz Claiborne, Inc., 189 F.3d 460 (2d Cir.1999) (unpublished opinion) (vague statements of optimism are not actionable); Werbowsky v. American Waste Services, Inc., 172 F.3d 51 (6th Cir.1998) (general statements relating to growth potential for industry were not material misrepresentations of company's growth prospects).

108. *E.g.,* Freedman v. Value Health, Inc., 34 Fed.Appx. 408, 2002 WL 825982 (2d Cir.2002) (unpublished disposition) (statement by CEO of a merger target in a press release that the company's business was "thriving" was supported by evidence, and was, at worst, non-actionable puffery); Nathenson v. Zonagen, Inc., 267 F.3d 400 (5th Cir.2001) (statements in press release that drug was a "fast-acting" "improved formulation" was inactionable puffery but statements concerning the scope of patents were materially misleading).

110. *E.g.,* In re Medimmune, Inc. Securities Litigation, 873 F.Supp. 953 (D.Md.1995) (statement that "there was absolutely no question about the efficacy" of a product could be actionable).

111. Newman v. L.F. Rothschild, Unterberg, Towbin, 662 F.Supp. 957 (S.D.N.Y.1987).

114. *See, e.g.,* In re Phillips Petroleum Securities Litigation, 881 F.2d 1236, 1245 (3d Cir.1989).

119. *See* § 3.9 *supra.*

120. United States v. Mylett, 97 F.3d 663, 667 (2d Cir.1996), relying on Basic Inc. v. Levinson, 485 U.S. 224, 238, 108 S.Ct. 978, 987, 99 L.Ed.2d 194 (1988).

121. Abromson v. American Pacific Corp., 114 F.3d 898 (9th Cir.1997) (nondisclosure of disagreement regarding effect of early loan repayment was not material in light of extremely low probability).

§ 12.9[6] Materiality of Merger Negotiations

Especially difficult questions of materiality relate to the question of whether preliminary merger negotiations or other control-related transactions must be disclosed.[127] It is the general view that Rule 10b–5 does not impose an affirmative duty of disclosure, and thus silence cannot be actionable.[128] Thus, absent some independent basis for the duty, the existence of preliminary negotiations will not have to be disclosed. However, when a material development is covered by a line-item in a document that needs to be filed with the Commission or otherwise publicly disseminated,[130] silence will not suffice and it must be decided whether preliminary negotiations need be disclosed. Similarly, once an issuer, rather than maintaining silence, voluntarily makes a statement—such as in response to an inquiry from the press or securities analysts—all statements must be totally devoid of material misstatements. As the Supreme Court has pointed out, arguments based on the premature nature of the disclosure are not pertinent in determining the materiality of a particular misstatement; "[t]he secrecy rationale is merely inapposite to the definition of materiality."[131] In addition to the corporation's disclosure obligations, the materiality of merger negotiations can be important in determining whether insiders have traded in violation of the securities laws.[132]

Some courts were of the view that preliminary acquisition negotiations need not be disclosed until there has been an agreement in principle as to the transaction's price and structure.[133] However, the SEC and many courts took a contrary position reasoning the "price and structure" threshold frequently would provide too late a materiality date, especially when the issue is a denial of such negotiations when in fact they are taking place.[134] In Basic Inc. v. Levinson,[135] the Supreme Court accepted the SEC's view in holding that

---

127. *E.g.,* SEC v. Poirier, 140 F.Supp.2d 1033 (D.Ariz.2001) ("By failing to disclose their control of [the corporation, the defendants] made a material omission in connection with the offer of securities; reasonable investors would find the existence of a control group important when deciding whether to purchase Garcis stock"); *relying on* Nelson v. Serwold, 576 F.2d 1332 (9th Cir.1978) (failure to disclose the existence of a control group that is the driving force behind a public company is a material omission that violates the anti-fraud provisions).

128. *E.g.,* Taylor v. First Union Corp. of South Carolina, 857 F.2d 240 (4th Cir.1988). *See* § 12.19 *infra.*

130. Thus, for example, if negotiations are taking place during a proxy solicitation, the proxy rules would require line-item disclosure of all material facts. *See* § 11.2–11.4 *supra.* Similarly, negotiations taking place as a defense to a hostile takeover might have to be disclosed in connection with management's response to the hostile offer. *See* 17 C.F.R. § 240.14e–2 and Schedule 14D–9 which are discussed in §§ 11.14–11.15 *supra.* Material negotiations taking place during a public offering would trigger the line-item disclosure requirement. *See* § 3.2–3.7 *supra.* Finally, if the negotiations are material when the issuer's periodic reports become due, line item disclosure will be required. *See* § 9.3 *supra.*

See also, e.g., Richard Rosen, Liability for "Soft Information": New Developments and Emerging Trends, 23 Sec. Reg. L.J. 3 (1995).

131. Basic Inc. v. Levinson, 485 U.S. 224, 235, 108 S.Ct. 978, 985, 99 L.Ed.2d 194, 211 (1988).

132. *See* Blanchard v. EdgeMark Financial Corp., 1999 WL 59994, [1999 Transfer Binder] Fed. Sec. L. Rep. (CCH) ¶ 90,439 (N.D. Ill. 1999). Insider trading is discussed in § 12.17 *infra.*

133. *See, e.g.,* Flamm v. Eberstadt, 814 F.2d 1169 (7th Cir.), *cert. denied,* 484 U.S. 853, 108 S.Ct. 157, 98 L.Ed.2d 112 (1987) (applying price and structure to find preliminary negotiations not material); Greenfield v. Heublein, Inc., 742 F.2d 751 (3d Cir.1984), *cert. denied,* 469 U.S. 1215, 105 S.Ct. 1189, 84 L.Ed.2d 336 (1985) (no duty under Rule 10b–5 to disclose merger negotiations where price had not yet been worked out).

134. *See, e.g.,* In re Carnation Co., Exch.Act Rel. No. 34–22214, 1985 WL 547371 [1985–1986 Transfer Binder] Fed.Sec.L.Rep. (CCH) ¶ 83,801 (July 8, 1985).

135. 485 U.S. 224, 108 S.Ct. 978, 99 L.Ed.2d 194 (1988).

whether preliminary merger negotiations have crossed the materiality threshold is a question of fact. Whether a fact is material depends upon whether a reasonable investor would consider it significant in making his or her investment decision.[136] As discussed earlier, materiality generally is based on a highly factual inquiry and thus is difficult to predict. The thrust of the Supreme Court decision in *Basic* seems to favor a finding of materiality in borderline cases of preliminary negotiations.[137] It is clear that the fact that the impending merger is contingent does not preclude a finding of materiality and reliance.[138] The ultimate decision on materiality in this context depends upon an evaluation of the magnitude of the event discounted by the improbability of occurrence.[139] This calculus is a good measure of materiality generally.

Questions concerning the need to disclose information may also arise when the issuer, its officers, or directors are questioned by the press or by securities analysts. In such situations a "no comment" response will avoid liability. "No comment" is the only safe harbor (other than giving a full and honest disclosure), as any other response will trigger the highly factual materiality inquiry.[140] While it is true that there are business reasons for keeping certain information confidential, it does not follow that management should be allowed to respond to inquiries with "white lies." As a result of the *Basic* decision, it is imperative that issuers maintain control of their information.[141] It is wise to limit the people who are authorized to speak on the issuer's behalf and to instruct everyone else to follow a "no comment" policy.

Once acquisition negotiations have been publicly disclosed, management must be careful in making statements about the progress of the negotiations. Although statements that progress is being made may not always be actionable,[142] comments that cover up negative events may result in liability.

§ 12.9[7] Predictions, Projections, and Other "Soft" Information; Management Discussion and Analysis

Another issue relating to materiality that is getting increased attention is with regard to predictions and other "soft information."[143] There are two questions that frequently arise regarding disclosure of soft information. One question is the extent to which there is an obligation to make a prediction or

136. *Id.*, TSC Industries, Inc. v. Northway, Inc., 426 U.S. 438, 96 S.Ct. 2126, 48 L.Ed.2d 757 (1976). Materiality under the proxy rules is discussed in § 11.4 *supra.*

137. *See, e.g.*, Glazer v. Formica Corp., 964 F.2d 149 (2d Cir.1992) (reversing finding of immateriality as a matter of law; however, silence was not actionable).

138. Semerenko v. Cendant Corp., 223 F.3d 165, 180 (3d Cir.2000).

139. *See, e.g.*, United States v. Mylett, 97 F.3d 663, 667 (2d Cir.1996), relying on Basic Inc. v. Levinson, 485 U.S. 224, 238, 108 S.Ct. 978, 987, 99 L.Ed.2d 194 (1988).

140. *See e.g.*, In re Western Waste Securities Litigation, 1994 WL 561165 [1994–1995 Transfer Binder] Fed. Sec. L. Rep. (CCH) ¶ 98,378 (C.D.Cal.1994). *Cf.* LB Partners, L.P. v. Neutrogena Corp., 1995 WL 714447 [1995–1996 Transfer Binder] Fed. Sec. L. Rep. (CCH) ¶ 98,913 (C.D.Cal.1995) ("no news release" was the equivalent of a "no comment" response).

141. Maintaining control of information is also important in order to prevent insider trading problems. Insider Trading is discussed in § 12.17 *infra.*

142. Grossman v. Novell, Inc., 120 F.3d 1112 (10th Cir.1997) (statements that merger presented a "compelling set of opportunities" and was "moving faster than we had thought" were immaterial statements of vague optimism); Eisenstadt v. Centel Corp., 113 F.3d 738 (7th Cir.1997) (repeated statements that auction process was going smoothly were not actionable).

143. *See, e.g.*, United States v. Smith, 155 F.3d 1051 (9th Cir.1998) (soft information can be material).

other disclosures of soft information. A second issue that arises is whether an incorrect opinion, projection, or prediction is actionable.[144]

Following the traditional common law rule, vague opinions and predictions[146] are not actionable.[147] However, the mere fact that a statement is couched in the form of soft information, such as a prediction or projection, does not preclude a finding of materiality.[148] Additionally, management's opinion as to the fairness of a transaction, although opinion, can be material.[149]

§ 12.9[7][B] Management Discussion & Analysis

There have been significant changes in the Commission's attitude towards projections. There currently are many line-item disclosure requirements that call for certain types of soft information. For example, under Item 303 of Regulation S–K,[159] in the course of its Management Discussion and Analysis (MD&A) of financial condition and report of operations, management is directed to analyze operations. This analysis must include disclosure of trends and uncertainties likely to have a material effect on the company.[161] The MD&A also should contain discussion of any positive trends that management foresees. The SEC has taken a vigorous enforcement stance on these disclosures.[163] The MD&A disclosure mandate can result in material misstatements or omissions that will give rise to liability.[164]

Although the MD&A disclosures contained in Item 303 or Regulation S–K require disclosure of "known trends or uncertainties," MD&A does not alter the basic rule that projections are not required.[174]

As pointed out above, once a prediction, projection, or valuation is made, it must withstand materiality scrutiny if there are any inaccuracies.[177] The

---

144. *See, e.g.,* Hillson Partners L.P. v. Adage, Inc., 42 F.3d 204 (4th Cir.1994) (Chief executive officer's statements in press release that the year would produce "excellent" results were merely predictions and thus not actionable misrepresentations of fact).

146. *See, e.g.,* Poth v. Russey, 99 Fed. Appx. 446 (4th Cir. 2004) (predictions relating to share price of anticipated IPO was not actionable as fraud).

147. *See, e.g.,* Rosenzweig v. Azurix Corp., 332 F.3d 854 (5th Cir. 2003) (generalized statements were immaterial).

148. *E.g.,* United States v. Smith, 155 F.3d 1051 (9th Cir.1998).

149. *E.g.,* Virginia Bankshares, Inc. v. Sandberg, 501 U.S. 1083, 111 S.Ct. 2749, 115 L.Ed.2d 929 (1991).

159. Regulation S–K contains the SEC's basic disclosure guidelines (Regulation S–B is a parallel guide for small business issuers). 17 C.F.R. §§ 228.10, 229.10 et seq., 7 Fed. Sec. L. Rep. (CCH) ¶¶ 71,001 et seq. Violations of Regulation S–K or S–B disclosure requirements are not *per se* actionable but can be used to support a Rule 10b–5 claim. *See* Feldman v. Motorola, Inc., 1994 WL 160115 [1993–1994 Transfer Binder] Fed. Sec. L. Rep. (CCH) ¶ 98,133 (N.D.Ill.1994).

161. *See* Management Discussion and Analysis of Financial Condition, Sec. Act Rel. No. 33–6835 (SEC May 18, 1989).

163. *See* In re Caterpillar, Inc., Exch. Act Rel. No. 34–30532, 6 Fed.Sec.L.Rep. (CCH) ¶ 73,829 (SEC March 31, 1992) (settlement order involving MD&A analysis and failure to adequately discuss the possible risk of lower earnings in the future).

164. *See, e.g.,* In re Scholastic Corp. Securities Litigation, 252 F.3d 63 (2d Cir. 2001) (adequately alleging actionable misstatements in connection with discussion relating to trends in sales of children's books).

174. *E.g.,* Glassman v. Computervision Corp., 90 F.3d 617 (1st Cir.1996) (fact that quarter's results lagged behind internal projections did not trigger a duty of disclosure).

177. *E.g.,* Raab v. General Physics Corp., 4 F.3d 286 (4th Cir.1993) (statement that company was poised to carry past success into the future was commercial puffery and thus was not actionable).

mere fact that a projection turns out to be wrong is not sufficient to state a Rule 10b–5 claim.[178]

§ 12.9[7][C] Safe Harbor for Forward–Looking Statements

As part of the Private Securities Litigation Reform Act of 1995,[179] Congress enacted section 21E of the 1934 Act,[180] which provides a safe harbor for forward-looking statements.[181] Section 2 is premised on 1933 Act Rule 175,[182] 1934 Act Rule 3b–6,[183] and the "bespeaks caution" doctrine created by the federal courts. The section 21E safe harbor allows corporate management to disclose forward-looking information[185] and projections to investors, while retaining protection under the safe harbor.[186] Section 21E applies to 1934 Act reporting companies, persons acting on behalf of such companies, outside reviewers retained by such companies, and underwriters deriving or obtaining forward-looking information from such companies. Section 21E applies to forward looking statements but not to statements of fact.[188] It has been held, for example, that a statement that a company was "on target" to meet its expectations for the quarter was a statement of present fact and therefore was not a forward-looking statement subject to the protection of the safe harbor.[189] In other words, "[i]n order to be eligible for safe harbor, the forward-looking statements must either (1) be identified as forward-looking and be accompanied by meaningful cautionary language; (2) be immaterial; or (3) not be made with actual knowledge that the statement was false or misleading."[190] Once established, the statutory safe harbor will protect the defendant from liability in a private suit. In an enforcement action, the defendant can seek the safe harbor provided in Rule 3b–6.

§ 12.9[7][D] Analysts' Opinions and Estimates

Ordinarily, a company's management will not be held responsible for opinions, projections, and estimates of security analysts even though management may have supplied the analysts with some of the information they used

---

178. *E.g.*, Grassi v. Information Resources, Inc., 63 F.3d 596 (7th Cir.1995) (earnings projections which turned out to be inaccurate did not amount to securities fraud); Wielgos v. Commonwealth Edison Co., 892 F.2d 509 (7th Cir.1989).

179. Pub. Law No. 104–67, 109 Stat. 737 (104th Cong. 1st Sess. December 22, 1995) (HR 1058).

180. 15 U.S.C.A. § 78u–5(c). A parallel provision was added to the 1933 Act. 15 U.S.C.A. § 77z–2. *See* § 3.7 *supra.*

181. *See, e.g.*, Helwig v. Vencor, Inc., 251 F.3d 540 (6th Cir.2001) (statements regarding effect of federal Balanced Budget Act on company's financial prospects were subject to but not protected by the statutory safe harbor for forward-looking statements).

182. 17 C.F.R. § 230.175.

183. 17 C.F.R. § 240.3b–6.

185. *See, e.g.*, Ehlert v. Singer, 245 F.3d 1313 (11th Cir.2001) (section of prospectus concerning risks of technological change was forward-looking despite inclusion of some statements of present conditions).

186. *See, e.g.*, Eizenga v. Stewart Enterprises, Inc., 124 F.Supp.2d 967 (E.D.La.2000) (forward-looking statements were not actionable).

188. *See, e.g.*, Franklin High Yield Tax–Free Income Fund v. County of Martin, Minnesota, 152 F.3d 736 (8th Cir.1998) (false statement that company would use "best efforts" to cover operating deficits with a tax levy was not protected by cautionary language).

189. In re Secure Computing Corp. Securities Litigation, 120 F.Supp.2d 810 (N.D.Cal.2000).

190. In re Sun Healthcare Group Securities Litigation, 181 F.Supp.2d 1283, 1288 (D.N.M. 2002).

to formulate their estimates.[201] A company will be held responsible if it passes on misinformation to analysts with the intention that the analysts communicate the misinformation to the market.[202] In the absence of such an intent to defraud the market, a company will not be held accountable for analysts' opinions unless the company has "adopted or endorsed" the analysts' reports[203] or unless the company or its management influenced or controlled the analysts' projections.[204] Thus, for example, it has been said that neither an issuer nor its management will be held accountable for an analyst's projection unless the issuer has adopted the projection or has otherwise "entangled" itself with the analyst's opinions.[205]

A statement by a company official that he is "comfortable" with analysts' estimates can form the basis of liability for over-optimism.[212] Such a statement can operate as an adoption of the analyst's opinion.[213] Also, management's statement that it is comfortable with analysts' projections may not be protected by the safe harbors discussed above.[214] However, merely stating that it is comfortable with analysts' estimates does not make the company liable simply because the estimate turns out to be wrong.[215]

In a related development, in 1999, the Commission proposed Regulation FD in order to require a fair disclosure policy for public companies.[216] As regulation FD was adopted in 2000 modified by the Commission in response to public comment. Under Regulation FD,[217] selective corporate disclosure is no longer permitted. Companies who make disclosures to analysts now have to make prompt public announcements so that all investors can have access to the same information. Regulation FD applies only to "communications by the

---

201. Raab v. General Physics Corp., 4 F.3d 286, 288 (4th Cir.1993) ("The securities laws require [a company] to speak truthfully to investors; they do not require the company to police statements made by third party for inaccuracies, even if the third party attributes the statement to [the company]").

202. Cooper v. Pickett, 122 F.3d 1186 (9th Cir.1997), *amended and superseded on denial of rehearing*, 137 F.3d 616 (9th Cir.1997).

203. In re Burlington Coat Factory Securities Litigation, 114 F.3d 1410, 1428–29 (3d Cir. 1997).

204. Warden v. Crown American Realty Trust, 1999 WL 476996, [1999 Transfer Binder] Fed. Sec. L. Rep. (CCH) ¶ 90,525 (W.D. Pa. 1999) (analysts' statements could not be attributed to company's management).

205. *See, e.g.,* Eisenstadt v. Allen, 113 F.3d 1240 (9th Cir. 1997) (unpublished opinion) (entanglement not found where there is no evidence that corporate insiders reviewed or endorsed analysts' projections in articles before publication); In re Syntex Corp. Securities Litigation, 95 F.3d 922 (9th Cir.1996) (explicit statement that analysts' statements should not be attributed to company and one-way flow of information sufficient to avoid entanglement); Elkind v. Liggett & Myers, 635 F.2d 156 (2d Cir.1980) (policy of examining projections but refraining from comment were not sufficient entanglement to impose duty to correct false information).

212. In re Burlington Coat Factory Securities Litigation, 114 F.3d 1410, 1428 (3d Cir.1997), *relying on* Virginia Bankshares, Inc. v. Sandberg, 501 U.S. 1083, 111 S.Ct. 2749, 115 L.Ed.2d 929 (1991), for the proposition that opinions of management can be actionable.

213. In re Burlington Coat Factory Securities Litigation, 114 F.3d 1410, 1429 (3d Cir.1997).

214. *See, e.g.,* In re QLT Inc. Securities Litigation, 312 F.Supp.2d 526, 533 (S.D.N.Y. 2004).

215. Plevy v. Haggerty, 38 F.Supp.2d 816 (C.D.Cal.1998) (statement that company was "comfortable" with analysts' estimates did not make company liable in absence of showing that it made material misrepresentations to the analysts).

216. *See* Sec. Exch. Act Rel. No. 34–24259 (SEC Dec. 20, 1999); Proposed Rules Would Bar Leaks to Analysts; Clarify Basis for SEC Action, 31 Sec. Reg. & L. Rep. (BNA) 1649 (Dec. 20, 1999).

217. 17 C.F.R. §§ 243.100–243.103. *See* Selective Disclosure and Insider Trading, Sec. Exch. Act Rel. No. 34–43154, 2000 WL 1201556 (SEC Aug. 15, 2000) (adopting release).

company's senior management, its investor relations professionals, and others who regularly communicate with market professionals and security holders." Regulation FD further applies only to a company's "communications with market professionals, and holders of the issuer's securities under circumstances in which it is reasonably foreseeable that the security holders will trade on the basis of the information." Accordingly, Regulation FD does not apply when the company is communicating with the press, rating agencies, and during ordinary business communications with customers and suppliers.

Regulation FD is purely a disclosure rule and does not create liability for fraud. It is enforced by the SEC. Regulation FD applies only to intentional or reckless conduct.[220] Disclosure is required only when "the person making the selective disclosure knows or is reckless in not knowing that the information disclosed was both material and nonpublic." Finally, Regulation FD does not apply to communications made in connection with most public offerings registered under the 1933 Act. Nor does it apply to foreign issuers.

§ 12.9[8] The "Bespeaks Caution" Doctrine and Materiality

A number of courts have adopted what is referred to as the "bespeaks caution" doctrine.[221] Congress codified the bespeaks caution doctrine as part of the Private Securities Litigation Reform Act of 1995.[222]

The doctrine holds that sufficient cautionary language may preclude misstatements from being actionable.[223] Courts invoking the doctrine have tended to do so, in cases involving projections in prospectuses and other offering documents, as a basis for dismissing the misrepresentation claim.[224] Similarly, since the test of materiality is based upon the total mix of information, it follows that cautionary language could be considered even outside the context of projections. Thus, whether under the rubric of bespeaks caution or the normal test of materiality, cautionary language may go a long way towards defeating a Rule 10b–5 claim. The doctrine has frequently been referred to in the context of judging whether the plaintiff's reliance is reasonable, but it also necessarily relates to materiality in the sense that it addresses the question of whether the misstatements are materially misleading when judged in light of the total mix of information available to the investor.[225]

---

220. *See, e.g.,* In the Matter of Siebel Systems, Inc., Sec. Exch. Act Rel. No. 34–46896, 2002 WL 31643027 (SEC Nov. 25, 2002) (consent order admitting to intentional violations of Regulation FD).

221. *See, e.g.,* Saltzberg v. TM Sterling/Austin Associates, Ltd., 45 F.3d 399 (11th Cir.1995); In re Worlds of Wonder Securities Litigation, 35 F.3d 1407 (9th Cir.1994); Ambrosino v. Rodman & Renshaw, Inc., 972 F.2d 776 (7th Cir.1992).

222. Section 21E(c)(2), 15 U.S.C.A. § 78u–5(c)(2); 1933 Act section 27A(c)(2).

223. *E.g.,* Halperin v. EBanker USA.com, Inc., 295 F.3d 352 (2d Cir.2002) ("When read in their entirety, these documents not only bespeak caution, they shout it from the rooftops, so to speak").

224. *See, e.g.,* In re Donald J. Trump Casino Securities Litigation–Taj Mahal Litigation, 7 F.3d 357, 371 (3d Cir.1993):

> when an offering document's forecasts, opinions or projections are accompanied by meaningful cautionary statements, the forward-looking statements will not form the basis for a securities fraud claim if those statements did not affect the "total mix" of information the document provided investors. In other words, cautionary language, if sufficient, renders the alleged omissions or misrepresentations immaterial as a matter of law.

225. *See, e.g.,* Gray v. First Winthrop Corp., 82 F.3d 877 (9th Cir.1996) (cautionary language was not sufficiently specific to invoke bespeaks caution doctrine).

The bespeaks caution doctrine applies to both material misstatements and omissions.[227] The cases invoking the bespeaks caution doctrine generally have involved projections or other soft information. The First and Seventh Circuits have held that the bespeaks caution doctrine is limited to projections and thus will not offset material misstatements regarding hard facts.[230] The 1995 legislation that codified the bespeaks caution doctrine expressly applies the doctrine to both oral and written "forward-looking statements,"[231] and should not be extended to material misstatements or omissions of fact.[232]

The bespeaks caution doctrine cannot be applied to protect statements that were known to have been inaccurate when made.[233] Also, the statutory safe harbor applies only to "meaningful" cautionary language.[234]

A review of disclosure documents both before and after the 1995 legislation revealed widespread use of cautionary language in both 1933 and 1934 Act filings.[248] Unfortunately, most such statements were couched in such general terms as to render them ineffective. As noted above, it is not sufficient to simply use a caution to the effect that projections and the like may not reflect actual performance. Similarly, trying to cover all disclosures with a general cautionary statement is unlikely to be effective. In order to be effective, the cautionary language should not only alert the reader to the risk factors, but should briefly summarize each of the risk factors. Cautionary language about one risk will not be effective with regard to other risks.[252] Issuers seeking to rely on the bespeaks caution doctrine must thus be careful to couch the cautionary language in terms of the specific risks and uncertainties involved. The cautionary language must directly relate to the alleged

---

227. *See, e.g.,* In re Donald J. Trump Casino Securities Litigation–Taj Mahal Litigation, 7 F.3d 357, 371 (3d Cir.1993).

230. Shaw v. Digital Equipment Corp., 82 F.3d 1194 (1st Cir.1996) (bespeaks caution doctrine would apply only if statements related to future events rather than present facts); Harden v. Raffensperger, Hughes & Co., 65 F.3d 1392 (7th Cir.1995) (bespeaks caution doctrine does not apply to hard facts).

231. 1933 Act § 27A(c)(2), 15 U.S.C.A. § 77z–3(c)(2); 1934 Act § 21E(c)(2), 15 U.S.C.A. § 78u–5(c)(2).

232. *See, e.g.,* EP Medsystems, Inc. v. EchoCath, Inc., 235 F.3d 865 (3d Cir.2000).

233. *See, e.g.,* Asher v. Baxter International Inc., 377 F.3d 727 (7th Cir. 2004).

234. *See, e.g.,* Asher v. Baxter International Inc., 377 F.3d 727 (7th Cir. 2004):

The fundamental problem is that the statutory requirement of "meaningful cautionary statements" is not itself meaningful. What must the firm say? Unless it is possible to give a concrete and reliable answer, the harbor is not "safe"; yet a word such as "meaningful" resists a concrete rendition and thus makes administration of the safe harbor difficult if not impossible. It rules out a caution such as: "This is a for-ward-looking statement: caveat emptor." But it does not rule *in* any particular caution, which always may be challenged as not sufficiently "meaningful" or not pinning down the "important factors that could cause actual results to differ materially"—for if it *had* identified all of those factors, it would not be possible to describe the for-ward-looking statement itself as materially misleading. A safe harbor matters only when the firm's disclosures (including the accompanying cautionary statements) are false or misleadingly incomplete; yet whenever that condition is satisfied, one can complain that the cautionary statement must have been inadequate. The safe harbor loses its function. Yet it would be unsound to read the statute so that the safe harbor never works; then one might as well treat § 77z–2 and § 78u–5 as defunct.

248. Bar Association of the City of New York, Committee on Securities Regulation, A Study of Current Practices–Forward–Looking Statements and Cautionary Language After the 1995 Private Securities Litigation Reform Act, 53 Record 725 (1998); SEC Report to the President on the Private Securities Litigation Reform Act of 1995, Fed. Sec. L. Rep. (CCH) Bull. 1763 (April 23, 1997).

252. *See* Hunt v. Alliance North American Government Income Trust, Inc., 159 F.3d 723 (2d Cir. 1998).

misstatements in question.[254] As is the case with issues of materiality generally, the adequacy of a particular cautionary statement will thus be a highly factual determination.

§ 12.9[9] Materiality In Financial Statements; Accounting Issues

Accountants have their own definition of materiality in the context of the presentation of financial information. While the accountants' concept of materiality is significant with the profession, materiality under the securities laws is determined by the same test of materiality that applies to other disclosure issues. In particular, the test of materiality is whether a reasonable investor would consider the information significant in making an investment decision.[255] The financial disclosures form an important part of any securities disclosure filing, as investors need to be able to have faith in the numbers put forth by management in their SEC reports and filings. The securities laws underscore the importance of financial disclosures through the requirement that there be audited financial statements.

In 1999, the Commission issued Staff Accounting Bulletin no. 99 to clarify its position on accounting and materiality issues. Following the highly factual approach to materiality generally, the SEC in SAB No. 99 reinforced the "facts and circumstances" test of materiality. Although more frustrating than a bright-line test would be, the SEC approach properly recognizes the difficulties of generalizing rules for materiality. The SEC release offered significant guidance for evaluating materiality in the context of financial statements.

The SEC rejects a numerical test of materiality of accounting items. This includes rejection of the five-percent threshold that frequently is cited in the accounting profession. Instead, the Commission reaffirms that even relatively small deviations can be material, especially if they are intentional.[258] The potential materiality of even relatively small accounting errors is not a new development, as it reflects the long-standing views of the courts and the SEC.[259] However, not every financial misstatement will cross the materiality threshold.

§ 12.9[10] Duty to Correct or Update

Absent a specific line-item requirement in an SEC filing, there is no affirmative duty to disclose merely because a fact is material.[266] This result is mandated by the terms of Rule 10b–5, which prohibits omissions of a material fact only if the fact was "necessary to make the statements made," not materially misleading.[267] The rule thus does not address the omission of facts in the absence of affirmatively making a statement. However, once a statement of fact (as opposed to a projection[268]) has been made, the person making

---

254. In re Donald J. Trump Casino Securities Litigation, 7 F.3d 357, 371 (3d Cir.1993).

255. Basic Inc. v. Levinson, 485 U.S. 224, 108 S.Ct. 978, 99 L.Ed.2d 194 (1988); TSC Industries, Inc. v. Northway, Inc., 426 U.S. 438, 449, 96 S.Ct. 2126, 2132, 48 L.Ed.2d 757 (1976).

258. *Id.*

259. *See, e.g.,* SEC v. Jos. Schlitz Brewing Co., 452 F.Supp. 824 (E.D.Wis.1978) (nondisclosure of kickback scheme was material because, inter alia, it reflected on the lack of management integrity).

266. *See, e.g.,* Blanchard v. Edgemark Financial Corp., 2001 WL 587861 (N.D. Ill. 2001).

267. Rule 10b–5(b), 17 C.F.R. § 240.10b–5(b).

268. 1933 Act section 27A(d), 15 U.S.C.A. § 7z–2(d) ("Nothing in this section shall impose upon any person a duty to update a forward-looking statement"). *Accord* 1934 Act section 21E(d),

the statement is then under a duty to correct any misstatements that person also perhaps has a duty to update the public as to any material changes.[269] The courts have drawn a distinction between the duty to correct misinformation and the absence of a duty to update information that was accurate when disseminated.[270]

Until the mid 1990s, the law was unclear concerning the extent to which companies making projections and other forward-looking statements had an obligation to correct and/or update misinformation. However, the Private Securities Litigation Reform Act of 1995 specifically addresses this issue. Section 21E(d) of the 1934 Act[273] specifically states that no person making a forward-looking statement is under any duty to update the statement. The exact impact of this provision remains to be seen. In all likelihood, claims based on a duty to update will try to characterize the initial disclosures as factual in nature in order to avoid the impact of section 21E(d). Nevertheless, it is clear that if all that is involved is a good faith projection that turns out not to be realized, there is no duty to update.

There are times when a company's disclosures will trigger a duty to update. There is an important but difficult distinction to be made, however, between the duty to correct misleading factual information and the absence of a duty to update a forward looking statement. Thus, for example, there is a duty to correct when the factual information contained therein remains "alive" in the minds of investors.[275] However, when the original disclosure simply is a projection made in good faith that turns out not to be correct, there is no duty to update.[276] When projections are made there is no implication that they will be updated. Instead, the only implication is that they were made on a reasonable basis and in good faith.[278]

§ 12.10 Reliance in Rule 10b–5 Actions; Fraud on the Market

The reliance requirement is a corollary of materiality.[1] As is true under common law, the reliance requirement applies in securities fraud cases. As observed by the Second Circuit, "to the requirement that the individual plaintiff must have acted upon the fact misrepresented, is added the parallel requirement that a reasonable man would also have acted upon the fact

---

15 U.S.C.A. § 78u–5(d). *See also, e.g.,* Mercury Air Group, Inc. v. Mansour, 237 F.3d 542, 547 (5th Cir.2001) (failure to update projections did not violate Rule 10b–5).

269. Weiner v. Quaker Oats Co., 129 F.3d 310 (3d Cir.1997) (company had duty to update debt-equity ratio that would result from pending purchase of another company; however, slight variation from original projection was immaterial); Stransky v. Cummins Engine Co., 51 F.3d 1329 (7th Cir.1995) (stating cause of action for failure to update after predictions of better profit margins).

270. Gallagher v. Abbott Laboratories, 269 F.3d 806 (7th Cir.2001); ("a statement may be 'corrected' only if it was incorrect when made"). *Compare, e.g.,* Stransky v. Cummins Engine Co., 51 F.3d 1329 (7th Cir.1995) (finding a duty to correct).

273. 15 U.S.C.A. § 78u–5.

275. *See* In re Burlington Coat Factory Securities Litigation, 114 F.3d 1410, 1432 (3d Cir.1997); In re Time Warner Inc. Securities Litigation, 9 F.3d 259, 267 (2d Cir.1993).

276. In re International Business Machines Corporate Securities Litigation, 163 F.3d 102 (2d Cir.1998).

278. In re Burlington Coat Factory Securities Litigation, 114 F.3d 1410, 1433 (3d Cir.1997).

§ 12.10

1. *See, e.g.,* Semerenko v. Cendant Corp., 223 F.3d 165, 180 (3d Cir.2000) (relying on this treatise).

misrepresented."[2] Thus, in order to recover damages in an action under Rule 10b–5, the reliance element must be satisfied. It is not clear, however, that reliance is also an element of a suit under the proxy rules' Rule 14a–9.[3]

Reliance is an element of a private claim under Rule 10b–5, but not in enforcement actions brought by the government.[4] Thus, it is not necessary for the SEC to establish reliance in an enforcement action.[5] Similarly, reliance need not be shown in a criminal prosecution. Furthermore, even in private suits, in some instances that are discussed below the courts have not required proof of actual reliance.[7] The fact that the statement made related to contingent events does not prevent the plaintiff from establishing reliance.[8] Proof of reliance is an especially difficult problem in an omission case where the question is how the plaintiff would have acted had the required information been disclosed.[9] If the transaction takes place prior to the disclosures in question, reliance cannot be established.[10]

Following the same pattern as cases involving materiality, questions of reliance are highly factual and thus courts are properly reluctant to dismiss on the pleadings.[29] Similarly, claims that reliance was unreasonable will often be highly factual and thus inappropriate for dismissal before trial.[30]

The Supreme Court in Affiliated Ute Citizens of Utah v. United States[34] has held that in a face-to-face transaction between seller and purchaser where the defendant purchaser failed to state material facts, the plaintiff's reliance can be presumed from the materiality of the omissions. The Court there held that upon a finding of materiality it is then up to the defendant to prove that the plaintiff had not in fact relied on the material omissions. Many subsequent district court and court of appeals decisions have followed this presumption of reliance in omission cases but have refused to extend this ruling to the extent of eliminating the reliance requirements from the securities laws even in the case of face-to-face transactions.

The courts in recognizing the presumption in favor of reliance will allow the defendants to rebut the presumption.[37] The *Affiliated Ute* presumption

---

2. List v. Fashion Park, Inc., 340 F.2d 457, 462 (2d Cir.1965), *cert. denied*, 382 U.S. 811, 86 S.Ct. 23, 15 L.Ed.2d 60 (1965).

3. 17 C.F.R. § 240.14a–9; Stahl v. Gibraltar Financial Corp., 967 F.2d 335 (9th Cir.1992).

4. *See* SEC v. Alliance Leasing Corp., 28 Fed.Appx. 648, 2002 WL 10482 (9th Cir.2002).

5. *E.g.,* SEC v. Rana Research, Inc., 8 F.3d 1358 (9th Cir.1993).

7. *See, e.g.,* Fulco, Inc. v. American Cable Systems, 1989 WL 205356 [1989–1990 Transfer Binder] Fed.Sec.L.Rep. 94,980 (D.Mass.1989) (limited partners need not show reliance since they were forced sellers). However, in other contexts actual reliance must be shown. *E.g.,* Levine v. Prudential Bache Properties, Inc., 855 F.Supp. 924 (N.D.Ill.1994) (complaint failed to plead actual reliance on prospectus).

8. Semerenko v. Cendant Corp., 223 F.3d 165, (3d Cir.2000).

9. *See, e.g.,* Affiliated Ute Citizens v. United States, 406 U.S. 128, 150–54, 92 S.Ct. 1456, 1470, 1472, 31 L.Ed.2d 741 (1972), *rehearing denied*, 407 U.S. 916, 92 S.Ct. 2430, 32 L.Ed.2d 692 (1972) (applying a presumption of reliance in an omission case).

10. Integrated Technology & Development, Inc. v. Rosenfield, [1999–2000 Transfer Binder] Fed. Sec. L. Rep. (CCH) ¶ 91,038 (E.D.N.Y. 2000).

29. *See, e.g.,* Provenz v. Miller, 102 F.3d 1478 (9th Cir.1996) amending earlier opinion at 95 F.3d 1376 (9th Cir.1996).

30. *See, e.g.,* Castellano v. Young & Rubicam, Inc., 257 F.3d 171 (2d Cir.2001).

34. 406 U.S. 128, 153–154, 92 S.Ct. 1456, 1472, 31 L.Ed.2d 741 (1972), *rehearing denied*, 407 U.S. 916, 92 S.Ct. 2430, 32 L.Ed.2d 692 (1972).

37. *See* Basic Inc. v. Levinson, 485 U.S. 224, 108 S.Ct. 978, 99 L.Ed.2d 194 (1988).

arose in the context of an omission case. Some courts have held that this presumption of reliance[38] does not apply in the case of misstatements (as opposed to omissions) to the extent that the plaintiff is in a better position to prove reliance.[39] It has been reasoned that the presumption is based on the difficulty of proving a negative—namely, the fact that someone relied on something that was not said.[41]

In what has been described as "an absurdity"[43] in light of its cost and impracticability, the Second Circuit once indicated that in a class action separate trials might be necessary in order to resolve the issue of reliance with regard to transactions in a faceless market.[44] On the other hand, typicality for class action purposes does not mean that the claims must be identical; and class actions will be permitted to proceed unless it is clear that the common questions of fact do not predominate.[45] Plaintiffs in a class action, for example, may not be proper representatives with regard to transactions and statements made subsequent to the plaintiff's purchases.[46]

The clear trend is to favor continuation of the class. For example, it has been pointed out that the question of whether individual trials on the reliance issue are necessary is itself a question that is common to the whole class.[48] Accordingly, the proper approach is to let the litigation continue as a class action until it becomes apparent that the common issues no longer predominate.[49]

Public markets are generally efficient markets. In an efficient market, securities prices are determined by the total mix of available information. The integrity of the securities markets is premised on the dissemination of accurate information about companies and their securities. When misleading information is injected into the market, it can move securities prices in an artificial manner. Investors in publicly traded securities rely on securities prices as the reflection of accurate pricing mechanisms. When the pricing mechanisms are rendered inaccurate because of material misinformation, something that is tantamount to a fraud has taken place. Fraud on the market recognizes the impact of false information by providing a presumption of reliance for investors who are able to establish the other elements of securities fraud.

In applying the presumption of reliance and economic theory, a number of courts fashioned a fraud-on-the-market presumption for proving reliance.

---

38. In contrast, the fraud-on-the-market presumption of reliance applies in cases of material misstatements. Fraud on the market is discussed later in this section.

39. *See* Joseph v. Wiles, 223 F.3d 1155 (10th Cir.2000).

41. Binder v. Gillespie, 184 F.3d 1059, 1063 (9th Cir.1999).

43. Richard W. Jennings & Harold Marsh, Jr., Securities Regulation: Cases and Materials 1049 (5th ed. 1982).

44. Green v. Wolf Corp., 406 F.2d 291 (2d Cir.1968), *cert. denied*, 395 U.S. 977, 89 S.Ct. 2131, 23 L.Ed.2d 766 (1969).

45. *E.g.*, Krogman v. Sterritt, 202 F.R.D. 467 (N.D. Tex. 2001).

46. *See e.g.*, In re Donald J. Trump Casino Securities Litigation, 793 F.Supp. 543, 565 (D.N.J.1992).

48. *E.g.*, In re Western Union Securities Litigation, 120 F.R.D. 629 (D.N.J.1988).

49. In re K Mart Corp. Securities Litigation, 1996 WL 924811 [1997 Transfer Binder] Fed. Sec. L. Rep. (CCH) ¶ 99,511 (E.D. Mich. 1996) (although evidence relating to rebuttal of fraud-on-the-market presumption of reliance would vary among defendants, this was not a basis for refusing to certify the class).

Simply put, the courts find that the reliance requirement in a securities fraud action can be satisfied by a showing that the market price was affected by the misstatement or omission and the plaintiff's injury is due to a purchase or sale at the then fraudulently induced market price.

The fraud-on-the-market presumption of reliance has three basic requirements. First, the information in question must have been material. Second, the market must have been sufficiently active to be deemed to be efficient. Third, the misinformation must have been disseminated publicly.

The fraud on the market theory was adopted by the Supreme Court in a sharply divided opinion.[64]

In Basic, Inc. v. Levinson,[67] the Supreme Court adopted the fraud-on-the-market theory in cases involving affirmative misrepresentations. *Basic* involved alleged materially misleading denials of preliminary merger negotiations. The Court viewed the fraud-on-the-market presumption of reliance as a natural inference "supported by common sense and probability."[68] The Court also recognized the importance of the fraud on the market presumption in allowing class action claims to proceed.[69]

The fraud-on-the-market presumption of reliance is a driving force that permits a finding that common issues predominate in class actions based on publicly disseminated statements.[71] For example, in fraud-on-the-market cases, some courts have held that proof that the market price was affected will prove reliance by the market,[72] even if the plaintiff never saw the statements in question.[73] The fraud-on-the-market analysis does not conclusively establish reliance. It merely serves as a presumption of reliance that, for example, can be rebutted by proof that the plaintiff would have purchased the stock even if the information had been fully and accurately disclosed.[74] Merely establishing a material misrepresentation, however, will not trigger the fraud-on-the-market presumption unless it can also be shown that the market reacted to the misstatements.[75] Sufficient cautionary information available to the public may preclude a fraud-on-the-market claim.[76] However, once the presumption is established, the defendant must show that the price was not causally affected.[77] Conversely, evidence of a precipitous decline in the stock upon

---

64. Basic Inc. v. Levinson, 485 U.S. 224, 108 S.Ct. 978, 99 L.Ed.2d 194 (1988).

67. 485 U.S. 224, 108 S.Ct. 978, 99 L.Ed.2d 194 (1988).

68. 485 U.S. at 246, 108 S.Ct. at 991, 99 L.Ed.2d at 218.

69. The Court quoted the district court in explaining that "the presumption of reliance created by the fraud-on-the-market theory provide[s] 'a practical resolution to the problem of balancing the substantive requirement of proof of reliance in securities cases against the procedural requisites of [Fed.Rule Civ.Proc.] 23.' " *Id.* at 242, 108 S.Ct. at 989, 99 L.Ed.2d at 215. *See also, e.g.,* Seidman v. American Mobile Systems, Inc., 813 F.Supp. 323 (E.D.Pa.1993).

71. *See, e.g.,* Pinker v. Roche Holdings Ltd., 292 F.3d 361 (3d Cir.2002).

72. *E.g.,* Zweig v. Hearst Corp., 594 F.2d 1261, 1271 (9th Cir.1979).

73. *E.g.,* In re Control Data Corp. Securities Litigation, 933 F.2d 616 (8th Cir.1991), *cert. denied,* 502 U.S. 967, 112 S.Ct. 438, 116 L.Ed.2d 457 (1991).

74. *E.g.,* In re K Mart Corp. Securities Litigation, 1996 WL 924811 [1997 Transfer Binder] Fed. Sec. L. Rep. (CCH) ¶ 99,511 (E.D. Mich. 1996).

75. *See* Lee v. Sierra On–Line, 1994 WL 655898 [1994–1995 Transfer Binder] Fed. Sec. L. Rep. (CCH) ¶ 98,420 (E.D.Cal.1994).

76. Kaplan v. Rose, 49 F.3d 1363 (9th Cir.1994).

77. Basic Inc. v. Levinson, 485 U.S. 224, 248, 108 S.Ct. 978, 992, 99 L.Ed.2d 194 (1988).

disclosure of the facts that were previously misstated will support the fraud-on-the-market presumption of reliance.[78]

The fraud-on-the-market presumption is borrowed from economic theory and the Efficient Capital Market Hypothesis.[79] A necessary element of the hypothesis is that the market is in fact efficient.[80] Accordingly, the fraud-on-the-market presumption depends on the existence of an active market.[81]

It would appear that the absence of an efficient market should be sufficient to rebut any presumption of reliance based solely on market impact. However, the Eleventh Circuit has held that even undeveloped markets can provide a basis for the "fraud-on-the-market" presumption of reliance, at least where the defendants knew that there would be no market but for their scheme to defraud.[94] This type of case does not really involve a fraud *on* the market but rather a fraudulent scheme depicting the existence of a market which in fact would not exist upon full and accurate disclosure. Some courts have referred to this as a fraud-created-the-market theory of recovery.[95] Some courts have rejected the fraud-created-the-market theory of recovery.[98] The Tenth Circuit has accepted the fraud-created-the-market theory, but only if the plaintiff establishes that the securities were in fact unmarketable or worthless but for the fraud.[99] Others courts have limited its application.[100]

A number of courts have referred to a "truth on the market" defense to a fraud-on-the-market theory of liability.[103] The origins of this defense can be found in the Supreme Court decision in Basic, Inc. v. Levinson.[104] In *Basic*, the Court noted that even in the face of materially misleading statements, if accurate information "credibly entered the market and dissipated the effects of the misstatements," then the misstatements would not be actionable.[105]

78.　Greenberg v. Crossroads Systems, Inc., 364 F.3d 657 (5th Cir. 2004).

79.　Broadly speaking, the hypothesis maintains that in an efficient market, pricing will be reflective of the sum total of investors' and analysts' evaluation of publicly available information about the company. For discussion of the hypothesis, *see, e.g.,* Thomas L. Hazen, Rational Investments, Speculation, or Gambling: Derivative Securities and Financial Futures and Their Effect on the Underlying Capital Markets, 86 Nw.U.L.Rev. 987 (1992); Donald C. Langevoort, Theories, Assumptions, and Securities Regulation: Market Efficiency Revisited, 140 U.Pa.L.Rev. 151 (1992).

80.　*See e.g.,* Feinman v. Dean Witter Reynolds, Inc., 84 F.3d 539 (2d Cir.1996) (the presumption of reliance attaches only to open-market transaction where investors rely on the integrity of the market).

81.　*See, e.g.,* In re Livent, Inc., 210 F.R.D. 512 (S.D.N.Y. 2002).

94.　Shores v. Sklar, 844 F.2d 1485 (11th Cir.1988).

95.　*See, e.g.,* Joseph v. Wiles, 223 F.3d 1155 (10th Cir.2000), relying on Ockerman v. May Zima & Co., 27 F.3d 1151, 1160 (6th Cir.1994) and Ross v. Bank South, 885 F.2d 723, 729 (11th Cir.1989) (en banc).

98.　*See* Eckstein v. Balcor Film Investors, 8 F.3d 1121 (7th Cir.1993).

99.　Joseph v. Wiles, 223 F.3d 1155 (10th Cir.2000) ("Thus, we require the securities to be unmarketable in order to invoke the presumption of reliance based on fraud creating the market;" plaintiff failed to meet that burden).

100.　*See* Rosenthal v. Dean Witter Reynolds, Inc., 945 F.Supp. 1412 (D.Colo.1996) (fraud-created-the-market presumption is limited to worthless securities and thus was inapplicable where securities had some value).

103.　*See, e.g.,* In re Seagate Technology II Securities Litigation, 843 F.Supp. 1341, 1368–69 (N.D.Cal.1994). *See also, e.g.,* Heliotrope General, Inc. v. Ford Motor Co., 189 F.3d 971 (9th Cir.1999).

104.　485 U.S. 224, 108 S.Ct. 978, 99 L.Ed.2d 194 (1988), *on remand*, 871 F.2d 562 (6th Cir.1989).

105.　485 U.S. at 248–49, 108 S.Ct. at 992.

Although sounding more like a question of causation[106] or materiality,[107] many courts have labeled the availability of adequate accurate public information as a truth-on-the-market defense.[108] Regardless of the nomenclature of the defense, a showing that the misstatements or nondisclosures did not affect the market price will rebut the fraud-on-the-market presumption of reliance.[109] The fact that the true information is publicly available will not preclude liability when that information is not easily accessible.[110] Furthermore, it must be established that the truth in the market was sufficient to counteract the alleged fraudulent impact of the statements in question.[111]

Any reliance by the plaintiff must be reasonable.[112] Thus, for example, once accurate information has been disclosed publicly, it is not reasonable for an investor to rely on representations to the contrary.[113] An investor who is aware of the wrongful conduct cannot succeed in a Rule 10b–5 claim.[114] Thus, an investor with knowledge of the untruth or omission cannot justifiably rely on a statement.[115]

Issuing warnings as to the reliability of information may preclude a showing of reasonable reliance on the information. It has been held, for example, that a plaintiff claiming reliance on alleged material misstatements will be charged with knowledge of warnings in the private placement memorandum concerning the investment risks, thus making reliance unreasonable.[116] In contrast, oral statements minimizing the significance of the written materials will still be actionable.[117] Although general blanket disclaimers of reliance will not be effective, a specific disclaimer will preclude a fraud action.[118] This is especially true where the specific disclaimers are a result of face-to-face negotiations.[119] Similarly, warnings in connection with a merger

---

106. Causation is discussed in § 12.11 *infra.*

107. One could say that the injection of truth into the market made the misstatements or omissions not material in light of the total mix of information available.

108. In re Seagate Technology II Securities Litigation, 802 F.Supp. 271, 275 (N.D.Cal.1992), *relying on* In re Convergent Technologies Securities Litigation, 948 F.2d 507, 513 (9th Cir.1991) *and* In re Apple Computer Securities Litigation, 886 F.2d 1109, 1115 (9th Cir.1989).

109. Heliotrope General, Inc. v. Ford Motor Co., 189 F.3d 971 (9th Cir.1999); Fine v. American Solar King Corp., 919 F.2d 290, 299 (5th Cir.1990).

110. Berry v. Valence Technology, Inc., 175 F.3d 699, 706 (9th Cir.1999) (statement in a magazine article critizing a company and its stock did not demonstrate that the market already knew of the company's fraud).

111. Ganino v. Citizens Utilities Co., 228 F.3d 154 (2d Cir.2000).

112. *See, e.g.,* Banca Cremi, S.A. v. Alex Brown & Sons, Inc., 132 F.3d 1017 (4th Cir.1997) (reliance by sophisticated investor on broker-dealer recommendations was not reasonable).

113. *See, e.g.,* Semerenko v. Cendant Corp., 223 F.3d 165 (3d Cir.2000).

114. Gurary v. Winehouse, 190 F.3d 37 (2d Cir.1999).

115. *E.g.,* Koehler v. Bank of Bermuda (New York), 209 F.3d 130 (2d Cir. 2000).

116. Ambrosino v. Rodman & Renshaw, Inc., 972 F.2d 776 (7th Cir.1992) (written disclosures precluded reliance on oral misrepresentations that were at variance with the writing).

117. *See, e.g.,* Parkhurst v. North American Financial Services Cos., 919 F.Supp. 270 (E.D.Mich.1996).

118. *See, e.g.,* Chavin v. McKelvey, 182 F.3d 898 (2d Cir.1999); Silva Run Worldwide Ltd. v. Gaming Lottery Corp., 2001 WL 396521, [2001–2002 Transfer Binder] Fed. Sec. L. Rep. (CCH) ¶ 91,417 (S.D.N.Y.2001) (upholding disclaimer of reliance by sophisticated investor). *Cf.* Tirapelli v. Advanced Equities, Inc., 215 F.Supp.2d 964 (N.D.Ill.2002) (upholding clause disclaiming reliance on statements made outside of share subscription agreement).

119. Chavin v. McKelvey, 182 F.3d 898 (2d Cir.1999).

will negate reliance on the statements that were the subject of the warnings.[120]

As noted earlier, many courts have referred to the effect of warnings as the "bespeaks caution" doctrine which, on appropriate facts, will preclude a finding of reasonable reliance.[121] However, blanket warnings and disclaimers in offering materials cannot preclude reliance on otherwise materially misleading statements. The cautionary language must be sufficient to adequately negate any reasonable implication to the contrary from the projection or prediction.[123]

The Tenth Circuit has summarized the relevant factors considered by the courts in assessing the reasonableness of reliance:

> the following are all relevant factors in determining whether reliance was justifiable: (1) the sophistication and expertise of the plaintiff in financial and securities matters; (2) the existence of long standing business or personal relationships; (3) access to the relevant information; (4) the existence of a fiduciary relationship; (5) concealment of the fraud; (6) the opportunity to detect the fraud; (7) whether the plaintiff initiated the stock transaction or sought to expedite the transaction; and (8) the generality or specificity of the misrepresentations.[125]

A plaintiff's sophistication will be considered a factor in determining whether his or her reliance was reasonable.[130] However, the fact that an investor is sophisticated will not preclude a finding that he or she reasonably relied on the misstatements in question.[131] The courts will consider the surrounding circumstances in determining the extent to which an investor's sophistication will bear upon the reasonableness of any reliance. The objective requirement of reasonable reliance may not apply when the defendant intentionally targets a naive or careless investor. The naivety or carelessness of a targeted investor will not preclude a finding of materiality when the defendant knew or should have known of the investor's frailties.[133]

§ 12.11 Causation in Actions Under Rule 10b–5

As in other areas of the law, causation embodies two distinct concepts: (1) cause in fact and (2) legal cause. Legal cause is frequently dealt with in terms of proximate cause. Cause-in-fact questions are frequently stated in terms of the sine qua non rule: but for the act or acts complained of, the injury would not have occurred. Legal cause represents the law's doctrinal basis for limiting liability even though cause in fact may be proven. Courts in both tort and contract cases frequently speak in terms of foreseeability in order to determine the extent of proximate or legal cause. Causation in securities law

---

120. *See* Kaplan v. Lazard Freres & Co., 2000 WL 145958, [1999–2000 Transfer Binder] Fed. Sec. L. Rep. (CCH) ¶ 90,760 (S.D.N.Y. 2000), *affirmed in relevant part, reversed in part*, 234 F.3d 1262 (2d Cir.2000).

121. The genesis of the doctrine is found in Polin v. Conductron Corp., 552 F.2d 797, 806 n. 28 (8th Cir.), *cert. denied*, 434 U.S. 857, 98 S.Ct. 178, 54 L.Ed.2d 129 (1977).

123. *E.g.,* Rubinstein v. Collins, 20 F.3d 160 (5th Cir.1994).

125. Zobrist v. Coal–X, Inc., 708 F.2d 1511, 1516 (10th Cir.1983).

130. *See, e.g.,* Emergent Capital Investment Management LLC v. Stonepath Group, Inc., 343 F.3d 189 (2d Cir. 2003).

131. Rubin v. Schottenstein, Zox & Dunn, 143 F.3d 263 (6th Cir.1998).

133. United States v. Davis, 226 F.3d 346, 358 (5th Cir.2000) ("the naivety, carelessness, negligence, or stupidity of a victim" does not preclude criminal liability for fraud).

involves the same analysis of cause in fact and legal cause that was developed under the common law.[8] However, notwithstanding the similarity of analysis, the courts have developed their own rubric for causation in securities cases.

Courts have broken down the causation analysis in securities cases into two categories: "transaction causation" and "loss causation."[9] As is true with any causation analysis, these concepts are but a means to an end. Transaction causation and loss causation are difficult concepts, and careless use of these terms is likely to hinder rather than facilitate understanding.[10]

To begin with, the plaintiff must prove "transaction causation," which means that, but for the wrongful conduct, the transaction would not have gone through, at least in the form that it eventually took.[11] The concept of transaction causation has been properly characterized as "nothing more than 'but for' causation," and more questionably as "merely another way of describing reliance."[12] Although reliance and causation constitute distinct elements of a Rule 10b–5 claim, transaction causation may be established by facts that establish reliance.[13] Transaction causation does not represent the strictest form of "but for" causation because it requires only that the terms of the transaction have been significantly affected by the material misstatement or omission.[14] It is not necessary to prove that the transaction would not have occurred but for the alleged 10b–5 violation.[15] It must be shown, however, that there was a direct causal nexus between the alleged violation and the resulting transaction.[16] Furthermore, as is the case with proximate cause generally, in applying the transaction causation analysis, intervening causes can preclude a Rule 10b–5 recovery; however, not all intervening causes will prevent recovery.[17] Many courts are willing to infer or presume transaction causation once it has been established that an omission of fact is material.[18]

A 1991 Supreme Court decision involving causation under the proxy rules undoubtedly has implications for fraud actions brought under Rule 10b–5. In

---

§ 12.11

8. *E.g.,* First Interstate Bank of Nevada v. Chapman & Cutler, 837 F.2d 775 (7th Cir.1988) (dismissing 10b–5 claim; although there was "but for" cause, the violation was not a "proximate cause" of plaintiff's loss).

9. *E.g.,* Suez Equity Investors, L.P. v. Toronto–Dominion Bank, 250 F.3d 87, 95–97 (2d Cir.2001).

10. *See* LHLC Corp. v. Cluett, Peabody & Co., 842 F.2d 928, 931 (7th Cir.1988) (citing this treatise).

11. *See, e.g.,* Gannon v. Continental Ins. Co., 920 F.Supp. 566 (D.N.J.1996).

12. Castellano v. Young & Rubicam, Inc., 257 F.3d 171, 186 (2d Cir.2001).

13. Arduini/Messina Partnership v. National Medical Financial Services Corp., 74 F.Supp.2d 352, 360 (S.D.N.Y.1999).

14. *See, e.g.,* Suez Equity Investors, L.P. v. Toronto–Dominion Bank, 250 F.3d 87 (2d Cir.2001).

15. *See, e.g.,* Schutzky Distributors, Inc. v. Kelly, 643 F.Supp. 57 (N.D.Cal.1986) (a showing that transactions were partially induced by misstatements was sufficient causation). *See also, e.g.,* Mills v. Electric Auto–Lite Co., 396 U.S. 375, 90 S.Ct. 616, 24 L.Ed.2d 593 (1970) which is discussed in § 10.5 *supra.*

16. *E.g.,* Grace v. Rosenstock, 228 F.3d 40 (2d Cir.2000).

17. *See* Rankow v. First Chicago Corp., 678 F.Supp. 202 (N.D.Ill.1988), *reversed on other grounds,* 870 F.2d 356 (7th Cir.1989) (market fluctuations were found to be an intervening cause between the alleged fraudulent conduct and the plaintiff's loss; the Seventh Circuit on appeal pointed out that not every intervening cause will preclude a finding of loss causation).

18. Castellano v. Young & Rubicam, Inc., 257 F.3d 171, 186 (2d Cir.2001).

Virginia Bankshares, Inc. v. Sandberg,[26] the Supreme Court held that alleged misstatements that were made in connection with a shareholder vote that was not required to effectuate the transaction in question could not form the basis of a private damage action.[27] The Court therefore held that material misstatements or omissions which affect the transaction only in a collateral sense fail to establish the type of direct causal connection that is required to state a claim under the proxy rules. The Court thus applied a rule that seems to call for a requirement of direct transaction causation as a precondition to liability.

Once the plaintiff has proven the requisite transaction causation, it will be necessary to prove loss causation. Difficult problems of proof may arise regarding the causal relationship of the conduct to both the transaction and injury in question.[31] In large part, the problems of proving loss causation are the same as those involved in demonstrating the extent of the plaintiff's actual loss.[32] Unless the loss was due to ordinary investment risks, it is sufficient if the plaintiff establishes that the fraud induced the transactions and the plaintiff suffered a loss as a result of the transactions that would not have occurred but for the defendant's fraud. Unforeseeable losses will not satisfy the loss causation requirement.[36]

The plaintiff must be able to prove "loss causation:" namely that the plaintiff's injury (generally the diminution in the value of his or her investment) is directly attributable both to the wrongful conduct and the form and manner in which the challenged transaction occurred.[37] Loss causation provides the necessary connection between the challenged conduct and the plaintiff's pecuniary loss.[38] Loss causation does not require that the material misstatement or omission be the exclusive cause of the loss; it is sufficient to show that it was a significant contributing factor to the loss.[39] The concept of loss causation was expressly codified in 1995. Section 21D(b)(4) of the 1934 Act now provides that loss causation is an element of a private suit for securities fraud.[40] Loss causation issues can be highly factual, thus frequently precluding judgment on the pleadings.[41] However, because of the enhanced pleading requirements for securities fraud, failure to specifically allege facts showing loss causation will result in dismissal.[42]

In 1990, the Seventh Circuit, in an opinion by Chief Judge Posner, took a relatively narrow view of loss causation.[55] As part of the Private Securities

26. 501 U.S. 1083, 111 S.Ct. 2749, 115 L.Ed.2d 929 (1991). *See* the discussion in § 10.5 *supra.*

27. *See* 501 U.S. 1083, 111 S.Ct. 2749, 115 L.Ed.2d 929 (1991).

31. *See, e.g.,* Blackie v. Barrack, 524 F.2d 891, 905 (9th Cir.1975), *cert. denied,* 429 U.S. 816, 97 S.Ct. 57, 50 L.Ed.2d 75 (1976); Dura–Bilt Corp. v. Chase Manhattan Corp., 89 F.R.D. 87, 99 (S.D.N.Y.1981).

32. *See* § 12.12 *infra* for a discussion of damages in Rule 10b–5 actions.

36. AUSA Life Insurance Co. v. Ernst & Young, 119 F.Supp.2d 394 (S.D.N.Y.2000).

37. *E.g.,* Franklin High Yield Tax–Free Income Fund v. County of Martin, Minnesota, 152 F.3d 736 (8th Cir. 1998).

38. *See* Rothman v. Gregor, 220 F.3d 81, 95 (2d Cir.2000).

39. *See, e.g.,* Broudo v. Dura Pharmaceuticals, Inc., 339 F.3d 933 (9th Cir. 2003).

40. 15 U.S.C.A. § 78u–4(b)(4).

41. *E.g.,* Emergent Capital Investment Management LLC v. Stonepath Group, Inc., 343 F.3d 189 (2d Cir. 2003).

42. *E.g.,* In re QLT Inc. Securities Litigation, 312 F.Supp.2d 526 (S.D.N.Y. 2004).

55. Bastian v. Petren Resources Corp., 892 F.2d 680, 685 (7th Cir.1990), *cert. denied,* 496 U.S. 906, 110 S.Ct. 2590, 110 L.Ed.2d 270 (1990) (" 'Loss causation' is an exotic name—perhaps an

Litigation Reform Act of 1995,[56] Congress codified this standard by providing that "the plaintiff shall have the burden of proving that the act or omission of the defendant alleged to have violated the Act caused the loss for which the plaintiff seeks to recover damages."[57] In another opinion by Judge Posner, it was held that in the absence of other evidence, studies showing that the stock in question moved in tandem with the stock of competitors precluded a finding of loss causation.[58]

In Dura Pharmaceuticals, Inc. v. Broudo,[58.1] the Supreme Court held that change in the stock price following the allegedly misleading disclosures may not be sufficient to show the loss causation necessary to establish a private remedy. The Court thus held that a plaintiff cannot establish loss causation merely by alleging that security price was inflated because of misrepresentation.

§ 12.12   The Measure of Damages in Rule 10b–5 Actions

The assessment of damages in Rule 10b–5 cases, like any quantification of economic loss, has been a challenging task for the courts. Evaluating the current state of the law is also difficult because most 10b–5 litigation does not proceed to final judgment on the merits. As a result, there is a relative paucity of decisions dealing with the question of damages. In addition, the courts have taken a number of approaches to the damages issue. The variety of approaches, combined with the scarcity of cases, makes it difficult to identify solid trends in the law of damages in securities cases.

Notwithstanding the various approaches to damages in Rule 10b–5 actions, a few generalizations can be made. First, the cases agree that punitive damages are not available in 10b–5 suits.[11] However, punitive damages may be available in 10b–5 litigation, when common law fraud claims are brought into the case under the doctrine of pendent, or supplemental, jurisdiction.[12] Even in the absence of a state law permitting punitive damages, punitive damages may be awarded in an arbitration proceeding.[13]

The plaintiff's measure of recovery under federal securities law is limited to damages actually and proximately caused by the violations in question.[18]

---

unhappy one—for the standard rule of tort law, that the defendant must allege and prove that, but for the defendant's wrongdoing, the plaintiff would not have incurred the harm of which he complains").

56.   Pub. Law No. 104–67, 109 Stat. 737 (104th Cong. 1st Sess. December 22, 1995) (HR 1058).

57.   Section 21D(b)(4), 15 U.S.C.A. § 78d–u(b)(4).

58.   Law v. Medco Research, Inc., 113 F.3d 781 (7th Cir.1997).

58.1   544 U.S. 336, 125 S.Ct. 1627, 161 L.Ed.2d 577 (2005).

§ 12.12

11.   *See, e.g.,* Manufacturers Hanover Trust Co. v. Drysdale Securities Corp., 801 F.2d 13, 29 (2d Cir.1986), *cert. denied*, 479 U.S. 1066, 107 S.Ct. 952, 93 L.Ed.2d 1001 (1987).

12.   *See, e.g.,* Mastrobuono v. Shearson Lehman Hutton, Inc., 514 U.S. 52, 115 S.Ct. 1212, 131 L.Ed.2d 76 (1995) (punitive damages under a state claim were available in arbitration proceedings subject to the Federal Arbitration Act, even though those damages would not have been permitted under state arbitration proceedings).

13.   *See, e.g.,* Mastrobuono v. Shearson Lehman Hutton, Inc., 514 U.S. 52, 115 S.Ct. 1212, 131 L.Ed.2d 76 (1995) (a state procedural rule barring punitive damages in arbitration proceedings must yield to the procedural rules of the Federal Arbitration Act which permit the award of punitive damages).

18.   *E.g.,* Abbey v. Control Data Corp., 933 F.2d 616 (8th Cir.1991), *cert. denied,* 502 U.S. 967, 112 S.Ct. 438, 116 L.Ed.2d 457 (1991).

Limiting recovery to actual damages is required by the terms of section 28(a) of the Exchange Act.[20] The fact that damages are limited to actual damages means, for example, that a plaintiff will not be able to participate in a double recovery.[21]

There is no universally recognized unitary theory of damages in actions brought under SEC Rule 10b–5. As one court put it, "Anyone researching the issue of Rule 10b–5 damages would be immediately confronted with the repeated observation that this is a confused area of the law where courts, forced to rely on their own wits, have crafted a myriad of approaches."[33] The proper measure of damages at common law is an equally elusive concept.[34] Under common law fraud, "benefit-of-the-bargain" damages will be allowed on appropriate facts.[35] In Rule 10b–5, cases most courts have rejected a benefit-of-the-bargain measure of damages[36] in lieu of an out-of-pocket measure,[37] in large part because in most instances proof of benefit-of-the-bargain damages is speculative.[38] However, in appropriate cases some courts have looked to the benefit-of-the-bargain.[39] There have been still other approaches to Rule 10b–5 damages. Some other courts in federal securities cases have adopted a rescission measure[41] while still others in insider trading cases require the disgorgement of ill-gotten gains.[42]

Lost profits may be available where out-of-pocket damages are difficult to prove.[44] Difficulty of proving out-of-pocket loss is not a prerequisite to establishing expectation damages in a fraud case. There is no doubt that benefit-of-the-bargain will be an available measure of damages in appropriate cases.[45]

---

20. 15 U.S.C.A. § 78bb(a).

21. Ambassador Hotel Co. v. Wei–Chuan Investment, 189 F.3d 1017 (9th Cir.1999).

33. Koch v. Koch Industries, Inc., 6 F.Supp.2d 1192, 1204–1205 (D.Kan.1998).

34. *See* W. Page Keeton, Dan B. Dobbs, Robert E. Keeton & David G. Owen, Prosser and Keeton on Torts § 110 (5th ed. 1984).

35. *E.g.,* Farley v. Henson, 11 F.3d 827 (8th Cir.1993) (benefit of bargain was appropriate in common law fraud action in connection with merger).

36. *But cf.* In the Matter of Arbitration Between Eljer Manufacturing, Inc. v. Kowin Development Corp., 14 F.3d 1250 (7th Cir.1994) (award of lost profits as element of damages was inconsistent with federal law to the contrary; however, the arbitration award would not be overturned on the basis of this "mere error" in interpreting the federal law).

37. *See, e.g.,* Wool v. Tandem Computers Inc., 818 F.2d 1433 (9th Cir.1987) (awarding out-of-pocket loss).

38. *See, e.g.,* Panos v. Island Gem Enterprises, Ltd., 880 F.Supp. 169, 175 (S.D.N.Y. 1995)

39. *E.g.,* McMahan & Co. v. Wherehouse Entertainment, Inc., 65 F.3d 1044 (2d Cir.1995) (benefit-of-the-bargain damages are available under Rule 10b–5 but not under section 11 of the 1933 Act).

41. *See, e.g.,* Glick v. Campagna, 613 F.2d 31 (3d Cir.1979); Western Federal Corp. v. Davis, 553 F.Supp. 818 (D.Ariz.1982), *order affirmed,* 739 F.2d 1439 (9th Cir.1984).

42. *See* Financial Industrial Fund, Inc. v. McDonnell Douglas Corp., 474 F.2d 514 (10th Cir.), *cert. denied,* 414 U.S. 874, 94 S.Ct. 155, 38 L.Ed.2d 114 (1973).

44. Gould v. American–Hawaiian Steamship Co., 535 F.2d 761, 781 (3d Cir.1976). *See also, e.g.,* Hershock v. Fiascki, 1992 WL 164739 at *7 (E.D.Pa.1992).

45. By way of further example, in a recent unpublished decision, the Second Circuit noted:

In analyzing the enabling theory, we are mindful that the purpose of the laws prohibiting securities fraud is to restore to a defrauded individual the "benefit of the bargain," i.e., "the excess of what he paid over the value of what he got." *McMahan & Co. v. Wherehouse Entm't, Inc.,* 65 F.3d 1044, 1049 (2d Cir.1995), quoting *Levine v. Seilon,* Inc., 439 F.2d 328, 334 (2d Cir. 1971) (Friendly, J.).

Ausa Life Ins. Co. v. Ernst & Young, 39 Fed.Appx. 667, 2002 WL 1467546 *3 (2d Cir. 2002).

One of the purposes of Rule 10b–5 is to assure that purchasers of securities are getting what they have been led to believe they are getting.[46]

It may fairly be said that benefit-of-the-bargain should be the exception rather than the rule, because it is in essence a contract remedy that is based on a breach of promise rather than the traditional out-of-pocket tort remedy. Thus, absent appropriate circumstances, benefit-of-the-bargain damages based on the purchaser's expected profit is not likely to be the appropriate measure under Rule 10b–5. As noted above, however, those appropriate circumstances exist when the Rule 10b–5 claim is based on a breach of promise to sell or purchase particular securities.[48] In breach of promise cases, benefit-of-the-bargain is applicable when that measure can be established with reasonable certainty.[49]

The measure of damages adopted in any particular case is dependent to a large extent upon the theory of recovery. When the essence of the plaintiff's claim is fraud in the inducement—namely, that he or she would not have entered into the transaction but for the defendant's fraud, rescission is arguably the proper measure of damages. In such a case, rescission would restore the status quo.[54] Rescission would not be appropriate, however, when the defendant is not on the other side of the transaction (either as a broker or principal). When the essence of the claim is not that the defendant induced the transaction, but rather, that the plaintiff's injury is attributable to the defendant's fraudulent inflation or deflation of the security's price, then the appropriate remedy would seem to be the out-of-pocket measure. In other words, rescission rests on a claim that the transaction should be undone due to fraud in the inducement, while a claim for fraud generally leads to out-of-pocket recovery.[56] Rescission has been rejected in favor of out-of-pocket loss when other factors contributed to the diminution in value of the stock.[57] In any event, rescission damages are not appropriate unless the defendant returns or has disposed of the securities in question.[58]

There are additional instances in which a measure of damages other than out-of-pocket loss may be available. Disgorgement of ill-gotten gain may be appropriate when the remedy is based in terms of restitution, and unjust enrichment rather than any compensable loss to the plaintiff. Thus, for example, a suit against someone who has traded on inside information in

---

46. *See, e.g.,* Chemical Bank v. Arthur Andersen & Co., 726 F.2d 930, 943 (2d Cir. 1984) (Friendly, J.).

48. *See, e.g.,* Panos v. Island Gem Enterprises, Ltd., 880 F.Supp. 169, 175 (S.D.N.Y. 1995) ("equating actual damages with compensatory damages, courts have interpreted the statute as permitting all forms of loss-based relief, whether articulated under out-of-pocket, benefit-of-the-bargain, or other loss theories").

49. As explained by the Second Circuit, "giving the plaintiff the benefit-of-the-bargain damages is appropriate only when they can be established with reasonable certainty." Osofsky v. Zipf, 645 F.2d 107 (2d Cir. 1981).

54. Hatrock v. Edward D. Jones & Co., 750 F.2d 767, 773 (9th Cir.1984).

56. Soderberg v. Gens, 652 F.Supp. 560, 565 (N.D.Ill.1987) ("Rescission and damages are normally mutually exclusive remedies. Rescission rests on a disaffirmance of the transaction and return to the status which existed before the transaction was made. For damages one accepts the contract but sues for the loss caused by the fraud.").

57. *E.g.,* Huddleston v. Herman & MacLean, 640 F.2d 534 (5th Cir.1981), *affirmed in part and reversed in part on other grounds,* 459 U.S. 375, 103 S.Ct. 683, 74 L.Ed.2d 548 (1983).

58. *See* Ambassador Hotel Co. v. Wei–Chuan Investment, 189 F.3d 1017 (9th Cir.1999).

breach of a duty to the plaintiff[59] is often said to be in the nature of restitution, and thus disgorgement of profits is the proper measure.[60] When the plaintiff can state a claim under more than one provision of the securities laws, he or she is entitled to the measure of damages that will result in the higher recovery.[61]

In assessing the plaintiff's actual loss, the courts have not always limited recovery to the out-of-pocket loss resulting directly from the transaction in shares. For example, it has been held that promised, but unrealized, tax losses are properly considered in assessing the measure of damages.[62] However, the Second Circuit has taken a contrary view in ruling that Rule 10b–5 is limited to actual damages and that awarding damages for hoped-for but unrealized tax savings would be an impermissible grant of expectation damages.[63] It seems that the court there took an unreasonably restrictive reading of section 28(a)'s limitation to actual damages. On appropriate facts, such as in a breach of contract case, expectation damages are the actual damages.[64] As noted above, in rare instances when the fraud results in unfulfilled promises, expectation is appropriate under the federal securities laws as well.

There is a Supreme Court ruling that comes to bear on the effects of tax consequences in securities damage actions. In Randall v. Loftsgaarden,[65] the Court held that intangible tax benefits are to be treated differently from tangible property and thus are not income which needs to be deducted in the calculation of rescissory damages under section 12 of the 1933 Act.

§ 12.13 Pleading Fraud With Particularity

Although pleading rules in federal court are generally quite permissive, special rules apply in the case of fraud. By virtue of Rule 9(b) of the Federal Rules of Civil Procedure,[1] fraud must be pleaded with particularity. The enhanced pleading requirements have been codified by the Private Securities Litigation Reform Act of 1995.[2] Rule 10b–5 claims are subject to this enhanced pleading requirement.[4]

---

59. Because of the necessity of proving a duty to the plaintiff, it is unlikely that many open market insider trading cases will result in damages in a Rule 10b–5 action. *E.g.*, Moss v. Morgan Stanley Inc., 719 F.2d 5 (2d Cir.1983).

60. This is also the measure adopted for computing the civil penalty in SEC enforcement actions under the Insider Trading Sanctions Act of 1984. 15 U.S.C.A. § 78u(d)(3)(B). The disgorgement measure has also been incorporated into the private right of action in the hands of contemporaneous traders, which was enacted as part of the Insider Trading and Securities Fraud Enforcement Act of 1988. 15 U.S.C.A. § 78t–1. *See* § 12.17 *infra*.

61. Cyrak v. Lemon, 919 F.2d 320 (5th Cir.1990) (plaintiff with claims under section 12(2) of the 1933 Act and Rule 10b–5 may recover the higher amount, and then in order to avoid double recovery, the lesser claim is extinguished), *relying on* Grogan v. Garner, 806 F.2d 829, 839 (8th Cir.1986).

62. Sharp v. Coopers & Lybrand, 649 F.2d 175 (3d Cir.1981), *cert. denied*, 455 U.S. 938, 102 S.Ct. 1427, 71 L.Ed.2d 648 (1982).

63. Freschi v. Grand Coal Venture, 767 F.2d 1041 (2d Cir.1985), *vacated and remanded for further consideration*, 478 U.S. 1015, 106 S.Ct. 3325, 92 L.Ed.2d 731 (1986), *on remand*, 800 F.2d 305 (2d Cir.1986).

64. *See, e.g.*, John D. Calamari & Joseph M. Perillo, Hornbook on the Law of Contracts ch. 14 (3d ed. 1987); Robert Cooter & Melvin Aron Eisenberg, Damages for Breach of Contract, 73 Calif.L.Rev. 1432 (1985).

65. 478 U.S. 647, 106 S.Ct. 3143, 92 L.Ed.2d 525 (1986).

§ 12.13

1. Fed.R.Civ.P. 9(b).

2. *See, e.g.*, Desaigoudar v. Meyercord, 223 F.3d 1020 (9th Cir.2000) (failure to plead claim resulted in dismissal with prejudice). The 1995 Litigation Reform Act is discussed in § 12.15[1] *infra*.

4. *See, e.g.*, GSC Partners CDO Fund v. Washington, 368 F.3d 228 (3d Cir. 2004) (insufficient specificity).

The particularity requirement has been said to serve three purposes.[6] First, sufficient particularity is necessary to provide defendants with adequate notice so as to permit them to formulate a response to the charges.[7] Second, the particularity requirement prevents fishing expeditions designed to uncover suspected but unknown wrongs. Third, the particularity requirement is designed to protect defendants from baseless accusations of wrongful and immoral conduct.

In order to satisfy the particularity requirement, the plaintiff must allege with sufficient specificity the acts constituting the fraud.[27] Conclusory allegations of fraudulent or deceptive conduct are not sufficient.[28]

§ 12.15　Securities Class Actions; Litigation Reform

§ 12.15[0]　Overview

Congress enacted the litigation reform legislation in response to perceived abuses involving securities class actions.[6] First, the Private Securities Litigation Reform Act of 1995[7] addressed many areas of private securities litigation including procedural reforms, enhanced pleading standards, and increased protection for disclosures involving soft information and projections. Second, Congress enacted the Securities Litigation Uniform Standards Act of 1998,[8] which prevents most class actions based on securities fraud from being brought in state court. Each of the changes to the securities laws brought in by the litigation reform initiatives are discussed in this section throughout this treatise as appropriate.

§ 12.15[1]　Private Securities Litigation Reform Act of 1995

A number of observers had become increasingly concerned with abuses of class actions in securities litigation. Among other things, there was concern over the use of then-existing class action procedures to bring strike suits in order to exact "extortionate settlements."[10] No doubt there were instances of litigation abuses, but it was highly questionable whether those abuses were sufficient to warrant broad-based legislation with the potential for reducing the efficacy of legitimate efforts to recoup losses resulting from securities fraud. In any event, Congress responded with legislation designed to limit the suspected abuses. The Private Securities Litigation Reform Act of 1995 added section 21D of the 1934 Act,[11] which purports to discourage frivolous lawsuits by establishing special procedures for instituting private class actions under

6. In re Checkers Securities Litigation, 858 F.Supp. 1168, 1175 (M.D.Fla.1994).

7. *See, e.g.,* Double Alpha, Inc. v. Mako Partners, LP, 2000 WL 1036034, [1999–2000 Transfer Binder] Fed. Sec. L. Rep. (CCH) ¶ 91,033 (S.D.N.Y. 2000).

27. For a "primer" on how a complaint should be pleaded, *see* Ciena Corp. Securities Litigation, 1999 WL 1027051, [1999 Transfer Binder] Fed. Sec. L. Rep. (CCH) ¶ 90,600 (D.Md. 1999).

28. *E.g.,* Adams v. Kinder–Morgan, Inc., 340 F.3d 1083 (10th Cir. 2003).

§ 12.15

6. *See, e.g.,* In re VISX, Inc. Securities Litigation, 2001 WL 210481, [2000–2001 Transfer Binder] Fed. Sec. L. Rep. (CCH) ¶ 91,336 (N.D. Cal. 2001).

7. Pub. Law No. 104–67, 109 Stat. 737 (104th Cong. 1st Sess. December 22, 1995) (HR 1058).

8. Pub. Law No. 105–353, 112 Stat. 3227 (105th Cong.–2d Sess. November 3, 1998) (S 1260).

10. H.R. Conf. Rep. No. 104–369, 104th Cong., 1st Sess. at 31–32 (1995).

11. 15 U.S.C.A. § 78u–4(e). A parallel provision was added to the 1933 Act. *See* § 7.17 *supra.* The 1995 Act contained other provisions which are discussed elsewhere. For example, there is now a statutory safe harbor for financial projections. *See* §§ 3.9, 12.9 *supra.*

the securities laws. Section 21D of the Exchange Act covers a wide range of topics, including restrictions on the class representative, limits on attorneys' fees, pleading requirements, pretrial discovery, and the burden of proof on some issues. There are parallel provisions for claims made under the Securities Act of 1933.[13]

§ 12.15[1][A] Qualifications of Lead Plaintiff

The traditional approach in class actions is to determine the lead plaintiff by looking to the first claim that is filed. The lead plaintiff and lead counsel provisions are part and parcel of the Reform Act's intent to prevent the "race to the courthouse" phenomenon sometimes associated with the first-to-file rule. The Litigation Reform Act creates a presumption in favor of the shareholder with the largest financial interest[20] as lead plaintiff; this is designed to encourage the appointment of institutional investors as lead plaintiffs. Accordingly, courts often will favor lead plaintiff applications by institutional investors.[22] However, the statutorily mandated preference for institutional investors does not mean that institutional investors will always prevail in their applications to serve as lead plaintiff.[23]

§ 12.15[1][B] Selection of Lead Counsel

Frequently, the same transaction will give rise to multiple class action filings in various federal district courts. This results not only in several candidates for lead plaintiff, but also in several candidates for lead counsel. In addition to the selection of the most appropriate lead plaintiff according to the provisions discussed directly above, issues arise as to how to select the lead counsel.[76] The presumptive lead plaintiff's choice of lead counsel is not automatic.[77]

There are a number of possible approaches a court could take in selecting or approving lead counsel. One possible approach would be to approve whichever counsel is selected by the plaintiff who is selected to lead the class.[78] An alternative is for the court to appoint a consortium of counsel from the various plaintiffs in the consolidated actions.[79] While some courts have

---

13.   Section 27, 15 U.S.C.A. § 77z–1. *See* § 7.17 *supra.*

20.   For a detailed analysis of the size of a plaintiff's financial interest in the context of a claim against specialists for alleged front running, *see* Pirelli Armstrong Tire Corp. v. LaBranche & Co., Inc., 229 F.R.D. 395 (S.D.N.Y. 2004).

22.   *See, e.g.,* Local 144 Nursing Home Pension Fund v. Honeywell International, Inc., 2000 WL 33173017 [2000–2001 Transfer Binder] Fed. Sec. L. Rep. (CCH) ¶ 91,261 (D.N.J.2000) (appointing group of 5 largest institutional investors as lead plaintiff).

23.   *See* Netsky v. Capstead Mortgage Corp., 2000 WL 964935, [1999–2000 Transfer Binder] Fed. Sec. L. Rep. (CCH) ¶ 91,020 (N.D.Tex.2000) (appointing group of investors rather than one of two institutional investors as lead plaintiff).

76.   For example, a conflict of interest will disqualify an attorney from serving as lead counsel. A lawyer may not be able to represent two different classes suing the same defendant, but he or she may represent two different classes in two different actions where each action is suing different defendants. *See* Dietrich v. Bauer, 192 F.R.D. 119 (S.D.N.Y.2000). Also, misconduct by lead counsel can result in disqualification. *Cf.* Stearns v. Navigant Consulting, Inc., 89 F.Supp.2d 1014 (N.D.Ill.2000) (co-lead counsel who contacted class members of another lead counsel "narrowly" avoided being disqualified).

77.   *See, e.g.,* In re Comdisco Securities Litigation, 141 F.Supp.2d 951 (N.D.Ill.2001).

78.   The determination of lead plaintiff and lead counsel are two separate decisions. *See, e.g.,* Mayo v. Apropos Technology, Inc., 2002 WL 193393, Fed. Sec. L. Rep. ¶ 91717 (N.D.Ill.2002).

79.   *See, e.g.,* Metro Services, Inc. v. Wiggins, 158 F.3d 162 (2d Cir.1998) (upholding appointment of co-lead plaintiffs).

appointed a team of lead counsel,[80] others have recognized the extra cost involved[81] and have refused to do so.[82] Courts can control the way in which lead counsel conducts the litigation. For example, one court did not condone putative co-lead counsel's decision to parcel out the work and ordered the co-lead plaintiffs to resubmit their petition for appointment of lead counsel.[83]

Yet another approach in selecting lead counsel is for the court to consider applications and select the counsel it decides would most adequately, efficiently, and competently be able to represent the class. The 1995 Litigation Reform Act provides that: "[t]he most adequate lead plaintiff shall, subject to the approval of the court, select and retain counsel to represent the class."[85] This means that the court's approval is subject to the court's discretion in determining "that lead plaintiff's choice of representative best suits the needs of the class."[86] In exercising this discretion, the courts should consider both the quality and the cost[87] of the legal representation. In addition to the cost of representation, courts will consider a firm's experience, size, and financial resources available for the action.[89] Other courts have questioned the propriety of determining lead counsel by auction.[90]

§ 12.15[1][C] Attorneys' Fees

The 1995 Reform Act also addressed the issue of attorneys' fees in securities class actions. Section 21D(a)(6)[104] states that attorneys' fees in class action cases are limited to a reasonable amount, but discretion in determining what is reasonable is left to the courts.[105] Attorneys' fees may be calculated according to the lodestar approach—multiplying an attorney's hours by a reasonable fee and increasing the amount due to relevant factors. Class action settlements are subject to court approval, as is the allocation of attorneys' fees out of the settlement fund. The Private Securities Litigation Reform Act of 1995 does not mandate a particular method of calculating the attorneys' fees.[107]

§ 12.15[1][D] Pretrial Motions and Pretrial Discovery

The Reform Act attempts to limit the use of pretrial discovery as a fishing expedition. Section 21D(b)(3)[108] provides that all discovery be stayed during

---

80. *See, e.g.,* In re Lernout & Hauspie Securities Litigation, 138 F.Supp.2d 39 (D.Mass.2001).

81. In re Nortel Networks Corp. Securities Litigation, 34 Sec. Reg. & L. Rep. (BNA) 346 (S.D.N.Y. 2002) (eliminating co-lead counsel in favor of single lead counsel since co-counsel created extra cost and also confusion).

82. Weltz v. Lee, 199 F.R.D. 129, [2000–2001 Transfer Binder] Fed. Sec. L. Rep. (CCH) ¶ 91,342 (S.D.N.Y. 2001) (rejecting consortium of lead counsel to represent lead plaintiff group consisting of 7 unrelated investors; giving 30 days to propose one firm to act as lead counsel).

83. Laborers Local 1298 Pension Fund v. Campbell Soup Co., [1999–2000 Transfer Binder] Fed. Sec. L. Rep. (CCH) ¶ 90,963, 2000 WL 486956 (D.N.J.2000).

85. 15 U.S.C.A. § 78u–4(a)(2)(A)(v). *See also* 15 U.S.C.A. § 77z–1(a)(3)(B)(v).

86. In re Cendant Corp. Litigation, 182 F.R.D. 144, 149 (D.N.J.1998).

87. *See, e.g.,* Tarica v. McDermott International, Inc., 2000 WL 377817 [1999–2000 Transfer Binder] Fed. Sec. L. Rep. (CCH) ¶ 90,946 (E.D.La.2000).

89. *See, e.g.,* Wenderhold v. Cylink Corp., 191 F.R.D. 600 (N.D.Cal.2000).

90. In re Cendant Corp. PRIDES Litigation, 243 F.3d 722 (3d Cir.2001).

104. 15 U.S.C.A. § 78u–4(a)(6). *Cf.* In re Quantum Health Resources, Inc., 962 F.Supp. 1254 (C.D.Cal.1997) (court found 10%, rather than 30%, was appropriate).

105. *E.g.,* Powers v. Eichen, 229 F.3d 1249 (9th Cir.2000) (district court failed to adequately explain the reasonableness of a fee based on 30% of the settlement fund).

107. Powers v. Eichen, 229 F.3d 1249 (9th Cir.2000) (section 21D of the 1934 Act does not mandate that fees be based on net recovery rather than the gross amount).

108. 15 U.S.C.A. § 78u–4(b)(3).

the pendency of a motion to dismiss or a motion for summary judgment, in order to alleviate discovery expenses on defendants.[109] The stay is mandatory.[110] However, the stay will be lifted if necessary to avoid "undue prejudice."[111]

§ 12.15[1][E] Projections and Forward Looking Statements

Section 27A of the 1933 Act[122] and Section 21E of the 1934 Act[123] provide a safe harbor for forward-looking statements and the "bespeaks caution" doctrine created by the federal courts. The safe harbor allows corporate management to disclose forward-looking information and projections to investors with a presumption that there was a reasonable basis[124] for the projections.[125] The bespeaks caution doctrine provides that specific cautionary language can render inaccurate projections not actionable.[126]

§ 12.15[1][F] Enhanced Pleading Requirements Regarding Defendants' State of Mind

In suits involving money damages predicated on proof that a defendant acted with a certain state of mind, plaintiffs must plead with particularity that the defendant acted with such state of mind with respect to each act or omission.[127] Plaintiffs further must provide facts that indicate a "strong inference" that a defendant acted with a particular state of mind.[128] A "reasonable inference" of scienter is not sufficient.[129] In order to withstand the scrutiny imposed by the Private Securities Litigation Reform Act of 1995, the inference of scienter must be both reasonable and strong.[130]

§ 12.15[1][G] Notice of Class Action Settlements

Notice of final or proposed settlement agreements in class actions must be provided to class members.[140] A summary of the agreement must appear on the cover page of the notice. The notice must also include the average amount

---

109. S. Rep. No. 104–98, 104th Cong., 1st Sess. at 14 (1995) (finding that discovery costs often force defendants to settle securities class action suits).

110. SG Cowen Securities Corp. v. U.S. District Court, 189 F.3d 909, 31 Sec. Reg. & L. Rep. (BNA) 1199 (9th Cir.1999) (limited discovery order was improper in light of mandatory stay of all discovery).

111. "Undue prejudice" has been interpreted to include something less than irreparable injury. Vacold LLC v. Cerami, 2001 WL 167704 *6, [2000–2001 Transfer Binder] Fed. Sec. L. Rep. (CCH) ¶ 91,334 (S.D.N.Y. 2001) (lifting discovery stay).

122. 15 U.S.C.A. § 77z–2.

123. 15 U.S.C.A. § 78u–5(c).

124. *See, e.g.,* Ehlert v. Singer, 245 F.3d 1313 (11th Cir.2001).

125. *See* SEC Rules 175 and 3b–6, 17 C.F.R. §§ 230.175, 240.3b–6 and § 12.9 *supra*.

126. *Id.*

127. 1934 Act § 21D(b)(2), 15 U.S.C. § 78u–4(b)(2).

128. Scienter is discussed in § 12.8, *supra*.

129. *E.g.,* Greebel v. FTP Software, Inc., 194 F.3d 185 (1st Cir.1999).

130. *See, e.g.,* Gompper v. VISX, Inc., 298 F.3d 893 (9th Cir.2002) (allegations did not satisfy the Reform Act's standards for pleading scienter).

140. *See, e.g.,* Krangel v. Golden Rule Resources, Ltd., 194 F.R.D. 501 (E.D.Pa.2000) (notice was adequate).

of damages per share that will be recovered; explanations of attorneys' fees and costs; the name, address, and telephone number of the lead counsel; and a statement outlining the reasons for settlement. As in the case with class actions generally, courts will review settlements in order to determine fairness to class members.[141]

§ 12.15[1][H] Security Deposit

In private suits involving class action claims, the court may require an undertaking from the attorneys for the plaintiff or defendant, the parties themselves, or both. The court may use equitable principles to ascertain whether to require an undertaking and to determine the relevant proportions.

§ 12.15[1][I] Review of Proceedings for Possible Sanctions

In order to dissuade abusive litigation, courts are directed to perform a mandatory review at the final adjudication[143] of the action to determine whether any party or attorney violated Rule 11(b) of the Federal Rules of Civil Procedure.[144] In the event that the mandatory review reveals any violation by an attorney or party, the Act directs the court to impose sanctions on the attorney or party pursuant to Rule 11 unless the violator can establish a proper basis for not imposing the sanctions.[145] Once a Rule 11 violation is established, the attorney or party is given an opportunity for a hearing. Prior to the imposition of sanctions, the court must give the attorney or party notice and an opportunity to respond. In the event that the court finds a plaintiff or attorney has violated Rule 11 in filing a complaint, there is a presumption in favor of awarding all attorneys' fees and costs incurred in the action. Similarly, there is a presumption in favor of awarding the prevailing party attorneys' fees and costs incurred as a direct result of the violation that arises when a party's responsive pleading or dispositive motion violates Rule 11(b). However, the presumption in favor of awarding attorneys' fees and costs is a rebuttable one. Once there has been a finding of a violation of Rule 11 and the statutory presumptions have come into play, the Act requires that the court give the violator an opportunity to offer rebuttal evidence in order to show that an award of attorneys' fees and costs is unreasonable or that the Rule 11 violation was de minimis. If the rebuttal evidence is not persuasive, sanctions are to be imposed pursuant to the standards set forth in Rule 11. In order to warrant the imposition of sanctions, the complaint must have been frivolous. Once a party moves for the imposition of Rule 11 sanctions, by virtue of the Reform Act, a court cannot deny the motion without making explicit findings regarding compliance with Rule 11(b).[147]

---

141. *See, e.g.,* In re Mego Financial Corp. Securities Litigation, 213 F.3d 454 (9th Cir.2000) (approving class action settlement).

143. The statutory command for a mandatory Rule 11 review at the end of the proceedings means at the end of the district court's adjudication of the matter; it does not include exhaustion of appellate remedies. *See* DeMarco v. Depotech Corp., 131 F.Supp.2d 1185 (S.D.Cal.2001).

144. Section 27 of the 1933 Act, 15 U.S.C.A. § 77z–1; Section 21D of the 1934 Act, 15 U.S.C.A. § 78u–4.

145. *See, e.g.,* Gurary v. Winehouse, 235 F.3d 792 (2d Cir.2000)*vacated on other grounds,* 303 F.3d 212 (2d Cir.2002) (sanctions imposed where the transaction in question took place in advance of the alleged wrongdoing).

147. Gurary v. Winehouse, 190 F.3d 37, 46–47 (2d Cir.1999). *See also, e.g.,* Gurary v. Winehouse, 235 F.3d 792 (2d Cir.2000)*vacated on other grounds,* 303 F.3d 212 (2d Cir.2002) (affirming award of sanctions).

§ 12.15[1][J] Calculation of Damages

The 1995 Reform Act contained a provision designed to assure that damages are limited to losses caused by the material misstatement or omission. Section 21D(e) sets forth the method for calculating damages in civil actions, which is based on the mean trading price of the security at issue.[152] The mean trading price includes the original value of the security on the date the plaintiff purchased or sold the security and the value of the security during the 90-day period after corrective information has been disseminated. If during the 90-day period the plaintiff sells or repurchases the security, damages are determined according to the price of that transaction and the value of the security immediately following the dissemination of the corrective information.

§ 12.15[1][K] Impact of the 1995 Reform Act

In 1997, the SEC delivered to the President a report[154] on the effects of the 1995 Litigation Reform Act. The Commission noted a drop in the number of cases being filed during the twelve month period following the Act's adoption. It was noted that most of the cases filed contained detailed allegations. There seems to have been a slowing of the "race to the courthouse," as most cases were filed at least several weeks following the release of negative news forming the basis of the law suit. The Reform Act's heightened pleading standards and discovery stay provisions appear to have been successful in making it more difficult for plaintiffs to bring securities law claims. Class action complaints contain many fewer secondary defendants, including accountants and lawyers.[155] The study further indicated that institutional investors have not played a significant role in class action litigation notwithstanding the Reform Act's provisions encouraging such involvement. The Commission also noted an increase in state court filings, perhaps in an attempt to overcome the federal discovery stay or because of a migration of the weaker cases to state court. Although the 1997 SEC study indicated a drop in securities litigation, more recent evidence is that this decrease has not continued. In recent years, there has been an upswing in securities litigation.[157] This increase in litigation, which is attributable to the weak market in the beginning of the new millennium, shows that the Reform Act has not unduly restricted litigation.

A study released in 2002 indicated that 2001 brought with it a huge increase in securities litigation.[158] The suits filed in 2001 doubled the number

---

152.   15 U.S.C.A. § 78u–4(e).

154.   *See* Litigation Reform: SEC Adopts Staff Conclusion No Legislative Changes Now Needed, 29 Sec. Reg. & L. Rep. (BNA) 523 (April 18, 1997); Fed. Sec. L. Rep. (CCH) Report Bull. 1763 (April 23, 1997).

155.   This may also have been due to the Supreme Court's decision in Central Bank of Denver v. First Interstate Bank of Denver, 511 U.S. 164, 114 S.Ct. 1439, 128 L.Ed.2d 119 (1994), which eliminated liability of aiders and abettors in private actions. *See* § 12.25 *infra*.

157.   *See, e.g.,* Tamara Loomis, In Spite of Reform Law, Milberg Weiss Emerges as Winner in Securities Suits, N.Y.L.J. A1 (April 22, 2003).

158.   *See* Alex Viall, Survey Unearths $5.4B Surge in Securities Litigation, Complinet, http://www.complinet.com/securities-na/dailynews/display.html?ref=36112 (June 11, 2002). *See also, e.g.,* James A. Kassis, The Private Securities Litigation Reform Act of 1995: A Review of its Key Provisions and an Assessment of its Effects at the Close of 2001. 26 Seton Hall Legis. J. 119 (2001).

filed in each of the two preceding years.[159] Most of the suits involved the allocation of shares in initial public offerings.[160] Another common claim involved accounting issues.[161] A report by Cornerstone Research and the Stanford Law School Securities Class Action Clearinghouse for 2005 indicates a decline in the number of securities class actions filed. The study found that the number of securities class actions filed in 2005 fell from 213 filings to 176 filings, resulting in a decrease of 17% as compared the 2004. The 2005 filing rate was nearly 10% below the average number of annual filings in the years following the enactment of the PSLRA historic average. The decrease in filings may not so much be a reflection of increased success of PSLRA. The report suggests that the decrease in overall filings may be the result of the large majority of suits related to the boom-and-bust cycle of the late 1990s-early 2000s having already been filed, improvements in corporate governance, and less stock market volatility. There thus is considerable evidence that the 1995 Reform Act has not met its goal of decreasing securities litigation.[162]

§ 12.15[2] Securities Litigation Uniform Standards Act of 1998

The class action procedural reforms of the 1995 Reform Act apply only to class actions[163] brought in federal court. Private actions under sections 11 and 12 of the Securities Act of 1933 can be brought in either federal or state court.[164] Jurisdiction over 1934 Act claims is exclusively federal;[165] however, state securities law and common law fraud could provide alternative forums for class action plaintiffs trying to avoid the provisions of the 1995 Reform Act. Congress largely eliminated these alternatives in the Securities Litigation Uniform Standards Act of 1998 (SLUSA),[167] which mandates that most class actions involving publicly traded securities be brought in federal court.[168]

Class actions involving state securities law and class actions based on common law fraud with regard to covered securities are preempted.[173] Covered securities are defined in such a way as to include most publicly traded securities.[174] SLUSA preemption provisions are applied to all securities fraud claims involving covered securities and are not limited to claims against issuers and thus, for example, apply to suits against broker-dealers.[175]

---

159. Alex, Viall, Survey Unearths $5.4B Surge in Securities Litigation, Complinet, http://www.complinet.com/securities-na/dailynews/display.html?ref=36112 (June 11, 2002).

160. *Id.*

161. *Id.*

162. *See, e.g.,* Michael A. Perino, Did the Private Securities Litigation Reform Act Work?, 2003 ILL. L. REV. 913 (2003) (concluding that the Act did not work as intended but that it may have improved overall case quality).

163. *See, e.g.,* Behlen v. Merrill Lynch, 311 F.3d 1087 (11th Cir. 2002) (SLUSA applies to claims brought as class actions and removal to federal court is appropriate even before the state court actually certifies the class).

164. 1933 Act § 22(a), 15 U.S.C.A. § 77v(a) which is discussed in § 17.1 *infra.*

165. 1933 Act § 27, 15 U.S.C.A. § 77aa.

167. Pub. Law No. 105–353, 112 Stat. 3227 (105th Cong.–2d Sess. November 3, 1998) (S 1260).

168. 15 U.S.C.A. § 78bb(f).

173. *See* Riley v. Merrill Lynch, Pierce, Fenner & Smith, Inc., 168 F.Supp.2d 1352 (M.D.Fla. 2001) (upholding constitutionality of Uniform Standards Act's preemption of state law).

174. 15 U.S.C.A. § 78bb(f)(5)(E) refers to section 18(b) of the 1933 Act for the definition of covered securities.

175. Prager v. Knight/Trimark Group, Inc., 124 F.Supp.2d 229 (D.N.J.2000) (securities class action against market-maker was properly removed to federal court).

SLUSA is not complete in its elimination of state court class actions since the Act preempts only those actions involving publicly traded securities.[178] SLUSA also applies only to fraud and misrepresentation claims that are based on conduct "in connection with the purchase or sale" of a covered security. Even though 1933 Act claims under section 11[181] or 12(a)(2)[182] do not require scienter,[183] they appear to be subject to SLUSA's preemption. In contrast, section 12(a)(1)[184] is based on a violation of the 1933 Act's registration provisions and should remain removable to state court since they are not subject to the language of the SLUSA's preemption.[185]

It is important to note further that SLUSA applies only to class actions and thus not to individual or derivative suits.[191] There also is an exclusion for actions brought in the state of incorporation involving certain corporate transactions. The preemption only applies to fraud related claims and thus does not preclude state law claims on other theories such as conversion,[192] breach of contract,[193] or breach of fiduciary duty.[194]

In Merrill Lynch, Pierce, Fenner & Smith v. Dabit,[194.1] the Supreme Court held that SLUSA preempts state law claims that could be brought by someone who held rather than sold securities. The Court noted that the absence of a Rule 10b–5 remedy reinforced the application n of SLUSA's preemptive effect.[194.2]

§ 12.16 Statutes of Limitations in Rule 10b–5 Actions

§ 12.16[1] Overview

The 1934 Act does not set forth a statute of limitations applicable to implied rights of action such as suits under Rule 10b–5. The courts, however, have identified four alternatives: (1) apply by analogy the statutes of limitation applicable to private remedies under Section 13 of the 1933 Act;[1] (2) apply the forum state's statute of limitations for common law fraud; (3) apply the statute of limitations for securities fraud under the forum state's blue sky law; or (4) apply the limitations period from section 9(e),[2] section 16(b),[3] or

---

178. Thus, for example, the National Securities Markets Improvement Act of 1996, which preempted certain types of state substantive regulation, did not preempt state law fraud actions. Zuri–Invest AG v. Natwest Finance Inc., 177 F.Supp.2d 189 (S.D.N.Y.2001).

181. 15 U.S.C.A. § 77k. *See* §§ 7.3–7.5 *supra*.

182. 15 U.S.C.A. § 77l(a)(2). *See* § 7.6 *supra*.

183. The scienter requirement is discussed in § 12.8 *supra*.

184. 15 U.S.C.A. § 77l(a)(1). *See* § 7.2 *supra*.

185. *See, e.g.,* In re Tyco International Securities Litigation, 322 F.Supp.2d 116 (D.N.H. 2004); In re King Pharmaceuticals, 36 Sec. Reg. & L. Rep. (BNA) 444 (E.D. Tenn. 2004); In re Waste Management Securities Litigation, 194 F. Supp.2d 590 (S.D. Tex. 2002).

191. *See, e.g.,* Central Laborers' Pension Fund v. Chellgren, 2004 WL 1348880 (E.D. Ky. 2004) (SLUSA preemption does not apply to derivative actions).

192. Burns v. Prudential Securities, 116 F.Supp.2d 917 (D.Ohio 2000).

193. Green v. Ameritrade, Inc., 279 F.3d 590 (8th Cir.2002).

194. *See, e.g.,* Alessi v. Beracha, 244 F.Supp.2d 354 (D.Del. 2003).

194.1 ___ U.S. ___, 126 S.Ct. 1503, 164 L.Ed.2d 179 (2006).

194.2 *See* § 12.7 *supra* for a discussion of Rule 10b–5 standing.

§ 12.16

1. 15 U.S.C.A. § 77m (one year from discovery or reasonable discovery but no more than three years after the sale or, if applicable, from the public offering).

2. 15 U.S.C.A. § 78i(e) (action for manipulation of exchange-listed securities; one-year from discovery, three years after the violation). Section 9(e) is discussed in § 12.1 *supra*.

3. 15 U.S.C.A. § 78p(b) (disgorgement of insider short-swing profits; two years from the date the profit was realized). Section 16(b) liability is discussed in chapter 13 *infra*.

section 18(a)[4] of the Exchange Act. With the enactment of the Insider Trading and Securities Fraud Enforcement Act's[5] private remedy against illegal insider trading, there became a fifth alternative. This express insider trading remedy contains a five-year limitations period.[6] The weight of scholarly authority consistently has favored the application of a federal limitations period in order to promote uniformity.[7] In 1991, the Supreme Court overturned years of lower court precedent in holding that the one-year federal statute of limitations with a three-year repose period applies in implied actions under Rule 10b–5.[10] The former one-year (now two-year) limitations period begins to run after plaintiff discovered or reasonably should have discovered "the facts constituting the violation."[11]

As part of the reform legislation[13] following in the wake of the corporate fraud scandals of 2001 and 2002, Congress expanded the limitations period to two years after the date of discovery (instead of the one-year period borrowed from the former version of section 18 of the 1934 Act), and the repose period to five years (rather than the former three-year repose period).[14]

Notwithstanding the existence of an analogous (and, at that time, potentially applicable) state statute of limitations, some courts have held that the defense of laches is available to bar a dilatory plaintiff from bringing suit under section 10(b).[114] It has been reasoned that where there is no federal statute of limitations, Congress did not intend to exclude this traditional equitable defense.[115] As one court put it, laches requires a showing of "(1) a lack of diligence by the party against whom the defense is asserted, and (2) prejudice to the party asserting the defense."[116] Because of the highly factual nature of laches, as well as its questionable application in the face of a relevant statute of limitations, it would seem to be a long shot to advance this defense where the statute of limitations has not yet run.[117] If anything, the

---

4.   15 U.S.C.A. 78r(a) (liability for misstatements or omissions in documents filed with the SEC; one year from discovery, three years after the violation). Section 18(a) is discussed in § 12.18 *infra*.

5.   Pub.L. No. 100–704, 102 Stat. 4677 (1988).

6.   Section 20A(b)(4) of the Exchange Act, 15 U.S.C.A. § 78t–1(b)(4). This new remedy is discussed in § 12.17 *infra*. Section 20A's five-year limitation period—as the most recent congressional statement—might be a good yardstick for 10b–5 actions. On the other hand, the insider trading remedy is based on restitutionary principles rather than fraud and thus may not be as analogous as the one-year/three-year statute of limitations which applies under the express antifraud provisions. *See* 15 U.S.C.A. § 77m, 78r(a). *See also* § 7.10 *supra*.

7.   *See, e.g.,* Louis Loss Fundamentals of Securities Regulation 995 (2d ed. 1988).

10.   Lampf, Pleva, Lipkind, Prupis & Petigrow v. Gilbertson, 501 U.S. 350, 111 S.Ct. 2773, 115 L.Ed.2d 321 (1991).

11.   CSI Investment Partners II, L.P. v. Cendant Corp., 180 F.Supp.2d 444, 461 (S.D.N.Y. 2001), quoting from section 9(e) of the 1934 Act, 15 U.S.C.A. § 78*i*(e).

13.   Sarbanes–Oxley Act of 2002, Pub. Law 107–204 (July 30, 2002).

14.   28 U.S.C.A. § 1658(b).

114.   *See, e.g.,* Mihara v. Dean Witter & Co., Inc., 619 F.2d 814 (9th Cir.1980).

115.   The equitable defenses of unclean hands and *in pari delicto* are discussed in § 12.21 *infra*.

116.   Mihara v. Dean Witter & Co., Inc., 619 F.2d 814 (9th Cir.1980); Hecht v. Harris, Upham & Co., 430 F.2d 1202 (9th Cir.1970).

117.   *See* Richard W. Jennings & Harold Marsh, Jr., Securities Regulation: Cases and Materials 1335 (6th Ed.1987) ("it would seem that the doctrine of laches should be applied only where the plaintiff asks for rescission rather than damages"), relying on Baumel v. Rosen, 412 F.2d 571 (4th Cir.1969), *cert. denied*, 396 U.S. 1037, 90 S.Ct. 681, 24 L.Ed.2d 681 (1970).

viability of the laches defense seems even more questionable in the wake of the *Lampf* decision and the 2002 legislation.

§ 12.17   Insider Trading and Rule 10b–5

§ 12.17[1]   Overview

Over the past forty years, there have been many celebrated cases involving trading in securities based on nonpublic confidential or proprietary information. There have been some highly publicized insider trading cases.[1] Defendants in insider trading cases have not been limited to corporate insiders and have included a wide range of people, including psychiatrists,[2] football coaches,[3] former athletes,[4] newspaper columnists,[5] printers,[6] leading arbitrageurs,[7] golfing partners,[8] and most unfortunately, lawyers[9] and, professional relationships.[10] Several instances have involved law firms. In one situation a partner of a major law firm with an active tender offer practice frequently made purchases in the targets of his firm's client's takeover attempts.[11] The partner was not working on any part of the takeovers, but the information somehow filtered down to him. Although these facts raise questions about the internal controls at law firms and other businesses dealing with confidential inside information, no action was taken against the firm.

In analyzing the law of what traditionally has been called insider trading, many cases do not involve corporate insiders but rather deal with outsiders.[12] Outsider trading involves what has for a long time been referred to as trading on market information.[13] This occurs when someone who is not an insider of the company whose shares are traded finds out information that will affect the market price of the shares. This occurs, for example when someone has

---

§ 12.17

1.   Consider, for example, the obstruction of justice conviction of Martha Stewart in 2004 that resulted from investigation of allegedly improper trading on nonpublic information she received from the CEO of Imclone.

2.   *See* United States v. Willis, 737 F.Supp. 269 (S.D.N.Y.1990).

3.   *See* SEC v. Switzer, 590 F.Supp. 756 (W.D.Okl.1984).

4.   *See* SEC v. Tarkenton, 2000 WL 63477, 71 S.E.C. Docket 1219, Release No. AE–12, (SEC Accounting & auditing Enforcement Rel. 2000).

5.   *See* United States v. Carpenter, 791 F.2d 1024 (2d Cir.1986), *affirmed by an equally divided court*, 484 U.S. 19, 108 S.Ct. 316, 98 L.Ed.2d 275 (1987).

6.   Chiarella v. United States, 445 U.S. 222, 100 S.Ct. 1108, 63 L.Ed.2d 348 (1980); SEC v. Materia, 745 F.2d 197 (2d Cir.1984), *cert. denied*, 471 U.S. 1053, 105 S.Ct. 2112, 85 L.Ed.2d 477 (1985).

7.   *See* In re Ivan F. Boesky Securities Litigation, 36 F.3d 255 (2d Cir.1994), *affirming*, 825 F.Supp. 623 (S.D.N.Y.1993).

8.   *See, e.g.,* SEC v. King, Civ. Action No. 7:00CV00622, 32 Sec. Reg. & L. Rep. (BNA) 1140 (W.D. Va. 2000).

9.   *E.g.,* United States v. O'Hagan, 521 U.S. 642, 117 S.Ct. 2199, 138 L.Ed.2d 724 (1997).

10.   In one instance reported in the popular press, a financier was passing information on to a prostitute that he visited. In a similar situation in a different big-city firm, a paralegal working on corporate takeovers tipped her boyfriend, a stock broker, who in turn purchased the target companies' shares in advance of the announcement of the tender offers.

11.   United States v. O'Hagan, 521 U.S. 642, 117 S.Ct. 2199, 138 L.Ed.2d 724 (1997).

12.   *See, e.g.,* Ian Ayres & Stephen Choi, Internalizing Outsider Trading, 101 Mich. L. Rev. 313 (2002).

13.   *See, e.g.,* Chiarella v. United States, 445 U.S. 222, 231, 100 S.Ct. 1108, 1116, 63 L.Ed.2d 348 (1980).

advance knowledge of a pending tender offer[14] an impending news article that is likely to affect the company's stock.[15] It is in such instances of outsider trading that the courts have come to rely on the misappropriation theory[16] for imposing liability under SEC Rule 10b–5.

The SEC has repeatedly declared that the eradication of trading on inside information is one of its top priority enforcement targets.[17] Trading on inside information destroys the integrity of the market place by giving an informational advantage to a select group of corporate insiders and others having an informational advantage.[18] The practice of insider trading is especially pernicious[19] in light of the federal securities laws' thrust of full disclosure, which is designed to create and maintain an informed market and a level playing field in securities transactions. Some commentators have argued that insider trading does not have, significant adverse market impact,[20] but fortunately, the courts, Congress, and the SEC have, not joined in that position. On the other hand, it is generally recognized that there is a positive value in encouraging corporate officers, directors, and other employees to invest in the shares of their company. Accordingly, there are a number of instances in which trading by insiders is permissible. Unfortunately, the law regarding the use of nonpublic material information when trading in shares has not developed systematically. Nor has it evolved in such a way as to produce bright-line tests of when it is permissible to trade.

It is ironic that, as important as regulating trading on the basis of inside information may be under the securities laws, there is no express statutory prohibition. Most insider trading cases are based on Rule 10b–5's general antifraud provisions,[21] which do not specifically mention insider trading. Section 16(b)'s prohibition against *short-swing* profits by designated statutory insiders[22] is the one of three sections in the Exchange Act that expressly deal with insider trading. The remaining two sections deal only with remedies for

---

14. *Compare, e.g.,* United States v. O'Hagan, 521 U.S. 642, 117 S.Ct. 2199, 138 L.Ed.2d 724 (1997) *with* United States v. Chestman, 947 F.2d 551 (2d Cir.1991), *cert. denied,* 503 U.S. 1004, 112 S.Ct. 1759, 118 L.Ed.2d 422 (1992).

15. United States v. Carpenter, 791 F.2d 1024 (2d Cir.1986), *affirmed by an equally divided court,* 484 U.S. 19, 108 S.Ct. 316, 98 L.Ed.2d 275 (1987).

16. *See* § 12.17[4] *infra.*

17. One example of this push is the legislation enacted by Congress. *See* the Insider Trading Sanctions Act of 1984 (Pub. L. No. 98–376, 98 Stat. 1264 (1984)) and the Insider Trading and Securities Fraud Enforcement Act of 1988 (Pub.L. No. 100–704, 102 Stat. 4677 (1988)).

18. *E.g.,* William H. Painter, Federal Regulation of Insider Trading, ch. XI (1968); Roy A. Schotland, Unsafe at Any Price: A Reply to Manne, "Insider Trading and the Stock Market", 53 Va.L.Rev. 1425 (1967); Alan Strudler and Eric W. Orts, "Moral Principle in the Law of Insider Trading," 78 Tex. L. Rev. 375 (1999); William K.S. Wang & Marc I. Steinberg, Insider Trading (1996). For a critique of the current state of the law, *see* Saikrishna Prakash, Our Dysfunctional Insider Trading Regime, 99 Colum. L. Rev. 1491 (1999).

19. *See. e.g.,* Kim Lane Scheppele, "It's Just Not Right": The Ethics of Insider Trading, 18 Law & Contemp. Probs. 123 (1993).

For an interesting suggestion that issuer self tender offers are frequently a way to disguise insider trading, *see* Jesse M. Fried, Insider Signalling and Insider Trading with Repurchase Tender Offers, 67 U. Chi. L. Rev. 421 (2000).

20. *See, e.g.,* Henry G. Manne, Insider Trading and the Stock Market (1966); Jeffrey F. Jaffe, The Effect of Regulation Changes on Insider Trading, 5 Bell.J.Econ. & Mgt.Sci. 93 (1974).

21. 17 C.F.R. § 240.10b–5. Insider trading investigations can result in criminal prosecutions. *See, e.g.,* United States v. O'Hagan, 521 U.S. 642, 117 S.Ct. 2199, 138 L.Ed.2d 724 (1997) (upholding criminal conviction for insider trading); United States v. Mooney, 2004 WL 1636960 (8th Cir. 2004) (same).

22. 15 U.S.C.A. § 78p(b). *See* chapter 13 *infra.*

insider trading rather than addressing the substantive question of what types of conduct comprise improper trading on nonpublic information. In 1984, Congress enhanced the SEC's enforcement capabilities and bolstered the penalties for insider trading.[23] In 1988, Congress supplemented Rule 10b–5 with an express private right of action.[24] Nevertheless, the fact remains that there is no statutory definition to precisely identify which types of insider trading are permissible and which are not.

The primary basis of the prohibitions on trading while in possession of nonpublic material information has been SEC Rule 10b–5.[26] Rule 10b–5, which does not expressly address the question of insider trading, has frequently been used to regulate trading by insiders who possess confidential inside information concerning their company's stock. Necessarily couched in terms of section 10(b)'s prohibitions against manipulative and deceptive conduct.[29] In most cases, accountability for trading on inside information has been premised upon Rule 10b–5(c)'s ban on acts or practices that operate as fraud.

As discussed more fully below, the prohibition of 10b–5(c) has been utilized to craft a rule of law that subjects certain persons in possession of material nonpublic information to a "disclose or abstain" rule. The disclose or abstain rule means that when potential securities traders have obtained the material information in such a way as to subject them to Rule 10b–5's reach, they must either abstain from trading or disclose the information prior to trading.[34] In most instances, disclosure is not a reasonable option; therefore, the practical mandate is to abstain from trading until the information has been disclosed. Since insider trading prohibitions are based on a rule that does not even mention insider trading, the courts for years have been plagued with the difficulties of trying to ascertain the proper scope of insider trading prohibitions. One consequence is that the law continues to change as the courts' view of insider trading evolves.

§ 12.17[2] The Basis of the Prohibition: The Development of Rule 10b–5 in Insider Trading Cases

In the seminal decision of Cady, Roberts & Co.,[55] the Securities and Exchange Commission imposed disciplinary sanctions against a registered broker-dealer who directed his customers to liquidate their holdings in Curtiss–Wright stock because he had advance knowledge of a dividend cut. The broker, tipped by a corporate insider, was merely a tippee who in turn tipped his customers. The SEC found that this conduct "violated [10b–5(c)] as a

---

23. Pub. L. No. 98–376, 98 Stat. 1264 (1984). The 1984 legislation that was supported by the SEC includes a fine based on treble damages against certain persons trading on inside information. In 1988, Congress added an express right of action by contemporaneous traders. 15 U.S.C.A. § 78t–1.

24. 15 U.S.C.A. § 78t–1. *See* Pub.L. No. 100–704, 102 Stat. 4677 (1988).

26. 17 C.F.R. § 240.10b–5. The SEC subsequently adopted Rule 14e–3, which directly addresses trading in advance of tender offers. 17 C.F.R. § 240.14e–3. *See* discussion *infra* and § 11.6 *supra*.

29. 15 U.S.C.A. § 78j(b). Section 10(b) and the other SEC rules promulgated thereunder are discussed in § 12.3 *supra*.

34. Trading on inside information does not violate Rule 10b–5 unless there is a duty to abstain from trading. *See, e.g.,* Abrams v. Prudential Securities, Inc., 2000 WL 390494, [2000–2001 Transfer Binder] Fed. Sec. L. Rep. (CCH) ¶ 91,292 (N.D.Ill.2000).

55. 40 S.E.C. 907, 1961 WL 60175 (SEC 1961).

practice which operated as * * * fraud or deceit upon the purchasers."[56] The Commission's opinion explained that "analytically, the obligation [to disclose or abstain from trading] rests on two principal elements; first, the existence of a relationship giving access, directly or indirectly, to information intended to be available only for a corporate purpose and not for the personal benefit of anyone, and second, the inherent unfairness involved where a party takes advantage of such information knowing it is unavailable to those with whom he is dealing."[57]

Following the SEC's *Cady, Roberts* decision, the Second Circuit in SEC v. Texas Gulf Sulphur Co.[58] held that corporate insiders who purchased stock on the open market with knowledge of a valuable mineral find that had not yet been publicly announced had violated Rule 10b–5 because the information not disclosed at the time of the transactions would have been "material" to a reasonable person's investment decision. The fact that the insiders began purchasing stock and options raised a strong inference that they considered the information material.[60] One lesson that can be learned from the court's reasoning is that when purchasing the shares of their own company, corporate insiders should adopt a regular and periodic plan of purchases. Otherwise, it is likely that the fact finder might infer that the information available to the insider was in fact material,[61] and thus induced illegal insider trading.

Following the lead of *Texas Gulf Sulphur*, it has been held that a tip of inside information will give rise to liability for fraud on the market.[62] One court has even held that non-insider tippees who sell in reliance on confidential inside information will be liable and held accountable by disgorging their profits.[63] Subsequent Supreme Court decisions have been narrowing the scope of tippee liability.[64]

Outside of the insider trading context, however, "fraud on the market" remains a basis for Rule 10b–5 liability.[65] A variation of fraud on the market has arisen in several insider trading cases. In a Ninth Circuit case,[66] a financial columnist who purchased stock prior to publishing his buy recommendation was held liable to a forced purchaser who did not rely on the

56. 40 S.E.C. at 913.

57. *Id.* at 912.

58. 401 F.2d 833 (2d Cir.1968), *cert. denied*, 394 U.S. 976, 89 S.Ct. 1454, 22 L.Ed.2d 756 (1969).

60. In determining the "materiality date" of the insiders' information, the court relied heavily on substantial increases in insider trading, reasoning that this presented circumstantial evidence that at least the insider deemed the information to be material.

61. *See, e.g.*, SEC v. Shared Medical Systems Corp., 1994 WL 201858, [1993–1994 Transfer Binder] Fed. Sec. L. Rep. (CCH) ¶ 98,247 (E.D.Pa.1994) (insider trading in suspicious amounts or at suspicious times is probative of scienter).

62. Shapiro v. Merrill Lynch, Pierce Fenner & Smith, Inc., 495 F.2d 228 (2d Cir.1974). *Accord, e.g.*, Elkind v. Liggett & Myers, Inc., 635 F.2d 156 (2d Cir.1980).

63. Financial Industrial Fund, Inc. v. McDonnell Douglas Corp., 474 F.2d 514 (10th Cir.1973), *cert. denied*, 414 U.S. 874, 94 S.Ct. 155, 38 L.Ed.2d 114 (1973).

64. Dirks v. SEC, 463 U.S. 646, 103 S.Ct. 3255, 77 L.Ed.2d 911 (1983); Chiarella v. United States, 445 U.S. 222, 100 S.Ct. 1108, 63 L.Ed.2d 348 (1980).

65. *E.g.*, Kumpis v. Wetterau, 586 F.Supp. 152 (E.D.Mo.1983). Fraud on the market is discussed in § 12.10 *supra*.

66. Zweig v. Hearst Corp., 594 F.2d 1261 (9th Cir.1979). The activity complained of—purchasing a security prior to publicly recommending it—is known as "scalping." *See* SEC v. Capital Gains Research Bureau, Inc., 375 U.S. 180, 84 S.Ct. 275, 11 L.Ed.2d 237 (1963). Scalping is discussed in § 14.17 *infra*.

column. The recommendation was based on an overly optimistic view of the company. The court reasoned that the defendant's failure to disclose his scalping activities defrauded the market by causing an artificially high price, and that the plaintiffs' injury arose from having to pay that price. The "fraud on the market" theory, however, is at best a longshot in the insider trading context. For example, the Sixth Circuit has held that a tippee trading on information obtained from his father, a corporate insider, is not liable to purchasers in a faceless market because of the plaintiff's inability to prove the causation requirement necessary to recover damages under a fraud theory.[69]

Perhaps an even more formidable impediment to implied private actions under Rule 10b–5 by open market purchasers or sellers against persons trading on inside information is the Supreme Court's ruling that the mere possession of inside information does not create a duty to market participants.[70] Market participants thus cannot state a claim unless the person trading on the information is a corporate official who owes an independent duty to the shareholders who were trading on the other side of the insiders' transactions.[71]

In 1988, Congress supplemented any remedy that may exist under Rule 10b–5 with an express private right of action by contemporaneous traders against persons making improper use of material, nonpublic information.[72] Under this express remedy, contemporaneous traders are permitted to sue for a disgorgement of the improper profits (or loss avoided).

§ 12.17[3] Causation in Insider Trading Cases—"Use" Versus "Possession"

Another question that has arisen is to what extent it must be shown that the inside information in fact caused the transactions in question. This issue has arisen, for example, in the context of the argument that it must be shown that the trader in fact used the information in question; namely, that he or she would not have traded but-for the confidential information. This debate arose in the course of Congressional deliberation over whether to define insider trading. In another case the issue was raised by a defendant being prosecuted for improper trading on confidential information. The Second Circuit indicated that actual use need not be shown; rather, it was sufficient to show that the trader, under a duty of confidentiality, entered into the transactions while *knowingly possessing*[76] material nonpublic information.[77] However, as discussed directly below, this ruling has been altered by SEC rulemaking. It can be argued that even in the face of the SEC's rulemaking, the Second Circuit rule is correct. In a decision following the SEC rulemaking, the Seventh Circuit did not reach the question of whether trading while in

69. Fridrich v. Bradford, 542 F.2d 307 (6th Cir.1976), *cert. denied*, 429 U.S. 1053, 97 S.Ct. 767, 50 L.Ed.2d 769 (1977).

70. Chiarella v. United States, 445 U.S. 222, 100 S.Ct. 1108, 63 L.Ed.2d 348 (1980).

71. *See* Moss v. Morgan Stanley, Inc., 719 F.2d 5 (2d Cir.1983). *Cf.* Goldman v. Belden, 754 F.2d 1059 (2d Cir.1985). Wilson v. Comtech Telecommunications Corp., 648 F.2d 88, 94–95 (2d Cir.1981).

72. 15 U.S.C.A. § 78t–1. *See* Pub.L. No. 100–704, 102 Stat. 4677 (1988).

76. Whether or not the defendant acted in knowing possession of material nonpublic information may depend upon the extent to which a reasonable person would have realized that the information was nonpublic. *See, e.g.,* SEC v. Thrasher, 152 F.Supp.2d 291 (S.D.N.Y.2001).

77. United States v. Teicher, 987 F.2d 112 (2d Cir.1993), *cert. denied*, 510 U.S. 976, 114 S.Ct. 467, 126 L.Ed.2d 419 (1993).

knowing possession of the information was sufficient to establish liability because, on the facts presented to the jury and under the instruction given by the judge, one could infer use from possession.[78] The court went on to say that the defendant can point to a legitimate reason for entering into the trades in question is not sufficient to counteract other evidence from which one could reasonably infer that the defendant actually used the nonpublic information in making the decision to trade.[79]

In a subsequent decision, the 11th Circuit held that it is not sufficient to establish that the defendant possessed inside information when the trades in question were made.[80] Instead, it must be shown that the use of the information actually caused the trades. The Ninth Circuit followed suit in adopting a use rather than a possession test of causation in insider trading cases.[82] It was argued that a use test imposed too high a burden of proof, but both courts pointed out that proof of trades while in possession of the information creates a very strong inference that the defendant in fact used the information.[83] The burden would then shift to the defendant to show that he or she did not use the information when making the trades.[84]

Rule 10b5–1 requires that the defendant have used the information in making the challenged securities transactions.[89] The rule thus rejects liability based merely on showing that the defendant and subject to a disclose or abstain obligation merely possessed material non public information. In addition to adopting the "use" test for liability, Rule 10b5–1 presumes that someone who trades while in possession of material nonpublic information has in fact used the information in making the trade. The presumption of use that follows from trading while in possession may be rebutted by a showing that the defendant (1) had a preexisting binding contract to enter into the transaction in question, (2) executed a prior instruction to a third party to execute the transaction in question, or (3) had previously adopted a written plan specifying the transactions in question.[90]

Rule 10b5–1(c) establishes two affirmative defenses that rebut the presumption that the insider has in fact used the material nonpublic information in making the trades in question.

The first defense is set forth in Rule 10b5–1(c)(1). Rule 10b5–1(c) protects individuals or entities, and applies in situations where material nonpublic information was not a factor in a trading decision because a trade was carried out pursuant to a pre-existing contract, instruction, or plan. Rule 10b5–1(c)(1)

---

78. SEC v. Lipson, 278 F.3d 656 (7th Cir.2002).

79. Judge Posner, speaking for the court, described it as "absurd" to suggest that a legitimate alternative purpose for making the trade is sufficient to negate liability. *Id.* at 661.

80. SEC v. Adler, 137 F.3d 1325 (11th Cir.1998).

82. United States v. Smith, 155 F.3d 1051 (9th Cir.1998).

83. United States v. Smith, 155 F.3d 1051 (9th Cir.1998); SEC v. Adler, 137 F.3d 1325 (11th Cir.1998). *Cf.* Stevelman v. Alias Research Inc., 174 F.3d 79 (2d Cir.1999) (insider's trades while company's stock was inflated by false financial information presented a strong inference of scienter).

84. *See, e.g.,* SEC v. Lipson, 278 F.3d 656 (7th Cir.2002) (use could be inferred from possession).

89. 17 C.F.R. § 240.10b5–1. *See* Selective Disclosure and Insider Trading, Sec. Exch. Act Rel. No. 34–43154, 2000 WL 1201556 (SEC Aug. 15, 2000). *See generally* Peter J. Romeo & Alan L. Dye, The SEC's New Insider Trading Rules, 34 Rev. Sec. & Commod. Reg. 1 (2001).

90. *Id.*

provides that a purchase or sale of securities is not deemed to be made on the basis of material nonpublic information if the individual or entity making the purchase or sale can show that, prior to becoming aware of the material nonpublic information, the individual or entity had entered into a binding contract for the purchase or sale of the security, or instructed a third party to purchase or sell the security for its account, or adopted a written plan for trading securities. Furthermore, the trading plan must specify the "amount"[91] of securities to be purchased or sold and the "price"[92] and "date"[93] on which the securities were to be purchased or sold, or include a written formula for determining the amount, price and date of the transaction, or does not permit the individual or entity to exercise any subsequent influence over how, when and whether to conduct the purchases or sales, and delegated those decisions to a person who did not possess material nonpublic information.

Having established the existence of a trading plan, the defendant must show that the purchase or sale at issue occurred "pursuant to the contract, instruction or plan," which means that the individual or entity that entered into the trading plan did not alter or deviate from the plan or enter into or alter a corresponding or hedging transaction with respect to the securities. A trading plan may be modified at any time provided that the insider is not in possession of material nonpublic information. A defendant's ability to rely on a Rule 10b5–1(c)(1) trading plan is explicitly conditioned on the good faith of the individual or entity in entering into the trading plan. The affirmative defense thus is not available where the trading plan was entered into "as part of a plan or scheme to evade" the rule.

The second affirmative defense to the Rule 10b5–1 presumption of use of inside information is available only to entities and thus not to individuals. Rule 10b5–1(c)(2) permits an entity to demonstrate that a trade was not on the basis of material nonpublic information by demonstrating (1) that the individual who made the investment decision on behalf of the entity was not aware of the information, and (2) the entity had implemented reasonable policies and procedures, in light of the nature of the entity's business, to ensure that those making investment decisions on its behalf would not violate the insider trading laws.[94]

Even beyond the presumptions and defenses established by Rule 10b5–1, the SEC or a private plaintiff claiming insider trading can establish an inference that improper trading has taken place if the insider has engaged in unusual trading patterns. In such a case, the plaintiff has the burden of showing the existence of an unusual trading pattern.[95] Some courts have

---

91. "Amount" is defined as either a specified number of shares or dollar value of securities.

92. "Price" is defined as the market price on a particular date, a limit price, or a particular dollar price.

93. "Date" is defined, in the case of a market order, as the day of the year on which the order is to be executed or as soon thereafter as possible under principles of best execution, and, in the case of a limit order, as any day of the year on which the limit order is in force.

94. 17 C.F.R. § 240.10b5–1(c)(2). The "policies and procedures" may include arrangements designed to prevent individuals who make investment decisions on behalf of an entity from acquiring material nonpublic information, as well as policies designed to restrict trading by those who have come into possession of such information. The requirement that these policies and procedures be designed "to ensure" that violations do not occur does not mean that the defense is unavailable if a violation does in fact occur, but instead requires that the policies and procedures be reasonably designed to prevent insider trading.

95. In re Silicon Graphics, Inc. Securities Litigation, 183 F.3d 970, 986–987 (9th Cir.1999); In re Peritus Software Services, Inc. Securities Litigation, 52 F.Supp.2d 211, 224 (D.Mass.1999). *See*

indicated that this requires a showing that the insiders' transactions were "dramatically different" from their prior trading patterns.[96] As explained by the Ninth Circuit, "[a]mong the relevant factors to consider are: (1) the amount and percentage of shares sold by insiders; (2) the timing of the sales; and (3) whether the sales were consistent with the insider's prior trading history."[97]

§ 12.17[4] Refining Rule 10b–5's Insider Trading Prohibitions; Developments in the Supreme Court and Elsewhere— The Misappropriation Theory

In Affiliated Ute Citizens of Utah v. United States,[101] the first Supreme Court case on point, it was held that, in a face-to-face transaction, a purchaser possessing material inside information about a company has a duty to disclose such information to the seller before consummating a transaction.[102] Showing the necessary causation in that case was not a problem because the purchaser dealt directly with the seller. The Court further held that reliance on the nondisclosure could be presumed from the materiality of the information in the absence of any evidence of actual nonreliance.[103] Subsequently, however, in Chiarella v. United States,[104] the Court held that, in a market transaction, there was no duty to disclose based solely on the possession of inside information, at least when that information was "market information" rather than fundamental information related to the issuer's condition.

The defendant, Chiarella, was an employee of a printing firm hired to produce documents for various tender offers.[105] The target company's identity was concealed in the galleys sent to the printer in an effort to maintain confidentiality. Chiarella, however, identified the target company by reading the other information in the tender offer material. Armed with this knowledge, he purchased the target company's stock and sold it at a profit after the tender offer was publicly announced.[106] Chiarella's indictment was framed in

---

also, e.g., In re FVC.COM Securities Litigation, 136 F.Supp.2d 1031 (N.D.Cal.2000) (failure to establish scienter).

96. In re Silicon Graphics, Inc. Securities Litigation, 183 F.3d 970, 986 (9th Cir.1999) ("insider trading is suspicious only when it is 'dramatically out of line with prior trading practices at times calculated to maximize the personal benefit from undisclosed inside information' "), *quoting* In re Apple Computer Securities Litigation, 886 F.2d 1109, 1117 (9th Cir.1989).

97. In re Silicon Graphics, Inc. Securities Litigation, 183 F.3d 970, 986 (9th Cir.1999), *relying on* Provenz v. Miller, 102 F.3d 1478, 1491 (9th Cir.1996).

See also, e.g., United States v. Pileggi, 202 F.3d 255 (3d Cir.1999) (evidence of trades by defendant's relatives was admissible to show unusual trading pattern).

101. 406 U.S. 128, 92 S.Ct. 1456, 31 L.Ed.2d 741 (1972), *rehearing denied*, 407 U.S. 916, 92 S.Ct. 2430, 32 L.Ed.2d 692 (1972).

102. *Id. Accord, e.g.,* List v. Fashion Park, Inc., 340 F.2d 457 (2d Cir.1965), *cert. denied*, 382 U.S. 811, 86 S.Ct. 23, 15 L.Ed.2d 60 (1965), *rehearing denied*, 382 U.S. 933, 86 S.Ct. 305, 15 L.Ed.2d 344 (1965).

The duty to make such a disclosure, of course, depends upon a showing of materiality. *See, e.g.,* McCormick v. Fund American Cos., 26 F.3d 869 (9th Cir.1994) (parent corporation purchasing its stock from former chief executive officer of subsidiary did not have duty to disclose preliminary merger negotiations involving parent).

103. The element of plaintiff's reliance is considered in § 12.9 *supra.*

104. 445 U.S. 222, 100 S.Ct. 1108, 63 L.Ed.2d 348 (1980).

105. This paragraph is adapted from Thomas L. Hazen, The Supreme Court and the Securities Laws; Has the Pendulum Slowed?, 30 Emory L.J. 3, 20–23 (1981).

106. The defendant engaged in five similar transactions and realized an aggregated profit of approximately $30,000.

terms of Rule 10b–5's requirement that insiders possessing confidential material information must either disclose the information or abstain from trading. The Court reversed the defendant's conviction on the grounds that he had no legal duty to speak and thus was not subject to the disclose or abstain obligation.

The Court, in *Chiarella*, first distinguished the SEC's ruling in *Cady, Roberts*[107] on the grounds that, in the later decision the SEC had imposed sanctions against a broker-dealer who had wrongfully obtained information from corporate insiders. The Supreme Court reasoned that the SEC's opinion in *Cady, Roberts* "recognized a relationship of trust and confidence between the shareholder of a corporation and those insiders who have obtained confidential information by reason of their position with that *corporation*."[108] The Court also explained that the *Texas Gulf Sulphur*[109] "disclose or abstain" rule was limited to persons—both insiders and others—who are subject to a duty to disclose apart from the mere possession of confidential inside information.[110] As noted above, another point of distinction between the facts in *Chiarella* and prior decisions recognizing 10b–5 violations is that *Chiarella* involved market information rather than information "belonging" to the target company.[111] This type of trading is often characterized as "outsider trading" because someone who is not a corporate insider is taking advantage of information that will affect the company's stock price.[112] The misappropriation theory thus permits the SEC and private plaintiffs to pursue trading on nonpublic information, but only if the trader is guilty of the same type of conduct as an insider in the classic insider trading context.[113]

The Supreme Court in *Chairella* held that the absence of a wrongful conversion or misappropriation of the information meant that no violation of Rule 10b–5 had occurred because there was no legal duty to disclose such information prior to trading.[114] The Court pointed out, however, that the only issue before it was whether a duty to disclose under 10b–5 was created vis-à-vis the target company by the mere possession of nonpublic information that would affect the price of its stock. The Supreme Court in *Chiarella* did not decide whether the printer's relationship to the acquiring corporation created a duty to abstain from trading.[115] Justice Stevens, in his concurrence, empha-

107. 40 S.E.C. 907 (SEC 1961).

108. 445 U.S. at 228, 100 S.Ct. at 1114, 1115 (footnote omitted; emphasis supplied).

109. SEC v. Texas Gulf Sulphur Co., 401 F.2d 833 (2d Cir.1968), *cert. denied*, 394 U.S. 976, 89 S.Ct. 1454, 22 L.Ed.2d 756 (1969).

110. 445 U.S. at 231, 100 S.Ct. at 1116.

111. 445 U.S. at 231, 100 S.Ct. at 1116 (The "market information upon which he relied did not concern the earning power or operations of the target company, but only the plans of the acquiring company").

112. *See, e.g.,* Ian Ayres & Stephen Choi, Internalizing Outsider Trading, 101 Mich. L. Rev. 313 (2002).

113. SEC v. Yun, 327 F.3d 1263, 1276 n.27 (11th Cir. 2003) ("The dichotomization of insider trading liability based on the classical and misappropriation theories has grown over the last decade, with the SEC utilizing the misappropriation theory with increasing regularity. We disagree with the way the SEC and several courts have come to put insider trading cases in separate and discrete classical and misappropriation boxes. Congress did not intend to create a scheme of law that depends on the label or theory under which the SEC brings its case").

114. 445 U.S. at 231–235, 100 S.Ct. at 1116–1118.

115. 445 U.S. at 235–36, 100 S.Ct. at 1118, 1119. For a strong indication that it might not, *see* Moss v. Morgan Stanley Inc., 719 F.2d 5 (2d Cir.1983), *cert. denied*, 465 U.S. 1025, 104 S.Ct. 1280, 79 L.Ed.2d 684 (1984).

sized that this latter theory was not decided,[116] while Justice Brennan's concurrence[117] and the dissent[118] would have upheld the conviction had the conversion theory been presented to the jury. It thus appears that at least four of the Justices would have affirmed the conviction had these alternative theories been presented to the jury.[119] The Court's subsequent ruling in Dirks v. SEC[120] may provide a basis for a narrow view of the proper scope of Rule 10b–5 in insider trading cases. However, one post-*Chiarella* decision upheld an SEC complaint seeking injunctive relief and disgorgement of profits in an action against a proofreader who allegedly "misappropriated" tender offer information from a financial printer.[121] Unlike in *Dirks*, the defendant had been entrusted with information and used that information to his own advantage in breach of a duty. The essence of the misappropriation theory thus is the misuse of the information in breach of a duty to the source of the information. As the Supreme Court explained in a later decision, Rule 10b–5 is violated when, in breach of a duty to the source of confidential information, someone misappropriates that information for securities trading purposes.[123]

Difficult questions can arise in determining which relationships establish a fiduciary duty of confidentiality. As discussed elsewhere in this section, Rule 10b5–2 provides some guidance as to when the disclose or abstain obligation will apply. Of course, not every relationship is a fiduciary one creating such a position of trust and confidence. For example in one leading case, it was held that the relationship of a customer to his stock broker did not create a duty of confidentiality.[135] In another case, the court explained that a fiduciary relationship requires "some measure of superiority, dominance, or control." The court then went on to hold that co-members of an entrepreneurs' society did not create such a relationship.[136] In so ruling, the court indicated that not every confidentiality agreement will trigger the obligation. For example, insider trading liability will not arise out of a confidentiality agreement that is not taken as legally binding but rather as a statement of ethical and moral obligation.[137]

It is clear that a legally binding confidentiality agreement such as those routinely signed by investment bankers and other professionals can form the basis of liability for trading on the basis of information so provided. As

---

116.　445 U.S. at 238, 100 S.Ct. at 1119, 1120 (Stevens, J., concurring).

117.　*Id.* at 239, 100 S.Ct. at 1120 (Brennan, J., concurring).

118.　*Id.* at 240, 100 S.Ct. at 1120, 1121 (Burger, J., dissenting); *see also id.* at 245, 100 S.Ct. at 1123 (Blackmun and Marshall, dissenting).

119.　Justice Blackmun in his dissent, with Marshall joining, would have affirmed on the issues presented to the jury without reaching the other theories supported by Justices Brennan and Burger.

120.　463 U.S. 646, 103 S.Ct. 3255, 77 L.Ed.2d 911 (1983).

121.　SEC v. Materia, 745 F.2d 197 (2d Cir.1984), *cert. denied*, 471 U.S. 1053, 105 S.Ct. 2112, 85 L.Ed.2d 477 (1985).

123.　United States v. O'Hagan, 521 U.S. 642, 652, 117 S.Ct. 2199, 2207, 138 L.Ed.2d 724 (1997) ("The 'misappropriation theory' holds that a person commits fraud 'in connection with' a securities transaction, and thereby violates § 10(b) and Rule 10b–5, when he misappropriates confidential information for securities trading purposes in breach of a duty owed to the source of the information").

135.　United States v. Chestman, 947 F.2d 551 (2d Cir.1991), *cert. denied*, 503 U.S. 1004, 112 S.Ct. 1759, 118 L.Ed.2d 422 (1992).

136.　United States v. Kim, 173 F.Supp.2d 1035 (N.D.Cal.2001), *amended by,* 184 F.Supp.2d 1006 (N.D.Cal.2002).

137.　*Id.*

pointed out in SEC Rule 10b5–2, the duty to abstain from trading on information can arise form a contractual confidentiality obligation. Thus, for example, a brokerage firm's policy against employees trading on proprietary information can form the basis of insider trading violations.[138]

Another Supreme Court case reemphasized the principles of the *Chiarella* decision in conjunction with its analysis of tippee liability. In Dirks v. SEC,[139] the Court found that "a tippee assumes a fiduciary duty to the shareholders of a corporation * * * only when the insider has breached his fiduciary duty to the shareholders * * * and the tippee knows or should know that there has been a breach."[140] The Court explained further that insiders have not breached their fiduciary duty unless the purpose of their passing on the information was to obtain, directly or indirectly, some personal or economic benefit. The six-to-three decision in *Dirks* contained a vigorous dissent that would have applied the disclose-or-abstain rule.

Although the Supreme Court was equally divided on the 10b–5 claim in *Carpenter v. United States,* the Court was unanimous in finding that the misappropriation of information constituted a violation of federal Mail Fraud Act.[151] In affirming the mail fraud conviction, the Court reasoned that the information concerning the Heard on the Street column was clearly property belonging to Dow Jones, and that the reporter had a duty to safeguard that information. The breach of that duty accordingly amounted to a deprivation of Dow Jones' property right in contravention of the Mail Fraud Act. In reaching its decision under the Mail Fraud Act, the Supreme Court embraced the rationale underlying the New York decision in Diamond v. Oreamuno[152] allowing a corporation to recover the profits of insiders who traded on confidential information.

The long wait for the Supreme Court's resolution of the issue ended in 1997 with its decision in United States v. O'Hagan,[155] which upheld misappropriation as a basis for imposing Rule 10b–5 liability for trading on nonpublic information.

O'Hagan arose out of the prosecution of a partner in a law firm that was retained by a would-be tender offeror. The attorney, after having learned of the firm's client's planned takeover, purchased call options in the target company prior to the announcement of the tender offer. The indictment charged that the attorney had violated Rule 10b–5 and Rule 14e–3, which prohibits trading in advance of a tender offer;[156] he was also charged with violating the mail fraud statute. The Eighth Circuit overturned a conviction on all three counts.[157] The court of appeals's rejection of the Rule 10b–5 claim

138. *See, e.g.,* In the Matter of Goldman Sachs & Co., Sec. Exch. Act Rel. No. 34–48436, 2003 WL 22056978 (SEC Sept. 4, 2003) (settlement order).

139. 463 U.S. 646, 103 S.Ct. 3255, 77 L.Ed.2d 911 (1983).

140. 463 U.S. at 660, 103 S.Ct. at 3264. The Court went on to explain: "Thus, the test is whether the insider personally will benefit, directly or indirectly, from his disclosure. Absent some personal gain, there has been no breach of duty to stockholders. And absent a breach by the insider, there is no derivative breach [by the tippee]." *Id.*

151. Carpenter v. United States, 484 U.S. 19, 108 S.Ct. 316, 98 L.Ed.2d 275 (1987).

152. 24 N.Y.2d 494, 301 N.Y.S.2d 78, 248 N.E.2d 910 (1969).

155. 521 U.S. 642, 117 S.Ct. 2199, 138 L.Ed.2d 724 (1997).

156. 17 C.F.R. § 240.14e–3. Rule 14e–3 is discussed *infra.*

157. United States v. O'Hagan, 92 F.3d 612 (8th Cir.1996), rev'd 521 U.S. 642, 117 S.Ct. 2199, 138 L.Ed.2d 724 (1997).

was based on two grounds. First, the court stated that Rule 10b–5 requires a misrepresentation or nondisclosure. Secondly, the Eighth Circuit held that a duty owed to the source of the nonpublic information was not sufficient to satisfy section 10(b)'s requirement that the fraud be "in connection with the purchase or sale" of a security. The Supreme Court rejected both objections to the imposition of liability. The Court responded to the first objection by pointing out that trading on nonpublic information involves deceptive nondisclosure.[158] The deception that results from the misappropriation of information is based on a "feigning fidelity" to the source of the information and the fiduciary's failure to disclose plans to trade on the information.[159] Second, in addition to being premised on the necessary deceptive conduct, liability based on misappropriation satisfies the requirement that the violation be "in connection with the purchase or sale of *any* security" because it is not necessary to make a further link to "identifiable purchasers or sellers of securities."[160] The *O'Hagan* decision accordingly clarified that the duty which forms the basis of the Rule 10b–5 violation need not be owed to a purchaser or seller of securities. It is sufficient that the breach of duty is carried out through securities trading. The use of a securities transaction to effectuate the breach of the duty is a sufficient connection.

Were Congress to adopt a law prohibiting trading on material nonpublic information, the law would be much clearer. We could then have a precise definition of when such conduct will violate the law. However, until Congress acts, the misappropriation doctrine is a necessary evil considering the fact that Rule 10b–5 is the primary source of the insider trading prohibition. There is an unevenness in the application of the doctrine. For example, a broker who trades on information supplied by a customer has been held not to have violated Rule 10b–5[161] while a psychiatrist who trades on information supplied by a patient has violated the law. This is because there is not a duty of confidentiality attaching to the broker/customer relationship,[162] while a psychiatrist is subject to an obligation of patient confidentiality.[163] To say the least, it is strange that the securities laws uphold the Hippocratic oath and punish the psychiatrist for breaching it, but do not capture the equally guilty stock broker. The obvious irony here is that the securities laws were enacted to protect investors and regulate the brokerage industry, not to uphold concepts of medical ethics. Relying on Rule 10b–5 as the primary source of the insider trading prohibition causes this irony since the rule is based on fraud and thus requires a duty not to trade on the nonpublic information independent of the mere possession of the information. Whether a particular relation-

158. 521 U.S. at 653, 117 S.Ct. at 2208, 138 L.Ed.2d at 1274. The Court explained that the defendant's failure to disclose his personal trading to his law firm and his firm's client rendered that conduct "deceptive." *Id.*

159. 521 U.S. at 655, 117 S.Ct. at 2209, 138 L.Ed.2d at 1274.

160. 521 U.S. at 660, 117 S.Ct. at 2111, 138 L.Ed.2d at 1274.

161. United States v. Chestman, 947 F.2d 551 (2d Cir.1991), *cert. denied*, 503 U.S. 1004, 112 S.Ct. 1759, 118 L.Ed.2d 422 (1992). The court in *Chestman* also held that the husband/wife relationship did not create a duty of confidentiality. *Id.* This result was questioned in SEC v. Yun, 327 F.3d 1263 (11th Cir. 2003), which found that the spousal relationship on the facts before the court did create an expectation of confidentiality. In addition, SEC Rule 10b5–2 creates a presumption of confidentiality from a spousal relationship. 17 C.F.R. § 240.10b5–2.

162. United States v. Chestman, 947 F.2d 551 (2d Cir.1991), *cert. denied*, 503 U.S. 1004, 112 S.Ct. 1759, 118 L.Ed.2d 422 (1992).

163. SEC v. Brody, 1999 WL 1425401, [1999–2000 Transfer Binder] Fed. Sec. L. Rep. (CCH) ¶ 90,667 (D.D.C. 1999); United States v. Willis, 737 F.Supp. 269 (S.D.N.Y.1990).

ship is fiduciary in nature so as to trigger Rule 10b–5's disclose-or-abstain rule can depend on the facts of the particular case.[164]

In 1999, the SEC proposed Rule 10b5–2 to establish a nonexclusive safe harbor rule as to the scope of misappropriation liability.[165] The rule was adopted in 2000.[166] Under Rule 10b5–2, there are "three non-exclusive bases for determining that a duty of trust or confidence was owed by a person receiving information: (1) when the person agreed to keep information confidential; (2) when the persons involved in the communication had a history, pattern, or practice of sharing confidences that resulted in a reasonable expectation of confidentiality; and (3) when the person who provided the information was a spouse, parent, child, or sibling of the person who received the information, unless it were shown affirmatively, based on the facts and circumstances of that family relationship, that there was no reasonable expectation of confidentiality."[167] Family relationships thus can provide the basis for a confidential relationship sufficient to trigger insider trading liability.[168] The Eleventh Circuit did not go so far as to uphold Rule 10b5–2's presumption of confidentiality, but if, nevertheless held that a family relationship can create a sufficient expectation of confidentiality so as to trigger Rule 10b–5's disclose or abstain obligation.[169] It remains to be seen whether the rule's presumption will be upheld.

Rule 10b5–2 establishes a non-exclusive list of three situations in which a person has a duty of trust or confidence for purposes of the misappropriation theory of insider trading liability.[171] By its terms, Rule 10b5–2 applies to any insider trading allegation that is "based on the purchase or sale of securities on the basis of, or the communication of, material nonpublic information misappropriated in violation of a duty of trust or confidence."[172] A "duty of trust or confidence" exists where a person (1) obtains material nonpublic information from his or her spouse, parent, child or sibling, (2) has a history, pattern or practice of sharing confidences with the recipient of the material nonpublic information such that the recipient "knows or reasonably should know" that the person communicating the information to the recipient expects that the recipient will maintain the information in confidence; or (3) agrees to maintain information in confidence.[173] Accordingly, breach of a

---

164. SEC v. Sargent, 229 F.3d 68, 75–76 (1st Cir.2000) (jury question whether defendant making a promise not to divulge the information had a preexisting fiduciary duty).

165. *See* Selective Disclosure and Insider Trading, Sec. Exch. Act Rel. No. 34–42259 (SEC Dec. 20, 1999) (proposing release).

166. 17 C.F.R. § 240.10b5–2. *See* Selective Disclosure and Insider Trading, Sec. Exch. Act Rel. No. 34–43154, 2000 WL 1201556 (SEC Aug. 15, 2000) (adopting release). *See generally* Peter J. Romeo & Alan L. Dye, The SEC's New Insider Trading Rules, 34 Rev. Sec. & Commod. Reg. 1 (2001).

167. Selective Disclosure and Insider Trading, Sec. Exch. Act Rel. No. 34–42259 (SEC Dec. 20, 1999).

168. *See, e.g.,* SEC v. Yun, 327 F.3d 1263 (11th Cir. 2003) (whether communications between spouses were confidential was a jury question), *vacating,* SEC v. Yun, 130 F.Supp.2d 1348 (M.D.Fla.2001) (post-nuptial negotiations created confidential relationship so as to support insider trading liability can be based on a tip of information between husband and wife). *See also, e.g.,* Ray J. Grzebielski, Friends, Family Fiduciaries: Personal Relationships as a Basis for Insider Trading Violations, 51 Cath. U. L. Rev. 467 (2002).

169. SEC v. Yun, 327 F.3d 1263 (11th Cir. 2003)

171. 17 C.F.R. § 240.10b5–2.

172. 17 C.F.R. § 240.10b5–2.

173. *I*17 C.F.R. § 240.10b5–2.

confidentiality agreement can result in a violation of the insider trading prohibitions.[174]

Rule 10b5–2 thus establishes a bright-line rule under which the receipt of information from a spouse, parent, child or sibling will provide a sufficient basis for insider trading liability, assuming that all other elements are satisfied.[175] The rule further provides an affirmative defense that permits the family member to rebut the presumption that a duty of confidence exists by showing that he or she did not know, and reasonably should not have known, that the insider-family member communicating the information had an expectation of confidentiality.

§ 12.17[5] Insider Trading—Passing on Non–Public Information—Tipper and Tippee Liability

As discussed above, the Supreme Court in Dirks v. SEC[176] held that "a tippee assumes a fiduciary duty to the shareholders of a corporation * * * only when the insider has breached his fiduciary duty to the shareholders * * * and the tippee knows or should know that there has been a breach."[177] Corporate insiders do not breach a fiduciary duty unless the purpose of their passing on the information was to obtain, directly or indirectly, some personal or economic benefit.[178] The actions of the defendant in Dirks were major factors in exposing the massive Equity Funding fraud.[179] In Dirks, the insid-

---

174. See SEC v. Kirch, 263 F.Supp.2d 1144 (N.D. Ill. 2003). Cf., e.g., United States v. Kim, 173 F.Supp.2d 1035 (N.D.Cal.2001) amended, 184 F.Supp.2d 1006 (N.D.Cal.2002) (membership in group did not create confidential relationship).

175. See also, e.g., SEC v. Yun, 327 F.3d 1263 (11th Cir. 2003) (whether communications between spouses were confidential was a jury question), vacating, 130 F.Supp.2d 1348 (M.D.Fla. 2001) (post-nuptial negotiations created confidential relationship so as to support insider trading liability based on a tip of information between husband and wife).

176. 463 U.S. 646, 103 S.Ct. 3255, 77 L.Ed.2d 911 (1983).

177. 463 U.S. at 660, 103 S.Ct. at 3264. The Court went on to explain: "Thus, the test is whether the insider personally will benefit, directly or indirectly, from his disclosure. Absent some personal gain, there has been no breach of duty to stockholders. And absent a breach by the insider, there is no derivative breach [by the tippee]." Id.

178. See, e.g., SEC v. Yun, 327 F.3d 1263 (11th Cir. 2003) (jury question as to whether wife who tipped husband had the requisite intent to benefit so as to trigger tipper liability; also rejecting a different standard of liability for misappropriation cases as opposed to classic insider trading cases).

179. The defendant, an investment analyst, was investigating Equity Funding Corp. After an investigation including talks with various employees he realized that the company's assets had been fraudulently inflated. As described by the Court,

While Dirks was in Los Angeles, he was in touch regularly with William Blundell, the *Wall Street Journal's* Los Angeles bureau chief. Dirks urged Blundell to write a story on the fraud allegations. Blundell did not believe, however, that such a massive fraud could go undetected and declined to write the story. He feared that publishing such damaging hearsay might be libelous.

During the two-week period in which Dirks pursued his investigation and spread word of Secrist's charges, the price of Equity Funding stock fell from $26 per share to less than $15 per share. This led the New York Stock Exchange to halt trading on March 27. Shortly thereafter California insurance authorities impounded Equity Funding's records and uncovered evidence of the fraud. Only then did the Securities and Exchange Commission (SEC) file a complaint against Equity Funding and only then, on April 2 did the Wall Street Journal publish a front-page story based largely on information assembled by Dirks. Equity Funding immediately went into receivership.

The SEC began an investigation into Dirks' role in the exposure of the fraud. After a hearing by an administrative law judge, the SEC found that Dirks had aided and abetted violations of § 17(a) of the Securities Act of 1933, 15 U.S.C.A. § 77q(a), § 10(b) of the Securities Exchange Act of 1934, 15 U.S.C.A. § 78j(b) and SEC Rule 10b–5, 17 CFR § 240.10b–5 (1982), by

ers—former employees of the company in question—were motivated by a desire to expose the company's fraud; therefore, Dirks was not obligated to abstain from passing on the inside information disclosed to him.[180]

In order for a tippee to be held liable, there must have been some benefit to the tipper in making the tip.[181] The benefit does not have to be a tangible one, and thus a gift of the information to a friend or relative for purpose of making the trades is sufficient.[182] It is possible to establish liability based on a tip on the basis of circumstantial evidence. Thus, for example, circumstantial evidence supported a criminal conviction even absent any direct evidence of a conversation involving inside information.[183]

The application of tippee liability is not limited to cases of true insiders. Tippee and tipper liability also applies in the misappropriation context.[184] This is true even if the tippee is remote from the tipper so long as there is a direct tainted chain of information. Thus, a tip from a magazine employee about an upcoming article to a printer and then to three intermediaries nevertheless resulted in a Rule 10b–5 violation under the misappropriation theory.[185] In order to establish tippee liability, contact between a tipper and the tippee must be established.[186] If a tippee knows or has reason to know of the taint from the tipper, there is no additional need to show that the tippee owed a fiduciary duty to the tipper.[187]

The conflict has continued between a broad and narrow view of tipper and tippee liability. For example, some courts have fashioned the concept of "temporary insider" to deal with tippee accountability.[188] On the other hand, where defendant traded after having overheard a family conversation that conveyed inside information, there was no 10b–5 liability because the tipper had not breached a duty, and therefore there could be no derivative liability

---

repeating the allegations of fraud to members of the investment community who later sold their Equity Funding stock. The SEC concluded: "Where 'tippees'—(regardless of their motivation or occupation)—come into possession of material 'information that they know is confidential and know or should know came from a corporate insider,' they must either publicly disclose that information or refrain from trading." 21 S.E.C. Docket 1401, 1407 (1981) (footnote omitted) (quoting Chiarella v. United States, 445 U.S. 222, 230 n. 12, 100 S.Ct. 1108, 1115 n. 12, 63 L.Ed.2d 348 (1980)). Recognizing, however, that Dirks "played an important role in bringing [Equity Funding's] massive fraud to light," 21 S.E.C. Docket, at 1412, the SEC only censured him.

463 U.S. at 649–652, 103 S.Ct. at 3259–3260. *See also* Raymond L. Dirks & Leonard Gross, The Great Wall Street Scandal—Inside Equity Funding (1974).

180. The six-to-three decision in *Dirks* contained a vigorous dissent that would have applied the disclose or abstain rule.

181. Dirks v. SEC, 463 U.S. 646, 662, 103 S.Ct. 3255, 77 L.Ed.2d 911 (1983).

182. SEC v. Sargent, 229 F.3d 68, 79 (1st Cir.2000); SEC v. Warde, 151 F.3d 42, 48–49 (2d Cir.1998); United States v. Libera, 989 F.2d 596, 600 (2d Cir.1993), *cert. denied*, 510 U.S. 976, 114 S.Ct. 467, 126 L.Ed.2d 419 (1993).

183. United States v. McDermott, 245 F.3d 133 (2d Cir.2001).

184. This, of course, was the situation in United States v. Carpenter, 791 F.2d 1024 (2d Cir.1986), *affirmed by an equally divided court*, 484 U.S. 19, 108 S.Ct. 316, 98 L.Ed.2d 275 (1987) which is discussed in § 12.17[4] *supra*.

185. United States v. Falcone, 97 F.Supp.2d 297 (E.D.N.Y.2000).

186. *See* SEC v. Truong, 98 F.Supp.2d 1086 (N.D.Cal.2000) (insider was held to have violated Rule 10b–5, but lack of proof of contact precluded liability of insider's friend).

187. SEC v. Lambert, 38 F.Supp.2d 1348, 1351 (S.D.Fla.1999).

188. SEC v. Tome, 833 F.2d 1086 (2d Cir.1987), *affirming*, 638 F.Supp. 596 (S.D.N.Y.1986); SEC v. Lund, 570 F.Supp. 1397 (C.D.Cal.1983).

on behalf of the tippee.[189] Conversely, when the tipper has breached a duty and the tippee has reason to know of the breach, the tippee would be guilty of sufficient scienter to violate Rule 10b–5.[190] Similarly, a tippee will be held liable for trading on a tip that was a "gift" of confidential information passed on with the tippee's trading in mind.[191] Insider trading liability has been based on a tip from husband to wife and then in turn to a third party.[192]

In the words of one court, "It is not accurate to say that *Dirks* wrote the book on insider or outsider trading; it wrote one chapter with respect to one type of fraudulent trading."[193]

§ 12.17[6] Insider Trading in Advance of Tender Offers: Rule 14e–3

Following the Supreme Court's decision in Chiarella v. United States,[200] the SEC tried to avoid Rule 10b–5's duty requirement by adopting Rule 14e–3[201] to prohibit anyone other than the tender offeror from trading on the basis of advance information pertaining to a not-yet-announced tender offer. In one case, the Fourth Circuit upheld a preliminary injunction against a tender offer where the offer was based upon information that had been allegedly misappropriated from the target company, in violation of Rule 14e–3.[202] That rule, which has been challenged as going beyond the scope of the statute, was upheld by the Second, Seventh, and Ninth Circuits.[203]

The impact of Rule 14e–3 was further bolstered by the Supreme Court's decision in *United States v. O'Hagan*.[212] The Court there upheld the conviction of an attorney who traded on advance knowledge of a tender offer where the source of the information was a client of the firm. There was a companion conviction based on the misappropriation of the information in violation of Rule 10b–5. The decision in *O'Hagan* left open a significant question concerning the scope of Rule 14e–3, as it did not reach the question of whether the SEC's power to define prohibited conduct under Rule 14e–3 is broader than its authority under Rule 10b–5.[214] However, the case certainly invites the broad reading of Rule 14e–3.[215]

Also, Rule 14e–3 has been used to capture tippers as well as those who

189. SEC v. Switzer, 590 F.Supp. 756 (W.D.Okl.1984).

190. *See, e.g.,* SEC v. Warde, 151 F.3d 42 (2d Cir.1998).

191. SEC v. Maio, 51 F.3d 623 (7th Cir.1995).

192. SEC v. Yun, 327 F.3d 1263 (11th Cir. 2003) (whether communications between spouses were confidential was a jury question).

193. United States v. Winans, 612 F.Supp. 827, 842 (S.D.N.Y.1985), *affirmed,* 791 F.2d 1024 (2d Cir.1986), *affirmed,* 484 U.S. 19, 108 S.Ct. 316, 98 L.Ed.2d 275 (1987).

200. 445 U.S. 222, 100 S.Ct. 1108, 63 L.Ed.2d 348 (1980).

201. 17 C.F.R. § 240.14e–3.

202. Burlington Industries, Inc. v. Edelman, 1987 WL 91498, [1987 Transfer Binder] Fed.Sec. L.Rep. (CCH) ¶ 93,339 (4th Cir.1987), *affirming on the basis of the opinion below,* 666 F.Supp. 799 (M.D.N.C.1987).

203. SEC v. Maio, 51 F.3d 623 (7th Cir.1995) (reaffirming Rule 14e–3 as a valid exercise of rulemaking authority); SEC v. Peters, 978 F.2d 1162 (10th Cir.1992); United States v. Chestman, 947 F.2d 551 (2d Cir.1991), *cert. denied,* 503 U.S. 1004, 112 S.Ct. 1759, 118 L.Ed.2d 422 (1992).

212. 521 U.S. 642, 117 S.Ct. 2199, 138 L.Ed.2d 724 (1997).

214. 521 U.S. at 672, 117 S.Ct. at 2217, 138 L.Ed.2d at 1274.

215. *See, e.g.,* SEC v. Mayhew, 121 F.3d 44 (2d Cir.1997).

trade on the information.[216] It is not necessary that the defendant know that the nonpublic information in his or her possession relates to a tender offer.[217] It is sufficient to establish that the defendant had reason to know that the information related to a tender offer.[218] It has further been held that if the defendant traded while in knowing possession of nonpublic information concerning a pending tender offer, it is not necessary to establish that the defendant acted in breach of a fiduciary duty.[219]

In order to hold someone criminally accountable for a violation of Rule 14e–3, it must be established that the defendant knew that the shares that were purchased were the target of a tender offer.[220] A violation of Rule 14e–3 can form the basis of a private right of action under section 20A of the 1934 Act.[221] The private action may be brought by contemporaneous traders who sold while the illegal purchases were taking place.[222]

§ 12.17[7] Insider Trading: Private Remedies Under Rule 10b–5; Enhanced SEC Sanctions

Following on the heels of the Supreme Court's ruling in Dirks v. SEC,[228] the Second Circuit in Moss v. Morgan Stanley Inc.[229] held that someone who sells a target company's stock in the open-market prior to the tender offer's announcement does not have a 10b–5 claim against a non-insider tippee who purchased shares using nonpublic material information obtained from the tender offeror's investment advisor. In so holding, the court rejected the idea of a non-insider's duty to disclose to an open market seller based on a misappropriation theory or on the fact that the defendant owed a special duty to the plaintiff due to its status as a broker-dealer.

By 1988, the existence of a meaningful private remedy under Rule 10b–5 to redress insider trading violations was at best questionable. Congress was concerned with the apparently increasing number of instances in which individuals were taking undue advantage of nonpublic material information. Accordingly, Congress responded with two important pieces of legislation. The Insider Trading Sanctions Act of 1984[236] (ITSA) enhanced the government's ability to pursue insider trading. The Insider Trading and Securities Fraud Enforcement Act of 1988[237] continued this trend and also added an express private remedy. These important remedial provisions are discussed below.

---

216. SEC v. Falbo, 14 F.Supp.2d 508 (S.D.N.Y.1998).

217. SEC v. Sargent, 229 F.3d 68, 78, 79 (1st Cir.2000).

218. United States v. O'Hagan, 139 F.3d, 641, 650 (8th Cir.1998).

219. *See, e.g.,* SEC v. Thrasher, 152 F.Supp.2d 291, [2000–2001 Transfer Binder] Fed. Sec. L. Rep. (CCH) ¶ 91,367 (S.D.N.Y. 2001).

220. United States v. Cassese, 290 F. Supp.2d 443 (S.D.N.Y. 2003).

221. 15 U.S.C.A. § 78t–1(a). *See* § 12.17[7][B] *infra.*

222. Brody v. Transitional Hospitals Corp., 280 F.3d 997 (9th Cir.2002).

228. 463 U.S. 646, 103 S.Ct. 3255, 77 L.Ed.2d 911 (1983).

229. 719 F.2d 5 (2d Cir.1983), *cert. denied,* 465 U.S. 1025, 104 S.Ct. 1280, 79 L.Ed.2d 684 (1984).

236. Pub. L. No. 98–376, 98 Stat. 1264 (1984).

237. Pub.L. No. 100–704, 102 Stat. 4677 (1988).

§ 12.17[7][A] Enhanced Remedies and Penalties—The Insider Trading Sanctions Act of 1984

One backlash of the *Chiarella* and *Dirks* decisions has been a push for congressional enactment of stronger insider trading penalties. Legislation by Congress (The Insider Trading Sanctions Act of 1984,[238] or ITSA) permits the SEC to bring suit against anyone violating the 1934 Act or rules "by purchasing or selling a security while in possession of material nonpublic information."[239] The enhanced sanctions apply not only to the person who violates the Act by trading on the information, but also to someone who violates the Act by passing on the information to someone else to facilitate his or her trading on the information. The enhanced set of remedies for illegal insider trading further provide for both the disgorgement of any profit and the imposition of a civil penalty. The civil penalty in such a suit, which can be granted in addition to disgorgement of the ill-gotten gain, can be as high as trebling the profits gained or loss avoided by the defendant.[242] In addition, the 1984 amendments to the Exchange Act also increased the criminal penalties for insider trading.

The Insider Trading Sanctions Act of 1984 raises a number of interesting questions. For example: do successive actions for civil penalties under ITSA and for criminal violations based on the same transactions violate the constitutional prohibition against double jeopardy? Since the treble damage provision is a penalty (although denominated as civil in nature), there would appear to be an argument that it should be treated as criminal so that double jeopardy would apply. On the other hand, a Supreme Court decision subsequently held that there is a strong presumption to be given to a congressional designation of a sanction as civil.[247] Under the current approach, it is doubtful that even a treble penalty for insider trading violations would be considered criminal. In any event, it is clear that double jeopardy would not apply to a criminal action followed by an SEC suit for disgorgement of profits.[248] This is the case because it is recognized that a criminal fine is a different matter from the remedial considerations underlying a disgorgement action.[249]

§ 12.17[7][B] Controlling Person Liability; Private Remedies—Insider Trading and Securities Fraud Enforcement Act of 1988

Congress bolstered the remedies provided by the Insider Trading Sanction Act amendments of 1984 when it enacted the Insider Trading and Securities Fraud Enforcement Act of 1988[254] (ITSFEA). This legislation specifically addresses liability of employers and controlling persons.[255] Under the Insider Trading and Securities Fraud Enforcement Act of 1988, a court can

---

238. Pub. L. No. 98–376, 98 Stat. 1264 (1984).

239. 15 U.S.C.A. § 78u–1(a)(1), 78ff(a).

242. *See, e.g.*, SEC v. Lipson, 129 F.Supp.2d 1148, 1159 (N.D.Ill.2001) (imposing maximum treble penalty).

247. Hudson v. United States, 522 U.S. 93, 118 S.Ct. 488, 139 L.Ed.2d 450 (1997).

248. SEC v. Bilzerian, 814 F.Supp. 116 (D.D.C.1993).

249. *Id.*

254. Pub.L. No. 100–704, 102 Stat. 4677 (1988).

255. Controlling person liability under the Exchange Act generally is governed by section 20(a) of the Act. 15 U.S.C.A. § 78t(a). *See* § 12.24 *infra*.

impose the treble damage penalties for insider trading violations on a controlling person only if: (1) the controlling person knew or acted in reckless disregard of the fact that the controlled person was likely to engage in illegal insider trading and (2) the controlling person failed to take adequate precautions to prevent the prohibited conduct from taking place.[256] It is further provided that general principles of respondeat superior and section 20(a)[257] controlling person liability do not apply to actions brought for illegal insider trading activities.[258]

Perhaps the most significant aspect of the Insider Trading and Securities Fraud Enforcement Act is its applicability to private enforcement. The Insider Trading and Securities Fraud Enforcement Act of 1988 created an express private right of action in the hands of contemporaneous traders. Section 20A of the Exchange Act provides that anyone violating the Act or SEC rules while trading in possession of material, nonpublic information shall be liable to contemporaneous traders trading on the other side of the insider trader's transactions.[262] Thus, if the violator is selling, all contemporaneous purchasers can sue, while if the violator is purchasing, all contemporaneous sellers can sue.

Section 20A does not define precisely who qualifies as a contemporaneous trader. Arguably, in light of the remedy's prophylactic (rather than compensatory) purpose, that phrase should be construed relatively broadly.[264] Most decisions seem to agree that establishing trading within a week of the defendant's improper trading will be sufficient to satisfy the contemporaneous trading requirement.[265] However, others have utilized a shorter period of time.[266] Although there are a number of pre-ITSFEA decisions that take a narrow view of what constitutes contemporaneous transactions,[267] their relevance is at best questionable. Prior to the enactment of section 20A, civil liability for insider trading was based upon Rule 10b–5 and some direct or indirect duty running from the trader to the plaintiff. By contrast, in 1988, when Congress enacted this statutory basis of liability, it eliminated the need for such a duty running to the plaintiff. More importantly, the remedy focuses on preventing the insider from retaining his or her ill-gotten profits rather than upon compensation for any supposed injury to contemporaneous traders.

There is authority to support the proposition that option holders can have standing under section 20A with regard to the defendant's contemporaneous trading in the underlying stock.[268] One court held that a plaintiff whose only trades are with the defendant may not sue under section 20A as a supplement

---

256. 15 U.S.C.A. § 78u–1(b)(1).

257. 15 U.S.C.A. § 78t(a). *See* § 12.24 *infra.*

258. 15 U.S.C.A. § 78u–1(b)(2).

262. 15 U.S.C.A. § 78t–1(a).

264. In re American Business Computers Corp. Securities Litigation, 1994 WL 848690, [1995 Transfer Binder] Fed. Sec. L. Rep. (CCH) ¶ 98,839 (S.D.N.Y.1994) ("contemporaneously" may embrace the entire period while relevant inside information remains undisclosed).

265. *See, e.g.,* Feldman v. Motorola, Inc., 1994 WL 160115, [1993–1994 Transfer Binder] Fed. Sec. L. Rep. (CCH) ¶ 98,133 (N.D.Ill.1994).

266. *E.g.,* In re MicroStrategy Securities Litigation, 115 F.Supp.2d 620 (E.D.Va.2000) (purchase of stock three days after officer's sale at higher price was not "contemporaneous").

267. *See, e.g.,* Backman v. Polaroid Corp., 540 F.Supp. 667, 671 (D.Mass.1982) (trades two days apart were not sufficient).

268. *E.g.,* Samuelson Trading Corp. v. Waksal, 2004 WL 813534 (N.D. Ill. 2004).

to the Rule 10b–5 action.[269] However, when the plaintiff has other trades in addition to those with the defendant, he or she may bring a section 20A claim as a contemporaneous trader.[270]

Damages in an action under the express insider trading private remedy are limited to the profits or losses avoided by the illegal transactions[274] and are to be diminished by any disgorgement (as opposed to penalty) ordered in an SEC enforcement action.[275] Controlling person liability in such a private suit is governed by section 20(a) of the Act[276] rather than by the specific controlling person provisions applicable to SEC enforcement actions.[277] Liability under the express private remedy for illegal insider trading extends to both tippers and tippees who violate the act; the act further provides that their liability is joint and several.[278]

This relatively express private remedy supplements any other existing express or implied remedies.[279] The Act also provides that the private remedy does not limit the Commission's or Attorney General's authority to recover penalties (as opposed to disgorgement of profits) for improper use of material, nonpublic information.[280]

Section 21A(e) of the Exchange Act permits the payment of a bounty of up to ten percent of the penalty to private individuals who provide information leading to the imposition of the penalty.[281] The decision to award a bounty lies in the sole discretion of the SEC, except that persons associated with the Commission, Department of Justice, or a self-regulatory organization are not eligible to receive a bounty award.

§ 12.17[9] Summary—The Need for Clarification

The precise scope of Rule 10b–5 liability for trading on nonpublic information remains unclear. Although it is clear that scienter is required for a Rule 10b–5 violation,[304] the courts have been struggling with the extent of the knowledge required. Thus, for example, it is sufficient that a tipper knowingly breached a fiduciary duty, and it is not necessary that he or she was aware of the trader's intent to trade.[305] Similarly, it is sufficient that a tippee knows the information has been improperly communicated; it need not be shown that the tippee knew the precise source of the information.[306] It is not necessary to show that the tipper benefited from the transaction, it is sufficient to show that the tipper intended that the tippee trade on the information.[307]

---

269. Fujisawa Pharmaceuticals Co. v. Kapoor, 115 F.3d 1332, 1337 (7th Cir.1997).

270. *See* Samuelson Trading Corp. v. Waksal, 2004 WL 813534 (N.D. Ill. 2004).

274. 15 U.S.C.A. § 78t–1(b)(1).

275. 15 U.S.C.A. § 78t–1(b)(2).

276. 15 U.S.C.A. § 78t(a).

277. 15 U.S.C.A. § 78u–1(b).

278. 15 U.S.C.A. § 78t–1(c).

279. 15 U.S.C.A. § 78t–1(d).

280. 15 U.S.C.A. § 78t–1(e).

281. 15 U.S.C.A. § 78u–1(e).

304. *See* § 12.8 *supra.*

305. United States v. Libera, 989 F.2d 596 (2d Cir.1993), *cert. denied*, 510 U.S. 976, 114 S.Ct. 467, 126 L.Ed.2d 419 (1993).

306. United States v. Chestman, 947 F.2d 551 (2d Cir.1991), *cert. denied*, 503 U.S. 1004, 112 S.Ct. 1759, 118 L.Ed.2d 422 (1992) (decided under Rule 14e–3).

307. SEC v. Warde, 151 F.3d 42 (2d Cir.1998), (relying on *Dirks*). *See also, e.g.*, SEC v. Maio, 51 F.3d 623 (7th Cir.1995) (gift of information was sufficient to create tipper liability); Stevens v.

As discussed earlier, in two of its insider trading decisions, the Supreme Court made it clear that the mere possession of inside information will not trigger insider trading liability. There must be some actual wrongdoing by an insider or a tippee acting in furtherance of the improper use of confidential information.[308] The Court has yet to deal with the question of who is an insider.

§ 12.18 Liability for Material Misstatements and Omissions of Fact in Documents Filed With the SEC—Section 18(a) of the Exchange Act

Section 18(a) of the Exchange Act[1] imposes liability upon anyone responsible for material misstatement or omission of fact in connection with any document required to be filed with the Commission under the terms of the Exchange Act.[2] The section 18(a) cause of action is available to any investor who, after having read the faulty document filed, actually relies upon statements in the document and is therefore injured. The courts have held that section 18(a) requires an "eyeball" test; that is, the plaintiff must have actual knowledge of and reliance upon the materials filed with the Commission, or a copy thereof; it is not sufficient that the plaintiff saw similar information contained in other documents prepared by the issuer.[3] Reliance based on a "fraud on the market" theory may be the foundation for a remedy under Rule 10b–5,[4] but will not satisfy section 18(a)'s requirements.

Section 18(a) applies to documents that must be filed with the Commission pursuant to section 15(d),[6] as well as to the Act's registration and periodic reporting requirements and SEC rules promulgated thereunder.[7] Although courts have imposed the "eyeball" requirement under section 18(a), it is not necessary that the plaintiff see the actual document on file; a copy will suffice.

Section 18(a) does not apply, however, to annual reports that must be sent to shareholders and filed with the SEC, unless the report is incorporated into the proxy statement or other proxy solicitation materials which are considered "filed" documents under section 18(a).[9] Not all required disclo-

---

O'Brien Environmental Energy, Inc., 1999 WL 310550, [1999 Transfer Binder] Fed. Sec. L. Rep. (CCH) ¶ 90,475 (E.D. Pa. 1999) (sufficiently alleging tipper/tippee liability).

308. *See also* Rule 10b5–1, 17 C.F.R. § 240.10b5–1, which requires that the defendant have used the information in making the trades; mere possession is not sufficient.

§ 12.18

1. 15 U.S.C.A. § 78r(a).

See § 1.8 *supra* for an overview of private remedies available under the 1933 and 1934 Acts.

2. Section 18(a) applies to documents "filed pursuant to this title," but does not apply to filing under the 1933 Act or any other of the securities laws. Nor does section 18(a) apply to the annual report disseminated to shareholders under the proxy rules. 17 C.F.R. §§ 240.14a–3(c), 14c–3(b).

3. Ross v. A.H. Robins Co., 607 F.2d 545, 552 (2d Cir.1979); Heit v. Weitzen, 402 F.2d 909, 916 (2d Cir.1968), *cert. denied*, 395 U.S. 903, 89 S.Ct. 1740, 23 L.Ed.2d 217 (1969).

4. *See, e.g.,* Panzirer v. Wolf, 663 F.2d 365 (2d Cir.1981), *vacated as moot*, 459 U.S. 1027, 103 S.Ct. 434, 74 L.Ed.2d 594 (1982).

6. 15 U.S.C.A. § 78o(d).

7. 15 U.S.C.A. §§ 78*l*, 78m(a). *See* §§ 9.2, 9.3 *supra*.

9. *See* 17 C.F.R. § 240.14a–3(c). *See also* section 14(c), 15 U.S.C.A. § 78n(c) (information to be furnished to securities holders in lieu of proxy statement). *See* §§ 10.6, 10.8 *supra*. The broad definition of proxy solicitation materials is discussed in § 10.2 *supra*. *See* 17 C.F.R. § 240.14a–1.

sures are contained in filed documents. Thus, for example, a company's annual report to shareholders[10] is not a filed document and thus cannot form the basis for section 18 liability unless the reader gathers the information in question from reading the 10K annual report that is filed with the Commission. Even with respect to disclosures contained in SEC filings, the SEC has identified certain disclosures as not constituting filed documents.[11] Thus, for example, financial information required by Part I of Form 10–Q and Form 10–QSB are deemed not to be "filed" documents for the purpose of section 18(a) liability.[12]

Since section 18(a) applies only to documents that must be filed with the Commission under the Exchange Act, it is necessarily limited to companies reporting under the Act. Section 18(a) not only imposes liability upon the issuer or other person filing the document, but also upon "any person who shall make or cause to be made" any misstatement or omission in "any application, report, or document filed. * * * "[13]This means that liability will extend to the company's officers and directors and especially to those who must sign the filed documents. A significant development here is that, in addition to the issuer's principal executive officers, now a majority of the board of directors must sign the annual 10K filing.

§ 12.19 Corporate Affirmative Disclosure Obligations and Accountability

§ 12.19[1] Affirmative Disclosure Obligations

As was pointed out in an earlier chapter of this treatise,[1] issuers subject to the registration requirements of section 12 of the Exchange Act[2] must file periodic reports with the Commission pursuant to section 13 of the Act.[3] Section 16(a)[4] further requires officers, directors, and ten percent beneficial owners of registered reporting companies to file reports of all transactions in the issuer's shares. In addition, section 13(d)[5] requires filings by any person acquiring five percent of an equity security subject to the registration and reporting requirements, and section 14(d)[6] imposes filing requirements in connection with tender offers. These filings are publicly available.

In the absence of a filing requirement, there is no affirmative obligation to disclose material information until the next quarterly report is due, except for the limited number of items that must be disclosed in interim reports on Form 8–K. The mandatory disclosure items in these interim reports has

10. 17 C.F.R. § 240.14a–3(b). *See* § 10.6[2] *supra.*

11. 17 C.F.R. § 240.13a–13(d).

12. *Id. See* In re Stone & Webster, Inc., Securities Litigation, 253 F.Supp.2d 102 (D. Mass. 2003).

13. 15 U.S.C.A. § 78r(a).

§ 12.19

1. *See* chapter 9 *supra.*

2. 15 U.S.C.A. § 78l. *See* § 9.2 *supra.*

3. 15 U.S.C.A. § 78m. *See* § 9.3 *supra.*

4. 15 U.S.C.A. § 78p(a). *See* § 13.2 *infra.*

5. 15 U.S.C.A. § 78m(d). *See* § 11.2 *supra.*

6. 15 U.S.C.A. § 78n(d). *See* § 11.5 *supra.*

expanded. Section 409 of the Sarbanes–Oxley Act of 2002[9] provides that the SEC should promulgate rules, as it deems "necessary or useful for the protection of investors and in the public interest," to provide for "real-time" disclosure of "information concerning material changes in the financial condition or operations of the issuer, in plain English, which may include trend and qualitative information and graphic presentations."[10] Even before this legislative impetus, the Commission began moving more towards a system of continuous rather than periodic reporting when it proposed expanding the items that have to be disclosed promptly on Form 8–K.[11] As of this writing, the Form 8–K mandatory disclosures have expanded and are likely to continue to be amended to include additional items.

Until the adoption of section 13(a)(*l*) of the 1934 Act,[23] the Exchange Act did not contain an express requirement for prompt disclosure. Section 13(a)(*l*) authorizes SEC rulemaking to require real time disclosure of material changes in financial condition,[24] but is not an across-the-board-requirement that a corporation report material information that is not otherwise required by the periodic reporting and shareholder information requirements. Thus, there is no affirmative duty to disclose many types of material developments until the next quarterly report. In contrast, the rules of the major stock exchanges expressly require corporations to make timely disclosure of all information that would be material to the reasonable investor.[25] However, the violation of the exchange listing requirements can lead only to sanctions by the exchange which have rarely been imposed for this type of violation alone. The SEC does not have enforcement power to pursue violations of the exchange listing requirements.

The above-mentioned interim prompt disclosure requirements are not supplemented by additional requirement to be implied from Rule 10b–5. Whether Rule 10b–5 alone is sufficient to trigger a similar affirmative duty of disclosure is, at most, highly doubtful. As discussed below, the language of Rule 10b–5 does not provide any basis for such an affirmative disclosure requirement. The absence of an affirmative disclosure requirement in Rule 10b–5 is particularly significant with regard to companies which are not subject to the New York or American Stock Exchange rules.

SEC Rule 10b–5 embodies the 1934 Act's general antifraud proscription. It prohibits fraud and material misstatements in connection with the purchase or sale of a security.[33] As discussed more fully below, the overwhelming majority of authority supports the position that the rule does not by itself impose an affirmative duty to speak, and this most certainly is the proper view.

---

9.   Sarbanes–Oxley Act of 2002, Pub. Law 107–204, § 409 (July 30, 2002).

10.   *Id.,* adding 1934 Act § 13(a) (*l*), 15 U.S.C.A. § 78m(*l*).

11.   *See* Proposed Amendments to Form 8–K, Sec. Act Rel. No. 33–8106; Sec. Exch. Act Rel. No. 34–46084; 67 FR 42914–01, 2002 WL 1361660 (F.R.) (SEC June 25, 2002).

23.   15 U.S.C.A. § 78m(*l*), added by the Sarbanes–Oxley Act of 2002, Pub. Law 107–204, § 409 (July 30, 2002).

24.   *Id.*

25.   N.Y.S.E. Company Manual, Fed.Sec.L.Rep. (CCH) ¶ 23,121 (1977); American Stock Exchange Company Guide (CCH) ¶ 10,121; Sec.Exch.Act Rel. No. 34–8995 (Oct. 15, 1970).

33.   17 C.F.R. § 240.10b–5. *See* § 12.3 *supra.*

SEC Rule 10b–5(a) and (c)[34] deal with acts and practices that constitute fraud or deceit. Rule 10b–5(b) prohibits materially misleading statements and materially misleading omissions from statements made. Rule 10b–5 does not by itself impose affirmative disclosure requirements absent some independent duty to disclose, such as one imposed by a line-item disclosure requirement of an applicable SEC required filing.[35] Mere nondisclosure, absent an independent duty such as a line-item disclosure mandate, contemporaneous insider trading,[36] or some other collateral activity, is insufficient to establish a violation of Rule 10b–5.[37] For example, Rule 10b–5 has been interpreted to impose a "disclose or abstain rule"[38] in insider trading cases. Nevertheless, unless a company is trading in its own shares, the disclose or abstain rule does not trigger a duty of disclosure. It follows that in the ordinary course of conducting company business, there is no duty to disclose. Even the corporate law that imposes fiduciary duties on corporate directors is not sufficient, standing alone, to impose an affirmative obligation to speak under Rule 10b–5.[39] However, when a corporation repurchases its own shares, it stands in a fiduciary relationship to the selling shareholders that is sufficient to trigger a Rule 10b–5 disclosure obligation.[40]

In relevant part, Rule 10b–5(b) provides that it is unlawful "to omit to state a material fact necessary *in order to make the statements made,* in light of the circumstances under which they were made, not misleading."[41] These words clearly seem to contemplate that in order to create liability for omission there must be some statement in which the material facts do not appear. Thus, even though some observers may have taken a more expansive view of the rule and have indicated that an affirmative disclosure duty should be found to exist,[42] the company may avoid liability for keeping silent absent an independent basis for the duty to disclose the information.

This absence of an affirmative company disclosure obligation under Rule 10b–5 is further strengthened by the Supreme Court's rule that the mere

---

34. 17 C.F.R. § 240.10b–5(a), (c). Rule 10b–5(c) prohibits conduct that operates as a fraud. It can be argued that mere silence and nondisclosure of material information is not a fraud but nevertheless has the same impact as fraud and thus operates as a fraud in violation of Rule 10b–5(c). There is no reported decision adopting such a view.

35. *See, e.g.,* Blanchard v. Edgemark Financial Corp., 2001 WL 587861 *5, [2000–2001 Transfer Binder] Fed. Sec. L. Rep. (CCH) ¶ 91,349 (N.D. Ill. 2001) quoting James D. Cox, Thomas Lee Hazen & F. Hodge O'Neal, Corporations § 12.11 (2000).

36. *See* § 12.17 *supra.*

37. *See, e.g.,* National Union Fire Insurance Co. v. Turtur, 892 F.2d 199 (2d Cir.1989).

38. *See* § 12.17 *supra.*

39. Blanchard v. Edgemark Financial Corp., 158 F.Supp.2d 297, 302 [2000–2001 Transfer Binder] Fed. Sec. L. Rep. (CCH) ¶ 91,349 (N.D. Ill. 2001). *But cf., e.g.,* Powers v. British Vita, P.L.C., 57 F.3d 176, 189 (2d Cir.1995) (directors owed fiduciary duty to plaintiff minority shareholder to disclose recapitalization plan that affected value of options issued to plaintiff); Rizzo v. MacManus Group, Inc., 158 F.Supp.2d 297, 2001 WL 314624 *5 (S.D.N.Y.2001).

40. Jordan v. Duff & Phelps, Inc., 815 F.2d 429, 435 (7th Cir.1987) ("[c]lose corporations buying their own stock, like knowledgeable insiders of closely held firms buying from outsiders, have a fiduciary duty to disclose material facts"); Rizzo v. MacManus Group, Inc., 158 F.Supp.2d 297, 302, 2001 WL 314624 *5 (S.D.N.Y.2001).

41. 17 C.F.R. § 240.10b–5(b) (emphasis supplied).

42. This was the contention of the issuer in *Texas Gulf Sulphur* with regard to why it issued a press release regarding a mineral find before all the facts were in. The court never reached this issue because it found the press release to have been materially misleading. SEC v. Texas Gulf Sulphur, 401 F.2d 833 (2d Cir.1968), *cert. denied,* 394 U.S. 976, 89 S.Ct. 1454, 22 L.Ed.2d 756 (1969). *Cf.* Comment, Liability Under Rule 10b–5 for Negligently Misleading Corporate Releases: A Proposal for the Apportionment of Losses, 122 U.Pa.L.Rev. 162 (1973).

possession of confidential inside information is not sufficient to trigger the duty to disclose or abstain from trading.[44] As one court has aptly explained, "[a]bsent a specific duty to disclose, even the most material information imaginable may be withheld from the public."[45]

In the absence of an independent duty[48] to disclose material information, the inability of 10b–5 to impose an affirmative disclosure obligation permits continued corporate silence.[49]

Once a company chooses to make a statement, Rule 10b–5 comes into play. Thus, for example, once a statement has been made by the issuer or one of its representatives, there may be a continuing duty to update and/or correct the information that was previously disseminated.[62] Furthermore, when the initial disclosure has been made in an SEC filing pursuant to a line-item disclosure requirement, the curative disclosure must be made in the appropriate manner, which frequently will require the filing of an amended disclosure form.[63] The duty to correct erroneous information does not mean that once some disclosures have been made, all facts that might be of interest to investors must be disclosed. The duty of further disclosure applies only when failure to do so would make the statement previously made materially misleading in light of subsequent developments.[64] Although Rule 10b–5 standing alone may not trigger an affirmative duty to disclose, a company that wants to suppress information that would be relevant to investors must be mindful of the above-mentioned disclosure requirements.

§ 12.19[2] Responding to Market Rumors

Particularly knotty disclosure problems face publicly traded issuers when there are market rumors concerning a company's securities, its fundamental condition, or possible takeover activity.[65] As discussed above, Rule 10b–5 does not create an affirmative disclosure obligation. However, when approached by exchange officials, the press, market researchers, or securities analysts, the company and its representatives are faced with a dilemma. In light of the repeated reaffirmation of a materiality standard based upon those facts that a reasonable investor would deem significant in making an investment decision,[67] denying that negotiations are taking place is not a viable alternative.

---

44. Dirks v. SEC, 463 U.S. 646, 103 S.Ct. 3255, 77 L.Ed.2d 911 (1983); Chiarella v. United States, 445 U.S. 222, 100 S.Ct. 1108, 63 L.Ed.2d 348 (1980).

45. Polak v. Continental Hosts, Ltd., 613 F.Supp. 153, 156 (S.D.N.Y.1985).

48. See, e.g., Blanchard v. Edgemark Financial Corp., 192 F.R.D. 233, 2000 WL 433491, 2000 WL 1060827, [1999–2000 Transfer Binder] Fed. Sec. L. Rep. (CCH) ¶ 90,991 (N.D. Ill. 2000) (bank directors owned duty of disclosure to holders of voting trust certificates).

49. See, e.g., Cooperman v. Individual, Inc., 171 F.3d 43, 47 (1st Cir.1999).

62. See, e.g., Stransky v. Cummins Engine Co., 51 F.3d 1329 (7th Cir.1995).

63. See, e.g., Kaufman v. Cooper Cos., Inc., 719 F.Supp. 174 (S.D.N.Y.1989) (quarterly report did not cure misstatements in proxy material sent out 15 days earlier).

64. Weiner v. The Quaker Oats Co., 129 F.3d 310 (3d Cir.1997) (company had duty to update debt-equity ratio that would result from pending purchase of another company; however, slight variation from original projection was immaterial); Backman v. Polaroid Corp., 910 F.2d 10 (1st Cir.1990).

65. E.g., In re Time Warner, Inc. Securities Litigation, 9 F.3d 259 (2d Cir.1993).

67. Basic, Inc. v. Levinson, 485 U.S. 224, 108 S.Ct. 978, 99 L.Ed.2d 194 (1988), on remand, 871 F.2d 562 (6th Cir.1989).

It seems clear that issuers have no independent obligation to correct rumors that cannot be traced back to the issuer or its representatives.[68] However, the situation is different when the issuer elects to speak. Once a statement has been made, the duty to correct may arise. When presented with a question about market rumors, companies have two alternatives. The company can, of course, respond with full disclosure, which in the case of preliminary negotiations or other sensitive business developments, might be counterproductive. Alternatively, the company can issue a "no comment" response. It has been observed that while the "no comment" response may be necessary for business reasons, as issuers develop increasing "no comment" policies, less information will be filtered into the market.[69] On the other hand, the absence of information clearly is preferable to the presence of misleading information.

Even a "no comment" response will not always be a safe harbor. If the issuer, or its agents, is responsible for leaks of sensitive information or market rumors, the SEC takes the position that the company is under a duty to correct any misinformation.[70] Although this proposition has not been definitively tested in the courts, it reflects a proper reading of the company's obligations. Thus, companies must take care to manage their proprietary information, not only for insider trading reasons but also to prevent being forced into premature disclosures by the existence of market rumors due to leaked information. Caution dictates that public companies not only develop information policies, including the creation of an information ombudsman, but also it is wise to limit the issuer's personnel who are authorized to divulge information or respond to outside questions.

Companies are thus placed in a very difficult position. When approached by a member of the press or a securities analyst, the issuer may not be able to get away with a "no comment" response. If a company is engaged in merger negotiations and, for example, has an upcoming meeting with securities analysts and decides to cancel the meeting, if the cancellation results in rumors, is the company in a position that it now has to come forward and clarify the facts behind the rumors? Some attorneys suggest that as a preventive measure, public companies adopt a policy of not commenting on acquisitions negotiations. Thus, when a question is posed, silence by the company can be supported by a recitation of the policy.

Another possible solution that has been suggested is for the SEC to adopt a safe harbor rule governing companies' responses to such inquiries. However, it seems difficult, if not impossible, to fashion a meaningful safe harbor (other than implementation of a "no comment" policy) in light of the highly factual nature of each situation. In the absence of such a rule, any response other than silence or "no comment" may result in a securities law violation. Of course, periodic reporting obligations may in and of themselves trigger the duty to disclose once the materiality threshold has been reached. There is

---

68. *See, e.g.,* Raab v. General Physics Corp., 4 F.3d 286, 288 (4th Cir.1993); Electronic Specialty Co. v. International Controls Corp., 409 F.2d 937 (2d Cir.1969) (no duty for company to correct published misstatement not directly attributable to it) Warshaw v. Xoma Corp., 856 F.Supp. 561 (N.D.Cal.1994), *reversed on other grounds,* 74 F.3d 955 (9th Cir.1996) (no duty to correct misinformation from a third party).

69. *See, e.g.,* Little Can be Done to Stop Rumors, Exchange Officials, Others Tell Forum, 18 Sec. Reg. & L. Rep. (BNA) 253 (Feb. 25, 1986).

70. *See* In re Carnation Co., Sec. Exch. Act Rel. No. 34–22214, [1985–86 Transfer Binder] Fed. Sec. L. Rep. (CCH) ¶ 83,801 (July 8, 1985).

thus a different process that applies in determining the necessity of disclosure when dealing with line-item disclosures in required filings as opposed to under the antifraud provisions generally.

§ 12.19[3] Adoption of and Entanglement With Statements by Third Parties

Just as issuers have no duty to respond to rumors, they do not have a duty to respond to analysts' statements so long as the issuer had no involvement with the analyst making the statement. In order to be held accountable as a primary violator, the issuer or its representative must have either created the misstatement or have had the misstatement publicly attributed to it.[73] Thus, for example, there is no duty with regard to an analyst's projection unless the issuer has adopted the projection or has otherwise "entangled" itself with the analyst's opinions.[74] However, once the company or a representative responds to the analyst's statements, liability can follow if there is sufficient involvement by the company. On the other hand, the mere fact that a third party obtained information from company insiders is not by itself sufficient to create entanglement so as to hold the company liable for the third party's materially misleading statements.[75] Entanglement is established, however, "when company officials 'intentionally foster a mistaken belief concerning a material fact.' "[76]

Liability can exist even without an express adoption of the analysts' or other third party statements if a company's management knowingly conveys materially misleading information to the analysts or other third party making a materially misleading statement or projection.[77] However, when the analysts' statements are based primarily on their own interpretation, vague statements of optimism by the company's executives will not make the company liable.[78] Similarly, a blanket statement in a third party's statement that the report was approved by management will not in itself be sufficient to hold management accountable for the analyst's report.[79] Mere allegations that management was in contact with analysts is not sufficient to hold management or the company liable for the analysts' statements.[80] However, such contact can be a first step in establishing entanglement so as to hold the company accountable for third-party statements about the company.

A statement by a company official that he is "comfortable" with analysts' estimates can form the basis of liability for over-optimism.[81] Such a statement

---

73. *E.g.,* Cooper v. Pickett, 137 F.3d 616, 624 (9th Cir.1997) (company could be held liable for misleading analysts into making materially false statements).

74. *See, e.g.,* In re Navarre Corp. Securities Litigation, 299 F.3d 735 (8th Cir.2002), (failure to allege linkage between analysts' statements and the company).

75. In re Cabletron Systems, Inc. Securities Litigation, 311 F.3d 11, 38 (1st Cir. 2002) (but upholding claim of entanglement).

76. In re Cabletron Systems, Inc. Securities Litigation, 311 F.3d 11, 38 (1st Cir. 2002), quoting from Elkind v. Liggett & Myers, Inc., 635 F.2d 156, 163–164 (2d Cir. 1980).

77. In re Allaire Corp. Securities Litigation, 224 F.Supp.2d 319, 339–340 (D. Mass. 2002).

78. In re Northern Telecom Ltd. Securities Litigation, 42 F.Supp.2d 234, 236–237 (S.D.N.Y. 1998).

79. Copperstone v. TCSI Corp., 1999 WL 33295869 (N.D.Cal.1999).

80. In re Number Nine Visual Technology Corp. Securities Litigation, 51 F. Supp. 2d 1 (D.Mass.1999).

81. In re Burlington Coat Factory Securities Litigation, 114 F.3d 1410, 1428 (3d Cir.1997), relying on Virginia Bankshares, Inc. v. Sandberg, 501 U.S. 1083, 111 S.Ct. 2749, 115 L.Ed.2d 929 (1991) for the proposition that opinions of management can be actionable.

can operate as an adoption of the analyst's opinion.[82] However, merely stating that it was comfortable with analysts' estimates does not make the company liable simply because the estimate turns out to be wrong.[83]

§ 12.19[4] SEC Regulation FD—Prohibition on Selective Disclosure

SEC Regulation FD was adopted in 2000 in order to level the playing field concerning access to information about a company that comes from the company.[84] Under Regulation FD,[85] selective disclosure by a company to analysts or other third parties is no longer permitted. Regulation FD requires companies who make disclosures to analysts to make prompt public announcements so that all investors can have access to the same information. Regulation FD, although controversial,[87] is not a novel idea. For example, the New York Stock Exchange has for a long time had a policy against selective disclosure to analysts.[88]

Regulation FD applies only to "communications by the company's senior management, its investor relations professionals, and others who regularly communicate with market professionals and security holders." Further, Regulation FD applies only to a company's "communications with market professionals, and holders of the issuer's securities under circumstances in which it is reasonably foreseeable that the security holders will trade on the basis of the information." Accordingly, Regulation FD does not apply when the company is communicating with the press, rating agencies, and ordinary-course business communications with customers and suppliers.

§ 12.19[5] Company Web Sites

An issue related to entanglement is the accountability of corporate management for material that appears on the Internet. It is clear that companies that maintain web sites must be careful to monitor the content of the sites. Material misstatements and omissions will satisfy the "in connection with" requirement. There thus can be serious securities law consequences for the content on company sponsored web sites. Another issue is the extent to which links on a company sponsored web site to third party sites will constitute an adoption of the statements contained on those sites.[109] At the very least, management should be careful to disclaim responsibility for statements that may appear in third party web sites that are linked to the company web site.

In 2000, the SEC issued an interpretative release that among other things, addressed company web sites.[110] The Commission announced that it will consider a number of factors in determining whether a hyperlink on a

---

82. In re Burlington Coat Factory Securities Litigation, 114 F.3d 1410, 1429 (3d Cir.1997).

83. Plevy v. Haggerty, 38 F.Supp.2d 816 (C.D.Cal.1998).

84. 17 C.F.R. §§ 243.100–243.103. *See* Selective Disclosure and Insider Trading, Sec. Exch. Act Rel. No. 34–43154, 2000 WL 1201556 (SEC Aug. 15, 2000) (adopting release).

85. 17 C.F.R. § 243.100–243.103.

87. For example, SEC Commissioner Unger dissented from the regulation's adoption.

88. NYSE Listed Company Manual ¶ 202.02(A).

109. *See, e.g.,* Eileen Smith Ewing, Fraud on the Cybermarket: Liability for Hyperlinked Misinformation Under Rule 10b–5, 56 Bus. Law. 375 (2000).

110. Use of Electronic Media, Sec. Act Rel. No. 33–7856, 2000 WL 502290 (SEC April 28, 2000).

company sponsored web site that links to a third party's web site will operate as the company's adoption of the information contained on the third party web site. The context of the hyperlink must be considered. Specifically, does the corporation expressly adopt or endorse the statements that may be contained on the third party web site that is hyperlinked to the company web site? If there is such an endorsement, then the corporation may be held accountable by statements made on the third party web site.[111] The Commission further takes the position that if the hyperlink exists within a portion of the web site that constitutes a document that satisfies delivery requirements under the federal securities laws, the company will be deemed to have adopted the statements contained on the hyperlinked third party web site.[112] Additionally, if the company is embarking on an offering of securities and is "in registration" under the Securities Act of 1933,[113] then there is a strong presumption that the company has adopted statements that are contained in web sites that are hyperlinked to the company's web site.[114]

Another factor in determining whether information contained in a third-party web site will be attributed to the company is the likelihood of confusion. For example, if the hyperlink from the company-sponsored web site presents a separate screen announcing that the viewer is leaving the company's web site, there is less likelihood that the company will be deemed to have adopted the statements on the third party's web site.[115] Company disclaimers of liability for statements contained in hyperlinked third-party web sites will not in and of themselves insulate the company from liability if there are other indications that the company has somehow endorsed the statements.[116]

The manner in which the hyperlinked information is presented will be considered in determining whether hyperlinked information from third-party web sites should be attributed to the company whose web page contains the hyperlink. A company's selectivity in determining which third-party sites are hyperlinked to the company web site may act in favor of attributing the information on the third-party site to the company. For example, if the hyperlinked web sites do not represent the broad range of information that may be available, this selective screening process for hyperlinked sites may result in attribution of third-party web site content to the company. The screen design for a company's web site that provides hyperlinks will also be a

---

111. *Id.*

112. *Id.*

113. The period during which an issuer is "in registration" begins "at least from the time an issuer reaches an understanding with the broker-dealer which is to act as managing underwriter prior to the filing of a registration statement and the period ... during which dealers must deliver a prospectus." Sec.Act Rel. No. 33–5180, Fed.Sec.L.Rep. (CCH) ¶ 3056 (Aug. 16, 1971).

114. Use of Electronic Media, Sec. Act Rel. No. 33–7856, 2000 WL 502290 (SEC April 28, 2000).

115. *Id.*:

Hyperlinked information on a third-party web site may be less likely to be attributed to an issuer if the issuer makes the information accessible only after a visitor to its web site has been presented with an intermediate screen that clearly and prominently indicates that the visitor is leaving the issuer's web site and that the information subsequently viewed is not the issuer's. Similarly, there may be less likelihood of confusion about whether an issuer has adopted hyperlinked information if the issuer ensures that access to the information is preceded or accompanied by a clear and prominent statement from the issuer disclaiming responsibility for, or endorsement of, the information. In contrast, the risk of investor confusion is higher when information on a third-party web site is framed or inlined.

116. *Id.*

factor. The more attention that is drawn to a hyperlink to a third party web site, the more likely it is that the information on that web site will be deemed to have been adopted by the company providing the hyperlink.[118]

An issue related to corporate web sites is the treatment of chat rooms that allow real-time online conversations. Questions can arise with respect to comments, projections and statements that may be made in a chat room sponsored by the company.

§ 12.20 Corporate Mismanagement, Rule 10b–5 and the Deception Requirement

§ 12.20[1] When Corporate Mismanagement Can be Securities Fraud

Although directed at securities fraud, over its history Rule 10b–5 has had a role to play in preventing corporate mismanagement that results in deception in connection with a purchase or sale of securities. While the high-water mark for Rule 10b–5 in mismanagement cases seems to be well in the past, the rule still may have some impact in regulating corporate management practices. In 2002, Congress enacted the Sarbanes–Oxley Act,[2] which instated various reforms in response to corporate scandals such as those involving Enron Corp. and Worldcom. Some of the Sarbanes–Oxley amendments may be relevant in setting a new tone for the role of Rule 10b–5 in dealing with governance issues. In relevant part, Sarbanes–Oxley addressed corporate governance, including the role of independent directors and audit committees,[3] as well as the establishment of corporate codes of ethics.[4] This may signal a new Congressional policy, opening the door once again for the use of Rule 10b–5 to monitor corporate governance. As discussed below, the cases to date make it clear that a breach of fiduciary duty, without more, is not a securities law violation.[5] It remains to be seen whether the pendulum will begin to swing to the other direction.

Although under current law, corporate mismanagement alone will not state a Rule 10b–5 claim, the courts must look to the substance rather than form of the claims. Thus, for example, a defendant's characterization of the plaintiff's claim as one based on corporate mismanagement will not defeat an otherwise valid securities fraud claim.[6]

As pointed out earlier in this chapter, section 10(b) prohibits "manipulative or deceptive" practices as defined by SEC rules.[7] In 1971, in Superintendent of Insurance v. Bankers Life & Casualty Co.,[8] the Supreme Court announced that Rule 10b–5 is violated when there is deception touching the

---

118. *Id.*

§ 12.20

2. Sarbanes–Oxley Act of 2002, Pub. Law 107–204 (July 30, 2002).

3. *See* § 9.6[2] *supra.*

4. *See* § 9.6[7] *supra.*

5. *See, e.g.,* Minzer v. Keegan, 218 F.3d 144 (2d Cir.2000); Fitzer v. Security Dynamics Technologies, Inc., 119 F.Supp.2d 12 (D.Mass.2000).

6. Krim v. pcOrder.com, Inc., 2002 WL 1185913, Fed. Sec. L. Rep. ¶ 91786 (W.D.Tex.2002).

7. 15 U.S.C.A. § 78j(b). Rule 10b–5 is not the only such rule. The other rules promulgated under section 10(b) are discussed in § 12.1 *supra.*

8. 404 U.S. 6, 92 S.Ct. 165, 30 L.Ed.2d 128 (1971).

purchase or sale of a security even if the acts complained of amount to no more than corporate mismanagement. The defendants, management of an insurance company, caused the company to part with its assets that consisted of marketable securities. The Court upheld the 10b–5 claim since the corporation was forced to part with its securities and thus the "seller was duped into believing that it ... would receive the proceeds."[9] As a result of the Court's ruling, 10b–5 became a potential remedy to redress corporate mismanagement. The 10b–5 mismanagement remedy continued to garner great support until the Supreme Court's ruling in Santa Fe Industries, Inc. v. Green.[11]

The *Santa Fe* case involved a claim by a shareholder who was frozen out by the majority pursuant to a short-form merger. The parent corporation complied with the requirements set out by the applicable Delaware short-form merger statute and disclosed all of the required information to both the minority shareholders and the independent appraiser. The plaintiff claimed that since the cash-out price was low, the transaction operated as a fraud or deceit upon him within the meaning of Rule 10b–5(c). The Supreme Court responded that, in order to state a 10b–5 claim the plaintiff must show an element of "deception" that was lacking in the allegations in *Santa Fe*. The Court pointed out that a number of states did not provide a cause of action for breaches of fiduciary duty in connection with freeze-out transactions, and thus to rule otherwise in the case at hand would be to federalize the corporate law of directors' obligation;[12] it further refused to impose a higher standard than the applicable state law.[13]

In the wake of the *Santa Fe* decision, commentators were quick to predict a demise of 10b–5's role in the area of corporate mismanagement. However, there were five post-*Santa Fe* court of appeals decisions that took an expansive reading of Rule 10b–5 and a correspondingly narrow reading of the Supreme Court's decision.[17] Under these and other decisions, it is clear that the fact that mismanagement is involved does not preclude a Rule 10b–5 claim for material misrepresentations.[18] However, it is also clear that, standing alone, a breach of fiduciary duty is not a securities law violation.[19] Similarly, a

---

9. *Id.* at 9, 92 S.Ct. at 167.

11. 430 U.S. 462, 97 S.Ct. 1292, 51 L.Ed.2d 480 (1977).

12. 430 U.S. at 479 n. 16, 97 S.Ct. at 1304 n. 16. Delaware subsequently recognized such a remedy under its state law. However, the Delaware remedy was shortlived. Weinberger v. UOP, Inc., 457 A.2d 701 (Del.1983), *appeal after remand*, 497 A.2d 792 (1985) (severely limiting the state remedy).

Santa Fe might well come out differently today in states recognizing a remedy for freeze-outs. *See, e.g.,* Goldberg v. Meridor, 567 F.2d 209 (2d Cir.1977), *cert. denied*, 434 U.S. 1069, 98 S.Ct. 1249, 55 L.Ed.2d 771 (1978). *But see* Biesenbach v. Guenther, 588 F.2d 400 (3d Cir.1978).

13. The Court also pointed out that scrutiny of "fairness" under Rule 10b–5 is "at best a subsidiary purpose" of the federal securities laws. 430 U.S. at 478, 97 S.Ct. at 1303, 1304. Any such expansion of the 10b–5 remedy would, according to the Court, have been in conflict with restrictions on implied remedies. *See* § 12.2 *supra.*

17. Healey v. Catalyst Recovery of Pennsylvania, 616 F.2d 641 (3d Cir.1980); Kidwell v. Meikle, 597 F.2d 1273 (9th Cir.1979); Alabama Farm Bureau Mutual Casualty Co. v. American Fidelity Life Insurance Co., 606 F.2d 602 (5th Cir.1979), *rehearing denied*, 610 F.2d 818 (5th Cir.1980); Wright v. Heizer Corp., 560 F.2d 236 (7th Cir.1977), *cert. denied*, 434 U.S. 1066, 98 S.Ct. 1243, 55 L.Ed.2d 767 (1978); Goldberg v. Meridor, 567 F.2d 209 (2d Cir.1977), *cert. denied*, 434 U.S. 1069, 98 S.Ct. 1249, 55 L.Ed.2d 771 (1978). *See also* Madison Consultants v. FDIC, 710 F.2d 57 (2d Cir.1983). *But cf.* Biesenbach v. Guenther, 588 F.2d 400 (3d Cir.1978); Valente v. PepsiCo, Inc., 454 F.Supp. 1228 (D.Del.1978).

18. *See, e.g.,* Minzer v. Keegan, 218 F.3d 144 (2d Cir.2000).

19. *See, e.g.,* Grace v. Rosenstock, 23 F.Supp.2d 326 (E.D.N.Y.1998).

lapse in a board of directors' business judgment alone cannot form the basis of a securities law violation.[20]

In Goldberg v. Meridor,[21] the defendant parent corporation caused a controlled subsidiary to issue common stock and convertible debentures. The offering raised seven million dollars in cash that was in turn loaned to its direct parent corporation. The public offering was followed by an exchange of assets whereby the controlling parent sold its assets to the subsidiary in return for stock in the subsidiary. After the transactions were completed, the direct parent's sole asset was the stock of the subsidiary, in which the plaintiff was a minority shareholder, and the subsidiary had acquired all of the parent's assets and liabilities (including the seven million dollar debt running to the subsidiary). The plaintiff brought suit under Rule 10b–5, claiming that the defendant caused its subsidiary to issue stock in the public offering for the benefit of the controlling parents, and that the subsequent exchange of assets was inadequate consideration and thus operated as a fraud against the subsidiary in the issuance of its own shares.[22] The Second Circuit applied the "controlling influence" doctrine.[23] Under the controlling influence doctrine, for a transaction in which the decision-makers are controlled directors, the standard of disclosure is measured by what would have been material to a disinterested director dealing at arms length. Although disclosure to the shareholders would not have directly affected the corporate decision in question, the court reasoned that, armed with material facts of the transactions, shareholders would have been able to avail themselves of a remedy at state law.[25] Accordingly, the Second Circuit in *Goldberg* held that disclosure of the unfair exchange would have been the basis of an injunction under New York law, and thus the plaintiffs were deceived into not seeking that relief.[26] As a second justification for the requisite deception and causation elements, the court pointed out that public disclosure of all relevant facts might have shamed the subsidiary's directors into voting against the transactions with its parents rather than hanging its dirty linen out in public.[27]

Four other circuit courts followed the Second Circuit's ruling that material non-disclosure that denied minority shareholders their opportunity to seek an injunction under state law is sufficient to satisfy the deception requirement of *Santa Fe*.[29] However, in a subsequent decision by Judge Posner, the

---

20. Isquith v. Caremark International, Inc., 136 F.3d 531 (7th Cir.1998).

21. 567 F.2d 209 (2d Cir.1977), *cert. denied*, 434 U.S. 1069, 98 S.Ct. 1249, 55 L.Ed.2d 771 (1978).

22. *Id.* at 211.

23. *See* Schoenbaum v. Firstbrook, 405 F.2d 200 (2d Cir.1968), *cert. denied*, 395 U.S. 906, 89 S.Ct. 1747, 23 L.Ed.2d 219 (1969).

25. 567 F.2d at 218–19. The court also noted the allegation that the transaction involved "wholly inadequate consideration."

26. *Id.* at 219–20.

27. *Id.* at 218–19.

29. Healey v. Catalyst Recovery of Pennsylvania, 616 F.2d 641 (3d Cir.1980); Kidwell v. Meikle, 597 F.2d 1273 (9th Cir.1979); Alabama Farm Bureau Mutual Casualty Co. v. American Fidelity Life Insurance Co., 606 F.2d 602 (5th Cir.1979), *rehearing denied*, 610 F.2d 818 (5th Cir.1980); Wright v. Heizer Corp., 560 F.2d 236 (7th Cir.1977), *cert. denied*, 434 U.S. 1066, 98 S.Ct. 1243, 55 L.Ed.2d 767 (1978). *See also, e.g.*, McCoy v. Goldberg, 883 F.Supp. 927 (S.D.N.Y. 1995) (partnership's alleged failure to disclose misconduct of general partner that injured plaintiff stated a claim since a jury could find that the failure to disclose management's misconduct induced purchases); In re PHLCORP Securities Tender Offer Litigation, 700 F.Supp. 1265 (S.D.N.Y.1988) (failure to disclose appraisal remedy stated a Rule 10b–5 claim). *But see* Weill v.

Seventh Circuit indicated that it had rejected the *Goldberg* method of analysis.[30]

As noted elsewhere in this treatise,[51] Congress instituted significant corporate governance reforms with the various amendments to the securities laws that were embodied in the Sarbanes–Oxley Act of 2002.[52] It is conceivable that courts will view this federal law of corporate governance as a signal that the line between investor protection under the securities laws and corporate governance is not as clear as it was formerly.

Section 10(b)'s deception requirement received additional attention from the Supreme Court in Schreiber v. Burlington Northern, Inc.,[53] wherein it was held that manipulative conduct does not violate section 14(e)'s tender offer antifraud provision[54] unless the conduct complained of is also deceptive.[55] In so ruling, the Court emphasized that the thrust of the deception requirement is to address materially misleading statements and omissions. The *Schreiber* decision reinforces the fact that attempting to characterize a breach of fiduciary duty as manipulative will not elevate it to a Rule 10b–5 violation absent the type of deception required in the *Santa Fe Industries* case.

§ 12.21   The Effect of Plaintiff's Conduct on Implied Civil Liability; Due Diligence; In Pari Delicto

In order to recover in an action for common law fraud, plaintiffs are required to prove that their reliance was reasonable.[1] As a corollary to the reliance element, the federal courts developed a requirement that the plaintiff in a Rule 10b–5 action have acted with due diligence with regard to the transaction in question.[2] The plaintiff's due diligence requirement developed initially along negligence lines.[3] However, in Rule 10b–5 cases, it seems unquestionable that this has been changed by the Supreme Court's imposition of a scienter requirement upon defendant's conduct, which impliedly should carry over to the plaintiff's standard of conduct.[4] It would make little sense to

Dominion Resources, Inc., 875 F.Supp. 331 (E.D.Va.1994) (failure to disclose mismanagement was not actionable since there was no deception).

30. Isquith v. Caremark International, Inc., 136 F.3d 531, 534 (7th Cir.1998), relying on LHLC Corp. v. Cluett, Peabody & Co., 842 F.2d 928, 931–32 (7th Cir.1988); Harris Trust & Savings Bank v. Ellis, 810 F.2d 700, 704 (7th Cir.1987).

51. *See, e.g.*, § 9.6 *supra* for discussion of the accounting reforms and increased responsibility of audit committees.

52. Sarbanes–Oxley Act, Pub. L. 107–204, 116 Stat. 745 (2002).

53. 472 U.S. 1, 105 S.Ct. 2458, 86 L.Ed.2d 1 (1985).

54. 15 U.S.C.A. § 78n(e). *See* § 11.6, 11.10 *supra*.

55. *See also* the discussion in § 12.1 *supra*.

§ 12.21

1. Restatement, Second, Torts § 537 (1976); W. Page Keeton, Dan B. Dobbs, Robert E. Keeton & David G. Owen, Prosser and Keeton on Torts § 108 (5th ed. 1984). The reliance requirement is discussed in § 12.10 *supra*.

2. *E.g.*, Thompson v. Smith Barney, Harris Upham & Co., 709 F.2d 1413 (11th Cir.1983); Dupuy v. Dupuy, 551 F.2d 1005 (5th Cir.), *cert. denied*, 434 U.S. 911, 98 S.Ct. 312, 54 L.Ed.2d 197 (1977).

3. Rochez Brothers v. Rhoades, 491 F.2d 402 (3d Cir.1973).

4. *E.g.*, Stephenson v. Paine Webber Jackson & Curtis, Inc., 839 F.2d 1095 (5th Cir.1988) (investor's delay in reporting unlawful trades after having become aware of improprieties in his account was more than mere negligence and thus satisfied the reckless standard for showing a lack of due diligence).

say that an investor's negligence is sufficient to negate the defendant's more culpable intentional conduct.[5]

The Supreme Court in Bateman Eichler, Hill Richards, Inc. v. Berner,[15] held that the *in pari delicto* defense cannot be invoked in a Rule 10b–5 action unless it can be said that the plaintiff was indeed truly as culpable as the defendant. Although it has been suggested that this ruling abolishes the due diligence defense, the courts have not agreed.[16]

In a related development, in Pinter v. Dahl,[18] the Supreme Court extended the *Bateman Eichler* rationale in defining equal fault under the 1933 Act. The Court, echoing the investor-protection thrust of the securities, laws held that "the *in pari delicto* defense may defeat recovery in a § 12(a)(1) action only where the plaintiff's role in the offering or sale of nonexempted, unregistered securities is more as a promoter than as an investor."[20] It might be argued that the *Pinter* decision adds further strength to the argument that the Court will not recognize even the due diligence defense unless the same type of equal fault can be shown.

§ 12.22 Is There an Implied Remedy Under Section 17(a) of the 1933 Act?

As noted in an earlier section of this treatise,[1] SEC Rule 10b–5[2] was modeled upon section 17(a) of the 1933 Act.[3] There are three principal differences between the 1934 Act rule and section 17(a). First, Rule 10b–5 applies to any "purchase or sale" of a security,[4] whereas section 17(a) covers the "offer or sale" of any security. Second, section 17(a) does not contain the phrase "manipulative or deceptive device" that is found in section 10(b) of the Exchange Act[5] and has formed a basis of the scienter[6] and deception[7] requirements. Third, by virtue of the jurisdictional provisions of the 1933 and 1934 Acts,[8] the federal courts are vested with exclusive jurisdiction over Rule 10b–5, actions, while section 17(a) actions may be brought either in state or federal court with no right of removal from state to federal court.

Notwithstanding the arguments that might favor recognition of the section 17(a) remedy, the courts have found the contrary position to be more

5. *Cf.* Bateman Eichler, Hill Richards, Inc. v. Berner, 472 U.S. 299, 105 S.Ct. 2622, 86 L.Ed.2d 215 (1985).

15. 472 U.S. 299, 105 S.Ct. 2622, 86 L.Ed.2d 215 (1985).

16. Stephenson v. Paine Webber Jackson & Curtis, Inc., 839 F.2d 1095 (5th Cir.1988).

18. 486 U.S. 622, 108 S.Ct. 2063, 100 L.Ed.2d 658 (1988).

20. 486 U.S. at 639, 108 S.Ct. at 2074, 100 L.Ed.2d at 677.

§ 12.22

1. *See* § 12.3 *supra.*

2. 17 C.F.R. § 240.10b–5.

3. 15 U.S.C.A. § 77q(a).

4. In Blue Chip Stamps v. Manor Drug Stores, 421 U.S. 723, 95 S.Ct. 1917, 44 L.Ed.2d 539 (1975), *rehearing denied*, 423 U.S. 884, 96 S.Ct. 157, 46 L.Ed.2d 114 (1975), the Supreme Court held that this statutory language limited 10b–5 private-damage plaintiffs to purchasers and sellers of the securities in question. *See* § 12.7 *supra.*

5. 15 U.S.C.A. § 78j(b).

6. Ernst & Ernst v. Hochfelder, 425 U.S. 185, 96 S.Ct. 1375, 47 L.Ed.2d 668 (1976), *rehearing denied*, 425 U.S. 986, 96 S.Ct. 2194, 48 L.Ed.2d 811 (1976). *See* § 12.8 *supra.*

7. Santa Fe Industries, Inc. v. Green, 430 U.S. 462, 97 S.Ct. 1292, 51 L.Ed.2d 480 (1977). *See* § 12.20 *supra.*

8. 15 U.S.C.A. § 77v, 78aa. The jurisdictional provisions of both the 1933 and 1934 Acts are discussed in § 17.1 *infra.*

compelling.[23] The decline of implied remedies in the Supreme Court and elsewhere cannot be ignored and accordingly there certainly is a persuasive argument which has been accepted by an increasingly large number of courts that no section 17(a) remedy should be recognized.

§ 12.23 Waiver of Claims; Voiding of Contracts in Violation of the Securities Laws

§ 12.23[1] Waiver of Claims

Under common law and equitable principles, a party who voluntarily relinquishes a known right can be found to have waived his or her claim for relief.[1] Section 14 of the Securities Act of 1933 provides that contracts and stipulations purporting to waive compliance with any provision of the Act or SEC rules promulgated thereunder are void.[2] The Exchange Act's counterpart is found in section 29(a).[3] It is clear that the prohibition against waivers does not preclude releases of liability issued for consideration in connection with settlements of litigation or incipient suits.[4] However, to be valid, such a release must be for consideration and the parties must have had knowledge of the claim.[5] Thus, waivers that have been secured before there is reason to suspect that a claim may exist are not valid.[6] The rule is to the contrary when the waiver arises in the context of a bona fide settlement.

§ 12.23[2] Voiding of Contracts Waiving Compliance with the Securities Laws

Section 29(b) of the Exchange Act[26] goes further than the anti-waiver prohibitions discussed above. While the anti-waiver provisions merely preclude certain defenses to conduct that violates the securities acts, section 29(b) can be viewed as providing an affirmative remedy for parties who have entered into contracts with provisions contrary to the securities laws.[27] Section 29(b) provides that contracts involving performance that would be in violation of the Act are void. In the first instance, this means that since a contract in violation of the act is void, a party to that contract will have a successful defense to an action to enforce the contract.[29]

---

23. *E.g.,* Barnes v. Resource Royalties, Inc., 795 F.2d 1359 (8th Cir.1986); Landry v. All American Assurance Co., 688 F.2d 381 (5th Cir.1982); Citizens State Bank v. FDIC, 639 F.Supp. 758 (W.D.Okl.1986).

§ 12.23

1. *E.g.,* Bass v. Janney Montgomery Scott, Inc., 210 F.3d 577, 589–590 (6th Cir.2000) (but finding that defendant failed to establish a waiver).

2. 15 U.S.C.A. § 77n.

3. 15 U.S.C.A. § 78cc(a).

4. *See, e.g.,* Petro–Ventures, Inc. v. Takessian, 967 F.2d 1337 (9th Cir.1992).

5. Hamilton v. Harrington, 807 F.2d 102, 106–7 (7th Cir.1986).

6. *See, e.g.,* McMahan & Co. v. Wherehouse Entertainment, Inc., 859 F.Supp. 743 (S.D.N.Y. 1994), *affirmed in part, reversed in part,* 65 F.3d 1044 (2d Cir.1995).

26. 15 U.S.C.A. § 78cc(b). *See* Comment, A Structural Analysis of Section 29(b) of the Securities Exchange Act, 56 U.Chi.L.Rev. 865 (1989).

27. *E.g.,* Mills v. Electric Auto–Lite Co., 396 U.S. 375, 385–388, 90 S.Ct. 616, 622–624, 24 L.Ed.2d 593 (1970).

29. *See, e.g.,* Couldock & Bohan, Inc. v. Societe Generale Securities Corp., 93 F.Supp.2d 220 (D.Conn.2000) (clearing broker was justified in canceling contract to act as clearing broker for unregistered broker-dealer).

In addition to being used defensively, section 29(b) can be used affirmatively by a party challenging a contract in violation of the Act. The Supreme Court has held that a similar provision contained in the Investment Advisers Act of 1940[30] supports a private right of action for rescission.[31] It seems clear that a correlative private remedy must exist under section 29(b) for contracts in violation of the Exchange Act or applicable SEC rules.

As part of the 1990 Penny Stock Reform Act,[37] Congress empowered the Commission to designate section 15(c)(2) rules that if violated, would not result in avoidable transactions under section 29(b) of the Act.[38] This evidences a congressional intent of the rescission remedy in other circumstances.

§ 12.24 Multiple Defendants in Actions Under the Securities Exchange Act of 1934: Controlling Person Liability

§ 12.24[1] Controlling Person Liability Defined

Section 20(a) of the 1934 Act[1] states that "[e]very person who, directly or indirectly, controls any person liable under any provision of this chapter or of any rule or regulation thereunder shall also be liable jointly and severally with and to the same extent as such controlled person...."[2] Thus, for a controlling person to be liable, the person over who control was exercised must have committed a primary violation of the securities laws.[3] Section 20(a) of the Exchange Act closely parallels section 15 of the 1933 Act,[5] except that the 1933 Act provision is limited to actions under section 11 or 12 of that Act.[6]

For a plaintiff to have a prima facie case that the defendant was a controlling person within the meaning of section 20(a), the plaintiff must show that (1) the defendant had actual power or influence over the controlled person, and (2) the defendant induced or participated in the alleged illegal activity.[9] Several circuits hold that under the second prong of the test, the defendant must have been a "culpable participant" in the alleged illegal activity.[10]

§ 12.24[2] What Constitutes Control?

Although the term "control" is not defined in section 20(a), the SEC has defined the term "control" generally (including the terms "controlling", "controlled by", and "under common control with") to mean "the possession,

---

30. Section 215, 15 U.S.C.A. § 80b–15. The Investment Advisers Act is discussed in chapter 21 *infra.*

31. Transamerica Mortgage Advisors, Inc. v. Lewis, 444 U.S. 11, 100 S.Ct. 242, 62 L.Ed.2d 146 (1979), *on remand,* 610 F.2d 648 (9th Cir.1979) which is discussed in § 12.2 *supra.*

37. *See* § 14.19 *infra.*

38. 15 U.S.C.A. § 78cc(b). Section 15(c)(2) is discussed in § 12.1 *supra.*

§ 12.24

1. 15 U.S.C.A. § 78t(a).

2. 15 U.S.C.A. § 78t(a).

3. *E.g.,* Rosenzweig v. Azurix Corp., 332 F.3d 854, 865 (5th Cir. 2003).

5. 15 U.S.C.A. § 77o. *See* § 7.7 *supra.*

6. 15 U.S.C.A. § 77k, 77l. *See* § 7.2–7.5 *supra.*

9. *See, e.g.,* Wallace v. Buttar, 239 F.Supp.2d 388 (S.D.N.Y. 2003).

10. *See* Seymour v. Summa Vista Cinema, Inc., 817 F.2d 609 (9th Cir.1987).

direct or indirect, of the power to direct or cause the direction of the management and policies of a person whether through the ownership of voting securities, by contract, or otherwise."[23] In addition, the scope of power and degree of influence necessary to hold a defendant liable as a controlling person are not spelled out in section 20(a).[24]

The most common relationship in which control is presumed is that of the employer-employee.[29] However, controlling person liability is limited to transactions taking place on behalf of the employer. Thus, for example, when the investor deals with an employee other than in his or her capacity as an employee without relying on any affiliation with the employer, the employer will not be held accountable as a controlling person.[30] On the other hand, when an employee is acting under the employer's auspices, controlling person liability and control depends upon control over the employee; control with regard to the particular transaction in question need not be shown.[31]

Controlling shareholders can be found to be control persons.[32] Corporate officers are usually presumed to possess the requisite power to control the actions of their employees and are often held accountable as controlling persons.[33]

In contrast to officers, corporate directors are not automatically liable as controlling persons.[34] Thus, "[t]here must be some showing of actual participation in the corporation's operation or some influence before the consequences of control may be imposed."[35]

The Eleventh Circuit adopted its own articulation of the test for controlling person liability where the primary violator is an entity.[38] The court, adopting the approach that had been taken by the district court, focused on three factors. The court explained that controlling person liability exists: (1) if the alleged control person had the power to control the general affairs of the entity at the time of the alleged securities law violations, (2) the alleged control person possessed the power to control the specific company policy that resulted in primary liability, and (3) the controlled entity committed a securities law violation.[39] This test, which would be applicable to corporate officers and directors, among others, seems to be a fair restatement of the general principles of controlling person liability.

Controlling person liability does not depend upon the actual exercise of the power to control.[40] Thus, all that is necessary is to establish the possession of the power of control over the primary violator.[41]

---

23.   17 C.F.R. § 230.405.

24.   Wool v. Tandem Computers Inc., 818 F.2d 1433, 1441 (9th Cir.1987).

29.   *See* Noland v. Gurley, 566 F.Supp. 210, 220 (D.Colo.1983).

30.   *E.g.,* Kohn v. Optik, Inc., 1993 WL 169191, [1992–1993 Transfer Binder] Fed.Sec.L.Rep. (CCH) ¶ 97,435 (C.D.Cal.1993).

31.   Hauser v. Farrell, 14 F.3d 1338 (9th Cir.1994).

32.   Dietrich v. Bauer, 198 F.R.D. 397 (S.D.N.Y.2001).

33.   Wool v. Tandem Computers Inc., 818 F.2d 1433, 1441 (9th Cir.1987).

34.   *See, e.g.,* Paracor Finance v. General Electric Capital Corp., 96 F.3d 1151 (9th Cir.1996).

35.   Burgess v. Premier Corp., 727 F.2d 826, 832 (9th Cir.1984) (quoting Herm v. Stafford, 663 F.2d 669, 684 (6th Cir.1981)).

38.   Brown v. Enstar Group, Inc., 84 F.3d 393 (11th Cir.1996).

39.   *Id.*

40.   *E.g.,* IBS Financial Corp. v. Seidman & Associates, 136 F.3d 940 (3d Cir.1998).

41.   *Id.*

Under the statute, a defendant has two affirmative defenses to a controlling person liability claim. First, the defendant can try to establish that he or she acted in "good faith."[64] The defendant will have the burden of proving his or her own good faith, which "requires not only the establishment of a proper system of supervision, but also its diligent enforcement."[65] Secondly, the defendant can also try to establish that he or she did not induce the alleged violation, or in other words, that he or she did not participate in the violation.[66]

As a general proposition, controlling person liability is distinct from other forms of secondary liability.[67] It has different elements, and in some respects it is broader, while in others it is narrower. Questions have arisen as to the extent that controlling person liability is the exclusive basis of secondary liability under the securities laws.[68]

Much debate has occurred over whether section 20(a) is an exclusive remedy, so that common law claims based on agency theories such as respondeat superior cannot be brought by plaintiffs. A number of circuit courts have held that section 20(a) is not an exclusive remedy.[69] The Ninth and Third Circuits decided differently, and have held that section 20(a) is an exclusive remedy.[70] The Ninth Circuit, however, has since changed its position and is now aligned with a majority of cases permitting the common law claim to proceed.[71]

Although the controlling person liability provision of section 20(a) applies to private actions for improper trading on non-public information,[114] it does not apply under SEC enforcement provisions dealing with insider trading. In SEC actions brought under the Insider Trading Sanctions Act (ITSA),[115] controlling person liability is limited to controlling persons and employers who knew or recklessly disregarded the likelihood of misuse of confidential information and failed to take adequate precautions.[116] Specifically, by virtue

64. *See, e.g.,* Ash v. Ameritreat, 189 F.3d 463 (3d Cir.1999).

65. Harrison v. Dean Witter Reynolds, Inc., 79 F.3d 609 (7th Cir.1996).

66. Federal Savings and Loan Insurance Corp. v. Shearson–American Express, 658 F.Supp. 1331, 1343 (D.Puerto Rico 1987).

67. *See, e.g.,* SEC v. Militano, 1994 WL 558040, [1994–1995 Transfer Binder] Fed. Sec. L. Rep. (CCH) ¶ 98,441 (S.D.N.Y.1994) (SEC complaint alleging aiding and abetting liability could not be amended three weeks before trial to include a claim of controlling person liability).

68. This issue has become even more significant since the Supreme Court's ruling that there is no implied aiding and abetting liability under the securities laws. See Central Bank of Denver v. First Interstate Bank of Denver, 511 U.S. 164, 114 S.Ct. 1439, 128 L.Ed.2d 119 (1994), which is discussed in § 12.25 *infra.*

69. *See* In re Villa, 261 F.3d 1148, 1152 (11th Cir.2001); In re Atlantic Financial Management, Inc., 784 F.2d 29 (1st Cir.1986); Henricksen v. Henricksen, 640 F.2d 880, 887 (7th Cir.1981), *cert. denied,* 454 U.S. 1097, 102 S.Ct. 669, 70 L.Ed.2d 637 (1981); Paul F. Newton & Co. v. Texas Commerce Bank, 630 F.2d 1111 (5th Cir.1980).

70. *See* Zweig v. Hearst Corp., 521 F.2d 1129 (9th Cir.1975), *cert. denied,* 423 U.S. 1025, 96 S.Ct. 469, 46 L.Ed.2d 399 (1975); Rochez Brothers, Inc. v. Rhoades, 527 F.2d 880 (3d Cir.1975); and Sharp v. Coopers & Lybrand, 649 F.2d 175 (3d Cir.1981).

71. Hollinger v. Titan Capital Corp., 914 F.2d 1564 (9th Cir.1990), *cert. denied,* 499 U.S. 976, 111 S.Ct. 1621, 113 L.Ed.2d 719 (1991).

114. 15 U.S.C.A. § 78t–1(b)(3). *See* § 12.17 *supra.*

115. Pub. L. No. 98–376, 98 Stat. 1264 (1984). *See* 15 U.S.C.A. §§ 78u, 78u–1.

116. 15 U.S.C.A. § 78u–1(b)(1).

of the amendments in the Insider Trading and Securities Fraud Enforcement Act of 1988,[117] a court can impose ITSA penalties on a controlling person of a primary violator only if: (1) the controlling person knew or acted in reckless disregard of the fact that the controlled person was likely to engage in illegal insider trading, and (2) the controlling person failed to take adequate precautions to prevent the prohibited conduct from taking place.[118] It is further provided that general principles of respondeat superior and section 20(a)[119] controlling person liability expressly do not apply to SEC and criminal actions brought under ITSA.[120]

§ 12.25 Multiple Defendants in Actions Under the Securities Exchange Act of 1934: Aiding and Abetting Liability

§ 12.25[1] The Decline of Aiding and Abetting Liability

In cases involving violations of the securities laws, plaintiffs often brought suit against not only the person who was the primary violator of the specific statute, but also any persons who may have assisted in the wrongful act. Aiding and abetting is an outgrowth of criminal law.[1] Until 1994, private suits against aiders and abettors were most often brought to assure a solvent defendant. Aiders and abettors formerly were generally held to be jointly and severally liable to plaintiffs for violations and were often viewed as better sources from which to seek monetary awards. A 1994 Supreme Court decision[3] eliminated private aiding and abetting claims. Aiding and abetting remains an important issue in criminal and SEC enforcement actions. In the private litigation arena, there is an increasing tendency of plaintiffs to try to characterize participants in a securities fraud as primary violators.

Aiding and Abetting in Enforcement Actions and Criminal Prosecutions

The denial of an implied private right of action against collateral participants[56] did not directly address the ability of the SEC to pursue aiders and abettors. In 1995, Congress restored any SEC authority to pursue aiders and abettors that may have been taken away by the Supreme Court's decision in the *Central Bank* case.[57] Similarly, the *Central Bank* decision leaves untouched the viability of aiding and abetting in criminal prosecutions.[58]

117. Pub.L. No. 100–704, 102 Stat. 4677 (1988).

118. 15 U.S.C.A. § 78u–1(b)(1). In addition, broker-dealers are specifically directed to establish, maintain, and enforce written policies designed to prevent insider trading violations by their employees. 15 U.S.C.A. § 78o(f). A similar provision exists for investment advisers. 15 U.S.C.A. § 80b–4a. Investment advisers are discussed in chapter 21 *infra*.

119. 15 U.S.C.A. § 78t(a).

120. 15 U.S.C.A. § 78u–1(b)(2).

§ 12.25

1. *See* 18 U.S.C.A. § 2. *See, e.g.,* United States v. Bradstreet, 135 F.3d 46 (1st Cir.1998) (upholding criminal conviction for aiding and abetting).

3. Central Bank of Denver, N.A. v. First Interstate Bank of Denver, 511 U.S. 164, 114 S.Ct. 1439, 128 L.Ed.2d 119 (1994).

56. Central Bank of Denver, N.A. v. First Interstate Bank of Denver, 511 U.S. 164, 114 S.Ct. 1439, 128 L.Ed.2d 119 (1994).

57. 15 U.S.C.A. § 78t(e); Private Securities Litigation Reform Act of 1995, Pub. Law No. 104–67, 109 Stat. 737 (104th Cong. 1st Sess. December 22, 1995) (HR 1058).

58. 18 U.S.C.A. § 2. *See, e.g.,* United States v. Bradstreet, 135 F.3d 46 (1st Cir.1998) (upholding criminal conviction for aiding and abetting).

Distinction Between Primary and Secondary Violations

To the extent that an accountant or an attorney actually prepares documents containing materially misleading statements, then primary liability may well be appropriate.[77] Thus, for example, when a law firm makes public materially misleading statements that investors might rely upon, the law firm may be held accountable as a primary violator.[79] An attorney's drafting of disclosure can lead to primary liability if the disclosure is found to have violated the securities laws[80] and the person drafting the disclosure created the fraud.[81] However, primary liability for violation of Rule 10b–5 necessarily depends upon knowledge or willful ignorance regarding the falsity of the statement.[82]

Primary liability is not always dependent on the defendant having actually participated in the drafting of the materially misleading statement. For example, a chief executive officer and a chief operating officer could be classified as primary violators for having allowed the inaccurate filings to be filed.[85] Some courts have required that the defendant have actually made the statement in order to be held liable as a primary violator.[86] Other courts, however, have held that other types of substantial assistance can be sufficient to establish primary liability under the securities laws.[87]

§ 12.26 Multiple Defendants in Actions Under the Securities Exchange Act of 1934: Joint and Several and Proportional Liability

Section 21D(g) of the 1934 Act,[2] which was enacted as part of the Private Securities Litigation Reform Act of 1995,[3] changes the prior rule of joint and several liability for defendants in 1934 Act suits. The statute institutes a system of proportionate liability for defendants who do not knowingly commit

---

77. *See, e.g.,* Ziemba v. Cascade International, Inc., 256 F.3d 1194 (11th Cir.2001).

79. In re Enron Corp. Securities, Derivative and ERISA Litigation, 235 F.Supp.2d 549 (S.D. Tex. 2002). In contrast, the claims were dismissed against another law firm in the same case that did not make any public statements. *Id.*

80. *See, e.g.,* In re Enron Corp. Securities, Derivative & ERISA Litigation, 235 F.Supp.2d 549 (S.D.Tex. 2002).

81. *See* Annual Review of Federal Securities Regulation, 59 Bus. Law. 689, 877 (2004).

82. *See, e.g.,* In re Enron Corp. Securities, Derivative & ERISA Litigation, 235 F.Supp.2d 549 (S.D.Tex. 2002).

85. Kaufman v. Motorola, Inc., 1999 WL 688780, [1999 Transfer Binder] Fed. Sec. L. Rep. (CCH) ¶ 90,481 (N.D.Ill.1999).

86. *See, e.g.,* Anixter v. Home–Stake Production Co., 77 F.3d 1215, 1225 (10th Cir.1996) ("The critical element separating primary liability from aiding and abetting violations is the existence of a representation, either by statement or omission made by the defendant, that is relied on by plaintiff. Reliance only on representations made by others cannot itself form the basis of liability").

87. *See, e.g.,* SEC v. First Jersey Securities, 101 F.3d 1450, 1471 (2d Cir.1996) (primary liability may be imposed "not only on persons who made fraudulent misrepresentations but also on those who had knowledge of the fraud and assisted in its perpetration").

§ 12.26

2. 15 U.S.C.A. § 78u–4(g). A somewhat more modest change was made with regard to liability under section 11 of the 1933 Act which applies these provisions only to outside directors, while other defendants remain jointly and severally liable unless fraud was involved. *See* text accompanying notes 57–60 in § 7.3 *supra.*

3. Pub. Law No. 104–67, 109 Stat. 737 (104th Cong. 1st Sess. December 22, 1995) (HR 1058).

violations of the Act.[4] Proportionate liability is also applicable to outside directors in actions under section 11 of the 1933 Act.[5] The fair share rule of liability that is imposed by section 21D(g) does not create a new cause of action or in any way change the requisite states of mind for 1933 or 1934 Act suits.

Defendants engaging in "knowing" violations of the securities laws are subject to joint and several liability. Knowing violations include material misrepresentations or omissions made with actual knowledge of false information, and do not include reckless conduct. Defendants not meeting the standard of knowledge are responsible only for their proportionate share of a judgment. Courts in private actions are required to instruct juries to answer special interrogatories or make findings in non-jury suits with respect to each defendant. The court or jury must determine (1) whether each defendant violated any securities law; (2) the percentage of each defendant's responsibility; and (3) whether each defendant's violation(s) was knowing.

Non-knowing defendants may still be held jointly and severally liable under certain provisions relating to the uncollectible shares of other defendants. If a plaintiff establishes: (1) that the recoverable damages under the judgment are more than ten percent of the net worth of the plaintiff; and (2) that the net worth of the plaintiff is less than $200,000, a non-knowing defendant will be held jointly and severally liable for any uncollectible shares. Additionally, non-knowing defendants may be held jointly and severally liable for up to fifty percent of another defendant's share who is unable to pay due to insolvency.

However, defendants paying additional amounts due to uncollectible shares may, within six months of the date of payment, seek contribution. All defendants held liable in an action may seek contribution within six months of the final judgment from parties not named in the suit. Additionally, any defendant who settles prior to final judgment may not seek a right of contribution and the court is required to reduce the final judgment by the amount the settling defendant paid to the plaintiff.[6]

In addition to the foregoing rules on liability, the 1995 Reform Act requires bar orders with regard to partial settlement of securities law claims.[7]

§ 12.27 Multiple Defendants in Actions Under the Securities Exchange Act of 1934: Contribution and Indemnity

Defendants found liable for violations of securities laws are often jointly and severally liable to plaintiffs for their fraudulent acts under Rule 10b–5,[1] and consequently, the entire damage award can be collected from one or more

---

4. S. Rep. No. 104–98, 104th Cong., 1st Sess. at 20 (1995).

5. 15 U.S.C.A. § 77k(f).

6. *See, e.g.,* Lucas v. Hackett Associates, Inc., 18 F.Supp.2d 531 (E.D.Pa.1998) (settling defendants denied order barring non-settling defendants' contribution claims).

7. *See* § 12.27 *infra. Cf.* State of Wisconsin Investment Board v. Ruttenberg, 300 F.Supp.2d 1210 (N.D. Ala. 2004) (PSLRA's bar order requirement does not preclude a settlement fashioning its own bar order).

§ 12.27

1. 17 C.F.R. § 240.10b–5. Joint and several liability under the 1933 Act is discussed in § 7.12 *supra.*

defendants, assuming joint liability is found. Under the tort principle of contribution, the court may distribute the loss among the joint tortfeasors by requiring each defendant to pay his or her portion of the damages.[2] A person seeking contribution may do so either by the use of third party practice (impleader) or by bringing a separate action.

In Musick, Peeler & Garrett v. Employers Insurance of Wausau,[37] the Court held that a right of contribution was an appropriate part of the implied right of action that has long existed under Rule 10b–5. In so ruling, the Court distinguished cases decided under other federal statutes containing an express right of action but no right of contribution. Although a number of decisions caution against the implication of additional federal remedies,[38] once the courts have recognized an implied right of action, then it is appropriate to flesh it out so as to render it a reasonable remedy.[39] Furthermore, sections 9(e) and 18(a) of the Act[40] both contain an express right of action and further provide for a right of contribution. The Court reasoned that the similarities between sections 9(e), 18(a), and 10(b) support the recognition of an implied right of contribution under Rule 10b–5. Although the Court has recognized the existence of an implied right of contribution, other questions remain concerning the scope of such a right. For example, presumably, unlike a primary damage action under Rule 10b–5, it is not necessary that one violator seeking contribution from another have been a purchaser or seller of securities.[41] All that need be shown is that the third party may be liable for all or part of the liability incurred by the plaintiff seeking contribution.

Section 11 of the 1933 Act contains a right of contribution.[46] In contrast, section 12 of the 1933 Act[47] does not contain an express right of contribution and, especially in light of the Court's reasoning, it remains unclear whether an implied right of contribution would exist there. A right of contribution under section 12 may be less significant, however, since secondary liability is based on controlling person liability[48] or vicarious liability, in which case principles of indemnity should apply.

While indemnity generally has not been permitted in federal securities claims, contribution has routinely been allowed.[49]

---

2. See, e.g., In re Olympia Brewing Co. Securities Litigation, 674 F.Supp. 597 (N.D.Ill.1987).

37. Musick, Peeler & Garrett v. Employers Insurance of Wausau, 508 U.S. 286, 113 S.Ct. 2085, 124 L.Ed.2d 194 (1993).

38. See § 12.2 supra.

39. See 508 U.S. at 292–293, 113 S.Ct. at 2089, relying on Virginia Bankshares, Inc. v. Sandberg, 501 U.S. 1083, 111 S.Ct. 2749, 115 L.Ed.2d 929 (1991) and Blue Chip Stamps v. Manor Drug Stores, 421 U.S. 723, 95 S.Ct. 1917, 44 L.Ed.2d 539 (1975).

40. 15 U.S.C.A. § 78i(e), 78r(a). See § 12.1, 12.8 supra.

41. See Axel Johnson, Inc. v. Arthur Andersen & Co., 830 F.Supp. 204 (S.D.N.Y.1993).

46. 15 U.S.C.A. § 77k(f). See §§ 7.3, 7.4 supra.

47. 15 U.S.C.A. § 77l. Section 12(a)(1) and section 12(a)(2) actions are discussed in § 7.2, 7.5–7.5.4 supra.

48. See Odette v. Shearson, Hammill & Co., 394 F.Supp. 946, 958 (S.D.N.Y.1975) (section 12(a)(2) of the 1933 Act); Getter v. R.G. Dickinson & Co., 366 F.Supp. 559, 569 (S.D.Iowa 1973) (section 12(a)(2) of the 1933 Act).

49. E.g., In re Del–Val Financial Corp. Securities Litigation, 868 F.Supp. 547 (S.D.N.Y.1994) (permitting contribution but not indemnification). See also the cases in footnote 25 supra. The few cases that did not permit contribution in an action under section 10(b) arose out of situations in which the third-party defendant was not alleged to be a joint tortfeasor in the 10(b) violation. See Stratton Group, Ltd. v. Sprayregen, 466 F.Supp. 1180 (S.D.N.Y.1979) and Index Fund, Inc. v. Hagopian, 417 F.Supp. 738 (S.D.N.Y.1976). But see In re Professional Financial Management, Ltd., 683 F.Supp. 1283 (D.Minn.1988).

The Private Securities Litigation Reform Act of 1995 provides for proportional rather than joint and several liability in the case of many defendants.[76] The same rule applies to an outside director who is a defendant in an action brought under section 11 of the 1933 Act.[77]

The Litigation Reform Act also codifies what had become the emerging rule regarding partial settlements of cases involving multiple defendants and or potential defendants.[78] Section 21D(f)(7) of the 1934 Act[79] sets forth the settlement bar rule for pretrial settlements. If a defendant in a Rule 10b–5 action settles prior to trial, the court is directed to enter a bar order which will preclude all future claims for contribution against the settling defendant arising out of the action.[80] The bar order is bilateral in that it prohibits not only contribution claims against the settling defendant, but also any contribution claims the settling defendant might have, except claims against someone whose liability was extinguished by the settlement.[81] The Reform Act further provides that any judgment subsequently obtained against non-settling defendants shall be reduced by the greater of (1) an amount corresponding to the settling defendant's percentage responsibility, or (2) the dollar amount paid by the settling defendant to the plaintiff.[82] The specific prohibitions of the Reform Act bar contribution for liability arising out of settlements even with regard to claims where a right of contribution might be found under other provisions of the securities laws.[83]

---

76. 15 U.S.C.A. § 78u–4(f).

77. 15 U.S.C.A. § 77k. *See* §§ 7.3–7.4.2 *supra.*

78. *See* David Kaplan, Note, The Scope of Bar Orders in Federal Securities Fraud Settlements, 52 Duke L.J. 211 (2002).

79. 15 U.S.C.A. § 78u–4(f)(7).

80. *Id. See* Harden v. Raffensperger, Hughes & Co., 933 F.Supp. 763 (S.D.Ind.1996) (proportionate share method requires assessing relative fault of each defendant and then limiting nonsettling defendant's share of damage to his or her degree of blameworthiness).

81. 15 U.S.C.A. § 78u–4(g)(7).

82. 15 U.S.C.A. § 78u–4(g)(7).

83. *See, e.g.,* In re Cendant Corp. Securities Litigation, 139 F.Supp.2d 585 (D.N.J.2001) (Litigation Reform Act precludes contribution after settlement even though contribution might otherwise be permitted under section 11 of the 1933 Act).

Chapter 13

INSIDER REPORTING, SHORT–SWING TRADING, AND FALSE SEC FILINGS

Table of Sections

§ 13.1 Reporting Requirements for Insiders and Their Transactions in Shares—Section 16(a)

§ 13.1[1] Overview of Section 16 Filing Requirements

By virtue of section 16(a) of the Exchange Act,[1] all officers, directors, and beneficial owners of more than ten percent of any class of equity security registered under section 12 of the Act[3] must file appropriate notice with the Commission within ten days of becoming an officer, director, or beneficial owner. The section 16(a) notice must include disclosure of all ownership interest in any of the issuer's equity securities. Further, when there has been a change in an officer's, director's, or beneficial owner's share holdings, notice must also be filed with the Commission, generally on Form 4.[4] The Sarbanes–Oxley Act of 2002 mandates more rapid reporting of insider transaction than formerly was the case under section 16(a).[5] Section 16(a) was amended to require Form 4 reports of changes in beneficial ownership to be filed with the SEC by the end of the second business day after the day of execution of the transaction.[6] The Act permits the SEC to set another deadline if it determines the two-day period is not feasible.[7] Prior to this change, the deadline was the

---

§ 13.1

1. 15 U.S.C.A. § 78p(a).

3. 15 U.S.C.A. § 78*l*.

4. 15 U.S.C.A. § 78p(a).

5. Sarbanes–Oxley Act of 2002, Pub. Law 107–204 (July 30, 2002). *See also, e.g.,* Ownership Reports, Sec. Exch. Act Rel. No. 34–46313, 2002 WL 1792168 (SEC Aug. 6, 2002).

6. 15 U.S.C.A. § 78p(a)(2).

7. *Id.*

tenth day of the month following the end of the month in which the ownership change occurred. The Act also requires that Form 4 be filed electronically starting no later than one year after enactment of the 2002 amendments to the Act.[8]

Section 16(a) reports are publicly available at the Commission's office in Washington, D.C. The Commission also publishes official monthly summaries of the section 16(a) reports. Some investment analysts, by watching insider transactions, try to get a sense of how the issuer's securities are likely to fare in the future. Insider sales in the aggregate for any particular company are viewed as one indicator of the issuer's health. Similarly, on a macro level, the market's overall health is judged at least in part by the balance between aggregate insider purchases and aggregate insider sales.

In addition to its reporting requirements, section 16(a) also determines who is subject to section 16(b)'s provisions for disgorgement of insider short-swing profits.[24]

The initial section 16(a) filing must be made on Form 3, while all subsequent filings indicating a change in beneficial ownership must be filed on Form 4.[25] In 1991, the Commission adopted Form 5 to be filed annually to disclose any reportable section 16 transactions that were not reported on Form 3 or 4 because of an exemption or that should have been reported during the year on Form 3 or 4 but were not so reported.[26] If a Form 5 is due, it must be made within forty-five days after the close of the issuer's fiscal year. A delay in making the applicable section 16(a) reports will toll the limitations period for disgorgement of short-swing profits under section 16(b).[27] Under the insider trading reporting regime that was introduced, transactions which are exempt and thus eligible for reporting on Form 5 may voluntarily use Form 4.[28]

In deciding whether a particular transaction is reportable on Form 4, it is important to distinguish between the various types of exemptions available under the rules. Transactions that are exempted from section 16(b)'s short-swing profit provisions need not be reported on Form 4, but if not so reported must be reported on Form 5.[29] A limited exemption from Form 4 filings exists for acquisitions of equity securities not exceeding $10,000; these transactions do not trigger a Form 4 filing obligation, but must be reported on the next Form 4 or Form 5, whichever is due sooner.[30]

---

8. 15 U.S.C.A. § 78p(a)(4).

24. 15 U.S.C.A. § 78p(b); § 13.2 *infra.*

25. Rule 16a–3(a), 17 C.F.R. § 240.16a–3(a).

26. *See* Rule 16a–3(f), 17 C.F.R. § 240.16a–3 (1991).

27. *See, e.g.,* Tristar Corp. v. Freitas, 84 F.3d 550 (2d Cir.1996).

28. *See* Gibson, Dunn & Crutcher, 23 Sec.Reg. & L.Rep. (BNA) 966 (SEC No Action Letter available June 12, 1991).

29. The exemptions from section 16(b) include transactions approved by a regulatory authority (Rule 16b–1); acquisitions made through dividend or interest reinvestment plans (Rule 16b–2); qualifying employee benefit plan transactions (Rule 16b–3); acquisition of securities issued in certain issuer redemptions (Rule 16b–4); bona fide gifts and inheritance (Rule 16b–5); certain exercises of derivative securities (Rule 16b–6(b)); certain securities acquired as a result of qualifying mergers, reclassifications, or consolidations (Rule 16b–7); and deposit or withdrawal of securities from a voting trust (Rule 16b–8). 17 C.F.R. §§ 240.16b–1–240.16b–8. *See* § 13.3 *infra.* Some of these exemptions are highly conditional and thus the rules must be consulted before any reliance is placed on them.

30. Rule 16a–6, 17 C.F.R. § 240.16a–6.

The foregoing transactions thus do not result in complete exemptions from section 16(a)'s requirements. In contrast, there are other transactions that are exempted from section 16(a) reporting or from section 16 in its entirety.[31] For example, transactions effected in connection with a distribution where the securities were acquired with a view to distribute are specifically exempt from section 16(a);[32] accordingly no section 16(a) reports are required[33] because the insider's holdings are only transitory. There are exemptions from section 16 in its entirety for stock splits, stock dividends, and rights issued pro rata.[34] There are also statutory exemptions for market maker transactions[35] and for pure arbitrage transactions.[36]

In addition to filing with the Commission, the appropriate forms must also be sent to the exchange, if any, upon which the security is traded. When a security is traded on more than one national exchange, the issuer may designate one exchange as a recipient of the section 16(a) reports.[37]

The periodic reporting requirements for transactions in the issuer's equity securities extend beyond the statutory insider's tenure in office with the issuer. Thus, absent an exemption, an officer or director who resigns must continue to file Form 4 reports with respect to any change in his or her beneficial ownership of the issuer's equity securities that occurs within the six months following the last transaction made before resignation.[38]

Nowhere in the Exchange Act is the concept of beneficial ownership explicitly defined, and therefore its scope has been limited to judicial interpretation and administrative rulemaking. Prior to 1991, the applicable rules defined some but not all of the issues relating to the determination of beneficial ownership within the context of section 16. Over the years, there was increasing dissatisfaction with the section 16(a) reporting requirements. On the one hand, the Commission was concerned with widespread noncompliance. On the other hand, there was increasing concern that the existing rules did not supply sufficiently clear definitions and were not up to date with current developments, such as the proliferation of derivative investment instruments. After more than two years of rule proposals,[40] in 1991 the Commission adopted a completely revised series of reporting rules.[41]

The revised reporting rules deal with questions relating to who must file section 16 reports, the identification and computation of ten percent beneficial

---

31. In 1994, the SEC proposed broadening the exemptions. *See* Ownership Reports and Trading by Officers, directors and Principal Security Holders, Exch. Act Rel. No. 34–34514 (SEC Aug. 10, 1994).

32. Rule 16a–7, 17 C.F.R. § 240.16a–7.

33. An exemption is also provided for odd lot transactions by odd lot dealers. 17 C.F.R. § 240.16a–5.

34. Rule 16a–9, 17 C.F.R. § 240.16a–9.

35. Section 16(d), 15 U.S.C.A. § 78p(d) which is discussed in § 13.6 *infra*.

36. Section 16(e), 15 U.S.C.A. § 78p(e) which is discussed in § 13.6 *infra*.

37. Rule 16a–3(c), 17 C.F.R. § 240.16a–3(c).

38. Rule 16a–2(b), 17 C.F.R. § 240.16a–2(b). This does not represent a change from former Rule 16a–1(e), 17 C.F.R. § 240.16a–1(e) (1990).

40. *See* Sec.Exch. Act Rel. No. 34–26333, [1988–1989 Transfer Binder] Fed.Sec.L.Rep. (CCH) ¶ 84,343 (Dec. 2, 1988) (the initial proposing release); Sec.Exch. Act Rel. No. 34–27148, [1989 Transfer Binder] Fed.Sec.L.Rep. (CCH) ¶ 84,439 (Aug. 18, 1989) (the reproposing release).

41. *See* Sec.Exch. Act Rel. No. 34–28869, [1990–1991 Transfer Binder] Fed.Sec.L.Rep. (CCH) ¶ 84,709 (Feb. 8, 1991).

ownership, and the applicability of the reporting requirements to derivative securities.

§ 13.1[2] Who Must File Section 16 Reports

§ 13.1[2][A] Officers and Directors

There has been a good deal of litigation involving the question of who is an "officer" so as to be subject to section 16 of the Act. The revised rules take the position that section 16 should not be applied to individuals who are officers only in name. As such, the rules should put to rest a lot of the uncertainty that has previously existed in trying to determine who qualifies as an officer so as to trigger section 16 responsibilities. Rule 16a–1(f) expands upon the definition of "executive officer" used elsewhere in the rules.[43] Specifically included in the rule as revised are the president, principal financial officer, principal accounting officer,[44] any vice president in charge of a principal business unit, division, or function[45] as well as any other officer or other person who performs policy-making functions.[46] However, "policy-making function" is not meant to include activities that are not significant.[47] Furthermore, officers of the issuer's parent or subsidiary who perform policy-making functions of the issuer are deemed to be officers of the issuer for section 16 purposes.[48] In the event that the issuer is a limited partnership or a trust, officers or employees of the general partner or trustee who perform duties similar to those outlined above are officers of the issuer.[49] With regard to advisory, emeritus, or honorary directors, the Commission has announced that it has carried forth its previous policy and thus does not treat them as subject to the regulation.[50]

Once it has been determined that someone is an officer or director required to file reports, what about transactions occurring before he or she takes office or after resignation? Someone who becomes an officer is not required to report transactions occurring prior to that date. In contrast, someone who has been an officer or director of a company before it became subject to section 12's registration requirements has filing obligations with respect to transactions prior to the effective date of the reporting obligation. In such a case, the officer or director must make reports with regard to transactions occurring within the six months prior to the issuer's 1934 Act registration provided those transactions occurred within six months of the transaction that triggered the Form 4 filing obligation.[51] As noted above, the revised provisions continue the former practice of requiring reports of trans-

---

43. Rule 3b–7, 17 C.F.R. § 240.3b–7. *See also* Rule 3b–2, 17 C.F.R. § 240.3b–2 (definition of officer).

44. Or the comptroller if there is no principal accounting officer.

45. The Commission lists sales, administration, and finance as specific examples.

46. 17 C.F.R. § 240.16a–1(f).

47. Note to 17 C.F.R. § 240.16a–1(f).

48. 17 C.F.R. § 240.16a–1(f).

49. *Id.*

50. Sec.Exch. Act Rel. No. 34–28869, [1990–1991 Transfer Binder] Fed.Sec.L.Rep. (CCH) ¶ 84,709, n. 27 and accompanying text (Feb. 8, 1991).

51. Rule 16a–2(a), 17 C.F.R. § 240.16a–2(a). The reason for treating these transaction differently from those occurring prior to the time the officer or director takes office is that in the latter case access to inside information is not presumed until the officer or director takes office.

actions following an officer or director leaving office so long as the transaction occurred within six months of the last transaction while in office.[52]

§ 13.1[2][B] Ten Percent Beneficial Owners

With respect to reporting based on beneficial ownership, the 1991 revisions of the section 16 reporting rules parallel the rules applicable to section 13(d) of the Williams Act.[53] The Commission notes that, as is the case with section 13(d), "[s]ection 16, as applied to ten percent holders, is intended to reach those persons who can be presumed to have access to inside information because they can influence or control the issuer as a result of their equity ownership."[54] In making the ten percent holder determination under section 16, nonvoting securities are excluded and derivative securities are included only if they are convertible or exercisable within sixty days.[55] It is clear that the Commission intended to create parallel definitions of beneficial ownership under sections 16 and 13(d).[56]

It is not always easy to determine if and when a shareholder reached the ten percent threshold. For example, in the case of issuers who periodically repurchase their shares, the threshold can be a moving target. Further, at least one court has held that if someone does not know (and does not have reason to know) of his or her ten percent ownership status, section 16(b) liability will not be imposed.[63] When section 16 insider status is based on the formation of a group, only transactions occurring after formation of the group, as opposed to contemporaneously with the group's formation, will be matched against other transactions for the purpose of determining section 16(b) liability.[64]

Rule 16a–1(a)(2)[65] begins by setting forth the basic rule that, for reporting purposes, beneficial ownership hinges upon the direct or indirect pecuniary interest in the shares,[66] and that that interest may be the result of "any contract, arrangement, understanding, relationship, or otherwise."[67] This includes the opportunity to participate, directly or indirectly, in any profit attributable to transactions in the shares in question. The rule then goes on

---

52. Rule 16a–2(b), 17 C.F.R. § 240.16a–2(b).

53. 15 U.S.C.A. § 78m(d) which is discussed in § 11.2 *supra*. This brings with it section 13(d)'s "group theory" which is discussed *id.*

54. Sec.Exch. Act Rel. No. 34–28869, [1990–1991 Transfer Binder] Fed.Sec.L.Rep. (CCH) ¶ 84,709 (Feb. 8, 1991).

55. Rules 13d–3, 16a–1(a)(1), 17 C.F.R. §§ 240.13d–3, 240.16a–1(a)(1). *See, e.g.,* Decker v. Advantage Fund, Ltd., 362 F.3d 593 (9th Cir. 2004).

56. C.R.A. Realty Corp. v. Enron Corp., 842 F.Supp. 88, 91 (S.D.N.Y.1994), relying on Exch. Act Rel. No. 34–28869, [1990–1991 Transfer Binder] Fed.Sec.L.Rep. (CCH) ¶ 84,709 (Feb. 8, 1991).

63. C.R.A. Realty Corp. v. Enron Corp., 842 F.Supp. 88 (S.D.N.Y.1994).

64. Rosenberg v. XM Ventures, 129 F.Supp.2d 681 (D.Del.2001).

65. Rule 16a–1(a)(2), 17 C.F.R. § 240.16a–1(a)(2). *See* Feder v. Frost, 220 F.3d 29 (2d Cir.2000) (upholding the validity of Rule 16a–1(a)(2)).

66. The "pecuniary interest" analysis set forth in Rule 16a–1(a)(2) applies to the determination of which transactions are subject to section 16(a)'s reporting requirements and also which transactions may be subject to section 16(b)'s disgorgement provisions. *See* Rosen v. Brookhaven Capital Management Co., 113 F.Supp.2d 615, 627–628 (S.D.N.Y.2000). This is distinct from the application of the ten percent beneficial ownership threshold to determine whether someone qualifies as a statutory insider and thus is subject to the reporting requirements and disgorgement provisions. *Id.*

67. Rule 16a–1(a)(2), 17 C.F.R. § 240.16a–1(a)(2).

to list examples of an "indirect pecuniary interest" that triggers section 16. Securities held by immediate family members sharing the same household are included.[68] A general partner's proportional interest in securities held by a general or limited partnership are similarly included.[69] In contrast, a shareholder does not have a pecuniary interest in the portfolio securities held by a corporation, limited partnership, or similar entity, so long as he or she is not a controlling shareholder of the entity and does not possess, either alone or with others, investment control over the entity's portfolio securities.[70] As a general rule, subject to some exceptions, performance-based fees (other than asset-based fees) received by any broker, dealer, investment adviser, investment manager, trustee, or person performing a similar function constitute an indirect pecuniary interest.[71] A person's right to dividends is not considered an indirect pecuniary interest unless the right to dividends is separated or separable from the underlying security.[73] An indirect pecuniary interest also exists with regard to securities held by a trust, although the beneficiaries without investment control will not ordinarily have section 16 reporting obligations.[74] A settlor of a trust who reserves the right to revoke the trust without anyone else's consent is a beneficial owner of the securities held by the trust and is also subject to the reporting and short-swing profit provisions with regard to the securities held by the trust.[75] The right to acquire equity securities through the exercise of any derivative security creates a pecuniary interest even if the rights are not presently exercisable.[76] Rule 16a–1(a)(2)'s validity was upheld by the Second Circuit in the case of indirect pecuniary interest being premised on the ownership of a corporation, which in turn held and sold shares in a corporation whose stock was subject to section 16(b)'s disgorgement provisions.[77]

Included in the definition of "equity security" are participation in profit-sharing agreements, preorganization certificates or subscriptions, voting trust certificates, and beneficial interests in business trusts.[81] It previously has been held that stock appreciation rights, or phantom stock, is an equity security for purposes of section 16.[82] The revised rules in their inclusion of derivative securities codify this result. Stock appreciation rights that are settled for stock (or stock and/or cash) are derivative securities and are subject to section 16.[84] However, stock appreciation rights that may be settled only for cash are exempt from section 16.[85]

---

68. 17 C.F.R. § 240.16a–1(a)(2)(ii)(A).

69. 17 C.F.R. § 240.16a–1(a)(2)(ii)(B).

70. 17 C.F.R. § 240.16a–1(a)(2)(iii). Portfolio securities are all securities owned by an entity except for securities issued by the entity. 17 C.F.R. § 240.16a–1(g).

See also, e.g., Mayer v. Chesapeake Ins. Co., Ltd., 698 F.Supp. 52 (S.D.N.Y.1988) (investor receiving proceeds of corporation's sale of stock was beneficial owner).

71. 17 C.F.R. § 240.16a–1(a)(2)(ii)(C).

73. 17 C.F.R. § 240.16a–1(a)(2)(ii)(D).

74. Rule 16a–1(a)(2)(ii)(E), 17 C.F.R. § 240.16a–1(a)(2)(ii)(E).

75. Rule 16a–8(b), 17 C.F.R. § 240.16a–8(b).

76. Rule 16a–1(a)(2)(ii)(F), 17 C.F.R. § 240.16a–1(a)(2)(ii)(F).

77. Feder v. Frost, 220 F.3d 29 (2d Cir.2000).

81. 17 C.F.R. § 240.3a11–1.

82. Matas v. Siess, 467 F.Supp. 217 (S.D.N.Y.1979).

84. *See, e.g.,* Magma Power Co. v. Dow Chemical Co., 136 F.3d 316 (2d Cir.1998), affirming 1997 WL 23186, [1997 Transfer Binder] Fed. Sec. L. Rep. (CCH) ¶ 99,419 (S.D.N.Y.1997).

85. Rule 16a–1(c)(3), 17 C.F.R. § 240.16a–1(c)(3).

The determination of beneficial ownership, as between an insider and spouse frequently presents difficult factual questions. For example, within the context of a 16(b) action to recover proscribed short-swing profits, it has been held that a wife's sale of securities is attributed to her husband who is a director of the issuer even where the husband and wife maintain separate brokerage accounts but engaged in some joint planning.[86]

§ 13.1[2][C] Definition of Equity Security

The former rules required inclusion in the ten percent ownership computation of all equity securities which the holder had the right to acquire by exercising presently exercisable rights, warrants, or conversion rights.[87] However, in light of the revised rules' treatment of derivative instruments generally, the requirement that there be a present right has been deleted.[88] Section 3(a)(11) and Rule 3a11–1 of the Act define equity security to include "any security convertible, with or without consideration" into an equity security;[89] this definition also includes warrants and rights to subscribe to or purchase an equity security. The Second Circuit has held that convertible debentures do not themselves constitute a separate class of equity security for purposes of section 16.[90] The court explained that the ten percent beneficial ownership threshold for section 16 reporting is computed with regard to the underlying security assuming "full dilution" of the underlying security which would result from exercise of all conversion rights.[91] This would include other warrants and rights as well.[92] The Second Circuit's rule has been codified by the Commission.[93]

Under Rule 16a–4(a),[94] convertible securities are not considered a separate class of equity security, but rather part of the class of the underlying security which would be acquired upon the exercise of the conversion rights. This computation of ten percent beneficial ownership applies to convertible securities conversion rights, and derivative securities that are currently exercisable without contingencies.[95] However, when the conversion rights have material contingencies and therefore are not presently exercisable, the shares underlying convertible securities will not be aggregated with other direct holdings in the underlying securities.[97]

The Commodity Futures Modernization Act of 2000[100] permitted trading in security future products for the first time. Since a security futures product

---

86. Whiting v. Dow Chemical Co., 523 F.2d 680 (2d Cir.1975).

87. Former Rule 16a–2(b), 17 C.F.R. § 240.16a–2(b) (1990).

88. *See* § 13.1[2][D] *infra.*

89. 15 U.S.C.A. § 78c(a)(11); 17 C.F.R. § 240.3a11–1.

90. Chemical Fund, Inc. v. Xerox Corp., 377 F.2d 107 (2d Cir.1967). *See also, e.g.,* Foremost–McKesson, Inc. v. Provident Securities Co., 423 U.S. 232, 96 S.Ct. 508, 46 L.Ed.2d 464 (1976).

Computation of beneficial ownership based on conversion and other rights includes the right to acquire securities within sixty days. Rule 13d–3(d)(1)(i), 17 C.F.R. § 240. 13d–3(d)(1)(i).

91. Chemical Fund, Inc. v. Xerox Corp., 377 F.2d 107 (2d Cir.1967).

92. Warrants and rights are included in the general definition of equity security under the Act. 15 U.S.C.A. § 78c(a)(11).

93. Rule, 16a–4(a), 17 C.F.R. § 240.16a–4(a).

94. *Id.*

95. *Id.*

97. *See* Levner v. Saud, 903 F.Supp. 452 (S.D.N.Y.1994).

100. Pub. Law No. 106–554, 114 Stat. 2763 (Dec. 21, 2000).

is not convertible into the underlying security until the settlement date for the contract, the underlying securities are not counted in an owner's long position until settlement.[101]

§ 13.1[2][D] Treatment of Derivative Securities

One of the more significant changes implemented by the Commission with its revised section 16 rules is the applicability of the reporting requirements to derivative securities. The proliferation of put and call options has made it possible for investors to take a derivative position with regard to underlying equity securities. In many ways, investment positions in these derivative investment vehicles are functionally equivalent to positions in the underlying security in terms of the potential for trading profits. Accordingly, the Commission has reversed its long-standing policy by making the acquisition of a derivative security, rather than its exercise, the significant event for section 16 purposes.[103] Derivative securities are covered not only by the section 16(a) reporting requirements, but also by the short-swing profit provisions of section 16(b). The revised rules view transactions in derivative securities as matchable not only against each other, but also against transactions in the underlying security.[104] The revised rules thus equate ownership of a derivative security with ownership of the underlying security and recognize that, as is the case with convertible securities, exercise merely changes ownership from indirect to direct ownership of the underlying security.

As a result of the 1991 Rule amendments, the purchase or sale of options and other derivative investments occurs for section 16 purposes on the date the option is received rather than on the date it is exercised.[109] This is consistent with the approach taken with respect to reporting obligations although it represented a reversal of the position the SEC took prior to 1991. How is the expiration of a derivative security treated under section 16? If the expiration occurs within six months of any premium received for writing the option, then the insider realizes a section 16(b) profit that must be disgorged.[111] The expiration of a put option[112] or a call option[113] more than six months after the option was written is not subject to disgorgement under section 16(b).

§ 13.1[3] Exemptions From Section 16 Filing Requirements

The revised rules contain various exemptions from the reporting and/or short-swing profit provisions of section 16. Although revised as compared to their predecessors, the revised rules continue the exemption for qualifying

---

101. *See* Commission Guidance on the Application of Certain Provisions of the Securities Act of 1933, the Security Exchange Act of 1934, and Rules Thereunder to Trading in Security Futures Products, Sec. Act Rel. No. 33–8107, Sec. Exch. Act Rel. No. 34–46101, 67 Fed. Reg. 43233, 2002 WL 1377488 (SEC June 27, 2002).

103. Sec.Exch.Act Rel. No. 34–28869, [1990–1991 Transfer Binder] Fed.Sec.L.Rep. (CCH) ¶ 84,709 (Feb. 8, 1991).

104. Rule 16b–6(a), 17 C.F.R. § 240.16b–6(a). *See* § 13.2 *infra*

109. Rule 16b–6(a), 17 C.F.R. § 240.16b–6(a).

111. Rule 16b–6(d), 17 C.F.R. § 240.16b–6(d).

112. *See* Baker Botts, LLP, 32 Sec. Reg. & L. Rep. (BNA) 1009, 2000 WL 972990 (SEC No Action Letter July 13, 2000).

113. *See* Sullivan & Cromwell, [1993 Transfer Binder] Fed. Sec. L. Rep. (CCH) ¶ 76,721 (June 24, 1993).

employee benefit plans from the short-swing profit provisions.[114] Rule 16a–9 exempts from section 16 stock splits or stock dividends applying equally to all members of a class of equity securities.[115] Also exempted are pro rata grants of rights to all holders of a class of equity securities;[116] this would cover the grant of many poison pills. Although the acquisition of the rights is exempt, the exercise or sale of the rights is a reportable event.

§ 13.2 Disgorgement of Insider Short–Swing Profits—Section 16(b)

§ 13.2[1] Overview of Section 16(b)

Section 16(b)[1] imposes liability for short-swing profits in the issuer's stock upon all persons required to file reports under section 16(a) of the Act.[2] Thus, officers, directors, and beneficial owners of ten percent of a class of equity securities subject to the Exchange Act's reporting requirements are subject to the short-swing profit prohibitions. These listed statutory insiders must disgorge to the issuer any "profit" realized as a result of a purchase and sale or sale and purchase of covered equity securities occurring within a six month period. Section 16(b) is not designed as a compensatory remedy. The preamble to section 16(b) indicates that this civil liability is imposed "for the purpose of preventing the unfair use of information which may have been obtained by such beneficial owner, director, or officer by reason of his relationship to the issuer."[4] The legislative history reveals congressional recognition of such a great potential for abuse of inside information so as to warrant the imposition of strict liability. The statute was viewed as a "crude rule of thumb" or objective method of preventing "the unscrupulous employment of [corporate] inside information."[5] Accordingly, in light of its broad remedial purpose, section 16(b) will require disgorgement of insider short-swing profits even in the absence of any wrongdoing. The liability so imposed is often referred to as prophylactic in nature. Section 16(b) thus does not make moral distinctions as it penalizes insiders who commit a technical violation but are still "pure of heart" while at the same time a more culpable insider may be able to avoid liability by going beyond the letter of the statute.[6]

In 2002, Congress enacted the Sarbanes–Oxley Act to combat corporate fraud.[17] That Act contained provisions designed to strengthen the prohibitions on insider trading.[18] The Act prohibits directors and executive officers are

---

114.   Rule 16b–3, 17 C.F.R. § 240.16b–3.

115.   Rule 16a–9(a), 17 C.F.R. § 240.16a–9(a).

116.   Rule 16a–9(b), 17 C.F.R. § 240.16a–9(b).

§ 13.2

1.   15 U.S.C.A. § 78p(b).

2.   *See* § 13.1 *supra.*

4.   15 U.S.C.A. § 78p(b).

5.   Hearings on S.Res. 84, S.Res. 97 Before The Senate Comm. on Banking and Currency, 73d Cong., 1st Sess. pt. 15 at 6557 (1934).

6.   *See* Magma Power Co. v. Dow Chemical Co., 136 F.3d 316, 320–21 (2d Cir.1998) (section 16(b) "operates mechanically, and makes no moral distinctions, penalizing technical violators of pure heart, an bypassing corrupt insiders who skirt the letter of the prohibition").

17.   Sarbanes–Oxley Act of 2002, Pub. Law 107–204 (July 30, 2002).

18.   15 U.S.C.A. § 7244. As is the case with section 16(b), intent of the insider is not a precondition to recovery.

prohibited from purchasing or selling company equity securities during black-out periods under 401(k) and other similar retirement funds.[19] The company may recover (including through a shareholder derivative-type action) any profits realized from such prohibited purchases or sales.[20] Unlike Section 16 of the 1934 Act, this disgorgement action does not require a matching transaction within the black-out period.

§ 13.2[2] Issuers Covered

As noted above, the applicability of section 16(b)'s disgorgement provisions is determined by reference to section 16(a)'s reporting requirements.[25] Accordingly, section 16(b) liability attaches to officers, directors, and ten percent beneficial owners of a class of equity securities registered under section 12 of the Exchange Act.[27]

§ 13.2[3] Securities Covered

Section 16(a)'s reporting provisions determine the parameters of section 16(b)'s coverage.[35] By virtue of Rule 16a–10 the exemptions from 16(a) carry over to 16(b).[36] Similarly, the definition of equity security is equally broad under section 16(b) as under 16(a) and extends to conversion rights, warrants, and even stock appreciation rights.[37] Also, the same rules apply to the determination of beneficial ownership under sections 16(a) and 16(b).[38]

§ 13.2[4] Procedural Aspects; Standing; Demand Requirement; Right to Jury Trial; Statute of Limitations

The private remedy embodied in section 16(b) is self contained, sui generis, and is a hybrid variety of derivative suit. For example, the statute on its face requires that the shareholder make a demand upon directors prior to being sued.

Standing to bring a suit under section 16(b) has three basic requirements. First, the plaintiff must be an owner of an equity security covered by section 16. Second, the security so owned must be the same class of security traded by the section 16(b) defendant. Third, the plaintiff must own the security at the time that the section 16(b) action is instituted.[40] There is no requirement comparable to derivative actions generally[41] imposing a contemporaneous ownership rule requiring that the plaintiff owned the security at the time of the violation. Instead, section 16(b) requires "only that he has 'some continu-

---

19.   15 U.S.C.A. § 7244(a)(1).

20.   15 U.S.C.A. § 7244(a)(2).

25.   15 U.S.C.A. § 78p(a),(b). Section 16(a)'s reporting provisions are discussed in § 13.1 *supra.*

27.   15 U.S.C.A. § 78*l*.

35.   *See* § 13.1 *supra.*

36.   17 C.F.R. § 240.16a–10.

37.   *See* 15 U.S.C.A. § 78c(a)(11).

38.   *See* § 13.3 *infra*; § 13.1 *supra.*

40.   Gollust v. Mendell, 501 U.S. 115, 123–124, 111 S.Ct. 2173, 115 L.Ed.2d 109 (1991); DiLorenzo v. Edgar, 2004 WL 609374 *2 (D. Del. 2004).

41.   *See* Fed. R. Civ. P. 23.1. *See generally* 2 James D. Cox & Thomas Lee Hazen, Cox & Hazen on Corporations § 15.09 (2d ed. 2003).

ing financial stake in the litigation' so as to satisfy minimum standing requirements imposed by the jurisdictional limitations of Article III.''[42]

In 1991, the Supreme Court addressed the question of whether a shareholder of a corporation that was subsequently merged into another can bring suit under section 16(b) against officers, directors, or ten percent beneficial holders of the merged disappearing corporation. In *Gollust v. Mendell*,[43] the plaintiff was a shareholder of a merged corporation, and under the terms of the merger agreement he received a combination of stock and cash. Plaintiff instituted his section 16(b) claim prior to the merger and the court held that he had standing under the statute since he owned a security of the issuer at the time he instituted the suit. In reaching this result, the Court emphasized that while section 16(b) sets forth a narrow class of potential defendants, it sets forth a broad class of plaintiffs—much broader than would apply under the contemporaneous ownership rule applicable to derivative suits generally. The Court in *Gollust* set forth two requirements for standing under section 16(b): first, the suit must have been initiated at a time that plaintiff was a shareholder; and second, the plaintiff must have a continuing interest in the corporation (or its assets) so as to allow him or her to benefit from any recovery.

Notwithstanding the possible champerty implications, the courts have held that it is no defense to an action under section 16(b) that the suit was motivated primarily by an attorney's desire to obtain the attorneys' fees that may be awarded to the successful plaintiff.[46] Attorneys' fees are awarded out of the fund created by the recovery and are not added to the defendant's liability.[47]

It is generally a requirement of derivative suits that the plaintiff must first make a demand on directors to bring suit on behalf of the corporation.[51] As noted above, section 16(b) contains its own demand requirement. The corporation, through its directors, then has sixty days to decide whether or not to bring suit.[52] However, no demand is required when it would be a futile gesture due to the self-interest of the directors.

The section 16(b) action may be brought either in law or in equity. It has been held that the plaintiff's failure to demand a jury trial renders the action one in equity, thus denying the defendant the right of election.[60]

The statute contains a two-year limitation period which begins to run from the date of the second transaction, that is, the one that creates the section 16(b) profits. However, the statute of limitations period may be extended until the time of reasonable discovery where there has been a failure

---

42. DiLorenzo v. Edgar, 2004 WL 609374 *2 (D. Del. 2004), quoting from Gollust v. Mendell, 501 U.S. 115, 125, 111 S.Ct. 2173, 115 L.Ed.2d 109 (1991).

43. 501 U.S. 115, 111 S.Ct. 2173, 115 L.Ed.2d 109 (1991).

46. Magida v. Continental Can Co., 231 F.2d 843 (2d Cir.1956), *cert. denied* 351 U.S. 972, 76 S.Ct. 1031, 100 L.Ed. 1490 (1956).

47. *See* Super Stores, Inc. v. Reiner, 737 F.2d 962, 965 (11th Cir.1984).

51. *See* Fed. R. Civ. P. 23.1. *See generally* 2 James D. Cox & Thomas Lee Hazen, Cox & Hazen on Corporations §§ 15.06–15.07 (2d ed. 2003).

52. Weisman v. Spector, 158 F.Supp. 789 (S.D.N.Y.1958); Netter v. Ashland Paper Mills, Inc., 19 F.R.D. 529 (S.D.N.Y.1956).

60. Arbetman v. Playford, 83 F.Supp. 335 (S.D.N.Y.1949). *See also* Dottenheim v. Emerson Elec. Manufacturing Co., 7 F.R.D. 343 (E.D.N.Y.1947).

to file timely section 16(a) reports.[62] The statute of limitations will not be tolled beyond the filing of the Form 4 or 5.[63]

§ 13.2[5] Jurisdictional Aspects

Jurisdiction over section 16(b) actions is exclusively within the federal courts.[67] The 16(b) action may be brought in a district where the violation occurred or where "the defendant is found or is an inhabitant or transacts business."[68] Once jurisdiction is established, there is nationwide service of process.[69]

Although resulting in civil damages, section 16(b) violations do not give rise to criminal sanctions, nor are they within the purview of SEC enforcement actions or proceedings. In contrast, violations of section 16(a)'s reporting requirements may result in both criminal sanctions[70] and SEC action.[71]-

§ 13.2[6] Section 16(b) Timing (the "Short Swing"[72])

Section 16(b) was intended to be straightforward in application, thus providing the predictability necessary for sound planning. However, the terms of the statute have given rise to much litigation. It is not always clear whether a particular person comes within the section's reach. Similarly it is frequently difficult to determine whether and when a purchase or sale occurs.[74] The computation of the six-month period has not escaped judicial scrutiny. It is clear that the prohibitions of section 16(b) extend to six months both prior and subsequent to the date of any particular transaction,[75] assuming, of course, that insider status attaches. Furthermore, the statute speaks in terms of a "period of *less* than six months" in which the transactions are prohibited and thus two transactions occurring within exactly six months of each other are not subject to section 16(b)'s disgorgement provisions.[76] In order to determine when a purchase or sale takes place, the courts look to the time at which the purchaser or seller became irrevocably obligated.[77]

---

62. Tristar Corp. v. Freitas, 84 F.3d 550 (2d Cir.1996) (two-year period was tolled from time Form 4 filing became overdue until the date it was actually filed).

63. *See, e.g.*, Donoghue v. American Skiing Co., 155 F.Supp.2d 70 (S.D.N.Y.2001).

67. Section 27, 15 U.S.C.A. § 78aa.

68. *Id.*

69. *See, e.g.*, A+ Network, Inc. v. Shapiro, 960 F.Supp. 123 (M.D.Tenn.1997) (claim for underlying legal fees should be made where violations occurred not where the legal fees were incurred).

70. *E.g.* United States v. Guterma, 281 F.2d 742 (2d Cir.), *cert. denied* 364 U.S. 871, 81 S.Ct. 114, 5 L.Ed.2d 93 (1960); Section 32(a), 15 U.S.C.A. § 78ff.

71. Section 21, 15 U.S.C.A. § 78u.

72. Log On America v. Promethean Asset Management, 223 F.Supp.2d 435, 449–450 (S.D.N.Y. 2001) (dismissing section 16(b) claim due to failure to allege matching purchase and sale); Portnoy v. Seligman & Latz, Inc., 516 F.Supp. 1188, 1200 (S.D.N.Y.1981) ("It don't mean a thing if it ain't got that swing," quoting E.K. "Duke" Ellington).

74. *See* § 13.4 *infra*. Generally, a sale occurs when the seller has become irrevocably bound to dispose of the securities. Seinfeld v. Hospital Corp. of America, 685 F.Supp. 1057 (N.D.Ill.1988) ("lock up" option is a purchase); Colan v. Brunswick Corp., 550 F.Supp. 49 (N.D.Ill.1982).

75. Gratz v. Claughton, 187 F.2d 46 (2d Cir.), *cert. denied* 341 U.S. 920, 71 S.Ct. 741, 95 L.Ed. 1353 (1951).

76. Morales v. Reading & Bates Offshore Drilling Co., 392 F.Supp. 41 (N.D.Okl.1975); R. Jennings & H. Marsh, Securities Regulations Cases and Materials 1352 (5th ed. 1982).

77. Riseman v. Orion Research, Inc., 749 F.2d 915 (1st Cir.1984).

§ 13.2[7] Determination of "Profit"

There has also been significant question as to the method of computing a "profit" within the meaning of section 16(b). Someone who sells stock and subsequently repurchases the amount sold for a lower price within a six-month period realizes a section 16(b) profit. One court had held that in order for a court to require disgorgement, the defendant must have actually realized a profit rather than simply receiving an increase in value of shares held.[81] The Second Circuit reversed this ruling since the increase in value was due to sales by a corporation of shares that resulted in a profit within six months. Since the defendant owned all of the shares of the corporation that sold the shares in question, the defendant in fact benefited from the sale and realized the economic effects of a profit through the increase in value to the shares he owned in the selling corporation.[82]

Many courts have taken a broad view of what constitutes a section 16(b) "profit" when there have been a series of transactions within a six-month period. The apparent majority view is to match the lowest purchase price against the highest sales price within that period.[83] This method is the harsher of the alternative interpretations since it captures a "profit" even in situations where an out-of-pocket loss for all transactions entered into during the six-month period may exist.[84] There is a strong argument that this measure of damages is unnecessarily punitive and cannot be justified by section 16(b)'s remedial purpose. As is pointed out elsewhere,[85] punitive damages are generally not available in actions arising under the federal securities laws. Imposing liability for excess "profits" which in fact exceed actual profits can be viewed as unjustifiably punitive and thus contrary to the spirit of section 28(a) of the Exchange Act, which limits damages to actual damages.[86]

The matching problem described above applies only when there are multiple purchases and sales within a six month period. It does not arise when there is a series of purchases followed by a single sale (or vice versa). For example, when there are multiple purchases and one block sale, it is sufficient to simply aggregate the purchase price and then subtract the sum from the sale price.[87]

81. Feder v. Frost, 1999 WL 163174, 31 Sec. Reg. & L. Rep. (BNA) 465 (S.D.N.Y. 1999), reversed 220 F.3d 29 (2d Cir.2000).

82. Feder v. Frost, 220 F.3d 29 (2d Cir.2000).

83. Arrow Distributing Corp. v. Baumgartner, 783 F.2d 1274, 1277–78 (5th Cir.1986); Whittaker v. Whittaker Corp., 639 F.2d 516, 530–32 (9th Cir.1981), *cert. denied* 454 U.S. 1031, 102 S.Ct. 566, 70 L.Ed.2d 473 (1981); Gratz v. Claughton, 187 F.2d 46 (2d Cir.1951); Smolowe v. Delendo Corp., 136 F.2d 231 (2d Cir.1943), *cert. denied* 320 U.S. 751, 64 S.Ct. 56, 88 L.Ed. 446 (1943).

84. *See* Smolowe v. Delendo Corp., 136 F.2d 231, 239 (2d Cir.1943), *cert. denied* 320 U.S. 751, 64 S.Ct. 56, 88 L.Ed. 446 (1943).

85. *See* §§ 7.5, 7.8, 12.12 *supra.*

86. 15 U.S.C.A. § 78bb(a). Section 28(a) does not directly apply, since a section 16(b) recovery is not based on damage to the plaintiff but rather upon the desire to create a prophylactic remedy. The section 16(b) recovery can be analogized to restitutionary relief which likewise need not be based on actual damage. However, where such relief exceeds the defendant's ill-gotten gain, it is punitive rather than restitutionary.

87. Mayer v. Chesapeake Ins. Co. Ltd., 877 F.2d 1154 (2d Cir.1989), *cert. denied* 493 U.S. 1021, 110 S.Ct. 722, 107 L.Ed.2d 741 (1990).

There is some authority to the effect that dividends declared on shares that are sold at a profit will be considered part of the section 16(b) profit, provided that the dividend recipient had insider status at the time of declaration of the dividend.[88] However, there is considerable authority to the contrary, holding that dividends are excluded from the section 16(b) computation absent evidence that the defendant manipulated the dividend.[89]

Difficult questions can arise concerning the computation of a profit when faced with transactions involving derivative securities. In 1991, the Commission addressed the computation of profits resulting from acquisitions and dispositions of derivative securities. If an acquisition of a derivative security is matched with the disposition of the same derivative security within a six-month period, the section 16(b) recovery is based on the profit received from the matching transactions.[94] If an acquisition or disposition of a derivative security is matched with a transaction in the underlying security or different derivative security, the maximum section 16(b) profit is based on the difference in the market value of the underlying security on the transaction dates, but the court may award a lesser recovery in the event the insider can demonstrate that the amount of profit was less.[95]

Notwithstanding some Tax Court rulings to the contrary, the federal courts of appeals have uniformly held that profits disgorged under section 16(b) cannot be deducted by the insider as an ordinary or necessary business expense.[96] From the issuer's perspective, a section 16(b) recovery will constitute taxable income.[97]

§ 13.2[8] Actual Use of Inside Information Not Necessary

In light of section 16(b)'s remedial and prophylactic purposes, it is not necessary that the defendant have utilized inside information in planning the transactions. Nor is it necessary that the transactions have resulted in injury to the issuer. The rule of the statute is absolute, imposing strict liability for short-swing profits by statutory insiders of Exchange Act reporting companies. Notwithstanding the clear congressional intent to provide a catch-all, prophylactic remedy, not requiring proof of actual misconduct,[104] the statute is not always strictly applied. When dealing with traditional cash-for-stock purchases and sales, the courts uniformly employ an objective approach, not looking beyond the terms of the statute. However, when faced with "unorthodox" transactions, the courts will look behind the transaction under a pragmatic mode of analysis.[105] Under the pragmatic approach courts will include or exclude unorthodox transactions from section 16(b)'s reach depend-

88. Western Auto Supply Co. v. Gamble–Skogmo, Inc., 348 F.2d 736 (8th Cir.1965), *cert. denied* 382 U.S. 987, 86 S.Ct. 556, 15 L.Ed.2d 475 (1966).

89. *See, e.g.,* Blau v. Lamb, 363 F.2d 507, 528 (2d Cir.1966), *cert. denied* 385 U.S. 1002, 87 S.Ct. 707, 17 L.Ed.2d 542 (1967); Adler v. Klawans, 267 F.2d 840, 849 (2d Cir.1959).

94. Rule 16b–6(c), 17 C.F.R. § 240.16b–6(c).

95. Rule 16b–6(c), 17 C.F.R. § 240.16b–6(c).

96. Cummings v. C.I.R., 506 F.2d 449 (2d Cir.1974), *cert. denied* 421 U.S. 913, 95 S.Ct. 1571, 43 L.Ed.2d 779 (1975); Anderson v. C.I.R., 480 F.2d 1304 (7th Cir.1973).

97. General American Investors Co. v. Commissioner, 348 U.S. 434, 75 S.Ct. 478, 99 L.Ed. 504 (1955).

104. *See* Hearings on S.Res. 84, S.Res. 97 Before The Senate Comm. on Banking and Currency, 73d Cong., 1st Sess. pt. 15 at 6557 (1934).

105. *See* § 13.4 *infra; see also* Thomas L. Hazen, The New Pragmatism Under Section 16(b) of the Securities Exchange Act, 54 N.C.L.Rev. 1 (1975).

ing upon the presence or absence of the potential for speculative abuse. In any event, the section presents severe limitations on insider trading in stock subject to the Exchange Act's reporting requirements. To a large extent section 16(b) remains a trap for the unwary.

§ 13.2[9] Equitable Defenses Rejected

The generally accepted rule is that equitable defenses will not defeat an action brought under section 16(b).[106] Thus, for example, equitable estoppel will not be a defense to a section 16(b) action.[107] *In pari delicto* is not a defense to section 16(b) liability.[108] Thus, the fact that the issuer has participated in the transaction does not preclude recovery,[109] even where the issuer may have been the impetus for the transaction.[110] As is the case with securities law claims generally,[111] waiver will not constitute a defense to section 16(b) liability.[112] The anti-waiver provision does not apply to settlement of existing or threatened litigation.[113] Accordingly, release of liability under section 16 will be upheld if supported by valid consideration. However, if there is no knowledge of the section 16(b) liability at the time of the purported release, the waiver will not be effective.[114]

§ 13.2[10] Exemptions From 16(b)'s Disgorgement Provisions

The SEC has provided a number of exemptions from section 16(b) liability. The section 16 rules adopted in 1991 retained many of the former exemptions.[116] Section 16 does not apply to many foreign issuers.[117] Section 16(b) does not apply to transactions in registered investment company shares that are exempt from the Investment Company Act's short-swing prohibitions.[118] Similarly exempt are transactions exempted from the comparable provisions of the Public Utility Holding Company Act of 1935,[119] and certain

106. *See, e.g.,* Texas International Airlines v. National Airlines, Inc., 714 F.2d 533, 536 (5th Cir.1983), *cert. denied* 465 U.S. 1052, 104 S.Ct. 1326, 79 L.Ed.2d 721 (1984); Roth v. Fund of Funds, Ltd., 405 F.2d 421, 422–23 (2d Cir.1968), *cert. denied* 394 U.S. 975, 89 S.Ct. 1469, 22 L.Ed.2d 754 (1969).

107. *E.g.,* Texas International Airlines v. National Airlines, Inc., 714 F.2d 533, 536 (5th Cir.1983), *cert. denied* 465 U.S. 1052, 104 S.Ct. 1326, 79 L.Ed.2d 721 (1984).

108. *See, e.g.,* Donoghue v. Natural Microsystems Corp., 198 F.Supp.2d 487 (S.D.N.Y.2002).

109. *E.g.,* Texas International Airlines v. National Airlines, Inc., 714 F.2d 533, 536 (5th Cir.1983), *cert. denied* 465 U.S. 1052, 104 S.Ct. 1326, 79 L.Ed.2d 721 (1984).

110. *E.g.,* Roth v. Fund of Funds, Ltd., 405 F.2d 421, 422–23 (2d Cir.1968), *cert. denied* 394 U.S. 975, 89 S.Ct. 1469, 22 L.Ed.2d 754 (1969).

111. *See* § 12.23 *supra.*

112. Section 29(a) of the Exchange Act provides that contracts and stipulations purporting to waive compliance with any provision of the Act or SEC rules promulgated thereunder are void. 15 U.S.C.A. § 78cc(a). Section 14 of the 1933 Act contains a similar provision. 15 U.S.C.A. § 77n.

113. *See, e.g.,* Petro–Ventures, Inc. v. Takessian, 967 F.2d 1337 (9th Cir.1992).

114. Synalloy Corp. v. Gray, 816 F.Supp. 963 (D.Del.1993).

116. *See* Sec.Exch.Act Rel. No. 34–28869, [1990–1991 Transfer Binder] Fed.Sec.L.Rep. (CCH) ¶ 84,709 (Feb. 8, 1991).

In 1994, the SEC proposed broadening the exemptions. *See* Ownership Reports and Trading by Officers, Directors and Principal Security Holders, Exch. Act Rel. No. 34–34514 (SEC Aug. 10, 1994).

117. Many foreign private issuers are exempted by Rule 3a12–3, 17 C.F.R. § 240.3a12–3.

118. Rule 16b–1(a), 17 C.F.R. § 240.16b–1(a). *See* 15 U.S.C.A. § 80a–17(a); Chapter 18 *infra.*

119. Rule 16b–1(b), 17 C.F.R. § 240.16b–1(b).

transactions involving railroads that have been approved by the Interstate Commerce Commission.[120]

Acquisitions of securities resulting from reinvestment of dividends or interest may be exempt from section 16(b). The exemption is conditioned upon the existence of a plan providing for regular reinvestment, and further upon availability of that plan to all holders of the class of securities in question.[121]

Qualifying employee benefit plans, including those involving stock appreciation rights or phantom stock, may qualify for an exemption from section 16(b). SEC Rule 16b–3 divides employee benefit plan transactions into two principal categories: grant/award transactions and participant-directed transactions.[123] The grant and award of securities under qualifying plans are exempt so long as the securities are held for at least six months.[124] Shareholder approval continues to be a requirement for most exempt plans.[125] Rule 16b–3(d)(1) further provides that that stock transactions from an issuer to insiders "involving a grant, award or other acquisition" of issuer equity securities shall be exempt from Section 16(b) liability if the transaction is "approved by the board of directors of the issuer."[126] It is not necessary that each transaction be individually approved so long as the plan authorizing the transaction is approved by the board.[127] The rule also contains two conditions that apply to all plan transactions involving employer securities: (1) the transaction must be pursuant to a written plan and (2) with limited exceptions, the plan must require any derivative securities to be nontransferable.[128] Another condition for the exemption is that any grants of options or other rights to insiders have to be made either (1) by a disinterested committee of directors that makes all substantive decisions with regard to timing, eligibility, pricing, and the amount of the awards or (2) pursuant to an automatic formula which specifies those terms.[129] The reason for this condition is to preclude insiders from influencing key terms, thereby taking advantage of inside information.[130]

Other exemptions from section 16(b) include securities acquired through certain issuer redemptions. There is an exemption for redemption of other securities where the securities so acquired replace securities of an issuer whose assets consist of cash, government securities, and equity securities of the issuer whose securities were acquired.[131] The SEC rules continue the

---

120. Rule 16b–1(c), 17 C.F.R. § 240.16b–1(c).

121. Rule 16b–2, 17 C.F.R. § 240.16b–2.

123. *See* Sec.Exch.Act Rel. No. 34–28869, [1990–1991 Transfer Binder] Fed.Sec.L.Rep. (CCH) ¶ 84,709 (Feb. 8, 1991).

124. Rule 16b–3(c), 17 C.F.R. § 240.16b–3(c).

125. Sec.Exch.Act Rel. No. 34–28869, [1990–1991 Transfer Binder] Fed.Sec.L.Rep. (CCH) ¶ 84,709 (Feb. 8, 1991).

126. 17 C.F.R. § 240.16b–3(d)(1).

127. Gryl v. Shire Pharmaceuticals Group PLC, 298 F.3d 136 (2d Cir.2002).

128. Rule 16b–3(a), 17 C.F.R. § 240.16b–3(a).

129. Rule 16b–3(c), 17 C.F.R. § 240.16b–3(c).

130. *See* Sec.Exch.Act Rel. No. 34–28869, [1990–1991 Transfer Binder] Fed.Sec.L.Rep. (CCH) ¶ 84,709 (Feb. 8, 1991).

131. Rule 16b–4, 17 C.F.R. § 240.16b–4. The new securities must also have a value equivalent to the securities acquired in the redemption. *See also* Levy v. Oz Master Fund, Ltd., 2001 WL 767013 (S.D.N.Y. 2001) (redemption within six months of purchase did not result in § 16(b) liability).

exemption for bona fide gifts[132] and inheritance.[133] Securities acquired in certain mergers also are exempt.[134] The SEC had indicated that Rule 16b–7's exemption is not limited to mergers and might also apply to other share exchanges effectuated through a statutory procedure.[135] This does not mean, however, that every reclassification is exempt under Rule 16b–7.[136]

Rule 16b–8 exempts acquisitions and dispositions resulting from the deposit to or withdrawal of securities from a voting trust.[140] However, the exemption does not apply if there has been a non-exempt purchase or sale of an equity security of the class deposited within six months.[141] Rule 16a–9 provides an exemption from section 16 for acquisitions of rights pursuant to a pro rata grant to all holders of a class of securities.[142]

Two additional exemptions are set forth in the statute. Section 16(d)[143] provides that bona fide market making transactions[144] are not subject to section 16(b), nor are they subject to section 16(a)'s reporting requirements[145] or section 16(c)'s prohibitions[146] regarding short sales and sales against the box. Section 16(e)[147] exempts from section 16 pure arbitrage transactions that are carried out in accordance with applicable SEC rules. SEC Rule 16e–1[148] exempts arbitrage transactions by ten percent beneficial owners who are not also officers and directors of the issuer, while officers' and directors' arbitrage transactions are subject to section 16(a) reporting and 16(b), disgorgement, but not to section 16(c)'s prohibitions against short sales and sales against the box.[149]

In addition to the foregoing exemptions from the disgorgement provisions, section 16(b) excludes from its coverage securities "acquired in good faith in connection with a debt previously contracted."[150] This exemption from section 16(b)'s coverage should be narrowly construed to avoid extending it to transactions where the potential for speculative abuse exists. The exemption accordingly does not apply to shares that were not necessary for retirement of the debt and thus were not directly attributable to the previously acquired debt.[151]

---

132. *See* Dreiling v. Kellett, 281 F.Supp.2d 1215, 1224 (W.D. Wash. 2003) (gift exception to section 16 did not apply to transfer pursuant to escrow arrangement).

133. Rule 16b–5, 17 C.F.R. § 240.16b–5.

134. Rule 16b–7, 17 C.F.R. § 240.16b–7.

135. Interpretive Release on Rules Applicable to Insider Reporting and Trading, Exchange Act Release No. 34–18114, 46 Fed.Reg. 48147, 48176–77 (Sept. 24, 1981).

136. Levy v. Sterling Holding Co., 314 F.3d 106 (3d Cir. 2002).

140. 17 C.F.R. § 240.16b–8.

141. *Id.*

142. 17 C.F.R. § 240.16a–9(b).

143. 15 U.S.C.A. § 78p(d).

144. Market makers are discussed in § 14.10 *infra.*

145. 15 U.S.C.A. § 78p(a).

146. 15 U.S.C.A. § 78p(c).

147. 15 U.S.C.A. § 78p(e).

148. 17 C.F.R. § 240.16e–1.

149. *See* § 12.7 *infra.*

150. 15 U.S.C.A. § 78p(b).

151. C.R.A. Realty Corp. v. Fremont General Corp., 5 F.3d 1341 (9th Cir.1993).

§ 13.2[11] No Indemnification for Liability Under Section 16(b)

In First Golden Bancorporation v. Weiszmann,[152] a director held liable under section 16(b) sought indemnification from his investment advisor. The court rejected the claim for indemnification as contrary to the public policy underlying section 16(b). The court noted that section 16(b) imposes strict liability as a means to deter improper conduct and that the policy of deterrence would be undermined by permitting indemnification. This result is consistent with the SEC's long-time contention that agreements to indemnify individuals and entities from liability for misstatements in a 1933 Act registration statement are void.

§ 13.3 Who Is Subject to Sections 16(a) and (b)? When Does Insider Status Attach?

Section 16(b)'s damage provisions, like section 16(a)'s filing requirements, apply to officers, directors, and ten percent beneficial owners of any class of equity security subject to section 12's registration requirements. Section 16 identifies three classes of persons whose relationship to the issuer is sufficiently close to conclusively presume access to inside information. The Act does not precisely define officer, director, or ten percent beneficial owner; and, as a result numerous questions have arisen as to the scope of section 16's coverage.

§ 13.3[1] Officers and Directors

For example, when dealing with a business trust or other unincorporated form of business association, does a trustee or partner qualify as a director under section 16? Presumably the issue would be approached by asking whether the person performs functions similar to those of a director.[3] While there is no explicit definition of director under the Exchange Act, SEC Rule 3b–2 provides that an " 'officer' means a president, vice president, treasurer, secretary, comptroller, and any other person who performs for an issuer, whether incorporated or unincorporated, functions corresponding to those performed by the foregoing officers." Reasoning by analogy, "director" should include the functional equivalent regardless of title; this view is confirmed by other SEC rules.

When a person, although not holding a formal office, performs the functions of an officer and therefore has access to inside information, section 16(b) will require disgorgement of all short-swing profits.[6] Although expressly refusing to pass on the validity of Rule 3b–2, the Second Circuit adopted a functional equivalency test under the terms of the statute.[7] The SEC's rule was upheld in two subsequent decisions, both of which held that, on the facts

---

152. 942 F.2d 726 (10th Cir.1991).

§ 13.3

3. Section 6(a) of the 1933 Act, which specifies who must sign the registration statement, explicitly addresses this alternative. 15 U.S.C.A. § 77f(a). *Cf.* 17 C.F.R. § 240.3b–2 (definition of "officer").

6. Colby v. Klune, 178 F.2d 872, 873 (2d Cir.1949).

7. 178 F.2d at 875. *Accord* C.R.A. Realty Corp. v. Crotty, 878 F.2d 562, 567 (2d Cir.1989) ("it is the duties of an employee—especially his access to inside information—rather than his corporate title which determine whether he is an officer subject to the short-swing trading restrictions of § 16(b) of the 1934 Act").

of each case, statutory insider status did not attach to an assistant secretary or assistant comptroller.[8]

In the early cases defining "officer," the courts were faced with the issue of whether to subject a person not holding an officer's title to section 16(b) liability. In two subsequent cases the issue was whether a person, although denominated an officer by title, is properly treated as officer" for purposes of section 16(b). In the first case,[9] the court approved a settlement at a discount below the section 16(b) profit because of the strength of the defense that the defendant, although vested with a vice president's title, was not a section 16(b) "officer." The Ninth Circuit held that where a company had three hundred and fifty "executive vice presidents" the title merely created an inference of "opportunities for confidential information."[10] The court went on to say that the defendant vice president was not subject to section 16(b) liability since he met the burden of proof "that the title was merely honorary and did not carry with it any of the executive responsibilities that might otherwise be assumed."[11]

Obligations imposed by section 16 can be seen as one of the burdens of taking such an honorary title. On the other hand, placing the section 16 reporting obligations on middle management can be seen as an undue burden. Courts formerly were reluctant to undertake a detailed factual examination and generally would not look behind the title.[14] Some courts have spoken in terms of a presumption of access to inside information that results from having an officer's title.[15] Such an approach allows the non-executive "officer" to prove that section 16 should not apply because of the lack of access to inside information. The Commission and state corporate law have gone a long way toward doing away with figurehead or "dummy" directors by imposing standards of care.[16] The rationale for not permitting director titles and positions without concomitant obligations is that the title is a "holding out" and thus justifies imposition of fiduciary obligations. The same may not be true of honorary or purely titular officers. Unlike figure-head directors, merely making someone a vice president may not confer any authority nor impose any special fiduciary obligation. Nor, in such a case would the conferring of a title provide any access to inside information. As discussed below, this is the approach taken by current SEC rules.

In addition to the definition of officer contained in Rule 3b–2, Rule 3b–7 defines "executive officer" to include the president, any vice president in charge of a principal unit or division as well as "any other officer who performs a policy making function," or any other person performing "similar

---

8. Lockheed Aircraft Corp. v. Campbell, 110 F.Supp. 282 (S.D.Cal.1953); Lockheed Aircraft Corp. v. Rathman, 106 F.Supp. 810 (S.D.Cal.1952).

9. Schimmel v. Goldman, 57 F.R.D. 481 (S.D.N.Y.1973).

10. Merrill Lynch, Pierce, Fenner & Smith, Inc. v. Livingston, 566 F.2d 1119, 1122 (9th Cir.1978).

11. *Id.*

14. National Medical Enterprises, Inc. v. Small, 680 F.2d 83, 84 (9th Cir.1982).

15. *See* National Medical Enterprises, Inc. v. Small, 680 F.2d 83, 84 (9th Cir.1982); C.R.A. Realty Corp. v. Crotty, 663 F.Supp. 444 (S.D.N.Y.1987).

16. *E.g.* Escott v. BarChris Construction Corp., 283 F.Supp. 643 (S.D.N.Y.1968) (liability under section 11 of the 1933 Act); ABA, Corporate Director's Guidebook, 33 Bus.Law. 1591, 1619–27 (1978). *See* § 7.4 *supra.*

policy making functions.''[18] In 1991, the SEC revamped its section 16 reporting rules and in doing so adopted a definition of officer that is modeled on but expands upon Rule 3b–7's definition of executive officer.[19] Rule 16a–1(f) begins with the basic definition of executive officer and then adds principal financial and accounting officers as well as officers of a parent organization having policy-making functions with respect to the issuer.[20] Consistent with the cases discussed above, the Commission has stated that a person's title alone should not determine whether he or she is subject to section 16. The focus should be on whether, in discharging his or her duties, the individual is likely to obtain information that would be helpful in his or her personal market transactions.[21]

§ 13.3[1][A] Deputization as the Basis of Insider Status

Another problem in determining who is subject to section 16(b) arises in the context of deputization. The Supreme Court has explained that where a partnership has profited from short-swing transactions in a corporation's stock and has designated or "deputized" one of its partners to sit on that corporation's board of directors, the partnership will be deemed to be a "director" under the doctrine of deputization.[22] Even in the absence of deputization, the director-partner's pro rata share of the partnership profits would necessarily have to be disgorged under section 16(b).[23] The Court held that the mere possibility of inside information flowing to the partnership was not sufficient and gave the plaintiff the burden of proving an actual deputizing or agency relationship.[24]

The Second Circuit seems to have retreated from the Supreme Court's heavy burden of proof on the deputization issue. Where a corporation's president and chief executive officer sat on the issuer's board and where that person had a say in the corporation's investment interest, and further where the president resigned as a director of the issuer after the decision to sell within six months of a purchase, deputization was established and the corporation had to disgorge its short-swing profit.[25] The Second Circuit pointed out that although there was no actual proof of a formal or a de facto deputization, the corporation had a recurring pattern of placing a representative on the board of any company in which it owned a substantial number of shares. The defendant's representative on the issuer's board was not only its president and chief executive officer but also had participated in discussions with other corporate personnel about its investment holdings. Deputization was found notwithstanding the lack of evidence of any actual communication

---

18.   17 C.F.R. § 240.3b–7.

19.   Rule 16a–1(f), 17 C.F.R. § 240.16a–1(f). *See* Sec.Exch. Act Rel. No. 34–28869, [1990–1991 Transfer Binder] Fed.Sec.L.Rep. (CCH) ¶ 84,709 (Feb. 8, 1991).

20.   17 C.F.R. § 240.16a–1(f). The rule expressly includes the controller when the issuer has no principal accounting officer.

21.   Sec.Exch. Act Rel. No. 34–28869, [1990–1991 Transfer Binder] Fed.Sec.L.Rep. (CCH) ¶ 84,709 (Feb. 8, 1991), relying on Colby v. Klune, 178 F.2d 872, 873 (2d Cir.1949).

22.   Blau v. Lehman, 368 U.S. 403, 82 S.Ct. 451, 7 L.Ed.2d 403 (1962). *See* Caroll J. Wagner, Jr., Deputization Under Section 16(b): The Implications of Feder v. Martin Marietta Corporation, 78 Yale L.J. 1151 (1969).

23.   Blau v. Lehman, 368 U.S. 403, 82 S.Ct. 451, 7 L.Ed.2d 403 (1962).

24.   *Id.* at 411, 82 S.Ct. at 455.

25.   Feder v. Martin Marietta Corp., 406 F.2d 260 (2d Cir.1969), *cert. denied* 396 U.S. 1036, 90 S.Ct. 678, 24 L.Ed.2d 681 (1970).

of inside information since the potential for abuse was more than a mere possibility. The Second Circuit's approach was quite realistic, given the circumstances surrounding the case.

Although it is clear that the mere presence of an interlocking director will not be sufficient to create a section 16(b) deputization,[27] the subjective or case-by-case nature of analysis means that each situation must be determined on its own facts.

§ 13.3[1][B] Family Relationships

Somewhat akin to the question of deputization is the question whether a spouse's holdings are to be attributed to the other spouse who is a section 16(b) insider. In one case,[31] it was held that a wife's sales were to be matched against her husband's exercise of stock options where the husband was a director. The husband/director did not control the wife's investments; the couple maintained separate brokerage accounts but engaged in joint estate planning. The court reasoned that the wife, by virtue of her relationship and investment related conversations with her husband, had access to inside information. Federal rather than state law determines the question of beneficial ownership with regard to securities held by husband and wife.[32]

With regard to stock held by a spouse or child of an insider or trusts for either, the Seventh Circuit has required a "direct pecuniary benefit" to the insider in order to find section 16(b) liability. "[T]ies of consanguinity," "an enhanced sense of well-being" or the insider's being "led to reduce his gift giving" to the stock owner or its beneficiary will not alone lead to attribution under section 16(b).[33] Reading these two cases together, the courts quite properly will attribute beneficial ownership when it appears that the potential for speculative abuse exists.

§ 13.3[1][C] Timing and Director or Officer Liability; Effect of Resignation

Another question under section 16 is the effect of the timing of the transactions with regard to an officer's or a director's assumption of office or resignation. For example, it has been held that a director who resigned prior to a sale at a profit within six months of his purchase was held subject to section 16(b).[34] Similarly, it was held that section 16(b) liability attaches to a short-swing profit where the defendant became an officer after his purchase but prior to his sale within six months of the purchase.[35] Notwithstanding some dicta to the contrary,[36] these rulings still had substantial following until

---

27. *See* Popkin v. Dingman, 366 F.Supp. 534 (S.D.N.Y.1973).

31. Whiting v. Dow Chemical Co., 523 F.2d 680 (2d Cir.1975).

32. Walet v. Jefferson Lake Sulphur Co., 202 F.2d 433 (5th Cir.1953), *cert. denied* 346 U.S. 820, 74 S.Ct. 35, 98 L.Ed. 346 (1953).

33. C.B.I. Industries, Inc. v. Horton, 682 F.2d 643, 646–47 (7th Cir.1982).

34. Feder v. Martin Marietta Corp., 406 F.2d 260 (2d Cir.1969), *cert. denied* 396 U.S. 1036, 90 S.Ct. 678, 24 L.Ed.2d 681 (1970).

35. Adler v. Klawans, 267 F.2d 840 (2d Cir.1959); Marquette Cement Manufacturing Co. v. Andreas, 239 F.Supp. 962 (S.D.N.Y.1965). *But cf.* Gryl v. Shire Pharmaceuticals Group PLC, 298 F.3d 136 (2d Cir.2002) *affirming* 33 Sec. Reg. & L. Rep. (BNA) 1366 (S.D.N.Y.2001) (for directors who received shares before they became directors the pre-directorship acquisitions were not subject to section 16(b) disgorgement).

36. Allis-Chalmers Manufacturing Co. v. Gulf & Western Industries, Inc., 527 F.2d 335, 346–348 (7th Cir.1975), *cert. denied* 423 U.S. 1078, 96 S.Ct. 865, 47 L.Ed.2d 89 (1976).

subsequent SEC rulemaking.[37] Rule 16a–2 provides that under most circumstances, transactions effectuated by an officer or director prior to becoming subject to section 16(a)'s reporting requirements are not subject to section 16.[38] The only instance in which the reporting requirements apply to this period is when the reporting obligation began as a result of the issuer's having to comply with section 12's registration requirements.[39] Accordingly, when the reporting requirements are occasioned by the appointment or election to office, transactions occurring prior to the appointment or election need not be reported. At least one court has held that this carries over to liability under section 16(b).[40] The SEC rules go on to clarify that officers and directors remain subject to section 16's requirements for the six months following the last sale before cessation of officer or director status.[42]

§ 13.3[2] Ten Percent Beneficial Ownership

§ 13.3[2][A] Who is a Ten Percent Beneficial Owner?

In order to be found to be a beneficial owner of the stock, the purported owner was required by the cases to have a direct pecuniary interest in those shares.[47] The SEC rules define who is considered a beneficial owner, for the purpose of matching purchases and sales, and include in the definition of beneficial owner anyone who has a direct or indirect pecuniary interest.[49] As discussed more fully below, courts and the SEC have extended to concept of beneficial ownership to a group owning more than ten percent in the aggregate and that has agreed to act together in exercising control.[50] This interpretation is consistent with the purposes underlying section 16(b).

What happens if the owner is not made aware that his or her holdings have crossed the ten percent threshold? Especially in the case of issuers who periodically repurchase their shares, the threshold can be a moving target. If an owner is not at least put on inquiry notice that his or her holdings have reached the threshold, then there should be no section 16(b) liability until those facts come to light.[51] In contrast to the cases dealing with officers and directors, section 16(b) on its face provides that where insider status attaches by virtue of ten percent beneficial equity ownership, the section applies only where such person was a beneficial owner "both at the time of the purchase and sale, or the sale and purchase."[52] Notwithstanding some lower court decisions to the contrary, the Supreme Court held that the threshold purchase that pushes the defendant over ten percent beneficial ownership does not qualify as a "purchase" subject to section 16(b) and that only purchases made

---

37. *See* Foremost–McKesson, Inc. v. Provident Securities Co., 423 U.S. 232, 243, n. 16, 96 S.Ct. 508, 515, n. 16, 46 L.Ed.2d 464 (1976).

38. 17 C.F.R. § 240.16a–2.

39. 17 C.F.R. § 240.16a–2(a).

40. Gryl v. Shire Pharmaceuticals Group PLC, 298 F.3d 136 (2d Cir.2002) *affirming* 33 Sec. Reg. & L. Rep. (BNA) 1366 (S.D.N.Y.2001).

42. 17 C.F.R. § 240.16a–2(b).

47. Mayer v. Chesapeake Ins. Co., 877 F.2d 1154, 1160 (2d Cir.1989), *cert. denied* 493 U.S. 1021, 110 S.Ct. 722, 107 L.Ed.2d 741 (1990).

49. Rule 16a–1(a)(2), 17 C.F.R. § 240.16a–1(a)(2).

50. Morales v. Freund, 163 F.3d 763 (2d Cir.1999); Schaffer ex rel. Lasersight Inc. v. CC Investments, LDC, 2002 WL 31869391, Fed.Sec.L.Rep. ¶ 92248 (S.D.N.Y. 2002).

51. C.R.A. Realty Corp. v. Enron Corp., 842 F.Supp. 88 (S.D.N.Y.1994).

52. 15 U.S.C.A. § 78p(b).

after that date will give rise to liability when matched with subsequent sales occurring within six months and resulting in a profit.[55] Thus, the initial purchase that places a non-officer or director shareholder over the ten percent threshold is a "lock-in event" that only gives rise to short-swing liability with respect to additional shares.[56]

In another case,[58] the Court has held that where a ten percent beneficial owner first sells just enough shares to put him below the ten percent threshold, and on the next day liquidates the remainder of his holdings, the second sale cannot be subject to section 16(b) because of the statute's express "at the time of" requirement. This ruling was based on an objective reading of the statute rather than a subjective evaluation of the statutory insider's motives in so structuring the two-step sale.[59]

§ 13.3[2][B] Group Theory and Beneficial Ownership

As discussed in an earlier section of this treatise, when a group of shareholders agree to act together to exercise control, they are treated as a "group" and thus subject to the filing requirements of section 13(d) if their aggregate holdings exceed five percent of a class of equity securities[62] (as compared to section 16's ten percent threshold): This rationale has been extended to section 16(b). In Morales v. Freund,[63] the Second Circuit affirmed a finding that a group of shareholders acting together would be classified as a group and thus as a beneficial owner subject to section 16(b)'s disgorgement requirements. The court reasoned that the application of "group" analysis to the provisions of section 16 is consistent with the purposes of the Act. It certainly is true that if the statute presumes access to inside information because one person owns ten percent of a class of equity securities, that a group acting in concert should also be presumed to have the same access. However, a strict reading of the statutory language may lead to a different result. Section 16 of the Act defines beneficial owner in terms of "every *person* who is directly or indirectly the beneficial owner of more than 10 per centum of any class of equity security."[64]

The existence of a group depends upon a finding that the shareholders comprising the group had an agreement to acquire, hold, or dispose of the securities in question[69] or, alternatively, to exert control over the issuer of the securities.[70] The existence of a group depends an agreement among the group members concerning the control of the shares. As such, the existence of a group will often depend upon findings of fact and thus often will not be

---

55. Foremost-McKesson, Inc. v. Provident Securities Co., 423 U.S. 232, 96 S.Ct. 508, 46 L.Ed.2d 464 (1976).

56. Schaffer ex rel. Lasersight, Inc. v. CC Investments, LDC., 2003 WL 22480052 (S.D.N.Y. 2003).

58. Reliance Electric Co. v. Emerson Electric Co., 404 U.S. 418, 92 S.Ct. 596, 30 L.Ed.2d 575 (1972).

59. In his dissent Justice Douglas argued that a pragmatic view should be taken. 404 U.S. at 427 *et seq.*

62. 15 U.S.C.A. § 78m(d). *See* § 11.2 *supra.*

63. 163 F.3d 763 (2d Cir.1999). *See also, e.g.,* Strauss v. Kopp Investment Advisors, Inc., 1999 WL 787818, [1999–2000 Transfer Binder] Fed. Sec. L. Rep. (CCH) ¶ 90,666 (S.D.N.Y.1999).

64. 15 U.S.C.A. § 78p(a) (emphasis supplied).

69. *See* Schaffer v. CC Investments, LDC, 153 F.Supp.2d 484 (S.D.N.Y.2001).

70. Morales v. Quintel Entertainment, Inc., 249 F.3d 115 (2d Cir.2001).

appropriate for determination on a motion to dismiss.[71] Section 16(b) liability will attach to transactions occurring after the group has been formed but not with regard to transactions occurring contemporaneously with the group's formation.[72] A district court has held that the fact that some members of the group are exempt from section 16 will not provide an exemption unless each member of the group qualifies for an exemption.[73]

§ 13.3[2][E] Convertible Securities

What about convertible securities? The convertible securities do not themselves qualify as a separate class of equity securities, so that ownership of ten percent of the convertible securities will not classify the holder as a ten percent beneficial owner unless it can be said that he or she is a ten percent owner of the underlying security, assuming full dilution.[84] The owner of convertible securities becomes a ten percent beneficial owner with regard to the underlying securities when his or her ownership of the underlying securities if his or her conversion rights were exercised would result in ten percent ownership of the underlying security.[85] Once that threshold is crossed, if the owner converts and then sells the underlying shares within six months, it has been held that the conversion will count as a section 16(b) purchase that can be matched against a subsequent sale within six months for the purpose of finding a section 16(b) profit.[86]

§ 13.4 The Definition of "Purchase" and "Sale" and the Pragmatic Approach Under Section 16(b)[1]

Following the same pattern as section 2(a)(3) of the 1933 Act's definition of "sale,"[2] section 3(a)(13) of the 1934 Act defines "purchase" to "include any contract to buy, purchase, or otherwise acquire."[3] The definition is not limited to normal day-to-day cash for stock transactions. Accordingly courts have had to decide whether other transactions such as exercise of stock options or

---

71. *See, e.g.,* Hollywood Casino Corp. v. Simmons, 2002 WL 1610598 (N.D.Tex.2002) (there were issues of fact as to whether there was agreement between former officers and outside investors to take control of the company).

72. Rosenberg v. XM Ventures, 129 F.Supp.2d 681 (D.Del.2001). As a general proposition, the purchase or other transaction that places the defendant over the 10 percent ownership line will not be matched against subsequent sales for section 16(b) purposes. Foremost–McKesson, Inc. v. Provident Securities Co., 423 U.S. 232, 96 S.Ct. 508, 46 L.Ed.2d 464 (1976).

73. Strauss v. Kopp Investment Advisors, Inc., 1999 WL 787818, [1999–2000 Transfer Binder] Fed. Sec. L. Rep. (CCH) ¶ 90,666 (S.D.N.Y.1999).

84. Medtox Scientific, Inc. v. Morgan Capital, L.L.C., 258 F.3d 763 (8th Cir.2001); Chemical Fund, Inc. v. Xerox Corp., 377 F.2d 107 (2d Cir.1967); Levy v. Oz Master Fund, Ltd., 2001 WL 767013, [2001–2002 Transfer Binder] Fed. Sec. L. Rep. (CCH) ¶ 91,503 (S.D.N.Y.2001) (but the exercise of the conversion right was not a purchase or sale as defined by section 16).

85. Medtox Scientific, Inc. v. Morgan Capital L.L.C., 258 F.3d 763 (8th Cir. 2001) *affirming* 50 F.Supp.2d 896 (D.Minn.1999). *But see,* Levy v. Oz Master Fund, Ltd., 2001 WL 767013 (S.D.N.Y. 2001) (defendant was not beneficial owner at the time of purchase).

86. Medtox Scientific, Inc. v. Morgan Capital L.L.C., 258 F.3d 763 (8th Cir. 2001), *affirming* 50 F.Supp.2d 896 (D. Minn. 1999).

§ 13.4

1. Parts of this section were adapted from Thomas L. Hazen, The New Pragmatism Under Section 16(b) of the Securities Exchange Act, 54 N.C.L.Rev. 1 (1975).

2. 15 U.S.C.A. § 77b(a)(3). *See* § 5.1 *supra. See also* § 12.6 *supra* for discussion of what constitutes a purchase or sale under SEC Rule 10b–5.

3. 15 U.S.C.A. § 78c(a)(13).

conversion rights and exchanges of securities pursuant to a merger—so called "unorthodox transactions"[4]—fall within section 16(b)'s reach.

A number of early section 16(b) cases raised the question of whether a voluntary conversion of stock constituted a purchase of the new security or, alternatively, a sale of the convertible security, so as to have section 16(b) consequences. The cases were in conflict,[5] although they tended not to find a purchase or sale unless the surrounding circumstances created a potential for the type of speculative abuse that section 16(b) was designed to prevent. It was out of the conversion cases that the pragmatic or subjective trend arose, with the courts looking at the facts to determine if section 16 evils were present.

The opportunity to realize a profit begins the moment an insider purchases or is granted a derivative security. It follows that the acquisition of a derivative security not only is a reportable event under section 16(a),[10] it can be matched against dispositions of either the derivative or underlying security occurring within the preceding or following six months.[11] Thus for example, an acquisition of a call option may be matched with any disposition of either the underlying security or other equivalent call option.[12] Conversely, an acquisition of a put option may be matched with an acquisition of the underlying security or disposition of an equivalent put position.[13] Just as acquisitions of derivative securities are reportable and matchable events, dispositions of derivative securities have similar section 16 implications.[14]

In the leading case of Kern County Land Co. v. Occidental Petroleum Corp.,[21] the Supreme Court addressed the applicability of section 16(b) to sales of the target company's shares by a defeated tender offeror. The management of Kern, the target company, had opposed the takeover by defendant Occidental, and within two weeks responded with a defensive stock for stock merger with Tenneco. Rather than sell its holdings immediately, two weeks after approval of the merger, Occidental entered into an agreement with Tenneco to issue to Tenneco an option to purchase the Tenneco preferred shares received pursuant to the merger in six months at one hundred and five dollars per share. In return, Tenneco agreed to pay Occidental a premium of ten dollars per option which would be applied to the exercise price. More than six months after both Occidental's purchase of the Old Kern stock and its

---

4. The term "unorthodox" has been "applied to stock conversions, exchanges pursuant to mergers and other corporate reorganizations, stock reclassifications, and dealings in options, rights and warrants." Kern County Land Co. v. Occidental Petroleum Corp., 411 U.S. 582, 594, n. 24, 93 S.Ct. 1736, 1744, n. 24, 36 L.Ed.2d 503 (1973). It has been applied to sales pursuant to tender offers prior to merger, Makofsky v. Ultra Dynamics Corp., 383 F.Supp. 631, 637 (S.D.N.Y.1974).

5. *Compare, e.g.,* Heli–Coil Corp. v. Webster, 352 F.2d 156 (3d Cir.1965) (conversion is a section 16(b) purchase; applying objective test) *with* Petteys v. Butler, 367 F.2d 528 (8th Cir.1966), *cert. denied* 385 U.S. 1006, 87 S.Ct. 712, 17 L.Ed.2d 545 (1967) (finding no purchase, utilizing "pragmatic" analysis).

10. Rule 16a–4(a), 17 C.F.R. § 240.16a–4(a). *See* § 13.1 *supra.*

11. Rule 16a–6(a), 17 C.F.R. § 240.16b–6(a).

12. Sec.Exch.Act Rel. No. 34–28869, [1990–1991 Transfer Binder] Fed.Sec.L.Rep. (CCH) ¶ 84,709 (Feb. 8, 1991).

13. *Id.*

14. Thus, for example, dispositions of call positions may be matched against acquisitions of the underlying security or acquisitions of another call equivalent position. Similarly, dispositions of put positions may be matched against dispositions of the underlying security or call equivalent positions of the underlying security. *Id.*

21. 411 U.S. 582, 93 S.Ct. 1736, 36 L.Ed.2d 503 (1973).

acquisition via the exchange of the Tenneco stock,[22] Tenneco exercised the option. The district court held that Occidental's acquisition of Tenneco stock pursuant to the Old Kern–Tenneco merger was a section 16(b) "sale" within six months of its Kern purchases pursuant to the original tender offer, and further that the subsequent option agreement was a "sale" of the revised securities and thus also within the reach of section 16(b).[23] The Second Circuit reversed since, *inter alia,* Occidental's obligation to dispose of the shares had not been fixed until Tenneco exercised the option more than six months after the purchase.

The Supreme Court affirmed the Second Circuit's ruling and its adherence to a pragmatic analysis of the transaction:

> In deciding whether borderline [unorthodox] transactions are within the reach of the statute, the courts have come to inquire whether the transaction may serve as a vehicle for the evil which Congress sought to prevent—the realization of short-swing profits based upon access to inside information—thereby endeavoring to implement congressional objectives without extending the reach of tha statute beyond its intended limits.[25]

The Court's opinion recognized that Occidental was in a very difficult position at the time that the Old Kern–Tenneco merger had been announced since the only realistic alternative to participating in the exchange and subsequent sale to Tenneco would have been to dispose of the Old Kern stock on the open market via a garden variety cash-for-stock sale which clearly would have resulted in certain 16(b) liability.

Proceeding on the theory that there had not been a statutory sale by virtue of the share exchange,[26] the next question for decision was whether Occidental "sold" its new Tenneco shares on the date of the option agreement or at the later date it was exercised. The Court reasoned that Occidental's obligation to dispose of the stock did not become fixed until Tenneco's exercise of the option on December 11. The Court also pointed out that as of June 2, Occidental had not locked in a profit since, had the stock price declined sufficiently in value by the exercise date, the defendant would have been left with Tenneco holdings worth less than the "purchase" price, notwithstanding the option premium.[27] Although this pragmatic analysis creates some uncertainty in the section 16(b) analysis, it gives the courts the ability to achieve the statute's purpose.[28]

The apex of the pragmatic approach was achieved by the Fourth Circuit in Gold v. Sloan[29] where the court held one selling director liable under section 16(b) while exonerating three others. The issue was whether an

---

22. As a holder of Kern stock under the merger, Occidental received shares of Tenneco, one of its largest competitors.

23. Abrams v. Occidental Petroleum Corp., 323 F.Supp. 570, 579–80 (S.D.N.Y.1970), *reversed* 450 F.2d 157 (2d Cir.1971).

25. 411 U.S. at 594–95, 93 S.Ct. at 1744–45 (footnotes omitted).

26. *Accord* Heublein, Inc. v. General Cinema Corp., 722 F.2d 29 (2d Cir.1983), *affirming* 559 F.Supp. 692 (S.D.N.Y.1983).

27. 411 U.S. at 602, 93 S.Ct. at 1748.

28. *See, e.g.,* Transcontinental Realty Investors, Inc. v. Gotham Partners, L.P., 218 F.Supp.2d 415 (S.D.N.Y. 2002) (option arrangement was unorthodox transaction but was not subject to speculative abuse).

29. 486 F.2d 340 (4th Cir.1973), *cert. denied* 419 U.S. 873, 95 S.Ct. 134, 42 L.Ed.2d 112 (1974).

exchange of stock pursuant to a merger between the Atlantic Research and Susquehanna corporations constituted a "purchase" under 16(b).[30] Within less than six months after the merger had been consummated, the defendant insiders sold their newly acquired Susquehanna holdings at a profit. The Fourth Circuit pointed to the Supreme Court's decision in *Kern County* as having "resolved [the] conflict and adopted what had earlier been described as a 'pragmatic rather than technical' test"[31] for unorthodox transactions. It was thus necessary "to examine the particular situation of each defendant as it relates to the merger."[32] Three of the defendants had no contact whatsoever with the merger negotiations and thus were held to have had no access to Susquehanna's inside information.[33] In contrast, the fourth defendant, Atlantic's chief executive officer, had been "in complete charge of the negotiations" and "had access to the books and records * * *."[34] Accordingly, this access created a potential for abuse and thus warranted finding the merger exchange to have been a section 16(b) purchase by the inside director. Although certainly consistent with the Supreme Court's rationale in *Kern*, the *Gold* decision has been criticized as running contrary to the straightforward, crude rule of thumb that section 16(b) was designed to provide.[35] Critics of the *Gold* decision were particularly upset with the ruling that the same transaction produces differing treatment for individuals falling within the statute's objective reach. However, the pragmatic trend continued to flourish.[36]

Involuntariness often is an important element of an unorthodox transaction. Therefore, since a sale pursuant to a tender offer is not involuntary, section 16(b) applies to an exchange offer.[58] Furthermore, since a sale pursuant to a *cash* tender offer is equally voluntary, the pragmatic analysis would be equally inapplicable.

§ 13.5 Prohibitions Against Short Sales by Insiders—Section 16(c)

Section 16(c) of the Exchange Act[1] prohibits certain speculative activity by insiders who must file reports under the reporting provisions of section

---

30. Atlantic Research Corporation had merged into the Susquehanna Corporation via an exchange of stock; the defendants in *Gold* had been holders of Atlantic stock for more than six months prior to the merger negotiations, thus eliminating the problem of whether the exchange was a section 16(b) "sale," which had been dealt with in the *Kern County* decision. The defendants were also officers and directors of Atlantic and under the terms of the merger agreement occupied similar positions with respect to Susquehanna, the surviving corporation.

31. 486 F.2d at 343.

32. *Id.* at 344.

33. *Id.*.

34. 486 F.2d at 351–52.

35. *See. e.g.,* Note, Securities Exchange Act § 16(b): Fourth Circuit Harvests Some Kernels of Gold, 42 Fordham L.Rev. 852 (1974); Recent Developments, Securities-' 16(b)-Mergers as a "Purchase," 20 Wayne L.Rev. 1415 (1974).

36. *See, e.g.,* Portnoy v. Revlon, Inc., 650 F.2d 895 (7th Cir.1981) (finding no sale in merger agreement); Heublein, Inc. v. General Cinema Corp., 559 F.Supp. 692 (S.D.N.Y.1983) (no sale in defensive merger), *affirmed* 722 F.2d 29 (2d Cir.1983); Reece Corp. v. Walco National Corp., 565 F.Supp. 158 (S.D.N.Y.1981) (two-step transaction treated as one "sale" in violation of § 16(b)); Colan v. Cutler–Hammer, Inc., 516 F.Supp. 1342 (N.D.Ill.1981) (finding a sale pursuant to a merger, following the rationale of Gold).

58. Colan v. Mesa Petroleum Co., 941 F.2d 933 (9th Cir.1991), *amended* 951 F.2d 1512 (9th Cir.1991), *cert. denied* 504 U.S. 911, 112 S.Ct. 1943, 118 L.Ed.2d 548 (1992).

§ 13.5

1. 15 U.S.C.A. § 78p(c).

16(a)[2] (*i.e.*, officers, directors, and ten percent beneficial owners of any class of equity securities subject to the Exchange Act's reporting requirements).[3] The section is aimed at two types of speculative transactions: (1) short sales,[4] or selling the security of the issuer without owning the underlying security, and (2) sales against the box,[5] where the seller delays in delivering the securities.[6] In both instances, the investor's hope is that the price will decline from the time of sale, thus enabling the seller to cover at a lower price. Both short sales and sales against the box are permissible trades, provided there is compliance with the applicable SEC rules[7] and margin requirements.[8] Both short sales and sales against the box present the potential for speculative abuse where the seller has access to inside information and thus both are prohibited by section 16(c) just as short-swing profits based on long positions in securities must be disgorged under section 16(b).[9] It has been held that the section applies only to shares beneficially owned by the insider, but not to shares sold by an insider acting merely as an agent for the true owners.[10]

Section 16(c) operates to make it unlawful to sell the security if the selling insider either (1) does not own the security or (2) if he or she owns the security but does not deliver it within twenty days or deposit it in the mail within five days. The section provides that "no person shall be deemed to have violated this subsection if he proves that notwithstanding the exercise of good faith he was unable to make such delivery or deposit within such time, or that to do so would cause undue inconvenience or expense."[11]

Although they are certainly legitimate speculating devices in certain instances, the practices of selling short[12] and selling against the box are high risk transactions which, as in the case with the short-swing profit,[13] are subject to speculative abuse and are therefore declared improper for insiders.[14] It has been held that section 16(c) was not intended to create a private remedy parallel to the one provided by section 16(b).[15]

---

2. 15 U.S.C.A. § 78p(a). *See* § 13.1 *supra*.

3. 15 U.S.C.A. § 78*l*. *See* § 9.2 *supra*.

4. Short sale: When a seller believes the price of a stock will fall, he or she borrows stock from a lender and sells the borrowed shares to the buyer. Later, he or she buys similar stock to pay back the lender, hopefully at a lower price than he or she received on sale to the buyer.

5. Sale against the box: When the seller anticipates a decline in the price of stock he or she owns, he or she will sell it to a buyer at the present market price, but deliver it later, when hopefully the market price will have fallen below the sales price, thus creating a paper profit for the seller.

6. *See, e.g.,* SEC v. Le Duc, CV–1185 02–CV–1185, SEC News Digest 2002–109, 2002 SECDIG 2002–109–9, 2002 WL 1225527 (D. Minn. 2002) (consent order to § 16(c) violations).

7. 17 C.F.R. §§ 240.10a–1, 10a–2. *See* § 14.22 *infra*.

8. The margin requirements address the extension of credit for securities transactions. *See* § 14.9 *infra*. It is clearly unlawful to enter a sell order without owning the underlying security in the absence of full disclosure. *See* United States v. Naftalin, 441 U.S. 768, 99 S.Ct. 2077, 60 L.Ed.2d 624 (1979).

9. *See* § 13.2 *supra*.

10. Rogers v. Valentine, 306 F.Supp. 34 (S.D.N.Y.1969), *affirmed* 426 F.2d 1361 (2d Cir.1970).

11. 15 U.S.C.A. § 78p(c). *See* Fuller v. Dilbert, 244 F.Supp. 196 (S.D.N.Y.1965), *affirmed sub nom.* Righter v. Dilbert, 358 F.2d 305 (2d Cir.1966) (seller showed inconvenience).

12. *See, e.g.,* Short Sales, Sec. Exch. Act Rel. No. 34–50103, 2004 WL 1697019 (SEC 2004) (adopting Regulation SHO that regulates short sales generally).

13. 15 U.S.C.A. § 78p(b). *See* §§ 13.1–13.4 *supra*.

14. 15 U.S.C.A. § 78p(c).

15. Executive Telecard, Ltd. v. Mayer, 941 F.Supp. 435 (S.D.N.Y.1996).

SEC Rule 16c–1[16] provides that section 16(c)'s prohibition against short sales and sales against the box will not affect the validity of transactions executed by a broker in which the broker has no interest. The purpose of this exemption is to assure that the purchaser of the security in question will not be subject to having the sale set aside where the broker has executed the order even though the insider has violated the Act. In such a case, the loss if any will have to fall on the broker.

Rule 16c–2[18] exempts from the prohibition against insider short sales and sales against the box, all sales made by or on behalf of a dealer in connection with distributions of a substantial block of securities (1) if the sales are traceable to an over-allotment and the dealer is participating as a member of the underwriting group or selling group, or (2) if a nonparticipating dealer in good faith intends to offset the sale with a security to be acquired by or on behalf of the dealer as an underwriter, participant, or member of the selling group. Former Rule 16c–2(b) provided that the exemption is available only if other persons not covered by section 16(c) are participating in the distribution of the block of securities on terms at least as favorable as those of the insider and dealer claiming the exemption.

There is a third exemption from section 16(c); this exemption applies to certain securities which the seller is about to acquire. Rule 16c–3[19] exempts from the section's coverage sales of securities not yet acquired where the seller, as an "incident to ownership of an issued security and without the payment of consideration, [has a right] to receive another security 'when issued' or 'when distributed'." Rule 16c–3's exemption is available only if (1) the sale of the security to be acquired is made subject to the same conditions attaching to the right of acquisition, (2) the seller exercises reasonable diligence to deliver the security promptly after the right of acquisition matures, and (3) the seller has filed appropriate reports on the applicable form under section 16(a). Further, Rule 16c–3 is not available as an exemption for transactions combining sales of when-issued securities with other securities where in the aggregate the total amount sold exceeds the number of units owned by the seller plus those he is entitled to receive on a when-issued basis.[20]

The prohibition of section 16(c) against short sales and sales against the box is strictly construed because of the speculative abuse that can arise out of such transactions. On the other hand, it has been held that a statutory insider's issuance of a naked "call" option, which if exercised would have triggered an obligation to sell and deliver the securities within twenty days after the sale, was not in itself a sale and therefore did not violate section 16(c).[21]

The SEC clarified the treatment of derivative securities for the purposes of section 16(c)'s short sale prohibitions. Rule 16c–4,[22] which was adopted in

---

16. 17 C.F.R. § 240.16c–1.

18. 17 C.F.R. § 240.16c–2.

19. 17 C.F.R. § 240.16c–3.

20. *Id.*

21. Silverman v. Landa, 306 F.2d 422 (2d Cir.1962), *affirming* 200 F.Supp. 193 (S.D.N.Y. 1961).

22. 17 C.F.R. § 240.16c–4.

connection with the Commission's adoption of the revised section 16 rules,[23] provides that establishing or increasing a put equivalent position is exempt from section 16(c) so long as it is a covered position (the put position does not exceed the amount of underlying securities owned). This exemption makes clear that an uncovered put equivalent should be treated as a short sale, as, at least in the context of section 16(c)'s prohibitions, an uncovered put option is functionally equivalent from an investment standpoint.[24]

---

23. *See* Sec.Exch. Act Rel. No. 34–28869, [1990–1991 Transfer Binder] Fed.Sec.L.Rep. (CCH) ¶ 84,709 (Feb. 8, 1991).

24. *But cf.* Baker Botts, LLP, 32 Sec. Reg. & L. Rep. (BNA) 1009, 2000 WL 972990 (SEC No Action Letter July 13, 2000) (expiration of put option more than six months after it was written does not violate section 16(b); there was no mention of any impact of section 16(c)'s prohibition against insider short sales).

Chapter 14

MARKET REGULATION;
BROKER–DEALERS

Table of Sections

---

§ 14.1   Market Regulation—An Overview

Regulation of securities brokers is not new. Securities broker regulation can be traced back to the thirteenth century. This early regulation took the form of licensing securities brokers in London.[1] Notwithstanding this regula-

---

1. Statute of Edward I, in 1285.

tory structure, stock exchange dealings, with speculation subject to alternate booms and panics, became a part of the English markets in the latter part of the seventeenth century. There were periods of speculation and wild fluctuations in the market.[2] This was followed by English legislation by the end of the seventeenth century, which was enacted to protect investors against unscrupulous manipulation by stock jobbers and stock brokers.[4] Many of the U.S. states adopted similar stock jobber and stock broker regulation. For example, in 1829, in reaction to speculative fever, New York enacted a Stock Jobbing Act[5] which was designed to control "the more shadowy forms of financial speculation."[6] This and similar legislation proved to be ineffective, and there was no comprehensive regulation of securities brokers in this country until the adoption of the Securities Exchange Act of 1934. Among other things, the Exchange Act created the SEC and charged this federal agency with regulating the securities markets. As discussed in the sections that follow, over the years this has developed into a comprehensive system of SEC regulation and self regulation by the securities exchanges and the National Association of Securities Dealers.

§ 14.1[1] How The Markets Operate—An Overview

SEC regulation is supplemented by its oversight of the self-regulatory organizations (SROs). An exchange is a securities market that is formally organized as an exchange in contrast to the "over-the-counter" markets which is a term that describes the trading of securities other than on a formal centralized exchange. At one time there were two major stock exchanges— The New York Stock Exchange and the American Stock Exchange—and several regional stock exchanges. In addition to exchange-traded securities, there is the over-the-counter market where non-exchange listed securities are traded. At one time, most "prestige" securities were traded on the New York Exchange, or "big board" which carries the most prestige of the United States securities markets. One reason for the higher prestige of the New York Stock Exchange is the listing requirements for securities, with the New York's listing standards being more difficult for a company to satisfy. Over the years, the over-the-counter markets gained in their prestige and today many "blue chip" companies in the technology field are traded in those markets. Microsoft and Intel are two notable examples.

There are also seven regional exchanges which at one time only traded secondary stocks and provided regional trading for New York and American Exchange listed securities.[11] Today some of the regional exchanges such as the Chicago, Pacific, and Philadelphia exchanges are major centers for options trading.

An exchange, as the name implies, provides a central clearing house for the trading of its listed securities. Originally all transactions took place

---

2. Promoters of both incorporated and unincorporated companies foisted doubtful schemes on the investing public. *See* 1 James D. Cox & Thomas Lee Hazen Cox & Hazen on Corporations § 2.2 (3d 2002).

4. 8 & 9 Wm. 3, ch. 32 (1697) ("An act to restrain the number and ill practice of brokers and stock jobbers"); see Lane, The Years Before the Stock Exchange, 7 Hist. Today 760, 761 (1957).

5. Stock Jobbing Act, 1 N.Y. REV. STAT. 710, tit. 19, art. 2, § 6 (1829)

6. See The Development of the Law of Gambling 1776–1976 150 (National Institute for Law Enforcement and Criminal Justice Grant No. 74–NI–99–0030, Nov. 1977).

11. *See* J. Walter, The Role of the Regional Security Exchanges (1958).

physically on the floor of the exchange. While this in large part is still true today, there has been some movement towards more of a national market system with automated quotations and a consolidated tape reflecting all transactions and volume whether or not the transactions are made on the exchange floor. Trading on the exchange floor is carried out by "specialists" in each listed security, whose job it is to help maintain an orderly market.[14] By the end of the twentieth century, the mechanics of many trading processes had been automated and computerized.

Securities not traded on one or more of the national exchanges[15] are traded in the over-the-counter markets[16] which are coordinated by the NASD. There is no central exchange floor but merely a matching of bid and asked quotes for each security. The matching of these offers to buy and offers to sell securities is carried out by market-makers with respect to each security.[17] With its national market quotation system, the NASD has moved toward a national market system.[18] This national market system has been successful in keeping many companies in the over-the-counter markets that in the past would have moved to the New York Stock Exchange. NASDAQ is not a national securities exchange as that term is used in the 1934 Act.[19] In another attempt to strengthen its competitive position, the NASD acquired the American Stock Exchange. The exchange was acquired by the NASD but as a subsidiary and continued to be operated as a separate entity. In 2003, the NASD entered into an agreement to sell the American Stock Exchange to GTCR Golder Rauner LLC (GTCR), a Chicago-based private equity firm. The NASD did not abandon its acquisitive activities. In 2006, NASDAQ acquired a substantial stake in the London Stock Exchange. That same year, the NASDAQ national market became registered under the Exchange Act as a national securities exchange. The New York Stock Exchange also made major acquisitions. It acquired Archipelago, one of the leading ECNs. As a result of the NYSE—Archipelago merger, the New York Stock Exchange became a publicly traded company. Subsequently the NYSE eyed international expansion when it entered into an agreement to merge with Euronext—a major offshore market.

Prior to 1976, the exchanges prohibited "off-board" trading of listed securities. This prohibition has now been abolished as part of the movement towards coordinated national markets, thereby permitting off-exchange transactions in exchange-listed securities. The SEC initiated proposals for a national market system.[21] There is not yet a single, unified national market system, and there may never be. However, strides have been made in this direction through the consolidated reports of transactions in exchange-listed securities provided by the automated Intermarket Trading System (ITS), a communica-

---

14. *See* § 14.11 *infra.*

15. Frequently there are dual or multiple listings on regional exchanges for New York and American Stock Exchange listed securities. Dual listing between the New York and American Exchanges has happened on occasion but is exceedingly rare.

16. *See* Irwin Friend, G. Wright Hoffman, Willis J. Winn, Morris Hamberg & Stanley Schor, The Over-the-Counter Securities Markets (1958).

17. *See* § 14.2[1] *infra.*

18. *See* 17 C.F.R. §§ 240.11Aa–1–11Ac–2.

19. *See* Fezzani v. Bear, Stearns & Co., Inc., 2004 WL 744594 (S.D.N.Y.2004).

21. *See* SEC Statement on the Future Structure of the Securities Markets (1972).

tions network that helps centralize activity among the exchanges.[22] The NASD now lists several hundred of its most frequently traded securities in its national market. Section 12(f) of the Exchange Act permits unlisted trading privileges through the medium of an exchange for securities listed on another exchange or traded in the over-the-counter markets.[24] Additionally under Rule 19c–3,[25] the SEC permits off-exchange trading of exchange listed securities. There has thus been continued movement towards facilitating trading in securities across various markets.[27] Also, the SEC for a long time has taken the position that exchanges may not prevent its member broker-dealers from trading on other securities exchanges.[28]

Although a completely unified national market system might arguably benefit investors and promote market efficiency,[29] old institutions die hard and thus the exchange system and over-the-counter markets are likely to remain the bulwarks of the securities markets for quite a long period of time. Furthermore, there are some indications that the centralized exchanges perform a function, including policing of their members and listed companies, that is not accomplished through an automated quotation system.

One development in the move toward a world-wide market was the move by a number of stock exchanges to permit twenty-four hour trading of securities. The New York Stock Exchange historically prohibited off-hours trades except in connection with foreign markets. As a first step in this new direction, the major exchanges expanded the length of their trading day. The SEC now permits after hours trading through the exchanges[32] and various electronic communications networks that have been approved as public trading markets.[33] As noted above, the New York Stock Exchange acquired Archipelago, one of the leading ECNs. As a result of the NYSE—Archipelago merger, the New York Stock Exchange became a publicly traded company. The NYSE eyed international expansion when it entered into an agreement to merge with Euronext—a major offshore market.

Technological advancements have now created an environment in which electronic trading systems can facilitate off-exchange trading.[37] Another outgrowth of this technology was the approval, originally on a one-year pilot basis, of an NASD electronic bulletin board for computerized quotations for stocks not listed on a national exchange or in the NASDAQ system.[38] The electronic bulletin board is not an established part of the NASD's over-the-

---

22. *See* Sec.Exch. Act Rel. No. 34–15671 (March 22, 1979); SEC, A Monitoring Report on the Operation of the Intermarket Trading System 5–9 (1981).

24. 1934 Act § 12 (f)(1)(A), 15 U.S.C.A. § 78*l*(f)(1)(A).

25. 17 C.F.R. § 240.19c–3.

27. *See, e.g.,* Yakov Amihud & Haim Mendelson, A New Approach to The Regulation of Trading Across Securities Markets, 71 N.Y.U.L. Rev. 1411 (1996).

28. See In the Matter of the Rules of the New York Stock Exchange, 10 S.E.C. 270, 292, 1941 WL 36871 (1941).

29. The national market system is discussed in § 14.2 *infra*.

32. Exchange after hours trading has been limited to institutional investors and large block transactions.

33. *See, e.g.,* C.F.R. §§ 240.11Ac1–1, 11Ac1–4.

37. Off-exchange trading permits large institutions to bypass the exchange. Bypassing the exchange can decrease transaction costs for large investors. It has been predicted that before long about twenty of the nation's largest investment funds will bypass the exchanges and trade between themselves.

38. Sec.Exch.Act Rel. No. 34–27975 (May 1, 1990).

counter network. Also, in conjunction with its adoption of Rule 144A,[39] the SEC approved the NASD's screen-based computer and communication system called PORTAL (Private Offerings, Resales and Trading through Automated Linkages) to facilitate secondary trading of Rule 144A securities.

Another major development of the securities markets has been the move toward demutualization. For most of their history, the exchanges and the NASD were organized as mutual membership organizations. In the late 1990s, the New York Stock Exchange announced its intent to demutualize and transform into a profit-making corporation. When eventually undertaken, this will involve placing the regulatory operations in a separate entity that will not be part of the for-profit corporation. No concrete steps in this direction have yet been taken. However, the NASD has demutualized and has spun off its regulatory functions to NASDR (National Association of Securities Dealers Regulation). In addition, the International Securities Exchange and the Pacific Stock Exchange have demutualized.

§ 14.1[2] Options Trading and Other Derivatives

In addition to the stock and bond markets, the SEC regulates the options markets wherein there is public trading of put and call options for securities and indexes. The options themselves qualify as securities which are separate and distinct from the underlying securities.[43] Accordingly, the public trading of options contracts on stock, stock indexes, and other securities is subject to SEC regulation. Options on securities and certain indexes are publicly traded on the American Stock Exchange as well as many of the regional exchanges— primarily the Midwest, Pacific, and Philadelphia Exchanges. Rather than have the exchanges separately register each option that is publicly traded, the Options Clearing Corporation files applicable disclosure documents governing the generic options—*i.e.*, put and call options on individual securities. These disclosure documents not only reveal the mechanics of options trading but also the risks peculiarly associated with options trading.[44] These options-related disclosures are also designed to help inform investors as to the various option investment strategies.

As noted elsewhere in this treatise,[47] the Commodity Futures Trading Commission (CFTC) regulates financial futures. Options and index futures have been cited as the cause of increased volatility.[48] As a result various proposals have been considered, including earlier options and futures expiration and the disclosure of open orders.

In 2000, there was a massive overhaul of commodities regulation.[51] The revolutionary legislation introduced three tiers of commodities markets and parallel tiers of regulation.[52] The 2000 overhaul of commodities regulation also

---

39. 17 C.F.R. § 230.144A, which is discussed in § 4.29 *supra*.

43. 15 U.S.C.A. § 77b(a)(1); 15 U.S.C.A. § 78c(a)(10). *See* § 1.6 *supra*.

44. 17 C.F.R. § 240.9b–1 (options disclosure document). *See also* NASD Manual (CCH) 2183–84.

47. *See* § 22.7 *infra*.

48. *See, e.g.,* Franklin R. Edwards, Stock Index Futures and Stock Market Volatility: Evidence and Implications, 6 Commod.L. Letter 3 (Nov.-Dec. 1986).

51. Commodity Futures Modernization Act of 2000, Pub. Law No. 106–554, 114 Stat. 2763 (Dec. 21, 2000).

52. The highest degree of regulation remains with the designated commodities contract markets where retail futures trading takes place. The 2000 legislation created a type of contract

formally recognized the over-the-counter commodities markets and these markets which are virtually unregulated except for antifraud proscriptions[53] are open only to the largest institutional investors dealing in certain types of swap and other hybrid contracts.[54] At the same time, both the securities and commodities laws were amended to provide that securities-based swap agreements are not securities,[55] although they remain subject to the securities laws' antifraud provisions.[56] The degree of CFTC involvement in derivatives markets thus depends on the nature of the investors that are permitted to participate and the types of commodities based products being offered.

Until 2001, futures instruments on individual stocks were not permitted. However, the commodities markets wanted a share of the trading volume and the Commodities Futures Trading Commission agreed. In September 2000, the SEC and CFTC agreed on a proposal for submission to Congress.[57] This legislation was enacted in December that same year.[58] Futures on individual stocks thus are subject to both SEC and CFTC regulation.[59]

§ 14.1[3] Market Regulation—History, Background, and Overview

§ 14.1[3][A] Background

While the Securities Act of 1933 regulates the distribution of securities,[60] the Securities Exchange Act of 1934 charges the SEC with the authority to supervise daily market activity. In addition to imposing disclosure requirements upon issuers of publicly traded securities,[61] the Exchange Act of 1934 regulates the market place. Regulating the market place means regulating broker-dealers, securities exchanges, clearing organizations, and the over-the-counter markets. Although the SEC has direct authority, a great deal of market regulation is carried out through its oversight of national exchanges and self-regulatory organizations.[62] The SEC oversight responsibilities include the review of rulemaking by self-regulatory organizations.

---

market for the trading of futures contracts—an "exempt board of trade." An exempt board of trade can be recognized as a derivatives transaction execution facility and is subject to fewer regulatory requirements than CFTC designated contract markets. The third tier is the formal recognition of over-the-counter derivatives instruments for institutional investors. *See* § 22.6 *infra*.

53. The 2000 legislation also provided that although excluded from the definition of security under the securities acts, commodities based swap agreements are subject to the securities laws' antifraud provisions.

54. Commodity Futures Modernization Act of 2000, Pub. Law 106–554, 114 Stat. 2763 (December 21, 2000).

55. 15 U.S.C.A. §§ 77b(a)(1), 78c(a)(10).

56. 15 U.S.C.A. §§ 77q(a), 78j(b).

57. *See* Single Stock Futures Would be Securities Under Agencies' Agreement for Lifting Ban, 32 Sec. Reg. & L. Rep. (BNA) 1256, 1256 (September 18, 2000).

58. Pub. Law No. 106–554, 114 Stat. 2763 (Dec. 21, 2000).

59. *Id.*

60. *See* chapters 2–3 *supra*.

61. *See* chapter 9 *supra*.

62. *See* § 14.3 *infra*. For a detailed history of broker-dealer operations and regulation generally, *see* Jerry W. Markham & Thomas L. Hazen, Broker–Dealer Operations Under Securities and Commodities Law: Financial Responsibilities, Credit Regulation, and Customer Protection, chs. 1, 2 (2d ed. 2003).

§ 14.1[3][B] Nature of Broker–Dealer Regulation

A substantial portion of the SEC's activity is devoted to regulation of firms engaged in the securities business.[70] The three principal capacities in which firms act in that business are as broker, dealer, and investment adviser. The 1934 Act defines a "broker" as a "person engaged in the business of effecting transactions in securities for the account of others,"[71] while a "dealer" is a "person engaged in the business of buying and selling securities for such person's own account."[72] An "investment adviser" is defined in 202(a)(11) of the Investment Advisers Act of 1940 as a "person who, for compensation, engages in the business of advising others . . . as to the advisability of investing in, purchasing or selling securities,"[73] but broker-dealers who render such advice as part of their brokerage activities are exempt from the definition.[74]

Under section 15(a) of the 1934 Act,[75] no person may engage in business as a broker or dealer in securities (unless he does exclusively intrastate business or deals only in exempted securities) unless he is registered with the Commission. Under section 15(b),[76] the SEC may revoke or suspend a broker-dealer's registration, or impose a censure, if the broker-dealer is found to have violated any of the federal securities laws or committed other specified misdeeds.

In spelling out the substantive obligations of these securities "professionals" in dealing with public investors, the SEC has proceeded largely under the general anti-fraud provisions of sections 10(b)[77] and 15(c)[78] of the 1934 Act, section 17(a) of the 1933 Act,[79] and section 206 of the Investment Advisers Act.[80] The SEC's attention has been focused on two broad areas: (a) conflicts between the firm's obligations to its customers and its own financial interests,[81] and (b) trading in or recommending securities in the absence of adequate information about the issuer.[82] Violation of the anti-fraud provisions in these two areas has given rise to lawsuits by aggrieved customers[83] as well as disciplinary actions by the SEC.[84]

A number of the sections in this chapter exemplify the approaches taken by the SEC and the courts in regulating (1) excessive prices for over-the-

---

70. Some of the discussion in the next several paragraphs are adapted from David L. Ratner & Thomas L. Hazen, Securities Regulation: Cases and Materials 842–844 (5th ed. 1996).

71. 1934 Act § 3(a)(4), 15 U.S.C.A. § 78c(a)(4).

72. 1934 Act § 3(a)(5), 15 U.S.C.A. § 78c(a)(5).

73. 15 U.S.C.A. § 80b–3(a). *See* § 21.2[1] *infra*.

74. 15 U.S.C.A. § 80b–2(a)(11)(C).

75. 15 U.S.C.A. § 78*o*(a).

76. 15 U.S.C.A. § 78*o*(b).

77. 15 U.S.C.A. § 78j(b). *See* § 12.1 *supra* and § 14.3[6] *infra*.

78. 15 U.S.C.A. § 78*o*(c). *See* § 12.1 *supra* and § 14.3[6] *infra*.

79. 15 U.S.C.A. § 77q(a). *See* § 7.11 *supra*.

80. 15 U.S.C.A. § 80b–6. *See* § 21.4[1] *infra*.

81. *See* §§ 14.3, 14.10 *infra*.

82. *See* §§ 14.15–14.18 *infra*.

83. *See* § 14.26 and chapter 15 *infra*.

84. *See* § 14.3 *infra*. The SEC's enforcement authority generally is discussed in chapter 16 *infra*.

counter securities;[85] (2) activities of market-makers who deal directly with individual customers;[86] (3) generation of commissions by excessive trading in customers' accounts;[87] and (4) undisclosed interests of investment advisers in the stocks they recommend.[88]

Market regulation includes the establishment of fair market practices and minimum capital requirements for broker-dealers in order to minimize the risk of insolvency.[89] A major goal of this regulation is to assure orderly markets.[90] There are also severe prohibitions against fraudulent and manipulative broker-dealer conduct.[91] Additionally, the SEC and the Federal Reserve Board work together in regulating the extension of credit for securities transactions.[92]

§ 14.1[3][C] Self Regulation[93]

SEC regulation of the industry is supplemented by a system of "self regulation". Sections 6 and 15A of the 1934 Act[94] delegate to "national securities exchanges" and "national securities associations," respectively, substantial authority over their members, including the power to expel, suspend, or discipline them for certain specified kinds of activities or for "conduct ... inconsistent with just and equitable principles of trade."[95] In order to exercise such powers, an exchange or association must register with the SEC, which, under section 19 of the Act,[96] is given certain oversight powers with respect to its disciplinary proceedings and adoption and amendment of its rules.

In general, a securities firm must become a member of one or more exchanges in order to execute transactions in listed securities on an exchange, and must become a member of the National Association of Securities Dealers (NASD), the only registered association, to transact business effectively in the over-the-counter market.

§ 14.1[3][C][1] Stock Exchanges

When Congress created the SEC in 1934, stock exchanges, as private associations, had been regulating their members for up to one hundred and forty years. Rather than displace this system of "self regulation," Congress superimposed the SEC on it as an additional level of regulation. The effect of section 5[97] is to require every "national securities exchange" to register with

---

85. *See* § 14.14 *infra.*

86. *See* § 14.10 *infra.*

87. *See* § 14.20 *infra.*

88. *See* § 14.18 *infra.*

89. *See* § 14.8 *infra.*

90. *See* §§ 14.3, 14.10–14.11 *infra.*

91. *See* §§ 14.3[6], 14.15–14.23 *infra.*

92. *See* § 14.9 *infra.*

93. *See* § 14.3 *infra.*

94. 15 U.S.C.A. §§ 78f, 15o–1.

95. *See also, e.g.,* NASD Manual Conduct Rule 2110 (available on Westlaw) ("a member in the conduct of its business, shall observe high standards of commercial honor and just and equitable principles of trade").

96. 15 U.S.C.A. § 78s.

97. 15 U.S.C.A. § 78e.

the SEC. Under section 6(b) of the Act,[98] an exchange cannot be registered unless the SEC determines that its rules are designed, among other things, to "prevent fraudulent and manipulative acts and practices, to promote just and equitable principles of trade,"[99] and to provide for appropriate discipline of its members for any violations of its own rules or the securities laws.

Under the authority of section 6 of the Act, the various exchanges, of which the New York Stock Exchange (NYSE) is by far the largest and most important, have maintained and enforced a large body of rules for the conduct of their members. As noted above, in 2006, the NASDAQ national market became a registered national securities exchange. These rules fall into two categories: rules relating to transactions on the particular exchange, and rules relating to the internal operations of the member firms and their dealings with their customers.

In the first group are found rules governing: criteria for listing securities on the exchange and provisions for delisting or suspension of trading in particular securities; obligations of issuers of listed securities; bids and offers on the exchange floor; activities of "specialists" (designated market-makers in listed securities); transactions by members in listed securities for their own account; conditions under which transactions in listed securities may be effected off the exchange; clearing and settlement of exchange transactions; and rules for the governance and operation of the exchange itself.[100]

In the second category are rules governing: the form of organization of member firms and qualifications of their partners or officers; qualifications of salesmen and other personnel; handling of customers' accounts; advertising; and financial statements and reports. In the case of firms which are members of more than one exchange, there is a kind of "pecking order" with respect to regulatory responsibility: the New York Stock Exchange has principal responsibility for regulation of the internal affairs of all of its members (which includes almost all of the largest firms in the industry), the American Stock Exchange has principal responsibility for those of its members that are not also New York Stock Exchange members, and the various "regional" exchanges in cities other than New York have responsibility over their "sole" members.

Section 19 of the Exchange Act, as originally enacted, gave the SEC power to suspend or withdraw the registration of an exchange, to suspend or expel any member of an exchange, to suspend trading in listed securities, and to require changes in exchange rules with respect to a wide range of matters. However, it did not require SEC approval for changes in stock exchange rules, nor did it provide for SEC review of disciplinary actions by exchanges against their members. Section 19, as amended in 1975, expanded and consolidated the SEC's authority over *all* self regulatory organizations. The SEC's increased authority with respect to exchanges and the National Association of Securities Dealers (NASD) with respect to the over-the-counter markets is roughly comparable to, but even broader than, its previous authority over the NASD.[101] In particular, since 1975, the SEC must give advance approval for

---

98. 15 U.S.C.A. § 78f(b).

99. *See, e.g.,* In the Matter of Hazelgrove–Mulkerrins, Exchange Hearing Panel Decision 00–211, 2000 WL 33158159 (N.Y.S.E. Nov. 28, 2000).

100. *See* § 14.11 *infra.*

101. *See* Marianne K. Smythe, Self Regulation and the Antitrust Laws: Suggestions for An Accommodation, 62 N.C.L.Rev. 475, 505–506 (1984).

any exchange rule changes, and has review power over exchange disciplinary actions. The 1975, amendments also confirmed the SEC action terminating the power of exchanges to fix minimum rates of commission[102] (which both Congress and the SEC found to have been a major cause of market distortion), and directed the SEC to eliminate any other exchange rules which imposed unwarranted restraints on competition.

§ 14.1[3][C][2] National Association of Securities Dealers

When Congress decided to extend federal regulation over the nonexchange, or over-the-counter (OTC) market, it followed the pattern already established with respect to exchanges. Section 15A,[103] added by the "Maloney Act" of 1938,[104] authorized the establishment of "national securities associations" to be registered with the SEC. Like an exchange, any such association must have rules designed "to prevent fraudulent and manipulative acts and practices [and] to promote just and equitable principles of trade" in transactions in the over-the-counter market.[105] Only one such association has been established, the National Association of Securities Dealers (NASD). The NASD has adopted a substantial body of "Rules of Fair Practice," dealing with various problems in the over-the-counter markets. Among the most important are: its rule that a dealer may not recommend a security unless it has reason to believe the security is "suitable" to the customer's financial situation and needs;[107] its interpretation of its "fair spread or profit" rule to bar mark-ups in excess of five percent on principal transactions;[108] its procedures for reviewing underwriting compensation and provisions for assuring that members make a bona fide public offering of underwritten securities;[109] and its rules with respect to execution of orders in the over-the-counter market and disclosure in confirmations to customers.[110]

From time to time, the NASD promulgates rules and issues interpretations directed to specially described prohibited practices. Although the NASD rules and interpretations identify a number of impermissible practices, those specifically identified practices do not comprise an exclusive list of prohibited practices. The rules and interpretations that identify specific practices are not exclusive. In other words, the NASD can invoke general antifraud principles as well as the general concept of just and equitable principles of trade to invalidate improper conduct that is not specifically defined in NASD or SEC rulemaking.[112]

The self-regulation of the securities industry by and large has been successful. However, not all fraudulent conduct gets detected by the system. A

---

102. *See* Adoption of Securities Exchange Act Rule 19b–3, Sec. Exch. Act Rel. No. 34–11203, 6 SEC Docket. 147, 1975 WL 18377 (SEC Jan. 23, 1975).

103. 15 U.S.C.A. § 78o.

104. Pub. L. No. 75–719, 52 Stat. 1070 (1938).

105. *See, e.g.,* NASD Manual Conduct Rule 2110 (available on Westlaw) ("a member in the conduct of its business, shall observe high standards of commercial honor and just and equitable principles of trade").

107. *See* § 14.16 *infra.*

108. *See* § 14.14[3] *infra.*

109. NASD Manual Rule 2710 (Corporate Finance Rule) (available on Westlaw).

110. *See* § 14.13 *infra.*

112. *See* In the Matter of Kunz, Admin. Proc. File No. 3–9960, Sec. Exch. Act Rel. No. 34–45290 n. 2, 2002 WL 54819 at *9 n. 2 (SEC Jan. 16, 2002).

cynic might attribute this to the fact that there may be a self interest in permitting certain profitable practices to continue. The fact that an industry practice has been followed for a long period of time does not mean that it is compliant with NASD and SEC standards of fair and equitable conduct.[114] Similarly, the fact that a certain type of conduct has been long-standing industry practice does not prevent it from being fraudulent.[115]

The scandals following the turn of the twentieth century led to increased concern over the effectiveness of self regulation. As noted elsewhere in this chapter, one response was to adopt rules specifically directed to the abuses in connection with IPOs and with respect to research analyst recommendations. One other response was to expand the NASD's enforcement authority. In 2003, the NASD was given increased enforcement authority when it was given cease and desist powers with respect to certain securities law violations.[116]

§ 14.1[8] Regulation of Online Trading and Day Trading

An outgrowth of technological advancements has been the advent of online securities trading. The growing use of the Internet for stock trading created a new arena for securities fraud. One variety of online trading that has drawn attention has been day trading. Problems relating to day trading are likely to get increasing attention because of the publicity given to a day trader's shooting spree in Atlanta in 1999.

For the most part, rather than creating new regulatory rules, online trading and day trading have simply led to new applications for well established regulatory doctrine. The NASD has, however, adopted online trading suitability standards[164] and special rules for providing trading facilities to day trading customers.[165] The SEC has also pursued fraudulent day trading operations.[166] The rapidity of day trading and resulting account and value changes has implications for margin accounts and margin maintenance requirements.[167]

§ 14.1[9] Antitrust Laws and Market Regulation

The federal antitrust laws are designed to curb anticompetitive activities.[169] From time to time, the anticompetitive consequences of various activities in the securities markets have been brought into question. For example, since the definition of securities manipulation depends upon artificially pegging or fixing the price of securities, manipulative conduct by definition has

---

114. *See* Newton v. Merrill, Lynch, Pierce, Fenner & Smith, 135 F.3d 266, 274 (3d Cir.1998).

115. *See* SEC v. Dain Rauscher, Inc., 254 F.3d 852, 857 (9th Cir.2001).

116. *See* NASD Special Notice to Members 03–35, http://www.nasdr.com/pdf-text/0335ntm.txt (NASDR June 23, 2003).

164. *See, e.g.,* NASD Notice to Members 01–23 Online Suitability, 2001 WL 278614 (March 19, 2001); § 14.16[2] *infra*.

165. NASD Rule 2360. *See* § 14.16[2] *infra*.

166. *See* SEC Charges iCapital Markets LLC, Successor to Datek Securities, with Securities Fraud; Firm Will Pay $6.3 Million Penalty to Settle Charges, SEC News Digest 2002–16, 2002 WL 89854 (Jan. 24, 2002).

167. Margin regulation is discussed in § 14.9 *infra*.

169. *See, e.g.,* section 1 of the Sherman Antitrust Act, 15 U.S.C.A. § 1 which, among other things, prohibits contracts in restraint of trade. *See also, e.g.,* Section 2 of the Sherman Antitrust Act address monopolies as they violate the antitrust laws. 15 U.S.C.A. § 2. Section 5 of the Clayton Antitrust Act, 15 U.S.C.A. § 15.

an anticompetitive effect on securities prices.[172] The former practice of fixed brokerage commission rates imposed by the New York Stock Exchange is another example of anticompetitive activity challenged under the antitrust laws.[173] Additionally, many of the rules of the SEC and of the self regulatory organizations permit conduct that otherwise would violate the antitrust laws.[174] From time to time, antitrust challenges have been made and the question arises whether the pervasive regulatory framework imposed by the securities laws on the securities markets operates as an implied repeal of the antitrust laws. The implied repeal argument has been met with considerable success in challenging antitrust scrutiny of the securities markets.[175] On the other hand, it is clear that the antitrust laws will not be preempted simply because the alleged anticompetitive conduct involves the securities markets.[176]

§ 14.3   Regulation of Broker–Dealers—The SEC, Self Regulatory Organizations, National Exchanges, and the NASD

§ 14.3[1] Nature of Market Regulation

While the SEC exercises some direct jurisdiction over broker-dealers, the overwhelming bulk of broker-dealer regulation is attributable to the Commission's oversight of the activities of self regulatory organizations ("SRO"s) and of national securities exchanges. Section 15(a) of the Exchange Act requires registration with the Commission of all broker-dealers who are engaged in interstate business involving securities transactions.[1] The only complete exemption from the registration requirements is for a broker-dealer "whose business is exclusively intrastate and who does not make use of any facility of a national exchange."[2] An individual who is a registered associated person with a registered broker-dealer may himself or herself be exempt from

---

172. *See, e.g.,* Friedman v. Salomon/Smith Barney, Inc., 313 F.3d 796 (2d Cir. 2002), *affirming* 2000 WL 1804719, [2000–2001 Transfer Binder] Fed. Sec. L. Rep. (CCH) ¶ 91,273, 2000–2 (S.D.N.Y. 2000), rehearing denied, 2001 WL 64774 (S.D.N.Y.2001) (but holding that the SEC pervasive regulation of manipulation scheme precluded attacking manipulation under the antitrust laws).

173. *See* Gordon v. New York Stock Exchange, Inc., 422 U.S. 659, 95 S.Ct. 2598, 45 L.Ed.2d 463 (1975).

174. For example, the market-maker regulations by imposing barriers to entry, limit which firms can act as market makers for over-the-counter securities. Market-maker regulation is discussed in § 14.10 *infra.* Similarly, the specialist system for exchange based trading is a form of permissible monopoly. Specialist and exchange trading are discussed in § 14.11 *infra.*

175. *See, e.g.,* United States v. NASD, 422 U.S. 694, 95 S.Ct. 2427, 45 L.Ed.2d 486 (1975); Gordon v. New York Stock Exchange, Inc., 422 U.S. 659, 95 S.Ct. 2598, 45 L.Ed.2d 463 (1975); In re Stock Exchanges Options Trading Antitrust Litigation, 317 F.3d 134 (2d Cir. 2003); Friedman v. Salomon/Smith Barney, Inc., 313 F.3d 796 (2d Cir. 2002).

176. Silver v. New York Stock Exchange, 373 U.S. 341, 359, 83 S.Ct. 1246, 1258, 10 L.Ed.2d 389 (1963).

§ 14.3

1. 15 U.S.C.A. § 78*o*(a). Registration involves disclosure of the broker-dealer's business and principal officers on Form BD. The broker-dealer registration and disclosure requirements are handled through a central registration depositary (CTD) that is operated by the National Association of Securities Dealers.

2. 15 U.S.C.A. § 78*o*(a). The intrastate exemption is as restrictive as its counterpart under the 1933 Act. *See* § 4.12 *supra.*

registration.[3] However, the exemption will not be available when the registered representative is conducting business on his or her own.[4]

§ 14.3[2] State Regulation of Broker–Dealers—Limited Preemption

In 1996, Congress, as part of the National Securities Markets Improvement Act of 1996,[5] took away from the states the power to regulate certain areas of broker-dealer activity. In particular, the states may not impose regulations relating to the extension of credit (margin requirements), net capital requirements, or recordkeeping and reporting requirements.[6]

In addition to this substantive preemption of state law, class actions based on securities fraud are preempted by the Securities Litigation Uniform Standards Act of 1998 (SLUSA).[7]

Notwithstanding this preemptive legislation, many states play a significant role in broker-dealer regulation. The preemption of broker-dealer regulation imposed by National Securities Markets Improvement Act of 1996 is limited. It does not affect the states' ability to regulate broker dealers generally through registration requirements.[10] A number of states have been aggressive in enforcing their antifraud provisions in broker-dealer prosecutions.[11] Furthermore, the existence of exclusive federal jurisdiction under the Securities Exchange Act of 1934[12] does not preclude state law claims against broker dealers.[13] Nor does it preempt state law fraud claims generally.[14]

§ 14.3[3] Self–Regulation: The National Association of Securities Dealers and the National Exchanges

By virtue of section 15A,[18] the NASD operates as the largest of the self regulatory organizations subject to SEC oversight. Although the Commission has, pursuant to Section 15 of the Act, the direct authority to regulate broker-dealers who are members of the NASD, as a practical matter the bulk of the day-to-day regulation is generally delegated to the self regulatory organization. The NASD is a nationwide organization and has extensive rules governing its members and employees which relate both to organizational structure and standards of conduct.[20]

In addition to the NASD, as observed earlier, there a number of self regulatory organizations that qualify and are registered as national exchanges

---

3. Section 15(a)(1), 15 U.S.C.A. § 78o(a)(1). Associated person is a broad concept and is not limited to natural persons. *Cf., e.g.,* McMahan Securities Co. L.P. v. Forum Capital Markets L.P., 35 F.3d 82 (2d Cir.1994) (entity that was a partner of the member firm was an associated person under NASD bylaws).

4. Roth v. SEC, 22 F.3d 1108 (D.C.Cir.1994).

5. Pub. L. No. 104–290, 110 Stat. 3416 (1996).

6. 1934 Act section 15(h), 15 U.S.C. § 78o(h).

7. Pub. Law No. 105–353, 112 Stat. 3227 (105th Cong.–2d sess. November 3, 1998) (S 1260).

10. *See* A.S. Goldmen & Co. v. New Jersey Bureau of Securities, 163 F.3d 780 (3d Cir.1999) (upholding constitutionality of state registration requirements for broker-dealers doing business within the state).

11. *E.g.,* People v. Schwartz, 34 Sec. Reg. & L. Rep. (BNA) 532 (N.Y.Sup.Ct. March 27, 2002).

12. *See* § 17.2 *infra.*

13. *See* Roskind v. Morgan Stanley Dean Witter & Co., 165 F.Supp.2d 1059, 1065–1066 (N.D.Cal.2001).

14. *See* Zuri–Invest AG v. Natwest Finance Inc., 177 F.Supp.2d 189 (S.D.N.Y.2001).

18. 15 U.S.C.A. § 78o–3.

20. The NASD constitution and rules are compiled in NASD Manual (CCH).

under section 6 of the Act.[22] The number of national securities exchanges is likely to increase. In 2000, the SEC approved the application of the International Securities Exchange to be registered as a national securities exchange.[23] The ISE is the first attempt to adapt the auctions system applicable to securities exchange to an entirely electronic environment.[24] Also, in 2001, the NASDAQ filed an application with the SEC to be recognized as a national securities exchange.[25] That registration became effective in 2006. Additionally, as a result of the Commodity Futures Modernization Act of 2000,[26] there are likely to be new exchanges recognized for the limited purpose of trading securities futures products.[27]

By virtue of section 19 of the Act,[32] the Commission has oversight responsibility with respect to all rulemaking activity of national exchanges.[33] Similar authority exists with regard to the NASD.[34] Section 19(b)(1) requires that all self regulatory associations file proposed rule changes with the Commission.[35] If the SEC does not institute disapproval proceedings within thirty-five days of the proposed rules' publication (unless extended by the SEC to ninety days), the proposed rules become effective.[36] Section 19(c)[37] empowers the SEC to "abrogate, add to, and delete from" the rules of self regulatory organizations. However, this power is exercised only on a very infrequent basis.

Section 19(a)(1) gives the Commission the authority to register national exchanges.[38] Under section 19(h), the Commission has the authority to discipline national exchanges for violating the securities Acts' provisions.[39] There is also the express authority of exchanges to discipline persons associated with an exchange, including power to remove from office or censure its officers or directors for willful violations of the Act.[40] The Commission has exercised its statutory authority[41] to expel a national exchange on only one occasion.[42] But

---

22. 15 U.S.C.A. § 78f.

23. Approval of Application for Exchange Registration International Securities Exchange LLC, SEC News Digest 2000–36, 2000 WL 218366 (S.E.C.) (SEC February 25, 2000).

24. *See* Notice of Filing of Proposed Rule Change by the International Securities Exchange LLC, 66 FR 36353–01, 2001 WL 768983 (F.R.) (SEC July 11, 2001); Commission Grants ISE Exemption to Accommodate its Electronic Market in the Marketwide Data System, SEC News Digest 2000–101, 2000 WL 681095 (S.E.C.) (SEC May 26, 2000).

25. Fed. Sec. L. Rep. (CCH) Report Bulletin No. 1981 p. 4 (June 13, 2001).

26. Pub. Law 106–554, 114 Stat. 2763 (December 21, 2000).

27. *See* Registration of National Securities Exchanges Pursuant to Section 6(g) of the Securities Exchange Act of 1934 and Proposed Rule Changes of National Securities Exchanges and Limited Purpose National Securities Associations, Sec. Exch. Act Rel. No. 34–44279, 2001 WL 491727 (SEC May 10, 2001).

32. 15 U.S.C.A. § 78s.

33. *See generally* Paul G. Mahoney, The Exchange as Regulator, 83 Va. L. Rev. 1453 (1997).

34. *See* 15 U.S.C.A. § 78o–3.

35. 15 U.S.C.A. § 78s(b)(1).

36. 15 U.S.C.A. § 78s(b)(2). *Cf.* Higgins v. SEC, 866 F.2d 47 (2d Cir.1989) (upholding SEC approval of New York Stock Exchange rule change).

37. 15 U.S.C.A. § 78s(c).

38. 15 U.S.C.A. § 78s(a)(1).

39. 15 U.S.C.A. § 78s(h).

40. 15 U.S.C.A. § 78f(d).

41. 15 U.S.C.A. § 78s(h)(1).

42. San Francisco Mining Exchange v. SEC, 378 F.2d 162 (9th Cir.1967).

the Commission has with more frequency exercised its authority under subsection (h) to uphold expulsion of members from the exchange.[43] The power to discipline and sanction members is given directly to the exchange with a right of appeal to the SEC which may in its discretion review the record de novo.[44] The SEC decision is then subject to review by a federal court of appeals. The NASD has similar status and authority. The Commission can suspend or revoke the securities association's registration.[46] The NASD has the power to hold hearings and issue sanctions against members and associated persons, including expulsion of its members from the association for conduct in violation of the Act or the NASD's rules.[47]

In addition to the sanctions imposed by the SROs, the Commission can institute its own proceedings. The Commission is empowered to suspend or revoke broker-dealer registration for violations of the securities laws.[48] The Commission can also bar any person from associating with a broker-dealer,[49] a member of a registered securities association (*i.e.* the NASD),[50] or an investment adviser,[51] as well as barring that person from serving in various capacities with a registered investment company.[52] Additionally, with respect to all of the powers outlined above, the Commission can, of course, impose less severe sanctions, including suspension for a definite period of not more than twelve months, or merely censuring persons involved.[53] Section 19(d) sets out the SEC's authority with regard to disciplinary actions by self regulatory organizations.[54] Sections 19(e) and 19(f) set out the standards for commission review of disciplinary proceedings and sanctions imposed by self regulatory organizations.[55]

Over and beyond the regulatory structure outlined above, agreements between members of self regulatory agencies that their disputes be arbitrated are generally enforceable.[59] This supplements the general rule that federal securities claims are arbitrable.[60]

Although the federal securities laws do not regulate commodities transactions directly, since stock brokers frequently trade in commodities, improper conduct can run afoul of both the federal securities and commodities regulatory framework.[61] In some instances commodities transactions may be directly

---

43. *See, e.g.,* Archer v. SEC, 133 F.2d 795 (8th Cir.1943), *cert. denied,* 319 U.S. 767, 63 S.Ct. 1330, 87 L.Ed. 1717 (1943).

44. 15 U.S.C.A. § 78f; *see* 15 U.S.C.A. § 78s(h).

46. 15 U.S.C.A. § 78o–3(h).

47. 15 U.S.C.A. § 78s(h)(2).

48. 15 U.S.C.A. § 78o(b)(5).

49. 15 U.S.C.A. § 78o(b)(6).

50. 15 U.S.C.A. § 78s(h)(3).

51. 15 U.S.C.A. § 80b–3(f).

52. 15 U.S.C.A. § 80a–9(b).

53. *See* Sec.Exch.Act Rel. No. 34–14761 (May 15, 1978).

54. 15 U.S.C.A. § 78s(d). *See* 17 C.F.R. §§ 240.19d–1, .19d–2, .19d–3.

55. 15 U.S.C.A. §§ 78s(e), s(f).

59. 15 U.S.C.A. § 78bb(b).

60. *See* chapter 15 *infra.*

61. *See, e.g.,* Smoky Greenhaw Cotton Co. v. Merrill Lynch, Pierce, Fenner & Smith, Inc., 785 F.2d 1274 (5th Cir.1986), *on remand* 650 F.Supp. 220 (W.D.Tex.1986).

regulated by the securities laws, such as is the case with pooled managed commodities accounts.[62]

There have been a number of significant developments in the operation of the markets. The New York Stock Exchange has departed from precedent in permitting after-hours trading. Perhaps even more significant than the extension of the trading day into two after hours sessions is the fact that these sessions are operated through a screen-based execution system instead of taking place on the floor of the exchange. The New York Stock Exchange's screen-based after hours system is open to all investors for forty-five minutes beginning fifteen minutes after the close of trading.[66] A second screen-based system is open to large program traders dealing in baskets of stocks and lasts for one hour and fifteen minutes after the close of exchange trading. The significance of the screen-based system is that it bypasses the specialist system that has been the core of the exchange mechanism for so many years.[67]

The fact that exchange operations can be conducted through a screen-based trading system does not mean that every screen-based system will be classified as an exchange.[69] As noted above, an automated quotation system which does not involve the actual execution of trades is clearly not an exchange. A screen-based system for trading options on government securities was held not to be an exchange.[70] Judge Posner of the Seventh Circuit reasoned that since the screen-based system involved only three firms each of whom was actively and comprehensively regulated by the SEC, additional regulation was unnecessary. Thus, although the system differed "only in degree and detail from an exchange," the regulation of the three participants and the absence of regulatory gaps led the majority to hold that this was not an exchange under the Act.[71] It was further noted that requiring the extra level of regulation that would ensue from classifying the system as an exchange would "destroy" it.[72] Judge Flaum, dissenting, pointed out that the size of an operation should not affect whether it is classified as an exchange.[73] Judge Flaum's functional approach seems preferable not only in light of the statutory language, but also in terms of the ramifications of permitting the SEC to establish an appropriate regulatory policy. Classifying screen-based systems as exchanges would simply give the SEC the task of determining which, if any, should be granted exemptions from registration.

SEC Rules 11Ac–1–1 and 11Ac–4 permit electronic communications networks ("ECN"s) for providing electronic quotations and facilitating transactions in the over-the-counter markets.[75] These and other alternative trading systems[76] have opened up competition in the electronic markets[77] but have

---

62. *See* § 1.6 *supra*. The courts are split as to whether an individual managed commodities account falls within the definition of "security" so as to subject it to regulation under the securities laws. *Id.*

66. *See* Wall St.J. p. C1 (May 22, 1991).

67. Specialists are discussed in § 14.11 *infra*.

69. Cantor Fitzgerald G.P., [1993–1994 Transfer Binder] Fed. Sec. L. Rep. (CCH) ¶ 76,837 (SEC No Action Letter Oct. 1, 1993).

70. Board of Trade v. SEC, 923 F.2d 1270 (7th Cir.1991).

71. 923 F.2d at 1273.

72. *Id.*

73. 923 F.2d at 1274–75.

75. 17 C.F.R. §§ 240.11Ac1–1, 11Ac1–4.

76. *See* Regulation ATS. Securities Exchange Act Release No. 40760 (Dec. 8, 1998), 63 FR 70844 (December 22, 1998).

77. *See, e.g.,* NASD Rule 6540, as amended in May 2002, which permits ECNs and other alternative trading systems (ATS) to list over-the-counter bulletin board stocks provided that

also engendered some criticism as being too restrictive and not being as competitive as some observers had hoped.[78]

§ 14.3[4] Substance of Self Regulation

Section 15(b)(4)[79] of the Exchange Act empowers the Commission to hold a hearing and impose disciplinary sanctions ranging from censure to revocation of the registration of broker-dealers engaging in certain types of proscribed conduct. The Act lists the following situations in which the SEC may impose sanctions after an administrative hearing: (1) when a broker-dealer makes false filings with the Commission;[81] (2) when the broker-dealer within the past ten years has been convicted of certain crimes or misdemeanors involving moral turpitude or breaches of fiduciary duty;[82] (3) when the person involved has been enjoined from being a broker-dealer or investment adviser or from engaging in or continuing to engage in any conduct or practice in connection with such activity or in connection with the purchase or sale of any security;[83] (4) when a broker-dealer has willfully violated any provision of the Securities Act of 1933, the Exchange Act of 1934, the Investment Company Act of 1940, or the Investment Advisers Act of 1940, or any rules promulgated thereunder;[84] (5) when the broker-dealer has willfully aided, abetted, counseled, commanded, induced, or procured any violation of any of the foregoing statutes or rules;[85] (6) when the broker-dealer is subject to an SEC order barring or suspending his right to be associated with a broker or dealer;[86] and (7) when the broker-dealer has violated any foreign securities law or regulation.[87] Section 15(b)(6)[88] empowers the Commission to impose similar sanctions for the same types of conduct with regard to persons who, although not themselves broker-dealers, are associated or seek to become associated with broker-dealers.[89] Brokerage firms have a duty to supervise their personnel and can be held liable and subject to SEC or self regulatory organization sanctions for breach of the duty to supervise.[90]

§ 14.3[4][A] Self Regulatory Disciplinary Authority

In addition to direct SEC enforcement, the self regulatory organizations—the exchanges and the NASD—can investigate suspected violations and disci-

---

certain conditions are met. One of those conditions is the the ECN or ATS will have to obtain current information about a company that complies with SEC Rule 15c2–11, 17 C.F.R. § 240.15c2–11 before listing a quotation.

78. Mark Klock, The SEC's New Regulation ATS: Placing the Myth of Market Fragmentation Ahead of Economic Theory and Evidence, 51 Fla. L. Rev. 753 (1999).

79. 15 U.S.C.A. § 78o(b)(4).

81. 15 U.S.C.A. § 78o(b)(4)(A).

82. 15 U.S.C.A. § 78o(b)(4)(B).

83. 15 U.S.C.A. § 78o(b)(4)(C).

84. 15 U.S.C.A. § 78o(b)(4)(D).

85. 15 U.S.C.A. § 78o(b)(4)(E).

86. 15 U.S.C.A. § 78o(b)(5)(F). *See* 15 U.S.C.A. 78o(b)(6).

87. 15 U.S.C.A. § 78o(b)(4)(G).

88. 15 U.S.C.A. § 78o(b)(6).

89. *See, e.g.,* Alderman v. SEC, 104 F.3d 285 (9th Cir.1997) (NASD Rule requiring associated person to conform to just and equitable principles of trade was not void for vagueness).

90. *E.g.,* Kersh v. General Council of the Assemblies of God, 804 F.2d 546 (9th Cir.1986).

pline their members for violations of self regulatory organization rules. The exchanges and the NASD are given broad investigatory and disciplinary powers. Self regulatory organization disciplinary actions are subject to SEC review and, in turn, to review by a federal court of appeals.[94] The doctrine of exhaustion of remedies applies to self regulatory organization disciplinary proceedings. This means that disciplinary and other self regulatory action must proceed through the self regulatory agency's appeals process before there can be review by the SEC or by a court.[95] Courts generally will not permit collateral attack as an alternative to the statutory review process for disciplinary proceedings.[96] Additionally, self regulatory organizations and their employees enjoy immunity from private suits seeking damages resulting from alleged improprieties in the disciplinary process.[97] SEC approval of sanctions for violation of self regulatory organization rules will be affirmed unless there has been an abuse of discretion.[98] In 2003, the NASD was given cease and desist powers with respect to certain securities law violations.[99]

§ 14.3[4][B] Broker–Dealer Operations

In addition to imposing sanctions arising out of the SEC's direct broker-dealer regulation, the Commission is charged with the supervision of a firm's structure and taking measures to ensure the broker-dealer's solvency. Section 15(b)(7) requires broker-dealers to meet such operational and financial competence standards as the Commission may establish.[118] Perhaps the most significant of these requirements is the Commission's net capital rule which sets out the minimum standards of broker-dealer solvency based on the balance sheet. The net capital rule, Rule 15c3–1, is among the longest and most complex of the Commission's rules.[119] In short, the rule requires that a broker-dealer's balance sheet reflect a sufficient asset base as well as mandating the applicable accounting standards for determining that asset base.[120] The net capital rule is complicated not only because of its formulas but also because of the rules regarding "haircuts"—the discounted value of the securities before the computation is made. The competence requirements imposed by the Act include provisions for maintenance of adequate records[121] and imposition of standards for supervisory and associated personnel,[122] as well as a number of

---

94. Since the statute vests judicial review in the courts of appeals, federal district courts have no jurisdiction to hear such an appeal. *See* Maschler v. National Association of Securities Dealers, 827 F.Supp. 131 (E.D.N.Y.1993).

95. Marchiano v. NASD, 134 F.Supp.2d 90 (D.D.C.2001) (action for injunction against NASD disciplinary proceedings was dismissed due to failure to exhaust administrative remedies).

96. *See, e.g.,* First Jersey Securities, Inc. v. Bergen, 605 F.2d 690 (3d Cir.1979), *cert. denied,* 444 U.S. 1074, 100 S.Ct. 1020, 62 L.Ed.2d 756 (1980).

97. D'Alessio v. New York Stock Exchange, Inc., 258 F.3d 93 (2d Cir.2001), *affirming* 125 F.Supp.2d 656 (S.D.N.Y.2000).

98. *See, e.g.,* Krull v. SEC, 248 F.3d 907 (9th Cir.2001) (upholding one year suspension for recommendations involving short-term switching of mutual fund investments).

99. *See* NASD Special Notice to Members 03–35, http://www.nasdr.com/pdf-text/0335ntm.txt (NASDR June 23, 2003).

118. 15 U.S.C.A. § 78*o*(b)(7).

119. 17 C.F.R. § 240.15c3–1.

120. For a more detailed analysis *see* Jerry W. Markham & Thomas L. Hazen, Broker-dealer Operations Under Securities and Commodities Law: Financial Responsibilities, Credit Regulation, and Customer Protection, ch. 5 (2d ed. 2003).

121. *See* the recordkeeping requirements of section 17(h), 15 U.S.C.A. § 78q(h).

122. *See, e.g.,* In re White, [1991–1992 Transfer Binder] Fed.Sec.L.Rep. (CCH) ¶ 84,949 (SEC 1992).

related requirements that go into more detail than is appropriate here. One of the other more important regulatory structures is the SEC's customer protection rule, which requires segregation of customers' funds from the brokerage firm's propriety funds and accounts.[124]

Section 15(c)(1)[125] prohibits securities broker-dealers from engaging in fraudulent practices and conduct. Section 15(c)(1) applies to all registered broker-dealers.[126] It is also specifically declared illegal to misuse customers' funds and securities.[127]

§ 14.3[4][C] Potential Conflicts of Interest and The Chinese Wall (or "Fire Wall") Requirement

Over the years, there has been an increased concern about the potential conflicts of interest resulting from the varied activities of multiservice brokerage firms. For example, when a firm acts as an underwriter or investment adviser for publicly traded issuers it will have access to nonpublic information that would be of interest to its retail customers who may be purchasing or selling the securities in question. The traditional response has been to establish a Chinese Wall (or "firewall") between the firm's various departments and thus to eliminate the potential conflict within each department.[150] Another response to potential conflicts of interest has been for firms to place securities on a "restricted list" when the investment banking or underwriting department becomes involved in a proposed public offering or acquisition. The required information barriers go beyond separating the research and underwriting functions from each other and from the retail operations. When a broker-dealer acts as a market maker for over-the-counter securities, the market making activities must be carried on independently of other operations including the firm's own trading department as well as the departments mentioned above.

Conflicts of interest and information barriers are discussed in a later section of this treatise.[151] Broker-dealer firms encounter conflicts of interest in other areas as well. For example, conflicts of interest arise in the over-the-counter markets between a firm's retail operations and its market making functions.[152] There has been considerable controversy over the conflicts of securities analysts.[153] Another concern of the regulators has been some brokerage firms' commercial loans to corporate clients to the firm's investment banking services. The NASD has reminded its members that such tying arrangements are illegal.[154]

---

124. Rule 15c3–3, 17 C.F.R. § 240.15c3–3.

125. 15 U.S.C.A. § 78o(c)(1).

126. SEC v. Lorin, 1991 WL 576895, [1993–1994 Transfer Binder] Fed. Sec. L. Rep. (CCH) ¶ 98,188 (S.D.N.Y.1991) (rejecting contention that 15(c)(1) applies only to exchange members; the language of the statute clearly provides otherwise).

127. 15 U.S.C.A. § 78o(c)(3).

150. *See, e.g.,* SEC v. First Boston Corp., [1985–1986 Transfer Binder] Fed. Sec. L. Rep. (CCH) ¶ 92712 (S.D.N.Y.1986) (consent order disgorging $132,238 in profits plus civil penalty of $264,276; defendant also agreed to review its restricted list and Chinese Wall procedures).

151. *See* § 14.12 *infra.*

152. *See* § 14.10[4] *infra.*

153. *See* § 14.16[6] *infra. See also, e.g.* Phillip Ballard Kennedy, Comment, Investment Banking Conflicts: Research Analysts and IPO Allocations, 7 N.C. Banking Inst. 199 (2003).

154. *See* NASD Advises Securities Firms on Tying Arrangements, http://www.nasdr.com/news/pr2002/release_02_044.html (Sept. 19, 2002). These types of tying arrangements violate The Bank Holding Company Act Amendments of 1970. *Id.*

§ 14.3[4][D] Maintaining an Orderly Securities Market

The Market Reform Act of 1990[155] was enacted in response to concerns over various market disruptions that have occurred over the past several years. The Act set forth additional SEC powers in times of market disruptions. The Commission was given the emergency power to close a securities exchange for a period of up to ninety days,[156] as well as the power to summarily suspend trading in any security for a period up to ten business days.[157] The Act also gave the SEC the emergency power to suspend, alter, or impose rules on a self regulatory organization for a maximum of ten business days.[158]

Sections 12(j)[159] and 12(k)[160] of the Exchange Act provide the SEC with the power to revoke or suspend the registration of a security under the Exchange Act. This in effect gives the Commission the ability to suspend trading in that security either on an exchange or in the over-the-counter markets. One of the grounds for suspending trading is the absence of an orderly market.

§ 14.3[4][E] Large Trader Reporting

In addition to the foregoing emergency powers given to the SEC, the 1990 amendments to the Exchange Act also impose identification and reporting requirements for major market participants. Section 13(h) of the Exchange Act[163] grants the SEC the authority to impose these reporting requirements on "large traders." The large trader reporting requirements are a result of concerns that arose following the market break of 1987. Specifically, Congress was concerned that market swings and increasing volatility generally could be attributed, at least in part, to the impact of large traders and their participation in the derivatives and underlying securities markets. Accordingly, the Exchange Act now empowers the SEC to promulgate rules "[f]or the purpose of monitoring the impact on the securities markets of securities transactions involving a substantial volume or large fair market value or exercise value."[164] These large trader reporting requirements, which are to be implemented by SEC rulemaking, are modeled upon and parallel the large trader reporting system that is administered with respect to the commodities markets by the Commodity Futures Trading Commission.[165] Under the Exchange Act, the SEC is granted the authority to impose reporting requirements on broker-dealers that maintain and carry accounts for large traders.[166] The Act gives the Commission broad discretion in defining who is a large trader and in framing the reporting requirements to be imposed, subject to, among other

---

155. *See* § 14.1 *supra.*

156. 15 U.S.C.A. § 78l(k)(1)(B).

157. 15 U.S.C.A. § 78l(k)(1)(A).

158. 15 U.S.C.A. § 78l(k)(2). These emergency orders are subject to presidential disapproval.

159. 15 U.S.C.A. § 78l(j).

160. 15 U.S.C.A. § 78l(k).

163. 15 U.S.C.A. § 78m(h).

164. *Id.*

165. 17 C.F.R. Part 15. *See* Philip McBride Johnson & Thomas Lee Hazen, Derivatives Regulation (2004).

166. 15 U.S.C.A. § 78m(h)(2).

things, the cost of creating and implementing the system.[167] The Commission is given additional authority with regard to examination of broker-dealer records.[168] The SEC is further given broad power to promulgate rules requiring disclosures relating to the financial condition of broker-dealer affiliates and holding companies.[169]

Under Rule 17a–25,[176] which was adopted in 2001,[177] the SEC imposes reporting obligations on broker-dealers that provide the necessary information with respect to large trader transactions. The rule requires broker-dealers to report standard transactions information that parallels the information that may be requested by the self regulatory organizations in their inquiries relating to surveillance and enforcement, including the account number and customer name for nonproprietary trades.[178]

§ 14.3[4][F] Broker–Dealer Registration Requirements

Section 15(b)(1) requires that broker-dealers register with the SEC.[184] Section 15(b)(8) requires that all broker-dealers be members of a qualifying self regulatory organization (either a national exchange or registered securities association).[185]

The broker-dealer registration requirements apply only to persons who as a firm or as individuals engage in broker-dealer activities.[188] Associated persons who work for the registered broker-dealer firm do not have to register as a broker dealer.[189] The exemption from the broker-dealer registration requirements does not insulate registered representatives and other associated persons from SEC regulation. Thus, for example, employees of brokerage firms who have regular contact with the public as order takers have to qualify as registered representatives.[190] Furthermore, associated persons who do not have to register in any capacity are subject nevertheless to SEC and NASD disciplinary authority.[191]

---

167. 15 U.S.C.A. § 78m(h)(5).

168. 15 U.S.C.A. § 78m(h)(4).

169. *See* 15 U.S.C.A. § 78q(h).

176. 17 C.F.R. § 240.17a–25.

177. Electronic Submission of Securities Trading Data by Exchange Members, Brokers and Dealers, Sec. Exch. Act Rel. No. 34–44494, 66 Fed. Reg. 35843, 2001 WL 758385 (SEC July 9, 2001).

178. Specifically, this information includes: (1) Clearing house number or alpha symbol used by the broker-dealer submitting the information; (2) clearing house number(s) or alpha symbol(s) of the broker-dealer(s) on the opposite side to the trade; (3) security identifier; (4) execution date; (5) quantity executed; (6) transaction price; (7) account number; and (8) identity of the exchange or market where each transaction was executed. 17 C.F.R. § 240.17a–25(a).

184. 15 U.S.C.A. § 78o(b)(1).

185. 15 U.S.C.A. § 78o(b)(8). Up until 1983, broker-dealers could submit themselves to direct SEC control, but the Act was amended to abolish SECO ("SEC Only") regulation.

188. *See, e.g.,* Roth v. SEC, 22 F.3d 1108 (D.C.Cir.1994) (associated person had to register as a broker-dealer where she was engaged in the securities business on her own and not through a registered broker-dealer)

189. *But see id.*

190. *See, e.g.,* Exchange Services, Inc. v. SEC, 797 F.2d 188 (4th Cir.1986) (order takers for discount brokers must register as general securities representatives).

191. Haberman v. SEC, 205 F.3d 1345 (8th Cir.2000) (upholding disqualification of associated person).

§ 14.3[4][G] Government and Municipal Securities Dealers

None of the regulation discussed above relates to the increasingly large markets for federal, state, and local government securities. Persons who deal solely in those securities are not covered by section 15's regulatory structure as described above. In 1975, Congress created the Municipal Securities Rulemaking Board to regulate dealers of municipal securities.[193] In 1986, Congress created a regulatory structure for dealers in federal government securities such as Treasury bonds, bills, and notes.[194]

§ 14.3[4][H] Banking and the Securities Laws

Until 1999, the Glass–Steagall Act prohibited national banks from dealing in investment securities.[198] The Gramm–Leach–Bliley Act[199] repealed the Glass–Steagall barriers between commercial and investment banking. Even prior to its repeal, Glass–Steagall's separation of commercial and investment banking eroded. For example, bank holding companies acquired discount brokerage services. Many full service securities brokerage firms purchased regional banks. There is ever-increasing competition between banks and broker-dealers with money market funds and interest-bearing checking accounts. A related development was the acquisition of brokerage firms by companies offering other financial services. In the post-Glass–Steagall era, there is a system of functional regulation. This means, for example, that the SEC has regulatory authority over securities activities of all financial institutions.

§ 14.3[4][I] Money Laundering Provisions[212]

As major financial instructions, broker-dealers are frequently used by the unscrupulous to engage in money laundering operations. The activities that can lead to money laundering include organized crime operations, drug trafficking, and financial fraud generally. There are several federal statutes that address illegal money laundering operations.[213] As a result of increased efforts to enforce the federal anti-money laundering rules, broker-dealers, like other financial instructions, are subject to regulations and compliance programs designed to detect and in turn prevent money laundering operations from being filtered through these institutions.[214] The required compliance programs include reporting of certain transactions.[215] In 2002, the New York Stock Exchange and the NASD set forth rules designed to strengthen their anti-money laundering compliance programs.[216] In particular, these rules require member firms to establish compliance programs that at a minimum: (1) establish and implement policies and procedures that can be reasonably

---

193. See § 14.6 *infra*.

194. Government Securities Act of 1986, Public Law 99–571, 100 Stat. 3208.

198. 12 U.S.C.A. § 24 (repealed).

199. Pub. Law. 106–102, 1999 U.S.C.C.A.N. (113 Stat.) 1338 (1999).

212. See also the discussion in § 22.5 *infra*.

213. *E.g.*, 18 U.S.C.A. § 1952 (the Travel Act); 31 U.S.C.A. §§ 5311–5313 (Foreign Corrupt Practices Act); 31 U.S.C.A. § 5313(a); 31 C.F.R. § 103.22(a) (Bank Secrecy Act).

214. *See generally* Jerry W. Markham & Thomas Lee Hazen, Broker–Dealer Operations Under Securities and Commodities Law ch. 11 (2002).

215. 31 U.S.C.A. § 5318(g). *See* § 22.4.1 for additional discussion of the anti-money-laundering laws.

216. Sec. Exch. Act Rel. No. 34–45487, 2002 SEC LEXIS 478 (SEC Feb. 28, 2002).

expected to detect and cause the reporting of transactions required under 31 U.S.C.A. § 5318(g); (2) establish and implement policies, procedures, and internal controls reasonably designed to achieve compliance with the Bank Secrecy Act; (3) provide for independent testing for compliance to be conducted by member or member organization personnel or by a qualified outside party; (4) designate, and identify to the Exchange (by name, title, mailing address, e-mail address, telephone number, and facsimile number) a person or persons responsible for implementing and monitoring the day-to-day operations and internal controls of the program and provide prompt notification to the Exchange regarding any change in such designation(s); and (5) provide ongoing training for appropriate persons.[217] The exchanges now require broker-dealers to establish anti-money laundering compliance programs.[218]

In the wake of the terror attacks of September 11, 2001, Congress enacted the USA Patriot Act[219] which, among other things, broadens the list of financial institutions subject to the anti-money laundering laws. The Treasury Department has promulgated rules implementing the new provisions.[220] The rules apply to mutual funds that are regulated under the Investment Company Act of 1940,[221] and it is unclear whether their coverage extends to hedge funds as well.

§ 14.3[5] SEC Administrative Sanctions for Broker–Dealers

Section 15(b)(4) of the Exchange Act gives the Commission authority to impose various sanctions against registered broker-dealers who violate the Act.[233] Registered brokers and dealers who violate the Act can suffer a wide range of consequences, ranging from censure to revocation of registration.[234] Depending on the severity of the violations, the SEC can also place limits on the registrant's activities.[235] In addition to sanctions against registered brokers and dealers, the Commission has similar authority with respect to persons associated with registered brokers and dealers.[236] Section 15(b)(6)(A) of the 1934 Act grants the SEC broad administrative authority over such associated persons.[237] The SEC is empowered to hold hearings and impose sanctions for violations of the Act upon associated persons of broker-dealers. These sanctions can range from censure to suspension for up to twelve months and also include the power to issue an order barring the violator from

217. *Id. See also, e.g.,* NASD Board Approves Proposed Rule on Requirements of Anti–Money Laundering Compliance Programs, http://www.nasdr.com/news/pr2002/release_02_008.html (Jan. 30, 2002).

218. *See, e.g.,* American Stock Exchange to Require Members and Member Organizations to Establish Anti–Money Laundering Compliance Programs, Sec. Exch. Act Rel. No. 34–46075, 2002 WL 1308329 (SEC June 13, 2002).

219. Pub. L. No. 107–56 (2001).

220. Financial Crimes Enforcement Network; Anti–Money Laundering Programs for Financial Institutions, 67 Fed. Reg. 21,110, 2002 WL 737165 (April 29, 2002); 31 C.F.R. Part 103.

221. 15 U.S.C.A. § 80a–5(a)(1). Investment company regulation is discussed in chapter 20 *infra.*

233. 15 U.S.C.A. § 78o(b)(4).

234. *Id.*

235. *Id.*

236. *See, e.g.,* Haberman v. SEC, 205 F.3d 1345 (8th Cir.2000) (unpublished opinion) (upholding disqualification of associated person).

237. 15 U.S.C.A. § 78o(b)(6)(A).

associating with a broker or dealer.[238] The Commission can also place limitations on the activities of such associated persons.[239] The Commission can impose similar sanctions against municipal securities dealers[240] and government securities dealers.[241] In addition, the Commission can impose an administrative penalty for each violation of the act or rules of up to $50,000 for natural persons and $250,000 for entities.[242] The SEC also has cease and desist authority which permits cease and desist orders, after notice and opportunity for a hearing, against any person who violates the Act or rules promulgated under the Act.[243]

§ 14.3[6] Prohibitions Against Deceptive and Manipulative Conduct

Sections throughout this chapter discuss various SEC and NASD prohibitions that address fraudulent and deceptive practices generally as well as particular types of misconduct by broker dealers. This section discusses and introduces the manipulative practices that are prohibited by the securities laws. The SEC has also issued industry bar orders as part of its cease and desist authority.[244]

§ 14.3[6][A] Prohibited Practices Generally

SEC Rule 15c1–2[245] generally prohibits fraudulent, manipulative, and deceptive practices in connection with securities brokerage transactions.[246] Broker-dealers and their employees are also subject to the anti-manipulation provisions contained in section 9 of the Exchange Act[247] as well as Rule 10b–5's general antifraud proscriptions that prohibit any person from engaging in deceptive conduct in connection with a purchase or sale of a security.[248] Because they result from artificial activity, manipulated prices are in and of themselves unfair.[249] Conduct that is designed to artificially restrict supply is manipulative because it is designed to artificially raise prices as a result of the limited supply.[250] Manipulative activity can consist of both fraudulent and

---

238. 15 U.S.C.A. § 78o(b)(6)(A).

239. 15 U.S.C.A. § 78o(b)(6)(A).

240. Securities Exchange Act section 15–(c)(2), 15 U.S.C.A. § 78o–4(c)(2).

241. Securities Exchange Act section 15C(c)(1), 15 U.S.C.A. § 78o–5(c)(1). The Commission also has similar powers with regard to investment advisers (Investment Advisers Act § 203(f), 15 U.S.C.A. § 80b–3(e); *See* § 21.1 *infra*) and clearing agencies (Securities Exchange Act section 17A, 15 U.S.C.A. § 78q–1).

242. Securities Exchange Act section 21B, 15 U.S.C.A. § 78u–2.

243. Securities Exchange Act section 21C, 15 U.S.C.A. § 78u–3.

244. *E.g.,* In the Matter of Carmel Equity Partners, 2001 WL 603883, Sec. Act Rel. No. 33–7981, Sec. Exch. Act Rel. No. 34–44378 (SEC June 1, 2001).

245. 17 C.F.R. § 240.15c1–2.

246. *See, e.g.,* In the Matter of Bressman, Administrative Proceedings File No. 3–9168, Sec. Exch. Act Rel. No. 34–43188, 2000 WL 1201587 (SEC Aug. 22, 2000) ("conduct of a broker or dealer of the type prohibited by Section 9(a) also violates Section 15(c)(1) of the Exchange Act and Rule 15c1–2 thereunder with respect to securities traded over-the-counter").

247. 15 U.S.C.A. § 78i. Section 9 of the Act prohibits certain manipulative practice involving exchange-listed securities. *See* § 12.1 *supra*.

248. 17 C.F.R. § 240.10b–5. *See* §§ 12.3–12.12 *supra*.

249. *See, e.g.,* Universal Heritage Investments Corporation, 47 S.E.C. 839, 843 (1982).

250. For example, withholding securities from the market is a manipulative practice. *See, e.g.,* In the Matter of Silverman, Sec. Act Rel. No. 33–45407, Sec. Exch. Act Rel. No. 34–45407, 2002 WL 185905, SEC News Digest 2002–26, 2002 WL 189036 (SEC Feb. 6, 2002) (consent order for

nonfraudulent conduct.[251] Manipulation standing alone can create liability to the victims of the manipulation under SEC Rule 10b–5.

Manipulation generally does not consist of a single act, but rather is usually accomplished through a combination of various activities. As discussed below, there are virtually an infinite variety of manipulations. However, many manipulations have a number of common characteristics. For example, the following factors frequently are "classic elements" of a market manipulation: (i) restriction of the "float" or floating supply of the securities in the public market; (ii) price leadership by the manipulator; (iii) dominating and controlling the market for the security; and (iv) a collapse of the market for the security after the manipulative activity has ceased.[254] The foregoing factors are indicia of market manipulation but are not necessarily present in every manipulation case.[255]

Although it can take many forms, manipulation consists of any intentional interference with supply and demand.[261] As discussed in the subsections that follow, fictitious trades frequently form the basis of manipulative activity. However, it is not necessary that the transactions in question be fictitious. Manipulation can infect bona fide transactions.[262] The determination of whether a manipulation exists depends upon a combination of the foregoing factors. The presence of one or two of the factors does not by itself establish manipulation.[263]

§ 14.3[6][B] Wash Sales, Fictitious Trades, Matched Orders, and Cross Trades

Section 9 of the Act not only prohibits manipulative practices generally but also certain well known manipulative practices. These include wash sales, fictitious trades, and matched orders. Related to a fictitious trade is a fictitious order or "spoof" that is designed to drive the quoted price higher.[264] Fictitious orders can also be used to artificially depress the market price of a security.[265] By their very nature, fictitious orders are deceptive.[266]

A wash sale is a fictitious sale where there is no change in beneficial ownership.[267] The evil of a wash sale is that it is a transaction without the

---

manipulation based on withholding). Withholding is a manipulation that is sometimes associated with new and hot issues. *See* § 6.3[2] *supra.*

251. Markowski v. SEC, 274 F.3d 525, 529 (D.C.Cir.2001).

254. *See, e.g.,* SEC v. Resch–Cassin & Co., 362 F.Supp. 964, 976 (S.D.N.Y.1973); In the Matter of Monroe Parker Securities, Inc., Disciplinary Proceeding No. CAF970011, 1999 WL 33261827 (N.A.S.D.R. June 18, 1999).

255. *See, e.g.,* In the Matter of Swartwood, Hesse, Inc., 50 S.E.C. 1301, 1307, Admin. Proc. No. 3–6985 Sec. Act Rel. No. 34–31212, 52 S.E.C. Docket 1557, 1992 WL 252184 (SEC 1992).

261. *See, e.g.,* Brooklyn Capital & Securities Trading, Inc., 52 S.E.C. 1286, Sec. Exch. Rel. No. 34–38454, 64 S.E.C. Docket 483, 1997 WL 144843 *3 (SEC 1997) (manipulation is the "intentional interference with the forces of supply and demand") (quoting Pagel, Inc., 48 S.E.C. 223, 226 (1985), aff'd, 803 F.2d 942 (5th Cir. 1986)).

262. *E.g.,* Markowski v. SEC, 274 F.3d 525, 529 (D.C.Cir.2001).

263. In the Matter of Robert J. Setteducati, Sec. Act Rel. No. 33–8334, Sec. Exch. Act Rel. No. 34–48759, 2003, WL 22570689 (SEC Nov. 7, 2003).

264. Spoofing is a practice whereby someone enters an order in order to drive the price up and then cancels the order before it is executed. *See* In the Matter of Monski, Administrative Proceeding File No. 3–10465, Sec. Exch. Act Rel. No. 34–44250, 2001 WL 460744 *2 (SEC May 3, 2001).

265. *See, e.g.,* In the Matter of the Application of Nickolaou, Administrative Proceeding File No. 3–5542 Sec. Exch. Act Rel. No. 34–16210, 18 S.E.C. Docket 409, 1979 WL 170308 (SEC Sept. 18, 1979).

266. *See* In the Matter of Jawitz, Complaint No. CMS960238, 1999 WL 1022138 (N.A.S.D.R. July 9, 1999).

267. *See, e.g.,* Ernst & Ernst v. Hochfelder, 425 U.S. 185, 205, n. 25, 96 S.Ct. 1375, 47 L.Ed.2d 668 (1976); Dietrich v. Bauer, 76 F.Supp.2d 312, 339 (S.D.N.Y.1999).

usual profit motive and is designed to give the false impression of market activity when in fact there is none.[268] A matched order occurs when orders are entered simultaneously to buy and sell the same security.[269] The mere fact that a broker crosses trades[270] or enters into matched orders does not violate the Act.[271] In fact, cross trades can actually benefit the firms' customers if the savings on commissions are passed on to the customers.[272] Thus, in some instances cross trades can result in price improvement for the firms customers.[273] In fact, specialists and market makers may violate their best execution obligation[274] if they interposition themselves between customer orders that could be matched or crossed for the benefit of both customers.[275]

Although beneficial under some circumstances, cross trades become problematic when the cost savings are not passed on to the customer. Cross trades can violate the best execution obligation, as evidenced by New York Stock Exchange Rule 91 which "prohibits a member from crossing trades of a customer with an account in which the member or its member organization, among others, 'is directly or indirectly interested,' without first ensuring that the order has an opportunity for an improved price on the Exchange floor and providing notification to, and obtaining acceptance of the trade from, the member who placed the order."[278] When a broker's compensation is based on an account's profitability, the broker has an interest in the account and cross trades are thus prohibited.[280]

---

268. *See* 2 Philip McBride Johnson & Thomas Lee Hazen, Derivatives Regulation § 5.07[3] (2004) ("these trades contribute to the appearance of trading volume but are economic neuters").

269. *E.g.,* Dietrich v. Bauer, 76 F.Supp.2d 312, 340 (S.D.N.Y.1999).

270. *See, e.g.,* Michelson v. Merrill Lynch, Pierce, Fenner & Smith, Inc., 669 F.Supp. 1244, 1252 (S.D.N.Y.1987) ("A 'cross trade' is understood to mean a noncompetitive trade made by matching the orders of two customers, either directly or through an intermediary, without offering them openly").

271. In the Matter of Meehan, File No. 4–232, 2 S.E.C. 588, 1937 WL 1551 (SEC July 31, 1937).

272. *See* In the Matter of Strong/Corneliuson Capital Management, Administrative Proceeding File No. 3–8411, 57 S.E.C. Docket 394, Inv. Adv. Act Rel. No. IA–1425, 1994 WL 361971 n10 (SEC June 12, 1994) ("cross trades can be beneficial to both the purchaser and seller because no brokerage commission is paid").

273. *See, e.g.,* In re Self-Regulatory Organizations; Notice of Filing of Amendment No. 2 to Proposed Rule Change by National Ass'n of Securities Dealers, Inc. Relating to Nasdaq's Proposed Separation from NASD and Establishment of NASD Alternative Display Facility, Sec. Exch. Act Rel. No. 34–45991, 77 S.E.C. Docket 2101, 2002 WL 1072081 n. 7 (SEC May 28, 2002) ("If a Designated Dealer holds for execution on the Exchange a customer buy order and a customer sell order that can be crossed, the Designated Dealer shall cross them without interpositioning itself as a dealer.").

274. *See* § 14.13 *infra.*

275. *See, e.g.,* In re Self Regulatory Organizations; Notice of Filing of Amendment No. 2 to Proposed Rule Change by National Ass'n of Securities Dealers, Inc. Relating to Nasdaq's Proposed Separation from NASD and Establishment of NASD Alternative Display Facility, Sec. Exch. Act Rel. No. 34–45991, 77 S.E.C. Docket 2101, 2002 WL 1072081 n. 7 (SEC May 28, 2002) ("If a Designated Dealer holds for execution on the Exchange a customer buy order and a customer sell order that can be crossed, the Designated Dealer shall cross them without interpositioning itself as a dealer.")

278. *See* In the Matter of Sohmer, Sec. Exch. Act Rel. No. 34–49052, 2004 WL 51681 *7 (SEC 2004) (upholding sanctions against broker and firm).

280. *See* In the Matter of McCarthy, Admin. Proc. No. 3–10999, Sec. Exch. Act Rel. No. 34–48554, 81 S.E.C. Docket 465, 2003 WL 22233276 (SEC 2003) (affirming New York Stock Exchange disciplinary sanctions).

Failure to disclose that trades entered on customer's behalf were cross trades can constitute deceptive conduct in violation of the Exchange Act.[281] Cross trades must be recorded as such in the broker-dealer's records.[283]

Another variety of market manipulation that can involve wash sales is "marking the close."[299] Marking the close consists of attempting to influence a security's closing price by executing purchase or sale orders at or near the close of normal trading hours. If successful, the placing of an order to peg the price will artificially inflate or depress the closing price for the security and thus will determine the price of "market-on-close" orders placed by customers or other third parties.

§ 14.3[6][C] Other Manipulative Practices: High Pressure Sales, Deceptive Recommendations, Excessive Commissions, Order Execution Obligations, Parking

The types of specific conduct that are addressed in other broker-dealer rules include market manipulation,[309] high pressure sales tactics,[310] deceptive recommendations,[311] generation of excessive commissions,[312] unauthorized trading,[313] improper order executions,[314] improper extension of credit for securities transactions,[315] and misuse of customer funds or securities.[316]

Parking

Another manipulative practice is known as "parking" which consists of transferring record ownership of securities in order to hide the true identity of the beneficial owner.[318] All of the foregoing practices are prohibited by section 9 with regard to exchange-traded securities and by rules promulgated under sections 10(b)[319] and 15[320] of the Exchange Act with regard to securities traded in the over-the-counter markets as well as on the exchanges.

Trading ahead of customers is an impermissible practice whereby a broker enters an order for his or her own account in advance of placing an order for customers. The object of this manipulative practice is to give the broker a preferential price. Trading ahead of customers ordinarily contravenes the NASD's fair and equitable principles of trade. Front running is a

Front running)

---

281. *See* Sartain v. SEC, 601 F.2d 1366, 1370 (9th Cir.1979).

283. *See, e.g.,* In the Matter of Robert Schwarz, Inc., Administrative Proceeding File No. 3–7377 No. 34–1248, 46 S.E.C. Docket 20, Release No. IA–28400, 1990 WL 310672 (SEC Aug. 31, 1990) (failure to report cross trades).

299. *See, e.g.,* In the Matter of Chema, Sec. Exch. Act Rel. No. 34–40719, 68 S.E.C. Docket 1911, 1998 WL 820658 (SEC Nov. 30, 1998).

309. *See* §§ 6.2–6.3 *supra* (manipulation in connection with public offerings) § 12.1 *supra* (manipulation generally), and § 14.10[5] *infra* (manipulation by market makers).

310. *See* § 14.18 *infra.*

311. *See* §§ 14.16, 14.17 *infra.*

312. *See* § 14.20 *infra. See also* 14.21 *infra.*

313. *See* § 14.21 *infra.*

314. *See* § 14.13 *infra.*

315. *See* § 14.9 *supra.*

316. *See* § 14.8[2] *supra.*

318. *See, e.g.,* Yoshikawa v. SEC, 192 F.3d 1209 (9th Cir.1999).

319. 15 U.S.C.A. § 78j(b). *See* § 12.1[3][B] *supra* for an overview of the rules promulgated under section 10(b). These rules are also discussed in various sections throughout this treatise.

320. 15 U.S.C.A. § 78o. *See* § 12.1[3][C] *supra* for an overview of the rules promulgated under section 15. These rules are also discussed in various sections throughout this treatise and especially in the sections that follow in this chapter.

Front running-

manipulative practice that is based on a form of insider trading.[322] Front running exists in many forms. For example, front running can consist of trading ahead of customers' orders in order to take advantage of inside information pertaining to others that will have an effect on the price. If the broker knows of a large sell order that will move the price downward once it is entered and executed, and if the broker sells for his or her own account ahead of that order, the broker gets the advantage of the market price determined without the market's consideration of the large pending sell order. Front running is manipulative and also is inconsistent with the NASD's requirement that brokers' conduct be consistent with fair and equitable principles of trade.

Various manipulative practices can occur in connection with public offerings. For example, artificially preparing the market or stimulating the aftermarket will run afoul of the anti-manipulation rules.[325] Additionally, Regulation M[326] severely restricts purchases by persons participating in a distribution in the course of the distribution. Another deceptive practice that can take place in the context of a public offering is "free riding,"[327] which involves purchasing securities in a public offering without the intent or the funds to pay for the purchase with a view toward taking a free ride on a rising market.[328] Free riding also violates the margin requirements that govern the extension of credit for securities transactions.[329] In any context, entering an order to purchase a security without any intent to pay for it other than through a free ride is deceptive conduct.[330] In contrast, where a customer's nonpayment for the securities is a simple breach of contract without deception, the securities laws will not be implicated.[331]

Beyond these specific manipulative broker-dealer activities and the general anti-manipulation and deception rules, the SEC makes it clear that violation of its rules is not limited to violation of any specified SEC rules, but rather covers all conduct that operates as a deceptive or manipulative device.[332] This broad coverage of SEC regulation thus is not limited to conduct that is specifically identified in SEC rules. Broker-dealers have an obligation to act in a professional manner and failure to do so can be a deceptive practice in violation of the generalized antifraud prohibitions.[333]

The SEC has taken the position in various contexts that it can regulate conduct that would be manipulative even if the concern is not based on activity that is explicitly prohibited by existing rules.[334]

---

322. *See, e.g.,* John v. Journal Communications, Inc., 801 F.Supp. 210, 211 (E.D.Wis.1992).

325. *See* § 6.3 *supra.*

326. 17 C.F.R. §§ 242.101 *et seq.*; *See* Anti-Manipulation Rules Concerning Securities Offerings, Sec. Rel. Nos. 33-7375; 34-38076; IC-22412 (Dec. 20, 1996), 62 Fed. Reg. 520 (1997). *See* § 6.2 *supra.*

327. *See, e.g.,* In the Matter of Wu, Administrative Proceeding File No. 3-9024, 70 S.E.C. Docket 386, Rel. No. ID-144, 1999 WL 518983 *13 n. 8 (SEC July 22, 1999).

328. *See* § 6.3[2] *supra.*

329. *See* § 14.9 *infra.*

330. *See, e.g.,* A.T. Brod & Co. v. Perlow, 375 F.2d 393 (2d Cir.1967).

331. *See* A.T. Brod & Co. v. Perlow, 375 F.2d 393, 398 (2d Cir.1967).

332. Rule 15c1-2 (c), 17 C.F.R. § 240.15c1-2(c).

333. As explained in one opinion, "Under the shingle theory, investors are entitled to rely on the implied representation that they will be dealt with fairly, honestly and in accord with industry standards." In the Matter of Gartz, Administrative Proceeding File No. 3-9060, 65 S.E.C. Docket 351, Release No. ID-113, 1997 WL 441913 n. 33 (SEC Initial Decision Aug. 6, 1997) relying on Charles Hughes & Co. v. SEC, 139 F.2d 434, 437 (2d Cir.1943), *cert. denied*, 321 U.S. 786, 64 S.Ct. 781, 88 L.Ed. 1077 (1944).

334. *See, e.g.,* In the Matter of Hazel Bishop, Inc., 40 S.E.C. 718, 1961 WL 65108 (SEC 1961) which is discussed in § 4.28 *supra*, wherein the Commission held up a registration statement

§ 14.4   Broker–Dealer Registration; Definitions and Exemptions

Section 15(a)(1) of the Exchange Act[1] provides that securities brokers and dealers must be registered in order to conduct their business, unless their business is exclusively intrastate or unless otherwise exempted from registration.

§ 14.4[1]   Broker–Dealer Registration: Definitions

§ 14.4[1][A]   Definitions of Broker and Dealer

Broker is defined in the Exchange Act to include any person, other than a bank,[2] in the business of buying and selling securities for others.[3] To fall within the definition, it is not necessary that the broker deal directly with customers; thus, for example, clearing brokers are subject to SEC regulation.[4] A dealer is defined by the Exchange Act to be any person other than a bank who is in the business of purchasing securities for his or her own account.[5]

The Act's registration requirements, as well as the definitions of broker and dealer, are drafted broadly to include a wide range of securities professionals. Key terminology in the definitions of broker and dealer is the phrase "engaged in the business."[6] Merely providing information that may facilitate investors will not classify the provider as a broker-dealer. Thus, a company that merely provided information on the Internet regarding offerings did not itself classify the provider as a broker-dealer.[7] However, another company that made this type of information available for a fee calculated on the basis of securities purchased would be operating as a broker-dealer.[8] Furthermore, a website that is organized in order to bring investors and companies together must either operate under the supervision of a broker-dealer,[9] or else register as a broker-dealer.[10]

---

because of the potential for manipulation in connection with an at market secondary offering. *See also* chapter 6 *supra.*

§ 14.4

1.   15 U.S.C.A. § 78*o*(a)(1).

2.   Banks used to be prohibited from engaging in commercial securities brokerage by the Glass–Steagall Act (12 U.S.C.A. §§ 24, 378(a)). However, there has been erosion and eventual repeal of the prohibition. *See* § 22.5 *infra.*

3.   15 U.S.C.A. § 78c(a)(4)(A).

4.   *See generally* Henry F. Minnerop, The Role and Regulation of Clearing Brokers, 48 Bus.Law. 841 (1993).

5.   Section 3(a)(5)(A), 15 U.S.C.A. § 78c(a)(5)(A).

6.   Sections 3(a)(4), 3(a)(5); 15 U.S.C.A. §§ 78c(a)(4), 78c(a)(5).

7.   *See* StockPower, Inc., 1998 WL 767495 (SEC No Action Letter July 13, 1998).

8.   In the Matter of Flannigan, Admin. Proc. File No. 3–10530, Sec. Exch. Act Rel. No. 34–47142, 79 S.E.C. Docket 842, 2003 WL 60764 (SEC Jan. 8, 2003).

9.   *See* IPONET, 1996 WL 431821 (SEC No Action Letter July 26, 1996), relied on in Progressive Technology, Inc., [2000–2001 Transfer Binder] Fed. Sec. L. Rep. (CCH) ¶ 78,009, 2000 WL 1508655 (SEC No Action Letter Oct. 11, 2000).

10.   Progressive Technology, Inc., [2000–2001 Transfer Binder] Fed. Sec. L. Rep. (CCH) ¶ 78,009, 2000 WL 1508655 (SEC No Action Letter Oct. 11, 2000).

In deciding whether a firm is acting as a broker-dealer, a number of factors are considered. The relevant factors include whether the firm (1) receives transaction-based compensation, such as commissions or referral fees, (2) is involved in negotiations between an issuer of securities and investors, (3) makes valuations as to the merits of the investment or gives advice, and (4) is active rather than passive in locating investors.[19] Participating in a public offering as an underwriter or dealer requires registration as a broker-dealer under the Exchange Act.[20]

Although the Exchange Act does not define the phrase "engaged in the business," case law and no-action letters have outlined the fact that "regularity of participation" is a primary indication of being "engaged in the business" and therefore of acting as a broker-dealer.[23] When someone participates in securities transactions "at key points in the chain of distribution,"[24] he or she will be considered to be acting as a broker-dealer.[25]

§ 14.4[1][B] Banks and Subsidiaries of Banks

The exclusion from the broker-dealer definition for banks (but not subsidiaries of banks) applies only to corporations that in fact are banks, and thus does not apply to non-banking subsidiaries.[55] When Congress repealed the Glass Steagall Act in 1999, the Gramm–Leach–Bliley Act[56] enacted a system of functional regulation. Subsidiaries of banks can engage in all sorts of securities related activities and their activities are subject to SEC control. Similarly, financial holding companies can engage in banking, securities and insurance activities and their securities activities are regulated by the SEC.

The functional regulation introduced by the Gramm–Leach–Bliley Act means that the securities affiliates of banks are regulated by the SEC as broker-dealers rather than by bank regulators.[57] This legislation thus adopted two categories of activities that would be exempt from broker-dealer registration under the Securities Exchange Act of 1934. These two types of activities are bank securities activities that relate to functions traditionally performed by banks and transactions that relate to traditional bank products. The banking exemptions from broker-dealer regulation for traditional banking activities include such things as trust activities (unless the bank customer has discretionary trading authority), stock purchase plans, sweep accounts, private securities placements, and municipal securities.

As noted above, the passage of Graham–Leach–Bliley opened up additional opportunities for banks to engage in activities that traditionally were left to

---

19. *See, e.g.,* SEC v. Zubkis, No. 97 Civ. 8086, 2000 WL 218393, *9 (S.D.N.Y.2000).

20. *See, e.g.,* SEC v. Milan Capital Group Inc., 2000 WL 12467 (S.D.N.Y. 2000). *See also, e.g.,* In the Matter of Paul A. Barrios, 2000 WL 279232 (SEC 2000) (participation in unregistered offerings).

23. Massachusetts Fin. Servs., Inc. v. Securities Investor Protection Corp., 411 F.Supp. 411, 415 (D.Mass.1976), *affirmed* 545 F.2d 754 (1st Cir.1976), *cert. denied,* 431 U.S. 904, 97 S.Ct. 1696, 52 L.Ed.2d 388 (1977).

24. *Id.*

25. *See, e.g.,* BD Advantage, Inc., 2000 WL 1742088 (SEC No Action Letter Oct. 11, 2000).

55. *See, e.g.,* Securities Exchange Act of 1934 Section 3(a)(4), 2002 WL 925039 (SEC No Action Letter April 1, 2002).

56. Pub. Law. 106–102, 1999 U.S.C.C.A.N. (113 Stat.) 1338 (1999).

57. *See generally* Jerry W. Markham, Banking Regulation: Its History & Future, 4 N.C. Bank. Instit. 221,264 (2000).

securities brokers and thus fall under SEC jurisdiction. The SEC took several years evolving its rules on banks as broker-dealers, including the establishment of a temporary exemption. In 2003, the SEC adopted a rule addressing banks as securities dealers under the Exchange Act.[60] The SEC amended its rule granting an exemption from dealer registration to banks whose securities activity consists solely of a de minimis number of riskless principal transactions. The SEC also adopted changes to its rule that defines terms used in the exception to dealer registration for banks engaged in asset-backed transactions. The Commission adopted a new exemption for banks with respect to certain securities lending transactions. The exemption applies to non-custodial lending transactions to qualified investors.[65]

§ 14.5   Broker–Dealer Registration Requirements

§ 14.5[1]   Broker–Dealer Registration Generally

As is pointed out in the preceding section, section 15(a)(1) of the Exchange Act[1] provides that securities brokers and dealers must be registered in order to conduct their business, unless their business is exclusively intrastate or otherwise exempted from registration.

The broker-dealer registration requirements are found in section 15(b) of the Exchange Act[3] and the SEC rules promulgated thereunder.[4] The registration process is commenced by an applicant's completion of SEC Form BD. The information to be supplied in the registration materials includes a detailed description of the broker-dealer's assets and financial condition, including a showing of compliance with the Commission's net capital rule.[7] Nonresident broker-dealers, general partners of broker-dealers, and managing agents of broker-dealers must file an irrevocable power of attorney designating the SEC as agent for service of process.

After the Form BD has been filed, the SEC may grant or deny the registration.[9] In the event that the Commission is inclined to deny an application for registration, it is directed by statute to institute formal proceedings by giving notice of the grounds for the proposed denial and giving the applicant an opportunity to be heard.[10] Once a broker-dealer's registration has been granted, the Commission can also institute formal proceedings to

---

60. *See* Definition of Terms in and Specific Exemptions for Banks, Savings Associations, and Savings Banks Under Sections 3(a)(4) and 3(a)(5) of the Securities Exchange Act of 1934, Sec. Exch. Act Rel. No. 34–47364, 79 S.E.C. Docket 1838, 2003 WL 328058 (SEC Feb. 13, 2003).

65. *Id.* The investor must be a "qualified investor" as that term is used in section 3(a)(4) of the Exchange Act, 15 U.S.C.A. § 78c(a)(4). Qualified investors are limited to large institutions as well as individuals having at least $10 million. *Id.*

§ 14.5

1. 15 U.S.C.A. § 78o(a)(1).

3. 15 U.S.C.A. § 78o(b).

4. The broker-dealer registration and disclosure requirements are handled through a central registration depositary (CTD) that is operated by the National Association of Securities Dealers. *See, e.g.,* Broker–Dealer Registration and Reporting Monday, 58 Fed. Reg. 11–01, 1993 WL 362 (SEC Jan. 4, 1993).

7. *See* 17 C.F.R. § 240.15c3–1. *See also* Steven L. Molinari & Nelson S. Kibler, Broker–Dealers' Financial Responsibility under the Uniform Net Capital RuleCA Case for Liquidity, 72 Geo.L.J. 1 (1983).

9. 15 U.S.C.A. § 78o(b).

10. 15 U.S.C.A. § 78o(b)(1)(B).

revoke the registration for noncompliance with the registration or other requirements of the Act.[11] The SEC may suspend a broker-dealer's registration pending a determination of whether the registration should be revoked.[12] As an alternative to ordering a revocation of registration, for less severe violations, the Commission has the option of censuring or placing limitations upon the broker-dealer's activities.[13] Additionally, the Commission may suspend a broker-dealer for a period of up to one year.[14]

Once a broker-dealer is registered under the Act, cancellation may be effected by a filing of a formal withdrawal from registration.[16] Registration can also be suspended or revoked as a result of disciplinary action by the SEC or a self regulatory organization.

§ 14.5[2] Registration of Foreign Broker–Dealers

The language of section 15(a)(1) requires registration of foreign broker-dealers who utilize the mails or other means of interstate commerce to effect transactions in nonexempt securities.[24] "Interstate commerce" is defined to include commerce between a foreign country and any state.[25] Section 30(b) of the 1934 Act relieves foreign brokers from the broker-dealer registration requirements imposed by section 15 so long as the foreign broker is operating outside of the jurisdiction of the United States.[26]

§ 14.6 Municipal Securities Dealers

Municipal securities, as referred to in the Securities Exchange Act of 1934, comprise a wide variety of obligations, primarily bonds issued by state, local or other political subdivisions or their agencies, including industrial development bonds.[1] Because of their governmental issue or guarantee, municipal securities are generally exempt from the registration and reporting provisions of both the 1933 and 1934 Acts.[2] Proponents of the municipal exemption from registration and reporting requirements cite several arguments in favor of the current legal status: (1) independent audits of municipal issuers and SEC registration are claimed to be undue cost burdens which would decrease municipal bond marketability and impair the municipality's ability to borrow for a public purpose; and (2) the 1934 Act sought to prevent speculative abuse, which had not occurred in the municipal area, and would

11. 15 U.S.C.A. § 78o(b)(4).

12. 15 U.S.C.A. § 78o(b)(5).

13. 15 U.S.C.A. § 78o(b)(4).

14. 15 U.S.C.A. § 78o(b)(4).

16. 17 C.F.R. § 240.15b6–1.

24. 15 U.S.C.A. § 78o(a)(1). Jurisdiction over foreign broker-dealers is discussed in § 17.4[10] *infra.*

25. 15 U.S.C.A. § 78c(a)(17).

26. 15 U.S.C.A. § 78dd(b). Section 10(b) has been found to apply to transactions in securities which occur outside the United States between foreign buyers and sellers when the subject securities were registered on an American exchange and there was concern about welfare of domestic markets or domestic investors. AVC Nederland B.V. v. Atrium Investment Partnership, 740 F.2d 148 (2d Cir.1984); *compare* Zoelsch v. Arthur Andersen & Co., 824 F.2d 27 (D.C.Cir. 1987).

§ 14.6

1. 15 U.S.C.A. § 78c(a)(29).

2. 15 U.S.C.A. §§ 77c(a)(2), 78c(a)(12). *See* § 4.3 *supra.*

not arise since institutional investors dominated that market and held the bonds for investment, not speculative, objectives.[3]

Transactions in municipal securities generally take place in more specialized markets by brokers and dealers dealing exclusively with municipal securities and who are, therefore, exempt from the general broker-dealer regulation and rules of the Securities and Exchange Commission. There is no organized exchange subject to SEC oversight nor is there NASD coverage regarding persons dealing only in municipal securities. Furthermore, prior to 1975, the Securities and Exchange Commission had no jurisdiction over these transactions except in circumstances involving fraud. The antifraud provisions that are applicable to municipal securities[4] provide some protection to investors, but significantly less than investors in securities of private issuers. Even with municipal securities regulation that was added to the Exchange Act in 1975, the 1933 Securities Act's exemptions and the lack of an organized exchange leave investors with less protection than with the regular securities market for private issuers. However, notwithstanding the exemption from 1933 Act registration, when municipal securities are initially offered to the general public, municipal securities dealers must provide a disclosure document that somewhat parallels those that would be required in a 1933 Act registration. The required disclosure document has been criticized as inadequate. In addition to the required disclosure document, although exempt from registration, municipal securities are not exempt from the antifraud provisions. Thus, for example, failure to disclose mark-ups for municipal securities transactions can support a private action for violations of SEC Rule 10b–5.[9]

The early 1970s witnessed a lack of investor confidence in the municipal securities markets.[10] At the same time, the SEC instituted several fraud actions involving municipal securities dealers which were unregulated but nevertheless subject to the Exchange Act's antifraud proscriptions.[11] These and other factors led Congress to conclude in 1975 that "[e]xpanding the protections generally available under the federal securities laws to investors in municipal securities is * * * appropriate."[12]

§ 14.7   Regulation of Government Securities Dealers

As discussed earlier, brokers and dealers who deal solely in exempted securities need not register under section 15 of the Exchange Act.[1] Municipal securities dealers, who are also exempt from broker-dealer registration, are

3. *See* Note, Municipal Bonds, and the Federal Securities Laws: The Results of Forty Years of Indirect Regulation, 28 Vand. L. Rev. 561, 583–85 (1975).

4. *See, e.g.,* SEC v. Cochran, 214 F.3d 1261 (10th Cir.2000) (nondisclosure of bid rigging regarding temporary investment of proceeds from municipal bond offering could be material).

9. Grandon v. Merrill Lynch & Co., 2001 WL 826092, [2001–2002 Transfer Binder] Fed. Sec. L. Rep. (CCH) ¶ 91,497 (S.D.N.Y.2001). *See also* Grandon v. Merrill Lynch & Co., 208 F.R.D. 107 (S.D.N.Y.2002) (plaintiff charging excessive mark ups of municipal bonds was entitled to discovery of algorithm that the firm used to compute mark ups).

10. *See, e.g.,* Sen.Rep. No. 94–75 pp. 3–4 (Banking, Housing and Urban Affairs Committee April 25, 1975).

11. *See* Municipal Securities Rulemaking Board Manual (CCH) ¶ 101.

12. Sen.Rep. No. 94–75 p. 3 (Banking, Housing and Urban Affairs Committee April 25, 1975).

§ 14.7

1. 15 U.S.C.A. § 78o–4(c). *See* §§ 14.2, 14.4 *supra*.

regulated through the Municipal Securities Rulemaking Board,[2] but there was no comparable regulation for government securities dealers until 1986. Following the insolvency of a number of government securities dealers, Congress enacted legislation to require the regulation of government securities dealers. The government securities dealer registration requirements more closely parallel that of broker-dealers generally than of municipal securities dealers.

Government securities are those securities which are issued or guaranteed by the federal government or a federal agency.[3] Treasury securities, such as savings bonds, "T–Bills," and "Treasury Notes" are familiar government securities. Lesser-known government-guaranteed securities are those issued by federally-owned agencies, for example Government National Mortgage Obligations or "Ginnie Maes." Finally, there are money market instruments such as "federal funds," and "repurchase agreements." Federal funds are cash reserves which the Federal Reserve Board requires banks to maintain for liquidity purposes and which are manipulated by the Federal Reserve Board to effectuate monetary policy.[4] "Repurchase agreements" or "repos" are investment schemes by which institutional investors and government securities dealers exchange cash for government securities.[5]

The market for United States government securities has been described as the world's largest, most efficient and liquid securities market.[6] The United States Treasury uses the market to finance the national debt, while the Federal Reserve Board conducts monetary policy through the market.[7] As such, the market is "the cornerstone of the U.S. capital market system," and its integrity must be insured.[8] However, between July 1975 and April 1985, failures of unregistered government securities dealers threatened this integrity.[9] Certain problems were common to many of the failures. In some cases the failed firm had issued false and misleading financial statements; or in some cases a firm would mask its troubled status through complex relationships and transactions with affiliated companies; and finally, customer losses often occurred because the customer failed to secure control of or collateralize securities underlying a repurchase (or "repo") transaction with a problem dealer. Congress identified the weakness of the regulatory framework for the government securities market as a major cause of these failures. To bolster this framework, Congress enacted the Government Securities Act of 1986.[12]

The Government Securities Act of 1986 added section 15C to the Exchange Act of 1934 and provided for conforming amendments to the Exchange Act, the Investment Company Act of 1940, and the Investment Advisers Act of 1940.[13] The Government Securities Act of 1986 was developed to overcome the problems which caused investor losses in the government securities market. The Act seeks to eliminate those problems by: (1) requiring registration of

2. See 15 U.S.C.A. § 78o–4. The regulation of municipal securities dealers is discussed in § 14.6 supra.

3. 15 U.S.C.A. § 78c(a)(42).

4. See, e.g., Note, The Government Securities Market: In the Wake of ESM, 27 Santa Clara L.Rev. 587, 589–91 (1987).

5. See id.

6. Senate Report No. 99–426, S. 1416, Government Securities Act of 1986, Fed.Sec.L.Rep. (CCH) No. 1195 at 5 (Sept. 17, 1986).

7. Id. at 4.

8. Id. at 2.

9. Id. at 6.

12. 15 U.S.C.A. § 78o–5(a)(1)(A).

13. Senate Report No. 99–426, S. 1416, Government Securities Act of 1986, Fed.Sec.L.Rep. (CCH) No. 1195 at 11 (Sept. 17, 1986).

government securities brokers and dealers with the Commission or with appropriate regulatory agencies; (2) establishing financial responsibility safeguards such as capital adequacy and reporting requirements; (3) mandating procedures for the acceptance and use of customers' securities; and (4) allowing on-site inspection and enforcement by federal regulators.[15] The Government Securities Act of 1986 is also designed not to impose regulation that will adversely affect the liquidity and efficiency of the government securities market.[16]

§ 14.8 Broker–Dealer Net Capital and Reserve Requirements

The solvency of broker-dealer firms has long been a concern for investors and for the investment markets generally. As discussed in a later section, in reaction to a number of firm failures, Congress enacted the Securities Investor Protection Act of 1970 to provide for customers' insurance against losses due to brokerage firm insolvency.[1] However, other regulatory protections focused on preventing brokerage firm insolvencies have been in place much longer. For example, the SEC has had its long-standing net capital requirements for broker-dealer firms. A companion set of protections are found in the reserve requirements. Both the net capital and reserve requirements are discussed below.

§ 14.8[1] Net Capital Requirements

In 1942, the SEC adopted its net capital rule which is designed to assure a safe balance between a brokerage firm's securities holdings, cash, and liabilities.[2] The current net capital rule imposes extremely complicated accounting and solvency requirements for a brokerage firm's assets and liabilities.[3] The discussion that follows will present a brief overview of the net capital requirements.[4] For more detailed discussion, the reader should consult other sources.[5]

The basic financial responsibility standards for broker-dealers are found in the "net capital" rules adopted by the SEC under authority of section 15(c)(3) of the 1934 Act.[6] Prior to the financial debacle suffered by the securities industry from 1968 to 1970, securities firms belonging to exchanges which had "net capital" rules deemed to be more stringent than those of the SEC were exempt from the SEC's requirements. However, after SEC and Congressional investigations showed how flexibly the exchanges had interpreted their rules to allow member firms to continue in business with inadequate capital, the SEC revoked this exemption and made all broker-dealers subject to its requirements.

---

15. *Id.* at 14.

16. *Id.*

§ 14.8

1. 15 U.S.C.A. §§ 78ccc *et seq. See* the discussion in § 14.24 *infra.*

2. Sec. Exch. Act Rel. No. 34–3323 (SEC Oct. 29, 1942).

3. SEC Rule 15c3–1, 17 C.F.R. § 240.15c3–1.

4. A portion of this discussion has been adapted from David L. Ratner & Thomas Lee Hazen, Securities Regulation: Cases and Materials 970–971 (5th ed. 1996).

5. *See* 23A Jerry W. Markham & Thomas Lee Hazen, Broker–Dealer Operations Under Securities and Commodities Law: Financial Responsibilities, Credit Regulation and Customer Protection ch. 5 (2d ed. 2003).

6. 15 U.S.C.A. § 78o(c)(3).

Under the SEC net capital rule, if the broker-dealer opts out of the aggregate indebtedness test that is described below, a broker-dealer must maintain "net capital" of at least $250,000. "Net capital" is defined as "net worth" (excess of assets over liabilities), subject to many special adjustments prescribed in the rule. One of the more important special adjustments is the "haircut" or discount that must be applied in valuing securities listed on the asset side of the balance sheet. The net capital rule requires that securities be discounted by a specified amount; this amount varies depending on the type of security. The haircut is designed to provide an additional margin of safety in light of the volatility of securities prices.

The alternative to the net capital rule's net worth test is the rule's aggregate indebtedness test under which a broker-dealer may not let its aggregate indebtedness exceed 1500% of its net capital (800% during its first year of business). A broker-dealer can alternatively qualify under Rule 15c3–1(f), which is designed to test its general financial integrity and liquidity and its ability to meet its continuing commitments to its customers.

On occasion unscrupulous brokers have attempted to evade the net capital requirements by contrived and deceptive transactions known as parking. Parking consists of transferring securities for the purpose of hiding their true ownership.[8]

§ 14.8[2] Customers' Funds and Securities: The Customer Protection Rule and the Reserve Requirements[13]

Customers leave large amounts of cash and securities with their brokers. The securities are of two types: securities purchased "on margin"[14] (i.e., with the broker advancing part of the purchase price to the customer), which (under the standard margin agreement) the broker is entitled to hold as security for the loan and to repledge to secure its own borrowings; and "fully-paid" securities, which the broker holds solely as a convenience for the customer and is supposed to "segregate" from the broker's own securities.[15] The cash "free credit balances" arise principally from two sources: a deposit of cash by a customer prior to giving his broker a purchase order, and receipt by the broker of proceeds of a sale of securities, or interest or dividend income, which has not yet been reinvested or delivered to the customer.

§ 14.9 The Margin Rules and Extension of Credit for Securities Transactions

§ 14.9[1] Margin Transactions Explained

Not all securities are purchased in a straight cash transaction. A large number of securities transactions, especially those by speculative investors,

---

8. *See, e.g.,* Yoshikawa v. SEC, 192 F.3d 1209 (9th Cir.1999) (remanding for determination of whether transfer of securities between accounts was parking).

13. A portion of this discussion has been adapted from David L. Ratner & Thomas Lee Hazen Securities Regulation: Cases and Materials 971–972 (5th ed. 1996).

14. The margin requirements are discussed in § 14.9 *infra.*

15. SEC Rule 15c2–1(a), 17 C.F.R. § 240.15c2–1(a). These rules require segregation of customers securities and are designed to prevent the broker's hypothecation of such securities. *See* 23 Jerry W. Markham & Thomas Lee Hazen, Broker–Dealer Operations Under Securities and Commodities Law: Financial Responsibilities, Credit Regulation and Customer Protection § 4.07 (2d ed. 2003). *See also* Michael P. Jamroz, The Customer Protection Rule, 57 Bus. Law. 1069 (2002).

are entered into by the broker extending credit to the purchaser while the lender holds the purchased securities as collateral. Securities purchases on credit are referred to as margin transactions. A margin purchase gives the security holder leverage and thus while significantly increasing the risk of investment, also increases the potential gain. Excessive credit balances create undue investor risk. In addition, brokerage firms that extended high levels of credit in the 1920s were wiped out by the stock market crash of 1929. The margin requirements were designed to curb such excesses.

The effect of price changes on a margin account can be understood from examining how an increase in the loan value of a securities account will increase the likelihood of a margin call. Assume that an investor has a stock portfolio consisting entirely of marginable securities[2] with a current market value of $100,000. The risk of a margin maintenance call is greatly reduced the less the investor borrows against his or her portfolio. For example, if the investor borrows thirty percent of the value of stocks (i.e., $30,000), the stocks would have to decline in value by more than fifty-seven percent before the investor would be subject to a maintenance call, assuming a margin maintenance requirement of thirty percent imposed by the investor's brokerage firm.[3] The following table[4] demonstrates the effects of margin borrowing against $100,000 worth of stock:

If investor borrows:	A maintenance call will be issued if the portfolio value declines to:	Percentage decline before maintenance call occurs:
$50,000　(50%)	$71,429	29%
$40,000　(40%)	$57,143	43%
$30,000　(30%)	$42,857	57%
$20,000　(20%)	$28,571	71%
$10,000　(10%)	$14,286	85%

The examples that follow demonstrate the calculation of permissible margin levels for an initial purchase of securities. If an investor wants to buy 10,000 shares of ABC Corp. stock which is trading at $10 per share (for a total $100,000 for 10,000 shares) and wants to make the purchase with only $75,000 cash, he or she can do so by borrowing the remaining $25,000 that is necessary to complete the purchase. The margin calculation for the account would be as follows:

> The investor purchases 10,000 shares of ABC Corp. at $10 per share for a total cost of $100,000. The investor would then deposit the $75,000 cash with the broker and borrow the remaining $25,000 from the broker.
>
> $100,000 (value of stock) − ($25,000) (debit balance) = $75,000 (net equity) $75,000 (net equity) ÷ $100,000 (value of stock) = 75% net equity

---

§ 14.9

2. Accordingly, all equity in the account is available as collateral for a margin loan.

3. Although, as discussed below, the self regulatory organizations impose a 25% maintenance requirement for most securities, many brokerage firms impose a higher requirement for their own protection. The margin maintenance requirement may in fact be higher for more volatile and/or less liquid securities.

4. This table is found at http://www.smithbarney.com/prodsvc/credlend/portfolio.html

The next example demonstrates the calculation of the maximum loan permitted under the Federal Reserve Board's fifty percent limit under its margin rules for the extension of credit.[5] An investor wants to purchase 10,000 shares of ABC Corp. stock which is trading at $10 per share (a total of $100,000 for the 10,000 shares). The investor can purchase on fifty percent margin by purchasing the stock for $100,000, using $50,000 cash and borrowing $50,000 from the broker:

> 10,000 shares ABC Corp. @ $10 = $100,000 total equity $50,000 cash + $50,000 margin loan

This is the maximum that the investor may purchase with $50,000 cash, since it puts the investor at the Federal Reserve Board's fifty percent margin limit for the extension of credit.[6] Each time an investor purchases additional securities on margin, it is considered another extension of credit so that the 50% maximum credit balance (or minimum fifty percent margin) will apply to each purchase. Thus, for example, after making the first purchase of the 10,000 ABC Corp. shares, if the investor now wants to purchase an additional $10,000 of stock, he or she must deposit at least an additional $5,000 cash (or at least an additional $10,000 worth of other marginable collateral) in order to make the second purchase.

The following are examples of the operation of the margin maintenance requirements of at least twenty-five percent[7] that are imposed by the self regulatory organizations[8]:

An investor's securities account has a $50,000 debit on which the investor will be charged interest by the lending brokerage firm. The interest on the investor's debt will in turn be added to the account's debit balance. For example, if the $10 per share price of the 10,000 shares of ABC Corp. stock remains constant, assuming 6% interest (1/2% per month), after one month the investor's account would incur an additional $250 debit. The investor's account would still consist of 10,000 shares ABC Corp. at $10 per share for a total of $100,000. There would be the initial $50,000 debit plus an additional $250 resulting from the interest charged over the first month. This would result in a total debit balance of $50,250. The margin computation would then be as follows:

> $100,000 (value of stock) − $50,250 (debit balance) = $49,750 (net equity) $49,750 (net equity) ÷ $100,000 (value of stock) = 49.75% margin

The foregoing example would be in compliance with the self regulatory organization margin maintenance requirements[9] but not with the Federal Reserve Board's extension of credit requirements. Assume that after the first month, the price of ABC Corp. has dropped to $8 per share. The investor's account would then consist of 10,000 shares of ABC Corp. at $8 per share for a total of $80,000. The account would have the $50,000 initial debit plus the

5. *See* § 14.9[2] *infra.*

6. *Id.*

7. As pointed out *supra*, many brokerage firms impose a higher requirement for their own protection.

8. *See* § 14.9[3] *infra.*

9. *Id.*

$250 interest for a total debit of $50,250. The account would still be in compliance with the minimum margin maintenance requirement:

$80,000 (value of stock) − $50,250 (debit balance) = $29,750 (net equity)
$29,750 (net equity) ÷ $80,000 (value of stock) = 37.1875% margin

However, if during the first month, the price of ABC has dropped to $6 (instead of the $8 per share in the previous example), then the investor's account would be computed as follows. There would be 10,000 shares of ABC Corp. at $6 per share for a total of $60,000. The account would have the $50,000 initial debit plus the $250 interest for a total debit of $50,250. The account would not be in compliance with the minimum margin maintenance requirement:

$60,000 (value of stock) − $50,250 (debit balance) = $9,750 (net equity)
$9,750 (net equity) ÷ $60,000 (value of stock) = 16.25% margin

This example results in a total that is below the New York Stock Exchange, American Stock Exchange, and NASD minimum margin maintenance requirements[10] and the investor would be subject to a margin call. Either additional collateral would have to be supplied or the securities in the account would be liquidated to pay off the debit balance.

§ 14.9[2] Limitations on the Extension of Credit for Securities Transactions

Section 7 of the Exchange Act sets out a complex system of regulation with regard to the extension of credit for securities transactions, but does not apply to exempt securities.[11] By virtue of section 7(a),[12] the Federal Reserve System Board of Governors is delegated the authority to promulgate rules governing the extension of credit where securities are used as collateral to secure the loan. Various regulations have been adopted with regard to broker-dealers, banks, and other persons so extending credit. Broker-dealer margin rule enforcement lies with the SEC through injunctions, criminal proceedings, revocation of registration, or suspension from membership in self regulatory organizations. In 1996, Congress preempted the states' ability to regulate the extension of credit in securities transactions.[13]

The credit extension rules are not limited to traditional margin accounts. As discussed more fully below, the credit extension rules also apply to late payments in cash accounts.[14]

The maximum limits for the extension of credit are set forth in the statute, but the statutory limits have been further cut back by the Federal Reserve Board. Section 7(a) of the Exchange Act states that the initial

---

10. *Id.*

11. 15 U.S.C.A. § 78g. Exempt securities under the 1934 Act parallel many of the 1933 Act exemptions. *See* 15 U.S.C.A. § 77c; chapter 4 *supra.* 1934 Act registration and reporting requirements are discussed in § 9.2–9.3 *supra.*

12. 15 U.S.C.A. § 78g(a).

13. 1934 Act section 15(h), 15 U.S.C.A. § 78o(h).

14. The settlement period for equity securities formerly was five business days but this has been shortened to three business days. Rule 15c6–1, 17 C.F.R. § 240.15c6–1. *See* Securities Transactions Settlement, Sec. Exch. Act Rel. No. 34–33023, 55 S.E.C. Docket 332, 1993 WL 403275 (SEC Oct. 6, 1993); NASD Notice to Members 93–77, 1993 WL 1434168 (Nov. 1993). Options transactions have a one-day settlement and thus must be settled on the next business day.

extension of credit may not be for an amount greater than the higher of (1) fifty-five percent of the security's then current market price or (2) one hundred percent of the lowest market price of the security during the preceding thirty-six calendar months but no more than seventy-five percent of the current market price. Certain exempt governmental securities trade with a much higher margin. For example, United States Treasury bills can have up to a ninety percent margin at the time of purchase.[17] This more highly leveraged transaction for federal government notes is more in line with the margin requirements for the more speculative commodity markets.[18] Notwithstanding the statutory fifty-five percent ceiling on credit, the Federal Reserve Board has imposed an even lower credit ceiling of fifty percent for the extension of credit as opposed to the margin maintaining requirements.[19]

The applicable rules of the Federal Reserve Board for broker-dealers' extension of credit are found in Regulation T.[22]

In order to qualify for an extension of credit under Regulation T, the securities must either be traded on a national securities exchange[30] or be actively traded in the over-the-counter market. Formerly, there was a list of margin equity securities established by the Federal Reserve Board.[31] The Federal Reserve Board now provides for the automatic marginability of over-the-counter stocks that are part of the NASD's National Market System.[32] Additionally, foreign sovereign debt securities are marginable to the extent of their "good faith" loan value. The current level of the margin securities cannot exceed a fifty percent debit balance in connection with the purchase of any additional securities.[33] The Federal Reserve Board is statutorily empowered to impose minimum levels for maintaining margin accounts under section 7(a), as well as initial levels, but it has never exercised this authority. Accordingly, a "margin call," whereby the customer is required to come up with additional collateral lest the margined securities be sold, will never be required by operation of law unless a new security is purchased for the account.[34] This is thus left to the broker-dealer's discretion[35] and the twenty-five percent minimum required by exchange rules and by the NASD.[36] Most brokerage firms have established their own policies for margin calls, many of which are more stringent than the NASD and exchange rules. Brokers'

17. Section 7 of the Act does not apply to exempted securities. 15 U.S.C.A. § 78g(a).

18. One way to achieve comparable leverage in the securities markets is to trade listed "put" and "call" options. *See* SEC Report of the Special Study of the Options Markets, 96th Cong., 1st Sess. (1978).

19. *See, e.g.,* Supplement to Regulation T, 12 C.F.R. § 220.18.

22. 12 C.F.R. § 220.1–220.131.

30. *See* section 6 of the Act, 15 U.S.C.A. § 78f. *See* § 14.2 *supra.*

31. 15 U.S.C.A. § 78g(c)(2). *Cf.* Mark A. Guinn & William L. Harvey, Taking OTC Derivative Contracts as Collateral, 57 Bus. Law. 1127 (2002).

32. *See* Bd. of Governors of the Federal Reserve System Docket No. R–0512 (March 7, 1984).

33. 12 C.F.R. §§ 220.3(c), (d), 220.18(a). Regulation T does not avail itself of the fifty-five percent statutory maximum. Instead, it imposes a lower ceiling of fifty percent. Supplement to Regulation T, 12 C.F.R. § 220.18.

34. *Cf.* In re Weisberg, 136 F.3d 655 (9th Cir.1998) (brokerage firm liquidated margin position in bankrupt customer's account in order to meet margin calls without violating automatic stay provisions of Bankruptcy Act).

35. *See* SEC Report of the Special Study of the Options Markets, 96th Cong., 1st Sess. pt. 4 at 5–6 (1978).

36. *Cf.* Nevitsky v. Manufacturers Hanover Brokerage Services, 654 F.Supp. 116, 119–20 (S.D.N.Y.1987) (dismissing Rule 10b–5 action claiming improper margin call).

guidelines may also depend in part not only upon the value of the collateral but also on the diversification of the margined securities as well as their reliability.

In addition to the credit limitations for margin accounts, the margin rules require that whenever a security is purchased in a cash account, payment must be made within a specified settlement period after the date of purchase or else the broker-dealer must cancel or otherwise liquidate the transaction.[37] In mid–1993, the settlement period for most securities was shortened to three business days.[38] The settlement date for options remains the business day following the transaction. A broker's delay in liquidating the account will not relieve the customer of the obligation to pay for the securities.[39] A rapid sale of the securities before the settlement date will not enable the customer to take a free ride. Free riding is the entering into a transaction without the intent to pay with the hope that the purchase price will be covered by a quick sale. As discussed in an earlier section of this treatise,[40] free riding violates the securities laws. Under the Federal Reserve Board rules, if a customer sells securities within three days of purchase and without having paid for the securities, for the next ninety days the customer cannot purchase securities unless the account contains enough cash to cover the purchase price.[41]

§ 14.9[3] Margin Maintenance Requirements

The statutory (and Federal Reserve Board) limits on margin accounts apply only to the *initial* extension of credit and do not deal with an increase in the ratio of the debit of the margin account in relation to the value of the securities due to the decline in the price of securities used as collateral after their initial purchase. In other words, under both SEC and Federal Reserve Board regulation it lies purely within the lender's discretion to decide at what point additional securities as collateral or cash will be needed to fortify a margin account where the value of the current collateral is declining. However, the exchanges and the NASD impose margin maintenance requirements. Under these margin maintenance rules, the current market value of the collateral must be at least twenty-five percent of the account's total value. Thus, there are minimum margin maintenance requirements for all accounts. Generally, brokerage firms assure compliance with the margin maintenance requirements by instituting an internal policy for "house calls" at a level above the regulatory minimum.[43] The higher house call level thus provides a safety zone in the event that the market is unusually volatile or the customer delays in providing the necessary additional collateral. Violation of the margin requirements will result in disciplinary sanctions.

---

37. 12 C.F.R. § 220.8(b)(1), (4).

38. Rule 15c6–1, 17 C.F.R. § 240.15c6–1. *See* Securities Transactions Settlement, Sec. Exch. Act Rel. No. 34–33023, 55 S.E.C. Docket 332, 1993 WL 403275 (SEC Oct. 6, 1993); NASD Notice to Members 93–77, 1993 WL 1434168 (Nov. 1993).

39. Shearson Lehman Brothers, Inc. v. M & L Investments, 10 F.3d 1510 (10th Cir.1993) (broker-dealer's failure to liquidate account after purchaser failed to pay for stock was not a defense to breach of contract action).

40. *See* § 6.3 *supra*.

41. 12 C.F.R. § 220.105.

43. The brokerage firm can raise the house call level without prior notice to the customer. *See, e.g.,* Sec. Exch. Act Rel. No. 34–44223, 2001 WL 431540 (SEC April 26, 2001); NASD Rule 2341.

§ 14.9[4] Margin Disclosure Requirements; Suitability

In addition to the substantive margin regulation set forth in the Federal Reserve Board and self regulatory organization regulations, margin accounts trigger special disclosure obligations.[45] The customer must be given a margin disclosure statement when the margin account is opened and must also receive a disclosure statement annually.[46] The disclosure statement is designed to alert customers to the risks associated with margin accounts. The required disclosure at the opening of a margin account is designed to inform the customer of margin related risks.[48] The annual disclosure requirement is designed to remind the customer of these risks. By themselves, margin trades are high risk transactions.[50] The advent of online trading[51] and increased market volatility can heighten those risks.[52]

Failure to fully inform the client of margin risks can result in liability for losses caused as a result thereof.[53] However, when a customer understands the nature of margin risks, he or she will not be able to state a claim for relief.[54]

The SEC has evidenced significant concern about investors' misunderstanding of the significant risks associated with margin transactions. In addition to the foregoing disclosure requirements, SEC Rule 10b–16[55] requires broker-dealers to adequately disclose the cost to the customer of any securities transaction where credit is extended. In 2001, the SEC initiated a special link on its official website to better inform investors as to the risks of purchasing securities on credit.[56]

The risks associated with margin accounts are such that margin transactions are not suitable for all investors. A broker who uses margin trading in violation of the suitability requirements has violated broker-dealer conduct rules.[58]

§ 14.9[5] Remedies for Violations of the Margin Rules

At one time, some courts recognized a private remedy in the hands of the customer who is injured by violation of the credit extension rules.[64] However,

---

45. *See* NASD Rule 2341. *See, e.g.,* Sec. Exch. Act Rel. No. 34–44223, 2001 WL 431540 (SEC April 26, 2001). *See also, e.g.* NASD Notice to Members Notice 01–31, 2001 WL 568064 (NASD May 4, 2001).

46. *Ibid.*

48. NASD Rule 2341(a).

50. *See, e.g.,* In the Matter of Zessinger, Administrative Proceeding File No. 3–8838, 62 S.E.C. Docket 1482, Release No. ID–94, 1996 WL 464154 (SEC Initial Decision Aug. 2, 1996) (sanctions imposed for opening margin accounts for customers who did not understand risks).

51. *See* § 14.1[8] *supra* and § 14.16[2] *infra.*

52. *See, e.g.,* NASD Guidance Regarding Stock Volatility, NASD Notice 99–11, 1999 WL 33176494 (NASDR Feb. 1999).

53. *See, e.g.,* Burton v. Wheat First Securities, Inc., Docket Number 99–03729, 2000 WL 33171709 (N.A.S.D. Dec. 20, 2000) (arbitration award in excess of $200,000).

54. *See, e.g.,* Podgoretz v. Evans & Co., Inc., 1997 WL 138989 (E.D.N.Y.1997).

55. 17 C.F.R. § 240.10b–16.

56. *See* http://www.tradeworx.com/sec/cgi-bin/tutorialmargin.cgi.

58. *See, e.g.,* In the Matter of Canady, Administrative Proceeding File No. 3–8531, Sec. Exch. Act Rel. No. 34–41250, 69 S.E.C. Docket 1158, 1999 WL 183600 (SEC April 5, 1999).

64. *E.g.* Pearlstein v. Scudder & German, 429 F.2d 1136 (2d Cir.1970), *cert. denied,* 401 U.S. 1013, 91 S.Ct. 1250, 28 L.Ed.2d 550 (1971); Remar v. Clayton Securities Corp., 81 F.Supp. 1014 (D.Mass.1949).

the overwhelming majority of more recent decisions is to the contrary.[65] The absence of an implied remedy under the margin rules is bolstered by the amendment to section 7(f) and ensuing Federal Reserve Board Regulation X rendering the customer himself or herself in violation of the Act.

As noted above, SEC Rule 10b–16[69] requires disclosure of the customer's cost in any securities transaction where credit is extended. A substantial number of courts recognize the existence of a private remedy under Rule 10b–16 for misleading margin related disclosures.[70]

§ 14.10   Market Makers in the Over-the-Counter Markets

§ 14.10[1]   Market Making in Context

Since the over-the-counter markets by definition do not have a central exchange for the entering of buy and sell orders, it is necessary to have some sort of central clearing mechanism to perform a comparable function. The National Association of Securities Dealers Automated Quotation System (NASDAQ) is merely an electronic means of transmitting, disseminating, and publicizing the latest quotes but it is not a vehicle for effecting transactions. NASDAQ generally gives both "bid" and "asked" quotes for over-the-counter securities. Several hundred of the more actively traded over-the-counter securities are listed on a "national market" with only one quoted price. A number of smaller over-the-counter companies listed in NASDAQ which do not qualify for the national market system have their securities listed in the NASDAQ small capitalization system.

Lower volume stocks and many of the lowest priced[4] over-the-counter securities have their quotations listed on an electronic bulletin board or in the "pink sheets." Traditionally, quotations for securities not traded through the national market system or automated quotation system were found in the "pink sheets." The SEC approved, originally on a one-year pilot basis, a NASD electronic bulletin board for computerized quotations for stocks not listed on a national exchange or in the NASDAQ system.[5] It was anticipated that the electronic bulletin boards will replace the pink sheets. Although "pink sheets" continue to exist for some securities, many small capitalization companies that formerly would have been listed in the pink sheets are now traded through the NASD bulletin board.

In 1996, there was some controversy over the emergence of the use of the Internet for securities trading. For example, the SEC was concerned about a small brewery which used the Internet to accomplish an initial public offering and then make a market in its shares. The SEC seriously questioned this and the activities were subsequently halted, but after negotiations, the Commis-

---

65. *E.g.* Useden v. Acker, 947 F.2d 1563 (11th Cir.1991), *cert. denied,* 508 U.S. 959, 113 S.Ct. 2927, 124 L.Ed.2d 678 (1993).

69. 17 C.F.R. § 240.10b–16.

70. *E.g.,* Angelastro v. Prudential–Bache Securities, Inc., 764 F.2d 939 (3d Cir.1985), *cert. denied,* 474 U.S. 935, 106 S.Ct. 267, 88 L.Ed.2d 274 (1985).

§ 14.10

4. Many of these lowest priced stocks would are commonly referred to as microcap stocks and brokers dealing in these stocks may be subject to the heightened requirement of the penny stock rules. The penny stock rules are discussed in § 14.19 *infra.*

5. Sec.Exch.Act Rel. No. 34–27975 (May 1, 1990). *See* SEC Approves One–Year Pilot Program for NASD's OTC Electronic Bulletin Board, 22 Sec.Reg. & L.Rep. (BNA) 672 (May 4, 1990).

sion permitted trading to resume with certain safeguards. Additionally, the Commission has since issued a no action letter permitting a company to make a market in its own shares using the Internet.[8] Beyond Internet offerings, considerable problems can occur when a market maker is also acting as an underwriter for the company in a public offering. Although this is a perfectly permissible dual role, it does present all sorts of opportunities for illegal manipulation.[9]

Most NASDAQ and over-the-counter trades take place through online communications among securities dealers and using quotations provided by market makers. The enhanced technology presents the opportunity for magnifying the effects of human error by transferring that misinformation more rapidly and efficiently into the marketplace.

§ 14.10[2] Mechanics of Market Making Activities—Some Basic Concepts

A broker-dealer acts as a market maker for a particular security or securities. Many securities have more than one market maker. A market maker for a particular security not traded on a national exchange must enter "bid" and "asked" quotes in or over the automated quotation system (NASDAQ), over the NASD's bulletin board for less actively traded small capitalization stocks or in the "pink sheets" with respect to stocks not listed on an automated quotation system. There must be at least three market makers in order for a security to be listed through NASDAQ.[12] Some market makers are more active than others in maintaining current quotations. In addition to general market maker qualifications, the NASD rules provide that a market maker can qualify as a Primary NASDAQ Market Maker ("PNMM").[13]

A market maker is responsible for making "two-way" bids on the securities for which it makes a market. In other words, the market maker has the responsibility of quoting both a bid price (the price which someone is willing to pay for the security) or an offer wanted (OW) as well as an asked price (the price at which someone is willing to sell the security) or a bid wanted (BW). The difference between the bid and asked price is known as the spread and represents the market maker's compensation with respect to transactions executed at the bid and asked price. To the extent that trades are to be made in transactions that exceed the size of the bid and asked quotes, there is no published spread.

---

8. Real Goods Trading Corp., 28 Sec. Reg. & L. Rep. (BNA) 850 (SEC No Action Letter available June 25, 1996).

9. See § 6.3 *supra.*

12. NASD Manual & 4310(c)(1). Once a stock is listed on NASDAQ, there must be at least two market makers for continued listing. *Id.* Except that there must be four active market makers for the more active NASDAQ stocks listed in its National Market System. NASD Rule 4450(e).

13. For example, there are the following thresholds for being designated as a Primary Nasdaq Market Maker: (I) it must be at the best bid or best offer as shown in the NASDAQ quotation system at least thirty-five percent of the time, (II) it must maintain a spread no greater than one hundred and two percent of the average dealer spread, and (III) no more than fifty percent of the market maker's quotation updates may occur without being accompanied by at least one unit of trading.

A firm may continue as a market maker only so long as it carries out its market making functions properly. *Cf.* In the Matter of Tower Trading, L.P., Sec. Exch. Act Rel. No. 34–47537, 2003 WL 1339179 (SEC 2003) (NASD revoked permission to act as primary market maker but SEC reversed the order, citing irregularities in the hearing process).

Published bid and asked quotations are qualified by the quantity of shares for any quote. In other words a bid or asked quote at a stated price would be for a stated number of shares (which could range, for example, from 100 shares to thousands of shares). As such, the market maker must be willing to stand behind these price quotations.[14] The market maker thus must be willing and prepared to both buy the stock and sell it as principal according to the quantities covered in any bid or asked price that the market maker posts. Accordingly, the market maker is frequently in the position of holding long and short positions in the securities in which he or she makes the market. To the extent that a market maker executes transactions beyond the amount of shares currently in inventory or outside the size parameters of the current quotations, the market maker is taking a risk, depending upon the demands of the market. The SEC rules require that the market maker is financially able to fulfill its market making obligations.[15] As a general proposition, market makers are subject to significant regulation by both the NASD and SEC.[16] The SEC rules also give the NASD supervisory power over market makers which includes the ability to withdraw a broker-dealer's market making authority.[17]

Actively traded stocks have multiple active market makers. Competition for orders among active market makers results in competitive prices although there may be price variations between and among market makers.

A market maker's obligations include the posting of reliable quotations that are not the result of market manipulation.[18] The market maker is also obligated to honor the quotations that it posts to the market. Accordingly, it is a violation of NASD rules for a market maker to fail to honor posted quotes.[19]

When there are multiple market makers, the national best bid/best offer ("NBBO") is representative of the best price available based on current quotations. This is a constantly moving target which can change on a second-by-second basis. The NBBO represents the highest bid and the lowest asked quotation that is available at a particular point in time.[20] The NBBO, as is the case with any published bid or asked price, is generally qualified by the number of shares being offered. In other words, the NBBO price reflects quotations or offers with respect to a specified number of shares. The availability of the both the NBB (national best bid) and the NBO (national best offer) thus necessarily is in large part dependent upon a transaction size falling within the NBBO share quantity parameters. In rare instances, even for trades within the NBBO share quantity parameters, brokers may be able

---

14. Similarly, requests for bids wanted and offers wanted may also be qualified by the quantity of shares.

15. 17 C.F.R. § 240.15c3–1(a)(4). They must maintain net capital in an amount not less than $2,500 for each security in which they make a market, and an aggregate net capital not less than $25,000 though not required to be more than $100,000.

16. *See* § 14.10[4] *infra.*

17. *See* 15 U.S.C.A. § 78o–3(b)(7), following procedures set out in 15 U.S.C.A. § 78o–3(h)(i).

18. Manipulation by market makers is considered in § 14.10[5].

19. *See, e.g.,* NASD Regulation Directs Knight Securities to Pay $1.5 Million For Market Violations, *http://www.nasdr.com/news/pr2002/release_02_001.html* (Jan. 7, 2002) (imposing a $700,000 fine and requiring $800,000 in payments to customers for failing to honor posted quotes and other market making violations).

20. *See, e.g.,* Geman v. S.E.C., 334 F.3d 1183, 1186 n.5 (10th Cir. 2003) ("More specifically, the NBBO is the highest quoted bid price and lowest quoted offer price from among all quotations entered in the Consolidated Quotation Service.")

to get a better execution. For example, price improvement may be possible when there are available cross trades within the firm. It is to be noted, however, that cross trades in many situations may be problematic as they are susceptible to claims of manipulation.[21]

§ 14.10[3] Maintaining an Orderly Market

The national securities exchanges, modeled on an auction paradigm, operate in such a way as to match customers seeking to sell securities with those seeking to buy.[29] The NASDAQ and over-the-counter markets do not operate as a traditional exchange as they are not a centralized organization. In order to maintain a market for securities without a central exchange, designated broker-dealers operate as "market makers" in the NASDAQ and over-the-counter markets, buying and selling as principals for their own account rather than as agents for customers.

The concept of market maker is defined broadly to include dealers who hold themselves out as willing to purchase and sell a particular security for their own account "on a regular or continuous basis."[31] It is not necessary that the dealer so hold itself out in any particular manner,[32] thus raising the possibility of inadvertent market maker status. Attainment of market maker status will exempt the dealer from some provisions of the securities laws that otherwise would apply, such as section 16(b)'s prohibitions against short-swing profits.[33] Additionally, market making activities are closely scrutinized by the SEC and NASD.

§ 14.10[4] Premise of NASD Regulation of Market Makers

As noted above, market makers are subject to both SEC and NASD regulation. This regulation includes inspection of records in order to assure that they are not abusing their market making positions. The NASD's oversight of market making activity includes the authority to disqualify a broker-dealer from acting as a market maker.[35]

The NASD Rules of Fair Practice establish standards of conduct for market makers to ensure that they carry out their operations in an appropriate manner. Thus, for example, a broker-dealer who accepts payment for its decision to act as a market maker has compromised its position of neutrality and therefore will be subject to SEC sanctions. The acceptance of compensation interferes with the normal factors a broker-dealer should consider in deciding whether to act as market maker; such factors include attributes that affect the security's liquidity and intrinsic value. The market maker's obli-

---

21. *See, e.g.,* SEC v. Sayegh, 906 F.Supp. 939 (S.D.N.Y.1995) (trader whose firm was market maker violated Rule 10b–5 by consistently posting high bids and entering into cross trades for the purpose of creating the illusion of an active market). Cross trades as a manipulative device are discussed in § 14.3[6][B] *supra.*

29. *See generally,* Birl E. Schultz, The Securities Market-and How It Works (rev. ed.1963); Robert Sobel, N.Y.S.E. History of the New York Stock Exchange (1975); Amex: A History of the American Stock Exchange, 1921–1971 (1972); Peter Wyckoff, Wall Street and the Stock Markets (1972).

31. 15 U.S.C.A. § 78c(a)(38).

32. *See* C.R.A. Realty Corp. v. Tri–South Investments, 568 F.Supp. 1190 (S.D.N.Y.1983).

33. *Id.;* 15 U.S.C.A. § 78p(b). *See* §§ 13.2–13.5 *supra.*

35. *See* 15 U.S.C.A. § 78o–3(b)(7), following procedures set out in 15 U.S.C.A. § 78o–3(h)(i).

gation is to maintain an orderly market. However, when the market maker is executing customer orders, its primary obligation is to those customers.[37]

§ 14.10[5] Market Makers' Conflict of Interest; Disclosure Obligations

In an attempt to promote the more efficient execution of customer orders and more accurate pricing, as well as to eliminate potential conflicts of interest, the SEC approved the NASD's prohibition against market makers trading ahead of certain customer orders.[38] The interpretation of NASD Rules of Fair Practice[39] applies to all NASDAQ-traded securities and prohibits broker-dealers acting in their market making capacity from trading ahead of their customers' limit orders.[40] This interpretation represented a change of policy which permitted market makers not to give priority to customers' limit orders so long as appropriate disclosures were made.

In addition to conducting market making transactions in which the broker-dealer acts as principal, he or she may also enter into riskless transactions upon a customer's order or upon orders of other broker-dealers.[42] The individual risk that attaches to his or her transactions as a principal puts the market maker in a potential conflict of interest situation vis-à-vis his or her responsibilities as an agent for retail customers. It has been held that a broker-dealer who recommends a security without disclosing that he or she is a market maker has made a material misrepresentation so as to give rise to a private right of action for violation of Rule 10b–5.[43] In order to prevail in such an action, plaintiff must prove all the elements normally required to state a Rule 10b–5 claim.[44] Thus, for example, nondisclosure of the market maker's

---

37. Eichler v. SEC, 757 F.2d 1066 (9th Cir.1985).

38. Exch. Act Rel. No. 34–34279, 59 Fed. Reg. 34,883 (SEC July 7, 1994).

39. Interpretation of Rules of Fair Practice, Article III, Section 1.

40. A limit order is one in which a customer specifies a minimum price that he or she will accept in payment for securities being sold or a maximum price that he or she will pay for securities being purchased. The limit order is an alternative to an "at market" order which simply instructs a broker to purchase or sell a security at the market price.

42. "In Nasdaq, a riskless principal trade is one in which a broker/dealer, after having received an order to buy (sell) a security, purchases (sells) the security as principal, at the same price, to satisfy that order. The broker/dealer generally charges its customer a mark up, markdown, or commission equivalent for its services, which is disclosed on the confirmation required by Securities Exchange Act (Exchange Act) Rule 10b–10." See Guidance on Compensation and Mixed Capacity Trading, Special NASD Notice to Members 01–85 (Dec. 24, 2001) (question 3). For further guidance on riskless principal trade reporting obligations for Nasdaq securities, see NASD, Notice to Members 00–79; NASD Notice to Members 99–66; NASD Notice to Members 99–65.

This is in contrast to an agency trade: "An agency trade is a trade in which a broker/dealer, authorized to act as an intermediary for the account of its customer, buys (sells) a security from (to) a third party (e.g., another customer or broker/dealer). Such a trade is not executed in, or does not otherwise pass through, the broker/dealer's proprietary account. When executing an agency trade, the broker/ dealer generally charges the customer a commission for its services." Guidance on Compensation and Mixed Capacity Trading, Special NASD Notice to Members 01–85 (Dec. 24, 2001) (question 2).

"A riskless principal transaction occurs when a dealer receives from its customer an order to purchase (or sell) a security and purchases (or sells) that security to another person in a transaction that is proximate in time and designed to offset the customer's order." In re Lynch, Sec. Exch. Act Rel. No. 34–46439, 78 S.E.C. Docket 1055, 78 S.E.C. Docket 1058, 2002 WL 1997953 (SEC Aug. 30, 2002), relying on Strategic Resource Management, Inc., 52 S.E.C. 542, 544 n.8 (1995).

43. Chasins v. Smith, Barney & Co., 438 F.2d 1167 (2d Cir.1970). Liability was imposed even though the sales confirmation disclosed the broker's market making activity. See also, Magnum Corp. v. Lehman Brothers Kuhn Loeb, Inc., 794 F.2d 198 (5th Cir.1986); Bischoff v. G.K. Scott & Co., 687 F.Supp. 746 (E.D.N.Y.1986).

44. See §§ 12.2–12.12 supra.

acting as principal did not result in liability in the absence of proof that the price of the stock was affected.[45] It has been held, however, that a market maker who purchases stock from a customer at a price below the market will be liable for fraud in the transaction.[46]

In addition to imposing civil liability for material omissions in connection with recommendations, the SEC rules require disclosure of market maker status. SEC Rule 10b–10[52] makes it unlawful for a broker or dealer to effect a transaction for any customer or to induce any purchase or sale of a security without disclosing whether the broker is acting as the agent for the customer or as agent for someone else, including whether or not the broker is acting as a market maker or principal. It has been held that the mere fact that the dealer's role is disclosed in the transaction confirmation slip will be insufficient to preclude a violation of Rule 10b–10 if the customer does not understand the significance of the disclosure. It is to be noted, however, that not every nondisclosure of a conflict of interest will violate Rule 10b–10.[54]

A broker-dealer is subject to disciplinary sanctions for failure to disclose his or her market maker status in violation of Rule 10b–10. It is one thing to show a failure to disclose market maker or principal status in a given transaction; however, it is quite another thing for the customer to show materiality, reliance, and scienter so as to give rise to a Rule 10b–5 cause of action.[55] A Second Circuit decision recognized a 10b–5 claim for nondisclosure of market maker status in connection with a broker-dealer's recommendation since the market maker status was a material factor in the customer's decision to invest.[56] As noted above, some courts have required proof of actual loss causation in terms of a differential in market price.[57] In the context of an unsolicited transaction, it is not as significant for the investor to know that the broker-dealer effecting the customer's offer is a market maker, except perhaps for the purpose of determining the commission.[58] When a broker's firm acts as a market maker it may be possible for the customer to get a slight break on the commission.[59]

---

45. Shivangi v. Dean Witter Reynolds, Inc., 825 F.2d 885 (5th Cir.1987). *But see* Chasins v. Smith, Barney & Co., 438 F.2d 1167 (2d Cir.1970) (where the court permitted rescission without a specific showing of loss causation). *Cf.* Geman v. SEC, 334 F.3d 1183 (10th Cir. 2003) (affirming sanctions against brokerage firm for failing to disclose it was trading as principal at favorable prices).

46. Weiner v. Rooney Pace, Inc., [1987 Transfer Binder] Fed.Sec.L.Rep. (CCH) ¶ 93,174 (S.D.N.Y.1987). *See also* Ettinger v. Merrill Lynch, Pierce, Fenner & Smith, Inc., 835 F.2d 1031 (3d Cir.1987) (denying broker's motion for summary judgment on claim that market maker failed to disclose allegedly excessive mark-ups on bonds).

52. 17 C.F.R. § 240.10b–10.

54. *See* Press v. Quick & Reilly, Inc., 218 F.3d 121 (2d Cir.2000).

55. *See* Cant v. A.G. Becker & Co., 374 F.Supp. 36 (N.D.Ill.1974), *opinion supplemented* 379 F.Supp. 972 (N.D.Ill.1974) (decided under Rule 15c1–4c which was rescinded in 1978 but is to the same effect as Rule 10b–10).

56. Chasins v. Smith, Barney & Co., 438 F.2d 1167 (2d Cir.1970). *But see* Shivangi v. Dean Witter Reynolds, Inc., 825 F.2d 885 (5th Cir.1987).

57. Shivangi v. Dean Witter Reynolds, Inc., 825 F.2d 885 (5th Cir.1987). *See also, e.g.,* Eichler v. SEC, 757 F.2d 1066 (9th Cir.1985) (affirming disciplinary sanctions against underwriter and market maker which failed to obtain the best executions for its retail customers).

58. *Cf.* Manela v. Garantia Banking, Ltd., 5 F.Supp.2d 165 (S.D.N.Y.1998) (broker's failure to disclose it owned bonds that were sold to investor was not in itself actionable).

59. When a broker goes through a third party market maker they split the commission. Although a brokerage firm's market making and retail operations are distinct, acting through a broker which is also a market maker does eliminate a middleman.

Although Rule 10b–10 establishes disclosure obligations in connection with confirmation of securities transactions, compliance with its requirements does not preclude liability for fraud.[60] It has thus been held that compliance with Rule 10b–10 did not preclude a market maker's liability for failing to disclose allegedly excessive mark-ups.[61]

§ 14.10[6] Market Makers and Manipulation

The market making obligations place market makers in control of market prices. As such, unscrupulous market makers can abuse their positions by engaging in manipulative practices.[69] Due to the potential for manipulation, regulators scrutinize market making activities. The NASD watches closely to assure that the market maker in fact maintains an orderly market and is not engaging in manipulative practices; if so, the market maker will be subject to losing approval to act as market maker. The risk of market maker manipulation is much greater when a broker-dealer acts as the sole active market maker for the stock in question. When brokerage firms have such "house stocks,"[71] there is no independent free market to gauge the legitimacy of their market making and other activities. Brokerage houses handling house stocks are thus in a very good position to manipulate the market. Thus, although there is nothing illegal per se about concentrating in house stocks, doing so is one of the common benchmarks of a controlled market manipulation.[73] Other manipulative activities can also occur in connection with house stocks.[74] For example, account representatives may be given higher commissions for pushing "house stocks."[75] They may also be given disincentives for having customers enter sell orders in house stocks.[76] In extreme instances, customer sell orders may even be ignored.[77] These practices designed to dissuade customer sales orders constitute illegal manipulation and also violate broker-dealer standards of fair dealing.

In part because of the potential for abuse resulting from control of the market, NASDAQ stocks must be handled by at least three market makers in order to be listed on NASDAQ.[79] Continued listing requires only two active market makers,[80] except for the largest National Market System securities, which must have at least four active market makers.[81] The presence of

---

60. *E.g.,* Ettinger v. Merrill Lynch, Pierce, Fenner & Smith, Inc., 835 F.2d 1031 (3d Cir.1987).

61. *Id.*

69. *E.g.,* United States v. Haddy, 134 F.3d 542 (3d Cir.1998).

71. Stocks that are traded solely among the clients of that brokerage house. *See, e.g.,* United States v. DiStefano, 129 F.Supp.2d 342 (S.D.N.Y.2001).

73. *See, e.g.,* SEC v. Graystone Nash, Inc., Civ. Action 91–4327 (AMW), Litigation Release No. 13624, 53 S.E.C. Docket 2721, 1993 WL 133729 (D.N.J. April 29, 1993).

74. *See, e.g.,* SEC v. Hasho, 784 F.Supp. 1059 (S.D.N.Y.1992).

75. *See, e.g.,* SEC v. Wellshire Securities, 737 F.Supp. 251 (S.D.N.Y.1990). *See also, e.g.,* In the Matter of Olde Discount Corp., Administrative Proceeding File No. 3–9699, Sec. Act Rel. No. 33–7577, 67 S.E.C. Docket 2045, 1998 WL 575171 (SEC September 10, 1998).

76. *See, e.g,* In the Matter of Demaio, Administrative Proceeding File No. 3–7912, 54 S.E.C. Docket 1509, Release No. ID–37, 1993 WL 300297 (SEC Aug. 4, 1993).

77. *E.g.,* United States v. Matthews, 34 Sec. Reg. & L. Rep. (BNA) 601 (S.D.N.Y.2002).

79. NASD Manual & 4310(c)(1).

80. NASD Rule 4310(c)(1).

81. NASD Rule 4450(e).

multiple market makers does not eliminate the potential for collusion and thus a dealer with only a small percentage of the total market float can be participating in manipulative market making practices.[82] Collusion is not the only way that one market maker can dominate the market. Some market makers may simply decide to concentrate on other stocks that they make markets in and thus remain passive with regard to securities that end up being handled by a dominant market maker. In this way one market maker can dominate the market without conscious collusion with the remaining market makers.

Control over the market is not in itself a violation of the Act.[84] However, it violates the antifraud provisions to fail to disclose control over the market for securities handled by the market-maker and broker-dealer.[85] Also, by controlling and cornering[87] the market by reducing the market float,[88] or executing market squeezes,[89] broker-dealers can illegally maintain artificially high prices in the stocks they are manipulating.[90] Market domination is thus a common starting point for manipulative scheme.[91]

Regardless of the absence of market dominance, a market maker's bad faith in publishing quotations is a breach of the market maker's obligations. Thus, for example, a market maker's pattern of backing away from published quotes can establish manipulation.[95] A market maker's backing away from published quotations will often be in violation of the so-called "firm quote" rule[96] that requires market makers to stand behind their published quotations. Market maker improprieties can easily develop into manipulative conduct. However, not every questionable act by a market maker amounts to a manipulation. Thus, for example, although backing away from quotations may be evidence of a manipulative scheme, the mere fact that a market maker backed away is not sufficient to establish a manipulation.[97]

82. In the Matter of Hibbard, Brown & Co. Admin. Proc. File No. 3–8418 March 13, 1995 Release No. 34–35476, 58 S.E.C. Docket 2561, 1995 WL 116488 n. 20 (SEC March 13, 1995).

84. Pagel, Inc, 48 S.E.C. 223, 226 (1985), aff'd sub nom. Pagel, Inc. v. SEC, 803 F.2d 942 (8th Cir.1986).

85. SEC v. First Jersey Securities, 101 F.3d 1450, 1467–1468 (2d Cir.1996) (violation of 1933 Act § 17(a) and 1934 Act § 10(b)).

87. Cornering the market consists of acquiring sufficient supply of the securities or commodities in question so as to establish control over the market. For a description of cornering the market, *See* 2 Philip McBride Johnson & Thomas Lee Hazen, Derivatives Regulation § 5.02[4] (2004).

88. *See, e.g,* SEC v. National Bankers Life Ins. Co., 334 F.Supp. 444, 446 (N.D.Tex.1971), affirmed 477 F.2d 920 (5th Cir.1973).

89. *See, e.g.,* In the Matter of Goldman, Administrative Proceeding File No. 3–7866, Sec. Exch. Act Rel. No. 34–31210, 52 S.E.C. Docket 1551, 1992 WL 252182 (SEC Sept. 22, 1992).

90. *See, e.g.,* In the Matter of AMR "Tony" Elgindy Key West Securities, Inc., Complaint No. CMS000015, 2003 WL 21203080 (N.A.S.D.R. May 7, 2003).

91. *See, e.g.,* S.E.C. v. First Jersey Securities, Inc., 890 F.Supp. 1185, 1197 (S.D.N.Y.1995), affirmed and reversed on other grounds, 101 F.3d 1450 (2d Cir.1996).

95. *See, e.g.,* In re The Chicago Stock Exchange, Sec. Exch. Act Rel. No. 34–48566, 81 S.E.C. Docket 490, 2003 WL 22245922 (SEC 2003).

96. The SEC's firm quote requirement is found in SEC Rule 11 Ac1, 17 C.F.R. § 240. 11 Ac1–1.–1.

97. In the Matter of Elgindy, Admin. Proc. File No. 3–11145, Sec. Exch. Act Rel. No. 34–49389, 2004 WL 865791 (SEC 2004) (reversing NASD's finding of manipulation).

§ 14.11   Trading on Stock Exchanges; The Specialist System

§ 14.11[1]   Trading by Exchange Members[1]

§ 14.11[1][A]   Exchange Trading Generally

The principal function and purpose of a national securities exchange is to provide a marketplace in which member firms, acting as brokers, can purchase and sell securities for the account of their customers. The question addressed in section 11 of the Exchange Act[2] is the extent to which stock exchange members and their firms should be permitted to trade in listed securities for their own account, in view of the possibly unfair advantages they may have over public customers when engaging in such trading.

Section 11(a),[3] as amended in 1975, prohibits an exchange member from effecting any transactions on the exchange for its own account, or any account with respect to which it exercises investment discretion,[4] with certain specified exceptions, including transactions as a market maker (specialist) or odd-lot dealer, stabilizing transactions in connection with distributions, bona fide arbitrage transactions, and other transactions which the SEC concludes should be exempt from the prohibition. Traditionally, the inquiry has focused on three special categories of transactions: (a) "floor trading" and "off-floor trading" by members and their firms, (b) transactions by "odd-lot dealers," and (c) transactions by specialists. The increasing domination of New York Stock Exchange trading by institutional customers has focused attention on two additional categories: (d) "block positioning" by member firms, and (e) transactions for "managed institutional accounts."

§ 14.11[1][B]   "Floor Trading" and "Off–Floor Trading"

The primary purpose of 11(a), as originally enacted, was to authorize the SEC to write rules (1) "to regulate or prevent floor trading" by exchange members, and (2) to prevent excessive off-floor trading by members if the Commission found it "detrimental to the maintenance of a fair and orderly market."[5]

Floor practices are scrutinized to enable the prevention of manipulative practices. For example, trading ahead of customer orders is prohibited and can result in disciplinary action including expulsion.[6] One such practice, also known as "flipping"[7] or "trading for eighths," occurs when a broker simultaneously trades for a customers account, at a fractionally different price in

---

§ 14.11

1. This subsection is adapted from David L. Retner & Thomas Lee Hazen, Securities Regulation: Cases and Materials 976–978 (5th ed. 1996).

2. 15 U.S.C.A. § 78k.

3. 15 U.S.C.A. § 78k(a).

4. 15 U.S.C.A. § 78k(a)(1). *See* SEC Rule 11a–1, 17 C.F.R. § 240.11a–1.

5. 15 U.S.C.A. § 78k(a).

6. *See, e.g.,* MFS Securities Corp. v. New York Stock Exchange, Inc., 277 F.3d 613 (2d Cir.2002) (challenging the Exchange procedure used in disciplinary proceeding); In the Matter of Savarese Exchange Hearing Panel Decision 99–112, 1999 WL 988116 (N.Y.S.E.1999). Trading ahead of customers also violates the NASD rules governing market makers. *See § 14.13* infra.

7. This is to be distinguished from the frequently challenged practice of flipping in connection with initial public offerings, whereby someone purchasing securities as part of an initial offering, flips his or her investment by selling in the aftermarket at a price above the IPO price. *See* § 6.3[2] *supra.*

order to take advantage of the spread between the bid and the asked price.[8] Typically the broker will also charge a commission on these transactions.[9]

"Floor trading" was the specialty of a small percentage of New York Stock Exchange members who maintained their memberships for the sole or primary purpose of roaming around the exchange floor and trading for their own account in whatever securities caught their fancy. The SEC adopted some mild restrictions on floor trading in 1945, but nothing significant was done until 1963, when the Commission's Special Study of the Securities Markets concluded that floor trading was a vestige of the pre–1934 "private club" atmosphere of the exchanges, and should be abolished. In 1964, the Commission adopted Rule 11a–1,[10] prohibiting all floor trading by members, unless conducted in accordance with a plan adopted by an exchange and approved by the Commission. The New York Stock Exchange simultaneously adopted a plan, which was then approved by the Commission, requiring floor traders to register with the exchange, to maintain minimum capital and pass a qualifying examination, and to comply with special restrictions on their trading activity.

Among other things, Rule 11a–1 prohibits a floor trader from trading for a customer's account over which the trader exercises discretion.[11] The rule is violated when a floor trader ignores the instructions on an order ticket and instead uses his or her discretion in executing the trade.[12]

"Off-floor" trading by member firms (i.e., transactions initiated by decisions at the firm's offices, rather than on the floor) accounts for a much greater proportion of activity than floor trading, having amounted to roughly 14% of total New York Stock Exchange volume in 1989. In 1999, off-floor trading amounted to 11.1% of the New York Stock Exchange's total volume.[13] From January to June 2006, specialists participated in 6.3% to 7.4% on a monthly basis.[13.5]

§ 14.11[1][C] Specialists

The specialist firm occupies a unique dual role in the operation of the New York Stock Exchange, which is also the case with the other securities exchanges. First, a specialist firm acts as a "broker's broker," maintaining a "book" on which other brokers can leave customers' "limit orders" (i.e., orders to buy or sell at a price at which they cannot currently be executed). Second, a specialist acts as the exclusive franchised dealer, or "market maker" in its assigned stocks, buying and selling shares from other brokers

8. In the Matter of D'Alessio, Sec. Exch. Act Rel. No. 34–47627, 2003 WL 1787291 n.42 (SEC 2003).

9. *See, e.g.,* MFS Securities Corp. v. New York Stock Exchange, Inc., 277 F.3d 613 (2d Cir.2002) (challenging the Exchange procedure used in disciplinary proceeding).

10. 17 C.F.R. § 240.11a–1.

11. 17 C.F.R. § 240.11a–1. A similar prohibition is found in NYSE Rule 95(a). *See, e.g., See* In the Matter of McCarthy, Admin. Proc. No. 3–10999; Sec. Exch. Act Rel. No. 34–48554, 81 S.E.C. Docket 465, 2003 WL 22233276 (SEC 2003) (affirming NYSE disciplinary sanctions).

12. *See, e.g., See* In the Matter of McCarthy, Admin. Proc. No. 3–10999; Sec. Exch. Act Rel. No. 34–48554, 81 S.E.C. Docket 465, 2003 WL 22233276 (SEC 2003).

13. NYSE Fact Book (2000), http://www.nyse.com/pdfs/activity99.pdf, at 19.

13.5 *See* NYSE Website, http://www.nysedata.com/nysedata/Default.aspx?tabid=115 (visited July, 26, 2006).

when there are no customer orders on its book against which they can be matched.

The functions of the specialist can be illustrated by the following example. A firm is the specialist in an actively-traded stock, in which the market is $40 to $40.10. This means that customer orders are on the specialist's book to buy specified numbers of shares at $40 or less, and other orders are on his book to sell at $40.10 or more (for historical reasons, shares formerly were quoted in halves, quarters and eighths, rather than cents but now are traded in decimals). A broker who comes to the specialist with an order to sell "at the market" will sell to the customer with the first buy order on the book at $40, and a broker who comes with a market order to buy will buy from the customer with the first sell order on the book at $40.10. The specialist acts solely as a subagent, receiving a portion of the "book" customer's commission to his broker.

Now assume the same firm is also specialist in an inactively traded stock. The only orders on the book are an order to buy at $38 and an order to sell at $42. If the specialist acted solely as agent, a broker who came in with a market order to sell would receive $38, and another broker who came in an hour later with a market order to buy would pay $42. The report of these two trades on the "tape" would indicate the stock had risen 4 points, or 10%, in an hour. The exchange therefore imposes an obligation on the specialist to maintain an "orderly market" in his assigned stocks, buying and selling for his own account to even out swings which would result from buyers and sellers not appearing at his post at the same time. In this case he might make his market at $40 to $40.25, trading for his own account as long as necessary, but yielding priority to customers' orders on his book whenever they provide as good a price to the party on the other side.

In essence, exchange trading and the specialist system is based on a "continuous two-way agency auction market" in which the firms acting as specialists "are responsible for the quality of the markets" for the securities in which they specialize.[15] The specialist's obligation is also phrased in terms of the duty to maintain a fair and orderly market. The SEC has explained that a fair and orderly market is one that is not marred by manipulation or deception and characterized by reliable price continuity.[17]

Specialists on an exchange are viewed as having two primary duties: to secure the best execution[18] of orders with "minimal dealer intervention" and at the same time to manage supply and demand imbalances.[19] Specialists carry out these obligations by participating in the market both as a broker or agent in acting as an intermediary between two matching orders and also as a dealer or principal when there is no available counter party to the transaction. Thus, specialists should not interposition themselves between matching offsetting orders. In other words, specialists may obtain the best execution by

---

15. *See, e.g.,* In the Matter of Van Der Moolen Specialists USA, LLC, Sec. Exch. Act Rel. No. 34–49502, 2004 WL 626564 (SEC Mar 30, 2004).

17. *See* In the Matter of Van Der Moolen Specialists USA, LLC, Sec. Exch. Act Rel. No. 34–49502, 2004 WL 626564 (SEC Mar 30, 2004).

18. The best execution obligation in the over-the-counter markets is discussed in § 4.10 *supra* and § 4.13 *infra.*

19. *See* In the Matter of Van Der Moolen Specialists USA, LLC, Sec. Exch. Act Rel. No. 34–49502, 2004 WL 626564 (SEC Mar 30, 2004).

matching transactions and crossing customer orders.[21] In fact, it is the specialist's obligation to do so if possible.[22]

Irrespective of whether a specialist is acting as agent or principal, their obligation to maintain a fair and orderly market takes priority over any self interest that the specialist may have in a particular transaction. As described by the SEC: "When matchable customer buy and sell orders arrive at specialists' trading posts—generally either through the NYSE's Super Designated Order Turnaround System ('DOT') to an electronic display book (the 'Display Book'), or by floor brokers gathered in front of the specialists' trading posts ('the crowd')—specialists are required to act as agent and cross or pair off those orders and to abstain from participating as principal or dealer."[24]

While this combination of a specialist's functions has obvious advantages, it also offers possibilities for abuse. With his monopoly trading position and knowledge of the "book," the specialist, by moving the price of his specialty stocks up and down, can guarantee himself profits in both his "broker" and "dealer" functions. The SEC has from time to time studied and expressed its concern about this potential manipulation by specialists but has never undertaken direct regulation of specialists' activities. In 1965, it adopted Rule 11b–1,[25] requiring the principal exchanges to maintain and enforce rules designed to curb abuses by specialists, but SEC and Congressional studies expressed continuing dissatisfaction with NYSE surveillance and regulation of specialist activities. In recent years, however, the NYSE has disciplined a number of specialists for improper trades or reports of trades, failure to maintain orderly markets, and other violations.

In 1975, Congress amended 11(b) of the Exchange Act[26] to make clear that the SEC had authority to limit specialists to acting either as brokers or dealers, but not both, but the Commission has not yet taken any action pursuant to this authority.

§ 14.11[1][D] Block Positioning

Institutional investors (principally pension funds, mutual funds, and insurance companies) have increased their investments in common stocks to the point that they currently account for sixty to seventy percent of the trading on the New York Stock Exchange. Institutions often trade in large blocks (10,000 shares or more), which in 1999 accounted for a bit over one half of total New York Stock Exchange trading volume.[27] These block transactions put special strains on exchange market-making mechanisms. If a member firm which specializes in institutional business has a customer that wishes

---

21. Outside the context of specialist or legitimate market making activity, matching of orders and cross trading may be manipulative practices. *See* § 14.3[6][B] *supra.*

22. *See, e.g.,* In re Self–Regulatory Organizations; Notice of Filing of Amendment No. 2 to Proposed Rule Change by National Ass'n of Securities Dealers, Inc. Relating to Nasdaq's Proposed Separation from NASD and Establishment of NASD Alternative Display Facility, Sec. Exch. Act Rel. No. 34–45991, 77 S.E.C. Docket 2101, 2002 WL 1072081 n. 7 (SEC May 28, 2002).

24. *See* In the Matter of Van Der Moolen Specialists USA, LLC, Sec. Exch. Act Rel. No. 34–49502, 2004 WL 626564 (SEC Mar 30, 2004).

25. 17 C.F.R. § 240.11b–1.

26. 15 U.S.C.A. § 78k(b).

27. In 1989 block trades accounted for 51% of the volume. In 1999, these trades accounted for 50.2% of total New York Stock Exchange volume. NYSE Fact Book,available at http://www.nyse.com/pdfs/historical99.pdf, at 93.

to sell 100,000 shares of a particular stock, but can only find buyers for 80,000, the firm itself will "position" the remaining 20,000 shares, and then sell them off over a period of time as the market can absorb them. Section 11(a)(1)(A)[28] recognizes this "market making" function as a legitimate exception to the prohibition against trading by members for their own account.

§ 14.12   Multiservice Brokerage Firms; Information Barriers; The Chinese Wall or Fire Wall

At the time that the federal securities laws were originally enacted, the functions of the various professionals in the securities industry were relatively distinct. However, the last quarter of the twentieth century witnessed not only the elimination of clear distinctions between the permissible activities of banks and securities firms, but also the proliferation of multiservice firms providing a wide variety of financial services. Thus, for example, today, a multiservice securities firm combines the functions of investment banking and corporate counseling with investment advisory, investment management and retail broker-dealer services.

Brokerage firms that offer a wide variety of services will have to separate the operations of many of those services. This separation is not limited to operations but also to accounting and recordkeeping issues. Furthermore, information barriers known as "Chinese walls" or "fire walls" may have to be established in order to avoid conflict of interest problems.

A typical multiservice firm performs numerous functions. These functions typically include: (1) investment banking (including underwriting and rendering advice to corporate issuers); (2) research (which services all of the firm's departments); (3) sales, which includes both retail sales and investment management; and (4) generally firms will have their own trading desk which operates in the over-the-counter markets and also performs arbitrage for their own account. The following simplified graphic depicts a prototypical multiservice securities brokerage firm:

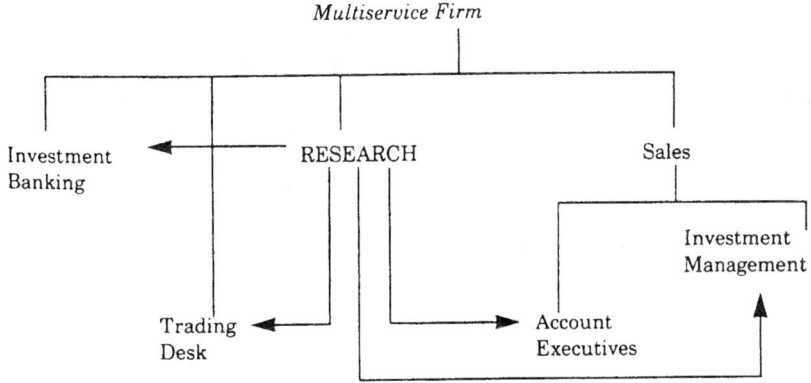

These varied functions give rise to conflicts of interest as the firm has a duty to guard the confidentiality of any non-public information it receives from a corporate client. A major problem is that while the research depart-

---

28.   15 U.S.C.A. § 78k(a)(1)(A).

ment is supplying information to each of the other departments, the research department should be basing its evaluation on independent research, not from confidential information acquired from the firm's other departments. The antifraud provisions of the security laws require the firm to disclose all material non-public information it has or abstain from using it in trading or recommending the security in question.[3] This "disclose or abstain" rule further obligates firms to refrain from executing or recommending transactions unless justified in light of all information known to the firm. In response to these conflicting duties, multiservice financial institutions have established internal policies and procedures to restrict the flow of material nonpublic information from the department in which it originates. These procedures are colloquially referred to as "Chinese Walls" or "fire walls."[5]

The required information barriers involve every aspect of a brokerage firms operations. Information barriers are not limited to separating the research and underwriting functions from each other and from the retail operations. When a broker-dealer acts as a market maker.[6] for over-the-counter securities, there are a number of potential conflicts of interest that can arise. For example, market makers may also be acting as underwriters with respect to a public offering.[7] A brokerage firm's market making activities must be carried on independently of other operations including the firm's own trading department as well as the firm's other departments that are mentioned above.

§ 14.13   Execution of Customer Orders

§ 14.13[1] The Best and Prompt Execution Obligations

Assuring fair execution of customer orders is a concern of the SEC in overseeing the operation of the securities markets.[1] Customers can enter various types of orders. For example, a market order directs the broker (through the floor trader or market maker) to execute the transaction at the market price. As discussed below in this section, broker-dealers have obligations to ensure that customers receive a fair execution of these market orders. As an alternative to committing to purchase or sell at the market price, a customer can let the market come to him or her by placing a limit order and giving the broker specific limits. For example, a limit order would authorize purchase at a particular price or lower but in no event higher than the price specified in the limit order. Broker-dealers have duties with regards to these orders as well. For example, there is the question of priority of limit orders. There are prohibitions against broker-dealers trading ahead of their customer's limit orders.[2] This is designed to prevent the broker from putting

---

§ 14.12

3. *See* § 12.17 *supra.*

5. *See generally* David A. Lipton & Robert B. Mazur, The Chinese Wall Solution to the Conflict Problems of Securities Firms, 50 N.Y.U.L.Rev. 459 (1975); Larry L. Varn, The Multiservice Securities Firm and the Chinese Wall: A New Look in the Light of the Federal Securities Code, 63 Neb.L.Rev. 197 (1984).

6. Market makers are discussed in § 14.10 *supra.*

7. *See* §§ 6.3, 14.3[6], 14.10 *supra*

§ 14.13

1. *See, e.g.,* Order Execution Obligations File No. S7–30–95, Sec. Exch. Act Rel. No. 34–36310, 60 S.E.C. Docket 919, 1995 WL 600238 (SEC Sept. 29, 1995).

2. *See, e.g.,* NASD IM–2110–2 (available on Westlaw).

its order (and therefore its interests) above that of the customer.[3] In addition to violating trading standards, undisclosed trading ahead of customers perpetrates a deception upon those customers. This type of deception is in violation of a broker-dealer's obligations even in the absence of an express prohibition on undisclosed trading ahead of customer orders.[5] In addition, it has been held that trading ahead of customer orders can violate state unfair trade practices prohibitions.[6]

Over the past several years, there has been increasing concern over whether brokers, especially in the NASDAQ and over-the-counter markets, were securing the best order executions for their customers.[7] There were charges that brokers and market makers were conspiring on setting the spread between bid and asked quotes so as to deny customers the benefit of competitive quotes for stocks having multiple market makers. SEC investigation of the problem led to charges of antitrust violations.[9] On the heels of these proceedings, the SEC established a series of requirements designed to improve the execution of customer orders in the over-the-counter markets.[10] The Commission adopted Rule 11Ac1–4,[11] known as the "display rule." Rule 11Ac1–4 requires market makers and specialists to display the price and the full size of customer limit orders that reflect buying and selling interest at a better price than a specialist's or market maker's public quote. The rule also requires market makers and specialists to increase the size of their quote for a particular security to reflect a limit order when the limit order is priced equal to the specialist's or market maker's disseminated quote and that quote is equal to the national best bid or offer.[12] The Commission also amended its "quote rule"[13] which requires market makers and specialists to publicly disseminate the best prices that they enter into an electronic communications network.[14]

The best execution obligation extends beyond broker-dealers. Thus, for example, investment advisers owed their customers a duty to obtain the best execution in transactions directed by the adviser.[19] This means that an

---

3. *See* Order Approving National Association of Securities Dealers, Inc.'s Limit Order Protection on Nasdaq, File No. SR–NASD–94–62, Sec. Exch. Act Rel. No. 34–35751, 59 S.E.C. Docket 867, 1995 WL 325939 (SEC May 22, 1995).

5. In the Matter of E.F. Hutton & Co., Admin. Proc. File No. 3–6490, 49 S.E.C. 829, Sec. Exch. Act Rel. No. 34–25887, 41 S.E.C. Docket 413, 1988 WL 239506 (SEC July 6, 1988).

6. Roskind v. Morgan Stanley Dean Witter & Co., 80 Cal.App.4th 345, 95 Cal.Rptr.2d 258 (2000).

7. *See, e.g.,* Introducing Firms Must Monitor Best Execution by Clearing Brokers, 32 Sec. Reg. & L. Rep. (BNA) 567 (May 5, 2000).

9. *See, e.g.,* Molly Baker, NASDAQ Fights Back on Pricing Allegations, Wall St. J., Apr. 6, 1995 at C1, 1995 WL–WSJ 2125237. *See* Court Approves Distribution of Settlement in Nasdaq Market–Makers Antitrust Litigation, 32 Sec. Reg. & L. Rep. (BNA) 148 (Feb. 7, 2000).

10. *See* Order Execution Obligations, 60 Fed. Reg. 52,792 (SEC 1995).

11. 17 C.F.R. § 240.11Ac1–4.

12. The size must be increased only when the customer limit order is "greater than de minimis." *See* Order Execution Obligations, Sec. Exch. Act Rel. No. 34–37619A, 61 Fed. Reg. 48,290 (SEC Sept. 12, 1996).

13. Rule 11Ac1–1, 17 C.F.R. § 240.11Ac1–1.

14. *See* Order Execution Obligations, Exch. Act Rel. No. 34–37619A, 61 Fed. Reg. 48,290, 1996 WL 513729 (SEC Sept. 12, 1996).

19. *See, e.g.,* In the Matter of Portfolio Advisory Services, Inv. Adv. Act Rel. No. IA–2038, 2002 WL 1343823 (SEC June 20, 2002).

investment adviser should "periodically and systematically" evaluate the execution they are receiving for their clients.[20]

Whether the NASD's order execution requirements directly translate into a broker's obligation to secure the best possible execution for his or her customer has been described as "ambiguous."[28] Accordingly, a three judge panel of the Third Circuit held that a broker's executions of trades only with reference to NASDAQ's National Best Bid and Offer (NBBO) electronic quotations were not actionable simply because the broker failed to disclose to the customer that the broker relied on only one quotation system and thus the trades may not have been executed at the best possible price.[29] However, in an en banc decision, the court reinstated the claim that the broker could be held liable for executing trades at the NBBO[30] if the broker could have secured a better execution on private on-line services such as SelectNet and Instinet.[31] That precise issue is unlikely to arise again since ECN quotes are now subject to the SEC's display rule and thus should be included in the NBBO. Nevertheless, price improvement over and beyond the NBBO may still be possible through the crossing or matching of complementary orders. In such a case, a market maker's interpositioning itself could result in denying one or both customers the best reasonably available price.[32] The same is true of specialists operating on an exchange.

A corollary to the best execution obligation is the requirement that orders be executed promptly. Some leeway in this regard may exist when a customer consents to a "not held order" which grants discretion with respect to order execution.[35] This discretion is not absolute as the best execution obligations still apply to the extent that all steps must be taken to obtain the best available price for the customer.[36]

§ 14.13[2] Exchange Trading—Floor Broker Obligations

Many transactions taking place on an exchange take place through a floor broker. Just as brokers in the over the counter markets and other brokers

---

20. *Id.*

28. Newton v. Merrill, Lynch, Pierce, Fenner & Smith, 115 F.3d 1127 (3d Cir.1997), *reversed* (3d Cir. 1998) (en banc).

29. Newton v. Merrill, Lynch, Pierce, Fenner & Smith, 115 F.3d 1127 (3d Cir.1997), *reversed*, 135 F.3d 266 (3d Cir. 1998) (en banc).

30. *See, e.g.,* Geman v. S.E.C., 334 F.3d 1183, 1186 n.5 (10th Cir. 2003) ("the NBBO is the highest quoted bid price and lowest quoted offer price from among all quotations entered in the Consolidated Quotation Service.")

31. Newton v. Merrill, Lynch, Pierce, Fenner & Smith, 135 F.3d 266 (3d Cir.1998) (en banc).

32. *See, e.g.,* In re Self–Regulatory Organizations; Notice of Filing of Amendment No. 2 to Proposed Rule Change by National Ass'n of Securities Dealers, Inc. Relating to Nasdaq's Proposed Separation from NASD and Establishment of NASD Alternative Display Facility, Sec. Exch. Act Rel. No. 34–45991, 77 S.E.C. Docket 2101, 2002 WL 1072081 n. 7 (SEC May 28, 2002) ("If a Designated Dealer holds for execution on the Exchange a customer buy order and a customer sell order that can be crossed, the Designated Dealer shall cross them without interpositioning itself as a dealer.").

35. "A 'not-held' order is generally an order in which the broker is given time and place discretion but is not responsible for losses." Jerry W. Markham, Prohibited Floor Trading Activities Under the Commodity Exchange Act, 58 Fordham L. Rev. 1 (1989), relying on Thomas Hieronymus, Economics of Futures Trading 63 (1977).

36. *See, e.g.,* Notice of Filing of Proposed Rule Change by the New York Stock Exchange, Inc., SR–NYSE–99–25, Sec. Exch. Act Rel. No. 34–42381, 71 S.E.C. Docket 1343, 2000 WL 126910 (SEC 2000) ("A[n exchange] member representing a 'not held' order is not permitted to 'miss the market,' and must execute the order pursuant to its terms.").

generally are subject to best and prompt execution obligations, floor brokers' are subject to similar requirements. Section 11(a) of the 1934 Act,[45] subject to exceptions,[46] prohibits a member of a national securities exchange[47] (from effecting transactions on that exchange for its own account, the account of an associated person, or an account over which it or its associated person exercises investment discretion).[48] Section 11(a) applies both to transaction taking place on the floor of the exchange as well as off-exchange transaction by exchange members. This dual trading[49] prohibition is designed to free the exchanges from member firms' conflicts of interest in the execution of transactions. Floor brokers[51] on an exchange are supposed to operate with a degree of independence that rids them of conflicts of interest in executing transactions. Thus, for example, SEC Rule 11a–1 prohibits a floor trader from trading for a customer's account over which the trader exercises discretion.[52]

There are exemptions to the dual trading prohibition of section 11(a) of the 1934 Act.[53] The Act sets forth exemptions from the dual trading prohibition for certain types of transactions that "... contribute to the fairness and orderliness of exchange markets or which have not given rise to serious problems."[54] For example, section 11(a)(1)(A) exempts from the section 11(a)'s prohibitions any transaction by a dealer acting in the capacity of a market maker.[55]

---

45. 15 U.S.C.A. § 78k(a)(1). Similar prohibitions are contained in exchange rules. For example, New York Stock Exchange (NYSE) Rule 90(a) prohibits a member or member organization from effecting any transaction in any security "for his or its account, the account of an associated person, or an account with respect to which the member, member organization or an associated person thereof exercises investment discretion." NYSE Rule 95(a) provides that "[n]o member while on the Floor shall execute or cause to be executed on the Exchange, ... any transaction for the purchase or sale of any stock with respect to which transaction such member is vested with discretion as to (1) the choice of security to be bought or sold, (2) the total amount of any security to be bought or sold, or (3) whether any such transaction shall be one of purchase or sale." NYSE Rule 111(a) provides that "[n]o member shall initiate transactions, while on the Floor, for an account in which he has an interest." NYSE Rule 91 prohibits a member from crossing trades of a customer with an account in which the member or its member organization, among others, "is directly or indirectly interested," without first ensuring that the order has an opportunity for an improved price on the Exchange floor and providing notification to, and obtaining acceptance of the trade from, the member who placed the trade. NYSE Rule 92 prohibits a member from purchasing or selling a security for an account in which the member or its member organization, among others, "is directly or indirectly interested" while holding an unexecuted order for a customer on the same side of the market.

46. 15 U.S.C.A. § 78k(a)(1).

47. Other than a notice-registered exchange. *Id.*

48. "any compensation arrangement that results in the exchange member sharing in the trading performance of an account, however structured, makes the account that member's 'own account,' or constitutes an 'interest' in the account." New York Stock Exchange, Inc., Sec. Exch. Act Rel. No. 34–41574, 70 SEC Docket 153, 157, 1999 WL 430844 (June 29, 1999).

49. Dual trading traditionally was severely restricted on commodities exchanges. *See* Philip McBride Johnson & Thomas Lee Hazen, Commodities Regulation § 2.05[15] (3d Ed. 1998)

51. *See, e.g.,* In the Matter of D'Alessio, Sec. Exch. Act Rel. No. 34–47627, 2003 WL 1787291 (SEC 2003) ("Independent floor brokers are agents who execute orders on the floor of the Exchange, typically for other members or brokerage firms").

52. 17 C.F.R. § 240.11a–1. A similar prohibition is found in NYSE Rule 95(a).

53. *See* 15 U.S.C.A. § 78k(a)(1).

54. Securities Acts Amendments of 1975, Report of the Senate Comm. on Banking, Housing and Urban Affairs to Accompany S. 249, S. Rep. No. 94–75, 9th Cong., 1st Sess. 99 (1975).

55. 15 U.S.C.A. § 78k(a)(1)(A). Another type of transaction specifically exempted from Section 11(a) is "any bona fide hedge transaction involving a long or short position in an equity security and a long or short position in a security entitling the holder to acquire or sell such equity security...." 15 U.S.C. § 78k(a)(1)(D).

§ 14.14 Brokerage Commissions—Disclosure, Payment for Order Flow, Excessive Mark-Ups

As discussed in subsequent sections, broker-dealers owe fiduciary duties to their customers.[1] These duties arise when brokers recommend securities to their customers.[2] Execution of these fiduciary duties and recommendations often revolve around brokers' conflicts of interest. One such conflict of interest arises from the fact that if a customer follows a broker's recommendation to buy or sell a security, the broker ordinarily receives a sales commission. Accordingly, brokers have a self-interest in encouraging customer transactions and thus are faced with a conflict of interest.

§ 14.14[1] Disclosure of Broker–Dealer Commissions

SEC Rule 10b–10[4] requires broker-dealers to confirm securities transactions in writing before the transaction is completed. In reality, however, the confirmation is not sent until after the investor makes the investment decision and becomes committed to the transaction. Rule 10b–10 imposes certain specific disclosure requirements in the sales confirmation. Among the disclosures required is the compensation to be received by the broker-dealer in connection with the transaction.[6] The compensation need not be disclosed in the confirmation; however, it is determined other than on a per transaction basis in accordance with a prior written agreement between the broker and the customer.[7] Rule 10b–10 applies to the disclosures required in the sales confirmation. This is an after-the-fact disclosure obligation and does not address the disclosure obligations prior to or at the time of the transaction. In fact, Rule 10b–10 specifically admonishes that the rule does not govern the broker-dealer's obligation to make additional disclosures that may be required by the antifraud rules.[8] Failure to fully disclose the compensation will not only violate Rule 10b–10, it can also form the basis of liability under Rule 10b–5.[9] The fiduciary duty that a broker owes to his or her customers requires disclosure of excessive commissions.[11] In addition, failure to disclose the true amount of the compensation for executing the trade or the true identity of the person receiving the sales commission[12] can run afoul of the antifraud provisions. It has long been established that charging an excessive mark-up can result in a misrepresentation of the true market price.[13] Similarly, as discussed directly below, the mark-up or commission that a customer is charged may include a payment that is made for directing the order flow to a particular dealer or market maker.

---

§ 14.14

1. *See* § 14.15 *infra.*

2. *See* § 14.16 *infra.*

4. 17 C.F.R. § 240.10b–10.

6. 17 C.F.R. § 240.10b–10(a)(2)(i)(B).

7. *Id.*

8. Preliminary note to SEC Rule 10b–10, 17 C.F.R. § 240.10b–10.

9. 17 C.F.R. § 240.10b–5. *See, e.g.,* Grandon v. Merrill Lynch & Co., 147 F.3d 184 (2d Cir.1998).

11. *E.g.,* United States v. Szur, 289 F.3d 200 (2d Cir.2002).

12. *See, e.g.,* In the Matter of Vailati, Sec. Act Rel. No. 33–8159, Sec. Exch. Act Rel. No. 34–46978, 2002 WL 31749940 (SEC 2002) (failure to disclose that commission was being paid to someone who was not a licensed broker-dealer; consent order).

13. *See, e.g.,* Barnett v. United States, 319 F.2d 340 (8th Cir.1963).

The mark-up or commission will be divided between the broker and the employing firm. Generally, commission splitting arrangements between a broker-dealer firm and its registered representatives are not of concern unless they are so unusual that they create a conflict of interest or are otherwise material, thus requiring disclosure.[14]

Mark-ups[18] and mark downs[19] consist of charges added to the transaction price and represent the way that sales commissions are generally described with respect to transactions in the over-the-counter markets.

Ordinarily, the terms commission, mark-up, and mark-down apply to payments to broker-dealers in connection with agency transactions.[20] However, commissions and commission equivalent charges can also exist when the broker-dealer firm is acting in other capacities as well.[21]

In addition to the obligations regarding disclosure and the size of commissions, the NASD takes the position that brokers who offer wrap accounts, where the customer is charged a fee based on the size of accounts as opposed to the more traditional transaction-based compensation, must take steps to ensure that those accounts are suitable for the customers to whom they are offered.[25] Fee-based brokerage accounts eliminate the risk of churning[26] and other temptations to encourage trades to generate commissions.

§ 14.14[2] Payment for Order Flow

Brokers sometimes charge other brokers a fee for directing orders to them. These payments, known as payment for order flow, are permissible subject to certain disclosure requirements.[30] Payment for order flow has long

---

14. *See, e.g.,* NASD Notice to Members 99–81, 1999 WL 33176581 (NASDR Sept. 2, 1999).

18. A mark-up is the sales commission that is added to the market price of a security when a customer purchases a security. Thus, for example, it the transaction takes place at $5 per share and the broker-dealer charges a 2% mark-up, the customer will pay a total of $5.10 for each share of the security purchased, with the broker-dealer firm receiving a 10per share mark-up that generally will be shared with the account executive dealing with the customer.

19. A mark-down is the sales commission that is deducted from the market price of a security when a customer sells a security. Thus, for example, it the transaction takes place at $5 per share and the broker-dealer charges a 2% mark-down, the customer will receive a total of $4.90 for each share of the security sold, with the broker-dealer firm receiving a 10¢ per share mark-down that generally will be shared with the account executive dealing with the customer. Note that in this context if the customer buys and sells the security at the same market price, there will be a total 20¢ in brokerage commissions—the 10¢ per share mark-up for the purchase and the 10¢ mark-down for the sale. It is further to be noted that in an over the counter market there also will be a spread between the bid and the asked price meaning that a customer wanting to purchase the security will pay a higher price than the customer will receive for selling a security. *See* the discussion of market making in § 14.10 *supra.*

20. "An agency trade is a trade in which a broker/dealer, authorized to act as an intermediary for the account of its customer, buys (sells) a security from (to) a third party (e.g., another customer or broker/dealer). Such a trade is not executed in, or does not otherwise pass through, the broker/dealer's proprietary account. When executing an agency trade, the broker/dealer generally charges the customer a commission for its services." Guidance on Compensation and Mixed Capacity Trading, Special NASD Notice to Members 01–85 (Dec. 24, 2001) (question 2).

21. *E.g.,* Guidance on Compensation and Mixed Capacity Trading, Special NASD Notice to Members 01–85 (Dec. 24, 2001).

25. *See* NASD Reminds Members That Fee–Based Compensation Programs Must Be Appropriate, NASD Notice to Members 03–68, http://www.nasdr.com/pdf-text/0368ntm.pdf (Nov. 2003).

26. *See* § 14.20 *infra* for a discussion of churning.

30. Rules 10b–10(a)(2)(i)(c) and 11Ac1–3, 17 C.F.R. §§ 240.10b–10(a)(2)(i)(c); 240.11Ac1–3.

been a part of the equities markets but is a relatively new development in the options markets.[31]

The SEC has indicated that it has concerns about the practice of payment for order flow as having led to less vigorous quote competition and isolation of investor limit orders.[37] The SEC's concern is reflected in various payment for order flow requirements. Rule 11Ac1-3 requires that when opening a new account, broker-dealers who will be acting as the customer's agents to make written disclosures of their policies regarding payment for order flow.[38] The NASD has also indicated its concern with the practice and responded by requiring disclosure of payment for order flow on confirmations of customer transactions.[39] In addition, the SEC confirmation rule, Rule 10b-10 requires disclosure of payment for order flow in transactions where the broker is acting as the customer's agent.[40]

Directing orders pursuant to a payment for order flow arrangement can be viewed as contrary to the broker's obligation to seek the best execution for the customer.[41] Some courts have indicated that the duties of stockbrokers are governed by federal, not state law.[42] Other courts have disagreed.[43] There is considerable authority to the effect that the Securities Exchange Act preempts any fiduciary duty claims associated with failure to inform the customer of payments for order flow.[44]

§ 14.14[3] Excessive Mark–Ups

§ 14.14[3][A] Mark–Ups Generally

At one time, brokerage firms charged uniform commission rates. This custom ceased as we moved into a competitive era with the abolition of fixed brokerage commission rates. The absence of fixed commission rates was designed to promote competition. With regard to exchange traded securities, the commission is usually based on a percentage of the transaction price, or alternatively, in the case of discount brokers at a set fee per trade or per share

---

31. *See* Norman S. Poser, Broker–Dealer Law and Regulation § 16.03 (3d ed. 1999).

37. Disclosure of Order Execution and Routing Practices, Sec. Exch. Act Rel. No. 34–43590, 2000 WL 1721163 (SEC Nov. 17, 2000).

38. 17 C.F.R. § 240.11Ac1–3.

39. Notice of Amendment to Proposed Rule Change by National Association of Securities Dealers, Inc. Relating to Disclosure of Payment for Order Flow Arrangements on Customer Confirmations, Sec. Exch. Act Rel. No. 34–28774, 47 S.E.C. Docket 1475, 1991 WL 286831 (SEC Jan. 14, 1991).

40. 17 C.F.R. § 240.10b–10(a)(2)(i)(c).

41. NASD Notice 01–22, 2001 WL 278615 (NASD March 16, 2001) ("The traditional non-price factors affecting the cost or efficiency of executions should also continue to be considered; however, broker-dealers must not allow an order routing inducement, such as payment for order flow or the opportunity to trade with that order as principal, to interfere with its duty of best execution"). The "best execution" obligation is discussed in § 14.9 *supra*.

42. *See, e.g.,* Smith Barney, Inc. v. Painters Local Union No. 109 Pension Fund, 254 Neb. 758, 579 N.W.2d 518, (1998).

43. *E.g.,* Levin v. Kilborn, 756 A.2d 169 (R.I.2000) (neither Rhode Island's security law, nor federal securities law, supersedes common law causes of action regarding breach of fiduciary duty, misrepresentation, etc.).

44. Gilman v. BHC Securities, Inc., 1995 WL 747738, [1995–1996 Transfer Binder] Fed. Sec. L. Rep. (CCH) ¶ 99,051 (S.D.N.Y.1995), *vacated on the other grounds* 104 F.3d 1418 (2d Cir.1997); McKey v. Charles Schwab & Co., 67 Cal.App.4th 731, 79 Cal.Rptr.2d 213 (Cal.App.1998); Eirman v. Olde Discount Corp., 697 So.2d 865 (Fla.App.1997); Orman v. Charles Schwab & Co., 179 Ill.2d 282, 227 Ill.Dec. 927, 688 N.E.2d 620 (1997); Dahl v. Charles Schwab & Co., Inc., 545 N.W.2d 918 (Minn.1996); Guice v. Charles Schwab & Co., 89 N.Y.2d 31, 674 N.E.2d 282, 651 N.Y.S.2d 352 (1996); Shulick v. PaineWebber, Inc., 554 Pa. 524, 722 A.2d 148 (1998).

block. Unlike the exchanges, in the over-the-counter markets there is no centralized exchange and shares are traded through market makers who purchase shares and then resell them. The difference between the bid price[51] and asked price[52] in the over-the-counter markets thus reflects a market maker's mark up.

Although increased competition in commission rates generally favors customers, some less scrupulous broker-dealers have tried to gouge customers by charging excessive mark-ups. In the case of a customer's purchase of a security, the mark-up is the difference between the price the broker paid for the security and the price at which it is resold to the customer. In the case of a sale, the mark-down is the difference between the price at which the broker purchased the security and the price at which he or she resells it to the customer. Brokers will generally add a commission to any mark-up that may be received through the firm's market making activities.[53] The charging of excessive brokerage commissions usually involves disguising all or a portion of the true mark-up that is being charged. This is a deceptive and manipulative practice that will result in disciplinary action against the offending broker-dealer.[54]

Failure to disclose an excessive mark-up is fraudulent conduct that violates SEC Rule 10b–5.[55] In addition, excessive mark-ups can form the basis of fraud and fiduciary duty claims under state law.[56] Some courts have held, however, that failure to disclose an excessive mark-up although in violation of the securities laws, is not actionable as common law fraud[57] Nevertheless, a scheme of undisclosed excessive mark-ups can form the basis of state criminal prosecutions for securities fraud.[58]

The SEC and self regulatory organizations seek to prevent the charging of excessive commissions. For example, the SEC not only determines the types of entities that can receive remuneration from securities trades,[68] it also imposes disclosure requirements regarding the basis of customer charges.[69] The SEC also in the interest of investor protection tries to assure that the competitive rate system works smoothly. Additionally, the NASD through its

---

51. The price at which the market maker is willing to purchase the securities.

52. The price at which the market maker is willing to sell the securities.

53. If the broker executing the transaction is not with a firm that makes a market in the security, then the broker will have to look to another firm to act as market maker.

54. *See, e.g.,* In the Matter of Castle Securities Corp., Administrative Proceeding File No. 3–9188, Sec. Exch. Act Rel. No. 34–39523, 66 S.E.C. Docket 531, 1998 WL 3456 (SEC Jan. 7, 1998).

55. *See* Grandon v. Merrill Lynch & Co., 147 F.3d 184, 189–90 (2d Cir.1998).

56. *See, e.g.,* City of Vista v. Robert Thomas Securities, Inc., 84 Cal.App.4th 882, 101 Cal.Rptr.2d 237 (Cal.App. 2000).

57. Lehman Bros. Commercial Corp. v. Minmetals International Non–Ferrous Metals Trading Co., 179 F.Supp.2d 159 (S.D.N.Y.2001) (New York law); Granite Partners, L.P. v. Bear, Stearns & Co. Inc., 58 F.Supp.2d 228, 263 (S.D.N.Y.1999) (same).

58. *E.g.,* New York v. Downey, 33 Sec. Reg. & L. Rep. (BNA) 1548 (N.Y.Sup.Ct. Oct. 22, 2001) (conviction for high pressure sales and nondisclosure of excessive mark-ups); People v. A.S. Goldmen & Co., 33 Sec. Reg. & L. Rep. (BNA) 1122 (N.Y.Sup.Ct. July 23, 2001) (conviction for excessive mark-ups and high pressure sales operations; sentences running as long as 10–25 years).

68. *See, e.g.,* In re Financial Charters & Acquisitions, Inc., 17 Sec.Reg. & L.Rep. (BNA) 27 (SEC No–Action Letter Nov. 25, 1984) (unregistered firms may get commissions for referrals to registered broker-dealers).

69. 17 C.F.R. § 240.10b–10(a)(7), (8).

mark-up policy provides guidelines as to what would constitute an excessive brokerage commission.[71]

§ 14.14[3][B] The Five Percent Mark–Up Policy

The NASD has established a "five percent" policy as a guide for determining the fairness of the mark-up.[76] The NASD stresses that this is a guide, not a per se rule nor a safe harbor rule.[78] Thus, the markup must be considered in conjunction with other factors. Some of the factors considered in determining the fairness of a mark-up are the type, availability, and price of the security, the amount of money involved in the transaction, the disclosures made to the customer, the broker-dealer's general pattern of mark-ups, and the nature of the broker-dealer's business.[80] Mark-ups in excess of five percent are not per se illegal. However, the SEC has "consistently" taken the position that undisclosed mark-ups on equity securities in excess of ten percent violate the law.[81] The NASD takes the position that mark-ups in excess of five percent "generally" are excessive.[82] Mark-ups below the threshold have been found to be excessive.[83] Mark-ups in excess of ten percent are per se violations of the antifraud rules.[84]

In computing the mark-up, the best evidence of prevailing market price is the dealer's contemporaneous cost for the securities.[86] However, identifying the true mark-up is not always an easy task, especially in less liquid markets when there can be a time lag between a market maker's purchase of the security and its resale. In riskless transactions, mark-ups should be based on the cost of acquisition rather than the prevailing market price.[88] The dealer's cost will thus be the appropriate measure of market price when faced with an integrated dealer who controls the market of the securities in question. However, in such a situation, the interdealer market is a better indicator of the true market price than the price that the integrated dealer paid in a transaction with a retail customer.[90] The interdealer price ordinarily is the

71. NASD Rules of Fair Practice, Art. III, sec. 4, NASD Manual (CCH) ¶ 2154.

76. NASD Rules of Fair Practice, Art. III, sec. 4, NASD Manual (CCH) ¶ 2154.

78. *See* Lehl v. S.E.C., 90 F.3d 1483, 1488 n. 4 (10th Cir.1996).

80. *Id.*

81. *See* Bank of Lexington & Trust Co. v. Vining–Sparks Securities, Inc., 959 F.2d 606, 613 (6th Cir.1992); S.E.C. v. Rauscher Pierce Refsnes, Inc., 17 F.Supp.2d 985, 998 (D.Ariz.1998); SEC v. Charles A. Morris & Assocs., 386 F.Supp. 1327, 1334 n. 5 (W.D.Tenn.1973).

82. S.E.C. v. Rauscher Pierce Refsnes, Inc., 17 F.Supp.2d 985, 998 (D.Ariz.1998).

83. *See* In Re Lehman Bros., Inc., Administrative Proceeding File No. 3–9079, Sec. Exch. Act Rel. No. 34–37673, 1996 WL 519914, at *5 (SEC Sept. 12, 1996) (holding that mark-ups of 3.5 to 4.7% were excessive); In Re Investment Planning, Inc., Admin. Proc. File No. 3–7388, 51 S.E.C. 592, Sec. Exch. Act Rel. No. 34–32687, 54 S.E.C. Docket 1362l 1993 WL 289728, at *2 (SEC July 28, 1993) (mark-ups on municipal bonds between 4 and 5.99% were excessive). *See also, e.g.,* S.E.C. v. Rauscher Pierce Refsnes, Inc., 17 F.Supp.2d 985, 998 (D.Ariz.1998) (based on industry practice with respect to zero coupon bonds, "under some circumstances, markups as high as 3 1/2% may not be excessive, but under other circumstances markups above 1/32 of one percent may be excessive").

84. *See, e.g.,* In the Matter of Mazzeo, Sec. Act Rel. No. 33–8060, Sec. Exch. Act Rel. No. 34–45329, 2002 WL 89041 (SEC Jan. 24, 2002).

86. *E.g.,* Lehl v. SEC, 90 F.3d 1483 (10th Cir.1996).

88. *E.g.,* G.K. Scott & Co., Inc. v. S.E.C., 56 F.3d 1531, 1995 WL 364671 (D.C.Cir.1995) (unpublished opinion on Westlaw).

90. In the Matter of Sanders, Administrative Proceedings File No. 3–9195, Sec. Exch. Act Rel. No. 34–40600, 68 S.E.C. Docket 745, 1998 WL 741105 (SEC Oct. 26, 1998).

best indicator[91] and will be rejected only when there is reason to believe that it took place in an artificially manipulated market.[92]

§ 14.14[4] Recommendations Induced by Commissions or Other Incentive

The preceding discussion addresses the effect of excessive commissions on a broker's obligations. Even in the absence of excessive commissions, a commission structure can interfere with the impartiality of brokers in recommending securities for their customers.

Where a brokerage firm's commission rate structure encourages sales representatives to recommend selected securities, those recommendations will run afoul of the securities laws to the extent they are motivated by the sales representative's self interest rather than the best interests of the customer. Thus, for example, undisclosed differential sales commissions, when used as an incentive to recommend particular stocks, is a material omission from the broker's recommendation.[116] While it is true that neither Rule 10b–10 nor the NASD rules explicitly require disclosure of the compensation paid to individual brokers,[117] when the size of the commission on selected stocks is an incentive for brokers to recommend that stock, nondisclosure is problematic. The NASD makes it clear that commissions are not limited to a portion of the transaction price charged to the customer. NASD Conduct Rule 3040 thus defines selling compensation to include any compensation that is paid directly or indirectly from whatever source as a result of the purchase or sale of a security.[119]

Recommendations that are induced by compensation violate the broker-dealer's obligations that generally attach to recommendations.[127] In addition, recommendations are subject to the implied representation that brokers will deal fairly and professionally with their customers.[128] Even beyond sales incentives, high pressure brokerage firms may unduly pressure their sales representatives to solicit transactions.[129] The foregoing broker-dealer prohibitions are supplemented by section 17(b) of the Securities Act of 1933,[130] which declares illegal recommending securities for compensation without disclosing the compensation paid in connection with the making of the recommendation.[131] A recommendation that is bought and paid for violates the securities laws.[132] In fact, the SEC has explained that it is "egregious" for a broker to

---

91. In the Matter of Salloum, Sec. Exch. Act Rel. No. 34–35563, 59 SEC Docket 4349 (SEC April 5, 1995).

92. *See* In the Matter of Sanders, Administrative Proceedings File No. 3–9195, Sec. Exch. Act Rel. No. 34–40600, 68 S.E.C. Docket 745, 1998 WL 741105 (SEC Oct. 26, 1998).

116. *E.g.*, Platsis v. E.F. Hutton & Co., 1990 WL 640492 (W.D.Mich.1990), affirmed in part, reversed in part 946 F.2d 38 (6th Cir.1991).

117. *See, e.g.*, United States v. Alvarado, 2001 WL 1631396 at **8–9 (S.D.N.Y.2001).

119. NASD Conduct Rule 3040. *See* In the Matter of Goldsworthy, Sec. Exch. Act Rel. No. 34–45926, 2002 WL 987627 n. 40 (SEC May 15, 2002).

127. *See* § 14.16 *infra*.

128. *See* § 14.15 *infra*.

129. *See, e.g.*, Varljen v. H.J. Meyers, Inc., 1998 WL 395266, *1 (S.D.N.Y.1998).

130. 15 U.S.C.A. § 77q(b).

131. *See, e.g.*, SEC v. Heredia, 2002 SECDIG 2002–43–2, 2002 WL 339431 (M.D.Fla.2002).

132. *See, e.g.*, In the Matter of Wenger, Administrative Proceeding File No. 3–10444, Sec. Exch. Act Rel. No. 44105, 2001 WL 333197 (SEC March 27, 2001).

accept compensation in exchange for recommending a particular security to his customers.[133]

Conduct that violates section 17(b) ordinarily will be a violation of section 17(a)'s and 1934 Act's Rule 10b–5.[134]

Section 17(b) of the 1933 Act is not invalidated by the First Amendment since the prohibition is addressed to commercial speech.[138] Among other things, the anti-touting provisions of section 17(b) are reasonably related to governmental interests in protecting the deception of investors.[139]

§ 14.15 Broker–Dealers and Fiduciary Obligations; The Shingle Theory

§ 14.15[1] Effect of Arbitration on the Law of Brokers' Obligations

Before exploring the range of duties that comprise broker-dealers' obligations to their customers, it is important to understand one effect that the current trend favoring arbitration of customer disputes has had on the law. Since most disputes between brokers and their customers are now subject to arbitration, much of the law relating to broker-dealer obligations is likely to be frozen in a state of suspended animation, preserved in much the state that it was in the pre-arbitration era. Arbitration awards generally do not contain long discussions of the law. Furthermore, the standard of judicial review gives so much leeway to the arbitrators' decision that additional judicial decisions will be few and far between. Much of the law relating to broker-dealer obligations will thus be found primarily in the older decisions arising out of customer litigation, the relatively few customer suits that may still be litigated in court, plus the SEC administrative decisions (and any subsequent judicial review) arising out of broker-dealer regulation.

§ 14.15[2] Fiduciary Obligations of Securities Brokers

There are various SEC and NASD prohibitions addressing particular types of misconduct by broker dealers. For example, Rule 15c1–2[1] generally prohibits fraudulent, manipulative, and deceptive practices in connection with securities brokerage transactions. Broker-dealers and their employees are also subject to Rule 10b–5's general antifraud proscriptions relating to deceptive conduct in connection with a purchase or sale of a security.[2] The types of specific conduct that are addressed in other rules include market manipulation,[3] high pressure sales tactics,[4] deceptive recommendations,[5] generation of

---

133. In the Matter of DuBois, Sec. Act Rel. No. 33–8264, Sec. Exch. Act Rel. No. 34–48332, 2003 WL 21946858 (SEC Aug. 13, 2003).

134. See, e.g., United States v. Blitz, 533 F.2d 1329, 1338 (2d Cir. 1976).

138. United States v. Wenger, 292 F. Supp.2d 1296, 1303–1307 (D. Utah 2003).

139. Id. See also SEC v. Wall Street Publishing, 851 F.2d 365 (D.C. Cir. 1988).

§ 14.15

1. 17 C.F.R. § 240.15c1–2.

2. 17 C.F.R. § 240.10b–5. See §§ 12.3–12.12 supra.

3. See §§ 6.2–6.3 supra (manipulation in connection with public offerings) § 12.1 supra (manipulation generally), and § 14.10[5] supra (manipulation by market makers).

4. See § 14.18 infra.

5. See §§ 14.15–14.18 infra.

excessive commissions,[6] unauthorized trading,[7] improper order executions,[8] improper extension of credit for securities transactions,[9] and misuse of customer funds or securities.[10] Beyond these specific activities and the general anti-manipulation and deception rules, the SEC makes it clear that violation of its rules is not limited to violation of any specified SEC rules, but rather covers all conduct that operates as a deceptive or manipulative device.[11] This broad coverage thus is not limited to specific SEC rules. The SEC has taken the position elsewhere that it can regulate conduct that would be manipulative even if the concern is not based on any specified violation of existing rules.[12] Even beyond SEC rules, the rules of the various self regulatory organizations impose standards of conduct on broker dealers.[13]

In addition to SEC rules and requirements of the applicable self regulatory organizations,[14] broker-dealers are, of course, subject to common law duties and fiduciary obligations. Federal courts have recognized the existence of the fiduciary relationship in federal securities cases.[16] However, the implied representations arising out of a fiduciary duty will not violate the securities laws' antifraud provisions in the absence of a showing that the defendant acted with the requisite scienter.[17]

Some courts have spoken in terms of an "inherent" fiduciary duty running from the stock broker to the customer.[18] This is so because the brokerage relationship is an agency relationship which is fiduciary in nature. However, the fact that the relationship is a fiduciary one only takes one so far. They key question is to determine what actual duties arise out of the relationship. The answer to that question depends on the particular broker-customer relationship and the functions performed by the broker. Thus, for example, a clearing broker that does not perform the retail functions normally associated with introducing and full-service brokers and has been said not to owe fiduciary duties to the customer[20] unless the clearing broker has reason to know of wrongdoing by the introducing broker.[21]

---

6. *See* § 14.20 *infra.*

7. *See* § 14.21 *infra.*

8. *See* § 14.13 *supra.*

9. *See* § 14.9 *supra.*

10. *See* § 14.8[2] *supra.*

11. Rule 15c1–2(c), 17 C.F.R. § 240.15c1–2(c):

   The scope of this rule shall not be limited by any specific definitions of the term "manipulative, deceptive, or other fraudulent device or contrivance" contained in other rules adopted pursuant to section 15(c)(1) of the Act.

12. *See, e.g.,* In the Matter of Hazel Bishop, Inc., 40 S.E.C. 718 (SEC 1961).

13. For example, the NASD imposes on its members the obligation to adhere to fair and equitable principles of trade.

14. *See* § 14.3 *supra.*

16. *See, e.g.,* United States v. Santoro, 302 F.3d 76 (2d Cir.2002) (broker's recommendation created "position of trust" pursuant to federal sentencing guidelines).; Rolf v. Blyth Eastman Dillon & Co., Inc., 424 F.Supp. 1021, 1036 (S.D.N.Y.1977).

17. *E.g.,* In the Matter of Flanagan, Administrative Proceeding File No. 3–9784, 71 S.E.C. Docket 1415, Release No. ID–160, 2000 WL 98210 *24 (SEC Initial Decision Jan. 31, 2000).

18. *E.g.,* French v. First Union Securities, Inc., 209 F.Supp.2d 818, 825 (M.D.Tenn.2002).

20. *E.g.,* Lesavoy v. Lane, 304 F. Supp.2d 520, 526 (S.D.N.Y. 2004) (applying New York law).

21. *See, e.g.,* Fezzani v. Bear, Stearns & Co., Inc., 2004 WL 744594 (S.D.N.Y.,2004) and the discussion below.

Although there is authority to the contrary, the apparent majority view of the cases applying state common law is that a blanket fiduciary relationship[23] between broker-dealer and client does not arise as a matter of law,[24] but that additional facts can suffice to create a fiduciary duty.[25] Chief among these factors which may create a fiduciary relationship is "a reposing of faith, confidence and trust,"[26] often evidenced by a broker-dealer having either prior authorization to trade for the client's account on a discretionary basis, or de facto control of the account. Representing oneself to have investment and advisory expertise will give rise to fiduciary obligations.[28] When a broker makes investment recommendations to a customer, the broker is acting in a position of trust vis-a-vis the customer, and as such is acting as a fiduciary.[29]

In contrast to the narrow view of securities brokers' fiduciary duties, a number of decisions have taken a broader view.[55] For example, since a brokerage relationship is a principal/agent relationship, some courts have recognized fiduciary duties that accompany agency relationships generally.[56] When the broker claims to have special skills in handling a customer's account, fiduciary duties will attach.[57] The experience and sophistication of the customer will be a factor in judging the extent of the broker's fiduciary duty.[58]

§ 14.15[3] The Shingle Theory

Common law principles have been borrowed in formulating SEC policy in many areas. These common law principles may also form the basis of liability under state law. The discussion that follows focuses on the "shingle theory" which holds that by hanging up a shingle, the broker implicitly represents that he or she will conduct business in an equitable and professional manner.[82] A breach of the implied representation that a broker will deal fairly with the customer will be actionable under Rule 10b–5 only if the plaintiff can show a causal relationship between the alleged breach and an injury to the plaintiff.[83] A breach of fiduciary duty will not by itself support a claim under

---

23. *See, e.g.,* Press v. Chemical Investment Services Corp., 166 F.3d 529 (2d Cir.1999), affirming 988 F.Supp. 375, 386–87 (S.D.N.Y. 1997) ("naked allegation" that broker was a fiduciary of customer was insufficient).

24. *See, e.g.,* Associated Randall Bank v. Griffin, Kubik, Stephens & Thompson, Inc., 3 F.3d 208 (7th Cir.1993).

25. *See, e.g.,* Press v. Chemical Investment Services Corp., 166 F.3d 529 (2d Cir.1999).

26. McCracken v. Edward D. Jones & Co., 445 N.W.2d 375, 381 (Iowa App.1989).

28. *See, e.g.,* Burdett v. Miller, 957 F.2d 1375, 1381 (7th Cir.1992).

29. United States v. Hart, 273 F.3d 363, 376 (3d Cir.2001), relying on United States v. Hussey, 254 F.3d 428 (2d Cir.2001).

55. *E.g.,* Goodrich v. E. F. Hutton Group, 542 A.2d 1200 (Del.Ch.1988).

56. *E.g.,* Glisson v. Freeman, 243 Ga.App. 92, 532 S.E.2d 442 (Ga.App.2000).

57. Patsos v. First Albany Corp., 433 Mass. 323, 741 N.E.2d 841 (2001) *affirming* 48 Mass.App.Ct. 266, 719 N.E.2d 882 (1999).

58. *Compare, e.g.,* McCracken v. Edward D. Jones & Co., 445 N.W.2d 375, (Iowa Ct.App.1989) (broker owed a fiduciary duty to the customer, relying in large part on the customer's inexperience) *with* Williams v. Edward D. Jones & Co., 556 So.2d 914 (La.Ct.App.1990) (finding no breach of duty to a sophisticated customer).

82. *See, e.g.,* Brennan v. Midwestern United Life Ins. Co., 286 F.Supp. 702, 707 (N.D.Ind. 1968), *affirmed* 417 F.2d 147 (7th Cir.1969), *cert. denied,* 397 U.S. 989, 90 S.Ct. 1122, 25 L.Ed.2d 397 (1970); Charles Hughes & Co., Inc. v. SEC, 139 F.2d 434 (2d Cir.1943) *cert. denied,* 321 U.S. 786, 64 S.Ct. 781, 88 L.Ed. 1077 (1944).

83. *See, e.g.,* Gruntal & Co., Inc. v. San Diego Bancorp, 901 F.Supp. 607, 618 (S.D.N.Y.1995).

Rule 10b–5.[84] The shingle theory will thus be the basis of a Rule 10b–5 violation only to the extent that it amounts to a fraudulent implied misrepresentation in connection with the purchase or sale of a security.[85]

Although often attributed to the common law, the shingle theory is well grounded under the federal securities laws as well. The shingle theory has been applied in both SEC enforcement[86] actions and private damage actions under the federal securities laws.[87]

The shingle theory arose in the context of a broker's charging excessive mark-ups[91] but is not limited to mark-up cases. When brokers hold themselves out as experts either in investments in general or in the securities of a particular issuer, they will be held to a higher standard of care in making recommendations.[93] In applying this aspect of shingle theory, a broker who makes a recommendation is viewed as making an implied representation that he or she has adequate information on the security in question for forming the basis of the broker's opinion.[94] This concept of implied representation has also been expressed in terms of a broker-dealer "implicitly warrant[ing] the soundness of the statements of stock value,"[95] but this is too strong a statement of the rule. The concept of implied warranty has not to date been extended to brokers' recommendations, and the appropriate standard of care, whether under the shingle theory or otherwise, is necessarily based upon the broker-dealer's factual basis and reasonable belief in the opinions that form the basis of the recommendation.

The shingle theory is sometimes applied to bring activities of the broker which otherwise might not fall within the literal application of the SEC antifraud rules within the ambit of those rules. In many of these cases brokers have held themselves out as having complied with SEC regulations. These activities that have then given rise to accountability, and in some cases liability, include undisclosed insolvency,[96] egregious failures to comply with SEC bookkeeping requirements,[97] and noncompliance with net capital requirements.[98]

---

84. *See* Santa Fe Industries, Inc. v. Green, 430 U.S. 462, 479–80, 97 S.Ct. 1292, 1304, 51 L.Ed.2d 480 (1977), which is discussed in § 12.20 *supra*.

85. Bissell v. Merrill Lynch & Co., Inc., 937 F.Supp. 237, 246 n. 7 (S.D.N.Y.1996).

86. *See, e.g.*, Charles Hughes & Co. v. SEC, 139 F.2d 434, 437–438 (2d Cir.1943), *cert. denied*, 321 U.S. 786, 64 S.Ct. 781, 88 L.Ed. 1077 (1944); S.E.C. v. Great Lakes Equities Co., 1990 WL 260587 *6 (E.D.Mich.1990); Duker & Duker, 6 S.E.C. 386, 388, Sec. Exch. Act Rel. No. 34–2350, 1939 WL 36426 (SEC Dec. 19, 1939).

87. Granite Partners, L.P. v. Bear, Stearns & Co. Inc., 58 F.Supp.2d 228, 262 (S.D.N.Y.1999), relying on Grandon v. Merrill Lynch & Co., 147 F.3d 184, 189–90, 192–93 (2d Cir.1998).

91. Charles Hughes & Co. v. SEC, 139 F.2d 434 (2d Cir.1943), *cert. denied*, 321 U.S. 786, 64 S.Ct. 781, 88 L.Ed. 1077 (1944).

93. *See also, e.g.*, United States v. Santoro, 302 F.3d 76 (2d Cir.2002) (broker's recommendation created "position of trust" pursuant to federal sentencing guidelines).

94. *See, e.g.*, Filloramo v. Johnston, Lemon & Co., 697 F.Supp. 517 (D.D.C.1988).

For a discussion of materiality generally *see* § 12.9 *supra*.

95. Kahn v. SEC, 297 F.2d 112, 115 (2d Cir.1961) (Clark J., concurring).

96. SEC v. Resch–Cassin & Co., 362 F.Supp. 964 (S.D.N.Y.1973). *But see* Brennan v. Midwestern United Life Insurance Co., 286 F.Supp. 702, 707 (N.D.Ind.1968), *affirmed* 417 F.2d 147 (7th Cir.1969), *cert. denied*, 397 U.S. 989, 90 S.Ct. 1122, 25 L.Ed.2d 397 (1970).

97. Joseph v. Shields, Jr., [1967–1969 Transfer Binder] Fed.Sec.L.Rep. (CCH) & ¶ 77,643 (Jan. 3, 1969).

98. SEC v. Charles Plohn & Co., 433 F.2d 376 (2d Cir.1970); Joseph v. Shields, Jr., [1967–1969 Transfer Binder] Fed.Sec.L.Rep. (CCH) ¶ 77,643 (SEC Jan. 3, 1969).

The shingle theory intertwines with the suitability and "know your customer" doctrines that are discussed in the next section.

§ 14.16 A Broker's Obligation to Customers With Regard to Recommendations: The Know Your Security, Suitability, and Know Your Customer Obligations

§ 14.16[1] Recommendations and Suitability Generally

Securities brokers and brokerage firms that render advice incidental to their brokerage activities are exempted from the coverage of the Investment Advisers Act of 1940 that regulates those persons and entities in the business of rendering investment advice.[1] Accordingly, this type of incidental advice rendered by brokerage firms is regulated pursuant to the applicable provisions of the 1934 Exchange Act, SEC rules, and the rules of the self regulatory organizations as supplemented by common law principles. Many brokerage firms also register as investment advisers (or have advisory divisions or subsidiaries) in which case the 1934 Act regulation will be supplement by the Investment Advisers Act.

§ 14.16[1][A] Recommendations Generally

The securities laws prohibit a broker-dealer from recommending a security unless he or she has actual knowledge of the characteristics and fundamental facts relevant to the security in question; furthermore, the recommendation must be reasonably supported by the facts. This is but one example of the way in which existence of the broker-customer relationship can establish special duties with regard to the securities broker.[4] In the context of a securities brokerage relationship, whenever a broker recommends a security to a customer, there is an implied representation that the broker is informed as to the security and that the recommendation has a reasonable factual basis.[5] When a broker recommends a security for purchase there is said to be an implied representation that the broker "has made a thorough investigation."[6] The obligation to have a basis for the recommendation sometimes is referred to as the "know the security" obligation. The broker's responsibilities do not end with this obligation. Consideration must also be given to whether the broker has a conflict of interest when making the recommendation. A broker's or securities analyst's recommendation should not be unduly influenced by special incentives from the brokerage firm or from others.[7] This obligation is sometimes referred to as the "know or security" obligation.[8] It also is sometimes called "reasonable basis suitability."[9]

---

§ 14.16

1. 15 U.S.C.A. § 80b–2(a)(11). *See* § 21.2 *infra*.

4. *See* the discussion of fiduciary duties and the shingle theory in § 14.15 *supra*.

5. *E.g.*, SEC v. Dain Rauscher, Inc., 254 F.3d 852, (9th Cir. 2001).

6. *See, e.g.*, Alton Box Bd. Co. v. Goldman, Sachs & Co.,560 F.2d 916, 922 (8th Cir.1977).

7. *See, e.g.*, In the Matter of Flanagan, Administrative Proceeding File No. 3–9784, 71 S.E.C. Docket 1415, Release No. ID–160, 2000 WL 98210 (SEC Initial Decision Jan. 30, 2000).

8. *See, e.g.*, Nancy C. Libin & James S. Wrona, The Securities Industry and the Internet: A Suitable Match? 01 Colum. Bus. L. Rev. 601, 620 (2001); *See also, e.g.*, In the Matter of F.J. Kaufman and Co., 1989 WL 259961, 50 S.E.C. 164 (1989).

9. *See* Thomas Lee Hazen & David L. Ratner, Securities Regulation Cases and Materials 1008 (6th ed. 2002).

§ 14.16[1][B] Suitability Generally

In addition to the broker-dealer's knowledge of the security,[21] there are also obligations imposed with regard to the broker-dealer's duty to know his or her customer. This is most commonly referred to as the suitability obligation. The suitability obligation was originally derived from the antifraud rules. Specifically, it was said that a recommendation to a customer implies that the security recommended is consistent with the customer's investment objectives and thus is suitable. The SEC has not established express suitability requirements applicable to broker-dealers generally, but such an obligation can be found in the rules of the self-regulatory organizations.[22]

The suitability obligation takes various forms depending on the applicable self regulatory organization. Unsuitability violations often result in severe administratively imposed sanctions.[30] It is unlikely that a violation of these rules without more will provide an independent basis for private relief by an injured investor, although it may be relevant in an action brought under SEC Rule 10b–5.[31] The essence of a Rule 10b–5 claim is deception, which generally means misrepresentation or nondisclosure. A broker's recommendation of a security will give rise to damages to the customer for an unsuitable recommendation only if the recommendation contains an express or implied material misrepresentation of the risks involved. As explained by one court: "the plaintiff asserting unsuitability must show (1) the investment was incompatible with the plaintiff's investment objectives; and (2) the broker recommended the investment although (3) the broker knew or reasonably believed the investment was inappropriate."[35] Brokers and advisers who materially misrepresent risks of an investment will be held accountable for their misstatements or implied misrepresentations.[36]

The NASD in its so-called "suitability rule" requires that in recommending a purchase or sale of a particular security to a customer, the broker-dealer must have "reasonable grounds for believing that the recommendation is suitable for such customer upon the basis of the facts, if any, disclosed by such customer as to his other security holdings and as to his financial situation and needs."[39] Interestingly, the suitability rule on its face does not impose upon the broker any affirmative duty of investigating the customer's investment objective, but merely requires the broker-dealer to act reasonably based upon the information, if any, that the customer provides. Nevertheless, the NASD in a policy statement by its Board of Governors goes further by requiring the broker to obtain information concerning the customers' other securities holdings before recommending speculative, low-priced securities.[40]

---

21. As discussed in the preceding section and again in § 4.18 *infra* s securities broker's recommendation of a security carries with it an implicit recommendation that the broker has an adequate basis for the recommendation. *See, e.g.,* Hanly v. SEC, 415 F.2d 589, 596 (2d Cir.1969).

22. *See, e.g.,* the NASD's suitability rule. NASD Rule 2310.

30. *See, e.g.,* In the Matter of Alacan, Admin. Proc. No. 3–10765, Sec. Act Rel. No. 33–8436, Sec. Exch. Act Rel. No. 34–49970, 2004 WL 1496843 (SEC July 06, 2004) (imposing industry bar for suitability violations).

31. 17 C.F.R. § 240.10b–5.

35. Keenan v. D.H. Blair & Co., 838 F.Supp. 82, 87 (S.D.N.Y.1993).

36. *See, e.g.,* In re Piper Capital Management, Inc., SEC Admin Proc. File No. 3–9657, 32 Sec. Reg. & L. Rep. (BNA) 1674 (SEC Initial decision 2000).

39. NASD Rule 2310.

40. *Id.*.

The suitability and know your customer obligations have arisen in the context of broker-dealer recommendations. There has been some suggestion that the concept should be extended to the broker's suggested obligation to monitor the investor's own decisions. However, there is considerable authority to the contrary, holding that the broker does not have a duty to intercede when the investment is the customer's choice rather than on the basis of the broker's recommendation.[42]

The NASD has issued an interpretation applying its suitability rule to advice given institutional investors.[44] Under the NASD interpretation there are two important considerations in invoking the suitability doctrine for institutional investors. The first consideration is the institutional customer's ability to comprehend and independently evaluate the risks involved. The second factor is the extent to which the customer will be exercising independent judgment in evaluating the recommendation.[46] Suitability rules regarding recommendations to institutional investors are especially timely in light of many crises involving derivative investments.[47] Because of the high level of risk involved in hedge fund investments, in 2003, the NASD reminded its members of suitability issues regarding hedge fund recommendations.[48] As with any recommendation, the broker must use due diligence in investigating the security or fund being recommended.

In addition to the NASD's suitability rule, Rule 405[52] of the New York Stock Exchange expressly imposes obligations on broker-dealers.[53] Rather than talk in terms of suitable investments, the New York Stock Exchange Rule expressly places upon member broker-dealers an affirmative obligation to "know your customer"[54] with regard to sales or offers as well as recommendations.[55]

From time to time, the NASD has identified investments that are particularly susceptible to suitability concerns. For example, as discussed in later sections, the NASD has targeted online trading and day trading,[60] low priced securities,[61] and mutual fund sales practices.[62] Additionally, in a notice to members, the NASD issued a reminder of suitability obligations as they related to hedge-fund recommendations.[63]

---

42. *See* Associated Randall Bank v. Griffin, Kubik, Stephens & Thompson, Inc., 3 F.3d 208, 212 (7th Cir.1993).

44. *See* NASD Approves New Interpretation of Suitability Obligations to Institutions, 27 Sec. Reg. & L. Rep. (BNA) 1220 (July 21, 1995).

46. *Id.*

47. *See also, e.g.,* Banca Cremi, S.A. v. Alex Brown & Sons, Inc., 132 F.3d 1017 (4th Cir.1997).

48. NASD Notice to Members 03–07, http://www.nasdr.com/pdf-text/0307ntm.txt.

52. NYSE Rule 405, New York Stock Exchange Guide (CCH) ¶ 2405.

53. "Rule 405 of the New York Stock Exchange ... was originally intended in part to protect customers against poor credit risks and unauthorized transactions. As interpreted over the years, it has served as protection for customers against unsuitable recommendations." Nicholas Wolfson, Richard M. Phillips & Thomas A. Russo, Regulation of Brokers, Dealers and Securities Markets 2–33 (1977).

54. NYSE Rule 405, New York Stock Exchange Guide (CCH) ¶ 2405.

55. *See, e.g.,* In re Nicholaou, 1994 WL 398705, SEC Admin. Proc file 1994 WL 398705, Sec. Reg. & L. Rep. (BNA) (SEC July 28, 1994), affirmed 81 F.3d 161 (6th Cir.1996).

60. *See* § 14.16[2] *infra.*

61. *See* § 14.16[3] *infra.*

62. *See* § 14.16[4] *infra.*

63. NASD Notice to Members 03–07, Obligations When Selling Hedge Funds, http://www.nasdr. com/pdf-text/0307ntm.pdf (Feb. 2003).

§ 14.16[2] Suitability: Online Trading and Day Trading

The growing use of the Internet for stock trades has created a new arena for fraud and for suitability issues in particular. In this regard, the NASD has issued a notice to its members cautioning that the suitability requirements apply to online recommendations of securities.[86]

The SEC has approved NASD rules relating to day trading. Among other things, the NASD rule[91] requires that the broker-dealer make an investigation into the suitability of the customer for day trading before opening an account.[92] Before approving an account for day trading, a firm must "have reasonable grounds for believing that the day-trading strategy is appropriate for the customer."[93]

§ 14.16[3] Special Suitability Problems Associated With Low Priced Securities

Over the past several years, there has been increasing concern over low priced securities that are not marketed through a national exchange or the NASD national market system. Many investors have been injured as a result of high pressure sales techniques in connection with these so-called "penny stocks." In response, in 1989, the Commission proposed special regulation of penny stocks.[98] As discussed more fully below,[99] the penny stock regulations were implemented in 1990 and expanded in 1992. Congress reinforced the SEC's concerns with penny stocks with the enactment of the Securities Enforcement and Penny Stock Reform Act of 1990.[100] Section 3(a)(51) of the Exchange Act now provides a statutory definition of "penny stock" which excludes most exchange-listed and NASDAQ securities.[101]

§ 14.16[4] Suitability and Mutual Fund Sales Practices

In 1995, the NASD issued a directive concerning the obligations of member broker-dealers with respect to mutual fund sales practices.[104] There is an obligation to assure that when recommending mutual funds all material facts be disclosed to investors. Material facts include: the fund's investment objectives, portfolio, performance history, expense ratio, and sales charges. The risks of investing in the recommended fund as compared with other investment products also is material and must be disclosed. Violation of suitability rules with regard to mutual fund investments can result in the imposition of NASD sanctions.[105] There are also specific disclosures relating to breakpoint pricing of mutual fund shares. The SEC's rules regarding mutual

---

86. Executive summary, NASD Notice to Members 01–23 Online Suitability, 2001 WL 278614 (March 19, 2001).

91. NASD Rule 2360.

92. *See* Securities Exchange Act Release No. 34–43021, 2000 WL 955176 (SEC July 10, 2000).

93. *Id.*

98. Sec.Exch.Act Rel. No. 34–26,529, [1988–1989 Transfer Binder] Fed.Sec.L.Rep. (CCH) ¶ 84,352 (Feb. 8, 1989).

99. *See* § 14.19 *infra*.

100. Pub.L. No. 101–429 (1990).

101. 15 U.S.C.A. § 78c(a)(51).

104. Special NASD Notice to Members 95–80 (Sept. 26, 1995).

105. *See, e.g.,* In the Matter of Koppel–Heath, Complaint No. C02950044, 1998 WL 1084579 (N.A.S.D.R. Jan. 6, 1998) ($59,000 fine, 30–day suspension).

fund pricing focus on disclosures sufficient to inform investors regarding breakpoint pricing.[106]

Mutual funds are generally considered to be long-term investments. Recommendations regarding frequent switching of mutual funds can run afoul of the NASD's suitability requirements.[111] In 2004, cognizant of abuses in connection with market timing of mutual fund shares, the SEC amended its rules to require mutual fund disclosures regarding frequent trading in mutual fund shares.[112] For the similar reasons, recommendations calling for frequent switching of variable annuity investments is not proper.[113]

§ 14.16[5] Suitability and Investment Advisers

In 1994, the SEC proposed a rule that would expressly prohibit an investment adviser from making recommendations of securities that are unsuitable for his or her clients.[116] However, that rule was never adopted. In light of the proposal not having been adopted, the only formal suitability requirement would be the one that is recognized with regard to broker-dealer recommendations.[117] Nevertheless, the Commission has taken the position that the antifraud provisions of the Investment Advisers Act can be used to enforce a suitability requirement.[118]

§ 14.16[6] Recommendations and Conflicts of Interest; Analysts' Recommendations

Another problem that arises in connection with securities recommendations is nondisclosure of potential conflicts of interest. Most brokerage firms engage in a wide variety of activities and some of those activities create internal conflicts of interest. One such example is the conflict between the brokerage retail department and research analysts who supposedly are making their recommendations independent of any incentive for the retail brokerage business. It is impermissible to receive compensation for making a recommendation of a particular security without disclosing that compensa-

---

106. Disclosure of Breakpoint Discounts by Mutual Funds, Sec. Act Rel. No. 33–8427; Sec. Exch. Act rel. No. 34–49817; Inv. Co. Act Rel. No. IC–26464 (SEC 2004). In particular, the SEC rules require that in the prospectus mutual funds provide a brief description of arrangements resulting in sales load breakpoints. The disclosures relating to breakpoints must include a summary of eligibility requirements. Mutual fund prospectuses must also contain a description of the methods used to value accounts in order to determine whether a shareholder qualifies for sales load breakpoints. The pricing disclosures in the prospectus must also state any requirement that in order to obtain a breakpoint, it may be necessary for a shareholder to provide information and records, such as account statements, to a mutual fund or financial intermediary. In addition the SEC rules require a mutual fund to state in its prospectus whether breakpoint information is made available on the mutual fund's website.

111. *See, e.g.,* Krull v. SEC, 248 F.3d 907 (9th Cir.2001).

112. *See* Disclosure Regarding Market Timing and Selective Disclosure of Portfolio, Sec. Act Rel. No. 33–8408; Inv. Co. Act Rel. No. IC–26418, 69 FR 22300–01, 2004 WL 865628 (SEC April 23, 2004).

113. *See* Former President of South Florida Investment Adviser is Barred From Association with any Broker, Dealer or Investment Adviser Based on his Variable Annuity Switching, SEC News Digest 2002–14, 2002 WL 77624 (Jan. 22, 2002).

116. Inv. Adv. Act Rel. No. IA–1406, [1993–1994 Transfer Binder] Fed. Sec. L. Rep. (CCH) ¶ 85,327 (SEC March 16, 1994). *See also, e.g.,* MLC Limited 1997 WL 408759 n. 2 (SEC No Action Letter July 21, 1997).

117. The only formalized suitability requirements for broker-dealers are embodied in the NASD suitability rule and in the New York Stock Exchange's know your customer rule. These rules could be applied by analogy to investment advisers.

118. MLC Limited, 1997 WL 408759 n. 2 (SEC No Action Letter July 21, 1997).

tion.[124] The violation extends to nondisclosure of any economic self interest that could have an influence on the broker, analyst, or other person making the recommendation.[125]

The SEC approved the adoption of the NASD's rules regarding analysts' recommendations.[136] The NASD's rules addressing analysts' recommendations are in large measure a codification of prior NASD policy in light of the implications drawn from the NASD's more general rules regarding fair practice and disclosure obligations. The NASD rules on analysts' recommendations make more explicit the requirements that have traditionally been imposed under the more generalized requirements that NASD members adhere to fair and equitable principles of trade. The NASD specifically addressed analysts' compensation, the relationship between a firm's investment banking and research departments, the personal trading activities of analysts, and disclosures relating to the firm's and the analyst's ownership of securities. The rules also impose a quiet period on recommendations following a firm's underwriting activities. The NASD proposal was drafted in consultation with the New York Stock Exchange, which agreed to impose similar requirements upon its members.

The rules explicitly provide than an analyst's compensation may not be tied to specific investment banking transactions. Furthermore, if the analyst's compensation is based in any degree upon the investment banking revenues, the research reports must disclose this. Disclosure is also required if the firm or its affiliates received compensation from that company within the previous 12 months; disclosure is also required if the firm or affiliates expect to receive compensation from the company within the next three months following publication of the report. Additionally, when an analyst recommends a security in a public appearance, the analyst must disclose if the issuer is a client of the firm.

The requirements relating to analysts' independence preclude a research analyst from being supervised or controlled by a firm's investment banking department. The research department must act independently of the investment banking department and may only have reports checked for factual accuracy by either the investment banking department or the company that is the subject of the report.

The independence requirements preclude an analyst or member of the analyst's household from purchasing or receiving a company's securities prior to its IPO, if the company is engaged in the same business that the analyst follows and issues reports about. The rules also impose a trading moratorium so that no analyst or household member may trade securities issued by companies the analyst follows for thirty days prior to the issuance of the research report and ending five days after the date of the research report. The rules also prohibit analysts and household members from making trades contrary to the analyst's most current recommendations.

The NASD rules require that when making a public appearance an analyst would have to disclose (and a firm must disclose in research reports) if

124. Section 17(b) of the 1933 Act, 15 U.S.C.A. § 77q(b).

125. *See, e.g.,* In re Richmark Capital Corp., Sec. Act Rel. No. 33–8333, Sec. Exch. Act Rel. No. 34–48758, 2003 WL 22570712 *3 (SEC Nov. 7, 2003).

136. Sec. Exch. Act Rel. No. 34–45908, 2002 WL 970848 (SEC May 10, 2002). *See also* NASD Notice to Members 02–39, 2002 WL 1447486 (NASD July 2002).

the analyst or a household member has a financial interest in the securities of a recommended company. Any other known conflict of interest must also be disclosed in the research report or during the public appearance. Additionally, if a firm, as of five business days before the public appearance or publication of a research report, owns one percent or more of any equity class of the company, there must be disclosure in the research report or during the appearance.

The NASD rules also impose a quiet period for securities offerings registered under the Securities Act of 1933 where the analyst's firm participates as an underwriter.[138] The rules as proposed and adopted require quiet periods, during which a firm acting as manager or co-manager of a securities offering may not issue a report on a company within forty days after an initial public offering or within ten days after a secondary offering. The rules also prohibit a firm from offering or threatening to withhold favorable research to induce business.

The concern over analysts' conflicts of interest has spread beyond the NASD proposed rules. Thus, for example, Merrill Lynch agreed in a settlement with the New York Attorney General to create a website to list all of its relevant banking relationships with companies discussed in its research reports during the preceding twelve months and also to include this same information directly in its research reports. Additionally, Merrill Lynch agreed to state on the cover of every research report that investors should assume the firm is seeking, or will seek, investment banking business from the covered company.[147] Following on the heels of the actions of the New York Attorney General, the SEC announced that it was investigating problems relating to analysts' recommendations and conflicts of interest.[148] The investigation was conducted jointly by the New York Stock Exchange, the National Association of Securities Dealers, the New York Attorney General, the North American Securities Administrators Association, and the states.[149] After considerable negotiations, the investigation culminated in a global settlement that included the largest monetary settlement resulting from securities law violations—1.4 billion dollars.[150]

Even beyond the staggering monetary payment, the global settlement included reforms in the ways investment bankers operate. The reforms instituted by the settlement include a more rigid separation of brokerage firms' research and investment banking activities. For example, under the terms of the settlement, research analysts may no longer solicit business or accompany investment bankers on road shows or other promotional activities. Research analysts may not assist in identifying potential investment banking customers. Compensation and evaluation of research analysts must be completely independent of a firm's investment banking activities. Analysts' com-

---

138. *See* §§ 2.3[6], 2.4[4], 2.5[8] *supra* for discussion of broker and analyst recommendations while a security is in registration.

147. *See* Merrill Lynch, Spitzer Reach Interim Deal; New Securities Research Offered, 34 Sec. Reg. & L. Rep. (BNA) 647 (April 22, 2002); Merrill Lynch Stock Rating System Found Biased by Undisclosed Conflicts of Interest, http://www.oag.state.ny.us/press/2002/apr/apr08b_02.html (N.Y. Dept. Law Press Release April 8, 2002).

148. *See* SEC Launches Inquiry into Research Analyst Conflicts, http://www.sec.gov/news/press/2002–56.htm (SEC Press Release April 25, 2002).

149. *Id.*

150. *See* Joint Press Release, http://www.sec.gov/news/press/2003–54.htm.

pensation must be based on the success of their research rather than on factors such as investment banking or other brokerage firm revenue.

The settlement also contained provisions designed to increase the transparency of rating information. The settlement also prohibited certain practices that created undue conflicts of interest within a firm's integrated operations. For example, the settlement banned spinning of IPO shares. This means that a firm may no longer allocate officers or directors of public companies preferential access to valuable IPO shares of corporations from which they have sought or obtained investment banking business.

The Sarbanes–Oxley Act of 2002[151] contains provisions designed to preserve the objectivity of research analysts by enhancing the separation between investment bankers and research analysts.[153] Shortly after the enactment of the new analyst provisions, the SEC proposed Regulation Analyst Certification (AC) to require that any research report disseminated by broker or dealer include certifications by the research analyst that the views expressed in the research report accurately reflect the analyst's personal views, and whether the analyst received compensation or other payments in connection with his or her specific recommendations or views.[155] The new rules would further require a research analyst to provide certifications and disclosures in connection with public appearances.[156] In 2003, the SEC adopted Regulation AC.[158]

§ 14.17　Scalping

Scalping consists of a broker's or investment adviser's purchasing a security in advance of making a buy recommendation, with the knowledge that a buy recommendation will help drive up the price of the stock. The stock is sold at a profit once the scalper's recommendation has been issued and the price has risen in reaction thereto.

In SEC v. Capital Gains Research Bureau, Inc.,[2] the Supreme Court held that failure to disclose an intention to scalp operates as a fraud or deceit upon an investment adviser's prospective clients under the terms of section 206 of the Investment Advisers Act of 1940.[3] The Court ruled that the concept of fraud or deceit in section 206 of the Act is not limited to material misstatements but also extends to omissions of material fact. The Court explained: "The high standards of business morality exacted by our laws regulating the securities industry do not permit an investment adviser to trade on the market effect of his own recommendations without fully and fairly revealing his personal interest(s) in these recommendations to his clients."[4] On balance, it was held that this is a relatively low burden to place upon the investment

---

151.　Sarbanes–Oxley Act of 2002, Pub. Law 107–204 (July 30, 2002).

153.　15 USCA § 78o–6.

155.　Regulation Analyst Certification, Sec. Act Rel. No. 33–8119, Sec. Exch. Act Rel. No. 34–46301, 2002 WL 1781118 (SEC 2002).

156.　*Id.*

158.　*See* Regulation Analyst Certification, Sec. Act Rel. No. 33–8193, Sec. Exch. Act Rel. No. 34–47384, 68 Fed. Reg. 9482–01, 2003 WL 535908 (SEC Feb. 27, 2003), codified in 17 C.F.R. §§ 242.500–242.505.

§ 14.17

2.　375 U.S. 180, 84 S.Ct. 275, 11 L.Ed.2d 237 (1963).

3.　15 U.S.C.A. § 80b–6. The Investment Advisers Act is discussed in chapter 21 *infra*.

4.　375 U.S. at 201, 84 S.Ct. at 287.

adviser (or anyone else whose investment opinions are likely to be relied upon by others). The Court further explained that this burden is justified when viewed in relation to the necessity of preserving a climate of fair dealing that is essential to maintain confidence in the securities markets.

It is interesting to note that the Supreme Court's reasoning in *Capital Gains Research Bureau* appears to make undisclosed scalping a violation of Rule 10b–5(c)'s[5] prohibition against acts and practices that operate as a fraud as well as Rule 10b–5(b)'s proscription against making material misstatements or omissions in connection with the purchase or sale of securities.[6] The Ninth Circuit in Zweig v. Hearst Corp.[7] has followed up on the Supreme Court's lead in holding that undisclosed scalping is in violation of Rule 10b–5. The 10b–5 scalping violation is not based on the conduct alone, but rather only when the conduct is viewed together with the actionable nondisclosure of the scalper's trading in the securities being recommended. In *Zweig* the defendant, a financial columnist, received unjustifiably optimistic information about a corporation directly from the corporation's officers and directors, whom he interviewed in preparation for a column on the company. After receiving this favorable information, and apparently making no effort to investigate its accuracy, the defendant purchased five thousand shares of stock directly from the issuer at a substantial discount below the market price. Two days later in his column, the defendant published a buy recommendation for the stock in question, causing the market price of the stock to increase by more than fifty percent. The day after the column appeared, the defendant recovered his entire initial investment by selling two thousand shares, thus retaining three thousand shares as sheer profit.[8] The court, following the reasoning of *Capital Gains Research Bureau,* held that defendant's activities were in violation of Rule 10b–5, saying "[w]hile Rule 10b–5 should not be extended to require every financial columnist or reporter to disclose his or her portfolio to all of his or her readers, it does cover the activities of one who uses a column as part of a scheme to manipulate the market and deceive the investing public."[9]

The court in *Zweig* held the defendant liable in damages to those readers who had purchased the securities at the artificially high price as well as to shareholders of another company who had not read the column but had suffered a loss when the artificially high price of the recommended stock decreased the number of shares they received in a merger. The rationale was that the defendant had perpetrated a fraud on the market.[10] The court explained that the plaintiffs had "relied on the free and unmanipulated market that the federal securities laws were designed to foster * * *."[11] The court acknowledged that the defendant did not owe any common law duty to non-readers, but to deny them recovery while allowing the readers a recourse

---

5. 17 C.F.R. § 240.10b–5(c).

6. *See id. See also* chapter 12 *supra.*

7. 594 F.2d 1261 (9th Cir.1979).

8. Defendant had a "long history of similar dealings." 594 F.2d at 1265. In one two-year period he purchased the stock of twenty-one companies just prior to publishing columns pertaining to those companies. In twenty-one of twenty-two sales taking place inside of five days after publication defendant profited from an increase in the price of the stock. *Id.* at 1264 n. 4.

9. *Id.* at 1271.

10. *Id.* at 1270.

11. *Id.* at 1270.

would be a "wholly incongruous result."[12] The defendant was thus held liable despite the fact that the plaintiffs' aggregate losses far exceeded the defendant's gain.[13] The court couched its decision wholly in terms of the defendant's failure to disclose his purchase of the stock prior to making his recommendation.[14]

In addition to violation of the Securities Exchange Act of 1934, and the Investment Advisers Act of 1940, scalping necessarily triggers the potential for sanctions under the broker-dealer registration provisions of the Exchange Act.[18] Additionally, scalping violates the rules of self regulatory organizations such as the traditional exchanges and NASD.[19]

Section 17(b) of the Securities Act of 1933[20] outlaws practices similar to scalping. As explained in an earlier section of this treatise,[22] section 17(b) prohibits the making of recommendation to sell a security without disclosing any compensation that may have been paid to the person making the recommendation.

§ 14.18   High Pressure Sales Tactics: Boiler Room Operations

In making his or her recommendation to the customer, the broker-dealer is under an obligation not only to know and consider the customer's investment objectives, but also to have some familiarity with the security being recommended. As detailed further below, high pressure sales tactics can take various forms and are carried our using a variety of tactics. For example, one unfortunate practice that has developed with some of the more unscrupulous securities brokers and dealers is a concerted high pressure sales campaign which frequently includes the cold calling of individuals who are not regular customers. Cold calling is but one example of the tactics that can create the backdrop for improper high pressure sales campaigns by securities brokers. Brokerage firms sponsoring such high pressure sales campaigns typically pressure their sales representatives to push the securities in question through the use of sales incentives[3] or other tactics.[4] Although boiler rooms appear

---

12.   549 F.2d at 1270–71.

13.   For a discussion of the measure of damages under rule 10b–5 *see* § 12.12 *supra.*

14.   594 F.2d at 1271.

18.   15 U.S.C.A. § 78*o. See* § 14.3 *supra.*

19.   *See, e.g.,* N.Y.S.E.Guide (CCH) ¶ 2472.40 (October 1998); Am.Stock Ex.Guide (CCH) ¶ 9491A.40 (June 6, 1997). *See also, e.g.,* Rule 2210(d)(2)(B), NASD Manual (CCH) ¶ (2000).

20.   15 U.S.C.A. § 77q(b).

22.   *See* §§ 7.11[2], 14.14[4] *supra.*

§ 14.18

3.   *See* § 14.14[4] *supra.*

4.   In one case:

H.J. Meyers sponsored incentive programs that offered rewards such as television sets for high volumes of sales. The firm also provided brokers with various scripts that could be used in cold calls to potential customers to pressure customers to purchase Palomar stock. As negative reinforcement, for example, the managers subjected brokers who did not meet target sales to a ritual called the "walk of shame," wherein the broker was required to walk around the floor of the brokerage office while other brokers threw objects at him or her. In addition, brokers were subjected to the "ten or ten" rule, meaning that they were required to make at least ten successful cold calls to sell Palomar stock, or to stay in the office until ten o'clock at night.

Varljen v. H.J. Meyers, Inc., 1998 WL 395266, *1 (S.D.N.Y.1998).

boiler room

with more frequency in active bull markets, they also spring up in market down turns where the boiler room operators are still able to find customers.[5]

The movie "Boiler Room"[6] accurately depicted many of the tactics used in the perpetration of securities brokers' high pressure sale frauds. The extreme measures portrayed in that movie were not exaggeration. In fact, they reflect many of the tactics found in the SEC and NASD decisions. These tactics are not new. In fact, similar overreaching brokerage sales programs were behind the regulation that Congress imposed in 1934. For example, many of these operations "lent a carnival tone to securities marketing."[8] In particular, Congress was concerned with sales contests for brokers, awarding liberal prizes to the brokers and/or offices with the most securities sales.[9] These types of sales campaigns are thus clearly inconsistent with the fair and equitable principles of trade that apply to securities brokers under the 1934 Act and system of self regulation that exists thereunder.[10] Conduct that may be acceptable in other sales intensive business simply is not to be tolerated for securities brokers. High pressure sales operations often result in criminal convictions and imprisonment.

In the context of these problematic high pressure sales campaigns, the sales personnel making the calls typically recommend purchases of large blocks of speculative securities in new companies, predicting dramatic earnings and rapid increases in the market prices of the securities. Where there is a conscious plan of high pressure sales tactics, the situation is referred to as a "boiler room" operation.[15] The term boiler room reflects the former practice of locating such operations in back rooms or boiler rooms.[16] One notable location for making telephone solicitations was from a prison cell.[17]

Sometimes the term "bucket shop" is used interchangeably with "boiler room." The bucket shop has many of the same high pressure sales tactics as a boiler room but has a different history. The bucket shops that operated long ago were based on a failure to enter customer orders on an exchange,[20] and

bucket shop

---

5. *See, e.g.,* Brokers From Garden City, N.Y. Firm Indicted Over Alleged Boiler Room Fraud, 36 Sec. Reg. & L. Rep. (BNA) 948 (May 24, 2004).

6. New Line Cinema (2000).

8. Joel Seligman, The Transformation of Wall Street 24 (1982).

9. *See,* Jerry W. Markham & Thomas L. Hazen, Broker-Dealer Operations Under Securities and Commodities Law: Financial Responsibilities, Credit Regulation, and Customer Protection pp. 1–64 (2d ed. 2003).

10. *See, e.g.,* §§ 14.3[6], 14.5[3] *supra.*

15. *See, e.g.,* Berko v. SEC, 316 F.2d 137 (2d Cir.1963).

16. *See, e.g.,* In the Matter of Josephthal & Co., Disciplinary Proceeding No. C3A990071, 2001 WL 1886873 n. 58 (NASDR May 15, 2001) ("A 'boiler room' is defined as a 'place where high-pressure salespeople use banks of telephones to call lists of potential investors (known in the trade as sucker lists) in order to peddle speculative, even fraudulent, securities. They are called boiler rooms because of the high-pressure selling.' Barron's Dictionary of Finance and Investment Terms 54 (4th ed.1995)").

In one instance, a boiler room operation was compared to high pressure television marketing campaigns. In the Matter of Blinder, Robinson & Co., Complaint No. NEW–737 1991 WL 840282 (N.A.S.D.R. Sept. 18, 1991) ("... the managers got up and it was like a Jerry Lewis telethon. Everyone in the office was selling this blind pool. We didn't know what they were. We were given a pitch to use, and it was a sales pitch. We were sales people. We were not stockbrokers. We were told to tell people that our clients made money. And if you wanted to make money, you do this or that. We basically were boiler room people.")

17. SEC v. Monas, 33 Sec. Reg. & L. Rep. (BNA) 338 (S.D.N.Y. 2001).

20. *See, e.g.,* Board of Trade of City of Chicago v. Christie Grain & Stock Co., 198 U.S. 236, 246, 25 S.Ct. 637, 638, 49 L.Ed. 1031 (1905) (describing bucket shops as "places wherein is

thus turning the apparent transactions into illegal difference contracts[21] or simply wagers.[22] The essence of the bucket shop is the fictitious nature of the transactions. In contrast, boiler rooms use high pressure sales with respect to real transactions.

Bucket shops and boiler room operations as high pressure sales campaigns are inconsistent with the broker-dealer's implied representation under the shingle theory to conduct its business in a professional (i.e., fair and equitable) manner.[24]

In the context of a boiler room, high pressure sales campaigns can constitute securities fraud and illegal manipulative activity. Thus, for example, boiler room activities and other high pressure sales tactics can violate SEC Rule 10b–5 and can also form the basis for NASD disciplinary sanctions.[26] One benchmark of the boiler room variety of high pressure sales tactics is heavy reliance on telephone solicitations and usually concentrating on long-distance cold calling operations. Another common high pressure tactic that implicates the anti-manipulation rules is the use of pre-written scripts including prepared rebuttals to customer objections.[27] This is often accompanied by high commissions to sales representatives for pushing the stocks in question. Many boiler room operations routinely use unregistered sales representatives.[29] Frequently, boiler room operations involve shell companies or other scam stocks.[30]

Brokers and others who sell securities are often very aggressive in their marketing techniques. However, not every instance of high pressure sales tactics will violate the securities laws.[33] Material misrepresentations and omissions can of course expose brokers and others to potential liabilities under the securities laws, but high pressure sales tactics alone will not rise to the requisite level of fraud.[34] On the other hand, when brokers and brokerage firms cross the line between permissible accepted sales tactics and impermissible manipulative or deceptive conduct, they can be held accountable for this conduct under the securities laws. A common manipulative device is for a brokerage firm to compensate brokers in such a way as to encourage high pressure sales.[35] In extreme cases, customer sell orders may even be ignored.

---

permitted the pretended buying and selling of grain, etc., without any intention of receiving and paying for the property so bought, or of delivering the property so sold.'').

21. *See,* Davis v. Fleshman, 245 Pa. 224, 227, 91 A. 489, 490 (1914).

22. *See,* Streeter v. Lowe, 184 F. 263, 264 (1st Cir.1911).

24. *See,* In the Matter of Mac Robbins & Co., 41 S.E.C. 116, Release No. 34–6846, 1962 WL 3592 *2 (SEC July 11, 1962).

26. *See, e.g.,* In the Matter of Goodman, Complaint No. C9–960013, 1999 WL 1489030 (N.A.S.D.R. Nov. 9, 1999).

27. In the Matter of Olde Discount Corp., Administrative Proceeding File No. 3–9699, Sec. Act Rel. No. 33–7577, 67 S.E.C. Docket 2045, 1998 WL 575171 (SEC September 10, 1998).

29. *See, e.g.,* In the Matter of M. Rimson & Co., Administrative Proceeding File No. 3–8772, 63 S.E.C. Docket 2494, Release No. ID–106, 1997 WL 93628 (S.E.C. Feb. 25, 1997).

30. *See, e.g.,* SEC v. Mersky, Civ. Ac. No. 93–CV–5200, Litigation Release No. 13812, 55 S.E.C. Docket 307, 1993 WL 387105 (E.D.PA. Sept. 30, 1993). *See also, e.g.,* Gary Weiss, The Mob on Wall Street, Business Week p.92 (Dec. 16, 1996).

33. *See, e.g.,* In re Westcap Enterprises, 230 F.3d 717, 727–728 (5th Cir.2000).

34. *Id.*

35. *See, e.g.,* SEC v. Wellshire Securities, 737 F.Supp. 251, 254–255 (S.D.N.Y.1990).

One of the features of a boiler room operation is aggressive cold calling programs whereby a broker calls someone with whom there has been no prior business relationship and tries to enlist him or her as a client. The practice of cold calling has not been limited to boiler room operations and has been utilized by many of the more established retail brokerage firms. In 1994, Congress enacted the Telemarketing and Consumer Fraud and Abuse Prevention Act.[38] As part of that legislation the SEC was authorized to impose limitations on telephone solicitations. In 1995, the SEC approved New York Stock Exchange and NASD rules requiring member firms to maintain and preserve "do not call lists."[39] Among other things, the rules require firms to honor requests not to be called by the firm or its sales agents. The rules also contain sanctions for violations of the requirement that a list be maintained and also for failure to honor customers' requests to be left alone. Many states have their own telemarketing laws that supplement the federal law and in some cases go further.

The SEC disclaims that there is any *per se* violation of the antifraud provisions resulting from boiler room activities.[43] However, liability is readily imposed under either the shingle theory or the antifraud provisions.[44] The Commission requires that a broker find out certain minimum information about the customer and the security before entering into a transaction.[45] This duty of investigation prior to making a recommendation has been phrased in terms of an obligation of "due diligence." In contrast, the duty of investigation of the security is higher in a sale of unseasoned securities; in such a case, before recommending purchase (or sale), the broker should make a "searching inquiry."[46] In addition, an individual's knowing participation in a high pressure sales campaign fraught with improper sales techniques and recommendations will result in a violation of the Act notwithstanding the defense that he or she relied upon information furnished by the employer broker-dealer.[47] The cases deal mostly with SEC- or NASD- imposed sanctions on participants in boiler room activities rather than in terms of private rights of action by injured investors. Private remedies for boiler room operations can be based upon the antifraud provisions of SEC Rule 10b–5 provided that there have been material misrepresentations in connection therewith. Similarly, boiler room operations can result in liability for fraud.[49]

38. Pub. L. No. 103–297, 108 Stat. 1545 (1994).

39. Sec. Exch. Act Rel. No. 34–35831 (SEC June 9, 1995) (approving NASD rule requiring maintenance of do not call lists); Sec. Exch. Act Rel. No. 34–35832 (SEC June 7, 1995) (approving New York Stock Exchange rule requiring maintenance of do not call list).

43. *E.g.*, Kahn v. SEC, 297 F.2d 112 (2d Cir.1961); In re Palombi Securities Co., 41 S.E.C. 266 (SEC 1962).

44. Richard J. Buck & Co., 43 S.E.C. 998 (1968), *aff'd sub nom.* Hanly v. SEC, 415 F.2d 589 (2d Cir.1969).

45. *See* Sec.Exch.Act Rel. No. 34–9671 (July 26, 1972).

46. R.A. Holman & Co., 42 S.E.C. 866 (1965), *affirmed* 366 F.2d 446 (2d Cir.1966), *modified on other grounds* 377 F.2d 665 (2d Cir.1967), *cert. denied* 389 U.S. 991, 88 S.Ct. 473, 19 L.Ed.2d 482 (1967).

47. Berko v. SEC, 316 F.2d 137 (2d Cir.1963); SEC v. Macon, 28 F.Supp. 127, 129 (D.Colo. 1939); 2 L.Loss, Securities Regulation 1316 *et seq.* (2d ed. 1961).

49. *See, e.g.*, In the Matter of the Arbitration Between Johnston v. Investors Associates, Inc., Docket Number 98–03685, 2000 WL 1919877 (N.A.S.D. Arbitration Nov. 10, 2000) (arbitration award of $688,000 damages for fraud and common law fraud in connection with high pressure telephone sales).

§ 14.19   Penny Stock Regulation; Microcap Fraud

§ 14.19[1]   Penny Stock Regulation

As discussed in the preceding section,[1] issues relating to the suitability of broker-dealer recommendations can apply to a wide variety of investments. However, suitability problems are particularly acute when dealing with low-priced securities (frequently referred to as "penny stocks"). For example, the NASD in its suitability rule has highlighted the particular concern for low priced securities.[2] In August 1989, the SEC adopted the penny stock rule which became effective on January 1, 1990.[3] The penny stock regulations, which are discussed below, contain special investor protections applicable to certain dealers in low priced securities. Although not directly applicable to all transactions involving any broker-dealers, the SEC's increased focus on suitability probably has implications, at least by analogy, for all brokers and for all recommendations.

Congress reinforced the SEC's concerns with penny stocks with the enactment of the Securities Enforcement and Penny Stock Reform Act of 1990.[18] Section 3(a)(51) of the Exchange Act now provides a statutory definition of "penny stock" which excludes most exchange-listed and NASDAQ securities.[19] However, the 1990 legislation gave the SEC rulemaking power to include as "penny stock" one that is listed only on a regional exchange or a NASDAQ security that is not listed in the national market system.[20] In addition to giving the SEC the authority to promulgate rules defining "penny stock," the 1990 amendments also imposed substantive disclosure and regulatory requirements upon broker-dealers dealing in penny stocks.

The 1990 legislation required broker-dealers entering into penny stock transactions to provide substantial risk-disclosure documents to prospective customers before any transactions can take place.[21] Broker-dealers must disclose with respect to each penny stock transaction the spread between the bid and asked price, the depth and liquidity of the market for the stock, and the broker-dealers' compensation for effectuating the transaction. The broker-dealer must also provide the customer with monthly statements indicating the value of the account's penny stock holdings. The Commission is directed to adopt rules establishing additional disclosure requirements.[22] The Commission is also given the authority to provide exemptions from the disclosure requirements "by rule, regulation, or order."[23] It is unlawful to violate any of the above disclosure requirements as well as any SEC rules "reasonably designed to prevent fraudulent, deceptive, or manipulative acts and practices with

---

§ 14.19

1.   *See* § 14.16 *supra.*

2.   NASD Rule 2310. *See also* former Art. III, Sec. 2 NASD Rules of Fair Practice.

3.   Sec.Exch.Act Rel. No. 34–27160, [1989 Transfer Binder] Fed.Sec.L.Rep. (CCH) ¶ 84,440 (Aug. 22, 1989).

18.   Pub.L. No. 101–429 (1990). *See* H.R. Rep. No. 101–617, 101st Cong., 2d Sess. (1990). *See also, e.g.,* Randolph Beatty & Padma Kadiyala, Impact of the Penny Stock Reform Act of 1990 in the Initial Public Offering Market, 46 J.L. & Econ. 5127 (2003). The provisions of the Penny Stock Reform Act that relate to SEC enforcement generally are discussed in § 16.2, 16.5 *infra.*

19.   15 U.S.C.A. § 78c(a)(51).

20.   15 U.S.C.A. § 78c(a)(51)(B).

21.   15 U.S.C.A. § 78o(g)(2).

22.   15 U.S.C.A. § 78o(g)(3).

23.   15 U.S.C.A. § 78o(g)(4).

respect to penny stocks," in order to protect investors or to maintain fair and orderly markets.[24] The penny stock legislation permits the SEC to designate any section 15(c)(2)[25] rules which if violated will not result in a voidable transaction under section 29(b) of the Act.[26] The 1990 reform legislation also prevents a person subject to statutory disqualification from acting as a promoter, consultant, or broker-dealer that underwrites penny stocks.[27] The 1990 penny stock legislation gave the SEC administrative sanctioning authority against persons associated with anyone offering penny stocks.[28]

In addition to the disclosure and regulatory reform described above, the Penny Stock Reform Act enacted section 17B of the Exchange Act[29] which is designed to encourage the development of automated quotation systems for penny stocks. There were also amendments to the 1933 Act regarding "blank check" offerings. A "blank check" company is any company issuing penny stock as defined in section 3(a)(51) of the Exchange Act[30] that either has no specific business plan or purpose or has indicated that it plans to merge with an unidentified company or companies.[31] The 1990 legislation not only created this new definition, it also directed the Commission to promulgate rules imposing special disclosure requirements for offerings by blank check companies.[32] Furthermore, it also empowered the Commission to place restrictions on the use of the proceeds until such disclosure requirements have been met.[33] The 1990 amendments further authorized the SEC to impose a right of rescission by purchasers of securities sold in violation of the blank check company disclosure requirements.[34] As is the case with the broker-dealer disclosure requirements, the Commission was given exemptive power with regard to blank check offerings.[35]

§ 14.19[3] Microcap Fraud

In the 1990s, "microcap" fraud stole the spotlight from the penny stock problems of the late 1980s and early 1990s. Microcap became the term that is now often used when referring to *very small* capitalization companies. The Internet has been used for many microcap offerings and has led to several abuses and securities law violations.[53] For example, the Commission became concerned with the use of the exemption from registration under 1933 Act Rule 504[54] for unregistered Internet offerings of microcap securities.[55] In

---

24. 15 U.S.C.A. § 78o(g)(5).

25. 15 U.S.C.A. § 78o(c)(2).

26. 15 U.S.C.A. § 78cc(b). The voidability of contracts entered into in violation of the Act is discussed in § 12.23[2] *supra.*

27. 15 U.S.C.A. § 78o(b)(6)(C). The SEC's power over broker-dealers is discussed in § 14.3 *supra.*

28. Securities Exchange Act § 15(b)(6)(A), 15 U.S.C.A. § 78o(b)(6)(A) expressly includes anyone "participating, in an offering of any penny stock." *Id. See* §§ 9.5, 10.2 *supra.*

The authority to impose sanctions against violators did not extend to conduct prior to 1990. Koch v. SEC, 177 F.3d 784 (9th Cir.1999) (overturning lifetime bar of penny stock broker because the conduct in question occurred prior to 1990).

29. 15 U.S.C.A. § 78q–2.

30. 15 U.S.C.A. § 78c(a)(51).

31. 15 U.S.C.A. § 77g(b)(3).

32. 15 U.S.C.A. § 77g(b)(1)(A).

33. 15 U.S.C.A. § 77g(b)(1)(B).

34. 15 U.S.C.A. § 77g(b)(1)(C).

35. 15 U.S.C.A. § 77g(b)(2).

53. *See, e.g.,* Special Report, Microcap Fraud over the Internet Seen as Trend by Enforcement Officials, 30 Sec. Reg. & L. Rep. (BNA) 1224 (Aug. 14, 1998).

54. 17 C.F.R. § 230.504. *See* § 4.19 *supra.*

55. *See* Sec. Act Rel. No. 33–7300 (May 31, 1996).

particular, the Commission was concerned with so-called "pump and dump" offerings[56] where Rule 504 frequently was used for Internet offerings (to "pump" the securities into the market) and then creating a secondary market (so that the securities could be "dumped" by the initial purchasers). In 1999, the Commission amended Rule 504 to prohibit the use of the exemption for public offerings unless registered under state law.[57] The SEC has also focused enforcement efforts on microcap fraud.[58] Another microcap abuse was the utilization of the short Form S–8 for 1933 Act registration of offerings to employees, advisors, and consultants for microcap securities.[59] In an effort to deter these microcap abuses, the Commission eliminated the availability of Form S–8 for offerings to advisors and consultants whose services involve selling or making a market in the issuer's securities.[60] Pump and dump schemes also arise outside of initial offerings, where the perpetrators of the scheme manipulate the price of a security to create a frothy market.[61]

NASD Rule 2315 applies to recommendations of securities that are published in a "quotation medium"[66] and are either (1) not listed on NASDAQ or a national securities exchange or (2) are listed on a regional securities exchange and are not included in transaction reports over the Consolidated Tape. NASD Rule 2315 requires that before making a purchase or short sale recommendation, the broker-dealer must review the company's "current financial statements" and "current material business information." The Rule applies to recommendations of a purchase or short sale of covered microcap securities, but does not apply to recommended sales out of a long position.

§ 14.20 Excessive Trading in Securities—Churning

§ 14.20[1] Basis of Violation

SEC Rule 15c1–7[1] prohibits excessive trading by a broker for any account in which he or she holds discretionary trading powers. When a broker in a

---

56. *See, e.g.,* In the Matter of Scacci, Administrative Proceeding File No. 3–10012, Sec. Exch. Act Rel. No. 34–41873, 70 S.E.C. Docket 1290, 1999 WL 710848 (SEC Sept. 14, 1999).

57. A general solicitation can be used in a Rule 504 offering only if one of two conditions is met. A general solicitation can be used for a Rule 504 offering if the transaction is registered under a state securities law that requires public filing and delivery of a substantive disclosure document. Rule 504(b)(1)(i), (ii), 17 C.F.R. § 230.504(b)(1)(i), (ii). Alternatively, a general solicitation can be used for an offering only to accredited investors (as that term is defined in Regulation D, 17 C.F.R. §§ 230.501 *et seq.*) under a state law exemption that permits a general solicitation. Rule 504(b)(1)(iii), 17 C.F.R. § 230.504 (b)(1)(iii).

58. *See* SEC Brings Action Against Microcap Firms; 82 Charged in Actions Involving $12 Million, 31 Sec. Reg. & L. Rep. (BNA) 1040 (Aug. 6, 1999).

59. Form S–8 does not impose the detailed disclosure requirements that are found with other registration forms. *See* § 3.3 *supra.* This then allowed microcap issuers taking advantage of the form to issue securities without the level of disclosure that would ordinarily be required.

60. *See* Sec. Act Rel. No. 33–7645 (SEC Feb. 25, 1999).

61. *See, e.g.,* In the Matter of Terrell, Administrative Proceeding File No. 3–10154, Sec. Exch. Act Rel. No. 34–42483, 71 S.E.C. Docket 1863, 2000 WL 248549 (SEC March 2, 2000).

66. The Rule defines "quotation medium" as (1) any system of general circulation to brokers or dealers that regularly disseminates quotation or indications of interest of identified brokers or dealers or (2) any publication, alternative trading system or other device that is used by brokers or dealers to disseminate quotations or indication of interest to others.

§ 14.20

1. 17 C.F.R. § 240.15c1–7.

discretionary trading account enters into transactions for the purpose of generating commissions, the broker unjustifiably gains from the customer's loss or transaction costs. This practice is generally referred to as "churning" the customer's account. Rule 15c1–7 declares churning to be a "manipulative, deceptive or other fraudulent device or contrivance." The SEC rule is limited by its terms to trading accounts where the broker has the discretion to enter into transactions, but the account overall need not be formally discretionary. A 1949 SEC ruling took the position that the "handling of a customer's account may become fraudulent whenever the broker or dealer is in a position to determine the volume and frequency of transactions by reason of the customer's willingness to follow the suggestions of the broker or the dealer and he abuses the customer's confidence by overtrading."[4] In contrast to a fraudulent pattern of recommendations, a churning claim requires more than asserting a pattern of the customer having followed the broker's advice; it must be shown that the broker had "control" over the account.[5] In addition to violating the broker's standards of conduct embodied in section 15(c)(1), churning can form the basis of a violations of the 1934 Act's general antifraud provisions contained in Rule 10b–5.[7]

There are few, if any, substantive defenses to a churning claim once a prima facie case has been established. It has further been held that the customer's opportunity to complain about the transactions by virtue of his having viewed the transaction confirmations does not in itself create an estoppel so as to preclude a churning action under Rule 10b–5.[26] Similarly, it is not a defense to a churning claim that the plaintiff's failure to object to the trades in question operated as a ratification of the trades.

When analyzing the private remedy for churning, it must be remembered that additional judicial developments are likely to be slow to arrive, if at all. Formerly, most customer disputes were litigated in court. However, now most disputes between brokers and their customers are subject to arbitration.[29] Arbitration awards do not generally contain long discussions of the law. Furthermore, there is a relatively narrow basis for judicial review. Much of the law relating to churning, as is the case with other broker-dealer obligations, will be found primarily in the older decisions arising out of customer litigation. In addition some guidance may be found in the relatively few customer suits that may still be litigated in court, plus the SEC administrative decisions (and any subsequent judicial review) arising out of broker-dealer regulation.

§ 14.20[2] Establishing a Churning Claim

In order to establish churning it generally will be necessary to prove substantial disparity between the turnover in the account in question and the

---

4. In re Norris & Hirshberg, 21 S.E.C. 865, 890 (1946), *affirmed sub nom.* Norris & Hirshberg v. SEC, 177 F.2d 228 (D.C.Cir.1949).

5. *See, e.g.,* Hotmar v. Lowell H. Listrom & Co., Inc., 808 F.2d 1384 (10th Cir.1987) (failure to establish control).

7. *E.g.,* Arceneaux v. Merrill Lynch, Pierce, Fenner & Smith, Inc., 767 F.2d 1498 (11th Cir.1985); Costello v. Oppenheimer & Co., 711 F.2d 1361 (7th Cir.1983).

26. Mihara v. Dean Witter & Co., Inc., 619 F.2d 814, 822–23 (9th Cir.1980); Hecht v. Harris, Upham & Co., 430 F.2d 1202, 1208 (9th Cir.1970).

29. *See, e.g.,* Rodriguez de Quijas v. Shearson/American Express, 490 U.S. 477, 109 S.Ct. 1917, 104 L.Ed.2d 526 (1989); Shearson/American Express, Inc. v. McMahon, 482 U.S. 220, 107 S.Ct. 2332, 96 L.Ed.2d 185 (1987).

normal trading activity for similar accounts. For example, in one case the plaintiff prevailed by showing that an account which amounted to less than one-tenth of one percent of the local office's portfolio value generated 4.7 percent of its commission income.[30] Although the damaging turn-over rate must necessarily be decided on a case by case basis, it appears that a given account's annual turn-over rate in excess of six times is considered generally to reflect excessive trading.[31]

§ 14.20[3] Measure of Damages in Churning Cases

The appropriate measure of damages[44] is not always easy to identify in a churning case. The general rule appears to be that the defendant is liable only for the losses due to the excessive commissions plus accrued interest.[45] However, some courts have assessed the measure of damages as the excess of the average decline in market values over the decline in value of the plaintiff's portfolio.[46] Since churning does not necessarily result in less prudent investments, it quite properly has been suggested that the better view would be to award damages for diminution in investment value only in situations where the broker-dealer has also violated the suitability requirements.[48] Since the evil involved is the generation of excessive commissions, the fact that the customer's account increased in value does not preclude a churning claim.[49] At least one court has allowed consideration of the lost profits that would have accrued to the investor had the churning and accompanying unsuitable investments not occurred.[50]

§ 14.21 Unauthorized Trading

An unauthorized trade is simply the purchase or sale of stock by a broker on behalf of a customer who has not authorized the transaction. Unauthorized trading differs from churning in that under a churning claim, the plaintiff will attempt to show that excessive trading has occurred on his account simply to generate brokerage fees or commissions.[1] The plaintiff in churning cases need

---

30. Hecht v. Harris, Upham & Co., 430 F.2d 1202 (9th Cir.1970). *See also* Adams v. Swanson, 652 F.Supp. 762 (D.Or.1985) (120 trades on 150 trading days, inadequate notice to customer); Donald A. Winslow & Seth C. Anderson, A Model for Determining the Excessive Trading Element in Churning Claims, 68 N.C.L.Rev. 327 (1990).

31. *See* Mihara v. Dean Witter & Co., Inc., 619 F.2d 814, 821 (9th Cir.1980).

44. *See* § 12.12 *supra* for discussion of the measure of damages in Rule 10b–5 actions generally.

45. Hecht v. Harris, Upham & Co., 430 F.2d 1202 (9th Cir.1970); Sebbag v. Shearson Lehman Brothers, Inc., 1991 WL 12431, [1990–1991 Transfer Binder] Fed.Sec.L.Rep. (CCH) ¶ 95,775 (S.D.N.Y.1991) (upholding arbitration award denying the change in portfolio value but awarding damages based on commissions and interest attributable to churning); Zaretsky v. E.F. Hutton & Co., Inc., 509 F.Supp. 68 (S.D.N.Y.1981).

46. *E.g.*, Miley v. Oppenheimer & Co., 637 F.2d 318 (5th Cir.1981).

48. Nesbit v. McNeil, 896 F.2d 380, 385 (9th Cir.1990); Miley v. Oppenheimer & Co., 637 F.2d 318, 326 (5th Cir.1981); In re Thomson McKinnon Securities, Inc., 191 B.R. 976 (Bkrtcy.S.D.N.Y. 1996) (churning damages limited to excess commissions since there was no suitability claim). *See* Richard W. Jennings & Harold Marsh, Jr., Securities Regulation, Cases and Materials 569–70 (5th ed.1982). The suitability requirements and the limited availability of a private remedy for violation thereof are discussed in § 14.16 *supra*.

49. Davis v. Merrill Lynch, Pierce, Fenner & Smith, Inc., 906 F.2d 1206 (8th Cir.1990); Nesbit v. McNeil, 896 F.2d 380 (9th Cir.1990).

50. *See* Scalp & Blade, Inc. v. Advest, Inc., 765 N.Y.S.2d 92, 309 A.D.2d 219 (2003).

§ 14.21

1. The elements of a plaintiff's cause of action for churning are (1) that excessive trading has occurred; (2) the stocks were purchased or sold to generate commissions and not with the

not argue that the trading was per se unauthorized. Usually, the customer authorizes trading on his or her account; the evil in churning cases is the broker's excessive trading in order to generate commissions. A variation on unauthorized trading is the ignoring of customer sell orders. Ignoring customer orders obviously is not to generate sales commissions but rather may be part of a scheme to manipulate and thereby inflate the price of the stock in question.

Unauthorized trading claims can arise in many contexts. The only defense to unauthorized trading claims is that the broker in fact had the authority or discretion to execute the transactions in question. The broker can get such authority from a specific customer order or from a grant of discretionary trading authority. Grants of discretionary trading authority require prior written authorization. Specifically, NASD Rule of Conduct 2510 provides that a registered representative may not exercise without written authorization.[3] Unauthorized trades similarly place a broker in violation of New York Stock Exchange Rules.[4]

Claims of unauthorized trading can arise in a variety of contexts. For example, a broker's exercise of discretion of an account without proper authorization from the customer is a form of unauthorized trading. Unauthorized trading claims sometimes arise in connection with liquidation of margin positions, but authorization for these liquidations ordinarily is included in the customer's margin agreement.[6]

§ 14.22   Regulation of "Short Sales"

If an investor believes that the price of a security is likely to decline, there are several potential investment strategies. Most such strategies are linked to dealing with put and call options.[1] Another alternative is to enter an order to sell the security at the current price with the understanding that the investor is to fulfill that obligation at a later date by purchasing the security at a lower price. This practice, known as selling short, is extremely risky since every increase in the price causes loss to the investor until he or she covers the short sale. An alternative method is "selling against the box" where securities are borrowed as collateral for delivery for sale at a later date.

customer's best interests in mind; and (3) that the plaintiff relied on his or her broker to make sound investment decisions on his or her behalf. Marshak v. Blyth, Eastman, Dillon & Co., Inc., 413 F.Supp. 377, 379 (N.D.Okl.1975); Mark C. Jensen, Abuse of Discretion Under Rule 10b–5: Churning, Unsuitability and Unauthorized Transactions, 18 Sec.Reg.L.J. 374 (1991).

3.   NSAD Rule of Conduct 2510.

4.   *See, e.g.,* In the Matter of Koos, NYSE Hearing Panel Decision 01–122 2002 WL 799395 (N.Y.S.E. August 1, 2001).

6.   Margin transactions are discussed in § 14.9 *supra.*

§ 14.22

1.   For example, by purchasing a "put" option, the investor gets the right to put the security to the option seller at the exercise price on or before the expiration date. The hope is that the security can be purchased at a low enough price to offset the premium paid for the right to "put" it (*i.e.,* sell it) to the option writer at the higher price. Options are traded on several of the national securities exchanges under the supervision of the SEC, the applicable exchange and the Options Clearing Corporation. *See* SEC, Report of the Special Study of the Options Market, 96th Cong., 1st Sess. (1979).

Another strategy, of course, is selling the security if it is owned in order to prevent loss resulting from the anticipated price deterioration.

The mechanics of a short sale are as follows. The customer sells securities that he or she does not own. The customer then borrows the security from the broker in order to be able to deliver the security to the purchaser in the short sale transaction.[3] In turn, the customer pays interest on the loan[4] until he or she closes the transaction by purchasing the security in question and restoring that stock to the broker.[5] As pointed out above, an alternative method to effectuate the transaction is known as "selling against the box" where rather than borrowing securities from the broker, the customer uses securities that he or she already owns as collateral for the short sale.[6] When the customer posts collateral for the short sale or sale against the box, the brokerage firm may earn profits from the collateral so held.[7] It is not securities fraud to fail to inform the customer of these profits.[8]

Because of the speculative nature of and potential for abuse associated with short sales and sales against the box, insiders of publicly traded securities are strictly prohibited from engaging in such transactions.[9] Also, short sales are not meant for the ordinary investor both because of the risk involved and the level of sophistication that should exist before an investor embarks upon such a transaction. An investor can take the same investment strategy with the use of options. For example, purchasing a put option on a particular security gives the investor the right (before the option expires) to sell the security at the exercise price to the writer of the put option. If the price of the security declines below the option exercise price, then the option is "in the money" since if the option is exercised and the underlying security is then sold, the investor would realize a profit. There would cease to be a profit once the price of the stock climbs above the option exercise price since the investor could purchase the security more cheaply on the open market than by exercising his or her put option.

When an investor writes (or sells) a put option, the investor takes a "short" investment position, and therefore this involves similar risks as short sales and sales against the box. However, the writing of put options is not expressly covered by most of the short sale regulations.

Because of the risky nature of a short sale investment strategy, a broker has a duty to explain the transaction in a manner understandable to the investor.[10] This is equally true of a short position in options. A material misrepresentation concerning the risks of a short sale transaction (or option transaction) can form the basis of a private suit under SEC Rule 10b–5.

---

3. Since the securities that are borrowed for the short sale are delivered for sale, from the purchaser's perspective a purchase of securities from a short sale is no different that an ordinary purchase.

4. The loan transaction is regulated by the margin rules which govern the extension of credit where securities are held as collateral. *See* § 10.11 *supra.*

5. *See, e.g.,* Levitin v. PaineWebber, Inc. 159 F.3d 698 (2d Cir.1998).

6. *See* Bissell v. Merrill Lynch & Co., 157 F.3d 138 (2d Cir.1998) ("In 'trading against the box,' the customer posts as collateral shares he owns that are identical to or convertible into those being sold short").

7. Bissell v. Merrill Lynch & Co., 157 F.3d 138 (2d Cir.1998); Levitin v. PaineWebber, Inc., 159 F.3d 698 (2d Cir.1998).

8. Bissell v. Merrill Lynch & Co., 157 F.3d 138 (2d Cir.1998).

9. 15 U.S.C.A. § 78p(c). *See* § 13.5 *supra.*

10. Vucinich v. Paine, Webber, Jackson & Curtis, Inc., 803 F.2d 454 (9th Cir.1986).

Short selling has the potential to be manipulative and can be used as part of a scheme to manipulate the market. However, short selling by itself is not manipulative.[13] The fact that there is a large amount of short selling that necessarily has the effect of depressing a stock's price does not make the short sales manipulative.[14] As discussed elsewhere in this treatise,[15] the key question in any manipulation case is not whether the activity in fact affected the price of the stock but whether the activity was entered into for the purpose of affecting the price.

The SEC, which has regulated short sales since 1938,[16] adopted rules governing short sales in general. Formerly short sales were regulated by Rule 10a–1 and former Rule 10a–2. In 2004, the SEC adopted Regulation SHO,[17] which amended Rule 10a–1[18] and repealed Rule 10b–2,[19] incorporating their terms into the more comprehensive short sale regulations. Regulation SHO and Rule 10a–1 combine to provide a quite complex and technical regulation of short sales.

Rule 10a–1 applies to short sale transactions with regard to securities on a national securities exchange and requires that a short sale not be entered below the last sales price.[20] Furthermore, the short sale cannot be at the last sale price "unless such price is above the next preceding different price."[21] Thus, except for certain narrow exceptions, short sales cannot be executed on a minus tick based on the immediately preceding sale price, or if the most recent price was the same, the previous immediately proceeding sale price.[22]

Regulation SHO, which supplements Rule 10a–1 in regulating short sales, defines ownership of securities, specifies aggregation of long and short positions, and requires broker-dealers to identify sales in all equity securities "long," "short," or "short exempt."[34] Regulation SHO also includes a temporary rule embodying a pilot program which establishes procedures for the SEC to temporarily suspend operation of the current "tick" test, as well as any

---

13.   *See* GFL Advantage Fund, Ltd. v. Colkitt, 272 F.3d 189, 207–210 (3d Cir.2001); Sullivan & Long, Inc. v. Scattered Corp., 47 F.3d 857, 864 (7th Cir.1995).

14.   GFL Advantage Fund, Ltd. v. Colkitt, 272 F.3d 189, 209 (3d Cir.2001).

15.   *See* § 12.1 *supra*.

16.   *See* Sec.Exch.Act Rel. No. 34–1548 (Feb. 8, 1938).

17.   17 C.F.R. § 242.200–242.203, adopted in Short Sales, *See, e.g.,* Short Sales, Sec. Exch. Act Rel. No. 34–50103, 2004 WL 1697019 (SEC 2004).

18.   17 C.F.R. § 240.10a–1.

19.   17 C.F.R. § 230.10a–2 (repealed 2004), replaced by Rule 203 of Regulation SHO. 17 C.F.R. § 242.203.

20.   17 C.F.R. § 240.10a–1(a)(1)(i)(A). Specifically, the rule prohibits transactions below that previous price (as reported per an effective transaction reporting plan under Rule 11Aa3–1). For an interpretive release *see* Sec.Exch.Act Rel. No. 34–1571 (Feb. 5, 1938).

21.   17 C.F.R. § 240.10a–1(a)(1)(i)(B). As explained by Professor Loss, "after sales at 49⅞ and 50 an indefinite number of short sales may be effected at 50; but after sales at 49⅞ and 49¾ the minimum price at which a short sale may be effected is 49⅞." Louis Loss, Fundamentals of Securities Regulation 716 (1983).

22.   *See* In the Matter of Andover, Release No. 47228, Release No. 34–47228, 79 S.E.C. Docket 1183, 2003 WL 147555 (SEC Release No., Jan 22, 2003) (NO. 3–11013) ("A minus tick refers to a price below the immediately preceding sale price. A zero-minus tick refers to a price which is the same as the immediately preceding sale price, but which is less than the most immediate different preceding sale price.") (order instituting cease and desist proceedings).

34.   *See* Short Sales, Sec. Exch. Act Rel. No. 34–50103, 2004 WL 1697019 (SEC 2004) (adoption of Regulation SHO).

short sale price test of any exchange or the NASD.[35] Regulation SHO provides further that short sellers of equity securities must locate securities to borrow before selling.[36]

When it adopted Regulation SHO, the SEC replaced former Rule 3b-3's[38] short sale definition with Rule 200.[39] Among other things, Rule 200 requires broker dealers to identify sell orders in all equity securities as "long," "short," or "short exempt."[40]

Rule 203(a) relates to delivery requirements applicable with respect to long sales of securities.[47] Among other things, Rule 203(a) requires that if a broker-dealer knows or should know that a sale of an equity security is marked long, the broker-dealer must make delivery when due and cannot use borrowed securities to do so.

Short selling prior to or in connection with a distribution can make it difficult for issuers to complete public offerings. Short sales in anticipation of a public offering do not involve the same market risks as short sales generally.[59] Since the pending offering will bring additional supply into the market, there will be downward price pressure. Such guaranteed downward price pressure is not ordinarily present in the securities markets. Limiting short sales during distributions necessarily has an adverse impact on short sellers. Notwithstanding the arguments to the contrary, the Commission concluded that this is justified in light of the potential for manipulation resulting from short sales in connection with public offerings.[60]

Under Rule 105 of Regulation M[78] there is a period following the effective date during which short sales of securities made prior to the effective date may not be covered with securities issued in a cash offering that have been acquired from an underwriter or dealer participating in the offering. The rule's prohibition applies to short sales made during the shorter of two periods: (a) the period beginning five days before the pricing of the offering and ending when the offering is priced[79] or (b) the period beginning with the initial filing of the registration statement of Regulation A's Form 1–A and ending with the pricing of the offering.[80] Securities issued pursuant to a shelf registration under 1933 Act Rule 415[81] or otherwise not offered under a firm commitment underwriting agreement, are excluded from Rule's 105's purview.[82] In addition to the foregoing exemption, either upon request or upon its

---

35.   *See id.*

36.   *See id.*

38.   17 C.F.R. § 240.3b–3 (repealed 2004).

39.   17 C.F.R. § 242.200. *See* Short Sales, Sec. Exch. Act Rel. No. 34–50103, 2004 WL 1697019 (SEC 2004) (adoption of Regulation SHO).

40.   17 C.F.R. § 242.200(g).

47.   17 C.F.R. § 242.203(a).

59.   *See, e.g.,* Sec.Act Rel. No. 33–6798, Sec.Exch.Act Rel. No. 34–26028, [1988–1989 Transfer Binder] Fed.Sec.L.Rep. (CCH) ¶ 84,315 (SEC Aug. 25, 1988).

60.   *Id.* at p. 89,390.

78.   17 C.F.R. § 242.105. *See* Anti-manipulation Rules Concerning Securities Offerings, Sec. Rel. Nos. 33–7375; 34–38076; IC–22412 (Dec. 20, 1996), 62 Fed. Reg. 520 (1997). [See main volume]. The rest of Regulation M is discussed in § 6.1 *supra.*

79.   Rule 105(a)(1), 17 C.F.R. § 242.105(a)(1).

80.   Rule 105(a)(1), 17 C.F.R. § 242.105(a)(1).

81.   17 C.F.R. § 230.415 which is discussed in § 3.8 *supra.*

82.   Rule 105(b), 17 C.F.R. § 242.105(b).

own initiative, the Commission may grant an exemption from Rule 105.[83] This general exemptive authority may be invoked with or without specified terms and conditions.[84]

§ 14.23 Parking

A practice that is clearly deceptive and also can be manipulative is known as "parking." Parking occurs when an investor or broker transfers his or her securities to a third party for the purpose of hiding the true ownership.[1] The SEC has described parking as "the sale of securities subject to an agreement or understanding that the securities will be repurchased by the seller at a later time and at a price which leaves the economic risk on the seller."[2] When this type of transfer occurs, it clearly qualifies as deceptive within the meaning of section 10(b) of the 1934 Act.[3] Parking is a "sham" transaction[4] and thus in addition to constituting deceptive conduct is also properly characterized as manipulation.[5]

Usually, the critical issue in a parking case is establishing whether the arrangements relating to the transactions in question involve bona fide purchases and sales, or, instead, are sham transactions designed to conceal true ownership.

§ 14.24 Broker–Dealer Bankruptcy—The Securities Investor Protection Act

During the 1960s, a large number of brokerage firms experienced various types of severe financial problems, including insolvency. Since many investors allow their securities to be held by their brokers in "street name,"[1] the broker's insolvency creates a substantial risk of harm in addition to that resulting from the broker-dealer's inability to honor or follow through with customer orders. Congress responded to these risks with the Securities Investor Protection Act of 1970.[2] The Act established the Securities Investor Protection Corporation (SIPC), a nonprofit corporation whose membership is made up of most broker-dealers registered under the 1934 Exchange Act.

The Securities Investor Protection Corporation, which operates under SEC supervision,[5] has two primary functions. First, SIPC is responsible for

---

83. Rule 105(c), 17 C.F.R. § 242.105(c).

84. *Id.*

§ 14.23

1. Yoshikawa v. SEC, 192 F.3d 1209 (9th Cir.1999); SIPC v. Vigman, 74 F.3d 932, 933 n. 3 (9th Cir.1996); United States v. Jones, 900 F.2d 512, 515 (2d Cir.1990).

2. In re Barlage, 63 S.E.C. 1060, 1996 WL 733756 at *1 n. 2 (SEC 1996). *See also, e.g.,* In re Hibbard & O'Connor Securities, Inc., 46 S.E.C. 328, 1976 WL 20109 at *2 (SEC 1976).

3. 15 U.S.C.A. § 78j(b). *See, e.g.,* United States v. Russo, 74 F.3d 1383 (2d Cir.1996).

4. In re Cotzin, 45 S.E.C. 575, 1974 WL 11424 at *2 (SEC 1974); In re Capital Securities Co., 43 S.E.C. 758, 1968 WL 3996 at *2 (SEC 1968) ("not in fact bona fide purchases").

5. *See* § 12.1 *supra* for discussion of manipulation. *See also* § 6.1 *supra* for discussion of manipulation in the context of public offerings.

§ 14.24

1. *See* SEC, Street Name Study; § 10.10 *supra.*

2. 15 U.S.C.A. §§ 78aaa–78*lll.*

5. 15 U.S.C.A. §§ 78ccc(a)(2)(B), 78ggg.

establishing and maintaining a fund for the benefit of injured investors.[6] The SIPC fund is designed to protect customer claims for both cash and securities that are lost due to a brokerage firm's insolvency.[7]

In many respects, SIPC is similar in nature to the Federal Deposit Insurance Corporation (FDIC), which protects depositors in commercial banks,[8] and formerly the Federal Savings and Loan Insurance Corporation (FSLIC), the counterpart for depositors in savings and loan associations.[9] Second, the SIPC becomes a party to proceedings to liquidate insolvent brokerage firms,[10] which are conducted in a manner similar to that provided under the federal bankruptcy laws,[11] including the appointment of a trustee.[12] Unlike the federal bankruptcy laws, however, there is no provision under the Securities Investor Protection Act for reorganization as an alternative to liquidation.[13] SIPC may bring suit against third parties on behalf of the customers of the insolvent brokerage firm.[14] SIPC's standing to bring suit exists notwithstanding the statute's failure to expressly list the authority to sue, since bringing a suit for damages falls within SIPC's authority to pursue the insolvent brokerage firm's revenue in the ordinary course of business.[15]

The SIPC fund is maintained by both initial and periodic assessment of the members.[16] The fund is available to provide cash advances to injured customers who have valid claims[17] against the insolvent broker-dealer in the liquidation proceedings.[18] Any such advance is limited to five hundred thousand dollars per customer, but is not to exceed one hundred thousand dollars if the customer has a claim only for cash as opposed to a claim for securities.[19] SIPC may also, in its discretion, advance to the trustee for the liquidation proceedings funds (1) to pay or guarantee indebtedness to a bank or other lender,[20] (2) to secure indemnification of SIPC members against cash short-

---

6. 15 U.S.C.A. § 78ddd. *See* 15 U.S.C.A. §§ 78fff–3, 78fff–4.

7. *See, e.g.*, In re New York Times Securities Services, Inc., 371 F.3d 68 (2d Cir. 2004).

8. *See* SEC v. Albert & Maguire Securities Co., 560 F.2d 569 (3d Cir.1977).

9. The Federal Deposit Insurance Corporation (FDIC) was created by the Banking Act of 1933, Act of June 16, 1933, ch. 89, § 8, 48 Stat. 168, which is now the Federal Deposit Insurance Act, codified as amended at 12 U.S.C.A. §§ 1811–1832.

10. 15 U.S.C.A. § 78eee(d).

11. 15 U.S.C.A. §§ 78fff–1—78fff–2. *See* Redington v. Touche Ross & Co., 612 F.2d 68 (2d Cir.1979).

12. 15 U.S.C.A. § 78eee(b)(3). The trustee has the same powers and title and the same rights to avoid preferences as a trustee in bankruptcy. 15 U.S.C.A. § 78fff–1(a). *See* Securities Investor Protection Corp. v. Christian–Paine & Co., 755 F.2d 359 (3d Cir.1985) (SIPA trustee has powers similar to a trustee in bankruptcy); SIPC v. Poirier, 653 F.Supp. 63 (D.Or.1986) (semble). Thus, for example, SIPC can bring securities fraud claims as subrogee of customers' claims. SIPC v. Vigman, 803 F.2d 1513 (9th Cir.1986).

13. *See* SEC v. Securities Northwest, Inc., 573 F.2d 622 (9th Cir.1978).

14. *See, e.g.*, SIPC v. BDO Seidman, 222 F.3d 63, 68–69 (2d Cir. 2000).

15. SIPC v. BDO Seidman, 232 F.3d 63, 69–70 (2d Cir. 2000); 15 U.S.C.A. § 78ddd.

16. 15 U.S.C.A. § 78ddd(c).

17. A SIPA claim requires that the customer be able to identify cash or property held in an account by the insolvent broker-dealer in order to recover. *See, e.g.*, In re MJK Clearing, Inc., 371 F.3d 397 (8th Cir. 2004) (failure to establish SIPA claim).

18. 15 U.S.C.A. § 78fff–3.

19. 15 U.S.C.A. § 78fff–3(a)(1).

20. 15 U.S.C.A. § 78fff–3(c)(1). *See* 15 U.S.C.A. § 78fff–1(b)(2).

ages,[21] and (3) to purchase securities for the satisfaction of customer claims against the insolvent broker-dealers.[22]

The protection of the Securities Investor Protection Act is generally reserved for customers of broker-dealers. Not every transaction effected through a securities broker that may happen to involve securities will classify someone delivering securities to a broker-dealer as a customer with regard to the transaction in question.[24]

§ 14.25 Private Remedies Against Exchanges and the NASD for Damages Resulting From Nonenforcement of Their Own Rules

On occasion, a self regulatory organization will fail to enforce its own rules. In such situations can the self regulatory organization be held accountable for losses resulting from the failure to enforce?[1] The case law under the Exchange Act is relatively sparse, although there is some authority for the existence of a private remedy in appropriate cases to redress nonenforcement of securities exchange's customer protection[2] rules. Analogies can be made to the more substantial body of law that recognized a private remedy against commodity exchanges for enforcement lapses.[3] The federal regulatory patterns which govern the securities and commodities industries have obvious parallels. It follows that the decisions recognizing a right of action under the Commodity Exchange Act may add support to the existence of a comparable remedy under the Exchange Act. The courts have been in conflict as to the existence of an implied remedy against exchanges under the Exchange Act.[4] The Third Circuit in Walck v. American Stock Exchange, Inc.,[12] denied the existence of an implied right of action against a securities exchange.[13]

The Eighth Circuit has held that a mere negligent failure to supervise its members will not support a private suit against the NASD.[30] It has also been

21. 15 U.S.C.A. § 78fff–3(c)(2). *See* 15 U.S.C.A. § 78fff–2(f).

22. 15 U.S.C.A. § 78fff–3(c)(3). *See* 15 U.S.C.A. § 78fff–2(d).

24. *See, e.g.,* In re Stalvey & Associates, Inc., 750 F.2d 464 (5th Cir.1985).

§ 14.25

1. *See, e.g.,* Charles E. Dropkin, National Securities Exchange Liability to Public Investors: Time to Overcome Inertia?, 56 Notre Dame Law. 419 (1981).

2. Any such private right of action should necessarily be limited to customer protection. Exchange "housekeeping" rules do not relate directly to the Exchange Act's primary focus and goal-investor protection. *See, e.g.,* Kakar v. Chicago Board Options Exchange, Inc., 681 F.Supp. 1039 (S.D.N.Y.1988); Geyer v. Paine, Webber, Jackson & Curtis, Inc., 389 F.Supp. 678, 683 (D.Wyo.1975). Cf. Birotte v. Merrill Lynch, Pierce, Fenner & Smith, Inc., 468 F.Supp. 1172 (D.N.J.1979) (no cause of action against broker for violation of housekeeping rules).

3. *See generally* 3 Philip McBride Johnson & Thomas Lee Hazen, Derivatives Regulation (2004).

4. *See, e.g.,* Raymond James & Associates v. National Association of Securities Dealers, 844 F.Supp. 1504 (M.D.Fla.1994) (dictum recognizing implied remedy).

12. 687 F.2d 778 (3d Cir.1982), *cert. denied* 461 U.S. 942, 103 S.Ct. 2118, 77 L.Ed.2d 1300 (1983). *See also, e.g.,* Lenowitz v. Philadelphia Stock Exchange, 502 F.Supp. 428 (E.D.Pa.1980) (denying implied right of action to exchange member claiming damages as a result of exchange's enforcement lapse).

13. *See also, e.g.,* Ferreri v. Mainardi, 690 F.Supp. 411 (E.D.Pa.1988) (no implied remedy against exchange for failure to enforce its own rules).

30. FDIC v. National Association of Securities Dealers, 747 F.2d 498 (8th Cir.1984). *See also, e.g.,* Honn v. NASD, 182 F.3d 1014 (8th Cir.1999) (upholding NASD's arbitral immunity); Hawkins v. NASD, 149 F.3d 330 (5th Cir.1998) (NASD protected by arbitral immunity against claim that arbitration proceeding was biased); Olson v. NASD, 85 F.3d 381 (8th Cir.1996) (arbitral immunity protects NASD from claim that it appointed a biased arbitrator); Barton v. Horowitz, 31 Sec. Reg. & L. Rep. (BNA) 462 (D. Colo. 1999).

held that an action will not lie against the NASD for an alleged wrongful refusal to enforce its own rules.[33] As is the case with the exchanges, the NASD enjoys immunity with regard to challenges to the exercise of it oversight responsibility.[34]

§ 14.26   Private Remedies Against Market Professionals; Secondary Liability

Broker-dealers, like anyone else, can be subject to liability for a violation, Rule 10b–5's general antifraud provisions.[1] Rule 10b–5 and the general antifraud provisions are discussed in chapter 12 of this treatise. It is significant that the Supreme Court has taken a broad view of Rule 10b–5's requirement that for the rule to apply the fraud be in connection with the purchase or sale of a security.[2] The fraud does not have to occur with respect to a particular securities transaction, but can involve a course of conduct relating to securities transactions generally.[3] Since by definition broker-dealers' contact with their customers generally relates to securities transactions, the securities antifraud provisions are likely to be implicated.[4]

As for violations of exchange or NASD rules, it is generally held that violation of a rule of a self regulatory organization will not, by itself, support a private right of action.[28] However, a violation of an exchange or NASD rule can form the basis of a 10b–5 action, provided, of course, that all of the elements of a 10b–5 claim can be established. Thus, for example, it is well established that a broker-dealer who churns a customer's account can be held accountable for damages under Rule 10b–5.[30] Broker-dealers may, of course, be held liable under Rule 10b–5 for material misstatements or omissions in connection with their customers' purchases and sales of securities.[31]

In addition to the duty to supervise that exists under agency principles, the securities laws and the rules of the self regulatory organizations impose upon broker-dealers a duty to supervise their employees.[104] Although this

---

33. Raymond James & Associates v. National Association of Securities Dealers, 844 F.Supp. 1504 (M.D.Fla.1994) (dictum recognizing implied remedy) (no implied remedy under section 19 even though one may exist against exchanges under section 6(b)).

34. Sparta Sugical Corp. v. NASD, 159 F.3d 1209 (9th Cir.1998).

§ 14.26

1. 17 C.F.R. § 240.10b–5. *See* chapter 12, §§ 14.15–14.21 *supra.*

2. SEC v. Zandford, 535 U.S. 813, 122 S.Ct. 1899, 153 L.Ed.2d 1 (2002), reversing 238 F.3d 559 (4th Cir 2001) (which had held that a broker's conversion of a customer's funds was not fraud "in connection with" a securities transaction and thus not subject to rule 10b–5). The in connection with requirement is discussed in § 12.5[1] *supra.*

3. SEC v. Zandford, 535 U.S. 813, 122 S.Ct. 1899, 153 L.Ed.2d 1 (2002); *See also, e.g.,* United States v. O'Hagan, 521 U.S. 642, 117 S.Ct. 2199, 138 L.Ed.2d 724 (1997) (the "in connection with" requirement does not require that the fraud be linked to identifiable purchasers or sellers of securities).

4. SEC v. Zandford, 535 U.S. 813, 122 S.Ct. 1899, 153 L.Ed.2d 1 (2002).

28. *See, e.g.,* Spicer v. Chicago Board Options Exchange, Inc., 977 F.2d 255 (7th Cir.1992).

30. *See* cases collected in § 14.20 *supra.*

31. Liability under Rule 10b–5 is discussed in §§ 12.2–12.12 *supra. See, e.g.,* Filloramo v. Johnston, Lemon & Co., 697 F.Supp. 517 (D.D.C.1988).

104. *See, e.g.,* Gliksman, Complaint No. C02960039, 1999 WL 515762 (N.A.S.D.R. March 31, 1999) (NASD sanctions imposed for failure to supervise registered representative who committed suitability violations); In the Matter of Stevens, Complaint No. C3A960009, 1998 WL 1735133 (N.A.S.D.R. June 10, 1998) (failure to supervise with regard to suitability obligations).

provides the basis for administrative sanctions[106] and does not extend expressly to private litigation, a failure to supervise can be the basis of controlling person liability.[107] In a 1992 SEC administrative action, the Commission set forth some helpful guidelines for establishing a sufficient supervision system.[108] In addition to the consequences under federal law, inadequate supervision of brokerage employees can result in violation of state law.[109]

If a brokerage firm's employees in supervisory positions are put on inquiry notice that an employee may be acting improperly, the supervisor must see that the matter is investigated promptly and then take steps to follow up on the investigation. If the supervisor does not initiate his or her own investigation, he or she must direct someone else to investigate. It, thus, is not sufficient to rely simply on the employee's representations that no misconduct took place. The investigation should determine whether the conduct in fact occurred and whether there have been similar occurrences.

In the event that multiple supervisors may be involved, it is important to promptly and clearly define the responsibility of each of the supervisors in responding to the suspected wrongdoing. Again, it will be necessary to follow up in order to assure that appropriate investigatory and preventive measures have been taken. Additionally, simply reporting the suspected misconduct to a higher supervisor will not be sufficient unless the supervisor's superiors instruct him or her not to take any action. The Commission explained that appropriate supervisory action should be taken even after the matter is reported.

Instituting the investigation does not end the supervisor's responsibilities. Prompt action should be taken to prevent repetition of the suspected misconduct. This would include increased supervision of the suspected employee. Thus, it is not sufficient simply to tell the employee that the matter is under investigation and that his or her career may be in jeopardy.

The duty to supervise is not satisfied by the supervisor's merely relying on a trader's experience.[110] The presence of "red flags" imposes on the supervisor a duty to make an affirmative inquiry or investigation.[111] Thus, someone in a supervisory position cannot simply ignore or disregard "red flags" or "suggestions of irregularities"; instead, the supervisor must "act decisively to detect and prevent" improper activity.[112]

---

106. *See, e.g.,* Patrick v. SEC, 19 F.3d 66 (2d Cir.1994) (brokerage firm's president held responsible for failing to supervise trader); SEC v. Yu, 231 F.Supp.2d 16 (D.D.C. 2002) (preliminary injunction against brokerage firm president's flagrant violations of supervisory bar).

107. *See, e.g.,* Jairett v. First Montauk Securities Corp., 153 F.Supp.2d 562, 572–573 (E.D.Pa. 2001). Controlling person liability is discussed in §§ 12.24, 14.26[6][A] *supra.*

108. In the Matter of Gutfreund, Exch.Act Rel. No. 34–31554 (Dec. 3, 1992).

109. *See, e.g.,* New York v. Justin, 237 F.Supp.2d 368 (W.D.N.Y. 2002) (federal law does not preempt state's ability to prosecute securities broker for improper supervision of registered sales representative).

110. *See, e.g.,* In the Matter of Grady, Sec. Exch. Act Rel. No. 34–41309, 69 S.E.C. Docket 1392, 1999 WL 222640 (SEC Apr. 19, 1999).

111. *Id.*

112. *E.g.,* In the Matter of Grady, Sec. Exch. Act Rel. No. 34–41309, 69 S.E.C. Docket 1392, 1999 WL 222640 (SEC Apr. 19, 1999).

Chapter 15

ARBITRATION OF BROKER–DEALER DISPUTES

Table of Sections

---

§ 15.1 The Enforceability of Arbitration Agreements in Federal and State Securities Cases

§ 15.1[1] Enforcement of Broker–Dealer Arbitration Agreements

At one time, predispute arbitration agreements were unenforceable with regard to claims arising under the federal securities laws. This meant that virtually all claims by customers against their securities brokers were resolved in court or by settlement. In subsequent years there was a major reversal of this earlier situation. As a result of this major shift of position by the Supreme Court,[1] most brokerage firms routinely require customers to sign predispute arbitration agreements. Accordingly, most disputes between customers[2] and their brokers now are decided in arbitral forums rather than in court.[3] One consequence of this shift has been that much of the law relating to broker-dealer litigation has been placed in a state of suspended animation as it existed in the pre-arbitration era. This is the case because of the relatively few private disputes that will continue to be litigated in court and the narrow standard of judicial review of arbitrators' decisions.

---

§ 15.1

1. *See* Rodriguez de Quijas v. Shearson/American Express, 490 U.S. 477, 109 S.Ct. 1917, 104 L.Ed.2d 526 (1989); Shearson/American Express, Inc. v. McMahon, 482 U.S. 220, 107 S.Ct. 2332, 96 L.Ed.2d 185 (1987).

2. The category of customers is a broad one. Thus, for example, conducting trades through a broker is sufficient to establish a customer relationship even if no account was ever formally opened. *See,* Vestax Securities Corp. v. McWood, 280 F.3d 1078 (6th Cir. 2002), *affirming* Vestax Securities Corp. v. Skillman, 32 Sec. Reg. & L. Rep. (BNA) 1291 (N.D. Ohio 2000).

Although expansive, the definition of customer is not all-inclusive. Thus, for example, under NASD rules an entity that was owed funds in connection with investment advice rendered to a brokerage firm is not a customer so as to fall within the NASD's arbitration program. Fleet Boston Robertson Stephens, Inc. v. Innovex, Inc., 264 F.3d 770 (8th Cir.2001).

3. The arbitration agreement typically applies to transactions arising out of the brokerage relationship even if those transactions do not involve securities. Financial Network Investment Corp. v. Becker, 305 A.D.2d 187, 762 N.Y.S.2d 25 (2003), *affirming* 191 Misc.2d 297, 741 N.Y.S.2d 837 (2002).

§ 15.1[1][A] The Rise of the *Wilko* Doctrine

In Wilko v. Swan,[5] the Supreme Court held that a court could not compel arbitration of claims asserted under section 12(a)(2)[6] of the Securities Act of 1933, despite the existence of an arbitration agreement between the plaintiff and the defendant broker. The court relied on the language of section 14 of the 1933 Act which states that: "Any condition, stipulation or provision binding any person acquiring any security to waive compliance with any provision of this subchapter or of the rules and regulations of the Commission shall be void."[7] Thus, agreements to arbitrate securities law claims were held void as stipulations requiring the waiver of judicial trial and review. Because Congress specifically granted persons asserting federal securities claims the right to bring suit in federal court, the Court decided that the intention of Congress would be best effectuated by invalidating arbitration agreements with respect to Securities Act claims.[8] Following *Wilko,* courts at first were consistent in holding that agreements to arbitrate claims arising under the Securities Exchange Act of 1934 were equally invalid, because the 1934 Act contains an anti-waiver provision[9] almost identical to the one found in the 1933 Act.[10]

§ 15.1[1][B] The Decline of the *Wilko* Doctrine

In a number of decisions, it was held that a Supreme Court ruling upholding the arbitrability of pendent state claims[13] brought into question the vitality of *Wilko* and, accordingly, the federal securities claims often were submitted to arbitration along with the state claims.[14] One basis for such rulings was that as implied rights of action, Rule 10b–5 claims do not incorporate the "special right" that the Court found to be present with regard to the 1933 Act claims involved in *Wilko.* These decisions took their lead from Justice White's concurrence in Dean Witter Reynolds, Inc. v. Byrd.[15] Although a great number of decisions seem to have followed Justice White's suggestion, a split developed and many cases continued to adhere to the view that 1934 Act claims are not arbitrable.[16] The Supreme Court has now made it clear that claims subject to a predispute arbitration agreement arising under Rule 10b–5 are arbitrable.[17]

The Court in Shearson/American Express, Inc. v. McMahon pointed out that the basis of the *Wilko* decision was the belief that arbitration did not

---

5. 346 U.S. 427, 74 S.Ct. 182, 98 L.Ed. 168 (1953).

6. 15 U.S.C.A. § 77*l*(a)(2) (prohibits false representations made to induce a securities sale). Section 12(a)(2) is discussed in § 7.6 *supra.* At the time of the *Wilko* decision, the section was numbered 12(1), 15 U.S.C.A. § 77*l*(2) (1952).

7. 15 U.S.C.A. § 77n.

8. 346 U.S. 427, 438, 74 S.Ct. 182, 188, 189, 98 L.Ed. 168 (1953).

9. 15 U.S.C.A. § 78cc(a).

10. Sibley v. Tandy Corp., 543 F.2d 540, 543 (5th Cir.1976), *cert. denied* 434 U.S. 824, 98 S.Ct. 71, 54 L.Ed.2d 82 (1977).

13. Dean Witter Reynolds, Inc. v. Byrd, 470 U.S. 213, 105 S.Ct. 1238, 84 L.Ed.2d 158 (1985).

14. *E.g.* Phillips v. Merrill Lynch, Pierce, Fenner & Smith, Inc., 795 F.2d 1393 (8th Cir.1986).

15. 470 U.S. 213, 224, 105 S.Ct. 1238, 1244, 84 L.Ed.2d 158 (1985), *on remand* 760 F.2d 238 (9th Cir.1985).

16. *E.g.* Jacobson v. Merrill Lynch, Pierce, Fenner & Smith, Inc., 797 F.2d 1197 (3d Cir.1986), *cert. granted and judgment vacated* 482 U.S. 923, 107 S.Ct. 3204, 96 L.Ed.2d 691 (1987).

17. Shearson/American Express, Inc. v. McMahon, 482 U.S. 220, 107 S.Ct. 2332, 96 L.Ed.2d 185 (1987).

adequately safeguard the parties' interest, thus implicating the anti-waiver provisions. However, as commercial arbitration has become more widely accepted, the procedures are now viewed more favorably than before. Additionally the major exchanges and the NASD have arbitration rules that are subject to SEC oversight.[20] Accordingly, the premise of *Wilko* became highly suspect, at least with regard to predispute arbitration agreements between brokers and customers. Although the *McMahon* ruling is limited to implied remedies of the Exchange Act, there is strong dictum that seemed to signal *Wilko's* demise. A number of later decisions held 1933 Act claims (as well as other Exchange Act claims) to be arbitrable and the Supreme Court agreed.[21] The Supreme Court explicitly overruled *Wilko* in Rodriguez de Quijas v. Shearson/American Express, Inc.[22]

As the decline of *Wilco* was complete, it became apparent that courts will give a broad interpretation to the scope of arbitration agreements.[26]

§ 15.1[2] The Federal Arbitration Act: Policies Favoring Arbitration

The Federal Arbitration Act[28] embodies a strong public policy favoring arbitration.[29] There are limits, however, to the Act's impact. For example, the Federal Arbitration Act does not create a basis for federal jurisdiction independent of that which might be available under the federal securities laws.[30] Similarly, although the Federal Arbitration Act applies to claims involving interstate commerce, it does not apply to a transaction which is wholly intrastate.[31] On the other hand, when the jurisdictional reach of the Federal Arbitration Act is implicated, that act may preempt the applicable state law.[32]

§ 15.1[8] Waiver of Right to Arbitrate

Resort to the courts can be viewed, on appropriate facts, as a waiver of the right to have the dispute resolved by arbitration,[93] but participation in pretrial discovery has been held not to act as a waiver of the arbitration agreement.[94] Similarly, participation in an arbitration does not in and of itself

20. American Stock Exch. Guide (CCH) ¶¶ 9540–575; NASD Manual (CCH); N.Y.Stock Exch. Guide ¶¶ 4311–17. *See, e.g.,* The Practitioner's Edition of this Treatise.

21. Rodriguez De Quijas v. Shearson/Lehman Brothers, Inc., 845 F.2d 1296 (5th Cir.1988) (section 12(2) claim held arbitrable), *affirmed* 490 U.S. 477, 109 S.Ct. 1917, 104 L.Ed.2d 526 (1989).

22. 490 U.S. 477, 109 S.Ct. 1917, 104 L.Ed.2d 526 (1989).

26. *See, e.g.,* Daugherty v. Washington Square Securities, Inc., 271 F.Supp.2d 681 (W.D. Pa. 2003) (dispute involving investment sold by broker-dealer was subject to arbitration even if investments were not "securities").

28. 9 U.S.C.A. §§ 1 *et seq.*

29. *See, e.g.*, Boss v. Salomon Smith Barney Inc., 263 F.Supp.2d 684 (S.D.N.Y. 2003).

30. Baltin v. Alaron Trading Corp., 128 F.3d 1466 (11th Cir.1997).

31. Ex parte Jones, 628 So.2d 316 (Ala.1993).

32. Olde Discount Corp. v. Tupman, 1 F.3d 202 (3d Cir.1993) (Federal Arbitration Act may preclude state action seeking rescission pending outcome of arbitration).

93. *E.g.*, Hoxworth v. Blinder, Robinson & Co., 980 F.2d 912 (3d Cir.1992) (active litigation for over a year, including extensive pretrial discovery and lengthy memorandum opposing class certification operated as a waiver of arbitration agreement).

94. PaineWebber Inc. v. Faragalli, 61 F.3d 1063 (3d Cir.1995).

waive any objections to the proceedings, especially where the participation consists of motions objecting to continuation.[95] Failure to object to litigation and delay in making a motion to compel arbitration can result in a waiver of the right to arbitrate.[96] A party asserting that the right to arbitrate has been waived has a "heavy" burden of proof.[97]

§ 15.1[9] Other Factors Affecting Enforcement of Predispute Arbitration Agreements[102]

Section 2 of the Federal Arbitration Act provides that arbitration agreements can be invalidated upon such grounds as exist at law or equity for the invalidity of any contract.[103] Thus, a court cannot compel arbitration unless there is a valid contractual obligation.[104] Brokerage customers frequently seek to avoid predispute arbitration agreements by claiming that the arbitration clause is an invalid contract of adhesion.[105] It is generally held that if the claims of invalidity go to the contract as a whole, they should be resolved by the arbitrator.[107]

The contract interpretation issues will generally be determined under state law, keeping in mind the federal policy favoring arbitration. However, rules of the self regulatory organizations may also affect the validity of arbitration clauses. Accordingly, failure to comply with the NASD and New York Stock Exchange disclosure obligations, including the requirement that any agreement containing an arbitration clause be specifically acknowledged by the customer,[112] can result in the invalidity, and hence unenforceability, of the arbitration agreement.[113]

The essence of the adhesion contract claim is that the use of arbitration clauses is an industry-wide practice and that it is unfair to force them upon customers. However, the majority of courts have held that there is nothing inherently unfair about arbitration clauses[115] and thus the clause does not place the customer in an unfair position.[116] Arbitration clauses have been upheld even when appearing on the reverse side of the brokerage agreement.[117]

---

95. *See* Prudential Securities Inc. v. Hornsby, 865 F.Supp. 447 (N.D.Ill.1994).

96. *See, e.g.,* Hales v. ProEquities, Inc., 2003 WL 21569859 (Ala. 2003).

97. *See, e.g.,* Britton v. Co–op. Banking Group, 916 F.2d 1405 (9th Cir.1990).

102. For further discussion of these issues *see* § 15.2 of the Practitioner's Edition.

103. 9 U.S.C.A. § 2.

104. *See, e.g.,* Jolley v. Welch, 904 F.2d 988 (5th Cir.1990), *cert. denied* 498 U.S. 1050, 111 S.Ct. 762, 112 L.Ed.2d 781 (1991).

105. *See* Kenneth R. Davis, The Arbitration Claws: Unconscionability in the Securities Industry, 78 B.U. L. Rev. 255 (1998).

107. *See, e.g.,* Houlihan v. Offerman & Co., 31 F.3d 692 (8th Cir.1994); Bhatia v. Johnston, 818 F.2d 418 (5th Cir.1987); Benoay v. Prudential–Bache Securities, Inc., 805 F.2d 1437 (11th Cir.1986).

112. NASD Rules of Fair Practice, Art. III, § 21; NYSE Rule 637.

113. *See* Mueske v. Piper, Jaffray & Hopwood, Inc., 260 Mont. 207, 859 P.2d 444 (1993).

115. *See, e.g.,* Coleman v. Prudential Bache Securities, Inc., 802 F.2d 1350 (11th Cir.1986).

116. *See, e.g.,* Shotto v. Laub, 632 F.Supp. 516 (D.Md.1986).

117. *See* Speck v. Oppenheimer & Co., Inc., 583 F.Supp. 325 (W.D.Mo.1984). In 1989, the SEC approved new arbitration rules which provide that prominence should be given to predispute arbitration agreements. *See* Sec.Exch.Act Rel. No. 34–26805 (May 16, 1989).

§ 15.1[10] Judicial Review of Arbitration Decisions[122]

Arbitration decisions under the federal securities laws are reviewable by federal district courts.[123] In addition to the statutory grounds of corruption, fraud, and evident partiality,[124] arbitration decisions are subject to the judicially created standard of "manifest disregard of the law."[125] The arbitrators' mere misapplication of law is not enough to warrant reversal by a court.[126] A number of decisions have spoken in terms of a "clearly erroneous"[127] or "completely irrational" standard for judicial review of arbitration decisions.[128] The scope of judicial review thus is "extremely limited."[129]

---

122. For further discussion *see* § 15.10 of the Practitioner's Edition of this Treatise.

123. 9 U.S.C.A. § 9 provides that the arbitration agreement may establish the appropriate court for making the review and if no court is selected, it is the federal district court in the district where the award was made.

124. 9 U.S.C.A. § 10.

125. *E.g.,* GMS Group, LLC v. Benderson, 326 F.3d 75, 77–78 (2d Cir. 2003).

126. *See, e.g.,* Wallace v. Buttar, 378 F.3d 182 (2d Cir. 2004) (upholding punitive damage arbitration award).

127. As explained by the Supreme Court, arbitrators' findings of fact are accepted unless they were clearly erroneous; however, there is a *de novo* review on questions of law. First Options of Chicago, Inc. v. Kaplan, 514 U.S. 938, 115 S.Ct. 1920, 131 L.Ed.2d 985 (1995). The Court noted that the courts give "considerable leeway" to the decisions of arbitrators. It does not follow, however, that the appellate courts should give "extra leeway" to a lower court that upholds the arbitrator's decision. *Id.*

128. *See, e.g.,* Nordahl Development Corp. v. Salomon Smith Barney, 309 F.Supp.2d 1257 (D. Or. 2004) (upholding arbitration decision); Sidarma Societa Italiana Di Armamento Spa, Venice v. Holt Marine Industries, Inc., 515 F.Supp. 1302, 1308 (S.D.N.Y.1981).

129. Merrill Lynch, Pierce, Fenner & Smith v. Bobker, 808 F.2d 930, 934 (2d Cir.1986).

Chapter 16

OPERATION OF THE SECURITIES AND EXCHANGE COMMISSION

Table of Sections

---

§ 16.2 Civil and Criminal Enforcement: SEC Injunctions, Investigations, Parallel Proceedings; Administrative Hearings and Disciplinary Sanctions

The Securities and Exchange Commission has a panoply of administrative powers. In fact, the Commission has all administrative powers save one: the SEC does not adjudicate disputes between private parties. The Securities and Exchange Commission has a wide variety of enforcement roles under the various securities acts.[1] With regard to registration statements under the Securities Act of 1933, the Commission has the power to issue stop orders and refusal orders with regard to defective registration statements.[2] In addition, the Commission can impose disciplinary sanctions against broker-dealers registered under section 15 of the Exchange Act,[3] against municipal securities dealers pursuant to section 15B,[4] and against government securities dealers under section 15C.[5] Beyond these administrative enforcement powers, its oversight of regulatory and self-regulatory organizations,[6] and its rulemaking responsibilities,[7] the Commission is given broad investigatory and enforcement powers in the courts.

The SEC may cooperate with other parties or agencies in litigation under the securities laws. Section 21(g) of the 1934 Act prohibits the consolidation of SEC actions with any other action, even though those actions involve the same factual determinations, without the Commission's consent.[9] Since sec-

---

§ 16.2

1. The work of the SEC is discussed in § 1.4 *supra*. The commission is also discussed in the remainder of chapter 16. *See also, e.g.,* Roberta S. Karmel, Creating Law at the Securities and Exchange Commission: The Lawyer as Prosecutor, 61 Law & Contemp. Probs. 33 (Winter 1998).

2. 15 U.S.C.A. § 77h. *See* § 3.6 *supra*.

3. 15 U.S.C.A. § 78o–1. *See* § 14.3 *supra*.

4. 15 U.S.C.A. § 78o–4. *See* § 14.12 *supra*.

5. 15 U.S.C.A. § 78o–5. *See* § 14.13 *supra*.

6. *See* § 14.3 *supra*.

7. *See* §§ 1.3, 1.4 *supra*.

9. 15 U.S.C.A. § 78u(g).

tion 21(g) provides for consolidation with other actions only with the SEC's consent, it was improper for a federal court in one case to enjoin an SEC injunction suit in another federal court.[10] Third parties can move to intervene in SEC actions[11] in order to protect their interests, but this does not mean that they have a right to intervene,[12] nor do third parties have a right to enforce consent, decrees between the SEC and a violator of the Act.[13] Section 21(g) which, as mentioned above, precludes consolidations without the SEC's consent, has been held to preclude intervention without the Commission's consent.[14]

In 2001, the SEC announced a major shift in its enforcement program.[18] In order to encourage more self-policing by 1934 Act reporting companies, the SEC announced that it will proceed with leniency against companies that, after an internal investigation admit and correct past violations. The Commission announced that in deciding whether to seek punishment for violations of reporting requirements, the SEC would consider four factors. The SEC will consider: (1) whether a company has a system of internal controls that provides an effective self-policing mechanism; (2) whether the company promptly reported the violations in question; (3) the extent of the company's cooperation with law enforcement agencies; and (4) whether the company disciplined the persons responsible, improved internal control procedures, and compensated investors who were injured by the violations.[19] This increased emphasis on self-policing means that companies should seriously review their internal compliance procedures and ensure that adequate procedures and compliance personnel are in place.

§ 16.2[1] SEC Administrative Hearings

Section 15(b)(4) of the Act gives the Commission authority to sanction registered broker dealers by imposing a variety of consequences ranging from censure to revocation of registration.[25] Depending on the severity of the violations, the SEC can also place limits on the registrants' activities.[26] Section 15(b)(6)(A) of the 1934 Act grants the SEC broad administrative authority over persons associated with brokers and dealers.[27] In particular, the Commission is empowered to hold hearings and impose sanctions against associated persons of broker-dealers, ranging from censure to suspension for up to twelve months and also including bar orders.[29] The Commission can also place

---

10. Smith v. SEC, 129 F.3d 356 (6th Cir.1997).

11. *See, e.g.,* SEC v. Credit Bancorp., Ltd., 103 F.Supp.2d 223 (S.D.N.Y.2000), s.c. 124 F.Supp.2d 824 (S.D.N.Y.2000) (permitting intervention, denying interlocutory appeal).

12. *E.g.,* SEC v. Homa, [2000–2001 Transfer Binder] Fed. Sec. L. Rep. (CCH) ¶ 91,223, 2000 WL 1468726 (N.D.Ill.2000).

13. SEC v. Prudential Securities, Inc., 171 F.R.D. 1 (D.D.C.1997).

14. SEC v. Homa, [2000–2001 Transfer Binder] Fed. Sec. L. Rep. (CCH) ¶ 91,223, 2000 WL 1468726 (N.D.Ill.2000).

18. Report of Investigation Pursuant to Section 21(a) of the Securities Exchange Act of 1934 and Commission Statement of the Relationship of Cooperation to Agency Enforcement Decisions, Sec. Exch. Act Rel. No. 34–44969, 2001 WL 1301408 (SEC Oct. 23, 2001).

19. *Id.*

25. 15 U.S.C.A. § 78o(b)(4).

26. *Id.*

27. 15 U.S.C.A. § 78o(b)(6).

29. 15 U.S.C.A. § 78o(b)(6)(A).

limitations on the activities of such associated persons.[30] The Commission has similar powers with regard to investment advisers.[31] The Commission can impose similar sanctions against municipal securities dealers,[32] government securities dealers,[33] and clearing agencies.[34] In addition to the power to impose these administrative sanctions, the Commission can impose an administrative penalty for each violation of the act or rules.[35] The SEC also has cease and desist authority, which permits cease and desist orders, after notice and opportunity for a hearing, against any person who violates the Act or rules promulgated under the Act.[36]

Relying on the rule applied in SEC injunctive actions in the courts, the SEC has taken the position that there is no statute of limitations that is generally applicable to the Commission's institution of administrative proceedings to enforce the Act.[37] However, where the SEC invokes its own administrative process by instituting an administrative proceeding to seek imposition of a civil fine or penalty, then a five-year statute of limitations applies in administrative proceedings.[38]

It is quite common for SEC enforcement actions, both those initiated in court as well as those taking the form of administrative proceedings, to end in settlement. Generally, when the defendant in an SEC enforcement proceeding consents to SEC sanctions, he or she does so without either admitting or denying guilt. It has become standard Commission policy to include a statement to the effect that the settling defendant will not deny the allegations of the complaint.

§ 16.2[2] SEC Injunctions

§ 16.2[2][A] Power to Seek Injunctive Relief

Under each of the securities acts, the SEC has the authority to seek either temporary or permanent injunctive relief in the courts "whenever it shall appear to the Commission that any person is engaged or about to engage in any acts or practices which constitute or will constitute a violation."[41] Frequently, the SEC will announce the initiation of an enforcement action by publicly issuing a litigation release. It has been held that the issuance of such a release does not violate the defendant's due process.[43] The enhanced

---

30.   15 U.S.C.A. § 78*o*(b)(6)(A).

31.   Investment Advisers Act § 203(f), 15 U.S.C.A. § 80b–3(e). *See* § 21.1 *infra.*

32.   Securities Exchange Act section 15B(c)(2), 15 U.S.C.A. § 78*o*–4(c)(2).

33.   Securities Exchange Act section 15C(c)(1), 15 U.S.C.A. § 78*o*–5(c)(1).

34.   Securities Exchange Act section 17A, 15 U.S.C.A. § 78q–1.

35.   Securities Exchange Act section 21B, 15 U.S.C.A. § 78u–2.

36.   Securities Exchange Act section 21C, 15 U.S.C.A. § 78u–3.

37.   In the Matter of Patricia A. Johnson, Exch. Act Rel. No. 34–33664, [1993–1994 Transfer Binder] Fed. Sec. L. Rep. (CCH) ¶ 85,323 (SEC 1994).

38.   24 U.S.C.A. § 2462 (applicable to fines, civil penalties, and forfeitures in federal administrative proceedings generally).

41.   1933 Act section 20(b), 15 U.S.C.A. § 77t(b). Similar provisions are found in the 1934 Exchange Act, the 1935 Public Utility Holding Company Act, the Trust Indenture Act of 1939, and the Investment Company and Investment Advisers Acts of 1940. 15 U.S.C.A. §§ 78u(d), 79r(f), 80b–9(e).

43.   SEC v. Rivlin, 1999 WL 1455758, [1999–2000 Transfer Binder] Fed. Sec. L. Rep. (CCH) ¶ 90,725 (D.D.C. 1999).

pleading requirements of the Private Securities Litigation Reform Act of 1995[44] do not apply in SEC actions.[45]

Courts have observed that the injunctive power should not be used without "positive proof of a reasonable likelihood that past wrongdoing will occur" and proof that there is "something more than the mere possibility which keeps the case alive."[46] Accordingly, even in the face of proof of past violations, failure to prove a reasonable likelihood of future violations is likely to mean that no injunction will be granted.[47] In light of the severe consequences that can flow from an SEC injunction, the Tenth Circuit has indicated that a violation based merely on negligence and not resulting in a profit or other undue benefit to the defendant may not be sufficient to support an injunction.[48]

Once a permanent injunction has been issued, the burden is on the defendant to establish reasons why it should be lifted. The party seeking to remove the injunction must establish that "it is no longer equitable that the judgment should have prospective application."[49] This type of relief is viewed as "extraordinary relief" which will be granted only under extraordinary circumstances.[50] Lifting of a permanent injunction, including one incorporated in a consent decree, places on the moving party the burden of showing a significant change in circumstances that warrants modification of the decree.[51] Thus, for example, the mere passage of time will not be sufficient to warrant the lifting of an injunction.[52]

§ 16.2[2][B] Preliminary Injunctive Relief

In deciding whether to issue an injunction, courts will look to the seriousness of the securities law violations[53] and the requested injunction's impact on the defendant.[54] Other factors include the degree of the defendant's culpability[55] and the length of time between the acts complained of and time of suit. In deciding whether to order a preliminary injunction, courts will thus consider "the egregiousness of the defendant's actions, the isolated or recurrent nature of the infraction, the degree of scienter involved, the sincerity of

---

44. Pub. Law No. 104–67, 109 Stat. 737 (104th Cong. 1st Sess. December 22, 1995) (HR 1058). The Private Securities Litigation Reform Act is discussed in § 12.15 *supra*.

45. *See, e.g.,* SEC v. ICN Pharmaceuticals, Inc., 84 F.Supp.2d 1097 (C.D.Cal.2000).

46. SEC v. Bausch & Lomb, Inc., 565 F.2d 8, 18 (2d Cir.1977) (quoting United States v. W.T. Grant Co., 345 U.S. 629, 633, 73 S.Ct. 894, 897, 97 L.Ed. 1303 (1953)).

47. *See e.g.,* S.E.C. v. Sargent, 329 F.3d 34 (1st Cir. 2003).

48. SEC v. Pros International, Inc., 994 F.2d 767 (10th Cir.1993) (affirming district court's denial of injunctive relief for negligent violations of section 17(a) of the 1933 Act).

49. Fed. R. Civ. P. 60(b)(5).

50. Transgo, Inc. v. Ajac Transmission Parts Corp., 911 F.2d 363, 365 (9th Cir.1990).

51. Rufo v. Inmates of Suffolk County Jail, 502 U.S. 367, 383, 112 S.Ct. 748, 760, 116 L.Ed.2d 867 (1992); SEC v. Coldicutt, 258 F.3d 939, 942 (9th Cir.2001) (failure to show changed circumstances warranting modification of injunction) SEC v. Worthen, 98 F.3d 480, 482 (9th Cir.1996).

52. SEC v. Worthen, 98 F.3d 480, 482 (9th Cir.1996) (passage of 22 years since injunction was issued did not justify removal of injunction).

53. SEC v. Advance Growth Capital Corp., 470 F.2d 40, 53–54 (7th Cir.1972); SEC v. Manor Nursing Centers, Inc., 458 F.2d 1082, 1102 (2d Cir.1972).

54. *E.g.,* SEC v. Manor Nursing Centers, Inc., 458 F.2d 1082, 1102 (2d Cir.1972).

55. *See* SEC v. Spence & Green Chemical Co., 612 F.2d 896, 903 (5th Cir.1980), *cert. denied* 449 U.S. 1082, 101 S.Ct. 866, 66 L.Ed.2d 806 (1981).

the defendant's assurances against future violations, the defendant's recognition of the wrongful nature of his conduct, and the likelihood that the defendant's occupation will present opportunities for future violations."[57] Before granting a preliminary injunction, the court will consider both the likelihood of proving the current violation as well as the likelihood of future violations.[58] In SEC v. Unifund SAL,[59] the Second Circuit reconsidered the appropriate standard for a court in deciding whether to issue preliminary relief. The court began by rejecting a requirement that the Commission establish a "strong prima facie case"[60] as a precondition to issuing a preliminary injunction. The court also rejected the SEC's contention that the test applicable to private litigants—a substantial likelihood of success on the merits in addition to a showing of irreparable harm that would result in the absence of an injunction[61]—should be utilized. Instead, the court required not only a likelihood of success on the merits, but also a showing that there is a risk of future violations and that the seriousness of the violation warrants the preliminary relief. The court made it clear that the more burdensome the relief requested, the more substantial must be the showing of violation and risk of recurrence.[62] However, it has been held that in deciding whether to issue preliminary relief, a court should view the evidence "in a light most favorable to the Commission" and further that the SEC is "entitled to all reasonable inferences."[63]

§ 16.2[4] Ancillary Relief in SEC Injunction Actions

§ 16.2[4][A] Varieties of Ancillary Relief

The statutory enabling provisions speak solely in terms of the SEC's power to enjoin violations. However, the SEC and the courts have fashioned remedies ancillary to the traditional injunctive decree relying on "the general equitable powers of the federal courts."[100] Ancillary relief has taken many forms, ranging from disgorgement of ill-gotten profits[101] to more imaginative corrective or remedial action. Among such imaginative remedies are the appointment of an independent majority on the board of directors,[102] the appointment of a receiver,[103] prohibitions against exercising voting control in a

---

57. SEC v. International Heritage, Inc., 4 F.Supp.2d 1368, 1372 (N.D.Ga.1998).

58. SEC v. Princeton Economic International, Ltd., 73 F.Supp.2d 420 (S.D.N.Y.1999).

59. 910 F.2d 1028 (2d Cir.1990), *rehearing denied* 917 F.2d 98 (1990).

60. This standard had been enunciated in prior decisions. *See, e.g.,* SEC v. Management Dynamics, Inc., 515 F.2d 801, 807 (2d Cir.1975); SEC v. Boren, 283 F.2d 312, 313 (2d Cir.1960).

61. The standard applicable for private preliminary relief is discussed in §§ 11.9, 11.10 *supra.*

62. The court thus vacated a preliminary injunction against future insider trading violations in light of the gaps in the SEC's showing of a prima facie case. On the other hand, the court upheld the lower court's asset freeze that had been issued in order to protect possible disgorgement and penalties. The court thus viewed the freeze order as less burdensome than an injunction against future violations.

63. SEC v. International Heritage, Inc., 4 F.Supp.2d 1368, 1372 (N.D.Ga.1998), relying on SEC v. Blatt, 583 F.2d 1325 (5th Cir.1978).

100. James R. Farrand, Ancillary Remedies in SEC Civil Enforcement Suits, 89 Harv.L.Rev. 1779, 1781 (1976).

101. *E.g.,* SEC v. Musella, 1992 WL 420902, [1992–1993 Transfer Binder] Fed.Sec.L.Rep. (CCH) ¶ 97,205 (S.D.N.Y.1992).

102. *See* SEC v. Vesco, 571 F.2d 129 (2d Cir.1978).

103. *E.g.,* SEC v. Elliott, 953 F.2d 1560 (11th Cir.1992).

proxy battle,[104] the appointment of "special professionals" to assure compliance with securities laws,[105] the imposition of additional reporting requirements,[106] fashioning of orders designed to protect remaining assets,[107] and prohibitions against continued participation as an officer or director of any public company.[108] Refusal to comply with orders of ancillary relief can result in contempt of court and also can form the basis of incarceration.[109]

Ancillary relief will sometimes include relief that is designed to compensate injured investors. An example is ordering a disgorgement of profits. Although investors may thus have an interest in the outcome of SEC litigation, they are not parties to the proceedings. However, at least in the Fifth Circuit which has an admittedly lenient rule[110] for standing to appeal, an injured investor may be able to appeal an order entered in an SEC enforcement action.[111] The court applied a three-part test to grant a private party standing to appeal from an order in an SEC enforcement action. The court relied on (1) the private parties' participation in the district court proceedings by filing a notice that they were interested parties, (2) the equities weighed in their favor since they would be affected by the distribution of funds ordered below, and (3) therefore, they had a personal stake in the outcome of the SEC suit.[112]

The SEC can pursue ancillary relief against so-called "nominal defendants."[113] A nominal defendant is an intermediary who has not been a knowing participant in the securities law violation but has possession of illegally obtained funds.[114] The enforcement action against such a nominal defendant is for the purpose of collecting funds rather than to impose any sanctions against the nominal defendant.[115]

§ 16.2[4][B] Disgorgement of Profits

Disgorgement of ill-gotten gain is common in insider trading cases and can be based on specific statutory authority.[116] The disgorgement remedy has

---

104. *E.g.,* SEC v. Westgate California Corp., SEC Litigation Release No. 6142, 3 SEC Docket 30 (S.D.Cal. Nov. 9, 1978) (settlement order).

105. *E.g.,* SEC v. Beisinger Industries Corp., 552 F.2d 15, 18–19 (1st Cir.1977), *affirming* 421 F.Supp. 691 (D.Mass.1976); SEC v. Joseph Schlitz Brewing Co., 452 F.Supp. 824 (E.D.Wis.1978) (consent decree).

106. *See generally* James R. Farrand, Ancillary Remedies in SEC Civil Enforcement Suits, 89 Harv.L.Rev. 1779, 1792–1793(1976).

107. *E.g.,* SEC v. Hickey, 322 F.3d 1123 (9th Cir. 2003).

108. SEC v. Cosmopolitan Inv. Funding Co., SEC Litigation Release No. 7366 (April 23, 1976); 42 SEC Ann.Rep. 119 (1976).

109. SEC v. Princeton Economic International Ltd., 152 F.Supp.2d 456 (S.D.N.Y.2001) (upholding continued confinement for civil contempt); SEC v. Bilzerian, 131 F.Supp.2d 10 (D.D.C. 2001) (incarceration ordered due to defendant's failure to comply with disgorgement order).

110. *See also, e.g.,* In re Beef Industry Antitrust Litigation, 589 F.2d 786, 788 (5th Cir.1979).

111. SEC v. Forex Asset Management LLC, 242 F.3d 325 (5th Cir. 2001). *See also, e.g.,* CFTC v. Topworth International Ltd., 205 F.3d 1107, 1113 (9th Cir.1999) (allowing nonparty creditor to object to receivership).

112. *Id.*

113. SEC v. Cavanagh, 155 F.3d 129, 136 (2d Cir.1998); SEC v. Colello, 139 F.3d 674, 675–677 (9th Cir.1998). *See also, e.g.,* CFTC v. Kimberlynn Creek Ranch, 276 F.3d 187, 191–192 (4th Cir.2002).

114. CFTC v. Kimberlynn Creek Ranch, 276 F.3d 187, 191–192 (4th Cir.2002) (discussing nominal defendant status).

115. SEC v. Colello, 139 F.3d 674, 676 (9th Cir.1998).

116. Congress has expressly empowered the SEC to seek disgorgement plus a treble damage penalty for insider trading violations. 15 U.S.C.A. § 78u–1(a)(1), 78ff(a). *See also, e.g.,* SEC v.

been utilized in the context of other violations as well.[117] Courts have continued to become increasingly receptive to the disgorgement remedy. Thus, for example, it is not necessary that the disgorgement amount be proven with absolute precision; it is sufficient to reasonably approximate the profits attributable to the illegal transaction.[118] Also, disgorgement is remedial in nature and is not to be awarded for punitive purposes.[119] The remedial nature of the remedy does not mean, however, that it is essentially compensatory in nature. The primary function of the remedy is to deny the wrongdoer the fruits of ill-gotten gains.[120] Although distribution of the disgorgement proceeds to investors may be appropriate in many cases, disgorgement is not appropriate when there are a large number of investors with relatively small claims.[121] The SEC simply is not equipped to act as a collection agency in every case that results in compensable losses to investors. Unless distributed to investors, the disgorgement fund goes to the United States Treasury.[122]

It is common for disgorgement to the SEC to be followed by a disbursement of the funds to provide restitution to injured investors. However, restitution is not required and will not be granted when it would constitute a windfall and not compensate the true victims of the fraud.[123]

The disgorgement remedy is not limited to violators and may be used against non-violators holding illegally obtained profits where the defendants have no legitimate claim to the proceeds.[125] Section 20(f) of the 1933 Act and section 21(d)(4) of the 1934 Act prohibit any funds received in a disgorgement action, either by the SEC in federal court or in an administrative proceeding, from being used to pay attorneys' fees in private actions seeking a distribution of the disgorged funds.[126]

Musella, 1992 WL 420902, [1992–1993 Transfer Binder] Fed.Sec.L.Rep. (CCH) ¶ 97,205 (S.D.N.Y. 1992).

In 1988, Congress supplemented the SEC remedy with an express private right of action by contemporaneous traders against persons making improper use of material, nonpublic information. 15 U.S.C.A. § 78t–1.

117. *See, e.g.,* SEC v. First Jersey Securities, 101 F.3d 1450 (2d Cir.1996) (disgorgement was appropriate in a series of manipulations and nondisclosure of fraudulent practices).

118. *See, e.g.,* SEC v. Friendly Power Co., 49 F.Supp.2d 1363 (S.D.Fla.1999).

119. SEC v. Risman, 7 Fed.Appx. 30 (2d Cir. 2001).

120. SEC v. McCaskey, 34 Sec. Reg. & L. Rep. (BNA) 559, 2002 WL 850001 (S.D.N.Y. 2002) (magistrate's recommendation) (" 'the primary purpose of disgorgement [to the SEC] is not to compensate investors,' but rather to force 'a defendant to give up the amount by which he was unjustly enriched.' "), quoting SEC v. Commonwealth Chem. Sec., Inc., 574 F.2d 90, 102 (2d Cir.1978).

121. S.E.C. v. Lange, 2002 WL 475130 (E.D.Pa.2002)¢, relying on SEC v. Drexel Burnham Lambert, Inc., 956 F.Supp. 503, 507 (S.D.N.Y.1997); *SEC v. Lorin,* 869 F.Supp. 1117, 1129 (S.D.N.Y.1994), 76 F.3d 458 (2d Cir.1996).

122. S.E.C. v. Lange, 2002 WL 475130 (E.D.Pa.2002)¢, relying on SEC v. Drexel Burnham Lambert, Inc., 956 F.Supp. 503, 507 (S.D.N.Y.1997); *SEC v. Dimensional Entertainment Corp.,* 1996 WL 107290 at *2 (S.D.N.Y.1996); *SEC v. Lund,* 570 F.Supp. 1397, 1404–05 (C.D.Cal.1983).

123. SEC v. Fischbach Corp., 133 F.3d 170 (2d Cir.1997).

125. SEC v. Seibald, 1997 WL 605114, [1997 Transfer Binder] Fed. Sec. L. Rep. (CCH) ¶ 99,586 (S.D.N.Y.1997). However, a broker with a bona fide security interest in violator's securities will not be required to disgorge the violator's profits. SEC v. Lehman Brothers, Inc., 157 F.3d 2 (1st Cir.1998).

126. 15 U.S.C.A. §§ 77tk; 78u(d).

§ 16.2[4][D] Civil Penalty Under the Insider Trading Sanctions Act of 1984 (ITSA)

In 1984, Congress gave the Commission additional enforcement power in terms of the ability in a case of insider trading to seek a civil penalty of up to three times the amount of the insider's ill-gotten profits.[153] This statutory civil remedy given to the SEC, which, to some extent, has been further clarified and supplemented by the Insider Trading and Securities Fraud Sanctions Act of 1988,[154] raised a number of interesting questions. For example, is the treble penalty, the proceeds of which go to the United States Treasury, a criminal proceeding so as to preclude an action under the Insider Trading Sanctions Act following or followed by a criminal prosecution? More specifically, can the treble damage penalty be invoked in addition to imprisonment and/or the statutory criminal fine (or both)? Even putting the constitutional issues aside, it would certainly seem to be a case of overkill to allow the Justice Department and the SEC in successive actions to exact cumulative penalties. The statutory remedy raises other questions as well. For example, does the statutory treble damage penalty have any effect on the SEC's ability to obtain ancillary relief in an injunction action, such as ordering a disgorgement of profits to a private party? The SEC practice in most cases has been to bring an action for disgorgement, combined with its request for a penalty. Combining disgorgement with the penalty has been a practice reflected in SEC settlements. As discussed more fully below, as a result of 1990 legislation, the Commission can order disgorgement in its own administrative proceedings and thus can bypass judicial relief.[157]

Another issue raised by the Insider Trading Sanctions Act is the defendant's right to a jury trial. The Supreme Court has held that there is a constitutional right to a jury trial in governmental action for liability under the Clean Water Act, but any penalties are to be fixed by the Court.[158] Thus, by analogy, there is no constitutional right to a jury trial for civil penalties imposed under the Insider Trading Sanctions Act.[159] Additionally, since an SEC disgorgement action is equitable in nature, it would appear that there is no right to a jury trial in the SEC action.[160] However, the Seventh Circuit indicated that it is "erroneous" to assume that civil penalties in SEC actions

---

153. 15 U.S.C.A. § 78u(d)(2)(A). *Cf.*

154. Pub.L. No. 100–704, 102 Stat. 4677 (1988).

157. For example, the SEC can order disgorgement in conjunction with a cease and desist order. *See* 16.2[11], 16.5 *infra*.

158. Tull v. United States, 481 U.S. 412, 107 S.Ct. 1831, 95 L.Ed.2d 365 (1987).

159. Pub. L. No. 98–376, 98 Stat. 1264 (1984). *But see* United States v. Marcus Schloss & Co., Inc., 724 F.Supp. 1123 (S.D.N.Y.1989) ($20,000 penalty in civil ITSA proceeding did not amount to punishment and thus the criminal prosecution was permitted to proceed).

160. The *Tull* decision involved a government claim for liability, injunctive relief, and civil penalty. The court characterized the liability claim as in law rather than equity. Such a characterization of SEC disgorgement actions would apparently give a right to a jury trial. However, this seems unlikely as disgorgement has been viewed as equitable in nature. Furthermore, disgorgement in insider trading cases may be based on a constructive trust or accounting of profits, both of which are equitable claims. *See* § 12.17.

See also, e.g., SEC v. Rind, 991 F.2d 1486 (9th Cir.1993), *affirming* 1991 WL 214267, [1991 Transfer Binder] Fed.Sec.L.Rep. (CCH) ¶ 96,167 (C.D.Cal.1991); Comment, The Seventh Amendment Right to Jury Trial in Civil Penalties Actions: A Post–*Tull* Examination of the Insider Trading Sanctions Act of 1984, 43 U.Miami L.Rev. 361 (1988).

to redress insider trading are not "a form of legal relief."[161] But then the court went on to find that once the jury finds liability, the questions relating to the nature of the equitable relief and the amount of the penalty are both properly matters for the judge.[162] In the course of its opinion, the court indicated that disgorgement is a form of equitable relief[163] and thus would be an issue for the judge rather than a jury.

§ 16.2[5] Civil Penalties in Other SEC Enforcement Actions

In 1990, Congress expanded the scope and amount of civil penalties that can be ordered in judicial proceedings brought by the SEC.[164] As discussed more fully below, at the same time, the SEC was given the power to impose civil penalties in administrative proceedings.[165] While those administrative proceedings are limited to market professionals registered with or otherwise regulated under the supervision of the SEC,[166] the Commission can institute a civil action in federal court against anyone who is in violation of the securities laws or rules promulgated thereunder. In assessing penalties, it is appropriate to consider the public statements by the defendant which tended to trivialize the violations.[168]

If it appears to the Commission that a person has violated an SEC rule or regulation, or a cease and desist order, other than a violation which is subject to a penalty under the Insider Trading Sanctions Act of 1984, the SEC may bring a civil action seeking a civil penalty against the violator by virtue of its general enforcement authority.[169] The amount of the penalty is discretionary so long as it fits within the three-tiered system established by the statute.[170] The second and third tiers permit larger penalties in the case of more culpable conduct. The general rule (established in the first tier) is that the penalty is not to exceed the greater of (i) five thousand dollars for a natural person or fifty thousand dollars for any other person, or (ii) the gross amount of pecuniary gain to the defendant as a result of the violation. Second-tier penalties may be imposed against more culpable defendants. If the violation involved fraud, deceit, manipulation, or deliberate or reckless disregard of a regulatory requirement, the penalty amount may not exceed the greater of (i) fifty thousand dollars for a natural person or two hundred and fifty thousand dollars for any other person, or (ii) the gross amount of pecuniary gain to the

161. SEC v. Lipson, 278 F.3d 656, 662 (7th Cir.2002) (criticizing SEC v. Clark, 915 F.2d 439, 442 (9th Cir.1990) for making that assumption). This was dictum since the defendant was tried before a jury.

162. *Id.*

163. *Id.* at 663.

164. Pub.L. No. 101–429 (1990).

165. The Commission was also given cease and desist authority.

166. The power to impose civil penalties applies to proceedings against a broker-dealer, associated person, municipal securities dealer, government securities dealer, or registered clearing agent, as well as to persons registered under the Investment Company or Investment Advisers Acts of 1940. 15 U.S.C.A. §§ 78u–2, 80a–9(d), (e), § 80b–3(i). *See* 15 U.S.C.A. §§ 78o(b)(4), 78o(b)(6), 78o–4, 78o–5, 78q–1.

168. Civil penalties can be substantial. *See, e.g.,* Arthur Andersen LLP Agrees to Settlement Resulting in First Antifraud Injunction in More Than 20 Years and Largest–Ever Civil Penalty ($7 Million) in SEC Enforcement Action Against a Big Five Accounting Firm, 2001 WL 684751 (S.E.C.) (SEC June 19, 2001).

169. 15 U.S.C.A. §§ 77t(d)(1), 78u(d)(3)(A), 80a–12(e)(1), 80b–9(e)(1). The SEC further has the power to impose civil penalties in the course of administrative proceedings. Section 21B, 15 U.S.C.A. § 78u–2.

170. *See, e.g.,* SEC v. Interlink Data Network of Los Angeles, Inc., 1993 WL 603274, [1993–1994 Transfer Binder] Fed. Sec. L. Rep. (CCH) ¶ 98,049 (C.D.Cal.1993) (penalty of more than $12 million, representing the aggregate amount raised in the fraudulent offering under attack was an appropriate penalty).

defendant as a result of the violation. Third-tier penalties may be imposed against such culpable conduct if it has a significant impact on other persons. If the violation (1) involved fraud, deceit, manipulation, or deliberate or reckless disregard of a regulatory requirement and (2) directly or indirectly resulted in substantial losses or created a significant risk of substantial losses to other persons, the maximum amount of the penalty is increased to the greater of (i) one hundred thousand dollars for a natural person or five hundred thousand dollars for any other person, or (ii) the gross amount of pecuniary gain to the defendant as a result of the violation.[171]

The foregoing civil penalties are payable to the United States Treasury. If a defendant fails to pay a penalty within the time prescribed, the SEC may refer the matter to the Attorney General, who is directed to file an action in the United States district court for the payment of such penalty.

There are special penalties applicable to judicial actions to enforce cease and desist orders. In an action to enforce a cease and desist order, each separate violation of such order shall be a separate offense, and in the case of violation through a continuing failure to comply with such an order, each day of noncompliance is deemed a separate offense.[172]

§ 16.2[6] Bar Orders

The penalty provisions were only part of the expansion of the SEC's enforcement authority. The 1990 legislation also empowers the SEC to seek judicial orders prohibiting certain violators from serving as officers and directors of 1934 Act reporting companies.[173] In any action by the SEC for an injunction or criminal prosecution under section 20(b) of the 1933 Act[174] or section 21(d)(1) of the 1934 Act,[175] the court may prohibit, conditionally or unconditionally, permanently or temporarily, any person who has violated section 17(a)(1) of the 1933 Act[176] or section 10(b) of the 1934 Act,[177] from acting as an officer or director of any issuer that has a class of securities registered under the Securities Exchange Act of 1934[178] or that is required to file periodic reports under that Act.[179] The bar order may be issued if the violator's conduct demonstrates substantial unfitness to serve as an officer or director of any such issuer.[180] The SEC can also go to court to secure an order barring violators from associating with broker-dealers.[181] In 2002, the SEC

---

171. 15 U.S.C.A. §§ 77t(d)(2), 78u(d)(3)(B)k, 80a–12(e)(2), 80b–9(e)(2).

172. 15 U.S.C.A. §§ 77t(d)(4), 78u(d)(3)(D), 80a–12(e)(4), 80b–9(e)(4).

173. *See, e.g.,* SEC v. First Pacific Bancorp, 142 F.3d 1186 (9th Cir. 1998) (CEO subjected to lifetime ban from serving as an officer of a public company).

174. 15 U.S.C.A. § 77t(b).

175. 15 U.S.C.A. § 78u(d)(1).

176. 15 U.S.C.A. § 77q(a). Section 17(a), which prohibits any person in the offer or sale of securities, by any means of transportation or communication in interstate commerce or by mail, from employing any device or scheme to defraud. *See* § 7.11 *supra.*

177. 15 U.S.C.A. § 78j(b). Section 10(b) prohibits manipulative or deceptive acts or practices in connection with a purchase or sale of a security (and also with regard to security-based swap agreements). *See* chapter 12 *supra.*

178. 15 U.S.C.A. § 78g. *See* § 9.2 *supra.*

179. 15 U.S.C.A. §§ 77t(e), 78u(d)(2). *See* 15 U.S.C.A. § 78o(d), which is discussed in § 9.3 *supra.*

180. 15 U.S.C.A. §§ 77t(e), 78u(d)(2).

181. *See, e.g.,* Rizek v. SEC, 215 F.3d 157, [1999–2000 Transfer Binder] Fed. Sec. L. Rep. (CCH) ¶ 90,998 (1st Cir. 2000) (permanently barring broker from securities industry); S.E.C. v. Zahareas, 100 F.Supp.2d 1148 (D.Minn.2000).

714 **SECURITIES & EXCHANGE COMMISSION** **Ch. 16**

decided to request that Congress grant the Commission the authority to impose bar orders against officers and directors in administrative proceedings.[182] The SEC already has the authority with respect to broker dealers.[183]

In addition to the ability to seek a bar order by judicial decree, the SEC can issue bar orders in the course of its administrative proceedings. The Commission's general sanctioning authority over associated persons of broker-dealers in section 15(b)(6) of the Act[184] contains the express authority to bar violators from associating with brokers or dealers.[185] The SEC has long taken the position that it has the ability to issue a bar order in an administrative proceeding, barring the defendant from participation in any of the branches of the securities industry for which the Commission administers an occupational licensing regime. This became known as a collateral bar order. However, in 1999, the Court of Appeals for the District of Columbia ruled that the statute limits to the SEC's authority to a bar in connection with the violators licensed occupation.[187]

§ 16.2[7] SEC Investigations[188]

Prior to instigating formal action, the SEC generally investigates possible securities law violations that have been brought to its attention. There are generally two stages of any SEC investigation. First, the SEC staff conducts an informal investigation. There is no requirement that targets of preliminary administrative investigations be given either actual or constructive notice of the investigation.[191] Frequently, an informal investigation will lead to the second stage—an SEC order instituting a formal investigation. The SEC is vested with broad discretionary powers of investigation. The decision to commence an investigation is not a final order subject to review and, thus, it is not appropriate to enjoin a continuing investigation.[192] Similarly, the Commission's decision not to institute a proceeding is not judicially reviewable.[193]

Formal investigations are authorized when the Commission believes that there is a "likelihood" of a violation. The issuance of an order authorizing a formal investigation gives the SEC staff subpoena power.[195] It has been held that the appropriate procedure for challenging an investigative subpoena is to

182. *See* Pitt Says Commission to Seek Bar Authority in Agency Proceedings, 34 Sec. Reg. & L. Rep. (BNA) 333 (March 4, 2002).

183. Section 15(b)(6), 15 U.S.C.A. § 78o(b)(6). *See* § 14.4[3] *supra*.

184. 15 U.S.C.A. § 78o(b)(6)(A).

185. There is a parallel authority for sanctions against investment advisers. Investment Advisers Act § 203(f), 15 U.S.C.A. § 80b–3(e). The authority to issue sanctions such as bar orders against investment advisers applies to both registered and unregistered investment advisers. Teicher v. SEC, 177 F.3d 1016 (D.C.Cir.1999).

187. Teicher v. SEC, 177 F.3d 1016 (D.C.Cir.1999).

188. *See* §§ 16.28–16.31 of the Practitioner's Edition of this Treatise.

191. RNR Enterprises, Inc. v. SEC, 122 F.3d 93, 98 (2d Cir.1997); Wells v. SEC, 113 F.3d 1230 (2d Cir.1997) (due process does not require that target be named); Gold v. SEC, 48 F.3d 987, 991 (7th Cir.1995) ("[d]ue process does not require notice, either actual or constructive, of an administrative investigation into possible violations of the securities laws").

192. Hunter v. SEC, 1994 WL 580096, [1995 Transfer Binder] Fed. Sec. L. Rep. (CCH) ¶ 98,601 (E.D.Pa.1994).

193. Block v. SEC, 50 F.3d 1078 (D.C.Cir.1995) (shareholders tried to challenge SEC's decision not to hold hearing to determine whether investment company directors were "interested persons").

195. 15 U.S.C.A. § 78u(b).

refuse to comply and then raise the issue in the ensuing SEC enforcement action.[196] Courts will generally enforce any such subpoena unless it is shown that the Commission was not acting in good faith and, thus, enforcement would constitute an abuse of the court's process.[197] As stated by the Ninth Circuit, a subpoena directed to the target of a formal investigation will be upheld upon the SEC's showing: "(1) the agency has a legitimate purpose for the investigation; (2) the inquiry is relevant to that purpose; (3) the agency does not possess the information sought; and (4) the agency has adhered to administrative steps required by law."[198] The Supreme Court held that in many cases the SEC does not have to give notice of third-party subpoenas.[201]

The SEC practice has been to invite targets of investigations to respond informally to the Commission. These responses have come to be known as "Wells submissions."[209] This informal process[210] gives a person under investigation the opportunity to present his or her position to the SEC before the SEC decides whether to initiate formal proceedings.[211] This presents the target of an informal investigation with the opportunity to try to dissuade the Commission from proceeding further. Although the SEC has indicated that the Wells submission process may be most useful in providing an opportunity to be heard with respect to law or policy,[213] Wells submissions are frequently used to deal with factual matters as well.[214]

§ 16.2[8] Parallel Civil and Criminal Proceedings

SEC investigations that reveal wrongdoing may result in SEC injunction actions brought in federal district court. Alternatively, the SEC can refer the case to the Department of Justice to determine if criminal sanctions are appropriate.[225] The Commission and the Department of Justice may cooperate in their parallel proceedings.[226]

Double jeopardy problems will not ordinarily affect the ability to impose both SEC civil sanctions and criminal penalties in separate actions. Similarly, even though the SEC has review power over NASD sanctions, the double

---

196. 15 U.S.C.A. § 78u(c).

197. *See* SEC v. Wheeling–Pittsburgh Steel Corp., 648 F.2d 118 (3d Cir.1981).

198. Jerry T. O'Brien, Inc. v. SEC, 704 F.2d 1065, 1067 (9th Cir.1983), *reversed on other grounds* 467 U.S. 735, 104 S.Ct. 2720, 81 L.Ed.2d 615 (1984), *on remand* 773 F.2d 1070 (9th Cir.1985) relying on United States v. Powell, 379 U.S. 48, 57–58, 85 S.Ct. 248, 254–55, 13 L.Ed.2d 112 (1964).

201. SEC v. Jerry T. O'Brien, Inc., 467 U.S. 735, 104 S.Ct. 2720, 81 L.Ed.2d 615 (1984).

209. The practice was initiated in response to the recommendations of a special advisory committee appointed by the SEC that was chaired by a lawyer named John Wells. *See* Arthur F. Mathews, Effective Defense of SEC Investigations: Laying the Foundation for Successful Disposition of Subsequent Civil, Administrative and Criminal Proceedings, 24 Emory L.J. 567, 618 n. 172 (1975). For a discussion of the history and use of Wells submissions, *see generally* Joshua A. Naftalis, Note "Wells Submissions" to the SEC as Offers of Settlement Under Federal Rule of Evidence 408 and Their Protection from Third–Party Discovery, 102 Colum. L. Rev. 1912 (2002).

210. *See* Sec. Act Rel. No. 33–5320, 37 Fed. Reg. 23,829 (SEC Nov. 9, 1972) (discussing the process).

211. *See* In re Initial Public Offering Securities Litigation, 2004 WL 60290 *1 (S.D.N.Y. 2004).

213. *See* Sec. Act Rel. No. 33–5310, 1972 WL 18218 *1 (SEC Sept. 27, 1972).

214. *See* William R. McLucas, J. Lynn Taylor & Susan A. Mathews, A Practitioner's Guide to the SEC's Investigative and Enforcement Process, 70 Temp. L. Rev. 53, 112 (1997).

225. 15 U.S.C.A. § 78u(d).

226. *See, e.g.,* SEC v. Dresser Industries, Inc., 628 F.2d 1368 (D.C.Cir.1980), *cert. denied* 449 U.S. 993, 101 S.Ct. 529, 66 L.Ed.2d 289 (1980).

jeopardy clause does not preclude the SEC from bringing an enforcement action notwithstanding prior NASD sanctions for the same activity.[228] For the same reason, the existence of a parallel criminal investigation did not excuse the targets of an NASD investigation from responding to a subpoena compelling testimony in connection with the NASD investigation.[229]

Collateral estoppel may preclude the defendant from relitigating in an SEC enforcement action facts determined in a prior criminal action resulting in conviction for the same violations.[230] The Supreme Court has long recognized the availability of collateral estoppel in a civil action that was preceded by a criminal conviction.[231]

§ 16.2[10] Section 21(a) Reports

Securities and Exchange Commission investigations do not always culminate in enforcement actions, even when the Commission concludes that the securities laws have been violated. The SEC can publicize the results of its investigations. Section 21(a) of the 1934 Act expressly authorizes such public reports.[251] The institution of civil litigation in a matter does not limit the Commission's ability to continue with a section 21(a) investigation parallel to the law suit.[252]

Section 21(a) thus supplements the SEC's already broad investigatory powers. However, the section 21(a) power to issue public reports has not been utilized to what some view as its optimal extent.[253] In fact, section 21(a) has formed the basis of much controversy. For example, in In re Spartek, Inc.,[254] the Commission issued a section 21(a) report of a staff investigation including the acceptance of the registrant's offer of settlement. Commissioner Karmel vigorously dissented, considering the report to be in excess of the SEC's jurisdiction.[255] She reasoned that the publicity function could not properly be used as an alternative to SEC enforcement actions.[256] Notwithstanding Commissioner Karmel's concern, the SEC has since used the section 21(a) publicity function in this manner, albeit relatively sparingly.[257] Additionally, the SEC issued a statement of practice supporting the use of section 21(a) reports and asserting that "where it appears to be in the public interest," settlement statements given to the Commission should be submitted "with the expecta-

---

228. Jones v. SEC, 115 F.3d 1173 (4th Cir.1997), *cert. denied* 523 U.S. 1072, 118 S.Ct. 1512, 140 L.Ed.2d 666 (1998).

229. D.L. Cromwell Investments, Inc. v. NASD Regulation, Inc., 132 F. Supp.2d 248 (S.D.N.Y. 2001).

230. *See* SEC v. Westerfield, 1997 WL 282241, [1997 Transfer Binder] Fed. Sec. L. Rep. (CCH) ¶ 99,530 (S.D.N.Y.1997).

231. *See* Emich Motors Corp. v. General Motors Corp., 340 U.S. 558, 568, 71 S.Ct. 408, 95 L.Ed. 534 (1951). *See also, e.g.,* SEC v. Zandford, 238 F.3d 559, 562 (4th Cir.2001).

251. 15 U.S.C.A. § 78u(a). *See* Dennis L. Block & Nancy E. Barton, Securities Litigation: Section 21(a): A New Enforcement Tool, 7 Sec.Reg.L.J. 265 (1979).

252. *See* SEC v. F.N. Wolf & Co., [1993–1994 Transfer Binder] Fed. Sec. L. Rep. (CCH) ¶ 98,015 (S.D.N.Y.1993).

253. *See* BNA Interview: Pollack Questions Advisability of Passing Federal Securities Code at This Time. 484 Sec.Reg. & L.Rep. (BNA) AA–1 (Jan. 3, 1979).

254. Sec.Exch.Act Rel. No. 34–15567, 491 Sec.Reg. & L.Rep. (BNA) E–1 (February 21, 1979).

255. *Id.* at E–4.

256. *Id.* at E–5.

257. *E.g.,* Report of Investigation Pursuant to Section 21(a) of the Securities Exchange Act of 1934 Concerning The Conduct of Certain Former Officers and Directors of W.R. Grace & Co., Sec. Exch. Act Rel. No. 34–39157, 65 S.E.C. Docket 1240, 1997 WL 597984 (Sept. 30, 1997).

tion that the Commission may make the statements public."[258] Once again, Commissioner Karmel voiced her dissent, pointing, *inter alia,* to possible due process objections.[259] The SEC has used section 21(a) as a vehicle for announcing policy shifts. For example, in 2001, the SEC announced a new approach to enforcement proceedings in instance when companies' self-policing efforts led to discovery of securities law violations.[260]

In 2002, the SEC invoked the power to issue reports under section 21(a) to impose the requirement that CEOs and CFOs certify the accuracy of financial statements.[261] Some members of the bar voiced their objection to the use of this procedure to bypass formal rulemaking.[262] The certification requirements were subsequently incorporated into the Sarbanes–Oxley Act.[263]

§ 16.2[11] Section 15(c)(4) Orders

As part of the Insider Trading Sanctions Act of 1984,[264] Congress significantly expanded the SEC's administrative powers with regard to an individual or entity who was a "cause" of a failure to comply with the act's reporting requirements. Prior to the amendment, the section 15(c)(4) power was limited in its coverage to persons who were the actual violators of the Act. The 1984 legislation thus expanded the SEC's power, after notice and opportunity for a hearing, to issue an order calling for compliance or steps toward compliance with any SEC Rule or Regulation.[265] The section 15(c)(4) order extends the SEC's administrative power beyond broker-dealers and thus gives the Commission power to issue administrative sanctions against issuers subject to the 1934 Act, as well as against officers, directors, and employees of such issuer, or anyone else responsible for, or who could have prevented, the violation.[266] Further, since the section 15(c)(4) order applies to anyone subject to the provisions of section 12, 13, 14, or 15(d) of the Act, it also extends to persons and entities required to make Williams Act filings in connection with the acquisition of reporting company shares.[267] The broad terms of section 15(c)(4) do not place any limits on the types of orders that the Commission may issue. Thus, for example, the SEC could rely on section 15(c)(4) to issue an order barring an individual from being associated with a 1934 Act reporting company.[268] The bar order is but one example of the potential of this expanded

---

258. Sec.Exch.Act Rel. No. 34–15664 [1979 Transfer Binder] Fed.Sec.L.Rep. (CCH) ¶ 82,014 at pp. 81,557–558 (March 21, 1979).

259. *Id.* at p. 81,558.

260. *See* Report of Investigation Pursuant to Section 21(a) of the Securities Exchange Act of 1934 and Commission Statement of the Relationship of Cooperation to Agency Enforcement Decisions, Sec. Exch. Act Rel. No. 34–44969, 2001 WL 1301408 (SEC Oct. 23, 2001).

261. Order Requiring the Filing of Sworn Statements Pursuant to Section 21(a)(1) of the Securities Exchange Act of 1934, SEC Order File No. 4–460, http://www.sec.gov/rules/other/4–460.htm (SEC June 27, 2002).

262. *See* Lawyers Question SEC's Use of § 21(a) to Impose CEO Certification Requirement, 34 Sec. Reg. & L. Rep. (BNA) 1185 (July 22, 2002).

263. Sarbanes–Oxley Act of 2002, Pub. Law 107–204 (July 30, 2002). *See* § 9.3[2][A] *supra.*

264. Pub. L. No. 98–376, 98 Stat. 1264 (1984).

265. 15 U.S.C.A. § 78*o*(c)(4).

266. *See, e.g.,* In re Runge, Sec.Exch.Act Rel. No. 34–23066 (March 26, 1986).

267. 15 U.S.C.A. §§ 78m(d), (e), 78n(d), (e), (f). The Williams Act is discussed in chapter 11 *supra.*

268. *Cf.* In re Blinder, Robinson & Co., Admin.Proc.File No. 3–6380, [1985–86 Transfer Binder] Fed.Sec.L.Rep. (CCH) ¶ 83,911 (SEC 1985). This, of course, is supplemented by the Commission's authority to seek bar orders in judicial proceedings.

administrative enforcement power. The SEC has used section 15(c)(4) proceedings to deal with a wide variety of violations.

A significant exercise of the Commission's authority under section 15(c)(4) occurred in In the Matter of George Kern,[270] wherein the administrative law judge indicated that an attorney whose negligence resulted in the filing of a false document might be found to have been a cause of a violation of the Act. The ALJ held that he was without power to issue any bar order because at the time of the decision, the respondent was no longer associated with the company in question. The full Commission has affirmed the ALJ's decision solely on the grounds that it was beyond the ALJ's authority once the respondent was no longer in a position to control the company's future compliance. The *Kern* proceeding nevertheless stands as an example of the expansive potential of the section 15(c)(4) remedy.

§ 16.2[12] Cease and Desist Authority

A major part of the 1990 enforcement legislation was the granting to the Commission of its cease and desist power.[271] If the SEC finds, after notice and opportunity to be heard, that a regulated securities professional is violating, has violated, or is about to violate any rule or regulation, the SEC may issue a cease and desist order against that person for any current or future violations and against any other person who causes the violation due to an act or omission that the person knew or should have known would contribute to such violation.[272] The authority to issue a cease and desist order may be invoked against any person who violates the Act. In addition, the Commission may order an asset freeze if the proceeding is against a respondent who acts, or during the alleged misconduct acted, as a broker, dealer, investment advisor, investment company, municipal securities dealer, government securities broker, government securities dealer, transfer agent, or associate of any of the foregoing.[273]

In deciding whether a cease and desist order should issue, the administrative law judge must consider the possibility of a recurrence of the alleged violation.[274] The seriousness of the violation may also be a factor. A "weak" risk of future violation will not be sufficient to support a cease and desist order.[276]

§ 16.2[13] SEC Administrative Proceedings

The SEC is empowered to hold administrative hearings in the course of exercising its supervisory authority over broker-dealers,[291] national ex-

---

270. [1991 Transfer Binder] Fed.Sec.L.Rep. (CCH) ¶ 84,815 (SEC 1991), *affirming* [1988–1989 Transfer Binder] Fed.Sec.L.Rep. (CCH) ¶ 84,342 (SEC Initial Decision 1987).

271. Securities Act of 1933 § 8A, 15 U.S.C.A. § 77h–1; Securities Exchange Act of 1934 §§ 21C, 23(d), 15 U.S.C.A. §§ 78u–3, 78w(d); Investment Company Act of 1940 § 9(f), 15 U.S.C.A. § 80a–9(f); Investment Advisers Act of 1940 § 203(k), 15 U.S.C.A. § 80b–3(k).

In addition to the SEC's cease authority, the NASD can issue cease and desist orders with respect to certain securities law violations. *See* NASD Special Notice to Members 03–35, http://www.nasdr.com/pdf-text/0335ntm.txt (NASDR June 23, 2003).

272. *See, e.g.,* In the Matter of Haeglin, Acc. & Audit. Enforcement Rel. No. 461, Fed.Sec. L.Rep. (CCH) 73,920 (SEC 1993).

273. 15 U.S.C.A. § 77h–1(c)(2); 15 U.S.C.A. § 78u–2; 15 U.S.C.A. § 80a–9(f)(3)(B); 15 U.S.C.A. § 80b–3(k)(3)(B).

274. *See, e.g.,* WHX Corp. v. SEC, 362 F.3d 854 (D.C. Cir. 2004).

276. *See, e.g., Id.*

291. 15 U.S.C.A. § 78o–1. *See* § 14.3 *supra.*

changes,[292] investment companies and advisers,[293] municipal securities dealers,[294] government securities dealers,[295] and public utility holding companies.[296] These are generally disciplinary proceedings.[297]

Pursuant to section 6 of the 1934 Act, the Commission is charged with overseeing national securities exchanges.[303] Although the power has been exercised only once,[304] the SEC may suspend or revoke registration of an exchange.[305] The SEC also has the power to expel individual broker-dealers from a national exchange.[306] The 1934 Act additionally charges the SEC with overseeing registered securities associations and other broker-dealer self-regulatory organizations.[307] The Commission can suspend or revoke an association's registration,[308] as well as suspend or expel a member of the association.[309] Also, by virtue of its registration of broker-dealers,[310] the Commission has the power to suspend or revoke such registration.[311] The Commission can bar any person from associating with a broker-dealer,[312] a member of a registered securities association,[313] or an investment adviser,[314] or bar that person from serving in various capacities with a registered investment company.[315] In addition, in a divided decision, the SEC has held that it has the power to issue collateral or industry-wide bar orders against securities professionals.[316] With respect to all of the powers discussed above, the Commission can impose the less drastic sanction of censure.[318]

The Supreme Court has held that in reviewing SEC sanctions, the courts of appeals should affirm the Commission's findings if they are supported by a

---

292. 15 U.S.C.A. §§ 78*l*, 78s. *See* §§ 14.1, 14.3 *supra.*

293. *See* 15 U.S.C.A. § 80a–1 *et seq.,* 80b–1 *et seq. See* chapters 20, 21 *infra.*

294. 15 U.S.C.A. § 78*o*–4. *See* § 14.12 *supra.*

295. 15 U.S.C.A. § 78*o*–5. *See* § 14.13 *supra.*

296. 15 U.S.C.A. § 79a *et seq. See* chapter 18 *infra.*

297. *See generally* Daniel Hirsch & Kenneth Winer, SEC Administrative Enforcement Proceedings—Parts I and II, 29 Rev. Sec. & Commod. Reg. 243, 259 (1996).

303. 15 U.S.C.A. § 78f.

304. San Francisco Mining Exchange v. SEC, 378 F.2d 162 (9th Cir.1967).

305. 15 U.S.C.A. § 78s(h)(1).

306. 15 U.S.C.A. § 78s(h)(2). *See, e.g.,* Archer v. SEC, 133 F.2d 795 (8th Cir.1943).

307. 15 U.S.C.A. §§ 78*o*–3, 78q–1, 78s, 78c(a)(26), 78c(a)(34). The Commission is the reviewing authority for sanctions imposed by the exchanges, the National Association of Securities Dealers (NASD), and other self-regulatory organizations pursuant to §§ 6(d), 15A(h), 17A(b)(5), and 19(d)–(f) of the Exchange Act, 15 U.S.C.A. §§ 78f(d), 78*o*–3h, 78*l*–1(b)(5), 78o(d)–(f) (1976).

308. 15 U.S.C.A. § 78s(h)(1).

309. 15 U.S.C.A. § 78s(h)(2). *See, e.g.,* Mister Discount Stockbrokers, Inc. v. SEC, 768 F.2d 875 (7th Cir.1985) (expelling brokerage firm from NASD).

310. 15 U.S.C.A. § 78*o*.

311. 15 U.S.C.A. § 78*o*(b)(5). *See, e.g.,* Svalberg v. SEC, 876 F.2d 181 (D.C.Cir.1989) (permanently barring brokers from serving as principals in any NASD member firm).

312. 15 U.S.C.A. § 78*o*(b)(6). *See, e.g.,* Elliott v. SEC, 36 F.3d 86 (11th Cir.1994) (barring individual convicted of 37 counts of mail fraud from associating with any broker-dealer).

313. 15 U.S.C.A. § 78s(h)(3).

314. 15 U.S.C.A. § 80b–3(f).

315. 15 U.S.C.A. § 78a–9(b).

316. In re Blinder, SEC Admin. Proc. File No. 3–8305, 29 Sec. Reg. & L. Rep. (BNA) 1406 (SEC 1997).

318. *See* Sec.Exch.Act Rel. No. 34–14761 (May 15, 1978).

preponderance of the evidence.[319] Many courts have stated the standard of review in terms of substantial evidence,[320] which requires something less than a preponderance of the evidence.[321] Also, any review of SEC decisions is to be made on a deferential basis.[322] For the purpose of determining the timeliness of an appeal, the period begins to run from the caption date on the SEC final order.[323]

Direct appeal to the SEC is the proper method of review for NASD disciplinary sanctions, and the sanctions are not reviewable by way of collateral attack in a subsequent SEC judicial enforcement action.[325] The normal review process is from the NASD to the SEC and then to a federal court of appeals.[326] The same procedure applies in the case of sanctions imposed by a securities exchange.

§ 16.2[14] Civil Penalties in Administrative Actions

The Securities Enforcement Remedies and Penny Stock Reform Act of 1990[327] empowers the Commission to impose civil penalties in administrative proceedings.[328] The power to impose civil penalties applies to proceedings against a broker-dealer,[329] associated person,[330] municipal securities dealer,[331] government securities dealer,[332] or registered clearing agent.[333] The SEC has similar authority over persons registered under the Investment Company or Investment Advisers Act of 1940.[334] If, after notice and opportunity to be heard, the Commission finds: (1) a willful violation of the securities laws, (2) a willful violation of the rules of an applicable self regulatory organization, (3) that the respondent has willfully made material misstatements or omissions in required reports, or (4) that the respondent has willfully failed to adequately supervise persons,[335] then it may impose a civil penalty according to a three-

---

319. Steadman v. SEC, 450 U.S. 91, 101 S.Ct. 999, 67 L.Ed.2d 69 (1981), *rehearing denied* 451 U.S. 933, 101 S.Ct. 2008, 68 L.Ed.2d 318 (1981).

320. L.C. Wegard & Co. v. SEC, 189 F.3d 461 (2d Cir.1999) (unpublished opinion), *relying on* Cellular Telephone Co. v. Town of Oyster Bay, 166 F.3d 490 (2d Cir.1999).

321. "Substantial evidence, in the usual context, has been construed to mean less than a preponderance, but more than a scintilla of evidence. 'It means such relevant evidence as a reasonable mind might accept as adequate to support a conclusion.' Universal Camera v. NLRB, 340 U.S. 474, 477, 71 S.Ct. 456, 95 L.Ed. 456 (1951)." Cellular Telephone Co. v. Town of Oyster Bay, 166 F.3d 490, 494 (2d Cir.1999).

322. *E.g.*, Valicenti Advisory Services, Inc. v. SEC, 198 F.3d 62 (2d Cir.1999).

323. Newell v. SEC, 812 F.2d 1259 (9th Cir.1987).

325. *See, e.g.*, SEC v. Waco Financial, Inc., 751 F.2d 831 (6th Cir.1985), *cert. denied* 474 U.S. 818, 106 S.Ct. 65, 88 L.Ed.2d 53 (1985).

326. *See, e.g.*, Maschler v. National Association of Securities Dealers, 827 F.Supp. 131 (E.D.N.Y.1993). Since judicial review is vested in the courts of appeals, federal district courts cannot assert jurisdiction. *Id.*

327. Pub.L. No. 101–429.

328. Securities Exchange Act of 1934 § 21B, 15 U.S.C.A. § 78u–2; Investment Company Act § 9(d), (e), 15 U.S.C.A. § 80a–9(d), (e); Investment Advisers Act § 203(i), 15 U.S.C.A. § 80b–3(i).

329. *See* section 15(b)(4), 15 U.S.C.A. § 78*o*(b)(4).

330. *See* section 15(b)(6), 15 U.S.C.A. § 78*o*(b)(6).

331. *See* section 15B, 15 U.S.C.A. § 78*o*–4.

332. *See* section 15C, 15 U.S.C.A. § 78*o*–5.

333. *See* section 17A, 15 U.S.C.A. § 78q–1.

334. 15 U.S.C.A. §§ 80a–9(d), (e), 80b–3(i).

335. *See* section 15(b)(4)(E), 15 U.S.C.A. § 78*o*(b)(4)(E).

tiered maximum, depending upon the degree of the respondent's culpability and the impact of the violations.[336] In considering whether the imposition of a penalty is warranted, and if so the appropriate amount of the penalty, the Commission is directed to consider a number of factors. The Commission must consider the degree of culpability, the harm to others, the extent to which the violator was unjustly enriched, whether the violator has previously run afoul of the securities laws (or similar laws), the need to deter such conduct, "and other matters as justice may require."[337] In considering whether to impose such a penalty, the Commission must consider any evidence the respondent chooses to introduce that relates to his or her ability to pay.[338] In addition to a penalty, the Commission is empowered to order a disgorgement or accounting of profits.[339]

§ 16.2[15] Administrative Proceedings and Double Jeopardy

In 1997, the Supreme Court in Hudson v. United States[344] overruled the position that it had previously taken in one case and reinstated the law as it was under an earlier ruling[345]—namely, that there is a strong presumption resulting from a congressional designation of a sanction as civil. It is thus clear that there should be a strong presumption that double jeopardy would not be implicated by administrative sanctions.

§ 16.2[16] Collateral Estoppel Effect of SEC Proceedings

Frequently, private litigation will coincide with or follow either SEC injunctive relief or administrative proceedings, whether these proceedings involve the SEC or one of the self regulatory organizations.[346] In such cases, the question may arise as to the preclusive effect to be given to the prior determination. In general, the federal district courts have a wide range of discretion in deciding whether to apply collateral estoppel.[347] Thus, collateral estoppel effect may be given in a private suit to a prior SEC injunctive action notwithstanding the absence of a jury trial in the first action. When there is an identity of issues, collateral estoppel will be applied to preclude relitigation in an SEC civil action of facts that had been determined in a prior criminal prosecution.[349] Although nonjudicial determination such as agency decisions are less formal than judicial proceedings, courts have given a preclusive effect to such decisions when it is shown that there was the opportunity to fully and fairly litigate the issue.[350]

---

336. *See* section 21B of the Exchange Act, 15 U.S.C.A. § 78u–3.

337. Section 21C, 15 U.S.C.A. § 78u–3(c).

338. Section 21C(d). 15 U.S.C.A. § 78u–3(d).

339. Section 21C(e), 15 U.S.C.A. § 78u–3(e).

344. 522 U.S. 93, 118 S.Ct. 488, 139 L.Ed.2d 450 (1997).

345. United States v. Ward, 448 U.S. 242, 100 S.Ct. 2636, 65 L.Ed.2d 742(1980).

346. Collateral estoppel is limited to formal agency actions and does not apply to positions taken outside of a formal adjudication. *See, e.g.,* Graham v. SEC, 222 F.3d 994 (D.C.Cir.2000) (SEC not equitably estopped by previous position).

347. *E.g.,* Parklane Hosiery Co. v. Shore, 439 U.S. 322, 99 S.Ct. 645, 58 L.Ed.2d 552 (1979).

349. SEC v. Gruenberg, 989 F.2d 977 (8th Cir.1993).

350. *E.g.,* Bowen v. United States, 570 F.2d 1311, 1322 (7th Cir.1978); Campbell v. Superior Court, 18 Ariz.App. 287, 501 P.2d 463 (1972).

§ 16.2[18] Suspension of the Right to Practice Before the Commission—SEC Rule 102(e)[359]

Under SEC Rule of Practice 102(e)[360] the Commission may suspend, limit, or bar *"any* person" from practicing before it "in *any* way."[361] Rule 102(e) has been used by the SEC to discipline professionals. The Rule 102(e) power has been used against both accountants[363] and lawyers.[364] Although use of Rule 102(e)'s sanctions has been questioned in light of the absence of express statutory authority, the Second Circuit has upheld the rule as consistent with the Commission's overall statutory mandate.[365]

In 1988, the Commission amended Rule 2(e) so that unless the SEC orders otherwise, Rule 2(e) proceedings shall be public. Prior to the controversial amendments, Rule 2(e) proceedings were presumed to be nonpublic unless the SEC ordered that they be public. The SEC has also indicated that scienter must be shown in order to discipline attorneys for violations of the antifraud rules.[368]

However, the Commission must exercise that power consistently.[369] The District of Columbia Court of Appeals took the Commission to task for indicating that in some instances negligence would be sufficient to support a Rule 2(e) sanction while in others it would not.[370] The Commission responded by amending Rule 2(e) to clarify that in some instances, negligence will be sufficient. In 1999, the SEC amended Rule 102(e) of its Rules of Practice to make it clear that the Commission can suspend or bar professionals from practicing before the Commission if they engage in "improper professional conduct."[371] Under the rule as amended, accountants can be disciplined for intentional, reckless, and in some cases, negligent conduct. The Commission explained that it can issue Rule 102(e) sanctions against a professional who has demonstrated that he or she is not competent to practice before the SEC. Specifically, the rule as amended provides that "improper professional conduct" means intentional or reckless conduct that violates applicable pro-

---

359. *See also* the discussion of lawyers and the SEC in § 9.8 *supra.*

360. Rule 102(e) formerly was designated Rule 2(e). Those descriptions are used interchangeably throughout this section.

361. 17 C.F.R. § 201.102(e)(3). *See* § 16.4 *infra.*

363. *E.g.,* Potts v. SEC, 151 F.3d 810 (8th Cir.1998).

364. *E.g.,* In the Matter of Carter & Johnson, Sec.Exch.Act Rel. No. 34–17597, [1981 Transfer Binder] Fed.Sec.L.Rep. (CCH) ¶ 82,847 (Feb. 28, 1981)(dismissing case because of lack of scienter).

365. Touche Ross & Co. v. SEC, 609 F.2d 570, 579 (2d Cir.1979). *Accord,* Sheldon v. SEC, 45 F.3d 1515 (11th Cir.1995). (upholding constitutionality of Rule 2(e)'s use against attorneys).

368. In re Carter & Johnson, Administrative Proceeding File No. 3–5464, 47 S.E.C. 471, Sec. Exch. Act Rel. No. 34–17597, 47 S.E.C. 471, [1981 Transfer Binder] Fed.Sec.L.Rep. (CCH) ¶ 82,847 (SEC Feb. 28, 1981). *See also, e.g.,* Checkosky v. SEC, 23 F.3d 452 (D.C.Cir.1994) (remanding SEC suspension of accountants for failing to distinguish the *Carter & Johnson* scienter requirement). Curiously, in *Checkosky,* the SEC had indicated that the accountants' GAAP and GAAS violations warranted Rule 2(e) sanctions even if they had not acted with scienter. The Commission found, however, that they had acted recklessly. On appeal, the D.C. Circuit remanded for further explanation of the scienter issue. *See* § 12.8 *supra* for a discussion of scienter generally.

369. Checkosky v. SEC, 139 F.3d 221 (D.C.Cir.1998).

370. *Id.*

371. Rule 102(e)(1)(ii), 17 C.F.R. § 210.102(e)(1)(ii). *See* Sec. Act Rel. No. 33–7593, 1998 WL 729201 (SEC Oct. 19, 1998). The phrase "improper professional conduct" is not unconstitutionally vague. *See* Marrie v. SEC, 374 F.3d 1196 (D.C. Cir. 2004).

fessional accounting standards.[372] Additionally, improper conduct includes negligent conduct when such conduct is either a single instance of highly unreasonable conduct or repeated instances of unreasonable conduct.[373]

In 2002, Congress enacted the Sarbanes–Oxley Act in response to the corporate fraud scandals of 2001 and 2002.[374] There was considerable concern that more vigilant representation by attorneys could have prevented or at least minimized the fraud involved in such celebrated failures as Enron and WorldCom. As a result, Congress expanded attorney responsibility by calling on attorneys to report serious wrongdoing to high ranking corporate officials.[375] The Act mandates that the SEC promulgate rules setting forth minimum standards of professional conduct for attorneys appearing and practicing before the SEC in connection with their representation of issuers.[376] The SEC rules must contain a requirement that attorneys report evidence of a material violation of securities laws or breach of fiduciary duty or similar violation by a company, including an agent of the company, to the chief legal counsel or the chief executive officer and, if that officer does not respond appropriately, to the audit committee (or other committee composed entirely of outside directors).[377] The statute makes no distinction between inside and outside counsel advising a reporting company.

In announcing its proposed rules regulating attorney conduct, the SEC set forth a broad definition of what constitutes practice before the Commission.

Rule 102(e) is not the only means for pursuing attorneys and other professionals. For example, the SEC has used its power under section 15(c)(4) of the Act[384] against attorneys who caused a violation of the securities laws.[385] In 2001, the SEC announced that as an alternative to Rule 102(e) proceedings, it was considering the use of its cease and desist power[386] to deal with attorney misconduct.[387] The SEC followed through with this policy and has used cease and desist proceedings to sanction improper professional conduct.[388]

---

372. Rule 102(e)(1)(iv)(A), 17 C.F.R. § 201.102(e)(1)(iv)(A). The amendment to include reckless conduct could not be applied retroactively. Marrie v. SEC, 374 F.3d 1196 (D.C. Cir. 2004).

373. Rule 102(e)(iv)(B), 17 C.F.R. § 201. 102(e)(iv)(B).

374. Sarbanes–Oxley Act of 2002, Pub. Law 107–204 (July 30, 2002).

375. 15 U.S.C.A. § 7245. *See generally* Thomas Lee Hazen, Administrative Law Controls on Attorney Practice Before the Securities and Exchange Commission, 55 Admin. L. Rev. 323 (2003).

376. *Id.*

377. *Id.* For a fuller discussion *see* § 9.8 *supra.*

384. 15 U.S.C.A. § 78*o*(c)(4).

385. In the Matter of George C. Kern, Jr. Administrative Proceeding File No. 3–6869, 52 S.E.C. Docket 451, 1988 WL 357006, (SEC Initial decision March 21, 1988), *reversed as not applying to future violations,* 1991 WL 284804, 50 S.E.C. 596, Sec. Exch. Act Rel. No. 34–29356, 49 S.E.C. Docket 422 (SEC Jun 21, 1991).

386. *See* § 16.2[12] *supra.*

387. *See* SEC May Consider Cease-and-Desist to Sanction Attorneys for Misconduct, 33 Sec. Reg. & L. Rep. (BNA) 358 (March 12, 2001).

388. *See, e.g.,* In The Matter of Seymour, Administrative Proceeding File No. 3–10521, 2001 WL 698371, Sec. Exch. Act Rel. No. 34–44461, Release No. AE–1413 (SEC June 21, 2001).

§ 16.2[19] SEC Oversight Authority

The self regulatory organizations for the securities industry—the exchanges and the NASD—are subject to SEC oversight.[393] As part of this oversight responsibility, by virtue of section 19 of the Act,[394] the Commission has oversight responsibility with respect to all rulemaking activity of national exchanges.[395] Similar authority exists with regard to the NASD.[396] One consequence of the SEC oversight authority is that when it provides a pervasive regulatory scheme, the regulation will operate as an implied repeal of the antitrust laws as an alternative way to scrutinize the activity in question.[397]

The self regulatory organizations have disciplinary authority over their members to redress violations of self regulatory organization rules. Self regulatory organization disciplinary actions[399] are subject to SEC review and, in turn, to review by a federal court of appeals.[400] The doctrine of exhaustion of remedies means that disciplinary and other self regulatory action must proceed the self regulatory agency before review by the SEC or by a court.[401]

The SEC also has the authority to proceed directly against the self regulatory organization should they fail to adequately enforce their rules. For example, in a widely publicized conclusion of a long-standing investigation, in 1996, the SEC censured the NASD for its failures in self-regulatory oversight with regard to NASD market makers' quotation practices.[402]

---

393. *See* § 14.3 *supra.*

394. 15 U.S.C.A. § 78s.

395. *See generally* Paul G. Mahoney, The Exchange as Regulator, 83 Va. L. Rev. 1453 (1997).

396. *See* 15 U.S.C.A. § 78o–3.

397. *See* United States v. NASD, 422 U.S. 694, 95 S.Ct. 2427, 45 L.Ed.2d 486 (1975); Gordon v. New York Stock Exchange, Inc., 422 U.S. 659, 95 S.Ct. 2598, 45 L.Ed.2d 463 (1975). *See also, e.g.,* Silver v. New York Stock Exchange, 373 U.S. 341, 83 S.Ct. 1246, 10 L.Ed.2d 389 (1963). The impact of the antitrust laws generally is discussed in § 14.1[9] *supra.*

399. The exchanges and the NASD are given broad investigatory and disciplinary powers. *See, e.g.,* Gold v. SEC, 48 F.3d 987 (7th Cir.1995) (due process does not require exchange to give notice to former brokerage employee that his conduct with the firm was under investigation).

400. *See, e.g.,* L.H. Alton & Co. v. SEC, [1999–2000 Transfer Binder] Fed. Sec. L. Rep. (CCH) ¶ 91,021, 2000 WL 975183 (9th Cir.2000) (unpublished) (affirming NASD sanctions).

401. *See, e.g.,* Marchiano v. NASD, 134 F.Supp.2d 90 (D.D.C.2001) (action for injunction against NASD disciplinary proceedings was dismissed due to failure to exhaust administrative remedies).

402. *See* Fed. Sec. L. Rep. (CCH) (Report no. 1727, Aug. 27, 1996).

Chapter 17

JURISDICTIONAL ASPECTS

Table of Sections

---

§ 17.1 Exclusive Federal Jurisdiction Under the Exchange Act; Concurrent Jurisdiction Under the 1933 and Other Securities Acts

§ 17.1[1] The Jurisdictional Mosaic

The federal securities laws provide a mosaic approach to jurisdiction. The Securities Act of 1933 and most of the other acts comprising the battery of securities laws provide for concurrent jurisdiction of federal and state courts, thus giving private parties a choice of forum.[1] In contrast, the Securities Exchange Act of 1934 provides that jurisdiction is exclusively federal, which means that all private suits must be brought in federal court. All criminal prosecutions under the securities laws and judicial enforcement actions by the Securities and Exchange Commission must be maintained only in federal court.[2] Similarly, jurisdiction over appeals from SEC administrative decisions is exclusively federal.[3] When dealing with private remedies, however, the six securities acts present three different approaches to jurisdictional allocation.

---

§ 17.1

1. Even among the acts providing for concurrent jurisdiction, there are variations regarding the right of removal to federal court. Furthermore, in 1998, Congress took away from the states' jurisdiction over securities fraud class actions involving more than fifty plaintiffs. Securities Litigation Uniform Standards Act of 1998, Pub. Law No. 105–353, 112 Stat. 3227 (105th Cong.– 2d sess. November 3, 1998) (S 1260). *See* 1933 Act § 16(f), 15 U.S.C.A. § 77p(f); 1934 Act § 28(f), 15 U.S.C.A. § 78bb(f). *See* §§ 7.17[2], 12.15[2] *supra*.

2. Securities Act of 1933, § 22(a), 15 U.S.C.A. § 77v(a); Securities Exchange Act of 1934, § 27, 15 U.S.C.A. § 78aa; Public Utility Holding Company Act of 1935, § 25, 15 U.S.C.A. § 79y; Trust Indenture Act of 1939, § 322(b), 15 U.S.C.A. § 77vvv(b); Investment Company Act of 1940, § 44, 15 U.S.C.A. § 80a–43; Investment Advisers Act of 1940, § 214, 15 U.S.C.A. § 80b–14.

3. Securities Act of 1933, § 9, 15 U.S.C.A. § 77i; Securities Exchange Act of 1934, § 25, 15 U.S.C.A. § 78y; Public Utility Holding Company Act of 1935, § 24, 15 U.S.C.A. § 79x; Trust Indenture Act of 1939, § 322(a), 15 U.S.C.A. § 77vvv(a); Investment Company Act of 1940, § 43, 15 U.S.C.A. § 80a–42; Investment Advisers Act of 1940, § 213, 15 U.S.C.A. § 80b–13.

A state court does not have the power to interfere with SEC proceedings. First Jersey Securities, Inc. v. SEC, 194 N.J.Super. 284, 476 A.2d 861 (1984), *appeal dismissed*, 101 N.J. 208, 501 A.2d 893 (1985).

First, the Securities Exchange Act of 1934 provides for exclusive federal jurisdiction over all suits in law or equity to enforce liabilities arising under the Act or applicable SEC rules.[4] Thus, only under the Exchange Act is all jurisdiction exclusively federal. Second, the other five federal securities acts provide for concurrent federal and state jurisdiction over private civil actions while granting exclusive federal jurisdiction over criminal proceedings and SEC enforcement actions.[5] The third approach, which actually is a variation of the second and is found in the Securities Act of 1933[6] and the Trust Indenture Act of 1939,[7] is concurrent state and federal jurisdiction, provided, however, that suits initiated in state courts are not removable to federal court.[8] As is the case with the other acts, jurisdiction over criminal actions and SEC judicial enforcement proceedings under the 1933 Act and Trust Indenture Act is exclusively federal.

Securities claims can form the basis of other rights of action. The courts were divided as to whether there is exclusive or concurrent jurisdiction for claims brought under the Racketeering Influenced and Corrupt Organizations Act (RICO).[9] The Supreme Court resolved the issue when it held that there is concurrent state and federal jurisdiction over civil RICO claims.[11]

Most federal statutes that grant concurrent state and federal jurisdiction typically also provide for a right of removal to federal court.[12] Denial of the right of removal is generally limited to federal legislation involving matters of strong local, as opposed to national, interests.[13] Thus, the ban on removal in the 1933 and 1939 Acts is surprising in light of the strong federalizing strains running through securities regulation.[14] One justification for the denial of the right of removal is the facilitation of private enforcement[15] by giving the plaintiff an absolute choice of forum; especially since, in many cases, state court litigation may prove less complex and less expensive than suits in federal court. Accordingly, complaints framed solely in terms of the 1933 or 1939 Acts can guarantee a state court forum and avoid the exclusive federal jurisdiction of the 1934 Exchange Act[16] or the removal to federal court that would be permitted under the other acts.

---

4. 15 U.S.C.A. § 78aa.

5. *See* footnote 2 *supra.*

6. 15 U.S.C.A. § 77v(a).

7. 15 U.S.C.A. § 77vvv(b).

8. The non-removal provisions of the securities laws must yield to the more specific removal provision found in the bankruptcy laws. California Public Employees' Retirement System v. WorldCom, Inc., 368 F.3d 86 (2d Cir. 2004); 28 U.S.C.A. § 1452(a).

9. 18 U.S.C.A. § 1961 *et seq. See* § 22.3 *infra.*

11. Tafflin v. Levitt, 493 U.S. 455, 110 S.Ct. 792, 107 L.Ed.2d 887 (1990), *rehearing denied,* 495 U.S. 915, 110 S.Ct. 1942, 109 L.Ed.2d 305 (1990).

12. *E.g.,* Federal Employers' Liability Act, 28 U.S.C.A. § 1445(a); Jones Act, 46 U.S.C.A. § 688; Magnuson–Moss Federal Warranty Act, 15 U.S.C.A. § 2310(d).

13. *See, e.g.,* McKnett v. St. Louis & San Francisco Railway Co., 292 U.S. 230, 54 S.Ct. 690, 78 L.Ed. 1227 (1934); Mondou v. New York, New Haven & Hartford Railroad, 223 U.S. 1, 32 S.Ct. 169, 56 L.Ed. 327 (1911). *Cf.* Missouri ex rel. Southern Railway v. Mayfield, 340 U.S. 1, 71 S.Ct. 1, 95 L.Ed. 3 (1950) (upholding the state court's right to invoke *forum non conveniens* as a basis for dismissal).

14. *See, e.g.,* Edgar v. MITE Corp., 457 U.S. 624, 102 S.Ct. 2629, 73 L.Ed.2d 269 (1982) (federal preemption of state tender offer statute). *See* § 11.13 *supra.*

15. Many securities violations give rise to cumulative express and implied private rights of action under the 1933 and 1934 Acts. *See* chapters 7, 10, 11, 12, 13 *supra.*

16. Drexel Burnham Lambert, Inc. v. Merchants Investment Counseling, Inc., 451 N.E.2d 346 (Ind.App.1983).

The ability to take advantage of state court forums has been severely limited by the preemptive effect of the Securities Litigation Uniform Standards Act of 1998 (SLUSA).[17] The federal preemption is not total but, as described in an earlier section of this treatise,[18] it does extend to most securities fraud class actions involving publicly traded securities, even if the complaint includes claims under state law.[19] Even though 1933 Act claims under section 11[20] or 12(a)(2)[21] do not require scienter,[22] they appear to be subject to SLUSA's preemption. In contrast, section 12(a)(1)[23] is based on a violation of the 1933 Act's registration provisions and should remain removable to state court since the claim is not based on fraud or misrepresentation and thus is not subject to the language of the SLUSA's preemption.[24]

§ 17.1[2] Exclusive Federal Jurisdiction Under the Exchange Act

State courts are bound to dismiss any claim based on the Securities Exchange Act of 1934 in light of its grant of exclusive federal jurisdiction.[33] As discussed below, there has been some disagreement as to whether this also extends to those instances in which the alleged federal violation of federal law is raised as a defense to a state law cause of action that was brought in a state court forum.

It is one thing to say that jurisdiction over affirmative claims is exclusively federal, and it may be another to preclude the Securities Exchange Act from being raised as a defense in a state court. Although a large number of states will entertain 1934 Act claims raised defensively,[34] a few influential courts, including Delaware's, have ruled that they lack jurisdiction in such cases.[35] This harsh minority view has been criticized,[36] as well it should be. The mere fact that the success of a state law claim may be dependent on an interpretation of an SEC rule is not sufficient to transform a state law cause of action into a federal claim.[37] Conversely, a plaintiff cannot disguise a federal claim as one under state law.[38] The "artful pleading rule" prevents a plaintiff

---

17.　Pub. Law No. 105–353, 112 Stat. 3227 (105th Cong., 2d Sess. November 3, 1998) (S 1260).

18.　*See* § 12.15[2] *supra.*

19.　15 U.S.C.A. §§ 77p(b), 78bb(f).

20.　15 U.S.C.A. § 77k. *See* §§ 7.3–7.5 *supra.*

21.　15 U.S.C.A. § 77l(a)(2). *See* § 7.6 *supra.*

22.　The scienter requirement is discussed in § 12.8 *supra.*

23.　15 U.S.C.A. § 77l(a)(1). *See* § 7.2 *supra.*

24.　*See, e.g.,* In re Tyco International Multidistrict Litigation, 322 F.Supp.2d 116 (D.N.H. 2004); In re King Pharmaceuticals, 36 Sec. Reg. & L. Rep. (BNA) 444 (E.D. Tenn. 2004); In re Waste Management Securities Litigation, 194 F. Supp.2d 590 (S.D. Tex. 2002).

33.　*See, e.g.,* Evans v. Dale, 896 F.2d 975 (5th Cir.1990).

34.　*See, e.g.,* Gregory–Massari, Inc. v. Purkitt, 1 Cal.App.3d 968, 82 Cal.Rptr. 210 (1969).

35.　*See, e.g.,* Investment Associates v. Standard Power & Light Corp., 29 Del.Ch. 225, 238–39, 48 A.2d 501, 508–09 (1946), *affirmed,* 29 Del.Ch. 593, 606, 51 A.2d 572, 579 (1947).

36.　2 Louis Loss, Securities Regulation 973–1000 (2d ed.1961); *see generally* Thomas L. Hazen, Allocation of Jurisdiction Between the State and Federal Courts for Remedies Under the Federal Securities Laws, 60 N.C.L. Rev. 707, 722–724 (1982).

37.　Petrie v. Pacific Stock Exchange, 982 F.Supp. 1390 (N.D.Cal.1997).

38.　*E.g.,* Herman v. Salomon Smith Barney, Inc., 266 F.Supp.2d 1208 (S.D. Cal. 2003) (allegations of violations of California unfair trade practices law was really based in violations of the Municipal Securities Rulemaking Board rules and thus was a federal claim).

from omitting necessary federal questions from the complaint.[40] However, the fact that the same facts may give rise to both federal and state claims does not implicate the artful pleading doctrine so as to defeat the state court's jurisdiction.[41]

§ 17.1[4] Federal Supplemental (or Pendent) Jurisdiction Over State Claims

What about the plaintiff with 1934 Act claims and related state causes of action? All related claims can be heard together in federal court when the court invokes supplemental pendent jurisdiction over the state law claims.[58] Even after the federal claim is dismissed, a federal court can retain jurisdiction over the state claim.[59] If the federal claim fails, however, the federal court is likely to dismiss the state law cause of action.[60]

§ 17.1[6] Preemption of State Jurisdiction in Securities Class Actions

The Uniform Standards Act of 1998,[85] which amended both the Securities Act of 1933 and the Securities Exchange Act of 1934, requires that most class actions involving publicly traded securities be brought in federal court.[86]

§ 17.2 Subject Matter Jurisdiction—Use of the Jurisdictional Means

The Exchange Act's registration and reporting requirements are triggered by offerings or issuers having sufficient interstate contact to support federal regulation.[1] In contrast, the 1933 Act registration requirements are implicated

---

40. "A state-created cause of action can be deemed to arise under federal law (1) where federal law completely preempts state law; (2) where the claim is necessarily federal in character; or (3) where the right to relief depends on the resolution of a substantial, disputed federal question." ARCO Environmental Remediation, LLC v. Department of Health and Environmental Quality of the State of Montana, 213 F.3d 1108 (9th Cir.2000).

41. Lippitt v. Raymond James Financial Services, Inc., 340 F.3d 1033 (9th Cir. 2003) (state unfair advertising claim arising out of brokerage firm's marketing of charitable organization's certificates of deposit was not preempted by federal law).

58. United Mine Workers v. Gibbs, 383 U.S. 715, 86 S.Ct. 1130, 16 L.Ed.2d 218 (1966); Chapman v. Merrill Lynch, Pierce, Fenner & Smith, Inc., 1983 WL 1340, [1984–1984 Transfer Binder] Fed.Sec.L.Rep. (CCH) ¶ 99,419 at p. 96,410–11 (D.Md.1983).

Nation-wide service of process applies to pendent state claims. *See* Gill v. Three Dimension Systems, Inc., 87 F.Supp.2d 1278 (M.D.Fla.2000).

59. *See, e.g.,* United International Holdings, Inc. v. Wharf (Holdings) Ltd., 210 F.3d 1207, 1219–1220 (10th Cir.2000), *affirmed on other grounds,* 532 U.S. 588, 121 S.Ct. 1776, 149 L.Ed.2d 845 (2001).

60. United Mine Workers v. Gibbs, 383 U.S. 715, 725–27, 86 S.Ct. 1130, 1138–1140, 16 L.Ed.2d 218 (1966).

85. Securities Litigation Uniform Standards Act of 1998, Pub. Law No. 105–353, 112 Stat. 3227 (105th Cong.–2d sess. November 3, 1998) (S 1260). *See* 1933 Act § 16(f). 15 U.S.C.A. § 77p(f); 1934 Act§ 28(f), 15 U.S.C.A. § 78bb(f). *See* §§ 7.17[2], 12.15[2] *supra*

86. *See* § 12.15 *supra.*

§ 17.2

1. Thus, for example, the Exchange Act's registration requirements are based on the securities being listed on a national securities exchange or the issuer having more than ten million dollars in assets and five hundred or more holders of record of a class of equity securities. 15 U.S.C.A §§ 78*l*(a), (g); 17 C.F.R. § 240.12g–1.

by a nonexempt offer or sale of securities through an instrumentality of interstate commerce.[2] Although not required as a matter of jurisdictional limitation, Congress elected to exempt from 1933 Act registration offerings that originate and take place within the confines of a single state.[3]

The jurisdictional requirements are easily satisfied. However, in order to state a claim and establish jurisdiction, the complaint must refer to federal law.

Typically, the securities acts' antifraud provisions are triggered by the use of an instrumentality of interstate commerce.[5] The language of the various jurisdictional provisions is varied. However, the courts' focus in interpreting these provisions has centered on the use of an instrumentality of interstate commerce for some part of the transaction. Furthermore, in interpreting the reach of the statute, the federal courts have taken a broad view of the securities laws' jurisdictional reach. The broad language regarding the necessary jurisdictional nexus when combined with the courts' expansive interpretation means that most securities transactions will be covered. Thus, for example, an intrastate telephone call will support jurisdiction.[7] Similarly, it has been held that the particular communication containing the actionable statement need not be made through an instrumentality of interstate commerce so long as the transaction in question was effectuated through the use of such an instrumentality.[8] Accordingly, although the language of the jurisdictional provisions seems to focus on the communication forming the basis of the securities law violations,[9] the courts have tended to look to the transaction as a whole.[10]

While a face-to-face conversation, standing alone, will not satisfy the jurisdictional requirements, there may be jurisdiction under Rule 10b–5, if the conversations are part of a transaction that utilizes an instrumentality of interstate commerce.[11] Thus, for example, a face-to-face conversation followed by a transaction utilizing an instrumentality of interstate commerce generally has been held to subject the speaker to Rule 10b–5 scrutiny.

---

2. Section 5 of the Act makes it unlawful to make offers and sales "mak[ing] use of any means or instrumentality of transportation or communication in interstate commerce or of the mails to sell such security" unless the securities are registered (or exempt). 15 U.S.C.A. § 77e. *See* chapter 2 *supra*. The exemptions are discussed in chapter 4 *supra*.

3. 15 U.S.C.A. § 77c(a)(11); 17 C.F.R. § 230.147. *See* § 4.12 *supra*.

5. *E.g.,* 15 U.S.C.A. § 77*l* (referring back to violations of section 5's prohibitions); 15 U.S.C.A. § 77q(a) ("offer or sale of any securities by the use of any means or instruments of transportation or communication in interstate commerce or by use of the mails, directly or indirectly * * * "); 15 U.S.C.A. § 78j(b) ("by the use of any means or instrumentality of interstate commerce, or of the mails, or of any facility of any national securities exchange"); 17 C.F.R. § 240.10b–5 ("by the use of any means or instrumentality of interstate commerce, or of the mails, or of any facility of any national securities exchange"). *Cf.* United States v. Cashin, 281 F.2d 669, 673 (2d Cir.1960) (jurisdictional reach of section 12(1) and 17(a) of the 1933 Act are the same).

7. *E.g.,* Loveridge v. Dreagoux, 678 F.2d 870, 874 (10th Cir.1982); Dupuy v. Dupuy, 511 F.2d 641, 642–44 (5th Cir.1975).

8. *See, e.g.,* Leiter v. Kuntz, 655 F.Supp. 725, 726–27 (D.Utah 1987).

9. *E.g.,* 15 U.S.C.A. § 78j(b).

10. *E.g.,* Franklin Savings Bank of New York v. Levy, 551 F.2d 521, 524 (2d Cir.1977).

11. *E.g., Id.*

§ 17.4 Extraterritorial Application of the Securities Laws; Their Relevance to Foreign Issuers and to Transactions in Foreign Markets; Antifraud Provisions

Geographic and geopolitical borders have had increasingly less significance in the operation of securities markets around the globe. This has led to increasingly complex questions about which countries should be regulating transactions in the increasingly multinational securities markets.

This section addresses the securities laws' extraterritoriality in two contexts. First, to what extent do the antifraud provisions apply to foreign issuers and to transactions taking place, at least in part, abroad? Second, what reporting and disclosure provisions apply to foreign issuers?

Most American case law dealing with the extraterritorial application of United States securities laws focuses on the antifraud provisions of the 1934 Exchange Act.[2] The courts have developed two tests for subject-matter jurisdiction in securities fraud cases. One test is based on the conduct[3] of foreign persons within the United States; the other focuses on the effects[4] within the United States of conduct occurring in foreign countries. These tests do not always lead to predictable results.[5]

The increased use of the Internet for securities offerings and trading increases the potential for extraterritorial impact.[6] The Commission has taken the position that Internet communications that are targeting only foreign investors will be considered offshore so long as the web site takes precautions to guard against sales to United States residents.[7]

§ 17.4[1] Extraterritorial Jurisdiction Under the Antifraud Provisions

In Schoenbaum v. Firstbrook,[8] the Second Circuit held that an extraterritorial transaction involving foreign securities, listed on the American Stock Exchange and held by American citizens, affected the domestic securities market. The court thus found the assertion of subject-matter jurisdiction

---

§ 17.4

2. *E.g.*, 17 C.F.R. § 240.10b–5. *See* chapter 12 *supra*.

3. *See, e.g.*, Kauthar SDN BHD v. Sternberg, 149 F.3d 659 (7th Cir.1998); IIT v. Vencap, Ltd., 519 F.2d 1001, 1017 (2d Cir.1975), *on remand*, 411 F.Supp. 1094 (S.D.N.Y.1975); Paraschos v. YBM Magnex International, Inc., 2000 WL 325945, [1999–2000 Transfer Binder] Fed. Sec. L. Rep. (CCH) ¶ 90,923 (E.D. Pa. 2000).

4. *See, e.g.*, Des Brisay v. Goldfield Corp., 549 F.2d 133 (9th Cir.1977); Reingold v. Deloitte Haskins & Sells, 599 F.Supp. 1241 (S.D.N.Y.1984).

5. *See, e.g.*, Lewis D. Lowenfels & Alan R. Bromberg, U.S. Securities Fraud Across the Border: Unpredictable Jurisdiction, 55 Bus. Law. 1023 (2000).

6. *See, e.g.*, SEC v. Golds–Ventures Club, Case No. 1:02–CV–1434 (CAP), 2002 SECDIG 2002–103–3, 2002 WL 1062134, Litigation Release No. 17537, 2002 WL 1058847 (N.D. Ga. 2002) (emergency order including asset freeze against foreign website attempting to lure U.S. investors through fraudulent promotion).

7. Statement of the Commission Regarding Use of Internet Web Sites to Offer Securities, solicit Securities Transactions or Advertise Investment Services Offshore, International Series Release No. 1125, Sec. Act Rel. No. 33–7516, 1998 WL 135626 (F.R.) (SEC March 27, 1998). The SEC Release suggests a disclaimer that the web site offering is not available to United States residents, and further, that there be some procedures to assure that offers are not made to United States residents. *See also, e.g.*, Richard Cameron Blake, Advising Clients on Using the Internet to Make Offers of Securities in Offshore Offerings, 55 Bus. Law. 177 (1999).

8. 405 F.2d 200 (2d Cir.1968), *modified en banc on other grounds*, 405 F.2d 215 (2d Cir.1968), *cert. denied*, 395 U.S. 906, 89 S.Ct. 1747, 23 L.Ed.2d 219 (1969).

proper under the federal securities laws due to the domestic effects of the challenged transaction. The Ninth Circuit has similarly found jurisdiction over an international stock transaction under the "effects" test.[9] Jurisdiction can be based on misrepresentations made here, although involving foreign securities that were traded only in foreign markets.[10] However, activities within the United States that are "merely preparatory" to the actual fraud are clearly insufficient to confer subject-matter jurisdiction.[11] In one case, extraterritorial jurisdiction existed over foreign defendants with regard to fraudulent off-shore sales of promissory notes of foreign issuer where both plaintiff and defendant were also offshore; jurisdiction existed because the off-shore issuer was controlled from within the United States.[12] Where the fraudulent conduct takes place in the United States, jurisdiction will exist even though the transaction takes place outside the United States.[13]

It has, thus, been said that the antifraud provisions of the federal securities laws:

(1) Apply to losses from sales of securities to Americans resident in the United States whether or not acts * * * of material importance occurred in this country; and

(2) Apply to losses from sales of securities to Americans resident abroad if * * * acts * * * of material importance in the United States have significantly contributed thereto; but

(3) Do not apply to losses from sales of securities to foreigners outside the United States unless acts * * * within the United States directly caused such losses.[14]

§ 17.4[2] 1933 Act Registration and 1934 Act Reporting Requirements for Foreign Issuers

A common method for domestic trading of foreign issues is through American Depositary Receipts (ADR's). The foreign securities are placed in a central depository and ADR certificates, representing a share of the depository's holdings, are traded in the American securities markets. When ADRs are first offered to the American public, registration of the depositary shares (ADSs) is required under the 1933 Act on Form F–6.[54] ADSs registered on

9. Des Brisay v. Goldfield Corp., 549 F.2d 133 (9th Cir.1977) (takeover of Canadian corporation by American corporation involved improper use of the American corporation's securities, which were registered and listed on a national exchange, and adversely affected both the foreign plaintiffs and the American securities market).

10. Leasco Data Processing Equipment v. Maxwell, 468 F.2d 1326 (2d Cir.1972), *on remand* 63 F.R.D. 94 (S.D.N.Y.1973) (the court premised jurisdiction upon domestic conduct and the direct effect on American investors).

11. Zoelsch v. Arthur Andersen & Co., 824 F.2d 27 (D.C.Cir.1987); Bersch v. Drexel Firestone, Inc., 519 F.2d 974 (2d Cir.1975), *cert. denied* 423 U.S. 1018, 96 S.Ct. 453, 46 L.Ed.2d 389 (1975); IIT v. Vencap, Ltd., 519 F.2d 1001 (2d Cir.1975), *on remand*, 411 F.Supp. 1094 (S.D.N.Y.1975).

12. SEC v. Princeton Economic International, Ltd., 94 F.Supp.2d 396 (D.N.J.2000) (opinion withdrawn).

13. *See, e.g.,* Paraschos v. YBM Magnex International, Inc., 2000 WL 325945, [1999–2000 Transfer Binder] Fed. Sec. L. Rep. (CCH) ¶ 90,923 (E.D. Pa. 2000). *See also, e.g.,* SEC v. Banner Fund Intern., 211 F.3d 602 (D.C. Cir. 2000) (fraudulent conduct occurred in the United States and United States investors were defrauded).

14. Bersch v. Drexel Firestone, Inc., 519 F.2d 974, 993 (2d Cir.1975), *cert. denied*, 423 U.S. 1018, 96 S.Ct. 453, 46 L.Ed.2d 389 (1975).

54. For discussion of 1933 Act registration forms, *see* § 3.4 *supra*. The distinction between ADRs and ADSs has been described as follows:

Form F–6 have been exempted from the 1934 Act's registration and reporting requirements.[55]

In 1994, the Commission made significant moves towards streamlining its registration and reporting requirements applicable to foreign issuers.[64] Part of that initiative included the adoption of a safe harbor rule to permit public announcement of certain exempt offerings of foreign issuers. Rule 135c[65] permits an announcement of a pending offering, provided that the announcement is not calculated to condition the market in the United States. The contemplated offering must be one that will not be registered, and the information in the permitted statement must explain that the securities will not be sold in the United States without registration or, alternatively, an exemption from registration.[66] The permitted announcement may then briefly describe the general nature of the offering, but may not be so specific as to be deemed an offer for sale in the United States.[67] In setting forth the information that may be contained in such an announcement, Rule 135c(3) of the 1933 Act permits much the same information as the general prefiling publicity safe harbor that is applicable generally to registered offerings in the United States.[68]

Rule 135e,[69] adopted by the SEC in 1997, provides a safe harbor for private foreign issuers and private governmental issuers contacting journalists offshore in connection with offerings outside the United States. The safe harbor applies to "providing any journalist with access to its press conferences held outside the United States, to meetings with the issuer or selling security-holder representatives conducted outside the United States," and "to written press-related materials released outside the United States," even though the materials or meetings relate to a proposed offering of securities so long as the securities will not be offered solely within the United States.[70] The rule thus applies both to offerings made wholly outside the United States as well as to foreign issuer offerings taking place both in the United States and abroad; the only exclusion is for offerings made solely within the United States.

The Commission has also addressed the applicability of Regulation D to transactions occurring outside the United States. As a general proposition, registration is not required for sales to nonresident purchasers where the

---

American Depositary Shares are shares of a foreign corporation that are deposited with an American financial institution. The depositary institution issues American Depositary Receipts ("ADRs") to the beneficial owners of the ADSs, who are then free to sell the ADSs on American securities exchanges. Essentially, ADSs and ADRs allow American investors to trade foreign securities within the United States.

55. 17 C.F.R. § 240.12g3–2(c).

64. Simplification of Registration and Reporting Requirements for Foreign Companies; Safe Harbors for Public Announcements of Unregistered Offerings and Broker–Dealer Research Reports, Sec. Act Rel. No. 33–7053, [1993–1994 Transfer Binder] Fed. Sec. L. Rep. (CCH) ¶ 85,331 (SEC April 19, 1994).

65. 17 C.F.R. § 230.135c.

66. Rule 135c(a)(2), 17 C.F.R. § 230.135c(a)(2).

67. Rule 135c(a)(3), 17 C.F.R. § 230.135c(a)(3).

68. *See* Rule 135, 17 C.F.R. § 230.135, which is discussed in § 2.3 *supra*.

69. 17 C.F.R. § 230.135e.

70. Rule 135e(a), 17 C.F.R. § 230.135e(a). *See* Offshore Press Conferences, Meetings with Company Representatives Conducted Offshore and Press–Related Materials Released Offshore, Sec. Act Rel. No. 33–7470, 62 Fed. Reg. 53,948 (SEC Oct. 17, 1997).

sales are made outside of the United States and effected in a manner that should result in the securities coming to rest outside the United States.[83] This rule may be relied upon even if Regulation D sales are contemporaneously being made in the United States.[84] The Commission has made it clear in Regulation D that an issuer's providing information to journalists outside of the United States will not be deemed to have violated the requirement that the issuer not be engaged in a general solicitation of purchasers.[85] Issuers can take advantage of this provision so long as the materials or meetings offshore are in compliance with Rule 135e's safe harbor.[86]

§ 17.4[3] Offshore Offerings of United States Securities—Regulation S

In 1988, the Commission proposed Regulation S as a way to deal with offshore offerings.[87] The Regulation is discussed in an earlier section.[88]

In 1997, the SEC amended Regulation S to permit United States issuers engaging in offshore offerings to participate in press conferences and meetings with journalists outside the United States.[92] The regulation as amended not only permits participation in offshore press conferences, it also permits offshore meetings with company representatives and the release of information to the press offshore without violating Regulation S's requirement that the selling efforts be directed outside the United States.

§ 17.4[6] Multijurisdictional Disclosure System for Canadian Issuers

In 1991, the Commission adopted a multijurisdictional disclosure system (MJDS) to facilitate registration and reporting of qualifying securities of Canadian issuers.[105] In adopting the MJDS, four registration forms were added. 1933 Act registration Form F–7 is available to an issuer organized in Canada, which is either a foreign private issuer or a Crown corporation, provided that the issuer has a class of securities listed on either the Toronto Stock Exchange, Montreal Exchange, or Senior Board of the Vancouver Stock

83. Regulation D, Preliminary Note 7, 17 C.F.R. § 230.501, relying on Sec.Act Rel. No. 33–4708 (July 9, 1964). *See also* § 4.19 *supra.*

84. Regulation D, Preliminary Note 7, 17 C.F.R. § 230.501. *Cf.* G.T. Global Financial Services, Inc., 20 Sec.Reg. & L.Rep. (BNA) 1820 (SEC No Action Letter avail. Aug. 2, 1988).

85. Rule 502(c)(2), 17 C.F.R. § 230.502(c)(2). *See* Offshore Press Conferences, Meetings with Company Representatives Conducted Offshore and Press–Related Materials Released Offshore, Sec. Act Rel. No. 33–7470, 62 Fed. Reg. 53,948 (SEC Oct. 17, 1997).

86. Rule 502(c)(2), 17 C.F.R. § 230.502(c)(2). *See* 17 C.F.R. § 230.135e.

87. Sec.Act Rel. No. 33–6779, [1987–88 Transfer Binder] Fed.Sec.L.Rep. (CCH) & 84,242 (June 10, 1988).

88. *See* § 4.33 *supra.*

92. Rule 902(b)(8), 17 C.F.R. § 230.902(b)(8). *See* Offshore Press Conferences, Meetings with Company Representatives Conducted Offshore and Press–Related Materials Released Offshore, Sec. Act Rel. No. 33–7470, 62 Fed. Reg. 53,948 (SEC Oct. 17, 1997).

Regulation S was amended in 1998 to provide that securities issued under the regulation are subject to the resale restrictions of SEC Rule 144. *See* Sec. Act Rel. No. 33–7505 (SEC Feb. 18, 1998). SEC Rule 144 is discussed in § 4.29 *supra.*

105. Sec.Exch.Act Rel. No. 33–6902, [1991 Transfer Binder] Fed.Sec.L.Rep. (CCH) ¶ 84,812 (SEC June 21, 1991). *See also* the proposing releases. Sec.Act Rel. No. 33–6897 [1990–1991 Transfer Binder] Fed.Sec.L.Rep. (CCH) ¶ 84,701 (SEC Oct. 16, 1990); Sec.Act Rel. No. 33–6841 (July 26, 1989).

Exchange.[106] The required disclosures under Form F–7 consist of those disclosures that are required by the home jurisdiction to be delivered to shareholders. Form F–8 is also available to issuers qualifying for Form F–7 for mergers and other reorganization transactions. Form F–9 is designed for investment grade debt or preferred securities. Form F–10 is available to qualifying issuers for registration of any class of securities, provided that certain conditions are met. Issuers must satisfy five conditions in order to qualify for use of Form F–10.

When the Commission embarked on the Multijurisdictional Disclosure System, it was the Commission's intent to pursue similar arrangements with countries other than Canada. However, the SEC appears to have abandoned that original plan.

§ 17.4[7] Rule 144A—A Secondary Domestic Market for Unregistered Securities of Foreign Issuers

Another significant development was the creation of a trading system for unregistered foreign securities.[110] In conjunction with its adoption of Rule 144A,[111] the SEC approved the NASD's screen-based computer and communication system called PORTAL (Private Offerings, Resales and Trading through Automated Linkages) to facilitate secondary trading of Rule 144A securities. Accordingly, there now is a formalized market to facilitate sales of unregistered securities to qualifying institutional investors. It was anticipated that Rule 144A will be especially significant for investments in securities of foreign issuers.[112]

---

106. The shares must have been listed on one of these exchanges for the thirty-six months preceding SEC registration. Furthermore the issuer must presently be in compliance with the exchange's listing obligations.

110. Rule 144A is discussed in § 4.30 *supra.*

111. 17 C.F.R. § 230.144A.

112. *See, e.g.,* Louis F. Moreno Trevino, Access to U.S. Capital Markets for Foreign Issuers: Rule 144A Private Placements, 16 Houst. J. Int'l L. 159 (1993).

Chapter 19

DEBT SECURITIES AND PROTECTION OF BONDHOLDERS—THE TRUST INDENTURE ACT OF 1939

Table of Sections

§ 19.1 Introduction to the Trust Indenture Act of 1939[1]

Corporations, like other forms of business, frequently raise capital through debt financing. Debt represents borrowed capital that must be repaid.[2] In essence, bonds or debentures are promissory notes, but contain more elaborate provisions than ordinary commercial loans. Corporate debentures are generally long-term obligations, but in times of fluctuating interest rates, shorter-term instruments are not uncommon. In order to borrow funds from a large number of investors, corporations and other public issuers contract with a third party to administer a bond issue. This third party acts as the indenture trustee.

There are two parts to every bond issue; there is the trust indenture (the counterpart of the loan agreement) and the separate bonds (the counterpart of the promissory note). The trust indenture has two distinct parts. The first part of the indenture sets forth all the obligations and restrictions on the bonds' issuer; the second part not only sets forth the bondholders' rights on default of the conditions set forth in the first part, but also, by tracking the standards embodied in the Trust Indenture Act of 1939, sets forth the relationship between the indenture trustee and the bondholders. The trust indenture, also contains provisions related to amendment of the indenture, as well as protection of any conversion privilege.

§ 19.1

1. Act of August 3, 1939, 53 Stat. 1149.

2. For discussion of corporate capital structures, *see* 2 James D. Cox & Thomas L. Hazen, Cox & Hazen on Corporations ch. 18 (2d ed.2003).

The contract, or "indenture," identifies the rights of all parties concerned, as well as the duties of the trustee (a third-party administrator), the obligations of the borrower, and the remedies available to the investors ("indenture securities holders").[3]

The provisions of the Trust Indenture Act are supplemented by the other federal securities laws. For example, privately issued debt instruments[4] generally are securities, whether they be in the form of bonds or notes, are securities[5] that are subject to the 1933 Securities Act's exemption[6] and the 1934 Exchange Act's exclusion[7] for short-term commercial paper. Accordingly, the issuance of bonds as well as notes (other than short-term obligations issued in commercial transactions) implicates the registration provisions of the 1933 Act.[8] Corporate bonds that are listed on a national securities exchange must be registered under section 12 of the 1934 Act.[9] A class of equity securities of issuers having at least ten million dollars in assets and more than five hundred securities holders of record of that class also must be registered under the Exchange Act.[10] However, there is no comparable registration requirement for over-the-counter debt instruments, unless they are convertible into equity securities, in which case the convertible bonds themselves qualify as "equity securities."[11] Although there is no registration requirement under the Exchange Act for straight debt securities that are not listed on a national exchange, any such security that was issued under a 1933 Act registration statement is subject to the periodic reporting requirements by virtue of section 15(d) of the Exchange Act, so long as there remain at least three hundred holders of the security.[12] Additionally, trading in corporate bonds is subject to Rule 10b–5's antifraud proscriptions, regardless of whether the bonds are subject to the Exchange Act's registration or reporting requirements.[13] Finally, broker-dealers handling trading in privately issued debt securities are subject to the normal broker-dealer regulations,[14] while separate regulation exists regarding dealers in municipal securities[15] and federal government securities.[16] Thus, debt securities are subject to considerable regulation outside the context of the Trust Indenture Act. However, that regulation

---

3. *See* 15 U.S.C.A. § 77ccc(7). Substantive rights are thus governed by the indenture and the Act. In contrast, SEC Rule 10b–5 imposes disclosure obligations, it does not affect the issuer's obligations under the terms of the indenture. *See* Lorenz v. CSX Corp., 1 F.3d 1406 (3d Cir.1993); LNC Investments, Inc. v. First Fidelity Bank, 1994 WL 73648, [1993–1994 Transfer Binder] Fed. Sec. L. Rep. (CCH) ¶ 98,151 (S.D.N.Y.1994) (since action is based on contract, state contract law governs).

4. Government issued and guaranteed securities are exempt from both the 1933 Act's registration requirements and the 1934 Act's registration and reporting requirements. 15 U.S.C.A. §§ 77c(a)(2), 78c(a)(12). *See* § 4.3 *supra*.

5. 15 U.S.C.A. § 77b(a)(1). *See* § 1.6 *supra*.

6. 15 U.S.C.A. § 77c(a)(3). *See* § 4.4 *supra*.

7. 15 U.S.C.A. § 78c(a)(10).

8. 15 U.S.C.A. §§ 77e, 77f. *See* chapter 2 *supra*.

9. 15 U.S.C.A. § 78l(g). *See* § 9.2 *supra*.

10. 15 U.S.C.A. § 78l(g)(1); 17 C.F.R. §§ 240.12g–1.

11. 15 U.S.C.A. § 78c(a)(11) (equity security includes any security convertible, with or without consideration, into an equity security).

12. 15 U.S.C.A. § 78o(d). *See* § 9.3 *supra*.

13. 17 C.F.R. § 240.10b–5. *See* §§ 12.2–12.11 *supra*.

14. *See* chapter 14 *supra*.

15. 15 U.S.C.A. § 78o–4. *See* § 14.6 *supra*.

16. 15 U.S.C.A. § 78o–5. *See* § 14.7 *supra*.

does not address the special situation created by the relationship between the issuer and the indenture trustee.

The Trust Indenture Act of 1939[17] was enacted to protect "the national public interest and the interest of investors."[18] The necessity for federal legislation became apparent after years of judicial conflict over the duties of trustees to bondholders[19] and the lack of financial protection afforded even secured bondholders in the chaos that followed the 1929 stock market crash.[20] Exculpatory clauses were included in most indentures and rendered bondholders impotent to hold trustees liable even in those instances in which the trustee's acts or omissions directly resulted in an injury.[21] The federal legislation addressed itself to these and to other issues as well.[22]

Unlike the Securities Act of 1933 and the Exchange Act of 1934 which are generally limited to disclosure issues, the Trust Indenture Act goes beyond disclosure and imposes regulation over the substance of corporate and other private debt securities. The Act lists six separate instances wherein a public offering of private debt securities could prove harmful to investor interests: (1) when the obligor fails to provide a trustee; (2) when the trustee is without adequate rights, powers, or duties to protect and enforce the rights of investors; (3) when the trustee is without adequate resources to fulfill its duties; (4) when the flow of information from obligor to trustee is inadequate; (5) when the indenture contains misleading provisions; and (6) when the obligor prepares the indenture without investor participation or understanding.[23] The Act addresses these problems.

§ 19.2 Operation of the Trust Indenture Act of 1939; Exemptions

The Trust Indenture Act of 1939 focuses primarily upon the terms of the indenture as the means to its end of bondholder protection.[1] In the absence of the Act's coverage, rights and obligations under the indenture would be purely a matter of state law. The Trust Indenture Act applies to notes, bonds, debentures, and other evidences of indebtedness, whether or not secured, and

17. 15 U.S.C.A. §§ 77aaa *et seq.*

18. 15 U.S.C.A. § 77bbb(a).

19. Sturges v. Knapp, 31 Vt. 1, 58 (1858) (trustee required to act as the "prudent man" would); York v. Guaranty Trust Co., 143 F.2d 503 (2d Cir.1944), *reversed on other grounds,* 326 U.S. 99, 65 S.Ct. 1464, 89 L.Ed. 2079 (1945) (relationship between trustee and bondholders is that of a fiduciary); First Trust Co. v. Carlsen, 129 Neb. 118, 261 N.W. 333 (1935) (relationship one of agency); Hazzard v. Chase National Bank, 159 Misc. 57, 287 N.Y.S. 541 (Sup.Ct.1936) *motion granted,* 258 App.Div. 709, 14 N.Y.S.2d 1021 (1939) (relationship primarily contractual). *See generally* Louis S. Posner, Liability of the Trustee Under the Corporate Indenture, 42 Harv.L.Rev. 198, 199–200 (1928).

20. SEC Report on the Study and Investigation of the Work, Activities, Personnel and Functions of Protective and Reorganization Committees, pt. VI Trustees Under Indentures (1936). For an excellent summary of the Report's findings, *see* Morris v. Cantor, 390 F.Supp. 817, 820 (S.D.N.Y.1975).

21. *See generally,* 2 Louis Loss, Securities Regulation 719–725 (2d ed. 1961).

22. Although the federal law imposes minimum requirements, as a general matter, actions under the Indenture Act are contract actions and thus are governed substantively by state law. LNC Investments, Inc. v. First Fidelity Bank, 1994 WL 73648, [1993–1994 Transfer Binder] Fed. Sec. L. Rep. (CCH) ¶ 98,151 (S.D.N.Y.1994).

23. 15 U.S.C.A. § 77bbb.

§ 19.2

1. The background and purpose of the Act is considered in § 19.1 *supra.*

to all certificates representing such an interest.[2] Most of these securities, when issued, are also subject to registration under the Securities Act of 1933.[3] Thus, there is an interrelationship between the disclosure provisions of the 1933 Act and the more substantive regulation of the Trust Indenture Act. For example, if there is noncompliance with the provisions of the Trust Indenture Act, the SEC may refuse to permit the issuer's 1933 Act registration statement to become effective.[4] Once issued, the bonds are also subject to regulation under the Securities Exchange Act of 1934.

In 1990, Congress enacted comprehensive amendments to the Trust Indenture Act.[5] The revisions were designed to modernize the Act and to make it more efficient in light of current market conditions and industry practices.[6] Among other things, the 1990 amendments eliminated the requirement of certain boilerplate language in the trust agreements which serve only to increase administrative costs without providing additional investor protection.[7] Additionally, debenture holders will receive statutory protection notwithstanding contrary language in the indenture.

Exemptions From the Act's Coverage

Section 304 of the Trust Indenture Act exempts from its coverage a number of debt securities that would otherwise fall within the Act's purview.[8] Section 304(a)(9) of the Act[9] exempts securities issued under an indenture where the aggregate amount of debt within a thirty-six month period does not exceed ten million dollars unless the Commission prescribes a lower dollar ceiling. The Commission has exercised this rulemaking authority, to lower the ceiling, in Rule 4a–2.[10] Rule 4a–2 exempts securities issued pursuant to an indenture limiting the aggregate principal outstanding indebtedness to five million dollars and provided further that for thirty-six consecutive months the issuer has not had outstanding securities with more than five million dollars in aggregate principal indebtedness. Also exempted are most securities ex-

---

2. 15 U.S.C.A. § 77ddd(a)(1).

3. 15 U.S.C.A. §§ 77a–77bbb. *See* § 19.1 and chapters 1–7 *supra*.

4. 15 U.S.C.A. § 77eee(b).

5. P.L. 101–550, 101st Cong. 2d Sess. *See* Fed.Sec.L.Rep. (CCH) Report Bulletin no. 1420 (Nov. 7, 1990).

As articulated in this Senate Committee report, which accompanied the reform bill, modernization was the primary focus of the Amendments:

During this period, however, the public market for debt securities has undergone significant change. Innovations in the forms of debt instruments have produced securities, such as collateralized mortgage obligation, [which] were not contemplated in 1939. Technological developments and regulatory changes have resulted in new distribution methods including shelf offerings, direct placements and "dutch auctions." In addition, public securities markets have been profoundly changed by the increasing internationalization of securities markets. Thus, current market practices conflict with many of the assumptions underlying the Act, which were based on financial customs prevailing in 1939. . . . Enactment of Title IV would conform the Act to the present realities of the market and make it adaptable to future developments, while easing the administration of the Act.

Id. at 29.

6. *Id.*

7. *Id.*

8. 15 U.S.C.A. § 77ddd.

9. 15 U.S.C.A. § 77ddd(a)(9). *Compare* section 4(a)(8)'s limited exemption for securities not issued under an indenture. *See* 17 C.F.R. §§ 260.0–7, 260.4a–2.

10. 17 C.F.R. § 260.4a–2.

empted from 1933 Act registration[11]; these include securities issued or guaranteed by the federal government (or any state or foreign government), notes with a maturity date less than nine months from the date of issuance, bonds issued by non-profit organizations, any indebtedness of a savings and loan association due to bonds issued, common carrier certificates, securities offered only within a particular state, securities issued by a trustee in bankruptcy, and commercial paper.[12]

Also exempt from the Trust Indenture Act are certificates of interest or participation in more than one security where the pooled securities have "substantially different rights and privileges."[13] Debt securities that were issued prior to six months after the Act's effective date are exempt, but the exemption does not apply to any new offering of such securities.[14] Debt securities issued under a mortgage insured under the National Housing Act[15] are exempt from the Trust Indenture Act.[16] Debt securities issued by foreign governments or their agencies, departments, subdivisions, or instrumentalities are also exempt.[17] The Act further provides an exemption for guarantees of any of the above securities exempted by section 304(a).[18]

A further exemption is provided in section 304(a)(8) of the Trust Indenture Act[21] for debt securities that are not issued under an indenture, provided that the aggregate offering of any such securities within a twelve-month period does not exceed the dollar limit established by section 3(b) of the 1933 Act[22] (which currently is five million dollars), unless the SEC sets a lower ceiling. The Commission formerly had lowered the limit in Rule 4a–1[23] so that the exemption applied only if during a period of twelve consecutive months the issuer had not had more than two million dollars aggregate principal amount of *any* securities of that issuer, but in 1992, the ceiling was raised to five million dollars.

In 1990, Congress greatly expanded the Commission's exemptive authority under the Act. Section 304(d) of the Act now empowers the Commission to exempt from all or part of the Act any person, registration statement, indenture, security, or transaction from the Act to the extent that the exemption is "necessary or appropriate in the public interest and consistent with the protection of investors and the purposes fairly intended" by the Act.,[24] The SEC is further specifically permitted to exercise its discretion to refuse to consider an application for such an exemption.[25] SEC Rule 4d–7 sets

11. 15 U.S.C.A. §§ 77c(a)(2), (3), (4), (5), (6), (7), (8), (11). *See* chapter 4 *supra.*

12. 15 U.S.C.A. § 77ddd(a)(4). *See* 17 C.F.R. §§ 260.0–7, 260.4a–2.

13. 15 U.S.C.A. § 77ddd(a)(2). Also included in the exemption are temporary certificates of the same type.

14. 15 U.S.C.A. § 77ddd(a)(3). *See* 15 U.S.C.A. § 77ddd(c).

15. 12 U.S.C.A. §§ 1701 *et seq.*

16. 15 U.S.C.A. § 77ddd(a)(5), (a)(10).

17. 15 U.S.C.A. § 77ddd(a)(6).

18. 15 U.S.C.A. § 77ddd(a)(7).

21. 15 U.S.C.A. § 77ddd(a)(8). *Compare* section 304(a)(9)'s exemption for securities issued under an indenture where the aggregate principal indebtedness does not exceed five million dollars within thirty-six consecutive months, as provided in Rule 4a–2.

22. 15 U.S.C.A. § 77c(b). *See* § 4.16 *supra.*

23. 17 C.F.R. § 260.4a–1.

24. 15 U.S.C.A. § 78ddd(d).

25. *Id.*

forth the technical requirements with regard to filing an application for an exemption pursuant to section 304(d).[26] The application to the Commission requesting the exemption must contain the name, address, and telephone number of each applicant and each other person to whom questions concerning the application should be directed.[27] In addition to stating the relevant facts, the application must contain a justification for the requested exemption as well as a statement of any benefits that could be expected to accrue as a result thereof to security holders, trustees, and/or obligors.[28]

In addition to the foregoing exclusions from the Trust Indenture Act of 1939, all of the transaction exemptions found in section 4 of the 1933 Act apply as well to registration under sections 305 and 306 of the Trust Indenture Act.[29] These transaction exemptions are: (1) transactions by a person other than an issuer, underwriter or dealer,[30] (2) transactions not involving a public offering,[31] (3) certain transactions by dealers,[32] (4) unsolicited brokers transactions,[33] (5) transactions involving certain real estate mortgage notes,[34] and (6) transactions involving accredited investors,[35] as defined in section 2(a)(15) of the 1933 Act.[36]

In addition, the SEC may, on application from the issuer and after a hearing, exempt debt securities issued by private foreign issuers.[37] Also, the Commission may by rule exempt securities issued by a small business investment company pursuant to the Small Business Investment Company Act of 1958.[38]

§ 19.3 Qualification Under the Trust Indenture Act

Debt securities that are not exempt from the Trust Indenture Act by virtue of section 304,[1] whether or not also subject to the 1933 Act, must be "qualified" under the Trust Indenture Act before they may be offered for public sale.[2] In order to be so qualified under the Act, issuers must disclose, to

---

26. 17 C.F.R. § 260.4d–7.

27. 17 C.F.R. § 260.4d–8.

28. *Id.*

29. 15 U.S.C.A. § 77ddd(b). *See* 15 U.S.C.A. §§ 77eee, 77fff.

30. 15 U.S.C.A. § 77d(1). *See* § 4.26 *supra.* The Trust Indenture Act further provides that persons selling on behalf of control persons are not underwriters. 15 U.S.C.A. § 77ddd(b). *Contra* 15 U.S.C.A. § 77b(a)(11). *See* § 4.27 *supra.*

31. 15 U.S.C.A. § 77d(2). *See* 4.24 *supra.* The fact that there are only a limited number of lenders may preclude a finding that a public offering has taken place. The fact that a trustee is not covered by the 1939 Act does not affect the applicability of state law relating to indenture trustees. *See, e.g.,* In re E.F. Hutton Southwest Properties II, Ltd., 953 F.2d 963 (5th Cir.1992) (New York law characterized the trustee as an indenture trustee notwithstanding absence of a public offering; but further holding that trustee's reliance on counsel precluded a finding of liability for negligence).

32. 15 U.S.C.A. § 77d(3). *See* § 4.31 *supra.*

33. 15 U.S.C.A. § 77d(4). *See* § 4.26 *supra.*

34. 15 U.S.C.A § 77d(5). *See* § 4.32 *supra.*

35. 15 U.S.C.A. § 77d(6). *See* § 4.23 *supra.*

36. 15 U.S.C.A. § 77b((a)15).

37. 15 U.S.C.A. § 77ddd(d). Private foreign issuers are discussed in § 17.4 *supra.*

38. 15 U.S.C.A. § 77ddd(e).

§ 19.3

1. 15 U.S.C.A. § 77ddd. *See* § 19.2 *supra.*

2. 15 U.S.C.A. §§ 77eee–77ggg.

the SEC through an application for qualification[3] and to investors through a prospectus,[4] the following information:

(1) whether the proposed trustee is eligible to serve as such;

(2) whether the trustee has a conflict of interest;[5]

(3) what will constitute a default under the indenture and under which circumstances the trustee may withhold information of such default from bondholders;

(4) the method of authentication and delivery of indenture securities and how their proceeds will be applied;

(5) provisions defining when the release or release and substitution of any property subject to the lien of indenture will be allowed;

(6) how satisfaction and discharge of the indenture will occur; and

(7) the evidence an obligor will be required to furnish in order to remain in compliance with the indenture's conditions and covenants.[6]

§ 19.4   Trustee Qualifications

Conflicts of Interest

The role of the trustee under the Act's provisions is perhaps its most controversial aspect. A qualified indenture must provide for one or more trustees, at least one of which is a corporation that is organized under the laws of the United States, or any single U.S. state, and further has a minimum combined capitalization and surplus of one hundred and fifty thousand dollars.[2] The Act further specifies that trustees may not have conflicting interests with those of indenture securities holders.[3] The statute enumerates a number of conflict of interest situations that preclude qualification of the trustee under the Trust Indenture Act. The conflicting interest situations that operate to disqualify a trustee are those where:

(1) the trustees serve as trustee under other indentures of the obligor;[4]

(2) the trustees, or any of their officers or directors, are the obligors or an underwriter for the obligor;

(3) the trustees control or are controlled by the obligor or its underwriter;

---

3. 15 U.S.C.A. § 77ggg.

4. 15 U.S.C.A. § 77fff(b) & (c).

5. As defined in 15 U.S.C.A. § 77jjj(b), discussed in § 19.4 *infra.*

6. 15 U.S.C.A. § 77eee(a).

§ 19.4

2. 15 U.S.C.A. § 77jjj(a). Corporations serving as trustees are known as institutional trustees. *Id.* § 77jjj(a)(1). Whether someone is an indenture trustee or a traditional trustee depends upon the functions performed, not upon the title of the position. *Cf.* In re E.F. Hutton Southwest Properties II, Ltd., 953 F.2d 963 (5th Cir.1992) (although not covered by the federal Act, a trustee agreeing to act for the benefit of other noteholders was an "indenture trustee" under state law).

3. 15 U.S.C.A. § 77jjj(b).

4. For a discussion of the significance of this provision, *see* Robert I. Landau, Corporate Trust: Administration and Management 59 (4th ed. 1992) ("The significance of the same trustee acting under separate indentures is apparent. Although before default the trustee might act under two indentures of the same obligor without encountering difficulty, the happening of an event of default will usually created a conflict and prevent the trustee from adequately representing holders under both indentures, for their interests are quite likely to be adverse.").

(4) the trustees, or their officers or directors, are directors or officers of the obligor or its underwriter, except that if there are more than nine directors, one may overlap;

(5) the obligor, or any of its officers or directors, beneficially owns ten percent of the trustee's voting securities, or twenty percent of such securities are owned by two such persons;

(6) the trustees beneficially own five percent of the obligor's voting securities or ten percent of any other class of securities of the obligor or the obligor's underwriter;

(7) the trustees beneficially own five percent or more of the voting securities of persons controlling or controlled by obligors or persons owning ten percent or more of the obligor's voting securities;

(8) the trustees beneficially own ten percent or more of any class of securities of any person who, to the trustee's knowledge, owns fifty percent or more of the obligor's voting securities; or

(9) the trustees own an aggregate of twenty-five percent or more of any class of securities in a representative capacity where beneficial ownership would constitute a conflict of interest under (6), (7), or (8) above.[6]

Once a trustee finds that it is in a conflict of interest situation, the trustee must eliminate the conflict within ninety days or resign.[7] The trustee's resignation under these circumstances is to be effective upon the appointment of a successor.[8] If the trustee does not resign in the face of a statutorily defined conflict of interest, the trustee must notify indenture security holders within ten days of the expiration of the ninety-day period.[9] Upon such notification, "any security holder who has been a bona fide holder of indenture securities for at least six months may, on behalf of himself and all others so situated, petition any court of competent jurisdiction for the removal of such trustee, and the appointment of a successor if such trustee fails, after a written request therefore by such holder, to [eliminate the conflict of interest or resign]."[10]

The Trust Indenture Reform Act of 1990[11] amended section 310(b) to provide that a trustee's conflict of interest does not arise until there has been a default under the indenture.[12] The Act thus permits the trustee with a conflict of interest to apply to the SEC, within ninety-days of certain defaults, for permission to continue to serve as trustee.[13] This application for permission to remain a trustee beyond the ninety-day period may be made for defaults not involving principal, interest, or sinking fund payments. This application will be granted if, after an opportunity for a hearing, the applicant has demonstrated that (1) the default may be cured or waived in accordance with procedures described in the application, and (2) a stay of the duty to

---

6. *Id.*

7. 15 U.S.C.A. § 77jjj(b)(1)(i).

8. *Id.*

9. 15 U.S.C.A. § 77jjj(b)(1)(iii).

10. *Id.*

11. P.L. 101–550, 101st Cong. 2d Sess.

12. 15 U.S.C.A. § 77jjj(b).

13. *Id.*

resign is not inconsistent with the interests of indenture security holders.[14] The contents of and procedures for such an application to the Commission are set forth in Rules 10b–4, 10b–5, and 10b–6.[15]

Trustees Who Are Also Creditors of the Issuer (Obligor)

Banks frequently serve as trustees under the Act. These banks also may be creditors of the issuer, but this relationship does not result in a per se disqualification under the Trust Indenture Act. The Trust Indenture Act does not consider the trustee to have a conflict of interest with bondholders substantial enough for disqualification simply because the trustee is also a creditor of the obligor.[16] This view may seem surprising since, according to the SEC, "however honest or conscientious a trustee may be, if it occupies a creditor position competitive with that of its beneficiaries, self-interest may lead to violations of fiduciary obligations."[17] The conflict of interest nevertheless is allowed in recognition of the economic realities governing the corporate and banking worlds wherein the most likely source of credit to a troubled obligor would be the institutional indenture trustee since it is already familiar with the obligor's business.[18] However, the Trust Indenture Act creates certain safeguards in order to reduce the potential abuse of debt collection by trustee creditors where an obligor has economic problems and its default or demise may be imminent. Section 311(a) of the Act[19] does not allow a trustee to retain any payment or property it receives as a creditor, whether secured or unsecured, within four months before, or any time subsequent to, a default on the issuer's obligation to the bondholders. The section contains disgorgement provisions to ensure that trustees do not receive "a greater percentage of their claims as creditors (after deducting non-preferential collections) than the investors receive on the unsecured portions of their claims."[20] These disgorgement provisions do not apply in all instances where the trustee is also a creditor of the obligor as there are exclusions in certain limited situations.[21]

---

14. *Id.*

15. Rule 10b–4 sets forth the technical filing requirements. Rule 10b–5 sets forth the contents of the application, including a statement of reasons why the exemption should be granted. Rule 10b–6 specifies the notice required and directs that the application contain a draft notice that will appear in the Federal Register and a notice for interested persons to appear to be heard. 17 C.F.R. §§ 260.10b–4—260.10b–6. Notice of applications for a stay will appear in the Federal Register. Also, the filing of an application automatically stays the duty to resign pending the Commission's decision. 15 U.S.C.A. § 77jjj(b).

16. *See* 15 U.S.C.A. § 77jjj(b).

17. SEC, Report on the Study and Investigation of the Work, Activities, Personnel and Functions of Protective and Reorganization Committees, pt. VI, Trustees Under Indentures at 88 (1936).

18. Hearings on H.R. 2191 & H.R. 5020 before a subcommittee of the committee on Interstate and Foreign Commerce, House of Representatives, 76th Congress, 1st session pp. 159–60, 170–71, 268–9 (1939).

19. 15 U.S.C.A. § 77kkk(a).

20. John P. Campbell & Robert Zack, Put a Bullet in the Poor Beast. His Leg is Broken and His Use is Past. Conflict of Interest in the Dual Role of Lender and Corporate Indenture Trustee: A Proposal to End It in the Public Interest, 32 Bus.Law. 1705, 1711 (1977), discussing 15 U.S.C.A. § 77kkk(a).

21. 15 U.S.C.A. § 77kkk(b). Excepted from the provisions of this section are creditor relationships arising from (1) the ownership of securities whose maturity is more than a year, (2) authorized advances made for the purpose of preserving the security, (3) minor disbursements made as trustee, and (4) certain temporary credits arising out of sales of goods and transactions in "self liquidating" paper such as drafts and acceptances. Note, The Trust Indenture Act of 1939, 25 Cornell L.Q. 105, 109 (1939).

§ 19.5 Qualification of the Indenture; Required Provisions

In order to qualify under the Act, the trust indenture must contain certain required provisions.[1] In cases of conflict, the statute's mandatory provisions control.[2] In 1990, Congress enacted comprehensive amendments to the Trust Indenture Act.[3] Among other things, the 1990 amendments to the Trust Indenture Act legislation eliminated the requirement of certain boiler-plate language in the trust agreements which served only to increase adminis-trative costs without providing additional investor protection.[4] Additionally, debenture holders will receive statutory protection notwithstanding contrary language in the indenture.

§ 19.6 Duties of Trustee When the Issuer Defaults

The duties of the indenture trustee change considerably upon a default by the obligor.[1] Upon default, trustees must use "the same degree of care and skill in their exercise as a prudent man would exercise or use under the circumstances in the conduct of his own affairs" to prevent injury to the bondholders' interests.[2] This "prudent man" standard of conduct is mitigated, however, by section 315(d)(2),[3] which absolves a trustee for errors made in good faith.

The term "default" is nowhere defined in the Act; presumably, its characteristics are instead left to the indenture provisions.[4] Generally, the trustee must notify the bondholders of a default.[5] The indenture may permit the trustee to withhold notice of known defaults not connected with defaults in principal, interest, or sinking fund payments.[6] In the event of default, a wide assortment of alternative actions are available to the trustee. The trustee has the power to accelerate the balance due if so authorized, or it might recover a judgment against the obligor, or it might sue to enforce the covenants of the indenture. The trustee, however, must also determine whether immediate resort to litigation will best serve the interests of the bondholders. A complete liquidation and sale, which is often the end result of many remedial actions, may not only destroy the obligor's business, but may also destroy much of the value of the bondholders' security.[8] The Act empow-ers trustees to excuse defaults on interest payments for up to three years, provided they secure the consent of seventy-five percent of the indenture

---

§ 19.5

1. 15 U.S.C.A. § 77fff(a), 77ggg.

2. 15 U.S.C.A. § 77aaaa.

3. P.L. 101–550, 101st Cong. 2d Sess. *See* Fed.Sec.L.Rep. (CCH) Report Bulletin no. 1420 (Nov. 7, 1990).

4. *Id.*

§ 19.6

1. Prior to default, the trustee's obligations are not as great. *See, e.g.,* 15 U.S.C.A. § 77*ooo* (a)(2).

2. 15 U.S.C.A. § 77*ooo* (c).

3. 15 U.S.C.A. § 77*ooo* (d)(2).

4. *See, e.g.,* Upic & Co. v. Kinder–Care Learning Centers, Inc., 793 F.Supp. 448 (S.D.N.Y. 1992).

5. 15 U.S.C.A. § 77*ooo* (b).

6. *Id.*

8. *See* Henry F. Johnson, The "Forgotten" Securities Statute: Problems in the Trust Inden-ture Act, 13 U. Toledo L.Rev. 92, 100–101 (1981).

security holders.[9] Upon default, the trustee must institute foreclosure proceedings whenever a majority of the bondholders instructs the trustee to institute such proceedings.[10] The trustee is insulated from liability for such actions taken at the bondholder's demand.[11]

§ 19.7 Enforcement of the Act; Remedies for Trustees' Breaches of Duties

Enforcement of the trustee's pre-default duties is qualified by the leeway in allowing reasonable reliance by the trustee upon third parties' representations.[1] Indeed, it has been held that no fiduciary obligations in this regard are imposed on the trustee by federal law beyond those stipulated in the trust indenture.[2]

The only express civil liability imposed by the Trust Indenture Act is found in section 323(a) and covers material misstatements and omissions in any report filed with the SEC pursuant to the Act's filing requirements.[9] Reliance by the plaintiff is a precondition to a finding of liability.[10] Additionally, as is the case with section 18(a) of the Exchange Act,[11] section 323 liability does not attach if the defendant can prove that he or she acted in good faith and without knowledge of the materially misleading defects.[12] The section 323 claim must be brought within one year of discovery of the violation, but in no event will an action lie more than three years after the violation.[13]

§ 19.8 Overview of the Trust Indenture Act's Registration and Disclosure Requirements

In addition to the indenture and trustee qualifications that are discussed above, the Trust Indenture Act imposes various informational and disclosure requirements. Section 305[1] requires disclosure in the registration statement and prospectus of information relating to the trustee's qualification and provisions in the indenture. With regard to debt securities being offered but not registered under the 1933 Act, unless exempt by virtue of section 304,[2] section 306[3] provides that the securities cannot be sold unless the indenture

---

9.   15 U.S.C.A. § 77ppp(a)(2).

10.   15 U.S.C.A. § 77ppp(a)(1).

11.   15 U.S.C.A. § 77ooo(d)(3).

§ 19.7

1.   Caplin v. Marine Midland Grace Trust Co., 406 U.S. 416, 92 S.Ct. 1678, 32 L.Ed.2d 195 (1972) (failure to ascertain certain facts does not create trustee liability where trustee relied upon statutorily sanctioned certificates and opinions).

2.   Browning Debenture Holders' Committee v. DASA Corp., 431 F.Supp. 959 (S.D.N.Y.1976), *affirmed in part* 560 F.2d 1078 (2d Cir.1977), *remanded*, 81 F.R.D. 407 (1978), *on remand* 454 F.Supp. 88 (S.D.N.Y.1978), *affirmed*, 605 F.2d 35 (2d Cir.1978).

9.   15 U.S.C.A. § 77www.

10.   In re Nucorp Energy Securities Litigation, 772 F.2d 1486 (9th Cir.1985), affirming 1983 WL 1374, Fed.Sec.L.Rep. (CCH) ¶ 99,539 (S.D.Cal.1983).

11.   15 U.S.C.A. § 78r(a). *See* § 12.18 *supra*.

12.   15 U.S.C.A. § 77www(a).

13.   *Id.*

§ 19.8

1.   15 U.S.C.A. § 77eee.

2.   15 U.S.C.A. § 77ddd. *See* § 19.2 *supra*.

3.   15 U.S.C.A. § 77fff.

has been qualified. Although not expressly limited, section 306, as explained by the legislative history and SEC, applies to debt securities issued in a reorganization or exchange with existing securities holders even though those securities are exempted from the 1933 Act by virtue of sections 3(a)(9)[4] or 3(a)(10)[5] of that Act.

Section 308 of the Trust Indenture Act[7] provides for integration of the informational requirements with those of the 1933 and 1934 Acts, as well as with the Public Utility Holding Company Act of 1935.[8] This integration is facilitated in Trust Indenture Act filings by permitting incorporation by reference to filings under the other acts.[9]

Section 312(a)[10] of the Trust Indenture Act requires that a qualified indenture provide that the trustee receive a list of current bondholders' names and addresses at regular intervals of not more than six months. A trustee must also be able to obtain a current list at any other time in response to a written request.[11] Analogous to the 1934 Act's proxy rules' right of access to other security holders,[12] the Trust Indenture Act confers similar rights. The indenture must provide that upon receiving a written request from three or more indenture security holders, the trustee must make available to them a current list or mail information to the other security holders.[13] However, the trustee need comply with such a request only when at least three requesting security holders have been owners for six months.[14] Also, the communication must relate either to proxy solicitations or security holders' rights under the indenture.

---

4. 15 U.S.C.A. § 77c(a)(9) (securities exchanged exclusively with security holders). *See* § 4.10 *supra.*

5. 15 U.S.C.A. § 77c(a)(10) (securities issued under judicially or administratively approved reorganizations). *See* § 4.11 *supra.*

7. 15 U.S.C.A. § 77hhh.

8. The Public Utility Holding Company Act is discussed in chapter 15 *supra.*

9. 15 U.S.C.A. § 77hhh(a).

10. 15 U.S.C.A. § 77*lll*(a).

11. *Id.*

12. 17 C.F.R. § 240.14a–7. *See* § 11.7 *supra.*

13. 15 U.S.C.A. § 77*lll*(b).Following the pattern of 1934 Act proxy Rule 14a–7, the trustee has the option of providing the list or mailing the communications at the expense of the requesting security holders.

14. 15 U.S.C.A. § 77*lll*(b).

Chapter 20

FEDERAL REGULATION OF INVEST-MENT COMPANIES—THE INVEST-MENT COMPANY ACT OF 1940

Table of Sections

§ 20.1   The Investment Company Act of 1940: Background and Scope

The Investment Company Act of 1940[1] was enacted to protect investors entrusting their savings to others for expert management and diversification of investments which would not be available to them as individuals. The most common type of investment company is the mutual fund. Investors wanting to invest in a mutual fund or investment company have relatively little protection under state law. State corporate law does not provide safeguards to the public, such as independent boards of directors[5] and a separate investment

---

§ 20.1

1. Act of Aug. 22, 1940, 54 Stat. 789, codified in 15 U.S.C.A. §§ 80a–1 through 80a–52.

5. As explained by the SEC:

To be truly effective, a fund board must be an independent force in fund affairs rather than a passive affiliate of management. Its independent directors must bring to the boardroom "a high degree of rigor and skeptical objectivity to the evaluation of management and its plans and proposals," particularly when evaluating conflicts of interest. They must commit their time and energy, and devote themselves to the principles set forth in the Investment Company Act and state corporate and trust law under which the fund is organized.

Investment Company Governance, Inv. Co. Act Rel. No. IC–26520, 2004 WL 1672374 (SEC 2004) (footnotes omitted).

advisor, which are among the requirements imposed by the Investment Company Act. Investment company assets most often consist of cash, securities which generally are liquid, mobile, and readily negotiable, and in some cases commodity futures and options. An entity such as a corporation that is formed to provide a pooling of investment funds to permit the entity to invest in securities (including securities options) ordinarily will be considered an investment company and, unless exempt, are subject to SEC regulation. Pooled investment funds where the investment objective focuses primarily on commodity-related investments (including futures and options) are known as commodity pools. Commodity Pool Operators (CPOs) are regulated by the Commodity Futures Trading Commission.[7]

Companies subject to the Investment Company Act are also governed by the Securities Act of 1933 and the Securities Exchange Act of 1934. In 1990, Congress enacted the Shareholder Communication Act, which extends the applicability of the proxy rules under the Securities Exchange Act of 1934 that apply to reporting companies generally to mutual funds and other investment companies that are registered under the Investment Company Act.[8]

The highly liquid nature of investment company assets creates an increased risk of management abuse that is not present with ordinary manufacturing and other operating companies. This led Congress to believe that investment companies would be easy prey for management abuse in the absence of comprehensive federal regulation.[18]

The basic impact of the Investment Company Act is to require registration of non-exempt investment companies and to protect against money managers' conflicts of interest. Section 7 of the Act[29] bars an investment company from engaging in any form of interstate commerce when there has been a failure to register under the Act, unless there is an applicable exemption.[30] There are criminal sanctions for willful violations of the Act,[31] and contracts of unregistered investment companies are rendered unenforceable and thus courts will not order performance by third parties.[32] The Act also

---

7.   7 U.S.C.A. §§ 6m, 6o. *See generally* Philip M. Johnson & Thomas L. Hazen, Derivatives Regulation (2004). The jurisdiction of the SEC and CFTC is discussed in § 1.5 *supra.*

8.   15 U.S.C.A. § 78n(b). The proxy rules under the Exchange Act are discussed in chapter 10 *supra.*

The SEC clarified that in reporting to shareholders, investment companies are subject to the enhance requirements imposed by the Sarbanes–Oxley Act of 2002, which include financial certifications by a company's chief executive officer and chief financial officer. *See* In re Management's Report on Internal Control Over Financial Reporting and Certification of Disclosure in Exchange Act Periodic Reports, Sec. Act Rel. No. 33–8238, Sec. Exch. Act Rel. No. 34–47986, Inv. Co. Act Rel. No. IC–26068, 2003 WL 21294970 (SEC June 5, 2003).

18.   Sen.Rep. No. 1775, 76th Cong., 3d Sess. (1940). An investment company differs from a holding company in that the latter is concerned mainly with the "control of productive wealth," *i.e.,* the means of producing, while the former is concerned with the yield from investments in the productive activity of others. Comment, The Investment Company Act of 1940, 50 Yale L.J. 44041 (1941).

29.   15 U.S.C.A. § 80a–7.

30.   *See, e.g.,* Europe & Overseas Commodity Traders v. Banque Paribas London, 147 F.3d 118 (2d Cir.1998) (section 7(d) did not apply to Bahamian investment company which had fewer than 100 United States shareholders).

31.   15 U.S.C.A. § 80a–48.

32.   15 U.S.C.A. § 80a–46.

regulates the investment company's relationship with its investment advisers.[33]

Interlocking Ownership of Investment Company Shares—The Antipyramiding Provisions

Another Investment Company Act provision that deserves mention is the antipyramiding rules imposed by section 12(d)(1) of the Act.[37]

First, section 12(d)(1) prohibits an investment company from acquiring more than three percent of the total outstanding voting securities of another investment company.[39] Second, section 12(d)(1) also prohibits an investment company from acquiring shares of another investment company when the shares so acquired would have a value in excess of five percent of the acquiring company's assets.[40] Third, section 12(d)(1) of the Investment Company Act prohibits an investment company from acquiring shares of another investment company when the aggregate of all shares in all investment companies owned by the acquiring company when calculated after the acquisition would exceed ten percent of the acquiring company's assets.[41] The antipyramidding provisions apply to share ownership by investment companies, but cannot be extended to cover situations in which affiliated investment companies are controlled by the same investment adviser even thought he investment adviser decides how to vote the fund's portfolio shares.[42] In addition to focusing on the acquiring company, section 12(d) makes it unlawful for any investment company, principal underwriter, or registered broker-dealer to knowingly sell or otherwise dispose of investment company shares when the result of the transaction would be to place the investment company acquiring the shares in violation of section 12(d)'s ownership limitations.[43] It has been held that violations of section 12(d)'s antipyramiding provisions will support an implied private right of action, at least for injunctive relief[44] but not all courts have agreed.[45] There are various provisions of the Act that are designed not only to assure the independence of directors but also to protect investment company shareholders from conflict of interest transactions.[46]

---

33. *See* §§ 20.2, 20.9 *infra.*

37. 15 U.S.C.A. § 80a–12(d). *See* Roger M. Klein, Who Will Manage the Managers? The Investment Company Act's Antipyramiding Provision and its Effect on the Mutual Fund Industry, 59 Ohio St. L.J. 507 (1998).

39. 15 U.S.C.A. § 80a–12(d)(1)(A)(i).

40. 15 U.S.C.A. § 80a–12(d)(1)(A)(ii).

41. 15 U.S.C.A. § 80a–12(d)(1)(A)(iii).

42. *See* meVC Draper Fisher Jurvetson Fund I, Inc. v. Millennium Partners, L.P., 260 F.Supp.2d 616 (S.D.N.Y. 2003).

43. 15 U.S.C.A. § 80a–12(d)(1)(B).

44. Bancroft Convertible Fund, Inc. v. Zico Investment Holdings, Inc., 825 F.2d 731 (3d Cir.1987) (action by the target company); Clemente Global Growth Fund, Inc. v. Pickens, 705 F.Supp. 958 (S.D.N.Y.1989) (semble, preliminary injunction issued).

45. *See* meVC Draper Fisher Jurvetson Fund I, Inc. v. Millennium Partners, L.P., 260 F.Supp.2d 616 (S.D.N.Y. 2003). *See also, e.g.,* Olmsted v. Pruco Life Ins. Co. of New Jersey, 283 F.3d 429 (2d Cir. 2002) (no private remedy under sections 26(f) and 27(i) of the Act); White v. Heartland High-Yield Municipal Bond Fund, 237 F.Supp.2d 982 (E.D. Wis. 2002) (no private remedy under sections 22 or 34(b) of the 1940 Act).

46. *See, e g.,* In the Matter of Coxon, Sec. Act Rel. No. 33–8271, Sec. Exch. Act Rel. No. 34–48385, Inv. Adv. Act Rel. No. IA–2161, Inv. Co. Act Rel. No. IC–26165, 2003 WL 21991359 (SEC Aug. 21, 2003) (imposing sanctions for managers who, among other things, entered into transactions that favored other customers rather than the fund).

As pointed out above, the antipyramiding prohibitions are designed to protect the shareholders of investment companies. Other substantive protections, as well as investment company registration and disclosure obligations, are discussed in the sections that follow.

As part of the National Securities Markets Improvement Act of 1996, Congress provided that investment companies registered under the Investment Company Act of 1940 are subject to exclusive federal jurisdiction with regard to regulatory requirements.[47] However, the states may still impose notice requirements.[48] The states' enforcement jurisdiction over fraudulent practices of federally registered investment companies is expressly preserved by the otherwise preemptive federal legislation.[49]

There were a number of improper mutual fund practices that came to light after the turn of the twenty-first century. These practices included late trading,[50] market timing,[51] and pricing practices.[52] Another improper mutual fund sales practice that came to light took another form of improper sales incentive. Some mutual funds make payments to securities brokers to obtain priority in "shelf space"[53] for their funds.[54] Payments for more prominent shelf space are designed to make it more likely that a broker's customer will purchase the targeted fund. As such, these payments for shelf space involve the same type of conflict of interest issues as do differential sales commissions and other hidden incentives that brokers receive to recommend particular securities to their customers.[55]

In the aftermath of the mutual fund practices unearthed by the SEC and New York Attorney General investigations, the SEC adopted some reforms.,[56] The reforms address problems with market timing of mutual funds. For example, the SEC instituted a requirement that a mutual fund set forth in its prospectus the risks that frequent purchases and redemptions of fund shares may present for other shareholders. Along the same lines, there is now a requirement that mutual funds state in their prospectus whether or not the fund's board of directors has adopted policies and procedures with respect to frequent purchases and redemptions of fund shares and, if the board has not adopted any such policies and procedures, state the specific basis for the view of the board that it is appropriate for the fund not to have such policies and procedures. In addition, there is a requirement that a mutual fund describe with specificity in its prospectus any policies and procedures for deterring frequent purchases and redemptions of fund shares. Also, if there are any

---

47. Section 18(b)(2) of the 1933 Act, 15 U.S.C.A. § 77r(b)(2).

48. *Id.*

49. *Id.*

50. *See* § 20.5[4][A] *infra*

51. *See* § 20.5[4][B] *infra*

52. *See* § 20.5[4][C] *infra*

53. Just as a store can feature products by the shelf space allocated to the products it wants to highlight, a securities sales person can favor selected funds by giving them more prominence and visibility when dealing with customers.

54. *See* Stuart Gittleman, In a First of a Kind, SEC Fines MFS $50m for Pay–To–Play Fraud, Complinet, http://www.complinet.com/securities-na/dailynews/display.html?ref=53476 (April 1, 2004).

55. For discussion of broker recommendations *see* § 14.16 *supra*.

56. *See* Disclosure Regarding Market Timing and Selective Disclosure of Portfolio, Sec. Act Rel. No. 33–8408; Inv. Co. Act Rel. No. IC–26418, 69 FR 22300–01, 2004 WL 865628 (SEC April 23, 2004).

arrangements permitting frequent purchases and redemptions of fund shares, these arrangements must be described in a Statement of Additional Information.

§ 20.2 The Relationship Between Investment Companies, Investment Advisers, and Underwriters

Functionally, an investment company has been described as "a shell, a pool of assets consisting of securities, belonging to the shareholders of the fund."[1] Investors depend upon prudent management of the investment company's securities holdings. In theory and in practice, recommendations concerning where to put the investment company's funds are made by an investment adviser to the investment company's board of directors. The investment adviser has a contractual relationship with the investment company.

Frequently, the investment adviser (or a parent company that controls the adviser) is the investment company's founder, appointing its initial board of directors[3] and providing its initial capitalization. Due to the potential for abuses of this close relationship between investment company and investment adviser, section 15 of the Investment Company Act requires a written contract between the two entities which, as discussed below, must be approved by the investment company shareholders.[5] The section also requires a written contract between investment companies and underwriters,[6] but these underwriting provisions are becoming less important in practice as more investment companies have become "no-load" and sell directly to the public.[7] The underwriting function remains significant, however, during the investment company's start-up period, when a maximum of twenty-five "responsible persons" must make firm commitments to buy at least an aggregate of one hundred thousand dollars worth of securities from the investment company before any securities may be issued by it.[8] The Act also prohibits and investment company from retaining a principal underwriter unless a majority of the investment company's board of directors are not considered interested persons of the underwriter.[9]

Section 15(a) of the Act requires that the contract between an investment company and an investment adviser be approved by a majority of the investment company's outstanding voting securities.[10] Section 15(a) appears to vest the investment company's board of directors with a great deal of responsibility, authority, and discretion in deciding whether or not to renew the advisory contract. While the directors clearly have a large amount of

---

§ 20.2

1. Zell v. InterCapital Income Securities, Inc., 675 F.2d 1041, 1046 (9th Cir.1982). *See* Leland E. Modesitt, Mutual Fund—A Corporate Anomaly, 14 U.C.L.A.L.Rev. 1252 (1967).

3. *See* 2 Tamar Frankel, The Regulation of Money Managers, 212–13 (1978).

5. 15 U.S.C.A. § 80a–15(a).

6. 15 U.S.C.A. § 80a–15(b).

7. *See, e.g.,* James H. Ellis, Going No Load, 6 Sec.Reg.L.J. 357 (1979).

8. 15 U.S.C.A. § 80a–14(a)(3).

9. Section 10(b)(2) of the Investment Company Act, 15 U.S.C.A. § 80a–10.

10. 15 U.S.C.A. § 80a–15(a). This requirement is largely negated regarding the investment company's initial advisory contract because the investment adviser generally controls the voting shares of a start-up investment company. For a discussion of shareholder voting on subsequent advisory contracts in connection with their assignment, *see* § 20.9 *infra*.

responsibility,[12] their authority and discretion are rarely exercised. For example, it would generally not be practical for an investment company to terminate its advisory contract because of the dominant role generally played by the investment adviser. Functionally, it is the adviser which "selects the fund's investments and operates its business, providing [the investment company with] expertise, personnel, and office space."[13] For many investment companies, in essence, the adviser runs the investment company.[14] Directors act primarily as "watchdogs" over adviser activity and do so for the benefit of fund shareholders.[15]

In 2003, a number of mutual fund abuses came to light that resulted in the strengthening of the roles of independent fund directors. The improper practices that came to light in these scandals included market-timing and late trading issues, breakpoint pricing of transaction fees, and other fee-related concerns. Late trading, which is discussed more fully below,[21] occurs when traders take advantage of open-end mutual funds' forward pricing by trading on the basis of news and events made public *after* the price of the shares has been fixed, thus allowing the late traders to take advantage of virtually guaranteed price movements in the fund shares the next day. The concern over breakpoints for transaction fees, which also is discussed more fully below, addresses pricing practices that failed to provide customers with the cheapest transaction fee consistent with their investment objectives.

In the aftermath of the focus on late trading, market timing, breakpoint pricing, and other questionable mutual fund practices, the SEC adopted new rules designed to insure better compliance by mutual funds and their investment advisers.[22] The SEC rules mandate that investment companies and investment advisers registered with the SEC adopt compliance programs. These compliance rules require investment companies[23] and investment advisers[24] to (1) adopt and implement written policies and procedures reasonably designed to prevent violations of the federal securities laws, (2) annually review those policies and procedures for adequacy and effectiveness of implementation, and (3) designate a chief compliance officer. In 2004, the SEC adopted a requirement that an investment company retain copies of written materials that the board considers when approving the fund's advisory contract.[26]

Investment company shareholders' major protection against mismanagement and imprudent investments is section 36(b)'s express cause of action against an investment adviser for breach of fiduciary duty to the investment company.[27] The investment company security holder bears the burden of proof

---

12. *See* authorities in §§ 20.6, 20.9, *infra.*

13. Zell v. InterCapital Income Securities, Inc., 675 F.2d 1041, 1046 (9th Cir.1982).

14. Report of the Securities and Exchange Commission on the Public Policy Implications of Investment Company Growth, H.R.Rep. No. 2337, 89th Cong. 2d Sess. (1966).

15. *See* § 20.6 *infra* for a discussion of investment company directors' duties.

21. *See* § 20.5 *infra.*

22. *See* Compliance Programs of Investment Companies and Investment Advisers, Inv. Adv. Act Rel. No. IA–2204, Inv. Co. Act Rel. No. IC–26299, 2003 WL 22971048 (SEC 2003).

23. Investment Company Act Rule 38a–1, 17 C.F.R. § 270.38a–1.

24. Investment Adviser Act Rule 206(4)–7, 17 C.F.R. § 275.206(4)–7.

26. Rule 31a–2, 17 C.F.R. § 270.31a–2. *See* Investment Company Governance, Inv. Co. Act Rel. No. IC–26520, 2004 WL 1672374 (SEC 2004).

27. 15 U.S.C.A. § 80a–35(b). *See* § 20.10 *infra.*

in such an action.[28] The adviser's fiduciary role is given further weight by section 15(c)'s affirmative obligation to provide investors with "such information as may reasonably be necessary to evaluate the terms of [the advisory] contract."[29] Directors of an investment company have a parallel affirmative duty to request this information.[30]

§ 20.3   The Definition of "Investment Company"; The Problem of the Inadvertent Investment Company

In relevant part, Section 3(a) of the Investment Company Act defines "investment company" to be any issuer which: "(1) is or holds itself out as being engaged primarily, or proposes to engage primarily, in the business of investing, reinvesting, or trading in securities ..."[1] As was indicated in the preceding section of this treatise, there are a number of companies inadvertently finding themselves subject to the Investment Company Act by virtue of section 3(a)(3).[2] Any company holding investment securities in excess of forty percent of its total non-cash asset value comes within the purview of section 3(a)(3). By virtue of the Act's definitional sections, "investment securities" do not include government securities,[5] securities issued by employees' securities companies,[6] or securities issued by non-investment company majority-owned subsidiaries of the holder.[7]

A business enterprise not intending to be an investment company is most likely to cross the forty percent threshold during its start-up period when the company invests the capital it does have in order to amass enough money to finance its own operating expenses, when it is selling off its assets and investing the proceeds pending ultimate use of them,[10] and when it is in the process of a final liquidation. The advent of Internet initial public offerings for start-up companies has added increased possibilities for inadvertent investment companies. There are, of course, other less common situations where one may encounter an inadvertent investment company. For example, an unsuccessful tender or exchange offer conceivably could turn the would-be acquirer into an inadvertent investment company.

Exclusions from section 3(a)(3) of the Investment Company Act are found in section 3(b).[14] Although sometimes referred to as exemptions,[15] the statutory language *excludes* certain categories of companies from the definition of investment company.

---

28.   15 U.S.C.A. § 80a–35(b)(1).

29.   15 U.S.C.A. § 80a–15(c).

30.   15 U.S.C.A. § 80a–15(c).

§ 20.3

1.   15 U.S.C.A. § 80a–3(a)(3).

2.   15 U.S.C.A. § 80a–3(a)(3).

5.   Defined in section 2(a)(16), 15 U.S.C.A. § 80a–2(a)(16).

6.   Defined in section 2(a)(13), 15 U.S.C.A. § 80a–2(a)(13).

7.   Defined in section 2(a)(24), 15 U.S.C.A. § 80a–2(a)(24).

10.   SEC v. Fifth Ave. Coach Lines, Inc., 289 F.Supp. 3 (S.D.N.Y.1968), *affirmed* 435 F.2d 510 (2d Cir.1970) (condemnation award pushed bus company over 40% line, but company given reasonable time to act in dispensing cash before held in violation of Investment Company Act); *Cf.* In the Matter of Real Silk Hosiery Mills, 36 S.E.C. 365 (1955).

14.   15 U.S.C.A. § 80a–3(b).

15.   Section 6 of the Act sets forth exemptions. 15 U.S.C.A. § 80a–6; *see* § 20.4[2] *infra.*

Though not as "safe" or reliable as a section 3(b)(2) exemption, an inadvertent investment company has the alternative of seeking a no-action letter from the SEC, provided that it plans to engage in a good faith effort to regain its non-investment company status within a six-month period. A number of these "transient" investment companies are excluded from sections 3(a)(1) and 3(a)(3) by virtue of Rule 3a–2.[27]

In addition to the foregoing instances in which a company may become an inadvertent investment company, Investment Company Act problems can arise when a company issues tracking stock. It is becoming increasingly common for companies in many lines of business to issue tracking stock in order to allow investors to share in the success or failure of specific lines of the company's business.[32] Companies that issue tracking stock can fall within the definition of an investment company. An SEC no action letter explains that, depending on the way that the tracking stock is established and defined, there may be multiple separate issuers within the operating company and thus investment company status may exist.[33] The existence of separate issuers of securities within a single operating company can result in the finding of in investment company.[34]

As noted above, start-up companies, which may invest in securities as their operating business is developing, need to be concerned as to whether these investments will result in status as an investment company. In order to minimize this trap for the unwary, the SEC adopted an exclusion from the investment company definition.[38] SEC Rule 3a–8[39] states that certain research and development companies will not be classified as an investment company.

§ 20.4 Companies Covered by the Investment Company Act— Statutory Definitions, Exemptions and Classification

A rather complex set of provisions govern the determination of which companies are "investment companies" subject to the Investment Company Act's provisions. The Act sets out basic definitions and exemptions from registration. The Act further classifies investment companies according to the form of organization and operation.

§ 20.4[3] Classification of Investment Companies

Companies deemed subject to the Investment Company Act are divided into three categories by section 4 of the Act. There are (1) face-amount

---

27. 17 C.F.R. § 270.3a–2.

32. For discussion of the corporate law implications of tracking stock. *See, e.g.,* Jeffrey J. Hass, Directorial Fiduciary Duties in a Tracking Stock Equity Structure: The Need for a Duty of Fairness, 94 Mich. L. Rev. 2089, 2091–93 (1996); Comment, Toward Transaction–Specific Standards of Directorial Fiduciary Duty in the Tracking–Stock Context, 75 Wash. L. Rev. 1365 (2000).

33. Comdisco, Inc., 32 Sec. Reg. & L. Rep. (BNA) 1537, 2000 WL 1585639 (SEC No Action Letter Oct. 25, 2000).

34. Prudential Insurance Company of America v. SEC, 326 F.2d 383 (3d Cir.1964), cert. denied, 377 U.S. 953, 84 S.Ct. 1629, 12 L.Ed.2d 497 (1964).

38. *See* Certain Research and Development Companies, Inv. Co. Act Rel. No. IC–26077, 2003 WL 21382916 (SEC June 16, 2003).

39. 17 C.F.R. § 270.3a–8.

certificate companies, (2) unit investment trusts,[113] and (3) management companies.[114]

The largest group of investment companies consists of management companies. The Act establishes two categories of management companies. Section 5 classifies management companies as either "open-end," that is, those offering for sale already-issued redeemable securities, or "closed-end" which includes all other management companies.[115] As discussed in subsequent sections, there are special regulations that apply to each of these categories. Traditionally, most mutual funds are open-end investment companies. Trading in shares of these open-end companies is primarily through redemption and reissuance by the company at the per share net asset value.[117] Closed-end management companies typically have a fixed number of shares outstanding which are traded as any other corporate stock might be, that is, on the exchanges or over-the-counter at a price established by the market.[118] A closed-end investment company repurchases its own shares from investors wanting to sell their investment company shares. This option ordinarily is constantly open to closed-end company shareholders. In order to avoid unnecessary entanglement with the tender offer laws, Rule 14e–6 of the Securities Exchange Act of 1934 exempts most closed-end management investment companies from the requirements of Rules 14e–2 and 14e–3.[119]

The Investment Company Act further categorizes companies according to the diversification of investments in their portfolios. Section 5 of the Act classifies management companies as "diversified" and "non-diversified."[120] In the former category, seventy-five percent of the management company's assets are "limited to securities representing not more than 10 percent of the outstanding voting securities of any one company and not more than 5 percent of its total assets [may be] in the securities of any one company."[121] Contrary to the popular meaning of the term, "diversification" refers to the concentration of investments in a single issuer, not in a single industry. Authorization by a majority of its outstanding voting securities is required before a diversified investment company may change its investment policy towards one of non-diversification.[123]

Another type of investment company falling within the purview of the Investment Company Act is the "special situation company."[124] A special

---

§ 20.4

113. A unit investment trust is a company that is (a) organized under a trust indenture or some similar instrument, (b) without a board of directors, and (c) issuing only redeemable securities (not including a voting trust.) 15 U.S.C.A. § 80a–4(2). The trust indentures are governed by the Trust Indenture Act of 1939, 15 U.S.C.A. § 77aaa *et seq.* which is discussed in chapter 19 *supra.*

114. All investment companies not fitting into the other categories are management companies, 15 U.S.C.A. § 80a–4(3).

115. 15 U.S.C.A. § 80a–5(a).

117. *See* Comment, The Distribution of Mutual Fund Shares—Recent Developments in SEC Regulation, 1975 Wash.U.L.Q. 1153, 1190 (1975).

118. A "closed-end" company is one with a set number of shares as compared to "open-end" companies which will issue additional shares as new investors or new capital is found. 15 U.S.C.A. § 80a–5.

119. 17 C.F.R. § 240.14e–6. Rules 14e–1 and 14e–2 are discussed in § 11.6 *supra.*

120. 15 U.S.C.A. § 80a–5(b).

121. Alan Rosenblatt & Martin E. Lybecker, Some Thoughts on the Federal Securities Laws Regulating External Management Arrangements and the ALI Federal Securities Code Project, 124 U.Pa.L.Rev. 587, 593 n. 16 (1976). A diversified company receives special treatment under Subchapter M of the Internal Revenue Code, *id.*

123. 15 U.S.C.A. § 80a–13(a)(1).

124. *See* Edmund H. Kerr, The Inadvertent Investment Company: Section 3(a)(3) of the Investment Company Act, 12 Stan.L.Rev. 29, 47 (1959).

situation company typically buys up controlling blocks of the securities of another corporation with the intent of boosting the value of these securities through more efficient management of the target corporation. Special situation companies do not have a long-term interest in managing the businesses acquired; the primary goal is to eventually sell all of the securities at a profit.[126]

Another special category of investment companies is comprised of certain enterprises devoted to financing small businesses. As part of the Small Business Incentive Act of 1980,[127] "business development companies" are afforded different treatment than regular investment companies. Business development companies principally invest in and provide managerial assistance to small, growing, and financially troubled businesses.[128]

Although money market funds are not classified as a separate type of investment company under the statute, the Commission has adopted special rules applicable to these funds.[131] One of the unique aspects of these funds is that the per share value remains constant. Variations in net asset value will thus, if anything, affect the dividends on the shares rather than the price of the shares.

§ 20.5 Regulating the Distribution and Pricing of Investment Company Shares

Open-end and closed-end investment companies[1] are subject to different provisions and regulations of the Investment Company Act regarding both the types of capital structure they may have and the methods they may use for the distribution and pricing of their shares. Nevertheless, there are similarities between the two types of companies. Neither type of investment company may make a public offering of its securities until it has a net worth of at least one hundred thousand dollars.[2] Section 18(i) requires, with some exceptions, that every share of stock issued by a registered management company must be voting stock with equal voting rights.[3] Further similarities between open-end and closed-end management/investment companies lie in the Investment

---

126. In the Matter of Frobisher Ltd., 1948 WL 28984, 27 S.E.C. 944, 950 (1948).

127. Pub.L. 96–477, 94 Stat. 2275 (1980).

128. 5 U.S. Code Cong. and Adm. News 4800, 4801 (1980).

131. For example, the Commission has imposed limits on the amount of money that money market funds can invest in debt instruments of any one issuer. Rule 2a–7, 17 C.F.R. § 270.2a–7; Inv.Co.Act Rel. IC–18005, [1990–1991 Transfer Binder] Fed.Sec.L.Rep. (CCH) ¶ 84,710 (Feb. 20, 1991). *See* SEC Adopts Changes to Help Ensure Safety of Money Market Funds, 23 Sec.Reg. & L.Rep. (BNA) 193 (Feb. 15, 1991). The SEC excluded tax exempt money market funds from the general money market fund requirement that money market fund directors approve the acquisition of securities that are either unrated or rated only by one rating agency. 17 C.F.R. § 270.2a–7. *See* Inv.Co.Act Rel. IC–18177, [1990–1991 Transfer Binder] Fed.Sec.L.Rep. (CCH) ¶ 84,741 (May 31, 1991).

§ 20.5

1. In a closed-end investment company, the issuer puts out a limited number of shares; with an open-end company, additional shares are usually issued to each new investor. In a closed-end company there may or may not be active secondary markets. 15 U.S.C.A. § 80a–5. *See* § 20.3 *supra.*

2. 15 U.S.C.A § 80a–14(a). Rule 14a–3 exempts unit investment trusts from this capitalization requirement if certain preconditions are met, 17 C.F.R. § 270.14a–3.

3. 15 U.S.C.A. § 80a–18(i). However, in 1993, the Commission proposed a rule that would permit open-end funds to issue multiple classes of stock. Investment Company Act Rel. No. IC–19995 (SEC Dec. 15, 1993).

Company Act's provisions prohibiting either type of company from issuing warrants or rights for its stock,[4] and the provisions prohibiting the payment of dividends for either type of company from a source other than accumulated undistributed net income unless the dividend is accompanied by a written statement identifying the source.[5] There are, however, significant differences in the regulations applicable to closed-end and open-end investment companies.

§ 20.5[1] Distribution and Pricing of Closed–End Investment Company Shares; Repurchases of Its Own Shares

Closed-end investment companies may issue debt securities and preferred stock; open-end companies may not. Section 18(a) of the Act provides that debt securities must have an asset coverage of three hundred percent and preferred stock must have an asset coverage of two hundred percent.[6] In addition, no more than one class of preferred stock may be issued by a single closed-end company.[7] Section 23(a) of the Act requires that the consideration received by a closed-end company for any stock it issues must be cash or securities, which may include its own securities, "except [shares issued] as a dividend or distribution to its securities holders or in connection with a reorganization."[8] Unlike most corporate enterprises,[9] past services are specifically disallowed as consideration for the issuance of closed-end investment company shares.[10]

The Investment Company Act places restrictions on the initial offering price of investment company shares. A closed-end company may not sell any shares of its common stock at a price below its current net asset value without the consent of a majority of its stockholders, or unless pursuant to a conversion privilege.[11] The stock of closed-end investment companies generally has a market price below net asset value.[12] Section 23(b) thus presents a serious impediment to additional offerings of closed-end investment company shares.[13]

The Investment Company Act also restricts a closed-end company's repurchase of its own shares. A closed-end company may purchase any of its own shares only upon notification to its shareholders of its intention to do so, given within the preceding six months, and in accordance with rules designated by the Commission.[14] Share repurchases may also be made pursuant to tender offers to all holders of the class of securities to be purchased and pursuant to any rules the Commission may promulgate to ensure fairness to

---

4. 15 U.S.C.A. § 80a–18(d).

5. 15 U.S.C.A. § 80a–19(a).

6. 15 U.S.C.A. § 80a–18(a). "Asset coverage" is defined in 15 U.S.C.A. § 80a–18(h).

7. 15 U.S.C.A. § 80a–18(c).

8. 15 U.S.C.A. § 80a–23(a).

9. *See generally* 2 James D. Cox & Thomas L. Hazen, Cox & Hazen on Corporations § 16.18 (2d ed. 2004); Harry G. Henn & John Alexander, Laws of Corporations § 167 (3d ed. 1983).

10. 15 U.S.C.A. § 80a–23(a).

11. 15 U.S.C.A. § 80a–23(b).

12. Among other things, this reflects the fact that the costs of liquidation will cut into the liquidation value of the assets.

13. *See, e.g.,* David L. Ratner & Thomas Lee Hazen, Securities Regulation in a Nutshell § 30(b) (7th ed. 2002).

14. 15 U.S.C.A. § 80a–23(c).

all securities holders of the class of shares to be purchased.[15] Rule 23c–1 operates independently of section 23's provisions and allows a closed-end company to purchase its own securities for cash upon either the satisfaction of eleven stated conditions or upon application and Commission permission to do so.[16] Rule 23c–2 permits the redemption of closed-end company shares that are redeemable according to their terms, provided that there is equal treatment of and adequate notice to all shareholders.[17] Rule 23c–3 allows repurchase offers at the net asset value at preestablished periodic intervals or, alternatively, on a discretionary basis not more than once every two years.[18]

§ 20.5[2] Distribution and Pricing of Open–End Investment Company Shares

While the provisions regulating the distribution of the shares of a closed-end investment company are relatively straightforward and have remained stable since the Investment Company Act's passage in 1940, such has not been the case for the provisions dealing with open-end investment companies. Section 22 of the Act regulates the distribution of open-end investment company shares. The section's complexity is partially necessitated by the fact that open-end companies are constantly issuing and distributing new shares to balance out the shares redeemed and to satisfy the demand created by new investors. The consideration requirements placed on open-end company shares are the same as those placed on the shares of closed-end companies.[20] No registered investment company may suspend the right of redemption of its securities except under the narrow circumstances delimited in section 22(e) of the Act.[21] Suspension of redemption rights is permitted only (1) when the New York Stock Exchange is closed or has restricted trading, (2) during an "emergency" rendering redemption "not reasonably practicable," or (3) in accordance with SEC rules.[22] The Commission has not provided any additional exceptions through its rule-making power.

Section 11(a) of the Act prohibits registered open-end companies and underwriters from making exchange offers to investment company shareholders on any basis other than the net asset value unless the exchange is approved by the Commission order or in accordance with applicable SEC rules.[23] In 1989, the Commission adopted Rule 11a–3 to permit exchange offers to shareholders of different funds in the same group of funds without seeking SEC approval.[24] Under the rule, the investment company is permitted to charge sales loads, redemption fees, administrative fees, or any combination thereof provided that certain conditions are met.

Section 22(d) of the Investment Company Act requires that the securities of all open-end investment companies be sold "at a current public offering

---

15. *Id.*

16. 17 C.F.R. § 270.23c–1.

17. 17 C.F.R. § 270.23c–2.

18. *See* Investment Co. Act Rel. No. IC–19399, [1993 Transfer Binder] Fed. Sec. L. Rep. (CCH) ¶ 85,125 (SEC April 7, 1993).

20. 15 U.S.C.A. § 80a–22(g).

21. 15 U.S.C.A. § 80a–22(e).

22. *Id.*

23. 15 U.S.C.A. § 80a–11(a).

24. 17 C.F.R. § 270.11a–3. *See* Inv. Co. Act Rel. No. 40–17097, [1989–1990 Transfer Binder] Fed.Sec.L.Rep. ¶ 84,435 (Aug. 3, 1989).

price described in the prospectus," whether to the public directly by the fund or through an underwriter.[26] Shares are sold at the first price calculated after an order to buy or sell is received.[27] Also, shares are valued twice daily.[28] This practice, adopted in 1968, is known as "forward pricing."[29]

The uniformity of price requirement imposed by section 22(d) of the Act prevents price competition between dealers selling shares of the same fund.[31] Most broker-dealers belong to the National Association of Securities Dealers (NASD).[32] The NASD may prescribe rules for its members regarding the purchase and sale of redeemable securities from investment companies "for the purpose of eliminating or reducing so far as reasonably practicable any dilution of the value of other outstanding securities of such company" or other practice "unfair to holders of such other outstanding securities."[33]

The NASD Rules of Fair Practice place a ceiling on the "sales load,"[37] or the sales commission, for transactions in shares of open-end companies that an NASD member may charge to investors.[38] The ceiling on sales loads is in accordance with section 22(b)'s mandate that the price allowed by NASD rules "shall not include an excessive sales load but shall allow for reasonable compensation for sales personnel, broker-dealers, and underwriters and for reasonable sales loads to investors."[40] Under these rules a fund is limited to a maximum sales charge of 7.25 percent, subject to mandatory quantity discounts, unless it offers additional services which in the aggregate carry a maximum additional 1.25 percentage point value.[41] Thus, in no event may the sales charge on any transaction exceed 8.5 percent of the offering price. Although this regime would seem to indicate a strict price control system, it is intended to foster "the preconditions necessary for effective price competition" between funds offering different services.[42] "Appropriate qualified exemptions" from these sales load rules are available for smaller companies subject to higher operating costs.[43] In 1985, the SEC relaxed its system of

---

26. 15 U.S.C.A. § 80a–22(d). The Act requires that all shares in open-end investment companies be redeemable. The SEC has given permission for the redemption to be in kind (*i.e.*, the portfolio securities) rather than cash. Signature Financial Group, 1999 WL 1261284 (SEC No Action Letter Dec. 28, 1999) (enumerating conditions under which such redemptions would be permitted).

See also 17 C.F.R. § 270.22d–1 permitting sales of redeemable investment company securities at a sales load.

27. 17 C.F.R. § 270.22c–1.

28. NASD Rules of Fair Practice, Art. III § 26. The National Association of Securities Dealers is discussed in § 14.3 *supra*.

29. *See* Inv.Co.Act Rel. No. 5519 (1968). For a summary of the "two price system" that forward pricing eliminated *see* United States v. NASD, 422 U.S. 694, 702–709, 95 S.Ct. 2427, 2434–2438, 45 L.Ed.2d 486 (1975).

31. James V. Heffernan & James F. Jorden, Section 22(d) of the Investment Company Act of 1940—Its Original Purpose and Present Function, 1973 Duke L.J. 975, 976 (1973).

32. *See* § 14.3 *supra* for a description of the role of the NASD in the regulation of broker-dealer activities.

33. 15 U.S.C.A. § 80a–22(a).

37. As defined in section 2(a)(35), 15 U.S.C.A. § 80a–2(a)(35).

38. NASD Rule 2830.

40. 15 U.S.C.A. § 80a–22(b)(1).

41. Rule 2830(d).

42. Comment, The Distribution of Mutual Fund Shares—Recent Development in S.E.C. Regulation, 1975 Wash.U.L.Q. 1153, 1186–7 (1975).

43. 15 U.S.C.A. § 80a–22(b)(1).

price control when it began to allow investment companies to sell shares under varying sales loads.[44] In addition to section 22(b)'s limitations on sales loads, section 12(b) of the Act[45] places limits on a funds marketing plan and prohibits charging fictitious operating fees.[46]

Volume discounts on sales loads for large purchases of shares in open-end investment companies are allowed if they are "available to all purchasers on a non-discriminatory basis."[47] The fund may set its own "breakpoint," that is, the purchase quantity required to qualify for the discount; the breakpoint is usually set at an amount between ten and twenty-five thousand dollars.[48] In response to the investment company industry's displeasure with the investor practice of grouping together to qualify for these quantity discounts, the SEC promulgated Rule 22d–1 in 1958.[49] As it currently reads, Rule 22d–1 allows funds the alternative of offering load discounts. Under the rule, underwriters and dealers in open-end investment company shares may offer variations in, and even eliminate, the sales load under certain conditions. The variation or elimination of sales loads can only be instituted if they are in accordance with a predetermined schedule, according to particular classes of investors or transactions.[50] The scheduled variations in sales loads must be applied uniformly to all offerees in the class specified by the schedule.[51] Existing shareholders and prospective investors must be furnished adequate information concerning the scheduled variations in sales loads; the information must be furnished in accordance with the standards set forth in the applicable registration statement form.[52] Before any scheduled variations in the sales load or changes in the schedule can be implemented, the prospectus must be amended to describe any new variation.[53] Finally, the investment company must advise existing shareholders of any new variation in the sales load within one year of the date on which it is first made available to the company.[54]

The SEC has rules requiring certain disclosures relating to mutual fund breakpoint share pricing.[56] The SEC's rules regarding mutual fund pricing focus on disclosures sufficient to inform investors regarding breakpoints.

§ 20.5[3] Secondary Markets for Investment Company Shares

This initial distribution system of mutual fund shares forms the primary market for these shares.[63] The "secondary market" for mutual funds shares

---

44. 17 C.F.R. § 270.22d–1. The rule does not permit investors to negotiate sales loads even though the SEC originally proposed such an amendment. *See* Inv.Co.Act Rel. No. IC–14390 [1984–1985 Transfer Binder] Fed.Sec.L.Rep. (CCH) & 83,740 (Feb. 27, 1985).

45. 15 U.S.C.A. § 80a–12(b).

46. In re Coxam, SEC Admin. Proc. File No. 3–9218, 31 Sec. Reg. & L. Rep. (BNA) 459 (SEC initial decision 1999) (ordering disgorgement of excessive disguised fees paid to mutual fund adviser). *See also* 15 U.S.C.A. §§ 80a–26(e), 80a–27(i), requiring that expenses, charges, and other fees be reasonable.

47. Inv.Co.Act Rel. No. 89 (Mar. 13, 1941).

48. SEC Report of the Division of Investment Management Regulation Mutual Fund Distribution and Section 22(d) of the Investment Company Act of 1940, p. 90 (Aug. 1974).

49. 17 C.F.R. § 270.22d–1.

50. 17 C.F.R. § 270.22d–1.

51. 17 C.F.R. § 270.22d–1(a).

52. 17 C.F.R. § 270.22d–1(b).

53. 17 C.F.R. § 270.22d–1(c).

54. 17 C.F.R. § 270.22d–1(d).

56. Disclosure of Breakpoint Discounts by Mutual Funds, Sec. Act Rel. No. 33–8427; Sec. Exch. Act rel. No. 34–49817; Inv. Co. Act Rel. No. IC–26464 (SEC 2004).

63. United States v. NASD, 422 U.S. 694, 699, 95 S.Ct. 2427, 2433, 45 L.Ed.2d 486 (1975).

refers to the trading of such shares other than through the investment company directly or its underwriter and broker-dealer network. Though still existing, elimination of this market where investors had little protection was among the primary goals of the Congress in enacting the Investment Company Act.[64] The Supreme Court has held that section 22(d) of the Act does not prohibit broker-dealers from matching buy and sell orders of individual investors, nor from acting as an agent in the sale of mutual fund shares at any price the investors agree upon.[65] This order matching practice is not subject to section 22(d)'s uniform price requirement because the section speaks only of "dealer transactions," that is, when securities are bought and sold for the agent's own account.[66] When merely acting as a broker for the accounts of others, the broker-dealer is not effecting a transaction for his own account and therefore escapes section 22(d)'s provisions.[67] The Court also dealt with section 22(f)'s provision allowing a mutual fund to restrict the transferability and negotiability of its shares in conformity with legends on the shares themselves and with the fund's registration statement. SEC rules under section 22(d) allow mutual funds to regulate the secondary market by private contractual agreements between the funds, the NASD, and brokers, dealers and underwriters, as well as by the terms of the funds' registration statements.[68] The SEC had held that this private method of regulating the secondary market was preferable to the promulgating of further administrative rules in the area.[69] The Supreme Court held these arrangements to be immunized from illegality under the Sherman Antitrust Act[70] due to the broad regulatory powers over mutual fund shares granted by Congress to the SEC in section 22(f) of the Investment Company Act.[71] The importance of this aspect of the decision is minimal due to the relatively insignificant size of the secondary mutual fund market of open-end companies today.

§ 20.5[4] Improper Trading and Pricing Practices

§ 20.5[4][A] Late Trading

One of the pernicious practices that came to light in 2003 was that many mutual funds engaged in late trading of open-end fund shares. Investigations by the SEC and the New York Attorney General revealed that many reputable mutual funds were engaging in fraudulent practices. The two most visible practices were late trading schemes and market timing.[72] Open-end mutual fund shares are based on forward pricing. Open-end fund shares are priced each day based on the net asset value of the fund's assets at the close of

---

64. *Id.* at 700, 95 S.Ct. at 2433–2434.

65. *Id.* at 711–19, 95 S.Ct. at 2438–2443.

66. As defined in 15 U.S.C.A. § 80a–2(a)(11).

67. As defined in 15 U.S.C.A. § 80a–2(a)(6). *See* 422 U.S. at 713, 95 S.Ct. at 2439–2440.

68. 422 U.S. at 720–28, 95 S.Ct. at 2443–2447.

69. *Id.*

70. 15 U.S.C.A. § 1.

71. 422 U.S. at 729–30, 95 S.Ct. at 2447–2448.

72. *See, e.g.,* SEC Chairman Donaldson Releases Statement Regarding Initiatives to Combat Late Trading and Market Timing of Mutual Funds, http://www.sec.gov/news/press/2003-136.htm (Oct. 9, 2003); Roberto M. Braceras, Late Trading and Market Timing, 37 Rev. Sec. & Commod. Reg. 61 (2004).

regular trading in the securities markets (4:00 p.m. eastern time). Late trading occurs when a trade is entered after the market's closed but is priced at the level fixed by the 4:00 calculation. This allows late traders to take advantage of events taking place after 4:00 that will move the net asset value either up or down. This allows the late trader to guarantee a profit by trading on news available to everyone but at a price available only to those who have access to late trading. All other investors desiring to trade on the news get to trade at the price fixed at 4:00 on the *next* trading day, after that news has affected the price of the securities in the fund's portfolio. Late trading thus operates just like insider trading. A group of insiders are able to take advantage of their access based on their position. In the case of insider trading, the violation consists of taking advantage of information not generally available at a transaction price available to the investing public. Conversely, late trading allows an insider to take advantage of pricing not available to the investing public in order to take advantage of price movements resulting from information that is generally available. Late trading practices unfairly advantage participating investors and have been the subject of SEC enforcement actions.[73] In late 2003, the SEC proposed a 4:00 p.m. cut-off for mutual fund trading in order to eliminate late trading issues.[74]

§ 20.5[4][B] Market Timing

Market timing transaction by the mutual fund industry is another way to take advantage of the forward pricing mechanism of open-end mutual fund shares. It provides another way for traders to take advantage of prices that have become stale because the mutual fund share price is fixed, notwithstanding events and news that will affect the fund share price once the next net asset valuation is made at the close of trading. Market timing permits traders to trade once during the course of business one day and then lock in a mutual fund share price based on the previous day's close and then sell the mutual fund shares the next day once the fund shares are trading at the price that reflects the new information. The mutual fund industry segments engaging in this practice claim that although it may have been questionable,[75] it is not illegal. Nevertheless, the SEC and the states have been pursuing certain market timing practices as securities law violations.[76] There are at least two instances in which institutional market timing of mutual fund shares is clearly improper. In the first instance, if a mutual fund, as it should, discourages short-term investment strategies but then enters into arrangements with market timers that encourage timing, the fund has breached obligations to the other fund shareholders. The second situation involves offshore funds where the varying time zones allow market timers to take advantage of forward pricing of mutual fund shares in much the same was as late traders in the United States. Improprieties also occur when a fund fails to

---

73. *See, e.g.,* SEC Sues Dallas Broker/Adviser, Mutuals.com, for Fraud in Fund Trading, 35 Sec. Reg. & L. Rep. (BNA) 2021 (Dec. 8, 2003).

74. *See* Compliance Programs of Investment Companies and Investment Advisers, Inv. Adv. Act Rel. No. IA–2204, Inv. Co. Act Rel. No. IC–26299, 2003 WL 22971048 (SEC 2003). *See also, e.g.,* SEC Adopts Fund, Adviser Compliance Rule, Proposes Rule to Curb Late Trading or Funds, 35 Sec. Reg. & L. Rep. (BNA) 2014 (Dec. 8, 2003).

75. As discussed in § 14.16[4] *supra,* regulators have long taken the position that market timing in mutual fund shares generally is not a suitable investment strategy.

76. *See, e.g.,* Invesco, Its CEO Face SEC, N.Y. Charges Over Market Timing, 35 Sec. Reg. & L. Rep. (BNA) 2020 (Dec. 8, 2003).

charge redemption fees in order to facilitate undisclosed or otherwise improper market timing by the account holder.[77]

§ 20.5[4][C] Breakpoint Pricing of Investment Company Shares

Mutual funds sometimes offer their shares in various classes with differing sales charges. For example, Class A mutual fund shares typically are based on front-end loaded sales charges. In contrast, sales charges on class B shares typically are back-end loaded. The size of the investment and the investor's investment objectives can bear upon the most appropriate class for a particular investment. Class C shares typically have back-end loaded sales charges that are lower than class B shares.[78]

---

77. *See* In the Matter of BancOne Investment Advisers Corp., Admin. Proc. No. 3–11530, Inv. Adv. Act Rel. No. IA–2254, Inv. Co. Act Rel. No. IC–26490, 2004 WL 1472043 (SEC June 29, 2004) (settlement of cease and desist proceedings).

78. Consider, for example, the following description of the differences between mutual fund share classes as found on a mutual fund website:

Class A Shares

Class "A" shares are sometimes called front-end loaded shares because a sales charge is paid immediately, before any principal is invested. For example, if you put $1,000 in an "A" share with a 5.5% sales charge, $55 would be deducted from your investment. The remaining $945 of principal would be invested in the fund. In addition to an upfront sales charge and other fund expenses, investors pay a 12b–1 fee. "A" Shares typically have lower overall expense ratios than other retail share classes.

Class B Shares

Class "B" shares are sometimes called back-end loaded shares because a sales charge is paid if you sell shares within a certain number of years (this charge is also known as a contingent deferred sales charge or CDSC). For example, if you invest $1,000 in a "B" share, the entire $1,000 is invested immediately. If you sell your shares within two years, a sales charge equal to 5% of the value of your assets is assessed. If your savings have appreciated during this time, you owe 5% of the current value of your account. The back-end sales charge declines by 1% each year after year two and after year five disappears.

Investors pay higher annual 12b–1 fees for class "B" shares than class "A" shares. After eight years, "B" shares convert into "A" shares and investors' 12b–1 fees are reduced.

"B" shares may be appropriate for investors with long-term goals. If you withdraw your savings during the first five years, you'll pay a back-end load. However, if you hold your shares for more than five years, you may be able to avoid paying a sales charge altogether.

Class C Shares

Class "C" shares have a low back-end sales charge that is assessed for a shorter period of time than "B" shares. If you sell shares within 18 months of purchase, a 1% contingent deferred sales charge or CDSC is assessed. An exception is made for dividends or distributions reinvested into "C" shares.

Class "C" shares charge a higher 12b–1 fee each year than Class "A" shares, and do not convert into "A" shares at any time.

"C" shares may be appropriate for investors with short-to intermediate-term goals. A higher 12b–1 fee is paid; however, there is no CDSC after 18 months, so investors can redeem without a charge after a shorter period of time, unlike "B" shares.

Class H shares

Class "H" shares are sometimes called hybrid shares because they combine a low front-end sales charge with a low back-end sales charge (CDSC) that is assessed if shares are redeemed within 18 months. Class "H" shares pay higher 12b–1 fees than Class "A" shares, and do not convert into "A" shares at any time.

"H" shares may be appropriate for investors with intermediate-term goals. A higher 12b–1 fee is paid each year, but there is no CDSC after 18 months, so investors can redeem without a charge after a shorter period of time, unlike "B" shares.

Class I Shares

Class "I" shares are sometimes called institutional shares because they are intended only for financial institutions purchasing shares for their own or their clients' accounts. Class "I"

Recommendations regarding fund purchases must adequately disclose the differing sales charges.[80] Suitability issues can arise in recommending a class of shares that may not have the charges suitable for the particular investor.[81]

In addition to multiple classes of shares, many mutual funds offer breakpoint discounts for investors based on the amount of money invested. An SEC study indicated that many firms have not been offering many investors the breakpoint discounts that could have been applicable.[82] The NASD, the Securities Industry Association, and the Investment Company Institute created a working group "to explore and recommend ways in which the mutual fund and broker-dealer industries can prevent breakpoint problems in the future, and improve systems and disclosure."[83] The NASD also issued a notice to members calling for the refund to customers of excess break point charges.[84]

§ 20.6   Fiduciary Duties; Independent Investment Company Directors

Unlike the 1933 and 1934 securities acts, the Investment Company Act of 1940 imposes substantive rules upon an issuer's internal governance structure. This represents a significant departure from the general thrust of most federal securities laws and regulations, which is to eschew direct involvement in the corporate chartering process. For example, the Securities Exchange Act of 1934 protects shareholder interests by requiring full disclosure and regulating proxy machinery in shareholder votes. These shareholder voting safeguards alone are considered inadequate methods of protecting investment company shareholders, due both to the nature of investment company activity and the fluctuations in the number of shares owned by any single shareholder as a result of dividend payments or daily cash needs.[2] Accordingly, there are additional duties imposed upon investment company directors by federal regulation under the 1940 Act.

The totality of investment company directors' duties is imposed by state corporate law, state blue sky laws, common law, and the Investment Company

---

shares have no front-end sales charge and low annual operating expenses and cannot be purchased by the general public.

Armada Funds, http://www.armadafunds.com/Funds/ShareClasses.asp (visited May 18, 2003).

80. *See, e.g.,* In the Matter of Hoffman, 71 S.E.C. Docket 1247, Release No. ID–158, 2000 WL 64976 (SEC Initial Decision Jan. 27, 2000) (disclosures were adequate).

81. *See* In the Matter of Belden, Adm. Proc. File No. 3–10888, Sec. Exch. Act Rel. No. 34–47859, 2003 WL 21088079 (SEC May 14, 2003), *affirming* 2002 WL 1967925 (N.A.S.D.R. Aug. 13, 2002) (affirming NASD sanctions for sales of Class B shares).

82. Joint SEC/NASD/NYSE Report of Examinations of Broker–Dealers Regarding Discounts on Front–End Sales Charges on Mutual Funds, http://www.sec.gov/news/studies/breakpoin-trep.htm (March 2003).

83. *Id. See, e.g.,* NASD Special Notice to Members 02–85, NASD Requires Immediate Member Firm Action Regarding Mutual Fund Purchases and Breakpoint Schedules, http://www.nasdr.com/pdf-text/0285ntm.pdf (NASD December, 2002); Paul F. Roye, A New Era of Accountability in Fund Regulation, 2003 WL 1902922 (Palm Desert, CA March 31, 2003). *See also, e.g.,* NASD IM–2830–1.

84. Refunds to Customers Who Did Not Receive Appropriate Breakpoint Discounts in Connection with the Purchase of Class A Shares of Front–End Load Mutual Funds and the Capital Treatment of Refund Liability, NASD Notice to Members 03–47 (August 2003).

§ 20.6

2. One example of the substantive protection is the antipyramiding rule of section 12(d)(1) 15 U.S.C.A. § 80a–12(d)(1) which is discussed in § 20.1 *supra.*

Act.[4] Directors who are engaged in fraudulent practices may also be subject to liability for violations of Exchange Act Rule 10b–5.[5] The Investment Company Act thus supplements federal and state regulation applicable to management generally.

§ 20.6[1] Composition of an Investment Company's Board of Directors

Independent directors serve primarily as "watchdogs" over an investment company to protect the interests of shareholders against abuses by investment advisers and others in a position to profit illegally from the company.[6] The SEC continues to stress the importance of investment company directors, especially in the face of scandals in the mutual fund industry.

Section 10(a) of the Investment Company Act ensures some degree of management independence by requiring registered investment companies' boards of directors to be composed of at least forty percent disinterested persons.[9] "Interested persons" are defined to include: (1) any affiliated person of the investment company; (2) the immediate family members of an affiliated natural person; (3) any person interested in the investment company's investment adviser or principal underwriter; (4) anyone who has acted as the investment company's legal counsel within the past two years; (5) certain brokers or dealers registered under the Securities Exchange Act who have a relationship to the investment company, or any affiliate thereof;[10] and (6) any person the Commission deems to be interested due to a material or professional relationship with the investment company within the previous two years.[11] An "affiliated person" is any person owning or holding with voting power five percent or more of the company's outstanding voting securities; any company of whose outstanding voting securities the investment company owns five percent or more; any person controlled by the investment company; any officer, director, partner, copartner, or employee of the investment company; and any investment adviser or member of the advisory board of the investment company.[12]

Membership on the board of directors of an investment company or ownership of less than five percent of the investment company securities does not in and of itself constitute grounds to classify a person as "interested."[13] Participation on multiple boards of funds within the same fund complex does not in itself not render directors "interested" in violation in violation of the Investment Company Act's definition of who is a disinterested director.[14] In the case of no-load mutual funds, only one member of the board need be a disinterested person with regard to the investment adviser.[15]

---

4. Blue sky laws are considered in chapter 8 *supra.*

5. 17 C.F.R. § 240.10b–5. *See* chapter 12 *supra.*

6. S.Rep.No. 184, 91st Cong., 1st Sess. 32 (1969).

9. 15 U.S.C.A. § 80a–10(a).

10. *See* 17 C.F.R. § 270.2a19–1.

11. 15 U.S.C.A. § 80a–2(a)(19)(A)(i)–(vi).

12. 15 U.S.C.A. § 80a–2(a)(3).

13. 15 U.S.C.A. § 80a–2(a)(19).

14. Krantz v. Prudential Investments Fund Management LLC, 305 F.3d 140 (3d Cir. 2002) (failure to show fees were excessive).

15. 15 U.S.C.A. § 80a–10(d)(3).

Control persons, affiliates, and employees of an investment company will qualify as interested persons under the Act.[16] There is a presumption that a natural person is not a control person.[17] This is a rebuttable presumption.[18] There is no comparable presumption for the more generalized concept of control person under the 1933 and 1934 Acts.[19] The independence of investment company directors will be judged by the substance of any relationship to the investment advisor rather than focusing on the form. Indirect compensation from the adviser will preclude a finding of independence. Thus, for example, a director who receives compensation from service on the board of multiple investment companies managed by a single adviser is not a disinterested person within the meaning of the Investment Company Act.[20] In contrast, when a director receives special consideration in IPO allocations, his independence may be compromised.[21]

When Congress enacted the Gramm–Leach–Bliley Act, which abolished former barriers between various financial institutions,[26] it amended section 2(a)(19) of the Investment Company Act[27] and established additional standards for determining investment company director independence based on affiliation with a broker-dealer; this amendment eliminated the need for further SEC rulemaking in this area.[28] The mutual fund scandals that emerged at the beginning of the twenty-first century[29] resulted in considerable efforts to further enhance the independence requirements.

The Sarbanes–Oxley Act[30] imposed additional independence requirements and monitoring obligations of directors of publicly held companies generally. In 2004, the SEC adopted rules to further enhance the director independence requirements.[31]

The SEC has ten exemptive rules[32] under the Investment Company Act that condition the exemptions for investment companies where (i) indepen-

16. Investment Company Act § 2(a)(9), 15 U.S.C.A. § 80a–2(a)(9).

17. Investment Company Act §§ 2(a)(3)(D), 2(a)(9), 15 U.S.C.A. §§ 80a–2(a)(3)(D), 80a–2(a)(9).

18. *See* Strougo v. BEA Associates, 2000 WL 45714, [1999–2000 Transfer Binder] Fed. Sec. L. Rep. (CCH) ¶ 90,742 (S.D.N.Y. 2000) (director was interested for purposes of demand requirement).

19. 15 U.S.C.A. §§ 77o, 78t. *See* §§ 7.12, 12.24 *supra*.

20. Strougo v. BEA Associates, 2000 WL 45714, [1999–2000 Transfer Binder] Fed. Sec. L. Rep. (CCH) ¶ 90,742 (S.D.N.Y. 2000).

21. *See* Monetta Financial Services, Inc., Sec. Act Rel. No. 33–8239, Sec. Exch. Act Rel. No. 34–48001, Inv. Adv. Act Rel. No. IA–2136, Inv. Co. Act Rel. No. IC–26070, 2003 WL 21310330 (SEC June 9, 2003).

26. The Gramm–Leach–Bliley Act is discussed in § 22.5 *infra*.

27. 15 U.S.C.A. § 80a–2(a)(19).

28. *See* Role of Independent Directors of Investment Companies, Sec. Exch. Act Rel. No. 34–43786, 2001 WL 6738 (SEC Jan. 2, 2001).

29. *See, e.g.,* Investment Company Governance, Inv. Co. Act Rel. No. IC–26520, 2004 WL 1672374 (SEC 2004).

30. Sarbanes–Oxley Act of 2002, Pub. Law 107–204 (July 30, 2002), codified in 15 U.S.C. § 7245 (2002 supp.).

31. *See* Investment Company Governance, Inv. Co. Act Rel. No. IC–26520, 2004 WL 1672374 (SEC 2004).

32. Those ten rules are: Rule 10f–3 (permitting funds to purchase securities in a primary offering when an affiliated broker-dealer is a member of the underwriting syndicate); Rule 12b–1 (permitting use of fund assets to pay distribution expenses); Rule 15a–4(b)(2) (permitting fund boards to approve interim advisory contracts without shareholder approval where the adviser or a

dent directors constitute a majority of their boards; (ii) independent directors select and nominate other independent directors; and (iii) any legal counsel for the fund's independent directors be an independent legal counsel.[33]

Supplementing all of the independence requirements described briefly above, the SEC imposes disclosure requirements on the directors so that the fund shareholders can evaluate who their directors are and the role that they play. The information must be contained in a table that appears in three places: the fund's annual report to shareholders, statements of additional information, and the proxy statement for the election of directors.[61] The table must provide the following information for each director: (1) name, address, and age; (2) current positions held with the fund; (3) term of office and length of time served; (4) principal occupations during the past five years; (5) number of portfolios overseen within the fund complex; and (6) other directorships held outside of the fund complex. For each interested director, as defined in Section 2(a)(19) of the Investment Company Act, the table must contain a description of the relationship, events, or transactions by reason of which the director is an interested person. In 2001, the SEC adopted enhanced conflict of interest disclosures for investment company act directors.[62]

§ 20.6[2] Duties of Investment Company Directors

As in the case of any corporation, the board of directors is responsible for overseeing the investment company's general management.[63] The Act does not impose strict liability upon directors, so long as the fiduciary duties imposed upon them by section 36(a)[64] have been fulfilled.[65]

It has been held that section 1(b) of the Act[66] codified the common law duties and obligations of corporate directors generally and applies them to investment company directors.[67] In Burks v. Lasker,[68] the Supreme Court expressly noted that the Investment Company Act was not intended to

---

controlling person receives a benefit in connection with the assignment of the prior contract); Rule 17a–7 (permitting securities transactions between a fund and another client of the fund's adviser); Rule 17a–8 (permitting mergers between certain affiliated funds); Rule 17d–1(d)(7) (permitting funds and their affiliates to purchase joint liability insurance policies); Rule 17e–1 (specifying conditions under which funds may pay commissions to affiliated brokers in connection with the sale of securities on an exchange); Rule 17g–1(j) (permitting funds to maintain joint insured bonds); Rule 18f–3 (permitting funds to issue multiple classes of voting stock); and Rule 23c–3 (permitting the operation of interval funds by enabling closed-end funds to repurchase their shares from investors).

33. *See* Role of Independent Directors of Investment Companies, Sec. Exch. Act Rel. No. 34–43786, 2001 WL 6738 (SEC Jan. 2, 2001). *See also* Jay C. Baris, The New Fund Governance Standards. 34 Rev.Sec. & Commod.Reg. 135 (2001).

61. *See* Role of Independent Directors of Investment Companies, Sec. Exch. Act Rel. No. 34–43786, 2001 WL 6738 (SEC Jan. 2, 2001).

62. *Id.*

63. SEC, Institutional Investor Study Report, H.R. Doc. No. 64, Vol. 2, 92d Cong. 1st Sess. 214 (1971).

64. 15 U.S.C.A. § 80a–35(a); Brouk v. Managed Funds, Inc., 286 F.2d 901, 918 (8th Cir.1961), *judgment vacated* 369 U.S. 424, 82 S.Ct. 878, 8 L.Ed.2d 6 (1962).

65. *See, e.g.,* Moses v. Burgin, 445 F.2d 369 (1st Cir.1971), *cert. denied* 404 U.S. 994, 92 S.Ct. 532, 30 L.Ed.2d 547 (1971); Fogel v. Chestnutt, 533 F.2d 731 (2d Cir.1975), *cert. denied* 429 U.S. 824, 97 S.Ct. 77, 50 L.Ed.2d 86 (1976); Tannenbaum v. Zeller, 552 F.2d 402 (2d Cir.1977).

66. 15 U.S.C.A. § 80a–1(b).

67. Aldred Investment Trust v. SEC, 151 F.2d 254, 260 (1st Cir.1945), *cert. denied* 326 U.S. 795, 66 S.Ct. 486, 90 L.Ed. 483 (1946).

68. 441 U.S. 471, 99 S.Ct. 1831, 60 L.Ed.2d 404 (1979).

supplant the "entire corpus of state corporation law" even where a plaintiff's cause of action arises solely out of Investment Company Act provisions.[69] *Burks* concerned the ability of investment company directors acting upon independent advice to terminate shareholder derivative suits. The Court reversed the overturning of the board action and stated that federal courts "should apply state law governing the authority of independent directors to discontinue derivative suits to the extent such law is consistent with the policies of the Investment Company Act and the Investment Advisers Act."[70] Suits claiming breaches of fiduciary duty under the Investment Company Act are derivative in nature and thus are subject to the demand requirement.

§ 20.6[3] Approval of the Advisory Contract

Some state courts have given undue deference to the decisions of unaffiliated boards of directors renewing advisory contracts.[75] To counteract this undue deference and potential for self-dealing, section 36(b) was added in 1970 to provide that investment advisers are also subject to a fiduciary duty to the investment company.[76] This is supplemented by section 15(c)'s requirement that the investment adviser provide the information requested by the board of directors that is reasonably necessary to evaluate the adviser's performance.[77] The investment company's board has a statutory duty to request this information and consider it in its deliberations of whether to renew the advisory contract.[78] The Investment Company Act further requires that for renewal of the advisory contract, a majority of the disinterested directors must approve the renewal in person at a special meeting called for that express purpose.[79] This approval is in addition to the majority shareholder consent that is required for the initial advisory contract or for a change in investment advisers.[80]

Investment company directorial responsibility does not diminish with a delegation of authority to an investment adviser.[81] The investment adviser's "contractual authority to direct the functions and activities of the investment company to the extent of portfolio selection,"[82] the restrictions placed upon investment company activity by section 12,[83] and the requirement of share-

---

69. *Id.* at 478, 99 S.Ct. at 1837.

70. *Id.* at 486, 99 S.Ct. at 1841.

The Court has also held that demand on directors is not necessary in an action under section 36(b) of the Act, complaining of excessive advisory fees. Daily Income Fund, Inc. v. Fox, 464 U.S. 523, 104 S.Ct. 831, 78 L.Ed.2d 645 (1984).

However, in a subsequent ruling, the Court held that in a derivative suit involving a registered investment company, a federal court must apply the demand futility exception to any demand requirement as that exception is defined by the law of the state of incorporation. Kamen v. Kemper Financial Services, Inc., 500 U.S. 90, 111 S.Ct. 1711, 114 L.Ed.2d 152 (1991).

75. *See, e.g.,* Saxe v. Brady, 40 Del.Ch. 474, 184 A.2d 602 (1962).

76. Investment Company Amendment Act, Pub.L. No. 91–547, 84 Stat. 1413 (1970); 15 U.S.C.A. § 80a–35(b). *See* § 20.10 *infra.*

77. 15 U.S.C.A. § 80a–15(c).

78. *Id.*

79. *Id.*

80. 15 U.S.C.A. § 80a–15(a). *See also* § 20.9 *infra.*

81. *See* 15 U.S.C.A. § 80a–15.

82. Joseph F. Krupsky, Role of Investment Company Directors, 32 Bus.Law. 1748 (1977).

83. 15 U.S.C.A. § 80a–12.

holder approval for changes in investment policy,[84] all combine to impose upon investment company directors a duty to continually oversee the adviser's portfolio supervision throughout the year. This obligation supplements the directors' duty to annually reconsider and reevaluate investment advisory contracts that continue in effect for more than two years from the making and execution of the advisory contract.[86] A "heavy duty of disclosure is imposed upon management in order to permit the directors to exercise informed discretion [in performing their duties]" since directors are not full-time employees and therefore probably not attuned to possible problems in the fund's day-to-day operation.[87]

In most instances, directors are entitled to rely upon the assertions and representations of management; however, there is an implied duty to make further inquiries when a director is alerted to, or charged with constructive knowledge of, a potential conflict of interest problem between advisers and fund shareholders. Conflict-of-interest problems most frequently occur when a major reason to increase the size of the fund is to increase the fee paid to the adviser rather than the earning power of the fund. The Supreme Court in *Burks* commented: "Congress consciously chose to address the conflict-of-interest problem through the Act's independent-directors section, rather than through more drastic remedies such as complete disaffiliation of the companies from their advisers or compulsory internalization of the management function."[90] Conflict-of-interest problems also arise in the affiliation of inside directors with the investment adviser; such a relationship creates a duty of disclosure to facilitate evaluation of their ability to serve as investment company directors.[91]

The actual protection afforded public shareholder interests by disinterested director requirements and shareholder voting in adopting the original advisory contract is questionable since the adviser controls the initial voting securities after it creates the fund.[92] Even with the expansion of investment company shareholders, the investment adviser continues to effectively control the company's proxy machinery. Voting rights as a protection of shareholder interests are therefore minimal, and the independent director emerges as the shareholders' only unbiased advocate.[93]

An investment company rarely has the option of terminating an advisory contract due to its inability to internalize management and further due to the financial disturbance which would be suffered by the fund with a change of investment adviser.[96] Indeed, a change of advisers may frustrate shareholder expectations since most shareholders decide to invest in a company based on

84. 15 U.S.C.A. § 80a–13.

86. 15 U.S.C.A. § 80a–15(a).

87. Clarke Randall, Fiduciary Duties of Investment Company Directors and Management Companies Under the Investment Company Act of 1940, 31 Okla.L.Rev. 635, 668 (1978).

90. 441 U.S. at 483, 99 S.Ct. at 1839–1840.

91. Joseph F. Krupsky, Role of Investment Company Directors, 32 Bus.Law. 1733, 1748 (1977).

92. Comment, Duties of the Independent Director in Open–End Mutual Funds, 70 Mich. L.Rev. 696, 699 (1972); Joseph F. Krupsky, Role of Investment Company Directors, 32 Bus.Law. 1733, 1743 (1977).

93. Richard M. Phillips, Deregulation Under the Investment Company Act—Reevaluation of the Corporate Paraphernalia of Shareholder Voting and Boards of Directors, 37 Bus.Law. 903, 909 (1982).

96. Joseph F. Krupsky, Role of Investment Company Directors, 32 Bus.Law. 1749–51 (1977).

the reputation of the adviser.[97] Therefore, the mandatory reporting of all investment adviser activity affecting the company's performance to the board of directors is the most efficacious method of keeping adviser activity honest and aboveboard. The investment company board of directors' decision to renew an advisory contract is given only as much weight as a court deems appropriate in an action against an adviser for breach of fiduciary duty.[98]

In 2004, the SEC adopted enhanced disclosure requirements regarding approval of the investment advisory contract. The SEC rules as amended require registered mutual funds to make disclosures in their reports to shareholders regarding the material factors and the conclusions with respect to those factors that formed the basis for the board's approval of advisory contracts during the most recent fiscal half-year.[99]

§ 20.6[4] Other Investment Company Board Obligations

The selection and supervision of an investment adviser is not the only function of the investment company's board of directors. Investment company directors must also choose an independent accountant for the fund—a choice which must be ratified by a majority of shareholders.[101] The independent accountants aid the investment company directors in discharging their duty to evaluate portfolio securities where market quotations are not readily available, since accountants presumably have more expertise to make such evaluations.[102] The choice of accountant is also important since it is the accountant who is required to report "inadequacies in the fund's accounting system and system of internal accounting control, along with an indication of any corrective action taken or proposed" in Form NBIR that is required under section 30 of the Investment Company Act.[103] Accountants therefore act as watchdogs for the watchdogs. Directors must also choose the investment company's attorney, although there are no statutory provisions for that procedure.

Investment company directors must ensure that the reports required by the various securities laws and SEC regulations are filed in a timely and accurate fashion. Directors of investment companies have a duty to fill board vacancies created by death or resignation prior to the expiration of a director's term.[104] However, at least two-thirds of the directors of an investment company must have been elected by the shareholders.[105] Directors are also responsible for assuring that proper proxy solicitation materials are submitted to the shareholders and the SEC, although this obligation is often satisfied by the investment adviser. Directors must also ensure that dividends are paid correctly and that conditions for maintaining Subchapter M tax treatment[106]

---

97. SEC, Public Policy Implications of Investment Company Growth, H.R. Rep. No. 2337, 89th Cong.2d Sess. 31 (1966).

98. 15 U.S.C.A. § 80a–35(b)(2).

99. Disclosure Regarding Approval of Investment Advisory Contracts by Directors of Investment Companies, Sec. Act Rel. No. 33–8433, Sec. Exch. Act Rel. No. 34–49909, Inv. Co. Act Rel. No. IC–26486 (SEC June 30, 2004) (adopting release).

101. 15 U.S.C.A. § 80a–31.

102. 15 U.S.C.A. § 80a–2(a)(41).

103. Michael J. Radmer, Duties of Directors of Investment Companies, 3 J.Corp.L. 61, 84 (1977).

104. 15 U.S.C.A. § 80a–15.

105. 15 U.S.C.A. § 80a–16(a).

106. 26 U.S.C.A. §§ 851–55.

are met. In sum, investment company directors are subjected to all common law directorial duties and a host of others by the Investment Company Act. As a means of implementing the additional duties imposed by the Act, a private cause of action will lie for breach of a director's fiduciary duty.[107]

Over the years, there has been increasing concern over the accountability of mutual fund managers to the mutual fund investors when exercising the voting rights arising out of the ownership of shares in the investment portfolio. In 2003, the SEC adopted new rules requiring investment companies to make disclosures relating to their voting of portfolio securities.[108] The SEC adopted Investment Company Act Rule 30b1–4[109] to require registered management investment companies to provide disclosure about how they vote proxies relating to portfolio securities they hold. The SEC adopted a new form N–PX for making the portfolio voting disclosures and also amended existing registration and disclosure forms to assure that similar disclosures are made at least annually. Specifically, it requires registered management investment companies to disclose the policies and procedures that they use to determine how to vote proxies relating to portfolio securities.[110] In addition, management investment companies must file with the SEC and make available to shareholders the specific proxy votes that they cast in shareholder meetings of issuers of portfolio securities.[111] The SEC adopted a parallel set of rules for investment advisers.[112]

§ 20.6[5] Enhanced Fiduciary Obligations; Investment Adviser Code of Ethics

As discussed earlier in this treatise, the Sarbanes–Oxley Act of 2002[113] introduced a number of corporate governance reforms applicable to publicly traded companies,[114] including disclosures relating to a company's code of ethics.[115] These disclosures apply as well to publicly traded mutual funds. In 2004, the SEC adopted rules requiring investment advisers to adopt and enforce codes of ethics applicable to persons they supervise.[116]

The SEC rules require investment advisers to report violations of their codes of ethics. Thus, an investment adviser's code of ethics must require supervised persons to report, promptly, any violations of the adviser's code of ethics to the firm's chief compliance officer or to other designated persons.

---

107. 15 U.S.C.A. § 80a–35(b). *See* § 20.10 *infra.*

108. *See* Disclosure of Proxy Voting, Policies and Proxy Voting Records by Registered Management Investment Companies, Sec. Act Rel. No. 33–8188, Sec. Exch. Act Rel. No. 34–47304, Inv. Co. Act Rel. No. IC–25922, 79 S.E.C. Docket 1638, 2003 WL 215451 (SEC Jan. 31, 2003).

109. 17 C.F.R. § 270.30b1–4.

110. *See* Disclosure of Proxy Voting, Policies and Proxy Voting Records by Registered Management Investment Companies, Sec. Act Rel. No. 33–8188, Sec. Exch. Act Rel. No. 34–47304, Inv. Co. Act Rel. No. IC–25922, 79 S.E.C. Docket 1638, 2003 WL 215451 (SEC Jan. 31, 2003).

111. *Id.*

112. *See* Proxy Voting By Investment Advisors, Inv. Adv. Act Rel. No. IA–2106, 79 S.E.C. Docket 1673, 2003 WL 215467 (SEC Jan. 31, 2003).

113. Sarbanes–Oxley Act of 2002, Pub. Law 107–204 (July 30, 2002).

114. *See* § 9.3[2] *supra.*

115. *See* § 9.4[8][F] *supra.*

116. Inv. Adv. Act Rule 204A–1, 17 C.F.R. § 280.204A–1. *See also* Inv. Co. Act Rule 17j–1, 17 C.F.R. § 270.17j–1; Inv. Adv. Act Rule 204–2, 17 C.F.R. § 280.204–2.

§ 20.7 Transactions Between an Investment Company and Affiliated Persons

Section 17 of the Investment Company Act[1] regulates the activities of those who, due to their connection with an investment company, stand to gain personally from the manipulation of the company's investments, perhaps to the detriment of shareholders. Section 17(a) thus protects "minority interests from exploitation by insiders of *their* 'strategic position' "[2] and assures that interested persons deal with the investment company "at arm's length in an endeavor to secure the best possible bargain for their respective stockholders."[3] "Affiliated person" is defined in section 2(a)(3).[4] Briefly stated, the statutory definition includes persons controlling, controlled by or in common control with the investment company.[5]

Section 17 of the Act contains numerous provisions regulating the conduct of interested persons. Subsections (e) through (j) are relatively straightforward in protecting shareholders on a basic level against such things as theft of securities. In contrast, subsections (a) through (d) regulate more complex transactions between affiliated persons and the investment company. Subsection (e) prohibits affiliated persons acting as agents from accepting payment for transactions in securities or other property by an investment company except as regular salary or commission in the course of its business as an underwriter or a broker.[6] Such fees may not exceed "the usual and customary broker's commission."[7] Because of the potential conflict of interest, the prohibitions of section 17(e) should be broadly construed.[8] Thus, for example, a portfolio manager was appropriately convicted of a section 17(e) violation when she accepted the opportunity to purchase warrants from a company, the securities of which she had purchased for the pension plans she managed.[9] The conviction was upheld without proof that the warrants were purchased at a discount since the jury could reasonably have concluded that the opportunity to purchase the warrants was itself a benefit.[10]

Section 17(f)[11] of the Investment Company Act requires that securities owned by investment companies be placed in a bank, with a member of a

§ 20.7

1. 15 U.S.C.A. § 80a–17. *See* Note, The Application of Section 17 of The Investment Company Act of 1940 to Portfolio Affiliates, 120 U.Pa.L.Rev. 983 (1972).

2. E.I. du Pont de Nemours & Co. v. Collins, 432 U.S. 46, 60 n. 6, 97 S.Ct. 2229, 2237 n. 6, 53 L.Ed.2d 100 (1977) (Brennan, J., dissenting), quoting SEC Report on Investment Trusts and Investment Companies, H.R. Doc. No. 279, 76th Cong., 1st Sess., 1414 (1940).

3. *Id. See also, e.g.,* In the Matter of Strong/Corneliuson Capital Management, Inc., [1994–1995 Transfer Binder] Fed. Sec. L. Rep. (CCH) ¶ 85,416 (SEC 1994) (mutual funds violated section 17(a) in series of transactions with other funds managed by the same investment adviser).

4. 15 U.S.C.A. § 80a–2(a)(3).

5. *Id. See also* § 20.6 *supra.*

6. 15 U.S.C.A. § 80a–17(e)(1).

7. 15 U.S.C.A. § 80a–17(e)(2).

8. *But cf.* Paine/Webber Managed Investments Trusts, 26 Sec. Reg. & L. Rep. (BNA) 1168 (SEC No Action Letter available Aug. 8, 1994) (permitting sales of illiquid securities to an affiliated person; the staff response agreed that in light of the unusual nature of the transaction and representations as to the value of the securities, the protections of the Act did not require invocation of the prohibition).

9. United States v. Ostrander, 999 F.2d 27 (2d Cir.1993).

10. *Id.*

11. 15 U.S.C.A. § 80a–17(f).

national securities exchange (as defined in the Securities Exchange Act of 1934[12]), or with the investment company. Securities may also be deposited in a central handling system established by any registered securities exchange.[13] No investment company may act as custodian of its own securities except pursuant to Rule 17f–2.[14] Rule 17f–2 requires the securities to be physically separated at all times from those of any other person,[15] unless the securities are serving as collateral for a loan.[16] There are further restrictions under Investment Company Act Rule 17f–2. Access to the securities is through resolution of the board of directors only; a maximum of five persons may be designated for access by each resolution and each must be an officer or "responsible employee" of the investment company.[17] An investment company officer must be present when access to the securities is permitted.[18] Additional precautionary measures against larceny and embezzlement appear in section 17(g)'s bonding requirements for those with access to the investment company's securities.[19] The minimum permissible bond varies with the investment company's gross assets.[20]

Section 17(h) prohibits certain types of indemnification agreements. An investment company's charter, certificate of incorporation, articles of association, indenture of trust, or bylaws cannot indemnify or otherwise protect a director or officer against liability for "willful misfeasance, bad faith, gross negligence or reckless disregard of the duties involved in the conduct of his office."[21] Section 17(i) similarly prohibits any investment adviser or principal underwriter from contracting away its liability.[22] Prior to 1987, sections 17(h) and 17(i) both provided that if such clauses do appear in the specified documents, a written waiver of the indemnification clause in the document will preclude violation of these subsections of the Act.[23] However, those provisions have since been repealed.

Section 17(j) of the Investment Company Act[24] parallels section 10(b) of the Securities Exchange Act[25] as the general antifraud provision applicable to affiliated persons. Enacted in 1970, section 17(j) is directed at insider trading for the insider's personal account in the investment company's portfolio

---

12.   Section 6, 15 U.S.C.A. § 78f. There are currently nine active national exchanges: the New York Stock Exchange, the American Stock Exchange, the Boston Stock Exchange, the Philadelphia Stock Exchange, the Midwest Stock Exchange, the Chicago Board Options Exchange, the Pacific Stock Exchange, the Intermountain Stock Exchange, and the Cincinnati Stock Exchange. *See* §§ 14.1, 14.3 *supra*.

13.   17 C.F.R. § 270.17f–4 (1982). *See* § 14.2 *supra*.

14.   17 C.F.R. § 270.17f–2.

15.   17 C.F.R. § 270.17f–2(b).

16.   17 C.F.R. § 270.17f–2(c).

17.   17 C.F.R. § 270.17f–2(d). Certain bank officers and employees and independent public accountants may also have access to the securities jointly with the investment company officers, *id*.

18.   *Id*.

19.   15 U.S.C.A. § 80a–17(g).

20.   17 C.F.R. § 270.17g–1(d)(1).

21.   15 U.S.C.A. § 80a–17(h). *Compare* the SEC's approach to indemnification in connection with 1933 Act registration statements. *See* § 7.14 *supra*.

22.   15 U.S.C.A. § 80a–17(i).

23.   15 U.S.C.A. § 80a–17(h), (i) (repealed).

24.   15 U.S.C.A. § 80a–17(j).

25.   15 U.S.C.A. § 78j(b); 17 C.F.R. § 240.10b–5. *See,* chapter 12 *supra*.

securities.[26] Rule 17j–1[27] is the Investment Company Act's counterpart to Rule 10b–5 in prohibiting material misrepresentation and fraudulent practices. Rule 17j–1 also requires each investment company to adopt a written code of ethics to be followed by each of the company's "access persons."[28] The term "access persons" is defined broadly in the rule to include persons who render investment advice.

Investment Company Act Rule 17j–1 also addresses the need for investment companies to adopt appropriate codes of ethics. In 1999, the SEC amended Rule 17j–1 of the Investment Company Act.[35] The Rule, as amended, requires that a majority of disinterested fund directors approve the investment company's code of ethics.[36] The rule also requires that a majority of disinterested directors approve the codes of ethics of the fund's investment adviser and principal underwriter.[37] Among other things, the 1999 amendments require each investment company and its investment adviser to review and give prior approval for investments in initial public offerings and limited offerings by investment company personnel participating in management of investment company's portfolio.[38]

Difficult problems of interpretation can arise in the application of subsections (a) through (d) of section 19. These are due to those subsections' effect on affiliates and section 2(a)(3)'s broad definition of an "affiliated person."[39] "Portfolio affiliation" is included in this definition.[40] "Upstream" portfolio affiliates refers to those owning five percent or more of the voting securities of an investment company or a company controlled by the investment company.[41] "Downstream" portfolio affiliates are defined as those companies, five percent or more of whose voting securities are held by an investment company or a company controlled by an investment company.[42] For example, if company X owns five percent of an investment company's voting securities and company Y owns five percent of company X's voting securities, company Y is an affiliate of an affiliate of the investment company and the provisions of subsections 17(a) through (d) will apply. Conversely, if an investment company owns five percent of company A's voting securities and company A owns five percent of company B's voting securities, company B is an affiliate of an affiliate of the investment company. The subsections further cloud the already murky test for determining inadvertent investment company status.[43]

---

26. 1970 U.S.Code Cong. and Adm.News 4897, 4923.

27. 17 C.F.R. § 270.17j–1. *See* Inv. Co. Act Rel. No. 11421, [1980 Transfer Binder] Fed.Sec. L.Rep. (CCH) ¶ 82,679 (Oct. 31, 1980).

28. 17 C.F.R. § 270.17j–1(b); As defined in 17 C.F.R. § 270.17j–1(e)(2).

35. Inv. Co. Act Rel. No. IC–23958 (SEC 1999). *See* Gregory N. Bressler, Amendments to the Code of Ethics Rule Under the Investment Company Act, 33 Rev. Sec. & Commod. Reg. 19 (2000).

36. Rule 17j–1(c)(1)(ii), 17 C.F.R. § 270.17j–1(c)(1)(ii).

37. Rule 17j–1(c)(1)(ii), 17 C.F.R. § 270.17j–1(c)(1)(ii).

38. Rule 17j–1(e), 17 C.F.R. § 270.17j–1(e).

39. 15 U.S.C.A. § 80a–2(a)(3).

40. *See generally* Milton P. Kroll, The "Portfolio Affiliate" Problem, PLI Third Annual Institute on Securities Regulation, 261–291 (1972); Comment, The Application of § 17 of the Investment Company Act of 1940 to Portfolio Affiliates, 120 U.Pa.L.Rev. 983 (1972).

41. 15 U.S.C.A. § 80a–2(a)(3)(A).

42. 15 U.S.C.A. § 80a–2(a)(3)(B).

43. *See* 15 U.S.C.A. § 80a–3(a)(3) which is discussed in § 20.4 *supra*.

It is frequently difficult for companies to identify whether they are indeed portfolio affiliates of an investment company since investment companies generally hold portfolio securities in the nominee names of their custodian banks.[44] Section 13(d)(1) of the Securities Exchange Act of 1934[45] alleviates the problem somewhat by requiring an investment company to notify an issuer once it acquires over five percent of the issuer's securities. Problems nevertheless arise when an investment company group owns an aggregate of over five percent, or a company controlled by an investment company does. For these reasons, and because the drafters of section 17 considered abuses in mergers and consolidations only where a shift in investment company control was involved (thereby directly affecting the investment company sharehold- ers),[46] it was forcefully argued that section 17 should only apply to upstream affiliates, that is, those in a position to maneuver investment company policy.[47] The SEC has not adopted this view, however, and has sought wider application of these subsections of the Act.

Section 17(a)(1) of the Investment Company Act prohibits the sale of securities to an investment company by any affiliated person, promoter, or underwriter of the investment company, or by any affiliate thereof.[48] Excep- tions to section 17(a)(1) are listed within the subsection; they include sales of investment company securities to the investment company which issued them (*i.e.* redemptions) and sales of securities issued by the affiliate, promoter, or underwriter (or affiliate thereof) which are part of a general securities offering to the public.[49]

Subsection 17(a)(2) of the Act prohibits an affiliate, promoter, underwrit- er, or affiliate of such parties from purchasing securities from an investment company or a company controlled by an investment company, or a controlled affiliate of an investment company.[50] Section 17(a)(2) excludes purchases of securities when the seller is the issuer.[51] Section 17(a)(2) therefore prohibits redemptions of an affiliate's securities held by an investment company, conversions of securities, and virtually every negotiated securities transaction between the two.

Investment Company Act Rule 17a–4[53] exempts from section 17(a) trans- actions made pursuant to a contract entered into before there was an affiliation. In order to avoid abuse, the rule further requires that during the preceding six months there was no affiliation between the parties. Other SEC

---

44. Milton P. Kroll, The "Portfolio Affiliate" Problem, PLI Third Annual Institute on Securities Regulation, 269 (1972).

45. 15 U.S.C.A. § 78m(d). *See* § 11.2 *supra. See also* 15 U.S.C.A. § 78m(f) dealing with similar filings by institutional investment managers, which is discussed in § 11.3 *supra.*

46. SEC Report on the Study of Investment Trusts and Investment Companies pt. 3 at 1024 (1939–42).

47. Comment, The Application of § 17 of the Investment Company Act of 1940 to Portfolio Affiliates, 120 U.Pa.L.Rev. 983, 998 (1972).

48. 15 U.S.C.A. § 80a–17(a)(1).

49. 15 U.S.C.A. § 80a–17(a)(1)(A), (B). Subsection (a)(1)(C) applies to unit investment trusts and periodic payment plans.

50. 15 U.S.C.A. § 80a–17(a)(2).

51. *Id.*

53. 17 C.F.R. § 270.17a–4. The rule was amended in 1970 to clearly include stock option and stock purchase plans of controlled companies. Investment Company Act Rel. No. IC–6154 (Aug. 10, 1970).

rules exempt certain underwriting transactions.[54] These include loans between banks and investment companies "of a commercial character rather than of an investment character,"[55] transactions between an investment company and its fully-owned subsidiaries or between fully-owned subsidiaries of an investment company,[56] and pro-rata distributions in cash or in kind to common stockholders.[57] Also exempt are mergers, consolidations, or purchases and/or sales of substantially all of the assets of companies affiliated solely through a common investment adviser, common directors, or common officers so long as a majority of the disinterested directors of each investment company participating finds that the best interests of the investment company will be served and that the interests of existing investment company shareholders "will not be diluted as a result of . . . the transaction."[58] Rule 17a–6 exempts transactions from section 17(a) of the Act where no one associated with the affiliated company is associated with the investment company.

Section 17(b) further complicates the application of section 17(a) by allowing the Commission to grant still additional exemptions for certain companies.[63]

Subsection 17(d) of the Investment Company Act prohibits "joint or joint and several" participation in transactions by an affiliated person or principal underwriter for an investment company and that investment company in contravention of rules prescribed by the Commission.[67]

§ 20.8   Registration and Disclosure Requirements; Civil Liability

§ 20.8[1] Investment Company Name

Investment Company Rule 35d–1[1] imposes limitations on the names of registered investment companies. The rule is designed to prevent investment companies from adopting names that are likely to mislead investors about the investment company's investments and risks.[2] Rule 35d–1 requires that a registered investment company with a name that suggests the company focuses on a particular type of investment or industry[3] to invest at least eighty percent of its assets in the type of investment suggested by its name. Rule 35d–1 also addresses investment company names suggesting that an investment company focuses its investments in a particular country or geographic

---

54. 17 C.F.R. § 270.17a–1.

55. 17 C.F.R. § 270.17a–2.

56. 17 C.F.R. § 270.17a–3. "Fully owned subsidiary" is defined in § 270.17a–3(b) as a subsidiary all of whose securities are owned by the parent corporation or other fully owned subsidiaries. This is in contrast to section 2(a)(43)'s definition of "wholly-owned subsidiary" which surprisingly requires only ninety-five percent ownership. 15 U.S.C.A. § 80a–2(a)(43).

57. 17 C.F.R. § 270.17a–5. The option for even one shareholder to choose specific assets for receipt makes the rule inoperative as to the distribution to all shareholders, *id.*

58. 17 C.F.R. § 270.17a–8.

63. 15 U.S.C.A. § 80a–17(b).

67. 15 U.S.C.A. § 17(d).

§ 20.8

1. 17 C.F.R. § 270.35d–1.

2. Investment Company Names, Inv. Co. Act Rel. IC–24828, 66 Fed. Reg. 8509–01, 2001 WL 81473 (F.R.) (SEC Feb. 1, 2001).

3. For example, if an investment company that calls itself the ABC Stock Fund, the XYZ Bond Fund, or the QRS U.S. Government Fund.

region, names indicating that a company's distributions are exempt from income tax, and names suggesting that a company or its shares are guaranteed or approved by the United States government.

§ 20.8[2] Registration Requirements

As is the case with all other federal securities laws, the Investment Company Act has numerous registration, disclosure, and antifraud provisions meant to protect the investing public by requiring information relating to the issuer's policies and activities. Unless an available exemption can be found, a domestic company deemed to be an investment company within the definitions of section 3(a) of the Act[12] must register under section 8.[13] Registration is initiated by the filing of Form N–8A,[14] which is a short-form notification of registration that will be followed by more detailed disclosures in subsequent filings.

In addition, the registrant must recite and describe all of its investment policies which may change only if authorized by a shareholder vote, those policies fundamental to the company, the name and address of each affiliated person of the registrant, the name and principal address of every company of which each such person is an officer, director or partner, and a brief statement of the business experience of each officer and director of the registrant for the past five years.[17]

As a final safety net for investors, the affirmative disclosure requirements of the Act are supplemented by broad antifraud prohibitions in Rule 8b–20.

The investment company must provide complete disclosure of all its relevant activities; there is, however, the disclaimer that "information required need be given only insofar as it is known or reasonably available to the registrant."[25] The issuer can be held criminally accountable[26] and civilly liable[27] for fraudulent statements made in connection with its registration and/or the reports which the investment company is required to file. Failure to file registration statements properly and/or omissions of material facts are grounds for the revocation of a company's registration.[29]

The Investment Company Act contains periodic reporting requirements in addition to the initial registration. Section 30 of the Act requires issuers to file periodic reports with the SEC and to send such to their shareholders.[30] Annual reports similar to those required by section 13(a) of the Securities Exchange Act[31] must be filed by the investment company issuer.[32] Formerly, issuers were required to file quarterly reports with the Commission and

---

12. 15 U.S.C.A. § 80a–3(a). *See* § 20.3 *supra.*

13. 15 U.S.C.A. § 80a–8. Foreign investment companies register through the provisions of Section 7(d). *Id.* at § 80a–7(d).

14. 17 C.F.R. § 274.10.

17. 15 U.S.C.A. § 80a–8(b)(2)–(4).

25. 17 C.F.R. § 270.8b–21.

26. 15 U.S.C.A. § 80a–33(b).

27. False filings under the 1934 Act will result in civil liability under section 18(a). 15 U.S.C.A. § 78r(a). *See* § 12.19 *supra.*

29. 15 U.S.C.A. § 80a–8(e).

30. 15 U.S.C.A. § 80a–29.

31. 15 U.S.C.A. § 78m(a). *See* § 9.3 *supra.*

32. 15 U.S.C.A. § 80a–29(a); 17 C.F.R. § 270.30a–1.

supply the Commission with copies of all information sent to their shareholders within ten days of the transmission.[33] In 1985 the SEC replaced the quarterly reporting requirement with semi-annual reports.[34] The reporting form, Form N–SAR, replaced the five quarterly reporting forms that formerly were used by most registered investment companies and thus is another step in the Commission's move towards simplification.[35] Also, the amended reporting system parallels the semi-annual reports that have to be made to shareholders. In 1990, the Shareholder Communication Act extended to mutual funds and other investment companies that are registered under the Investment Company Act the applicability of the 1934 Act proxy rules that govern Exchange Act reporting companies generally.[36]

§ 20.8[3] Reporting Requirements

Registered investment companies must send semi-annual reports to their shareholders.[38]

In 1993, 1933 Act Registration Form N–1A (for investment company securities) requires disclosures pertaining to fund managers, a discussion of the factors and strategies that had an effect on recent fund performance, and a line graph comparing the fund's performance to an index of the over-all market over a ten-year period.[39]

An open-end management company may substitute a currently effective prospectus under the Securities Act of 1933 if the remuneration information from item (5) and financial information for the half-year are also included.[40] The financial statements filed by an investment company must be signed or certified by an independent public accountant.[41] No controlling person, em-

---

33. 15 U.S.C.A. § 80a–30(b); 17 C.F.R. § 270.30b1–5(T) (1984).

34. 17 C.F.R. § 270.30b1–1. *See* Inv.Co.Act.Rel. No. IC–14299, [1984–1985 Transfer Binder] Fed.Sec.L.Rep. (CCH) ¶ 83,725 (Jan. 4, 1985).

35. The SEC, in yet another step towards integrated disclosure requirements, has also proposed a new form N–7 that would replace form N–8B–2 for investment trusts and would replace Form S–6 under the 1933 Act. Inv.Co.Act Rel. No. IC–15612, [1987 Transfer Binder] Fed.Sec.L.Rep. (CCH) ¶ 84,109 (March 9, 1987); Inv. Co. Act Rel. No. IC–14513, [1984–1985 Transfer Binder] Fed.Sec.L.Rep. (CCH) ¶ 83,774 (May 14, 1985).

36. 15 U.S.C.A. § 78n(b). The Exchange Act's proxy rules are discussed in chapter 10 *supra*.

38. These reports should include the following information compiled "as of a reasonably current date":

(1) a balance sheet accompanied by a statement of the investments' aggregate value;

(2) a listing of amounts and values of securities owned;

(3) an itemized income statement insofar as each item of income or expense exceeds five percent of the company's total income or expense;

(4) a statement of surplus itemized for each charge or credit representing over five percent of the total charges or credits in the report period;

(5) a statement of the aggregate remuneration paid during the report period to all directors and members of an advisory board for regular compensation, to each of the foregoing for special compensation, to all officers, and to each person of whom any officer or director of the investment company is an affiliated person; and

(6) a statement of the aggregate dollar amounts of sales and purchases of investment securities, other than government securities, during the report period.

15 U.S.C.A. § 80a–29(d).

39. *See* Inv. Co. Act. Rel. IC–19382, [1993 Transfer Binder] Fed. Sec. L. Rep. (CCH) ¶ 85,123 (SEC April 6, 1993).

40. 17 C.F.R. § 270.30d–1.

41. 15 U.S.C.A. § 80a–29(e).

ployee, or principal accounting officer of a management company or face-amount certificate company may participate in the preparation of financial statements without an affirmative vote to do so by a majority of the board or of the shareholders.[42]

Adoption of Rule 482 (formerly Rule 434d) under the Securities Act of 1933[43] in 1979 has allowed investment companies to advertise more freely than had been allowed previously.[44] This rule permits an investment company to advertise in newspapers and magazines and on radio and television some but not all of the information required to be included in its prospectus by section 10(a) of the Securities Act of 1933[45] so as to satisfy the requirement of section 5 of that Act that statutory prospectuses be distributed to investors along with the sale of registered securities.[46] The advertisement must conspicuously state "from whom a prospectus containing more complete information may be obtained and that the investor should read that prospectus carefully before investing."[47] Any representation by a money market fund of its yield must be computed according to the formula required by Form N–1[48] and identify the last day in the period used in compiling the quotation.[49]

Investment companies are required to file periodic reports[50] with the SEC and, further, must amend their registration statements annually.[51] Registration statements of open-end management companies, unit investment trusts, and face-amount certificate companies must be amended to reflect any increase in the number of securities offered.[52] If such a company sells more than the number of securities registered, it may be required to pay a treble registration fee and the securities will be deemed to have been registered.[53] To avoid this potentially expensive filing penalty, open-end companies may register to sell "an indefinite number of the securities."[54]

Prior to the mid-1990s, shareholders of investment companies were not taxed on their investment company's gains and income that were not passed through dividends or other distributions to the investment company shareholders. This all changed when investment companies became pass-through tax entities so that the company's gains and income would be passed on to the investment company shareholders for tax purposes. One consequence of this was that between 1994 and 1999, investors in diversified stock funds were required to pay an average of fifteen percent of their annual investment company's gains to taxes.[55] In order to give mutual fund investors a more

---

42. 15 U.S.C.A. § 80a–31(b).

43. 17 C.F.R. §§ 230.134(d), 482. *See* § 20.8[4] *infra.*

44. 15 U.S.C.A. § 77j(a).

45. 17 C.F.R. § 230.134(d).

46. The registration and prospectus provisions of the 1933 Act are discussed in chapter 2 *supra.*

47. 17 C.F.R. § 230.434(d)(a)(4).

48. 17 C.F.R. § 274.11.

49. 17 C.F.R. § 230.434(d)(a)(6).

50. 15 U.S.C.A. § 80a–29.

51. 17 C.F.R. § 270.8b–16.

52. 15 U.S.C.A. § 80a–24(e)(1).

53. 15 U.S.C.A. § 80a–24(f).

54. *Id.*

55. *See* Disclosure of Mutual Fund After–Tax Returns, Inv. Co. Act Rel. IC–24832, 66 Fed. Reg. 9002–01, 2001 WL 89496 (F.R.) (SEC Feb. 5, 2001).

accurate picture of the return on their investment, in 2001, the SEC amended its disclosure requirements to require investment companies to provide shareholders with after-tax performance information.[56] Mutual funds must disclose in their prospectuses the after-tax returns based on standardized formulas comparable to the formula currently used to calculate before-tax average annual total returns.[57] The amendments further require certain funds to include standardized after-tax returns in advertisements and other sales materials.

§ 20.8[5] Investment Company Sales Literature

The Securities Act of 1933 limits written materials during the waiting and post-effective periods during a 1933 Act registration to permissible prospectuses.[62] 1933 Act Rule 482[63] permits specified investment company advertising materials in compliance with the 1933 Act prospectus requirements.[64] As originally adopted, information that could be provided in advertisements was limited to the information that is permitted in a prospectus.[65] Limiting permissible advertising material to information that is in the prospectus operates as a limitation on investment company advertising, since usually not all matters are covered in the 1933 Act prospectus.[66] In 1996, Congress expanded the information that may be included in part to facilitate the advertising of funds using performance data which would not be permitted in a 1933 Act prospectus.[68] All sales literature used by open-end management companies, unit investment trusts, and face-amount certificate companies must be filed with the Commission within ten days of its being sent.[69]

§ 20.8[6] Civil Liability; Applicability of Antifraud Provisions

The date of the latest amendment to an investment company's registration statement is its effective date.[73] This is especially important in the case of an open-end management company which is constantly issuing and selling new shares, since under section 13 of the Securities Act of 1933,[74] a shareholder may have up to three years from the effective date to institute a suit for misleading registration statements under section 11 of that Act.[75] Under section 11 of the 1933 Act, suit for material misstatements or omissions in the registration statement generally must be brought within one year of the

---

56. *Id.*

57. Form N–1A, Item 21. Calculation of Performance Data *See* Disclosure of Mutual Fund After–Tax Returns, Inv. Co. Act Rel. IC–24832, 66 Fed. Reg. 9002–01, 2001 WL 89496 (F.R.) (SEC Feb. 5, 2001).

62. *See* §§ 2.4–2.5 *supra.*

63. 17 C.F.R. § 230.482.

64. The 1933 Act prospectus requirements are found in sections 5 and 10 of the 1933 Act. 15 U.S.C.A. §§ 77e, 77j. *See* chapter 2 *supra.*

65. 17 C.F.R. § 230.482(a)(2).

66. Testimony of Barry Barbash Concerning H.R. 1495, The Investment Company Act Amendments of 1995, Before the Subcommittee on Telecommunications and Finance, Committee on Commerce, U.S. House of Representatives 34 (Oct. 31, 1995), citing H.R. Rep. No. 1382, 91st Cong., 2d Sess. 10–11, 23–35 (1970) at 16.

68. 15 U.S.C.A. § 80a–24(g).

69. 15 U.S.C.A. § 80a–24(b).

73. 15 U.S.C.A. § 80a–24(e)(3).

74. 15 U.S.C.A. § 77m. *See also* § 7.10 *supra.*

75. 15 U.S.C.A. § 77k. *See* §§ 7.3–7.4 *supra.*

violation or reasonable discovery of the violation.[76] When the violation is not reasonably discoverable, the one-year limitations will be tolled, but in no event, for more than three years after the security was bona fide offered to the public.[77] In the event of a continuous offering, an unfortunate literal reading of the statute might unduly shorten this three-year repose period.

In addition to liability for misstatements and omissions in an investment company's registration statement, investment companies will be held accountable for misstatements and omissions in their reports to shareholders. 1934 Act Rule 10b–5[78] will provide a remedy to investment company investors who purchase[79] or sell investment company shares as a result of material misstatements or omissions in investment company reports.

§ 20.9   Limitations on Advisory Fees; Transfers of Control— The "Sale" of Investment Advisory Contracts

§ 20.9[1]   Investment Advisory Fees

Investment advisers that manage investment companies' assets generally are compensated through a management fee based on a percentage of the fund's average asset value. Typically this fee is annualized based on between one-half and one percent of the fund's average assets. During the start-up time, the adviser's fee may be quite modest but, as the fund grows, the fee can become "enormous."[1] Prior to the shareholders' annual approval of the advisory contract there must be full disclosure of the terms of compensation.[2] The limitations on the amount of compensation are found in the Act's general imposition of fiduciary duties,[3] and prohibition against unlawful conversion of investment company assets.[4] In addition, the Act prohibits the charging of unreasonable expenses and other charges in connection with the operation of the investment company.[5]

Section 37 of the Act[6] makes it unlawful for any person to steal, unlawfully "abstract," or convert investment company assets. A violation of this section seems to require more than merely excessive compensation and thus section 37 will not be very helpful in challenging excessive advisory fees.[7] Section 36(b), which supports an express private right of action,[8] imposes fiduciary obligations upon the investment adviser. Section 36(b)'s fiduciary

---

76. 15 U.S.C.A. § 77m.

77. *Id.*

78. 17 C.F.R. § 240.10b–5. Rule 10b–5 is discussed in chapter 12 *supra.*

79. Investment company shareholders who participate in dividend reinvestment programs so as to receive shares in lieu of dividends are making a new purchase each time the dividend is declares. *See* § 12.6 *supra.*

§ 20.9

1. Richard W. Jennings & Harold Marsh, Jr., Securities Regulation: Cases and Materials 1398 (5th ed.1982).

2. 15 U.S.C.A. § 80a–15(a)(1).

3. 15 U.S.C.A. § 80a–35(b).

4. 15 U.S.C.A. § 80a–36.

5. 15 U.S.C.A. §§ 80a–26(e), 80a–27(i).

6. 15 U.S.C.A. § 80a–36.

7. *See, e.g.,* Brown v. Bullock, 294 F.2d 415 (2d Cir.1961).

8. 15 U.S.C.A. § 80a–35(b).

obligations include refraining from charging and collecting excessive investment advisory fees.

The courts have long required under general corporate law that management compensation be fair and reasonable.[9] This rule has been followed under the Investment Company Act, which "subject[s] the transaction to rigorous scrutiny for fairness."[10] As noted in one decision, "the Court must consider the 'nature, quality and extent' of the services to the Fund in relation to the fee paid by the Fund."[11]

Although investment company advisory fees may be high, the courts have tended to validate the compensation in light of industry practices[13] as well as looking to the size of the fund.[14] A successful challenge to advisory fees requires a showing that the fees themselves are excessive.[15] This means that the courts will scrutinize the amount of the compensation and not the method of calculation. Thus, for example, the Second Circuit upheld a fee arrangement that gave the investment advisers incentive to maximize leverage in order to increase their advisory fees.[16] Even though this fee arrangement created the potential for a conflict of interest in selecting investments, it was not a *per se* breach of fiduciary duty.[17] Furthermore, it is not sufficient to establish that the fee structure created an incentive for the fund manager to consider its own interests when making leverage decisions for the funds.[18]

Another reason for the difficulty of proving excessive fees is the fact that shareholders or the board of directors ratify the contract annually.[19] There is a relatively high burden imposed for overcoming the effect of shareholder ratification.

In evaluating whether excessive fees are being charged, courts will look to six factors.[22] First, the courts will look to both the nature and the quality of

---

9. Rogers v. Hill, 289 U.S. 582, 53 S.Ct. 731, 77 L.Ed. 1385 (1933); Hingle v. Plaquemines Oil Sales Corp., 399 So.2d 646 (La.App.1981), *writ denied* 401 So.2d 987 (La.1981); Ruetz v. Topping, 453 S.W.2d 624 (Mo.App.1970). *See generally* 2 James D. Cox & Thomas L. Hazen, Cox and Hazen on Corporations, ch. 11 (2d ed. 2003).

10. Galfand v. Chestnutt, 545 F.2d 807, 811–812 (2d Cir.1976).

11. Gartenberg v. Merrill Lynch Asset Management, Inc., 528 F.Supp. 1038, 1047 (S.D.N.Y. 1981), *affirmed* 694 F.2d 923 (2d Cir.1982).

13. *E.g.* Krinsk v. Fund Asset Management, Inc., 875 F.2d 404 (2d Cir.1989); Saxe v. Brady, 40 Del.Ch. 474, 184 A.2d 602 (1962).

See also Bromson v. Lehman Management Co., 1986 WL 165, [1985–1986 Transfer Binder] Fed.Sec.L.Rep. (CCH) ¶ 92,521 (S.D.N.Y.1986) (refusing discovery of the management fees charged by defendant in connection with management of its thirty largest non investment company accounts but permitting discovery of compensation paid to affiliated directors).

14. *E.g.*, Meyer v. Oppenheimer Management Corp., 895 F.2d 861 (2d Cir.1990) (advisory and distribution fees were not excessive); Gartenberg v. Merrill Lynch Asset Management, Inc., 694 F.2d 923 (2d Cir.1982). *But see* Brown v. Bullock, 294 F.2d 415, 424 (2d Cir.1961) (Moore, J. dissenting), which is quoted in footnote 1 *supra*.

15. *See, e.g.*, Krantz v. Prudential Investments Fund Management LLC, 305 F.3d 140 (3d Cir. 2002) (failure to show fees were excessive); Migdal v. Rowe Price–Fleming Intern., Inc., 248 F.3d 321, 2001 (4th Cir.2001) (insufficient allegations of excessive fees).

16. Green v. Fund Asset Management, L.P., 286 F.3d 682 (3d Cir.2002).

17. *Id.*

18. Green v. Nuveen Advisory Corp., 295 F.3d 738 (7th Cir. 2002).

19. *See* 15 U.S.C.A. § 80a–15(a)(2).

22. Krinsk v. Fund Asset Management, 875 F.2d 404, 409 (2d Cir.1989); Gartenberg v. Merrill Lynch Asset Management, Inc., 694 F.2d 923, 929–930 (2d Cir.1982); Krantz v. Fidelity Management & Research Co., 98 F.Supp.2d 150, 159 (D.Mass.2000).

the advisory services that are being provided. A second factor is the fund's profitability to the adviser. Third, the court will look to the economics of scale that come into play in managing the fund as it grows larger. Fourth, comparative fee structures of comparable funds are to be considered in evaluating the advisory fee. Fifth, the courts look to any indirect profits that inure to the adviser that can be attributed in some way to the fund; these are known as "fall out benefits." Sixth, the independence and conscientiousness of the fund's directors are a factor in evaluating the advisory fees.

§ 20.9[2] Modification or Assignment of the Avisory Contract

A basic premise of the Investment Company Act is that the public interest, and that of an investment company's investors, is adversely affected by a change in the management of an investment company without the consent of its stockholders.[29] In most instances, modifications of the advisory agreement will require approval by the investment company's shareholders. A number of Investment Company Act provisions operate to limit potential abuses in connection with changes in investment advisers. Section 2(a)(4) of the Act provides that any "direct or indirect" transfer of a controlling block of shares in the investment adviser constitutes an assignment of the advisory contract.[31] The investment advisory contract automatically terminates upon its assignment.[32] Approval of the new contract with the new adviser by the investment company's shareholders is required to validate the contract.[33]

Section 15(f) of the Act allows, but at the same time places express limitations upon, the receipt of a premium based on the transfer of controlling interests in an investment adviser to a mutual fund or investment company.[34] When control in the adviser is sold at a premium and the investment company shareholders and directors ratify the new advisory contract, there is considered to be express approval of the transfer of control for a premium. Absent the Investment Company Act's provisions, this premium might be prohibited by the common law of most states because the former adviser is making a profit while choosing its successor—a decision that, at least in form, lies in the hands of the investment company's directors and shareholders. Section 15(f) was enacted in 1975[36] in response to the Second Circuit's decision in Rosenfeld v. Black,[37] which contained broad statements concerning the investment adviser's fiduciary duty and corresponding obligation not to profit personally from a sale of its office with the investment company.[38] Section 15(f) makes it clear that the investment adviser may make a profit either by selling a controlling block of its shares at a price above their net asset value or by facilitating the transfer of an advisory contract to a new adviser.

Section 15(f) affords a higher degree of protection for investment company shareholders by requiring seventy-five percent of the board to be disinter-

29. 15 U.S.C.A. § 80a–1(b)(6).

31. 15 U.S.C.A. § 80a–2(a)(4).

32. 15 U.S.C.A. § 80a–15(a)(4).

33. 15 U.S.C.A. § 80a–15(a).

34. 15 U.S.C.A. § 80a–15(f).

36. Act of June 4, 1975, Pub.L. No. 94–29, 89 Stat. 97 (1975).

37. 445 F.2d 1337 (2d Cir.1971), *cert. dismissed sub nom.* Lazard Freres & Co. v. Rosenfeld, 409 U.S. 802, 93 S.Ct. 24, 34 L.Ed.2d 62 (1972).

38. *See, e.g.,* 445 F.2d at 1343.

ested, as opposed to the regular forty percent requirement.[40] The seventy-five percent disinterested director requirement is does not apply when a controlling block of the adviser's securities is distributed to the public without changing the identity of those in actual control of the adviser, and where the transferee adviser has been in control of the transferor advisers (or shared control of the adviser) for the six months immediately preceding the transfer.[41]

§ 20.10 Private Causes of Action and Civil Liability for Violations of the Investment Company Act

§ 20.10[1] Implied Remedies Under the Investment Company Act

A number of Supreme Court cases have cast a looming shadow on implied remedies.[5] It remains to be seen whether this means the demise of the Investment Company Act remedies that have been implied by the lower federal courts.[6] Some decisions have refused to recognize implied remedies under the Act, but others have continued to recognize implied remedies.[7] There is nevertheless substantial precedent for the implication of private relief under the Act. An unregistered investment company has been held civilly liable under section 7 of the Act[8] for failure to comply with the registration requirements of section 8.[9] The sale of securities to an unregistered investment company has been held *voidable* at the seller's option, rather than automatically void under section 47 of the Act,[10] lest innocent sellers be penalized to the same extent as the culpable unregistered purchaser.[11] It is clear that an innocent shareholder/purchaser may rescind transactions with an investment company.[12] Private enforcement actions by "injured" plaintiffs have also been recognized (1) under section 17[13] for dealings between affiliates,[14] (2) under section 37[15] for the willful conversion of an investment

---

40. 15 U.S.C.A. § 80a–10(a). *See* § 20.6 *supra*.

41. 15 U.S.C.A. § 80a–15(f)(4).

§ 20.10

5. For a discussion of implied remedies generally, *see* § 12.2 *supra*.

6. *See, e.g.,* Green v. Fund Asset Management, L.P., 19 F.Supp.2d 227 (D.N.J.1998), later opinion reversed on other grounds 245 F.3d 214 (3d Cir.2001) (since there is an express right of action under section 36(b) for breach of an investment company's investment adviser's breach of fiduciary duty, there is no need for an implied remedy under sections 8(e), 34(b), and 36(a)).

7. *Compare, e.g.,* In re Merrill Lynch & Co., Research Reports Securities Litigation, 289 F.Supp.2d 429, 438 (S.D.N.Y. 2003) (there is no implied remedy under section 34(b) of the Investment Company Act) *with* Lessler v. Little, 857 F.2d 866 (1st Cir.1988) (recognizing an implied right of action under section 17(a)(2) which prohibits certain transactions between affiliated persons and the investment company).

8. 15 U.S.C.A. § 80a–7. *E.g.,* Blatt v. Merrill Lynch, Pierce, Fenner & Smith, Inc., 916 F.Supp. 1343 (D.N.J.1996).

9. 15 U.S.C.A. § 80a–8; Cogan v. Johnston, 162 F.Supp. 907 (S.D.N.Y.1958).

10. 15 U.S.C.A. § 80a–46.

11. Avnet, Inc. v. Scope Industries, 499 F.Supp. 1121 (S.D.N.Y.1980).

12. 15 U.S.C.A. § 80a–46(b); Mathers Fund, Inc. v. Colwell Co., 564 F.2d 780, 783–84 (7th Cir.1977).

13. 15 U.S.C.A. § 80a–19.

14. Langner v. Brown, 913 F.Supp. 260, 268–69 (S.D.N.Y.1996) (section 17 claim survived motion to dismiss).

15. 15 U.S.C.A. § 80a–36.

company's assets,[16] (3) under section 35(d)[17] for misleading use of an investment company name,[18] and (4) under section 48[19] for contravention of Investment Company Act provisions through the use of a third party.[20] However, many of these cases were decided prior to the more recent Supreme Court decisions curtailing implied remedies. As such, there is some question as to their continued vitality. More recently, the Second Circuit held that plaintiff could not bring a private right of action under either section 26(f) or 27(i) to recover allegedly excessive fees charged in connection with an insurance company's sale of variable annuity.[22]

The issues become thornier when suit is brought for a breach of the fiduciary duties imposed upon investment company directors and advisers by section 36 of the Act[30] and implemented by section 15.[31] Section 15(a) has been held to provide investment company shareholders with a private right of action for the failure of directors to approve an investment contract in a meaningful fashion.[32] Section 15(a) has also provided a private right of action against an investment adviser charged with self-dealing,[33] but not the recovery of excessive fees which is governed by section 36(b)'s express remedy.[34] Similarly, section 15(c), which provides a clearer duty of meaningful negotiations and disclosure between investment company directors and investment advisers, has been held not to provide a basis for a private shareholder right of action due to section 36(b)'s express cause of action for a breach of investment adviser fiduciary duty.[35] For similar reasons, sections 26(e) and 27(i) of Act[36] requiring that expenses, deductions and fees be reasonable do not support an implied private right of action.[37] As noted above, section 20 of the Act, which regulates the solicitation of proxies, has been held to support an implied right of action, provided that the claim is for something other than excessive advisory fees.[38]

Although federally regulated under the Investment Company Act of 1940, investment companies are incorporated or otherwise organized under state

---

16. Brown v. Bullock, 294 F.2d 415 (2d Cir.1961) (holding directors liable for willful conversion of assets rather than for a breach of any explicit fiduciary duty).

17. 15 U.S.C.A. § 80a–34(d).

18. Taussig v. Wellington Fund, Inc., 313 F.2d 472, 475–76 (3d Cir.1963), *cert. denied* 374 U.S. 806, 83 S.Ct. 1693, 10 L.Ed.2d 1031 (1963).

19. 15 U.S.C.A. § 80a–47. *See* Strougo v. Bassini, 282 F.3d 162 (2d Cir.2002) (private action under §§ 36(a) and 48).

20. Jerozal v. Cash Reserve Management, 1982 WL 1363, [1982–1983 Transfer Binder] Fed.Sec.L.Rep. (CCH) ¶ 99,019 (S.D.N.Y.1982).

22. Olmsted v. Pruco Life Ins. Co. of New Jersey, 283 F.3d 429 (2d Cir.2002).

30. 15 U.S.C.A. § 80a–35.

31. 15 U.S.C.A. § 80a–15.

32. *See, e.g.,* Brown v. Bullock, 294 F.2d 415, 420–21 (2d Cir.1961).

33. Fogel v. Chestnutt, 668 F.2d 100 (2d Cir.1981), *cert. denied* 459 U.S. 828, 103 S.Ct. 65, 74 L.Ed.2d 66 (1982).

34. Tarlov v. Paine Webber Cashfund, Inc., 559 F.Supp. 429 (D.Conn.1983).

35. 15 U.S.C.A. § 80a–35(a), (b)(3); Halligan v. Standard & Poor's/Intercapital, Inc., 434 F.Supp. 1082, 1084 (E.D.N.Y.1977).

36. 15 U.S.C.A. §§ 80a–26(e), 80a–27(i).

37. Olmsted v. Pruco Life Insurance Co., 134 F.Supp.2d 508 (E.D.N.Y.2000).

38. Kamen v. Kemper Financial Services, Inc., 659 F.Supp. 1153 (N.D.Ill.1987) (allowing section 20(a) claim to supplement section 36(b) claim for excessive fees); Krinsk v. Fund Asset Management, Inc., 654 F.Supp. 1227 (S.D.N.Y.1987); Schuyt v. Rowe Price Prime Reserve Fund, Inc., 622 F.Supp. 169 (S.D.N.Y.1985).

law. It follows that state law generally controls questions relating to breaches of fiduciary duty unless specifically preempted by federal law. In this regard, the Third Circuit has held that the Investment Company Act does not preempt state common law claims.[40] Depending on the theory underlying the claim, shareholders challenging director misconduct may be able to bring either a direct (e.g., class action) or a derivative suit.[41] The determination of whether a fiduciary duty claim with respect to investment companies is direct or derivative is a question of state law.[42]

In Moses v. Burgin,[43] affiliated directors were held to have a fiduciary duty to inform independent directors of the possibility of recapturing give-ups under the pre–1970 version of section 36 of the Investment Company Act. In Fogel v. Chestnutt,[44] a similar duty was held to exist under section 36(a) in its present form. The *Moses* and *Fogel* duty has been held to extend beyond the "give-up" situation.[45] In Cambridge Fund v. Abella[46] an affiliated director was held liable for a breach of fiduciary duty by personally trading in securities simultaneously with transactions by the investment company and for non-disclosure of the company's payment of that director's legal expenses in SEC proceedings against him.[47] The cases[48] and legislative comment[49] indicate that section 36(b)'s enactment did not curtail existing private rights of action under section 36(a) by a shareholder against investment company directors for breaching their fiduciary duty.[50] This is echoed by Supreme Court dictum in *Burks v. Lasker*,[51] which found no breach of section 36(a)'s fiduciary duty resulting from an investment company's board of directors terminating a shareholder's derivative suit if the applicable state law would allow such board action.[52] There is a requirement that a plaintiff in an action under Rule 10b–5 must have been a purchaser or seller of securities.[53] However, since a

---

40. Green v. Fund Asset Management, L.P., 245 F.3d 214 (3d Cir. 2001) (section 36(b) of the Investment Company Act does not preempt common law claims challenging investment advisory fees as a breach of fiduciary duty).

41. *See, e.g.,* 2 James D. Cox, & Thomas Lee Hazen, Cox & Hazen on Corporations § 15.3. (2d ed. 2003).

42. *E.g.,* Strougo v. Bassini, 282 F.3d 162 (2d Cir.2002).

43. 445 F.2d 369 (1st Cir.1971), *cert. denied* 404 U.S. 994, 92 S.Ct. 532, 30 L.Ed.2d 547 (1971).

44. 533 F.2d 731 (2d Cir.1975), *cert. denied* 429 U.S. 824, 97 S.Ct. 77, 50 L.Ed.2d 86 (1976). The "give-up" issue has been mooted by a change in New York Stock Exchange and SEC rules eliminating the practice. For a full discussion of the practice and the problem *see* Richard W. Jennings & Harold Marsh, Jr., Securities Regulation: Cases and Materials 481–485 (5th ed.1982).

45. *See, e.g.,* McLachlan v. Simon, 31 F.Supp.2d 731 (N.D.Cal.1998) (recognizing an implied remedy under section 36(a)).

46. 501 F.Supp. 598 (S.D.N.Y.1980).

47. *Id.* at 619–24.

48. Tannenbaum v. Zeller, 552 F.2d 402, 416 (2d Cir.1977), *cert. denied* 434 U.S. 934, 98 S.Ct. 421, 54 L.Ed.2d 293 (1977); Cambridge Fund, Inc. v. Abella, 501 F.Supp. 598 (S.D.N.Y.1980); Whitman v. Fuqua, 549 F.Supp. 315 (1982). The Supreme Court assumed without deciding, that a cause of action existed under section 36(a) in Burks v. Lasker, 441 U.S. 471, 99 S.Ct. 1831, 60 L.Ed.2d 404 (1979). *But cf.* Tarlov v. Paine Webber Cashfund, Inc., 559 F.Supp. 429 (D.Conn. 1983) (no section 36(a) remedy for excessive advisory fees).

49. " * * * the fact that subsection (b) [of Section 36] specifically provides for a private right of action should not be read by implication to affect subsection (a)," House Committee Report, H.R. No. 91–1382, 91st Cong. 2d Sess. (1970), at 38.

50. *See* Strougo v. Bassini, 282 F.3d 162 (2d Cir.2002) (private action under §§ 36(a) and 48).

51. 441 U.S. 471, 99 S.Ct. 1831, 60 L.Ed.2d 404 (1979).

52. *Id.* at 486, 99 S.Ct. at 1841.

53. Blue Chip Stamps v. Manor Drug Stores, 421 U.S. 723, 95 S.Ct. 1917, 44 L.Ed.2d 539 (1975). *See* § 12.7 *supra*.

claim under section 36(a) of the Investment Company Act is premised on a breach of fiduciary duty, rather than fraud in connection with the purchase or sale of securities, there is no comparable purchase/seller standing requirement.[54] Not all courts have recognized an implied remedy under section 36(a).[55]

The Supreme Court held that Rule 23.1's demand requirement does not apply in shareholder derivative actions brought under section 36(b) of the Investment Company Act.[88]

The demand controversy has thus been put to rest, except in the case of implied remedies. In such a case, the demand futility rule of the state of incorporation governs whether the demand is excused.[91]

§ 20.10[3] Standing to Sue Under Section 36(b); Right to Jury Trial

Liability under section 36 is based on a breach of duty to the investment company shareholders and thus will not support an action by someone else injured by the alleged wrongdoing.[92] The essence of a claim under section 36(b) is a classic case of breach of fiduciary duty, which historically has been an action in equity, and accordingly there is no right to a jury trial.[93] The realm of fiduciary duties covered by section 36(b) is relatively narrow and thus does not include, for example, violations of the Investment Company Act's proxy regulations.[94] Although as discussed above, an implied remedy may exist under the Investment Company Act and also under the Securities Exchange Act of 1934.

§ 20.10[4] Damages in Actions Under Section 36(b)

The amount recoverable in a section 36(b) action is limited to improper compensation paid within one year before the suit was instituted.[95] Only those who actually receive compensation from the investment company for advisory services may be held liable for breach of their fiduciary duties under section 36(b).[96] In making the determination whether the compensation paid was, in fact, excessive, courts will give great weight to approval by fully informed, properly qualified independent directors.[97]

---

54. *E.g.,* Strougo v. Scudder, Stevens & Clark, Inc., 964 F.Supp. 783 (S.D.N.Y.1997).

55. *See, e.g.,* Green v. Fund Asset Management, L.P., 19 F.Supp.2d 227 (D.N.J.1998), later opinion reversed on other grounds 245 F.3d 214 (3d Cir.2001) (since there is an express right of action under section 36(b) for breach of an investment company's investment adviser's fiduciary duty, there is no need for an implied remedy under sections 8(e), 34(b), and 36(a)).

88. Daily Income Fund, Inc. v. Fox, 464 U.S. 523, 542, 104 S.Ct. 831, 841–42 78 L.Ed.2d 645, 659 (1984).

91. Kamen v. Kemper Financial Services, Inc., 500 U.S. 90, 111 S.Ct. 1711, 114 L.Ed.2d 152 (1991).

92. *See* Index Fund, Inc. v. Hagopian, 609 F.Supp. 499, 505 (S.D.N.Y.1985).

93. Krinsk v. Fund Asset Management, Inc., 875 F.2d 404 (2d Cir.1989).

94. *See* Schuyt v. Rowe Price Prime Reserve Fund, Inc., 622 F.Supp. 169 (S.D.N.Y.1985) (recognizing a right to sue for the proxy violations under section 20(a) of the Act).

95. Section 36(b)(3), 15 U.S.C.A. § 80a–35(b); Halligan v. Standard & Poor's/Intercapital, Inc., 434 F.Supp. 1082, 1085 (E.D.N.Y.1977).

96. Halligan v. Standard & Poor's/Intercapital, Inc., 434 F.Supp. 1082, 1085 (E.D.N.Y.1977).

97. *See* §§ 20.6, 20.9 *supra.*

Chapter 21

INVESTMENT ADVISERS ACT OF 1940

Table of Sections

---

§ 21.1   Regulation of Investment Advisers; Terms and Conditions in Advisory Contracts

The Securities Exchange Act of 1934 regulates market professionals through its broker-dealer registration and oversight provisions.[1] The Exchange Act does not, however, address itself directly to non-broker-dealers who are in the business of rendering investment advice. This gap is filled by the Investment Advisers Act of 1940.[2]

Professional investment advisers frequently sell their services by disseminating advice through newsletters and other publications.[3] Others manage funds through an investment company or otherwise through custodial accounts. The Investment Advisers Act of 1940 addresses itself to many of these services. In 1999, with the enactment of the Gramm–Leach–Bliley Act,[4] Congress ended the long-time separation of investment banking and commercial banking when it repealed the Glass–Steagall Act of 1933.[5] This deregulatory effort will no doubt have an effect on bank-related investment advisory services.[6]

In 1985, the Supreme Court ruled that requiring registration of newsletters rendering investment advice on an impersonal basis does not fall within the Act's definition of investment adviser.[7] The Court held that the unregis-

---

§ 21.1

1.   15 U.S.C.A. §§ 78o, 78o–4. *See* § 14.3 *supra.*

2.   Act of Aug. 22, 1940 54 Stat. 847, codified in 15 U.S.C.A. § 80b–1 *et seq. See generally* James E. Anderson, Robert G. Bagnall & Marianne K. Smythe, Investment Advisers: Law and Compliance (2002).

3.   *See, e.g.,* Richard D. Harroch, The Applicability of the Investment Advisers Act of 1940 to Financial and Investment Related Publications, 5 J.Corp.L. 55 (1979).

4.   Pub. Law. 106–102, 1999 U.S.C.C.A.N. (113 Stat.) 1338 (1999). *See generally* Symposium, 4 N.C. Banking Inst. 1 (2000). *See* § 22.5 *infra.*

5.   The Banking Act of 1933, Ch. 89, 48 Stat. 184 (1933), codified in various sections of 12 U.S.C.A. (1999) *See* in particular 12 U.S.C.A. §§ 24, 378(a) (1999).

6.   Satish Kini, Impact of the 1999 Financial Modernization Act on Investment Advisers and Investment Companies, 33 Rev. Sec. & Commod. Reg. 69 (2000).

7.   Lowe v. SEC, 472 U.S. 181, 105 S.Ct. 2557, 86 L.Ed.2d 130 (1985). See § 21.2 *infra.*

tered status of such investment services did not justify restraining future publication. Notwithstanding the Supreme Court's holding, as of May 1986, of the approximately five to six thousand publishers of investment letters nevertheless registered as investment advisers, fewer than twenty had deregistered. Presumably, these publishers believed it would add to their credibility to be able to state that they were registered with the SEC.

Section 203(f) of the Investment Advisers Act gives the SEC the authority to hold hearings and impose sanctions against investment advisers and their associated persons who violate the securities laws. These sanctions range from censure to suspension.[9] This power includes the ability to limit the adviser's activities or to impose a bar order.[10] The Court of Appeals for the District of Columbia Circuit has held that this power extends to both registered and unregistered investment advisers.[11]

The Investment Advisers Act requires registration of all non-exempt investment advisers.[13] In addition to registration, non-exempt investment advisers must file periodic reports with the SEC and be available for periodic examination by the Commission.[14] Section 206 of the Act[15] prohibits material misrepresentations and fraudulent practices in connection with the rendering of investment advice. This antifraud provision applies to investment advisers even though they may be exempt from the Act's registration requirements. Section 206 applies to negligent misstatements, as well as to those made with the intent to defraud.[16]

The Act also regulates contracts between investment advisers and their clients.[17] The Act prohibits contracts whereby the adviser's compensation is dependent upon a share of the client's capital appreciation or gain.[18] Contingent fees are therefore prohibited. The theory is that such arrangements may lead the adviser to take undue risks with clients' funds.[19] The fee may be based on the total value of the fund taken at designated time periods.[20] In 1985, the SEC changed its long-time policy and now permits performance-based advisory fees for certain qualifying large advisory contracts.[21]

---

9.   15 U.S.C.A. § 80b–3(f).

10.   15 U.S.C.A. § 80b–3(f).

11.   Teicher v. SEC, 177 F.3d 1016 (D.C.Cir.1999). The court also held that the SEC does not have the authority under the Exchange Act to issue collateral bar orders covering any type of activity over which the SEC has occupational licensing authority. *Id. See* § 16.2 *supra*.

13.   *See* § 21.3 *infra*.

14.   15 U.S.C.A. § 80b–4.

15.   15 U.S.C.A. § 80b–6. Section 207 is addressed specifically to false filings with the Commission. 15 U.S.C.A. § 80b–7.

16.   *See* Morris v. Wachovia Securities, Inc., 277 F.Supp.2d 622, 644 (E.D. Va. 2003), relying on SEC v. Capital Gains Research Bureau, Inc., 375 U.S. 180, 194, 84 S.Ct. 275, 11 L.Ed.2d 237 (1963).

17.   15 U.S.C.A. § 80b–5.

18.   15 U.S.C.A. § 80b–5(a)(1).

19.   Inv.Adv.Act Rel. No. IA–721 (May 16, 1980).

20.   15 U.S.C.A. § 80b–5; 17 C.F.R. §§ 275.205–1, 275.205–2.

21.   An adviser can base fees on net realized capital gains and unrealized capital appreciation of a customer's funds for advisory contracts with a client that has at least $500,000 under the adviser's management or of a client with a net worth that exceeds one million dollars. In addition to the objective financial criteria, the client must be financially sophisticated and, in particular, the client must understand both the method of compensation and the risks presented by such a performance-based system of adviser compensation. 17 C.F.R. § 275.205–3. *See* Inv.Adv.Act Rel. No. IA–996 (Nov. 14, 1985).

An advisory contract must by its terms preclude assignment of the contract unless the client or customer consents.[22] This is designed to protect the investor against an unannounced change in the quality or character of the advisory services. If the investment adviser is a partnership, the advisory contract must provide for notice within a reasonable time of all changes in the composition of the partnership.[23] The sections that follow examine the registration and disclosure provisions of the Advisers Act.

§ 21.2   Who Is Subject to the Advisers Act—Definitions, Exclusions, and Exemptions

§ 21.2[1] Definition of Investment Adviser

Section 203(a) of the Investment Advisers Act requires registration of all investment advisers doing business through an instrumentality of interstate commerce unless exempted under section 203(b).[1] The Act defines "investment adviser" to include "any person who, for compensation, engages in the business of advising others, either directly or through publications or writings as to the value of securities or as to the advisability of investing in, purchasing, or selling securities * * *."[2] As discussed below, there are significant exclusions from the Investment Adviser Act's definition of investment adviser. Some of the more important exclusions are banks,[3] lawyers, accountants, engineers, or teachers rendering such advice incidental to their professions.[4] Broker-dealers who render advice incidental to their broker-dealer operations are excluded from the definition of investment adviser[5] There is another exclusion for publications which render impersonal investment advice.[6] Also excluded from the definition are financial planners and other professionals who may render generalized advice as to how people should manage their money—including their investment activities but do not render advice on individual securities or mutual funds. When the activities of an entity are purely administrative and do not involve rendering investment advice, the Act's definition of investment adviser will not be implicated.[7] However, the fact that an entity's primary function is not the rendering of investment advice will not preclude application of the Investment Advisers Act.[8]

---

22. 15 U.S.C.A. § 80b–5(a)(2).

23. 15 U.S.C.A. § 80b–5(a)(3).

§ 21.2

1. 15 U.S.C.A. § 80b–3(a), (b).

2. 15 U.S.C.A. § 80b–2(a)(11).

3. As it is currently written the exclusion applies only to banks, not to thrifts or savings and loans. There has been movement to broaden the exclusion. *See* H.R. 3951 (2002); House Panel approves Thrift Exemption from Advisers Act, Complinet, http://www.complinet.com/securities-na/dailynews/display.html?ref=36317 (June 17, 2002).

4. 15 U.S.C.A. § 80b–2(a)(11)(B).

5. 15 U.S.C.A. § 80b–2(a)(11)(A), (B).

6. 15 U.S.C. § 80b–2(a)(11). *See* Lowe v. SEC, 472 U.S. 181, 105 S.Ct. 2557, 86 L.Ed.2d 130 (1985).

7. *See, e.g.,* League Central Credit Union, 1987 WL 108069 (SEC No Action Letter August 21, 1987). *See also, e.g.,* National Football League Players Association, 2002 WL 100675 (SEC No Action letter Jan. 25, 2002) (union's providing a list of screened investment advisers to its members did not require union register as an investment adviser).

8. *See, e.g.,* Gary L. Pleger, 1977 WL 15164 (SEC No Action Letter September 9, 1977) (cautioning that business broker may be investment adviser); Bay Business Service, 1977 WL 14076 (SEC No Action Letter Feb. 14, 1977) (same)

As evidenced by the exclusions from the definition of investment adviser, simply because someone renders investment advice as part of their profession does not put them within the Investment Adviser Act's definition of investment adviser. This is true even for the professions not expressly listed in the exclusions from the Act.[13] Thus, for example, a sports agent who advises professional athletes on investment matters does not necessarily fall within the definition of investment adviser.[14] A number of factors will be considered in determining whether someone who renders investment advice as part of their profession will fall within the definition of investment adviser.

The more individualized the investment advice that is given, the more likely it is that someone will be classified as an investment adviser.[16] As pointed out above, one of the considerations is whether the person rendering the investment advice is "in the business of rendering such advice. Whether someone who renders advice is considered to be in the business of rendering investment advice depends on a number of factors. A significant factor is whether the person rendering advice holds himself or herself out as an investment adviser or someone providing investment advice.[17] A second factor weighing in favor of classifying someone as an investment adviser is whether he or she receives any separate or additional compensation representing 'a clearly definable charge' for those advisory services."[18] The SEC takes a broad view of what constitutes compensation for advisory services. Rendering of investment advice without compensation is likely to take the person rendering the advice out from under the purview of the Investment Advisers Act.[20]

As a third factor, if the person rendering specific investment advice does so other than on "rare, isolated and non-periodic" occasions, he or she is not likely to be considered to be in the business of rendering investment advice.[21]

The definition of investment adviser depends upon the advice being rendered with regard to securities as opposed to some other type of investment. However, it is to be recalled that the definition of security is an expansive one[22] and is not limited to traditional securities such as stocks and bonds. Thus, for example, someone who offers clients advice with regard to investment vehicles, such as tax-exempt repurchase agreements, stock income agreements, or collateral loan agreements can fall within the Act's definition of investment adviser.[23]

---

13. Those listed professions include banks, lawyers, accountants, engineers, or teachers. 15 U.S.C.A. § 80b–2(a)(11)(B).

14. Zinn v. Parrish, 644 F.2d 360, 364 (7th Cir.1981).

16. *See* United States v. Elliott, 62 F.3d 1304, 1309–1311 (11th Cir.1995).

17. *See Id.*

18. *Id.* at 1304, 1309–1311 (11th Cir.1995); Applicability of the Investment Advisers Act to Financial Planners, Pension Consultants, and Other Persons Who Provide Investment Advisory Services as a Component of Other Financial Services, Investment Advisers Act Release No. IA–1092, 52 Fed.Reg. 38400(Oct. 8, 1987). The SEC talked in terms of "a clearly definable charge for providing advice about securities, regardless of whether the compensation is separate from or included within any overall compensation, or receives transaction-based compensation if the client implements ... the investment advice." *Ibid. Compare, e.g.*, Wang v. Gordon, 715 F.2d 1187, 1192–93 (7th Cir.1983) (where the commission was received for selling an apartment building rather than for selling securities).

20. *See, e.g.*, Dominion Resources, Inc., 1985 WL 54428 (SEC No Action Letter 1985).

21. *See* United States v. Elliott, 62 F.3d 1304, 1311 (11th Cir.1995).

22. 15 U.S.C.A. §§ 77b(a)(1), 78c(a)(10). *See* § 1.6 *supra*.

23. *See* United States v. Elliott, 62 F.3d 1304, 1309–1310 (11th Cir.1995).

The use of the Internet has raised all sorts of challenging regulatory issues under the securities laws. One such issue relates to its use for investment advice. Investment advice can be rendered through web sites as well as through chat rooms. The use of the Internet for the rendering of investment advice will classify the person rendering the advice as an investment adviser, unless he or she can fit within the exclusion for publications that render impersonal investment advice.[24] The SEC has indicated that providing a "passive" electronic bulletin board to facilitate the posting of information about securities will not qualify as rendering investment advice for the purpose of having to register under the Investment Advisers Act.[25] In order to avoid having to register, the providers of passive bulletin boards (1) may not be involved in any purchase or sale negotiations arising from the bulletin board and (2) may not give advice regarding the merits or shortcomings of any particular trade.[26]

Following the wake of scandals in the mutual fund industry, the SEC adopted a series of new compliance requirements for investment companies and investment advisers.[27] Investment Adviser Act Rule 206(4)–7[28] requires registered investment advisers to adopt and implement written policies and procedures, reasonably designed to prevent violations of the Advisers Act. These policies and procedures at a minimum, to the extent that they are relevant, must address to address: portfolio management processes, including (1) allocation of investment opportunities and compliance with clients' investment objectives and restrictions; (2) trading practices, including best execution and soft dollar arrangements; (3) proprietary trading of the adviser and personal trading activities of its employees; (4) accuracy of disclosures; (5) safeguarding of client assets; (6) creation and maintenance of required records; (7) marketing services, including the use of solicitors; (8) valuation of client assets and the assessment of fees based on those valuations; (9) safeguards for client privacy protection; and (10) business continuity plans.

Rule 206(4)–7 further requires that registered investment advisers review their policies and procedures annually to determine their adequacy and the effectiveness of their implementation.[29] The rule also requires registered investment advisers to designate a chief compliance officer to administer its compliance policies and procedures.[30] This chief compliance officer should have sufficient seniority and authority to (1) be competent and knowledgeable regarding the Advisers Act and (2) be empowered with full responsibility and authority to develop and enforce appropriate policies and procedures.[31]

24. SEC v. Park, 99 F.Supp.2d 889 (N.D.Ill.2000) (defendants did not fall within the exclusion from the definition of investment adviser for general publications).

25. *See, e.g.,* Internet Capital Corp., 1998 WL 9357 (SEC No Action Letter Jan. 13, 1998). *See also, e.g.,* Progressive Technology Inc., 2000 WL 1508655 (SEC No Action Letter Oct. 11, 2000) (providing an online a resource for individuals or businesses that are interested in obtaining debt and/or equity financing).

26. *See, e.g.,* Internet Capital Corp., 1998 WL 9357 (SEC No Action Letter Jan. 13, 1998); Angel Capital Electronic Network, 1996 WL 636094 (SEC No Action Letter Oct. 25, 1996) (listing of small business offerings).

27. *See* Compliance Programs of Investment Companies and Investment Advisers, Inv. Adv. Act Rel No. IA—2204, Inv. Co. Act Rel. No. IC—26299, 2003 WL 22971048, (SEC 2003). *See* §§ 20.1, 20.5 *supra.*

28. 17 C.F.R. § 275.206(4)–7.

29. *Id.*

30. *Id.*

31. *Id.*

§ 21.2[2] Exclusions From the Definition of Investment Adviser

§ 21.2[2][A] Exclusions Generally; Exemptions Distinguished

The definition of investment adviser excludes banks, lawyers, accountants, engineers, or teachers rendering such advice incidental to their professions.[33] Also excluded from the Investment Advisers Act are advises who render advice solely with respect to government securities of the Untied States government.[37] An exclusion from the definition of Investment Adviser means that there is no regulation under any of the provisions of the Investment Advisers Act. In contrast, an exemption provides only an exemption from the Act's registration provisions.[38]

§ 21.2[2][B] Exclusion for Broker–Dealers

Another exclusion from the definition of investment adviser is any broker-dealer whose advisory service "is solely incidental to the conduct of his business as a broker or dealer" and without special compensation.[39] Once it is established that someone is a broker, the burden falls on the SEC (or other plaintiff) to show that the investment advice given was more than incidental to the brokerage activities and that special compensation was received for that advice.[41] Absent proof of such special compensation, a broker-dealer will not be classified as an investment adviser.[42] A broker-dealer's holding himself or herself out as a financial planner will not in itself implicate the Investment Advisers Act registration provisions.[43]

Although excluded from the Adviser's Act, brokers and dealers furnishing such incidental advice are subject to the suitability,[44] "know your customer," and "know your merchandise" requirements when making investment recommendations to customers.[45] When dealing with investment advice furnished by brokerage firms, a critical issue is whether the customer is paying specially for the advice or whether the advice is simply part of the brokerage service.[46]

---

33. 15 U.S.C.A. § 80b–2(a)(11)(B).

37. 15 U.S.C.A. § 80b–2(a)(11)(E).

38. *See, e.g.,* Teicher v. SEC, 177 F.3d 1016 (D.C.Cir.1999) (SEC could sanction associated person of investment adviser even if adviser was not registered under the Act).

39. 15 U.S.C.A. § 80b–2(a)(11)(C). *See* Applicability of the Investment Advisers Act to Certain Brokers and Dealers, Sec. Exch. Act Rel. No. 34–15215, 15 S.E.C. Docket 1211, 1978 WL 14788 (SEC 1978) (extending temporary exemption from Investment Advisers Act for broker-dealers exercising discretionary authority over accounts).

41. *See, e.g.,* SEC v. Kenton Capital, Ltd., 69 F.Supp.2d 1, 13 (D.D.C.1998) (also holding that offerors of securities had to register both as brokers and investment advisers).

42. Darrell v. Goodson, [1979–1980 Transfer Binder] Fed. Sec. L. Rep. (CCH) ¶ 97,349, 1980 WL 1392 (S.D.N.Y.1980); Kaufman v. Merrill Lynch, Pierce, Fenner & Smith, 464 F.Supp. 528, 537–538 (D.Md.1978); Parsons v. Hornblower & Weeks–Hemphill, Noyes, 447 F.Supp. 482, 487–488 (M.D.N.C.1977), aff'd, 571 F.2d 203 (4th Cir.1978); E. F. Hutton & Co., [1979 Transfer Binder] Fed. Sec. L. Rep. (CCH) ¶ 82,000 (SEC No Action Letter 1979). *See also, e.g.,* Washington v. Baenziger, 656 F.Supp. 1176(N.D.Cal.1987) (upholding complaint only as to those defendants who were claimed to have received compensation for their investment advice).

43. *See* Inv. Adv. Act Rel. No. IA–770 (Aug. 13, 1981).

44. *See* § 14.16 *supra* for discussion of the suitability requirements generally.

45. *See* §§ 14.15–14.18 *supra.*

46. Inv.Adv.Act Rel. No. IA–2 (Oct. 28, 1949).

Bona fide news media including financial publications of general circulation[47] and persons limiting such advice to securities issued or guaranteed by the federal government[48] are not subject to the Investment Advisers Act registration requirements, as are other persons excluded by SEC rule.[49] Unlike persons that are exempted from the registration requirements, persons excluded from the Act's coverage are not subject to section 206's[50] antifraud proscriptions.

§ 21.2[2][C] Financial Planners

The past several decades have witnessed the growth of financial planning as an industry. The emergence of the financial planning industry necessarily raises questions concerning the applicability of the Investment Advisers Act's registration provisions. Financial planners who render only generalized investment advice do not have to register under the Investment Advisers Act.[53] However, the SEC has indicated that registration may be required for a computer-generated financial planning service, although not recommending specific securities, which would nevertheless offer a service developed by an unaffiliated organization where the service identifies investments that would affect the generalized investment recommendations.[54]

§ 21.2[2][D] Exclusion for Publications Rendering Impersonal Investment Advice

The Act expressly excludes from the definition of investment advisor "the publisher of any bona fide newspaper, news magazine or business or financial publication of general and regular circulation."[55] The exemption does not, however, exclude every regular publication that contains investment advice.

In Lowe v. SEC,[57] the Supreme Court interpreted the exclusion for publications and investment newsletters. The Court explained that the exclusion is limited to publications that render impersonal investment advice, and then held that the publication in question did not fall within the Act's definition of investment adviser.[58] The Court reasoned that the essence of the activity which the Act seeks to regulate is the personal service of investment advising and that such regularly published investment letters are impersonal and thus not within the Act's target. The Court in relying on the statutory definition did not have to reach the question on which it originally granted certiorari—whether prohibiting publication of such newsletters without regis-

---

47. 15 U.S.C.A. § 80b–2(a)(11)(D). Lowe v. SEC, 472 U.S. 181, 105 S.Ct. 2557, 86 L.Ed.2d 130 (1985).

48. 15 U.S.C.A. § 80b–2(a)(11)(E).

49. 15 U.S.C.A. § 80b–2(a)(11)(F).

50. 15 U.S.C.A. § 80b–6.

53. The Commission excludes persons rendering investment advice pursuant to their activities as financial planners, pension planners and others who provide the advice "as in integral component of other financially related services." Inv. Adv. Act Rel. No. IA–770 (Aug. 13, 1981).

54. In re Computer Language Research, Inc., [1985–1986 Transfer Binder] Fed.Sec.L.Rep. (CCH) ¶ 78,185 (SEC No Action Letter Dec. 26, 1985).

55. 15 U.S.C.A. § 80b–2(a)(11)(D).

57. 472 U.S. 181, 105 S.Ct. 2557, 86 L.Ed.2d 130 (1985).

58. 15 U.S.C.A. § 80b–2(a)(11)(C). *Compare, e.g.,* SEC v. Park, 99 F.Supp.2d 889 (N.D.Ill. 2000) (defendants failed to establish that they did not provide personalized advice; accordingly they did not fall within the exclusion from the definition of investment adviser for general publications).

tration under the Act was an unconstitutional prior restraint, which violated the First Amendment's right of free speech.[59] The Court noted, however, that Congress' decision to focus investment adviser regulation on the providing of personal services was motivated in part "to keep the Act free of constitutional infirmities."[60] The Court identified the Investment Adviser Act's focus as having been "designed to apply to those persons engaged in the investment advisory profession—those who provide *personalized* advice attuned to a client's concerns, whether by written or verbal communication."[61]

In defining the scope of its holding in *Lowe*, the Court pointed out that it was limited to "bona fide" newsletters rendering impersonal investment advice. The exclusion from the definition of investment adviser, thus, for example, does not apply to tout sheets designed to generate commissions for the adviser; and, thus, when used as part of a "scalping scheme," the SEC arguably should still have jurisdiction to enjoin publication.[63] As observed in an earlier section of this treatise, the *Lowe* decision did not result in a significant number of investment newsletter deregistrations. It is unclear whether, standing alone, these newsletters' apparent consent to SEC regulation can effectively expand the Commission's jurisdiction.[65]

The *Lowe* decision does not mean that investment newsletters which are excluded from the Act escape all regulation under the securities laws. For example, section 17(b) of the 1933 Act prohibits recommending securities without disclosing any remuneration connected with the recommendation.[66] Section 17(b) is designed to prevent the appearance of an unbiased opinion when, in fact, the opinion has been "bought and paid for."[67] A 1988 court of appeals decision rejected a constitutional challenge and thus upheld this type of regulation of financial newsletters.[68] Recommendations that contain materially misleading factual information can run afoul of Rule 10b–5 regardless of whether the publisher is an investment adviser.[69] Accordingly, the *Lowe*

---

59. The constitutional attack, which was rejected by the Second Circuit in its opinion below simply went to the registration requirements and did not challenge the SEC's power to regulate materially misleading publications and disclosures. *Cf.* SEC v. Blavin, 760 F.2d 706 (6th Cir.1985) (involving materially misleading statements; decided before *Lowe v. SEC*).

60. 472 U.S. at 208, 105 S.Ct. at 2572, 86 L.Ed.2d at 149.

61. *Id.* (emphasis supplied; footnote omitted.). *Compare* SEC v. Park, 99 F.Supp.2d 889 (N.D.Ill.2000) (defendants failed to establish that they did not render personalized advice).

63. *See* Joel D. Ferber, The Narrow Holding of the *Lowe* Case, 19 Rev.Sec. & Commodities Reg. 29 (1986).

65. *Lowe* held that these entities are not investment advisers thus depriving the Commission of jurisdiction. By continuing their registration, newsletters are consenting to the Commission's jurisdiction. However, can a private party vest the Commission with jurisdiction not granted by the statute? Since an administrative agency exists only by virtue of enabling legislation, there is a strong argument that its jurisdiction cannot be expanded except by Congress.

66. 15 U.SC.A. § 77q(b). *See* § 7.11[2] *supra.*

67. H.R.Rep. No. 85, 73d Cong., 1st Sess. 24 (1933). *See* SEC v. Wall Street Publishing Institute, Inc., 851 F.2d 365 (D.C.Cir.1988); United States v. Amick, 439 F.2d 351, 365 (7th Cir.1971).

68. SEC v. Wall Street Publishing Institute, Inc., 851 F.2d 365 (D.C.Cir.1988). The First Amendment argument was based on the Supreme Court's decision in Lowe v. SEC, 472 U.S. 181, 105 S.Ct. 2557, 86 L.Ed.2d 130 (1985), which held that the Investment Advisers Act does not require registration of newsletters rendering investment advice. Although not decided directly on constitutional grounds, the Court's decision in *Lowe* was premised on finding an interpretation of the Investment Advisers Act that would not be unconstitutional.

69. *See, e.g.,* Zweig v. Hearst Corp., 594 F.2d 1261 (9th Cir.1979) (undisclosed purchases prior to making recommendation violated Rule 10b–5). *Cf.* SEC v. Capital Gains Research Bureau, Inc., 375 U.S. 180, 84 S.Ct. 275, 11 L.Ed.2d 237 (1963) (failure to disclose purchases of securities prior

decision relates only to the Investment Advisers Act registration and anti-fraud provisions, but not to the antifraud provisions contained in other securities acts.

§ 21.2[3] Exemptions from the Investment Advisers Act

The dividing line between exclusions and exemptions is not as clear as it might be since the SEC has exercised its exemptive authority with regard to persons and entities that at least come close to falling within one of the exclusions that are discussed above that negate the applicability of the Act's investment adviser definition. The Commission has utilized its exemptive power to exclude persons rendering investment advice pursuant to their activities as financial planners, pension planners, and others who provide the advice "as an integral component of other financially related services."[71] In contrast, a broker-dealer can hold himself or herself out as a financial planner without Adviser Act registration so long as the planning services are incidental to broker-dealer activities and are without additional compensation, and further that the planner would be recommending only products that were offered by the brokerage firm.[72] Similarly, an accountant who offers financial planning services that are purely incidental to his or her business does not have to register as an investment adviser so long as he or she does not mention specific investment products.[73] The SEC has issued an interpretative release which explains that many financial planners, pension consultants, sports, or entertainment representatives, and others providing financial advisory services are investment advisers and therefore subject to regulation both at the federal and state levels.[74]

In addition to the above-mentioned exclusions from the definition of investment adviser, the Act provides exemptions from registration.[75] These exemptions do not immunize the adviser from the Act's anti-fraud provisions.[76] Securities offerings to sophisticated investors are exempted from registration under the Securities Act of 1933.[77] There is no comparable exemption for investment advisers. The Investment Adviser Act thus applies to advisers who render advice only to sophisticated investors.[78] There are three exemptions from investment adviser registration.

---

to making recommendation constituted a violation of Investment Advisers Act § 206); SEC v. Suter, 832 F.2d 988 (7th Cir.1987) (someone committing securities fraud cannot escape liability by publishing a newsletter and claiming exclusion from the Act). *See* § 14.17 *supra*.

71. Inv. Adv. Act Rel. No. IA–770 (Aug. 13, 1981).

72. In re Robinson, [1985–86 Transfer Binder] Fed.Sec.L.Rep. (CCH) ¶ 78,188 (SEC No Action Letter Jan. 6, 1986) (the SEC also asked that the limitations on the financial planning service be fully disclosed to all customers).

73. In re Hauk, Soule & Fasani, P.C., [1986 Transfer Binder] Fed.Sec.L.Rep. (CCH) ¶ 78,311 (SEC No Action Letter April 2, 1986).

74. Inv.Act Rel. No. IA–1092, 5 Fed.Sec.L.Rep. (CCH) ¶ 56,156E (Oct. 8, 1987). *Cf.* Note, Financial Planning: Is It Time For a Self–Regulatory Organization?, 53 Brooklyn L.Rev. 143 (1987).

75. 15 U.S.C.A. § 80b–3(b).

76. 15 U.S.C.A. § 80b–6. *See* § 21.4 *infra*.

77. 1933 Act § 4(2), 15 U.S.C.A. § 77d(2). *See* § 4.24 *supra*.

78. As explained by the SEC:

There is no legislative history that explains why the private adviser exemption was enacted. We do know, however, that it was not intended to exempt advisers to wealthy or sophisticated clients. They were the primary clients of many advisers in 1940 when the provision was included in the Act. While provisions of the Securities Act (and its rules) provide exemptions

First, a local adviser—that is, one whose clients are residents of the state of its principal place of business—is exempt so long as the adviser does not furnish advice with regard to exchange—listed securities.[79] The exemption for local advisers became less meaningful after April 10, 1997. As of that date, advisers with less than twenty-five million dollars in assets under management who are not advisers to registered investment companies are subject to the exclusive regulatory jurisdiction of the states.[80]

The second exemption from investment adviser registration applies to advisers whose only clients are insurance companies.[81] The third exemption from form investment adviser registration applies to advisers who do not have more than fifteen clients and do not hold themselves out as advisers either to the public[82] or to investment companies.[83]

This third exemption for so-called private investment advisers was used to shield most hedge funds from regulation. Advisers of most hedge funds were not subject to the Act's registration requirements. The SEC tried to subject hedge fund advisers to the registration requirements of section 203 of the Act.[83.10] The exclusion for advisers that have a limited number of clients was amended to provide a "look-through" approach that no longer counts a fund as one advisory client but rather looks through to the fund's investors as advisory clients.[83.15]

---

from registration under that Act for securities transactions with persons, including institutions, that have such knowledge and experience that they are considered capable of fending for themselves and thus do not need the protections of the applicable registration provisions, the Advisers Act does not. When a client—even one who is highly sophisticated in financial matters—seeks the services of an investment adviser, he acknowledges he needs the assistance of an expert. The client may be unfamiliar with investing or the type of strategy employed by the adviser, or may simply not have the time to manage his financial affairs. The Advisers Act is intended to protect all types of investors who have entrusted their assets to a professional investment adviser. Today, thirty-nine percent of advisers registered with us report that they advise only institutional and wealthy clients.

Registration Under the Advisers Act of Certain Hedge Fund Advisers, Release No. IA–2266, 69 Fed. Reg. 45172–01, 2004 WL 1665899 (SEC July 20, 2004) (footnotes omitted).

79. 15 U.S.C.A. § 80b–3(b)(1). The exemption also forbids advice with regard to securities having unlisted trading privileges on a national exchange. There are currently nine active national exchanges registered under section 6 of the 1934 Act. 15 U.S.C.A. § 78f. *See* §§ 14.1, 14.3 *supra*.

80. Investment Advisers Act section 203A, 15 U.S.C.A. § 80b–203A. *See also, e.g.,* John H. Walsh, Federal Regulation of Financial Planners After the Investment Advisers Supervision Coordination Act, 10 DePaul Bus. L.J. 259 (1998).

81. 15 U.S.C.A. § 80b–3(b)(2). Prior to 1970, the exemption extended to advisers acting solely on behalf of investment companies.

82. *See, e.g.,* Lamp Technologies, Inc., 1998 WL 278984 (SEC No Action Letter May 29, 1998) (making information available on the Internet only to selected, prescreened qualified investors did not constitute "holding out to the public"). *See also, e.g.,* Lamp Technologies, Inc., 1997 WL 282988 (SEC No Action Letter May 29, 1997).

83. 15 U.S.C.A. § 80b–3(b)(3). In applying this exemption, the SEC has adopted a safe harbor rule under which a limited partnership counts as one client provided that the general partner is not related to or affiliated with a registered investment adviser. 17 C.F.R. § 275.203(b)(3)–1, adopted in Inv.Adv.Act Rel. No. IA–983 (July 12, 1985).

83.10 *See* Registration Under the Advisers Act of Certain Hedge Fund Advisers, Inv. Co. Act Rel. No. IA-2333, 2004 WL 2785492 (SEC 2004). These changes were implemented by amending the rules relating to the registration exemption for investment advisers who render advice to no more than fifteen persons. This exemption is found in section 203(b)(3) of the Act (15 U.S.C.A. § 80b–3(b)(3)). *See* § 21.2 *infra* for discussion of this and the other exemptions from registration.

83.15 *See* Registration Under the Advisers Act of Certain Hedge Fund Advisers, Inv. Co. Act Rel. No. IA–2333, 2004 WL 2785492 (SEC 2004).

However, the look-through approach was struck down as inconsistent with the statutory scheme.[83.20]

An exemption from the Investment Advisers Act does not necessarily eliminate all federal regulation. The antifraud provisions are still applicable to unregistered investment advisers unless the SEC uses its exempted authority to provide an across-the-board exemption from all the Investment Advisers Act's provisions.[88] Also, the SEC can impose sanctions for wrongdoing by persons associated with an investment adviser[89] even if the adviser is not registered under the Investment Advisers Act of 1940.[90]

§ 21.3 Investment Adviser Registration and Reporting Requirements

§ 21.3[1] Federal Registration and Reporting Requirements

All non-exempt investment advisers must register pursuant to section 203(c) of the Act[1] by filing Form ADV with the Commission.[2] Form ADV requires disclosure of the identity and background of the adviser and affiliated persons. The adviser must disclose its principal business[3] and the nature of such business.[4] It is also necessary to disclose the scope of the adviser's authority[5] and the basis of compensation,[6] and also to include a balance sheet. The adviser must further disclose any criminal record that would affect qualification for registration.[7] The disclosure must include the adviser's educational and business background,[8] as well as a description of any other business activities. Form ADV requires the adviser to set forth a list of the services provided, including a description of the types of clients served and the types of securities for which advice is rendered. Additional disclosures apply when the adviser manages discretionary accounts. As a general rule, all information in an adviser's registration statement is available to the public.[9] Much of the information disclosed in Form ADV must also be provided to existing and prospective advisory clients.[10]

After Form ADV has been filed, the SEC has forty-five days to either grant the application for registration or institute proceedings to determine

---

83.20 Goldstein v. SEC, 2006 WL 1715766 (D.C. Cir. 2006).

88. The SEC's broad exemptive authority is found in 15 U.S.C.A. § 80b–6a.

89. Section 203(f) of the Investment Advisers Act empowers the SEC to regulate associated persons of investment advisers. 15 U.S.C.A. § 80b–3(f).

90. *See* Teicher v. SEC, 177 F.3d 1016 (D.C.Cir.1999).

§ 21.3

1. 15 U.S.C.A. § 80b–3(c). *See* Kauffmann v. Yoskowitz, 1989 WL 79364, [1989 Transfer Binder] Fed.Sec.L.Rep. (CCH) ¶ 94,532 (S.D.N.Y.1989) (it is "well settled" that there is no private remedy against an investment adviser for failure to register).

2. *See* 17 C.F.R. § 275.203–1.

3. 15 U.S.C.A. § 80b–3(c)(1)(H).

4. 15 U.S.C.A. § 80b–3(c)(1)(C).

5. 15 U.S.C.A. § 80b–3(c)(1)(E).

6. 15 U.S.C.A. § 80b–3(c)(1)(F).

7. 15 U.S.C.A. § 80b–3(c)(1)(G). Disqualifications from registration are found in 15 U.S.C.A. § 80b–3(e)(3) which also sets out the grounds for suspension or revocation of an investment adviser's registration.

8. 15 U.S.C.A. § 80b–3(c)(1)(B).

9. 15 U.S.C.A. § 80b–10(a).

10. 17 C.F.R. § 275.204–3(a). *See* Inv.Adv.Act Rel. No. IA–767 (July 21, 1981).

whether the application should be denied.[13] The applicant is entitled to notice of the grounds being considered as the basis for denial.[14] The SEC's statutory mandate is to deny registration if it finds that the applicant, if registered, would be subject to suspension or revocation.[15]

Registered investment advisers must file annual reports with the SEC on Form ADV-S.[16] Although the Form ADV must be kept current, the Commission has also designated records that must be maintained and made available for periodic inspection.[17] These records include balance sheets, income statements, and a journal of all accounts;[18] copies of all communications sent and received relating to investment advice or the execution of orders;[19] copies of all notices, letters, reports, and advertisements distributed by the adviser to more than ten customers;[20] and records of all securities transactions.[21]

The SEC has the power to impose sanctions, ranging from censure to revocation of registration, for advisers who themselves have committed certain crimes or securities law violations, or have associated with persons having committed such crimes or violations of the securities laws.[24] The disqualifying violations include false SEC filings, perjury, and crimes involving larceny, embezzlement, extortion, forgery, counterfeiting, fraud, mail fraud, and fraudulent misappropriation of funds or securities.[25] These sanctions may be imposed only after notice and a hearing and in accordance with the public interest.[26] The Commission can similarly censure, suspend, or bar persons subject to similar disqualification who seek to become associated with a registered investment adviser.[27]

There are some additional requirements beyond the above-mentioned registration and reporting requirements. Investment advisers, other than those furnishing "impersonal advisory services" through newsletters or otherwise,[28] must comply with the "brochure rule" prior to signing up prospective customers other than a registered investment company.[29] Rule 204–3 requires that prospective advisory customers be furnished with a brochure or disclo-

---

13. 15 U.S.C.A. § 80b–3(c)(2).

14. *Id.*

15. 15 U.S.C.A. § 80b–3(c)(2).

16. *See* 15 U.S.C.A. § 80b–4. 17 C.F.R. § 275.204–1(c). This is much less lengthy than the Exchange Act's annual report requirements for issuers. *See* 17 C.F.R. §§ 240–14a–3(b), 14c–3 which are discussed in § 10.6 *supra.*

17. 15 U.S.C.A. § 80b–4 (SEC is empowered to require reports by registered investment advisers); 17 C.F.R. § 275.204–2.

The Adviser's Act's record-keeping requirements are analogous to the broker-dealer record-keeping requirements imposed by the Securities Exchange Act of 1934. *See* § 14.3 *supra.*

18. 17 C.F.R. §§ 275.204–2(a)(1), (2).

19. 17 C.F.R. § 275.204–2(a)(7).

20. 17 C.F.R. § 275.204–2(a)(11).

21. 17 C.F.R. § 275.204–2(a)(12).

24. 15 U.S.C.A. § 80b–3(e).

25. 15 U.S.C.A. § 80b–3(e)(2). Mail fraud is discussed in § 22.4.

26. 15 U.S.C.A. § 80b–3(e).

27. 15 U.S.C.A. § 80b–3(f).

28. Rule 204–3(g) defines "impersonal advisory services" as those not related to the investment objectives of specific individuals or accounts. 17 C.F.R. § 275.204–3(g).

29. 17 C.F.R. § 275.204–3. *See* Inv. Advisers Act Rel. No. IA–664 (Jan. 30, 1979). The relationship between investment companies registered under the Investment Company Act of 1940 and their investment advisers is discussed in §§ 20.2, 20.9 *supra.*

sure document containing the information required in Part II of Form ADV's registration statement.[30] Advisers providing impersonal advisory services charging two hundred dollars or more must also comply with the brochure delivery requirements.[31]

Institutional investors play an important role in corporate governance.[32] In 2003, the SEC adopted rules under the Investment Advisers Act[33] that require investment advisers to make information about their voting of portfolio securities available to advisory clients. In particular, Rule 206–4(6) provides that registered investment advisers must adopt proxy policies and procedures for voting shares held for advisory clients, to describe their proxy voting policies and procedures to their advisory clients; to furnish a copy of the voting policies and procedures upon request to advisory client; and to disclose how advisory clients can obtain information about how the adviser voted their proxies.[34] The SEC also adopted a parallel set of rules under the Investment Company Act that are require management investment companies to make disclosures relating to their voting of portfolio securities.[35]

§ 21.3[2] Division of Federal and State Jurisdiction

As a result of 1996 amendments to the Investment Advisers Act, there is now exclusive federal jurisdiction over larger advisers and those advising registered investment companies.[36] Effective April 10, 1997, investment advisers managing more than $25 million in assets and advisers to registered investment companies fall under the exclusive jurisdiction of the SEC. All other advisers are subject to the exclusive jurisdiction of the states. The Act further limits the regulation that can be imposed on those advisers by states other than the adviser's principal place of business. There have been attempts by some advisers covered by this exception to retain their registration under the Act.[37] Presumably, such a request is motivated by a preference for the federal rather than state regulatory regime. In 1998, the Commission amended its rules to permit federal registration of some investment advisers even though they do not reach the $25 million threshold. Investment Adviser Act Rule 203A–2 exempts advisers that otherwise would have to be registered in thirty or more states from the prohibition against SEC registration of advisers below the twenty-five million dollar threshold.[38] Thus, truly national advisers

---

30.   17 C.F.R. § 275.204–3.

31.   17 C.F.R. § 275.204–3(c)(3). Rule 206(4)–4 explicitly requires disclosure of adverse financial conditions as well as disciplinary or legal events questioning the adviser's integrity. 17 C.F.R. § 275.206(4)–4.

32.   The federal proxy rules, including their application to institutional investors are discussed in § 10.2[3] *supra.*

33.   *See* Proxy Voting By Investment Advisors, Inv. Adv. Act Rel. No. IA—2106, 79 S.E.C. Docket 1673, 2003 WL 215467 (SEC Jan. 31, 2003).

34.   *Id.*

35.   *See* Disclosure of Proxy Voting, Policies and Proxy Voting Records by Registered Management Investment Companies, Sec. Act Rel. No. 33–8188, Sec. Exch. Act Rel. No. 34–47304, Inv. Co. Act Rel. No. IC–25922, 79 S.E.C. Docket 1638, 2003 WL 215451 (SEC Jan. 31, 2003).

36.   Section 203A of the Investment Advisers Act of 1940, 15 U.S.C.A. § 80b–203A. *See* Mari-Anne Pisarri, The Investment Advisers Supervision Coordination Act, 30 Rev. Sec. & Commod. Reg. 185 (1997). *See also, e.g.,* John H. Walsh, Federal Regulation of financial Planners After the Investment Advisers Supervision Coordination Act, 10 DePaul Bus. L.J. 259 (1998).

37.   *See* Investment Advisers Seek to Remain Registered with the SEC, Fed. Sec. L. Rep. (CCH) Rep. No. 1772 (June 25, 1997).

38.   17 C.F.R. § 275.203A–2.

can register with the SEC regardless of the asset value of the accounts they manage. The Investment Adviser Act rule applies to newly formed investment advisers who reasonably expect that they will satisfy the thirty-state test within ninety days of registration with the SEC.[39] In 2002, the SEC amended its rules to provide that an Internet-based investment adviser that provides all of its investment advice through the Internet may register with the SEC regardless of the amount of funds under management.[40]

Investment advisers subject to the state registration requirements register electronically through the Investment Adviser Registration Depository (IARD). The registration depository is a joint effort of the SEC and the North American Securities Administrators Association (NASAA).[43] The registration depository for investment advisers became operational in March 2002 and as of August 2002, 102,000 individuals filed their investment adviser registration through IARD.[44]

§ 21.4   Prohibited Practices; Sanctions and Penalties

§ 21.4[1]   Prohibited Investment Adviser Practices

§ 21.4[1][A]   Fraudulent Practices

Section 206 of the Investment Advisers Act[1] sets out the Act's basic prohibitions beyond failure to register or fulfill the informational requirements.[2] Section 206(1) outlaws fraudulent practices.[3] Section 206(1) of the Investment Advisers Act is virtually identical to 17(a)(1) of the Securities Act of 1933[4] which, according to the Supreme Court, is violated only when there is a showing that the defendant acted with scienter.[5] Due to the similarity in statutory language, scienter is a necessary element of any violation of section 206(1) of the Investment Adviser's Act.[6] The similarity in language among the antifraud provisions also means that scienter under section 206 carries the same definition as it does under other sections: knowing or reckless conduct.[7] Section 206 of the Advisers Act covers a wide variety of conduct. Prohibited practices under section 206(1) include scalping[8] and misleading advertising.[9]

---

39.   Rule 203A–2, 17 C.F.R. § 275.203A–2.

40.   17 C.F.R. § 275.203A–2(f). *See* Exemption for Certain Investment Advisers Operating Through the Internet, Inv. Adv. Act Rel. No. IA–2091, 67 Fed. Reg. 77620–01, 2002 WL 31827219 (SEC Dec. 18, 2002).

43.   The IARD system is operated by the NASD as a counterpart to the NASD's Central Registration Depository (CRD) that it uses for broker-dealer registration.

44.   Letter from Joseph Borg, NASAA President to Harvey Pitt, SEC Chairman (Aug. 21, 2002), http://www.nasaa.org/nasaa/Files/File_Uploads/IARDLetter.37492–74525.pdf.

§ 21.4

1.   15 U.S.C.A. § 80b–6.

2.   Section 203 makes it unlawful for a non-exempt adviser to fail to register; section 207 prohibits material misstatements in required filings. 15 U.S.C.A. §§ 80b–3, 80b–7.

3.   15 U.S.C.A. § 80b–6(1) (prohibiting "any device, scheme or artifice to defraud any client or prospective client").

4.   15 U.S.C.A. § 77q(a)(1).

5.   Aaron v. SEC, 446 U.S. 680, 100 S.Ct. 1945, 64 L.Ed.2d 611 (1980).

6.   SEC v. Steadman, 967 F.2d 636 (D.C.Cir.1992).

7.   *See* Vernazza v. SEC, 327 F.3d 851 (9th Cir.2003).

8.   The Supreme Court has held that scalping (recommending securities after they have been purchased) constitutes a violation of section 206(1). SEC v. Capital Gains Research Bureau, Inc., 375 U.S. 180, 84 S.Ct. 275, 11 L.Ed.2d 237 (1963). *See also* Courtland v. Walston & Co., 340 F.Supp. 1076 (S.D.N.Y.1972).

9.   *E.g.*, SEC v. C.R. Richmond & Co., 565 F.2d 1101 (9th Cir.1977).

The Act specifically outlaws aiding and abetting as well as primary viola-tions.[10] This is significant in light of the Supreme Court's ruling that aiding and abetting liability may not be implied from the primary prohibitions of the securities laws.[11]

Section 206 also prohibits excessive trading,[12] undisclosed conflicts of interest,[13] and splitting fees with persons not registered under the Act.[14] In addition to fraud, the Act also prohibits conduct that *"operates* as a fraud or deceit upon any client or prospective client."[15] Presumably, scienter is not an element of such a violation.[16]

Section 206(3) of the Investment Adviser's Act prohibits an investment adviser from acting as a principal in a transaction with a client without disclosure and the client's consent.[17] Similarly, where the adviser represents both parties to a transaction, there must be full written disclosure and the clients' written consent must be obtained.[18] These provisions do not apply to broker-dealers giving investment advice as part of their brokerage services.[19]

Following the pattern of section 10(b) of the 1934 Exchange Act,[20] section 206(4) of the Advisers Act[21] prohibits "fraudulent, deceptive, or manipulative" acts or practices as defined by SEC rules. Investment Adviser Act Rule 206(4)–1[22] governs adviser advertising and, as noted above, prohibits certain types of advertising. In addition to forbidding material misstatements general-ly,[23] the SEC also prohibits the commingling of clients' funds and requires separate accounts and adequate record-keeping.[24] When funds or securities are held by the adviser, they must be kept in custodial accounts and the client is

10. *See, e.g.,* In the Matter of Seaboard Investment Advisers, Inc., [1994–1995 Transfer Binder] Fed. Sec. L. Rep. (CCH) ¶ 85,419 (SEC 1994).

11. Central Bank of Denver v. First Interstate Bank of Denver, 511 U.S. 164, 114 S.Ct. 1439, 128 L.Ed.2d 119 (1994), which is discussed in § 12.25 *supra.*

12. *E.g.,* In the Matter of Shearson, Hammill & Co., 42 S.E.C. 811 (SEC 1965).

13. *See, e.g.,* In the Matter of Patrick Clements d/b/a Patrick Clements & Associates, 42 S.E.C. 373 (SEC 1964).

14. Rhodes, King, Ruman & Farber, [1972–73 Transfer Binder] Fed.Sec.L.Rep. (CCH) ¶ 79,-121 (SEC 1972) (splitting fees with attorney).

15. 15 U.S.C.A. § 80b–206(2).

16. *See* Sheldon Co. Profit Sharing Plan and Trust v. Smith, 828 F.Supp. 1262, 1284 (W.D.Mich.1993). *Cf.* Aaron v. SEC, 446 U.S. 680, 100 S.Ct. 1945, 64 L.Ed.2d 611 (1980) (not requiring scienter under sections 17(a)(2), (3) of the 1933 Act, 15 U.S.C.A. § 77q(a)(2), (3)). *See* §§ 10.3, 12.8 *supra.*

17. 15 U.S.C.A. § 80b–6(3).

18. 17 C.F.R. § 275.206(3)–2. These are known as "agency cross transactions."

19. 15 U.S.C.A. § 80b–6(3). Broker-dealers must disclose principal status under Exchange Act Rule 10b–10, 17 C.F.R. § 240.10b–10.

20. 15 U.S.C.A. § 78j(b). An investment adviser is a fiduciary for the purposes of determining liability under Rule 10b–5. Laird v. Integrated Resources, Inc., 897 F.2d 826 (5th Cir.1990).

21. 15 U.S.C.A. § 80b–6(4). Section 206(4) applies only to advisory contracts and not to collateral agreements. *See* Paul S. Mullin & Associates, Inc. v. Bassett, 632 F.Supp. 532 (D.Del.1986).

22. 17 C.F.R. § 275.206(4)–1.

23. *See* 15 U.S.C.A. § 80b–6(1).

24. 17 C.F.R. § 275.206(4)–2.

entitled to receive an itemized statement at least once every three months.[25] In addition, all such funds must be subjected to annual inspection and certification by an independent public accountant.[26]

In what could have become an extremely significant development, the SEC proposed a rule that would expressly prohibit an investment adviser from making recommendations of securities that are unsuitable for his or her clients.[27] However, that rule was never adopted. As such, the only formal suitability requirement is the one that is recognized with regard to broker-dealer recommendations.[28] Nevertheless, the Commission has taken the position that the antifraud provisions of the Investment Advisers Act can be used to enforce a suitability requirement.[29] As is the case with broker-dealers, investment advisers owed their customers a duty to obtain the best execution in transactions directed by the adviser.[31] This means that an investment adviser should "periodically and systematically" evaluate the execution they are receiving for their clients.[32]

§ 21.4[1][B] Fraudulent Advertising

Investment Adviser Act Rule 206(4)–1[33] prohibits certain types of advertisements which are deceptive or fraudulent within the meaning of section 206. The rule prohibits (1) testimonials concerning the adviser's services,[35] (2) reference to selected past recommendations,[36] (3) the use of any graphs or charts without explaining the limitations on such charting methods,[37] (4) offering free services with hidden charges,[38] and (5) the making of "any untrue statement of a material fact, or which is otherwise false or misleading."[39]

Related to the hidden charges is the question of disclosing mark-ups in connections with securities transactions. Nondisclosure of mark-ups which

---

25.   17 C.F.R. § 275.206(4)–2(a)(2), (4).

26.   17 C.F.R. § 275.206(4)–2(a)(5).

27.   Inv. Adv. Act Rel. No. IA–1406, [1993–1994 Transfer Binder] Fed. Sec. L. Rep. (CCH) ¶ 85,327 (SEC March 16, 1994). *See also, e.g.,* MLC Limited, 1997 WL 408759 n. 2 (SEC No Action Letter July 21, 1997).

28.   *See* § 14.16 *supra.*

29.   MLC Limited, 1997 WL 408759 n. 2 (SEC No Action Letter July 21, 1997).

31.   *See, e.g.,* In the Matter of Portfolio Advisory Services, Inv. Adv. Act Rel. No. IA—2038, 2002 WL 1343823 (SEC June 20, 2002).

32.   In the Matter of Portfolio Advisory Services, Inv. Adv. Act Rel. No. IA—2038, 2002 WL 1343823 (SEC June 20, 2002), relying on Securities; Brokerage and Research Services, Sec. Exch. Act Rel. No. 34–23170, 35 S.E.C. Docket 703, 1986 WL 630442 (SEC April 23, 1986).

33.   17 C.F.R. § 275.206(4)–1.

35.   17 C.F.R. § 275.206(4)–1(a)(1). *See, e.g.,* Cambiar Investors, Inc., 1997 WL 528245 (SEC No Action Letter Aug. 28, 1997) (supplying list of clients' names did not violate rule prohibiting testimonials in advertising).

36.   17 C.F.R. § 275.206(4)–1(a)(2). The adviser may provide a list of *all* recommendations within the past year, describing the price at the time of recommendation and the current price. There must also be the following cautionary legend: "it shall not be assumed that recommendations made in the future will be profitable or will equal the performance of the securities in this list." *Id.*

37.   17 C.F.R. § 275.206(4)–1(a)(3).

38.   17 C.F.R. § 275.206(4)–1(a)(4).

39.   17 C.F.R. § 275.206(4)–1(a)(5).

allegedly were excessive violates the antifraud provisions of the securities laws.[40]

As discussed in the preceding chapter of this treatise, investment companies are subject to specific rules concerning presentation of historical performance data.[41] In contrast, there were no comparable formal rules under the Investment Adviser's Act. Formerly, the Commission took the position that it was *per se* materially misleading for an investment adviser to publish performance data without reflecting the actual fees charged to the accounts whose performance was summarized.[42] However, in 1996, the Commission reversed this policy by announcing that an adviser could use "model" fees, provided the adviser maintain a record of the way in which the model fee was calculated.[43] Also, as discussed in a later section, investment advisers can have a performance-based fee structure for qualified clients and accounts.[44]

In addition to section 206's prohibitions against fraudulent conduct, section 208 sets out general prohibitions.[45] An adviser can advertise his registered status but may not imply any governmental approval of his activities.[46] It is unlawful for registered advisers to describe themselves as "investment counsel" unless that is their principal business.[47] It is also unlawful to do indirectly any act prohibited by the statute.[48]

§ 21.4[1][C] Limitations on Cash Referral Fees

In its cash referral fee rule, the Commission limits payments by the adviser for client solicitation.[49] Such fees may be paid to others by advisers rendering impersonal investment advice, but must be pursuant to a written agreement, under which they can be paid only after a client has been informed of the fee arrangements and cannot be paid to persons who have run afoul of the securities acts and other "bad boy" provisions.[50] The SEC has been willing to waive these bad actor disqualifications for paid solicitors so long as the conduct in the past did not result in conduct that would disqualify the solicitor from serving as a registered investment adviser.

A correlative problem occurs when investment advisers divert business to brokers in exchange for client referrals. Thus, for example, when an adviser agrees to use a broker's services in exchange for client referrals, the advisory

---

40. *See* SEC v. Rauscher Pierce Refsnes, Inc., 17 F.Supp.2d 985 (D.Ariz.1998). *See* § 14.14 *supra.*

41. Investment company advertising is discussed in § 20.5 *supra.*

42. Securities Industry Association, 1989 WL 246550 (SEC No Action Letter Nov. 27, 1989) (model fees not permitted); Clover Capital Management, Inc., 1986 WL 67379 (S.E.C.), Fed. Sec. L. Rep. (CCH) ¶ 78,378 (SEC No Action Letter Oct. 28, 1986) (adviser cannot use performance data without deducting actual fees for the accounts in question).

43. J.P. Morgan Investment Management, Inc., 1996 WL 282573, (SEC No Action Letter May 7, 1996).

44. *See* § 21.4[D] *infra. See also* Rule 205–3, 17 C.F.R. § 275.205–3.

45. 15 U.S.C.A. § 80b–8.

46. 15 U.S.C.A. § 80b–8(a), (b).

47. 15 U.S.C.A. § 80b–8(c). *See* Inv.Adv.Act Rel. No. IA–8 (Dec. 12, 1940).

48. 15 U.S.C.A. § 80b–8(d).

49. 17 C.F.R. § 275.206(4)–3. *See* Thomas P. Lemke, Cash Referral Fees Under the Investment Advisers Act, 21 Rev.Sec. & Commodities Reg. 171 (1988).

50. 17 C.F.R. § 275.206(4)–3(a)(1).

client must be given adequate disclosure of the arrangement.[52] The advisory client is entitled to be informed of brokerage and custody options that could be less expensive than those offered pursuant to the investment adviser's referral arrangement with the broker.[53] These referral arrangements also interfere with the investment adviser's obligation to get the best execution for its customer.[54]

§ 21.4[1][D] Limitations on Advisory Fees

Section 205 of the Advisers Act[55] imposes a number of conditions on the advisory contract. Subject to exceptions permitted by the SEC, section 205(a)(1) of the Act prohibits performance-based compensation to the extent that the fee is based on a share of the capital gain or appreciation of the value of the client's account.[56] The adviser's compensation may, however, be based upon the average asset value of the client's account over a definite period of time.[57]

The rationale for the general rule prohibiting performance-based fees was to avoid encouraging the investment adviser to take undue risks with the client's funds.[58] In 1983, the Commission decided to reverse its early refusal to permit performance-based fees under any circumstances. Originally, the SEC had proposed that performance-based compensation be permitted with regard to accounts of more than one hundred and fifty thousand dollars when the customer meets subjective sophistication tests.[59] However, the Commission eventually selected more stringent standards when it adopted guidelines for performance-based adviser fees for clients having accounts that represent at least a five hundred thousand dollar value and for clients having a net worth of at least one million dollars.[60] The rule as adopted retained the financial sophistication test as well as the requirement that the client understand not only the method of compensation but also the risks presented by the performance-based formula.[61] In 1998, the Commission increased the threshold eligibility levels for performance based fees.[62]

§ 21.4[1][E] Investment Advisers and Misuse of Nonpublic Information

On occasion, investment advisers have been charged with misuse of nonpublic information. For example, during the late 1980s, there were many

---

52. *See* Jamison, Eaton & Wood, Inc., Sec. Exch. Act Rel. No. 2129, Inv. Adv. Act Rel. No. IA–2129, 2003 WL 21099127 (SEC May 15, 2003) (consent order).

53. Jamison, Eaton & Wood, Inc., Sec. Exch. Act Rel. No. 2129, Inv. Co. Act Rel. No. IA–2129, 2003 WL 21099127 (SEC May 15, 2003) (consent order).

54. *Id.*; In re Portfolio Advisory Services, LLC, Inv. Adv. Rel. No. IA–2038, 77 S.E.C. Docket 2759, 2002 WL 1343823 (SEC June 20, 2002) (consent order).

55. 15 U.S.C.A. § 80b–5. *See* § 21.1 *supra.*

56. 15 U.S.C.A. § 80b–5(a)(1).

57. 15 U.S.C.A. § 80b–5(b)(1).

58. Inv.Adv. Act Rel. No. IA–721 (May 16, 1980).

59. 15 Sec.Reg. & L.Rep. (BNA) 1019 (June 3, 1983).

60. 17 C.F.R. § 275.205–3. Investment advisers who use performance data in their advertising literature must maintain records to support the advertising claims. 17 C.F.R. § 275.204–2.

61. Rule 205–3(e), 17 C.F.R. § 275.25–3(e).

62. Rule 205–3, 17 C.F.R. § 275.205–3 (raising the eligibility requirements from clients with $1 million net worth or accounts with more than $500,000 under management to $1.5 million net worth or accounts with more than $750,000 under management).

celebrated cases involving the misuse of information relating to planned takeovers.[63] The primary weapon against the misuse of nonpublic information has been the antifraud provision contained in Rule 10b–5 of the Exchange Act.[64] The brokerage industry has attempted to deal with the misuse of information through the establishment of Chinese Walls and other procedures to monitor the flow of information within multiservice firms dealing with financial services and advice.[65]

21.4[1][F] Investment Adviser Supervisory Obligations

As is the case with securities broker-dealers firms,[72] investment advisers are under an obligation to supervise their personnel.[73] In addition, in 2004 the SEC adopted rules requiring investment advisers to adopt and enforce codes of ethics applicable to persons they supervise.[74] The SEC rules also require investment advisers to report violations of their codes of ethics. Thus, an investment adviser's code of ethics must require supervised persons to report, promptly, any violations of the adviser's code of ethics to the firm's chief compliance officer or to other designated persons.

§ 21.4[2] Absence of Implied Remedy for Fraud but Recognition of Implied Right of Rescission

The Supreme Court has held that section 206 does not give rise to implied private remedies.[77] Enforcement of section 206's prohibitions is thus limited to criminal prosecution for willful violations,[78] SEC injunctive actions,[79] and the imposition of sanctions in an administrative hearing ranging from censure to revocation of registration.[80] These are the sanctions available for all violations of the Act. The Supreme Court has recognized an implied right of rescission under section 215 of the Act,[81] which provides that contracts in violation of the Act are void.[82]

Since the section 215 remedy is rescissory, restitution under that section does not include damages for consequential losses.[83] It has also been held that the only proper parties in a section 215 claim are parties to the advisory contract.[84] Thus, for example, an investment company or mutual fund share-

---

63. *See* the discussion of insider trading in § 12.17 *supra.*

64. 17 C.F.R. § 240.10b–5.

65. *See* § 14.12 *supra.*

72. *See* §§ 14.3[7], 14.26[6][C] *supra.*

73. 15 U.S.C.A. § 80b–3.

74. Inv. Adv. Act Rule 204A–1, 17 C.F.R. § 280.204A–1. *See also* Inv. Co. Act Rule 17j–1, 17 C.F.R. § 270.17j–1; Inv. Adv. Act Rule 204–2, 17 C.F.R. § 280.204–2.

77. Transamerica Mortgage Advisors, Inc. v. Lewis, 444 U.S. 11, 100 S.Ct. 242, 62 L.Ed.2d 146 (1979). *See also, e.g.,* Frank Russell Co. v. Wellington Management Co., 154 F.3d 97 (3d Cir.1998) (no private remedy under section 206 of the Advisers Act).

See also, e.g., Rifkin v. Bear Stearns & Co., Inc., 248 F.3d 628 (7th Cir.2001) (taxpayers who did not purchase bonds did not have standing to bring suit under the Investment Advisers Act).

78. 15 U.S.C.A. § 80b–17.

79. 15 U.S.C.A. § 80b–9(e). *See* § 16.2 *supra.*

80. 15 U.S.C.A. § 80b–12. *See also* 15 U.S.C.A. § 80b–3(e).

81. 15 U.S.C.A. § 80b–15.

82. Transamerica Mortgage Advisors, Inc. v. Lewis, 444 U.S. 11, 100 S.Ct. 242, 62 L.Ed.2d 146 (1979).

83. Washington v. Baenziger, 656 F.Supp. 1176 (N.D.Cal.1987).

84. *See Id.*

holder may not sue the adviser directly for rescission since the fund, not the shareholder is a party to the contract.[86]

---

86. Shahidi v. Merrill Lynch, Pierce, Fenner & Smith, Inc., 2003 WL 21488228, [2003–2004 Transfer Binder] Fed. Sec. L. Rep. (CCH) ¶ 92,431 (M.D. Fla. 2003).

Chapter 22

SPECIAL PROBLEMS AND OVERVIEW OF RELATED LAWS

Table of Sections

---

§ 22.1 Related Laws—Introduction

The preceding chapters are devoted primarily to the federal securities laws. In addition to the seven federal securities acts that are discussed in the preceding chapters, there are a number of other laws—both federal and state laws—that in some major respects overlap with the federal securities laws. Many of those laws are referred to in the earlier chapters. This chapter provides a summary of the most significant of these related laws. After providing an overview of the relationship of the federal securities law to state law and to other federal laws, this chapter discusses some of the more prominent federal laws that have a significant relationship to securities regulation.

§ 22.1[1] Relationship of Federal Securities Law to State Law and How the Sarbanes–Oxley Act Altered the Balance

§ 22.1[1][A] Differing Coverage of State Corporate Law and Federal Securities Law

As a general proposition, federal securities law is premised on a system of full disclosure rather than scrutinize the merits of securities that are offered and sold. The SEC does not review the substance of the investment. Instead, the SEC is charged with ensuring that investors have sufficient information upon which to make an investment decision. As discussed in chapter 8 of this treatise, this is in contrast to the state securities laws which focus not only on disclosure, but may also regulate the merits or fairness of securities offered within the state.[3] State securities laws are supplemented in many respects by

---

§ 22.1

3. *See* the discussion of the approaches of state and federal securities laws in § 1.2 *supra*.

state corporate laws. State corporate laws focus on corporate formation, operation, and corporate governance. Corporate governance includes defining the respective roles of shareholders, officers, and directors. Among other things, state corporate law provides the rules governing shareholder voting rights, although there are the federal disclosure requirements that are discussed earlier in this treatise.[4] State law also establishes corporate officers' and directors' duty of care and loyalty[5] and defines what constitutes mismanagement.[6] These are areas that the federal securities laws have traditionally avoided.[7] As discussed below, this changed in 2002.

§ 22.1[1][B] The Sarbanes–Oxley Act of 2002

There was a departure from the traditional dichotomy of state corporate law and federal securities law in 2002 when Congress enacted the Sarbanes–Oxley Act.[8] The Sarbanes–Oxley Act, which is discussed throughout this treatise where applicable,[9] adopted comprehensive amendments to the federal securities laws and also adopted some notable corporate governance reforms in response to various corporate scandals including Enron and Worldcom. These reforms placed significant new compliance obligations on public companies.[10] Many of the Sarbanes–Oxley provisions are disclosure requirements combined with enhanced criminal penalties for securities law violations, but the clear thrust of these amendments enhancing disclosure and accountability was to improve corporate governance.

From a long-term perspective, perhaps the most significant aspect of Sarbanes–Oxley is not the enhanced disclosure requirements or criminal penalties, but rather that the Sarbanes–Oxley Act goes further than any of the earlier federal securities laws and amendments in dealing directly with corporate governance—an area that had traditionally been reserved to the states.[11] For example, the Sarbanes–Oxley Act addressed accounting and auditing reforms, the role of public corporations' audit committees,[12] heightened disclosure obligations,[13] increased accountability of executive officers[14] and corporate attorneys,[15] in addition to increased criminal penalties for

---

4. The federal proxy rules are discussed in chapter 10 *supra*.

5. *See e.g.,* § 11.11 *supra* discussing the states' role in regulating management's responses to takeover attempts. *See also, e.g.,* §§ 11.12–11.13 *supra* discussing the role of state tender offer legislation.

6. *See* § 12.20 *supra* for a discussion of the federal securities laws' fraud provisions' inability to address matters of corporate mismanagement.

7. *See, e.g.,* the discussion of state tender offer statutes and their constitutionality in §§ 11.11–11.13 *supra*.

8. Sarbanes–Oxley Act of 2002, Pub. Law 107–204 (July 30, 2002). *See* Senate Report No. 107–205 (July 3, 2002).

9. For a brief summary of the coverage of Sarbanes–Oxley, *see* § 1.2[3][D][3] *supra*.

10. *See, e.g.,* Dan Roberts, GE Says it Faces $30m Bill for Governance, Financial Times 1B (April 29, 2004).

11. *See, e.g.,* the discussion of the inability to use SEC antifraud rules to regulate corporate mismanagement in § 12.20 *supra*.

12. *See* § 9.6 *supra*.

13. *See* chapter 9 *supra*.

14. *See* § 9.3[2][A] *supra*.

15. Sarbanes–Oxley Act of 2002, Pub. Law 107–204 § 307 (July 30, 2002), which mandates SEC rulemaking to define what constitutes proper representation by attorneys practicing before the SEC. The rules must require, *inter alia*, that once an attorney has evidence of serious corporate wrongdoing, he or she must climb the corporate ladder, possibly to the audit committee

violations of the securities laws. The Sarbanes–Oxley Act created an accounting oversight board to oversee the accounting profession to police the self-regulatory system that previously existed.[16] The Sarbanes–Oxley Act also addressed auditor independence requirements.[17]

The Sarbanes–Oxley Act may prove to be more than a one-time reaction to major corporate scandals. It could be the beginning of a sea change by focusing federal law more and more on corporate governance and other areas of corporate law that have traditionally been left to the states.

§ 22.1[2] Related Federal Regulatory Laws—Overview

There are a number of related federal laws that affect securities law practitioners and their clients. There may be SEC involvement in some of these related areas. For certain regulated industries, the securities of regulated issuers are subject to other federal administrative agencies.[18] For example, the Comptroller of the Currency has jurisdiction over the distribution of securities issued by national banks,[19] although securities issued by bank holding companies are subject to SEC jurisdiction. A similar arrangement exists with regard to securities of savings and loan associations, that are subject to regulation by the Office of Thrift Supervision (formerly the Federal Home Loan Bank Board).[20] Other issuers of securities that are subject to the jurisdiction of additional federal regulatory agencies include interstate railroads and common carriers subject to the jurisdiction of the Interstate Commerce Commission[21] and electric utility companies not subject to state regulation but subject to supervision by the Secretary of Energy.[22]

The SEC and the self regulatory organizations under its oversight authority provide pervasive regulation of broker-dealers and the securities markets generally.[23] Over the years various questions have arisen concerning the effect of the SEC's regulatory and self regulatory oversight authority on the impact of the antitrust laws. When the SEC directly, or the self regulatory organizations under the direct oversight and supervision of the SEC, regulate and thereby approve of the conduct in question, this regulation under the Securities Exchange Act will operate as an implied repeal of the antitrust laws.[24] Not all SEC regulation of conduct in the securities markets has a similar preemptive effect on the antitrust laws. For example, conduct that is not expressly permitted by SEC Rule, self regulatory rule, or general regulations, in appropriate cases, may be scrutinized under the antitrust laws.[25]

---

and to the board of directors, until satisfied that the problem has been attended to. *See* § 9.8 *supra.*

   16.   Sarbanes–Oxley Act of 2002, Pub. Law 107–204 tit. I (July 30, 2002). *See* § 9.6 *supra.*

   17.   Sarbanes–Oxley Act of 2002, Pub. Law 107–204 tit. II (July 30, 2002).

   18.   *See* Harry G. Henn & John R. Alexander, Laws of Corporations § 304 (3d ed. 1983).

   19.   12 U.S.C.A. §§ 51 *et seq.*

   20.   12 U.S.C.A. §§ 1464 *et seq.*

   21.   49 U.S.C.A. § 11301.

   22.   42 U.S.C.A. § 7151(b); 16 U.S.C.A. § 824c.

   23.   *See* chapter 14 *supra.*

   24.   *See* United States v. NASD, 422 U.S. 694, 95 S.Ct. 2427, 45 L.Ed.2d 486 (1975); Gordon v. New York Stock Exchange, Inc., 422 U.S. 659, 95 S.Ct. 2598, 45 L.Ed.2d 463 (1975). *See also, e.g.,* Silver v. New York Stock Exchange, 373 U.S. 341, 83 S.Ct. 1246, 10 L.Ed.2d 389 (1963). The impact of the antitrust laws generally is discussed in § 14.1[9] *supra.*

   25.   *See* In re Nasdaq Market–Makers Antitrust Litigation, 1999 WL 395407 (S.D.N.Y.1999); In re Nasdaq Market–Makers Antitrust Litigation, 184 F.R.D. 506 (S.D.N.Y.1999); Court Ap-

For securities and issuers that are subject to SEC regulation, there are a number of other related federal statutes that may come into play in addition to the federal securities laws. The more important of these laws are taken up in the sections that follow. First, the Foreign Corrupt Practices Act of 1977 was enacted in response to widespread concern over the activities of domestic companies in their dealings abroad.[26] That act has implications that go beyond foreign activities and corrupt practices.

The Racketeer Influenced and Corrupt Organizations Act (RICO) was enacted in order to make for more efficient law enforcement with regard to organized crime and racketeering activities.[27] RICO not only includes certain types of securities fraud with regard to its criminal penalties, it also includes civil actions for a fraud-based RICO violation resulting in the award of treble damages.[28]

The federal Mail Fraud Act[29] and the federal Wire Fraud Act[30] can be potent weapons in the enforcement of the securities law. For example, while the Supreme Court was equally divided over criminal convictions under the securities laws for trading on confidential information, the Court was unanimous that the conduct was violative of the Mail Fraud Act.[31]

The federal money laundering laws have for a long time been useful in tracking organized crime activities. As discussed later in this chapter,[32] money laundering laws necessarily impose regulatory requirements on financial services firms, including securities broker-dealers. There was increased emphasis on the money laundering laws in the wake of various terrorist attacks.

During the 1960s there was a rash of stock brokerage firm bankruptcies. In response to the need for customer protection, Congress enacted the Securities Investor Protection Act of 1970.[33] As a result of that Act, the Securities Investor Protection Corporation ("SIPC") helps safeguard customer interests in cases of broker-dealer insolvency. The Securities Investor Protection Act is considered in an earlier section of this treatise.[34]

Perhaps the hottest topic in securities regulation at the end of the twentieth century was the increasing competition between banking and more traditional securities industries. Although the Glass–Steagall Act of 1933[35] prohibited commercial and savings banks from engaging directly in various aspects of investment banking, the line between investment banking and

proves Distribution of Settlement in Nasdaq Market–Makers Antitrust Litigation, 32 Sec. Reg. & L. Rep. (BNA) 148 (Feb. 7, 2000). *See* Peterson v. Philadelphia Stock Exchange, 717 F.Supp. 332 (E.D.Pa.1989).

26. Pub.L. 95–213, 95th Cong., 1st Sess. (1977). *See* § 22.2 *infra.*

27. Pub.L. No. 91–452, 84 Stat. 922 (1970).

28. 15 U.S.C.A. § 1964(c). *See* § 22.3 *infra.*

29. 18 U.S.C.A. § 1341.

30. 18 U.S.C.A. § 1343.

31. Carpenter v. United States, 484 U.S. 19, 108 S.Ct. 316, 98 L.Ed.2d 275 (1987). *See* Theodore A. Levine, Arthur F. Mathews & W. Hardy Callcott, 21 Rev.Sec. & Commod.Reg. 55 (1988). Insider trading is discussed in § 12.17 *supra.* The mail and wire fraud statutes are discussed in § 22.4 *infra.*

32. *See* § 22.5 *infra.*

33. Codified in 15 U.S.C.A. §§ 78aaa–78*lll.*

34. *See* § 14.24 *supra.*

35. The Banking Act of 1933, ch. 89, 48 Stat. 184 (1933), codified in various sections of 12 U.S.C.A.

commercial banking became increasingly blurred over time.[36] The developing competition between commercial and investment banking was highlighted not only by each offering competing services, but also by bank acquisition of stock brokerage operations and vice versa. In addition to the increased competition between the two industries, the SEC and various bank regulatory agencies, including the Comptroller of the Currency, were constantly engaged in jurisdictional disputes. In 1999, Congress eliminated the separation of commercial and investment activities that had been imposed by the Glass–Steagall Act.[37]

One other major area of jurisdictional dispute involves the regulation of commodities futures and commodities options. In 2000, Congress revamped regulation under the Commodity Exchange Act with the amendments brought in by the Commodity Futures Modernization Act of 2000.[42] This legislation brought with it a new regulatory framework for regulating derivative investments.

Another major legislative reform that has had a profound change on the regulatory landscape is the Sarbanes–Oxley Act.[43]

§ 22.2   The Foreign Corrupt Practices Act

In 1977, Congress enacted the Foreign Corrupt Practices Act amendments to the Securities Exchange Act of 1934.[1] These amendments were inspired by concerns over foreign kickbacks and other corrupt practices taking place abroad; in many cases the conduct, although illegal if it took place here, may not have been frowned upon in other countries.[3] The reach of the Foreign Corrupt Practices Act is not limited to domestic companies.[4] The Foreign Corrupt Practices Act contains both substantive prohibitions against these acts,[5] as well as disclosure provisions and accounting controls that are limited neither to foreign acts nor corrupt practices.[6]

The Foreign Corrupt Practices Act's internal controls and accounting requirements sparked a great deal of controversy.[7] For a number of years, the SEC did not take as broad a view of the Foreign Corrupt Practices Act as it once did. The SEC continues to vigorously enforce the disclosure provisions of Foreign Corrupt Practices Act and those provisions cover a variety of matters.

---

36. *See* § 22.6 *infra.*

37. The Banking Act of 1933, Ch. 89, 48 Stat. 184 (1933), codified in various sections of 12 U.S.C.A. (1999) *See* in particular 12 U.S.C.A. §§ 24, 378(a) (1999). The Glass–Steagall Act was repealed by Pub. Law. 106–102, 1999 U.S.C.C.A.N. (113 Stat.) 1338. *See generally* Symposium, 4 N.C. Banking Inst. 1 (2000); Michael K. O'Neal, Summary and Analysis of the Gramm–Leach–Bliley Act, 28 Sec. Reg. L.J. 95 (2000).

42. Pub. Law No. 106–554, 114 Stat. 2763 (Dec. 21, 2000).

43. Sarbanes–Oxley Act of 2002, Pub. Law 107–204 (July 30, 2002). *See* Senate Report No. 107–205 (July 3, 2002). *See* § 21.1[B] *supra.*

§ 22.2

1. Pub.L. 95–213, 95th Cong., 1st Sess., 91 Stat. 1494 (1977), codified in 15 U.S.C.A. §§ 78m(b), 78dd–1, 78dd–2. The 1977 amendments also contain amendments to the 1934 Act reporting requirements (The Domestic and Foreign Investment Improved Disclosure Act of 1977).

3. S.Rep. No. 114, 95th Cong., 1st Sess. 1977.

4. *See, e.g.,* Robert A. Bassett, Canadian Companies Beware: the U.S. Foreign Corrupt Practices Act Applies to You!, 36 Alberta L. Rev. 455(1998).

5. 15 U.S.C.A. §§ 78dd–1, 78dd–2.

6. 15 U.S.C.A. § 78m(b).

7. *See* Sec.Exch. Act Rel. No. 34–17500 (Jan. 29, 1981).

§ 22.2[1] Substantive Prohibitions of the Foreign Corrupt Practices Act

Section 30A of the Exchange Act[13] contains the substantive provisions of the Foreign Corrupt Practices Act which applies to issuers subject to the Exchange Act's registration and periodic reporting requirements[14] and prohibits those companies from engaging in specified corrupt practices. For example, the Act makes it unlawful to use an instrumentality of interstate commerce "corruptly in furtherance of an offer, payment, promise to pay, or authorization of the payment of any money, or offer, gift, promise to give, or authorization of the giving of anything of value to (1) any foreign official"[15] and, *inter alia,* for any person to participate in diverting funds to such persons for the purposes of assisting the issuer "in obtaining or retaining business."[16] The Act prohibits both corrupt giving and offering anything of value with the purpose of improper influence peddling. Specifically prohibited is a payment or offer of payment designed to influence an official act or decision.[17] The Foreign Corrupt Practices Act prohibits a payment or offer of payment designed to induce someone to act or fail to act in such a way as to violate that person's lawful duty.[18] The Act prohibits a payment or offer of payment designed to induce someone to influence a foreign government to act in a certain way.[19] The Act also prohibits the payment or offering of a payment designed to secure any improper advantage in order to obtain, retain, or direct business to any person.[20]

Improper payments to foreign officials can include payment of travel and entertainment expenses that are paid as a quid pro quo for special favors.[21] Section 104 of the Foreign Corrupt Practices Act[22] applies similar prohibitions to any "domestic concern"[23] other than an issuer subject to section 30A. Penalties for violation of section 104's anti-bribery provisions of the Foreign

---

13. 15 U.S.C.A. § 78dd–1.

14. 15 U.S.C.A. §§ 78*l*, 78m(a), 78*o*(d). *See* §§ 9.2, 9.3 *supra.* The Act's prohibitions are thus not limited to registered securities but also to securities subject to section 15(d)'s periodic reporting requirements.

15. 15 U.S.C.A. § 78dd–1(a)(1).

16. 15 U.S.C.A. § 78dd–1.

17. 15 U.S.C.A. § 78dd–1.

18. *Id.*

19. *Id.*

20. *Id.*

21. United States v. Metcalf & Eddy, No. 1:99CV125666 (D. Mass. Filed Dec. 14, 1999) (permanent injunction and $400,000 civil penalties for travel and entertainment expense payments to foreign officials); Foreign Corrupt Practices Act Rev. Proc. Rel. Nos. 82–01 (Jan. 27, 1982), 83–2 (July 26, 1983), 83–3 (July 26, 1983), 85–1 *http://www.usdoj.gov.criminal/fraud/fcps/revindx.htm*; The Foreign Trade Practices Act: Hearings on H.R. 2157 Before the Subcomm. On International Economic Policy and Trade of the House Comm. On Foreign Affairs, 98th Cong. 126 (1983) (statement of Jonathan C. Rose, Assistant Attorney General).

22. 15 U.S.C.A. § 78dd–2.

23. *See* 15 U.S.C.A. § 78dd–2(h):

The term "domestic concern" means (A) any individual who is a citizen, national, or resident of the United States; and (B) any corporation, partnership, association, joint-stock company, business trust, unincorporated organization, or sole proprietorship which has its principal place of business in the United States, or which is organized under the laws of a State of the United States or a territory, possession, or commonwealth of the United States.

Corrupt Practices Act include fines of up to two million dollars against a domestic concern other than an individual.[24]

§ 22.2[2] Internal Controls and Disclosure Obligations

Sections 30A of the Exchange Act and section 104 of the Foreign Corrupt Practices Act zero in directly on the types of conduct that led to the Act's passage—corrupt practices taking place in foreign countries. In contrast, the amendments to section 13 of the Exchange Act[31] have a much broader reach. As noted above, these disclosure and reporting requirements are not limited to corrupt practices and do not require involvement in a foreign country. The Foreign Corrupt Practices Act imposed two requirements on issuers subject to the periodic reporting requirements of sections 13(a) and 15(d) of the Exchange Act.[32] The issuer must make more accurate disclosure of corporate expenditures and also must establish a system of internal controls to monitor expenditures of corporate funds. The theory behind section 13(b) was that by imposing more stringent accounting methods, corporate management would have tighter controls on corporate expenditures and thus be able to prevent the types of conduct prohibited by sections 30A of the Exchange Act and section 104 of the Foreign Corrupt Practices Act.

Section 13(b)(1) of the Exchange Act empowers the Commission to prescribe reports for information required by section 13(b)(2).[37] At one time the Commission proposed extensive disclosure requirements that would have had far-reaching effects upon corporate governance.[38] These proposals raised tremendous controversy. These proposals were not adopted, and there are currently two much less controversial rules that have been promulgated and adopted under section 13(b). Rule 13b2–1 prohibits falsification of records required by section 13(b)(2)(A).[39] Rule 13b2–2 prohibits officers and directors from making material misstatements or omissions of fact in connection with any audit or preparation of reports pursuant to section 13(b)(2).[40]

The SEC views the basic thrust of these provisions of the Foreign Corrupt Practices Act as requiring more effective accounting controls,[41] and thus has backed away from more stringent corporate governance requirements.

As noted above, the Sarbanes–Oxley Act of 2002[53] enhanced the independence of audit committees and the auditors themselves. Sarbanes–Oxley also established a requirement that company filings be personally certified by the CEO and CFO.[54] These certifications include the accuracy of the disclosures relating to a company's internal controls and thus reinforce the requirements of the section 13(b)(2) disclosures.

---

24. 15 U.S.C.A. § 78dd–2(g)(1)(A). Criminal penalties for corporations violating the accounting provisions (*see* § 22.2[2] *infra*) can be as high as two-and-one-half million dollars.

31. 15 U.S.C.A. § 78m. The reporting requirements generally are discussed in § 9.3 *supra*.

32. 15 U.S.C.A. §§ 78m(a), 78o(d).

37. 15 U.S.C.A. § 78m(b)(1).

38. Sec.Exch.Act Rel. No. 34–15772 (April 30, 1979).

39. 17 C.F.R. § 240.13b2–1.

40. 17 C.F.R. § 240.13b2–2.

41. Sec.Exch.Act Rel. No. 34–17500 (Jan. 29, 1981) ("The primary thrust of the Act's accounting provisions, in short, was to require those public companies which lacked effective internal controls or tolerated unreliable recordkeeping to comply with the standards of their better managed peers. *That* is the context in which these provisions should be construed").

53. Pub. Law No. 106–554, 114 Stat. 2763 (Dec. 21, 2000).

54. 15 U.S.C.A. § 7241.

§ 22.3 Securities Fraud and the Racketeer Influenced and Corrupt Organizations Act (RICO)

§ 22.3[1] RICO: An Overview

In 1973, Congress passed the Racketeer Influenced and Corrupt Organizations Act,[1] which is more commonly known as RICO. A number of states have enacted parallel legislation that has come to be known as "little RICO" statutes. Although as the name indicates, the federal legislation was adopted with the express purpose of eradicating organized crime,[3] the statute has a broader reach, at least as both traditionally and currently interpreted by most courts.

§ 22.3[2] RICO Predicate Acts

The RICO statute expressly includes securities fraud in its delineation of predicate acts and violations that constitute racketeering activities.[5] Formerly, the RICO Act provided for treble damages in most such cases, but as a result of the Private Securities Litigation Reform Act of 1995, the private remedy[7] has been significantly restricted.[8] Once viewed as an impressive weapon in enforcing the federal securities laws, RICO's impact has been severely limited in securities cases, even though it remains broadly available in criminal prosecutions as well as in private suits based on other types of fraud.

§ 22.6 The Intertwining of Financial Services: Commercial Banks, Investment Banking, and Investment Services

§ 22.6[1] Repeal of Former Barriers to Intertwining of Financial Services

In 1933, Congress enacted the Glass–Steagall Act[1] in order to erect a barrier between commercial banking and investment banking in this country. In 1999, Congress repealed the structural impediments that were formerly imposed by the Glass–Steagall Act. The barriers that once existed between commercial banking, insurance, and investment banking activities have been eliminated. This means that securities activities of banks and other financial institutions are subject to SEC jurisdiction. Banking activities are regulated by the appropriate federal or state banking agency. Insurance activities are regulated by state insurance regulators.[3] There is a transitional period during which the appropriate regulatory responsibility will be assigned to the various federal regulators. It seems clear, however, that securities-related activities

---

§ 22.3

1. Pub.L. No. 91–452, 84 Stat. 922 (1970), codified in 18 U.S.C.A. §§ 1961–1968.

3. Pub.L. No. 91–452, 84 Stat. 922, 923 (1970).

5. 18 U.S.C.A. § 1961(1) contains the complete list of acts constituting racketeering activities.

7. 18 U.S.C.A. § 1964(c).

8. In order to be sued in a civil RICO action for securities fraud, the defendant must have already been criminally convicted of the underlying violation. 18 U.S.C.A. § 1964(c).

§ 22.6

1. The Banking Act of 1933, Ch. 89, 48 Stat. 184 (1933), codified in various sections of 12 U.S.C.A. (1999). *See* in particular 12 U.S.C.A. §§ 24, 378(a) (1999).

3. *See generally* Lissa L. Broome & Jerry W. Markham, Banking and Insurance: Before and After the Gramm–Leach–Bliley Act, 25 J. Corp. L. 691 (2000).

will remain under the jurisdiction of the Securities and Exchange Commission.

§ 22.7 Derivatives Regulation Under the Commodity Exchange Act

§ 22.7[1] Overview of Commodities Markets and Regulation

Commodities Markets

Originally developed as a means for hedging by producers, manufacturers, and large-scale buyers of commodities, public trading in commodities futures contracts has become a major investment vehicle for many investors.[1] Futures contracts embody a promise to deliver underlying commodities at a future date that will then be sold at the previously agreed-upon price.[2] This promise of future delivery must be honored either by delivery of the underlying commodity or by purchasing an off-setting futures contract. Although the commodities laws do not impose a suitability requirement, it is a fact of reality that investments in commodities futures are suitable only for sophisticated investors who are able to bear the loss of their entire investment. The commodities markets are highly volatile and investment is usually made with ten percent payment and ninety percent credit margin, which magnifies the speculative nature of an intrinsically volatile investment. Added to the high degree of leverage are the limits on daily price movements in many commodities, the result of which can be to lock-in the investor while his or her investment tumbles.

There is wide variety in the types of publicly traded commodities contracts, providing a broad range of investment alternatives, many of which compete directly with comparable securities options. The regulation of trading in commodity futures contracts has been increasing in intensity. One byproduct has been the development of jurisdictional disputes between the Commodity Futures Trading Commission (CFTC) and the Securities and Exchange Commission.[8] The discussion that follows is designed to give a very brief overview of the increasingly complex regulation of the commodities markets.

Overlap of Securities and Commodities Markets

The Commodity Exchange Act contains a number of provisions designed to protect investors in the highly speculative and volatile commodities markets.[9] The Act generally prohibits contracts that are designed to defraud investors.[10] The Act also prohibits certain "meretricious transactions," including wash sales, cross trades, accommodation trades and fictitious sales.[11]

---

§ 22.7

1. *See generally* 1,2 Philip M. Johnson & Thomas L. Hazen, Derivatives Regulation (2004).

2. Futures trading is thus different from the securities options market, where there is no promise to deliver; instead, there is an option which may be exercised.

8. *See* § 1.5 *supra.*

9. 7 U.S.C.A. § 6a. The statute is directed, *inter alia*, to the establishment of trading or position limits, as well as to cornering the market and other abusive speculative practices. The CFTC's regulations are found in 17 C.F.R. parts 1–180.

10. 7 U.S.C.A. § 6b.

11. 7 U.S.C.A. § 6c.

From its inception, the CFTC has been in conflict with the SEC with regard to jurisdiction over conduct and transactions that could be covered by either the securities laws or the Commodity Exchange Act.[12] For example, commodities pools are subject to regulation under both the securities laws and the Commodity Exchange Act.[13] Ordinarily, a commodity futures contract is not a security.[14] However, a security will exist when the underlying commodity is itself a security[15]—but, according to one district court decision, not where the underlying commodity is a stock index.[16] Also, although the courts are in conflict, there is authority supporting the view that discretionary managed commodity accounts constitute securities.[17] There is increasing support, however, for the view that a discretionary commodities account is not a security unless there is a pooling of customers' funds.[18]

The chairmen of the SEC and CFTC reached an accord concerning their conflicts with regard to overlapping jurisdiction, but the truce was a tenuous one.[19] There were legislative proposals attempting to strike an appropriate balance in determining the respective roles for the SEC and CFTC.[20] As the securities and futures markets continued to converge, increasing regulatory coordination between the SEC and CFTC developed. In 2000, several proposals were introduced into Congress to repeal the prohibition on futures on individual stocks and other securities.[21] In September 2000, the SEC and CFTC agreed on a proposal for submission to Congress.[22] This legislation was enacted in December 2000.[23] Futures on individual securities that formerly were not permitted may be traded on securities exchanges and on registered commodities contract markets. Futures on individual stocks thus are subject to both SEC and CFTC regulation.[24]

12. Joint Explanatory Statement of the SEC and CFTC, [1980–1982 Transfer Binder] Commodities Fut.L.Rep. (CCH) ¶ 21,332 (Feb. 2, 1982).

13. See H.R.Rep. no. 565 (pt. 1) 97th Cong., 2d Sess. (1982); S.Rep. no. 384, 97th Cong., 2d Sess. (1982).

14. E.g., Silverstein v. Merrill Lynch, Pierce, Fenner & Smith, Inc., 618 F.Supp. 436 (S.D.N.Y.1985) (commodity future contract is not a security); Mechigian v. Art Capital Corp., 612 F.Supp. 1421 (S.D.N.Y.1985) (sale of artwork financed by non-recourse promissory note held not a security).

15. Abrams v. Oppenheimer Government Securities, Inc., 737 F.2d 582 (7th Cir.1984) (when the object underlying the futures contract is itself a security, the futures contract is also a security).

16. Mallen v. Merrill Lynch, Pierce, Fenner & Smith, Inc., 605 F.Supp. 1105 (N.D.Ga.1985) (stock index futures are commodities and are *not* securities); In re Federal Bank & Trust Co., Ltd. Securities Litigation, 1984 WL 2445, [1984 Transfer Binder] Fed.Sec.L.Rep. (CCH) ¶ 91,565 (D.Or.1984) (semble).

17. See Smoky Greenhaw Cotton Co. v. Merrill Lynch, Pierce, Fenner & Smith, Inc., 785 F.2d 1274 (5th Cir.1986) (taking a broad view in treating managed accounts as securities).

18. E.g., Lopez v. Dean Witter Reynolds, Inc., 805 F.2d 880 (9th Cir.1986); Point Landing, Inc. v. Omni Capital Int'l, Ltd., 795 F.2d 415 (5th Cir.1986) *affirmed on other grounds,* 484 U.S. 97, 108 S.Ct. 404, 98 L.Ed.2d 415 (1987) (CFTC has exclusive jurisdiction).

19. See, e.g., Jerry W. Markham & Don L. Horwitz, Sunset on the Commodities Futures Trading Commission: Scene II, 39 Bus.Law. 67, 72–76 (1983).

20. 7 U.S.C.A. § 16(e).

21. See 32 Fed. Sec. & L. Rep. (BNA) 647 (May 15, 2000).

22. See Single Stock Futures Would be Securities Under Agencies' Agreement for Lifting Ban, 32 Sec. Reg. & L. Rep. (BNA) 1256 (1256 (September 18, 2000).

23. Pub. Law No. 106–554, 114 Stat. 2763 (Dec. 21, 2000).

24. Id.

Overview of Commodities Regulation

Until 1974 there was very sparse regulation of commodities markets, but this was changed by the enactment of the Commodity Futures Trading Commission Act Amendments[25] to the Commodity Exchange Act.[26] The 1974 amendments created the Commodity Futures Trading Commission (CFTC) which has "pervasive" regulatory authority over the public futures markets, the brokers, and other professionals in the commodities markets. Specifically, it is unlawful for any person to act as a commodity trading adviser or commodity pool operator unless registered with the CFTC.[28] Additionally, CFTC registration requirements extend to brokers and all persons associated with futures commission merchants who solicit or accept customer orders (or persons supervising others engaged in these activities).[29] As is the case under the securities acts, brokerage firms dealing with commodities have a duty to supervise their employees to assure compliance with the Act and applicable rules of conduct.[30]

Comparable to the SEC's regulation of national securities exchanges[31] is the CFTC's power to designate any qualifying board of trade as a "contract market."[32] These contract markets not only regulate the futures contracts offered on a retail basis to the investing public, but also professional traders and brokers who must be members of a board of trade.[33] In contrast to the SEC, the CFTC has jurisdiction to adjudicate disputes between private parties. Private parties who have been injured by fraud or other Commodity Exchange Act violations by registered commodities professionals may seek reparation in administrative proceedings before the CFTC.[34] The Supreme Court has since concurred in the Commodity Futures Trading Commission's position that, in its reparations proceedings, the CFTC has the power to adjudicate counterclaims not arising under the Commodities Act but based on common law.[35]

The CFTC's reparations proceedings' administrative remedy to resolve disputes between customers and brokers is in addition to the implied private remedy that the Supreme Court subsequently recognized for violations of the Act's general antifraud proscriptions.[36] Following the Court's recognition of

---

25. Pub.L. No. 93–463, 88 Stat. 1389 (1974).

26. 7 U.S.C.A. §§ 1–25.

28. 7 U.S.C.A. § 6n.

29. 7 U.S.C.A. § 6k.

30. 7 U.S.C.A. § 13c(b) (the Act's controlling person provision by its terms is limited to enforcement actions).

31. 15 U.S.C.A. § 78f. *See* §§ 14.1, 14.3 *supra.*

32. 7 U.S.C.A. § 7 (designation of board of trade as contract market; conditions and requirements). CFTC oversight of the rules of qualified boards of trade is different from that of the SEC and national securities exchanges since the boards of trade enforce only their own rules, leaving to the CFTC the enforcement of the Act's requirements. Under the Securities Exchange Act, national securities exchanges not only enforce their own rules, but also the requirements of that Act generally. *See* § 14.3 *supra.*

Boards of trade are subject to investigation by the CFTC, and the results of such investigations are to be reported to the public. 7 U.S.C.A. § 12.

33. 7 U.S.C.A. §§ 7a, 12a. In 2000, Congress enacted two other regulatory tiers.

34. 7 U.S.C.A. § 18.

35. Commodity Futures Trading Commission v. Schor, 478 U.S. 833, 106 S.Ct. 3245, 92 L.Ed.2d 675 (1986).

36. Merrill Lynch, Pierce, Fenner & Smith, Inc. v. Curran, 456 U.S. 353, 102 S.Ct. 1825, 72 L.Ed.2d 182 (1982).

implied remedies, Congress amended the Commodity Exchange Act to provide express private remedies.[37]

Not every breach of a commodities broker's fiduciary duty will give rise to a remedy under the Act, as the plaintiff must be able to show intentional or reckless misconduct.[38]

Also, like the SEC, the Commodity Futures Trading Commission has cease and desist power with regard to registered professionals.[45] The CFTC also has enforcement powers in the courts.[46] In addition to regulation of contract markets, other registered entities, and commodities professionals, the CFTC has oversight responsibilities with respect to registered futures associations.[47]

The Commodity Exchange Act prohibits public futures transactions other than through a member of a board of trade that is registered as a "contract market."[48] Publicly traded futures and commodities options contracts formerly could be traded only through designated contract markets registered with the Commodity Futures Trading Commission.[49] Traditionally, there was no retail over the counter market for commodities based products. In the 1980s and 1990s, various types of commodities-based investments took place between institutional investors other than through the facility of a regulated contract market,[50] in what can only be called an over-the-counter market. Increasing trading of swap and other hybrid products took place under exemptions from the statutorily imposed contract market monopoly. The ever-changing appearance of the commodities markets and special needs of institutional and other large investors led to the most significant change in commodities regulation since 1974.

In 2000, there was a massive overhaul of commodities markets regulation when a three-tiered layer of regulation was introduced.[51] The highest degree of regulation remains with the designated contract markets where retail futures trading takes place in the more traditional commodities products,

---

37. 7 U.S.C.A. § 25.

38. *E.g.,* Evanston Bank v. Conticommodity Services, Inc., 623 F.Supp. 1014, 1023–24 (N.D.Ill.1985) (also holding that employer may be liable for broker's violations); Griswold v. E.F. Hutton & Co., 622 F.Supp. 1397 (N.D.Ill.1985). This is comparable to the scienter requirement under the Securities Exchange Act of 1934. *See* § 12.8 *supra.*

45. 7 U.S.C.A. § 13b.

46. 7 U.S.C.A. § 13a–1. *See, e.g.,* CFTC v. Hunt, 591 F.2d 1211 (7th Cir.1979); CFTC v. Muller, 570 F.2d 1296 (5th Cir.1978). The states also have *parens patriae* enforcement actions for violations of the Commodities Exchange Act. 7 U.S.C.A. § 13a–2. *See* Robert C. Lower, State Enforcement of the Commodity Exchange Act, 27 Emory L.J. 1057 (1978). *See also, e.g.* Jerry W. Markham & Don L. Horwitz, Sunset on the Commodities Futures Trading Commission: Scene II, 39 Bus.Law. 67, 76–80 (1983).

47. 7 U.S.C.A. § 22. This is analogous to the SEC's power under the Securities Exchange Act of 1934 with regard to self regulatory organizations. *See* § 14.3 *supra.*

48. 7 U.S.C.A. § 6(a).

49. As pointed out *infra,* the contract market monopoly disappeared with the enactment of the commodity futures Modernization Act of 2000, Pub. Law No. 106–554, 114 Stat. 2763 (Dec. 21, 2000). Among other things, the 2000 amendments to the Commodity Exchange Act recognized derivatives transaction execution facilities as alternatives to the more traditional contract markets. In addition, the Act now permits over-the-counter bilateral contracts between large sophisticated investors.

50. *See* § 1.7 *supra* for discussion of derivative instruments generally.

51. Commodity Futures Modernization Act of 2000, Pub. Law No. 106–554, 114 Stat. 2763 (Dec. 21, 2000).

including agricultural commodities. The Commodity Futures Modernization Act of 2000[52] introduced a new category of futures markets for certain commodities-based products and is open not to retail investors generally (unless participating through a registered futures commission merchant), but only to specified qualified investors. The Modernization Act created two new categories. The Act created an "exempt board of trade" (X–OT) and also created a "derivatives transaction execution facility" ("DTEF"). DTEFs are subject to fewer regulatory requirements than CFTC-designated contract markets. DTEFs are open only to certain investors and those trading through registered futures commission merchants.[53] Permitting retail investors access only through registered futures commission merchants is designed to provide unsophisticated investors with adequate regulatory protection, should they decide to participate in this over-the-counter derivatives market.[54] In addition to limiting investor access to derivatives transaction execution facilities (as opposed to registered contract markets), the regulatory scheme ushered in by the Modernization Act imposed limits on what products may be offered on a DTEF.[55] The 2000 amendments also formally recognized the over the counter commodities markets; but these markets—which are virtually unregulated except for antifraud proscriptions[56]—are open only to the largest institutional investors dealing in certain types of swap and other hybrid contracts. These unregulated over the counter derivatives transactions must be bilateral private transactions between eligible traders, and the transactions must be on a principal-to-principal basis.

At the same time that Congress gave formal approval to the over the counter commodities markets for qualified participants, both the securities and commodities laws were amended to provide that securities-based swap

52. Pub. Law No. 106–554, 114 Stat. 2763 (Dec. 21, 2000).

53. The 2000 amendments to the Commodity Exchange Act introduced a new category of eligible contract participants ("ECPs") consisting of institutional and highly accredited customers. ECPs include financial institutions; insurance companies, registered investment companies; corporations, partnerships, trusts, and other entities having total assets exceeding $10,000,000; employee benefit plans subject to ERISA that have total assets exceeding $5,000,000; governmental entities; and others. Eligible commercial entity refers to a subset of ECPs including, among others, entities who have a demonstrable ability to make or take delivery of the underlying commodity, incur risk in addition to price risk related to the commodity, or are dealers regularly providing risk management or hedging services to or engaging in market-making activities with other eligible commercial entities.

Access to DTEFs must be confined to ECPs or to non-ECPs who trade through an FCM that is registered with the CFTC, is a member of a registered futures association (or, "in the case of securities futures products, a registered securities association), is a clearing member of a derivatives clearing organization, and has net capital of at least $20,000,000.

54. Perhaps, once the DTEFs are fully operational, they will operate in much the same way as NASDAQ does for over the counter securities when viewed in contrast to the national securities exchanges. For discussion of the securities markets, see chapter 14 supra.

55. DTEFs may trade only commodities--based contracts satisfying the following criteria: (1) the underlying commodity has a "nearly exhaustible" deliverable supply; (2) the underlying commodity has a deliverable supply that is sufficiently large that the contract is "highly unlikely to be susceptible" to the threat of manipulation; (3) the underlying commodity has no cash market; (4) the contract is a security futures product and the registered DTEF is a national securities exchange registered under the 1934 Act; (5) the CFTC determines, based on the market characteristics, surveillance history, self-regulatory record and capacity of the facility, that trading in the contract is highly unlikely to be susceptible to the threat of manipulation, or (6) the underlying commodity is not an agricultural commodity and trading access is limited to eligible commercial entities trading for their own accounts.

56. The 2000 legislation also provided that, although excluded from the definition of security under the securities acts, commodities-based swap agreements are subject to the securities laws' antifraud provisions.

agreements are not securities[57]—although they remain subject to the securities laws' antifraud provisions.[58] The degree of CFTC involvement in derivatives markets thus depends on the nature of the investors and the types of commodities-based products being offered.

The Commodity Exchange Act authorizes the CFTC to coordinate its regulatory efforts with other regulatory bodies. This coordination includes cooperation with the SEC in regulating products that overlap the securities and commodities markets.[59] The CFTC cooperates with other regulatory bodies as well. Thus, for example, the Commodity Futures Trading Commission may refer any transaction or matter subject to other Federal or State statutes to any department or agency administering such statutes for investigation, action, or proceedings that that department or agency shall deem appropriate.

An unusual aspect of the Commodity Exchange Act is its reauthorization process. Under the terms of the statute, the power of the Commodity Futures Trading Commission is subject to reauthorization by Congress. Frequently, the reauthorization process results in major substantive amendments. For example, in its 1986 reauthorization legislation, Congress expanded the variety of investments by permanently authorizing trading of options on futures.[60] The 1992 amendments also were far-reaching. However, on other occasions, as in 1994, reauthorization has not resulted in major change.

§ 22.7[2] Commodities Trading Professionals

With the increased integration of financial services,[61] many of the major securities brokerage firms operate both as securities brokers and commodities brokers. Although the commodities brokerage relationship functions in much the same way as securities brokerage, the nomenclature and regulatory structure are quite different.

The primary retail brokerage unit in the commodities world is known as a futures commission merchant (FCM).[62] FCMs must be registered with the National Futures Association as a result of authority delegated to it by the Commodity Futures Trading Commission.[63] Employees of a futures commission merchant who function as account executives are classified as "associated persons" (APs) of the FCM, and similarly must be registered with the CFTC.[64] An alternative arrangement exists in the case of "introducing brokers" (IBs),[65] who perform much the same functions as associated persons of futures commission merchants, but elect not to be registered as an associate person of the FCM. Introducing brokers, who must also register with the National Futures Association, act as agents of the FCM.

---

57. 15 U.S.C.A. §§ 77b(a)(1), 78c(a)(10).

58. 15 U.S.C.A. §§ 77q(a), 78j(b).

59. *See* § 1.5 *supra.*

60. Futures Trading Act of 1986 § 102. Prior to this enactment, the CFTC had been supervising a pilot options program.

61. *See* § 22.6 *supra.*

62. *See* section 1a(12) of the Commodity Exchange Act, 7 U.S.C.A. § 1a(12).

63. Section 4f of the Commodity Exchange Act addresses the registration of futures commission merchants. 7 U.S.C.A. § 6f.

64. Section 4k of the Commodity Exchange Act addresses the registration of associated persons. 7 U.S.C.A. § 6k.

65. *See* section 1a(14) of the Commodity Exchange Act, 7 U.S.C.A. § 1a(14).

In the commodities world, many floor traders are known as floor brokers (FBs). As is the case with other commodity trading professionals, floor brokers are subject to registration requirements.[66]

The commodities world's counterparts to investment companies[67] are known as commodity pools. Commodity pools are managed by commodity pool operators (CPOs). Unless they can find an exemption in the Commodity Exchange Act or the CFTC regulations promulgated thereunder, commodity pool operators must register with the National Futures Association.[68] In addition to the various exemptions, entities that are registered as investment companies under the Investment Company Act of 1940[69] are excluded from the Commodity Exchange Act's CPO registration requirements.[70]

Investment advisors who render advice with regard to commodities investments are known as commodity trading advisors (CTAs). Unless an exemption is available, commodity trading advisors are subject to registration requirements similar to those applicable to commodity pool operators.[71]

Two other varieties of commodities trading professionals deserve mention. Prior to exchange trading for commodity options, off-exchange options that originated from registered option grantors could be traded through commodity option dealers.[72] Although off-exchange commodity options may soon become a thing of the past in light of exchange trading, commodity option grantors that operated prior to exchange trading continue to operate subject to the Act's registration requirements.[73] Additionally, leverage transaction merchants (LTMs) who are registered under the Act[74] may deal in leveraged commodity contracts. Over the years, there has been a great deal of consideration given to phasing out leverage contract trading.[75]

§ 22.7[3] Investor Remedies Under the Commodity Exchange Act

The Commodity Exchange Act provides for a broader range of investor remedies than is found in the securities laws. An investor in commodities who has been injured as a result of fraud, manipulation or other wrongdoing by a commodities trading professional has three alternative avenues for relief. First, the injured investor may resort to the courts pursuant to an express right of action provided by section 22 of the Act.[76] Second, the investor may

---

66. Section 4f of the Commodity Exchange Act addresses the registration of floor brokers. 7 U.S.C.A. § 6f.

67. *See* chapter 20 *supra.*

68. Section 4m of the Commodity Exchange Act addresses the registration of commodity pool operators. 7 U.S.C.A. § 6m.

69. 15 U.S.C.A. § 80a–1 et seq. *See* chapter 20 *supra.*

70. 17 C.F.R. § 4.5(a)(1).

71. Section 4m of the Commodity Exchange Act addresses the registration of commodity trading advisors. 7 U.S.C.A. § 6m.

72. *See Id.*

73. 7 U.S.C.A. § 6c(d); 17 C.F.R. §§ 32.1–32.12.

74. 7 U.S.C.A. § 23; 17 C.F.R. §§ 31.1–31.26.

75. *See Id.* In 1989, the National Futures Association was given regulatory responsibility for Leverage Transaction Merchants.

76. 7 U.S.C.A. § 25. Section 22(a) provides for a remedy against registered trading professionals, while subsection (b) provides for a private right of action against a commodities exchange or the National Futures Association for a bad faith refusal to enforce its own rules.

have the dispute heard in a reparations proceeding before the Commodity Futures Trading Commission.[77] Third, if the investor so elects, he or she may demand that the dispute be arbitrated in accordance with an arbitration program administered by a registered commodities exchange or the National Futures Association.[78]

Private Remedies in the Courts

Prior to 1982, there was a substantial body of case law recognizing an implied remedy for violations of the Commodity Exchange Act, in much the same manner as the federal courts have implied remedies under SEC Rule 10b–5.[80] In 1982 the Supreme Court recognized such a remedy.[81] Shortly after the Court's decision, Congress replaced the implied remedy with an express right of action.[82]

Section 22(a) of the Commodity Exchange Act[83] provides a remedy against any person other than exchanges and registered futures associations. Section 22(b) sets forth a private right of action against exchanges and registered futures associations.[84]

Anyone suffering actual damages as a result of a violation of the Commodity Exchange Act by a person other than a designated self regulatory organization may bring suit under section 22(a).[85] In order to maintain such an action, it is generally required for a plaintiff to have been in privity with the defendant.[86] Willfulness is an element of secondary liability for aiding and abetting,[87] but it is not expressly mentioned in section 22 as an element of a primary claim. Accordingly, in order to determine whether a private right of action exists, it is necessary to look to the underlying statutory provisions that have been violated in order to determine the appropriate standard of culpability.[88] For example, the Commodity Exchange Act's general antifraud provision[89] has generally been interpreted as containing a scienter requirement.[90] In contrast, the antifraud provision applicable to commodity pool

---

77. See 7 U.S.C.A. § 18.

78. See 7 U.S.C.A. §§ 7a(11), 21(b)(10); 17 C.F.R. Part 180.

80. *See* §§ 12.2, 12.3 *supra.*

81. Merrill Lynch, Pierce, Fenner & Smith, Inc. v. Curran, 456 U.S. 353, 102 S.Ct. 1825, 72 L.Ed.2d 182 (1982).

82. 7 U.S.C.A. § 25. In enacting the private remedies, Congress codified the remedies that had been implied by the courts, and further made the express remedy exclusive. 7 U.S.C.A. §§ 25(a)(2), (b)(5).

83. 7 U.S.C.A. § 25(a).

84. 7 U.S.C.A. § 25(b).

85. 7 U.S.C.A. § 25(a).

86. 7 U.S.C.A. § 25(a)(1)(A)–(C). The privity requirement applies only to primary violators and not to other defendants who may be named as aiders and abettors. Nor does the privity requirement expressly apply to primary violators who are accused of market manipulation, as opposed to fraud or other wrongdoing.

87. Compare the discussion of aiding and abetting liability under the securities laws in §§ 7.13, 12.25 *supra.* In contrast, there is no civil liability of aiders and abettors under the securities laws. *See* § 12.25 *supra.*

88. See Michael S. Sackheim, Parameters of Express Private Rights of Action For Violations of the Commodity Exchange Act, 28 St.L.U.L.J. 51, 81–86 (1984).

89. 7 U.S.C.A. § 6b.

90. See, e.g., First National Monetary Corp. v. Weinberger, 819 F.2d 1334 (6th Cir.1987); McIlroy v. Dittmer, 732 F.2d 98 (8th Cir.1984); McCarthy v. PaineWebber, Inc., 618 F.Supp. 933 (N.D.Ill.1985).

operators and commodity trading advisors has been interpreted not to require scienter.[91]

As is the case with actions under the Securities Exchange Act,[92] damages in a section 22 action are limited to actual damages, and thus punitive damages are not available in such an action.[93] Again, as is the case under the securities laws, where an action complaining of commodities fraud is brought under state law, punitive damages may be available.[94] Section 22(a) of the Commodity Exchange Act makes no provision for attorney fees and thus in the absence of bad faith, attorney fees will not be awarded.[95]

Jurisdiction for claims arising under section 22(a) lies exclusively in the federal courts.[96] There is no provision for nation-wide service of process; thus, courts should look to the forum state's long-arm statute in determining whether personal jurisdiction can be obtained.[97]

There is a two-year statute of limitations for actions brought under section 22(a).[98] The weight of authority supports application of federal equitable tolling principles in cases where the plaintiff did not discover and reasonably could not have discovered the conduct supporting the cause of action.[99]

The section 22(a) remedy is exclusive,[100] except for the CFTC's reparations procedure, and the alternative dispute resolution process provided by commodities exchange or National Futures Association arbitration programs. Exclusivity refers only to actions brought under the Commodity Exchange Act, and thus, does not affect claims based on common law fraud or breach of fiduciary duty.[103] Additionally, the language of the exclusivity provision leaves room for the argument that violations by commodity professionals of contract market or registered futures association rules are not specifically preempted. However, the language of the statute strongly weighs against the recognition of any such right of action.[104] In contrast with the securities acts' silence,[105]

---

91. *E.g.*, First National Monetary Corp. v. Weinberger, 819 F.2d 1334 (6th Cir.1987).

92. Section 28(a), 15 U.S.C.A. § 78bb. See § 12.12 supra.

93. *See* Lopez v. Dean Witter Reynolds, Inc., 591 F.Supp. 581 (N.D.Cal.1984).

94. *See, e.g.,* E.F. Hutton & Co. v. Arnebergh, 775 F.2d 1061 (9th Cir.1985) (claim for breach of implied covenant of good faith); Lasker v. Bear, Stearns & Co., 757 F.2d 15 (2d Cir.1985) (fraud claim).

95. *See* Lopez v. Dean Witter Reynolds, Inc., 591 F.Supp. 581 (N.D.Cal.1984).

96. 7 U.S.C.A. § 25(c).

97. Omni Capital International v. Rudolf Wolff & Co., 484 U.S. 97, 108 S.Ct. 404, 98 L.Ed.2d 415 (1987).

98. 7 U.S.C.A. § 25(c).

99. *See* § 12.16 *supra*.

100. "Except as provided in subsection (b) of this section [actions against designated self regulatory organizations], the rights of action authorized by this subsection and by sections 5a(11), 14, and 17(b)(10) of this title shall be the exclusive remedies under this chapter available to any person who sustains a loss as a result of any alleged violation of this chapter." 7 U.S.C.A. § 25(a)(2).

103. *See, e.g.,* Irvine v. Cargill Investor Services, Inc., 799 F.2d 1461, 1462 (11th Cir.1986) (upholding verdict based on breach of fiduciary duty notwithstanding the existence of an implied remedy under the Act).

104. *See generally* 2 Philip M. Johnson & Thomas L. Hazen, Derivatives Regulation § 5.09 (2004).

105. *Cf.* Rodriguez de Quijas v. Shearson/American Express, Inc., 490 U.S. 477, 109 S.Ct. 1917, 104 L.Ed.2d 526 (1989) (claims arising under the Securities Act of 1933 are arbitrable); Shearson/American Express, Inc. v. McMahon, 482 U.S. 220, 107 S.Ct. 2332, 96 L.Ed.2d 185 (1987) (RICO claims and claims arising under SEC Rule 10b–5 are arbitrable). *See* chapter 15 *supra*.

section 22(a)(2) makes it clear that predispute arbitration agreements are enforceable.[106]

The section 22(a) cause of action is broader than the CFTC's reparations remedy, discussed below, which is limited to actions against persons registered under the Act.[107]

In addition to section 22(a)'s remedy against commodity trading professionals, section 22(b) of the Act provides a private right of action against commodity exchanges and self regulatory organizations.[108] If an exchange, clearing organization, or registered futures association, *acting in bad faith*,[109] refuses to enforce its own rules, it can be held liable in damages.[110] The right of action also extends to enforcement of a rule that violates the Commodity Exchange Act or CFTC rule, regulation or order.[111] Liability under section 22(b) extends not only to the self-regulatory organizations, but also to their officers, directors and employees who have willfully aided and abetted the violation. Damages in such an action are limited to actual losses sustained.[112]

CFTC Reparations Proceedings

Since 1975, the Commodity Futures Trading Commission has been available as an adjudicatory authority for disputes between members and their brokers.[113] There are three different types of reparations procedures. The dispute will normally be held through summary or formal proceedings unless the parties elect the voluntary decisional procedure.

When the customer's damage claim (or broker's counterclaim), exclusive of interest and costs, does not exceed ten thousand dollars, the dispute will be held pursuant to the summary procedure.[114] When damages exceed ten thousand dollars, the dispute will be held in accordance with formal procedures.[115] The parties by unanimous election may opt out of either the summary or formal procedures in favor of the voluntary decisional procedure.[116] Voluntary decisional proceedings are not reviewable by the CFTC.

With summary and formal reparations proceedings, the case is heard before an ALJ or other presiding officer who makes an initial decision, that is

---

106. 7 U.S.C.A. § 25(a)(2). The parties are not limited to exchanges' or the National Futures Association's arbitration programs.

107. 7 U.S.C.A. § 18(a).

108. 7 U.S.C.A. § 25(b).

109. 7 U.S.C.A. § 25(b)(4).

110. 7 U.S.C.A. § 25(b).

111. *Id.*

112. 15 U.S.C.A. §§ 25(b)(1), (2).

113. *See* 7 U.S.C.A. § 18. *See generally* 2 Philip M. Johnson & Thomas L. Hazen, Derivatives Regulation § 4.10 (2004).

114. 17 C.F.R. § 12.26(b). The procedures for summary proceedings are set out in CFTC Regulations §§ 12.1 through 12.36, 12.200 through 12.210, and 12.400 through 12.408. 17 C.F.R. §§ 12.1–12.36, 12.200–12.210, and 12.400–12.408.

115. 17 C.F.R. § 12.26(c). The procedures for formal proceedings are set out in CFTC Regulations §§ 12.1 through 12.36 and 12.300 through 12.408. 17 C.F.R. §§ 12.1–12.36, and 12.300–12.408.

116. 17 C.F.R. § 12.26(a). The procedures for voluntary decisional proceedings are set out in CFTC Regulations §§ 12.100 through 12.106. 17 C.F.R. §§ 12.100–12.106.

appealable to the full CFTC.[117] In addition a final decision in a reparations case is appealable to a federal court of appeals.[118]

The choice of remedies under the Commodity Exchange Act requires the claimant to make an election of which one to pursue. Reparations proceedings provide an alternative, but they cannot be pursued coincidentally with a law suit or arbitration proceedings.[119]

The advantages of the reparations procedure over seeking relief in federal court include more rapid resolution of disputes and a less expensive procedure since the vast federal discovery procedures are not available as dilatory, tactics.[120] On the other hand, at least with larger claims, an aggrieved customer may believe that his or her rights will more adequately be protected by a judicial hearing.

SRO Arbitration Programs

As discussed earlier, the securities laws make no mention of arbitration of customer disputes, but the Supreme Court has held that predispute arbitration agreements are enforceable with regard to claims arising under the Securities Act or the Exchange Act.[121] Sections 5a(11)[122] and 17(b)(10)[123] of the Commodity Exchange Act require commodities exchanges and the National Futures Association to maintain fair and equitable procedures for the resolution of customer disputes. While the exchanges and NFA must offer the arbitration procedure for all customer disputes, the procedure is voluntary from the customer's prospective. The customer can thus elect whether to invoke the arbitration procedures, seek reparations before the CFTC, or to bring suit under section 25 of the Commodity Exchange Act.[126] The applicable CFTC regulations require that the customer be informed of the alternative avenues for relief.[127] In enacting these statutory provisions, Congress obviously viewed these arbitration programs as a way of furthering investor protection by giving aggrieved customers the option of arbitration. In contrast to the developing body of law under the Securities Exchange Act,[128] the commodities laws do not permit a commodities broker to force a customer into arbitration.

---

117. *See* 17 C.F.R. §§ 12.401–12.408.

118. 7 U.S.C.A. § 18(e).

119. CFTC Regulation § 12.24 provides that if parallel proceedings have been instituted, the reparations claim should be dismissed. 17 C.F.R. § 12.24. Bankruptcy or receivership proceedings are also defined as parallel for purposes of this rule.

120. Although the reparations procedures do provide for limited discovery, it is far more limited than what is available in federal court. *See* 17 C.F.R. § 12.30.

121. Rodriguez de Quijas v. Shearson/American Express, Inc., 490 U.S. 477, 109 S.Ct. 1917, 104 L.Ed.2d 526 (1989) (1933 Act claims are arbitrable); Shearson/American Express, Inc. v. McMahon, 482 U.S. 220, 107 S.Ct. 2332, 96 L.Ed.2d 185 (1987) (RICO claims and claims arising under SEC Rule 10b–5 are arbitrable). *See* chapter 15 *supra*.

122. 7 U.S.C.A. § 7a(11).

123. 7 U.S.C.A. § 21(b)(10).

126. 7 U.S.C.A. § 25.

127. 17 C.F.R. § 180.3.

128. *See* chapter 15 *supra*.

Appendix

RESEARCHING SECURITIES LAW ON WESTLAW

Section 1.   Introduction

The Law of Securities Regulation provides a strong base for analyzing even the most complex problem involving issues related to securities law. Whether your research requires examination of case law, statutes, administrative decisions, expert commentary, or other materials, West books and Westlaw are excellent sources of information.

To keep you informed of current developments, Westlaw provides frequently updated databases. With Westlaw, you have unparalleled legal research resources at your fingertips.

Additional Resources

If you have not previously used Westlaw or if you have questions not covered in this appendix, call the West Reference Attorneys at 1–800–REF–ATTY (1–

800–733–2889). The West Reference Attorneys are trained, licensed attorneys, available 24 hours a day to assist you with your Westlaw search questions. To subscribe to Westlaw, call 1–800–344–5008 or visit westlaw.com at **www.westlaw.com**.

Section 2.   Westlaw Databases

Each database on Westlaw is assigned an abbreviation called an *identifier*, which you can use to access the database. You can find identifiers for Westlaw databases in the online Westlaw Directory and in the printed *Westlaw Database Directory*. When you need to know more detailed information about a database, use Scope. Scope contains coverage information, lists of related databases, and valuable search tips.

The following chart lists selected Westlaw databases that contain information pertaining to securities law. For a complete list of securities law databases, see the online Westlaw Directory or the printed *Westlaw Database Directory*. Because new information is continually being added to Westlaw, you should also check the tabbed Westlaw page and the online Westlaw Directory for new database information.

Selected Securities Law Databases on Westlaw

Database	Identifier	Coverage
Combined Federal Materials		
Federal Securities Law—Combined Materials	FSEC–ALL	Varies by source
Federal Securities Law—Code and Regulations	FSEC–CODREG	Varies by source
Federal Case Law		
Federal Securities Law—Cases	FSEC–CS	Begins with 1789
Federal Securities Law—Supreme Court Cases	FSEC–SCT	Begins with 1790
Federal Securities Law—Courts of Appeals Cases	FSEC–CTA	Begins with 1891
Federal Securities Law—District Courts Cases	FSEC–DCT	Begins with 1789
Briefs, Pleadings, and Other Court Documents		
Andrews Derivatives Litigation Reporter Court Documents	ANDERLR–DOC	Begins with 2000
Andrews Mergers and Acquisitions Litigation	ANMALR–DOC	Begins with 2000

Database	Identifier	Coverage
Reporter Court Documents		
Andrews Securities Litigation and Regulation Reporter Court Documents	ANSLRR–DOC	Begins with 2000
Federal Securities Briefs	FSEC–BRIEF	Begins with 1942
Securities Trial Motions	SEC–MOTIONS	Begins with 1997
Securities Trial Pleadings	SEC–PLEADINGS	Begins with 1997

Federal Statutes, Legislative History, and Rules

Database	Identifier	Coverage
Federal Securities Law—U.S. Code Annotated	FSEC–USCA	Current data
Federal Commodity Futures Trading Commission United States Code Annotated	FCFTC–USCA	Current data
Federal Securities Law—Legislative History	FSEC–LH	Begins with 1933
Arnold & Porter Legislative History: Government Securities Act of 1986	GOVSEC86–LH	Full history
Arnold & Porter Legislative History: Government Securities Reform Act of 1993	GOVSEC93–LH	Full history
Arnold & Porter Legislative History: Insider Trading Act	INSIDER–LH	Full history
Arnold & Porter Legislative History: Sarbanes–Oxley Act of 2002	SAROX–LH	Full history
Federal Securities Law—Rules	FSEC–RULES	Current data

Federal Administrative Materials

Database	Identifier	Coverage
Federal Commodity Futures Trading Commission Code of Federal Regulations	FCFTC–CFR	Current data
Federal Commodity Futures Trading Commission Federal Register	FCFTC–FR	Begins with July 1980

Database	Identifier	Coverage
Federal Securities Law—Administrative Materials	FSEC–ADMIN	Varies by source
Federal Securities Law—Arbitration Awards	FSEC–ARB	Begins with 1989
Federal Securities Law—Code of Federal Regulations	FSEC–CFR	Current data
Federal Securities Law—Commodity Futures Trading Commission Decisions	FSEC–CFTC	CFTC decisions: begins with 1976 Administrative law judge decisions: begins with 1983
Federal Securities Law—Commodity Futures Trading Commission Letters	FSEC–CFTCLTR	Begins with 1987
Federal Securities Law—Federal Register	FSEC–FR	Begins with July 1980
Federal Securities Law—Final, Temporary, and Proposed Regulations	FSEC–REG	Varies by source
Federal Securities Law—News Releases	FSEC–NR	SEC releases: begins with November 1991 CFTC releases: begins with January 1992
Federal Securities Law—SEC News Digest	FSEC–DIG	Begins with July 1987
Federal Securities Law—SEC No–Action Letters	FSEC–NAL	Begins with 1970
Federal Securities Law—Securities Releases	FSEC–RELS	Begins with 1933
Federal Securities Law—Stock Exchange Disciplinary Decisions	FSEC–DISP	Exchange Hearing Panel decisions: begins with 1972 Disciplinary Panel decisions: begins with 1985 National Adjudicatory Council decisions: begins with 1990
National Association of Securities Dealers (NASD)–Arbitration Awards	NASD–ARB	Begins with 1981

Database	Identifier	Coverage
National Association of Securities Dealers (NASD)–Code of Federal Regulations (Title 12 and Title 17)	NASD–CFR	Current data
National Association of Securities Dealers (NASD)—Disciplinary Decisions	NASD–DISP	Selected coverage begins with 1990; full coverage begins with 1992
National Association of Securities Dealers (NASD)—Federal Register	NASD—FR	Begins with July 1980
National Association of Securities Dealers (NASD)—Final, Temporary, and Proposed Regulations	NASD—REG	Varies by source
National Association of Securities Dealers (NASD) Manual	NASD–MANUAL	Current data
National Association of Securities Dealers (NASD)—Notices to Members	NASD—NOTICE	Begins with 1983
National Association of Securities Dealers (NASD)—Office of Hearing Officers	NASD—OHO	Begins with 1998

Combined State Materials

Blue Sky Statutes and Regulations—Combined	BLUESKY—COMBINED	Current data
Individual State Blue Sky Combined	XXSEC–COMBINED (where XX is a jurisdiction's two-letter postal abbreviation)	Current data

State Case Law

Multistate Securities and Blue Sky Law—Cases	MSEC—CS	Varies by state
Individual State Securities and Blue Sky Law Cases	XXSEC–CS (where XX is a state's two-letter postal abbreviation)	Varies by state

State Statutes

Blue Sky Statutes	BLUESKY—ST	Current data
Individual State Blue Sky Statutes	XXSEC—ST (where XX is a jurisdiction's two-letter postal abbreviation)	Current data

Database	Identifier	Coverage
State Administrative Materials		
Blue Sky Regulations	BLUESKY—REG	Current data
Individual State Blue Sky Regulations	XXSEC—REG (where XX is a jurisdiction's two-letter postal abbreviation)	Current data
Multistate Securities and Blue Sky Law—Administrative Decisions	MSEC—ADMIN	Varies by state
Individual State Securities Administrative Decisions	XXSEC—ADMIN (where XX is a state's two-letter postal abbreviation)	Varies by state
Public Records		
EDGAR—SEC Filings	EDGAR	Full-text EDGAR filings: begins with April 1993 Records of other filings: begins with 1968
Federal Securities Law—Sworn Certification of Financial Statements	FSEC—CERT	Begins with August 2002
Insider Stock Transactions	STOCK	Current data
Securities and Exchange Commission Corporate Filings	SEC–ONLINE	Begins with January 1987
Legal Texts, Periodicals, and Practice Materials		
Securities and Blue Sky Law—Law Reviews, Texts, and Bar Journals	SEC—TP	Varies by publication
Acquisitions and Mergers: Negotiated and Contested Transactions	SECACQMERG	Current data
Analysis of Key SEC No—Action Letters	SECKEYNAL	2003–2004 edition
Blue Sky Law	SECBLUE	Current data
Broker— Dealer Operations Under Securities and Commodities Law	SECBDOP	Current data
Bromberg and Lowenfels on Securities	SECBROMLOW	Second edition

Database	Identifier	Coverage
Fraud and Commodities Fraud		
Civil Liabilities: Enforcement and Litigation Under the 1933 Act	SECCIVIL	Current data
Commodities Regulation: Fraud, Manipulation, and Other Claims	SECCOMMREG	Current data
Corporate Compliance Series: Securities	CORPC—SEC	Current data
D & O Liability Handbook	DOLIABH	Current data
Disclosure and Remedies Under the Securities Laws	SECDRSL	Current data
Exempted Transactions Under the Securities Act of 1933	SECEXTRANS	Current data
Ferrera on Insider Trading and the Wall	INSIDETRADE	Current data
Fordham Journal of Corporate and Financial Law	FDMJCFL	Full coverage begins with 1997 (vol. 2)
International Capital Markets and Securities Regulation	SECINTCAP	Current data
Law of Securities Regulation	LAWSECREG	Fourth edition
Liability of Attorneys and Accountants for Securities Transactions	SECATTACC	Current edition
Limited Offering Exemptions: Regulation D	SECREGD	Current data
Manual of Corporate Forms for Securities Practice	SECMCORPF	Current data
Mutual Fund Regulation	PLIREF—MFR	Current data
Opinion Letters in Securities Matters: Texts— Clauses—Law	SECOPINION	Current data
Proxy Rules Handbook	PRXYRH	2003 edition
Regulation of Investment Advisers	SECREGINA	Current data
Sarbanes—Oxley Act in Perspective	SEC–SOAP	Current data
Sarbanes—Oxley Deskbook	PLIREF—SAROX	Current data

Database	Identifier	Coverage
Section 16 of the Securities Exchange Act	SEC16	Current data
Securities and Federal Corporate Law	SECFEDCORP	Current data
Securities Law Handbook	SECLAW—HB	Current data
Securities Litigation: Damages	SECLITD	Current data
Securities Litigation: Forms and Analysis	SECLITFRMS	Current data
Securities Practice: Federal and State Enforcement	SECPRACFSE	Current data
Securities: Public and Private Offerings	SECPUBPRIV	Current data
Securities Regulation Forms	SECREGFRM	Current data
Shareholder Derivative Litigation: Besieging the Board	SDLBTB	Current data
Shareholder Litigation	SHARELIT	Current data
Tax—Advantaged Securities Handbook	SECTAXAHB	Current data
U.S. Securities Law for International Financial Transactions and Capital Markets, Second Edition	SECINTFTCM	Current data
West Group Securities Law Series Online	SECSERIES	Varies by publication

News and Information

Andrews Civil RICO Litigation Reporter	ANCRLR	Begins with November 1996
Andrews Derivatives Litigation Reporter	ANDERLR	Begins with November 1996
Andrews Mergers and Acquisitions Litigation Reporter	ANMALR	Begins with December 1996
Andrews Securities Litigation and Regulation Reporter	ANSLRR	Begins with November 1996
Corporate Governance Expert Commentary	CORPGOV—EXP	Begins with January 2003
Futures and Derivatives Law Report	GLFDLR	Begins with May 1996
Internet Law and Strategy	INTERLSTR	Begins with January 2003
Martha Stewart Securities Trial	MARTHA	Begins with 2003

Database	Identifier	Coverage
Securities and Federal Corporate Law Report	SECFEDCLN	Begins with January 2003
Wallstreetlawyer.com: Securities in the Electronic Age	GLWSLAW	Begins with July 1997
Westlaw Topical Highlights–Securities Regulation	WTH—SEC	Current data

Directories		
West Legal Directory®—Securities	WLD—SEC	Current data

Section 3. Retrieving a Document with a Citation: Find and Hypertext Links

3.1 Find

Find is a Westlaw service that allows you to retrieve a document by entering its citation. Find allows you to retrieve documents from any page in westlaw.com without accessing or changing databases. Find is available for many documents, including case law (state and federal), the *United States Code Annotated*® (USCA®), state statutes, administrative materials, and texts and periodicals.

To use Find, simply type the citation in the *Find this document by citation* text box at the tabbed Westlaw page and click **GO**. The following list provides some examples:

To find this document:	Access Find and type:
United States v. O'Hagan 117 S. Ct. 2199 (1997)	**117 sct 2199**
In re SEC ex rel. Glotzer 374 F.3d 184 (2nd Cir. 2004)	**374 f3d 184**
15 U.S.C.A. § 7201	**15 usca 7201**
17 C.F.R. § 201.430	**17 cfr 201.430**
N.Y. Gen. Bus. Law § 352–c	**ny gen bus s 352–c**

For a complete list of publications that can be retrieved with Find and their abbreviations, click **Find** on the toolbar and then click **Publications List**.

3.2 Hypertext Links

Use hypertext links to move from one location to another on Westlaw. For example, use hypertext links to go directly from the statute, case, or law review article you are viewing to a cited statute, case, or article; from a headnote to the corresponding text in the opinion; or from an entry in a statutes index database to the full text of the statute.

Section 4. Searching with Natural Language

Overview: With Natural Language, you can retrieve documents by simply describing your issue in plain English. If you are a relatively new Westlaw user, Natural Language searching can make it easier for you to retrieve cases that are on point. If you are an experienced Westlaw user, Natural Language gives you a valuable alternative search method to the Terms and Connectors search method described in Section 5.

When you enter a Natural Language description, Westlaw automatically identifies legal phrases, removes common words, and generates variations of terms in your description. Westlaw then searches for the concepts in your description. Concepts may include significant terms, phrases, legal citations, or topic and key numbers. Westlaw retrieves the documents that most closely match the concepts in your description, beginning with the document most likely to match.

4.1 Natural Language Search

Access a database, such as the Federal Securities Law–Cases database (FSEC–CS). Click **Natural Language** and type the following description in the text box:

who is a ten percent beneficial owner

4.2 Browsing Search Results

Best Mode: To display the best portion (the portion that most closely matches your description) of each document in a Natural Language search result, click the **Best** arrows at the bottom of the right frame.

Term Mode: Click the **Term** arrows at the bottom of the right frame to display portions of the document that contain your search terms.

Previous/Next Document: Click the left or right **Doc** arrow at the bottom of the right frame to view the previous or the next document in the search result.

Section 5.   Searching with Terms and Connectors

Overview: With Terms and Connectors searching, you enter a query consisting of key terms from your issue and connectors specifying the relationship between these terms.

Terms and Connectors searching is useful when you want to retrieve a document for which you know specific details, such as the title or the fact situation. Terms and Connectors searching is also useful when you want to retrieve all documents containing specific terms.

5.1 Terms

Plurals and Possessives: Plurals are automatically retrieved when you enter the singular form of a term. This is true for both regular and irregular plurals (e.g., **child** retrieves *children*). If you enter the plural form of a term, you will not retrieve the singular form.

If you enter the nonpossessive form of a term, Westlaw automatically retrieves the possessive form as well. However, if you enter the possessive form, only the possessive form is retrieved.

Compound Words and Abbreviations: When a compound word is one of your search terms, use a hyphen to retrieve all forms of the word. For example, the term **along-side** retrieves *along-side*, *alongside*, and *along side*.

When using an abbreviation as a search term, place a period after each of the letters to retrieve any of its forms. For example, the term **s.e.c.** retrieves *SEC, S.E.C., S E C* and *S. E. C.* Note: The abbreviation does not retrieve the phrase *Securities and Exchange Commission*, so remember to add additional alternative terms such as **"securities and exchange commission"** to your query.

The Root Expander and the Universal Character: When you use the Terms and Connectors search method, placing the root expander (!) at the end of a root term generates all other terms with that root. For example, adding the ! to the root *fraud* in the query

fraud! /s transfer

instructs Westlaw to retrieve such terms as *fraud, fraudulent,* and *fraudulently*.

The universal character (*) stands for one character and can be inserted in the middle or at the end of a term. For example, the term

s**holder**

will retrieve *shareholder* and *stockholder*. Adding three asterisks to the root *elect*

elect***

instructs Westlaw to retrieve all forms of the root with up to three additional characters. Terms such as *elected* or *election* are retrieved by this query. However, terms with more than three letters following the root, such as *electronic,* are not retrieved. Plurals are always retrieved, even if the plural form of the term has more than three letters following the root.

Phrase Searching: To search for an exact phrase, place it within quotation marks. For example, to search for references to *junk bond*, type **"junk bond"**. When you are using the Terms and Connectors search method, you should use phrase searching only if you are certain that the terms in the phrase will not appear in any other order.

5.2 Alternative Terms

After selecting the terms for your query, consider which alternative terms are necessary. For example, if you are searching for the term *admissible*, you might also want to search for the term *inadmissible*. You should consider both synonyms and antonyms as alternative terms. You can also use the Westlaw thesaurus to add alternative terms to your query.

5.3 Connectors

After selecting terms and alternative terms for your query, use connectors to specify the relationship that must exist between search terms in your retrieved documents. The connectors are described below:

Type:	To retrieve documents with:	Example:
& (and)	both terms	**director & officer**
a space (or)	either term or both terms	**i.p.o. "initial public offering"**

Type: /p	To retrieve documents with: search terms in the same paragraph	Example: **pre-empt! /p state**
/s	search terms in the same sentence	**investment /s advis*r**
+s	the first search term preceding the second within the same sentence	**burden +s prov! proof**
/n	search terms within *n* terms of each other (where *n* is a number from 1 to 255)	**limited /3 liability**
+n	the first search term preceding the second by *n* terms (where *n* is a number from 1 to 255)	**plain +3 english**
" "	search terms appearing in the same order as in the quotation marks	**"class action"**
Type:	**To exclude documents with:**	**Example:**
% (but not)	search terms following the %symbol	**fraud %"statute of frauds"**

5.4   Field Restrictions

Overview: Documents in each Westlaw database consist of several segments, or *fields*. One field may contain the citation, another the title, another the synopsis, and so forth. Not all databases contain the same fields. Also depending on the database, fields with the same name may contain different types of information.

To view a list of fields and their contents for a specific database, see Scope for that database. Note that in some databases not every field is available for every document.

To retrieve only those documents containing your search terms in a specific field, restrict your search to that field. To restrict your search to a specific field, type the field name or abbreviation followed by your search terms enclosed in parentheses. For example, to retrieve a federal district court case titled *Escott v. BarChris Constr. Corp.*, access the Federal Securities Law–District Courts Cases database (FSEC–DCT) and search for your terms in the title field (ti):

ti(escott & barchris)

The fields discussed below are available in Westlaw case law databases you might use for researching issues related to securities law.

Digest and Synopsis Fields: The digest (di) and synopsis (sy) fields summarize the main points of a case. The synopsis field contains a brief description of a case. The digest field contains the topic and headnote fields and includes the complete hierarchy of concepts used by West's editors to classify the headnotes to specific West digest topic and key numbers. Restricting your search to the synopsis and digest fields limits your result to cases in which your terms are related to a major issue in the case.

Consider restricting your search to one or both of these fields if

• you are searching for common terms or terms with more than one meaning, and you need to narrow your search; or

• you cannot narrow your search by using a smaller database.

For example, to retrieve state cases that discuss whether promissory notes are exempt from registration requirements for securities, access the Multistate Securities and Blue Sky Law–Cases database (MSEC–CS) and type the following query:

sy,di(exempt! /s regist! /p promissory /5 note)

Headnote Field: The headnote field (he) is part of the digest field but does not contain the topic names or numbers, hierarchical classification information, or key numbers. The headnote field contains a one-sentence summary for each point of law in a case and any supporting citations given by the author of the opinion. A headnote field restriction is useful when you are searching for specific statutory sections or rule numbers. For example, to retrieve headnotes from federal courts of appeals cases that cite 15 U.S.C.A. § 77k, access the Federal Securities Law–Courts of Appeals Cases database (FSEC–CTA) and type the following query:

he(15 +s 77k)

Topic Field: The topic field (to) is also part of the digest field. It contains the hierarchical classification information, including the West digest topic names and numbers and the key numbers. You should restrict search terms to the topic field in a case law database if

● a digest field search retrieves too many documents; or

● you want to retrieve cases with digest paragraphs classified under more than one topic.

For example, the topic Securities Regulation has the topic number 349B. To retrieve U.S. Supreme Court cases that discuss insider trading by officers or directors, access the Federal Securities Law–Supreme Court Cases database (FSEC–SCT) and type a query like the following:

to(349b) /p inside* /s trad! information /p officer director

To retrieve cases classified under more than one topic and key number, search for your terms in the topic field. For example, to retrieve federal courts of appeals cases discussing broker-dealers, which may be classified to such topics as Brokers (65), Exchanges (160), and Securities Regulation (349B), access the FSEC–CTA database and type a query like the following:

to(broker-dealer)

For a complete list of West digest topics and their corresponding topic numbers, access the Custom Digest by choosing **Key Numbers and Digest** from the *More* drop-down list on the toolbar.

Note: Slip opinions and cases from topical services do not contain the West digest, headnote, and topic fields.

Prelim and Caption Fields: When searching in a database containing statutes, rules, or regulations, restrict your search to the prelim (pr) and caption (ca) fields to retrieve documents in which your terms are important enough to appear in a section name or heading. For example, to retrieve federal statutes regarding the registration of securities, access the Federal

Securities Law–U.S. Code Annotated database (FSEC–USCA) and type the following query:

pr,ca(regist! & securities)

5.5 Date Restrictions

You can use Westlaw to retrieve documents *decided* or *issued* before, after, or on a specified date, as well as within a range of dates. The following sample queries contain date restrictions:

da(2003) & due /5 diligence

da(aft 1998) & due /5 diligence

da(3/6/1990) & due /5 diligence

You can also search for documents *added to a database* on or after a specified date, as well as within a range of dates, which is useful for updating your research. The following sample queries contain added-date restrictions:

ad(aft 2002) & due /5 diligence

ad(aft 11/9/2001 & bef 6/23/2002) & due /5 diligence

Section 6. Searching with Topic and Key Numbers

To retrieve cases that address a specific point of law, use topic and key numbers as your search terms. If you have an on-point case, run a search using the topic and key number from the relevant headnote in an appropriate database to find other cases containing headnotes classified to that topic and key number. For example, to search for federal cases containing headnotes classified under topic 349B (Securities Regulation) and key number 193 (Fraudulent Transactions), access the FSEC–CS database and type the following query:

349bk193

For a complete list of West digest topics and their corresponding topic numbers, access the Custom Digest by choosing **Key Numbers and Digest** from the *More* drop-down list on the toolbar.

> *Note:* Slip opinions and cases from topical services do not contain the West topic, and key numbers.

6.1 Custom Digest

The Custom Digest contains the complete topic and key number outline used by West attorney-editors to classify headnotes. You can use the Custom Digest to obtain a single document containing all case law headnotes from a specific jurisdiction that are classified under a particular topic and key number.

Access the Custom Digest by choosing **Key Numbers and Digest** from the *More* drop-down list on the toolbar. Select up to 10 topics and key numbers from the easy-to-browse outline and click **Search selected**. Then follow the displayed instructions.

For example, to research issues involving securities regulation, scroll down the Custom Digest page until topic *349B Securities Regulation* is displayed. Click the plus symbols (+) to display key number information. Select the check box next to each key number you want to include in your search, then click **Search selected**. Select the jurisdiction from which you want to retrieve headnotes and, if desired, type additional search terms and select a date restriction. Click **Search**.

6.2   KeySearch

KeySearch is a research tool that helps you find cases and secondary sources in a specific area of the law. KeySearch guides you through the selection of terms from a classification system based on the West Key Number System® and then uses the key numbers and their underlying concepts to provide a query for you.

To access KeySearch, click **KeySearch** on the toolbar. Then browse the list of topics and subtopics and select a topic or subtopic to search by clicking the hypertext links. For example, to search for cases that discuss officer and director liability under the Sarbanes–Oxley Act, click **Securities Law** at the first KeySearch page. Then click **Officers and Directors** and **Liabilities under Sarbanes–Oxley** at the next two pages. Select the source from which you want to retrieve documents and, if desired, type additional search terms. Click **Search**.

Section 7.   Verifying Your Research with Citation Research Services

Overview: A citation research service, such as KeyCite, is a tool that helps you ensure that your cases, statutes, regulations, and administrative decisions are good law; retrieve cases, legislation, articles, or other documents that cite them; and verify the spelling and format of your citations.

7.1   KeyCite for Cases

KeyCite for cases covers case law on Westlaw, including unpublished opinions. KeyCite for cases provides the following:

- direct appellate history of a case, including related references, which are opinions involving the same parties and facts but resolving different issues

- negative indirect history of a case, which consists of cases outside the direct appellate line that may have a negative impact on its precedential value

- the title, parallel citations, court of decision, docket number, and filing date of a case

- citations to cases, administrative decisions, secondary sources, and briefs and other court documents on Westlaw that have cited a case

- complete integration with the West Key Number System so you can track legal issues discussed in a case

7.2   KeyCite for Statutes and Regulations

KeyCite for statutes and regulations covers the USCA, the *Code of Federal Regulations* (CFR), statutes from all 50 states, and regulations from selected states. KeyCite for statutes and regulations provides

- links to session laws or rules amending or repealing a statute or regulation

- statutory credits and historical notes

- citations to pending legislation affecting a statute

- citations to cases, administrative decisions, secondary sources, and briefs and other court documents that have cited a statute or regulation

7.3 KeyCite for Administrative Materials

KeyCite for administrative materials includes the following:

- National Labor Relations Board decisions beginning with 1935

- Board of Contract Appeals decisions (varies by agency)

- Board of Immigration Appeals decisions beginning with 1940

- Comptroller General decisions beginning with 1921

- Environmental Protection Agency decisions beginning with 1974

- Federal Communications Commission decisions beginning with 1960

- Federal Energy Regulatory Commission (Federal Power Commission) decisions beginning with 1931

- Internal Revenue Service revenue rulings beginning with 1954

- Internal Revenue Service revenue procedures beginning with 1954

- Internal Revenue Service private letter rulings beginning with 1954

- Internal Revenue Service technical advice memoranda beginning with 1954

- *Public Utilities Reports* beginning with 1974

- U.S. Merit Systems Protection Board decisions beginning with 1979

- U.S. Patent and Trademark Office decisions beginning with 1984

- U.S. Tax Court (Board of Tax Appeals) decisions beginning with 1924

- U.S. patents beginning with 1976

7.4 KeyCite Alert

KeyCite Alert monitors the status of your cases, statutes, regulations, and administrative decisions and automatically sends you updates at the frequency you specify when their KeyCite information changes.

Section 8. Researching with Westlaw: Examples

8.1 Retrieving Law Review Articles

Recent law review articles are often a good place to begin researching a legal issue because law review articles serve as an excellent introduction to a new topic or review for an old one, providing terminology to help you formulate a query; as a finding tool for pertinent primary authority, such as cases, statutes, and rules; and in some instances, as persuasive secondary authority.

Suppose you need to gain background information on the bespeaks caution doctrine in securities fraud claims.

Solution

- To retrieve law review articles relevant to your issue, access the Securities and Blue Sky Law–Law Reviews, Texts, and Bar Journals database (SEC–

TP). Using the Natural Language search method, type a description like the following:

application of bespeaks caution doctrine in securities fraud claim

- If you have a citation to an article in a specific publication, use Find to retrieve it. (For more information on Find, see Section 3.1 of this appendix.) For example, to retrieve the article found at 58 U. Pitt. L. Rev. 619, access Find and type

58 u pitt l rev 619

- If you know the title of an article but not the journal in which it was published, access the SEC–TP database and search for key terms in the title field. For example, to retrieve the article "Good Faith and the Bespeaks Caution Doctrine: It's Not Just a State of Mind," type the following Terms and Connectors query:

ti("good faith" & bespeaks)

8.2   Retrieving Case Law

Suppose you need to retrieve federal district court cases discussing due diligence as a defense under section 11 of the Securities Act of 1933.

Solution

- Access the FSEC–DCT database. Type a Terms and Connectors query such as the following:

due /5 diligence /p "section 11"

- When you know the citation for a specific case, use Find to retrieve it. For example, to retrieve *In re WorldCom, Inc. Securities Litigation,* 219 F.R.D. 267 (S.D.N.Y. 2003), access Find and type

219 frd 267

- If you find a topic and key number that is on point, run a search using that topic and key number to retrieve additional cases discussing that point of law. For example, to retrieve federal cases containing headnotes classified under topic 349B (Securities Regulation) and key number 25.21(4) (Good Faith; Due Diligence or Reasonable Investigation), access the FSEC–CS database and type the following query:

349bk25.21(4)

- To retrieve opinions written by a particular judge, add a judge field (ju) restriction to your query. For example, to retrieve federal district court opinions written by Judge Cote that contain headnotes classified under topic 349B (Securities Regulation), access the FSEC–DCT cases and type the following query:

ju(cote) & to(349b)

- You can also use KeySearch and the Custom Digest to retrieve cases and headnotes that discuss the issue you are researching.

8.3 Retrieving Statutes and Regulations

Suppose you need to retrieve federal statutes dealing with manipulative or deceptive practices with regard to securities.

Solution

- Access the FSEC–USCA database. Search for your terms in the prelim and caption fields using the Terms and Connectors search method:

pr,ca(manipulat! decepti! & securities)

- When you know the citation for a specific statute or regulation, use Find to retrieve it. For example, to retrieve 15 U.S.C.A. § 78j, access Find and type

15 usca 78j

- To look at surrounding sections, use the Table of Contents service. Click **Table of Contents** on the Links tab in the left frame. To display a section listed in the Table of Contents, click its hypertext link. You can also use Documents in Sequence to retrieve the sections following 15 U.S.C.A. § 78j even if the subsequent sections were not retrieved with your search or Find request. Choose **Documents in Sequence** from the Tools menu at the bottom of the right frame.

8.4 Retrieving Administrative Decisions

Suppose you need to retrieve recent Commodity Futures Trading Commission (CFTC) decisions discussing wash sales.

Solution

- Access the Federal Securities Law–Commodity Futures Trading Commission Decisions database (FSEC–CFTC) and type the following query:

wash /s sale

8.5 Using KeyCite

Suppose one of the cases you retrieve in your case law research is *United States v. O'Hagan*, 117 S.Ct. 2199 (1997). You want to make sure it is good law and retrieve a list of citing references.

Solution

- Use KeyCite to retrieve direct and negative indirect history for *O'Hagan*. Access KeyCite and type **117 sct 2199**.

- Use KeyCite to display citing references for *O'Hagan*. Click **Citing References** on the Links tab in the left frame.

8.6 Following Recent Developments

If you are researching issues related to securities law, it is important to keep up with recent developments. How can you do this efficiently?

Solution

One of the easiest ways to follow recent developments in securities law is to access the Westlaw Topical Highlights–Securities Regulation database (WTH–SEC). The WTH–SEC database contains summaries of recent legal developments, including court decisions, legislation, and materials released by administrative agencies. When you access the WTH–SEC database, you automatically retrieve a list of documents added to the database in the last two weeks.

You can also use the WestClip® clipping service to stay informed of recent developments of interest to you. WestClip will run your Terms and Connectors queries on a regular basis and deliver the results to you automatically. You can run WestClip queries in legal and news and information databases.

*

Table of Cases and Selected Administrative Materials

A

Belden, Matter of, 2003 WL 21088079 (SEC 2003)—§ **20.5, n. 81**.

Bell v. Health-Mor, Inc., 549 F.2d 342 (5th Cir.1977)—§ **1.6, n. 12**.

Benjamin, United States v., 328 F.2d 854 (2d Cir.1964)—§ **9.8, n. 81**.

Benoay v. Prudential-Bache Securities, Inc., 805 F.2d 1437 (11th Cir.1986)—§ **15.1, n. 107**.

Bent Creek Country Club, 1993 WL 380731 (SEC 1993)—§ **1.6, n. 121**.

Bentley v. Legent Corp., 849 F.Supp. 429 (E.D.Va.1994)—§ **3.9, n. 61**.

Berk v. Maryland Publick Banks, Inc., 6 F.Supp.2d 472 (D.Md.1998)—§ **12.6, n. 51**.

Berko v. Securities and Exchange Commission, 316 F.2d 137 (2d Cir.1963)—§ **14.18, n. 15, 47**.

Berry v. Valence Technology, Inc., 175 F.3d 699 (9th Cir.1999)—§ **12.9, n. 14; § 12.10, n. 110**.

Bersch v. Drexel Firestone, Inc., 519 F.2d 974 (2d Cir.1975)—§ **17.4, n. 11, 14**.

Bertoglio v. Texas Intern. Co., 488 F.Supp. 630 (D.Del.1980)—§ **10.3, n. 57**.

Bhatia v. Johnston, 818 F.2d 418 (5th Cir. 1987)—§ **15.1, n. 107**.

Biesenbach v. Guenther, 588 F.2d 400 (3d Cir. 1978)—§ **12.20, n. 12, 17**.

Billing v. Credit Suisse First Boston Corp., 33 Sec. Reg. & L. Rep. (BNA) 309 (S.D.N.Y. 2001)—§ **6.3, n. 49**.

Binder v. Gillespie, 184 F.3d 1059 (9th Cir. 1999)—§ **12.10, n. 41**.

Bingham, United States v., 992 F.2d 975 (9th Cir.1993)—§ **12.9, n. 37**.

Birdman v. Electro-Catheter Corp., 352 F.Supp. 1271 (E.D.Pa.1973)—§ **3.9, n. 29**.

Birnbaum v. Newport Steel Corp., 193 F.2d 461 (2d Cir.1952)—§ **12.7; § 12.7, n. 6, 85**.

Birotte v. Merrill Lynch, Pierce, Fenner & Smith, Inc., 468 F.Supp. 1172 (D.N.J. 1979)—§ **14.25, n. 2**.

Bischoff v. G.K. Scott & Co., Inc., 687 F.Supp. 746 (E.D.N.Y.1988)—§ **14.10, n. 43**.

Bissell v. Merrill Lynch & Co., Inc., 157 F.3d 138 (2d Cir.1998)—§ **14.22, n. 6, 7, 8**.

Bissell v. Merrill Lynch & Co., Inc., 937 F.Supp. 237 (S.D.N.Y.1996)—§ **14.15, n. 85**.

B.J. Tannenbaum, Jr., 18 Sec.Reg. & L.Rep. (BNA) 1826 (SEC 1986)—§ **1.6, n. 16**.

Black Box Incorporated, 1990 WL 286633 (SEC 1990)—§ **4.36, n. 63**.

Blackie v. Barrack, 524 F.2d 891 (9th Cir. 1975)—§ **12.11, n. 31**.

Blanchard v. Edgemark Financial Corp., 192 F.R.D. 233 (N.D. Ill. 2000)—§ **12.19, n. 48**.

Blanchard v. Edgemark Financial Corp., 158 F.Supp.2d 297 (N.D.Ill.2001)—§ **9.3, n. 5; § 12.9, n. 266; § 12.19, n. 35, 39**.

Blanchard v. EdgeMark Financial Corporation, 1999 WL 59994 (N.D.Ill.1999)—§ **12.9, n. 132**.

Blatt v. Merrill Lynch, Pierce, Fenner & Smith Inc., 916 F.Supp. 1343 (D.N.J.1996)—§ **20.10, n. 8**.

Blau v. Lamb, 363 F.2d 507 (2d Cir.1966)—§ **13.2, n. 89**.

Blau v. Lehman, 368 U.S. 403, 82 S.Ct. 451, 7 L.Ed.2d 403 (1962)—§ **13.3, n. 22, 23**.

Blimpie Corporation of America, Matter of, 44 S.E.C. 558 (1971)—§ **3.6, n. 41**.

Blinder, In re, 29 Sec. Reg. & L. Rep. (BNA) 1406 (SEC 1997)—§ **16.2, n. 316**.

Blinder, Robinson & Co., In re, [1985–86 Transfer Binder] Fed.Sec.L.Rep. (CCH) ¶ 83,911 (SEC 1985)—§ **16.2, n. 268**.

Blinder, Robinson & Co., Matter of, 1991 WL 840282 (N.A.S.D.R. 1991)—§ **14.18, n. 16**.

Blinder, Robinson & Co., Matter of, 1990 WL 321585 (SEC 1990)—§ **2.5, n. 20**.

Blitz, United States v., 533 F.2d 1329 (2d Cir. 1976)—§ **14.14, n. 134**.

Block v. S.E.C., 50 F.3d 1078 (D.C.Cir.1995)—§ **16.2, n. 193**.

Blue Chip Stamps v. Manor Drug Stores, 421 U.S. 723, 95 S.Ct. 1917, 44 L.Ed.2d 539 (1975)—§ **1.6, n. 245; § 1.7, n. 4; § 7.12, n. 21; § 10.3, n. 8; § 11.9, n. 17; § 11.10, n. 27; § 12.2, n. 4; § 12.3, n. 27, 31; § 12.4, n. 16, 19; § 12.7; § 12.7, n. 7, 89, 93; § 12.22, n. 4; § 12.27, n. 39; § 20.10, n. 53**.

BNS Inc. v. Koppers Co., Inc., 683 F.Supp. 454 (D.Del.1988)—§ **11.12, n. 78**.

Board of Trade of City of Chicago v. Christie Grain & Stock Co., 198 U.S. 236, 25 S.Ct. 637, 49 L.Ed. 1031 (1905)—§ **14.18, n. 20**.

Board of Trade of City of Chicago v. S.E.C., 883 F.2d 525 (7th Cir.1989)—§ **1.5, n. 58**.

Board of Trade of City of Chicago v. S.E.C., 923 F.2d 1270 (1991)—§ **1.5, n. 60; § 14.3, n. 70**.

Boeing Co., 2001 WL 128120 (SEC 2001)—§ **10.8, n. 66**.

Bolton v. Gramlich, 540 F.Supp. 822 (S.D.N.Y. 1982)—§ **10.3, n. 15**.

Boone v. Carlsbad Bancorporation, Inc., 972 F.2d 1545 (10th Cir.1992)—§ **10.3, n. 45, 47**.

Booth v. Peavey Co. Commodity Services, 430 F.2d 132 (8th Cir.1970)—§ **1.6, n. 151**.

Borland Finance Co., 19 Sec.Reg. & L.Rep. (BNA) 1769 (SEC 1987)—§ **5.2, n. 7, 43, 45**.

Bormann v. Applied Vision Systems, Inc., 800 F.Supp. 800 (D.Minn.1992)—§ **12.1, n. 128**.

Boss v. Salomon Smith Barney Inc., 263 F.Supp.2d 684 (S.D.N.Y.2003)—§ **15.1, n. 29**.

Botto and Associates, 1989 WL 245530 (SEC 1989)—§ **4.36, n. 31**.

Bowen v. United States, 570 F.2d 1311 (7th Cir.1978)—§ **16.2, n. 350**.

Boyd v. Merrill Lynch, Pierce, Fenner & Smith, 611 F.Supp. 218 (S.D.Fla.1985)—§ **7.2, n. 17**.

Bradford v. Moench, 809 F.Supp. 1473 (D.Utah 1992)—§ **1.6, n. 304**.

Bradstreet, United States v., 135 F.3d 46 (1st Cir.1998)—§ **12.4, n. 23; § 12.25, n. 1, 58**.

Brady Rules Out any Compromise on SEC–CFTC Jurisdictional Dispute, 22 Sec.Reg. & L.Rep. (BNA) 1031 (July 13, 1990)—§ **1.5, n. 53**.

Brannan v. Eisenstein, 804 F.2d 1041 (8th Cir.1986)—§ **12.7, n. 37**.

C

D

G

H

M

O

P

*

Index

We have included references to material that appears only in the Practitioner's Edition in order to guide the reader to sources beyond this Hornbook

†